Principles of
Managerial
Finance

Lawrence J. Gitman

San Diego State University

HARPER & ROW, PUBLISHERS, New York
Cambridge, Philadelphia, San Francisco,
London, Mexico City, São Paulo, Singapore, Sydney

FIFTH EDITION

Principles of Managerial Finance

Photo Credits (listed by page number)
14 Courtesy, Primerica Corporation; **92** Courtesy, Bethlehem
Steel Corporation; **148** AP/Wide World; **194** Courtesy, CSX
Corporation; **231** AP/Wide World; **259** AP/Wide World; **339**
Courtesy, USX Corporation; **390** Courtesy, NCR Corporation;
451 AP/Wide World; **481** AP/Wide World; **527** Courtesy,
MAXIMA Corporation; **586** UPI/Bettmann; **660** Courtesy,
General Motors; **692** AP/Wide World.

Sponsoring Editor: John Greenman
Development Editor: Mary Lou Mosher
Project Editor: David Nickol
Editor in Chief: Judy Rothman
Text Design: York Production Services/Rose Design
Cover Design: Tomoko Miho
Text Art: Fine Line Illustrations, Inc.
Production Manager: Jeanie Berke
Production Assistant: Beth Maglione
Compositor: York Graphic Services, Inc.
Printer and Binder: R. R. Donnelley & Sons, Company
Cover Printer: The Lehigh Press, Inc.

Principles of Managerial Finance, Fifth Edition

Library of Congress Cataloging in Publication Data

Gitman, Lawrence J.
  Principles of managerial finance.

  Includes index.
  1. Corporations—Finance. 2. Business enterprises—
Finance. I. Title.
HG4011.G5   1988   658.1'5   87-35075
ISBN 0-06-042412-5

  90 91 9 8 7 6 5 4 3

To my wife, Robin,
our son, Zachary,
and our daughter, Jessica

CONTENTS IN BRIEF

CONTENTS IN DETAIL

Principles of Managerial Finance is designed primarily for the introductory finance course at the undergraduate level. It may also be used with good results in the core MBA finance course, in management development programs, and in executive study programs. It is intended to make factual material as easily digestible as possible so that the instructor can concentrate on theories, concepts, and techniques that will help students make reasonable real-world financial decisions. Examples designed to amplify concepts and catch student interest are liberally provided throughout the text—the book has been written and revised with the student constantly in mind. The payoff of readability accrues not only to students but also to instructors, who should find their job of teaching simplified.

General Changes in the Fifth Edition

Three general changes help make this edition a leaner text that incorporates fresh pedagogy and up-to-date coverage.

Streamlined Length

The text has been compressed to 20 chapter (from 24 chapters) to enhance its effectiveness in courses of varying length. This tightening was achieved by better integrating the material on financial institutions, markets, and interest rates, capital budgeting techniques, sources of short-term financing, dividend policy, leasing, and expansion and failure. In addition, tabular presentations now more efficiently cover certain types of descriptive material

New Pedagogical Devices

In addition to the pedagogical features retained from earlier editions, a number of new pedagogical devices have been introduced into the fifth edition of *Principles of Managerial Finance*.

Fact or Fable? Sets of provocative true/false questions labeled "Fact or Fable?" appear at the beginnings of chapters to encourge students to really think about key topics. Correct answers are interspersed in **boldface** throughout the text as the corresponding topics are discussed.

Chapter-Opening Vignettes. In order to capture the student's attention, each chapter begins by relating timely real-company events to one or more of the chapter's concepts. Students are introduced to companies such as Federal Express, Wang Laboratories, McDonnell Douglas, and Reebok.

High-Interest Boxes. Each chapter includes two or three boxed essays that demonstrate text concepts through engaging real-life stories or events in four categories: "Careers in Finance" "Profiles" (include photos), "Small Business," and "Finance in Action." A few examples: a career as an investment banker; a profile of T. Boone Pickens; how a small business goes public abroad; how R. J. Reynolds revitalized its tobacco operation.

Running Glossary. Throughout the text, key terms and their definitions appear in the text margin when they are first introduced. These terms and others also appear in a separate end-of-book glossary.

New Self-Test Problems. At the end of each chapter (except Chapter 1) one or more self-test problems are included, along with completely worked-out solutions. These demonstration problems strengthen students' understanding of the techniques presented.

Added Problems and New Integrative Problems. All end-of-chapter problems have been carefully reviewed and revised, and many new problems have been added. A number of longer problems integrating several concepts are included when appropriate.

Integrative Part-Ending Cases. Located at the end of each of the seven parts of the text is an integrative case that ties together the concepts introduced in that part's chapters. These innovative cases eliminate the need for a supplemental casebook.

Fully Integrates the *Tax Reform Act of 1986*

The key tax and depreciation requirements of the *Tax Reform Act of 1986* are fully explained and thoroughly integrated into all applicable text discussions and end-of-chapter and ancillary materials.

Content Changes

A number of other important but less sweeping changes have also been made:

1. Discussion of the major areas of finance and related career opportunities was added to Chapter 1.
2. The agency issue is now introduced in Chapter 1 and incorporated in the discussions of capital structure and long-term debt financing in Chapters 12 and 16 respectively.
3. The operating environment of the firm, including discussion of financial institutions, markets, and interest rates, is now described in a single chapter (Chapter 2) that replaces two chapters in the fourth edition.
4. Chapter 3 includes an expanded discussion of cash flow with specific emphasis on the statement of changes in financial position.

5. Chapter 6 on the time value of money now includes a discussion of nominal and effective interest rates.

6. Capital budgeting is now covered in two (rather than three) chapters—Chapter 9 and 10. Discussions of the average rate of return and profitability index have been deleted, scenario analysis added, and unequal lives simplified.

7. In Chapter 11 on the cost of capital, the weighted marginal cost of capital discussion has been simplified in a fashion that retains the conceptual strength of the presentation.

8. The coverage of working capital management fundamentals and sources of short-term financing has been streamlined and integrated into a single chapter (Chapter 13).

9. A brief discussion of junk bonds is now included in Chapter 16 on long-term debt and investment banking.

10. The discussions of common stock and dividend policy have been improved and integrated into a single chapter (Chapter 17).

11. More efficient coverage of preferred stock (including discussion of adjustable-rate preferred stock), leasing, convertibles, warrants, and options is included in Chapter 18. This single chapter replaces three chapters in the fourth edition.

12. The merger discussion, which now covers divestiture and leveraged buyouts, and the business failure discussion, which has been updated and significantly shortened, have been merged into a single chapter (Chapter 19).

13. Chapter 20 replaces the ''Multinational Finance'' inserts included in earlier editions with a completely new chapter on international finance that provides more cohesive coverage of this important topic.

14. A new text appendix (Appendix B) on career opportunities in managerial finance and financial services profiles eighteen different financial careers—what they are, where to find them, and what they're paying—in order to help students get a ''feel'' for various career opportunities.

15. Text Appendix D on the use of computers and spreadsheets in managerial finance has been added in order to provide students with useful insights into the role and widespread use of the personal computer and various types of software—especially electronic spreadsheets—in managerial finance.

Pedagogical Features

In addition to the new pedagogical devices in this edition noted above, the text retains a structured yet flexible organization, presents numerous examples, includes useful end-of-chapter summaries, questions, and problems, and contains other support items.

Flexible Organization

The text's organization conceptually links the firm's actions and its value as determined in the securities markets. Housed within this framework is a simple balance-sheet structure with which to analyze many of the decisions confronting the financial manager. Each major decision area is presented in terms of both risk and return factors and their potential impact on the owner's wealth, as reflected by share value.

In organizing each chapter, I have adhered to a managerial decision-making perspective. That is, I have not merely described a concept such as present value or operating leverage, but have also related it to the financial manager's overall goal of wealth maximization. Once a particular concept has been developed, its application is illustrated so that the student is not left with just an abstract definition, but truly senses the decision-making considerations and consequences of each financial action. New terms are defined when first used, and the definitions are sometimes repeated in subsequent discussions to help the reader master the vocabulary of finance. Also, the marginal glossary and end-of-book glossary make terms and definitions accessbile in two other ways.

The fifth edition of *Principles of Managerial Finance* contains twenty chapters. It is designed to be read in sequence, but almost any chapter may be taken out of sequence and studied as a self-contained unit. The flexibility of the book makes it suitable for courses of various lengths, from one quarter to two full semesters, and it should be easily adaptable to various teaching preferences.

In-Text Examples

Over 400 well-marked examples occur throughout the text to demonstrate potentially troublesome concepts. The examples are detailed, and quite often the reason for using a particular approach is given along with the demonstration. Reviewers of this and earlier editions have remarked that the content, quality, placement, and method of presenting the examples contribute greatly to both teaching and learning this material well.

End-of Chapter Material

In addition to the self-test problems described earlier, each chapter ends with a bulleted summary, questions, and problems.

Bulleted Summaries. The summary at the end of each chapter appears as a bulleted list of major points for quick review.

Questions. Ten to fifteen questions serve as a review by which students may test their understanding of the key theories, concepts, and techniques within the chapter.

Problems. I am a strong believer in the use of many problems during all phases of the first finance course, at whatever level it is taught. Therefore, a comprehensive set of problems containing more than one problem for each concept or technique is included to assure students multiple self-testing opportunities and to give professors a wide choice of assignable material. A short tag line at the beginning of each problem identifies the concept that the problem has been designed to test. In addition, a disk symbol, , appears in

the margin next to all problems that can be solved using *The Gitman Disk*—a user-friendly menu-driven personal computer disk (described in detail later) that accompanies the text. As noted earlier, some of these problems are captioned as "integrative" since they are designed to tie together related topics. Answers to selected end-of-chapter problems appear in Appendix E; these answers help students evaluate their progress in preparing detailed problem solutions.

Other Support Items

A complete set of financial tables for percentage rates between 1 and 50 percent is included in Appendix A. Also included for students' convenience is a removable, laminated future- and present-value table card that may be used in working problems.

Supplemental Materials

A number of additional materials are available to aid and enrich the learning and teaching process.

Study Guide

The student review manual, *Study Guide to Accompany Principles of Managerial Finance,* Fifth Edition, coauthored with J. Markham Collins of The University of Tulsa, has been completely revised. Each chapter of the study guide contains a chapter summary, a chapter outline, a programmed self-test, and problems and detailed solutions. Where appropriate, discussions and problems are keyed to *The Gitman Disk.*

Managerial Finance with Lotus 1-2-3

Written by Daniel J. Kaufman, Jr., and M. Fall Ainina, both of Wright State University, this new software package (IBM and compatibles) teaches students how to use Lotus 1-2-3 (and compatible spreadsheets) while reinforcing concepts introduced in this text. The thirty templates in the program will only be partially filled in; students must enter the appropriate cell formula to get a solution. In addition, templates are included for use in solving the integrative part-ending cases. The perforated paperback manual that accompanies the disk contains documentation on how to use each template. Instructional material and problems for each template can be detached and handed in to the instructor with the student's computer printout.

Instructor's Manual

The comprehensive *Instructor's Manual* enables the professor to use the text easily and effectively in the classroom. Prepared by Cherie Mazer, for each chapter it includes an overview of the topics, a guide to classroom use of supplemental materials, a four to five page set of lecture outline transparency masters, a ready-to-copy master of a practice quiz covering a key issue in the chapter, and detailed answers and solutions to all text questions, problems, and integrative cases. Great care has been taken to ensure the accuracy of all answers and solutions. The chapter-by-chapter guide to supplemental materials includes reference to *The Gitman Disk, Managerial Finance with Lotus 1-2-3,* preprinted overhead transparencies (annotated) in a reduced-image format for easy reference, key problems in the *Study Guide* suitable for classroom use, and a statement of purpose and an overview for each of the integrative cases presented in the text.

Test Bank (Both in Printed and Computer Software Disk Form)

A completely new and accurate test bank containing 1,000 multiple-choice questions and 100 problems with worked-out solutions has been developed by Cherie Mazer and is available in a separate test-bank manual and on Harper Test, a computerized test-generation system with full word-processing capabilities. It produces customized tests and allows instructors to scramble questions and/or add new ones. Harper Test is available for the Apple, IBM, and some compatibles.

Acetate Transparencies

A set of 100 transparency acetates of key exhibits and problem solutions is available to adoptors.

The Gitman Disk

A computerized supplement for use with the Apple, IBM, and some compatibles, *The Gitman Disk* has been specifically developed and revised by Frederick Rexroad to accompany this text. All routines are written in BASIC and can be transferred easily to other computers with little or no modification. *The Gitman Disk* includes 11 short programs, presented in a user-friendly menu-driven format, for use in solving financial problems. Applicability of the disk throughout the text and study guide is always keyed by a printed disk symbol like that shown above. Each routine on the disk includes page references to the text discussion of the technique being applied. *The Gitman Disk* is available free to adoptors. A detailed description of the disk and its use is given in Appendix C.

Videotapes

A new visual presentation of concepts in the text has been developed by George Flowers of Houston Baptist University. These videotapes present lecture and visual material that may be used as a basis for a telecourse, for coverage of specific topics, or for students' self-study. These tapes, which cover all chapters of the text, may be purchased individually by chapter, in groups of chapters, or as a complete video course package. Content and ordering information concerning the tapes may be obtained from: George Flowers; Houston Baptist University; 7502 Fondren Road; Houston, Texas 77074-3298; telephone: (713) 774-7661 ext. 2280 or (713) 995-3325.

Acknowledgments

Many people have made significant contributions to this edition as well as to earlier editions. Without their classroom experience, guidance, and advice, this book could not have been written or revised. Receiving continual feedback from students, colleagues, and practitioners helps me create a truly teachable textbook. If you or your students are moved to write me about any matters pertaining to this text package, please do. I welcome constructive criticism and suggestions for the book's further improvement.

Harper & Row obtained the experienced advice of a large group of excellent reviewers. I appreciate their many suggestions and criticisms, which have had a strong influence on various aspects of this volume. My special thanks go to the following people, who reviewed all or part of the manuscripts for earlier editions:

Ronald F. Anderson	Patrick A. Casabona
Gary A. Anderson	Roger G. Clarke
David A. Arbeit	Thomas Cook
Richard E. Ball	Donnie L. Daniel
Russell L. Block	Joel J. Dauten
Calvin M. Boardman	Lee E. Davis
Robert J. Bondi	Richard F. DeMong
Kenneth J. Boudreaux	Peter A. DeVito
Ron Braswell	Vincent R. Driscoll
Omer Carey	David R. Durst

F. Barney English
Ross A. Flaherty
George W. Gallinger
Gerald D. Gay
Anthony J. Giovino
Philip W. Glasgo
Ron B. Goldfarb
David A. Gordon
I. Charles Granicz
Phil Harrington
Melvin W. Harju
George T. Harris
Roger G. Hehman
Harvey Heinowitz
Glenn Henderson
Douglas A. Hibbert
James Hoban
Keith Howe
Kenneth M. Huggins
Dale W. Janowsky
Nalina Jeypalan
Timothy E. Johnson
Terrance E. Kingston
Harry R. Kuniansky
William R. Lane
Michael A. Lenarcic
A. Joseph Lerro
Timothy Hoyt McCaughey
James C. Ma
William H. Marsh
John F. Marshall
Linda J. Martin
Vincent A. Mercurio
Joseph Messina
Gene P. Morris
Edward A. Moses
William T. Murphy
Randy Myers

Donald A. Nast
Dennis T. Officer
Jerome S. Osteryoung
Kathleen F. Oppenheimer
Don B. Panton
Ronda S. Paul
Gerald W. Perritt
Stanley Piascik
Gerald A. Pogue
Walter J. Reinhart
William B. Riley, Jr.
Ron Rizzuto
Gary Sanger
William L. Sartoris
Carl J. Schwendiman
Carl Schweser
Richard A. Shick
A. M. Sibley
Surendra S. Singhvi
Stacy Sirmans
Gerald Smolen
Ira Smolowitz
Lester B. Strickler
Gary Tallman
Harry Tamule
Richard Teweles
Robert D. Tollen
Kenneth J. Venuto
James A. Verbrugge
Jonathan B. Welch
Grant J. Wells
Howard A. Williams
Bernard J. Winger
Tony R. Wingler
John C. Woods
Charles W. Young
Joe W. Zeman
J. Kenton Zumalt

The following people provided extremely useful reviews and input to the fifth edition:

Saul H. Auslander, Bridgewater State College

William Brunsen, Northern Arizona University

Samuel B. Bulmash, University of South Florida

James P. D'Mello, Walsh College

Ronald L. Ehresman, Baldwin-Wallace College

R. H. Gilmer, Jr., The University of Oklahoma

John D. Harris, Harris Leasing Company

Hugh A. Hobson, James Madison Univesity

Jerry G. Hunt, East Carolina University

Rich Lanear, Mercer University

Scott Lee, University of Oregon

Christopher K. Ma, The University of Toledo

Charles E. Maxwell, Murray State University

Jay Meiselman, Ohio Printing Company

Tarun K. Mukherjee, University of New Orleans

Richard M. Osborne, Michigan State University

John Park, Frostburg State College

Gladys E. Perry, Kennesaw College

Jerry B. Poe, Arizona State University

R. Daniel Sadlier, Bank One, Dayton, NA

Hadi Salavitibar, SUNY-New Paltz

John W. Settle, Portland State University

Cheryl W. Shannon, Bank One, Dayton, NA

Rolf K. Tedefalk, University of North Dakota

Pieter A. Vandenberg, San Diego State University

Ronald P. Volpe, Youngstown State University

William H. Weber III, Arkansas College

Larry R. White, Mississippi State University

I am especially indebted to Mehdi Salehizadeh of San Diego State University for the outstanding job he did in preparing Chapter 20 on international finance. Special thanks is due Cherie Mazer for her splendid assistance in preparing the opening vignettes, boxes, and integrative cases, Appendix B on career opportunities, Appendix D on computer and spreadsheet usage, the *Instructor's Manual,* and the *Test Bank.* I also wish to thank Fred Rexroad for developing and revising *The Gitman Disk.* The assistance of Ronald S. Pretekin of Coolidge, Wall Co., LPA, in updating and shortening the discussions of business failure is greatly appreciated. Thanks is also due George Flowers for his feedback as well as developing and making available his videotapes. My colleagues, tax experts Russell H. Hereth and John C. Talbott, Peter W. Bacon, Elsie Fenic, Waldemar M. Goulet, Nicolas Gressis, and Richard E. Williams provided continued advice, assistance, and support for which I am most appreciative.

Special thanks is due J. Markham Collins for his useful feedback and for coauthoring the *Study Guide.* I also greatly appreciate the helpful input provided by my colleagues Daniel J. Kaufman, Jr., and M. Fall Ainina who together coauthored the innovative Lotus 1-2-3 package available with this edition. A special word of thanks is also due Michael D. Joehnk (Arizona State University), George E. Pinches (The University of Kansas), and Stephen W. Pruitt (University of Mississippi) for their help. Special mention is due Teresa Mayfield and Mimi Ross for their outstanding efforts in typing the manuscript, running numerous errands, and generally keeping things in order.

The staff of Harper & Row—particularly John Greenman, Mary Lou Mosher, David Nickol, Judy Rothman, Lauren Bahr, and Debra Bremer—deserve thanks for their professional expertise, creativity, enthusiasm, and commitment to this text. A special word of thanks is due Mary Lou Mosher and David Nickol for not only accommodating my obsessive behavior, but for professionally coordinating and orchestrating the timely publication of the text and its many ancillaries. I am also indebted to freelance editor Ann Torbert, whose outstanding work on this as well as an earlier edition is reflected in the text's overall clarity and conciseness. Finally, my wife, Robin, and our children, Zachary and Jessica, have played most important parts in patiently providing the support and understanding I needed during the writing of this book. To them I will be forever grateful.

Lawrence J. Gitman

Dear Student,

My main purpose in writing this book was to put on paper for you the important concepts and practices of managerial finance in both an understandable and lively way. Managerial finance is an essential course in the business curriculum, as well as a key ingredient in the professional training of business people. Learning and knowing about finance is a basic underpinning for a productive career in your chosen field of business. A course in managerial finance should also be a positive educational experience, and I have worked to make this fifth edition an accessible and enjoyable introduction to the subject.

One feature I've added to make this edition more interesting and engaging is "Fact or Fable?" teasers that begin each chapter. I hope these true or false statements will increase your interest in the subject matter that follows. Another new element that should broaden your practical insights into the activities of managerial finance is the boxed essays interspersed throughout the book. I've titled them "Careers in Finance," "Profiles," "Small Business," and "Finance in Action." Career boxes acquaint you with career opportunities in finance; they are augmented by a career appendix at the end of the text. Profile boxes describe the background and accomplishments of major financial business leaders, such as T. Boone Pickens and Karen Horn. Small Business boxes give you insight into important financial issues facing small businesses. Finance in Action boxes expose you to the recent financial actions, outcomes, and concerns of specific firms.

Other elements that should heighten your interest in and appreciation of the material in this book include chapter-opening vignettes relating a real-world experience to the material that is to be covered; numerous examples demonstrating concepts that may be hard to grasp; a running glossary that allows you to quickly learn the definitions of key terms as they are introduced; and self-test problems at the end of each chapter that can be used to reinforce what you've learned.

I hope this book achieves my twin objectives of giving you an understanding and appreciation of the role of finance and the financial manager in today's business, and also stimulating you to pursue further study—and possibly a career—in finance. The field of finance is exciting and dynamic. It offers many challenges and opportunities. Whatever career path you choose, I am sure that the knowledge gained from this text will prove beneficial. Best of luck in your studies.

Sincerely yours,

Lawrence J. Gitman

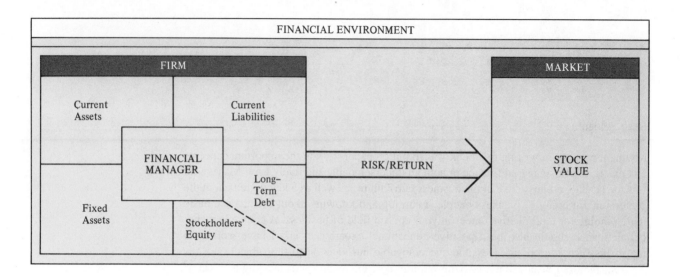

PART ONE

Financial Environment, Analysis, and Planning

CHAPTER 1

The Role of Finance and the Financial Manager

FACT OR FABLE?

Are the following statements fact *(true)* or fable *(false)*?

1

Managerial finance is the area of finance concerned with the design and delivery of financial products and advice to individuals, business, and government.

2

Both accountants and financial managers rely primarily upon the accrual method of funds recognition.

3

The primary activities of the financial manager are (1) financial analysis and planning, (2) managing the firm's asset structure, and (3) managing the firm's financial structure.

4

The goal of the financial manager is to maximize the owners' wealth rather than to maximize profits.

5

Agency costs are borne by creditors in order to assure that manager's actions are consistent with the goal of owner wealth maximization.

Federal Express was founded in 1973 by its chairman, Fred Smith, in the belief that there were lots of people who absolutely, positively had to have small packages delivered overnight. He was right. Sales were $160 million by 1978 and $2.6 billion by 1986.

In 1984 Federal Express introduced a new service called ZapMail in the belief that scores of businesses absolutely, positively had to have documents moved across country within two hours. By using a system of leased telephone lines, computer switches, and satellite links, Federal Express would be able to transmit, say, a legal document from the facsimile machine in an office in Maine to a facsimile machine in an office in California— all for a price of $35 for up to 10 pages. (Later the price dropped to $25 when "absolutely, positively" turned out to be "well, maybe" or "not yet.") In its short life of 26 months, ZapMail zapped Federal Express with an operating loss of $317 million.

What happened? First, the technology was good in theory but in practice it did not provide a consistently good picture. Second, forecasts about the demand for ZapMail were wrong. Smith was no doubt accurate in predicting the demand for almost-instant information at an affordable price. But he was probably five or ten years early. In October 1986 Fred Smith announced that Federal Express was discontinuing ZapMail because "it was not in the best interest of our shareholders, employees, or customers to continue on the present course."

Like Federal Express, all firms must consider the financial implications and outcomes of proposed actions on the achievement of their goals. This chapter sets the stage for the study of managerial finance by describing the role that finance and the financial manager play in achieving the firm's goals.

Finance as an Area of Study

The field of finance is broad and dynamic. It directly affects the lives of every person and every organization, financial or nonfinancial, private or public, profit-seeking or not-for-profit. There are many areas of finance for study, and a large number of career opportunities are available.

What Is Finance?

Finance can be defined as the art and science of managing money. Virtually all individuals and organizations earn or raise money and spend or invest money. Finance is concerned with the process, institutions, markets, and instruments involved in the transfer of money among and between individuals, businesses, and governments.

finance The art and science of managing money.

Major Areas and Opportunities in Finance

The major areas of finance can be summarized by reviewing the career opportunities in finance. These opportunities can, for convenience, be divided into two broad categories: financial services and managerial finance.

Financial Services

financial services The area of finance concerned with design and delivery of advice and financial products to individuals, business, and government.

Financial services is the area of finance concerned with the design and delivery of advice and financial products to individuals, business, and government. It is one of the fastest-growing areas of career opportunity in our economy. Financial services includes banking and related institutions, personal financial planning, investments, and real estate and insurance. Table 1.1 describes the career opportunities available in each of these areas.

Table 1.1
Career Opportunities in Financial Services

Opportunity	Description
Banking and related institutions	Banks, savings and loan associations, mutual savings banks, finance companies, and credit unions all offer challenging career opportunities for those trained in financial services. Because of the many services offered by these institutions, a wide choice of careers is available. Loan officers handle installment, commercial, real estate, and/or consumer loans. Trust officers administer trust funds for estates, foundations, and business firms. Many of these institutions have begun to offer new services in insurance brokerage, real estate, and personal financial planning.
Personal financial planning	Career opportunities for personal financial planners have increased dramatically in recent years, largely due to increasingly complicated tax laws, new investment vehicles, and a relaxed regulatory environment. Financial institutions, brokerage firms, insurance companies, and consulting firms are all interested in hiring individuals who can provide sound advice to consumers regarding the management of their personal financial affairs.
Investments	Careers in investments include working as a securities broker or as a securities analyst in a brokerage firm, insurance company, or other financial institution. Investment specialists are involved in analyzing securities and constructing portfolios that will achieve their clients' objectives. Related opportunities to work in investment banking, which involves developing and marketing security offerings for corporate and government issuers, are also available.
Real estate and insurance	Real estate is a field with varied career opportunities. Careers include real estate broker, appraiser, mortgage banker, and real estate developer. There are also highly rewarding career opportunities for insurance specialists, such as sales agents, statisticians, and underwriters. Insurance companies also need personnel well-trained in finance to help them manage their investment portfolios.

Managerial Finance

Managerial finance is concerned with the duties of the financial manager in the business firm. **Financial managers** actively manage the financial affairs of many types of business—financial and nonfinancial, private and public, profit-seeking and not-for-profit. They perform such varied tasks as budgeting, financial forecasting, cash management, credit administration, investment analysis, and funds procurement. In recent years the changing economic and regulatory environments have increased the importance and complexity of the financial manager's duties. As a result many top executives in industry and government have come from the finance area.

managerial finance
Concerns the duties of the financial manager in the business firm.

financial manager Actively manages the financial affairs of any type of business, whether financial or nonfinancial, private or public, profit or not-for-profit.

---

1 Managerial finance is the area of finance concerned with the design and delivery of financial products and advice to individuals, business, and government. *(Fable)*
Managerial finance is concerned with the duties of the financial manager in the business firm.

FACT OR FABLE?

The Study of Managerial Finance

An understanding of the theories, concepts, and techniques presented throughout this text will fully acquaint you with the financial manager's activities and decisions. As you study, you will learn about career opportunities in managerial finance. Boxed items highlighting specific career opportunities in managerial finance as well as financial services are included throughout the book. In addition, Appendix B of the text provides a summary of career opportunities in managerial finance and financial services. I hope that this first exposure to the exciting field of finance will provide the foundation and initiative for further study and possibly even a future career.

The Managerial Finance Function

Since most business decisions are measured in financial terms, the financial manager plays a key role in the operation of the firm. People in all areas—accounting, manufacturing, marketing, personnel, operations research, and so forth—need a basic understanding of the managerial finance function. To gain this understanding, we will now look at the organizational role of the finance function, its relationship to economics and accounting, and the key activities of the financial manager.

An Organizational View

The size and importance of the managerial finance function depend on the size of the firm. In small firms the finance function is generally performed by the accounting department. As a firm grows, the importance of the finance function typically results in the evolution of a separate department linked directly to the company president or chief executive officer (CEO) through a vice-president of finance, commonly called the chief financial officer (CFO). Figure 1.1 is an organizational chart showing the structure of the finance activity in a typical medium-to-large-size firm. Reporting to the vice-president of finance

Figure 1.1
Organization of the Finance Function

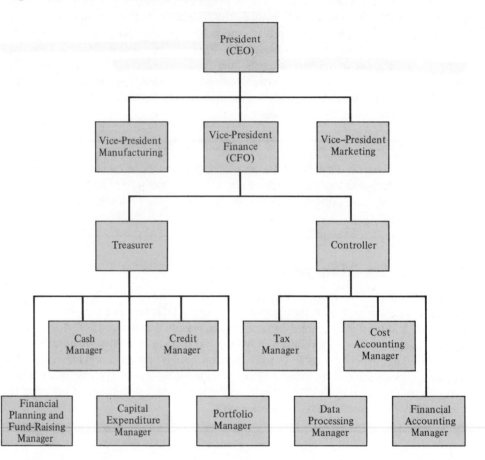

are the treasurer and the controller. The **treasurer** is commonly responsible for handling financial activities, such as financial planning and fund raising, managing cash, making capital expenditure decisions, managing credit activities, and managing the investment portfolio. The **controller** typically handles the accounting activities, such as tax management, data processing, and cost and financial accounting. The activities of the treasurer, or financial manager, are the primary concern of this text.

Relationship to Economics

The field of finance is closely related to economics. Since every business firm operates within the economy, the financial manager must understand the economic framework and be alert to the consequences of varying levels of economic activity and changes in economic policy. The financial manager must also be able to use economic theories as guidelines for efficient business operation. Examples include supply-and-demand analysis, profit-maximizing strategies, and price theory. The primary economic principle used

FINANCE IN ACTION

THE NEW CFO

"The traditional perception of the chief financial officer (CFO)—the introvert in green eyeshades, who works on the books and presents them to managers who then do things with them—is clearly out the window," says P. Anthony Price, a managing director with Russell Reynolds Associates, Inc., an executive research firm.

According to Price, the green eyeshades have clearly given way to Brioni suits, Turnbull & Asser shirts, Hermès ties, and Rolex watches. A foreign language or two and a knowing way with intricate interest rate swaps read better on the resumé than years at a Big Eight accounting firm.

"Our clients are asking us to find a much broader person, one who not only has good skills in the elements of the job, but one with much greater managerial and leadership skills," says Price. "This job is viewed as more important in major transactions, mergers, acquisi-

tions, and take-over defenses than was true in the past. A few years ago control was at the forefront of specifications. Now our clients want someone who not only knows Wall Street but understands the European money centers and, increasingly, Japan."

As an example, Price points to Charles R. Lee, who was placed as chief financial officer at GTE back in 1984. He has been behind the scenes of some of the creative financings in recent years. While CFO at Columbia Pictures, he helped stitch together complex moviemaking deals, then was immersed in the sale of the company to Coca-Cola. Prior to that he had spent nine years at Penn Central, where he played a key role in its turnaround. In addition, he had spent time in Europe, where he worked for U.S. Steel. That diversity of experience came in handy at GTE with major transactions like that company's formation of US Sprint in

1986 and in the firm's current takeover defenses.

Increasingly, Price says, clients are asking him to find someone who could move up to chief operating officer or even chief executive officer. In the past, the CFO at a company might have been a "young Turk," not necessarily strong in finance. "Doing time" in the finance function was a way station, part of his rounding out. No longer.

How does one train to become a top financial officer? Certified public accounting credentials or an advanced degree in business is still the most common educational credit. But as financial negotiations take on more importance, lawyers are beginning to show up in top financial spots, too, so a legal degree is also a plus. Acquiring the skills corporations want in a CFO usually means doing a variety of jobs, either at different companies or within the same corporation.

SOURCE: Adapted from Kathleen K. Wiegner, "CFOs Finally Get Some Respect," *Forbes*, December 1, 1986, p. 228. Excerpted by permission of *Forbes* magazine. © Forbes, Inc., 1986.

in managerial finance is **marginal analysis,** the principle that financial decisions should be made and actions taken only when the added benefits exceed the added costs. A basic knowledge of economics is therefore necessary to understand both the environment and the decision techniques of managerial finance.

marginal analysis States that financial decisions should be made and actions taken only when added benefits exceed added costs.

Relationship to Accounting

The firm's finance and accounting activities are typically within the control of the financial vice-president (CFO), as shown in Figure 1.1. These functions are closely related and generally overlap; indeed, managerial finance and accounting are not often easily distinguishable. In small firms the controller often carries out the finance function, and in large firms many accountants are intimately involved in various finance activities. However, there are two basic differences between finance and accounting; one relates to the method of funds recognition and the other to decision making.

Method of Funds Recognition

accrual method Recognizes revenue at the point of sale and recognizes expenses when incurred.

The accountant's primary function is to develop and provide data for measuring the performance of the firm, assessing its financial position, and paying taxes. Using certain standardized and generally accepted principles, the accountant prepares financial statements that recognize revenue at the point of sale and expenses when incurred. This approach is commonly referred to as the **accrual method.**

cash method Recognizes revenues and expenses only with respect to actual inflows and outflows of cash.

The financial manager, on the other hand, places primary emphasis on *cash flows*, the intake and outgo of cash. He or she maintains the firm's solvency by analyzing and planning the cash flows necessary to satisfy its obligations and to acquire assets needed to achieve the firm's goals. The financial manager uses this **cash method** to recognize the revenues and expenses only with respect to actual inflows and outflows of cash.

FACT OR FABLE?

2 Both accountants and financial managers rely primarily upon the accrual method of funds recognition. *(Fable)*

Accountants concentrate on the accrual method of recognizing revenues at the point of sale and recognizing expenses when incurred, whereas financial managers use the *cash method* to recognize revenues and expenses only with respect to actual inflows and outflows of cash.

A simple analogy may help to clarify the basic difference in viewpoint between the accountant and the financial manager. If we consider the human body as a business firm in which each pulsation of the heart represents a transaction, the accountant's primary concern is *recording* each of these pulsations as sales revenues, expenses, and profits. The financial manager is primarily concerned with whether the resulting flow of blood through the arteries reaches the cells and keeps the various organs of the whole body functioning. It is possible for a body to have a strong heart but cease to function due to the development of blockages or clots in the circulatory system. Similarly, a firm may be profitable but still may fail due to an insufficient flow of cash to meet its obligations as they come due.

> **Example**
> Nassau Corporation in the calendar year just ended made one sale in the amount of $100,000 for merchandise purchased during the year, at a total cost of $80,000. Although the firm paid in full for the merchandise during the year, at year end it has yet to collect the $100,000 from the customer to whom the sale was made. The accounting view and the financial view of the firm's performance during the year are given by the following income and cash flow statements, respectively.
> It can be seen that whereas in an accounting sense the firm is quite profitable, it is a financial failure in terms of actual cash flow. The Nassau Corporation's lack of cash flow resulted from the uncollected account receivable of $100,000. Without adequate cash inflows to meet its obligations the firm will not survive, regardless of its level of profits.

Accounting View

Nassau Corporation
Income Statement
for the Year Ended 12/31

Sales revenue	$100,000
Less: Expenses	80,000
Net profit	$ 20,000

Financial View

Nassau Corporation
Cash Flow Statement
for the Year Ended 12/31

Cash inflow	$ 0
Less: Cash outflow	80,000
Net cash flow	($80,000)

The example above shows that accrual accounting data do not fully describe the circumstances of a firm; thus the financial manager must look beyond financial statements to obtain insight into developing or existing problems. The financial manager, by concentrating on cash flow, should be able to avoid insolvency and achieve the firm's financial goals. Of course, while accountants are well aware of the importance of cash flows and financial managers use and understand accrual-based financial statements, the primary emphasis of accountants is on accrual methods and the primary emphasis of financial managers is on cash flow methods.

Decision Making

We come now to the second major difference between finance and accounting: decision making. Whereas the accountant devotes the majority of his or her attention to the collection and presentation of financial data, the financial manager evaluates the accountant's statements, develops additional data, and makes decisions based on subsequent analyses. The accountant's role is to provide consistently developed and easily interpreted data about the firm's past, present, and future operations. The financial manager uses these data, either in raw form or after certain adjustments and analyses, as an important input to the decision-making process. Of course, this does not mean that accountants never make decisions or that financial managers never gather data; but the primary focuses of accounting and finance are distinctly different.

Key Activities of the Financial Manager

The financial manager's activities can be evaluated in terms of the firm's basic financial statements. His or her primary activities are (1) financial analysis and planning; (2) managing the firm's asset structure; and (3) managing the firm's financial structure. Figure 1.2 relates each of these financial activities to the firm's balance sheet.

Figure 1.2
Key Activities of the Financial Manager

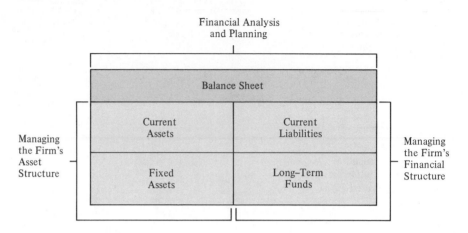

Financial Analysis and Planning

Financial analysis and planning is concerned with (1) transforming financial data into a form that can be used to monitor the firm's financial condition; (2) evaluating the need for increased productive capacity; and (3) determining what additional financing is required. These functions encompass the entire balance sheet as well as the firm's income statement and other financial statements.

Managing the Firm's Asset Structure

The financial manager determines both the mix and the type of assets found on the firm's balance sheet. This activity is concerned with the left-hand side of the balance sheet. *Mix* refers to the number of dollars of current and fixed assets. Once the mix is determined, the financial manager must establish and attempt to maintain certain optimal levels of each type of current asset. He or she must also decide which are the best fixed assets to acquire and know when existing fixed assets need to be modified or replaced.

Managing the Firm's Financial Structure

This activity deals with the right-hand side of the firm's balance sheet and involves two major decisions. First, the most appropriate *mix* of short-term and long-term financing must be determined. This decision is important because it affects the firm's profitability and overall liquidity. A second and equally important concern is which individual short-term or long-term sources of financing are best at a given point in time. Many of these decisions are dictated by necessity, but some require an in-depth analysis of the available alternatives, their costs, and their long-run implications.

FACT OR FABLE?   **3** The primary activities of the financial manager are (1) financial analysis and planning, (2) managing the firm's asset structure, and (3) managing the firm's financial structure. *(Fact)*

CAREERS IN FINANCE

CHIEF FINANCIAL OFFICER: In Charge of the Firm's Financial Activities

Richard Walters, 48, thinks that financial people get a bum rap. "I can laugh about being called a 'bean counter' or a 'number cruncher' because I know just how untrue those terms are. They were as untrue 25 years ago when I was the accountant, controller, planner, and everything else financial for a $10 million company as they are now that I'm CFO (chief financial officer) for one of the Fortune 1000. People in finance have to understand the total operations of a company, not just finance. And operations depend on people. When you get right down to it, my job is providing the financial base that allows people in the corporation to work most productively."

As CFO, Dick is responsible for the overall financial operation of his corporation. He is responsible for budgeting, short-term and long-term financing, capital expenditures, investor relations, cash management, financial reporting, pension management, bank relations, and a variety of other finance-related duties.

Among Dick's most important duties is financial planning. Using available data from the entire corporation, he establishes how much money the firm will need for more plant, more equipment, or more people. How will the company pay for what it needs? Will it borrow money? Will it pay a smaller dividend to stockholders and buy what it needs out of its earnings?

Right now Dick is working on the long-term financing for a major expansion of one of the company's fastest growing divisions. For this multi-million dollar loan, Dick is responsible for bringing together all the parties involved—the accountants, who have all the financial details; the lawyers; and the financiers, which could be banks or even insurance companies. Dick conducts these negotiations and makes sure the meetings move along smoothly and productively.

"I guess on paper my job sounds big time," says Dick, "but I also deal with short-term financial issues and even problems that occur on a day-to-day basis. Right now I want to look into the employees' pension fund to be sure the managers are getting the best return on the funds. We also have to improve planning our cash flow. Too often our quarterly predictions are off, and we have an immediate unpredicted need for short-term financing."

Where will Dick go from here? With an annual salary of over $140,000, he could already be considered a success. But his sights are set for the CEO's (chief executive officer's) job. The statistics say that one in five CEOs comes from the company's finance department. "It seems natural, since money is the language of business. As chief financial officer I'm in almost daily contact with my CEO and often with the board. If it happens, I'll be ready for it backed by my MBA and the years of experience. More importantly, my job as CFO has given me a broad picture of all the departments in the corporation. I think I'm right when I say that any good financial officer will have a broad outlook and be very aware of the human dimension that is at the heart of business success."

Goal of the Financial Manager

In the case of corporations, the owners of a firm are normally distinct from its managers. Actions of the financial manager related to financial analysis and planning, asset structure management, and financial structure management should be taken to achieve the objectives of the firm's owners, its stockholders. In most cases, if the managers are successful in this endeavor they will also achieve their own financial and professional objectives. In the sections that follow we first evaluate profit maximization, then describe wealth maximization, and finally discuss the *agency issue* related to potential conflicts between the goals of stockholders and the actions of management.

✳ Maximize Profit?

Some people believe that the <u>owner's objective is always to maximize profits</u>. To achieve the goal of profit maximization the financial manager takes only those actions that are expected to make a major contribution to the firm's overall profits. Thus, for each alternative being considered, the financial manager would select the one expected to result in the highest monetary return. For corporations, profits are commonly measured in terms of **earnings per share (EPS),** which represents the total earnings available for the firm's common stockholders—the firm's owners—divided by the number of shares of common stock outstanding.

earnings per share (EPS)
The total earnings available for a firm's common stockholders divided by the number of shares of common stock outstanding.

Example

The financial manager of Arnold's Delivery, Inc., is attempting to choose between two alternative investments, X and Y. Each is expected to provide the following earnings per share over its three-year life.

Investment	Earnings per share (EPS)			
	Year 1	Year 2	Year 3	Total for years 1, 2, and 3
X	$1.40	$1.00	$ .40	$2.80
Y	.60	1.00	1.40	3.00

Based on the profit-maximization goal, investment Y would be preferred over investment X since it results in higher earnings per share over the three-year period ($3.00 EPS for Y is greater than $2.80 EPS for X).

Profit maximization fails for a number of reasons: It ignores (1) the timing of returns, (2) cash flows available to stockholders, and (3) risk.

Timing

Because the firm can earn a return on funds it receives, *the receipt of funds sooner as opposed to later is preferred*. In our example, in spite of the fact that the total earnings from investment X are smaller than those from investment Y, X may be preferred due to the greater EPS it provides in the first year. These earlier returns could be reinvested in order to provide greater future earnings.

Cash Flows

A firm's earnings do *not* represent cash flows available to the stockholders. Owners receive realizable returns either through cash dividends paid them at regular intervals or by selling their shares for a higher price than initially paid. A greater EPS does not necessarily mean that dividend payments will increase, since the payment of dividends results solely from the action of the firm's board of directors. Furthermore, a higher EPS does not necessarily translate into a higher stock price. Firms often experience earnings increases without any correspondingly favorable change in stock price.

Risk

Profit maximization disregards **risk**—the chance that actual outcomes may differ from those expected. A basic premise in managerial finance is that a trade-off exists between return (profit) and risk. *Return and risk are in fact the key determinants of share price, which represents the wealth of the owners in the firm.* Profit and risk affect share price differently: Higher profit tends to result in a higher share price, whereas higher risk tends to result in a lower share price since the stockholder must be compensated for the greater risk. In general, stockholders are **risk averse**—that is, they want to avoid risk. Where risk is involved, stockholders expect higher returns from investments of higher risk and vice versa.

risk The chance that actual outcomes may differ from those expected.

risk averse Seeking to avoid risk.

Maximizing Shareholder Wealth ✳

The goal of the financial manager is to maximize the wealth of the owners for whom the firm is being managed. The wealth of corporate owners is measured by the share price of the stock, which in turn is based on the timing of returns, cash flows, and most important, on risk. In considering each decision alternative or possible action in terms of its impact on the share price of the firm's stock, only those actions that are expected to increase share price should be undertaken. Financial managers rely on the two dimensions, return and risk, to link decisions to share price. (Figure 1.3 depicts this process.) Since share price represents the owners' wealth in the firm, share-price maximization is consistent with owner-wealth maximization. Note that although profit (return) is considered in the wealth maximization process, it is not the key decision variable.

---

4 **The goal of the financial manager is to maximize the owners' wealth rather than to maximize profits.** *(Fact)*

FACT OR FABLE?

The Agency Issue

The control of the modern corporation is frequently placed in the hands of professional nonowner managers. We have seen that the goal of the financial manager should be to maximize the wealth of the owners of the firm; thus management can be viewed as *agents* of the owners who have hired them and given them decision-making authority to manage the firm for the owners' benefit. Technically, any manager owning less than 100 percent of the firm is to some degree an agent of the other owners.

Figure 1.3
Financial Decisions and Share Price

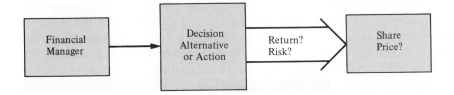

PROFILE

JERRY TSAI:
Making Good Deals for Stockholders

Primerica Corporation, which was American Can Company until spring of 1987, derives 80 percent of its revenues from financial services and 20 percent from retail operations. That means it doesn't manufacture cans anymore, which were the backbone of its business since it was founded in 1901. What caused the dramatic change in this venerable corporation, whose stock is included in the Dow Jones industrial average? In a word, survival. Primerica wasn't able to make cans profitably anymore. In fact, it lost $133 million in 1982 and its stock stood at $27.

By 1987 the company was in the black and its stock had climbed to over 80. The reason? Its new 57-year-old CEO and chairman was Jerry Tsai, who came to the United States from Shanghai in 1947 at the age of 17. According to Tsai, "We have only one job, and that's to maximize shareholder value." To do so, Tsai has been following a popular trend in modern business: move your old-line company away from its historic manufacturing base into the service sector. Along the way there will almost certainly be several mergers and acquisitions, so you'd better have your financial wits about you. Even if you're a financial whiz, you'd better have a CFO who can handle the financial and administrative details back at the store while you're out making deals.

Tsai's background prepared him to become the prototypical CEO for the 1980s, that is, the executive who manages a corporation the way he would manage a stock portfolio: by constantly evaluating the performance of subsidiaries and by being willing to buy, sell, or deal. Tsai emerged in the 1960s as an innovative money manager. Watching the performance of the so-called "go-go" stocks, many of which were quite speculative, he bought and sold for quick profits. In a time when mutual funds were hot, his company, the Manhattan Fund, dazzled Wall Street old-timers with its sizzling performance. Astute enough to see that go-go stocks were dancing into obliv-

ion, Tsai sold the Manhattan Fund to CNA Financial Corporation just before the sizzle went fizzle.

CNA introduced Tsai to the insurance business. He acquired his own company, Associated Madison, and was on the scene in 1982 when Primerica decided to sell a quarter of its manufacturing holdings in order to enlarge its financial services division. Primerica acquired Associated Madison and with it, Tsai, who took charge of Primerica's financial services and built it into the corporation's biggest revenue generator.

Tsai's performance convinced board members that he was right for the CEO's job. As CEO and chairman, Tsai seems unlikely to change the way he operates even if the company has changed its name. He depends a great deal on former Primerica CFO Kenneth A. Yarnell, who became president and chief operating officer of the corporation in 1987. This arrangement frees Tsai from day-to-day management of the corporation and allows him to do what he does best—increase the value of the stockholders' investment by improving the performance of the corporation. He will almost certainly do this by continuing his restructuring of Primerica Corporation through a series of mergers and acquisitions.

In theory, most financial managers would agree with the goal of owner wealth maximization. In practice, however, managers are also concerned with their personal wealth, job security, lifestyle, and perquisites (benefits such as country club memberships, chauffeured limousines, and impressive offices, all provided at company expense). Such concerns may make managers reluctant or unwilling to take more than moderate risk if they perceive that too much risk might result in a loss of job and damage to personal wealth. The result of such a "satisficing" approach (a compromise between satisfaction and maximization) is a less-than-maximum return and a potential loss of wealth for the owners.

Agency Costs

From this conflict of owner and personal goals arises what has been called the **agency problem**—the likelihood that managers may place personal goals ahead of corporate goals.[1] In order to prevent or minimize agency problems, stockholders incur **agency costs,** of which there are four types.

1. *Monitoring expenditures* prevent satisficing (rather than share-price-maximizing) behavior by management. These outlays pay for audits and control procedures that are used to assess and limit managerial behavior to those actions that tend to be in the best interest of the owners.

2. *Bonding expenditures* protect against the potential consequences of dishonest acts by managers. Typically the owners pay a third-party bonding company to obtain a **fidelity bond.** This bond is a contract under which the bonding company agrees to reimburse the firm for up to a stated amount if a specified manager's dishonest act results in financial loss to the firm.

3. *Structuring expenditures* typically involve managerial compensation that provides financial incentives for actions consistent with share price maximization. Popular incentive packages include (1) **stock options,** allowing management to purchase stock at a given, fixed price; (2) **performance shares,** shares of stock given to management as a result of meeting stated performance goals, typically measured in terms of return; and (3) **cash bonuses,** bonus money tied to achievement of certain performance goals in a fashion similar to performance shares.

4. *Opportunity costs* are attributable to the difficulties typically shown by large organizations in responding to new opportunities. The firm's necessary organizational structure, decision hierarchy, and control mechanisms may cause profitable opportunities to be foregone as a result of management's inability to seize upon them quickly.

A Practical View

Research on the agency issue suggests that the goals of managers and shareholders may not deviate too widely. More firms are tying management compensation to the firm's performance, and this incentive appears to motivate managers to operate in a manner reasonably consistent with stock price maximization.[2] Of course many firms incur additional agency costs for monitoring, bonding, and streamlining organizational decision-making in order to further assure congruence of management and owner objectives. Unconstrained, managers may have other goals in addition to share price maximization, but

agency problem The likelihood that managers may place personal goals ahead of corporate goals.

agency costs Costs borne by stockholders to prevent or minimize agency problems and to contribute to the maximization of the owners' wealth. They include monitoring, bonding, and structuring expenditures and opportunity costs.

fidelity bond A contract under which a bonding company agrees to reimburse a firm if a specified manager's dishonest act results in a financial loss to the firm.

stock options Incentive allowing management to purchase stock at a given, fixed price.

performance shares Shares of stock given to management as a result of meeting stated performance goals.

cash bonuses Bonus money paid to management for meeting stated performance goals.

---

[1] The agency problem and related issues were first addressed by Michael C. Jensen and William H. Meckling, ''Theory of the Firm: Managerial Behavior, Agency Costs and Ownership Structure,'' *Journal of Financial Economics* 3 (October 1976), pp. 305–360. For a comprehensive review of Jensen and Meckling and subsequent research on the agency problem, see Amir Barnea, R. Haugen, and L. Senbet, *Agency Problems and Financial Contracting* (Englewood Cliffs, N.J.: Prentice-Hall, 1985).

[2] See Wilbur G. Lewellen, ''Management and Ownership in the Large Firm,'' *Journal of Finance* 24 (May 1969), pp. 299–322; and Robert T. Masson, ''Executive Motivation, Earnings, and Consequent Equity Performance,'' *Journal of Political Economy* 79 (November-December 1971), pp. 1278–1292. Lewellen concluded that managers appear to make decisions that are largely consistent with share price maximization. Masson found that firms whose executives' compensation was closely tied to the performance of the firm's stock tended to outperform other firms in terms of stock returns.

much of the evidence suggests that share price maximization—the focus of this book—is the primary goal of most firms.

---

5 Agency costs are borne by creditors in order to assure that manager's actions are consistent with the goal of owner wealth maximization. *(Fable)*
Agency costs are borne by *stockholders* in order to prevent or minimize agency problems and to contribute to the maximization of the owners' wealth.

An Overview of the Text

The text's organization links the firm's activities to its value, as determined in the securities markets. Housed within this broad framework is a simple balance sheet structure that provides a basis for dissecting and investigating the various decisions that confront the financial manager. Each major decision area is presented in terms of both return and risk factors and their potential impact on the owner's wealth, as reflected by share value.

Keyed to various parts of the text is *The Gitman Disk,* a menu-driven computer disk compatible with most personal computers. It can be used as an aid in performing many of the routine financial calculations and procedures presented in the book. Appendix C describes this decision aid, which for convenience is keyed to text discussions and end-of-chapter problems that can be solved with it. These sections are clearly marked with a disk symbol: . As an additional aid, Appendix D includes a general description of the use

of computers and spreadsheets in managerial finance.

A brief description of each of the text's seven parts is given below. The linkage of each part to the text's overall structure is highlighted in the model of the text's conceptual structure appearing on the left page of each part-opening spread. At the end of each part an integrative case tying together the key topical material is included as a vehicle for synthesizing and applying concepts.

Part One: Financial Environment, Analysis, and Planning

Part One sets the stage for subsequent discussion of the managerial finance function. Chapter 1 has discussed finance as an area of study, described the managerial finance function, and presented the goal of the financial manager. Chapter 2 describes the operating environment of the firm. Chapters 3 and 4 present financial statements, depreciation, and cash flow and financial statement analysis. Chapter 5 emphasizes the role of cash budgeting and pro forma statements in financial planning.

Part Two: Basic Financial Concepts

Part Two presents the basic financial concepts underlying the principles and practices of going concerns. The time value of money, the concepts of risk and return, and the valuation process are discussed in Chapters 6, 7, and 8.

Part Three: Long-Term Investment Decisions

Part Three is concerned with long-term investment decisions (capital budgeting). The primary focus of Chapter 9 is on capital-budgeting cash flow principles and decision-making techniques under certainty. Chapter 10 discusses capital-budgeting decision making under risk and other topics in capital budgeting. A knowledge of each of these areas is necessary for a thorough understanding of the management and selection of fixed-asset investments.

Part Four: Cost of Capital, Leverage, and Capital Structure

Part Four is devoted to three important topics—the cost of capital, leverage, and capital structure. These closely related topics are directly linked to the firm's value. The cost of capital, discussed in Chapter 11, is an important input in the capital-budgeting process. Leverage and capital structure, presented in Chapter 12, affect the firm's cost of capital as well as its share value. These topics show how various suppliers of funds view the firm and enable the financial manager to recognize some important variables that must be considered when obtaining long-term funds.

Part Five: The Management of Working Capital

Part Five, Chapters 13 through 15, is devoted to the management of the firm's current accounts (working capital management). The focus is on management of the firm's key current assets (cash, marketable securities, accounts receivable, and inventory) and current liabilities (both unsecured and secured sources of short-term financing). The relationship between current assets and current liabilities is discussed along with strategies for their efficient management.

Part Six: Sources of Long-Term Financing

Part Six describes major sources of long-term financing. Chapters 16 through 18 discuss the cost, availability, inherent characteristics, and pros and cons of each of the following: long-term debt and investment banking; common stock and dividend policy; preferred stock, leasing, convertibles, warrants, and options.

Part Seven: Special Managerial Finance Topics

Part Seven, Chapters 19 and 20, discusses three other important managerial finance topics: external expansion through business combination, the alternatives available to the failed business firm, and the international dimensions of financial decision making.

Summary

● Finance, which is the art and science of managing money, affects the lives of every person and every organization.

● Major opportunities in finance exist in financial services—banking and related institutions, personal financial planning, investments, and real estate and insurance—and in managerial finance, which is concerned with the duties of the financial manager in the business firm.

● In large firms the managerial finance function might be handled by a separate department headed by the vice-president of finance (CFO), to whom both the treasurer and controller report;

in small firms the finance function is generally performed by the accounting department.

● The financial manager must have a knowledge of both economics and accounting. The accountant devotes primary attention to the accrual method of funds recognition and to gathering and presenting data; the financial manager concentrates on cash flow methods and decision making.

● The three key activities of the financial manager are (1) financial analysis and planning, (2) managing the firm's asset structure, and (3) managing the firm's financial structure.

● The goal of the financial manager is to maximize the owners' wealth (dependent on stock price) rather than profits. Profit maximization ignores the timing of profit, does not consider cash flows to owners, and most importantly, ignores risk.

● Return and risk are the key determinants of share price. Both must be assessed by the financial manager when evaluating decision alternatives or actions.

● An agency problem results from the fact that managers as agents for owners may place personal goals ahead of corporate goals. To minimize this problem shareholders incur agency costs related to (1) monitoring, (2) bonding, (3) structuring, and (4) opportunity loss. Regardless, evidence suggests that share price maximization remains the primary goal of most firms.

Questions

1-1   What is *finance?* Explain how this field affects the lives of everyone and every organization.

1-2   What is the *financial services* area of finance? Briefly describe each of the following areas of career opportunity:

   a. Banking and related institutions

   b. Personal financial planning

   c. Investments

   d. Real estate and insurance

1-3   Describe the field of *managerial finance*. Compare and contrast this field with financial services.

1-4   How does the finance function evolve within the business firm? What financial activities does the treasurer, or financial manager, perform in the mature firm?

1-5   Describe the close relationship between finance and economics, and explain why the financial manager should possess a basic knowledge of economics.

1-6   What are the major differences between accounting and finance with respect to:

   a. The method of funds recognition?

   b. Decision making?

1-7   What are the three key activities of the financial manager? Relate them to the firm's balance sheet.

1-8   Briefly describe three basic reasons why profit maximization is not consistent with wealth maximization.

1-9   What is *risk?* Why must risk as well as return be considered by the financial manager when evaluating a decision alternative or action?

1-10   What is the goal of the financial manager? Discuss how one measures achievement of this goal.

1-11   What is the *agency problem?* In this situation what are often the primary concerns of management? What should they be?

1-12   Why do firms incur *agency costs?* Are they effective in practice? Briefly describe each of the following categories of agency cost.

   a. Monitoring expenditures

   b. Bonding expenditures

   c. Structuring expenditures

   d. Opportunity costs

CHAPTER 2

The Operating Environment of the Firm

FACT OR FABLE?
Are the following statements fact *(true)* or fable *(false)*?

1
Most businesses in the United States are organized as corporations rather than as sole proprietorships or partnerships.

2
For corporations, both ordinary and capital gains income are treated the same for tax purposes under current law.

3
Financial institutions are intermediaries that channel the savings of individuals, businesses, and governments into loans or investments.

4
The money market is an organized exchange on which suppliers and demanders of long-term funds make marketable security transactions.

5
Securities exchanges—both organized and over-the-counter—act as the backbone of the capital market by providing a forum in which debt and equity transactions can be made.

6
An upward-sloping yield curve reflects an expectation of lower inflation and interest rates in the future.

Founded in 1860, J. P. Morgan & Co. has always been viewed as the grand old bank. Staid, conservative, the possessor of the most solid balance sheet of all big banks, Morgan's main business used to be lending money to prestigious clients.

But with the decline of profitability in commercial loans, Morgan has turned to more profitable fee-based businesses. In the United States, Morgan is involved in investment banking as well as mergers and acquisitions. In the less restricted international realm, Morgan is able to add more exotic lines, like Eurobond underwriting, foreign exchange trading, and interest rate and currency swaps.

In order to compete in today's information-hungry age, Morgan has invested $100 million in its global communications center in Delaware. This system allows Morgan offices throughout the world to stay in touch with each other and to have their finger at the pulse of their operating environment. At their fingertips are money market, capital market, and broad economic data.

With all of its innovations, Morgan retains the conservative values that have made it the envy of the banking world in a time when financial intermediaries are in a state of rapid change. For example, Morgan doesn't enter a business until it is sure it understands the venture. Morgan executives are more concerned with solid profitability than with broad diversification. Morgan chairman and CEO Lewis T. Preston says that Morgan will have to be very ''nimble'' in order to maintain its profitability. So far this venerable bank has shown herself to be very light on her feet.

Like J. P. Morgan & Co., to be competitive the financial manager must understand and adapt the firm's activities to changes in its operating environment. In this chapter some of the key aspects of the firm's financial operating environment are described.

Basic Forms of Business Organization

The three basic legal forms of business organization are the *sole proprietorship,* the *partnership,* and the *corporation.* The sole proprietorship is the most common form of organization; however, the corporation is by far the dominant form with respect to receipts and net profits. Corporations are given primary emphasis in this textbook.

sole proprietorship
A business owned by one person and operated for his or her own profit.

unlimited liability The condition imposed by a sole proprietorship (or general partnership) allowing the owner's total wealth to be taken to satisfy creditors.

Sole Proprietorships

A **sole proprietorship** is a business owned by one person who operates it for his or her own profit. About 75 percent of all business firms are sole proprietorships. The typical sole proprietorship is a small firm, such as a neighborhood grocery, auto-repair shop, or shoe-repair business. Typically the proprietor, along with a few employees, operates the proprietorship. He or she normally raises capital from personal resources or by borrowing and is responsible for all business decisions. The sole proprietor has **unlimited liability,** which means that his total wealth, not merely the amount originally invested, can be taken

Table 2.1
Strengths and Weaknesses of Legal Forms of Business Organization

	Legal form		
	Sole proprietorship	**Partnership**	**Corporation**
Strengths	• Owner receives all profits (as well as losses) • Low organizational costs • Income taxed as personal income of proprietor • Secrecy • Ease of dissolution	• Can raise more funds than sole proprietorships • Borrowing power enhanced by more owners • More available brain power and managerial skill • Can retain good employees • Income taxed as personal income of partners	• Owners have *limited liability,* which guarantees they cannot lose more than invested • Can achieve large size due to marketability of stock (ownership) • Ownership is readily transferable • Long life of firm—not dissolved by death of owners • Can hire professional managers • Can expand more easily due to access to capital markets • Receives certain tax advantages
Weaknesses	• Owner has *unlimited liability*—total wealth can be taken to satisfy debts • Limited fund-raising power tends to inhibit growth • Proprietor must be jack-of-all-trades • Difficult to give employees long-run career opportunities • Lacks continuity when proprietor dies	• Owners have *unlimited liability* and may have to cover debts of other less financially sound partners • When a partner dies, partnership is dissolved • Difficult to liquidate or transfer partnership • Difficult to achieve large-scale operations	• Taxes generally higher since corporate income is taxed and dividends paid to owners are again taxed • More expensive to organize than other business forms • Subject to greater government regulation • Employees often lack personal interest in firm • Lacks secrecy since stockholders must receive financial reports

to satisfy creditors. The majority of sole proprietorships are found in the wholesale, retail, service, and construction industries. The key strengths and weaknesses of sole proprietorships are summarized in Table 2.1.

Partnerships

partnership A business owned by two or more persons and operated for profit.

A **partnership** consists of two or more owners doing business together for profit. Partnerships, which account for about 9 percent of all businesses, are typically larger than sole proprietorships. Finance, insurance, and real estate firms are the most common types of partnership. Public accounting and stock brokerage partnerships often have large numbers of partners.

articles of partnership The written contract used to formally establish a business partnership.

Most partnerships are established by a written contract known as the **articles of partnership.** In a *general* (or *regular*) *partnership,* all the partners have unlimited liability. In a **limited partnership,** one or more partners can be designated as having limited liability as long as at least *one* partner has unlimited liability. A *limited partner* is normally prohibited from being active in the management of the firm. Strengths and weaknesses of partnerships are summarized in Table 2.1.

limited partnership Business relationship in which one or more partners can be assigned to have limited liability but in which one partner must assume unlimited liability.

Corporations

corporation An intangible business entity created by law (often called a "legal entity").

A **corporation** is an artificial being created by law. Often called a "legal entity," a corporation has the powers of an individual in that it can sue and be sued, make and be party to contracts, and acquire property in its own name. Although only 16 percent of all businesses are incorporated, the corporation is the dominant form of business organization. It accounts for 88 percent of business receipts and 78 percent of net profits. Since corporations employ millions of people and have many thousands of shareholders, their activities affect the lives of everyone. Although corporations are involved in all types of business, manufacturing corporations account for the largest portion of corporate business receipts and net profits. The key strengths and weaknesses of corporations are summarized in Table 2.1.

stockholders The true owners of the firm by virtue of their equity in the form of common and/or preferred stock.

FACT OR FABLE?

1 Most businesses in the United States are organized as corporations rather than as sole proprietorships or partnerships. *(Fable)*
Corporations make up only about 16 percent of all businesses, although they are the dominant form of business organization in terms of business receipts and net profits.

---

board of directors Group elected by the firm's stockholders and having ultimate authority to guide corporate affairs and make general policy.

The major parties in a corporation are the stockholders, the board of directors, and the president. Figure 2.1 depicts the relationship among these parties. The **stockholders** are the true owners of the firm by virtue of their equity in common and preferred stock. They vote periodically to elect the members of the board of directors and to amend the firm's corporate charter. The **board of directors** has the ultimate authority in guiding corporate affairs and in making general policy. The directors include key corporate personnel as well as outside individuals who typically are successful business persons and executives of other major organizations. Outside directors for major corporations are typically paid an annual fee of between $5,000 and $20,000. The **president** or **chief executive officer (CEO)** is responsible for managing day-to-day operations and carrying out the policies established by the board. He or she is required to report periodically to the firm's directors.

president or chief executive officer (CEO) Corporate official responsible for managing the firm's day-to-day operations and executing the policies established by the board of directors.

Figure 2.1
The General Organization of a Corporation

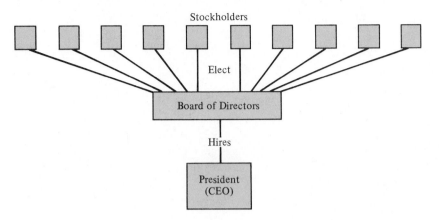

Business Taxation

Businesses, like individuals, must pay taxes on their income. The actual rates of taxation differ depending upon the form of business organization. Income can be subject to either individual or corporate income taxes. The income of sole proprietorships and partnerships is taxed as the income of the individual owners whereas corporate income is subject to corporate taxes. Regardless of their legal form, all businesses can earn either of two types of income—ordinary and capital gains. Both types of income are treated the same for tax purposes under current law. Because the corporation is financially dominant in our economy, *emphasis here is given to corporate taxation*.

Ordinary Income

The **ordinary income** of a corporation is income earned through the sale of a firm's goods or services. Ordinary income is currently taxed at the following rates:

> 15 percent on first $50,000
>
> 25 percent on next $25,000
>
> 34 percent on the amount over $75,000

Corporations with taxable income in excess of $100,000 must, in addition, increase the tax calculated from the above rate schedule by the lesser of $11,750 or 5 percent of the taxable income in excess of $100,000.

ordinary income Income earned through the sale of a firm's goods or services.

Example
Webster Manufacturing, Inc., has before-tax earnings of $250,000. The tax on these earnings can be found by taking:

$$
\begin{array}{lr}
.15 \times \$50,000 & = \$\ 7,500 \\
.25 \times\ \ 25,000 & =\ \ \ 6,250 \\
.34 \times (250,000 - 75,000) & =\ \ 59,500 \\
\text{Total} & \$73,250
\end{array}
$$

$$
\text{Plus lesser of:}\ \left[
\begin{array}{c}
\$11,750 \\
\text{or} \\
.05 \times (\$250,000 - \$100,000) \\
= .05 \times (\$150,000) = \$7,500
\end{array}
\right] =\ \ \ 7,500
$$

$$
\text{Total Taxes Due} \qquad \$80,750
$$

The firm's total taxes on its before-tax earnings are therefore $80,750. If the firm had earned only $20,000 before taxes, its total tax liability would have been .15 × $20,000, or $3,000.

Average Tax Rates

The *average tax rate* paid on the firm's ordinary income can be calculated by dividing its taxes by its taxable income. The average tax rate ranges from 15 to 34 percent, reaching 34 percent when taxable income equals or exceeds $335,000. The average tax rate paid by Webster Manufacturing, Inc., in our preceding example was 32.3 percent ($80,750 ÷ $250,000). Table 2.2 presents the firm's tax liability and average tax rate for various levels of pretax income; as income increases, the rate approaches and finally reaches 34 percent.

Marginal Tax Rates

marginal tax rate The rate at which additional income is taxed.

The **marginal tax rate** represents the rate at which additional income is taxed. In the current corporate tax structure, the marginal tax rate on income up to $50,000 is 15 percent; from $50,000 to $75,000 it is 25 percent; from $75,000 to $100,000 it is 34 percent; for income between $100,000 and $335,000 it is 39 percent (34 percent plus the 5 percent adjustment); and for income in excess of $335,000 it is 34 percent. To simplify calculations in the text, *a fixed 40 percent tax rate is assumed to be applicable to ordinary corporate income*.

Example

If Webster Manufacturing's earnings go up to $300,000, the marginal tax rate on the additional $50,000 of income will become 39 percent. The company will therefore have to pay additional taxes of $19,500 [(.34 × $50,000) + (.05 × $50,000)]. Total taxes on the $300,000, then, will be $100,250 ($80,750 + $19,500). To check this figure using the ordinary tax rates illustrated above, we would take: 15 percent of $50,000 plus 25 percent of $25,000 plus 34 percent of $225,000 (that is, $300,000 − $75,000) plus the lesser of (1) .05 × ($300,000 − $100,000) = $10,000 or (2) $11,750. This results in a total tax liability of $100,250 ($90,250 + $10,000)—the same value obtained by applying the marginal tax rate to the added income and adjusting the known tax liability.

A SCOOP OF THE ACTION

"I scream, you scream, we all scream for ice cream," as the saying goes, and lately a lot of people have been screaming for the "all-natural" gourmet ice cream made by Ben & Jerry's Homemade Inc. of Vermont. Indeed, so many people have been screaming for it that the company has had trouble keeping up with the demand. "We can't make enough," laments president Ben Cohen, who saw sales zoom to $1.8 million in 1983, double those of the year before. "We've had to turn down some orders from distributors in New York and Washington, D.C."

Finally, Cohen and co-founder, Jerry Greenfield, faced up to the fact that they had outgrown the 600,000-gallon-per-year capacity of their tiny plant. They definitely needed a bigger facility. But where would they get the money to pay for it?

As it happened, they didn't feel comfortable raising the money just anywhere. They felt a certain loyalty to the state in which they had launched Ben &

Jerry's back in 1977 with $8,000 of hard-earned savings. "Our product is very much identified with Vermont," says Cohen. "So I wanted to find a way for Vermonters to benefit from our growth. They're the ones who are most responsible for our success."

By "Vermonters," moreover, Cohen did not mean a few well-heeled vacationers from New York and Boston. Quite the contrary. "We're very community-oriented," he says, "and I wanted to give typical Vermonters a chance to participate." So Cohen and his attorney approached the local offices of several regional and national underwriters to discuss the prospect of a $600,000 public equity offering for Vermont residents only. While some of the underwriters seemed intrigued, "nobody wanted to do an intrastate offering," reports Cohen. "Nor were they willing to do anything that small."

But Cohen didn't give up. Rather, he went ahead and registered the offering—17.5 percent of the company's

common stock—with Vermont's Division of Banking and Insurance. (As an intrastate offering, it does not fall within the purview of the Securities and Exchange Commission.) The underwriter was none other than Ben & Jerry's Homemade Inc.

"Get a Scoop of the Action," read the announcements that ran in Vermont newspapers. The ads invited "bona fide" state residents to participate in Ben & Jerry's growth by purchasing the 73,500 shares being offered. Interested residents could request a copy of the prospectus by calling a toll-free number. The minimum investment was $126 for 12 shares.

Cohen hoped to raise the $600,000 in a month's time. It's an original way to make a stock offering, but it could sweeten the lives of the Vermonters who believed in Ben and Jerry when they first began to crank the ice-cream maker.

SOURCE: Adapted from Bruce G. Posner, "A Scoop of the Action," *Inc.*, July 1984, p. 123.

Table 2.2
Pretax Income, Tax Liabilities, and
Average Tax Rates

Pretax income (1)	Tax liability (2)	Average tax rate [(2) ÷ (1)] (3)
$ 50,000	$ 7,500	15.00%
75,000	13,750	18.33
100,000	22,250	22.25
200,000	61,250	30.63
335,000	113,900	34.00
500,000	170,000	34.00
1,000,000	340,000	34.00
2,500,000	850,000	34.00

Tax-Deductible Expenses

In calculating their taxes, corporations are allowed to deduct operating expenses, such as advertising expense, sales commissions, and bad debts as well as interest expense. The tax-deductibility of these expenses reduces their after-tax cost, making them less costly than they might at first appear. The following example illustrates the benefit of tax-deductibility.

Example

Companies X and Y each expect to have earnings before interest and taxes of $200,000 in the coming year. Company X during the year will have to pay $30,000 in interest, while Company Y has no debt and therefore will have no interest expense. Calculation of the earnings after taxes for these two firms, which pay a 40 percent tax on ordinary income, are shown below.

	Company X	Company Y
Earnings before interest and taxes	$200,000	$200,000
Less: Interest expense	30,000	0
Earnings before taxes	$170,000	$200,000
Less: Taxes (40%)	68,000	80,000
Earnings after taxes	$102,000	$120,000
Difference in earnings after taxes	$18,000	

The data demonstrate that while Company X had $30,000 more interest expense than Company Y, Company X's earnings after taxes are only $18,000 less than those of Company Y ($102,000 for Company X versus $120,000 for Company Y).

The tax-deductibility of certain expenses can be seen to reduce their actual (after-tax) cost to the profitable firm. Note that *interest is a tax-deductible expense, whereas dividends are not*. Because dividends are not tax-deductible, their after-tax cost is equal to the amount of the dividend. Thus a $30,000 cash dividend would have an after-tax cost of $30,000.

Capital Gains[1]

capital gain The amount by which the price at which an asset was sold exceeds the asset's purchase price.

If a firm sells a capital asset such as stock held as an investment for more than its initial purchase price, the difference between the sale price and the purchase price is called a **capital gain.** For corporations, capital gains are added to ordinary corporate income and taxed at the regular corporate rates, with a maximum marginal tax rate of 39 percent. To simplify the computations presented in later chapters of the text, like for ordinary income, *a 40 percent tax rate is assumed to be applicable to corporate capital gains.*

---

[1] To simplify the discussion, only capital assets are considered here. The full tax treatment of gains and losses on depreciable assets is presented as part of the discussion of capital-budgeting cash flows in Chapter 9.

> **Example**
> The Ross Company has operating earnings of $500,000 and has just sold for $40,000 a capital asset initially purchased two years ago for $36,000. Since the asset was sold for greater than its initial purchase price, there is a capital gain of $4,000 ($40,000 sale price − $36,000 initial purchase price). The corporation's taxable income will total $504,000 ($500,000 ordinary income plus $4,000 capital gain). Since this total is above $335,000, the capital gain will be taxed at the 34 percent rate, resulting in a tax of $1,360 (.34 × $4,000).

---

2 For corporations, both ordinary and capital gains income are treated the same for tax purposes under current law. *(Fact)*   **FACT OR FABLE?**

S Corporations

Subchapter S of the Internal Revenue Code permits corporations with 35 or fewer stockholders to be taxed like partnerships. That is, income is normally taxed as direct personal income of the shareholders, regardless of whether it is actually distributed to them. The **S corporation** is a tax-reporting entity rather than a tax-paying entity. The key advantage of this form of organization is that the shareholders receive all the organizational benefits of a corporation while escaping the double taxation normally associated with the distribution of corporate earnings. (**Double taxation** results when the already once-taxed earnings of a corporation are distributed as cash dividends to stockholders, who must pay taxes on these dividends.) S corporations do not receive other tax advantages accorded regular corporations.

S corporation A tax-reporting entity whose earnings are taxed not as a corporation but as the incomes of its shareholders, thus avoiding the usual double taxation on corporate earnings.

double taxation Occurs when the already once-taxed earnings of a corporation are distributed as dividends to the firm's stockholders, who are then taxed again on these dividends.

Tax Payment Dates

Corporations that expect to have an annual tax liability of $40 or more are required to make estimated tax payments. These payments are commonly made in four installments, each covering 25 percent of the estimated liability. Estimated tax payments for the calendar year are made on April 15, June 15, September 15, and December 15. Any additional tax payments or refunds resulting from an under- or overpayment of estimated taxes must be settled by March 15 of the following year. Certain penalties may be levied on corporations that significantly underestimate tax liability.

Financial Institutions and Markets: An Overview

Available funds can be transmitted to firms that require funds in three external ways. One is through a *financial institution* that accepts savings and transfers them to those needing funds. Another is through *financial markets,* organized forums where the suppliers and demanders of various types of funds can make transactions. A third is through private placement. Because of the unstructured nature of private placements, in this section we focus primarily on financial institutions and financial markets. However, private placement of funds is not unusual—especially in the case of debt instruments and preferred stock.

Financial Institutions

financial institution An intermediary that channels the savings of individuals, businesses, and governments into loans or investments.

Financial institutions are intermediaries that channel the savings of individuals, businesses, and governments into loans or investments. Many financial institutions directly or indirectly pay savers interest on deposited funds; others provide services for which they charge depositors (for example, the service charges levied on checking accounts). Some financial institutions accept savings and lend this money to their customers; others invest customers' savings in earning assets such as real estate or stocks and bonds; and still others both lend money and invest savings. Financial institutions are required by the government to operate within established regulatory guidelines.

Key Participants in Financial Transactions

The key suppliers and demanders of funds are individuals, businesses, and governments. The savings of individual consumers placed in certain financial institutions provide these institutions with a large portion of their funds. Individuals act not only as suppliers of funds to financial institutions but also demand funds from them in the form of loans. However, the important point here is that individuals as a group are the *net suppliers* for financial institutions: They save more money than they borrow.

Business firms also deposit some of their funds in financial institutions, primarily in checking accounts with various commercial banks. And firms, like individuals, also borrow funds from these institutions. As a group business firms, unlike individuals, are *net demanders* of funds: They borrow more money than they save.

Governments maintain deposits of temporarily idle funds, certain tax payments, and social security payments in commercial banks. They do not borrow funds directly from financial institutions, although by selling their securities to various institutions governments indirectly borrow from them. The government, like business firms, is typically a *net demander* of money: It borrows more than it saves.

Major Financial Institutions

The major financial institutions in the U.S. economy are commercial banks, mutual savings banks, savings and loans, credit unions, life insurance companies, pension funds, and mutual funds. These institutions attract funds from individuals, businesses, and governments, combine them, and perform certain services to make attractive loans available to individuals and businesses. They may also make some of these funds available to fulfill various government demands. Table 2.3 provides brief descriptions of the major financial institutions.

FACT OR FABLE?   **3** Financial institutions are intermediaries that channel the savings of individuals, businesses, and governments into loans or investments. *(Fact)*

Table 2.3
Major Financial Institutions

Institution	Description
Commercial bank	Accepts both demand (checking) and time (savings) deposits and also offers negotiable order of withdrawal (NOW) accounts, which are interest-earning savings accounts against which checks can be written. In addition, currently offers money market deposit accounts, which pay interest at rates competitive with other short-term investment vehicles. Makes loans directly to borrowers or through the financial markets.
Mutual savings bank	Similar to commercial banks except that it may not hold demand (checking) deposits. Obtains funds from savings, NOW, and money market deposit accounts. Generally lends or invests funds through financial markets, although some residential real estate loans are made to individuals. Located primarily in New York, New Jersey, and the New England states.
Savings and loan	Similar to mutual savings banks in that it holds savings deposits, NOW accounts, and money market deposit accounts. Also raises capital through the sale of securities in the financial markets. Lends funds primarily to individuals and businesses for real estate mortgage loans. Some funds are channeled into investments in the financial markets.
Credit union	A financial intermediary that deals primarily in transfer of funds between consumers. Membership is generally based on some common bond, such as working for a given employer. Accepts members' savings deposits, NOW account deposits, and money market deposit accounts and lends the majority of these funds to other members, typically to finance automobile or appliance purchases or home improvements.
Life insurance company	The largest type of financial intermediary handling individual savings. Receives premium payments that are placed in loans or investments to accumulate funds to cover future benefit payments. Funds are lent to individuals, businesses, and governments or channeled through the financial markets to those who demand them.
Pension fund	Set up so that employees of various corporations or government units can receive income after retirement. Often employers match the contributions of their employees. Money is sometimes transferred directly to borrowers, but the majority is lent or invested via the financial markets.
Mutual fund	A type of financial intermediary that pools funds of savers and makes them available to business and government demanders. Obtains funds through sale of shares and uses proceeds to acquire bonds and stocks issued by various business and governmental units. Creates a diversified and professionally managed portfolio of securities to achieve a specified investment objective, such as liquidity with a high return. Hundreds of funds, with a variety of investment objectives, exist. Money market mutual funds, which provide competitive returns with very high liquidity, are currently popular.

Changing Role of Financial Institutions

Passage of the **Depository Institutions Deregulation and Monetary Control Act of 1980 (DIDMCA)** signaled the beginning of the ''financial services revolution'' that continues to change the nature of financial institutions. By eliminating interest-rate ceilings on all accounts and permitting certain institutions to offer new types of accounts and services, the DIDMCA intensified competition and blurred traditional distinctions among these institutions. What is evolving is the **financial supermarket,** at which a customer can obtain a full array of financial services, such as checking, deposits, brokerage, insurance, and estate planning. The emergence of the financial supermarket is evidenced, for instance, by Sears, Roebuck and Company's ''Sears Financial Network.'' In addition to its credit and insurance (Allstate) and home mortgage (Sears Mortgage) operations, Sears now owns a national real estate brokerage firm (Coldwell Banker), a major stock brokerage firm (Dean Witter), and a West Coast savings and loan (Allstate Savings and Loan). It offers all these financial services in a growing number of ''financial network'' offices housed within its retail stores.

Financial Markets

Financial markets provide a forum in which suppliers of funds and demanders of loans and investments can transact business directly. Whereas the loans and investments of institutions are made without the direct knowledge of the suppliers of funds (savers), suppliers in the financial markets know where their funds are being lent or invested. The two key financial markets are the *money market* and the *capital market.* Transactions in short-term debt instruments, or marketable securities, take place in the money market. Long-term securities (bonds and stocks) are traded in the capital market.

All securities, whether in the money or capital markets, are initially issued in the **primary market.** This is the only market in which the corporate or government issuer is directly involved in the transaction and receives direct benefit from the issue—that is, the company actually receives the proceeds from the sale of securities. Once the securities begin to trade among individual, business, government, or financial institution savers and investors, they become part of the **secondary market.** The primary market is where ''new'' securities are sold; the secondary market can be viewed as a ''used'' or ''preowned'' securities market.

The Relationship Between Institutions and Markets

Financial institutions actively participate in the money market and the capital market as both suppliers and demanders of funds. Figure 2.2 depicts the general flow of funds through and between financial institutions and markets; private placement transactions are also shown. The individuals, businesses, and governments that supply and demand funds may be domestic or foreign. In some instances there may be legal constraints on the operations of certain institutions in the financial marketplace. We end this section with a brief description of the money market. The next major section of the chapter is devoted to discussion of the capital market because of its key importance to the firm.

The Money Market

The **money market** is created by a financial relationship between suppliers and demanders of *short-term funds,* which have maturities of one year or less. The money market is

Figure 2.2
Flow of Funds for Financial Institutions and Markets

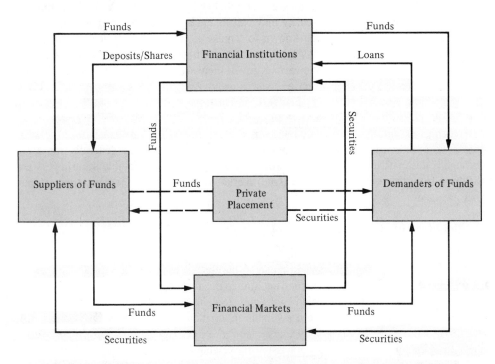

not an actual organization housed in some central location, such as a stock market, although the majority of money market transactions culminate in New York City. Most money market transactions are made in **marketable securities,** which are short-term debt instruments, such as U.S. Treasury bills, commercial paper, and negotiable certificates of deposit issued by government, business, and financial institutions, respectively. (Marketable securities are described in Chapter 14.)

The money market exists because certain individuals, businesses, governments, and financial institutions have temporarily idle funds that they wish to place in some type of liquid asset or short-term, interest-earning instrument. At the same time, other individuals, businesses, governments, and financial institutions find themselves in need of seasonal or temporary financing. The money market thus brings together these suppliers and demanders of short-term liquid funds.

The Operation of the Money Market

How are suppliers and demanders of short-term funds brought together in the money market? Typically, they are matched through the facilities of large New York banks, through government securities dealers, or through the Federal Reserve banks. The Federal Reserve banks become involved only in loans from one commercial bank to another; these loans are referred to as transactions in **federal funds.** A number of stock brokerage firms purchase various money market instruments for resale to customers. If a brokerage firm does not have an instrument that a customer has demanded, it will attempt to acquire it. In addition, financial institutions such as banks and mutual funds purchase money market

marketable securities
Short-term debt instruments, such as U.S. Treasury bills, commercial paper, and negotiable certificates of deposit issued by government, business, and financial institutions.

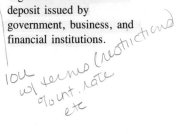

federal funds Loan transactions between commercial banks in which the Federal Reserve banks become involved.

instruments for their portfolios to provide attractive returns on their customers' deposits and share purchases.

Most money market transactions are negotiated by telephone. A firm wishing to purchase a certain marketable security may call its bank, which will then attempt to buy the security by contacting a bank known to "make a market" or to deal in the given security. The bank or the firm may also go directly to a **government security dealer,** an institution that purchases for resale various government securities and other money market instruments. Regardless of whether a business or government is *issuing* a money market instrument (demanding short-term funds) or *purchasing* a money market instrument (supplying short-term funds), one party must go directly to another party or use a middleperson, such as a commercial bank, government security dealer, or brokerage firm, to make a transaction. Individuals wishing to purchase marketable securities generally must go through a dealer firm. The secondary (or resale) market for marketable securities is no different from the primary (or initial issue) market with respect to the basic transactions that are made.

government security dealer
An institution that purchases for resale government securities and other money market instruments.

Participants in the Money Market

The key participants in the money market are individuals, businesses, governments, and financial institutions. Individuals participate as purchasers and as sellers of money market instruments. Their purchases are somewhat limited due to the large denominations traded—typically $100,000 or more. Certain banks and stock brokerage firms will "break down" marketable securities to make them available in smaller denominations. Individuals sell marketable securities in the money market not as issuers but to liquidate the securities prior to maturity. Individuals do not issue marketable securities.

Business firms, governments, and financial institutions both buy and sell marketable securities. They may be the primary issuers, or they may sell securities they have purchased and wish to liquidate prior to maturity. They therefore may act as primary or secondary sellers of these securities. Of course, each of these parties can issue only certain money market instruments; a business firm, for example, cannot issue a U.S. Treasury bill. Some financial institutions purchase marketable securities specifically for resale, whereas others purchase them as short-term investments. Businesses and governments purchase marketable securities solely to earn a return on temporarily idle funds.

FACT OR FABLE?   [4] The money market is an organized exchange on which suppliers and demanders of long-term funds make marketable security transactions. *(Fable)*
The money market is created by a financial relationship between suppliers and demanders of *short-term funds,* which have maturities of one year or less. Most transactions are made in marketable securities.

The Capital Market

The **capital market** is a financial relationship created by a number of institutions and arrangements that allows the suppliers and demanders of *long-term funds*—funds with maturities of more than one year—to make transactions. Included among long-term funds are securities issues of business and government. The backbone of the capital market is formed by the various securities exchanges that provide a forum for debt and equity transactions. The smooth functioning of the capital market, which is enhanced through the activities of *investment bankers,* is important to the long-run growth of business.

Key Securities

Major securities traded in the capital market include bonds (long-term debt) and both common and preferred stock (equity, or ownership). **Bonds** are long-term debt instruments used by business and government to raise large sums of money, generally from a diverse group of lenders. *Corporate bonds* typically pay interest *semiannually* (every six months) at a stated *coupon interest rate,* have an initial *maturity* of from 10 to 30 years, and have a *par,* or *face, value* of $1,000 that must be repaid at maturity. Bonds are described in detail in Chapter 16.

Example
Cato Industries has just issued a 12 percent coupon interest rate, 20-year bond with a $1,000 par value that pays interest semiannually. Investors who buy this bond receive the contractual right to (1) $120 annual interest (12 percent coupon interest rate × $1,000 par value) distributed as $60 at the end of each six months (½ × $120) for 20 years and (2) the $1,000 par value at the end of year 20.

Shares of **common stock** are units of ownership interest, or equity, in a corporation. Common stockholders expect to earn a return by receiving **dividends**—periodic distributions of earnings—or by realizing gains through increases in share price. **Preferred stock** is a special form of ownership that has features of both a bond and common stock. Preferred stockholders are promised a fixed periodic dividend that must be paid prior to payment of any dividends to the owners of common stock. In other words, preferred stock has "preference" over common stock. Common and preferred stock are described in detail in Chapters 17 and 18, respectively.

The Functions of Securities Exchanges

Capital markets permit the segments of the economy that need capital for plant and equipment to obtain funds from the savers in the economy. Thus, they enable the stock of capital goods in the economy to grow. Just as financial institutions collect savings from numerous parties and lend them to acceptable borrowers, so the capital markets permit the conversion of savings into investment, through loans or through the sale of ownership interests. The securities exchanges that make up the capital markets perform a number of important functions.

Creating a Continuous Market

The key function of securities exchanges is to create a continuous market for securities at a price that is not very different from the price at which they were previously sold. The continuity of securities markets provides the *liquidity* necessary to attract investors' funds. Without exchanges, investors might have to hold debt securities to maturity and equity securities indefinitely. It is doubtful that many people would be willing to invest under

capital market A financial relationship created by institutions and arrangements that allows suppliers and demanders of *long-term funds* to make transactions.

bond Long-term debt instrument used by businesses and government to raise large sums of money, generally from a diverse group of lenders.

common stock Collectively, units of ownership interest, or equity, in a corporation.

dividends Periodic distributions of earnings to the owners of stock in a firm.

preferred stock A special form of stock having a fixed periodic dividend that must be paid prior to payment of any common stock dividends.

such conditions. A continuous market also reduces the volatility of security prices, further enhancing their liquidity.

Allocating Scarce Capital

efficient market A market that allocates funds to the most productive uses.

The securities exchanges help allocate scarce funds to the best uses. That is, by disclosing the price behavior of securities and requiring the disclosure of certain corporate financial data, they allow investors to assess the securities' risk and return and to move their funds into the most promising investments. An **efficient market** is one that allocates funds to the most productive uses. The idea behind an efficient market is that the market price of securities always fully reflects available information and therefore is equal to the securities' value. This is especially true for securities that are actively traded on major exchanges, since the competition among profit-seeking investors tends to hold prices close to their correct level. Greater attention is given to this concept and its ramifications in Chapter 7.

Determining and Publicizing Security Prices

Securities exchanges both determine and publicize security prices. The price of an individual security is determined by what is bought and sold, or the demand and supply for the security. Figure 2.3 depicts the interaction of the forces of demand (represented by line D_0) and supply (represented by line S) for a given security currently selling at an equilibrium price P_0. At that price, Q_0 shares of the stock are traded.

A capital market brings together buyers and sellers from all geographic areas while affording them some anonymity. This trading forum helps to ensure an efficient market in which the price reflects the true value of the security. Changing evaluations of a firm, of course, cause changes in the demand for and supply of its securities and ultimately result in a new price for the securities. Suppose, for example, a favorable discovery by the firm

Figure 2.3
Supply and Demand for a Security

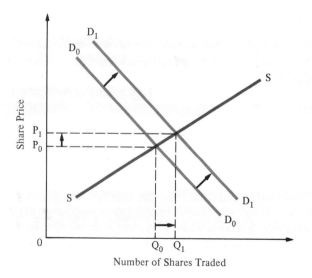

CAREERS IN FINANCE

MANAGER OF INVESTOR RELATIONS:
Marketing the Company's Financial Strengths

During her 8:00 A.M. drive to work at the home office of a major corporation, Janet reviews her schedule for the day. As manager of investor relations, her job is to gather information about her company and present it in the most favorable way to the entire investment community—from investment banking firms to individual stockholders. Her days are usually busy, but this one promises to be a whirlwind.

By 9:00 o'clock she will have quarterly sales projections for each subsidiary. At 10:00 four representatives from an investment banking firm will arrive for a briefing from the vice-president of finance. Janet has made all the arrangements for this meeting, which will last until 3:00 P.M. During that time, Janet and the CFO to whom she reports will explain to the investment bankers why and how the corporation wants to raise additional capital. The investment bankers then will return at a later date to discuss the possibility of handling the securities offering for the corporation.

By 4:30 Janet needs to be at the airport to pick up two pension fund managers. Janet wants them to know as much as possible about her corporation so that they will continue to view its stock as an attractive purchase candidate. It will, of course, be necessary to take these two people to dinner and then drive them to their hotel. This is just one of about 15 one-on-one meetings Janet has each month. Janet expects to cross her threshold about 10:30 tonight.

When asked about her 14-hour days, Janet makes light of them. "It happens only once or twice a week, and anyway," she says, "I enjoy it. What could be better than a job that keeps me continually busy and even gives me something of a social life?"

The main thrust of Janet's job is to make her company look good, especially to its investors or potential investors. To do so, she must understand accounting statements and interpret them for investors. She also has to keep up with external factors such as government regulations, tax laws, actions of

the Federal Reserve Board, the money and capital markets, and the competition. All these can affect the financial health of the corporation, and Janet and her staff communicate this information to investors. "We try to market our company so investors know the benefits of buying and holding our stock."

Many of these communications are written. Some go to stockholders, in the form of annual reports, quarterly reports, even individual letters. Other reports go regularly to the investment community—securities firms, analysts, pension fund managers—and require more detail and a more technical explanation.

Janet earns a little over $45,000 a year now and has access to the decision makers of the company. "If I can grow in this job and help put our company at the top, I'll be satisfied. Whatever I do, I want to stay somewhere where I can use my analytical and communications skills."

---

shown in Figure 2.3 is announced and investors in the marketplace increase their valuations of the firm's shares. The changing evaluation results in a shift in demand from D_0 to D_1; Q_1 shares will be traded; and a new, higher equilibrium price of P_1 will result. The competitive market created by the major securities exchanges provides a forum in which share price is continuously adjusted to changing demand and supply. Since the prices are readily available to interested parties, they can use this information to make better purchase and sale decisions.

Aiding in New Financing

Securities exchanges also provide firms with a method of obtaining new financing. Since the markets are continuous, thereby ensuring investor liquidity, new capital can be raised through new security issues. Of course, not all firms have access to those markets to raise new capital, but the presence of securities exchanges does give certain firms direct access to the savings of individuals, other firms, and financial institutions. Without these exchanges, new capital could be obtained only through direct negotiations with holders of large amounts of money. This effort obviously would be quite tedious.

Major Securities Exchanges

securities exchanges
Provide the marketplace in which firms raise funds through the sale of new securities and in which purchasers can resell securities.

As we noted earlier, **securities exchanges** provide the marketplace in which firms can raise funds through the sale of new securities and purchasers of securities can maintain liquidity by being able to easily resell them when necessary. Many people call securities exchanges ''stock markets,'' but this label is somewhat misleading because bonds, common stock, preferred stock, and a variety of other investment vehicles are all traded on these exchanges. The two key types of securities exchange are the organized exchange and the over-the-counter exchange.

Organized Securities Exchanges

organized securities exchanges Tangible organizations on whose premises outstanding securities are resold.

Organized securities exchanges are tangible organizations on whose premises outstanding securities are resold. Organized exchanges account for over 66 percent of *total* shares traded. The dominant organized exchanges are the New York Stock Exchange (NYSE) and the American Stock Exchange (AMEX), both headquartered in New York City. There are also regional exchanges, such as the Midwest Stock Exchange (in Chicago) and the Pacific Stock Exchange (in San Francisco).

Most exchanges are modeled after the New York Stock Exchange, which accounts for over 80 percent of the shares traded on organized exchanges. To make transactions on the ''floor'' of the New York Stock Exchange an individual or firm must own a ''seat'' on the exchange. There are a total of 1,366 seats on the NYSE, most of which are owned by brokerage firms. In order to be listed for trading on an organized stock exchange, a firm must file an application for listing and meet a number of requirements.

Trading is carried out on the floor of the exchange through an *auction process*. The goal of trading is to fill *buy orders* (orders to purchase securities) at the lowest price and to fill *sell orders* (orders to sell securities) at the highest price, thereby giving both purchasers and sellers the best possible deal. The general procedure for placing and executing an order can be described by a simple example.

Example
Kathryn Blake, who has an account with Merrill Lynch Pierce Fenner & Smith, wishes to purchase 200 shares of the NCR Corporation at the prevailing market price. Kathryn calls her account executive,[2] Howard Kohn of Merrill Lynch, and places her order. Howard immediately has the order transmitted to the New York headquarters of Merrill Lynch, which immediately forwards the order to the Merrill Lynch clerk on the floor of the exchange. The clerk dispatches the order to one of the firm's seat holders, who goes to the appropriate trading post, executes the order at the best possible price, and returns to the clerk, who then wires the execution price and confirmation of the transaction back to the brokerage office. Howard is given the relevant information and passes it along to Kathryn. Howard then has certain paperwork to do.

---

[2] The title *account executive* or *financial counselor* is often used to refer to an individual who traditionally has been called a *stockbroker*. These titles are believed to add respectability to the position and change the image of the stockbroker from that of a salesperson to that of a personal financial manager who provides diversified financial services to his or her clients.

Once placed, an order can be executed in minutes, thanks to sophisticated telecommunication devices. A sale of securities would have been handled in a similar manner. Information on the daily trading of securities is reported in various media, including financial publications such as *The Wall Street Journal*.

The Over-the-Counter Exchange

The **over-the-counter (OTC) exchange** is not an organization but an intangible market for the purchasers and sellers of securities not listed by the organized exchanges. Active traders in this market are linked by a sophisticated telecommunications network. The prices at which securities are traded ''over the counter'' are determined by competitive bids and negotiation. The OTC, in addition to creating a resale market for outstanding securities, is a *primary market* in which new public issues are sold. The OTC accounts for nearly 34 percent of *total* shares traded.

over-the-counter (OTC) exchange Not an organization, but an intangible market for the purchasers and sellers of securities not listed by the organized exchanges.

FACT OR FABLE?

5 Securities exchanges—both organized and over-the-counter—act as the backbone of the capital market by providing a forum in which debt and equity transactions can be made. *(Fact)*

The Role of the Investment Banker

In order to raise money in the capital market, firms can make either private placements or public offerings. **Private placement** involves the direct sale of a new security issue, typically debt or preferred stock, to an investor or group of investors, such as an insurance company or pension fund. However, most firms raise money through a **public offering** of securities; this takes the form of a nonexclusive issue of either bonds or stock. In making a securities offering, whether public or private, most firms hire an **investment banker** to find buyers for new security issues.

The term *investment banker* is somewhat misleading, because an investment banker is neither an investor nor a banker; furthermore, he or she neither makes long-term investments nor guards the savings of others. Instead, acting as a *broker* between the issuer and the buyer of new security issues, the investment banker purchases securities from corporations and governments and sells them to the public. Investment bankers, in addition to bearing the risk of selling a security issue, advise clients. In the United States, for example, Salomon Brothers and Merrill Lynch Capital Markets are two of the largest investment banking firms. (Detailed discussion of the functions, organization, and cost of investment banking is included in Chapter 16.)

private placement The direct sale of a new security issue, typically debt or preferred stock, to a selected investor or group of investors.

public offering A nonexclusive issue to the general public of either bonds or stock by a firm in order to raise funds.

investment banker An individual engaged by a firm to solicit buyers for new security issues.

Interest Rates and Required Returns

Financial institutions and markets create the mechanism through which funds flow between savers (funds suppliers) and investors (funds demanders). The level of funds flow between suppliers and demanders can significantly affect economic growth. Growth results from the interaction of a variety of economic factors, such as the money supply, trade balances, and economic policies, that are part of the cost of money—the interest rate or required return. The level of this rate acts as a regulating device that controls the flow of funds between suppliers and demanders. In general, the lower the interest rate, the greater the funds flow and therefore the greater the economic growth, and vice versa. Interest rates and required returns are key variables influencing the actions of the financial manager.

Interest Rate Fundamentals

The interest rate or required return represents the cost of money. It is the rent or level of compensation a demander of funds must pay a supplier. When funds are lent, the cost of borrowing the funds is the **interest rate.** When funds are invested to obtain an ownership, or equity interest—as in stock purchases—the cost to the demander is commonly called the **required return,** which reflects the level of expected return. In both cases the supplier is compensated for providing either debt or equity funds. Ignoring risk factors, the nominal or actual interest rate (cost of funds) results from the real rate of interest adjusted for inflationary expectations and **liquidity preferences**—general preferences of investors for shorter-term securities.

interest rate The compensation paid by a borrower of funds to the lender; from the borrower's point of view, the cost of borrowing funds.

required return The level of return expected on an investment.

liquidity preferences General preferences of investors for shorter-term securities.

real rate of interest That rate that creates an equilibrium between the supply of savings and the demand for investment funds in a perfect world, without inflation, where funds suppliers and demanders have no liquidity preference, and all outcomes are certain.

nominal rate of interest The actual rate of interest charged by the supplier of funds and paid by the demander.

The Real Rate of Interest

In a perfect world in which there is no inflation and where funds suppliers and demanders are indifferent to the term of loans or investments because they have no liquidity preference and all outcomes are certain,[3] there would be one cost of money—the **real rate of interest.** The real rate of interest creates an equilibrium between the supply of savings and the demand for investment funds. The real rate of interest in the United States is assumed to be stable and equal to around 2 percent.[4] This supply-demand relationship is shown in Figure 2.4 by the supply function (labeled S_0) and the demand function (labeled D). An equilibrium between the supply of funds and the demand for funds ($S_0 = D$) occurs at a rate of interest k_0^*, the real rate of interest.

Clearly, the real rate of interest changes with changing economic conditions, tastes, and preferences. A favorable international trade balance could result in an increased supply of funds, causing the supply function in Figure 2.4 to shift to, say, S_1. This could result in a lower real rate of interest, k_1^*, at equilibrium ($S_1 = D$). Likewise, a change in tax laws or other factors could affect the demand for funds, causing the real rate of interest to rise or fall to a new equilibrium level.

Nominal or Actual Rate of Interest (Return)

The **nominal rate of interest** is the actual rate of interest charged by the supplier and paid by the demander. It differs from the real rate of interest, k^*, as a result of two factors:

---

[3] These assumptions are made in order to describe the most basic interest rate, the real rate of interest. Subsequent discussions relax these assumptions in order to develop the broader concept of the interest rate and required return.

[4] The assumed 2 percent value for the real rate of interest is drawn from the findings of Roger G. Ibbotson and Rex A. Sinquefield, ''Stocks, Bonds, Bills and Inflation: Update,'' *Financial Analysts Journal,* July-August 1979, adjusted for more recent observations. They found that over the period 1926–1978, U.S. Treasury bills provided an average annual real rate of return of about 0 percent, while during the period 1952–1978, the real rate of return was about .5 percent. Because prior to 1951 T-bill rates were intentionally pegged artificially low, the post-1951 real rate of return of .5 percent is believed to be more accurate. In view of the post-1973 economy, many economists believe the real rate to be around 2 percent.

Figure 2.4
Supply of Savings and Demand for Investment Funds

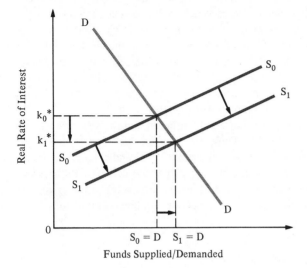

(1) inflationary expectations *(IE)* and (2) issuer and issue characteristics *(IC)*, such as default risk and contractual provisions. Using this notation, the nominal rate of interest for security 1, k_1, is given in Equation 2.1:

$$k_1 = \underbrace{k^* + IE}_{\substack{\text{risk-free} \\ \text{rate, } R_F}} + \underbrace{IC_1}_{\substack{\text{risk} \\ \text{premium}}}$$ (2.1)

As the horizontal braces in the equation indicate, the nominal rate, k_1, can be viewed as having two basic components: a risk-free rate of interest, R_F, plus a risk premium, IC_1:

$$k_1 = R_F + IC_1$$ (2.2)

To simplify the discussion, we will assume that the risk premium, IC_1, is equal to zero. We can therefore rewrite Equation 2.1[5] as

$$R_F = k^* + IE$$ (2.3)

Thus we concern ourselves only with the **risk-free rate of interest, R_F,** which is defined as the required return on a risk-free asset.[6] The risk-free rate (as shown in Equation 2.3) embodies the real rate of interest plus the inflationary expectation. Three-month **U.S. Treasury bills (T-bills),** which are short-term IOUs issued by the U.S. Treasury, are commonly considered the risk-free asset.

The premium for *inflationary expectations* represents the average rate of *inflation* (price-level change) expected over the life of the loan or investment. It is *not* the rate of

risk-free rate of interest, R_F The required return on a risk-free asset, typically a three-month U.S. Treasury bill.

U.S. Treasury bills (T-bills) Short-term IOUs issued by the U.S. Treasury; considered the risk-free asset.

[5] This equation is commonly called the *Fisher equation,* named for the renowned economist Irving Fisher, who first presented this approximate relationship between nominal interest and the rate of inflation. See Irving Fisher, *The Theory of Interest* (New York: Macmillan, 1930.)

[6] In a later part of this discussion, the risk premium and its effect on the nominal rate of interest will be discussed and illustrated.

inflation experienced over the immediate past; rather, it reflects the forecasted rate. Take, for example, the risk-free asset: During the week ended August 30, 1985, three-month Treasury bills earned a 7.10 percent rate of return. Assuming an approximate 2 percent real rate of interest, funds suppliers were forecasting a 5.10 percent (annual) rate of inflation (7.10% − 2.00%) over the following three months. This expectation was in striking contrast to the expected rate of inflation four years earlier in the week ended May 22, 1981. At that time, the three-month T-bill rate was 16.60 percent, which meant an expected (annual) inflation rate of 14.60 percent (16.60% − 2.00%). The inflationary expectation premium changes over time in response to many factors, including recent inflation rates, government policies, and international events.

Figure 2.5 illustrates the movement of the rate of inflation and the risk-free rate of interest during the 20-year period 1966–1986. During this period, the two rates tended to move in a similar fashion. Between the Arab oil embargo of 1973 and early 1980, inflation and interest rates were quite high, peaking at over 13 percent in 1980–1981. Since 1981 these rates have declined to levels comparable to those existing prior to the oil embargo. The data clearly illustrate the significant impact of inflation on the nominal rate of interest for the risk-free asset.

Term Structure of Interest Rates

Thus far we have concerned ourselves solely with the risk-free asset, represented by a three-month Treasury bill. In fact, all Treasury securities are *riskless* in terms of the chance that the Treasury will default on the issue by failing to make scheduled interest and

Figure 2.5
Relationship Between Annual Rate of Inflation and Three-Month U.S. Treasury Bill Average Yields

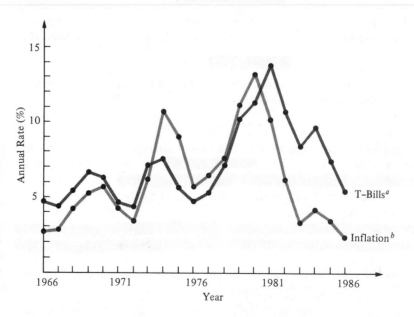

[a]Average annual rate of return on three-month U.S. Treasury bills.
[b]Annual percentage change in the consumer price index.

principal payments. Since it is believed to be easier to forecast inflation over shorter periods of time, the shorter-term three-month Treasury bill is considered the risk-free asset. Of course, differing inflation expectations associated with different maturities will cause nominal interest rates to vary, depending on the maturity of the security. Adding a maturity subscript, t, to it, Equation 2.3 can be rewritten as

$$R_{F_t} = k^* + IE_t \qquad (2.4)$$

In other words, for U.S. Treasury securities, the nominal, or risk-free, rate for a given maturity varies with the inflation expectation over the term of the security.

Example

The nominal interest rate, R_{F_t}, for four maturities of U.S. Treasury securities on August 30, 1985, is given in column 1 of the table below. Assuming the real rate of interest is 2 percent, as noted in column 2, the inflation expectation for each maturity is found in column 3 by solving Equation 2.4 for IE_t. It can be seen that while a 5.10 percent rate of inflation was expected over the three-month period beginning August 30, 1985, a 5.97 percent average rate of inflation was expected over the one-year period, and so on. An analysis of the inflation expectations in column 3 for August 30, 1985, suggests that at that time, a general expectation of increasing inflation existed.

Maturity, t	Nominal interest rate, R_{F_t} (1)	Real interest rate, k^* (2)	Inflation expectation, IE_t [(1) − (2)] (3)
3 months	7.10%	2.00%	5.10%
1 year	7.97	2.00	5.97
5 years	9.66	2.00	7.66
30 years	10.42	2.00	8.42

For any class of similar-risk securities, the **term structure of interest rates** relates the interest rate or rate of return to the time to maturity. For convenience we will continue to use Treasury securities as a class, but other classes could include securities that have similar overall quality or risk ratings such as Aaa utility bonds, Ba corporate bonds, and so on, as determined by independent agencies like Moody's and Standard & Poor's. The riskless nature of Treasury securities also provides a laboratory in which to develop the term structure. At any point in time the relationship between the rate of return or **yield to maturity**—the annual rate of interest earned on a security purchased on a given day and held to maturity—and the remaining time to maturity can be represented by the **yield curve.** In other words, the yield curve is a graphic depiction of the term structure of interest rates. Figure 2.6 shows two yield curves for all U.S. Treasury securities—one at May 22, 1981, and the other at August 30, 1985.

The yield curve reflects (1) the general supply-demand conditions for money, embodied in the real rate of interest, (2) the general preference of funds suppliers toward more liquid short-term securities, and (3) the general expectations of investors as to future interest rates. Interest rate expectations embody inflation expectations and reflect the fact that while short-term rates capture current behavior, long-term rates capture the level of expected future short-term interest rates. In Figure 2.6, it can be seen that on May 22,

term structure of interest rates The relationship between the interest rate or rate of return and the time to maturity.

yield to maturity Annual rate of interest earned on a security purchased on a given day and held to maturity.

yield curve A graph that shows the relationship between the yield to maturity of a security (y-axis) and the time to maturity (x-axis).

Figure 2.6
Yield Curves for U.S. Treasury Securities, May 22, 1981, and August 30, 1985

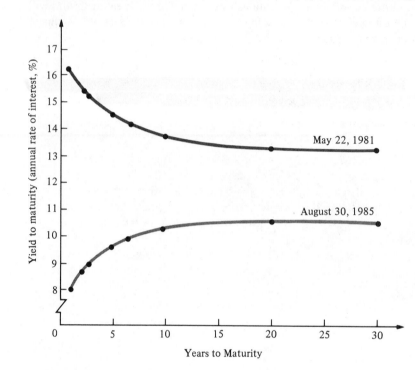

SOURCE: Data from *Federal Reserve Bulletin*, June 1981, p. A25, and December 1985, p. A24.

1981, the yield curve was *downward-sloping,* reflecting expected lower future interest rates. On August 30, 1985, the yield curve was *upward-sloping,* reflecting the expectation of higher future rates. Occasionally the yield curve is *flat,* indicating a stable expectation. The downward-sloping yield curve of May 1981 reflects an expectation of lower inflation and interest rates in the future. Figure 2.5 shows that in 1981 the inflation rate was over 10 percent, and the general expectation was for an economic recovery with reduced inflation. In August 1985, the upward-sloping yield curve reflected a slightly increasing rate of inflation from the less than 4 percent rate at that time. With the then-looming record budget deficit, the rate of inflation and interest rates were expected to rise.[7]

FACT OR FABLE?   6 An upward-sloping yield curve reflects an expectation of lower inflation and interest rates in the future. *(Fable)*
An upward-sloping yield curve reflects an expectation of *higher* inflation and interest rates in the future.

---

[7] It is interesting to note that the expectations reflected by the August 30, 1985, yield curve were not borne out by actual events. By November 1986 interest rates had declined to 5.31 percent for 3-month, 5.77 percent for 1-year, 6.66 percent for 5-year, and 7.42 percent for 30-year U.S. Treasury securities. The yield curve at that time had shifted downward although it still was generally upward-sloping, reflecting a continuing expectation of higher future interest rates.

FINANCE IN ACTION

THE FINANCIAL MANAGEMENT ASSOCIATION (FMA)

The Financial Management Association was established in 1970 in order to develop a continuing relationship between successful financial practitioners and leading academicians and to encourage the free exchange of ideas, techniques, and advances in the field of financial management and business finance. . . .

Financial Management

The quarterly journal of the Association, *Financial Management,* is dedicated to the common interests of financial managers and academicians. Articles report on and refine the most advanced academic research and review developments made by practitioners in many financially oriented fields. The journal's scope includes major business concerns operating in a variety of areas, regulated industries, non-profit organizations, financial institutions, and a variety of other public and private sector concerns. . . .

Annual Meetings

Participatory interaction is a central goal of the Association. The annual meeting draws from both practitioners and academicians to ensure that the FMA actively meets its objective of bringing theory and practice together. Recent meetings in San Diego, Atlanta, Denver, Cincinnati, New York, and Las Vegas have involved up to 1,400 participants. Future meeting sites include: New Orleans (1988), Boston (1989), Orlando (1990), Chicago (1991), and San Francisco (1992).

Student Chapters Program

FMA sponsors student finance clubs throughout the U.S. and Canada in order to provide students of finance, banking, and investments with an association that will encourage their professional development and increase the interaction between business executives, faculty, and students. FMA student chapters are a valuable link for

students to a successful future as professionals in finance. . . .

National Honor Society

The purpose of the National Honor Society is to encourage and reward scholarship and accomplishment in business and nonbusiness finance and banking among undergraduate and graduate students, to provide an association for college students actively interest in these fields, and to encourage an interaction between business executives and students of finance and banking. The National Honor Society is the *only* national honorary [organization] for students of finance. . . . For information on membership contact:

Financial Management Association
College of Business Administration
University of South Florida
Tampa, FL 33620
(813) 974-2084

SOURCE: *Careers in Finance* (Tampa, FL.: Financial Management Association, 1983), pp. 51, 52.

The financial manager needs to consider the yield curve when making a variety of decisions, since it provides information on current as well as future expectations for interest rates. While useful in the short-term investment process, the yield curve is of greatest importance in making financing decisions.

Risk Premiums: Issuer and Issue Characteristics

So far we have considered only risk-free U.S. Treasury securities. At this point we reintroduce the risk premium and assess it in view of risky non-Treasury issues. Recall that in Equation 2.1, restated here:

$$k_1 = \underbrace{k^* + IE}_{\text{risk-free rate, } R_F} + \underbrace{IC_1}_{\text{risk premium}}$$

the nominal rate of interest for security 1, k_1, is equal to the risk-free rate, which consists of the real rate of interest (k^*) plus the inflation expectation premium (IE), plus the risk premium. The *risk premium* varies with specific issuer and issue characteristics; it causes similar-maturity securities[8] to have differing nominal rates of interest.

Example

On August 30, 1985, the nominal rates on a number of classes of long-term securities were as noted below.[9]

Security	Nominal interest (%)
U.S. Treasury bonds (average)	10.46
Corporate bonds (by rating):	
Aaa	10.90
Aa	11.33
A	11.89
Baa	12.40
Utility bonds	11.73

Since the Treasury bond would represent the risk-free long-term security, we can calculate the risk premium associated with the other securities listed by subtracting the risk-free rate, 10.46 percent, from each yield.

Security	Risk premium (%)
Corporate bonds (by rating):	
Aaa	$10.90 - 10.46 = 0.44$
Aa	$11.33 - 10.46 = 0.87$
A	$11.89 - 10.46 = 1.43$
Baa	$12.40 - 10.46 = 1.94$
Utility bonds	$11.73 - 10.46 = 1.27$

These risk premiums reflect differing issuer and issue risks; the lower-rated corporate issues—A and Baa—have higher risk premiums than the higher-rated corporates—Aaa and Aa—while the utility issue has a risk premium comparable to the Aa and A corporates.

The risk premium, IC_1, consists of a number of issuer- and issue-related components including default risk, maturity risk, marketability risk, contractual provisions, and tax treatment. Each of these components is briefly defined in Table 2.4. In general, the highest risk premiums and therefore the highest nominal returns are to be found in securities issued by firms with a high risk of default and long maturities that are traded in thin markets, have unfavorable contractual provisions, and are not tax-exempt.

---

[8] To provide for the same risk-free rate of interest, $k^* + IE$, it is necessary to assume equal maturities. By doing this, the inflationary expectations, IE, and therefore R_F, will be held constant, and the issuer and issue characteristics become the key factor differentiating the nominal rates of interest on various securities.

[9] These yields were obtained from the *Federal Reserve Bulletin*, December 1985, p. A24.

Table 2.4
Issuer- and Issue-Related Risk Components *each have a % assigned*

Component	Description
Default risk	The possibility that the issuer of debt will not pay the contractual interest or principal as scheduled. The greater the uncertainty as to the borrower's ability to meet these payments, the greater the risk premium. High bond ratings reflect low default risk, and vice versa.
Maturity risk (also called *interest rate risk*)	The fact that a given change in interest rates will cause the value of the security to change by a greater amount the longer its maturity, and vice versa. If interest rates on otherwise similar-risk securities suddenly rise due to a change in the money supply, the prices of long-term bonds will decline by more than the prices of short-term bonds, and vice versa. The longer the time to maturity for a bond, the more significant is the effect of a movement in interest rates on the price of the security.[a]
Marketability risk	The ease with which securities can be converted into cash without experiencing a loss in value. Generally, securities actively traded on major exchanges and over-the-counter are marketable. Less actively traded securities that have a ''thin market'' have low marketability. Since a potential loss in value will result from the need to sell quickly a security with low marketability, it would have a high marketability risk.
Contractual provisions	Conditions often included in a debt agreement or a stock issue. Certain of these provisions reduce the risk of a security, while others may increase risk. For example, ignoring all other risks, a *freely callable bond* (one that can be retired any time at the issuer's option) would be more risky than a bond that does not have a call feature. The issuer of the freely callable bond will have to offer a higher return to compensate the bondholder for this risk.
Tax treatment	Tax treatment can be viewed as a component of the risk premium. Earnings on certain securities issued by agencies of state and local government are exempt from federal, and sometimes state and local, taxes.[b] Because of this benefit, their nominal interest rates tend to be reduced by an amount sufficient to allow their return to be equivalent to the after-tax return on a fully taxable issue with similar risk.

calling bonds "could be due to interest rates chging."

[a] A detailed discussion of the effects of interest rates on the price or value of bonds and other fixed-income securities is presented in Chapter 8.

[b] While all state and local issues are tax-exempt for federal income tax purposes, generally only those issued by the state or locality in which the taxpayer resides are exempt from state and local taxes, respectively. Securities that are exempt from federal, state, and local taxes are often called ''triple tax-exempts.''

Risk and Return

The fact that a positive relationship exists between risk and the nominal or actual return should be evident. After assessing the risk embodied in a given security, investors tend to purchase those securities that are expected to provide a return commensurate with the perceived risk. The actual return earned on the security will affect their subsequent actions—whether they sell, hold, or buy additional securities. In addition, most investors look to certain types of securities to provide a certain range of risk-return behaviors.

Figure 2.7
Risk-Return Profile for Popular Securities

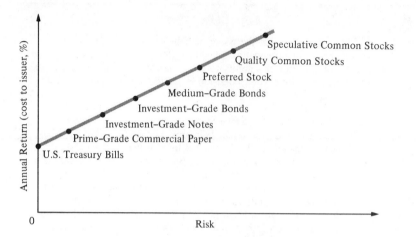

A **risk-return trade-off** exists such that investors must be compensated for accepting greater risk with the expectation of greater expected returns.[10] Figure 2.7 illustrates the typical relationship between risk and return for several popular securities. Clearly, higher returns (costs to the issuer) are expected with greater risk. Financial managers must attempt to keep revenues up and costs down, but they must also consider the risks associated with each investment and financing alternative. Decisions will ultimately rest on an analysis of the impact of risk and return on share price.

risk-return trade-off
The expectation that for accepting greater risk investors must be compensated with greater returns.

Summary

- The basic forms of business organization are the sole proprietorship, the partnership, and the corporation. Although there are more sole proprietorships than any other form of business organization, the corporation is dominant in terms of business receipts and net profits.

- Corporations are subject to corporate tax rates applicable to both ordinary income (after deducting allowable expenses) and capital gains. The average tax rate paid by a corporation ranges from 15 to 34 percent. For our purposes, a 40 percent marginal tax rate is assumed.

- Financial institutions, such as banks, savings and loans, and mutual funds, channel the savings of various individuals, businesses, and government into the hands of demanders of these funds. Their role is changing as the era of the "financial supermarket" is being ushered in by recent legislation.

- The financial markets—the money market and the capital market—provide a forum in which suppliers and demanders of loans and investments can transact business directly. In the money market, short-term debt instruments are traded; in the capital market, long-term debt and equity transactions are made.

- The backbone of the capital market is the organized securities exchanges and the over-the-counter exchange, which function to create a continuous market, allocate scarce capital, determine and publicize security prices, and aid firms in obtaining new financing.

- The organized securities exchanges provide secondary markets for securities. The over-the-counter exchange is a telecommunications network linking active participants in this market. In addition to creating a secondary market for securities, the over-

[10] The risk-return trade-off is discussed in detail in Chapter 7, where certain refinements are introduced to explain why investors are actually rewarded with higher returns for taking only certain types of "nondiversifiable" or inescapable risks.

the-counter exchange is a primary market in which new public issues are sold.

● Investment bankers are hired to bear the risk of finding buyers for new security issues as well as to advise clients. They help firms make both private placements and public offerings.

● The flow of funds between savers (suppliers) and investors (demanders) is regulated by the interest rate or required return. In a perfect, inflation-free, certain world there would be one cost of money—the real rate of interest.

● The nominal or actual interest rate is the sum of the risk-free rate, which is the sum of the real rate of interest and the inflation-ary expectation, and a risk premium reflecting issuer and issue characteristics including default risk, maturity risk, marketability risk, contractual provisions, and tax treatment.

● For any class of similar-risk securities, the term structure of interest rates reflects the relationship between the interest rate, or rate of return, and the time to maturity. Yield curves can be downward-sloping, upward-sloping, or flat.

● Since investors must be compensated for taking risks, they expect higher returns for greater risk. Each type of security offers a range of potential risk-return trade-offs.

Questions

2-1 What are the three basic forms of business organization? Which form is most common? Which form is dominant in terms of business receipts and net profits? Why?

2-2 Briefly define ordinary corporate income and capital gains and describe the tax treatments of each. What is the *average tax rate?* What is the *marginal tax rate?*

2-3 What benefit results from the tax-deductibility of certain corporate expenses? Compare and contrast the tax treatment of corporate interest and dividends.

2-4 What role do financial institutions play in our economy? Who are the key participants in these transactions? Indicate who are net savers and who are net borrowers.

2-5 Briefly describe each of the following financial institutions:

    a. Commercial banks

    b. Savings and loans

    c. Life insurance companies

    d. Mutual funds

2-6 Describe the changing role of financial institutions and explain how "financial supermarkets" fit into the evolving institutional environment.

2-7 What are *financial markets* and what role do they play in our economy? What relationship exists between financial institutions and financial markets?

2-8 What is the *money market?* Where it is housed? How does it differ from the capital market?

2-9 What is the *capital market?* What functions do securities exchanges play in this market? What are *primary* and *secondary* markets?

2-10 How does the over-the-counter exchange operate? How does it differ from the organized securities exchanges?

2-11 What is an *investment banker?* What role does he or she play in private placements and public offerings?

2-12 What is the *real rate of interest?* Differentiate it from the nominal rate of interest for the risk-free asset, a three-month U.S. Treasury bill.

2-13 What is the *term structure of interest rates* and how does it relate to the yield curve? For a given class of similar-risk securities, what expectation causes the yield curve to be downward-sloping, upward-sloping, or flat?

2-14 List and briefly describe the potential component risks embodied in the risk premium used to determine the nominal rate of interest on a risky security.

2-15 What is meant by the *risk-return trade-off?* How should this relationship affect the actions of financial managers?

Self-Test Problem

(Solution on page 53)

ST-1 Montgomery Enterprises, Inc., had operating earnings of $280,000 for the year just ended. During the year the firm sold stock it held in another company for $180,000 which was $30,000 above its original purchase price of $150,000, paid one year earlier.

handwritten notes in margin:

.15 x 50000
.25 x 25000
.34 x 235000
310,000

7500
6250
79900
93650 .05 x 210000
10500
1041 50

33.62

a. What is the amount, if any, of capital gains realized during the year?

b. How much total taxable income did the firm earn during the year?

c. Use the actual corporate tax rates given in the text to calculate the firm's total taxes due.

d. Calculate both the *average tax rate* and the *marginal tax rate* based upon your findings above.

Problems

2-1   **(Liability Comparisons)** Meredith Harper has invested $25,000 in the Southwest Development Company. This firm has recently become bankrupt and has $60,000 in unpaid debts. Explain the nature of payments, if any, by Ms. Harper in each of the following situations.

     a. The Southwest Development Company is a sole proprietorship owned by Ms. Harper.

     b. The Southwest Development Company is a 50-50 partnership of Ms. Harper and Christopher Black.

     c. The Southwest Development Company is a corporation.

2-2   **(Corporate Taxes)** Tantor Supply, Inc., is a small corporation acting as the exclusive distributor of a major line of sporting goods. During 1988 the firm earned $92,500 before taxes.

     a. Calculate the firm's tax liability using the actual tax rates given in the chapter.

     b. How much is Tantor Supply's 1988 after-tax earnings?

     c. What was the firm's average tax rate, based on your findings in **a?**

     d. What is the firm's marginal tax rate, based on your findings in **a?**

2-3   **(Average Corporate Tax Rates)** Using the corporate tax rates given in the text, perform the following:

     a. Calculate the tax liability, after-tax earnings, and average tax rates for the following levels of corporate earnings before taxes: $10,000; $80,000; $300,000; $500,000; $1.5 million.

     b. Plot the average tax rates (measured on the *y*-axis) against the pretax income levels (measured on the *x*-axis). What generalization can be made concerning the relationship between these variables?

2-4   **(Marginal Corporate Tax Rates)** Using the corporate tax rates given in the text, perform the following:

     a. Calculate the marginal tax rate for the following levels of corporate earnings before taxes: $15,000; $60,000; $90,000; $200,000; $400,000; $1 million.

     b. Plot the marginal tax rates (measured on the *y*-axis) against the pretax income levels (measured on the *x*-axis). Explain the relationship between these variables.

2-5   **(Interest versus Dividends)** The Michaels Corporation expects earnings before interest and taxes to be $40,000 for this period. Assuming an ordinary tax rate of 40 percent, compute the firm's after-tax net profits and earnings available for common stockholders under the following conditions:

a. The firm pays $10,000 in interest.

b. The firm pays $10,000 in preferred stock dividends.

2-6   **(Capital Gains Taxes)** Perkins Manufacturing is considering the sale of two nondepreciable assets, X and Y. Asset X was purchased for $2,000 and will be sold today for $2,250. Asset Y was purchased for $30,000 and will be sold today for $35,000. The firm is subject to a 40 percent tax rate on capital gains.

a. Calculate the amount of capital gain, if any, realized on each of the assets.

b. Calculate the tax on the sale of each asset.

2-7   **(Capital Gains Taxes)** The table below contains purchase and sale prices for the nondepreciable capital assets of a major corporation. The firm paid taxes of 40 percent on capital gains.

Asset	Purchase price	Sale price
A	$ 3,000	$ 3,400
B	12,000	12,000
C	62,000	80,000
D	41,000	45,000
E	16,500	18,000

a. Determine the amount of capital gain realized on each of the five assets.

b. Calculate the amount of tax paid on each of the assets.

2-8   **(Real Rate of Interest)** To estimate the real rate of interest, the economics division of Mountain Banks—a major bank holding company—has gathered the data summarized in the table below. Because there is a high likelihood that new tax legislation will be passed in the near future, current data as well as data reflecting the likely impact of passage of the legislation on the demand for funds are also included in the table. (*Note:* The proposed legislation will not have any impact on the supply schedule of funds.)

	Currently		With passage of tax legislation
Amount of funds supplied/demanded ($ billion)	Interest rate required by funds suppliers (%)	Interest rate required by funds demanders (%)	Interest rate required by funds demanders (%)
1	7	16	24
5	9	14	21
10	11	11	19
20	14	9	17
50	16	7	16
100	19	5	12

    a. Draw the supply curve and the demand curve for funds using the current data. (*Note:* Unlike Figure 2.4, these functions will not appear as straight lines.)

    b. Using your graph, label and note the real rate of interest using current data.

    c. Add to the graph drawn in **a** the new demand curve expected in the event the proposed tax legislation becomes effective.

    d. What is the new real rate of interest? Compare and analyze this finding in light of your analysis in **b.**

2-9   **(Yield Curve)** A firm wishing to evaluate interest rate behavior has gathered yield data on five U.S. Treasury securities, each having a different maturity and all measured at the same point in time. This data is summarized below.

U.S. Treasury security	Time to maturity	Yield (%)
A	1 year	12.6
B	10 years	11.2
C	6 months	13.0
D	20 years	11.0
E	5 years	11.4

    a. Draw the yield curve associated with the data given above.

    b. Describe the resulting yield curve in **a,** and explain the general expectations embodied in it.

2-10   **(Nominal Interest Rates and Yield Curves)** A recent study of inflationary expectations has disclosed that the consensus among economic forecasters yields the following average annual rates of inflation expected over the periods noted.

Period	Average annual rate of inflation (%)
3 months	5
1 year	6
5 years	8
10 years	8.5
20 years	9

    a. If the real rate of interest is currently 2.5 percent, find the nominal interest rate on each of the following U.S. Treasury issues: 20-year bond, 3-month bill, 1-year note, 5-year bond.

    b. If the real rate of interest suddenly drops to 2 percent without any change in inflationary expectations, what effect, if any, would this have on your answers in **a?** Explain.

    c. Using your findings in **a,** draw a yield curve for U.S. Treasury securities. Describe the general shape and expectations reflected by the curve.

2-11 (**Nominal and Real Rates and Yield Curves**) A firm wishing to evaluate interest rate behavior has gathered nominal rate of interest and inflationary expectation data on five U.S. Treasury securities, each having a different maturity and each measured at a different point in time during the year just ended. This data is summarized in the table below.

U.S. Treasury security	Point in time	Maturity	Nominal rate of interest (%)	Inflationary expectation (%)
A	Jan. 7	1 year	12.6	9.5
B	Mar. 12	10 years	11.2	8.2
C	May 30	6 months	13.0	10.0
D	Aug. 15	20 years	11.0	8.1
E	Dec. 30	5 years	11.4	8.3

   a. Using the data above, find the real rate of interest at each point in time.

   b. Describe the behavior of the real rate of interest over the year. What forces might be responsible for such behavior?

   c. Draw the yield curve associated with this data, assuming that the nominal rates were measured at the same point in time.

   d. Describe the resulting yield curve in **c** and explain the general expectations embodied in it.

2-12 (**Term Structure of Interest Rates**) The following yield data for a number of highest-quality corporate bonds existed at each of the three points in time noted.

Time to maturity (years)	Yield (%) 5 years ago	2 years ago	Today
1	9.1	14.6	9.3
3	9.2	12.8	9.8
5	9.3	12.2	10.9
10	9.5	10.9	12.6
15	9.4	10.7	12.7
20	9.3	10.5	12.9
30	9.4	10.5	13.5

   a. On the same set of axes, draw the yield curve at each of the three points of time given.

   b. Label each curve in **a** as to its general shape (downward-sloping, upward-sloping, flat).

   c. Describe the general inflationary and interest rate expectation existing at each of the three points in time.

2-13 **(Risk-Free Rate and Risk Premiums)** The real rate of interest is currently 3 percent; the inflationary expectations and risk premiums for a number of securities are given below.

Security	Inflationary expectation (%)	Risk premium (%)
A	6	3
B	9	2
C	8	2
D	5	4
E	11	1

a. Find the risk-free rate of interest, R_F, applicable to each security.

b. Although not noted, what factor must be the cause of the differing risk-free rates found in **a**?

c. Find the nominal rate of interest for each security.

2-14 **(Risk Premiums)** Eleanor Burns is attempting to find the nominal rate of interest for each of two securities—A and B—issued by different firms at the same point in time. She has gathered the following data:

Characteristic	Security A	Security B
Time to maturity	3 years	15 years
Inflationary expectation	9.0%	7.0%
Risk premium for:		
Default risk	1.0%	2.0%
Maturity risk	0.5%	1.5%
Marketability risk	1.0%	1.0%
Other risk	0.5%	1.5%

a. If the real rate of interest is currently 2 percent, find the risk-free rate of interest applicable to each security.

b. Find the total risk premium attributable to each security's issuer and issue risk.

c. Calculate the nominal rate of interest for each security. Compare and discuss your findings.

Solution to Self-Test Problem

ST-1 **a.** Capital gain = $180,000 sale price − $150,000 original purchase price = $30,000

b. Total taxable income = $280,000 operating earnings + $30,000 capital gain = $310,000

c. Firm's tax liability:

.15 × $50,000	= $ 7,500
.25 × $25,000	= 6,250
.34 × ($310,000 − $75,000)	= 79,900
Total	$93,650

$$\text{Plus Lesser of:} \begin{bmatrix} \$11,750 \\ \text{or} \\ .05 \times (\$310,000 - \$100,000) \\ = .05 \times (\$210,000) = \$10,500 \end{bmatrix} = \underline{\quad 10,500 \quad}$$

Total Taxes Due $104,150

d. Average tax rate = $\dfrac{\$104,150}{\$310,000} = \underline{\underline{33.6\%}}$

Marginal tax rate = 34% + 5% $= \underline{\underline{39\%}}$

CHAPTER 3

Financial Statements, Depreciation, and Cash Flow

FACT OR FABLE?

Are the following statements fact (true) or fable (false)?

1

Publicly held corporations are required by the Securities and Exchange Commission (SEC) to provide an annual stockholders' report.

2

The income statement presents a summary of the firm's financial position at a given time; the balance sheet summarizes the firm's operating results during a specified period.

3

Cash flow from operations can be found by subtracting all noncash charges such as depreciation from net profits after taxes.

4

From a strict financial viewpoint, straight-line depreciation is preferred over the accelerated cost recovery system (ACRS) for tax purposes since it results in higher profits.

5

Sources of cash include a decrease in any asset, an increase in a liability, net profits after taxes, depreciation and other noncash charges, and the sale of stock.

6

The statement of changes in financial position allows the financial manager and other interested parties to analyze the firm's past and possibly future funds flow.

It's an annual tradition. Each spring stockholders open their mailboxes to find over $4 billion dollars worth of stockholders' reports. AT&T, in 1987, sent over 4 million copies. The stockholders' report summarizes the company's most recent financial history and the expectations for the future.

Public companies are required by the SEC to report certain financial data to stockholders. Many companies view this requirement as an opportunity to communicate more than the no-frills financial statements to stockholders. They have added a large editorial section that tells the company's story: its activities, its aspirations, its plans for growth—all enhanced by a high-powered design, beautiful photography, and glossy paper stock.

A recent poll of CFOs shows that 60 percent of respondents feel the financial and editorial sections of the stockholders' report are equally important, and about half of the CFOs want to give greater emphasis to the stockholders' report as a marketing and image-building tool. No longer are annual reports predictable print media. Telerate, Inc., a financial information company, sent videocassettes in 1986. McCormick & Co., a spice maker, scents its reports with a different spice each year.

The most informative and best designed stockholders' reports are honored by the *Financial World* Louis Guenther Award. Among the top award winners have been the Dayton Hudson Corp., Avery International, and the Pillsbury Co.

Most people may be more interested in the editorial write-up concerning the company's products and plans and the traditional messages from the corporate officers than in the financial summary. But don't let the pretty pictures fool you—the story is still told in the numbers.

Because the numbers play an extremely important financial role, in this chapter we evaluate the financial statements included in the stockholders' report and discuss the closely related topics of depreciation and cash flow.

The Stockholders' Report

Every corporation has many and varied uses for the standardized records and reports of its financial activities. Periodically, reports must be prepared for regulators, creditors (lenders), owners, and management. Regulators, such as federal and state securities commissions, enforce the proper and accurate disclosure of corporate financial data. Creditors use financial data to evaluate the firm's ability to meet scheduled debt payments. Owners use corporate financial data in assessing the firm's financial condition and in deciding whether to buy, sell, or hold its stock. Management is concerned with regulatory compliance, satisfying creditors and owners, and monitoring the firm's performance.

The guidelines used to prepare and maintain financial records and reports are known as **generally accepted accounting principles (GAAP).** These accounting practices and procedures are authorized by the accounting profession's rule-setting body, the **Financial**

generally accepted accounting principles (GAAP) The practice and procedure guidelines used to prepare and maintain financial records and reports; authorized by the Financial Accounting Standards Board (FASB).

Financial Accounting Standards Board (FASB) The accounting profession's rule-setting body, which authorizes generally accepted accounting principles (GAAP).

publicly held corporations Corporations whose stock is traded on either an organized securities exchange or the over-the-counter exchange.

Accounting Standards Board (FASB). **Publicly held corporations** are those whose stock is traded on either an organized securities exchange or the over-the-counter exchange. These corporations are required by the **Securities and Exchange Commission (SEC)**—the federal regulatory body that governs the sale and listing of securities—and by state securities commissions to provide their stockholders with an annual **stockholders' report.** This report, which summarizes and documents the firm's financial activities during the past year, begins with a letter from the firm's president and/or chairman of the board followed by the key financial statements. In addition, other information about the firm is often included.

FACT OR FABLE?   1 Publicly held corporations are required by the Securities and Exchange Commission (SEC) to provide an annual stockholders' report. *(Fact)*

Securities and Exchange Commission (SEC) The federal regulatory body that governs the sale and listing of securities.

stockholders' report Annual report required of publicly held corporations that summarizes and documents for stockholders the firm's financial activities of the past year.

president's letter The first component of the annual stockholders' report, and the primary communication from management to the firm's owners.

The President's Letter

The **president's letter** is the primary communication from management to the firm's owners. Typically the first component of the stockholders' report, it describes the events considered to have had the greatest impact on the firm during the year. In addition, the letter generally discusses plans for the coming year and their anticipated effects on the firm's financial condition. Figure 3.1 includes excerpts from the president's letter to the stockholders of Eastman Kodak Company, from its 1985 stockholders' report. The letter summarizes key events of the fiscal year ended December 29, 1985, and discusses the outlook for 1986.

Financial Statements

Following the president's letter will be, at minimum, the four key financial statements required by the Securities and Exchange Commission (SEC). Those statements are (1) the income statement, (2) the balance sheet, (3) the statement of retained earnings, and (4) the statement of changes in financial position. The annual corporate report must contain these statements for at least the two most recent years of operation. Historical summaries of key operating statistics and ratios for the past five to ten years are also commonly included with the financial statements. (Financial ratios are discussed in Chapter 4.)

Other Features

The stockholders' reports of most widely held corporations also include discussions of the firm's activities, new products, research and development, and the like. Most companies view the annual report not only as a requirement but also as an important vehicle for influencing owners' perceptions of the company and its future outlook. Because of the information it contains, the stockholders' report may affect expected risk, return, stock price, and ultimately the viability of the firm.

Figure 3.1
Excerpt from Eastman Kodak Company's 1985 President's Letter

In financial terms, 1985 was a very disappointing year for Eastman Kodak Company. While sales advanced in real terms at a reasonable rate, the total in dollars—at $10,631 million—was only slightly higher. Unfavorable rates of currency exchange together with competitive pressure that restrained prices masked a gain in unit volume of about four percent. Earnings came under severe pressure due to the negative effect of the overvalued U.S. dollar, the depressed condition of the U.S. chemical industry, increased marketing costs and larger research and development expenditures. Absent an unusual charge relating mainly to the company's withdrawal from instant photography, net earnings would have been $634 million, down 31 percent from the year before—a result that prompted acceleration of cost-cutting measures now going forward in every part of the company.

While earnings fell short of our expectations, particularly in the final months of 1985, there was by the year-end a pervasive belief here that the company would make the turn in 1986. The earnings gyrations of the past few years were, we believed, a thing of the past. We were particularly encouraged by divisional forecasts of operating gains not only in 1986 but in each of the next several years. We continue to believe those forecasts are sound.

Exit From Instant Photography
An unexpected event early in 1986 significantly affected the prior year's earnings. The company made its exit from the instant photo business, notwithstanding its continuing appeal in the Kodak-Polaroid patent litigation. Federal courts had denied our request to stay an injunction that forced the company from this business. We moved promptly to retain the trust of our customers. In a voluntary effort unique in industrial history, we announced plans that would enable consumers to exchange their Kodak instant cameras for

a disk camera outfit or other options. The cost of this and other aspects of our withdrawal from instant photography accounted for $494 million of a $563 million charge to 1985 earnings (the balance was due to closure of a Kodak installation in France and termination of some Verbatim operations in this country). These charges lowered net earnings for 1985 to $332 million, a decline of 64 percent from 1984. On a per share basis, net earnings were $1.46 compared with $3.80, down 62 percent.

The company's withdrawal from instant photography should not be seen as threatening in financial terms or in the technological sense. In the near term, we expect to demonstrate alternative approaches to instant image-making for commercial and industrial applications, in keeping with the future of this market segment.

Financial Position Sound
The Kodak balance sheet remains one of the soundest in American industry, with $813 million in cash and marketable securities and 22.7 million common shares having been purchased during the past two years. In addition, the two leading debt-rating agencies in the United States, which had given Kodak their highest ratings, reaffirmed those ratings in January, 1986, with the knowledge that a "sizable write-off" related to the company's withdrawal from instant photography would be incurred.

Projected cash flows from internal sources should be adequate to support currently planned operations. External financing may become a requirement in the event of the commencement of a major project or acquisition.

Dividends
In 1985 cash dividends declared for shareowners totalled $553 million or $2.43 per share. While the total amount of dividends declared was down slightly from the previous year due to fewer

shares outstanding, the per share declarations showed an increase. Anticipated cash flows indicate a continuation of appropriate dividends. . . .

The Outlook for 1986
In terms of operating results, we believe the Kodak stage is set for several years of solid gains in sales and earnings. Nonetheless, two extraordinary factors must be considered.

First, our appeal in the litigation with Polaroid continues. If the decision is adverse to Kodak, a damages trial will ensue. Based on the advice of patent counsel retained to represent it in this case, the company does not believe that it is likely the amount of damages that might result will have a material adverse effect on the financial condition of the company. Any liability that may be sustained would be charged against earnings of the year of final resolution.

Second, we have outlined our commitment to a workforce reduction in 1986. Employees who leave Kodak under the reduction in force program will do so with enhanced retirement and separation benefits that permit them to make their exit with pride, dignity and a degree of economic protection. This process will have a negative effect on earnings before savings can be realized.

These factors notwithstanding, we expect 1986 to be a year of significant recovery in operating terms. And we expect this year to be the first in a series that will prove our resilience and our resolve. This company will be successful, in 1986 and in the years beyond.

Colby H. Chandler

Colby H. Chandler
Chairman and Chief Executive Officer

Kay R. Whitmore

Kay R. Whitmore
President

SOURCE: Eastman Kodak Company, *1985 Stockholders' Report*, pp. 2–3.

Basic Financial Statements

Our chief concern in this section is to understand the factual information presented in the four required corporate financial statements. The financial statements from the 1988 stockholders' report of a hypothetical firm, the Baker Corporation, are presented and briefly discussed below.

Income Statement

income statement Provides a financial summary of the firm's operating results during a specified period.

The **income statement** provides a financial summary of the firm's operating results during the period specified. Most common are income statements covering a one-year period ending at a specified date, ordinarily December 31 of the calendar year. (Many large firms, however, operate on a 12-month financial cycle, or *fiscal year,* that ends at a time other than December 31.) In addition, monthly statements are typically prepared for use by management, and quarterly statements must be made available to the stockholders of publicly held corporations.

Table 3.1 presents Baker Corporation's income statement for the year ended December 31, 1988. The statement begins with *sales revenue*—the total dollar amount of sales during the period—from which the *cost of goods sold* is deducted. The resulting *gross profits* of $700,000 represents the amount remaining to satisfy operating, financial, and tax costs after meeting the costs of producing or purchasing the products sold. Next *operating expenses,* which includes sales expense, general and administrative expense, and depreciation expense, is deducted from gross profits.[1] The resulting *operating profits* of $370,000 represents the profit earned from producing and selling products; it does not consider financial and tax costs. (Operating profit is often called *earnings before interest and taxes* or *EBIT*.) Next, the financial cost—interest expense—is subtracted from operating profits in order to find *net profits (or earnings) before taxes*. After subtracting $70,000 in 1988 interest, Baker Corporation had $300,000 of net profits before taxes.

After applying the appropriate tax rates to before-tax profits, taxes are calculated and deducted to determine *net profits (or earnings) after taxes*. Baker Corporation's net profits after taxes for 1988 were $180,000. Next, any preferred stock dividends must be subtracted from net profits after taxes to arrive at *earnings available for common stockholders*. This is the amount earned by the firm on behalf of the common stockholders during the period. Dividing earnings available for common stockholders by the number of shares of common stock outstanding, *earnings per share (EPS)* is obtained. EPS represents the amount earned during the period on each outstanding share of common stock. In 1988 Baker Corporation earned $170,000 for its common stockholders, which represents $1.70 for each outstanding share. (The earnings per share amount rarely equals the amount, if any, of common stock dividends paid to shareholders.)

Balance Sheet

balance sheet Summary statement of the firm's financial position at a given point in time.

The **balance sheet** presents a summary statement of the firm's financial position at a given point in time. The statement balances the firm's *assets* (what it owns) against its financing, which can be either *debt* (what it owes) or *equity* (what was provided by owners).

---

[1] Depreciation expense can be, and frequently is, included in manufacturing costs—costs of goods sold—in order to calculate gross profits. Depreciation is shown as an expense in this text in order to isolate it as an important cash flow component.

Table 3.1
Baker Corporation Income Statement ($000) for the Year
Ended December 31, 1988

Sales revenue		$1,700
Less: Cost of goods sold		1,000
Gross profits		$ 700
Less: Operating expenses		
Selling expense	$ 80	
General and administrative expense	150	
Depreciation expense	100	
Total operating expense		330
Operating profits		$ 370
Less: Interest expense[a]		70
Net profits before taxes		$ 300
Less: Taxes (rate = 40%)		120
Net profits after taxes		$ 180
Less: Preferred stock dividends		10
Earnings available for common stockholders		$ 170
Earnings per share (EPS)[b]		$ 1.70

[a] Interest expense includes the interest component of the annual financial lease payment as specified by the Financial Accounting Standards Board (FASB).

[b] Calculated by dividing the earnings available for common stockholders by the number of shares of common stock outstanding ($170,000 ÷ 100,000 shares = $1.70 per share).

Baker Corporation's balance sheets on December 31 of 1988 and 1987, respectively, are presented in Table 3.2. They show a variety of asset, liability, and equity accounts. An important distinction is made between short-term and long-term assets and liabilities. The **current assets** and **current liabilities** are *short-term* assets and liabilities. This means that they are expected to be converted into cash within one year or less. All other assets and liabilities, along with stockholders' equity, which is assumed to have an infinite life, are considered *long-term,* or *fixed,* since they are expected to remain on the firm's books for one year or more.

In reviewing Baker Corporation's balance sheets, a few points need to be highlighted. As is customary, the assets are listed beginning with the most liquid down to the least liquid. Current assets therefore precede fixed assets. *Marketable securities* represents very liquid short-term investments, such as U.S. Treasury bills or certificates of deposit, held by the firm. *Accounts receivable* represents the total monies owed the firm by its customers on credit sales made to them. *Inventories* includes raw materials, work-in-process (partially finished goods), and finished goods held by the firm. The entry for *gross fixed assets* is the original cost of all fixed (long-term) assets owned by the firm.[2] *Net fixed assets* represents the difference between gross fixed assets and *accumulated depreciation*— the total expense recorded for the depreciation of fixed assets. (The net value of fixed assets is called their *book value.*)

current assets Short-term assets, expected to be converted into cash within one year or less.

current liabilities Short-term liabilities, expected to be converted into cash within one year or less.

[2] For convenience the term *fixed assets* is used throughout this text to refer to what, in a strict accounting sense, is captioned "property, plant, and equipment." This simplification of terminology permits certain financial concepts to be more easily developed.

Table 3.2
Baker Corporation Balance Sheets ($000)

	December 31	
Assets	**1988**	**1987**
Current assets		
Cash	$ 400	$ 300
Marketable securities	600	200
Accounts receivable	400	500
Inventories	600	900
Total current assets	$2,000	$1,900
Gross fixed assets (at cost)		
Land and buildings	$1,200	$1,050
Machinery and equipment	850	800
Furniture and fixtures	300	220
Vehicles	100	80
Other (includes certain leases)	50	50
Total gross fixed assets (at cost)	$2,500	$2,200
Less: Accumulated depreciation	1,300	1,200
Net fixed assets	$1,200	$1,000
Total assets	$3,200	$2,900
Liabilities and stockholders' equity		
Current liabilities		
Accounts payable	$ 700	$ 500
Notes payable	600	700
Accruals	100	200
Total current liabilities	$1,400	$1,400
Long-term debt	$ 600	$ 400
Total liabilities	$2,000	$1,800
Stockholders' equity		
Preferred stock	$ 100	$ 100
Common stock—$1.20 par, 100,000 shares outstanding		
in 1988 and 1987	120	120
Paid-in capital in excess of par on common stock	380	380
Retained earnings	600	500
Total stockholders' equity	$1,200	$1,100
Total liabilities and stockholders' equity	$3,200	$2,900

Like assets, the liabilities and equity accounts are listed on the balance sheet from short-term to long-term. Current liabilities includes: *accounts payable,* amounts owed for credit purchases by the firm; *notes payable,* outstanding short-term loans, typically from commercial banks; and *accruals,* amounts owed for services for which a bill may not or will not be received. (Examples of accruals include taxes due the government and wages due employees.) *Long-term debt* represents debt for which payment is not due in the current year. *Stockholders' equity* represents the owners' claims on the firm. The *preferred stock* entry shows the historic proceeds from the sale of preferred stock ($100,000 for Baker Corporation). Next, the amount paid in by the original purchasers of common stock is shown by two entries—common stock and paid-in capital in excess of par on common stock. The *common stock* entry is the **par value** of common stock, an arbitrarily assigned per-share value used primarily for accounting purposes. **Paid-in capital in excess of par** represents the amount of proceeds in excess of the par value received from the original sale of common stock. The sum of the common stock and paid-in capital accounts divided by the number of shares outstanding represents the original price per share received by the firm on a single issue of common stock. Baker Corporation therefore received $5.00 per share [($120,000 par + $380,000 paid-in capital in excess) ÷ 100,000 shares] from the sale of its common stock. Finally, **retained earnings** represents the cumulative total of all earnings retained and reinvested in the firm since its inception. It is important to recognize that retained earnings *are not cash,* but rather have been utilized to finance the firm's assets.

Baker Corporation's balance sheets in Table 3.2 show that the firm's total assets increased from $2,900,000 in 1987 to $3,200,000 in 1988. The $300,000 increase was due primarily to the $200,000 increase in net fixed assets. The asset increase in turn appears to have been financed primarily by an increase of $200,000 in long-term debt. Better insight into these changes can be derived from the statement of changes in financial position, which we will discuss shortly.

par value Per-share value arbitrarily assigned to an issue of common stock primarily for accounting purposes.

paid-in capital in excess of par The amount of proceeds in excess of the par value received from the original sale of common stock.

retained earnings The cumulative total of all earnings retained and reinvested in the firm since its inception.

FACT OR FABLE?

2 The income statement presents a summary of the firm's financial position at a given time; the balance sheet summarizes the firm's operating results during a specified period. *(Fable)*

The **balance sheet** summarizes the firm's financial position at a given time; the **income statement** summarizes the firm's operating results during a specified period.

Statement of Retained Earnings

The **statement of retained earnings** reconciles the net income earned during a given year, and any cash dividends paid, with the change in retained earnings between the start and end of that year. Table 3.3 presents this statement for Baker Corporation for the year ended December 31, 1988. A review of the statement shows that the company began the year with $500,000 in retained earnings, had net profits after taxes of $180,000, from which it paid a total of $80,000 in dividends, resulting in year-end retained earnings of $600,000. Thus the net increase for Baker Corporation was $100,000 ($180,000 net profits after taxes minus $80,000 in dividends) during 1988.

statement of retained earnings Reconciles the net income earned in a given year, and any cash dividends paid, with the change in retained earnings between the start and end of that year.

Table 3.3
Baker Corporation Statement of Retained Earnings ($000) for the Year Ended December 31, 1988

Retained earnings balance (January 1, 1988)		$500
Plus: Net profits after taxes (for 1988)		180
Less: Cash dividends (paid during 1988)		
Preferred stock	($10)	
Common stock	(70)	(80)
Retained earnings balance (December 31, 1988)		$600

CAREERS IN FINANCE

SECURITIES BROKER: Providing Information and Making Transactions for Clients

"While the market is hitting record highs each day, being a securities broker is terrific. I know however when the bears hit Wall Street, I'll need a new strategy" comments Brenda, a 23-year-old stockbroker.

After graduating with a B.S. in finance, last year she went to work as a trainee in a brokerage firm in a Sun Belt city. "The firm's training program went on for four months," she says, "and the last week was spent in New York getting to know Wall Street and the New York Stock Exchange first hand."

Brenda's job is to give advice about securities investment—stocks and bonds—to her clients. She buys and sells according to the clients' wishes. Even though Brenda must have close familiarity with SEC regulations, her job is primarily a sales activity. She needs to bring in new clients for her firm. This involves getting out into the community and meeting people. Brenda attends lots of meetings, asks friends and relatives to recommend her, even offers to talk to different groups about investing. Finally, like all brokers, Brenda needs to do her homework. This involves learning about new investment opportunities as well as keeping up on important developments in the securities markets.

"After I passed my exam and received my license, I got my first client—my mother's uncle, Graham. Graham had $10,000 in a low-interest savings account; we put half in a certificate of deposit and the rest in common stock. This is the part of the job I'm really going to like. It's fitting the client to the right sort of investment. Graham doesn't need the interest to live on so we could afford to be a little speculative by entering the market. The stock's performance is as I predicted—steady price increases and solid dividends. Graham has been recommending me to his friends."

Brenda may seem a little starry-eyed about her job, but she is aware of the potential problems. "I know I'm going to have to convince a lot of peo-ple I'm competent," she says. "I'm young and I'm working in an area that has been almost exclusively male. I can't depend on Graham and his friends. I have to sell myself to the public as well."

As a trainee, Brenda earned $17,500, but now that she has her license, she's earning $20,000 plus commissions. With experience and the right clientele, her income could grow to $50,000 or more after 5 or 10 years.

Meanwhile she's keeping her options open. "Brokers also can work for mutual funds, insurance companies, investment banks, and even savings and loan companies and banks," she says. "They all have the same function: buying and selling securities. Most brokers have a computer on their desk and a telephone that seems to be growing out of their ear—at least during the hours when the market is open. And those tools are universal no matter where you work."

Statement of Changes in Financial Position

statement of changes in financial position Provides a summary of the flow of funds over the period of concern, typically the past year.

The **statement of changes in financial position** provides a summary of the flow of funds over the period of concern, typically the year just ended. The statement, which is sometimes called a "source and use statement," provides insight into operations and financing. Baker Corporation's statement of changes in financial position for the year ended December 31, 1988, is presented in Table 3.10 on page 74. However, before we look at the preparation of this statement it will be helpful to understand various aspects of depreciation.

Depreciation

not on exam but wants us to understand

Business firms are permitted to systematically charge a portion of the cost of a fixed asset against the annual revenues it generates. This allocation of historic cost over time is called

depreciation. For tax purposes, the depreciation of corporate assets is regulated by the Internal Revenue Code, which underwent major changes under the *Tax Reform Act of 1986*. Because the objectives of financial reporting are sometimes different from those of tax legislation, a firm often will use different depreciation methods for financial reporting than those required for tax purposes. (The student should thus not jump to the conclusion that a company is attempting to ''cook the books'' simply because it keeps two different sets of records.) Tax laws are used to accomplish economic goals such as providing incentives for corporate investment in certain types of assets, whereas the objectives of financial reporting are of course quite different.

Depreciation for tax purposes is determined using the **Accelerated Cost Recovery System (ACRS),**[3] whereas for financial reporting purposes a variety of depreciation methods are available. Before discussing the methods of depreciating an asset, we must understand the relationship between depreciation and cash flows, the depreciable value of an asset, and the depreciable life of an asset.

> **depreciation** The systematic charging of a portion of the cost of a fixed asset against the annual revenues generated by the asset.

> **Accelerated Cost Recovery System (ACRS)** Used to determine the depreciation of assets for tax purposes.

Depreciation and Cash Flows

The financial manager is concerned with cash flows rather than net profits as reported on the income statement. To adjust the income statement to show *cash flow from operations,* all noncash charges must be *added back* to the firm's *net profits after taxes.* **Noncash charges** are expenses that are deducted on the income statement but do not involve an actual outlay of cash during the period. Depreciation, amortization, and depletion allowances are examples. Since depreciation expenses are the most common noncash charges, we shall focus on their treatment; amortization and depletion charges are treated in a similar fashion.

> **noncash charges** Expenses deducted on the income statement that do not involve an actual outlay of cash during the period.

The general rule for adjusting net profits after taxes by adding back all noncash charges is expressed as follows:

$$\text{Cash flow from operations} = \text{net profits after taxes} + \text{noncash charges} \quad (3.1)$$

Applying Equation 3.1 to the 1988 income statement for Baker Corporation presented earlier in Table 3.1 yields a cash flow from operations of $280,000 due to the noncash nature of depreciation:

Net profits after taxes	$180,000
Plus: Depreciation expense	100,000
Cash flow from operations	$280,000

(This value is only approximate since not all sales are made for cash and not all expenses are paid when they are incurred.)

Depreciation and other noncash charges shield the firm from taxes by lowering taxable income. Some people do not define depreciation as a source of funds; however, it is a source of funds in the sense that it represents a ''nonuse'' of funds. Table 3.4 shows the Baker Corporation's income statement prepared on a cash basis as an illustration of how depreciation shields income and acts as a nonuse of funds. Ignoring depreciation, except in determining the firm's taxes, results in cash flow from operations of $280,000—the value obtained above. Adjustment of the firm's net profits after taxes by adding back

---

[3] This system was first established in 1981 with passage of the *Economic Recovery Tax Act*. The *Tax Reform Act of 1986* revised this system, which is sometimes referred to as the ''new'' or ''modified'' accelerated cost recovery system (ACRS). For convenience, the new system is called ''ACRS'' throughout this text.

Table 3.4
Baker Corporation Income Statement Calculated on a Cash
Basis ($000) for the Year Ended December 31, 1988

Sales revenue		$1,700
Less: Cost of goods sold		1,000
Gross profits		$ 700
Less: Operating expenses		
Selling expense	$ 80	
General and administrative expense	150	
Depreciation expense (noncash charge)	0	
Total operating expense		230
Operating profits		$ 470
Less: Interest expense		70
Net profits before taxes		$ 400
Less: Taxes (from Table 3.1)		120
Cash flow from operations		$ 280

noncash charges such as depreciation will be used on many occasions in this text to estimate cash flow.

FACT OR FABLE?

3   Cash flow from operations can be found by subtracting all noncash charges such as depreciation from net profits after taxes. *(Fable)*

Cash flow from operations can be found by *adding* all noncash charges such as depreciation to net profits after taxes.

Depreciable Value of an Asset

Under the basic ACRS procedures, the depreciable value of an asset (the amount to be depreciated) is its *full* cost including outlays for installation. No adjustment is required for expected salvage value.

> **Example**
> Baker Corporation acquired a new machine at a cost of $38,000, with installation costs of $2,000. Regardless of its expected salvage value, the depreciable value of the machine is $40,000: ($38,000 cost + $2,000 installation cost).

Depreciable Life of an Asset

depreciable life Time period over which an asset is depreciated.

The time period over which an asset is depreciated—its **depreciable life**—can significantly affect the pattern of cash flows. The shorter the depreciable life, the more quickly the cash flow created by the depreciation write-off will be received. Given the financial manager's preference for faster receipt of cash flows, a shorter depreciable life is preferred to a longer one. Unfortunately, the firm must abide by certain Internal Revenue

Table 3.5
First Four Property Classes under ACRS

Property class (Recovery period)	Definition
3-year	Research and experiment equipment and certain special tools.
5-year	Computers, typewriters, copiers, duplicating equipment, cars, light-duty trucks, qualified technological equipment, and similar assets.
7-year	Office furniture, fixtures, most manufacturing equipment, railroad track, and single-purpose agricultural and horticultural structures.
10-year	Equipment used in petroleum refining or in the manufacture of tobacco products and certain food products.

Service (IRS) requirements for determining depreciable life. These ACRS standards, which apply to both new and used assets, require the taxpayer to use as an asset's depreciable life the appropriate ACRS **recovery period,** except in the case of certain assets depreciated under the *alternative depreciation system.*[4] There are six ACRS recovery periods—3, 5, 7, 10, 15, and 20 years—excluding real estate. As is customary, the property classes (excluding real estate) are referred to in accordance with their recovery periods, as 3-year, 5-year, 7-year, 10-year, 15-year, and 20-year property. The first four property classes—those routinely used by business—are defined in Table 3.5.

recovery period The appropriate depreciable life of a particular asset as determined by ACRS.

Depreciation Methods

For *tax purposes,* using ACRS recovery periods, assets in the first four property classes are depreciated by the double-declining balance (200%) method using the half-year convention and switching to straight line when advantageous. Although tables of depreciation percentages are not provided by law, the *approximate* (i.e., rounded to nearest whole percent) *percentages* written off each year for the first four property classes are given in Table 3.6. Rather than using the percentages in Table 3.6, the firm can either use straight-line depreciation over the asset's recovery period with the half-year convention or use the alternative depreciation system. For purposes of this text, we will use the ACRS depreciation percentages given in Table 3.6, since they generally provide for the fastest write-off and therefore the best cash flow effects for the profitable firm.

Because ACRS requires use of the half-year convention, assets are assumed to be acquired in the middle of the year and therefore only one-half of the first year's depreciation is recovered in the first year. As a result, the final half year of depreciation is recovered in the year immediately following the asset's stated recovery period. In Table 3.6 the depreciation percentages for an *n*-year class asset are given for *n* + 1 years. For example, a 5-year asset is depreciated over 6 recovery years. (*Note:* The percentages in Table 3.6 have been rounded to the nearest whole percentage in order to simplify calculations while retaining realism.)

For *financial reporting purposes* a variety of depreciation methods—straight-line, double-declining balance, and sum-of-the-years'-digits[5]—can be used. Since primary

---

[4] For convenience, the depreciation of assets under the *alternative depreciation system* is ignored in this text.

[5] For a review of these depreciation methods as well as other aspects of financial reporting, see any recently published financial accounting text.

Table 3.6
Rounded Depreciation Percentages by Recovery Year
Using ACRS for First Four Property Classes

	Percentage by recovery year[a]			
Recovery year	3-year	5-year	7-year	10-year
1	33	20	14	10
2	45	32	25	18
3	15	19	18	14
4	7	12	12	12
5		12	9	9
6		5	9	8
7			9	7
8			4	6
9				6
10				6
11				4

[a] These percentages have been rounded to the nearest whole percentage in order to simplify
calculations while retaining realism. In order to calculate the *actual* depreciation for tax purposes,
be sure to apply the actual unrounded percentages or directly apply double-declining balance
(200%) depreciation using the half-year convention.

concern in managerial finance centers on cash flows, *only tax depreciation methods will
be utilized throughout this textbook.* The application of the tax depreciation percentages
given in Table 3.6 can be demonstrated by a simple example.

Example
The Baker Corporation acquired, for an installed cost of $40,000, a machine having a
recovery period of five years. Using the applicable percentages from Table 3.6, the
depreciation in each year is calculated below.

Year	Cost (1)	Percentages (from Table 3.6) (2)	Depreciation [(1) × (2)] (3)
1	$40,000	20%	$ 8,000
2	40,000	32	12,800
3	40,000	19	7,600
4	40,000	12	4,800
5	40,000	12	4,800
6	40,000	5	2,000
Totals		100%	$40,000

Column 3 shows that the new cost of the asset is written off over six recovery years.

4 From a strict financial viewpoint, straight-line depreciation is preferred over the accelerated cost recovery system (ACRS) for tax purposes since it results in higher profits. *(Fable)*
Because ACRS depreciation generally provides the fastest write-offs and therefore the best cash flow effects, financial managers prefer its use for tax purposes.

FACT OR FABLE?

Analyzing the Firm's Funds Flow

The statement of changes in financial position, briefly described earlier, summarizes the firm's funds flow over a given period of time. Because it can be used to capture historic cash flow, the statement is developed in this section. First, however, we need to discuss the definition of funds, cash flow through the firm, and the classification of sources and uses.

Definition of Funds: Cash or Net Working Capital?

Funds can be defined as either cash or net working capital. **Net working capital** is the numerical difference between total current assets and total current liabilities (net working capital = total current assets − total current liabilities). Both forms of funds are necessary for the firm to function effectively. Cash is needed to pay current bills. Net working capital—especially in a seasonal business—is needed to provide a cushion for the payment of bills due in the near future.

funds Either cash or net working capital.

net working capital The numerical difference between total current assets and total current liabilities.

Current corporate practice reflects a preference for the *net-working-capital-based* form of the statement of changes in financial position. However, the accounting profession has lately been urging the required inclusion of a *cash-based* form of this statement in the annual stockholders' report. Due to its greater detail, the cash-based statement is more informative and thus is emphasized here.

Cash Flow Through the Firm

Figure 3.2 illustrates the overall flow of cash through the firm. For convenience the cash flows are divided into (1) operating flows and (2) financial and legal flows. The **operating flows** are cash outlays and inflows that relate to the firm's production cycle. In carrying out this cycle a firm must utilize, and pay for, raw materials, labor, and fixed assets while also paying sales expenses and operating and administrative expenses and salaries. In turn the firm produces and sells its finished goods. As Figure 3.2 shows, not all expenses are made for cash; many are made on credit through an account payable or an accrual. Similarly, not all sales are made for cash; many are made on credit through accounts receivable.

operating flows Cash flows relating to the firm's production cycle.

financial and legal flows Cash flows that include receipt and payment of interest, payment and refund of taxes, incurrence and repayment of debt, payment of dividends and stock repurchases, and cash inflow from sale of stock.

The **financial and legal flows** depicted in Figure 3.2 include the receipt and payment of interest; the payment and refund of taxes; the incurrence and repayment of debt; the effect of distributions of equity through payment of dividends and stock repurchases; and cash inflow from the sale of stock.

Figure 3.2
Cash Flow Through the Firm

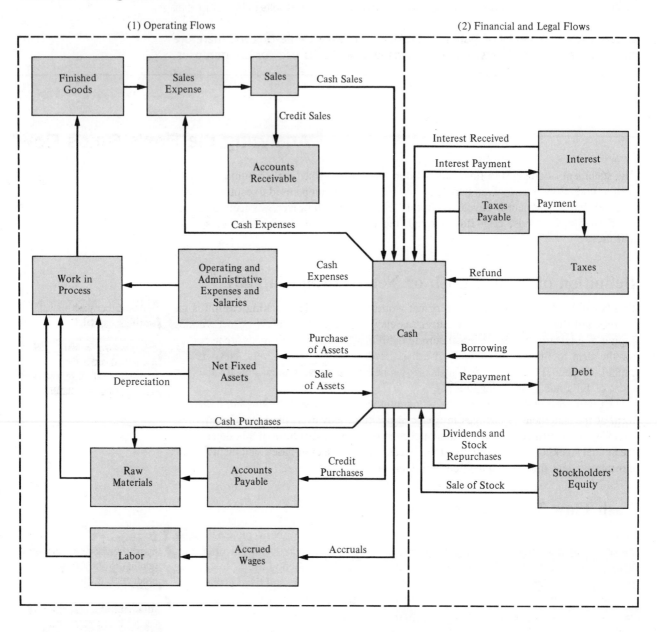

Classifying Sources and Uses of Cash

The cash-based statement of changes in financial position summarizes the sources and uses of cash during a given period. (Table 3.7 classifies the basic sources and uses.) For example, if a firm's accounts payable increased by $1,000 during the year, this change would be a *source of cash*. If the firm's inventory increased by $2,500 the change would be a *use of cash,* meaning that $2,500 was tied up in goods available for sale.

Table 3.7
The Sources and Uses of Cash ✳

Sources	Uses
Decrease in any asset	Increase in any asset
Increase in any liability	Decrease in any liability
Net profits after taxes	Net loss
Depreciation and other noncash charges	Dividends paid
Sale of stock	Repurchase or retirement of stock

A few additional points should be clarified with respect to the classification scheme in Table 3.7:

1. A *decrease* in an asset, such as the firm's cash balance, is a *source of cash flow* because cash is released for some purpose, such as adding to inventory. On the other hand, an *increase* in the firm's bank account is a *use of cash flow* since the cash must be drawn from somewhere.

2. Earlier, Equation 3.1 and the related discussion explained why depreciation and other noncash charges are considered cash inflows, or sources of cash. Adding noncash charges back to the firm's net profits after taxes gives cash flow from operations:

   Cash flow from operations = net profits after taxes + noncash charges

   A firm can have a *net loss* (negative net profits after taxes) and still have positive cash flow from operations when depreciation during the period is greater than the net loss. In the statement of changes in financial position, net profits after taxes (or net losses) and noncash charges are therefore treated as separate entries.

3. Because depreciation is treated as a separate source of cash, only *gross* rather than *net* changes in fixed assets appear on the statement of changes in financial position. This treatment avoids the potential double counting of depreciation.

4. Direct entries of changes in retained earnings are not classified as sources or uses of cash; instead, entries for items that affect retained earnings appear as net profits or losses after taxes and cash dividends.

---

5 Sources of cash include a decrease in any asset, an increase in a liability, net profits after taxes, depreciation and other noncash charges, and the sale of stock. *(Fact)*

FACT OR FABLE?

Developing the Statement of Changes in Financial Position

The statement of changes in financial position can be developed in two steps: (1) prepare a preliminary statement and (2) adjust the preliminary statement to obtain the final statement. Using this two-step procedure, the financial statements for Baker Corporation presented in Tables 3.1 and 3.2 can be used to demonstrate the preparation of its 1988 cash statement of changes in financial position.

FINANCE IN ACTION

CASH FLOW IS THE NAME OF THE GAME

Follow the money.

That's a guiding principle for the increasing number of stock analysts and investors who study corporate cash flows. While none of them advocates using cash-flow analysis by itself, they say it can be an important tool in piercing the camouflage that sometimes makes reported earnings misleading.
. . .

Take a company that spent $140 million on new machinery last year. If it depreciates the equipment over a seven-year period, it will be subtracting $20 million from reported profits each year.

Sheltering Earnings

But if the machines will stay up-to-date and useful for 25 years, the company's reported earnings may understate its true strength. In effect, says Norman Weinger, an analyst with Oppenheimer & Co., "companies with heavy depreciation can shelter earnings." . . .

Sometimes the reverse is true. If a company has been neglecting capital spending, its earnings may look good. But on a cash-flow basis, it will look no better, and perhaps worse, than its competitors.

Thus, focusing on cash flow makes the investor confront an important question: whether "the assets being depreciated really do wear out as rapidly as they are being depreciated," says Frank Williams, a vice president at Cantor, Fitzgerald & Co.

The simplest measure of corporate cash flow adds earnings and depreciation. This basic figure can be found in a company's financial statements, usually under the heading "working capital provided by operations." But Wall Street professionals don't stop there.

Thomas Mitchell, a research partner at Weiss, Peck & Greer, focuses on "free cash flow." This is basically cash flow minus the amount allocated for capital expenditures, but Mr. Mitchell also makes other adjustments.

Inventory and Receivables

First, he subtracts the amount of a company's additions to inventory; otherwise, he points out, a company might appear to have "great growth in cash flow" when, in fact, the money has already been spent on "six football fields of trucks." Next, he subtracts additions to receivables, since these might be dif-

ficult-to-collect bills. For most companies, he also subtracts dividends, because they verge on being non-discretionary expenditures.

Mr. Mitchell then calculates the ratio between a stock's price and its free cash flow. Using Mr. Mitchell's tough definition, only about 13 percent of all stocks have free cash flow equal to at least 5 percent of the stock's price. . . .

A company can also have negative cash flow. Mr. Williams of Cantor, Fitzgerald says that such companies can be good candidates for short selling, a strategy in which an investor sells borrowed shares in anticipation of a price decline.

Joseph Battipaglia, an analyst with Gruntal & Co., says that cash-flow trends gave alert investors an early warning of the auto industry's problems in the 1970s. . . .

Whatever cash-flow analysis shows about a company, the professionals say, further study is necessary. The main value of looking at cash flow, they add, may be that it can lead investors to consider stocks they might otherwise overlook.

SOURCE: John R. Dorfman, "Stock Analysts Increase Focus on Cash Flow," *The Wall Street Journal*, February 17, 1987, p. 37. Reprinted by permission of *The Wall Street Journal*, © Dow Jones & Company, Inc., 1987. All rights reserved.

The Preliminary Statement

A three-step procedure can be used to prepare a preliminary statement of changes in financial position.

Step 1: Calculate the balance sheet changes in assets, liabilities, and stockholders' equity over the period of concern. (*Note:* Calculate only the *net* fixed asset change for the fixed asset account.)

Step 2: Using the classification scheme in Table 3.7, classify each change calculated in Step 1 as either a source (S) or a use (U). (*Note:* Changes in stockholders' equity accounts are classified in the same way as changes in liabilities— increases are sources and decreases are uses.)

Step 3: List and sum all sources found in Steps 1 and 2 on the left and all uses found in

Steps 1 and 2 on the right to create a preliminary statement of changes in financial position. If this statement is prepared correctly, *total sources should equal total uses*.

Application of the three-step procedure to prepare a preliminary statement of changes in financial position is demonstrated in the following example.

Example

The Baker Corporation's balance sheets in Table 3.2 can be used to develop its 1988 preliminary statement of changes in financial position.

Step 1: The key balance sheet entries from Baker Corporation's balance sheet in Table 3.2 are listed in a stacked format in Table 3.8. Column (1) lists the account name and columns (2) and (3) give the 1988 and 1987 values, respectively, for each account. In column (4) the change in the balance sheet account between 1987 and 1988 is calculated. Note that for fixed assets, only the net fixed asset change of +$200,000 is calculated.

Step 2: Using the classification scheme from Table 3.7 and recognizing that changes in stockholders' equity are classified in the same way as changes in liabilities, the changes in column (4) of Table 3.8 are classified in column (5).

Step 3: The sources (S) and uses (U) from Table 3.8 are listed and totaled in Table 3.9 to create the preliminary statement of changes in financial position. *Note:* (1) All sources are listed on the left and all uses are listed on the right; (2) accounts for which no change (N) occurred are excluded from the statement; and (3) total sources ($900,000) equal total uses ($900,000).

Table 3.8
Balance Sheet Changes and Classification of Baker Corporation's Key Accounts ($000) Between 1987 and 1988

Account (1)	Account balance (from Table 3.2)		Change [(2) − (3)] (4)	Classification source (S); use (U); no change (N) (5)
	1988 (2)	1987 (3)		
Assets				
Cash	$ 400	$ 300	+$100	U
Marketable securities	600	200	+ 400	U
Accounts receivable	400	500	− 100	S
Inventories	600	900	− 300	S
Net fixed assets	1,200	1,000	+ 200	U
Liabilities				
Accounts payable	700	500	+ 200	S
Notes payable	600	700	− 100	U
Accruals	100	200	− 100	U
Long-term debts	600	400	+ 200	S
Stockholders' equity				
Preferred stock	100	100	0	N
Common stock at par	120	120	0	N
Paid-in capital in excess of par	380	380	0	N
Retained earnings	600	500	+ 100	S

Table 3.9
Preliminary Statement of Changes in Financial Position for Baker Corporation ($000) for the Year Ended December 31, 1988

Sources (S)[a]		Uses (U)[a]	
Decrease in accounts receivable	$100	Increase in cash	$100
Decrease in inventories	300	Increase in marketable securities	400
Increase in accounts payable	200	Increase in net fixed assets	200
Increase in long-term debts	200	Decrease in notes payable	100
Increase in retained earnings	100	Decrease in accruals	100
Total sources	$900	Total uses	$900

[a] Data from columns (4) and (5) of Table 3.8.

Adjustments to Get Final Statement

Although the preliminary statement of changes in financial position in Table 3.9 is in balance, it lacks important income statement information. Two of the entries in the statement—(1) the increase in retained earnings and (2) the increase in net fixed assets—contain important cash flow information. The two adjustments needed to convert the preliminary to the final statement involve these entries.

Retained Earnings Adjustment. The change in retained earnings reflects the *difference* between net profits and dividend payments during the period:

Net profits after taxes
Less: Dividends paid
—————————————
Change in retained earnings

Therefore in order to provide more useful information in the final statement of changes in financial position, net profits after taxes and dividends are substituted for the change in retained earnings on the preliminary statement.

Example
The Baker Corporation's change in retained earnings of +$100,000 during 1988 resulted from the following:

Net profits after taxes (from 1988 income statement in Table 3.1)	$180,000
Less: Dividends paid (from 1988 statement of retained earnings in Table 3.3)	80,000
Change in retained earnings	+$100,000

Note that the amount of dividends paid was obtained from the statement of retained earnings. If such a statement is not available, this value can be found by subtracting the change in retained earnings from net profits after taxes (dividends = $180,000 − $100,000 = $80,000).

In the final statement of changes in financial position in Table 3.10 the following two entries:

Net profits after taxes $180,000 (Source)
Dividends paid $ 80,000 (Use)

are substituted for:

Increase in retained earnings $100,000 (Source)

It can be seen that the net effect of the net profit and dividend entries is a $100,000 source ($180,000 source − $80,000 use), which is the amount of the retained earnings change eliminated.

Net Fixed Assets Adjustment. The change in net fixed assets reflects the *difference* between any change in gross fixed assets and depreciation expense. The depreciation expense from the income statement is generally equal to the change in accumulated depreciation during the period.[6]

Change in gross fixed assets
Less: Depreciation expense
Change in net fixed assets

In order to provide more useful information on the statement of changes in financial position, the change in gross fixed assets and depreciation expense are substituted for the change in net fixed assets on the preliminary statement.

Example
The Baker Corporation's change in net fixed assets of +$200,000 during 1988 resulted from the following:

Change in gross fixed assets (from 1988 and 1987 balance sheets in Table 3.2; $2,500,000 in 1988 − $2,200,000 in 1987)	+$300,000
Less: Depreciation expense (from 1988 income statement in Table 3.1)	100,000
Change in net fixed assets	+$200,000

Thus in the final statement of changes in financial position in Table 3.10, the following two entries:

Increase in gross fixed assets $300,000 (Use)
Depreciation expense $100,000 (Source)

---

[6] When the firm retires or sells fixed assets, the change in accumulated depreciation during the period will not equal the depreciation expense on the income statement. In this case special adjustments to gross fixed assets are required. To simplify, we will use depreciation expense that is assumed equal to the change in accumulated depreciation.

are substituted for:

Increase in net fixed assets $200,000 (Use)

The net effect of the gross fixed asset and depreciation entries is a $200,000 use ($300,000 use − $100,000 source), which is the amount of the net fixed asset entry eliminated.

The Final Statement. A number of important points relative to the statement of changes in financial position are to be noted in Table 3.10:

1. "Total sources" and "total uses" should be equal. If they are not, an error has been made somewhere. The amount of total sources and uses ($1,080,000) is not an important value.

2. Net profits after taxes are normally the first source listed, and dividends are normally the first use. Ordering items this way makes it easy to calculate the change in retained earnings.

3. Depreciation expense and increases in gross fixed assets are listed second to make it easy to compare them. Placing depreciation just below net profits after taxes also makes the firm's cash flow from operations easily calculable (see Equation 3.1).

4. The order of the remaining sources and uses does not matter; the only requirement is that sources appear on the left and uses on the right.

Net Working Capital Statement

The statement of changes in financial position in Table 3.10 is a cash statement summarizing the changes in all accounts during the period of concern. A more compact statement of changes is one in which *net working capital* rather than cash is the pivotal element. In this statement, instead of individual current asset and current liability changes, a summary entry—the change in net working capital—is made. (*Net working capital,* as noted ear-

Table 3.10
Final Cash Statement of Changes in Financial Position for Baker Corporation ($000) for the Year Ended December 31, 1988

Sources (S)		Uses (U)	
Net profits after taxes	$ 180	Dividends paid	$ 80
Depreciation expense	100	Increase in gross fixed assets	300
Decrease in accounts receivable	100	Increase in cash	100
Decrease in inventories	300	Increase in marketable securities	400
Increase in accounts payable	200	Decrease in notes payable	100
Increase in long-term debts	200	Decrease in accruals	100
Total sources	$1,080	Total uses	$1,080

Table 3.11
Calculation of Baker Corporation's Change in Net
Working Capital ($000), 1987 to 1988

	1988	1987
Total current assets	$2,000	$1,900
Less: Total current liabilities	1,400	1,400
Net working capital	$ 600	$ 500
Change in net working capital	+$100 (Use)	

lier, is the difference between total current assets and total current liabilities.) Changes in net working capital are classified in a fashion similar to changes in assets:

Decrease in net working capital (Source)
Increase in net working capital (Use)

To prepare the statement of changes in financial position on a net working capital basis, all noncurrent account entries are the same as for the cash statement.

Example
The first step in preparing the statement of changes in net working capital for Baker Corporation is to calculate the actual change in net working capital. Using the balance sheets in Table 3.2, the change in net working capital between 1987 and 1988 is calculated as shown in Table 3.11. Net working capital increased from $500,000 in 1987 to $600,000 in 1988, resulting in an increase of $100,000. As noted in Table 3.11, this change is a use of funds. Substituting the $100,000 increase in net working capital for all current account entries in the cash statement in Table 3.10 and retaining all other (noncurrent) entries results in the statement shown in Table 3.12.

Comparing the cash and net working capital statements for Baker Corporation in Tables 3.10 and 3.12, respectively, the more detailed nature of the cash statement is apparent. Most financial analysts prefer the detailed cash statement because it provides useful cash flow information. An understanding of the cash statement is therefore of prime importance to the financial manager.

Interpreting the Statement

The statement of changes in financial position allows the financial manager and other interested parties to analyze the firm's past and possibly future funds flow. The manager should pay special attention to the major sources and uses of funds in order to determine whether any developments have occurred that are contrary to the company's financial policies. In addition, the statement can be used to evaluate the fulfillment of projected goals. Specific links between sources and uses cannot be made using this statement, but it can be used to isolate inefficiencies. For example, increases in accounts receivable and inventories resulting in major uses of funds may respectively signal credit or inventory problems.

Table 3.12
Net Working Capital Statement of Changes in Financial Position for Baker Corporation ($000) for the Year Ended December 31, 1988

Sources (S)		Uses (U)	
Net profits after taxes	$180	Dividends paid	$ 80
Depreciation expense	100	Increase in gross fixed assets	300
Increase in long-term debts	200	Increase in net working capital	100
Total sources	$480	Total uses	$480

FACT OR FABLE?

6 The statement of changes in financial position allows the financial manager and other interested parties to analyze the firm's past and possibly future funds flow. *(Fact)*

In addition, the financial manager can prepare and analyze a statement of changes in financial position developed from projected, or pro forma, financial statements. This approach can be used to determine whether planned actions are desirable in view of the resulting cash flows.

Example
Analysis of Baker Corporation's cash statement of changes in financial position in Table 3.10 does not seem to indicate the existence of any major problems for the company. The sources and uses of funds seem to be distributed in a fashion consistent with prudent financial management. The firm seems to be growing since (1) less than half of its earnings ($80,000 out of $180,000) were paid to owners as dividends and (2) gross fixed assets increased by three times the amount of historic cost written off through depreciation expense ($300,000 increase in gross fixed assets versus $100,000 in depreciation expense). Major sources of funds were obtained by decreasing inventories and increasing accounts payable. The major use of funds—an increase in marketable securities—reflects improved liquidity. Other sources and uses by Baker Corporation tend to support the fact that the firm was well managed financially during the period. *An understanding of the basic financial principles presented throughout this text is a prerequisite to the effective interpretation of the statement of changes in financial position.*

Summary

The annual stockholders' report of a publicly traded corporation includes, in addition to the president's letter and various subjective and factual information, four key financial statements: (1) the income statement, (2) the balance sheet, (3) the statement of retained earnings, and (4) the statement of changes in financial position.

The income statement summarizes operating results during the period of concern. The balance sheet summarizes the firm's financial position at a given point in time. The statement of retained earnings reconciles income and cash dividends with retained earnings for the period. The statement of changes in financial position provides a summary of funds flow over the period.

● Depreciation, or the allocation of historic cost, is the most common type of corporate noncash expenditure. To estimate cash flow from operations, depreciation and any other noncash charges are added back to net profits after taxes.

● The depreciable value of an asset and its depreciable life are determined using the Accelerated Cost Recovery System (ACRS) standards set out in the federal tax codes. ACRS groups assets (excluding real estate) into six property classes based on length of recovery period—3, 5, 7, 10, 15, and 20 years—and can be applied over the appropriate period using a schedule of yearly depreciation percentages for each period.

● The funds flow of a firm can be measured either by cash or by net working capital. Sources of funds increase the firm's cash flow, and uses of funds result in a decrease in cash flow.

● A preliminary statement of changes in financial position can be developed by finding, classifying as sources or uses, and totaling changes in balance sheet accounts over the period.

● The final statement of changes in financial position is developed from the preliminary by replacing the change in retained earnings with net profits after taxes and dividends, and by replacing the change in net fixed assets with the change in gross fixed assets and depreciation expense.

● Interpretation of the statement of changes in financial position involves evaluation of the level of and relationship between various sources and uses of funds. An understanding of basic financial principles is a prerequisite to the effective interpretation of the statement.

Questions

3-1 What are *generally accepted accounting principles (GAAP)?* Who authorizes GAAP? What role does the *Securities and Exchange Commission (SEC)* play in the financial reporting activities of corporations?

3-2 Describe the basic contents, including the key financial statements, included in the stockholders' reports of publicly held corporations.

3-3 What basic information is contained in each of the following financial statements? Briefly describe each.

    a. Income statement

    b. Balance sheet

    c. Statement of retained earnings

3-4 In what sense does depreciation act as cash inflow? How can a firm's after-tax profits be adjusted to determine cash flow from operations?

3-5 Briefly describe the first four Accelerated Cost Recovery System (ACRS) property classes and recovery periods. Explain how the depreciation percentages are determined using the ACRS recovery periods.

3-6 Define *net working capital* and discuss its use as a measure of funds flow. What is the alternative and more popular definition of *funds flow?*

3-7 Describe the overall cash flow through the firms in terms of (a) operating flows and (b) financial and legal flows.

3-8 List and describe *sources of cash* and *uses of cash.* Discuss why a decrease in cash is a source and an increase in cash is a use.

3-9 Describe the three-step procedure used to develop a *preliminary* statement of changes in financial position. What two adjustments are required in order to obtain the *final* statement?

3-10 Describe the statement of changes in financial position, and explain the difference between the cash and the net working capital statement.

3-11 How is the statement of changes in financial position interpreted and used by the financial manager and other interested parties?

Self-Test Problem

(Solution on page 86)

ST-1 A firm expects to have earnings before depreciation and taxes (EBDT) of $160,000 in each of the next six years. It is considering the purchase of an asset costing $140,000, requiring $10,000 in installation costs, and having a recovery period of five years.

    a. Calculate the annual depreciation for the asset purchase using the ACRS depreciation percentages in Table 3.6 on page 66.

   b. Calculate the annual operating cash flows for each of the six years. Assume a 40 percent ordinary tax rate.

   c. Compare and discuss your findings in **a** and **b.**

Problems

3-1   **(Reviewing Basic Financial Statements)** The income statement for the year ended December 31, 1988, the balance sheets for December 31, 1988 and 1987, and the statement of retained earnings for the year ended December 31, 1988, for Technica, Inc. are given below and on page 79. Briefly discuss the form and informational content of each of these statements.

Income Statement Technica, Inc. for the Year Ended December 31, 1988		
Sales revenue		$600,000
Less: Cost of goods sold		460,000
Gross profit		$140,000
Less: Operating expenses		
General and administrative expense	$30,000	
Depreciation expense	30,000	
Total operating expense		60,000
Operating profit		$ 80,000
Less: Interest expense		10,000
Net profits before taxes		$ 70,000
Less: Taxes		27,100
Earnings available for common stockholders		$ 42,900
Earnings per share (EPS)		$2.15

Balance Sheets **Technica, Inc.**		
	December 31,	
Assets	**1988**	**1987**
Cash	$ 15,000	$ 16,000
Marketable securities	7,200	8,000
Accounts receivable	34,100	42,200
Inventories	82,000	50,000
Total current assets	$138,300	$116,200
Land and buildings	$150,000	$150,000
Machinery and equipment	200,000	190,000
Furniture and fixtures	54,000	50,000
Other	11,000	10,000
Total gross fixed assets	$415,000	$400,000
Less: Accumulated depreciation	145,000	115,000
Net fixed assets	$270,000	$285,000
Total assets	$408,300	$401,200
Liabilities and stockholders' equity		
Accounts payable	$ 57,000	$ 49,000
Notes payable	13,000	16,000
Accruals	5,000	6,000
Total current liabilities	$ 75,000	$ 71,000
Long-term debt	$150,000	$160,000
Stockholders' equity		
Common stock equity (20,000 shares outstanding)	$110,200	$120,000
Retained earnings	73,100	50,200
Total stockholders' equity	$183,300	$170,200
Total liabilities and stockholders' equity	$408,300	$401,200

Statement of Retained Earnings **Technica, Inc.** **for the Year Ended December 31, 1988**	
Retained earnings balance (January 1, 1988)	$50,200
Plus: Net profits after taxes (for 1988)	42,900
Less: Cash dividends (paid during 1988)	(20,000)
Retained earnings balance (December 31, 1988)	$73,100

3-2 **(Financial Statement Account Identification)** Mark each of the accounts listed in the table on page 80 as follows:

a. In column (1) indicate in which statement—income statement (IS) or balance sheet (BS)—the account belongs.

b. In column (2) indicate whether the account is a current asset (CA), current liability (CL), expense (E), fixed asset (FA), long-term debt (LTD), revenue (R), or stockholders' equity (SE).

Account name	(1) Statement	(2) Type of account
Accounts payable	————	————
Accounts receivable	————	————
Accruals	————	————
Accumulated depreciation	————	————
Administrative expense	————	————
Buildings	————	————
Cash	————	————
Common stock (at par)	————	————
Cost of goods sold	————	————
Depreciation	————	————
Equipment	————	————
General expense	————	————
Interest expense	————	————
Inventories	————	————
Land	————	————
Long-term debts	————	————
Machinery	————	————
Marketable securities	————	————
Notes payable	————	————
Operating expense	————	————
Paid-in capital in excess of par	————	————
Preferred stock	————	————
Preferred stock dividends	————	————
Retained earnings	————	————
Sales revenue	————	————
Selling expense	————	————
Taxes	————	————
Vehicles	————	————

3-3 **(Income Statement Preparation)** Use the *appropriate items* from those listed below to prepare in good form Perry Corporation's income statement for the year ended December 31, 1988.

Item	Values ($000) at or for year ended December 31, 1988
Accounts receivable	$350
Accumulated depreciation	205
Cost of goods sold	285
Depreciation expense	55
General and administrative expense	60
Interest expense	25
Preferred stock dividends	10
Sales revenue	525
Selling expense	35
Stockholders' equity	265
Taxes	rate = 40%

3-4   **(Income Statement Preparation)** Cathy Chen, a self-employed Certified Public Accountant (CPA), on December 31, 1988, completed her first full year in business. During the year she billed $135,000 in business. She had two employees, a bookkeeper and a clerical assistant. In addition to her *monthly* salary of $2,750, she paid annual salaries of $18,000 and $14,000, respectively, to the bookkeeper and the clerical assistant. Employment taxes and benefit costs for health insurance, etc., for Ms. Chen and her employees totaled $12,800 for the year. Expenses for office supplies, including postage, totaled $3,800 for the year. In addition, Ms. Chen spent $6,500 during the year on travel and entertainment associated with client visits and new business development. Lease payments for the office space rented (a tax-deductible expense) were $1,000 *per month*. Depreciation expense on the office furniture and fixtures was $6,200 for the year. During the year Ms. Chen paid interest of $6,900 on the $50,000 borrowed to start the business. She paid an average tax rate of 30 percent during 1988.

   a. Prepare an income statement for Cathy Chen, CPA for the year ended December 31, 1988.

   b. How much operating cash flow did Cathy realize during 1988?

   c. Evaluate her 1988 financial performance.

3-5   **(Calculation of EPS and Retained Earnings)** Philagem, Inc. ended 1988 with net profit *before* taxes of $218,000. The company is subject to a 40 percent tax rate and must pay $32,000 in preferred stock dividends prior to distributing any earnings on the 85,000 shares of common stock currently outstanding.

   a. Calculate Philagem's 1988 earnings per share (EPS).

   b. If the firm paid common stock dividends of $.80 per share, how many dollars would go to retained earnings?

3-6   **(Balance Sheet Preparation)** Use the *appropriate items* from those listed below to prepare in good form Owen Davis Company's balance sheet at December 31, 1988.

Item	Values ($000) at December 31, 1988
Accounts payable	$ 220
Accounts receivable	450
Accruals	55
Accumulated depreciation	265
Buildings	225
Cash	215
Common stock (at par)	90
Cost of goods sold	2,500
Depreciation expense	45
Equipment	140
Furniture and fixtures	170
General expense	320
Inventories	375
Land	100
Long-term debts	420
Machinery	420
Marketable securities	75
Notes payable	475
Paid-in capital in excess of par	360
Preferred stock	100
Retained earnings	210
Sales revenue	3,600
Vehicles	25

3-7   **(Initial Sale Price of Common Stock)** Beck Corporation has one issue of preferred stock and one issue of common stock outstanding. Given Beck's stockholders' equity account below, determine the original price per share at which the firm sold its single issue of common stock.

Stockholders' equity ($000)	
Preferred stock	$ 125
Common stock ($.75 par, 300,000 shares outstanding)	225
Paid-in capital in excess of par on common stock	2,625
Retained earnings	900
Total stockholders' equity	$3,875

3-8   **(Financial Statement Preparation)** The balance sheet for Rogers Industries for December 31, 1987, is given below. Information relevant to Rogers Industries 1988 operations is given in the table at the top of page 83. Using the data presented:

a. Prepare in good form an income statement for Rogers Industries for the year ended December 31, 1988. Be sure to show earnings per share (EPS).

b. Prepare in good form a balance sheet for Rogers Industries for December 31, 1988.

Balance Sheet ($000) Rogers Industries December 31, 1987			
Assets		**Liabilities and stockholders' equity**	
Cash	$ 40	Accounts payable	$ 50
Marketable securities	10	Notes payable	80
Accounts receivable	80	Accruals	10
Inventories	100	Total current liabilities	$140
Total current assets	$230		
Gross fixed assets	$890	Long-term debt	$270
Less: Accumulated		Preferred stock	40
depreciation	240	Common stock ($.75 par, 80,000 shares)	60
Net fixed assets	$650	Paid-in capital in excess of par	260
Total assets	$880	Retained earnings	110
		Total stockholders' equity	$470
		Total liabilities and stockholders' equity	$880

Relevant Information
Rogers Industries

1. Sales in 1988 were $1,200,000.
2. Cost of goods sold equals 60 percent of sales.
3. Operating expenses equals 15 percent of sales.
4. Interest expense is 10 percent of the total beginning balance of notes payable and long-term debts.
5. The firm pays 40 percent taxes on ordinary income.
6. Preferred stock dividends of $4,000 were paid in 1988.
7. Cash and marketable securities are unchanged.
8. Accounts receivable equals 8 percent of sales.
9. Inventory equals 10 percent of sales.
10. The firm acquired $30,000 of additional fixed assets in 1988.
11. Total depreciation expense in 1988 was $20,000.
12. Accounts payable equals 5 percent of sales.
13. Notes payable, long-term debt, preferred stock, common stock, and paid-in capital in excess of par remain unchanged.
14. Accruals are unchanged.
15. Cash dividends of $119,000 were paid to common stockholders in 1988.

3-9 **(Statement of Retained Earnings)** Hayes Enterprises began 1988 with a retained earnings balance of $928,000. During 1988 the firm earned $377,000 after taxes. From this amount preferred stockholders were paid $47,000 in dividends. At year-end 1988 the firm's retained earnings totaled $1,048,000. The firm had 140,000 shares of common stock outstanding during 1988.

  a. Prepare a statement of retained earnings for the year ended December 31, 1988, for Hayes Enterprises.

  b. Calculate the firm's 1988 earnings per share (EPS).

  c. How large a per share cash dividend did the firm pay on common stock during 1988?

3-10 **(Cash Flow)** A firm had earnings after taxes of $50,000 in 1988. Depreciation charges were $28,000, and a $2,000 charge for amortization of a bond discount was incurred. What was the actual cash flow from operations?

3-11 **(Depreciation)** On January 1, 1988, Norton Systems acquired two new assets. Asset A was research equipment costing $17,000 and having a three-year recovery period. Asset B was duplicating equipment having an installed cost of $45,000 and a five-year recovery period. Using the ACRS depreciation percentages in Table 3.6 on page 66, prepare a depreciation schedule for each of these assets.

3-12 **(Depreciation and Cash Flow)** A firm in the third year of depreciating its only asset, originally costing $180,000 and having a five-year ACRS recovery period, has gathered the following data relative to the given year's operations.

Accruals	$ 15,000
Current assets	120,000
Interest expense	15,000
Sales revenue	400,000
Inventory	70,000
Total costs before depreciation, interest, and taxes	290,000
Tax rate on ordinary income	40%

a. Use the *relevant data* above to determine the *cash flow from operations* for the current year.

b. Explain the impact that depreciation, as well as any other noncash charges, has on a firm's cash flows.

3-13 **(Classifying Sources and Uses)** Classify each of the following items as a source (S) or a use (U) of funds, or as neither (N).

Item	Change ($)	Item	Change ($)
Cash	+100	Accounts receivable	−700
Accounts payable	−1,000	Net profits	+600
Notes payable	+500	Depreciation	+100
Long-term debt	−2,000	Repurchase of stock	+600
Inventory	+200	Cash dividends	+800
Fixed assets	+400	Sale of stock	+1,000

3-14 **(Finding Dividends Paid)** Colonial Paint's net profits after taxes in 1988 totaled $186,000. The firm's year-end 1988 and 1987 retained earnings on its balance sheet totaled $812,000 and $736,000, respectively. How many dollars, if any, in dividends did Colonial pay in 1988?

3-15 **(Preparing Statements of Changes in Financial Position)** Given the balance sheets and selected data from the income statement of Keith Corporation at the top of page 85:

a. Prepare the firm's statement of changes in financial position on a *cash basis* for the year ended December 31, 1988.

b. Interpret the statement prepared in **a**.

c. Prepare the firm's statement of changes in financial position on a *net working capital basis* for the year ended December 31, 1988.

d. Compare and discuss the net working capital statement developed in **c** with the cash statement in **a**.

Balance Sheets Keith Corporation		
	December 31	
Assets	**1988**	**1987**
Cash	$ 1,500	$ 1,000
Marketable securities	1,800	1,200
Accounts receivable	2,000	1,800
Inventories	2,900	2,800
Total current assets	$ 8,200	$ 6,800
Gross fixed assets	$29,500	$28,100
Less: Accumulated depreciation	14,700	13,100
Net fixed assets	$14,800	$15,000
Total assets	$23,000	$21,800
Liabilities and stockholders' equity		
Accounts payable	$ 1,600	$ 1,500
Notes payable	2,800	2,200
Accruals	200	300
Total current liabilities	$ 4,600	$ 4,000
Long-term debt	$ 5,000	$ 5,000
Common stock	$10,000	$10,000
Retained earnings	3,400	2,800
Total stockholders' equity	$13,400	$12,800
Total liabilities and stockholders' equity	$23,000	$21,800
Additional data		
Depreciation expense	$ 1,600	
Net profits after taxes	1,400	

Handwritten annotations next to asset rows: 500, 600, 200, 100, 1400

3-16 **(Preparing Statements of Changes in Financial Position)** Using the 1988 income statement and the 1988 and 1987 balance sheets for Technica, Inc., given in Problem 3-1, do the following:

a. Prepare the firm's statement of changes in financial position on a *cash basis* for the year ended December 31, 1988.

b. Interpret the statement prepared in **a.**

c. Prepare the firm's statement of changes in financial position on a *net working capital basis* for the year ended December 31, 1988.

d. Compare and discuss the net working capital statement developed in **c** with the cash statement in **a.**

Solution to Self-Test Problem

ST-1 a. Depreciation schedule

Year	Cost* (1)	Percentages (from Table 3.6) (2)	Depreciation [(1) × (2)] (3)
1	$150,000	20%	$ 30,000
2	150,000	32	48,000
3	150,000	19	28,500
4	150,000	12	18,000
5	150,000	12	18,000
6	150,000	5	7,500
		100%	$150,000

*$140,000 asset cost + $10,000 installation cost.

b. Cash flow schedule

Year	EBDT (1)	Deprec. (2)	Net profits before taxes [(1) − (2)] (3)	Taxes [.4 × (3)] (4)	Net profits after taxes [(3) − (4)] (5)	Operating cash flows [(2) + (5)] (6)
1	$160,000	$30,000	$130,000	$52,000	$78,000	$108,000
2	160,000	48,000	112,000	44,800	67,200	115,200
3	160,000	28,500	131,500	52,600	78,900	107,400
4	160,000	18,000	142,000	56,800	85,200	103,200
5	160,000	18,000	142,000	56,800	85,200	103,200
6	160,000	7,500	152,500	61,000	91,500	99,000

c. The purchase of the asset allows the firm to use depreciation as a tax shield against income thereby causing operating cash flows (in column 6 of the table above) to exceed net profits after taxes (in column 5 of the table).

CHAPTER 4

The Analysis of Financial Statements

FACT OR FABLE?
Are the following statements fact *(true)* or fable *(false)*?

1
Cross-sectional analysis involves a comparison of a firm's current to past performance using ratio analysis.

2
Net working capital, the current ratio, and the quick (acid-test) ratio are measures of liquidity, which is the firm's ability to satisfy obligations as they come due.

3
Times interest earned and the fixed-payment coverage ratios are activity ratios which are used to measure the speed with which these obligations are paid.

4
The debt position of the firm can be assessed using ratios that measure its degree of indebtedness and/or its ability to service debts.

5
Profitability measures allow the analyst to evaluate the firm's earnings with respect to sales, assets, equity, or share value.

6
The appeal of the DuPont system is that it allows the firm to break its return on equity into a liquidity component (current ratio) and a profitability component (earnings per share).

Philips Industries, of Dayton, Ohio, is one of those companies that performs consistently well without generating the kind of excitement the business community seems to expect these days. In an era when technological innovations, mergers, and takeovers headline the business news, Philips goes its own way, churning out products and profits.

With a sales target of $1 billion a year by 1990, Philips is not known as a "star" in anything except performance. What, then, accounts for its success? The philosophy that runs the company says do the simple things but do them well and do them every day.

Among the simple things is "finding the niches," according to company founder Jesse Philips. That way, Philips avoids locking horns with big competitors. Among the products Philips produces are air diffusers, fans for heating and air conditioning systems, terminal boxes, bathtubs, even wheels for recreational vehicles. Nothing flashy or especially newsworthy—but all of it very necessary and much of it immune to economic downturns. Philips follows several other simple guidelines: expand your sales area, acquire only businesses that are in related product areas, and control costs at all levels.

In addition, the top management stays in close touch with operations. Jesse Philips and President Robert Brethen watch inventory at all locations, because high inventory levels can affect profits negatively. Philips management also insists on knowing whenever a problem is brewing in any area of the corporation.

Philips reported increasing sales and exceptional earnings during much of the mid-1980s—a time of slow or no growth for many industries. Combine this record of an average return on equity from 1983–1986 of 25 percent with a low debt load—14 percent of capital—and it's hard to believe there's no magic formula. Perhaps the magic is just what Jesse Philips says it is: concentrating on doing the ordinary things better than anyone else. It's an old-fashioned idea but it results in a rosy set of financial statements.

Financial managers as well as other interested parties must not only understand financial statements, but also be able to analyze them in order to gain clearer insight into the firm's financial condition, which is not always as rosy as that of Philips Industries. Here we describe how financial ratios can be used to analyze financial statements.

The Use of Financial Ratios

ratio analysis Involves the methods of calculating and interpreting financial ratios to assess the firm's performance and status.

In the preceding chapter we studied the format, components, and basic purpose of each of the firm's four basic financial statements. The information contained in these statements is of major significance to shareholders, creditors, and managers, all of whom regularly need to have relative measures of the company's operating efficiency and condition. *Relative* is the key word here since the analysis of financial statements is based on the knowledge and use of *ratios* or *relative values*.

Ratio analysis involves the methods of calculating and interpreting financial ratios in order to assess the firm's performance and status. The basic inputs to ratio analysis are the firm's income statement and balance sheet for the periods to be examined. However, before proceeding further we need to describe the various parties and the types of comparisons made using ratio analysis.

Interested Parties

Ratio analysis of a firm's financial statements is of interest to shareholders, creditors, and the firm's own management. Both present and prospective shareholders are interested in the firm's current and future level of risk and return. As will be explained in Chapters 7 and 8, these two dimensions directly affect share price. The firm's creditors are primarily interested in the short-term liquidity of the company and in its ability to make interest and principal payments. A secondary concern of creditors is the firm's profitability; they want assurance that the business is healthy and will continue to be successful. Management, like stockholders, must be concerned with all aspects of the firm's financial situation. Thus it attempts to operate in a manner that will result in financial ratios that will be considered favorable by both owners and creditors. In addition, management uses ratios to monitor the firm's performance from period to period. Any unexpected changes are examined in order to isolate developing problems.

Types of Comparisons

Ratio analysis does not merely involve the application of a formula to financial data in order to calculate a given ratio. More important is the *interpretation* of the ratio value. To answer such questions as, Is it too high or too low? Is it good or bad?, a meaningful standard or basis for comparison is needed. Two types of ratio comparisons can be made: cross-sectional and time-series.

Cross-Sectional Analysis

Cross-sectional analysis involves the comparison of different firms' financial ratios at the same point in time. The typical business is interested in how well it has performed in relation to its competitors. (If the competitors are also corporations, their reported financial statements should be available for analysis.) Often the firm's performance will be compared to that of the industry leader, and the firm may uncover major operating differences, which, if changed, will increase efficiency. Another popular type of comparison is to industry averages. These figures can be found in the *Almanac of Business and Industrial Financial Ratios, Dun & Bradstreet's Key Business Ratios, Dun's Business Month, FTC Quarterly Reports, Robert Morris Associates Statement Studies*, and other sources such as industry association publications.[1] A sample from one available source of industry averages is given in Table 4.1.

The comparison of a particular ratio to the standard is made in order to isolate any *deviations from the norm*. Many people mistakenly believe that in the case of ratios for which higher values are preferred, as long as the firm being analyzed has a value in excess of the industry average, it can be viewed favorably. However, this "bigger is better"

cross-sectional analysis
The comparison of different firms' financial ratios at the same point in time.

---

[1] Cross-sectional comparisons of firms operating in several lines of business are difficult to perform. The use of weighted-average industry average ratios based on the firm's product line mix or, if data are available, analysis of the firm on a product-line-by-product-line basis, can be performed to analyze a multiproduct firm.

Table 4.1
Industry Average Ratios for Selected Lines of Business[a]

Line of business (number of concerns reporting)	Quick ratio (X)	Current ratio (X)	Total liabilities to net worth (%)	Collection period (days)	Net sales to inventory (X)	Total assets to net sales (%)	Net sales to net working capital (X)	Return on net sales (%)	Return on total assets (%)	Return on net worth (%)
Computer related services (855)	2.8	3.9	31.9	20.8	46.7	25.9	20.0	18.2	28.0	65.8
	1.3	**1.7**	**79.0**	**38.5**	**16.1**	**40.0**	**8.9**	**9.1**	**15.7**	**35.0**
	0.6	1.1	205.4	66.4	6.7	72.9	4.4	3.5	5.9	17.2
Crude oil and natural gas (1244)	1.9	3.1	15.9	31.1	61.6	109.4	11.6	22.2	10.7	18.6
	0.9	**1.2**	**59.6**	**66.0**	**24.5**	**212.8**	**4.1**	**8.0**	**3.3**	**7.0**
	0.4	0.7	164.5	121.7	10.9	378.3	1.5	(2.4)	(1.3)	(2.4)
Grocery stores (2130)	1.2	3.9	34.3	1.0	23.1	13.0	32.9	3.7	13.4	32.2
	0.5	**2.1**	**86.1**	**2.9**	**16.3**	**18.8**	**16.3**	**1.6**	**6.5**	**14.2**
	0.2	1.3	221.5	6.5	10.4	30.3	9.0	0.5	2.1	5.0
Metal working machinery (77)	1.3	2.9	31.4	26.7	10.1	36.8	6.4	15.0	13.9	26.1
	0.9	**2.0**	**70.6**	**42.9**	**6.2**	**54.3**	**4.4**	**5.1**	**4.9**	**13.6**
	0.5	1.3	140.3	62.7	4.3	72.4	2.1	2.1	1.2	3.1
Petroleum products (1613)	1.8	2.8	40.9	12.5	60.8	12.7	41.3	2.6	10.2	23.6
	1.1	**1.7**	**103.3**	**20.8**	**34.0**	**19.0**	**18.8**	**1.3**	**6.1**	**12.5**
	0.7	1.2	238.5	33.5	19.0	30.9	8.7	0.5	2.1	5.3
Petroleum refining (73)	1.1	1.9	76.1	22.1	31.1	30.6	47.2	5.8	5.9	22.4
	0.6	**1.2**	**162.9**	**35.2**	**16.8**	**45.6**	**13.1**	**2.0**	**3.3**	**7.9**
	0.4	0.9	280.9	46.2	10.6	86.0	7.3	0.3	0.7	3.8
Variety stores (795)	1.0	6.2	19.4	1.8	5.1	32.1	7.4	8.2	18.8	32.2
	0.4	**3.2**	**54.7**	**4.7**	**3.6**	**44.0**	**4.3**	**3.7**	**8.7**	**16.4**
	0.2	2.0	131.3	12.4	2.4	66.1	2.6	1.1	3.4	6.4

[a] These values are given for each ratio for each line of business. The center value is the median, and the values immediately above and below it are the upper and lower quartiles, respectively.

SOURCE: Extracted from *Industry Norms and Key Business Ratios,* 1985–86 edition (New York: Dun & Bradstreet, Inc., 1986).

viewpoint can be misleading. Quite often a ratio value that has a large but positive deviation from the norm can be indicative of problems that may, upon more careful analysis, be more severe than had the ratio been below the industry average. It is therefore important for the analyst to further investigate significant *deviations to either side* of the industry standard.

The analyst must also recognize that ratio comparisons resulting in large deviations from the norm reflect only the *symptoms* of a problem. Further analysis of the financial statements coupled with discussions with key managers is typically required to isolate the *causes* of the problem. Once this is accomplished, the financial manager must develop prescriptive actions for eliminating such causes. The fundamental point is that *ratio analysis merely directs the analyst to potential areas of concern; it does not provide conclusive evidence as to the existence of a problem.*

Example

In early 1989 the chief financial analyst at Caldwell Manufacturing gathered data on the firm's financial performance during 1988, the year just ended. The analyst calculated a variety of ratios and obtained industry averages for use in making comparisons. One ratio she was especially interested in was inventory turnover, which reflects the speed with which the firm moves its inventory from raw materials through production into finished goods and to the customer as a completed sale. Generally, higher values of this ratio are preferred, since they indicate a quicker turnover of inventory. Caldwell Manufacturing's calculated inventory turnover for 1988 and the industry average inventory turnover were, respectively:

	Inventory turnover, 1988
Caldwell Manufacturing	14.8 *times during the year*
Industry average	9.7

The analyst's initial reaction to these data was that the firm had managed its inventory significantly better than the average firm in the industry. The turnover was in fact nearly 53 percent faster than the industry average. Upon reflection, however, the analyst felt there could be a problem, since a very high inventory turnover could also mean very low levels of inventory. In turn, the consequence of low inventory could be excessive stockouts (insufficient inventory). The analyst's review of other ratios and discussions with persons in the manufacturing and marketing departments did in fact uncover such a problem: The firm's inventories during the year were extremely low as a result of numerous production delays that hindered its ability to meet demand and resulted in lost sales. What had initially appeared to reflect extremely efficient inventory management was actually the symptom of a major problem.

Time-Series Analysis

Time-series analysis is applied when a financial analyst evaluates performance over time. Comparison of current to past performance utilizing ratio analysis allows the firm to determine whether it is progressing as planned. Developing trends can be seen by using multiyear comparisons, and knowledge of these trends should assist the firm in planning future operations. As in cross-sectional analysis, any significant year-to-year changes can be evaluated to assess whether they are symptomatic of a major problem. The theory behind time-series analysis is that the company must be evaluated in relation to its past performance, developing trends must be isolated, and appropriate action taken to direct the firm toward immediate and long-run goals. Time-series analysis is often helpful in checking the reasonableness of a firm's projected (pro forma) financial statements. A comparison of *current* and *past* ratios to those resulting from an analysis of *projected* statements may reveal discrepancies or overoptimism.

time-series analysis
Evaluation of the firm's financial performance over time utilizing financial ratio analysis.

DON TRAUTLEIN: Figures Don't Tell the Whole Story

"In the last two decades," says Don Trautlein, chairman and CEO of Bethlehem Steel, "the financial executive has changed substantially—both in the scope of his interests and in his view of his own role." While this officer must still look at the numbers, assess the financial soundness of major projects, and work out the bottom line for the organization, he is today much more people-oriented, and he looks at his whole organization in a much broader way than his predecessors did.

Don Trautlein has been a financial executive himself, and today presides over Bethlehem Steel, a major corporation hard hit by world competition. He is modernizing plants, restructuring the corporation, and dealing with agonizing changes. Trautlein emphasizes that change must be carefully managed. He says, "You cannot stampede or destroy those who have given of themselves to build the old structure and whose work and devotion will be required to make successful changes and build a new, more profitable structure." In moving a highly structured, centralized organiza-

tion toward greater flexibility, Trautlein must develop participative management, meet the needs of a more educated work force, and assess the forces molding his industry.

Don Trautlein underscores the importance of financial analysis. But in guiding the corporation into a new, more profitable era, he uses his financial skills in a new way. Cost effectiveness depends not just on amount

expended versus some immediate, quantifiable result, but also on the value of intangible benefits that can pay off only over an indeterminate time. "We have had to spend heavily," says Trautlein, "on training, on building morale, on breaking down 40-year-old adversarial union/management relationships." In one such move, Bethlehem took union leaders to visit competitors' plants here and abroad, so that they could see firsthand the kind of work practices and labor/management relationships they were competing against.

It is also difficult to foresee how acquisitions will help a company grow. A financial background, Trautlein believes, will be very useful in assessing possible acquisitions, but it must be supplemented with a vision of where one wants to go and a sense of both a company's culture and its capabilities.

In such tough decisions, input cannot always be quantified. The challenge is to integrate gut feelings and human judgment into decision-making. Today's CFO must look beyond a sheet of figures.

SOURCE: Adapted from "Donald Trautlein of Bethlehem Steel: How to Become a CEO," by George de Mare with Joanne Summerfield. Reprinted by permission of *FE: the magazine for financial executives,* April 1985, copyright 1985 by Financial Executives Institute.

Combined Analysis

The most informative approach to ratio analysis is one that combines cross-sectional and time-series analyses. A combined view permits assessment of the trend in the behavior of the ratio in relation to the trend for the industry. Figure 4.1 depicts this type of approach using Bartlett Oil Company's average collection period ratio in the years 1985–1988. Generally, lower values of this ratio, which reflects the average amount of time it takes the firm to collect bills, are preferred. A look at the figure quickly discloses that (1) Bartlett Oil's effectiveness in collecting its receivables is poor in comparison to the industry and (2) there is a trend toward longer collection periods. Clearly Bartlett Oil needs to shorten its collection period.

Figure 4.1
Combined Cross-Sectional and Time-Series View of Bartlett Oil Company's
Average Collection Period, 1985–1988

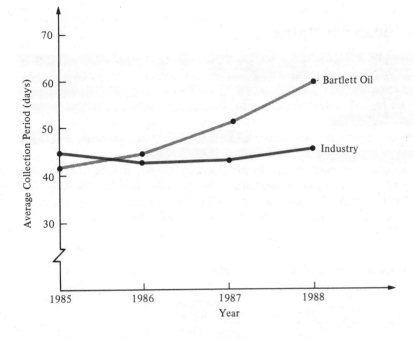

---

1 Cross-sectional analysis involves comparison of a firm's current to past performance using ratio analysis. *(Fable)*
Cross-sectional analysis involves comparison of different firms' financial ratios at the same point in time; *time-series analysis* **involves ratio comparison of a firm's current to past performance.**

FACT OR FABLE?

Some Words of Caution

Before discussing specific ratios, the following cautions are in order:

1. A single ratio does not generally provide sufficient information from which to judge the overall performance of the firm. Only when a group of ratios is used can reasonable judgments be made. If an analysis is concerned only with certain specific aspects of a firm's financial position, one or two ratios may be sufficient.

2. Be sure that the dates of the financial statements being compared are the same. If not, the effects of seasonality may produce erroneous conclusions and decisions.

3. It is preferable to use audited financial statements for ratio analysis. If the statements have not been audited, there may be no reason to believe that the data contained in them reflect the firm's true financial condition.

4. Be certain that the data being compared have all been developed in the same way. The use of differing accounting treatments—especially relative to depreciation and inventory—can distort the results of ratio analysis, regardless of whether cross-sectional or time-series analysis is used.

Groups of Financial Ratios

Financial ratios can be divided into four basic groups or categories: liquidity ratios, activity ratios, debt ratios, and profitability ratios. Liquidity, activity, and debt ratios primarily measure risk; profitability ratios measure return. In the near-term, the important elements are liquidity, activity, and profitability, since these provide the information critical to the short-run operation of the firm. (If a firm cannot survive in the short run, we need not be concerned with its longer-term prospects.) Debt ratios are useful primarily when the analyst is sure the firm will successfully weather the short run.

As a rule, the necessary inputs to an effective financial analysis include, at minimum, the income statement and the balance sheet. The 1988 and 1987 income statements and balance sheets for Bartlett Oil Company are presented in Tables 4.2 and 4.3, respectively, to demonstrate calculation of the ratios presented in the remainder of this chapter.

Table 4.2
Bartlett Oil Company Income Statements ($000)

	For the years ended December 31	
	1988	1987
Sales revenue	$3,074	$2,567
Less: Cost of goods sold	2,088	1,711
Gross profits	$ 986	$ 856
Less: Operating expenses		
Selling expense	$ 100	$ 108
General and administrative expenses	229	222
Depreciation expense	239	223
Total operating expense	$ 568	$ 553
Operating profits	$ 418	$ 303
Less: Interest expense[a]	93	91
Net profits before taxes	$ 325	$ 212
Less: Taxes (rate = 29%)[b]	94	64
Net profits after taxes	$ 231	$ 148
Less: Preferred stock dividends	10	10
Earnings available for common stockholders	$ 221	$ 138
Earnings per share (EPS)[c]	$ 2.90	$ 1.81

[a] Interest expense includes the interest component of the annual financial lease payment as specified by the Financial Accounting Standards Board (FASB).

[b] The 29 percent tax rate for 1988 results from the fact that the firm has certain special tax write-offs that do not show up directly on its income statement.

[c] Calculated by dividing the earnings available for common stockholders by the number of shares of common stock outstanding—76,262 in 1988 and 76,244 in 1987. Earnings per share in 1988: ($221,000 ÷ 76,262 = $2.90); in 1987: ($138,000 ÷ 76,244 = $1.81).

Table 4.3
Bartlett Oil Company Balance Sheets ($000)

	December 31	
Assets	**1988**	**1987**
Current assets		
Cash	$ 363	$ 288
Marketable securities	68	51
Accounts receivable	503	365
Inventories	289	300
Total current assets	$1,223	$1,004
Gross fixed assets (at cost)[a]		
Land and buildings	$2,072	$1,903
Machinery and equipment	1,866	1,693
Furniture and fixtures	358	316
Vehicles	275	314
Other (includes financial leases)	98	96
Total gross fixed assets (at cost)	$4,669	$4,322
Less: Accumulated depreciation	2,295	2,056
Net fixed assets	$2,374	$2,266
Total assets	$3,597	$3,270
Liabilities and stockholders' equity		
Current liabilities		
Accounts payable	$ 382	$ 270
Notes payable	79	99
Accruals	159	114
Total current liabilities	$ 620	$ 483
Long-term debts (includes financial leases)[b]	$1,023	$ 967
Total liabilities	$1,643	$1,450
Stockholders' equity		
Preferred stock—cumulative 5%, $100 par, 2,000 shares authorized and issued	$ 200	$ 200
Common stock—$2.50 par, 100,000 shares authorized, shares issued and outstanding in 1988: 76,262; in 1987: 76,244	191	190
Paid-in capital in excess of par on common stock	428	418
Retained earnings	1,135	1,012
Total stockholders' equity	$1,954	$1,820
Total liabilities and stockholders' equity	$3,597	$3,270

[a] In 1988, the firm has a six-year financial lease requiring annual beginning-of-year payments of $42,000. Four years of the lease have yet to run.

[b] Annual principal repayments on a portion of the firm's total outstanding debt amount to $71,000.

Analyzing Liquidity

liquidity A firm's ability to satisfy its short-term obligations as they come due.

The **liquidity** of a business firm is measured by its ability to satisfy its short-term obligations *as they come due*. Liquidity refers to the solvency of the firm's *overall* financial position. The three basic measures of liquidity are (1) net working capital, (2) the current ratio, and (3) the quick (acid-test) ratio.

Net Working Capital

net working capital A measure of liquidity calculated by subtracting total current liabilities from total current assets.

The firm's **net working capital,** as defined in Chapter 3, is calculated by subtracting total current liabilities from total current assets. The net working capital for Bartlett Oil in 1988 was as follows:

Net working capital = $1,223,000 − $620,000 = $603,000

This figure is *not* useful for comparing the performance of different firms, but it is quite useful for internal control.[2] Often the contract under which a long-term debt is incurred specifically states a minimum level of net working capital that must be maintained by the firm. This requirement is intended to force the firm to maintain sufficient operating liquidity and helps protect the creditor. A time-series comparison of the firm's net working capital is often helpful in evaluating its operations.

Current Ratio

current ratio A measure of liquidity calculated by dividing the firm's current assets by current liabilities.

The **current ratio,** one of the most commonly cited financial ratios, measures the firm's ability to meet its short-term obligations. It is expressed as follows:

$$\text{Current ratio} = \frac{\text{current assets}}{\text{current liabilities}}$$

The current ratio for Bartlett Oil in 1988 is

$$\frac{\$1,223,000}{\$620,000} = 1.97$$

A current ratio of 2.0 is occasionally cited as acceptable, but acceptability of the value depends on the industry in which a firm operates. For example, a current ratio of 1.0 would be considered acceptable for a utility but might be unacceptable for a manufacturing firm. The more predictable a firm's cash flows, the lower the acceptable current ratio. Since Bartlett Oil is in a business with a relatively predictable annual cash flow, its current ratio of 1.97 should be quite acceptable.

If the firm's current ratio is divided into 1.0 and the resulting quotient subtracted from 1.0, the difference multiplied by 100 represents the percentage by which the firm's current assets can shrink without making it impossible for the firm to cover its current liabilities.[3]

[2] To make cross-sectional as well as better time-series comparisons, *net working capital as a percent of sales* can be calculated. For Bartlett Oil in 1988 this ratio would be 19.6 percent ($603,000 ÷ $3,074,000). In general, the larger this value, the greater the firm's liquidity, and vice versa. Because of the relative nature of this measure, it is frequently used to make liquidity comparisons.

[3] This transformation actually results in the ratio of *net-working-capital-to-current-assets*. Clearly current assets can shrink by the amount of net working capital (i.e., their excess over current liabilities) while still retaining adequate current assets to just meet current liabilities.

For example, a current ratio of 2.0 means that the firm can still cover its current liabilities even if its current assets shrink by 50 percent ($[1.0 - (1.0 \div 2.0)] \times 100$).

A final point worthy of note is that whenever a firm's current ratio is 1.0, its net working capital is zero. If a firm has a current ratio of less than 1.0, it will have a negative net working capital. Net working capital is useful only in comparing the liquidity of the same firm over time and should not be used for comparing that of different firms; the current ratio should be used instead.

Quick (Acid-Test) Ratio

The **quick (acid-test) ratio** is similar to the current ratio except that it excludes inventory (generally the least liquid current asset). The quick ratio is calculated as follows[4]:

$$\text{Quick ratio} = \frac{\text{current assets} - \text{inventory}}{\text{current liabilities}}$$

The quick ratio for Bartlett Oil in 1988 is

$$\frac{\$1,223,000 - \$289,000}{\$620,000} = \frac{\$934,000}{\$620,000} = 1.51$$

A quick ratio of 1.0 or greater is occasionally recommended, but, as with the current ratio, an acceptable value depends largely on the industry. The quick ratio provides a better measure of overall liquidity only when a firm's inventory cannot easily be converted into cash. If inventory is liquid, the current ratio is a preferred measure of overall liquidity.

quick (acid-test) ratio
A measure of liquidity calculated by dividing the firm's current assets minus inventory by current liabilities.

---

2 Net working capital, the current ratio, and the quick (acid-test) ratio are measures of liquidity, which is the firm's ability to satisfy obligations as they come due. (Fact)

FACT OR FABLE?

Analyzing Activity

Activity ratios are used to measure the speed with which various accounts are converted into sales or cash. Measures of liquidity are generally inadequate because differences in the composition of a firm's current assets and liabilities can significantly affect the firm's "true" liquidity. For example, consider the current portion of the balance sheets for firms A and B in the table at the top of the next page.

activity ratios Used to measure the speed with which various accounts are converted into sales or cash.

---

[4] Sometimes the quick ratio is defined as (cash + marketable securities + accounts receivable) ÷ current liabilities. If a firm were to show as current assets items other than cash, marketable securities, accounts receivable, and inventory, its quick ratio might vary, depending on the method of calculation.

Firm A			
Cash	$ 0	Accounts payable	$ 0
Marketable securities	0	Notes payable	10,000
Accounts receivable	0	Accruals	0
Inventories	20,000	Total current liabilities	$10,000
Total current assets	$20,000		

Firm B			
Cash	$ 5,000	Accounts payable	$ 5,000
Marketable securities	5,000	Notes payable	3,000
Accounts receivable	5,000	Accruals	2,000
Inventories	5,000	Total current liabilities	$10,000
Total current assets	$20,000		

Although both firms appear to be equally liquid since their current ratios are both 2.0 ($20,000 ÷ $10,000), a closer look at the differences in the composition of current assets and liabilities suggests that *firm B is more liquid than firm A*. This results for two reasons: (1) firm B has more liquid assets in the form of cash and marketable securities than firm A, which has only a single and relatively illiquid asset in the form of inventories, and (2) firm B's current liabilities are in general more flexible than the single current liability— notes payable—of firm A.

It is therefore important to look beyond measures of overall liquidity to assess the activity (liquidity) of specific current accounts. A number of ratios are available for measuring the activity of the most important current accounts, which include inventory, accounts receivable, and accounts payable.[5] The activity of fixed and total assets can also be assessed.

Inventory Turnover

inventory turnover
Measures the activity, or liquidity, of a firm's inventory.

Inventory turnover commonly measures the activity, or liquidity, of a firm's inventory. It is calculated as follows:

$$\text{Inventory turnover} = \frac{\text{cost of goods sold}}{\text{inventory}}$$

Applying this relationship to Bartlett Oil in 1988 yields

$$\text{Inventory turnover} = \frac{\$2,088,000}{\$289,000} = 7.2$$

[5] For convenience, the activity ratios involving these current accounts assume that their end-of-period values are good approximations of the average account balance during the period—typically one year. Technically, when the month-end balances of inventory, accounts receivable, or accounts payable vary during the year, the average balance, calculated by summing the twelve month-end account balances and dividing the total by 12, should be used instead of the year-end value. This approach assures a ratio that on average better reflects the firm's circumstances. Because the data needed to find averages is generally unavailable to the external analyst, year-end values are frequently used to calculate activity ratios for current accounts.

The resulting turnover is meaningful only when compared with that of other firms in the same industry or to the firm's past inventory turnover. An inventory turnover of 20.0 would not be unusual for a grocery store, whereas a common inventory turnover for an aircraft manufacturer would be 4.0.

Inventory turnover can easily be converted into an **average age of inventory** by dividing it into 360—the number of days in a year.[6] For Bartlett Oil, the average age of inventory would be 50.0 days (360 ÷ 7.2). This value can also be viewed as the average number of days' sales in inventory.

average age of inventory
Average length of time inventory is held by the firm.

Average Collection Period

The **average collection period,** or average age of accounts receivable, is useful in evaluating credit and collection policies.[7] It is arrived at by dividing the average daily sales[8] into the accounts receivable balance:

average collection period
The average amount of time needed to collect accounts receivable.

$$\text{Average collection period} = \frac{\text{accounts receivable}}{\text{average sales per day}} = \frac{\text{accounts receivable}}{\dfrac{\text{annual sales}}{360}}$$

The average collection period for Bartlett Oil in 1988 is

$$\frac{\$503,000}{\dfrac{\$3,074,000}{360}} = \frac{\$503,000}{\$8,539} = 58.9 \text{ days}$$

On the average it takes the firm 58.9 days to collect an account receivable.

The average collection period is meaningful only in relation to the firm's credit terms. If, for instance, Bartlett Oil extends 30-day credit terms to customers, an average collection period of 58.9 days would indicate a poorly managed credit or collection department, or both. If it extended 60-day credit terms, the 58.9-day average collection period would be acceptable.

Average Payment Period

The **average payment period,** or average age of accounts payable, is calculated in the same manner as the average collection period:

average payment period
The average amount of time needed to pay accounts payable.

$$\text{Average payment period} = \frac{\text{accounts payable}}{\text{average purchases per day}} = \frac{\text{accounts payable}}{\dfrac{\text{annual purchases}}{360}}$$

The difficulty in calculating this ratio stems from the need to find annual purchases[9]—a value not available in published financial statements. Ordinarily, purchases are estimated as a given percentage of cost of goods sold. If we assume that Bartlett Oil's purchases

---

[6] Unless otherwise specified, a 360-day year consisting of twelve 30-day months is assumed throughout this textbook. This assumption allows some simplification of the calculations used to illustrate key concepts.

[7] A discussion of the evaluation and establishment of credit and collection policies is presented in Chapter 15.

[8] The formula as presented assumes, for simplicity, that all sales are made on a credit basis. If such is not the case, *average credit sales per day* should be substituted for average sales per day.

[9] Technically, annual *credit* purchases—rather than annual purchases—should be used in calculating this ratio. For simplicity, this refinement is ignored here.

equaled 70 percent of its cost of goods sold in 1988, its average payment period is

$$\frac{\$382,000}{\dfrac{.70(\$2,088,000)}{360}} = \frac{\$382,000}{\$4,060} = 94.1 \text{ days}$$

The above figure is meaningful only in relation to the average credit terms extended to the firm. If Bartlett Oil's suppliers, on the average, have extended 30-day credit terms, an analyst would give it a low credit rating. If the firm has been generally extended 90-day credit terms, its credit would be acceptable. Prospective lenders and suppliers of trade credit are especially interested in the average payment period, since it provides them with a sense of the bill-paying patterns of the firm.

Fixed Asset Turnover

fixed asset turnover
Measures the efficiency with which the firm has been using its *fixed,* or earning, assets to generate sales.

The **fixed asset turnover** measures the efficiency with which the firm has been using its *fixed,* or earning, assets to generate sales. It is calculated by dividing the firm's sales by its net fixed assets:

$$\text{Fixed asset turnover} = \frac{\text{sales}}{\text{net fixed assets}}$$

The fixed asset turnover for Bartlett Oil in 1988 is

$$\frac{\$3,074,000}{\$2,374,000} = 1.29$$

This means the company turns over its net fixed assets 1.29 times a year. Generally, higher fixed asset turnovers are preferred since they reflect greater efficiency of fixed asset utilization.

One caution with respect to use of this ratio and the total asset turnover described below stems from the fact that the calculations use the historical costs of fixed assets. Since some firms have significantly newer or older assets than others, comparing fixed asset turnovers of those firms can be misleading. Because of inflation and the historically based book values of assets, firms with newer assets will tend to have lower turnovers than those with older assets having lower book values.[10] The differences in these turnovers could result from more costly assets rather than from differing operating efficiencies. Therefore, the financial manager should be cautious when using these ratios for cross-sectional comparisons.

Total Asset Turnover

total asset turnover
Indicates the efficiency with which the firm uses all assets to generate sales.

The **total asset turnover** indicates the efficiency with which the firm is able to use all its assets to generate sales dollars. Generally, the higher a firm's total asset turnover, the

[10] This problem would not exist if firms were required to use current-cost accounting. Financial Accounting Standards Board (FASB) Statement No. 33, *Financial Reporting and Changing Prices,* issued in 1979 and amended by FASB Statement No. 82, *Financial Reporting and Price Changes: Elimination of Certain Disclosures,* issued in 1984, prescribes procedures for inflation accounting. The standard currently requires only large publicly held corporations to include such reporting as *supplementary information* in their stockholders' reports. For a good discussion of FASB Statements No. 33 and 82, see A. N. Mosich and E. John Larsen, *Intermediate Accounting,* 6th edition (New York: McGraw-Hill, 1986), pp. 1280–1299.

more efficiently its assets have been used. This measure is probably of greatest interest to management since it indicates whether the firm's operations have been financially efficient. Total asset turnover is calculated as follows:

$$\text{Total asset turnover} = \frac{\text{sales}}{\text{total assets}}$$

The value of Bartlett Oil's total asset turnover in 1988 is

$$\frac{\$3,074,000}{\$3,597,000} = 0.85$$

The company therefore turns its assets over .85 times a year.

---

3 Times interest earned and the fixed-payment coverage ratios are activity ratios which are used to measure the speed with which these obligations are paid. *(Fable)*
Activity ratios measure the speed with which various accounts are converted into sales or cash; times interest earned and the fixed-payment coverage ratio are measures of the ability to service debts, *not* activity.

FACT OR FABLE?

Analyzing Debt

The *debt position* of the firm indicates the amount of other people's money being used in attempting to generate profits. In general, the financial analyst is most concerned with long-term debts, since these commit the firm to paying interest over the long run as well as eventually repaying the principal borrowed. Since the claims of creditors must be satisfied prior to the distribution of earnings to shareholders,[11] present and prospective shareholders pay close attention to degree of indebtedness and ability to repay debts. Lenders are also concerned about the firm's degree of indebtedness and ability to service debts, since the more indebted the firm, the higher the probability that the firm will be unable to satisfy the claims of all its creditors. Management obviously must be concerned with indebtedness in recognition of the attention paid to it by other parties and in the interest of keeping the firm solvent.

In general, the more debt a firm uses in relation to its total assets, the greater its **financial leverage,** a term used to describe the magnification of risk and return introduced through the use of fixed-cost financing such as debt and preferred stock. In other words, the more fixed-cost debt, or financial leverage, a firm uses, the greater will be its risk and return.

financial leverage The magnification of risk and return introduced through the use of more fixed-cost financing relative to the firm's total assets.

Example
Michael Karp and Amy Parsons are in the process of incorporating a new business venture they have formed. After a great deal of analysis, they have determined that an

---

[11] The law requires that creditors' claims be satisfied prior to those of the firm's owners. This makes sense, since the creditor is providing a service to the owners and should not be expected to bear the risks of ownership.

initial investment of $50,000—$20,000 in current assets and $30,000 in fixed assets—is necessary. These funds can be obtained in either of two ways. The first is the no-debt plan, under which they would together invest the full $50,000 without borrowing. The other alternative, the debt plan, involves making a combined investment of $25,000 and borrowing the balance of $25,000 at 12 percent annual interest. Regardless of which alternative they choose, Michael and Amy expect sales to average $30,000, costs and operating expenses to average $18,000, and earnings to be taxed at a 40 percent rate. The balance sheets and income statements associated with the no-debt and debt plans are summarized in Table 4.4.

The no-debt plan results in after-tax profits of $7,200, which represent a 14.4 percent rate of return on Michael and Amy's $50,000 investment. The debt plan results in $5,400 of after-tax profits, which represent a 21.6 percent rate of return on their combined investment of $25,000. It therefore appears that the debt plan provides Michael and Amy with a higher rate of return, but the risk of this plan is also greater, since the annual $3,000 of interest must be paid prior to receipt of earnings.

From the example, it should be clear that *with increased debt comes greater risk as well as higher potential return;* therefore, the greater the financial leverage, the greater the potential risk and return, and vice versa. A detailed discussion of the impact of debt on the firm's risk, return, and value is included in Chapter 12. Here emphasis is given to the use of financial debt ratios to externally assess the degree of corporate indebtedness and the ability to meet fixed payments associated with debt.

Table 4.4
Financial Statements Associated with Michael and Amy's Alternatives

Balance sheets	No-debt plan	Debt plan
Current assets	$20,000	$20,000
Fixed assets	30,000	30,000
Total assets	$50,000	$50,000
Debt (12% interest)	$ 0	$25,000
(1) Equity	50,000	25,000
Total liabilities and equity	$50,000	$50,000

Income statements		
Sales	$30,000	$30,000
Less: Costs and operating expenses	18,000	18,000
Operating profits	$12,000	$12,000
Less: Interest expense	0	.12 × $25,000 = 3,000
Net profit before taxes	$12,000	$ 9,000
Less: Taxes (rate = 40%)	4,800	3,600
(2) Net profit after taxes	$ 7,200	$ 5,400
Return on equity [(2) ÷ (1)]	$\frac{\$7,200}{\$50,000} = 14.4\%$	$\frac{\$5,400}{\$25,000} = 21.6\%$

Measures of Debt

There are two general types of debt measures: measures of the degree of indebtedness and measures of the ability to service debts. The **degree of indebtedness** measures the amount of debt against other significant balance sheet amounts. Two of the most commonly used measures are the debt ratio and the debt-equity ratio, both of which are discussed below.

The second type of debt measure, the **ability to service debts,** refers to the ability of a firm to meet the contractual payments required on a scheduled basis over the life of a debt.[12] With debts come scheduled fixed-payment obligations for interest and principal. Lease payments as well as preferred stock dividend payments also represent scheduled obligations. The firm's ability to meet certain fixed charges is measured using **coverage ratios.** The lower the firm's coverage ratios, the more risky the firm is considered to be. "Riskiness" here refers to the firm's ability to meet fixed obligations; if a firm is unable to meet these obligations, it will be in default, and its creditors may seek immediate repayment. In most instances, this would force a firm into bankruptcy. Two ratios of coverage—times interest earned and the fixed-payment coverage ratio—are discussed below.[13] Actually, only the first of these ratios is concerned solely with debt; the second one considers other fixed-payment obligations in addition to debt service.

degree of indebtedness Measures amount of debt against other significant balance sheet amounts.

ability to service debts The ability of a firm to meet the contractual payments required on a scheduled basis over the life of a debt.

coverage ratios Ratios that measure the firm's ability to meet certain fixed charges.

Debt Ratio

The **debt ratio** measures the proportion of total assets provided by the firm's creditors. The higher this ratio, the greater the amount of other people's money being used in an attempt to generate profits. The ratio is calculated as follows:

debt ratio Measures the proportion of total assets provided by the firm's creditors.

$$\text{Debt ratio} = \frac{\text{total liabilities}}{\text{total assets}}$$

The debt ratio for Bartlett Oil in 1988 is

$$\frac{\$1,643,000}{\$3,597,000} = .457 = 45.7\%$$

This indicates that the company has financed 45.7 percent of its assets with debt. The higher this ratio, the more financial leverage a firm has.

The following ratio differs from the debt ratio by focusing on long-term debts. Short-term debts, or current liabilities, are excluded, since most of them are spontaneous (that is, they are the natural result of doing business) and do not commit the firm to the payment of fixed charges over a long period of time.

Debt-Equity Ratio

The **debt-equity ratio** indicates the relationship between the *long-term* funds provided by creditors and those provided by the firm's owners. It is commonly used to measure the degree of financial leverage of the firm and is calculated as follows:

debt-equity ratio Measures the ratio of long-term debt to stockholders' equity.

---

[12] The term *service* is used throughout this textbook to refer to the payment of interest and repayment of principal associated with a firm's debt obligations. When a firm services its debts, it pays, or fulfills, these obligations.

[13] Coverage ratios use data based on the application of accrual concepts (discussed in Chapter 1) to measure what in a strict sense should be measured with cash flows. This occurs since debts are serviced using cash flows, not the accounting values shown on the firm's financial statements. But because it is difficult to determine cash flows available for debt service from the firm's financial statements, the calculation of coverage ratios as presented here is quite common due to the ready availability of financial statement data.

$$\text{Debt-equity ratio} = \frac{\text{long-term debt}}{\text{stockholders' equity}}$$

The debt-equity ratio for Bartlett Oil in 1988 is

$$\frac{\$1,023,000}{\$1,954,000} = .524 = 52.4\%$$

The firm's long-term debts therefore are only 52.4 percent as large as stockholders' equity. This figure is meaningful only in light of the firm's line of business. Firms with large amounts of fixed assets, stable cash flows, or both typically have high debt-equity ratios, while less capital-intensive firms, firms with volatile cash flows, or both tend to have lower debt-equity ratios.

Times Interest Earned Ratio

times interest earned ratio Measures the firm's ability to meet contractual interest payments.

The **times interest earned ratio** measures the ability to meet contractual interest payments. The higher the value of this ratio, the better able the firm is to fulfill its interest obligations. Times interest earned is calculated as follows:

$$\text{Times interest earned} = \frac{\text{earnings before interest and taxes}}{\text{interest}}$$

Applying this ratio to Bartlett Oil yields the following 1988 value:

$$\text{Times interest earned} = \frac{\$418,000}{\$93,000} = 4.5$$

The value of earnings before interest and taxes is the same as the figure for operating profits shown in the income statements given in Table 4.2. The times interest earned ratio for Bartlett Oil seems acceptable; as a rule, a value of at least 3.0—and preferably closer to 5.0—is suggested. If the firm's earnings before interest and taxes were to shrink by 78 percent [(4.5 − 1.0) ÷ 4.5], the firm would still be able to pay the $93,000 in interest it owes. Thus it has a good margin of safety.

Fixed-Payment Coverage Ratio

fixed-payment coverage ratio Measures the firm's ability to meet all fixed-payment obligations.

The **fixed-payment coverage ratio** measures the firm's ability to meet all fixed-payment obligations, such as loan interest and principal and preferred stock dividends. Like the times interest earned ratio, the higher this value, the better. Principal payments on debt, scheduled lease payments, and preferred stock dividends[14] are commonly included in this ratio. Since financial (long-term) lease payments are written off in a fashion similar to owned assets, they do not require itemization. The formula for fixed-payment coverage ratio is as follows[15]:

---

[14] Although preferred stock dividends, which are stated at the time of issue, can be "passed" (not paid) at the option of the firm's directors, it is generally believed that the payment of such dividends is necessary. This text therefore treats the preferred stock dividend as if it were a contractual obligation, not only to be paid as a fixed amount, but also to be paid as scheduled.

[15] In the event a firm has operating (short-term) leases on its books, the fixed-payment coverage ratio would be

$$\frac{\text{earnings before oper. lease paymnts., int., and taxes}}{\text{oper. lease paymnts.} + \text{int.} + \{(\text{prin. paymnts.} + \text{pref. stock div.}) \times [1/(1 - T)]\}}$$

To simplify the text discussion, the presence of any operating leases is ignored.

$$\text{Fixed-payment coverage ratio} = \frac{\text{earnings before interest and taxes}}{\substack{\text{interest} + \{(\text{principal payments} + \\ \text{preferred stock dividends}) \times [1/(1 - T)]\}}}$$

where T is the corporate tax rate applicable to the firm's income. The term $1/(1 - T)$ is included to adjust the after-tax principal and preferred stock dividend payments back to a before-tax equivalent consistent with the before-tax value in the numerator. Applying the formula to Bartlett Oil's 1988 data yields

$$\text{Fixed-payment coverage ratio} = \frac{\$418,000}{\$93,000 + \{(\$71,000 + \$10,000) \times [1/(1 - .29)]\}}$$

$$= \frac{\$418,000}{\$207,000} = 2.0$$

Since the earnings available are twice as large as its fixed-payment obligations, the firm appears able to safely meet the latter.

Like the times interest earned ratio, the fixed-payment coverage ratio measures risk. The lower the ratio the greater the risk to both lenders and owners, and vice versa. This risk results from the fact that if the firm were unable to meet scheduled fixed payments, it could be driven into bankruptcy. An examination of the ratio therefore allows owners, creditors, and managers to assess the firm's ability to handle additional fixed-payment obligations such as debt.

---

4 **The debt position of the firm can be assessed using ratios that measure its degree of indebtedness and/or its ability to service debts.** *(Fact)*   **FACT OR FABLE?**

Analyzing Profitability

There are many measures of profitability. Each relates the returns of the firm to its sales, assets, equity, or share value. As a group, these measures allow the analyst to evaluate the firm's earnings with respect to a given level of sales, a certain level of assets, the owners' investment, or share value. Without profits a firm could not attract outside capital; moreover, present owners and creditors would become concerned about the company's future and attempt to recover their funds. Owners, creditors, and management pay close attention to boosting profits due to the great importance placed on earnings in the marketplace.

Common-Size Income Statements

A popular tool for evaluating profitability in relation to sales is the **common-size income statement.**[16] On this statement each item is expressed as a percentage of sales, thus enabling the relationship between sales and specific revenues and expenses to be easily evaluated. Common-size income statements are especially useful in comparing the performance for a particular year with that for another year. Three frequently cited ratios of

common-size income statement An income statement in which each item is expressed as a percentage of sales.

---

[16] This statement is sometimes called a "percent income statement." The same treatment is often applied to the firm's balance sheet to make it easier to evaluate changes in the asset and financial structures of the firm.

OPERATING MARGIN:
A Measure of Managerial Success

Shareholders are, logically, preoccupied with the bottom line. That tells them whether management is making them richer or poorer. But shareholders who want to know the how and the why need to look a little higher up on the profit and loss statement. There they will find operating income, which, divided by revenues, yields the operating margin. "There is no more important statistic than a company's operating margin to reveal how skillful management is in controlling operating costs and raising productivity," says Stephen Leeb, editor of the Jersey City (N.J.)-based *Investment Strategist*.

Why doesn't the net income figure capture managerial success? Because it reflects not only operating decisions, like what style of jeans to sell or where to locate the transmission factory, but also purely financial decisions, like how much leverage to put in the balance sheet. Moreover, a buyer of a business will be much more concerned with its operating income than with the net income. After all, the acquiring company can control leverage, interest costs, and taxes by the way it pays for the purchase, but it can't instantly transform a badly managed factory into a good one.

Take Wickes Co., the Santa Monica (Calif.)-based distributor of building materials. The company's operating margin doubled between 1980 and 1985. Earnings, however, shrank from 48 cents a share in 1980 to 11 cents in 1985 because of exorbitant interest and depreciation expenses. Wickes, which emerged from two and a half years in Chapter 11 procedures for reorganizing a failed firm in 1985, had a debt-to-equity ratio of over 225 percent by summer of 1986. But its strong operating margin, says Leeb, "makes it precisely the type of company a cash-rich takeover artist would be interested in."

Westmoreland Coal is an example of a company struggling to improve its operating margin. The operating margin climbed 2.4 percentage points between 1980 and 1985—but is still below the industry average of 14.4 percent. In 1985, despite an industry oversupply that forced it to reduce prices by 2 percent, Westmoreland reduced costs 8 percent and increased its operating margin to 8 percent. On the bottom line, however, write-offs from mine closings buried this improvement.

Can a firm have an operating margin that is too high? John Elliott, an associate professor of accounting at Cornell University, cautions, "If a firm's operating margin is considerably higher than the industry average, over time it will eventually creep back toward the average"—as competitors creep in.

Key to survival is a healthy operating margin—one that meets the industry standard and hopefully exceeds it. Almost every business decision, both daily and long-term, will have an impact on this financial statistic. For most firms, the operating margin is a true measure of success.

SOURCE: Adapted from Michael Ozanian, "How's Business," *Forbes*, August 11, 1986, pp. 120–122. Reprinted by permission of *Forbes* magazine. © Forbes Inc., 1986.

profitability that can be read directly from the common-size income statement are (a) the gross profit margin, (b) the operating profit margin, and (c) the net profit margin. These are discussed below.

Common-size income statements for 1988 and 1987 for Bartlett Oil are presented in Table 4.5. An evaluation of these statements reveals that the firm's cost of goods sold increased from 66.7 percent of sales in 1987 to 67.9 percent in 1988, resulting in a decrease in the gross profit margin from 33.3 to 32.1 percent. However, thanks to a decrease in operating expenses from 21.5 percent in 1987 to 18.5 percent in 1988, the firm's net profit margin rose from 5.8 percent of sales in 1987 to 7.5 percent in 1988. The decrease in expenses in 1988 more than compensated for the increase in the cost of goods sold. A decrease in the firm's 1988 interest expense (3.0 percent of sales versus 3.5 percent in 1987) added to the increase in 1988 profits.

Table 4.5
Bartlett Oil Company Common-Size Income Statements

	For the years ended December 31	
	1988	**1987**
Sales revenue	100.0%	100.0%
Less: Cost of goods sold	67.9	66.7
(a) Gross profit margin	32.1%	33.3%
Less: Operating expenses		
Selling expense	3.3%	4.2%
General and administrative expenses	7.4	8.6
Depreciation expense	7.8	8.7
Total operating expense	18.5%	21.5%
(b) Operating profit margin	13.6%	11.8%
Less: Interest expense	3.0	3.5
Net profits before taxes	10.6%	8.3%
Less: Taxes	3.1	2.5
(c) Net profit margin	7.5%	5.8%

Gross Profit Margin

The **gross profit margin** indicates the percentage of each sales dollar remaining after the firm has paid for its goods. The higher the gross profit margin the better, and the lower the relative cost of merchandise sold. Of course, the opposite case is also true, as the Bartlett Oil example shows. The gross profit margin is calculated as follows:

gross profit margin
Indicates the percentage of each sales dollar left after the firm has paid for its goods.

$$\text{Gross profit margin} = \frac{\text{sales} - \text{cost of goods sold}}{\text{sales}} = \frac{\text{gross profits}}{\text{sales}}$$

The value for Bartlett Oil's gross profit margin for 1988 is

$$\frac{\$3,074,000 - \$2,088,000}{\$3,074,000} = \frac{\$986,000}{\$3,074,000} = 32.1\%$$

This value is shown on line (a) of the common-size income statement in Table 4.5.

Operating Profit Margin

The **operating profit margin** represents what are often called the *pure profits* earned on each sales dollar. Operating profits are pure in the sense that they ignore any financial or government charges (interest or taxes) and measure only the profits earned on operations. A high operating profit margin is preferred. The operating profit margin is calculated as follows:

operating profit margin
Measures the percentage of profit earned on each sales dollar before interest and taxes.

$$\text{Operating profit margin} = \frac{\text{operating profit}}{\text{sales}}$$

The value for Bartlett Oil's operating profit margin for 1988 is

$$\frac{\$418,000}{\$3,074,000} = 13.6\%$$

This value is shown on line (b) of the common-size income statement in Table 4.5.

Net Profit Margin

net profit margin Measures the percentage of each sales dollar left after all expenses, including taxes, have been deducted.

The **net profit margin** measures the percentage of each sales dollar remaining after all expenses, including taxes, have been deducted. The higher the firm's net profit margin, the better. The net profit margin is a commonly cited measure of the corporation's success with respect to earnings on sales. "Good" net profit margins differ considerably across industries. A net profit margin of 1 percent or less would not be unusual for a grocery store, while a net profit margin of 10 percent would be low for a jewelry store. The net profit margin is calculated as follows:

$$\text{Net profit margin} = \frac{\text{net profits after taxes}}{\text{sales}}$$

Bartlett Oil's net profit margin for 1988 is

$$\frac{\$231,000}{\$3,074,000} = 7.5\%$$

This value is shown on line (c) of the common-size income statement in Table 4.5.

Return on Investment (ROI)

return on investment (ROI) Measures the overall effectiveness of management in producing profits from available assets.

The **return on investment (ROI),** which is often called the firm's *return on total assets,* measures the overall effectiveness of management in generating profits with its available assets. The higher the firm's return on investment, the better. The return on investment is calculated as follows:

$$\text{Return on investment} = \frac{\text{net profits after taxes}}{\text{total assets}}$$

Bartlett Oil's return on investment in 1988 is

$$\frac{\$231,000}{\$3,597,000} = 6.4\%$$

This value, which seems acceptable, could have been derived using the DuPont system of analysis, which will be described in a subsequent section.

Return on Equity (ROE)

return on equity (ROE) Measures the return on the owners' (preferred and common stockholders') investment in the firm.

The **return on equity (ROE)** measures the return earned on the owners' (both preferred and common stockholders') investment.[17] Generally, the higher this return, the better off the owners. Return on equity is calculated as follows:

[17] This ratio includes preferred dividends in the profit figure and preferred stock in the equity value, but because the amount of preferred stock and its impact on a firm are generally quite small, or nonexistent, this formula is a reasonably good approximation of the true owners'—that is, the common stockholders'—return.

$$\text{Return on equity} = \frac{\text{net profits after taxes}}{\text{stockholders' equity}}$$

This ratio for Bartlett Oil in 1988 is

$$\frac{\$231,000}{\$1,954,000} = 11.8\%$$

The above value, which seems to be quite good, could also have been derived using the DuPont system of analysis, to be described below.

Earnings per Share (EPS)

The firm's *earnings per share (EPS)* are generally of interest to present or prospective stockholders and management. The earnings per share represent the number of dollars earned on behalf of each outstanding share of common stock. They are closely watched by the investing public and are considered an important indicator of corporate success. Earnings per share, as noted in Chapter 1, are calculated as follows:

$$\text{Earnings per share} = \frac{\text{earnings available for common stockholders}}{\text{number of shares of common stock outstanding}}$$

The value of Bartlett Oil's earnings per share in 1988 is

$$\frac{\$221,000}{76,262} = \$2.90$$

This figure represents the dollar amount *earned* on behalf of each share outstanding. It does not represent the amount of earnings actually distributed to shareholders.

Price/Earnings (P/E) Ratio

Though not a true measure of profitability, the **price/earnings (P/E) ratio** is commonly used to assess the owners' appraisal of share value.[18] The P/E ratio represents the amount investors are willing to pay for each dollar of the firm's earnings. The level of the price/earnings ratio indicates the degree of confidence (or certainty) that investors have in the firm's future performance. The higher the P/E ratio, the greater investor confidence in the firm's future. The P/E ratio is calculated as follows:

price/earnings (P/E) ratio Represents the amount investors are willing to pay for each dollar of the firm's earnings.

$$\text{Price/earnings (P/E) ratio} = \frac{\text{market price per share of common stock}}{\text{earnings per share}}$$

If Bartlett Oil's common stock at the end of 1988 was selling at $32\frac{1}{4}$ (i.e., $32.25), using the earnings per share (EPS) of $2.90 from the income statement in Table 4.2, the P/E ratio at year-end 1988 is

$$\frac{\$32.25}{\$2.90} = 11.1$$

This figure indicates that investors were paying $11.10 for each $1.00 of earnings.

[18] Use of the price/earnings ratio to estimate the value of the firm is included as part of the discussion of popular approaches to common stock valuation in Chapter 8.

LOAN OFFICER ON A DISK

Business borrowers may not have their loan officers to kick around much longer. Across the country, banks are getting ready to turn much of their decision-making for small- and medium-sized business loans over to computer programs called *expert systems*. These systems are designed to do more than crunch numbers. They are programmed to make judgments about the soundness of a company's management, its business plan, and other subjective factors, much as a loan officer would do. Some wags call the systems "a banker on a diskette."

Among the banks that have installed or are considering installing expert systems are Security Pacific National Bank in Los Angeles, Wells Fargo Bank in San Francisco, Chemical Bank in New York, and Wachovia Bank & Trust Co. in Winston-Salem, N.C. "We think there's potential for making better [loan] decisions, making them faster, and improving the quality of our portfolios," says John H. Andren Jr., a

vice president at Manufacturers Hanover Trust Co. in New York, which is examining expert systems.

Most banks, though, won't talk about their expert systems. "An expert system is, by definition, expertise, and you don't want to give that away. That's your competitive edge," Mr. Andren says. Another banker notes that lenders would prefer if business customers didn't know their loan applications were being processed by computers, not people.

That brings up a sensitive issue. "What happens to the small-businessman who doesn't have the [financial] numbers [to justify a loan], but because he wins a place in the banker's heart, gets the loan and becomes the all-American success story?" says Edmon W. Blount, executive director of Astec Consulting Group, a New York company that advises banks on financial systems. "Probably, there will be less of those."

Software companies that write ex-

pert-system programs say they try hard to put some soul into the machine. Their programmers spend weeks with senior loan officers, getting them to articulate both the objective and subjective factors they use to make lending decisions. Then the programmers try to translate that reasoning process into quantitative terms a computer can understand.

Most bankers, for example, want to know how well a management team would cope with a financial crisis. An expert system arrives at such a judgment on the basis of answers to objective questions such as: How many years has the team been together? Has any team member bailed out a troubled company before? Does the company consistently meet its financial targets? Junior loan officers generally don't know how to make such judgments, so expert systems actually will improve lending decisions, software companies insist.

SOURCE: Steven P. Galante, "Your Loan Officer Next Time May Be an 'Expert' on a Disk," *The Wall Street Journal*, December 8, 1986, pp. 27, 29. Reprinted by permission of *The Wall Street Journal*, © Dow Jones & Company, Inc. 1986. All rights reserved.

FACT OR FABLE?   **5** **Profitability measures allow the analyst to evaluate the firm's earnings with respect to sales, assets, equity, or share value.** *(Fact)*

A Complete Ratio Analysis

As indicated earlier in the chapter, no single ratio is adequate for assessing all aspects of the firm's financial condition. Two popular approaches to a complete ratio analysis are (1) the DuPont system of analysis and (2) the summary analysis of a large number of ratios. Each of these approaches has merit. The DuPont system acts as a *search technique* aimed at finding the key areas responsible for the firm's financial performance. The summary analysis approach tends to view *all aspects* of the firm's financial activities in order to isolate key areas of responsibility.

DuPont System of Analysis

The **DuPont system of analysis** has for many years been used by financial managers as a structure for dissecting the firm's financial statements in order to assess its financial condition. The DuPont system merges the income statement and balance sheet into two summary measures of profitability: return on investment (ROI) and return on equity (ROE). Figure 4.2 depicts the basic DuPont system with Bartlett Oil's 1988 monetary and ratio values. The upper portion of the chart summarizes the income statement activities; the lower portion summarizes the balance sheet activities.

The DuPont system first brings together the *net profit margin,* which measures the firm's profitability on sales, with its *total asset turnover,* which indicates how efficiently the firm has used its assets to generate sales. In the **DuPont formula,** the product of these two ratios results in the *return on investment (ROI):*

$$ROI = \text{net profit margin} \times \text{total asset turnover}$$

Substituting the appropriate formulas into the equation and simplifying results in the formula given earlier,

$$ROI = \frac{\text{net profits after taxes}}{\text{sales}} \times \frac{\text{sales}}{\text{total assets}} = \frac{\text{net profits after taxes}}{\text{total assets}}$$

If the 1988 values of the net profit margin and total asset turnover for Bartlett Oil, calculated earlier, are substituted into the DuPont formula, the result is

$$ROI = 7.5\% \times 0.85 = 6.4\%$$

As expected, this value is the same as that calculated directly in an earlier section. The DuPont formula allows the firm to break down its return into a profit-on-sales and an efficiency-of-asset-use component. Typically, a firm with a low net profit margin has a high total asset turnover, which results in a reasonably good return on investment. Often, the opposite situation exists.

The second step in the DuPont system employs the **modified DuPont formula.** This formula relates the firm's return on investment (ROI) to the return on equity (ROE). The latter is calculated by multiplying the return on investment by the **equity multiplier,** which is the ratio of total assets to stockholders' equity[19]:

$$ROE = ROI \times \text{equity multiplier}$$

Substituting the appropriate formulas into the equation and simplifying results in the formula given earlier,

$$ROE = \frac{\text{net profits after taxes}}{\text{total assets}} \times \frac{\text{total assets}}{\text{stockholders' equity}} = \frac{\text{net profits after taxes}}{\text{stockholders' equity}}$$

Use of the equity multiplier to convert the ROI to the ROE reflects the impact of leverage (use of debt) on owners' return. Substituting the values for Bartlett Oil's ROI of 6.4%,

DuPont system of analysis System used by management as a framework for dissecting the firm's financial statements and assessing its financial condition.

DuPont formula Relates the firm's net profit margin and total asset turnover to its return on investment (ROI). The ROI is the product of the net profit margin and the total asset turnover.

modified DuPont formula Relates the firm's return on investment (ROI) to its return on equity (ROE) using the equity multiplier.

equity multiplier The ratio of the firm's total assets to stockholders' equity.

---

[19] The equity multiplier is equivalent to $\dfrac{1}{1 - \text{debt ratio}}$ and represents 1 divided by the percentage of total financing raised with equity. For computational convenience, the equity multiplier is utilized here rather than the seemingly more descriptive debt ratio.

Figure 4.2
The DuPont System of Analysis with Application to Bartlett Oil (1988)

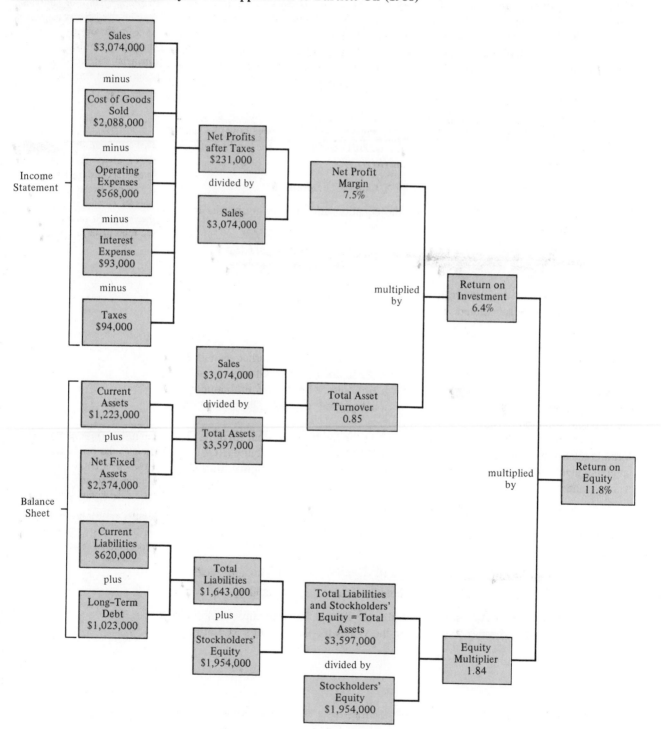

calculated earlier, and Bartlett's equity multiplier of 1.84 ($3,597,000 total assets ÷ $1,954,000 stockholders' equity) into the modified DuPont formula yields

$$ROE = 6.4\% \times 1.84 = 11.8\%$$

The 11.8 percent ROE calculated using the modified DuPont formula is the same as that calculated directly.

The considerable advantage of the DuPont system is that it allows the firm to break its return on equity into a profit-on-sales component (net profit margin), an efficiency-of-asset-use component (total asset turnover), and a use-of-leverage component (equity multiplier). The total return to the owners can therefore be analyzed in light of these important dimensions. As an illustration, let's look ahead to the ratio values summarized in Table 4.6. Bartlett Oil's net profit margin and total asset turnover increased between 1987 and 1988 to levels above the industry average. In combination, improved profit on sales and better asset utilization resulted in an improved return on investment (ROI). Increased investment return coupled with the increased use of debt reflected in the increased equity multiplier (not shown) caused the owners' return (ROE) to increase. Simply stated, it is clear from the DuPont system of analysis that the improvement in Bartlett Oil's 1988 ROE resulted from greater profit on sales, better asset utilization, and the increased use of leverage.

FACT OR FABLE?

6 The appeal of the DuPont system is that it allows the firm to break its return on equity into a liquidity component (current ratio) and a profitability component (earnings per share). *(Fable)*

The appeal of the DuPont system is that it allows the firm to break its return on equity into a *profit-on-sales component (net profit margin)*, an *efficiency-of-asset-use component (total asset turnover)*, and a *use-of-leverage component (equity multiplier)*.

Summarizing All Ratios

The 1988 ratio values calculated earlier and the ratio values calculated for 1986 and 1987 for Bartlett Oil, along with the industry average ratios for 1988, are summarized in Table 4.6. The table shows the formula used to calculate each ratio. Using these data, we can discuss the four key aspects of Bartlett's performance—(1) liquidity, (2) activity, (3) debt, and (4) profitability—on a cross-sectional and time-series basis.

Liquidity

The overall liquidity of the firm seems to exhibit a reasonably stable trend, having been maintained at a level that is relatively consistent with the industry average in 1988. The firm's liquidity seems to be good.

Activity

Bartlett Oil's inventory appears to be in good shape. Its inventory management seems to have improved, and in 1988 it performed at a level above that of the industry. The firm

Table 4.6
Summary of Bartlett Oil Company Ratios (1986–1988, including 1988 industry averages)

Ratio	Formula	Year			Industry average 1988[c]	Evaluation[d]		
		1986[a]	1987[b]	1988[b]		Cross-sectional 1988	Time-series 1986–1988	Overall
Liquidity								
Net working capital	total current assets − total current liabilities	$583,000	$521,000	$603,000	$427,000	good	good	good
Current ratio	$\dfrac{\text{current assets}}{\text{current liabilities}}$	2.04	2.08	1.97	2.05	OK	OK	OK
Quick (acid-test) ratio	$\dfrac{\text{current assets} - \text{inventory}}{\text{current liabilities}}$	1.32	1.46	1.51	1.43	OK	good	good
Activity								
Inventory turnover	$\dfrac{\text{cost of goods sold}}{\text{inventory}}$	5.1	5.7	7.2	6.6	good	good	good
Average collection period	$\dfrac{\text{accounts receivable}}{\text{average sales per day}}$	46.9 days	51.2 days	58.9 days	44.3 days	poor	poor	poor
Average payment period	$\dfrac{\text{accounts payable}}{\text{average purchases per day}}$	75.8 days	81.2 days	94.1 days	66.5 days	poor	poor	poor
Fixed asset turnover	$\dfrac{\text{sales}}{\text{net fixed assets}}$	1.50	1.13	1.29	1.35	OK	OK	OK
Total asset turnover	$\dfrac{\text{sales}}{\text{total assets}}$	0.94	0.79	0.85	0.75	OK	OK	OK

Ratio	Formula	Year			Industry average 1988[c]	Evaluation[d]		
		1986[a]	1987[b]	1988[b]		Cross-sectional 1988	Time-series 1986–1988	Overall
Debt								
Degree of indebtedness:								
Debt ratio	total liabilities / total assets	36.8%	44.3%	45.7%	40.0%	OK	OK	OK
Debt-equity ratio	long-term debt / stockholders' equity	44.2%	53.1%	52.4%	50.0%	OK	OK	OK
Ability to service debts:								
Times interest earned ratio	earnings before interest and taxes / interest	5.6	3.3	4.5	4.3	good	OK	OK
Fixed-payment coverage ratio	$\dfrac{\text{earnings before interest and taxes}}{\text{int.} + \{(\text{prin.} + \text{pref. div.}) \times [1/(1 - T)]\}}$	2.7	1.5	2.0	1.5	good	OK	good
Profitability								
Gross profit margin	gross profits / sales	31.4%	33.3%	32.1%	30.0%	OK	OK	OK
Operating profit margin	operating profit / sales	14.6%	11.8%	13.6%	11.0%	good	OK	good
Net profit margin	net profits after taxes / sales	8.8%	5.8%	7.5%	6.4%	good	OK	good
Return on investment (ROI)	net profits after taxes / total assets	8.3%	4.5%	6.4%	4.8%	good	OK	good
Return on equity (ROE)	net profits after taxes / stockholders' equity	13.1%	8.1%	11.8%	8.0%	good	OK	good
Earnings per share (EPS)	earnings available for common stockholders / number of shares of common stock outstanding	$3.26	$1.81	$2.90	$2.26	good	OK	good
Price/earnings (P/E) ratio	market price per share of common stock / earnings per share	10.5	10.0	11.1	12.5	OK	OK	OK

[a] Calculated from data not included in the chapter.

[b] Calculated using the financial statements presented in Tables 4.2 and 4.3.

[c] Obtained from sources not included in this chapter.

[d] Represent subjective assessments based on data provided.

may be experiencing some problems with accounts receivable. The average collection period seems to have crept up to a level above that of the industry. Bartlett also appears to be slow in paying its bills; it is paying nearly 30 days later than the industry average. Payment procedures should be examined to make sure that the company's credit standing is not adversely affected. While overall liquidity appears to be good, some attention should be given to the management of accounts receivable and payable. Bartlett's fixed asset turnover and total asset turnover reflect sizable declines in the efficiency of fixed and total asset utilization between 1986 and 1987. Although in 1988 the total asset turnover rose to a level considerably above the industry average, it appears that the pre-1987 level of efficiency has not yet been achieved.

Debt

Bartlett Oil's indebtedness increased over the 1986–1988 period and is currently at a level above the industry average. Although the increase in the debt ratio could be cause for alarm, the firm's ability to meet interest and fixed-payment obligations improved from 1987 to 1988 to a level that outperforms the industry. The firm's increased indebtedness in 1987 apparently caused a deterioration in its ability to pay debt adequately. However, Bartlett has evidently improved its income in 1988 so that it is able to meet its interest and fixed-payment obligations in a fashion consistent with the average firm in the industry. In summary, it appears that although 1987 was an off year, the company's ability to pay debts in 1988 adequately compensates for the increased degree of indebtedness.

Profitability

Bartlett's profitability relative to sales in 1988 was better than that of the average company in the industry, although it did not match the firm's 1986 performance. While the *gross* profit margin in 1987 and 1988 was better than in 1986, it appears that higher levels of operating and interest expenses in 1987 and 1988 caused the 1988 *net* profit margin to fall below that of 1986. However, Bartlett's 1988 net profit margin is quite favorable when compared to the industry average. The firm's return on investment, return on equity, and earnings per share behaved in a fashion similar to its net profit margin over the 1986–1988 period. Bartlett appears to have experienced either a sizable drop in sales between 1986 and 1987 or a rapid expansion in assets during that period. The owners' return, as evidenced by the exceptionally high 1988 level of return on equity, seems to suggest that the firm is performing quite well. In addition, although the firm's shares are selling at a price/earnings (P/E) multiple below that of the industry, some improvement occurred between 1987 and 1988. The firm's above-average returns—net profit margin, ROI, ROE, and EPS—may be attributable to its above-average risk as reflected in its below-industry-average P/E ratio.

In summary, it appears that the firm is growing and has recently undergone an expansion in assets, this expansion being financed primarily through the use of debt. The 1987–1988 period seems to reflect a phase of adjustment and recovery from the rapid growth in assets. Bartlett's sales, profits, and other performance factors seem to be growing with the increase in the size of the operation. In short, the firm appears to have done quite well in 1988.

Summary

● Ratio analysis allows present and prospective stockholders and lenders and the firm's management to evaluate the firm's performance and status. It can be performed on a cross-sectional or a time-series basis.

● Cautions in ratio analysis include: (1) a single ratio does not generally provide sufficient information; (2) ratios should be compared for similar time periods; (3) audited financial statements should be used; and (4) data should be checked for consistency of accounting treatment.

● The most common ratios can be divided into four basic groups: liquidity ratios; activity ratios; debt ratios; and profitability ratios.

● The liquidity, or ability of the firm to pay its bills as they come due, can be measured by the firm's net working capital, its current ratio, or its quick (acid-test) ratio.

● Activity ratios measure the speed with which various accounts are converted into sales or cash. The activity of inventory can be measured by its turnover, that of accounts receivable by the average collection period, and that of accounts payable by the average payment period. Fixed and total asset turnovers can be used to measure the efficiency with which the firm has used its fixed and total assets to generate sales.

● Financial debt ratios measure both degree of corporate indebtedness and the ability to pay debts. Commonly used measures of debt position are the debt ratio and the debt-equity ratio. The ability to pay contractual obligations such as interest, principal, and preferred stock dividends can be measured by times interest earned and fixed-payment coverage ratios.

● Measures of profitability can be made in various ways. The common-size income statement, which shows all items as a percentage of sales, can be used to determine gross profit margin, operating profit margin, and net profit margin. Other measures of profitability include return on investment, return on equity, earnings per share, and the price/earnings ratio.

● The DuPont system of analysis is a search technique aimed at finding the key areas responsible for the firm's financial performance. It allows the firm to break the return on equity into a profit-on-sales component, an efficiency-of-asset-use component, and a use-of-leverage component.

● By summarizing a large number of ratios, all aspects of the firm's activities can be assessed in order to isolate key areas of responsibility.

Questions

4-1   With regard to financial ratio analyses of a firm, how do the viewpoints held by the firm's present and prospective shareholders, creditors, and management differ? How can these viewpoints be related to the firm's fund-raising ability?

4-2   How can ratio analysis be used for *cross-sectional* and *time-series* comparisons? Which type of comparison would be more common for internal analysis? Why?

4-3   When performing cross-sectional ratio analysis, to what types of deviations from the norm should the analyst devote primary attention? Explain why.

4-4   Financial ratio analysis is often divided into four areas: *liquidity* ratios, *activity* ratios, *debt* ratios, and *profitability* ratios. Describe and differentiate each of these areas of analysis from the others. Which is of the greatest relative concern to present and prospective creditors?

4-5   Why is net working capital useful only in time-series comparisons of overall liquidity while the current and quick ratios can be used for both cross-sectional and time-series analysis?

4-6   In order to assess the reasonableness of the firm's average collection period and average payment period ratios, what additional information is needed in each instance? Explain.

4-7   What is *financial leverage?* What ratios can be used to measure the degree of indebtedness? What ratios are used to assess the ability of the firm to meet fixed payments associated with debt?

4-8   What is a *common-size income statement?* Which three ratios of profitability are found on this statement? How is the statement used?

4-9   How can a firm's having a high gross profit margin and a low net profit margin be explained? To what must this situation be attributable?

4-10   Define and differentiate between return on investment (ROI), return on equity (ROE), and earnings per share (EPS). Which measure is probably of greatest interest to owners? Why?

4-11   What is the *price/earnings (P/E) ratio?* How does its level relate to the degree of confidence (or certainty) of investors in the firm's future performance? Is the P/E ratio a true measure of profitability?

4-12   Three areas of analysis or concern are combined in the *DuPont system of analysis*. What are these concerns, and how are they combined to explain the firm's return on equity (ROE)? Can this formula yield useful information through cross-sectional or time-series analysis?

4-13   Describe how you would approach a complete ratio analysis of the firm on both a cross-sectional and a time-series basis by summarizing a large number of ratios.

Self-Test Problems

(Solutions on pages 129–130)

ST-1 Without referring to the text, indicate for each of the following ratios the formula for its calculation and the kinds of problems, if any, the firm is likely to be having if these ratios are too high relative to the industry average. What if they are too low relative to the industry? Create a table similar to that shown below and fill in the empty blocks.

Ratio	Too high	Too low
Current ratio =		
Inventory turnover =		
Times interest earned =		
Gross profit margin =		
Return on investment =		

ST-2 Complete the 1988 balance sheet for O'Keefe Industries using the information that follows it.

Balance Sheet O'Keefe Industries December 31, 1988			
Cash	$30,000	Accounts payable	$120,000
Marketable securities	25,000	Notes payable	
Accounts receivable	_____	Accruals	20,000
Inventories	_____	Total current liabilities	_____
Total current assets	_____	Long-term debt	
Net fixed assets	_____	Stockholders' equity	$600,000
Total assets	_____	Total liabilities and stockholders' equity	_____

Information (1988 values):
(1) Sales totaled $1,800,000.
(2) The gross profit margin was 25 percent.
(3) Inventory turnover was 6.0.
(4) There are 360 days in the year.
(5) The average collection period was 40 days.
(6) The current ratio was 1.60.
(7) The total asset turnover ratio was 1.20.
(8) The debt ratio was 60 percent.

Problems

4-1   (**Liquidity Management**) The Bauman Company's total current assets, net working capital, and inventory for each of the past four years are given below.

Item	1985	1986	1987	1988
Total current assets	$16,950 ⁹⁰⁰⁰	$21,900 ¹²⁶⁰⁰	$22,500 ¹²⁶⁰⁰	$27,000 ¹⁷⁴⁰⁰
Net working capital	7,950	9,300	9,900	9,600
Inventory	6,000	6,900	6,900	7,200

(handwritten: assets − liabilit = NWC)

a. Calculate the firm's current and quick ratios for each year. Compare the resulting time series of each measure of liquidity (i.e., net working capital, the current ratio, and the quick ratio).

b. Comment on the firm's liquidity over the 1985–1988 period.

c. If you were told that the Bauman Company's inventory turnover for each year in the 1985–1988 period and the industry averages were as follows, would this support or conflict with your evaluation in **b**? Why?

Inventory turnover	1985	1986	1987	1988
Bauman Company	⁵⁷ 6.3	⁵³ 6.8	⁵¹ 7.0	⁵⁶ 6.4
Industry average	³⁴ 10.6	³² 11.2	³³ 10.8	³³ 11.0

(handwritten below: 22   21   18   25)

4-2   (**Inventory Management**) Wilkins Manufacturing has sales of $4 million and a gross profit margin of 40 percent. Its *end-of-quarter inventories* are as follows:

Quarter	Inventory
1	$ 400,000
2	800,000
3	1,200,000
4	200,000

a. Find the average quarterly inventory and use it to calculate the firm's inventory turnover and the average age of inventory.

b. Assuming the company is in an industry with an average inventory turnover of 2.0, how would you evaluate the activity of Wilkins' inventory?

4-3   (**Accounts Receivable Management**) An evaluation of the books of Blair Trucking, shown in the table at the top of page 120, gives the end-of-year accounts receivable balance, which is believed to consist of amounts originating in the months indicated. The company had annual sales of $2.4 million. The firm extends 30-day credit terms.

Month of origin	Amounts receivable
July	$ 3,875
August	2,000
September	34,025
October	15,100
November	52,000
December	193,000
Year-end accounts receivable	$300,000

a. Use the year-end total to evaluate the firm's collection system.

b. If the firm's peak season is from July to December, how would this affect the validity of your conclusion above? Explain.

4-4 **(Debt Analysis)** The Springfield Bank is evaluating Creek Enterprises, which has requested a $4,000,000 loan, in order to assess the firm's financial leverage and financial risk. Based on the debt ratios for Creek, along with the industry averages and Creek's recent financial statements (presented below and on page 121), evaluate and recommend appropriate action on the loan request.

Income Statement Creek Enterprises for the Year Ended December 31, 1988		
Sales revenue		$30,000,000
Less: Cost of goods sold		21,000,000
Gross profits		$ 9,000,000
Less: Operating expenses		
Selling expense	$3,000,000	
General and administrative expenses	2,000,000	
Depreciation expense	1,000,000	
Total operating expense		6,000,000
Operating profits		$ 3,000,000
Less: Interest expense		1,000,000
Net profits before taxes		$ 2,000,000
Less: Taxes (rate = 40%)		800,000
Net profits after taxes		$ 1,200,000

Balance Sheet Creek Enterprises December 31, 1988	
Assets	
Current assets	
Cash	$ 1,000,000
Marketable securities	3,000,000
Accounts receivable	12,000,000
Inventories	7,500,000
Total current assets	$23,500,000
Gross fixed assets (at cost)	
Land and buildings	$11,000,000
Machinery and equipment	20,500,000
Furniture and fixtures	8,000,000
Gross fixed assets	$39,500,000
Less: Accumulated depreciation	13,000,000
Net fixed assets	$26,500,000
Total assets	$50,000,000
Liabilities and stockholders' equity	
Current liabilities	
Accounts payable	$ 8,000,000
Notes payable	8,000,000
Accruals	500,000
Total current liabilities	$16,500,000
Long-term debt[a]	$20,000,000
Stockholders' equity	
Preferred stock[b]	$ 2,500,000
Common stock (1 million shares at $5 par)	5,000,000
Paid-in capital in excess of par value	4,000,000
Retained earnings	2,000,000
Total stockholders' equity	$13,500,000
Total liabilities and stockholders' equity	$50,000,000

[a] Required annual principal payments are $800,000.

[b] 25,000 shares of $4.00 preferred stock is outstanding.

Industry averages	
Debt ratio	0.51
Debt-equity ratio	1.07
Times interest earned ratio	7.30
Fixed-payment coverage ratio	1.85

4-5 **(Common-Size Statement Analysis)** A common-size income statement for Creek Enterprises' 1987 operations is presented at the top of page 122. Using the firm's 1988 income statement presented in Problem 4-4, develop the 1988 common-size income statement and compare it to the 1987 statement. Which areas require further analysis and investigation?

Common-Size Income Statement Creek Enterprises for the Year Ended December 31, 1987		
Sales revenue ($35,000,000)		100.0%
Less: Cost of goods sold		65.9
Gross profits		34.1%
Less: Operating expenses		
Selling expense	12.7%	
General and administrative expenses	6.9	
Depreciation expense	3.6	
Total operating expense		23.2
Operating profits		10.9%
Less: Interest expense		1.5
Net profits before taxes		9.4%
Less: Taxes (rate = 40%)		3.8
Net profits after taxes		5.6%

4-6   **(DuPont System of Analysis)** Use the following ratio information for Johnson International and the industry averages for Johnson's line of business to

a. Construct the DuPont system for both Johnson and the industry.

b. Evaluate Johnson (and the industry) over the three-year period.

c. In which areas does Johnson require further analysis? Why?

Johnson	1986	1987	1988
Equity multiplier	1.75	1.75	1.85
Net profit margin	.059	.058	.049
Total asset turnover	2.11	2.18	2.34
Industry averages			
Equity multiplier	1.67	1.69	1.64
Net profit margin	.054	.047	.041
Total asset turnover	2.05	2.13	2.15

4-7   **(Cross-Sectional Ratio Analysis)** Use the financial statements provided on page 123 for Fox Manufacturing Company for the year ended December 31, 1988, along with the industry average ratios at the top of page 124, to:

a. Prepare and interpret a ratio analysis of the firm's 1988 operations.

b. Summarize your findings and make recommendations.

Income Statement
Fox Manufacturing Company
for the Year Ended December 31, 1988

Sales revenue		$600,000
Less: Cost of goods sold		460,000
Gross profits		$140,000
Less: Operating expenses		
General and administrative expenses	$30,000	
Depreciation expense	30,000	
Total operating expense		60,000
Operating profits		$ 80,000
Less: Interest expense		10,000
Net profits before taxes		$ 70,000
Less: Taxes		27,100
Net profits after taxes (Earnings available for common stockholders)		$ 42,900
Earnings per share (EPS)		$2.15

Balance Sheet
Fox Manufacturing Company
December 31, 1988

Assets

Cash	$ 15,000
Marketable securities	7,200
Accounts receivable	34,100
Inventories	82,000
Total current assets	$138,300
Net fixed assets	$270,000
Total assets	$408,300

Liabilities and stockholders' equity

Accounts payable	$ 57,000
Notes payable	13,000
Accruals	5,000
Total current liabilities	$ 75,000
Long-term debt	$150,000
Stockholders' equity	
Common stock equity (20,000 shares outstanding)	$110,200
Retained earnings	73,100
Total stockholders' equity	$183,300
Total liabilities and stockholders' equity	$408,300

Ratio	Industry average, 1988
Net working capital	$125,000
Current ratio	2.35
Quick ratio	.87
Inventory turnover	4.55
Average collection period	35.3 days
Fixed asset turnover	1.97
Total asset turnover	1.09
Debt ratio	.300
Debt-equity ratio	.615
Times interest earned ratio	12.3
Gross profit margin	.202
Operating profit margin	.135
Net profit margin	.091
Return on investment (ROI)	.099
Return on equity (ROE)	.167
Earnings per share (EPS)	$3.10

4-8   **(Financial Statement Analysis)** The financial statements of Zach Industries for the year ended December 31, 1988, are given below and on page 125.

Zach Industries
Balance Sheet
December 31, 1988

Assets

Cash	$ 500
Marketable securities	1,000
Accounts receivable	25,000
Inventories	45,500
Total current assets	$ 72,000
Land	$ 26,000
Buildings and equipment	90,000
Less: Accumulated depreciation	38,000
Net fixed assets	$ 78,000
Total assets	$150,000

Liabilities and stockholders' equity

Accounts payable	$ 22,000
Notes payable	47,000
Total current liabilities	$ 69,000
Long-term debt	$ 22,950
Common stock	$ 31,500
Retained earnings	$ 26,550
Total liabilities and stockholders' equity	$150,000

Zach Industries Income Statement for the Year Ended December 31, 1988	
Sales revenue	$160,000
Less: Cost of goods sold	106,000
Gross profits	$ 54,000
Less: Operating expenses	
Selling expense	$ 16,000
General and administrative expenses	11,000
Depreciation expense	10,000
Total operating expense	$ 37,000
Operating profits	$ 17,000
Less: Interest expense	6,100
Net profits before taxes	$ 10,900
Less: Taxes	4,360
Net profits after taxes	$ 6,540

a. Use the preceding financial statements to complete the table below. Assume that the industry averages given in the table are applicable for both 1987 and 1988.

Zach Industries Ratio Analysis

Ratio	Industry average	Actual 1987	Actual 1988
Current ratio	1.80	1.84	_____
Quick ratio	.70	.78	_____
Average collection period[a]	37 days	36 days	_____
Inventory turnover[a]	2.50	2.59	_____
Debt-equity ratio	50%	51%	_____
Times interest earned ratio	3.8	4.0	_____
Gross profit margin	38%	40%	_____
Net profit margin	3.5%	3.6%	_____
Return on investment	4.0%	4.0%	_____
Return on equity	9.5%	8.0%	_____

[a] Based on a 360-day year and on end-of-year figures.

b. Analyze Zach Industries' financial condition as it relates to (1) liquidity, (2) activity, (3) debt, and (4) profitability. Summarize the company's overall financial condition.

4-9 **(Integrative—Complete Ratio Analysis)** Given the financial statements, historical ratios, and industry averages below and on pages 127 and 128, calculate the Sterling Company's financial ratios for the most recent year. Analyze its overall financial situation from both a cross-sectional and a time-series viewpoint. Break your analysis into an evaluation of the firm's liquidity, activity, debt, and profitability.

Income Statement Sterling Company for the Year Ended December 31, 1988		
Sales revenue		$10,000,000
Less: Cost of goods sold		7,500,000
Gross profits		$ 2,500,000
Less: Operating expenses		
Selling expense	$300,000	
General and administrative expenses	700,000	
Depreciation expense	200,000	1,200,000
Operating profits		$ 1,300,000
Less: Interest expense[a]		200,000
Net profits before taxes		$ 1,100,000
Less: Taxes (rate = 40%)		440,000
Net profits after taxes		$ 660,000
Less: Preferred stock dividends		50,000
Earnings available for common stockholders		$ 610,000
Earnings per share (EPS)		$3.05

[a] Interest expense includes the interest component of the annual financial lease payment as specified by the Financial Accounting Standards Board (FASB).

Balance Sheet Sterling Company December 31, 1988		
Assets		
Current assets		
Cash		$ 200,000
Marketable securities		50,000
Accounts receivable		800,000
Inventories		950,000
Total current assets		$ 2,000,000
Gross fixed assets (includes financial leases)[a]	$12,000,000	
Less: Accumulated depreciation	3,000,000	
Net fixed assets		$ 9,000,000
Other assets		$ 1,000,000
Total assets		$12,000,000
Liabilities and stockholders' equity		
Current liabilities		
Accounts payable[b]		$ 900,000
Notes payable		200,000
Accruals		100,000
Total current liabilities		$ 1,200,000
Long-term debts (includes financial leases)[c]		$ 3,000,000
Stockholders' equity		
Preferred stock (25,000 shares, $2 dividend)		$ 1,000,000
Common stock (200,000 shares at $3 par)[d]		600,000
Paid-in capital in excess of par value		5,200,000
Retained earnings		1,000,000
Total stockholders' equity		$ 7,800,000
Total liabilities and stockholders' equity		$12,000,000

[a] The firm has an eight-year financial lease requiring annual beginning-of-year payments. Five years of the lease have yet to run.

[b] Annual credit purchases of $6,200,000 were made during the year.

[c] The annual principal payment on the long-term debt is $100,000.

[d] On December 31, 1988, the firm's common stock closed at $27½ (i.e., $27.50).

Historical and Industry-Average Ratios for Sterling Company

Ratio	1986	1987	Industry average, 1988
Net working capital	$760,000	$720,000	$1,600,000
Current ratio	1.40	1.55	1.85
Quick ratio	1.00	.92	1.05
Inventory turnover	9.52	9.21	8.60
Average collection period	45.0 days	36.4 days	35.0 days
Average payment period	58.5 days	60.8 days	45.8 days
Fixed asset turnover	1.08	1.05	1.07
Total asset turnover	0.74	0.80	0.74
Debt ratio	0.20	0.20	0.30
Debt-equity ratio	0.25	0.27	0.39
Times interest earned ratio	8.2	7.3	8.0
Fixed-payment coverage ratio	4.8	4.5	4.5
Gross profit margin	0.30	0.27	0.25
Operating profit margin	0.12	0.12	0.10
Net profit margin	0.067	0.067	0.058
Return on investment (ROI)	0.049	0.054	0.043
Return on equity (ROE)	0.066	0.073	0.072
Earnings per share (EPS)	$1.75	$2.20	$1.50
Price/earnings (P/E) ratio	12.0	10.5	11.2

Solutions to Self-Test Problems

ST-1

Ratio	Too high	Too low
Current ratio = current assets/current liabilities	May indicate firm is holding excessive cash, accounts receivable, or inventory.	May indicate poor ability to satisfy short-term obligations.
Inventory turnover = CGS/inventory	May indicate low level of inventory which may cause stockouts and lost sales.	May indicate poor inventory management, excessive inventory, or obsolete inventory.
Times interest earned = earnings before interest and taxes/ interest		May indicate poor ability to pay contractual interest payments.
Gross profit margin = gross profits/sales	Indicates the low cost of merchandise sold relative to the sales price; could indicate non-competitive pricing and potential lost sales.	Indicates the high cost of the merchandise sold relative to the sales price; May indicate either a low sales price or high cost of goods sold.
Return on investment = net profits after taxes/ total assets		Indicates ineffective management in generating profits with the available assets.

ST-2

O'Keefe Industries Balance Sheet December 31, 1988			
Cash	$ 30,000	Accounts payable	$ 120,000
Marketable securities	25,000	Notes payable	160,000[5]
Accounts receivable	200,000[1]	Accruals	20,000
Inventories	225,000[2]	Total current liabilities	$ 300,000[4]
Total current assets	$ 480,000	Long-term debt	$ 600,000[6]
Net fixed assets	$1,020,000[3]	Stockholders' equity	$ 600,000
Total assets	$1,500,000	Total liabilities and stockholders' equity	$1,500,000

[1] Average collection period (ACP) = 40 days
ACP = accounts receivable/average sales per day
40 = accounts receivable/($1,800,000/360)
40 = accounts receivable/$5,000
$200,000 = accounts receivable

[2] Inventory turnover = 6.0
Inventory turnover = cost of goods sold/inventory
6.0 = [sales × (1-gross profit margin)]/inventory
6.0 = [$1,800,000 × (1 − .25)]/inventory
$225,000 = inventory

[3] Total asset turnover = 1.20
Total asset turnover = sales/total assets
1.20 = $1,800,000/total assets
$1,500,000 = total assets
Total assets = current assets + net fixed assets
$1,500,000 = $480,000 + net fixed assets
$1,020,000 = net fixed assets

[4] Current ratio = 1.60
Current ratio = current assets/current liabilities
1.60 = $480,000/current liabilities
$300,000 = current liabilities

[5] Notes payable = total current liabilities − accounts payable − accruals
          = $300,000 − $120,000 − $20,000
          = $160,000

[6] Debt ratio = .60
Debt ratio = total liabilities/total assets
.60 = total liabilities/$1,500,000
$900,000 = total liabilities
Total liabilities = current liabilities + long-term debt
$900,000 = $300,000 + long-term debt
$600,000 = long-term debt

CHAPTER 5

Financial Planning

FACT OR FABLE?
Are the following statements fact *(true)* or fable *(false)*?

1
The financial planning process begins with the preparation of short-run (operating) plans and budgets which provide the basis for preparation of long-run (strategic) financial plans.

2
When preparing the cash budget it is important to include depreciation and any other noncash charges in the cash disbursements schedule.

3
The value for "required total financing" in the cash budget refers to the amount the firm would owe at the end of the period rather than the change in borrowing during the period.

4
When a simplified approach to pro forma income statement preparation is desired, breaking down costs and expenses into fixed and variable components improves on the use of a strict percent-of-sales approach.

5
The judgmental approach to the preparation of the pro forma balance sheet is attractive since it assures that the statement will automatically be in balance.

C ontextural Design was formed in 1977 by four men with a vision. They knew the manufacturing side of the wooden furniture business inside and out and planned to use that knowledge to find their fortune.

After getting together raw materials, the necessary equipment, and a labor force, they were ready to go. The only thing missing was a pricing strategy for the finished good. So they hastily estimated labor costs, added raw material costs, and multiplied by two. This was expected to cover overhead and return a handsome profit at the same time. The results seemed too good to be true. Sales were phenomenal. By 1983, Contextural Design was on *Inc.'s* list of the nation's fastest growing private companies.

Unfortunately, what had seemed to be too good to be true was proved to be just that. Financial statements had been badly neglected. When they were finally examined, they showed that the net worth of Contextural Design was spiraling downward. But how could this be with such high sales?

It went back to the pricing strategy. When the proper analysis was done, it showed that the estimated labor costs had been much too low. In addition, the overhead that had been left out of the pricing strategy actually amounted to one-and-a-half times labor. Of course, when costs exceeded price, the volume of sales became irrelevant.

Despite all this, the company might still have been saved if the proper action were taken soon enough. If financial statements were prepared on schedule, the problems may have been discovered before it was too late. Then Contextural Design could have examined options such as cost containment or a pricing restructure.

As it happened, though, all such measures came too little, too late. In 1985, Contextural Design filed for bankruptcy and was later bought out by Delta Design, Inc. These were the hard consequences of poor financial planning. Had Contextural Design carefully prepared and monitored financial plans, success, although not guaranteed, would have been much more likely. In this chapter the key aspects of financial planning—with primary emphasis on short-run plans and budgets—are presented.

The Financial Planning Process

Financial planning is an important aspect of the firm's operation and livelihood since it provides road maps for guiding, coordinating, and controlling the firm's actions in order to achieve its objectives. Two key aspects of the financial planning process are *cash planning* and *profit planning*. Cash planning involves the preparation of the firm's cash budget; profit planning is usually done by means of pro forma financial statements. These statements are useful not only for internal financial planning but also are routinely required by present and prospective lenders.

The **financial planning process** begins with long-run, or strategic, financial plans that in turn guide the formulation of short-run, or operating, plans and budgets. Generally, the short-run plans and budgets implement the firm's long-run strategic objectives. Although the major emphasis in this chapter is on short-run financial plans and budgets, a few comments on the long-run plans are appropriate here.

financial planning process Planning that begins with long-run (strategic) financial plans that in turn guide the formulation of short-run (operating) plans and budgets.

Long-Run (Strategic) Financial Plans

Long-run (strategic) financial plans are planned long-term financial actions and the anticipated financial impact of those actions. Such plans tend to cover periods ranging from two to ten years. The use of five-year strategic plans, which are periodically revised as significant new information becomes available, is common. Generally, firms that are subject to high degrees of operating uncertainty, relatively short production cycles, or both tend to use shorter planning horizons. Long-run financial plans consider proposed fixed-asset outlays, research and development activities, marketing and product development actions, and major sources of financing. Also included would be termination of existing projects, product lines, or lines of business; repayment or retirement of outstanding debts; and any planned acquisitions. Such plans tend to be supported by a series of annual budgets and profit plans.

long-run (strategic) financial plans Planned long-term financial actions and the anticipated financial impact of those actions.

Short-Run (Operating) Financial Plans

Short-run (operating) financial plans are planned short-term financial actions and the anticipated financial impact of those actions. These plans most often cover a one- to two-year period. Key inputs include the sales forecast and various forms of operating and financial data. Key outputs include a number of operating budgets, the cash budget, and pro forma financial statements. The short-run financial planning process, from the initial sales forecast through the development of the cash budget and pro forma income statement and balance sheet, is presented in the flow diagram in Figure 5.1.

From the sales forecast are developed production plans that take into account lead (preparation) times and include estimates of the required types and quantities of raw materials. Using the production plans, the firm can estimate direct labor requirements, factory overhead outlays, and operating expenses. Once these estimates have been made, the firm's pro forma income statement and cash budget can be prepared. With the basic inputs—pro forma income statement, cash budget, fixed-asset outlay plan, long-term financing plan, and current-period balance sheet—the pro forma balance sheet can finally be developed. Throughout the remainder of this chapter we will concentrate on the key outputs of the short-run financial planning process: the cash budget, the pro forma income statement, and the pro forma balance sheet.

short-run (operating) financial plans Planned short-term financial actions and the anticipated financial impact of those actions.

---

1 The financial planning process begins with the preparation of short-run (operating) plans and budgets which provide the basis for preparation of long-run (strategic) financial plans. *(Fable)*

The financial planning process *begins with long-run (strategic) financial plans* that in turn guide the formulation of short-run (operating) plans and budgets.

FACT OR FABLE?

Figure 5.1
The Short-Run (Operating) Financial Planning Process

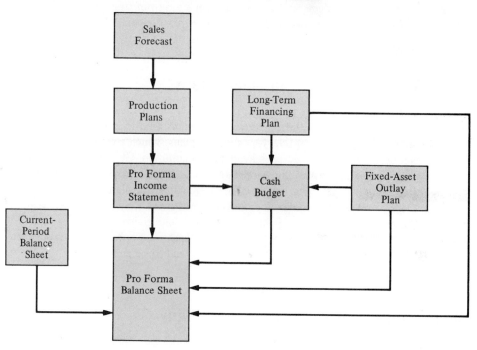

Cash Planning: Cash Budgets

cash budget (cash forecast)
Financial projection of the
firm's short-term cash
surpluses or shortages.

The **cash budget,** or **cash forecast,** allows the firm to plan its short-run cash needs. Attention is given to planning for surplus cash and for cash shortages. A firm expecting a cash surplus can plan short-term investments (marketable securities), whereas a firm expecting shortages in cash must arrange for short-term (notes payable) financing. The cash budget gives the financial manager a clear view of the timing of the firm's expected cash inflows and outflows over a given period.

Typically, the cash budget is designed to cover a one-year period, although any time period is acceptable. The period covered is normally divided into smaller time intervals. The number and type of intervals depend on the nature of the business. The more seasonal and uncertain a firm's cash flows, the greater the number of intervals. Since many firms are confronted with a seasonal cash flow pattern, the cash budget is quite often presented on a monthly basis. Firms with stable patterns of cash flow may use quarterly or annual time intervals. If a cash budget is developed for a period greater than one year, fewer time intervals may be warranted due to the difficulty and uncertainty of forecasting sales and other related cash items.

sales forecast The prediction
of the firm's sales over a
given period, based on
external and/or internal data,
and used as the key input to
the short-run financial
planning process.

The Sales Forecast

The key input to the short-run financial planning process and therefore any cash budget is the firm's **sales forecast.** This is the prediction of the firm's sales over a given period and is ordinarily furnished to the financial manager by the marketing department. On the basis of this forecast, the financial manager estimates the monthly cash flows that will result from projected sales receipts and from production-related, inventory-related, and sales-related outlays. The manager also determines the level of fixed assets required and the amount of financing, if any, needed to support the forecast level of production and sales. The sales forecast may be based on an analysis of external or internal data or on a combination of the two.[1]

External Forecasts

An **external forecast** is based on the relationships that can be observed between the firm's sales and certain key external economic indicators such as the gross national product (GNP), new housing starts, and disposable personal income. Forecasts containing these indicators are readily available. The rationale for this approach is that since the firm's sales are often closely related to some aspect of overall national economic activity, a forecast of economic activity should provide insight into future sales.

external forecast A sales forecast based on the relationships observed between the firm's sales and certain key external economic indicators.

Internal Forecasts

Internal forecasts are based on a buildup, or consensus, of sales forecasts through the firm's own sales channels. Typically, the firm's salespeople in the field are asked to estimate the number of units of each type of product they expect to sell in the coming year. These forecasts are collected and totaled by the sales manager, who may adjust the figures using his or her own knowledge of specific markets or of the salesperson's forecasting ability. Finally, adjustments may be made for additional internal factors, such as production capabilities.

internal forecast A sales forecast based on a buildup, or consensus, of forecasts through the firm's own sales channels.

Combined Forecasts

Firms generally use a combination of external and internal forecast data in making the final sales forecast. The internal data provide insight into sales expectations, while the external data provide a means of adjusting these expectations to take into account general economic factors. The nature of the firm's product also often affects the mix and types of forecasting methods used.

Preparing the Cash Budget

The general format of the cash budget is presented in Table 5.1. We will discuss each of its components individually.

Cash Receipts

Cash receipts includes all items from which cash inflows result in any given financial period. The most common components of cash receipts are cash sales, collections of accounts receivable, and other cash receipts.

cash receipts All items from which the firm receives cash inflows during a given financial period.

---

[1] A discussion of the calculation of the various forecasting techniques, such as regression, moving averages, and exponential smoothing, is not included in this text. The reader is referred to a basic statistics, econometrics, or management science text for a description of the technical side of forecasting. See, for example, Morris Hamburg, *Statistical Analysis for Decision Making,* 4th edition (San Diego: Harcourt Brace Jovanovich, Publishers, 1987) Ch. 1, or David R. Anderson, Dennis J. Sweeney, and Thomas A. Williams, *Quantitative Methods for Business,* 3d edition (St. Paul, MN: West Publishing Company, 1986), Ch. 7.

Table 5.1
The General Format of the Cash Budget

	Jan.	Feb.	. . .	Nov.	Dec.
Cash receipts					
Less: Cash disbursements	——	——	. . .	——	——
Net cash flow					
Add: Beginning cash	—— ↗ —— ↗ . . . ↗ —— ↗ ——				
Ending cash					
Less: Minimum cash balance	——	——	. . .	——	——
Required total financing					
Excess cash balance			. . .		

Example

Coulson Industries is developing a cash budget for October, November, and December. Coulson's sales in August and September were $100,000 and $200,000, respectively. Sales of $400,000, $300,000, and $200,000 have been forecast for October, November, and December, respectively. Historically, 20 percent of the firm's sales have been for cash, 50 percent have generated accounts receivable collected after one month, and the remaining 30 percent have generated accounts receivable collected after two months. Bad-debt expenses (uncollectible accounts) have been negligible.[2] In December, the firm will receive a $30,000 dividend from stock in a subsidiary. The schedule of expected cash receipts for the company is presented in Table 5.2. It contains the following items.

Forecast sales This initial entry is *merely informational*. It is provided as an aid in calculating other sales-related items.

Cash sales The cash sales shown for each month represent 20 percent of the total sales forecast for that month.

Collections of A/R These entries represent the collection of accounts receivable resulting from sales in earlier months.

Lagged one month These figures represent sales made in the preceding month that generated accounts receivable collected in the current month. Since 50 percent of the current month's sales are collected one month later, the collections of accounts receivable with a one-month lag shown for September, October, November, and December represent 50 percent of the sales in August, September, October, and November, respectively.

Lagged two months These figures represent sales made two months earlier that generated accounts receivable collected in the current month. Since 30 percent of sales are collected two months later, the collections with a two-month lag shown for October, November, and December represent 30 percent of the sales in August, September, and October, respectively.

---

[2] Normally it would be expected that the collection percentages would total slightly less than 100 percent to reflect the fact that some of the accounts receivable would be uncollectible. In this example the sum of the collection percentages is 100 percent (20% + 50% + 30%), which reflects the fact that all sales are assumed to be collected since bad debts are said to be negligible.

FINANCIAL ANALYST:
Preparer of Financial Analyses and Forecasts

When he isn't working as a financial analyst, you'll find Franco at one of his favorite hobbies: skydiving or training horses to jump hurdles. Do these leisure-time deeds of derring-do indicate a rift in Franco's personality: assertive at play but withdrawn at work? "Aw, come on," answers Franco. "I wish people would get over the notion that analysts are timid, inhibited types who never make a move unless we're sure how it will turn out. Almost anybody in business has to take a risk now and then. But it's my job to use the techniques of financial analysis to reduce the risk as much as possible. That way you're more likely to be in business tomorrow."

As a financial analyst at the home office of a national company, it's Franco's responsibility to study the financial feasibility of plans of various company divisions and to develop budgets that will accomplish those plans. If one division, for example, wants to add a piece of equipment that will increase productivity for an entire plant, Franco does a projection into the future to discover whether the resulting increased production will justify making the capital expenditure to acquire the machine.

Much of Franco's time is spent predicting the future, and his predictions are based on the best data he can find. He prepares pro forma statements, which show projected income and balance sheets for future years. Of course, in order to complete these, Franco must get sales projections as well as operating budgets from all the departments involved.

At 26, Franco thinks his career is ready to take off. "The danger in a company this size is that you get locked into one specialty too soon. Some financial analysts spend all their time on short-term borrowing, capital structure, liquidity, or even financial forecasting— my specialty. I don't want to be set in a career niche too soon." Franco is not worried about career-hopping to a smaller firm which will increase his opportunities to be exposed to various financial responsibilities. Financial analysis is a growing field. Some experts predict that the demand for analysts will increase by almost 40 percent between 1985 and 1995. It will be a very secure area and probably not nearly so exposed as the higher-level jobs like manager of capital budgeting or vice-president of finance.

Although the financial analyst makes a good wage, even the more experienced people don't earn huge salaries. With a year's experience and an MBA behind him, Franco earns $28,500 a year. Within five years that could be $40,000. To rise above the $40,000 salary threshold, Franco would need to move into a position involving a more direct decision-making role, such as cash manager or senior banking manager.

Even though Franco spends lots of time on his hobbies, his job demands more than the traditional 40 hours. Fifty-hour weeks are standard, and during busy periods, he works 60 or 65 hours. Does he get tired? "Not really," says Franco. "I think people get tired of a job when they're bored."

Other cash receipts   These are cash receipts expected to result from sources other than sales. Items such as dividends received, interest received, proceeds from the sale of equipment, stock and bond sale proceeds, and lease receipts may show up here. For Coulson Industries, the only other cash receipt is the $30,000 dividend due in December.

Total cash receipts   This figure represents the total of all the cash receipt items listed for each month in the cash receipt schedule. In the case of Coulson Industries, we are concerned only with October, November, and December; the total cash receipts for these months are shown in Table 5.2.

Table 5.2
A Schedule of Projected Cash Receipts for Coulson
Industries ($000)

	Aug.	Sept.	Oct.	Nov.	Dec.
Forecast sales	$100	$200	$400	$300	$200
Cash sales (.20)	$ 20	$ 40	$ 80	$ 60	$ 40
Collections of A/R:					
Lagged one month (.50)		50	100	200	150
Lagged two months (.30)			30	60	120
Other cash receipts					30
Total cash receipts			$210	$320	$340

Cash Disbursements

cash disbursements All cash
outlays by the firm during a
given financial period.

Cash disbursements include all outlays of cash in the period covered. The most common cash disbursements are:

> Cash purchases
>
> Payments of accounts payable
>
> Payments of cash dividends
>
> Rent expense
>
> Wages and salaries
>
> Tax payments
>
> Fixed-asset outlays
>
> Interest payments
>
> Principal payments (loans)
>
> Repurchases or retirements of stock

It is important to recognize that *depreciation and other noncash charges are NOT included in the cash budget* because they merely represent a scheduled write-off of an earlier cash outflow. The impact of depreciation, as noted in Chapter 3, is reflected in the level of cash outflow represented by the tax payments.

FACT OR FABLE?   **2** When preparing the cash budget it is important to include depreciation and any other noncash charges in the cash disbursements schedule. *(Fable)*

It is important to recognize that depreciation and other noncash charges are *not* included in the cash budget because they merely represent the write-off of an earlier cash outflow.

Example

Coulson Industries has gathered the following data needed for the preparation of a cash disbursements schedule for the months of October, November, and December.

Purchases The firm's purchases represent 70 percent of sales. Ten percent of this amount is paid in cash, 70 percent is paid in the month immediately following the month of purchase, and the remaining 20 percent is paid two months following the month of purchase.[3]

Cash dividends Cash dividends of $20,000 will be paid in October.

Rent expense Rent of $5,000 will be paid each month.

Wages and salaries The firm's wages and salaries can be estimated by adding 10 percent of its monthly sales to the $8,000 fixed-cost figure.

Tax payments Taxes of $25,000 must be paid in December.

Fixed-asset outlays New machinery costing $130,000 will be purchased and paid for in November.

Interest payments An interest payment of $10,000 is due in December.

Principal payments (loans) A $20,000 principal payment is also due in December.

Repurchases or retirements of stock No repurchase or retirement of stock is expected during the October–December period.

The firm's cash disbursements schedule, based on the data above, is presented in Table 5.3. Some items in Table 5.3 are explained in greater detail below.

Purchases This entry is *merely informational*. The figures represent 70 percent of the forecast sales for each month. They have been included to facilitate the calculation of the cash purchases and related payments.

Cash purchases The cash purchases for each month represent 10 percent of the month's purchases.

Payments of A/P These entries represent the payment of accounts payable resulting from purchases in earlier months.

Lagged one month These figures represent purchases made in the preceding month that are paid for in the current month. Since 70 percent of the firm's purchases are paid for one month later, the payments lagged one month shown for September, October, November, and December represent 70 percent of the August, September, October, and November purchases, respectively.

Lagged two months These figures represent purchases made two months earlier that are paid for in the current month. Since 20 percent of the firm's purchases are paid for two months later, the payments lagged two months for October, November, and December represent 20 percent of the August, September, and October purchases, respectively.

Wages and salaries These values were obtained by adding $8,000 to 10 percent of the *sales* in each month. The $8,000 represents the salary component; the rest represents wages.

The remaining items on the cash disbursements schedule are self-explanatory.

---

[3] Unlike the collection percentages for sales, the total of the payment percentages should equal 100 percent since it is expected that the firm will pay off all of its accounts payable. In line with this expectation, the percentages for Coulson Industries total 100 percent (10% + 70% + 20%).

Table 5.3
A Schedule of Projected Cash Disbursements for Coulson Industries ($000)

	Aug.	Sept.	Oct.	Nov.	Dec.
Purchases (.70 × sales)	$70	$140	$280	$210	$140
Cash purchases (.10)	$ 7	$ 14	$ 28	$ 21	$ 14
Payments of A/P:					
Lagged one month (.70)		49	98	196	147
Lagged two months (.20)			14	28	56
Cash dividends			20		
Rent expense			5	5	5
Wages and salaries			48	38	28
Tax payments			25		
Fixed-asset outlays				130	
Interest payments					10
Principal payments					20
Total cash disbursements			$213	$418	$305

Net Cash Flow, Ending Cash, Financing, and Excess Cash

net cash flow The mathematical difference between the firm's cash receipts and its cash disbursements in each period.

ending cash The sum of the firm's beginning cash and its net cash flow for the period.

required total financing Amount of funds needed by the firm if the ending cash for the period is less than the minimum cash balance.

excess cash balance The (excess) amount available for investment by the firm if the period's ending cash is greater than the minimum cash balance.

A firm's **net cash flow** is found by subtracting the cash disbursements from cash receipts in each period. By adding beginning cash to the firm's net cash flow, the **ending cash** for each period can be found. Finally, subtracting the minimum cash balance from ending cash yields the **required total financing** or the **excess cash balance.** If the ending cash is less than the minimum cash balance, *financing* is required. If the ending cash is greater than the minimum cash balance, *excess cash* exists.

Example

Table 5.4 presents Coulson Industries' cash budget, based on the cash receipt and cash disbursement data already developed for the firm. Coulson's end-of-September cash balance was $50,000, and the company wishes to maintain a minimum cash balance of $25,000.

For Coulson Industries to maintain its required $25,000 ending cash balance, it will need to have borrowed $76,000 in November and $41,000 in December. In the month of October the firm will have an excess cash balance of $22,000, which can be held in some interest-earning form. The required total financing figures in the cash budget refer to *how much will have to be owed at the end of the month;* they do *not* show the monthly changes in borrowing.

The monthly changes in borrowing as well as excess cash can be found by further analyzing the cash budget in Table 5.4. It can be seen that in October the $50,000 beginning cash, which becomes $47,000 after the $3,000 net cash outflow is deducted, results in a $22,000 excess cash balance once the $25,000 minimum cash is deducted. In November the $76,000 of required total financing resulted from the $98,000 net cash outflow less the $22,000 of excess cash from October. The $41,000 of total required financing in December resulted from reducing November's $76,000 of required total financing by the $35,000 of net cash inflow during December. Summarizing, the financial activities for each month would be as follows:

October: Invest $22,000 of excess cash.
November: Liquidate $22,000 of excess cash and borrow $76,000.
December: Repay $35,000 of amount borrowed.

Table 5.4
A Cash Budget for Coulson Industries ($000)

	Oct.	Nov.	Dec.
Total cash receipts[a]	$210	$320	$340
Less: Total cash disbursements[b]	213	418	305
Net cash flow	$ (3)	$ (98)	$ 35
Add: Beginning cash	50	47	(51)
Ending cash	$ 47	$ (51)	$(16)
Less: Minimum cash balance	25	25	25
Required total financing[c]	—	$ 76	$ 41
Excess cash balance[d]	$ 22	—	—

[a] From Table 5.2.

[b] From Table 5.3.

[c] Values are placed in this line when the ending cash is less than the minimum cash balance since in this instance financing is required.

[d] Values are placed in this line when the ending cash is greater than the minimum cash balance since in this instance an excess cash balance exists.

FACT OR FABLE?

3 The value for "required total financing" in the cash budget refers to the amount the firm would owe at the end of the period rather than the change in borrowing during the period. *(Fact)*

Evaluating the Cash Budget

The cash budget provides the firm with figures indicating the expected ending cash balance, which can be analyzed to determine whether a cash shortage or surplus is expected to result in each of the months covered by the forecast. Coulson Industries can expect a surplus of $22,000 in October, a deficit of $76,000 in November, and a deficit of $41,000 in December. Each of these figures is based on the internally imposed requirement of a $25,000 minimum cash balance and represents the total balance at the end of the month.

The excess cash balance in October can be invested in marketable securities. The deficits in November and December will have to be financed, typically, by short-term borrowing (notes payable). Since it may be necessary for the firm to borrow up to $76,000 for the three-month period evaluated, the financial manager should be sure that a line of credit is established or some other arrangement made to assure the availability of these

FINANCE IN ACTION

A TEN-GALLON HEADACHE: The Result of Poor Planning

Frances Gardner spent many of her days in a cubicle-size office in the Empire State Building, struggling with the Chapter 11 reorganization of the John B. Stetson hat company. A housewife who served on Stetson's board for seven years, Gardner took control of the business after her father, financier Ira Guilden, died in 1984. "What should have been a jewel of a business turned into a terrific headache," says Gardner.

Stetson stumbled when its since-dismissed president and chief executive attempted to transform the profitable business of licensing the Stetson name into a broad-based apparel company. In 1984 Stetson acquired a hatmaker, a millinery business, men's shirts, and an umbrella line. A Stetson retail store opened, and the company invested in a collection of women's sweaters. All lost money. At the same time, Stetson added dozens of employees, a $1 million computer system, and overhead designed to support a $38 million (sales) business. Result: $21 million in liabilities, $29 million in assets.

What happened? "We didn't have the right financial controls in place,"

says Gardner. Before Alan Feinberg, former president and chief executive got carried away, Stetson had $7 million in cash and receivables, no debt, and licensing and interest revenues of about $2 million. In 1985 Stetson lost about $5 million pretax. Feinberg was able to convince the board that the potential gains of expanding into new product areas justified the risks.

Besides, everyone knew that the hat industry had been in decline for the last 50 years. As men's hats went out of style in the early 1960s, dozens of manufacturers shut down. By 1971 business was so bad that Ira Guilden closed the Stetson factory in Philadelphia. He then licensed the Stetson name to the Stevens Hat Manufacturing Co., turning a hat company into quite a profitable licensing company.

In 1980 Guilden hired Feinberg. Feinberg quickly licensed the Stetson name to the Cody cosmetics division of Pfizer, Inc., which proceeded to launch one of the most successful men's fragrances in many years. Feinberg followed the Cody deal with a successful licensing agreement with Zyloware

Corp., an eyeglass maker. Feinberg, with Guilden's backing, was on a roll.

So how did the company end up with $21 million in debts? Guilden and Feinberg bought the Stevens Hat Manufacturing Co. in 1984, thus reversing the smart decision that Guilden had made 13 years earlier to get out of manufacturing. Overhead grew to over $11 million a year. Stetson salesmen were unable to sell the sweaters and the like, and complaints were heard that hat shipments were being delayed or missed. The Stevens Hat Manufacturing Co. had once contributed $700,000 in licensing revenues; now it was eating cash.

Frances Gardner then was elected president and chief executive, and the board fired Feinberg. The accessory businesses, with the exception of the men's hats, shut down, and the Stetson store in Stamford closed. Stetson's greatest asset remains intact: the famed old name, steeped in U.S. history. But exploiting these old names takes a deft touch.

SOURCE: Adapted from "Bad Judgment and Terrible Management," *Forbes,* September 22, 1986, pp. 184–186. Reprinted by permission of *Forbes* magazine. © Forbes, Inc., 1986.

funds. The manager will usually request or arrange to borrow more than the maximum financing indicated in the cash budget. This is necessary due to the uncertainty of the ending cash values, which are based on the sales forecast and other forecast values.

Coping with Uncertainty in the Cash Budget

Aside from care in preparation of sales forecasts and other estimates included in the cash budget, there are two ways of coping with the uncertainty of the cash budget.[4] One is to prepare several cash budgets—one based on a pessimistic forecast, one based on the most

[4] The term *uncertainty* is used here to refer to the variability of the cash flow outcomes that may actually occur. A thorough discussion of risk and uncertainty is presented in Chapter 7.

likely forecast, and a third based on an optimistic forecast. An evaluation of these cash flows allows the financial manager to determine the amount of financing necessary to cover the most adverse situation. The use of several cash budgets, each based on differing assumptions, should also give the financial manager a sense of the riskiness of alternatives so that he or she makes more intelligent short-term financial decisions. The sensitivity or "what if" analysis approach is often used to analyze cash flows under a variety of possible circumstances. Computers and spreadsheet programs (see Appendix D) are commonly used to greatly simplify the process of performing sensitivity analysis.

Example

Table 5.5 presents the summary results of Coulson Industries' cash budget prepared for each month of concern using a pessimistic, most likely, and optimistic estimate of cash receipts and cash disbursements. The most likely estimate is based on the expected outcomes presented earlier in Tables 5.2 through 5.4; the pessimistic and optimistic outcomes are based on the worst and best possible outcomes, respectively. During the month of October, Coulson will need a maximum of $15,000 of financing, while at best it will have a $62,000 excess cash balance available for short-term investment. During November, its financing requirement will be between $0 and $185,000. It could experience an excess cash balance of $5,000 during November. The December projections reflect maximum borrowing of $190,000 with a possible excess cash balance of $107,000. By considering the extreme values reflected in the pessimistic and optimistic outcomes, Coulson Industries should be better able to plan cash requirements. For the three-month period, the peak borrowing requirement under the worst circumstances would be $190,000, which happens to be considerably greater than the most likely estimate of $76,000 for this period.

A second and much more sophisticated way of coping with uncertainty in the cash budget is *computer simulation*.[5] By simulating the occurrence of sales and other uncertain events, a probability distribution of the firm's ending cash flows for each month can be developed. The financial decision maker can then use the probability distribution to determine the amount of financing necessary to provide a desired degree of protection against a cash shortage.

Cash Flow Within the Month

Since the cash budget shows cash flows only on a total monthly basis, the information provided by the cash budget is not necessarily adequate for assuring solvency. A firm must look more closely at its pattern of daily cash receipts and cash disbursements to make sure adequate cash is available for meeting bills as they come due. The following example illustrates the importance of monitoring daily cash flows.

---

[5] A more detailed discussion of the use of simulation is included as part of the discussion of capital budgeting under risk in Chapter 10.

Table 5.5
A Sensitivity Analysis of Coulson Industries' Cash Budget ($000)

	October			November			December		
	Pessi-mistic	Most likely	Opti-mistic	Pessi-mistic	Most likely	Opti-mistic	Pessi-mistic	Most likely	Opti-mistic
Total cash receipts	$160	$210	$285	$210	$320	$410	$275	$340	$422
Less: Total cash disbursements	200	213	248	380	418	467	280	305	320
Net cash flow	$(40)	$ (3)	$ 37	$(170)	$(98)	$(57)	$ (5)	$ 35	$102
Add: Beginning cash	50	50	50	10	47	87	(160)	(51)	30
Ending cash	$ 10	$ 47	$ 87	$(160)	$(51)	$ 30	$(165)	$(16)	$132
Less: Minimum cash balance	25	25	25	25	25	25	25	25	25
Required total financing	$ 15	—	—	$185	$ 76	—	$190	$ 41	—
Excess cash balance	—	$ 22	$ 62	—	—	$ 5	—	—	$107

Example
Coulson Industries found its actual pattern of cash receipts and cash disbursements during the month of October to be as shown in Table 5.6. Although the firm begins the month with $50,000 of cash and ends the month with $47,000 in cash, its cash balance is negative at various times within the month. Table 5.6 shows negative cash balances during the periods October 2–11 and October 17–22. The largest deficit, of $72,000, occurs on October 4.

Although the cash budget presented in Table 5.4 indicates that Coulson Industries will not require any financing during the month of October, since a $22,000 excess cash balance is expected, a look at the firm's daily cash flows during October shows that it will need additional financing in order to make payments as they come due. At the maximum, $72,000 is required to meet daily cash flow requirements.

The example makes it quite clear that the synchronization of cash flows in the cash budget at month-end does not ensure that the firm will be able to meet daily cash requirements. Since a firm's cash flows are generally quite variable when viewed on a daily basis, effective cash planning requires a look beyond the cash budget. Although Coulson Industries' cash budget (Table 5.4) suggests it does not need to borrow during October, the firm needs a maximum of $72,000 in additional funds, due to the nonsynchronized daily cash flows. The financial manager must therefore plan and monitor cash flow more frequently than on a monthly basis. The greater the variability of cash flows from day to day, the greater the attention required.

Table 5.6
Daily Cash Flows During October for Coulson Industries ($000)

Date	Amount received	Amount disbursed	Cash balance[a]
10/1	Beginning balance		$50
10/2		$100	−50
10/4		22	−72
10/5	$65	15	−22
10/11	74		52
10/12	10	12	50
10/16		40	10
10/17	3	21	−8
10/22	35		27
10/26	20	1	46
10/29	3		49
10/31		2	47
Total	$210	$213	

[a] These figures represent ending cash balances without any financing.

Profit Planning: Pro Forma Statement Fundamentals

The profit-planning process centers on the preparation of **pro forma statements,** which are projected, or forecast, financial statements—income statements and balance sheets. The preparation of these statements requires a careful blending of a number of procedures to account for the revenues, costs, expenses, assets, liabilities, and equity resulting from the firm's anticipated level of operations. The basic steps in this process were shown in the flow diagram presented in Figure 5.1. The financial manager frequently uses one of a number of simplified approaches to estimate the pro forma statements. The most popular are based on the belief that the financial relationships reflected in the firm's historical (past) financial statements will not change in the coming period. The commonly used approaches are presented in subsequent discussions.

The inputs required for preparing pro forma statements using the simplified approaches are financial statements for the preceding year and the sales forecast for the coming year. A variety of assumptions must also be made when using simplified approaches. The company we will use to illustrate the simplified approaches to pro forma preparation is Vectra Manufacturing, which manufactures and sells one product. It has two basic models—model X and model Y. Although each model is produced by the same process, each requires different amounts of raw material and labor.

pro forma statements
Projected, or forecast, financial statements: income statements and balance sheets.

Past Year's Financial Statements

The income statement for the firm's 1988 operations is given in Table 5.7. It indicates that Vectra had sales of $100,000, total cost of goods sold of $80,000, and net profits after taxes of $7,650. The firm paid $4,000 in cash dividends, leaving $3,650 to be transferred to retained earnings. The firm's balance sheet at the end of 1988 is given in Table 5.8.

Table 5.7
An Income Statement for Vectra Manufacturing for the Year Ended December 31, 1988

Sales revenue		
Model X (1,000 units at $20/unit)	$20,000	
Model Y (2,000 units at $40/unit)	80,000	
Total sales		$100,000
Less: Cost of goods sold		
Labor	$28,500	
Material A	8,000	
Material B	5,500	
Overhead	38,000	
Total cost of goods sold		80,000
Gross profits		$ 20,000
Less: Operating expenses		10,000
Operating profits		$ 10,000
Less: Interest expense		1,000
Net profits before taxes		$ 9,000
Less: Taxes (.15 × $9,000)		1,350
Net profits after taxes		$ 7,650
Less: Common stock dividends		4,000
To retained earnings		$ 3,650

Table 5.8
A Balance Sheet for Vectra Manufacturing (December 31, 1988)

Assets		Liabilities and equities	
Cash	$ 6,000	Accounts payable	$ 7,000
Marketable securities	4,000	Taxes payable	300
Accounts receivable	13,000	Notes payable	8,300
Inventories	16,000	Other current liabilities	3,400
Total current assets	$39,000	Total current liabilities	$19,000
Net fixed assets	$51,000	Long-term debts	$18,000
Total assets	$90,000	Stockholders' equity	
		Common stock	$30,000
		Retained earnings	$23,000
		Total liabilities and stockholders' equity	$90,000

Sales Forecast

Like the cash budget, the key input for the development of pro forma statements is the sales forecast. The sales forecast by model for the coming year, 1989, for Vectra Manufacturing is given in Table 5.9. This forecast is based on both external and internal data. The unit sales prices of the products reflect an increase from $20 to $25 for model X and from $40 to $50 for model Y. These increases are required to cover the firm's anticipated increases in the cost of labor, material, overhead, and operating expenses.

Table 5.9
1989 Sales Forecast for Vectra
Manufacturing

Unit sales	
Model X	1,500
Model Y	1,950
Dollar sales	
Model X ($25/unit)	$ 37,500
Model Y ($50/unit)	97,500
Total	$135,000

Preparing the Pro Forma Income Statement

A simple method for developing a pro forma income statement is to use the **percent-of-sales method,** which forecasts sales and then expresses the cost of goods sold, operating expenses, and interest expense as a percentage of projected sales. The percentages used are likely to be the percentage of sales for these items in the immediately preceding year. For Vectra Manufacturing, these percentages are as follows:

percent-of-sales method
A method for developing the pro forma income statement that expresses the cost of goods sold, operating expenses, and interest expense as a percentage of projected sales.

$$\frac{\text{Cost of goods sold}}{\text{Sales}} = \frac{\$80,000}{\$100,000} = 80.0\%$$

$$\frac{\text{Operating expenses}}{\text{Sales}} = \frac{\$10,000}{\$100,000} = 10.0\%$$

$$\frac{\text{Interest expense}}{\text{Sales}} = \frac{\$1,000}{\$100,000} = 1.0\%$$

The dollar values used are taken from the 1988 income statement (Table 5.7).

Applying these percentages to the firm's forecast sales of $135,000, developed in Table 5.9, and assuming that the firm will pay $4,000 in cash dividends in 1989, results in the pro forma income statement in Table 5.10. The expected contribution to retained earnings is $6,327, which represents a considerable increase over $3,650 in the preceding year.

Considering Types of Costs and Expenses

The technique used to prepare the pro forma income statement in Table 5.10 assumes that all the firm's costs are *variable*. This means that the use of the historical (1988) ratios of cost of goods sold, operating expenses, and interest expense to sales assumes that for a given percentage increase in sales, the same percentage increase in each of these expense components will result. For example, as Vectra's sales increased by 35 percent (from $100,000 in 1988 to $135,000 projected for 1989), its cost of goods sold also increased by 35 percent (from $80,000 in 1988 to $108,000 projected for 1989). Based on this assumption, the firm's net profits before taxes also increased by 35 percent (from $9,000 in 1988 to $12,150 projected for 1989).

In the approach just illustrated, the broader implication is that since the firm has no fixed costs, it will not receive the benefits often resulting from them.[6] Therefore, the use of past cost and expense ratios generally tends to understate profits, since the firm is in fact likely to have certain beneficial fixed operating and financial costs. The best way to adjust for the presence of fixed costs when using a simplified approach for pro forma income statement preparation is to break the firm's historical costs into *fixed* and *variable components* and make the forecast using this relationship.[7]

Example

Vectra Manufacturing's last-year (1988) and pro forma (1989) income statements broken into fixed- and variable-cost components, are given below.

Vectra Manufacturing's Income Statements		
	Last year (1988)	Pro forma (1989)
Sales revenue	$100,000	$135,000
Less: Cost of goods sold		
Fixed cost	40,000	40,000
Variable cost (.40 × sales)	40,000	54,000
Gross profits	$ 20,000	$ 41,000
Less: Operating expenses		
Fixed expense	5,000	5,000
Variable expense (.05 × sales)	5,000	6,750
Operating profits	$ 10,000	$ 29,250
Less: Interest expense (all fixed)	1,000	1,000
Net profits before taxes	$ 9,000	$ 28,250
Less: Taxes (.15 × net profits before taxes)	1,350	4,238
Net profits after taxes	$ 7,650	$ 24,012

By breaking Vectra's costs and expenses into fixed and variable components, its pro forma profit is expected to provide a more accurate projection. Had the firm treated all costs as variable, its pro forma (1989) net profits before taxes would equal 9 percent of sales, just as was the case in 1988 ($9,000 net profits before taxes ÷ $100,000 sales). As shown in Table 5.10, by assuming *all* costs as variable the net profits before taxes would have been $12,150 (9% × $135,000 projected sales) instead of the $28,250 of net profits before taxes obtained above by using the firm's fixed-cost–variable-cost breakdown.

[6] The potential returns as well as risks resulting from use of fixed (operating and financial) costs to create "leverage" are discussed in Chapter 12. The key point to recognize here is that when the firm's revenue is *increasing,* fixed costs can magnify returns.

[7] The application of *regression analysis*—a statistically based technique for measuring the relationship between variables—to past cost data as it relates to past sales could be used to develop equations that recognize the fixed and variable nature of each cost. Such equations could be employed in preparing the pro forma income statement from the sales forecast. The use of the regression approach in pro forma income statement preparation is widespread, and many computer software packages for use in pro forma preparation rely on this technique. Expanded discussions of the application of this technique can be found in most second-level managerial finance texts.

PROFILE

JACK WELCH: Restructuring for Profitability

General Electric was founded over a hundred years ago to manufacture Thomas Edison's remarkable discoveries and bring them to the American family. In the past 25 years, the manufacturing of many of these kinds of products has fled to developing nations where labor costs are lower than in the United States. As a result, GE was a giant with the ability to make everything from lightbulbs to hand mixers to jet engines, even though not all of these products could be made profitably anymore. So the giant grew slowly, or not at all.

That was the situation when Jack Welch was appointed CEO in 1981. Obviously the venerable company—third largest in the United States in market value—badly needed a restructuring if it was to become a contender once more. Welch brought along experience within the operation of GE. After receiving his doctorate in chemical engineering, he was hired to run a new department of the plastics division. Under him, it grew until it became a major supplier of plastics to the automobile industry. By 35, he was in charge of the division, and from there it was just a hop to the vice-presidency.

As CEO, Welch's plan was to get rid of low-profit operations, automate what was left, and acquire others that were either profitable or had potential.

Since 1981, GE has sold $6 billion worth of heavy industry and acquired $10 billion worth of service and technology businesses. This has helped put the company on the cutting edge of electronic, medical, and communications innovations, and has increased earnings by 54 percent in the years from 1980 to 1986.

Of course, there has been a heavy cost. Any strategy that converts a corporation from heavy industry to service and technology is destined to displace a significant number of employees. In GE's case, 100,000 jobs were wiped out—about a quarter of the company's work force. And they weren't blue-collar workers only. Many management levels were completely eliminated.

Any CEO who presides over such a titanic change is sure to earn an unflattering nickname. Welch was dubbed Neutron Jack because it was said that after he visited a GE plant the building remained but the workers would be gone. Welch thinks the name is unfair and believes that people who lost their jobs at GE were treated with dignity and compassion, and were provided as soft a landing as the company could possibly afford.

Welch has acquired definite guidelines that he believes will increase GE's profitability: a company must be first or second among all its competitors or it is ripe for divestment. He is, however, willing to invest corporate funds if he sees a way to make a company profitable. He has updated a plant that makes turbines, because every developing nation, he feels, will need to increase its power-generating capacity. An old-line dishwasher plant is the envy of the industry since it was completely automated. Welch's big opportunity—and his big challenge—is to continue his policy of resurrecting old companies when possible, merging them with new companies, and blending them all into a new, profitable GE.

The preceding example should make it clear that when using a simplified approach to pro forma income statement preparation, it is advisable to consider first breaking down costs and expenses into fixed and variable components. For convenience, the pro forma income statement prepared for Vectra Manufacturing in Table 5.10 was based on the assumption that all costs were variable—which is *not* likely to be the case. Therefore, Vectra's projected profits were understated using the percent-of-sales method.

Table 5.10
A Pro Forma Income Statement, Using the Percent-of-Sales Method, for Vectra Manufacturing for the Year Ended December 31, 1989

Sales revenue	$135,000
Less: Cost of goods sold (80.0%)	108,000
Gross profits	$ 27,000
Less: Operating expenses (10.0%)	13,500
Operating profits	$ 13,500
Less: Interest expense (1.0%)	1,350
Net profits before taxes	$ 12,150
Less: Taxes (.15 × $12,150)	1,823
Net profits after taxes	$ 10,327
Less: Common stock dividends	4,000
To retained earnings	$ 6,327

FACT OR FABLE?

4 When a simplified approach to pro forma income statement preparation is desired, breaking down costs and expenses into fixed and variable components improves on the use of a strict percent-of-sales approach. *(Fact)*

Preparing the Pro Forma Balance Sheet

judgmental approach
A method of developing the pro forma balance sheet in which the values of certain accounts are estimated while others are calculated, using the firm's external financing as a balancing, or "plug" figure.

A number of simplified approaches are available for preparing the pro forma balance sheet. Probably the best and most popular is the judgmental approach.[8] Under the **judgmental approach** for developing the pro forma balance sheet, the values of certain balance sheet accounts are estimated while others are calculated. When this approach is applied, the firm's external financing is used as a balancing, or "plug," figure. To apply the judgmental approach in order to prepare Vectra Manufacturing's 1989 pro forma balance sheet, a number of assumptions must be made:

1. A minimum cash balance of $6,000 is desired.

2. Marketable securities are assumed to remain unchanged from their current level of $4,000.

3. Accounts receivable will on average represent 45 days of sales. Since Vectra's annual sales are projected to be $135,000, accounts receivable should average $16,875 ($\frac{1}{8}$ × $135,000). (Forty-five days expressed fractionally is one-eighth of a year: $45/360 = \frac{1}{8}$.)

4. The ending inventory should remain at a level of about $16,000, of which 25 percent (approximately $4,000) should be raw materials, while the remaining 75 percent (approximately $12,000) should consist of finished goods.

[8] The judgmental approach represents an improved version of the often discussed *percent-of-sales approach* to pro forma balance sheet preparation. Because the judgmental approach requires only slightly more information and should yield better estimates than the somewhat naive percent-of-sales approach, it is presented here.

5. A new machine costing $20,000 will be purchased. Total depreciation for the year will be $8,000. Adding the $20,000 acquisition to the existing net fixed assets of $51,000 and subtracting the depreciation of $8,000 will yield net fixed assets of $63,000.

6. Purchases are expected to represent approximately 30 percent of annual sales, which in this case would be approximately $40,500 (.30 × $135,000). The firm estimates it can take 72 days on average to satisfy its accounts payable. Thus accounts payable should equal one-fifth (72 days ÷ 360 days) of the firm's purchases, or $8,100 ($\frac{1}{5}$ × $40,500).

7. Taxes payable are expected to equal one-fourth of the current year's tax liability, which would equal about $455 (one-fourth of the tax liability of $1,823 shown in the pro forma income statement presented in Table 5.10).

8. Notes payable are assumed to remain unchanged from their current level of $8,300.

9. No change in other current liabilities is expected. They will remain at the level of the previous year: $3,400.

10. The firm's long-term debts and its common stock are expected to remain unchanged, at $18,000 and $30,000, respectively, since no issues, retirements, or repurchases of bonds or stocks are planned.

11. Retained earnings will increase from the beginning level of $23,000 (from the balance sheet dated December 31, 1988, in Table 5.8) to $29,327. The increase of $6,327 represents the amount of retained earnings calculated in the year-end 1989 pro forma income statement in Table 5.10.

A 1989 pro forma balance sheet for Vectra Manufacturing based on these assumptions is presented in Table 5.11. A **"plug" figure**—called the **external funds required**—

external funds required ("plug" figure) Under the judgmental approach for developing a pro forma balance sheet, the amount of external financing needed to bring the statement into balance.

**Table 5.11
A Pro Forma Balance Sheet, Using the Judgmental Approach, for Vectra Manufacturing (December 31, 1989)**

Assets			Liabilities and equities	
Cash		$ 6,000	Accounts payable	$ 8,100
Marketable securities		4,000	Taxes payable	455
Accounts receivable		16,875	Notes payable	8,300
Inventories			Other current liabilities	3,400
Raw materials	$ 4,000		Total current	
Finished goods	12,000		liabilities	$ 20,255
Total inventory		16,000	Long-term debts	$ 18,000
Total current			Stockholders' equity	
assets		$ 42,875	Common stock	$ 30,000
Net fixed assets		$ 63,000	Retained earnings	$ 29,327
Total assets		$105,875	Total	$ 97,582
			External funds required[a]	$ 8,293
			Total liabilities and stockholders' equity	$105,875

[a] The amount of external funds needed to force the firm's balance sheet to balance. Due to the nature of the judgmental approach to preparing the pro forma balance sheet, the balance sheet is not expected to balance without some type of adjustment.

of $8,293 is needed to bring the statement into balance. This means that the firm will have to obtain about $8,293 of additional external financing to support the increased sales level of $135,000 for 1989. When this approach is used, under certain circumstances a negative external funds requirement might result. This would indicate that the firm's financing is in excess of its needs and that funds would therefore be available for repaying debt, repurchasing stock, or increasing the dividend to stockholders. Analysts sometimes use the judgmental approach to pro forma preparation as a technique for estimating financing needs, but for our purposes the approach is used to prepare the pro forma balance sheet.

FACT OR FABLE?   [5] The judgmental approach to the preparation of the pro forma balance sheet is attractive since it assures that the statement will automatically be in balance. *(Fable)*

A "plug" figure—called *external funds required*—is typically required to bring the statement into balance when using the judgmental approach to pro forma balance sheet preparation.

Evaluation of Pro Forma Statements

It is difficult to forecast the many variables involved in pro forma statement preparation. As a result, analysts—including investors, lenders, and managers—frequently use the techniques presented here in order to make rough estimates of pro forma financial statements. Although the growing availability and acceptance of personal computers and electronic spreadsheets is streamlining the financial planning process, simplified approaches to pro forma preparation are expected to remain popular. An understanding of the basic weaknesses of these simplified approaches is therefore important. Equally important is the ability to effectively use pro forma statements to make financial decisions.

Weaknesses of Simplified Approaches

The basic weaknesses of the simplified pro forma approaches shown in the chapter lie in two assumptions: (1) that the firm's past financial condition is an accurate indicator of its future and (2) that certain variables, such as cash, accounts receivable, and inventories, can be forced to take on certain "desired" values. These assumptions are questionable, but due to the ease of the calculations involved, the use of these approaches is quite common.

Other simplified approaches exist. Most are based on the assumption that certain relationships among income, costs and expenses, assets, liabilities, and equity will prevail in the future. For example, in preparing the pro forma balance sheet, all assets, liabilities, *and* equity are often increased by the percentage increase expected in sales. The financial analyst must know the techniques that have been used in preparing pro forma statements so that he or she can judge the quality of the estimated values and thus the degree of confidence he or she can have in them.

Using Pro Forma Statements

In addition to estimating the amount, if any, of external financing required to support a given level of sales, pro forma statements also provide a basis for analyzing in advance the level of profitability and overall financial performance of the firm in the coming year.

Using pro forma statements, the financial manager, as well as lenders, can analyze the firm's sources and uses of funds as well as various aspects of performance, such as liquidity, activity, debt, and profitability. Sources and uses can be evaluated by preparing a pro forma statement of changes in financial position. Various ratios can be calculated from the pro forma income statement and balance sheet to evaluate performance.

After analyzing the pro forma statements, the financial manager can take steps to adjust planned operations in order to achieve short-run financial goals. For example, if profits on the pro forma income statement are too low, a variety of pricing or cost-cutting actions, or both, might be initiated. If the projected level of accounts receivable shown on the pro forma balance sheet is too high, changes in credit policy may avoid this outcome. Pro forma statements are therefore of key importance in solidifying the firm's financial plans for the coming year.

Summary

● The two key aspects of the financial planning process are cash planning, which involves preparation of the cash budget or cash forecast, and profit planning, which relies on preparation of the pro forma income statement and balance sheet.

● Long-run (strategic) financial plans act as a guide for preparing short-run (operating) financial plans. Long-run plans tend to cover periods ranging from two to ten years and are updated periodically.

● Key inputs to short-run (operating) plans are the sales forecast and various forms of operating and financial data; key outputs include operating budgets, the cash budget, and the pro forma financial statements.

● The cash budget is typically prepared for a one-year period divided into months. It nets cash receipts and disbursements for each period in order to indicate net cash flow. Ending cash is estimated by adding beginning cash to the net cash flow. By subtracting the minimum cash balance from the ending cash, the required total financing or excess cash balance (whichever is the case) can be determined.

● To cope with uncertainty in the cash budget, sensitivity analysis or computer simulation can be used. A firm must also look beyond the cash budget and evaluate cash flows occurring within the month.

● A pro forma income statement can be developed by calculating past percentage relationships between certain cost and expense items and the firm's sales and then applying these percentages to forecasts. This process can be improved upon by first breaking down costs and expenses into fixed and variable components.

● A pro forma balance sheet can be estimated using the judgmental approach. Under this simplified technique, an entry for external funds required acts as a balancing, or "plug," figure.

● The use of simplified approaches for pro forma statement preparation, although quite popular, can be criticized for assuming the firm's past condition is an accurate predictor of the future and for assuming that certain variables can be forced to take on desired values.

● Pro forma statements are commonly used by financial managers and lenders to analyze in advance the firm's level of profitability and overall financial performance. Based on their analysis, financial managers adjust planned operations in order to achieve short-run financial goals.

Questions

5-1 What is the *financial planning process?* Define, compare, and contrast *long-run (strategic) financial plans* and *short-run (operating) financial plans.*

5-2 Which three statements result as part of the short-run (operating) financial planning process? Describe the flow of information from the sales forecast through the preparation of these statements.

5-3 What is the purpose of the *cash budget?* The key input to the cash budget is the sales forecast. What is the difference between *external* and *internal* forecast data?

5-4 Briefly describe the basic format of the cash budget, beginning with forecast sales and ending with required total financing or excess cash balance.

5-5   How can the two bottom lines of the cash budget be used to determine the firm's short-term borrowing and investment requirements?

5-6   What is the cause of uncertainty in the cash budget? What two techniques can be used to cope with this uncertainty?

5-7   What actions or analysis beyond preparation of the cash budget should the financial manager undertake to assure that cash is available when needed? Why?

5-8   What is the purpose of *pro forma financial statements?* Which of the pro forma statements must be developed first? Why?

5-9   Briefly describe the pro forma income statement preparation process using the percent-of-sales method. What are the strengths and weaknesses of this simplified approach?

5-10   Describe the judgmental approach for simplified preparation of the pro forma balance sheet. Contrast this with the more detailed approach shown in Figure 5.1.

5-11   What is the significance of the balancing (''plug'') figure, *external funds required,* used with the judgmental approach for preparing the pro forma balance sheet?

5-12   What are the two key weaknesses of the simplified approaches to pro forma statement preparation? In spite of these weaknesses, why do these approaches remain popular?

5-13   How may the financial manager wish to evaluate pro forma statements? What is his or her objective in evaluating these statements?

Self-Test Problems

(Solutions on pages 162–163)

ST-1   Jane McDonald, a financial analyst for Carroll Company, has prepared the following sales and cash disbursement estimates for the period February–June of the current year.

Month	Sales	Cash disbursements
February	$500	$400
March	600	300
April	400	600
May	200	500
June	200	200

Ms. McDonald notes that historically 30 percent of sales have been for *cash*. Of *credit sales,* 70 percent are collected one month after the sale, and the remaining 30 percent are collected two months after the sale. The firm wishes to maintain a minimum ending balance in its cash account of $25. Balances above this amount would be invested in short-term government securities, while any deficits would be financed through short-term bank borrowing. The beginning cash balance at April 1 is $115.

a. Prepare a cash budget for April, May, and June.

b. How much financing, if any, at a maximum would Carroll Company need to meet its obligations during this three-month period?

c. If a pro forma balance sheet dated at the end of June were prepared from the information presented, give the size of each of the following: cash, notes payable, marketable securities, and accounts receivable.

ST-2 Euro Designs, Inc., expects sales during 1989 to rise from the 1988 level of $3.5 million to $3.9 million. Due to a scheduled large loan payment, the interest expense in 1989 is expected to drop to $325,000. The firm plans to increase its cash dividend payments during 1989 to $320,000. The company's year-end 1988 income statement is given below.

Income Statement Euro Designs, Inc. for the Year Ended December 31, 1988	
Sales revenue	$3,500,000
Less: Cost of goods sold	1,925,000
Gross profits	$1,575,000
Less: Operating expenses	420,000
Operating profits	$1,155,000
Less: Interest expense	400,000
Net profits before taxes	$ 755,000
Less: Taxes (40%)	302,000
Net profits after taxes	$ 453,000
Less: Cash dividends	250,000
To retained earnings	$ 203,000

a. Use the percent-of-sales method to prepare a 1989 pro forma income statement for Euro Designs, Inc.

b. Explain why the statement may underestimate the company's actual 1989 pro forma income.

Problems

5-1 **(Cash Receipts)** A firm has actual sales of $65,000 in April and $60,000 in May. It expects sales of $70,000 in June and $100,000 in July and in August. Assuming that sales are the only source of cash inflows and that half of these are for cash and the remainder are collected evenly over the following two months, what are the firm's expected cash receipts for June, July, and August?

5-2 **(Cash Budget—Basic)** Grenoble Enterprises had sales of $50,000 in March and $60,000 in April. Forecast sales for May, June, and July are $70,000, $80,000, and $100,000, respectively. The firm has a cash balance of $5,000 on May 1 and wishes to maintain a minimum cash balance of $5,000. Given the following data, prepare and interpret a cash budget for the months of May, June, and July.

(1) Twenty percent of the firm's sales are for cash; 60 percent are collected in the next month, the remaining 20 percent are collected in the second month following sale.

(2) The firm receives other income of $2,000 per month.

(3) The firm's actual or expected purchases, all made for cash, are $50,000, $70,000, and $80,000 for the months of May through July, respectively.

(4) Rent is $3,000 per month.

(5) Wages and salaries are 10 percent of the previous month's sales.

(6) Cash dividends of $3,000 will be paid in June.

(7) Payment of principal and interest of $4,000 is due in June.

(8) A cash purchase of equipment costing $6,000 is scheduled in July.

(9) Taxes of $6,000 are due in June.

5-3 **(Cash budget—Advanced)** Xenocore, Inc.'s actual sales and purchases for September and October 1988, along with its forecast sales and purchases for the period November 1988 through April 1989, follow.

Year	Month	Sales	Purchases
1988	September	$210,000	$120,000
1988	October	250,000	150,000
1988	November	170,000	140,000
1988	December	160,000	100,000
1989	January	140,000	80,000
1989	February	180,000	110,000
1989	March	200,000	100,000
1989	April	250,000	90,000

The firm makes 20 percent of all sales for cash and collects on 40 percent of its sales in each of the two months following the sale. Other cash inflows are expected to be $12,000 in September and April, $15,000 in January and March, and $27,000 in February. The firm pays cash for 10 percent of its purchases. It pays for 50 percent of its purchases in the following month and for 40 percent of its purchases two months later.

Wages and salaries amount to 20 percent of the preceding month's sales. Rent of $20,000 per month must be paid. Interest payments of $10,000 are due in January and April. A principal payment of $30,000 is also due in April. The firm expects to pay cash dividends of $20,000 in January and April. Taxes of $80,000 are due in April. The firm also intends to make a $25,000 cash purchase of fixed assets in December.

a. Assuming that the firm has a cash balance of $22,000 at the beginning of November, determine the end-of-month cash balances for each month, November through April.

b. Assuming that the firm wishes to maintain a $15,000 minimum cash balance, determine the monthly total financing requirements or excess cash balances.

c. If the firm were requesting a line of credit to cover needed financing for the period November to April, how large would this line have to be? Explain your answer.

5-4 **(Cash Flow Concepts)** The following represent financial transactions that Johnsfield & Co. will be undertaking in the next planning period. For each transaction check the statement or statements that will be affected immediately.

	Statement		
Transaction	**Cash budget**	**Pro forma income statement**	**Pro forma balance sheet**
Cash sale	√	√	
Credit sale		√	√
Accounts receivable are collected	√		√
Asset with five-year life is purchased	√		√
Depreciation is taken		√	√
Amortization of goodwill is taken		√	√
Sale of common stock	√		√
Retirement of outstanding bonds	√		√
Fire insurance premium is paid for the next three years	√	√	√

5-5 **(Multiple Cash Budgets—Sensitivity Analysis)** Brownstein, Inc., expects sales of $100,000 during each of the next three months. It will make monthly purchases of $60,000 during this time. Wages and salaries are $10,000 per month plus 5 percent of sales. Brownstein expects to make a tax payment of $20,000 in the next month and a $15,000 purchase of fixed assets in the second month, and to receive $8,000 in cash from the sale of an asset in the third month. All sales and purchases are for cash. Beginning cash and the minimum cash balance are assumed to be zero.

a. Construct a cash budget for the next three months.

b. Brownstein's is unsure of the sales levels, but all other figures are certain. If the most pessimistic sales figure is $80,000 per month and the most optimistic is $120,000 per month, what are the monthly minimum and maximum ending cash balances the firm can expect for each of the one-month periods?

c. Briefly discuss how the data in **a** and **b** can be used by the financial manager to plan for his or her financing needs.

5-6 **(Pro Forma Income Statement)** The marketing department of Metroline Manufacturing estimates that its sales in 1989 will be $1.5 million. Interest expense is expected to remain unchanged at $35,000, and the firm plans to pay $70,000 in cash dividends during 1989. Metroline Manufacturing's income statement for the year ended December 31, 1988, is given on page 158, followed by a breakdown of the firm's cost of goods sold and operating expenses into its fixed- and variable-cost components.

a. Use the *percent-of-sales method* to prepare a pro forma income statement for the year ended December 31, 1989.

b. Used the *fixed- and variable-cost data* to develop a pro forma income statement for the year ended December 31, 1989.

c. Compare and contrast the statements developed in **a** and **b**. Which statement will likely provide the better estimates of 1989 income? Explain why.

7.14

Income Statement Metroline Manufacturing for the Year Ended December 31, 1988	
Sales revenue	$1,400,000
Less: Cost of goods sold	910,000
Gross profits	$ 490,000
Less: Operating expenses	120,000
Operating profits	$ 370,000
Less: Interest expense	35,000
Net profits before taxes	$ 335,000
Less: Taxes (40%)	134,000
Net profits after taxes	$ 201,000
Less: Cash dividends	66,000
To retained earnings	$ 135,000

handwritten notes: 1.5, 65%, 8.57, 35000, 2.5, 70000

Fixed- and Variable-Cost Breakdown Metroline Manufacturing for the Year Ended December 31, 1988	
Cost of goods sold	
Fixed cost	$210,000
Variable cost	700,000
Total cost	$910,000
Operating expenses	
Fixed expenses	$ 36,000
Variable expenses	84,000
Total expenses	$120,000

5-7 **(Pro Forma Balance Sheet—Basic)** Leonard Industries wishes to prepare a pro forma balance sheet for December 31, 1989. The firm expects 1989 sales to total $3,000,000. The following information has been gathered.

(1) A minimum cash balance of $50,000 is desired.

(2) Marketable securities are expected to remain unchanged.

(3) Accounts receivable represent 10 percent of sales.

(4) Inventories represent 12 percent of sales.

(5) A new machine costing $90,000 will be acquired during 1989. Total depreciation for the year will be $32,000.

(6) Accounts payable represent 14 percent of sales.

(7) Accruals, other current liabilities, long-term debt, and common stock are expected to remain unchanged.

(8) The firm's net profit margin is 4 percent and it expects to pay out $70,000 in cash dividends during 1989.

(9) The December 31, 1988, balance sheet is given below.

Leonard Industries Balance Sheet December 31, 1988			
Assets		**Liabilities and equities**	
Cash	$ 45,000	Accounts payable	$ 395,000
Marketable securities	15,000	Accruals	60,000
Accounts receivable	255,000	Other current liabilities	30,000
Inventories	340,000	Total current liabilities	$ 485,000
Total current assets	$ 655,000	Long-term debt	$ 350,000
Net fixed assets	$ 600,000	Common stock	$ 200,000
Total assets	$1,255,000	Retained earnings	$ 220,000
		Total liabilities and stockholders' equity	$1,255,000

a. Use the *judgmental approach* to prepare a pro forma balance sheet dated December 31, 1989, for Leonard Industries.

b. How much, if any, additional financing will be required by Leonard Industries in 1989? Discuss.

c. Could Leonard Industries adjust its planned 1989 dividend in order to avoid the situation described in **b**? Explain how.

5-8 **(Pro Forma Balance Sheet)** Peabody & Peabody has 1988 sales of $10 million. It wishes to analyze expected performance and financing needs for 1990—two years ahead. Given the following information, answer questions **a** and **b**.

(1) The percent of sales for items that vary directly with sales are as follows:
Receivables, 12 percent
Inventory, 18 percent
Accounts payable, 14 percent
Net profit margin, 3 percent

(2) Marketable securities and other current liabilities are expected to remain unchanged.

(3) A minimum cash balance of $480,000 is desired.

(4) A new machine costing $650,000 will be acquired in 1989 and equipment costing $850,000 will be purchased in 1990. Total depreciation in 1989 is forecast as $290,000, and in 1990 $390,000 of depreciation will be taken.

(5) Accruals are expected to rise to $500,000 by the end of 1990.

(6) No sale or retirement of long-term debt is expected.

(7) No sale or repurchase of common stock is expected.

(8) The dividend payout of 50 percent of net profits is expected to continue.

(9) Sales are expected to be $11 million in 1989 and $12 million in 1990.

(10) The December 31, 1988, balance sheet appears below.

Peabody & Peabody Balance Sheet December 31, 1988 ($000)			
Assets		**Liabilities and equities**	
Cash	$ 400	Accounts payable	$1,400
Marketable securities	200	Accruals	400
Accounts receivable	1,200	Other current liabilities	80
Inventories	1,800	Total current liabilities	$1,880
Total current assets	$3,600	Long-term debt	$2,000
Net fixed assets	$4,000	Common equity	$3,720
Total assets	$7,600	Total liabilities and stockholders' equity	$7,600

a. Prepare a pro forma balance sheet dated December 31, 1990.

b. Discuss the financing changes suggested by the statement prepared in **a**.

5-9 **(Integrative—Pro Forma Statements)** Red Queen Restaurants wishes to prepare financial plans. Use the financial statements below and the other information provided to prepare the financial plans.

a. Prepare a pro forma income statement using the *percent-of-sales method*.

b. Prepare a pro forma balance sheet using the *judgmental approach*.

c. Analyze these statements and discuss the resulting external funds required.

Income Statement Red Queen Restaurants for the Year Ended December 31, 1988	
Sales revenue	$800,000
Less: Cost of goods sold	600,000
Gross profits	$200,000
Less: Operating expenses	100,000
Net profits before taxes	$100,000
Less: Taxes (40%)	40,000
Net profits after taxes	$ 60,000
Less: Cash dividends	20,000
To retained earnings	$ 40,000

Balance Sheet Red Queen Restaurants December 31, 1988			
Assets		**Liabilities and equities**	
Cash	$ 32,000	Accounts payable	$100,000
Marketable securities	18,000	Taxes payable	20,000
Accounts receivable	150,000	Other current liabilities	5,000
Inventories	100,000	Total current liabilities	$125,000
Total current assets	$300,000	Long-term debt	$200,000
Net fixed assets	$350,000	Common stock	$150,000
Total assets	$650,000	Retained earnings	$175,000
		Total liabilities and stockholders' equity	$650,000

The following financial data are also available:

(1) The firm has estimated that its sales for 1989 will be $900,000.

(2) The firm expects to pay $35,000 in cash dividends in 1989.

(3) The firm wishes to maintain a minimum cash balance of $30,000.

(4) Accounts receivable represent approximately 18 percent of annual sales.

(5) The firm's ending inventory will change directly with changes in sales in 1989.

(6) A new machine costing $42,000 will be purchased in 1989. Total depreciation for 1989 will be $17,000.

(7) Accounts payable will change directly in response to changes in sales in 1989.

(8) Taxes payable will equal one-fourth of the tax liability on the pro forma income statement.

(9) Marketable securities, other current liabilities, long-term debt, and common stock will remain unchanged.

Solutions to Self-Test Problems

ST-1 **a.**

	Cash Budget Carroll Company April–June					Accounts receivable at end of June	
	February	March	April	May	June	July	Aug
Sales	$500	$600	$400	$200	$200		
Cash sales (.30)	$150	$180	$120	$ 60	$ 60		
Collections of A/R							
Lag 1 mo. [(.7 × .7) = .49]		245	294	196	98	$ 98	
Lag 2 mo. [(.3 × .7) = .21]			105	126	84	42	$42
						$140 + $42 = $182	
Total cash receipts			$519	$382	$242		
Less: Total cash disbursements			$600	$500	$200		
Net cash flow			$(81)	$(118)	$ 42		
Add: Beginning cash			115	34	(84)		
Ending cash			$ 34	$(84)	$(42)		
Less: Minimum cash balance			25	25	25		
Required total financing			—	$109	$ 67		
Excess cash balance			$ 9	—	—		

b. Carroll Company would need a maximum of $109 in financing over the three-month period.

c.

Account	Amount	Source of amount
Cash	$ 25	Minimum cash—June
Notes payable	67	Required total financing—June
Marketable securities	0	Excess cash balance—June
Accounts receivable	182	Calculation at right of cash budget statement

ST-2 a.

Pro Forma Income Statement Euro Designs, Inc. for the Year Ended December 31, 1989	
Sales revenue (given)	$3,900,000
Less: Cost of goods sold (55%)	2,145,000
Gross profits	$1,755,000
Less: Operating expenses (12%)	468,000
Operating profits	$1,287,000
Less: Interest expense (given)	325,000
Net profits before taxes	$ 962,000
Less: Taxes (40%)	384,800
Net profits after taxes	$ 577,200
Less: Cash dividends (given)	320,000
To retained earnings	$ 257,200

b. The percent-of-sales method may underestimate actual 1989 pro forma income by assuming all costs are variable. If the firm has fixed costs, which by definition would not increase with increasing sales, the 1989 pro forma income would likely be underestimated.

Steel Works, Inc.

A combination of mammoth investment and negative financial returns has plagued the steel industry since the late 1970s. Since then, steel consumption has dropped nearly 25 percent, and increasing numbers of products are being produced from alternative materials like aluminum and plastic. It is a dismal picture, but one that Steel Works, Inc., plans to meet head on.

Steel Works is a U.S. manufacturer of steel products serving the United States and foreign markets. The company's products directly compete with foreign imports, which over the last five years have captured a significant portion of the domestic market. Domestic consumption of steel imports continues to increase due to the low price per ton. Foreign producers are able to manufacture steel at a low cost when compared to U.S. firms due to lower labor costs and more technologically advanced manufacturing facilities.

Steel Works hopes to compete more effectively by implementing a modernization program which includes the construction of a state-of-the-art manufacturing facility. Betty West, an experienced budget analyst, has been assigned to evaluate the firm's current financial position. Steel Works plans to meet the industry's challenge by achieving productivity gains. Construction of a new facility will cost $400 million in 1989 and is expected to lower the variable cost per ton of steel. Both capacity and quality will improve with the addition of the new plant. Betty must also forecast the 1989 financial position based on these proposed capital outlays.

Betty has gathered the following financial statements and financial data for use in performing the needed analysis and developing the financial forecasts for 1989.

Steel Works, Inc.
Income Statement ($000)
for the Year Ended December 31, 1988

Sales revenue		$5,075,000	
Less: Cost of goods sold		3,704,000	73
Gross profits		$1,371,000	27
Less: Operating expenses			
Selling expense	$650,000	13	
General and administrative expenses	416,000	8	
Depreciation expense	152,000	3	
Total operating expense		1,218,000	24
Operating profits		$ 153,000	
Less: Interest expense		93,000	2
Net profits before taxes		$ 60,000	
Less: Taxes (40%)		24,000	
Net profits after taxes		$ 36,000	

Steel Works, Inc. Balance Sheets ($000)		
	December 31	
Assets	**1988**	**1987**
Current assets		
Cash	$ 25,000 ,5	$ 24,100
Accounts Receivable	805,556 16	763,900
Inventories	700,625 14	763,445
Total current assets	$1,531,181	$1,551,445
Gross fixed assets	$2,093,819 41	$1,691,707
Less: Accumulated depreciation	500,000 10	348,000
Net fixed assets	$1,593,819 31	$1,343,707
Total assets	$3,125,000	$2,895,152
Liabilities and stockholders' equity		
Current liabilities		
Accounts payable	$ 230,000 4.5	$ 400,500
Notes payable	311,000 6	370,000
Accruals	75,000	100,902
Total current liabilities	$ 616,000	$ 871,402
Long-term debts	$1,165,250	$ 700,000
Total liabilities	$1,781,250	$1,571,402
Stockholders' equity		
Preferred stock	$ 50,000	$ 50,000
Common stock (at par)	100,000	100,000
Paid-in capital in excess of par	193,750	193,750
Retained earnings	1,000,000	980,000
Total stockholders' equity	$1,343,750	$1,323,750
Total liabilities and stockholders' equity	$3,125,000	$2,895,152

Steel Works, Inc. Historical Ratios				
Ratio	**1986**	**1987**	**1988**	**Industry average**
Current ratio	1.7	1.8	2.5	1.5
Quick ratio	1.0	0.9	1.35	1.2
Inventory turnover (times)	5.2	5.0	5.29	10.2
Average collection period (days)	50	55	57	46
Fixed asset turnover (times)	3.2	3.5	3.2	4.1
Total asset turnover (times)	1.5	1.5	1.6	2.0
Debt ratio	45.8%	54.3%	57%	24.5%
Times interest earned	2.2	1.9	1.6	2.5
Gross profit margin	27.5%	28.0%	27%	26.0%
Net profit margin	1.1%	1.0%	.7%	1.2%
Return on investment	1.7%	1.5%	1.2	2.4%
Return on equity	3.1%	3.3%	2.7	3.2%

Required

1. Calculate the company's financial ratios for the most recent year (1988). Analyze its overall financial situation from both a cross-sectional and a time-series viewpoint. Break your analysis into an evaluation of the firm's liquidity, activity, debt, and profitability.

2. Prepare the firm's statement of changes in financial position on a cash basis for the year ended December 31, 1988.

3. Use the projected financial data provided below to prepare a pro forma income statement for the year ended December 31, 1989, and a pro forma balance sheet at December 31, 1989.

Steel Works, Inc. Key Projected Financial Data (1989) ($000)	
Data Item	**Value**
Sales revenue	$6,500,000
Cost of goods sold (as a percent of sales)	73.0%
Minimum cash balance	$25,000
Inventory turnover (times)	7.0
Average collection period (days)	50
Fixed assets purchases	$400,000
Dividend payments	$20,000
Depreciation expense	$166,000
Accounts payable increase	20%
Net profit margin	1.0%
Accruals and long-term debt	Unchanged
Preferred and common stock, notes payable	Unchanged

4. Comment on the firm's decision to modernize production facilities and assess its impact on the firm's financial performance. How would you recommend that the modernization be financed?

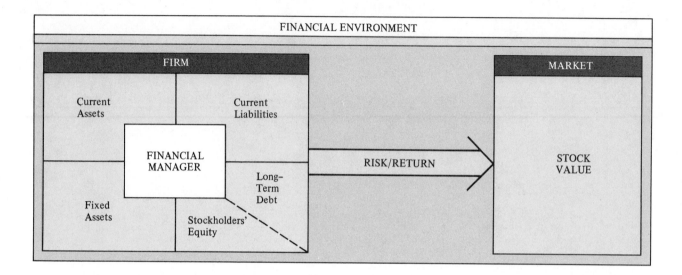

PART TWO

Basic Financial Concepts

CHAPTER 6

The Time Value of Money

FACT OR FABLE?

Are the following statements fact *(true)* or fable *(false)*?

1

The future value of a dollar decreases as the interest rate increases and decreases the farther in the future an initial deposit is to be received.

2

The more frequently interest is compounded at a given rate, the greater the amount of money accumulated and the higher the effective interest rate.

3

The future-value interest factor for an *n*-year annuity is found by adding the first *n*-1 future-value interest factors to 1.000.

4

The appropriate interest factor for the present value of one dollar can be found by dividing 1.0 by the future-value interest factor for the same interest rate and number of periods.

5

The present-value interest factor for an *n*-year annuity can be found by summing the first *n* present-value interest factors at the given rate.

6

When a loan is amortized, the portion of each payment representing interest increases, and the portion going to principal repayment declines over the repayment period.

T*he Cosby Show* has made quite a name for itself. The most successful television show on prime time during the mid-1980s, it is also responsible for the return of the network situation comedy. Although experts had predicted the demise of the sitcom, Bill Cosby has shown that it is not only alive and well, but prospering. Evidence of this success includes NBC's number one position among the networks for the first time ever during *The Cosby Show* years. This position is partially the result of the fact that the shows being aired after Cosby also reap the benefits of his success. One example is *Family Ties,* which was previously ranked low in the ratings. Riding the crest of Cosby's success, its advertising time sold for five times the previous rate.

The income this line-up has brought to NBC is phenomenal. Prospects also look great for the future as well. Although no one can predict the actual amount of money that the show will bring in during its prime-time years and its reruns, it is sure to be a large amount. Cosby has been called ''Billion-dollar Bill,'' based on figures from Robert Jacquemin, senior vice president at Walt Disney Productions. This billion-dollar figure is based on the earnings that *The Cosby Show* and the three shows following it should eventually realize.

But is this really a billion dollars? Because of the effect of the time value of money, the answer is no. The figure is based on the first cycle in syndication which actually spans five years. Assuming the required return on investment is 15 percent, the billion dollars is worth only $671 million today. Despite this discounting effect, most would agree that Cosby's success is still staggering. His show and the impact it continues to make may be responsible for a whole new era in television programming.

Like *The Cosby Show*'s one billion dollars, the time value of money can have a significant impact on expected returns. Here we present the important time value concepts and procedures which, as is demonstrated in subsequent chapters, are widely used in the financial decision-making process.

Future Value of a Single Sum

Imagine that at age 25 you begin making annual cash deposits of $2,000 into a savings account that pays 5 percent annual interest. At the end of 40 years, at age 65, you would have made deposits totaling $80,000 (40 years × $2,000 per year). Assuming you have made no withdrawals, what do you think your account balance would be then? $100,000? $150,000? $200,000? No, your $80,000 would have grown to $242,000! Why? Because

Note: Many of the computations introduced in this chapter and applied throughout the text can be streamlined using a calculator or personal computer. The reader is strongly urged to use these aids to simplify routine financial calculations once the basic underlying financial concepts are understood. With a little practice, both the speed and accuracy of financial computations using a calculator or personal computer can be improved.

future value The value of a present sum at a future date found by applying compound interest over a specified period of time.

the time value of money allowed the deposits to earn interest that was compounded over the 40 years. Because opportunities to earn interest on funds are readily available, the time value of money affects everyone—individuals, businesses, and government.

The **future value** of a present sum is found by applying compound interest over a specified period of time. Savings institutions advertise compound interest returns at a rate of x percent or x percent interest compounded annually, semiannually, quarterly, monthly, weekly, daily, or even continuously. The principles of future value are quite simple, regardless of the period of time involved.

The Concept of Future Value

compounded interest When the amount earned on a given deposit has become part of the principal at the end of a specified period.

principal The amount of money on which interest is paid.

We speak of **compounded interest** when we wish to indicate that the amount earned on a given deposit has become part of the principal at the end of a specified period. The term **principal** refers to the amount of money on which the interest is paid. Annual compounding is the most common type. The concept of future value with annual compounding can be illustrated by a simple example.

Example

If Rich Saver placed $100 in a savings account paying 8 percent interest compounded annually, at the end of one year he will have $108 in the account. This $108 represents the initial principal of $100 plus 8 percent ($8) in interest. The future value at the end of the first year is calculated using Equation 6.1:

$$\text{Future value at end of year 1} = \$100 \times (1 + .08) = \$108 \qquad (6.1)$$

If Rich were to leave this money in the account for another year, he would be paid interest at the rate of 8 percent on the new principal of $108. At the end of this second year, there would be $116.64 in the account. This amount would represent the principal at the beginning of year 2 ($108) plus 8 percent of the $108 ($8.64) in interest. The future value at the end of the second year is calculated using Equation 6.2:

$$\text{Future value at end of year 2} = \$108 \times (1 + .08) = \$116.64 \qquad (6.2)$$

Substituting the expression between the equal signs in Equation 6.1 for the $108 figure in Equation 6.2 gives us Equation 6.3.

$$\begin{aligned}
\text{Future value at end of year 2} &= \$100 \times (1 + .08) \times (1 + .08) \qquad (6.3)\\
&= \$100 \times (1 + .08)^2\\
&= \$116.64
\end{aligned}$$

The Calculation of Future Value

The basic relationship in Equation 6.3 can be generalized to find the future value after any number of periods. Let

F_n = the future value at the end of period n

P = the initial principal, or present value

k = the annual rate of interest paid

n = the number of periods—typically years—the money is left on deposit

Using this notation, a general equation for the future value at the end of period n can be formulated:

$$F_n = P \times (1 + k)^n \tag{6.4}$$

The usefulness of Equation 6.4 for finding the future value, F_n, in an account paying k percent interest compounded annually for n periods if P dollars were deposited initially can be illustrated by a simple example.

> **Example**
> Jane Frugal has placed $800 in a savings account paying 6 percent interest compounded annually. She wishes to determine how much money will be in the account at the end of five years. Substituting $P = \$800$, $k = .06$, and $n = 5$ into Equation 6.4 gives the amount at the end of year 5.
>
> $$F_5 = \$800 \times (1 + .06)^5 = \$800 \times (1.338) = \$1{,}070.40$$
>
> Jane will have $1,070.40 in the account at the end of the fifth year. This analysis can be depicted diagrammatically on a time line as shown in Figure 6.1.

Future-Value Interest Tables

Solving the preceding equation is quite time-consuming, since one must raise 1.06 to the fifth power. Using future-value interest tables simplifies the calculations. A table for the amount generated by the payment of compound interest on an initial principal of $1 is given as Appendix Table A-1 (at the back of the book). The table provides values for $(1 + k)^n$ in Equation 6.4[1]. This portion of Equation 6.4 is called the **future-value interest factor.** This factor is the multiplier used to calculate at a specified interest rate the future value of a present amount as of a given time. The future-value interest factor for an initial principal of $1 compounded at k percent for n periods is referred to as $FVIF_{k,n}$:

future-value interest factor The multiplier used to calculate at a specified interest rate the future value of a present amount as of a given time.

$$\text{Future-value interest factor} = FVIF_{k,n} = (1 + k)^n \tag{6.5}$$

By accessing the table with respect to the annual interest rate, k, and the appropriate periods,[2] n, the factor relevant to a particular problem can be found.

A sample portion of Table A-1 is shown in Table 6.1.[3] Because the factors in Table A-1 give the value for the expression $(1 + k)^n$ for various k and n combinations, by letting $FVIF_{k,n}$ represent the appropriate factor from Table A-1 we can rewrite Equation 6.4 as follows:

$$F_n = P \times (FVIF_{k,n}) \tag{6.6}$$

[1] This table is commonly referred to as a ''compound interest table'' or a ''table of the future value of one dollar.'' As long as the reader understands the source of the table values, the various names attached to it should not create confusion, since one can always make a trial calculation of a value for one factor as a check.

[2] Although we commonly deal with years rather than periods, financial tables are frequently presented in terms of periods to provide maximum flexibility.

[3] Occasionally, in the absence of tables of future-value interest factors, the financial manager will want to estimate how long a given sum must earn at a given annual rate in order to double the amount. The *Rule of 72* is used to make this estimate; dividing the annual rate of interest into 72 results in the approximate period it will take to double one's money at the given rate. For example, to double one's money at a 10 percent annual rate of interest, it will take about 7.2 years ($72 \div 10 = 7.2$). Looking at Table 6.1, it can be seen that the future-value interest factor for 10 percent and 7 years is slightly below 2 (1.949); this approximation therefore appears to be reasonably accurate.

Figure 6.1
Time Line for Future Value of a Single Amount ($800 Initial Principal, Earning 6 Percent Annual Interest, at End of 5 Years)

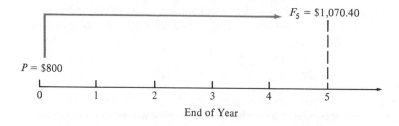

The expression indicates that to find the future value, F_n, at the end of period n of an initial deposit, we have merely to multiply the initial deposit, P, by the appropriate future-value interest factor from Table A-1. An example will illustrate the use of this table.

Example
Jane Frugal has placed $800 in her savings account at 6 percent interest compounded annually. She wishes to find out how much would be in the account at the end of five years and does so by the cumbersome process of raising $(1 + .06)$ to the fifth power. Using the table for the future value of one dollar (Table 6.1 or Table A-1), she could find the future-value interest factor for an initial principal of $1 on deposit for five years at 6 percent interest compounded annually without performing any calculations. The appropriate factor for 6 percent and 5 years, $FVIF_{6\%,5yrs}$, is 1.338. Multiplying this factor by her actual initial principal of $800 would then give her the future value at the end of year 5, which is $1,070.40.

Table 6.1
The Future-Value Interest Factors for One Dollar, $FVIF_{k,n}$

Period	5%	6%	7%	8%	9%	10%
1	1.050	1.060	1.070	1.080	1.090	1.100
2	1.102	1.124	1.145	1.166	1.188	1.210
3	1.158	1.191	1.225	1.260	1.295	1.331
4	1.216	1.262	1.311	1.360	1.412	1.464
5	1.276	1.338	1.403	1.469	1.539	1.611
6	1.340	1.419	1.501	1.587	1.677	1.772
7	1.407	1.504	1.606	1.714	1.828	1.949
8	1.477	1.594	1.718	1.851	1.993	2.144
9	1.551	1.689	1.838	1.999	2.172	2.358
10	1.629	1.791	1.967	2.159	2.367	2.594

NOTE: All table values have been rounded to the nearest thousandth. Thus the calculated values may differ slightly from the table values.

Four important observations should be made about the table for the future value of one dollar:

1. The factors in the table are those for determining the future value of one dollar *at the end of the given period*.
2. *The future-value interest factor for a single amount is always greater than 1*. Only if the interest rate were 0 would this factor equal 1.
3. *As the interest rate increases for any given period, the future-value interest factor also increases*. Thus the higher the interest rate, the greater the future value.
4. *For a given interest rate, the future value of a dollar increases with the passage of time*. Thus the longer the period of time, the greater the future value.

The relationship between various interest rates, the numbers of periods interest is earned, and future-value interest factors is illustrated in Figure 6.2. It clearly shows two relationships: (1) the higher the interest rate, the higher the future-value interest factor is, and (2) the longer the period of time, the higher the future-value interest factor is. Note that for an interest rate of 0 percent, the future-value interest factor always equals 1.00, and the future value therefore always equals the initial principal.

FACT OR FABLE?

1 The future value of a dollar decreases as the interest rate increases and decreases the farther in the future an initial deposit is to be received. *(Fable)*
The future value of an initial deposit *increases* both with increases in the interest rate and with the passage of time.

Figure 6.2
Interest Rates, Time Periods, and Future-Value Interest Factors Used to Find the Future Value of One Dollar

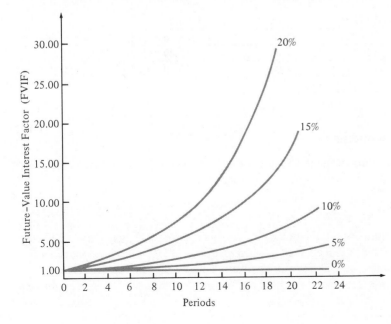

Compounding More Frequently than Annually

Interest is often compounded more frequently than once a year. Savings institutions compound interest semiannually, quarterly, monthly, weekly, daily, or even continuously. This section discusses semiannual and quarterly compounding and presents a general equation for compounding more frequently than annually. It also explains how to use future-value interest tables in these situations.

Semiannual Compounding

semiannual compounding
Compounding of interest over two periods within the year.

Semiannual compounding of interest involves two compounding periods within the year. Instead of the stated interest rate being paid once a year, one-half of the stated interest rate is paid twice a year.

> **Example**
> Rich Saver has decided to invest $100 in a savings account paying 8 percent interest *compounded semiannually*. If he leaves his money in the account for two years, he will be paid 4 percent interest compounded over four periods, each of which is six months long. Table 6.2 shows that at the end of one year, when the 8 percent interest is compounded semiannually, Rich will have $108.16; at the end of two years, he will have $116.99.

Table 6.2
The Future Value from Investing $100 at 8 Percent Interest Compounded Semiannually over Two Years

Period	Beginning principal (1)	Future-value interest factor (2)	Future value at end of period [(1) × (2)] (3)
6 months	$100.00	1.04	$104.00
1 year	104.00	1.04	108.16
18 months	108.16	1.04	112.49
2 years	112.49	1.04	116.99

Quarterly Compounding

quarterly compounding
Compounding of interest over four periods within the year.

Quarterly compounding of interest involves four compounding periods within the year. One-fourth of the stated interest rate is paid four times a year.

> **Example**
> Rich Saver, after further investigation of his savings opportunities, has found an institution that will pay him 8 percent *compounded quarterly*. If he leaves his money in this account for two years, he will be paid 2 percent interest compounded over eight periods, each of which is three months long. Table 6.3 presents the calculations required to

determine the amount Rich will have at the end of two years. As the table shows, at the end of one year, when the 8 percent interest is compounded quarterly, Rich will have $108.24; at the end of two years, he will have $117.16.

Table 6.4 presents comparative values for Rich Saver's $100 at the end of years 1 and 2 given annual, semiannual, and quarterly compounding at the 8 percent rate. As the table shows, the *more frequently interest is compounded, the greater the amount of money accumulated*. This is true for any interest rate for any period of time.

Table 6.3
The Future Value from Investing $100 at 8 Percent Interest Compounded Quarterly over Two Years

Period	Beginning principal (1)	Future-value interest factor (2)	Future value at end of period [(1) × (2)] (3)
3 months	$100.00	1.02	$102.00
6 months	102.00	1.02	104.04
9 months	104.04	1.02	106.12
1 year	106.12	1.02	108.24
15 months	108.24	1.02	110.40
18 months	110.40	1.02	112.61
21 months	112.61	1.02	114.86
2 years	114.86	1.02	117.16

Table 6.4
The Future Value from Investing $100 at 8 Percent for Years 1 and 2 Given Various Compounding Periods

End of year	Compounding period		
	Annual	Semiannual	Quarterly
1	$108.00	$108.16	$108.24
2	116.64	116.99	117.16

A General Equation for Compounding More Frequently than Annually

It should be clear from the preceding examples that, if *m* equals the number of times per year interest is compounded, Equation 6.4 (our formula for annual compounding) can be rewritten as

$$F_n = P \times \left(1 + \frac{k}{m}\right)^{m \times n}$$

(6.7)

If $m = 1$, Equation 6.7 reduces to Equation 6.4. Thus, if interest is compounded annually (once a year), Equation 6.7 will provide the same results as Equation 6.4. The general use of Equation 6.7 can be illustrated with a simple example.

Example

In the preceding examples, the amount that Rich Saver would have at the end of two years if he deposited $100 at 8 percent interest compounded semiannually and quarterly was discussed. For semiannual compounding, m would equal 2 in Equation 6.7, while for quarterly compounding m would equal 4. Substituting the appropriate values for semiannual and quarterly compounding into Equation 6.7 would yield

1. *For semiannual compounding*

$$F_2 = \$100 \times \left(1 + \frac{.08}{2}\right)^{2\times2} = \$100 \times (1 + .04)^4 = \$116.99$$

2. *For quarterly compounding*

$$F_2 = \$100 \times \left(1 + \frac{.08}{4}\right)^{4\times2} = \$100 \times (1 + .02)^8 = \$117.16$$

These results agree with the values for F_2 in Tables 6.2 and 6.3. If the interest were compounded monthly, weekly, or daily, m would equal 12, 52, or 365, respectively. In the case of **continuous compounding,** which implies compounding every microsecond, m would approach infinity and the use of calculus would be required to determine the future value.

continuous compounding
Compounding of interest an infinite number of times per year, at intervals of microseconds.

Using Table A-1

Table A-1, the table of future-value interest factors for one dollar, can be used to find the future value when interest is compounded m times each year. Instead of indexing the table for k percent and n years, as we do when interest is compounded annually, we index it for $(k \div m)$ percent and $(m \times n)$ periods. The usefulness of the table is usually somewhat limited, since only selected rates for a limited number of periods can be found. The table can commonly be used to calculate the results of semiannual ($m = 2$) and quarterly ($m = 4$) compounding, but when more frequent compounding is done, the aid of a financial calculator or personal computer may be necessary. The following example will clarify the use of the future-value interest factor table in situations where interest is compounded more frequently than annually.

Example

In the earlier examples, Rich Saver wished to find the future value of $100 invested at 8 percent compounded both semiannually and quarterly for two years. The number of compounding periods, m, was 2 and 4, respectively, in these cases. The values by which the table for the future value of one dollar is accessed, along with the future-value interest factor in each case, are given at the top of page 179.

Compounding period	m	Percentage interest rate ($k \div m$)	Periods ($m \times n$)	Future-value interest factor from Table A-1
Semiannual	2	$.08 \div 2 = .04$	$2 \times 2 = 4$	1.170
Quarterly	4	$.08 \div 4 = .02$	$4 \times 2 = 8$	1.172

The factor for 4 percent and four periods is used for the semiannual compounding, and the factor for 2 percent and eight periods is used for quarterly compounding. Multiplying each of the factors by the initial $100 deposit results in a value of $117.00 (1.170 × $100) for semiannual compounding and a value of $117.20 (1.172 × $100) for quarterly compounding. The corresponding values found by the long method are $116.99 and $117.16, respectively. The discrepancy can be attributed to the rounding of values in the table.

Nominal and Effective Interest Rates

It is important both for consumers and businesses to be able to make objective comparisons of interest rates. In order to compare loan costs or investment returns over different compounding periods, we must distinguish between nominal and effective interest rates. The **nominal**, or **stated**, **interest rate** is the contractual rate charged by a lender or promised by a borrower. The **effective**, or **true**, **interest rate** is the rate of interest actually paid or earned. In consumer finance the effective rate, commonly called the **annual percentage rate (APR)**, must by law be clearly stated to borrowers and depositors.

The effective rate differs from the nominal rate in that it reflects the impact of compounding frequency. In terms of interest earnings, it is probably best viewed as the *annual* interest rate that would result in the same future value as that resulting from application of the nominal rate using the stated compounding frequency. Reviewing Table 6.4 we can see that the future value using an 8 percent nominal interest rate increases with increasing compounding frequency. Clearly, the effective rate of interest must also increase with increased compounding frequency.

Using the notation introduced earlier, the effective interest rate, $k_{eff.}$, can be calculated by substituting the nominal interest rate, k, and the compounding frequency, m, into Equation 6.8.

$$k_{eff.} = \left(1 + \frac{k}{m}\right)^m - 1 \qquad (6.8)$$

Application of this equation can conveniently be demonstrated using data from the preceding examples.

nominal (stated) interest rate The rate of interest, agreed upon contractually, charged by a lender or promised by a borrower.

effective (true) interest rate The rate of interest actually paid or earned; commonly called the *annual percentage rate (APR)*.

annual percentage rate (APR) In consumer finance, the effective interest rate which must be clearly stated to borrowers and depositors.

Example
Rich Saver wishes to find the effective interest rate associated with an 8 percent nominal interest rate ($k = .08$) when interest is compounded (1) annually ($m = 1$); (2) semiannually ($m = 2$); and (3) quarterly ($m = 4$). Substituting these values into

Equation 6.8, we get

1. *For annual compounding*

$$k_{eff.} = \left(1 + \frac{.08}{1}\right)^1 - 1 = (1 + .08)^1 - 1 = 1 + .08 - 1 = .08 = 8\%$$

2. *For semiannual compounding*

$$k_{eff.} = \left(1 + \frac{.08}{2}\right)^2 - 1 = (1 + .04)^2 - 1 = 1.0816 - 1 = .0816 = 8.16\%$$

3. *For quarterly compounding*

$$k_{eff.} = \left(1 + \frac{.08}{4}\right)^4 - 1 = (1 + .02)^4 - 1 = 1.0824 - 1 = .0824 = 8.24\%$$

Two important points are demonstrated by these values: (1) the nominal and effective interest rates are equivalent for annual compounding, and (2) the effective rate of interest increases with increasing compounding frequency.

FACT OR FABLE? **2** The more frequently interest is compounded at a given rate, the greater the amount of money accumulated and the higher the effective interest rate. *(Fact)*

Future Value of an Annuity

annuity A stream of equal annual cash flows. These cash flows can be inflows of returns earned on investments or outflows of funds invested in order to earn future returns.

An **annuity** is a stream of equal annual cash flows. These cash flows can be *inflows* of returns earned on investments or *outflows* of funds invested in order to earn future returns. The calculations required to find the future value of an annuity on which interest is paid at a specified rate compounded annually can be illustrated by the following example.

Example
Fran Abrams wishes to determine how much money she will have at the end of five years if she deposits $1,000 annually in a savings account paying 7 percent annual interest. The deposits will be made at the end of each of the next five years. Table 6.5 presents the calculations required. This situation is depicted diagramatically on a time line in Figure 6.3. As the table and figure show, at the end of year 5 Fran will have $5,751 in her account. Column 2 of the table indicates that since the deposits are made at the end of the year, the first deposit will earn interest for four years, the second for three years, and so on. The future-value interest factors in column 3 correspond to these interest-earning periods and the 7 percent rate of interest.

FINANCE IN ACTION

THE WONDER OF COMPOUNDING

John Maynard Keynes supposedly called it magic. One of the Rothschilds is said to have proclaimed it the eighth wonder of the world. Today people continue to extol its wonder and its glory. The object of their affection is compound interest, a subject that bores or confuses as many people as it impresses.

Yet understanding compound interest can help people calculate the return on savings and investments, as well as the cost of borrowing. These calculations apply to almost any financial decision, from the reinvestment of dividends to the purchase of a zero-coupon bond for an individual retirement account.

"With all the time you spend working, saving, borrowing, and investing," says Richard P. Brief, a New York University business professor, "one could argue that the calculations [of compound interest] ought to be un-derstood by most people. And it is within reach of most people."

The power of compound interest has intrigued people for years. Early in the last century, an English astronomer, Francis Baily, figured that a British penny invested at an annual compound interest of 5 percent at the birth of Christ would have yielded enough gold by 1810 to fill 357 million earths. Benjamin Franklin was more practical. At his death in 1790, he left £1,000 each to the cities of Boston and Philadelphia on the condition they wouldn't touch the money for 100 years. Boston's bequest, which was equivalent to about $4,600, ballooned to $332,000 by 1890.

But savers and investors don't have to live to a hundred to reap its benefits. Consider an investment with a current value of $10,000 earning annual interest of 8 percent. After a year the investment grows to $10,800 (1.08 times $10,000). After the second year it's worth $11,664 (1.08 times $10,800). After three more years, the investment grows to $14,693. The same concept applies to consumer borrowing. A $10,000 loan, with an 8 percent interest charge compounded annually, would cost $14,693 to repay in a lump sum after five years.

Investors and savers can also take a rule-of-thumb shortcut to determine how long it would take to double a sum of money at a given interest rate with annual compounding: Divide 72 by the rate. For example, the $10,000 investment yielding 8 percent a year would double in about nine years (72 divided by 8).

But people should be aware that inflation compounds, too. Unless inflation disappears, that projected $20,000 investment nine years from now could be worth something less than that in today's dollars.

SOURCE: Robert L. Rose, "Compounding: It's Boring But a Wonder," *The Wall Street Journal*, June 17, 1985, p. 21. Reprinted by permission of *The Wall Street Journal*, © Dow Jones & Company, Inc., 1985. All rights reserved.

Table 6.5
The Future Value of a $1,000 Five-Year Annuity
Compounded at 7 Percent

End of year	Amount deposited (1)	Number of years compounded (2)	Future-value interest factors from Table A-1 (3)	Future value at end of year [(1) × (3)] (4)
1	$1,000	4	1.311	$1,311
2	1,000	3	1.225	1,225
3	1,000	2	1.145	1,145
4	1,000	1	1.070	1,070
5	1,000	0	1.000	1,000
Future value of annuity at end of year 5				$5,751

Figure 6.3

Time Line for Future Value of an Annuity ($1,000 End-of-Year Deposit, Earning 7 Percent, at End of 5 Years)

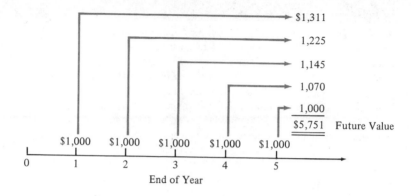

Simplifying Future-Value-of-Annuity Calculations

The calculations required in the preceding example can be simplified somewhat since each of the factors is actually multiplied by the same dollar amount. This is true only in the case of an annuity. The actual calculations required can be expressed as follows:

$$\text{Future value of annuity at end of year 5} = [\$1,000 \times (1.311)] \quad (6.9)$$
$$+ [\$1,000 \times (1.225)]$$
$$+ [\$1,000 \times (1.145)]$$
$$+ [\$1,000 \times (1.070)]$$
$$+ [\$1,000 \times (1.000)]$$
$$= \$5,751$$

Factoring out the $1,000, Equation 6.9 can be rewritten as

$$\text{Future value of annuity at end of year 5} = \$1,000 \times (1.311 + 1.225 \quad (6.10)$$
$$+ 1.145 + 1.070$$
$$+ 1.000) = \$5,751$$

Equation 6.10 indicates that to find the future value of the annuity, the annual amount must be multiplied by the sum of the appropriate future-value interest factors.

Using a Future-Value-of-an-Annuity Table

future-value interest factor for an annuity The multiplier used to calculate the future value of an annuity at a specified interest rate over a given period of time.

Annuity calculations can be further simplified using a **future-value interest factor for an annuity.** This factor is the multiplier used to calculate the future value of an annuity at a specified interest rate over a given period of time. A portion of Appendix Table A-2, which contains future-value interest factors for an annuity, is shown in Table 6.6. The factors included in the table are derived by summing the terms in parentheses in equations like Equation 6.10. In the case of Equation 6.10, summing the terms in parentheses results in Equation 6.11.

$$\text{Future value of an annuity at end of year 5} = \$1,000 \times (5.751) \quad (6.11)$$
$$= \$5,751$$

Table 6.6
The Future-Value Interest Factors for a One-Dollar Annuity, $FVIFA_{k,n}$

Period	5%	6%	7%	8%	9%	10%
1	1.000	1.000	1.000	1.000	1.000	1.000
2	2.050	2.060	2.070	2.080	2.090	2.100
3	3.152	3.184	3.215	3.246	3.278	3.310
4	4.310	4.375	4.440	4.506	4.573	4.641
5	5.526	5.637	5.751	5.867	5.985	6.105
6	6.802	6.975	7.153	7.336	7.523	7.716
7	8.142	8.394	8.654	8.923	9.200	9.487
8	9.549	9.897	10.260	10.637	11.028	11.436
9	11.027	11.491	11.978	12.488	13.021	13.579
10	12.578	13.181	13.816	14.487	15.193	15.937

The factors included in the table are based on the assumption that every deposit is made at the *end of the period*.[4]

The formula for the future-value interest factor for an *n*-year annuity with end-of-period cash flows when interest is compounded annually at *k* percent, $FVIFA_{k,n}$, is[5]

$$FVIFA_{k,n} = \sum_{t=1}^{n} (1 + k)^{t-1} \tag{6.12}$$

This formula merely states that the future-value interest factor for an *n*-year annuity is found by adding the sum of the first $n - 1$ future-value interest factors to 1.000 (i.e.,

$FVIFA_{k,n} = 1.000 + \sum_{t=1}^{n-1} FVIF_{k,t}$). This relationship can be easily verified by reviewing

the terms in Equation 6.10.[6]

Letting S_n equal the future value of an *n*-year annuity, *A* equal the amount to be deposited annually at the end of each year, and $FVIFA_{k,n}$ represent the appropriate *future-value interest factor for an n-year annuity compounded at k percent*, the relationship among these variables can be expressed as follows:

$$S_n = A \times (FVIFA_{k,n}) \tag{6.13}$$

[4] The discussions of annuities throughout this text concentrate on the more common form of annuity—the *ordinary annuity*, which is an annuity that occurs at the *end* of each period. An annuity that occurs at the *beginning* of each period is called an *annuity due*. The financial tables for annuities included in this book are prepared for use with ordinary annuities.

[5] The formula for the future-value interest factor for an *annuity due* (see footnote 4) is $\sum_{t=1}^{n} (1 + k)^t$, since in this case all deposits are made at the beginning of each period. The factor therefore merely represents the sum of the first *n* future-value interest factors, i.e., $\sum_{t=1}^{n} FVIF_{k,t}$. The future-value interest factor for an annuity due can be found by multiplying the future-value interest factor for an ordinary annuity, $FVIFA_{k,n}$ by $(1 + k)$.

[6] A mathematical expression that can be applied in order to more efficiently calculate the future-value interest factor for an ordinary annuity (see footnote 4) is:

$$FVIFA_{k,n} = [(1/k) \times ((1 + k)^n - 1)]$$

The use of this expression is especially attractive in the absence of the appropriate financial tables or a financial calculator or personal computer.

Equation 6.13 along with Table A-2 can be conveniently used to find the future value of an annuity. In Fran Abrams's case, the $1,000 deposit *(A)* can be multiplied by the interest factor for the future value of a one-dollar annuity at 7 percent for a five-year life $(FVIFA_{7\%,5yrs})$ obtained from Table A-2. Multiplying the $1,000 by the table value, 5.751, results in a future value for the annuity of $5,751. The following example further illustrates the usefulness of Table A-2.

Example
Fred Austin wishes to determine the sum of money he will have in his savings account, which pays 6 percent annual interest, at the end of ten years if he deposits $600 at the end of each year for the next ten years. The appropriate interest factor for the future value at 6 percent for a ten-year annuity, $FVIFA_{6\%,10yrs}$, is given in Table A-2 as 13.181. Multiplying this factor by the $600 deposit results in a future value of $7,908.60. The simple calculations required to find the future value of an annuity using Table A-2 should be clear from this example.

FACT OR FABLE?   **3** The future-value interest factor for an *n*-year annuity is found by adding the first *n*-1 future-value interest factors to 1.000. *(Fact)*

Present Value of a Single Sum

present value The current dollar value of a future sum. The amount that would have to be invested today at a given interest rate over the period in order to equal the future sum.

It is often useful to determine the "present value" of a future sum of money. **Present value** is the current dollar value of a future sum—the amount of money that would have to be invested today at a given interest rate over a specified period in order to equal the future sum. Present value, like future value, is based on the belief that a dollar today is worth more than a dollar that will be received at some future date. The actual present value of a dollar depends largely on the investment opportunities of the recipient and the point in time at which the earned return is to be received. This section explores the present value of a single sum.

The Concept of Present Value

discounting cash flows The process of finding present values; the inverse of compounding interest.

The process of finding present values is often referred to as **discounting cash flows.** This process is actually the inverse of compounding. It is concerned with answering the question "If I can earn *k* percent on my money, what is the most I would be willing to pay for an opportunity to receive F_n dollars *n* periods from today?" Instead of finding the future value of present dollars invested at a given rate, discounting determines the present value of a future amount, assuming that the decision maker has an opportunity to earn a certain return, *k*, on the money. This return is variously referred to as the *discount rate, required return, cost of capital,* or *opportunity cost.*[7] These terms will be used interchangeably in this text. The discounting process can be illustrated by a simple example.

[7] The theoretical underpinning of this "required return" is introduced in Chapter 7 and further refined in subsequent chapters.

Example

Paul Shorter has been given an opportunity to receive $300 one year from now. If he can earn 6 percent on his investments in the normal course of events, what is the most he should pay for this opportunity? To answer this question, we must determine how many dollars must be invested at 6 percent today to have $300 one year from now. Letting P equal this unknown amount, and using the same notation as in the compounding discussion, the situation can be expressed as follows:

$$P \times (1 + .06) = \$300 \tag{6.14}$$

Solving Equation 6.14 for P gives us Equation 6.15

$$P = \frac{\$300}{(1 + .06)} \tag{6.15}$$
$$= \$283.02$$

which results in a value of $283.02 for P. In other words, the "present value" of $300 received one year from today, given an opportunity cost of 6 percent, is $283.02. Paul should be indifferent to whether he receives $283.02 today or $300.00 one year from now. If he can receive either by paying less than $283.02 today, he should, of course, do so.

A Mathematical Expression for Present Value

The present value of a future amount can be found mathematically by solving Equation 6.4 for P. In other words, one merely wants to obtain the present value, P, of some future amount, F_n, to be received n periods from now, assuming an opportunity cost of k. Solving Equation 6.4 for P gives us Equation 6.16, which is the general equation for the present value of a future amount.

$$P = \frac{F_n}{(1 + k)^n} = F_n \times \left[\frac{1}{(1 + k)^n} \right] \tag{6.16}$$

Note the similarity between this general equation for present value and the equation in the preceding example (Equation 6.15). The use of this equation in finding the present value of a future amount can be illustrated by a simple example.

Example

Pam Valenti wishes to find the present value of $1,700 that will be received eight years from now. Pam's opportunity cost is 8 percent. Substituting $F_8 = \$1,700$, $n = 8$, and $k = .08$ into Equation 6.16 yields Equation 6.17.

$$P = \frac{\$1,700}{(1 + .08)^8} \tag{6.17}$$

To solve Equation 6.17, the term $(1 + .08)$ must be raised to the eighth power. The value resulting from this time-consuming calculation is 1.851. Dividing this value into $1,700 yields a present value for the $1,700 of $918.42. This analysis can be depicted diagramatically on a time line as shown in Figure 6.4.

Figure 6.4
Time Line for Present Value of a Single Amount ($1,700 Future Amount, Discounted at 8 Percent, from End of 8 Years)

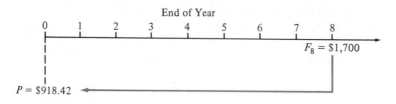

Present-Value Interest Tables

present-value interest factor The multiplier used to calculate at a specified discount rate the present value of an amount to be received in a future period.

The present-value calculation can be simplified using a **present-value interest factor.** This factor is the multiplier used to calculate at a specified discount rate the present value of an amount to be received in a future period. To further facilitate present-value operations, tables of present-value interest factors are available. The table for the present-value interest factor, $PVIF_{k,n}$, gives values for the expression $1/(1 + k)^n$ where k is the discount rate and n is the number of periods—typically years—involved.

$$\text{Present-value interest factor} = PVIF_{k,n} = \frac{1}{(1 + k)^n} \tag{6.18}$$

Table A-3 in the Appendix presents present-value interest factors for various discount rates and periods. A portion of Table A-3 is shown in Table 6.7. Since the factors in Table A-3 give the value for the expression $1/(1 + k)^n$ for various k and n combinations, we can, by letting $PVIF_{k,n}$ represent the appropriate factor from Table A-3, rewrite Equation 6.16 as follows:

$$P = F_n \times (PVIF_{k,n}) \tag{6.19}$$

This expression indicates that to find the present value, P, of an amount to be received in a future period, n, we have merely to multiply the future amount, F_n, by the appropriate present-value interest factor from Table A-3. An example should help clarify the use of Equation 6.19.

Table 6.7
The Present-Value Interest Factors for One Dollar, $PVIF_{k,n}$

Period	5%	6%	7%	8%	9%	10%
1	.952	.943	.935	.926	.917	.909
2	.907	.890	.873	.857	.842	.826
3	.864	.840	.816	.794	.772	.751
4	.823	.792	.763	.735	.708	.683
5	.784	.747	.713	.681	.650	.621
6	.746	.705	.666	.630	.596	.564
7	.711	.665	.623	.583	.547	.513
8	.677	.627	.582	.540	.502	.467
9	.645	.592	.544	.500	.460	.424
10	.614	.558	.508	.463	.422	.386

Example
Pam Valenti wishes to find the present value of $1,700 to be received eight years from now, assuming an 8 percent opportunity cost. Table A-3 gives us a present-value interest factor for 8 percent and eight years, $PVIF_{8\%,8yrs}$, of .540. Multiplying this factor by the $1,700 yields a present value of $918. This value is 42 cents less than the value obtained using the long method. This difference is attributable to the fact that the table values have been rounded to the nearest thousandth.

Four additional points with respect to present-value tables are also important:

1. The factors in the table are those for determining the present value of one dollar to be *received at the end of the given period.*

2. *The present-value interest factor for a single amount is always less than 1.* Only if the opportunity cost were 0 would this factor equal 1.

3. *The higher the discount rate for a given period, the smaller the present-value interest factor.* Thus the greater the potential return on an investment, the less an amount to be received in a specified future year is worth today.

4. *For a given discount rate, the present value of a dollar decreases with the passage of time.* Thus the longer the period of time, the smaller the present value.

The relationship among various discount rates, time periods, and present-value interest factors is illustrated in Figure 6.5. Everything else being equal, the figure clearly shows two relationships: (1) the higher the discount rate, the lower the present-value interest factor, and (2) the longer the period of time, the lower the present-value interest factor. The reader should also note that given a discount rate of 0 percent, the present-value interest factor always equals 1.00, and the future value of the funds therefore equals their present value.

Comparing Present Value and Future Value

A few important observations must be made with respect to present values. One is that the expression for the present-value interest factor for k percent and n periods, $1/(1 + k)^n$, is the inverse of the future-value interest factor for k percent and n periods, $(1 + k)^n$. This observation can be confirmed by dividing a present-value interest factor for k percent and n periods, $PVIF_{k,n}$, into 1.0 and comparing the resulting value to the future-value interest factor given in Table A-1 for k percent and n periods, $FVIF_{k,n}$. The two values should be equivalent. Because of the relationship between present-value interest factors and future-value interest factors, we can find the present-value interest factors given a table of future-value interest factors, and vice versa. For example, the future-value interest factor from Table A-1 for 10 percent and five periods is 1.611. Dividing this value into 1.0 yields .621, which is the present-value interest factor given in Table A-3 for 10 percent and five periods.

---

4 The appropriate interest factor for the present value of one dollar can be found by dividing 1.0 by the future-value interest factor for the same interest rate and number of periods. (*Fact*)   FACT OR FABLE?

Figure 6.5
Discount Rates, Time Periods, and Present-Value Interest Factors Used to Find the Present Value of One Dollar

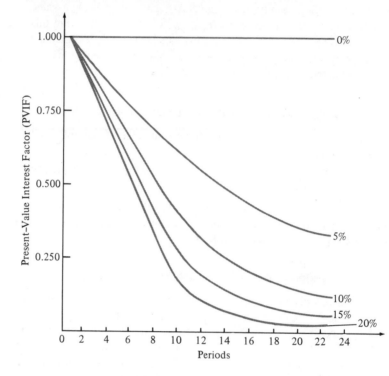

Present Value of Cash Flow Streams

mixed stream A group of cash flows that reflects no particular pattern.

Quite often in finance there is a need to find the present value of a stream of cash flows to be received in various future periods. Two basic types of cash flow streams are possible: the mixed stream and the annuity. A **mixed stream** of cash flows reflects no particular pattern, while, as stated earlier, an *annuity* is a pattern of equal annual cash flows. Since certain shortcuts are possible in finding the present value of an annuity, mixed streams and annuities will be discussed separately.

Table 6.8
The Present Value of a Mixed Stream of Cash Flows

Year (n)	Cash flow (1)	$PVIF_{9\%,n}$[a] (2)	Present value [(1) × (2)] (3)
1	$400	.917	$ 366.80
2	800	.842	673.60
3	500	.772	386.00
4	400	.708	283.20
5	300	.650	195.00
Present value of mixed stream			$1,904.60

[a] Present-value interest factors at 9 percent are from Table A-3.

Present Value of a Mixed Stream

To find the present value of a mixed stream of cash flows, determine the present value of each future amount in the manner described in the preceding section, then add all the individual present values to find the total present value of the stream.

Example

The Frey Company has been offered an opportunity to receive the following mixed stream of cash flows over the next five years:

Year	Cash flow
1	$400
2	800
3	500
4	400
5	300

If the firm must earn 9 percent, at minimum, on its investments, what is the most it should pay for this opportunity?

   To solve this problem, the present value of each cash flow discounted at 9 percent for the appropriate number of years is determined. The sum of all these individual values is then calculated to get the present value of the total stream. The present-value interest factors required are obtained from Table A-3. Table 6.8 presents the calculations needed to find the present value of the cash flow stream, which turns out to be $1,904.60.

   Frey should not pay more than $1,904.60 for the opportunity to receive these cash flows, since paying $1,904.60 would provide exactly a 9 percent return. This situation is depicted diagramatically on a time line in Figure 6.6.

Figure 6.6
Time Line for Present Value of a Mixed Stream (End-of-Year Cash Flows, Discounted at 9 Percent, over Corresponding Number of Years)

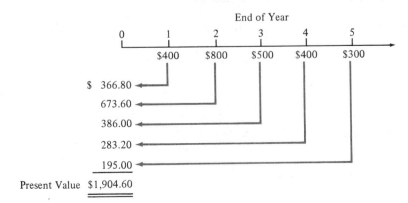

Present Value of an Annuity

The present value of an annuity can be found in a manner similar to that used for a mixed stream, but a shortcut is possible.

Example
The Braden Company is attempting to determine the most it should pay to purchase a particular annuity. The firm requires a minimum return of 8 percent on all investments, and the annuity consists of cash flows of $700 per year for five years. Table 6.9 shows the long way of finding the present value of the annuity, which is the same as the method used for mixed streams. This procedure yields a present value of $2,795.10, which can be interpreted in the same manner as for the mixed cash flow stream in the preceding example. Similarly, this situation is depicted graphically on a time line in Figure 6.7.

Simplifying Present-Value-of-Annuity Calculations

The calculations used in the preceding example can be simplified by recognizing that each of the five multiplications made to get the individual present values involved multiplying the annual amount ($700) by the appropriate present-value interest factor. This method of finding the present value of the annuity can also be written as an equation:

$$\text{Present value of annuity} = [\$700 \times (.926)] + [\$700 \times (.857)] \quad (6.20)$$
$$+ [\$700 \times (.794)] + [\$700 \times (.735)]$$
$$+ [\$700 \times (.681)] = \$2,795.10$$

Simplifying Equation 6.20 by factoring out the $700 yields Equation 6.21.

$$\text{Present value of annuity} = \$700 \times (.926 + .857 + .794 + .735 \quad (6.21)$$
$$+ .681) = \$2,795.10$$

Thus the present value of an annuity can be found by multiplying the annual amount received by the sum of the present-value interest factors for each year of the annuity's life.

Table 6.9
The Long Method for Finding the Present Value of an Annuity

Year (n)	Cash flow (1)	$PVIF_{8\%,n}$ [a] (2)	Present value [(1) × (2)] (3)
1	$700	.926	$ 648.20
2	700	.857	599.90
3	700	.794	555.80
4	700	.735	514.50
5	700	.681	476.70
	Present value of annuity		$2,795.10

[a] Present-value interest factors at 8 percent are from Table A-3.

Figure 6.7
Time Line for Present Value of an Annuity ($700 End-of-Year Cash Flows, Discounted at 8 Percent, over 5 Years)

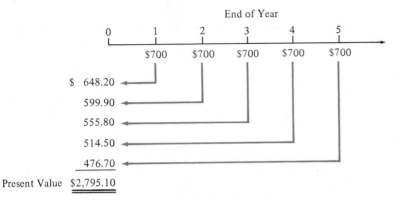

Using a Present-Value-of-an-Annuity Table

Annuity calculations can be further simplified by using a **present-value interest factor for an annuity.** This factor is the multiplier used to calculate the present value of an annuity at a specified discount rate over a given period of time. A portion of Appendix Table A-4, which contains present-value interest factors for an annuity, is shown in Table 6.10. The factors included in the table are derived by summing the terms in parentheses in equations like Equation 6.21. In the case of Equation 6.21, this results in Equation 6.22.

$$\text{Present value of annuity} = \$700 \times (3.993) = \$2,795.10 \qquad (6.22)$$

The interest factors in Table A-4 actually represent the sum of the first n present-value interest factors in Table A-3 for a given discount rate. The formula for the present-value interest factor for an n-year annuity with end-of-year cash flows[8] that are discounted at k

present-value interest factor for an annuity The multiplier used to calculate the present value of an annuity at a specified discount rate over a given period of time.

Table 6.10
The Present-Value Interest Factors for a One-Dollar Annuity, $PVIFA_{k,n}$

Period	5%	6%	7%	8%	9%	10%
1	.952	.943	.935	.926	.917	.909
2	1.859	1.833	1.808	1.783	1.759	1.736
3	2.723	2.673	2.624	2.577	2.531	2.487
4	3.546	3.465	3.387	3.312	3.240	3.170
5	4.329	4.212	4.100	3.993	3.890	3.791
6	5.076	4.917	4.767	4.623	4.486	4.355
7	5.786	5.582	5.389	5.206	5.033	4.868
8	6.463	6.210	5.971	5.747	5.535	5.335
9	7.108	6.802	6.515	6.247	5.995	5.759
10	7.722	7.360	7.024	6.710	6.418	6.145

[8] Consistent with the discussions of future value, our concern here is only with *ordinary annuities*—those with cash flows occurring at the *end* of each period.

percent, $PVIFA_{k,n}$, is[9]

$$PVIFA_{k,n} = \sum_{t=1}^{n} \frac{1}{(1 + k)^t}$$ (6.23)

This formula merely states that the present-value interest factor for an *n*-year annuity is found by summing the first *n* present-value interest factors at the given rate (i.e., $PVIFA_{k,n} = \sum_{t=1}^{n} PVIF_{k,t}$). This relationship can be verified by reviewing the terms in Equation 6.21.[10]

Letting P_n equal the present value of an *n*-year annuity, *A* equal the amount to be received annually at the end of each year, and $PVIFA_{k,n}$ represent the appropriate value for the *present-value interest factor for a one-dollar annuity discounted at* k *percent for* n *years,* the relationship among these variables can be expressed as follows:

$$P_n = A \times (PVIFA_{k,n})$$ (6.24)

The problem presented earlier involving the calculation of the present value of a five-year annuity of $700 assuming an 8 percent opportunity cost can be easily worked out with the aid of Table A-4 and Equation 6.24. The present-value interest factor for a one-dollar annuity in Table A-4 for 8 percent and five years, $PVIFA_{8\%,5yrs}$, is 3.993. Multiplying the $700 annuity by this factor provides a present value for the annuity of $2,795.10. A simple example may help clarify the usefulness of Table A-4 in finding the present value of an annuity.

Example
The Asheville Company expects to receive $160,000 per year at the end of each of the next 20 years. If the firm's opportunity cost of funds is 10 percent, how much is the present value of this annuity? The appropriate interest factor for the present value at 10 percent for a 20-year annuity, $PVIFA_{10\%,20yrs}$, is found in Table A-4 to be 8.514. Multiplying this factor by the $160,000 cash flow results in a present value of $1,362,240.

FACT OR FABLE?   [5] **The present-value interest factor for an *n*-year annuity can be found by summing the first *n* present-value interest factors at the given rate.** *(Fact)*

---

[9] The formula for the present-value interest factor for an *annuity due* (see footnote 4) is $\sum_{t=1}^{n} \frac{1}{(1 + k)^{t-1}}$, since in this case all cash flows occur at the beginning of each period. The factor therefore merely represents 1.0 plus the sum of the first $n - 1$ present-value interest factors. The present-value interest factor for an annuity due can be found by multiplying the present-value interest factor for an ordinary annuity, $PVIFA_{k,n}$, by $(1 + k)$.

[10] A mathematical expression that can be applied in order to more efficiently calculate the present-value interest factor for an ordinary annuity (see footnote 4) is:

$$PVIFA_{k,n} = \left[(1/k) \times \left(1 - \frac{1}{(1 + k)^n} \right) \right]$$

The use of this expression is especially attractive in the absence of the appropriate financial tables or a financial calculator or personal computer.

Special Applications of Time Value

Future-value and present-value techniques have a number of important applications. Four will be presented in this section: (1) the calculation of the deposits needed to accumulate a future sum, (2) the calculation of amortization on loans, (3) the determination of interest or growth rates, and (4) the calculation of the present value of perpetuities.

Deposits to Accumulate a Future Sum

Often an individual may wish to determine the annual deposit necessary to accumulate a certain amount of money so many years hence. Suppose a person wishes to purchase a house five years from now and recognizes that an initial down payment of $20,000 will be required at that time. She wishes to make equal annual end-of-year deposits in an account paying annual interest of 6 percent, so she must determine what size annuity will result in a lump sum equal to $20,000 at the end of year 5. The solution to this problem is closely related to the process of finding the future value of an annuity.

In an earlier section of this chapter, the future value of an n-year annuity, S_n, was found by multiplying the annual deposit, A, by the appropriate interest factor (from Table A-2), $FVIFA_{k,n}$. The relationship of the three variables has been defined by Equation 6.13, which is rewritten here as Equation 6.25.

$$S_n = A \times (FVIFA_{k,n}) \qquad (6.25)$$

We can find the annual deposit required to accumulate S_n dollars, given a specified interest rate, k, and a certain number of years, n, by solving Equation 6.25 for A. Isolating A on the left side of the equation gives us

$$A = \frac{S_n}{FVIFA_{k,n}} \qquad (6.26)$$

Once this is done, we have only to substitute the known values of S_n and $FVIFA_{k,n}$ into the right side of the equation to find the annual deposit required.

Example
In the problem just stated, a person wished to determine the equal annual end-of-year deposits required to accumulate $20,000 at the end of five years given an interest rate of 6 percent. Table A-2 indicates that the future-value interest factor for an annuity at 6 percent for five years, $FVIFA_{6\%,5yrs}$, is 5.637. Substituting $S_5 = \$20,000$ and $FVIFA_{6\%,5yrs} = 5.637$ into Equation 6.26 yields an annual required deposit, A, of $3,547.99 ($20,000 ÷ 5.637). If $3,547.99 is deposited at the end of each year for five years at 6 percent, at the end of the five years there will be $20,000 in the account.

Loan Amortization

The term **loan amortization** refers to the determination of the equal annual loan payments necessary to provide a lender with a specified interest return and repay the loan principal over a specified period. The loan amortization process involves finding the future payments (over the term of the loan) whose present value at the loan interest rate equals the

loan amortization The determination of the equal annual loan payments necessary to provide a lender with a specified interest return and repay the loan principal over a specified period.

HAYS WATKINS:
Staying on Track by Toeing the Bottom Line

"There is a common denominator for everyone—the bottom line. What is it worth? What does it cost? What's the return?" These words reflect the philosophy of Hays Watkins, chairman and chief executive officer of CSX, who turned a $250 million railroad from the 1940s into an $11 billion transportation and natural resources company in the 1980s.

Born on a small farm in Kentucky, Watkins was the only son of a banker. Even as a child, he was good with numbers. In college he majored in accounting and later earned an MBA from Northwestern University. Watkin's fascination with railroads began upon graduation. With an uncle who was a conductor and another relative who was an engineer, he landed his first job as an accountant on the Chesapeake & Ohio in 1949. "They say the bean counters and the lawyers are taking over the world, but I was a bean counter and proud of it. Still, the world of the railroad fascinated me, and I learned it well as an internal auditor."

Watkins progressed through the financial area of the organization to vice president-finance of the Chesapeake & Ohio–Baltimore & Ohio railroad. He learned a lot about his company and its operations then, but when he became

CEO, Watkins stepped into uncharted territory. "You can get to know the organization well in the financial area, and you are where it's at; but the hardest thing I faced in my career was the jump from this more or less structured position in a function I knew well to the chaos of the chief excutive's job—a jump from being accustomed to doing your own work to being wholly dependent on others in areas you do not know well. Being a financial executive can be excellent training for a chief executive, but nothing really prepares you for the pressures and uncertainties of trying to run an organization, especially during a

period of major change and tremendous growth."

For Watkins, the key to any large organization is people. "If I could sum up my operating philosophy, it would still get down to people. Do unto them as you would have them do to you if you were in their position. And what is important to people is important to me. I consider myself an old railroad man. We've built our organization beyond the railroads into a transportation company—rails, barges, trucking, and pipeline—a one-stop shipping organization using whatever transportation is best and most economical for the customer. But we have built on the special feeling old railroad people had for railroading and for each other in the times when this was the unique transportation mode in our country."

Watkin's successful management of people and money helped turn CSX into a multi-million dollar company. He stresses efficiency on the part of both management and the work force, as well as the utilization and returns earned from its asset base. Watkins states that he continues to rely on his background—and on toeing the bottom line. "We watch our numbers," he says. "I live with my computer all day."

SOURCE: George De Mare, "Hays Watkins," *Financial Executive*, June 1985, pp. 24–27.

---

loan amortization schedule
A schedule of equal payments to repay a loan. It shows the allocation of each loan payment to interest and principal.

amount of initial principal borrowed. Lenders use a **loan amortization schedule** to determine these payment amounts. In the case of home mortgages, these tables are used to find the equal *monthly* payments necessary to amortize, or pay off, the mortgage at a specified interest rate over a 15- to 30-year period.

Amortizing a loan actually involves creating an annuity out of a present amount. For example, an individual may borrow $6,000 at 10 percent and agree to make equal annual end-of-year payments over four years. To determine the size of the payments, the four-year annuity discounted at 10 percent that has a present value of $6,000 must be determined. This process is actually the inverse of finding the present value of an annuity.

Earlier in this chapter the present value, P_n, of an n-year annuity of A dollars was found by multiplying the annual amount, A, by the present-value interest factor for an annuity from Table A-4, $PVIFA_{k,n}$. This relationship, which was originally expressed as Equation 6.24, is rewritten here as Equation 6.27:

$$P_n = A \times (PVIFA_{k,n}) \tag{6.27}$$

To find the equal annual payment, A, required to pay off, or amortize, the loan, P_n, over a certain number of years at a specified interest rate, we need to solve Equation 6.27 for A. Isolating A on the left side of the equation gives us

$$A = \frac{P_n}{PVIFA_{k,n}} \tag{6.28}$$

Once this is done, we have only to substitute the known values of P_n and $PVIFA_{k,n}$ into the right side of the equation to find the annual payment required.

Example

In the problem just stated, a person wished to determine the equal annual end-of-year payments necessary to amortize fully a $6,000, 10 percent loan over four years. Table A-4 indicates that the present-value interest factor for an annuity corresponding to 10 percent and four years, $PVIFA_{10\%,4yrs}$, is 3.170. Substituting $P_4 = \$6,000$ and $PVIFA_{10\%,4yrs} = 3.170$ in Equation 6.28 and solving for A yields an annual loan payment of $1,892.74 ($6,000 ÷ 3.170). Thus, to repay the principal and interest on a $6,000, 10 percent, four-year loan, equal annual end-of-year payments of $1,892.74 are necessary.

The allocation of each loan payment to interest and principal in order to repay the loan fully can be seen in columns 3 and 4 of the *loan amortization schedule* given in Table 6.11. The portion of each payment representing interest (column 3) declines, and the portion going to principal repayment (column 4) increases over the repayment period. This is typical of amortized loans because with level payments, as the principal is reduced, the interest component declines, leaving a larger portion of each subsequent payment to repay principal.

Table 6.11
Loan Amortization Schedule ($6,000 Principal, 10 Percent Interest, 4-Year Repayment Period)

End of year	Loan payment (1)	Beginning-of-year principal (2)	Interest [.10 × (2)] (3)	Principal [(1) − (3)] (4)	End-of-year principal [(2) − (4)] (5)
1	$1,892.74	$6,000.00	$600.00	$1,292.74	$4,707.26
2	1,892.74	4,707.26	470.73	1,422.01	3,285.25
3	1,892.74	3,285.25	328.53	1,564.21	1,721.04
4	1,892.74	1,721.04	172.10	1,720.64	—[a]

[a] Due to rounding, a slight difference ($.40) exists between the beginning-of-year-4 principal (in column 2) and the year-4 principal payment (in column 4).

FACT OR FABLE?

6 When a loan is amortized, the portion of each payment representing interest increases, and the portion going to principal repayment declines over the repayment period. *(Fable)*

When a loan is amortized, the portion of each payment representing interest *declines,* and the portion going to principal repayment *increases* over the repayment period.

Interest or Growth Rates

It is often necessary to calculate the compound annual interest or growth rate associated with a stream of cash flows. In doing this, either future-value or present-value interest factors can be used. The approach using present-value interest tables is described in this section. The simplest situation is one in which a person wishes to find the rate of interest or growth in a cash flow stream.[11] This can be illustrated by the following example.

Example

Ray Noble wishes to find the rate of interest or growth of the following stream of cash flows.

Year	Cash flow	
1988	$1,520	4
1987	$1,440	3
1986	$1,370	2
1985	$1,300	1
1984	$1,250	

Using the first year (1984) as a base year, it can be seen that interest has been earned (or growth experienced) for four years. To find the rate at which this has occurred, the amount received in the earliest year is divided by the amount received in the latest year. This gives the present-value interest factor for four years, $PVIF_{k,4yrs}$, which is 0.822 ($1,250 ÷ $1,520). The interest rate in Table A-3 associated with the factor closest to 0.822 for four years is the rate of interest or growth rate associated with the cash flows. Looking across year 4 of Table A-3 shows that the factor for 5 percent is 0.823— almost exactly the 0.822 value. Therefore, the rate of interest or growth rate associated with the cash flows given is approximately (to the nearest whole percent)[12] 5 percent.

---

[11] Since the calculations required for finding interest rates and growth rates, given certain cash flow or principal flow streams, are the same, this section refers to the calculations as those required to find interest *or* growth rates.

[12] When making these and other types of interest or growth rate estimates using financial tables, *interpolation* can often be used to get a more exact answer. To illustrate, assume that for seven years of data, the quotient

Sometimes one wishes to determine the interest rate associated with an equal-payment loan. For instance, if a person were to borrow $2,000 to be repaid in equal annual end-of-year amounts of $514.14 for the next five years, he or she might wish to determine the rate of interest being paid on the loan. Using Equation 6.27, we find that $P_5 = \$2,000$ and $A = \$514.14$. Rearranging the equation and substituting these values results in a present-value interest factor for a five-year annuity, $PVIFA_{k,5yrs}$, of 3.890:

$$PVIFA_{k,5yrs} = \frac{P_5}{A} = \frac{\$2,000}{\$514.14} = 3.890 \qquad (6.29)$$

The interest rate for five years associated with a factor of 3.890 in Table A-4 is 9 percent; therefore, the interest rate on the loan is approximately (to the nearest whole percent) 9 percent.

Perpetuities

A **perpetuity** is an annuity with an infinite life—in other words, an annuity that never stops providing its holder with A dollars at the end of each year. It is sometimes necessary to find the present value of a perpetuity. The present value of an A-dollar perpetuity discounted at the rate k is defined by Equation 6.30.

perpetuity An annuity with an infinite life, making continual annual payments.

Present value of an A-dollar perpetuity discounted at k percent =

$$A \times (PVIFA_{k,\infty}) = A \times \left(\frac{1}{k}\right) \qquad (6.30)$$

As noted in the equation, the appropriate factor, $PVIFA_{k,\infty}$, is found merely by dividing the discount rate, k (stated as a decimal), into 1. The validity of this method can be seen by looking at the factors in Table A-4 for 8 percent, 10 percent, and 20 percent. As the

---

found by dividing the earliest by latest cash flow value is 0.575. Looking at the present-value interest table, Table A-3, for *six years* (the number of years of growth), the closest factors to 0.575 are 0.596 at 9 percent and 0.564 at 10 percent. Clearly, the growth rate is between 9 and 10 percent and is closer to the 10 percent value. To interpolate a more precise answer, the following steps are necessary:

1. Find the difference between the 9 and 10 percent present-value interest factors of 0.596 and 0.564. The difference is .032 (.596 − .564).
2. Find the *absolute* difference (i.e., ignore plus or minus sign) between the calculated quotient of .575 and the value of the present-value interest factor for the lower rate (9 percent), which is .596. This difference is .021 (.575 − .596).
3. Divide the value from step 2 by that found in step 1 to get the percent of total distance across the range attributable to the calculated value. The result is .6563 (.021 ÷ .032).
4. Multiply the percent found in step 3 by the interval width over which interpolation is being performed. In this case the interval width is 1 percent (10% − 9%); multiplying we get .6563 percent (.6563 × 1%). Note that when interpolation is being performed over a wider interval, this step becomes more important.
5. Add the value found in step 4 to the interest rate associated with the lower end of the interval. The result is 9.6563 percent (9% + .6563%). The growth or interest rate is therefore 9.6563 percent.

Of course, an even more accurate result could easily be obtained using a financially oriented calculator or personal computer. Using a financial calculator, the rate for this preceding problem is found to be 9.6618 percent.

Table 6.12
Summary of Key Definitions and Formulas for Time Value of Money

---

Variable definitions

F_n = future value or amount at the end of period n

P = initial principal, or present value

k = annual rate of interest

n = number of periods—typically years—over which money earns a return

m = number of times per year interest is compounded

t = period number index

$k_{eff.}$ = effective interest rate

S_n = future value of an n-year annuity

A = amount deposited or received annually at the end of each year

P_n = present value of an n-year annuity

Interest factor formulas

Future value of a single amount

$$FVIF_{k,n} = \left(1 + \frac{k}{m}\right)^{m \times n}$$ [Eq. 6.7]

for annual compounding, $m = 1$

$$FVIF_{k,n} = (1 + k)^n$$ [Eq. 6.5; factors in Table A-1]

to find the effective interest rate

$$k_{eff.} = (1 + k/m)^m - 1$$ [Eq. 6.8]

Future value of an (ordinary) annuity

$$FVIFA_{k,n} = \sum_{t=1}^{n} (1 + k)^{t-1}$$ [Eq. 6.12; factors in Table A-2]

Present value of a single amount

$$PVIF_{k,n} = \frac{1}{(1 + k)^n}$$ [Eq. 6.18; factors in Table A-3]

Present value of an annuity

$$PVIFA_{k,n} = \sum_{t=1}^{n} \frac{1}{(1 + k)^t}$$ [Eq. 6.23; factors in Table A-4]

Basic equations

Future value (single amount):	$F_n = P \times (FVIF_{k,n})$	[Eq. 6.6]
Future value (annuity):	$S_n = A \times (FVIFA_{k,n})$	[Eq. 6.13]
Present value (single amount):	$P = F_n \times (PVIF_{k,n})$	[Eq. 6.19]
Present value (annuity):	$P_n = A \times (PVIFA_{k,n})$	[Eq. 6.24]

number of years approaches 50, the value of these factors approaches 12.500, 10.000, and 5.000, respectively. Dividing .08, .10, and .20 (for k) into 1 gives factors for finding the present value of perpetuities at these rates of 12.500, 10.000, and 5.000. An example will help clarify the application of Equation 6.30.

Example

A person wishes to determine the present value of a $1,000 perpetuity discounted at 10 percent. The appropriate present-value interest factor can be found by dividing 1 by .10. As prescribed by Equation 6.30, the resulting factor, 10, is then multiplied by the annual perpetuity cash inflow of $1,000 to get the present value of the perpetuity, which is $10,000. In other words, the receipt of $1,000 every year for an indefinite period is worth only $10,000 today if a person can earn 10 percent on investments. The reason is that if the person had $10,000 and earned 10 percent interest on it each year, $1,000 a year could be withdrawn indefinitely without affecting the initial $10,000, which would never be drawn upon.

Summary

- The key concepts related to the time value of money are future value and present value. The key time-value definitions, formulas, and equations are given in Table 6.12.

- Future value relies on compound interest to measure the value of future sums. When interest is compounded, the initial principal or deposit in one period, along with the interest earned on it, becomes the beginning principal of the following period, and so on.

- Interest can be compounded annually, semiannually, quarterly, monthly, weekly, daily, or even continuously. The more frequently interest is compounded, the larger the future amount that will be accumulated and the higher the effective interest rate.

- The future value of an annuity, which is a pattern of equal annual cash flows, can be found using the future-value interest factor for an annuity.

- Present value represents the inverse of future value. In finding the present value of a future sum, we determine what amount of money today would be equivalent to the given future amount, considering the fact that we can earn a certain return on the current money.

- Occasionally it is necessary to find the present value of a stream of cash flows. For mixed streams, the individual present values must be found and summed. In the case of an annuity, the present value can be found by using the present-value interest factor for an annuity.

- By manipulating the equations for the future value and present value of single sums and annuities, the deposits needed to accumulate a future sum, loan amortization payments, interest or growth rates, and the present value of perpetuities can be calculated.

Questions

6-1 How is the *compounding process* related to the payment of interest on savings? What is the general equation for the future value, F_n, in period n if P dollars are deposited in an account paying k percent annual interest?

6-2 What effect would (a) a *decrease* in the interest rate or (b) an *increase* in the holding period of a deposit have on its future value? Why?

6-3 What effect does compounding interest more frequently than annually have on (a) the future value generated by a beginning principal and (b) the effective interest rate? Why?

6-4 Explain how one can conveniently determine the future value of an annuity that provides a stream of end-of-period cash inflows.

6-5 What is meant by the phrase "the present value of a future sum"? How are present-value and future-value calculations related?

6-6 What is the equation for the present value of a future amount, F_n, to be received in period n assuming that the firm requires a minimum return of k percent? How is this equation different from the equation for the future value of one dollar?

6-7 What effect do *increasing* (a) required return and (b) time periods have on the present value of a future amount? Why?

6-8 How can present-value tables be used to find the present value of a mixed stream of cash flows? How can the calculations required to find the present value of an annuity be simplified?

6-9 How can the size of the equal annual end-of-year deposits necessary to accumulate a certain future sum in a specified future period be determined? How might one of the financial tables discussed in this chapter aid in this calculation?

6-10 Describe the procedure used to amortize a loan into a series of equal annual payments. What is a *loan amortization schedule?*

6-11 Which financial table(s) would be used to find (a) the growth rate associated with a stream of cash flows and (b) the interest rate associated with an equal-payment loan? How would each of these be calculated?

6-12 What is a *perpetuity?* How might the present-value interest factor for such a stream of cash flows be determined?

Self-Test Problems

(Solutions on page 207)

ST-1 Delia Martin has $10,000 that she can deposit in any of three savings accounts for a three-year period. Bank A pays interest on an annual basis, bank B pays interest twice each year, and bank C pays interest each quarter. All three banks have a stated annual interest rate of 4 percent.

    a. What amount would Ms. Martin have at the end of the third year, leaving all interest paid on deposit, in each bank?

    b. What effective interest rate would she earn in each of the banks?

    c. Based on your findings in **a** and **b**, which bank should Ms. Martin deal with? Why?

ST-2 You have a choice of accepting either of two 5-year cash flow streams or lump-sum amounts. One cash flow stream is an annuity and the other is a mixed stream. You may accept alternative A or B—either as a cash flow stream or as a lump sum. Given the cash flow and lump-sum amounts associated with each, and assuming a 9 percent opportunity cost, which alternative (A or B) and in which form (cash flow stream or lump-sum amount) would you prefer?

	Alternative	
	A	B
End of year	**Cash flow stream**	
1	$ 700	$1,100
2	700	900
3	700	700
4	700	500
5	700	300
Lump-sum amount		
At time zero	$2,825	$2,800

ST-3 Judi Jordan wishes to accumulate $8,000 by the end of five years by making equal annual end-of-year deposits over the next five years. If Judi can earn 7 percent on her investments, how much must she deposit at the *end of each year* to meet this goal?

Problems

6-1 (**Future-Value Calculation**) *Without tables*, use the basic formula for future value along with the given interest rate, k, and number of periods, n, to calculate the future-value interest factor in each of the following cases. Compare the calculated value to the table value in Appendix Table A-1.

Case	Interest rate, k (%)	Number of periods, n
A	12	2
B	6	3
C	9	2
D	3	4

6-2 (**Future-Value Tables**) Use the future-value interest factors in Appendix Table A-1 in each of the following cases to estimate, to the nearest year, how long it would take an initial deposit, assuming no withdrawals,

a. To double.

b. To quadruple.

Case	Interest rate (%)
A	7
B	40
C	20
D	10

6-3 (**Future Values**) For each of the following cases, calculate the future value of the single cash flow deposited today that will be available at the end of the deposit period if the interest is compounded annually at the rate specified for the given period.

Case	Single cash flow ($)	Interest rate (%)	Deposit period (years)
A	200	5	20
B	4,500	8	7
C	10,000	9	10
D	25,000	10	12
E	37,000	11	5
F	40,000	12	9

(handwritten annotations:)
2.653   530.6
1.714   7713
2.367   23670
3.138
1.685   78450
2.773   62345
          110920

6-4 **(Single-Payment Loan Repayment)** A person borrows $200 to be repaid in eight years with 14 percent annually compounded interest. The loan may be repaid at the end of any earlier year with no prepayment penalty.

   a. What amount would be due if the loan is repaid at the end of year 1?

   b. What is the repayment at the end of year 4?

   c. What amount is due at the end of the eighth year?

6-5 **(Changing Compounding Frequency)** Using annual, semiannual, and quarterly compounding periods, for each of the following (1) calculate the future value if $5,000 is initially deposited and (2) determine the effective interest rate,

   a. At 12 percent for five years.

   b. At 16 percent for six years.

   c. At 20 percent for ten years.

6-6 **(Compounding Frequency, Future Value, and Effective Interest Rates)** For each of the following cases:

Case	Amount of initial deposit ($)	Nominal interest rate, k (%)	Compounding frequency, m (times/year)	Deposit period (years)
A	2,500	6	2	5
B	50,000	12	6	3
C	1,000	5	1	10
D	20,000	16	4	6

   a. Calculate the future value at the end of the specified deposit period.

   b. Determine the effective interest rate, k_{eff}.

   c. Compare the nominal interest rate, k, to the effective interest rate, k_{eff}. What relationship exists between compounding frequency and the nominal and effective interest rates?

6-7 **(Future Value of an Annuity)** For each of the following cases, calculate the future value of the annuity at the end of the deposit period, assuming that the annuity cash flows occur at the end of each year.

Case	Amount of annuity ($)	Interest rate (%)	Deposit period (years)
A	2,500	8	10
B	500	12	6
C	30,000	20	5
D	11,500	9	8
E	6,000	14	30

6-8 **(Annuities and Compounding)** Janet Boyle intends to deposit $300 per year in a credit union for the next ten years, and the credit union pays an annual interest rate of 8 percent.

Determine the future value Janet will have at the end of ten years given that end-of-period deposits are made and no interest is withdrawn if:

a. $300 is deposited annually and the credit union pays interest annually.

b. $150 is deposited semiannually and the credit union pays interest semiannually.

c. $75 is deposited quarterly and the credit union pays interest quarterly.

6-9 **(Future Value of a Mixed Stream)** For each of the following mixed streams of cash flows, determine the future value at the end of the final year if deposits are made at the *beginning of each year* into an account paying annual interest of 12 percent, assuming no withdrawals are made during the period.

	Cash flow stream		
Year	A	B	C
1	$ 900	$30,000	$1,200
2	1,000	25,000	1,200
3	1,200	20,000	1,000
4		10,000	1,900
5		5,000	

6-10 **(Present-Value Calculation)** *Without tables,* use the basic formula for present value along with the given opportunity cost, k, and number of periods, n, to calculate the present-value interest factor in each of the following cases. Compare the calculated value to the table value.

Case	Opportunity cost, k (%)	Number of periods, n
A	2	4
B	10	2
C	5	3
D	13	2

6-11 **(Present Values)** For each of the following cases, calculate the present value of the cash flow, discounting at the rate given and assuming that the cash flow will be received at the end of the period noted.

Case	Single cash flow ($)	Discount rate (%)	End of period (years)
A	7,000	12	4
B	28,000	8	20
C	10,000	14	12
D	150,000	11	6
E	45,000	20	8

6-12 **(Present Value)** Jim Nance has been offered a future payment of $500 three years from today. If his opportunity cost is 7 percent compounded annually, what value would he place on this opportunity?

6-13 **(Present Value)** An Iowa state savings bond can be converted to $100 at maturity six years from purchase. If the state bonds are to be competitive with U.S. Savings Bonds, which pay 8 percent annual interest (compounded annually), at what price will the state sell its bonds? Assume no cash payments on savings bonds prior to redemption.

6-14 **(Present Value—Mixed Streams)** Given the following mixed streams of cash flows:

	Cash flow stream	
Year	A	B
1	$ 50,000	$ 10,000
2	40,000	20,000
3	30,000	30,000
4	20,000	40,000
5	10,000	50,000
Totals	$150,000	$150,000

a. Find the present value of each stream using a 15 percent discount rate.

b. Compare the calculated present values and discuss them in light of the fact that the undiscounted total cash flows amount to $150,000 in each case.

6-15 **(Present Value—Mixed Streams)** Find the present value of the following streams of cash flows. Assume that the firm's opportunity cost is 12 percent.

A		B		C	
Year	Amount	Year	Amount	Year	Amount
1	−$2,000	1	$10,000	1–5	$10,000/yr.
2	3,000	2–5	5,000/yr.	6–10	8,000/yr.
3	4,000	6	7,000		
4	6,000				
5	8,000				

6-16 **(Relationship Between Future Value and Present Value)** Using *only* the following information:

Year (t)	Cash flow ($)	Future-value interest factor at 5 percent ($FVIF_{5\%,t}$)
1	800	1.050
2	900	1.102
3	1,000	1.158
4	1,500	1.216
5	2,000	1.276

a. Determine the *present value* of the mixed stream of cash flows using a 5 percent discount rate.

b. How much would you be willing to pay for an opportunity to buy this stream, assuming that you can at best earn 5 percent on your investments.

c. What effect, if any, would a 7 percent rather than 5 percent opportunity cost have on your analysis? (Explain verbally.)

6-17 **(Present Value of an Annuity)** For each of the following cases, calculate the present value of the annuity, assuming that the annuity cash flows occur at the end of each year.

Case	Amount of annuity ($)	Interest rate (%)	Period (years)
A	12,000	7	3
B	55,000	12	15
C	700	20	9
D	140,000	5	7
E	22,500	10	5

6-18 **(Cash Flow Investment Decision)** Tom Alexander has an opportunity to purchase any of the following investments. The purchase price, amount of the single cash inflow, and its year of receipt are given below for each investment. Which purchase recommendations would you make, assuming that Tom can earn 10 percent on his investments?

Investment	Price ($)	Single cash inflow ($)	Year of receipt
A	18,000	30,000	5
B	600	3,000	20
C	3,500	10,000	10
D	1,000	15,000	40

6-19 **(Accumulating a Growing Future Sum)** A retirement home at Deer Trail Estates now costs $85,000. Inflation is expected to cause this price to increase at 6 percent per year over the 20 years before C. L. Donovan retires. How large an equal annual end-of-year deposit must be made each year into an account paying an annual rate of 10 percent in order for Donovan to have the cash to purchase a home at retirement?

6-20 **(Loan Amortization)** Determine the equal annual end-of-year payment required each year over the life of the following loans in order to repay them fully during the stated term of the loan.

Loan	Principal ($)	Interest rate (%)	Term of loan (years)
A	12,000	8	3
B	60,000	12	10
C	75,000	10	30
D	4,000	15	5

6-21 **(Loan Amortization Schedule)** Joan Messineo borrowed $15,000 at a 14 percent annual rate of interest to be repaid over three years. The loan is amortized into three equal annual end-of-year payments.

   a. Calculate the annual end-of-year loan payment.

   b. Prepare a loan amortization schedule showing the interest and principal breakdown of each of the three loan payments.

   c. Explain why the interest portion of each payment declines with the passage of time.

6-22 **(Growth Rates)** You are given the following series of cash flows:

	Cash flows		
Year	A	B	C
1	$500	$1,500	$2,500
2	560	1,550	2,600
3	640	1,610	2,650
4	720	1,680	2,650
5	800	1,760	2,800
6		1,850	2,850
7		1,950	2,900
8		2,060	
9		2,170	
10		2,280	

   a. Calculate the compound growth rate associated with each cash flow stream.

   b. If year 1 values represent initial deposits in a savings account paying annual interest, what is the rate of interest earned on each account?

   c. Compare and discuss the growth rates and interest rates found in **a** and **b**, respectively.

6-23 **(Rate of Return)** Rishi Singh has $1,500 to invest. His investment counselor suggests an investment that pays no explicit interest but will return $2,000 at the end of three years.

   a. What annual rate of return will Mr. Singh earn with this investment?

   b. Mr. Singh is considering another investment, of equal risk, which earns a return of 8 percent. Which investment should he take, and why?

6-24 **(Rate of Return—Annuity)** What is the rate of return on an investment of $10,606 if the company expects to receive $2,000 each year for the next ten years?

6-25 **(Loan Rates of Interest)** John Fleming has been shopping for a loan to finance the purchase of his new car. He has found three possibilities that seem attractive and wishes to select the one having the lowest interest rate. The information available with respect to each of the three $5,000 loans follows.

Loan	Principal ($)	Annual payment ($)	Term (years)
A	5,000	1,352.81	5
B	5,000	1,543.21	4
C	5,000	2,010.45	3

a. Determine the interest rate that would be associated with each of the loans.

b. Which loan should Mr. Fleming take?

6-26 **(Perpetuities)** Given the following data, determine for each of the following perpetuities:

Perpetuity	Annual amount ($)	Discount rate (%)
A	20,000	8
B	100,000	10
C	3,000	6
D	60,000	5

a. The appropriate present-value interest factor.

b. The present value.

6-27 **(Annuity and Perpetuity)** You have decided to endow your favorite university with a scholarship in honor of your successful completion of managerial finance. It is expected that it will cost $6,000 per year to attend the university into perpetuity. You expect to give the university the endowment in ten years and will accumulate it by making annual (end-of-year) deposits into an account. The rate of interest is expected to be 10 percent for all future time periods.

a. How large must the endowment be?

b. How much must you deposit at the end of each of the next ten years to accumulate the required amount?

6-28 **(Integrative—Future and Present Value)** A major corporation wishes to accumulate funds to provide a retirement annuity for a key executive. The executive by contract will retire at the end of exactly 12 years. Upon retirement the executive is entitled to receive an annual end-of-year payment of $42,000 for exactly 20 years. In the event the executive dies prior to the end of the 20-year period, the annual payments will pass to his heirs. During the 12-year "accumulation period," the corporation wishes to fund the annuity by making equal annual end-of-year deposits into an account earning 9 percent interest. Once the 20-year "distribution period" begins, the corporation plans to move the accumulated monies into an account earning a guaranteed 12 percent per year. At the end of the distribution period, the account balance will equal zero. How large must the equal annual end-of-year deposits into the account be over the 12-year accumulation period in order to allow the $42,000 annual end-of-year distributions to be made over the 20-year period? Note that the first deposit will occur at the end of year 1 and the first distribution payment at the end of year 13. (*Hint:* It may be helpful to draw a time line of cash flows before solving this problem.)

Solutions to Self-Test Problems

ST-1 **a.** *Bank A*

$$F_3 = \$10,000 \times FVIF_{4\%,3yrs} = \$10,000 \times 1.125 = \underline{\$11,250}$$

Bank B

$$F_3 = \$10,000 \times FVIF_{4\%/2,2\times3yrs} = 10,000 \times FVIF_{2\%,6yrs}$$
$$= \$10,000 \times 1.126 = \underline{\$11,260}$$

Bank C

$$F_3 = \$10,000 \times FVIF_{4\%/4,\,4\times3\text{yrs}} = \$10,000 \times FVIF_{1\%,\,12\text{yrs}}$$
$$= \$10,000 \times 1.127 = \underline{\$11,270}$$

b. Bank A: $k_{\text{eff.}} = (1 + 4\%/1)^1 - 1 = (1 + .04)^1 - 1 = 1.04 - 1 = .04 = \underline{4\%}$

Bank B: $k_{\text{eff.}} = (1 + 4\%/2)^2 - 1 = (1 + .02)^2 - 1 = 1.0404 - 1 = .0404 = \underline{\underline{4.04\%}}$

Bank C: $k_{\text{eff.}} = (1 + 4\%/4)^4 - 1 = (1 + .01)^4 - 1 = 1.0406 - 1 = .0406 = \underline{\underline{4.06\%}}$

c. Ms. Martin should deal with Bank C: the quarterly compounding of interest at the given 4 percent rate results in the highest future value as a result of the corresponding highest effective interest rate.

ST-2 *Alternative A*
Cash flow stream:

$$P_5 = \$700 \times PVIFA_{9\%,\,5\text{yrs}}$$
$$P_5 = \$700 \times 3.890 = \underline{\$2,723}$$

Lump-sum: $\underline{\$2,825}$

Alternative B
Cash flow stream:

Year (n)	Cash flow (1)	$PVIF_{9\%,n}$ (2)	Present value [(1) × (2)] (3)
1	$1,100	.917	$1,008.70
2	900	.842	757.80
3	700	.772	540.40
4	500	.708	354.00
5	300	.650	195.00
		Present value	$2,855.90

Lump-sum: $\underline{\$2,800}$

Conclusion: Alternative B in the form of a cash flow stream is preferred since its present value of $2,855.90 is greater than the other three values.

ST-3 $S_5 = \$8,000$; $FVIFA_{7\%,\,5\text{yrs}} = 5.751$; $A = ?$
$S_n = A \times (FVIFA_{k,n})$ [Equation 6.13]
$\$8,000 = A \times (5.751)$
$A = \$8,000/5.751 = \underline{\$1,391.06}$

Judi should deposit $1,391.06 at the end of each of the five years in order to meet her goal of accumulating $8,000 at the end of the fifth year.

CHAPTER 7

Risk and Return

FACT OR FABLE?
Are the following statements fact *(true)* or fable *(false)*?

1

Risk refers to the variability of returns such that the less variable an asset's returns, the higher its risk, and vice versa.

2

Most financial managers are risk-indifferent since for a given increase in risk their required return does not change.

3

The coefficient of variation is more effective than the standard deviation in comparing the risk of assets that have different expected returns.

4

Generally, the lower (less positive and more negative) the correlation between two assets' returns, the lower the risk of the portfolio that would result from combining them.

5

The beta coefficient, *b*, is an index of the degree of movement of an asset's return in response to a change in the risk-free rate of return.

6

The capital asset pricing model (CAPM) reflects a positive relationship between an asset's nondiversifiable risk measured by beta and its required return.

S mart companies plan their future. They know if they just wait for the future to happen, it probably won't turn out the way they would like. Northrop Corporation and McDonnell Douglas Corporation are in the same business: building military aircraft. Yet both of them have gazed into the crystal ball and developed different plans to meet the future. Both plans include heavy investment that they believe will pay off in high returns.

Northrop plans to remain a defense contractor, so it will continue to put big dollars into research and development as well as the upgrading of production facilities. (Many defense contractors take steps to meet a military need only after it arises; Northrop tries to anticipate need.) Northrop has been successful with this philosophy in the past. The F5, a company-sponsored R&D project, became a 20-year product. Of course, Northrop is also a well-run company, with high productivity and a reputation for on-time, on-budget delivery. Will Northrop's success continue? The plan is to retain the formula: risk corporate resources to develop products the military will probably need. At the same time, however, Northrop will diversify—with military electronics equipment and guidance systems.

McDonnell Douglas, on the other hand, believes defense orders are not likely to grow rapidly, since there is a peacetime limit to the fighter planes and missiles that will be necessary. Instead of making heavy investments in the military area, McDonnell Douglas is focusing on commercial aircraft and computer information services. The company is, of course, experiencing the problems anyone would face in modifying its product line so significantly.

Both approaches—to stay with defense and to diversify into the civilian area—seem reasonable. They also require a large investment. Yet each company thinks it has made the right capital investment.

The strategies of Northrop and McDonnell Douglas appear to reflect conscious consideration of the trade-off between risk and return by each firm. In this chapter we develop and describe the relationship between risk and return, which, as will be shown in the next chapter, are the key determinants of stock value.

Risk and Return Fundamentals

In order to achieve the goal of share price maximization, the financial manager must learn to assess the two key determinants of share price: risk and return.[1] Each financial decision presents certain risk and return characteristics, and all major financial decisions must be viewed in terms of expected risk, expected return, and their combined impact on share

---

[1] Two important points should be recognized here: (1) While for convenience the publicly traded corporation is being discussed, the risk and return concepts presented apply equally well to all firms; and (2) concern centers only on common stockholders' wealth, since they in fact represent the "residual owners" whose returns are in no way specified in advance.

price. Risk can be viewed as it relates either to a single asset held in isolation or to a **portfolio,** or collection, of assets. Although portfolio risk is probably more important to the financial manager, the general concept of risk is more readily developed in terms of a single asset. Before considering risk in each of these forms, it is important to understand the fundamentals of risk, return, and risk preferences.

portfolio A collection, or group, of assets.

Risk Defined

In the most basic sense, **risk** can be defined as the chance of loss. Assets having greater chances of loss are viewed as more risky than those with lesser chances of loss. More formally, the term *risk* is used interchangeably with *uncertainty* to refer to the *variability of returns associated with a given asset.* For instance, a government bond that guarantees its holder $100 interest after 30 days has no risk, since there is no variability associated with the return. An equivalent investment in a firm's common stock that may earn over the same period anywhere from $0 to $200 is very risky due to the high variability of return. The more certain the return from an asset, the less variability and therefore the less risk.

risk The chance of financial loss or, more formally, the variability of returns associated with a given asset.

☐1☐ Risk refers to the variability of returns such that the less variable an asset's returns, the higher its risk, and vice versa. *(Fable)*

Risk refers to the variability of returns such that the *more* variable an asset's returns, the higher its risk, and vice versa.

FACT OR FABLE?

Return Defined

The **return** on an investment is measured as the total gain or loss experienced on behalf of the owner over a given period of time. It is commonly stated as the change in value plus any cash distribution, expressed as a percentage of the beginning-of-period investment value. The expression for calculating the rate of return earned on any asset over period t, k_t, is commonly defined as

return The change in value of an asset plus any cash distribution, expressed as a percentage of the beginning-of-period investment value.

$$k_t = \frac{P_t - P_{t-1} + C_t}{P_{t-1}} \tag{7.1}$$

where

k_t = actual, expected, or required rate of return[2] during period t

P_t = price (value) of asset at time t

P_{t-1} = price (value) of asset at time $t-1$

C_t = cash (flow) received from the asset investment in the time period $t-1$ to t

The return, k_t, reflects the combined effect of changes in value, $P_t - P_{t-1}$, and cash flow, C_t, realized over the period t.

Equation 7.1 is used to determine the rate of return over a time period as short as one day or as long as ten years or more. However, in most cases t is equal to one year, and k

[2] The terms *expected return* and *required return* are used interchangeably throughout this text since in an efficient market (discussed later) they would be expected to be equal. The actual return is an *ex post* value, while expected and required returns are *ex ante* values.

therefore represents an annual rate of return. The beginning-of-period value, P_{t-1}, and the end-of-period value, P_t, are not necessarily *realized values*. They are commonly *unrealized*, which means that although the asset was *not* actually purchased at time $t - 1$ and sold at time t, the values P_{t-1} and P_t could have been realized had they been.

Example

Robin Industries wishes to determine the actual annual rate of return on two assets, C and D. Asset C was purchased exactly one year ago for $20,000 and currently has a market value of $21,500. During the year it generated $800 of cash flow. Asset D was purchased four years ago, and its value at the beginning and end of the year just completed declined from $12,000 to $11,800. During the year it provided $1,700 of cash flow.

Substituting into Equation 7.1, the annual rate of return, k, for each asset is calculated.

Asset C

$$k_C = \frac{\$21,500 - \$20,000 + \$800}{\$20,000} = \frac{\$2,300}{\$20,000} = \underline{\underline{11.5\%}}$$

Asset D

$$k_D = \frac{\$11,800 - \$12,000 + \$1,700}{\$12,000} = \frac{\$1,500}{\$12,000} = \underline{\underline{12.5\%}}$$

Although the value of asset D declined during the year, its relatively high cash flow caused it to earn a higher rate of return than that earned by asset C during the same period. Clearly, it is the combined impact of changes in value and cash flow measured by the rate of return that is important.

Risk Preferences

risk-indifferent The attitude toward risk in which no change in return would be required for an increase in risk.

risk-averse The attitude toward risk in which an increased return would be required for an increase in risk.

risk-taking The attitude toward risk in which a decreased return would be accepted for an increase in risk.

Because of differing managerial (firm) preferences, it is important to specify a generally acceptable level of risk.[3] The three basic risk preference behaviors—risk-averse, risk-indifferent, and risk-taking—are depicted graphically in Figure 7.1. Note that as risk goes from x_1 to x_2, for the **risk-indifferent** manager the required return does not change. In essence, no change in return would be required for the increase in risk. In the case of the **risk-averse** manager, the required return increases for an increase in risk. For the **risk-taking** manager, the required return decreases for an increase in risk. *Most managers are risk-averse, since for a given increase in risk they require an increase in return.* Although in theory the risk disposition of each manager could be measured, in practice managers tend to accept only those risks with which they feel comfortable. And they generally tend to be conservative rather than aggressive when accepting risk.

[3] The risk preferences of the managers in theory should be consistent with the risk preferences of the firm. While the *agency problem* suggests that in practice managers may not behave in a manner consistent with the firm's risk preferences, it is assumed here that they do. Therefore, the manager's risk preferences and those of the firm are assumed to be identical.

Figure 7.1
Risk Preference Functions

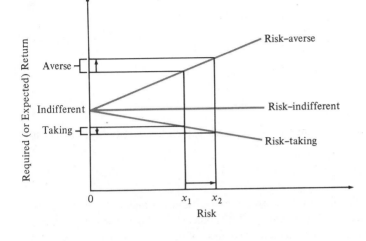

Basic Risk Concepts: A Single Asset

The concept of risk is most readily developed by first considering a single asset held in isolation. Such an approach creates a "white laboratory" in which the potential interactions of asset returns can be ignored. The relationship between risk and time is important in understanding the role of risk in financial decision making.

Risk of a Single Asset

Although the risk of a single asset is measured in much the same way as the risk of an entire portfolio of assets, it is important to differentiate between these two entities, since certain benefits accrue to holders of portfolios. It is also useful to assess risk from both a behavioral and a quantitative point of view.

Sensitivity Analysis

Sensitivity analysis is an approach that uses a number of possible return estimates to obtain a sense of the variability among outcomes. One common method involves the estimation of the pessimistic (worst), the most likely (expected), and the optimistic (best) returns associated with a given asset. In this case the asset's risk can be measured by the **range,** which is found by subtracting the pessimistic (worst) outcome from the optimistic

sensitivity analysis An approach in assessing risk that uses a number of possible return estimates to obtain a sense of the variability among outcomes.

range The extent of an asset's risk, which is found by subtracting the pessimistic (worst) outcome from the optimistic (best) outcome.

Table 7.1
Assets A and B

	Asset A	Asset B
Initial investment	$10,000	$10,000
Annual rate of return		
Pessimistic	13%	7%
Most likely	15%	15%
Optimistic	17%	23%
Range	4%	16%

(best) outcome. The greater the range for a given asset, the more variability, or risk, it is said to have.

Example

Norman Company is attempting to choose the best of two alternative investments, A and B, each requiring an initial outlay of $10,000 and each having a *most likely* annual rate of return of 15 percent. To evaluate the riskiness of these assets, management has made *pessimistic* and *optimistic* estimates of the returns associated with each. The three estimates for each asset, along with its range, are given in Table 7.1. It can be seen that asset A appears to be less risky than asset B since its range of 4 percent (17 − 13 percent) is less than the range of 16 percent (23 − 7 percent) for asset B. The risk-averse financial decision maker would prefer asset A over asset B since A offers the same most likely return as B (15%) but with lower risk (smaller range).

Although the use of sensitivity analysis and the range is rather crude, it does provide the decision maker with more than one estimate of return that can be used to assess roughly the risk involved.

Probabilities

probability The *percentage chance* that a given outcome will occur.

Probabilities can be used to assess more precisely the risk involved in an asset. The **probability** of an event occurring is the *percentage chance* of a given outcome. If an outcome has an 80 percent probability of occurrence, the given outcome would be expected to occur eight out of ten times. If an outcome has a probability of 100 percent, it is certain to occur. Outcomes having a probability of zero will never occur.

probability distribution A model that relates probabilities to the associated outcomes.

bar chart The simplest type of probability distribution showing only a limited number of outcomes and associated probabilities for a given event.

Example

An evaluation of Norman Company's past estimates indicates that the probabilities of the pessimistic, most likely, and optimistic outcomes' occurring are 25 percent, 50 percent, and 25 percent, respectively. The sum of these probabilities must equal 100 percent; that is, they must be based on all the alternatives considered.

Probability Distributions

A **probability distribution** is a model that relates probabilities to the associated outcomes. The simplest type of probability distribution is the **bar chart,** which shows only a

---

FINANCE IN ACTION

FINDING RISK/REWARD INEFFICIENCIES IN THE OTC MARKET

A bad day in the stock market gets people thinking risk again. Louis G. Navellier has a system that thinks risk as well as reward. Navellier is an earnest 28-year-old who took a crash course through college because he couldn't wait to get to work. Work on what? The stock market.

Navellier's $150-a-year monthly *OTC Insight* letter has a remarkable record. And he's doing it all with Modern Portfolio Theory (MPT), the rigorously quantitative, academically approved investment technique. *OTC Insight*'s performance is a matter of public record, because since 1985 it has been one of about 100 such advisory services monitored by the *Hulbert Financial Digest,* judge of the investment letter industry. "Navellier's nine model portfolios appreciated an average of 144.3 percent from January 1985 through the end of August 1986," says *HFD.* That's over twice the Dow's gain in the same period, and two-and-a-half times that of the Nasdaq OTC Composite Index.

The operating assumption of the *OTC Insight* system is that the stock

market is not completely efficient—it can be beaten with a disciplined approach that assesses the odds carefully, particularly with stocks that are traded in the less liquid over-the-counter market rather than on any exchange. Thus, Navellier concentrates on relatively obscure over-the-counter stocks.

Every month Navellier's computer begins by inspecting a database containing 1,100 over-the-counter stocks. For each one, it crunches out a "beta" and an "alpha." "Beta" is the extent to which a stock's fluctuation is related to the movement of the market. "Alpha" represents the stock's propensity to move independently of the market. Navellier's computer has been told to calculate betas and alphas over a 12-month period. The computer works out each stock's mean monthly rate of return—which, since OTC stocks pay minimal dividends, generally turns out to be the mean monthly capital appreciation. Additionally, it computes the variance from the mean monthly return, a statistical measure that tells you how likely the return is to occur.

Got that? Now, the crucial step: The computer divides each stock's alpha by its monthly variance of return. This gives a reward/risk ratio—the market-independent gain per unit of volatility. The computer then lists the top 98 stocks in order of reward/risk. This constitutes the *OTC Insight* Buy List—those stocks for which the reward potential is highest relative to the risk involved.

Navellier's methods have certainly turned up some hot stocks, some of which were just waiting to be discovered. Many of them catch Wall Street's attention only after someone issues a favorable research report. Navellier regards this as typical OTC inefficiency. No Big Board stock would wait so long to be discovered.

Navellier and his partner are now investigating the extension of his system to listed stocks. "But to be very frank with you," says Navellier, "the stock market is much more efficient in the listed stocks. There's no way that we are going to get the same returns."

SOURCE: Peter Brimelow, "An Alpha-Beta Man," *Forbes,* October 6, 1986. Reprinted by permission of *Forbes* magazine, October 6, 1986. © Forbes Inc., 1986.

---

limited number of outcome-probability coordinates. The bar charts for Norman Company's assets A and B are shown in Figure 7.2. Although both assets have the same most likely return, the range of return is much more dispersed for asset B than for asset A—16 percent versus 4 percent. If we knew all the possible outcomes and associated probabilities, a **continuous probability distribution** could be developed. This type of distribution can be thought of as a bar chart for a very large number of outcomes.[4] Figure 7.3 presents

continuous probability distribution A probability distribution showing all the possible outcomes and associated probabilities for a given event.

[4] To develop a continuous probability distribution, one must have data on a large number of historical occurrences. Then, by developing a frequency distribution indicating how many times each outcome has occurred over the given time horizon, one can convert these data into a probability distribution. Probability distributions for risky events can also be developed using *simulation*—a process discussed briefly in Chapter 10.

Figure 7.2
Bar Charts for Asset A's and Asset B's Returns

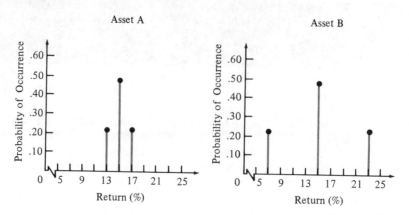

continuous probability distributions for assets A and B.[5] Note in Figure 7.3 that although assets A and B have the same most likely return (15 percent), the distribution of returns for asset B has much greater *dispersion* than the distribution for asset A. Clearly, asset B is more risky than asset A.

Standard Deviation

standard deviation, σ_k
The most common statistical indicator of an asset's risk, which measures the dispersion around the *expected* value.

expected value of a return, $\bar{k}$ The most likely return on a given asset.

The most common statistical indicator of an asset's risk is the **standard deviation, σ_k,** which measures the dispersion around the *expected* value.[6] The **expected value of a return, $\bar{k}$,** is the most likely return on an asset. This can be calculated using Equation 7.2:

$$\bar{k} = \sum_{i=1}^{n} k_i \times Pr_i \tag{7.2}$$

where

k_i = return for the ith outcome

Pr_i = probability of occurrence of the ith outcome

n = number of outcomes considered

[5] The continuous distribution's probabilities change due to the large number of additional outcomes considered. The area under each of the curves is equal to 1, which means that 100 percent of the outcomes, or all the possible outcomes, are considered. Often "probability density functions," such as those in Figure 7.3, are converted into *cumulative probability distributions,* which show the probability of obtaining *at least* a given value.

[6] Although risk is typically viewed as determined by the variability, or dispersion, of outcomes around an expected value, many people believe it is present only when outcomes are below the expected value, since only returns below the expected value are considered bad. Nevertheless, the common approach is to view risk as determined by the variability on either side of the expected value, since the greater this variability, the less confident one can be of the outcomes associated with an asset investment.

Figure 7.3
Continuous Probability Distributions for Asset A's and Asset B's Returns

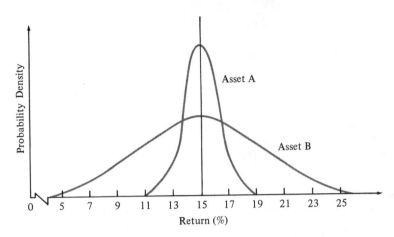

Table 7.2
Expected Values of Returns for Assets A and B

Possible outcomes	Probability (1)	Returns (%) (2)	Weighted value (%) [(1) × (2)] (3)
Asset A			
Pessimistic	.25	13	3.25
Most likely	.50	15	7.50
Optimistic	.25	17	4.25
Total	1.00	Expected return	15.00
Asset B			
Pessimistic	.25	7	1.75
Most likely	.50	15	7.50
Optimistic	.25	23	5.75
Total	1.00	Expected return	15.00

Example
The calculation of the expected values for Norman Company's assets A and B are presented in Table 7.2. Column 1 gives the Pr_i's and column 2 gives the k_i's, n equaling 3 in each case. The expected value for each asset's return is 15 percent.

The expression for the *standard deviation of returns*, σ_k, is given in Equation 7.3:[7]

$$\sigma_k = \sqrt{\sum_{i=1}^{n} (k_i - \bar{k})^2 \times Pr_i} \qquad (7.3)$$

In general, the higher the standard deviation, the greater the risk.

Example

Table 7.3 presents the calculation of standard deviations for Norman Company's assets A and B, based on the data presented earlier. The standard deviation for asset A is 1.41 percent, and the standard deviation for asset B is 5.66 percent. The higher risk of asset B is clearly reflected in its higher standard deviation.

---

normal probability distribution A symmetrical probability distribution whose shape resembles a bell-shaped curve.

A **normal probability distribution,** depicted in Figure 7.4, is one that always resembles a "bell-shaped" curve. It is symmetrical: From the peak of the graph, the curve's extensions are mirror images of each other. The symmetry of the curve means that half the curve's area lies to the left of the peak and half to the right. Therefore, half the probability is associated with the values to the left of the peak and half with values to the right. As noted on the figure, for normal probability distributions, 68 percent of the possible outcomes will lie between ± 1 standard deviation from the expected value, 95 percent of all outcomes will lie between ± 2 standard deviations from the expected value, and 99 percent of all outcomes will lie between ± 3 standard deviations from the expected value.[8]

Example

If we assume that the probability distribution of returns for the Norman Company is normal, 68 percent of the possible outcomes would be expected to have a return ranging between 13.59 and 16.41 percent for asset A and 9.34 and 20.66 percent for asset B; 95 percent of the possible return outcomes would range between 12.18 and 17.82 percent for asset A and 3.68 and 26.32 percent for asset B; and 99 percent of the possible return outcomes would range between 10.77 and 19.23 percent for asset A and -1.98 and 31.98 percent for asset B. From these ranges, the greater risk of asset B is clearly reflected by its much wider range of possible returns at a given level of confidence (68 percent, 95 percent, etc.).

---

[7] The formula commonly used to find the standard deviation of returns, σ_k, in a situation where *all* of the outcomes are known and their related probabilities are assumed equal, is

$$\sigma_k = \sqrt{\dfrac{\sum_{i=1}^{n} (k_i - \bar{k})^2}{n}}$$

where n is the number of observations. Because, when analyzing asset investments, returns and related probabilities are often available, the formula given in Equation 7.3 is emphasized in this chapter.

[8] Tables of values indicating the probabilities associated with various deviations from the expected value of a normal distribution can be found in any basic statistics text. These values can be used to establish confidence limits and make inferences about possible outcomes. Such applications are not discussed in this text but may be found in most basic statistics and upper-level managerial finance texts.

Table 7.3
The Calculation of the Standard Deviation of
the Returns for Assets A and B

				Asset A		
i	k_i	$\bar{k}$	$k_i - \bar{k}$	$(k_i - \bar{k})^2$	Pr_i	$(k_i - \bar{k})^2 \times Pr_i$
1	13%	15%	−2%	4%	.25	1%
2	15	15	0	0	.50	0
3	17	15	2	4	.25	1

$$\sum_{i=1}^{3} (k_i - \bar{k})^2 \times Pr_i = 2\%$$

$$\sigma_{k_A} = \sqrt{\sum_{i=1}^{3} (k_i - \bar{k})^2 \times Pr_i} = \sqrt{2\%} = \underline{1.41\%}$$

				Asset B		
i	k_i	$\bar{k}$	$k_i - \bar{k}$	$(k_i - \bar{k})^2$	Pr_i	$(k_i - \bar{k})^2 \times Pr_i$
1	7%	15%	−8%	64%	.25	16%
2	15	15	0	0	.50	0
3	23	15	8	64	.25	16

$$\sum_{i=1}^{3} (k_i - \bar{k})^2 \times Pr_i = 32\%$$

$$\sigma_{k_B} = \sqrt{\sum_{i=1}^{3} (k_i - \bar{k})^2 \times Pr_i} = \sqrt{32\%} = \underline{5.66\%}$$

Figure 7.4
Normal Probability Distribution, with Ranges

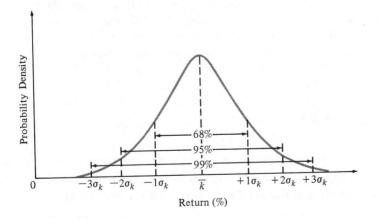

Coefficient of Variation

The **coefficient of variation,** *CV,* is a measure of relative dispersion that is useful in comparing the risk of assets with differing expected returns. Equation 7.4 gives the expression for the coefficient of variation:

$$CV = \frac{\sigma_k}{\bar{k}} \qquad (7.4)$$

The higher the coefficient of variation, the greater the risk.

Example
Substituting the standard deviation values (from Table 7.3) and the expected returns (from Table 7.2) for assets A and B into Equation 7.3, the coefficients of variation for A and B, respectively, are .094 (1.41% ÷ 15%) and .377 (5.66% ÷ 15%). Asset B has the higher coefficient of variation and is therefore more risky than asset A. Since both assets have the same expected return, the coefficient of variation has not provided any more information than the standard deviation.

The real utility of the coefficient of variation is in comparing assets that have *different* expected returns. A simple example will illustrate this point.

Example
A firm is attempting to select the less risky of two alternative assets—X and Y. The expected return, standard deviation, and coefficient of variation for each of these assets' returns is given below.

Statistics	Asset X	Asset Y
(1) Expected return	12%	20%
(2) Standard deviation	9%[a]	10%
(3) Coefficient of variation [(2) ÷ (1)]	.75	.50[a]

[a] Preferred asset using the given risk measure.

If the firm were to compare the assets solely on the basis of their standard deviations, it would prefer asset X, since asset X has a lower standard deviation than asset Y (9 percent versus 10 percent). However, comparing the coefficients of variation of the assets shows that management would be making a serious error in choosing asset X over asset Y, since the relative dispersion, or risk, of the assets as reflected in the coefficient of variation is lower for Y than for X (.50 versus .75). Clearly, the use of the coefficient of variation to compare asset risk is effective because it also considers the relative size, or expected return, of the assets.

FACT OR FABLE?   **3** **The coefficient of variation is more effective than the standard deviation in comparing the risk of assets that have different expected returns.** *(Fact)*

Figure 7.5
Risk as a Function of Time

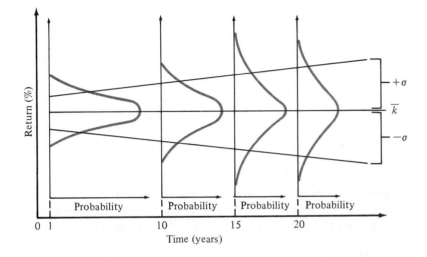

Risk and Time

Risk can be viewed not only with respect to the current time period but also as an *increasing function of time*. Figure 7.5 depicts probability distributions of returns for a 1-year, 10-year, 15-year, and 20-year forecast, assuming each year's expected returns are equal. A band representing $\pm$ 1 standard deviation, σ, from the expected return, $\bar{k}$, is indicated in the figure. It can be seen that the *variability of the returns, and therefore the risk, increases with the passage of time*. Generally, the longer-lived an asset investment, the greater its risk due to increasing variability of returns resulting from increased forecasting errors for distant years.[9]

Risk of a Portfolio

The risk of any single proposed asset investment should not be viewed independent of other assets. New investments must be considered in light of their impact on the risk and return of the *portfolio* of assets.[10] The financial manager's goal for the firm is to create an **efficient portfolio,** one that maximizes return for a given level of risk or minimizes risk for a given level of return. The statistical concept of correlation underlies the process of diversification that is used to develop an efficient portfolio of assets.

efficient portfolio A portfolio that maximizes return for a given level of risk or minimizes risk for a given level of return.

Correlation

Correlation is a statistical measure of the relationship, if any, between series of numbers representing any kind of data, from returns to test scores. If two series move in the same

correlation A statistical measure of the relationship, if any, between series of numbers representing data of any kind.

[9] These forecasting errors are normal since, in most situations, uncontrollable factors, such as strikes, wars, and inflation, are difficult, if not impossible, to predict but can have a very real effect on future returns.

[10] The portfolio of a firm, which would consist of its total assets, is not differentiated from the portfolio of an owner, which would likely contain a variety of different investment vehicles (i.e., assets). The differing characteristics of these two types of portfolios should become clear upon completion of Chapter 10.

Figure 7.6
The Correlation Between Series M and N

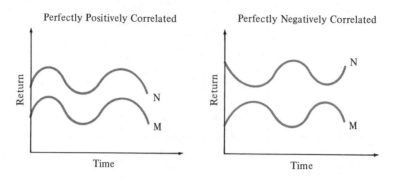

<table>
<tr><td>Perfectly Positively Correlated</td><td>Perfectly Negatively Correlated</td></tr>
</table>

positively correlated
Descriptive of two series
that move in the same
direction.

negatively correlated
Descriptive of two series
that move in opposite
directions.

correlation coefficient
A measure of the degree of
correlation between two
series.

**perfectly positively
correlated** Describes two
positively correlated series
having a correlation
coefficient of +1.

**perfectly negatively
correlated** Describes two
negatively correlated series
having a correlation
coefficient of −1.

uncorrelated Descriptive of
two series that lack any
relationship or interaction
and therefore have a
correlation coefficient of
zero.

direction, they are **positively correlated;** if the series move in opposite directions, they are **negatively correlated.** The degree of correlation is measured by the **correlation coefficient,** which has a range of +1 for **perfectly positively correlated** series and −1 for **perfectly negatively correlated** series. These two extremes are depicted for series M and N in Figure 7.6. The perfectly positively correlated series move exactly together, while the perfectly negatively correlated series move in exactly opposite directions.

Diversification

To reduce overall risk, it is best to combine or add to the portfolio assets that have a negative (or a low positive) correlation. By combining negatively correlated assets, the overall variability of returns, or risk, σ_k, can be reduced. Figure 7.7 shows that a portfolio containing the negatively correlated assets F and G, both having the same expected return, $\bar{k}$, also has the return, $\bar{k}$, but has less risk (variability) than either of the individual assets. Even if assets are not negatively correlated, the lower the positive correlation between them, the lower the resulting risk. Some assets are **uncorrelated,** that is, they are completely unrelated in the sense that there is no interaction between their returns. Combining uncorrelated assets can reduce risk—not as effectively as combining negatively correlated assets, but more effectively than combining positively correlated assets. The correlation

Figure 7.7
Combining Negatively Correlated Assets to Diversify Risk

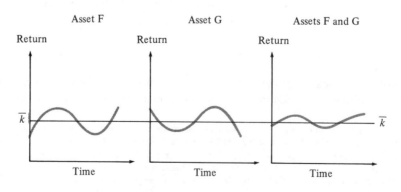

coefficient for uncorrelated assets is close to zero and acts as the midpoint between perfect positive and perfect negative correlation.

The creation of a portfolio by combining two assets having perfectly positively correlated returns *cannot* reduce the portfolio's overall risk below the risk of the least risky asset, whereas a portfolio combining two assets with less than perfectly positive correlation *can* reduce total risk to a level below that of either of the components, which in certain situations may be zero. For example, assume you are in the machine-tool manufacturing business which is very *cyclical,* having high sales when the economy is expanding and low sales during a recession. If you acquired another machine-tool company, which would have sales positively correlated with those of your firm, the combined sales would continue to be cyclical. As a result, risk would remain the same. As an alternative, however, you could acquire a sewing machine manufacturer which is *countercyclical,* having low sales during economic expansion and high sales during recession (since consumers are more likely to make their own clothes at such a time). Combination with the sewing machine manufacturer, which has negatively correlated sales, should reduce risk since the low machine tool sales during a recession would be balanced out by high sewing machine sales, and vice versa. A numeric example will provide a better understanding of the role of correlation in the diversification process.

Example

Table 7.4 presents the anticipated returns from three different assets—X, Y, and Z—over the next five years, along with their expected values and standard deviations. Each of the assets has an expected value of return of 12 percent and a standard deviation of 2.83 percent. The assets therefore have equal return and equal risk, although their return patterns are not necessarily identical. A comparison of the return patterns of assets X and Y shows that they are perfectly negatively correlated, since they move in exactly opposite directions over time. A comparison of assets X and Z shows that they are perfectly positively correlated, since they move in precisely the same direction. (Note that the returns for X and Z are identical.)[11]

Portfolio XY   By combining equal portions of assets X and Y—the perfectly negatively correlated assets—portfolio XY (shown in Table 7.4) is created.[12] The risk in the portfolio created by this combination, as reflected in the standard deviation, is reduced to 0 percent, while the expected return value remains at 12 percent. Since both assets have the same expected return values, are combined in equal parts, and are perfectly negatively correlated, the combination results in the complete elimination of risk. Whenever assets are perfectly negatively correlated, an optimum combination (similar to the 50–50 mix in the case of assets X and Y) exists for which the resulting standard deviation will equal 0.

[11] It is *not* necessary for return streams to be identical in order for them to be perfectly positively correlated. Identical return streams are used in this example to permit the concepts to be illustrated in the simplest, most straightforward fashion. Any return streams that move (i.e., vary) exactly together—regardless of the relative magnitude of the returns—are perfectly positively correlated.

[12] Although the assets are not divisible in actuality, for illustrative purposes it has been assumed that each of the assets—X, Y, and Z—can be divided up and combined with other assets in order to create portfolios. This assumption is made only to permit the concepts, again, to be illustrated in the simplest, most straightforward fashion.

Portfolio XZ   By combining equal portions of assets X and Z—the perfectly positively correlated assets—portfolio XZ (shown in Table 7.4) is created. The risk in this portfolio, as reflected by its standard deviation, which remains at 2.83 percent, is unaffected by this combination, and the expected return value remains at 12 percent. Whenever perfectly positively correlated assets such as X and Z are combined, the standard deviation of the resulting portfolio cannot be reduced below that of the least risky asset; the maximum portfolio standard deviation will be that of the riskiest asset. Since assets X and Z have the same standard deviation (2.83 percent), the minimum and maximum standard deviations are both 2.83 percent, which is the only value that could be taken on by a combination of these assets. This result can be attributed to the unlikely situation that X and Z are identical assets.

Table 7.4
Returns, Expected Values, and Standard Deviations for Assets X, Y, and Z and Portfolios XY and XZ

| | Assets | | | Portfolios | |
Year	X	Y	Z	XY[a] (50%X + 50%Y)	XZ[b] (50%X + 50%Z)
1989	8%	16%	8%	12%	8%
1990	10	14	10	12	10
1991	12	12	12	12	12
1992	14	10	14	12	14
1993	16	8	16	12	16
Statistics:					
Expected value	12%	12%	12%	12%	12%
Standard deviation[c]	2.83%	2.83%	2.83%	0%	2.83%

[a] Portfolio XY, which consists of 50 percent of asset X and 50 percent of asset Y, illustrates *perfect negative correlation*, since these two return streams behave in completely opposite fashion over the five-year period.

[b] Portfolio XZ, which consists of 50 percent of asset X and 50 percent of asset Z, illustrates *perfect positive correlation*, since these two return streams behave identically over the five-year period.

[c] Since the probabilities associated with the returns are not given, the formula given earlier in Equation 7.3 could not be used to calculate the standard deviations, σ_k. Instead the general formula

$$\sigma_k = \sqrt{\frac{\sum_{i=1}^{n} (k_i - \bar{k})^2}{n}}$$

where k_i = return i, $\bar{k}$ = expected value of return, and n = the number of outcomes considered, was used.

The portfolio standard deviations can be directly calculated from the standard deviations of the component securities using the following formula:

$$\sigma_k = \sqrt{x_1^2\sigma_1^2 + x_2^2\sigma_2^2 + 2x_1x_2r_{1,2}\sigma_1\sigma_2}$$

where x_1 and x_2 are the proportions of the component securities 1 and 2; σ_1 and σ_2 are the standard deviations of the component securities 1 and 2; and $r_{1,2}$ is the correlation coefficient between the returns of component securities 1 and 2.

Correlation, Diversification, Risk, and Return

In general, the lower (less positive and more negative) the correlation between asset returns, the greater the potential diversification of risk. (This should be clear from the behaviors illustrated in Table 7.4.) For each pair of assets there is a combination that will

Table 7.5
Correlation, Return, and Risk for Various Two-Asset Portfolio Combinations

Correlation coefficient	Range of return	Range of risk
+1 (perfect positive)	Between returns of two assets held in isolation	Between risk of two assets held in isolation
0 (uncorrelated)	Between returns of two assets held in isolation	Between risk of most risky asset and less than risk of least risky asset, but greater than 0
−1 (perfect negative)	Between returns of two assets held in isolation	Between risk of most risky asset and 0

result in the lowest risk (standard deviation) possible. The amount of potential risk reduction at this combination depends on the degree of correlation. This concept is a bit difficult to grasp since many potential combinations (assuming divisibility) could be made, given the expected return for each of two assets, the standard deviation for each asset, and the correlation coefficient. Note that only one combination of the infinite number of possibilities will minimize risk.

Three possible correlations—perfect positive, uncorrelated, and perfect negative—can be used to illustrate the effect of correlation on the diversification of risk and return. Table 7.5 summarizes the impact of correlation on the range of return and risk for various two-asset portfolio combinations. It should be clear from the table that as we move from perfect positive correlation to uncorrelated assets to perfect negative correlation, the ability to reduce risk is improved. Note that in no case will creating portfolios of assets result in greater risk than that of the riskiest asset included in the portfolio. An example may clarify this concept further.

---

4 Generally, the lower (less positive and more negative) the correlation between two assets' returns, the lower the risk of the portfolio that would result from combining them. *(Fact)*   **FACT OR FABLE?**

Example
A firm has carefully calculated the expected return, k, and risk, σ, for each of two assets—R and S—as summarized below:

Asset	Expected return, k	Risk (standard deviation), σ
R	6%	3%
S	8%	8%

From these data it can be seen that asset R is clearly a lower-risk, lower-return asset than asset S.

To evaluate possible combinations (assuming divisibility of the two assets), the firm considered three possible correlations—perfect positive, uncorrelated, and perfect negative. The results of the analysis are shown in frames A, B, and C and summarized in frame D of Figure 7.8. Each endpoint represents a portfolio consisting of 100 percent of the given asset and 0 percent of the other asset. All points on the line joining the two endpoints (R and S) represent portfolios consisting of various combinations of assets R and S.

The ranges of return and risk exhibited are consistent with those noted in Table 7.5. In all cases the return will range between the 6 percent return of R and the 8 percent return of S. The risk, on the other hand, ranges between the individual risks of R and S (from 3 percent to 8 percent) in the case of perfect positive correlation (frame A), ranges from below 3 percent (the risk of R) but greater than 0 to 8 percent (the risk of S) in the uncorrelated case (frame B), and ranges between 0 percent and 8 percent (the risk of S) in the perfectly negatively correlated case (frame C). Note that *only in the case of perfect negative correlation can the risk be reduced to 0*. It also can be seen in frame D, which includes all three cases plotted on the same set of axes, that as the correlation becomes less positive and more negative, the ability to reduce risk improves. Keep in mind that the amount of risk reduction achieved also depends on the proportions in which the assets are combined. While determination of the risk-minimizing combination is beyond the scope of this discussion, it is an important issue in developing portfolios of assets.

Risk and Return: The Capital Asset Pricing Model (CAPM)

The most important aspect of risk is the *overall risk* of the firm as viewed by investors in the marketplace. Overall risk significantly affects investment opportunities—and even more important, the owners' wealth. The basic theory that links together risk and return for all assets is commonly called the **capital asset pricing model (CAPM).** Here we will use CAPM to understand the basic risk-return trade-offs involved in all types of financial decisions.[13]

capital asset pricing model (CAPM) The basic theory that links together risk and return for all assets

Types of Risk

To understand the basic types of risk, consider what happens when we begin with a single security (asset) in a portfolio. Then we expand the portfolio by randomly selecting additional securities from, say, the population of all actively traded securities. Using the standard deviation, σ, to measure the total portfolio risk, Figure 7.9 depicts the behavior

[13] While CAPM has been widely accepted, an alternative theory, *Arbitrage Pricing Theory (APT),* first described by Stephen A. Ross, "The Arbitrage Theory of Capital Asset Pricing," *Journal of Economic Theory* (December 1976), pp. 341–360, has in recent years received a great deal of attention in the financial literature. The theory suggests that the risk premium on securities may result from a number of factors in addition to the market return used in CAPM. While testing of this theory confirms the importance of the market return, it has thus far failed to clearly identify other risk factors. We therefore concentrate our attention here on CAPM.

Figure 7.8
Portfolio Risk (σ) and Return (k) for Combinations of Assets R and S for Various Correlation Coefficients

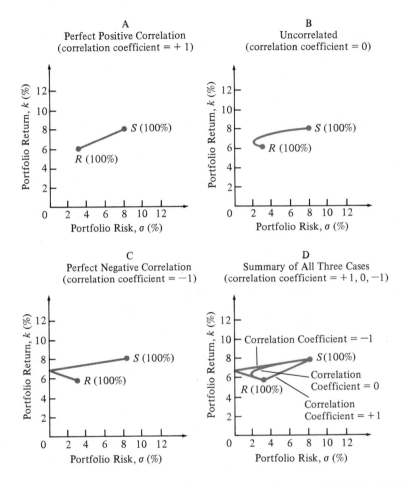

of the total portfolio risk (y-axis) as more securities are added (x-axis). With the addition of securities, the total portfolio risk declines, due to the effects of diversification (as explained in the previous section), and tends to approach a limit. Research has shown that virtually all the benefits of diversification, in terms of risk reduction, can be gained by forming portfolios containing 10 to 20 randomly selected securities.[14]

The **total risk** of a security can be viewed as consisting of two parts:

$$\text{Total security risk} = \text{nondiversifiable risk} + \text{diversifiable risk} \qquad (7.5)$$

Diversifiable risk, which is sometimes called *unsystematic risk,* represents the portion of an asset's risk associated with random causes that can be eliminated through diversification. It is attributable to firm-specific events, such as strikes, lawsuits, regulatory actions, loss of a key account, and so forth. **Nondiversifiable risk,** which is also called *systematic*

total risk The combination of a security's nondiversifiable risk and diversifiable risk.

diversifiable risk The portion of an asset's risk attributable to firm-specific, random events that can be eliminated through diversification.

nondiversifiable risk The relevant portion of an asset's risk attributable to factors that affect all firms; it cannot be eliminated through diversification.

[14] See, for example, W. H. Wagner and S. C. Lau, "The Effect of Diversification on Risk," *Financial Analysts Journal* 26 (November–December 1971), pp. 48–53, and Jack Evans and Stephen H. Archer, "Diversification and the Reduction of Dispersion: An Empirical Analysis," *Journal of Finance* 23 (December 1968), pp. 761–767.

Figure 7.9
Portfolio Risk and Diversification

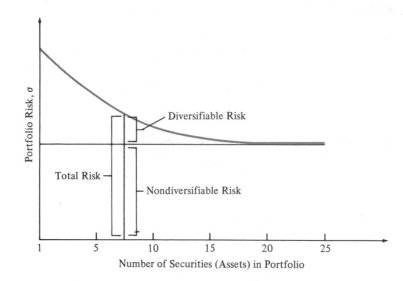

risk, is attributable to market factors that affect all firms. Factors such as war, inflation, international incidents, and political events account for nondiversifiable risk.

Because, as illustrated in Figure 7.9, any investor can create a portfolio of assets that will eliminate all, or virtually all, diversifiable risk, the *only relevant risk is nondiversifiable risk.* Any investor (or firm) must therefore be concerned solely with nondiversifiable risk, which reflects the contribution of an asset to the risk of the portfolio. The measurement of nondiversifiable risk is thus of primary importance in selecting those assets possessing the most desired risk-return characteristics.

The Model: CAPM

The capital asset pricing model (CAPM) links together nondiversifiable risk and return for all assets. We will discuss the model in four parts. The first part defines and describes the beta coefficient, which is a measure of nondiversifiable risk. The second part presents an equation of the model itself, and the third part graphically describes the relationship between risk and return. The final part presents some general comments on CAPM.

Beta Coefficient

beta coefficient, *b*
A measure of nondiversifiable risk. An index of the degree of movement of an asset's return in response to a change in the market return.

market return The return on the market portfolio of all traded securities.

The **beta coefficient, *b*,** is used to measure nondiversifiable risk. It is an *index* of the degree of movement of an asset's return in response to a change in the market return. The beta coefficient for an asset can be found by examining the asset's historical returns relative to the returns for the market.[15] The **market return** is the return on the market portfolio of all traded securities. The return on a portfolio of the stocks in *Standard & Poor's 500 Stock Composite Index* or some similar stock index is commonly used to

[15] The empirical measurement of beta is approached using regression analysis to find the regression coefficient (b_j) in the equation for the "characteristic line"

$$k_j = a_j + b_j k_m + e_j$$

Table 7.6
Beta Coefficients for Selected Stocks
(April 3, 1987)

Stock	Beta
Apple Computer	1.55
Avon Products	1.05
Briggs & Stratton	.70
CBS Inc.	1.10
Cascade Natural Gas	.60
Delta Air Lines	1.10
Exxon Corporation	.85
General Motors	1.10
Gerber Scientific	1.70
International Business Machines	1.05
Merrill Lynch & Company	1.75
NCR Corporation	1.30
Paine Webber Group	1.70
Reynolds & Reynolds	.95
Seagram Company	1.15
Standard Register	.85
Tandy Corporation	1.25
Union Electric	.75
USLIFE Corporation	1.05
Xerox Corporation	1.05

Source: *Value Line Investment Survey* (New York: Value Line, Inc., April 3, 1987).

measure the market return. Beta coefficients can be obtained for actively traded stocks from published sources, such as *Value Line Investment Survey,* or through brokerage firms. Betas for selected stocks are given in Table 7.6. The beta coefficient for the market is considered to be equal to 1.0; all other betas are viewed in relation to this value. Asset betas may take on values that are either positive or negative, but positive betas are the norm. The majority of beta coefficients fall between 0.5 and 2.0. Table 7.7 provides some selected beta values and their associated interpretations.

where

$$k_j = \text{the return on asset } j$$
$$a_j = \text{the intercept}$$
$$b_j = \text{the beta coefficient, which equals}$$
$$\frac{Cov\ (k_j,\ k_m)}{\sigma_m^2}$$

where

$Cov\ (k_j,\ k_m) = $ covariance of the return on asset j, k_j, and the market portfolio, k_m

$\sigma_m^2 = $ variance of the return on the market portfolio

$k_m = $ the required rate of return on the market portfolio of securities

$e_j = $ random error term, which reflects the diversifiable or unsystematic risk of asset j

Because of the somewhat rigorous calculations involved in finding betas, the interested reader is referred to an advanced managerial finance or investments text for a more detailed discussion of this topic.

Table 7.7
Selected Beta Coefficients and Their Interpretations

Beta	Comment	Interpretation[a]
2.0 ⎫	Move in same	⎧ Twice as responsive, or risky, as the market
1.0 ⎬	direction as	⎨ Same response or risk as the market (i.e., average risk)
.5 ⎭	market	⎩ Only half as responsive, or risky, as the market
0		Unaffected by market movement
− .5 ⎫	Move in opposite	⎧ Only half as responsive, or risky, as the market
−1.0 ⎬	direction to	⎨ Same response or risk as the market (i.e., average risk)
−2.0 ⎭	market	⎩ Twice as responsive, or risky, as the market

[a] A stock that is twice as responsive as the market will experience a 2 percent change in its return for each 1 percent change in the return of the market portfolio, whereas the return of a stock that is half as responsive as the market will change by $\frac{1}{2}$ of 1 percent for each 1 percent change in the return of the market portfolio.

FACT OR FABLE?

5 The beta coefficient, b, is an index of the degree of movement of an asset's return in response to a change in the risk-free rate of return. (*Fable*)
The beta coefficient is an index of the degree of movement of an asset's return in response to a change in the *market return*.

The Equation

Using the beta coefficient, b, to measure nondiversifiable risk, the *capital asset pricing model (CAPM)* is given in Equation 7.6:

$$k_j = R_F + [b_j \times (k_m - R_F)] \tag{7.6}$$

where

$$k_j = \text{required return on asset } j$$
$$R_F = \text{risk-free rate of return, commonly measured by the return on a U.S. Treasury bill}$$
$$b_j = \text{beta coefficient or index of nondiversifiable risk for asset } j$$
$$k_m = \text{market return; the return on the market portfolio of assets}$$

The required return on an asset, k_j, is an increasing function of beta, b_j, which measures nondiversifiable risk. In other words, *the higher the risk, the higher the required return, and vice versa*. The model can be broken into two parts: (1) the *risk-free rate, R_F*; and (2) the *risk premium, $b_j \times (k_m - R_F)$*. The $(k_m - R_F)$ portion of the risk premium is called the *market risk premium*, since it represents the premium the investor must receive for taking the average amount of risk associated with holding the market portfolio of assets. Let us look at an example.

Example

Benjamin Corporation wishes to determine the required return on an asset—asset Z—that has a beta, b_z, of 1.5. The risk-free rate of return is found to be 7 percent; the

---

PROFILE

TED TURNER:
Building an Empire on Risk

Ted Turner understands risk. Since 1964, when he inherited a billboard company deep in red ink, he has gambled over and over, building Turner Broadcasting System into an empire. His purchase of the MGM film library may be among his riskiest deals. The MGM deal was struck in March 1986. It was rooted in Turner's drive to protect the future of WTBS, the cable station that is his most valuable asset. The encroaching shadow Turner saw was increasingly expensive programming. Hollywood studios' rising fees for movies and other shows had become a threat to profits.

Turner moved to stem the tide. First, he attempted a hostile takeover of CBS. Owning CBS would have increased his power as a purchaser of movies, helping him negotiate lower prices. But the takeover became a costly debacle. Next Turner moved to buy the programming outright. His target was the huge MGM film library.

Turner's intentions brought him to the bargaining table with Kirk Kerkorian, who controlled Metro-Goldwyn-Mayer/United Artists Enter-

tainment. The unexpected happened when Turner, who had wanted only a film library, agreed to buy all of MGM/UA, assuming its huge indebtedness. As part of the deal, he sold a debt-free United Artists back to Kerkorian and stockholders. Net cost to Turner: $1.6 billion, more than twice MGM's market value.

The financing included an issue of 53 million shares of preferred stock in TBS, transferred to Kerkorian and

MGM/UA stockholders. To make an initial debt payment of $600 million, furthermore, Turner sold MGM, without the film library, back to Kerkorian and to Lorimar-Telepictures for a total of $490 million. Finally, Turner guaranteed the value of the preferred stock he issued. If its dividend falls below $1.45 per share, he must supplement it with new shares of TBS common stock. If the common falls below $15 in value, he must supplement it with preferred. A vicious cycle of stock issues could dilute Turner's control, leaving him without the cherished asset he set out to protect.

Has Kerkorian outwitted Turner? Kerkorian now has much of the original MGM/UA, new cash and securities, more money to come, and a chance to gain control of TBS. Turner has the hugely expensive films, a perhaps-temporary 81 percent of TBS, and crushing indebtedness. Yet Turner claims he has won the game. He has long familiarity with indebtedness and has built his empire on risk. Many still bet on Turner. But betting on him is not for the fainthearted.

---

return on the market portfolio of assets is 11 percent. Substituting $b_z = 1.5$, $R_F = 7$ percent, and $k_m = 11$ percent into the capital asset pricing model given in Equation 7.6 yields a required return:

$$k_z = 7\% + [1.5 \times (11\% - 7\%)] = 7\% + 6\% = \underline{13\%}$$

It can be seen that the market risk premium of 4 percent (11 percent − 7 percent), when adjusted for the asset's index of risk (beta) of 1.5, results in a risk premium of 6 percent (1.5 × 4%), which when added to the 7 percent risk-free rate, results in a 13 percent required return. Other things being equal, the higher the beta, the greater the required return, and vice versa.

The Graph: The Security Market Line (SML)

security market line (SML)
The depiction of the capital asset pricing model (CAPM) as a graph.

When the capital asset pricing model (Equation 7.6) is depicted graphically, it is called the **security market line (SML).** The SML will, in fact, be a straight line. It reflects for each level of nondiversifiable risk (beta) the required return in the marketplace. In the graph, risk as measured by beta, b, is plotted on the x-axis, and required returns, k, are plotted on the y-axis. The risk-return trade-off is clearly represented by the SML. Let us look at an illustration.

Example

In the preceding example for the Benjamin Corporation, the risk-free rate, R_F, was 7 percent, and the market return, k_m, was 11 percent. Since the betas associated with R_F and k_m, b_{R_F} and b_m, are by definition 0[16] and 1, respectively, the SML can be plotted using these two sets of coordinates (i.e., $b_{R_F} = 0$, $R_F = 7\%$, and $b_m = 1$, $k_m = 11\%$). Figure 7.10 presents the security market line that results from plotting the coordinates given. As traditionally shown, the security market line in Figure 7.10 presents the required return associated with all positive betas. The market risk premium of 4 percent (k_m of 11 percent minus R_F of 7 percent) has been highlighted. Using the beta for asset Z, b_z, of 1.5, its corresponding required return, k_z, is 13 percent. Also shown in the figure is asset Z's risk premium of 6 percent (k_z of 13% minus R_F of 7%). It should be clear that for assets with betas greater than 1, the risk premium is greater than that for the market; for assets with betas less than 1, the risk premium is less than that for the market.

FACT OR FABLE?

6 The capital asset pricing model (CAPM) reflects a positive relationship between an asset's nondiversifiable risk measured by beta and its required return. *(Fact)*

Some Comments on CAPM

The capital asset pricing model generally relies on historical data to estimate required returns. The betas, which are developed by using data for the given asset as well as for the market, may or may not actually reflect the *future* variability of returns. Therefore, the required returns specified by the model can be viewed only as rough approximations. Analysts and other users of betas commonly make subjective adjustments to the historically determined betas in order to reflect their expectations of the future when such expectations differ from the actual risk-return behaviors of the past.

efficient market An assumed "perfect" market in which there are many small investors, each having the same information with respect to securities; there are no restrictions on investment, no taxes, and no transaction costs; and all investors view securities similarly and prefer higher returns and lower risk.

The CAPM was actually developed to explain the behavior of security prices and provide a mechanism whereby investors could assess the impact of a proposed security investment on their portfolio's overall risk and return. It is actually based on an assumed **efficient market** in which there are many small investors, each having the same information with respect to securities; there are no restrictions on investment, no taxes, and no transaction costs; and all investors view securities similarly and prefer higher returns and lower risk. While this perfect world appears unrealistic, empirical studies have provided

---

[16] Since R_F is the rate of return on a risk-free asset, the beta associated with the risk-free asset, b_{R_F}, would equal 0. The 0 beta on the risk-free asset reflects not only its absence of risk but also that the asset's return is unaffected by movements in the market return.

Figure 7.10
The Security Market Line (SML) with Benjamin Corporation's Asset Z Data Shown

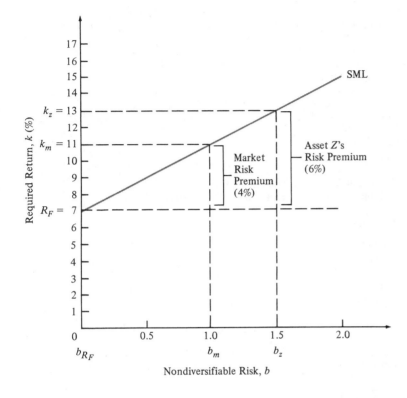

support for the existence of the relationships described by CAPM in active markets such as the New York Stock Exchange. In the case of real corporate assets, such as plant and equipment, research thus far has failed to prove the general applicability of CAPM because of indivisibility, relatively large size, limited number of transactions, and absence of an efficient market for such assets.

In spite of the fact that the risk-return trade-off described by CAPM is not generally applicable to all assets, it provides a useful conceptual framework for evaluating and linking risk and return. An awareness of this trade-off and an attempt to somehow capture and consider risk as well as return in financial decision making should aid the financial manager in achieving the goal of owner wealth maximization.

Summary

● The key risk and return definitions and formulas are given in Table 7.8.

● Risk is the chance of loss, or, more formally, refers to the variability of returns. Return is the change in value plus any cash distributions expressed as a percentage of the initial value. Most financial decision makers are risk-averse.

● The risk of a single asset is measured in much the same way as the risk of a portfolio, or collection, of assets, but it is often useful to differentiate between them, since certain benefits often accrue to holders of portfolios.

● Two approaches commonly used to get a sense of asset risk are sensitivity analysis and the use of probabilities. Probability

Table 7.8
Summary of Key Definitions and Formulas for Risk and Return

Variable definitions

k_t = actual, expected, or required return during period t

P_t = price (value) of asset at time t

P_{t-1} = price (value) of asset at time $t - 1$

C_t = cash received from the asset investment in the time period $t - 1$ to t

$\bar{k}$ = expected value of a return

k_i = return for the ith outcome

Pr_i = probability of occurrence of the ith outcome

n = number of outcomes considered

σ_k = standard deviation of returns

CV = coefficient of variation

k_j = required return on asset j

R_F = risk-free rate of return

b_j = beta coefficient or index of nondiversifiable risk for asset j

k_m = market return; the return on the market portfolio of assets

Risk and return formulas

Rate of return during period t

$$k_t = \frac{P_t - P_{t-1} + C_t}{P_{t-1}}$$
[Eq. 7.1]

Expected value of a return

$$\bar{k} = \sum_{i=1}^{n} k_i \times Pr_i$$
[Eq. 7.2]

Standard deviation of returns

$$\sigma_k = \sqrt{\sum_{i=1}^{n} (k_i - \bar{k})^2 \times Pr_i}$$
[Eq. 7.3]

Coefficient of variation

$$CV = \frac{\sigma_k}{\bar{k}}$$
[Eq. 7.4]

Capital asset pricing model (CAPM)

$$k_j = R_F + [b_j \times (k_m - R_F)]$$
[Eq. 7.6]

distributions—bar charts or continuous distributions—can be used to examine risk.

● Two statistics that can be used to measure an asset's risk—dispersion around the expected value—are the standard deviation and the coefficient of variation. Risk is an increasing function of time.

● New investments must be considered in light of their impact on the portfolio of assets. The correlation of asset returns affects the diversification process.

● The only relevant risk is nondiversifiable risk, since diversifi-

able risk can be easily eliminated through diversification. Nondiversifiable risk can be measured by the beta coefficient.

● The capital asset pricing model (CAPM) uses beta to relate an asset's risk relative to the market to the asset's required return. The graphic depiction of the CAPM is the security market line (SML).

● CAPM relies on historical data to estimate required returns. Because it best explains the behavior of security prices in efficient markets, it is used by the financial decision maker to provide a conceptual framework, rather than a quantitative tool, for evaluating and linking risk and return.

Questions

7-1 Define *risk* as it relates to financial decision making. Why is it important for a decision maker to have some sense of the risk or uncertainty associated with an investment in an asset? Do any assets have perfectly certain returns?

7-2 Describe the basic calculation involved in finding the return on an investment. Differentiate between realized and unrealized returns.

7-3 Compare and contrast the following risk-preference behaviors and indicate which is most commonly exhibited by the financial manager.

    a. Risk-averse

    b. Risk-indifferent

    c. Risk-taking

7-4 How can *sensitivity analysis* be used to assess asset risk? What is one of the most common methods of sensitivity analysis? Define and describe the role of the *range* as an aid in sensitivity analysis.

7-5 How does a plot of the *probability distribution* of outcomes allow the decision maker to get a sense of asset risk? What is the difference between a bar chart and a continuous probability distribution?

7-6 What does the *standard deviation* of a distribution of asset

returns indicate? What relationship exists between the size of the standard deviation and the degree of asset risk?

7-7 What is the *coefficient of variation?* How is it calculated? When is the coefficient of variation preferred over the standard deviation for comparing asset risk?

7-8 Why must assets be evaluated in a portfolio context? What is an *efficient portfolio?* Why is the *correlation* between asset returns important?

7-9 How does diversification of risk in the asset selection process allow the investor to combine risky assets so that the risk of the portfolio is less than the risk of the individual assets in it?

7-10 What is the relationship of total risk, nondiversifiable risk, and diversifiable risk? Why would someone argue that nondiversifiable risk is the only relevant risk?

7-11 What risk is measured by *beta?* Define beta. Where can betas be obtained?

7-12 What is the equation for the *capital asset pricing model (CAPM)?* Explain the meaning of each variable. Assuming a risk-free rate of 8 percent and a market return of 12 percent, graph the risk-return trade-off as defined by the CAPM.

7-13 Why do financial managers have difficulty applying CAPM in decision making? Generally, what benefit does CAPM provide them?

Self-Test Problems

(Solutions on page 243)

ST-1 You have been asked for your advice in selecting a portfolio of assets and have been supplied with the following data:

	Expected Return (%)		
Year	Asset A	Asset B	Asset C
1989	12	16	12
1990	14	14	14
1991	16	12	16

No probabilities have been supplied. You have been told that you can create two portfolios—one consisting of assets A and B and the other consisting of assets A and C—by investing equal proportions (i.e., 50 percent) in each of the two component assets.

a. What is the expected return for each asset over the three-year period?

b. What is the standard deviation for each asset's return?

c. What is the expected return for each of the two portfolios?

d. How would you characterize the correlations of returns of the two assets making up each of the two portfolios identified in **c**?

e. What is the standard deviation for each portfolio?

f. Which portfolio do you recommend? Why?

ST-2 Currently under consideration is a project with a beta, b, of 1.50. At this time the risk-free rate of return, R_F, is 7 percent and the return on the market portfolio of assets, k_m, is 10 percent. The project is actually *expected* to earn an annual rate of return of 11 percent.

a. If the return on the market portfolio were to increase by 10 percent, what would happen to the project's *required return?* What if the market return were to decline by 10 percent?

b. Use the capital asset pricing model (CAPM) to find the *required return* on this investment.

c. Based upon your calculation in **b,** would you recommend this investment? Why or why not?

Problems

7-1 (**Rate of Return**) Douglas Keel, a financial analyst for Orange Industries, wishes to estimate the rate of return for two similar-risk investments—X and Y. Keel's research indicates that the immediate past returns will act as reasonable estimates of future return. A year earlier, investment X had a market value of $20,000 and investment Y, of $55,000. During the year, investment X generated cash flow of $1,500 and investment Y, of $6,800. The current market values of investments X and Y are $21,000 and $55,000, respectively.

a. Calculate the expected rate of return on investments X and Y using the most recent year's data.

b. Assuming that the two investments are equally risky, which one should Keel recommend? Why?

7-2 (**Return Calculations**) For each of the following investments, calculate the rate of return earned over the unspecified time period.

Investment	Beginning-of-period value ($)	End-of-period value ($)	Cash flow during period ($)
A	800	1,100	−100
B	120,000	118,000	15,000
C	45,000	48,000	7,000
D	600	500	80
E	12,500	12,400	1,500

7-3   **(Risk Preferences)** Sharon Smith, the financial manager for Barnett Corporation, wishes to evaluate three prospective investments—X, Y, and Z. Currently the firm earns 12 percent on its investments, which have a risk index of 6 percent. The three investments under consideration are profiled below in terms of expected return and expected risk.

Investment	Expected return (%)	Expected risk index (%)
X	14	7
Y	12	8
Z	10	9

a. If Sharon Smith were *risk-indifferent,* which investments would she select? Explain why.

b. If Sharon Smith were *risk-averse,* which investments would she select? Explain why.

c. If Sharon Smith were a *risk taker,* which investments would she select? Explain why.

d. Given the traditional risk-preference behavior exhibited by financial managers, which investment would be preferred? Why?

7-4   **(Risk Analysis)** Solar Designs is considering an investment in an expanded product line. Two possible types of expansion are being considered. After investigating the possible outcomes, the following estimates were made:

	Expansion A	Expansion B
Initial investment	$12,000	$12,000
Annual rate of return		
Pessimistic	16%	10%
Most likely	20	20
Optimistic	24	30

a. Determine the range of the rates of return for each of the two projects.

b. Which project is less risky? Why?

c. If you were making the investment decision, which one would you choose? Why? What does this imply about your feelings toward risk?

d. Assume that expansion B's most likely outcome was 21 percent per year and all other facts remained the same. Does this change your answer to part **c**? Why?

7-5   **(Risk and Probability)** Micro-Pub, Inc., is considering the purchase of one of two micro-film cameras—R or S. Both should provide benefits over a ten-year period, and each requires an initial investment of $4,000. Management has constructed the following table of estimates of probabilities and rates of return for pessimistic, most likely, and optimistic results:

	Camera R		Camera S	
	Amount	**Probability**	**Amount**	**Probability**
Initial investment	$4,000	1.00	$4,000	1.00
Annual rate of return				
Pessimistic	20%	.25	15%	.20
Most likely	25	.50	25	.55
Optimistic	30	.25	35	.25

a. Determine the range for the rate of return for each of the two cameras.

b. Determine the expected rate of return for each camera.

c. Which camera is more risky? Why?

7-6 **(Bar Charts and Risk)** Swan's Sportswear is considering bringing out a line of designer jeans. Currently it is negotiating with two different well-known designers. Because of the highly competitive nature of the industry, the two designs have been given code names. After market research, the firm has established the following expectations about the annual rates of return:

		Annual rate of return	
Market acceptance	**Probability**	**Line J**	**Line K**
Very poor	.05	.0075	.010
Poor	.15	.0125	.025
Average	.60	.0850	.080
Good	.15	.1475	.135
Excellent	.05	.1625	.150

Use the table to:

a. Construct a bar chart for each line's annual rate of return.

b. Calculate the expected value of return for each line.

c. Evaluate the relative riskiness for each jean line's rate of return using the bar charts.

7-7 (Assessing Return and Risk) Swift Manufacturing must choose between two asset purchases. The annual rate of return and the related probabilities given below summarize the firm's analysis to this point.

Project 257		Project 432	
Rate of return	Probability	Rate of return	Probability
−10%	.01	10%	.05
10	.04	15	.10
20	.05	20	.10
30	.10	25	.15
40	.15	30	.20
45	.30	35	.15
50	.15	40	.10
60	.10	45	.10
70	.05	50	.05
80	.04		
100	.01		

a. For each project, compute:
   (1) The range of possible rates of return.
   (2) The expected value of return.
   (3) The standard deviation of the returns.
   (4) The coefficient of variation.

b. Construct a bar chart of each distribution of rates of return.

c. Which project would you consider the less risky? Why?

7-8 (Integrative—Expected Return, Standard Deviation, and Coefficient of Variation) Three assets—F, G, and H—are currently being considered by Perth Industries. The following probability distributions of expected returns for these assets have been developed.

	Asset F		Asset G		Asset H	
i	Pr_i	Return, k_i	Pr_i	Return, k_i	Pr_i	Return, k_i
1	.10	40%	.40	35%	.10	40%
2	.20	10	.30	10	.20	20
3	.40	0	.30	−20	.40	10
4	.20	− 5			.20	0
5	.10	−10			.10	−20

a. Calculate the expected value of return, $\bar{k}$, for each of the three assets. Which provides the largest expected return?

b. Calculate the standard deviation, σ_k, for each of the three assets' returns. Which appears to have the greatest risk?

c. Calculate the coefficient of variation, CV, for each of the three assets. Which appears to have the largest *relative* risk?

7-9   **(Normal Probability Distribution)** Assuming that the rates of return associated with a given asset investment are normally distributed and that the expected return, $\bar{k}$, is 18.9 percent and the coefficient of variation, CV, is 2.25, answer the following questions.

  a. Find the standard deviation of returns, σ_k.

  b. Calculate the range of expected return outcomes associated with the following probabilities of occurrence.
  (1) 68 percent
  (2) 95 percent
  (3) 99 percent

  c. Draw the probability distribution associated with your findings in **a** and **b**.

7-10 **(Correlation, Risk, and Return)** Matt Peters wishes to evaluate the risk and return behaviors associated with various combinations of assets V and W under three assumed degrees of correlation—perfect positive, uncorrelated, and perfect negative. The following expected return and risk values were calculated for each of the assets.

Asset	Expected return, $\bar{k}$ (%)	Risk (standard deviation), σ_k (%)
V	8	5
W	13	10

  a. If the returns of assets V and W are *perfectly positively correlated* (correlation coefficient = +1), describe the *range* of (1) expected return and (2) risk associated with all possible portfolio combinations.

  b. If the returns of assets V and W are *uncorrelated* (correlation coefficient = 0), describe the *approximate range* of (1) expected return and (2) risk associated with all possible portfolio combinations.

  c. If the returns of assets V and W are *perfectly negatively correlated* (correlation coefficient = −1), describe the *range* of (1) expected return and (2) risk associated with all possible portfolio combinations.

7-11 **(Total, Nondiversifiable, and Diversifiable Risk)** David Talbot randomly selected securities from all those listed on the New York Stock Exchange for his portfolio. He began with one security and added securities one by one until a total of 20 securities were held in the portfolio. After each security was added, David calculated the portfolio standard deviation, σ. The calculated values are given below:

Number of securities	Portfolio risk, σ (%)	Number of securities	Portfolio risk, σ (%)
1	14.50	11	7.00
2	13.30	12	6.80
3	12.20	13	6.70
4	11.20	14	6.65
5	10.30	15	6.60
6	9.50	16	6.56
7	8.80	17	6.52
8	8.20	18	6.50
9	7.70	19	6.48
10	7.30	20	6.47

a. On a set of number of securities in portfolio (*x*-axis)–portfolio risk (*y*-axis) axes, plot the portfolio risk data given in the preceding table.

b. Divide the total portfolio risk in the graph into its *nondiversifiable* and *diversifiable* risk components and label each of these on the graph.

c. Describe which of the two risk components is the *relevant risk* and explain why it is relevant. How much of this risk exists in David Talbot's portfolio?

7-12 **(Interpreting Beta)** A firm wishes to assess the impact of changes in the market return on one of its assets that has a beta of 1.20.

a. If the market return increased by 15 percent, what impact would this change have on the asset's return?

b. If the market return decreased by 8 percent, what impact would this change have on the asset's return?

c. If the market return did not change, what impact, if any, would there be on the asset's return?

d. Would this asset be considered more or less risky than the market? Explain.

7-13 **(Betas)** Answer the questions below for each of the following assets.

Asset	Beta
A	0.50
B	1.60
C	−0.20
D	0.90

a. What impact would a *10 percent increase* in the market return have on each asset's return?

b. What impact would a *10 percent decrease* in the market return have on each asset's return?

c. If you were certain that the market return would *increase* in the near future, which asset would you prefer? Why?

d. If you were certain that the market return would *decrease* in the near future, which asset would you prefer? Why?

7-14 **(Betas and Risk Rankings)** Stock A has a beta of 0.80, Stock B has a beta of 1.40, and Stock C has a beta of −0.30.

a. Rank these stocks from the most risky to the least risky.

b. If the return on the market portfolio increases by 12 percent, what change in the return for each of the stocks would you expect?

c. If the return on the market portfolio declines by 5 percent, what change in the return for each of the stocks would you expect?

d. If you felt the stock market was just ready to experience a significant decline, which stock would you likely add to your portfolio? Why?

e. If you anticipated a major stock market rally, which stock would you add to your portfolio? Why?

7-15 (**Capital Asset Pricing Model—CAPM**) For each of the following cases, use the capital asset pricing model to find the required return.

Case	Risk-free rate, R_F (%)	Market return, k_m (%)	Beta, b
A	5	8	1.30
B	8	13	.90
C	9	12	−.20
D	10	15	1.00
E	6	10	.60

7-16 (**Manipulating CAPM**) Use the basic equation for the capital asset pricing model (CAPM) to work each of the following:

a. Find the *required return* for an asset with a beta of 0.90 when the risk-free rate and market return are 8 percent and 12 percent, respectively.

b. Find the *risk-free rate* for a firm with a required return of 15 percent and a beta of 1.25 when the market return is 14 percent.

c. Find the *market return* for an asset with a required return of 16 percent and a beta of 1.10 when the risk-free rate is 9 percent.

d. Find the *beta* for an asset with a required return of 15 percent when the risk-free rate and market return are 10 percent and 12.5 percent, respectively.

7-17 (**Security Market Line—SML**) Assume that the risk-free rate, R_F, is currently 9 percent and that the market return, k_m, is currently 13 percent.

a. Draw the security market line (SML) on a set of nondiversifiable risk (*x*-axis)–required return (*y*-axis) axes.

b. Calculate and label on the axes in **a** the *market risk premium*.

c. Given the data above, calculate the required return on asset A having a beta of 0.80 and asset B having a beta of 1.30.

d. Draw in the betas and required returns from **c** for assets A and B on the axes in **a**. Label the *risk premium* associated with each of these assets and discuss them.

7-18 (**Integrative—Risk, Return, and CAPM**) Wolff Enterprises must consider several investment projects, A through E, using the capital asset pricing model (CAPM) and its graphic representation, the security market line (SML). Use the following table to answer the questions at the top of page 243.

Item	Rate of return (%)	Beta (b) value
Risk-free asset	9	0
Market portfolio	14	1.00
Project A	—	1.50
Project B	—	.75
Project C	—	2.00
Project D	—	0
Project E	—	−.50

a. Calculate the required return and risk premium for each project, given its level of nondiversifiable risk.

b. Graph the security market line (required rate of return relative to nondiversifiable risk) for all projects listed in the table.

c. Discuss the relative nondiversifiable risk of projects A through E.

Solutions to Self-Test Problems

ST-1 **a.** Expected return, $\bar{k} = \dfrac{\Sigma \text{Returns}}{3}$

$$\bar{k}_A = \frac{12\% + 14\% + 16\%}{3} = \frac{42\%}{3} = \underline{\underline{14\%}}$$

$$\bar{k}_B = \frac{16\% + 14\% + 12\%}{3} = \frac{42\%}{3} = \underline{\underline{14\%}}$$

$$\bar{k}_C = \frac{12\% + 14\% + 16\%}{3} = \frac{42\%}{3} = \underline{\underline{14\%}}$$

b. Standard deviation, $\sigma = \sqrt{\dfrac{\displaystyle\sum_{i=1}^{3} (k_i - \bar{k})^2}{n}}$

$$\sigma_A = \sqrt{\frac{(12\% - 14\%)^2 + (14\% - 14\%)^2 + (16\% - 14\%)^2}{3}} = \sqrt{\frac{4\% + 0\% + 4\%}{3}} = \sqrt{\frac{8\%}{3}} = \underline{\underline{1.63\%}}$$

$$\sigma_B = \sqrt{\frac{(16\% - 14\%)^2 + (14\% - 14\%)^2 + (12\% - 14\%)^2}{3}} = \sqrt{\frac{4\% + 0\% + 4\%}{3}} = \sqrt{\frac{8\%}{3}} = \underline{\underline{1.63\%}}$$

$$\sigma_C = \sqrt{\frac{(12\% - 14\%)^2 + (14\% - 14\%)^2 + (16\% - 14\%)^2}{3}} = \sqrt{\frac{4\% + 0\% + 4\%}{3}} = \sqrt{\frac{8\%}{3}} = \underline{\underline{1.63\%}}$$

c.

	Annual expected returns	
Year	**Portfolio AB**	**Portfolio AC**
1989	$(.50 \times 12\%) + (.50 \times 16\%) = 14\%$	$(.50 \times 12\%) + (.50 \times 12\%) = 12\%$
1990	$(.50 \times 14\%) + (.50 \times 14\%) = 14\%$	$(.50 \times 14\%) + (.50 \times 14\%) = 14\%$
1991	$(.50 \times 16\%) + (.50 \times 12\%) = 14\%$	$(.50 \times 16\%) + (.50 \times 16\%) = 16\%$

Over the three-year period:

$$\bar{k}_{AB} = \frac{14\% + 14\% + 14\%}{3} = \frac{42\%}{3} = \underline{\underline{14\%}}$$

$$\bar{k}_{AC} = \frac{12\% + 14\% + 16\%}{3} = \frac{42\%}{3} = \underline{\underline{14\%}}$$

d. AB is perfectly negatively correlated.
AC is perfectly positively correlated.

e. Standard deviation of portfolios

$$\sigma_{AB} = \sqrt{\frac{(14\% - 14\%)^2 + (14\% - 14\%)^2 + (14\% - 14\%)^2}{3}} = \sqrt{\frac{0\% + 0\% + 0\%}{3}} = \sqrt{\frac{0\%}{3}} = \underline{\underline{0\%}}$$

$$\sigma_{AC} = \sqrt{\frac{(12\% - 14\%)^2 + (14\% - 14\%)^2 + (16\% - 14\%)^2}{3}} = \sqrt{\frac{4\% + 0\% + 4\%}{3}} = \sqrt{\frac{8\%}{3}} = \underline{\underline{1.63\%}}$$

f. Portfolio AB is preferred since it provides the same return (14%) as AC but with less risk $[(\sigma_{AB} = 0\%) < (\sigma_{AC} = 1.63\%)]$.

ST-2 **a.** When the market return increases by 10 percent, the project's required return would increase by 15 percent ($10\% \times 1.50$). When the market return decreases by 10 percent, the project's required return would decrease by 15 percent ($-10\% \times 1.50$).

b. $k_j = R_F + [b_j \times (k_m - R_F)]$
$= 7\% + [1.50 \times (10\% - 7\%)]$
$= 7\% + 4.5\% = \underline{\underline{11.5\%}}$

c. No, the project should be rejected since its expected return of 11 percent is less than the 11.5 percent return required from the project.

CHAPTER 8

Valuation

FACT OR FABLE?
Are the following statements fact *(true)* or fable *(false)?*

1
The value of any asset regardless of its pattern of expected cash flow is the present value of all future cash flows it is expected to provide over the relevant time period.

2
When the required return on a bond is greater than its coupon interest rate, the bond sells at a premium; when the required return is less than the coupon rate, it sells at a discount.

3
The longer the period of time until a bond matures, the less responsive is its market value to a given change in the required return.

4
The value of a share of common stock is equal to the present value of all the dividends it is expected to provide over an infinite time horizon.

5
The variable growth common stock valuation model can be used to estimate the value of preferred stock, while the zero growth model is the most widely cited dividend valuation approach.

6
The decisions of financial managers, through their effect on expected return (measured using expected future dividends) and risk (measured using the required return), can cause the value of the firm to change.

What would you do if your company's profits plummeted from $210 million to $16 million in one year? If the value of your stock plunged to less than half its highest value as investors lost confidence in your ability to pay them a worthwhile return?

In 1984, this frightening scenario happened to An Wang, chairman and CEO of Wang Laboratories. From the production of calculators in the 1950s to word processing equipment in the 1960s, Wang built a business that in 1984 was valued at $2.4 billion. He employed about 30,000 people and maintained a growth rate of 30 percent a year. Wang Labs was tops in its market. Wang himself was one of the richest people in the United States.

What happened to destroy investor confidence? Analysts cite several reasons. First, the introduction of personal computers into the office gave word processors tough competition. Computer compatibility became increasingly important. Although most Wang customers used IBM or DEC equipment, Wang ignored their need to connect diverse machines. Then Wang decided to turn over leadership of the company to his oldest son, Fred. Both former president John Cunningham and his successor J. Carl Masi admit leaving because Fred Wang represented an impasse in their careers. Finally, morale problems and cost-cutting measures resulted in the exodus of much Wang talent.

The chips were down. Wang abandoned a short-lived retirement to return to the company's helm. Hand-holding key customers and bagging a $480 million minicomputer sale to the Air Force, he brought his company back into the black with $29 million in profits for the first six months of fiscal 1986. But problems persisted. Despite the layoff of 2,600 employees and severe austerity measures, the company showed about a $79 million loss for the last quarter of 1986. Wang began great efforts to revamp the product line and rebuild the company's credibility. First quarter 1987 sales showed an increase of 10 percent and Wang stock climbed from $11 to $16 a share.

Although Wang Laboratories has had major setbacks, its primary goal is to increase its stock price, thereby positively impacting its owners' wealth. Here we present the important concepts linking risk and return to value and describe their implications for financial decision making.

Valuation Fundamentals

valuation The process that links risk and return in order to determine the worth of an asset.

As noted in Chapter 7, all major financial decisions must be viewed in terms of expected risk, expected return, and their combined impact on share value. **Valuation** is the process that links risk and return in order to determine the worth of any asset. It is a relatively simple process that can be applied to expected streams of benefits from bonds, stocks, income properties, oil wells, and so on in order to determine their worth at a given point in time. To do this, the manager uses the time value of money techniques presented in Chapter 6 and the concepts of risk and return developed in Chapter 7.

Key Inputs

The key inputs to the valuation process include cash flows (returns), timing, and the discount rate (risk). Each is described briefly below.

Cash Flows (Returns)

The value of any asset depends on the cash flow(s) it is expected to provide over the ownership period. To have value an asset does not have to provide an annual cash flow; it can provide an intermittent cash flow or even a single cash flow over the period.

> **Example**
> Celia Sargent, the financial analyst for Groton Corporation, wishes to estimate the value of three assets—common stock in Michaels Enterprises, an interest in an oil well, and an original painting by a well-known artist. Her cash flow estimates for each were:
>
> *Stock in Michaels Enterprises:* Expect to receive cash dividends of $300 per year indefinitely.
>
> *Oil well:* Expect to receive cash flow of $2,000 at the end of one year, $4,000 at the end of two years, and $10,000 at the end of four years, when the well is to be sold.
>
> *Original painting:* Expect to be able to sell the painting in five years for $85,000.
>
> Having developed these cash flow estimates, Celia has taken the first step toward placing a value on each of these assets.

Timing

In addition to making cash flow estimates, the timing of the cash flows must be specified.[1] It is customary to specify the timing along with the amounts of cash flow. For example, the cash flows of $2,000, $4,000, and $10,000 for the oil well in the example were scheduled to occur at the end of years 1, 2, and 4, respectively. In combination, the cash flow and its timing fully define the return expected from the asset.

Discount Rate (Risk)

Risk, as noted in Chapter 7, describes the chance that an expected outcome will not be realized. The level of risk associated with a given cash flow can significantly affect its value. In general, the greater the risk of (or the less certain) a cash flow, the lower its value. In terms of present value (see Chapter 6), greater risk can be incorporated into an analysis by using a higher discount rate or required return. Recall that in the capital asset

---

[1] Although cash flows can occur at any time during a year, for computational convenience as well as custom, we will assume they occur at the *end* of the year unless otherwise noted.

pricing model (CAPM) presented in Chapter 7 (see Equation 7.6), the greater the risk as measured by beta, *b*, the higher the required return, *k*. In the valuation process, too, the discount rate is used to incorporate risk into the analysis—the higher the risk, the greater the discount rate (required return), and vice versa.

Example

Let's return to Celia Sargent's job of placing a value on Groton Corporation's original painting, which is expected to provide a single cash flow of $85,000 from its sale at the end of five years, and consider two scenarios.

Scenario 1—Certainty: A major art gallery has contracted to buy the painting for $85,000 at the end of five years. Because this is considered a certain situation, Celia views this asset as "money in the bank" and would use the prevailing risk-free rate, R_F, of 9 percent as the discount rate when calculating the value of the painting.

Scenario 2—High Risk: The value of original paintings by this artist has fluctuated widely over the past 10 years, and although Celia expects to be able to get $85,000 for the painting, she realizes its sale price in five years could range between $30,000 and $140,000. Due to the high uncertainty surrounding the painting's value, Celia believes a 15 percent discount rate is appropriate.

The preceding example and the associated estimates of the appropriate discount rate illustrate the role this rate plays in capturing risk. The often subjective nature of such estimates is also clear.[2]

The Basic Valuation Model

Simply stated, the value of any asset is *the present value of all future cash flows it is expected to provide over the relevant time period.* The time period can be as short as one year or as long as infinity. The value of an asset is therefore determined by discounting the expected cash flows back to their present value, using a discount rate commensurate with the asset's risk. Utilizing the present-value techniques presented in Chapter 6, the value of any asset at time zero, V_0, can be expressed as

$$V_0 = \frac{CF_1}{(1+k)^1} + \frac{CF_2}{(1+k)^2} + \cdots + \frac{CF_n}{(1+k)^n} \tag{8.1}$$

where

$$V_0 = \text{value of the asset at time zero}$$
$$CF_t = \text{cash flow expected at the end of year } t$$
$$k = \text{appropriate discount rate}$$
$$n = \text{relevant time period}$$

Using present-value interest factor notation, $PVIF_{k,n}$ from Chapter 6, Equation 8.1 can be

---

[2] Straightforward techniques for estimating discount rates do not exist. Actual practice tends to rely on subjective estimates based on the conceptual risk-return framework of the capital asset pricing model. Subsequent discussions describe some of these "practical" approaches.

rewritten as

$$V_0 = [CF_1 \times (PVIF_{k,1})] + [CF_2 \times (PVIF_{k,2})] + \cdots + [CF_n \times (PVIF_{k,n})] \quad (8.2)$$

Substituting the expected cash flows, CF_t, over the relevant time period, n, and the appropriate discount rate, k, into Equation 8.2, we can determine the value of any asset.

Example

Celia Sargent, using appropriate discount rates and Equation 8.2, calculated the value of each asset as shown in Table 8.1. The Michaels Enterprises stock has a value of $2,500, the oil well's value is $9,262, and the original painting has a value of $42,245. Note that regardless of the pattern of the expected cash flow from an asset, the basic valuation equation can be used to determine value.

Table 8.1
Valuation of Groton Corporation's Assets by Celia Sargent

Asset	Cash flow, CF	Appropriate discount rate (%)	Valuation
Michaels Enterprises stock[a]	$300/year indefinitely	12	$V_0 = \$300 \times (PVIFA_{12\%,\infty})$ $= \dfrac{\$300}{.12} = \$2,500$
Oil well[b]	Year (t) $\quad$ CF_t 1 $\quad$ \$ 2,000 2 $\quad$ 4,000 3 $\quad$ 0 4 $\quad$ 10,000	20	$V_0 = [\$2,000 \times (PVIF_{20\%,1})]$ $+ \ [\$4,000 \times (PVIF_{20\%,2})]$ $+ \ [\$0 \times (PVIF_{20\%,3})]$ $+ \ [\$10,000 \times (PVIF_{20\%,4})]$ $= [\$2,000 \times (.833)]$ $+ \ [\$4,000 \times (.694)]$ $+ \ [\$0 \times (.579)]$ $+ \ [\$10,000 \times (.482)]$ $= \$1,666 + \$2,776$ $+ \ \$0 + \$4,820$ $= \$9,262$
Original painting[c]	$85,000 at end of year 5	15	$V_0 = \$85,000 \times (PVIF_{15\%,5})$ $= \$85,000 \times (.497)$ $= \$42,245$

[a] This is a perpetuity (infinite-lived annuity), and therefore Equation 6.30 is applied.

[b] This is a mixed stream of cash flows and therefore requires a number of *PVIF*s as noted.

[c] This is a lump-sum cash flow and therefore requires a single *PVIF*.

---

1 The value of any asset regardless of its pattern of expected cash flow is the present value of all future cash flows it is expected to provide over the relevant time period. *(Fact)*   **FACT OR FABLE?**

Bond Valuation

The basic valuation equation can be customized for use in valuing specific securities—bonds, preferred stock, and common stock. Bonds and preferred stock are similar since they have stated contractual interest and dividend cash flows. The dividends on common stock, on the other hand, are not known in advance. Bond valuation is described in this section, and common stock valuation is discussed in the following section.

Bond Fundamentals

Bonds, which are discussed in detail in Chapter 16, are long-term debt instruments used by business and government to raise large sums of money, typically from a diverse group of lenders. As noted in Chapter 2, most corporate bonds pay interest *semiannually* (every six months), have an initial *maturity* of 10 to 30 years, and have a *par,* or *face, value* of $1,000 that must be repaid at maturity.[3] An example will illustrate the point.

Example

The Mills Company on January 1, 1989, issued a 10 percent coupon interest rate, 10-year bond with a $1,000 par value that pays interest semiannually. Investors who buy this bond receive the contractual right to (1) $100 annual interest (10 percent coupon interest rate × $1,000 par value) distributed as $50 ($\frac{1}{2}$ × $100) at the end of each six months and (2) the $1,000 par value at the end of the tenth year.

Using data presented for Mills Company's new issue, we look now at basic bond valuation and other issues.

Basic Bond Valuation

The value of a bond is the present value of the contractual payments its issuer is obligated to make from the current time until it matures. The appropriate discount rate would be the required return, k_d, which depends on prevailing interest rates and risk. The basic equation for the value, B_0, of a bond that pays *annual* interest of I dollars[4], has n years to maturity, has an M dollar par value, and for which the required return is k_d, is given by Equation 8.3:

$$B_0 = I \times \left[\sum_{t=1}^{n} \frac{1}{(1 + k_d)^t} \right] + M \times \left[\frac{1}{(1 + k_d)^n} \right] \tag{8.3}$$

$$= I \times (PVIFA_{k_d,n}) + M \times (PVIF_{k_d,n}) \tag{8.3a}$$

Example

Using the Mills Company data for the January 1, 1989, new issue and *assuming that interest is paid annually* and that the required return is equal to the bond's coupon interest rate, $I = \$100$, $k_d = 10$ percent, $M = \$1,000$, and $n = 10$ years. Substituting these values in Equation 8.3a yields

$$B_0 = \$100 \times (PVIFA_{10\%,10yrs}) + \$1,000 \times (PVIF_{10\%,10yrs})$$
$$= \$100 \times (6.145) + \$1,000 \times (.386)$$
$$= \$614.50 + \$386.00 = \underline{\$1,000.50}$$

The bond therefore has a value of approximately $1,000.[5] *Note that the value calculated above is equal to par value; this will always be the case when the required return is equal to the coupon interest rate.* The computations involved in finding the bond value are depicted graphically on the time line in Figure 8.1.

---

[3] Bonds often have features that allow them to be retired by the issuer prior to maturity; these *call* and *conversion* features are presented in Chapters 16 and 18. For the purpose of the current discussion, these features are ignored.

[4] The payment of annual rather than semiannual bond interest is assumed throughout the following discussion. This assumption simplifies the calculations involved while maintaining the conceptual accuracy of the valuation procedures presented.

[5] Note that a slight rounding error ($.50) results here due to the use of the table factors rounded to the nearest thousandth.

Figure 8.1
Graphic Depiction of Bond Valuation (Mills Company's 10 Percent Coupon Interest Rate, 10-Year Maturity, $1,000 Par, January 1, 1989, Issue Paying Annual Interest; Required Return = 10 Percent)

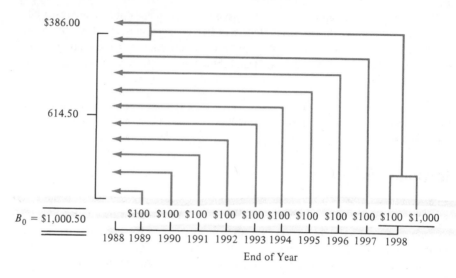

Bond Value Behavior

The value of a bond in the marketplace is rarely constant over its life. A variety of forces in the economy as well as the mere passage of time tend to affect value. Since these external forces are really in no way controlled by bond issuers or investors, it is useful to understand the impact that required return and time to maturity have on bond value.

Required Returns and Bond Values

Whenever the required return on a bond differs from the bond's coupon interest rate, the bond's value will differ from its par, or face, value. The required return on the bond is likely to differ from the stated interest rate either (1) because economic conditions have changed, causing a shift in the basic cost of long-term funds, or (2) the firm's risk has changed. Increases in the basic cost of long-term funds or in risk will raise the required return, and vice versa.

> **discount** The amount by which a bond sells at a value that is less than its par, or face, value.

> **premium** The amount by which a bond sells at a value that is greater than its par, or face, value.

Regardless of the exact cause, the important point is that when the required return is greater than the coupon rate of interest, the bond value, B_0, will be less than its par value, M. In this case the bond is said to sell at a **discount,** which will equal $M - B_0$. On the other hand, when the required rate of return falls below the coupon rate of interest, the bond value will be greater than par. In this situation the bond is said to sell at a **premium,** which will equal $B_0 - M$. An example will illustrate.

Example

In the preceding example it was shown that when the required return equaled the coupon rate of interest, the bond's value equaled its $1,000 par value. If for the same bond the required return were to rise to 12 percent, its value would be

$$B_0 = \$100 \times (PVIFA_{12\%,10yrs}) + \$1,000 \times (PVIF_{12\%,10yrs})$$
$$= \$100 \times (5.650) + \$1,000 \times (.322) = \underline{\$887.00}$$

The bond would therefore sell at a *discount* of $113.00 ($1,000 par value − $887.00 value).

If, on the other hand, the required return fell to, say, 8 percent, the bond's value would be

$$B_0 = \$100 \times (PVIFA_{8\%,10yrs}) + \$1,000 \times (PVIF_{8\%,10yrs})$$
$$= \$100 \times (6.710) + \$1,000 \times (.463) = \underline{\$1,134.00}$$

The bond would therefore sell at a *premium* of $134.00 ($1,134.00 value − $1,000 par value). These results are summarized in Table 8.2 and graphically depicted in Figure 8.2.

Table 8.2
Bond Values for Various Required Returns (10 Percent Coupon Interest Rate, 10-Year Maturity, $1,000 Par, Interest Paid Annually)

Required return, k_d (%)	Bond value, B_0	Status
12	$ 887.00	Discount
10	1,000.00	Par value
8	1,134.00	Premium

FACT OR FABLE?

2 When the required return on a bond is greater than its coupon interest rate, the bond sells at a premium; when the required return is less than the coupon rate, it sells at a discount. *(Fable)*

When the required return on a bond is greater than its coupon interest rate, the bond sells at a *discount*; when the required return is less than the coupon rate, it sells at a *premium*.

Time to Maturity

Whenever the required return is different from the coupon interest rate, the amount of time to maturity affects bond value, even if the required return remains constant until maturity. Two important relationships exist among time to maturity, required return, and bond value. They are concerned with constant required returns and changing required returns.

1. *Constant required returns*. When the required return is different from the coupon interest rate and assumed *constant until maturity*, the value of the bond will approach its par value as the passage of time moves the bond's value closer to maturity. Of

Figure 8.2
Bond Value and Required Return (Mills Company's 10 Percent Coupon Interest Rate, 10-Year Maturity, $1,000 Par, January 1, 1989, Issue Paying Annual Interest)

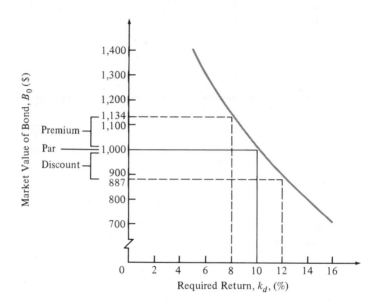

course, when the required return equals the coupon interest rate, the bond's value will remain at par until it matures.

Example
Figure 8.3 depicts the behavior of the bond values calculated earlier and presented in Table 8.2 for Mills Company's 10 percent coupon interest rate bond paying annual interest and having ten years to maturity. Each of the three required returns—12 percent, 10 percent, and 8 percent—is assumed to remain constant over the ten years to the bond's maturity. It can be seen that the bond's value in each case approaches and ultimately equals the bond's $1,000 par value at its maturity. At the 12 percent required return, the bond's discount declines with the passage of time as the bond's value increases from $887 to $1,000. When the 10 percent required return equals the bond's coupon interest rate, its value remains unchanged at $1,000 over its maturity. Finally, at the 8 percent required return, the bond's premium will decline as its value drops from $1,134 to $1,000 at maturity. With the required return assumed constant to maturity, the bond's value approaches its $1,000 par or maturity value as the time to maturity declines.

2. *Changing required returns.* The shorter the amount of time until a bond's maturity, the less responsive is its market value to a given change in the required return. In other words, short maturities have less "interest rate risk" than do long maturities when all other features—coupon interest rate, par value, and interest payment frequency—are the same.

Figure 8.3
Relationship Between Time to Maturity, Required Return, and Bond Value
(Mills Company's 10 Percent Coupon Interest Rate, 10-Year Maturity, $1,000
Par Issue Paying Annual Interest)

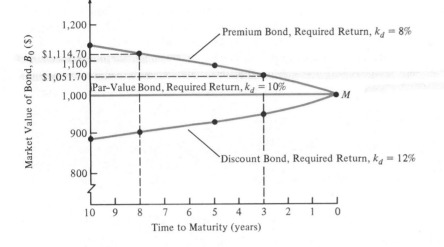

Example
The effect of changing required returns on bonds of differing maturity can be illustrated using Mills Company's bond and Figure 8.3. If, as noted by the dotted line at eight years to maturity, the required return declines from 10 to 8 percent, the bond's value rises from $1,000 to $1,114.70—an 11.47 percent increase. If the same change in required return had occurred with only three years to maturity, as noted by the dotted line, the bond's value would have risen to just $1,051.70—only a 5.17 percent increase. Similar types of responses can be seen in terms of the change in bond value associated with increases in required returns. The shorter the time to maturity, the smaller the impact on bond value caused by a given change in the required return.

FACT OR FABLE?

3 The longer the period of time until a bond matures, the less responsive is its market value to a given change in the required return. *(Fable)*
The *shorter* the period of time until a bond matures, the less responsive is its market value to a given change in the required return.

Yield to Maturity (YTM)

When investors evaluate and trade bonds they commonly consider **yield to maturity (YTM),** which is the rate investors earn if they buy the bond at a specific price, B_0, and hold it until maturity. The yield to maturity on a bond with a current price equal to its par, or face, value (i.e., $B_0 = M$) will always equal the coupon interest rate. When the

yield to maturity The rate of return investors earn if they buy a bond at a specific price and hold it until maturity.

bond value differs from par, the yield to maturity will differ from the coupon interest rate. In such situations the yield to maturity can be calculated precisely or approximated by formula.

Calculation of YTM

Assuming that interest is paid annually, the yield to maturity on a bond can be found by solving Equation 8.3 for k_d. In other words, the current value, B_0, the annual interest, I, the par value, M, and the years to maturity, n, are known, and the yield to maturity must be found. This calculation is difficult to perform by hand. It involves finding the value of the bond at various rates until the rate causing the calculated bond value to equal the current value is found. This trial-and-error process is best described using an example.

Example

The Mills Company bond, which currently sells for $1,080, has a 10 percent coupon interest rate and $1,000 par value, pays interest annually, and has ten years to maturity. Since $B_0 = \$1,080$, $I = \$100$ ($.10 \times \$1,000$), $M = \$1,000$, and $n = 10$ years, substituting into Equation 8.3a we get

$$\$1,080 = \$100 \times (PVIFA_{k_d,10\text{yrs}}) + \$1,000 \times (PVIF_{k_d,10\text{yrs}})$$

Since we know that a discount rate, k_d, of 10 percent would result in a value of $1,000, the discount rate that would result in $1,080 must be less than 10 percent. Trying 9 percent we get

$$\$100 \times (PVIFA_{9\%,10\text{yrs}}) + \$1,000 \times (PVIF_{9\%,10\text{yrs}})$$
$$= \$100 \times (6.418) + \$1,000 \times (.422)$$
$$= \$641.80 + \$422.00 = \$1,063.80$$

Since the 9 percent rate is not quite low enough to bring the value up to $1,080, we next try 8 percent and get

$$\$100 \times (PVIFA_{8\%,10\text{yrs}}) + \$1,000 \times (PVIF_{8\%,10\text{yrs}})$$
$$= \$100 \times (6.710) + \$1,000 \times (.463)$$
$$= \$671.00 + \$463.00 = \$1,134.00$$

Since the resulting value of $1,134 at the 8 percent rate is higher than $1,080 and the $1,063.80 value at the 9 percent rate is lower than $1,080, the bond's yield to maturity must be between 8 and 9 percent. Since the $1,063.80 is closer to $1,080, to the nearest whole percent the YTM is 9 percent. Using interpolation, the more precise value of YTM is 8.77 percent.[6] For convenience, a YTM slightly below 9 percent is assumed.

---

[6] To interpolate in this case, the following steps are involved:

1. Find the difference between the bond values at 8 and 9 percent. The difference is $70.20 ($1,134.00 − $1,063.80).

2. Find the absolute difference between the desired value of $1,080 and the value associated with the lower discount rate. The difference is $54 ($1,134 − $1,080).

3. Divide the value from step 2 by the value found in step 1 to get the percent of the distance across the discount rate range between 8 and 9 percent. The result is .77 ($54.00 ÷ $70.20).

A more practical alternative to the trial-and-error approach for finding the YTM is the approximate yield formula.

Approximate Yield Formula

The *approximate yield formula* is given in Equation 8.4.

$$\text{Approximate yield} = \frac{I + \dfrac{M - B_0}{n}}{\dfrac{M + B_0}{2}} \tag{8.4}$$

Use of this formula can best be illustrated via an example.

Example

Substituting the Mills Company bond data from the preceding example into Equation 8.4 we get

$$\text{Approximate yield} = \frac{\$100 + \dfrac{\$1,000 - \$1,080}{10}}{\dfrac{\$1,000 + \$1,080}{2}}$$

$$= \frac{\$100 + (-\$8)}{\$1,040} = \frac{\$92}{\$1,040} = .0885 = \underline{\underline{8.85\%}}$$

The approximate YTM is therefore 8.85 percent, which does not differ greatly from the 8.77 percent YTM calculated earlier.

This approach is often used to make quick and reasonably accurate estimates of YTM.

Semiannual Interest and Bond Values

The procedure used to value bonds paying interest semiannually is similar to that illustrated in Chapter 6 for compounding interest more frequently than annually—except that here we need to find present instead of future value. It involves

1. Converting annual interest, I, to semiannual interest by dividing it by 2.
2. Converting the number of years to maturity, n, to the number of six-month periods to maturity by multiplying n by 2.
3. Converting the required return from an annual rate, k_d, to a semiannual rate by dividing it by 2.

---

4. Multiply the percent found in step 3 by the interval width of 1 percent (9 percent − 8 percent) over which interpolation is being performed. The result is .77 percent (.77 × 1 percent).
5. Add the value found in step 4 to the interest rate associated with the lower end of the interval. The result is 8.77 percent (8 percent + .77 percent). The yield to maturity is therefore 8.77 percent.

Of course, quicker and more accurate results can be obtained using a financially oriented calculator. Using such a calculator, the yield to maturity in this case is found to be 8.7662 percent.

Substituting the three changes noted above into Equation 8.3 yields

$$B_0 = \frac{I}{2} \times \left[\sum_{t=1}^{2n} \frac{1}{\left(1 + \frac{k_d}{2}\right)^t} \right] + M \times \left[\frac{1}{\left(1 + \frac{k_d}{2}\right)^{2n}} \right] \qquad (8.5)[7]$$

$$= \frac{I}{2} \times \left(PVIFA_{\frac{k_d}{2}, 2n} \right) + M \times \left(PVIF_{\frac{k_d}{2}, 2n} \right) \qquad (8.5a)$$

Example

Assuming that the Mills Company bond pays interest semiannually and that the required return, k_d, is 12 percent, substituting into Equation 8.5a yields

$$B_0 = \frac{\$100}{2} \times \left(PVIFA_{\frac{12\%}{2}, 2 \times 10yrs} \right) + \$1,000 \times \left(PVIF_{\frac{12\%}{2}, 2 \times 10yrs} \right)$$
$$= \$50 \times (PVIFA_{6\%, 20 \text{ periods}}) + \$1,000 \times (PVIF_{6\%, 20 \text{ periods}})$$
$$= \$50 \times (11.470) + \$1,000 \times (.312) = \underline{\$885.50}$$

Comparing this result to that found using annual compounding, shown in Table 8.2, it can be seen that the value is less when semiannual interest is used. This will always occur when the bond sells at a discount. For bonds selling at a premium, the opposite will occur (value with semiannual interest is greater than with annual interest).

Common Stock Valuation

Common stockholders expect to be rewarded through the receipt of periodic cash dividends and an increasing—or at least nondeclining—share value. Like current owners, prospective owners and security analysts frequently estimate the firm's value. They choose to purchase the stock when they believe it to be *undervalued* (i.e., that its true value is greater than its market price) and to sell it when they feel it is *overvalued* (i.e., that its market price is greater than its true value).[8]

Popular Approaches

Many popular approaches for measuring value exist, but only one is widely accepted. The popular approaches to valuation include the use of book value, liquidation value, or some type of a price/earnings multiple.

---

[7] Although it may appear inappropriate to use the semiannual discounting procedure on the maturity value, M, this technique is necessary to find the correct bond value. One way to confirm the accuracy of this approach is to calculate the bond value in the case that the required return and coupon interest rate are equal; for B_0 to equal M, as would be expected in such a case, the maturity value must be discounted on a semiannual basis.

[8] A growing body of financial data tends to suggest that in an efficient market *widely held stocks that are actively traded* are always properly valued. In other words, the market price is always equal to the true share value. Such a conclusion tends to raise doubt about the recommendations of securities analysts. Because there remains much disagreement on the issue, further attention will not be given to it.

STEVE JOBS: Valuing and Financing a Dream

Steve Jobs, co-founder of Apple Computer, had wealth in excess of $100 million by age 31. Jobs is adept at financing. Even in 1976, when he and partner Steve Wosniak were mere garage tinkerers, Jobs was able to get financial support from the likes of Nolen Bushnell of Atari and venture capitalist Don Valentine. Jobs' silver tongue, his vision of an invention that would change the world, and his keen marketing judgment made all the difference. Jobs captured the imagination of those who listened. He sold his dream of the microcomputer revolution all along his way to the top of a billion-dollar corporation.

A decade later he could still work the old magic. In mid-1985, when Jobs found himself confined to an inactive role as chairman of the board at Apple, he discovered that wealth without work was not for him. Unsatisfied with travel and leisure, he left Apple. "I am but thirty," he said in his resignation letter, "and want still to contribute and achieve." Jobs decided to design, build, and market a whole new computer.

Jobs already had his next dream. In a long lunch with Paul Berg, Stanford's Nobel Prize-winning biochemist, Jobs had asked why scientists were not using computers to simulate time-consuming experiments with DNA and other unexplored mysteries. Berg replied that available hardware was not powerful enough and there was no suitable software. It was a vision for Jobs, who claimed the challenge as his next opportunity. Thus, Jobs' NeXT computer company was born. He wanted to create the "three-M" machine a group of scientists from Carnegie Mellon described several years ago—a computer powerful enough to simulate engineering designs, the human nervous system, and a host of other interesting realities. Furthermore, Jobs wanted to market the product for an affordable $3,000.

Investors, competitors, and scientists all watched with interest. When Jobs began looking around for capital, most analysts rejected his $126 million valuation of NeXT as too high. Then Texas billionaire H. Ross Perot bought in for $20 million, and so did Carnegie Mellon and Stanford Universities. Was Jobs' valuation too high or not? The answer is that value is often in the eye of the beholder. Track record is clearly important, but so was Jobs' persuasiveness. Faith in the dream is the most critical element in its value.

Book Value

Book value per share is simply the amount per share of common stock to be received if all assets are liquidated for their exact book (accounting) value and if the proceeds remaining after paying all liabilities (including preferred stock) are divided among the common stockholders. This method lacks sophistication and can be criticized on the basis of its reliance on historical balance sheet data. It ignores the firm's expected earnings potential and generally lacks any true relationship to the firm's value in the marketplace. Let us look at an example.

book value per share The amount per share of common stock to be received if all assets are liquidated for their book value, and if the proceeds remaining after paying all liabilities (including preferred stock) are divided among the common stockholders.

Example
The Lamar Company currently (December 31, 1988) has total assets of $6 million, total liabilities including preferred stock of $4.5 million, and 100,000 shares of com-

mon stock outstanding. Its book value per share would therefore be

$$\frac{\$6,000,000 - \$4,500,000}{100,000 \text{ shares}} = \underline{\underline{\$15 \text{ per share}}}$$

Since this value assumes that assets are liquidated for their book value, it may not represent the minimum share value. As a matter of fact, although most stocks sell above book value, it is not unusual to find stocks selling below book value.

Liquidation Value

liquidation value per share
The *actual* amount per share of common stock to be received if all the firm's assets are sold, liabilities (including preferred stock) are paid, and the remaining proceeds divided among the common stockholders.

Liquidation value per share is the *actual* amount per share of common stock to be received if all the firm's assets are sold, liabilities (including preferred stock) are paid, and any remaining money is divided among the common stockholders.[9] This measure is more realistic than book value, but it still fails to consider the earning power of the firm's assets. An example will illustrate.

Example

The Lamar Company found upon investigation that it would obtain only $5.25 million if it liquidated its assets today. The firm's liquidation value per share would therefore be

$$\frac{\$5,250,000 - \$4,500,000}{100,000 \text{ shares}} = \underline{\underline{\$7.50 \text{ per share}}}$$

Ignoring any expenses of liquidation, this would be the firm's minimum value.

Price/Earnings Multiples

Price/earnings (P/E) ratios were introduced in Chapter 4. The average P/E ratio in a particular industry can be used as the guide to a firm's value if it is assumed that investors value the earnings of a given firm in the same manner as they do the "average" firm in that industry. The **price/earnings multiple approach** to value is a popular technique whereby the firm's expected earnings per share (EPS) are multiplied by the average price/earnings (P/E) ratio for the industry to estimate the firm's share value. The average P/E ratio for the industry can be obtained from a source such as *Standard & Poor's Industrial Ratios*.

price/earnings multiple approach A technique whereby the firm's expected earnings per share (EPS) are multiplied by the average price/earnings (P/E) ratio for the industry to estimate the firm's share value.

The use of P/E multiples is especially helpful in valuing firms that are not publicly traded, whereas the use of market price may be preferable in the case of a publicly traded firm. In any case, the price/earnings multiple approach is considered superior to the use of book or liquidation values since it considers *expected* earnings.[10] Before we discuss the most widely accepted approach, let us consider an example of price/earnings multiples.

[9] In the event of liquidation, creditors' claims must be satisfied first, then those of the preferred stockholders. Anything left goes to common stockholders. A more detailed discussion of liquidation procedures is presented in Chapter 19.

[10] The price/earnings multiple approach to valuation does have a theoretical explanation. If we view 1 divided by the price/earnings ratio, or the earnings/price ratio, as the rate at which investors discount the firm's earnings, and if we assume that the projected earnings per share will be earned indefinitely, the price/earnings multiple approach can be looked on as a method of finding the present value of a perpetuity of projected earnings per share at a rate equal to the earnings/price ratio.

Example
The Lamar Company is expected to earn $2.60 per share next year (1989). This expectation is based on an analysis of the firm's historical earnings trend and expected economic and industry conditions. The average price/earnings ratio for firms in the same industry is 7. Multiplying Lamar's expected earnings per share (EPS) of $2.60 by this ratio gives us a value for the firm's shares of $18.20, assuming that investors will continue to measure the value of the average firm at 7 times its earnings.

The Basic Equation

Like bonds, the value of a share of common stock is equal to the present value of all future benefits it is expected to provide. Simply stated, *the value of a share of common stock is equal to the present value of all future dividends it is expected to provide over an infinite time horizon.*[11] Although by selling stock at a price above that originally paid, a stockholder can earn capital gains in addition to dividends, what is really sold is the right to all future dividends. Therefore, from a valuation viewpoint only dividends are relevant. Redefining terms, the basic valuation model in Equation 8.1 can be specified for common stock as given in Equation 8.6:

$$P_0 = \frac{D_1}{(1 + k_s)^1} + \frac{D_2}{(1 + k_s)^2} + \cdots + \frac{D_\infty}{(1 + k_s)^\infty} \qquad (8.6)$$

where

P_0 = value of common stock

D_t = per-share dividend expected at the end of year t

k_s = required return on common stock

The equation can be simplified somewhat by redefining each year's dividend, D_t, in terms of anticipated growth. Three cases are considered here—zero growth, constant growth, and variable growth.

---

4 The value of a share of common stock is equal to the present value of all the dividends it is expected to provide over an infinite time horizon. *(Fact)*

FACT OR FABLE?

Zero Growth

The simplest approach to dividend valuation, the **zero growth model,** assumes a constant, nongrowing dividend stream. In terms of the notation already introduced,

$$D_1 = D_2 = \cdots = D_\infty$$

Letting D_1 represent the amount of the annual dividend, Equation 8.6 under zero growth

zero growth model An approach to dividend valuation that assumes a constant, nongrowing dividend stream.

---

[11] The need to consider an infinite time horizon is not critical, since a sufficiently long period, say, 50 years, will result in about the same present value as an infinite period for moderate-sized required returns. For example, at 15 percent, a dollar to be received 50 years from now, $PVIF_{15\%, 50\text{yrs}}$, is worth only about $.001 today.

SMALL BUSINESS

PRESELLING A COMPANY: Finding Value in a Startup

No one paid much attention in 1985, when Ashton-Tate, a well-known software developer, bought Forefront Corporation, a smaller, obscure software firm. Yet the acquisition was unique, the consummation of an earlier deal in which one company purchased another not yet in existence.

The unusual story began in mid-1983, when Robert Carr and Martin Mazner were designing a sophisticated software package they called Fred. Carr and Mazner believed a minimum of $5 million would be necessary to bring Fred to a marketable condition. Certainly they could have approached venture capitalists. There were two reasons they did not. The first was a fear that venture capitalists would demand a huge payback, achievable only through rapid vertical growth. Carr and Mazner wanted instead to foster a work environment that would attract top talent and promote unpressured creativity. The second reason was the need for a corporate guardian that could provide an established name and reputation as well as marketing expertise.

They sought to sell Fred to an existing software publisher whose treasury might accelerate the development process. They presented their product to nearby Ashton-Tate first. They were granted a one-hour meeting that turned into a 48-hour marathon. When A-T offered to buy Fred outright, Carr and Mazner refused. They wanted to do something different: start a company around the product and then sell the company after a few years. A-T agreed to capitalize the company, now called Forefront, in return for an option to buy it three years later.

The terms were set up to motivate both buyer and seller to make the most of Forefront and to allow both to gain equitably from its success. A-T made an initial investment of $975,000: $750,000 for development, and $225,000 for a 15 percent stake in the new company. A-T would publish Fred, soon to be renamed Framework. In return for marketing rights, A-T would pay royalties to Forefront. Framework would be marketed as soon as it was complete, and A-T would spend a stipulated minimum on first-year advertising.

The formula for the final price of Forefront was based on three factors: the profitability of Forefront; an earn-out ratio showing Framework's performance among other A-T products; and A-T's average price/earnings ratio. Carr and Mazner believed the price formula was important to the team at Forefront. "We were more highly motivated because our price had not yet been determined than if we already had the money at a fixed price," Carr recalls.

By the turn of 1985, when Framework had been shipping only six months, it was providing 18 percent of A-T's annual revenues. A-T was ready to conclude the merger. Payment was made with 500,000 shares of A-T common stock, then at $10 per share. A few weeks later, the stock had risen to $20. Forefront's founders and employees, all of whom had traded equity in the small company for equity in the larger, had reason to rejoice and reflect. The acquisition had paid off for everyone.

SOURCE: Adapted from Robert A. Mamis, "Preselling the Company," *Inc.*, April 1986, pp. 115–116.

---

would reduce to

$$P_0 = D_1 \times \sum_{t=1}^{\infty} \frac{1}{(1 + k_s)^t} = D_1 \times (PVIFA_{k_s,\infty}) = \frac{D_1}{k_s} \qquad (8.7)$$

The equation shows that with zero growth, the value of a share of stock would equal the present value of a perpetuity of D_1 dollars discounted at a rate k_s. Let us look at an example.

Example
The Denham Company's dividend is expected to remain constant at $3 per share indefinitely. If the required return on its stock is 15 percent, the stock's value is $20 ($3 ÷ .15).

Since preferred stock typically provides its holder with a fixed annual dividend over its assumed infinite life, Equation 8.7 can be used to find the *value of preferred stock*. The value of preferred stock can be estimated by substituting the stated preferred dividend and the required return on the preferred stock for D_1 and k_s, respectively, in Equation 8.7. For example, a preferred stock paying a $5 stated annual dividend and having a required return of 13 percent would have a value of $38.46 ($5 ÷ .13). Detailed discussion of preferred stock is included in Chapter 18.

Constant Growth

The most widely cited dividend valuation approach, the **constant growth model,** assumes that dividends will grow at a constant rate, g, that is less than the required return, k_s $(g < k_s)$.[12] Letting D_0 represent the most recent dividend, Equation 8.6 can be rewritten as follows:

$$P_0 = \frac{D_0 \times (1 + g)^1}{(1 + k_s)^1} + \frac{D_0 \times (1 + g)^2}{(1 + k_s)^2} + \cdots + \frac{D_0 \times (1 + g)^\infty}{(1 + k_s)^\infty} \qquad (8.8)$$

If we simplify Equation 8.8, it can be rewritten as follows:[13]

$$P_0 = \frac{D_1}{k_s - g} \qquad (8.9)$$

The constant growth model in Equation 8.9 is commonly called the **Gordon model.** An example will show how it works.

constant growth model
A widely cited dividend valuation approach that assumes dividends will grow at a constant rate that is less than the required return.

Gordon model A common name for the *constant growth model* widely used in dividend valuation.

---

[12] One of the assumptions of the constant growth model as presented is that earnings and dividends grow at the same rate. This assumption is true only in cases where a firm pays out a fixed percentage of its earnings each year (has a fixed payout ratio). In the case of a declining industry, a negative growth rate ($g < 0$) might exist. In such a case the constant growth model, as well as the variable growth model presented in the next section, remains fully applicable to the valuation process.

[13] For the interested reader, the calculations necessary to derive Equation 8.9 from Equation 8.8 follow. The first step is to multiply each side of Equation 8.8 by $(1 + k_s)/(1 + g)$ and subtract Equation 8.8 from the resulting expression. This yields

$$\frac{P_0 \times (1 + k_s)}{1 + g} - P_0 = D_0 - \frac{D_0 \times (1 + g)^\infty}{(1 + k_s)^\infty} \qquad (1)$$

Since k_s is assumed to be greater than g, the second term on the right side of Equation 1 should be zero. Thus,

$$P_0 \times \left(\frac{1 + k_s}{1 + g} - 1\right) = D_0 \qquad (2)$$

Equation 2 is simplified as follows:

$$P_0 \times \left(\frac{(1 + k_s) - (1 + g)}{1 + g}\right) = D_0 \qquad (3)$$

$$P_0 \times (k_s - g) = D_0 \times (1 + g) \qquad (4)$$

$$P_0 = \frac{D_1}{k_s - g} \qquad (5)$$

Equation 5 equals Equation 8.9 above.

Example

The Lamar Company from 1983 through 1988 paid the per-share dividends shown below.

Year	Dividend ($)
1988	1.40
1987	1.29
1986	1.20
1985	1.12
1984	1.05
1983	1.00

Using Appendix Table A-3 for the present-value interest factor, *PVIF*, in conjunction with the technique described for finding growth rates in Chapter 6, the annual growth rate of dividends, which is assumed to equal the expected constant rate of dividend growth, *g*, is found to equal 7 percent.[14] The company estimates that its dividend in 1989, D_1, will equal $1.50. The required return, k_s, is assumed to be 15 percent. Substituting these values into Equation 8.9, the value of the stock is

$$P_0 = \frac{\$1.50}{.15 - .07} = \frac{\$1.50}{.08} = \underline{\$18.75 \text{ per share}}$$

Assuming that the values of D_1, k_s, and *g* are accurately estimated, Lamar Company's stock value is $18.75.

Variable Growth

variable growth model
A dividend valuation approach that allows for a change in the dividend growth rate.

The zero and constant growth common stock models presented in Equations 8.7 and 8.9, respectively, do not allow for any shift in expected growth rates. Because future growth rates might shift up or down due to changing expectations, it is useful to consider a **variable growth model** that allows for a change in the dividend growth rate.[15] To determine the value of a share of stock, given that a single shift in the growth rate occurs at the end of year *N*:

1. Find the value of the cash dividends at the end of *each year* during the initial growth

[14] The technique involves solving the following equation for *g*:

$$D_{1988} = D_{1983} \times (1 + g)^5$$
$$\frac{D_{1983}}{D_{1988}} = \frac{1}{(1 + g)^5} = PVIF_{g,5}$$

Two basic steps can be followed. First, dividing the earliest dividend ($D_{1983} = \$1.00$) by the most recent dividend ($D_{1988} = \$1.40$), a factor for the present value of one dollar, *PVIF*, of .714 ($\$1.00 \div \$1.40$) results. Although six dividends are shown, they reflect only five years of growth. Looking across the table at the present-value interest factors, *PVIF*, for five years, the factor closest to .714 occurs at 7 percent (.713). Therefore, the growth rate of the dividends, rounded to the nearest whole percentage, is 7 percent.

[15] Although more than one change in the growth rate can be incorporated in the model, to simplify the discussion we will consider only a single growth rate change. The number of variable growth valuation models is technically unlimited, but concern over all likely shifts in growth is unlikely to yield much more accuracy than a simpler model.

period. This step may require adjusting the most recent dividend, D_0, using the growth rate, g, expected during the initial period, in order to calculate the dividend amount for each year.

2. Find the present value of the dividends expected during the initial growth period. Using the notation presented earlier, this value can be given as

$$\sum_{t=1}^{N} \frac{D_t}{(1 + k_s)^t}$$

3. Find the value of the stock at the end of the initial growth period, $P_N = \dfrac{D_{N+1}}{k_s - g^*}$, which is the present value of all dividends expected from year $N + 1$ to infinity—assuming a constant dividend growth rate, g^*. This value is found by applying the constant growth model (presented as Equation 8.9 in the preceding section) to the dividends expected from year $N + 1$ to infinity. The present value of P_N would represent the value today of all dividends expected to be received from year $N + 1$ to infinity. This value can be represented by

$$\frac{1}{(1 + k_s)^N} \times \frac{D_{N+1}}{k_s - g^*} = PVIF_{k_s, N} \times P_N$$

4. Add the present-value components found in steps 2 and 3 to find the value of the stock, P_0, given in Equation 8.10.

$$P_0 = \underbrace{\sum_{t=1}^{N} \frac{D_t}{(1 + k_s)^t}}_{\substack{\text{Present value} \\ \text{of dividends} \\ \text{during initial} \\ \text{growth period}}} + \underbrace{\left(\frac{1}{(1 + k_s)^N} \times \frac{D_{N+1}}{k_s - g^*} \right)}_{\substack{\text{Present value of} \\ \text{price of stock at} \\ \text{end of initial} \\ \text{growth period}}} \tag{8.10}$$

The application of these steps to a variable growth situation with only one growth rate change is illustrated in the following example.

Example

Warren Industries' most recent (1988) annual dividend payment was $1.50 per share. The firm's financial manager expects that these dividends will increase at a 10 percent annual rate, g, over the next three years (1989, 1990, and 1991) due to the introduction of a hot new product. At the end of the three years (end of 1991) the firm's mature product line is expected to result in a slowing of the dividend growth rate to 5 percent per year forever (noted as g^*). The firm's required return, k_s, is 15 percent. To estimate the current (end-of-1988) value of Warren's common stock, $P_0 = P_{1988}$, the four-step procedure presented above must be applied to these data.

1. The value of the cash dividends in each of the next three years is calculated in columns 1, 2, and 3 of Table 8.3. The 1989, 1990, and 1991 dividends are $1.65, $1.82, and $2.00, respectively.

2. The present value of the three dividends expected during the 1989-to-1991 initial growth period is calculated in columns 3, 4, and 5 of Table 8.3. The sum of the present values of the three dividends is $4.14—the total of the column 5 values.

3. The value of the stock at the end of the initial growth period ($N = 1991$) can be found by first calculating $D_{N+1} = D_{1992}$:

$$D_{1992} = D_{1991} \times (1 + .05) = \$2.00 \times (1.05) = \$2.10$$

Using $D_{1992} = \$2.10$, $k_s = .15$, and $g^* = .05$, the value of the stock at the end of 1991 can be calculated:

$$P_{1991} = \frac{D_{1992}}{k_s - g^*} = \frac{\$2.10}{.15 - .05} = \frac{\$2.10}{.10} = \$21.00$$

Finally, in this step, the share value of $21 at the end of 1991 must be converted into a present (end-of-1988) value. Using the 15 percent required return we get

$$PVIF_{k_s,N} \times P_N = PVIF_{15\%,3} \times P_{1991} = .658 \times \$21.00 = \$13.82$$

4. Adding the present value of the initial dividend stream found in step 2 to the present value of the stock at the end of the initial growth period as specified in Equation 8.10, we get the current (end-of-1988) value of Warren Industries' stock.

$$P_{1988} = \$4.14 + \$13.82 = \$17.96$$

The stock is currently worth $17.96 per share; the calculation of this value is summarized diagramatically in Figure 8.4.

Table 8.3
Calculation of Present Value of Warren Industries' Dividends (1989–1991)

t	End of year	$D_0 = D_{1988}$ (1)	$FVIF_{10\%,t}$ (2)	D_t [(1) × (2)] (3)	$PVIF_{15\%,t}$ (4)	Present value of dividends [(3) × (4)] (5)
1	1989	$1.50	1.100	$1.65	.870	$1.44
2	1990	1.50	1.210	1.82	.756	1.38
3	1991	1.50	1.331	2.00	.658	1.32

$$\text{Sum of present value of dividends} = \sum_{t=1}^{3} \frac{D_t}{(1 + k_s)^t} = \quad \$4.14$$

Figure 8.4
Finding Warren Industries' Current (End-of-1988) Value with Variable Growth

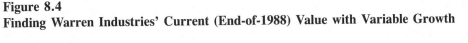

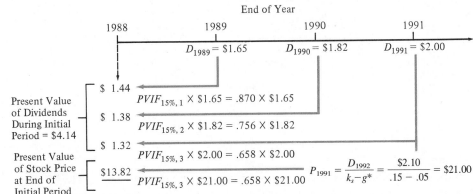

---

5 The variable growth common stock valuation model can be used to estimate the value of preferred stock, while the zero growth model is the most widely cited dividend valuation approach. *(Fable)*

The *zero* growth common stock valuation model can be used to estimate the value of preferred stock, while the *constant* growth model is the most widely cited dividend valuation model.

Decision Making and Common Stock Value

Valuation equations measure the stock value at a point in time based on expected return (D_1, g) and risk (k_s) data. The decisions of the financial manager, through their effect on these variables, can cause the value of the firm, P_0, to change. Figure 8.5 depicts the relationship among financial decisions, return, risk, and stock value.

Changes in Expected Return

Assuming that economic conditions remain stable, any management action that would cause current and prospective stockholders to raise their dividend expectations should increase the firm's value. In Equation 8.9[16] we can see that P_0 will increase for any increase in D_1 or g. Any action the financial manager can take that will increase the level of expected returns without changing risk (the required return) should be undertaken, since it will positively affect owners' wealth. An example will illustrate.

---

[16] To convey the interrelationship among financial decisions, return, risk, and stock value, the constant growth dividend valuation model is used. Other models—zero growth or variable growth—could be used, but the simplicity of exposition using the constant growth model justifies its use here.

Figure 8.5
Financial Decisions, Return, Risk, and Stock Value

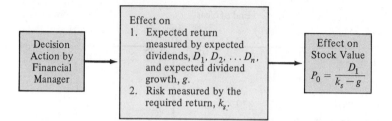

Example

Imagine that Lamar Company, which was found to have a share value of $18.75 in an earlier example, on the following day announced a major technological breakthrough that would revolutionize its industry. Current and prospective stockholders are not expected to adjust their required return of 15 percent, but they do expect that future dividends will be increased. Specifically, they feel that although the dividend next year, D_1, will remain at $1.50, the expected rate of growth will increase from 7 to 9 percent. Substituting $D_1 = \$1.50$, $k_s = .15$, and $g = .09$ into Equation 8.9, the resulting value is found to equal $25 [i.e., $1.50 ÷ (.15 − .09)]. The increased value therefore resulted from the higher expected future dividends reflected in the increase in the growth rate, g.

Changes in Risk

Although k_s is defined as the required return, it is, as pointed out in Chapter 7, directly related to the nondiversifiable risk, which can be measured by beta. The capital asset pricing model (CAPM) given in Equation 7.6 is restated as Equation 8.11.

$$k_s = R_F + [b \times (k_m − R_F)] \tag{8.11}$$

Reviewing the model, with the risk-free rate, R_F, and the required return on the market, k_m, held constant, the required return, k_s, depends directly on beta. In other words, any action taken by the financial manager that increases risk will also increase required return. In Equation 8.9 it can be seen that with all else constant, an increase in the required return, k_s, will reduce share value, P_0, and vice versa. Thus any action of the financial manager that increases risk contributes toward a reduction in value, and vice versa. An example will illustrate.

Example

Assume that the Lamar Company's 15 percent required return resulted from a risk-free rate, R_F, of 9 percent, a market return, k_m, of 13 percent, and a beta, b, of 1.50. Substituting into the capital asset pricing model, Equation 8.11, the 15 percent required return, k_s, results:

$$k_s = 9\% + [1.50 \times (13\% − 9\%)] = \underline{\underline{15\%}}$$

Using this return, the value of the firm, P_0, was calculated to be $18.75 in the earlier example.

Now imagine that the financial manager makes a decision that, without changing expected dividends, increases the firm's beta to 1.75. Assuming that R_F and k_m remain at 9 and 13 percent, respectively, the required return will increase to 16 percent (i.e., $9\% + [1.75 \times (13\% - 9\%)]$) to compensate stockholders for the increased risk. Substituting $D_1 = \$1.50$, $k_s = .16$, and $g = .07$ into the valuation equation, Equation 8.9, results in a share value of $16.67 [i.e., $\$1.50 \div (.16 - .07)$]. As expected, the owners, by raising the required return (without any corresponding increase in expected return), cause the firm's stock value to decline. Clearly the financial manager's action was not in the owners' best interest.

Combined Effect

A financial decision rarely affects return and risk independently; most decisions affect both factors. In terms of the measures presented, with an increase in risk (beta, b) one would expect an increase in return (D_1 or g, or both), assuming that R_F and k_m remain unchanged. Depending on the relative magnitude of the changes in these variables, the net effect on value can be assessed.

Example

If we assume that the two changes illustrated for Lamar Company in the preceding examples occur simultaneously as a result of an action of the financial decision maker, key variable values would be $D_1 = \$1.50$, $k_s = .16$, and $g = .09$. Substituting into the valuation model, a share price of $21.43 [i.e., $\$1.50 \div (.16 - .09)$] is obtained. The net result of the decision, which increased return (g from 7 to 9 percent) as well as risk (b from 1.50 to 1.75 and therefore k_s from 15 to 16 percent), is positive, since the share price increased from $18.75 to $21.43. Assuming that the key variables are accurately measured, the decision appears to be in the best interest of the firm's owners, since it increases their wealth.

---

6 **The decisions of financial managers, through their effect on expected return (measured using expected future dividends) and risk (measured using the required return), can cause the value of the firm to change.** *(Fact)*   **FACT OR FABLE?**

Summary

- The key valuation definitions and formulas are given in Table 8.4.

- Key inputs to the valuation process include cash flows (returns), timing, and the discount rate (risk). The value, or worth, of any asset is equal to the present value of all future cash flows it is expected to provide over the relevant time period.

- The value of a bond is the present value of interest payments plus the present value of its par, or face, value.

- The discount rate used to determine bond value is the required return, which may differ from the bond's coupon interest rate. A bond can sell at a discount, at par, or at a premium, depending upon whether the required return is respectively greater than, equal to, or less than its coupon interest rate.

    The amount of time to maturity affects bond values even if required return remains constant. When required return is constant, the value of a bond will approach its par value as the passage of time moves the bond closer to maturity. The shorter the amount of time until a bond's maturity, the less responsive is its market value to a given change in the required return.

    When investors evaluate and trade bonds, they commonly consider yield to maturity (YTM), which can be calculated precisely or approximated by formula.

    Popular approaches such as book value, liquidation value, and price/earnings (P/E) multiples are often used to estimate stock value, but the best approach defines the share value as the present value of all future dividends it is expected to provide over an infinite time horizon.

    Three cases of dividend growth—zero growth, constant

Table 8.4

Summary of Key Valuation Definitions and Formulas

Variable definitions

V_0 = value of the asset at time zero
CF_t = cash flow expected at the end of year t
k = appropriate discount rate
n = relevant time period, or number of years to maturity
B_0 = bond value
I = annual interest on a bond
k_d = required return on a bond
M = par, or face, value of a bond
P_0 = value of common stock
D_t = per-share dividend expected at the end of year t
k_s = required return on common stock
g = constant rate of growth in dividends (initial period of variable growth)
N = last year of initial growth period
g^* = constant rate of growth in dividends (subsequent period of variable growth)

Valuation formulas
Value of any asset

$$V_0 = \frac{CF_1}{(1+k)^1} + \frac{CF_2}{(1+k)^2} + \cdots + \frac{CF_n}{(1+k)^n}$$ [Eq. 8.1]

$$= [CF_1 \times (PVIF_{k,1})] + [CF_2 \times (PVIF_{k,2})] + \cdots + [CF_n \times (PVIF_{k,n})]$$ [Eq. 8.2]

Bond value

$$B_0 = I \times \left[\sum_{t=1}^{n} \frac{1}{(1+k_d)^t} \right] + M \times \left[\frac{1}{(1+k_d)^n} \right]$$ [Eq. 8.3]

$$= I \times (PVIFA_{k_d,n}) + M \times (PVIF_{k_d,n})$$ [Eq. 8.3a]

Common stock value

Zero growth: $P_0 = \dfrac{D_1}{k_s}$ [Eq. 8.7]

Constant growth: $P_0 = \dfrac{D_1}{k_s - g}$ [Eq. 8.9]

Variable growth: $P_0 = \displaystyle\sum_{t=1}^{N} \frac{D_t}{(1+k_s)^t} + \left(\frac{1}{(1+k_s)^N} \times \frac{D_{N+1}}{k_s - g^*} \right)$ [Eq. 8.10]

growth, and variable growth—can be considered in common stock valuation. The most widely cited model is the constant growth model.

● Because most financial decisions affect both return and risk, an assessment of their combined effect on value must be part of the financial decision-making process.

Questions

8-1 Define *valuation* and explain why it is important for the financial manager to understand the valuation process.

8-2 Briefly describe the three key inputs—cash flows, timing, and the discount rate—to the valuation process. Does the valuation process apply only to assets providing an annual cash flow? Explain.

8-3 Define and specify the general equation for the value of any asset, V_0, in terms of its expected cash flow, CF_t, in each year t, and the appropriate discount rate, k.

8-4 Describe the basic procedure used to value a bond that pays *annual* interest. What procedure is used to value bonds paying interest *semiannually?*

8-5 In terms of the required return and the coupon interest rate, what relationship between them will cause a bond to sell (a) at a discount? (b) at a premium? (c) at its par value? Explain.

8-6 If the required return on a bond differs from its coupon interest rate and is assumed constant until maturity, describe the behavior of the bond value as the passage of time moves the bond toward its maturity.

8-7 If you were a risk-averse investor, to protect against the potential impact of rising interest rates on bond value, would you prefer bonds with short or long periods until maturity? Explain why.

8-8 What is meant by the *yield to maturity (YTM)* on a bond?

Briefly describe both the precise and the approximate approach for calculating YTM.

8-9 Explain each of the three popular approaches—(a) book value, (b) liquidation value, and (c) price/earnings multiples—for estimating common stock value. Which of these is considered the best?

8-10 Describe, compare, and contrast each of the following common stock valuation models.

  a. Zero growth

  b. Constant growth

  c. Variable growth

8-11 Explain the linkages among financial decisions, return, risk, and stock value. How do the capital asset pricing model (CAPM) and the Gordon model fit into this basic framework? Explain.

8-12 Assuming that all other variables remain unchanged, what impact would *each* of the following have on stock price? Explain your answer.

  a. The firm's beta increases.

  b. The firm's required return decreases.

  c. The dividend expected next year decreases.

  d. The rate of growth in dividends is expected to increase.

Self-Test Problems

(Solutions on page 280)

ST-1 Lahey Industries has a $1,000 par value bond with an 8 percent coupon rate of interest outstanding. The bond has 12 years remaining to its maturity date.

  a. If interest is paid *annually,* what is the value of the bond when the required return is (1) 7 percent, (2) 8 percent, and (3) 10 percent?

  b. Indicate for each case in **a** whether the bond is selling at a discount, a premium, or at its par value.

  c. Using the 10 percent required return, find the bond's value when interest is paid *semiannually*.

ST-2 Elliot Enterprises' bonds currently sell for $1,150, have an 11 percent coupon rate of interest and a $1,000 par value, pay interest *annually,* and have 18 years to maturity.

  a. Calculate the bonds' yield to maturity (YTM) to the nearest whole percent.

  b. Estimate the bonds' YTM using the approximate yield formula.

  c. Compare and discuss your findings in **a** and **b.**

  d. Compare the YTM calculated in **a** to the bonds' coupon interest rate, and use a comparison of the bonds' current price and their par value to explain this difference.

ST-3 Perry Motors' common stock currently pays an annual dividend of $1.80 per share. The required return on the common stock is 12 percent. Estimate the value of the common stock under each of the following dividend growth rate assumptions.

  a. Dividends are expected to grow at an annual rate of 0 percent to infinity.

  b. Dividends are expected to grow at a constant annual rate of 5 percent to infinity.

  c. Dividends are expected to grow at an annual rate of 5 percent for each of the next three years followed by a constant annual growth rate of 4 percent from year four to infinity.

Problems

8-1 **(Valuation Fundamentals)** Imagine that you are trying to evaluate the economics of purchasing an automobile. Assume that you expect the car to provide annual after-tax cash benefits of $1,200 and that you can sell the car for after-tax proceeds of $5,000 at the end of the planned five-year ownership period. All funds for purchasing the car will be drawn from your savings, which are currently earning 6 percent after taxes.

  a. Identify the cash flows, their timing, and the discount rate applicable to valuing the car.

  b. What is the maximum price you would be willing to pay to acquire the car? Explain why.

8-2 **(Valuation of Assets)** Using the information provided, find the value of each of the following assets.

Asset	Cash flow End of year	Amount ($)	Appropriate discount rate (%)
A	1	5,000	18
	2	5,000	
	3	5,000	
B	1 through ∞	300	15
C	1	0	16
	2	0	
	3	0	
	4	0	
	5	35,000	
D	1 through 5	1,500	12
	6	8,500	
E	1	2,000	14
	2	3,000	
	3	5,000	
	4	7,000	
	5	4,000	
	6	1,000	

8-3 **(Asset Valuation and Risk)** Laura Drake wishes to estimate the value of an asset expected to provide cash inflows of $3,000 per year at the end of years 1 through 4 and $15,000 at the end of year 5. Her research indicates that she must earn 10 percent on low-risk assets, 15 percent on average-risk assets, and 22 percent on high-risk assets.

  a. What is the most Laura should pay for the asset if it is classified as (1) low risk? (2) average risk? or (3) high risk?

  b. If Laura is unable to assess the risk of the asset and wants to be certain she makes a good deal, based on your findings in **a,** what is the most she should pay? Why?

  c. All else being the same, what effect does increasing risk have on the value of an asset? Explain in light of your findings in **a.**

8-4 **(Basic Bond Valuation)** Complex Systems has an issue of $1,000-par-value bonds with a 12 percent coupon interest rate outstanding. The issue pays interest annually and has 16 years remaining to its maturity date.

  a. If bonds of similar risk are currently earning a 10 percent rate of return, how much will the Complex Systems bond sell for today?

  b. Describe the *two* possible reasons that similar-risk bonds are currently earning a return below the coupon interest rate on the Complex Systems bond.

  c. If the required return were at 12 percent instead of 10 percent, what would the current value of Complex Systems' bond be? Contrast this finding with **a** and discuss.

8-5 **(Bond Valuation—Annual Interest)** Calculate the value of each of the following bonds, all of which pay interest *annually*.

Bond	Par value ($)	Coupon interest rate (%)	Years to maturity	Required return (%)
A	1,000	14	20	12
B	1,000	8	16	8
C	100	10	8	13
D	500	16	13	18
E	1,000	12	10	10

8-6 **(Bond Value and Changing Required Returns)** Midland Utilities has outstanding a bond issue that will mature to its $1,000 par value in 12 years. The bond has a coupon interest rate of 11 percent and pays interest *annually*.

a. Find the value of the bond if the required return is
   (1) 11 percent
   (2) 15 percent
   (3) 8 percent

b. Plot your findings in **a** on a set of required return (*x*-axis)–market value (*y*-axis) axes.

c. Use your findings in **a** and **b** to discuss the relationship between the coupon interest rate on a bond and the required return and the market value of the bond relative to its par value.

d. What two reasons cause the required return to differ from the coupon interest rate?

8-7 **(Bond Value and Time—Constant Required Returns)** Pecos Manufacturing has just issued a 15-year, 12 percent coupon interest rate, $1,000-par bond that pays interest *annually*. The required return is currently 14 percent, and the company is certain it will remain at 14 percent until the bond matures in 15 years.

a. Assuming that the required return does remain at 14 percent until maturity, find the value of the bond with: (1) 15 years, (2) 12 years, (3) 9 years, (4) 6 years, (5) 3 years, and (6) 1 year to maturity.

b. Plot your findings on a set of time to maturity (*x*-axis)–market value of bond (*y*-axis) axes.

c. All else remaining the same, when the required return differs from the coupon interest rate and is assumed constant to maturity, what happens to the bond value as time moves toward maturity? Explain in light of the graph in **b.**

8-8 **(Bond Value and Time—Changing Required Returns)** Lynn Parsons is considering investing in either of two outstanding bonds. The bonds both have $1,000 par values and 11 percent coupon interest rates and pay *annual* interest. Bond A has exactly 5 years to maturity, while bond B has 15 years remaining until it matures.

a. Calculate the value of bond A if the required return is (1) 8 percent, (2) 11 percent, and (3) 14 percent.

b. Calculate the value of bond B if the required return is (1) 8 percent, (2) 11 percent, and (3) 14 percent.

c. From your findings in **a** and **b**, complete the following table and discuss the relationship between time to maturity and changing required returns.

Required return (%)	Value of bond A	Value of bond B
8	?	?
11	?	?
14	?	?

d. If Lynn wanted to minimize ''interest rate risk,'' which bond should she purchase? Why?

8-9 **(Yield to Maturity—Precise and Approximate)** The Salem Company bond currently sells for $955, has a 12 percent coupon interest rate and $1,000 par value, pays interest *annually*, and has 15 years to maturity.

a. Calculate the yield to maturity (YTM) on this bond using the more precise trial-and-error present-value-based approach.

b. Use the approximation formula to estimate the YTM on this bond.

c. Compare the yields calculated in **a** and **b** and discuss the relative utility of the approximation formula. Which approach would you recommend?

d. Explain the relationship that exists between the coupon interest rate and yield to maturity and the par value and market value of a bond.

8-10 **(Yield to Maturity)** Each of the following bonds pays interest *annually*.

Bond	Par value ($)	Coupon interest rate (%)	Years to maturity	Current value ($)
A	1,000	9	8	820
B	1,000	12	16	1,000
C	500	12	12	560
D	1,000	15	10	1,120
E	1,000	5	3	900

a. Use the approximation formula to find the yield to maturity (YTM) for each bond.

b. Calculate the YTM for each bond using the more precise trial-and-error present-value-based approach.

c. Compare and contrast your findings in **a** and **b** for each bond. Comment on the accuracy of your estimates from **a.**

d. What relationship exists between the coupon interest rate and yield to maturity and the par value and market value of the bond? Explain.

8-11 **(Bond Valuation—Semiannual Interest)** Find the value of a bond maturing in 6 years, with a $1,000 par value and a coupon interest rate of 10 percent (5 percent paid semiannually) if the required return on similar-risk bonds is 14 percent annual interest (7 percent paid semiannually).

8-12 (**Bond Valuation—Semiannual Interest**) Calculate the value of each of the following bonds, all of which pay interest *semiannually*.

Bond	Par value ($)	Coupon interest rate (%)	Years to maturity	Required return (%)
A	1,000	10	12	8
B	1,000	12	20	12
C	500	12	5	14
D	1,000	14	10	10
E	100	6	4	14

8-13 (**Bond Valuation—Quarterly Interest**) Calculate the value of a $5,000-par-value bond paying quarterly interest at an annual coupon interest rate of 10 percent and having 10 years until maturity if the required return on similar-risk bonds is currently a 12 percent annual rate paid *quarterly*.

8-14 (**Book and Liquidation Value**) The balance sheet for Gallinas Industries follows.

Balance Sheet Gallinas Industries December 31			
Assets		**Liabilities and stockholders' equity**	
Cash	$ 40,000	Accounts payable	$100,000
Marketable securities	60,000	Notes payable	30,000
Accounts receivable	120,000	Accrued wages	30,000
Inventories	160,000	Total current liabilities	$160,000
Total current assets	$380,000	Long-term debt	$180,000
Fixed assets	$400,000	Preferred stock	$ 80,000
Total assets	$780,000	Common stock (5,000 shares)	360,000
		Total liabilities and stockholders' equity	$780,000

Additional information with respect to the firm is available:
(1) Preferred stock can be liquidated for its book value.
(2) Accounts receivable and inventories can be liquidated at 90 percent of book value.
(3) The firm has 5,000 shares of common stock outstanding.
(4) All interest and dividends are currently paid up.
(5) Fixed assets can be liquidated at 70 percent of book value.
(6) Cash and marketable securities can be liquidated at book value.
Given this information, answer the following:

a. What is Gallinas Industries' book value per share?

b. What is the liquidation value per share?

c. Compare, contrast, and discuss the values found in **a** and **b**.

8-15 (**Valuation with Price/Earnings Multiples**) For each of the following firms, use the data given to estimate their common stock value employing price/earnings (P/E) multiples.

Firm	Expected EPS ($)	Price/earnings multiple
A	3.00	6.2
B	4.50	10.0
C	1.80	12.6
D	2.40	8.9
E	5.10	15.0

8-16 (**Common Stock Valuation—Zero Growth**) Scotto Manufacturing is a mature firm in the machine tool component industry. The firm's most recent common stock dividend was $2.40 per share. Due to its maturity as well as stable sales and earnings, the firm's management feels that dividends will remain at the current level for the foreseeable future.

a. If the required return is 12 percent, what is the value of Scotto's common stock?

b. If the firm's risk as perceived by market participants suddenly increases, causing the required return to rise to 20 percent, what will be the common stock value?

c. Based on your findings in **a** and **b,** what impact does risk have on value? Explain.

8-17 (**Preferred Stock Valuation**) Jones Design wishes to estimate the value of its outstanding preferred stock. The preferred issue has an $80 par value and pays an annual dividend of $6.40 per share. Similar-risk preferred stocks are currently earning a 9.3 percent annual rate of return.

a. What is the market value of the outstanding preferred stock?

b. If an investor purchases the preferred stock at the value calculated in **a,** how much would she gain or lose per share if she sells the stock when the required return on similar-risk preferreds has risen to 10.5 percent? Explain.

8-18 (**Common Stock Value—Constant Growth**) Use the constant growth valuation model (Gordon model) to find the value of each of the following firms.

Firm	Dividend expected next year ($)	Dividend growth rate (%)	Required return (%)
A	1.20	8	13
B	4.00	5	15
C	.65	10	14
D	6.00	8	9
E	2.25	8	20

8-19 **(Common Stock Value—Constant Growth)** Elk County Telephone has paid the following dividends over the past six years:

Year	Dividend per share ($)
1988	2.87
1987	2.76
1986	2.60
1985	2.46
1984	2.37
1983	2.25

The firm's dividend per share next year is expected to be $3.02.

a. If you can earn 13 percent on similar-risk investments, what is the most you would pay per share for this firm?

b. If you can earn only 10 percent on similar-risk investments, what is the most you would be willing to pay per share?

c. Compare and contrast your findings in **a** and **b** and discuss the impact of changing risk on share value.

8-20 **(Common Stock Value—Variable Growth)** Newman Manufacturing is considering a cash purchase of the stock of Grips Tool. During the year just completed, Grips earned $4.25 per share and paid cash dividends of $2.55 per share. Grips' earnings and dividends are expected to grow at 25 percent per year for the next three years, after which they are expected to grow at 10 percent per year to infinity. What is the maximum price per share Newman should pay for Grips if it has a required return of 15 percent on investments with risk characteristics similar to those of Grips?

8-21 **(Common Stock Value—Variable Growth)** Lawrence Industries' most recent annual dividend was $1.80 per share ($D_0 = \$1.80$), and the firm's required return is 10 percent. Find the market value of Lawrence's shares when:

a. Dividends are expected to grow at 8 percent annually for three years followed by a 5 percent constant annual growth rate from year 4 to infinity.

b. Dividends are expected to grow at 8 percent annually for each of three years followed by zero percent annual growth in years 4 to infinity.

c. Dividends are expected to grow at 8 percent annually for three years followed by a 10 percent constant annual growth rate in years 4 to infinity.

8-22 **(Common Stock Value—All Growth Models)** You are evaluating the potential purchase of a small business currently generating $42,500 of after-tax cash flow ($D_0 = \$42,500$). Based on a review of similar-risk investment opportunities, you must earn an 18 percent rate of return on the proposed purchase. Since you are relatively uncertain as to future cash flows, you have decided to estimate the firm's value using several possible cash flow growth rate assumptions.

a. What is the firm's value if cash flows are expected to grow at an annual rate of 0 percent to infinity?

b. What is the firm's value if cash flows are expected to grow at a constant annual rate of 7 percent to infinity?

c. What is the firm's value if cash flows are expected to grow at an annual rate of 12 percent for the first two years followed by a constant annual rate of 7 percent from year 3 to infinity?

8-23 **(Management Action and Stock Value)** REH Corporation's most recent dividend was $3 per share, its expected annual rate of dividend growth is 5 percent, and the required return is now 15 percent. A variety of proposals are currently being considered by management in order to redirect the firm's activities. For each of the proposed actions below, determine the resulting impact on share price and indicate the best alternative.

a. Do nothing, which will leave the key financial variables unchanged.

b. Invest in a new machine that will increase the dividend growth rate to 6 percent and lower the required return to 14 percent.

c. Eliminate an unprofitable product line, which will increase the dividend growth rate to 7 percent and raise the required return to 17 percent.

d. Merge with another firm, which will reduce the growth rate to 4 percent and raise the required return to 16 percent.

e. Acquire a subsidiary operation from another manufacturer. The acquisition should increase the dividend growth rate to 8 percent and increase the required return to 17 percent.

8-24 **(Integrative—Valuation and CAPM Formulas)** Given the following information for the stock of Foster Company, calculate its beta.

Current price per share of common	$50.00
Expected dividend per share next year	$ 3.00
Constant annual dividend growth rate	9%
Risk-free rate of return	7%
Required return on market portfolio	10%

8-25 **(Integrative—Risk and Valuation)** Giant Enterprises has a beta of 1.20, the risk-free rate of return is currently 10 percent, and the required return on the market portfolio is 14 percent. The company, which plans to pay a dividend of $2.60 per share in the coming year, anticipates that its future dividends will increase at an annual rate consistent with that experienced over the 1982-to-1988 period, when the following dividends were paid:

Year	Dividend per share ($)	Year	Dividend per share ($)
1988	2.45	1984	1.82
1987	2.28	1983	1.80
1986	2.10	1982	1.73
1985	1.95		

a. Use the capital asset pricing model (CAPM) to determine the required return on Giant Enterprises' stock.

b. Using the constant growth dividend valuation model and your finding in **a,** estimate the value of Giant Enterprises' stock.

c. Explain what effect, if any, a decrease in beta would have on the value of Giant's stock.

8-26 **(Integrative—Valuation and CAPM)** Hamlin Steel Company wishes to determine the value of Craft Foundry, a firm that it is considering acquiring for cash. Hamlin wishes to use the capital asset pricing model (CAPM) to determine the applicable discount rate to use as an input to the constant growth valuation model. Craft's stock is not publicly traded. After studying the betas of firms similar to Craft that are publicly traded, Hamlin believes that an appropriate beta for Craft's stock would be 1.25. The risk-free rate is currently 9 percent, and the market return is 13 percent. Craft's historical dividend per share for each of the past six years is given below:

Year	Dividend per share ($)
1988	3.44
1987	3.28
1986	3.15
1985	2.90
1984	2.75
1983	2.45

a. Given that Craft is expected to pay a dividend of $3.68 next year, determine the maximum cash price Hamlin should pay for each share of Craft.

b. Discuss the use of the CAPM for estimating the value of common stock, and describe the effect on the resulting value of Craft of:
   (1) A decrease in the dividend growth rate of 2 percentage points from that exhibited over the 1983–1988 period.
   (2) A decrease in the beta to 1.

Solutions to Self-Test Problems

ST-1 **a.** $B_0 = I \times (PVIFA_{k_d,n}) + M \times (PVIF_{k_d,n})$
$I = .08 \times \$1,000 = \$80$
$M = \$1,000$
$n = 12$ yrs.

(1) $k_d = 7\%$
$B_0 = \$80 \times (PVIFA_{7\%,12yrs}) + \$1,000 \times (PVIF_{7\%,12yrs})$
$= (\$80 \times 7.943) + (\$1,000 \times .444)$
$= \$635.44 + \$444.00 = \underline{\$1,079.44}$

(2) $k_d = 8\%$
$B_0 = \$80 \times (PVIFA_{8\%,12yrs}) + \$1,000 \times (PVIF_{8\%,12yrs})$
$= (\$80 \times 7.536) + (\$1,000 \times .397)$
$= \$602.88 + \$397.00 = \underline{\$999.88}$

(3) $k_d = 10\%$
$B_0 = \$80 \times (PVIFA_{10\%,12yrs}) + \$1,000 \times (PVIF_{10\%,12yrs})$
$= (\$80 \times 6.814) + (\$1,000 \times .319)$
$= \$545.12 + \$319.00 = \underline{\$864.12}$

b. (1) $k = 7\%$, $B_0 = \$1079.44$; sells at a *premium*
   (2) $k = 8\%$, $B_0 = \$999.88 \approx \$1,000.00$; sells at its *par value*
   (3) $k = 10\%$, $B_0 = \$864.12$; sells at a *discount*

c. $B_0 = \dfrac{I}{2} \times (PVIFA_{k_{d/2},2n}) + M \times (PVIF_{k_{d/2},2n})$

$ = \dfrac{\$80}{2} \times (PVIFA_{10\%/2,2\times12\text{periods}}) + \$1,000 \times (PVIF_{10\%/2,2\times12\text{periods}})$

$ = \$40 \times (PVIFA_{5\%,24\text{periods}}) + \$1,000 \times (PVIF_{5\%,24\text{periods}})$

$ = (\$40 \times 13.799) + (\$1,000 \times .310)$

$ = \$551.96 + \$310.00 = \underline{\underline{\$861.96}}$

ST-2 a. $B_0 = \$1,150$

$I = .11 \times \$1,000 = \$110$

$M = \$1,000$

$n = 18$ yrs.

$\$1,150 = \$110 \times (PVIFA_{k_d,18\text{yrs}}) + \$1,000 \times (PVIF_{k_d,18\text{yrs}})$

Since if $k_d = 11\%$, $B_0 = \$1,000 = M$, try $k_d = 10\%$.

$B_0 = \$110 \times (PVIFA_{10\%,18\text{yrs}}) + \$1,000 \times (PVIF_{10\%,18\text{yrs}})$

$ = (\$110 \times 8.201) + (\$1,000 \times .180)$

$ = \$902.11 + \$180.00 = \$1,082.11$

Since $\$1,082.11 < \$1,150$, try $k_d = 9\%$.

$B_0 = \$110 \times (PVIFA_{9\%,18\text{yrs}}) + \$1,000 \times (PVIF_{9\%,18\text{yrs}})$

$ = (\$110 \times 8.756) + (\$1,000 \times .212)$

$ = \$963.16 + \$212.00 = \$1,175.16$

Since the $1,175.16 value at 9 percent is higher than $1,150, and the $1,082.11 value at the 10 percent rate is lower than $1,150, the bond's yield to maturity must be between 9 and 10 percent. Since the $1,175.16 value is closest to $1,150, to the nearest whole percent the YTM is 9 percent. [Using interpolation, the more precise YTM value is 9.27 percent.]

b. Substituting into the *approximate yield formula:*

$$\text{Approximate yield} = \frac{I + \dfrac{M - B_0}{n}}{\dfrac{M + B_0}{2}}$$

$$= \frac{\$110 + \dfrac{\$1,000 - \$1,150}{18}}{\dfrac{\$1,000 + \$1,150}{2}} = \frac{\$110 - \$8.33}{\$1,075}$$

$$= \frac{\$101.67}{\$1,075} = \underline{\underline{9.46\%}}$$

c. The approximate yield of 9.46 percent is a reasonably good estimate of the actual yield (found using interpolation) of 9.27 percent. Comparing the 9.46 percent approximation to the 9.00 percent estimate to the nearest 1 percent, the use of the approximate yield formula seems appealing since its estimate is about as accurate (using the 9.27 percent value as the actual) as the use of the precise method rounded to the nearest whole percent.

d. The calculated YTM of 9+ percent is below the bond's 11 percent coupon interest rate since the bond's market value of $1,150 is above its $1,000 par value. Whenever a bond's market value is above its par value (it sells as a *premium*), its YTM will be below its coupon interest rate; when a bond sells at par, the YTM would equal its coupon interest rate; and when the bond sells for less than par (at a *discount*), its YTM will be greater than its coupon interest rate.

ST-3 $D_0 = \$1.80/\text{share}$
$\quad k_s = 12\%$

a. *Zero growth*

$$P_0 = \frac{D_1}{k_s} = \frac{D_1 = D_0 = \$1.80}{.12} = \underline{\underline{\$15/\text{share}}}$$

b. *Constant growth,* $g = 5\%$

$$D_1 = D_0 \times (1 + g) = \$1.80 \times (1 + .05) = \$1.89/\text{share}$$
$$P_0 = \frac{D_1}{k_s - g} = \frac{\$1.89}{.12 - .05} = \frac{\$1.89}{.07} = \underline{\underline{\$27/\text{share}}}$$

c. *Variable growth,* $g = 5\%$ for years 1 to 3 and $g^* = 4\%$ for years 4 to ∞.

$$D_1 = D_0 \times (1 + g)^1 = \$1.80 \times (1 + .05)^1 = \$1.89/\text{share}$$
$$D_2 = D_0 \times (1 + g)^2 = \$1.80 \times (1 + .05)^2 = \$1.98/\text{share}$$
$$D_3 = D_0 \times (1 + g)^3 = \$1.80 \times (1 + .05)^3 = \$2.08/\text{share}$$
$$D_4 = D_3 \times (1 + g^*) = \$2.08 \times (1 + .04) = \$2.16/\text{share}$$

$$P_0 = \sum_{t=1}^{3} \frac{D_t}{(1 + k_s)^t} + \left(\frac{1}{(1 + k_s)^N} \times \frac{D_{N+1}}{k_s - g^*} \right)$$

$$\sum_{t=1}^{3} \frac{D_t}{(1 + k_s)^t} = \frac{\$1.89}{(1 + .12)^1} + \frac{\$1.98}{(1 + .12)^2} + \frac{\$2.08}{(1 + .12)^3}$$
$$= [\$1.89 \times (PVIF_{12\%,1\text{yr}})] + [\$1.98 \times (PVIF_{12\%,2\text{yrs}})] + [\$2.08 \times (PVIF_{12\%,3\text{yrs}})]$$
$$= (\$1.89 \times .893) + (\$1.98 \times .797) + (\$2.08 \times .712)$$
$$= \$1.69 + \$1.58 + \$1.48 = \$4.75$$

$$\left(\frac{1}{(1 + k_s)^N} \times \frac{D_{N+1}}{k_s - g^*} \right) = \frac{1}{(1 + .12)^3} \times \frac{D_4 = \$2.16}{.12 - .04}$$
$$= (PVIF_{12\%,3\text{yrs}}) \times \frac{\$2.16}{.08}$$
$$= .712 \times \$27.00 = \$19.22$$

$$P_0 = \sum_{t=1}^{3} \frac{D_t}{(1 + k_s)^t} + \left(\frac{1}{(1 + k_s)^N} \times \frac{D_{N+1}}{k_s - g^*} \right) = \$4.75 + \$19.22 = \underline{\underline{\$23.97/\text{share}}}$$

Encore International

In the world of trend-setting fashion, instinct and marketing savvy are prerequisites to success. Jordan Ellis had both. His international casual-wear company, Encore, after ten years in business rocketed to $300 million in sales during 1988. His fashion line covered the young woman from head to toe, with hats, sweaters, dresses, blouses, skirts, pants, sweat shirts, socks, and shoes. In Manhattan, there was an Encore shop every five to six blocks, each featuring a different color focus. There were shops where the entire line was mauve, while others featured the entire line in canary yellow.

Encore had made it. The company's historical growth was so spectacular that no one could have predicted it. However, securities analysts speculated that Encore could not keep up the pace. They warned that competition is fierce in the fashion industry and that the firm might encounter little or no growth in the future. They estimated that stockholders also should expect no growth in future dividends.

Contrary to the conservative security analysts, Jordan Ellis, founder of Encore, felt the company could maintain a constant growth rate in dividends per share of 6 percent in the future, or possibly 8 percent for the next two years and 6 percent thereafter. Jordan Ellis based his estimates on an established long-term expansion plan into European and Latin American markets. By venturing into these markets, the risk of the firm as measured by beta was expected to immediately increase from 1.10 to 1.25.

In preparing the long-term financial plan, Encore's Chief Financial Officer (CFO) has assigned a junior financial analyst, Marc Scott, to evaluate the firm's current stock price. He has asked Marc to consider the conservative predictions of the securities analysts and the aggressive predictions of the company founder, Jordan Ellis.

Marc has compiled these 1988 financial data to aid his analysis.

Data Item	1988 Value
Earnings per share (EPS)	$6.25
Price per share of common stock	$40.00
Book value of common stock equity	$60,000,000
Total common shares outstanding	2,500,000
Common stock dividend per share	$4.00

Required

1. What is the firm's current P/E ratio?

2. What is the firm's current book value per share?

3. **a.** What are the required return and risk premium for Encore stock using the capital asset pricing model, assuming the beta of 1.10? (*Hint:* Use the Security Market Line—with data points noted—given in Figure 1 to find the market return.)

   b. What are the required return and risk premium for Encore stock using the capital asset pricing model assuming the beta of 1.25?

   c. What is the effect on the required return if the beta rises as expected?

4. If the securities analysts are correct and there is no growth in future dividends, what is the value per share of the Encore stock? (*Note:* Beta = 1.25.)

Figure 1
Security Market Line for Encore International

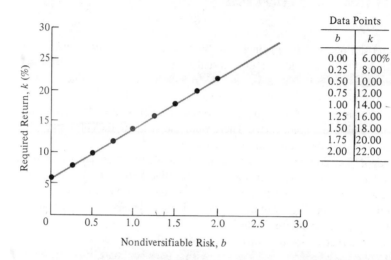

Data Points	
b	k
0.00	6.00%
0.25	8.00
0.50	10.00
0.75	12.00
1.00	14.00
1.25	16.00
1.50	18.00
1.75	20.00
2.00	22.00

5. **a.** If Jordan Ellis' predictions are correct, what is the value per share of Encore stock if the firm maintains a constant 6 percent growth rate in future dividends? (*Note:* Beta = 1.25.)
   b. If Jordan Ellis' predictions are correct, what is the value per share of Encore stock if the firm maintains a constant 8 percent growth rate in dividends per share over the next two years and 6 percent thereafter? (*Note:* Beta = 1.25.)

6. Compare the current (1988) price of the stock and the stock values found in questions **2, 4,** and **5.** Discuss why these values may differ. Which valuation method do you believe most clearly represents the true value of the Encore stock?

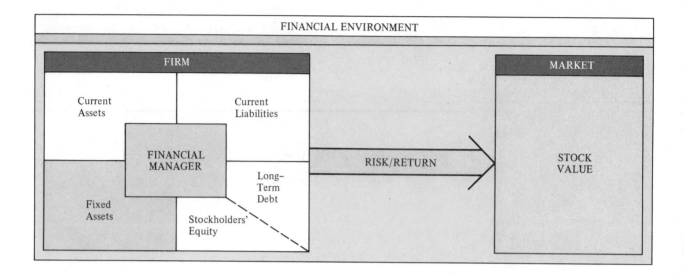

Long-Term Investment Decisions

CHAPTER 9

Capital Budgeting and Cash Flow Principles

FACT OR FABLE?
Are the following statements fact *(true)* or fable *(false)*?

1

Capital budgeting is the process of evaluating and selecting long-term investments (capital expenditures) consistent with the firm's goal of owner wealth maximization.

2

The capital budgeting process can be viewed as consisting of four distinct but interrelated steps—proposal generation, review and analysis, implementation, and follow-up.

3

The initial investment is calculated by subtracting installation costs and the after-tax proceeds from sale of an old asset from the cost of the new asset, and then adjusting for any change in net working capital.

4

When an asset held for a period of time is sold for more than its original purchase price, both a taxable capital gain and a taxable recapture of depreciation would result.

5

In a replacement decision, the relevant operating cash inflows are the after-tax cash inflows expected to result from the new asset, without regard to the cash inflows from the old asset.

6

The terminal cash flow is most often an inflow representing the after-tax cash flows, exclusive of operating cash inflows, occurring in the final year of a project.

Quality, upscale equipment has long kept Maytag the mighty grandmother of home appliances. The company's reputation for products that last longer and require fewer repairs has turned Newton, Iowa (Maytag headquarters), into "the washing-machine capital of the world."

Although Maytag doubled its sales and earnings in one five-year period and averages a 24.5 percent return on equity, outperforming bigger competitors such as General Electric and Whirlpool has not always been easy. When President and Chief Executive Officer Daniel J. Krumm took over in 1972, the company profits were beginning to look tattletale gray. The energy crisis had dealt a tough blow to the already-shrinking laundry appliance market. As Frigidaire and Westinghouse moved right out of the business, Wall Street questioned whether Maytag could survive.

Krumm had two answers. First, build up Maytag manufacturing and update technology. He invested $60 million in the modernization of the Newton plant, increasing its capacity by 75 percent. Second, diversify. In 1981, he purchased the Hardwick Stove Co. for $60 million and gave $50 million for Jenn-Air Corporation, a maker of top-line electric ranges. In 1984 and 1985, a $50-million-plus capital spending program brought an array of new products. Maytag was first in the industry to develop a stacked, full-sized washer and dryer with a space-saving capacity that makes them ideal for the rapidly growing condominium market.

Krumm predicts the future as "an age of great product innovation to meet the changing needs of the way people live." Estimating that two-thirds of the 450 million major appliances in U.S. homes are "ripe for replacement," he is sure of the size of Maytag's market and that his capital investment will pay off.

Maytag's highly successful spending program lends support to the adage "You have to spend money to make money!" It sounds easy, but a firm's major expenditure decisions must be based on carefully developed estimates of relevant cash flows, using procedures similar to those described in this chapter.

The Capital Budgeting Decision Process

Since long-term investments represent sizable outlays of funds that commit a firm to some course of action, procedures are needed to analyze and select them properly. Attention must be given to measuring relevant cash flows and applying appropriate decision techniques. As time passes, fixed assets may become obsolete or may require an overhaul; at these points, too, financial decisions may be required. **Capital budgeting** is the process of evaluating and selecting long-term investments consistent with the firm's goal of owner wealth maximization. Firms typically make a variety of long-term investments, but the most common such investment for the manufacturing firm is in *fixed assets,* which include property (land), plant, and equipment. These assets are quite often referred to as *earning assets* because they generally provide the basis for the firm's earning power and value.

capital budgeting The process of evaluating and selecting long-term investments consistent with the firm's goal of owner wealth maximization.

Capital budgeting (investment) and financing decisions are treated *separately* although it should become clear in the following chapter that the use of the cost of capital as a discount rate links these two decisions. Typically, once a proposed investment has been determined to be acceptable, the financial manager then chooses the best financing method. Therefore, here we concentrate on fixed asset acquisition without regard to the specific method of financing used. Chapters 11 and 12 and 16 to 18 address the key issues related to long-term financing of fixed assets. This section of the chapter discusses capital expenditure motives, the steps in the capital budgeting process, and basic capital budgeting terminology.

FACT OR FABLE?   1 **Capital budgeting is the process of evaluating and selecting long-term investments (capital expenditures) consistent with the firm's goal of owner wealth maximization.** *(Fact)*

Capital Expenditure Motives

capital expenditure An outlay of funds by the firm that is expected to produce benefits over a period *greater than* one year.

current expenditure An outlay of funds by the firm resulting in benefits received *within* one year.

A **capital expenditure** is an outlay of funds by the firm that is expected to produce benefits over a period of time *greater than* one year. A **current expenditure** is an outlay resulting in benefits received *within* one year. Fixed-asset outlays are capital expenditures, but not all capital expenditures are classified as fixed assets. A $60,000 outlay for a new machine with a usable life of 15 years is a capital expenditure that would appear as a fixed asset on the firm's balance sheet. A $60,000 outlay for advertising that produces benefits over a long period is also a capital expenditure. However, an outlay for advertising would rarely be shown as a fixed asset.[1]

Capital expenditures are made for many reasons, but although the motives differ, the evaluation techniques are the same. The basic motives for capital expenditures are to expand, replace, or renew fixed assets or to obtain some other less tangible benefit over a long period. Table 9.1 provides brief descriptions of the key motives for making capital expenditures.

Steps in the Process

capital budgeting process Consists of five distinct but interrelated steps: proposal generation, review and analysis, decision making, implementation, and follow-up.

The **capital budgeting process** can be viewed as consisting of five distinct but interrelated steps. It begins with *proposal generation*. This is followed by *review and analysis, decision making, implementation,* and *follow-up*. A brief description of each of these steps is given in Table 9.2. Each step in the process is important; major time and effort, however, are devoted to review and analysis and decision making. These are the steps given the most attention in this and the following chapter.

---

[1] Some firms do, in effect, capitalize advertising outlays if there is reason to believe the benefit of the outlay will be received at some future date. The capitalized advertising may appear as a deferred charge such as "deferred advertising expense," which is then amortized over the future. Expenses of this type are often deferred for reporting purposes in order to increase reported earnings, while for tax purposes the entire amount will be expensed in order to reduce the tax liability.

Table 9.1
Key Motives for Making Capital Expenditures

Motive	Description
Expansion	The most common motive for a capital expenditure is to expand the level of operations—usually through acquisition of fixed assets. A growing firm often finds it necessary to acquire new fixed assets rapidly; sometimes this includes the purchase of additional physical facilities, such as additional property and plant.
Replacement	As a firm's growth slows and it reaches maturity, most of its capital expenditures will be for the replacement or renewal of obsolete or worn-out assets. Each time a machine requires a major repair, the outlay for the repair should be evaluated in terms of the outlay to replace the machine and the benefits of replacement.
Renewal	Often an alternative to replacement. Renewal may involve rebuilding, overhauling, or retrofitting an existing machine or facility. For example, an existing drill press could be renewed by replacing its motor and adding a numeric control system, or a physical facility could be renewed by rewiring, adding air conditioning, and so on. Firms wishing to improve efficiency may find that both replacing and renewing existing machinery are suitable solutions.
Other purposes	Some capital expenditures do not result in the acquisition or transformation of tangible fixed assets shown on the firm's balance sheet. Instead, they involve a long-term commitment of funds by the firm in expectation of a future return. These expenditures include outlays for advertising, research and development, management consulting, and new products. Other capital expenditure proposals—such as the installment of pollution-control and safety devices mandated by the government—are difficult to evaluate because they provide intangible returns rather than clearly measurable cash flows.

(handwritten margin note: adjusting to the keep up with the competition)

(handwritten note next to "Other purposes" description: OSHA)

FACT OR FABLE?

2 The capital budgeting process can be viewed as consisting of four distinct but interrelated steps—proposal generation, review and analysis, implementation, and follow-up. *(Fable)*

The capital budgeting process can be viewed as consisting of *five* distinct but interrelated steps—proposal generation, review and analysis, *decision making*, implementation, and follow-up.

Basic Terminology

Before beginning to develop the concepts, tools, and techniques related to the review and analysis and decision-making steps in the capital budgeting process, it is useful to understand some of the basic terminology of these areas. In addition, we present a number of key assumptions used to simplify the discussion in the remainder of this chapter as well as in Chapter 10.

Independent versus Mutually Exclusive Projects

The two most common project types are (1) independent and (2) mutually exclusive projects. **Independent projects** do not compete with one another for the firm's invest-

independent projects
Projects that do not compete with one another for the firm's investment, so that the acceptance of one does not eliminate the others from further consideration.

Table 9.2
Steps in the Capital Budgeting Process

Steps (listed in order)	Description
Proposal generation	Proposals for capital expenditures are made by people at all levels within a business organization. To stimulate a flow of ideas that could result in potential cost savings, many firms offer cash rewards to employees whose proposals are ultimately adopted. Capital expenditure proposals typically travel from the originator to a reviewer at a higher level in the organization. Clearly, proposals requiring large outlays will be much more carefully scrutinized than less costly ones.
Review and analysis	Capital expenditure proposals are formally reviewed (1) to assess their appropriateness in light of the firm's overall objectives and plans and (2) more important, to evaluate their economic validity. The proposed costs and benefits are evaluated and then converted into a series of relevant cash flows to which various capital budgeting techniques are applied in order to measure the investment merit of the potential outlay. In addition, various aspects of the *risk* associated with the proposal are either incorporated into the economic analysis or rated and recorded along with the economic measures. Once the economic analysis is completed, a summary report, often with a recommendation, is submitted to the decision maker(s).
Decision making	The actual dollar outlay and the importance of a capital expenditure determine the organizational level at which the expenditure decision is made. Firms typically delegate capital-expenditure authority on the basis of certain dollar limits. Generally, the board of directors reserves the right to make final decisions on capital expenditures requiring outlays beyond a certain amount, while the authority for making smaller expenditures is given to other organizational levels. Inexpensive capital expenditures such as the purchase of a hammer for $15 are treated as operating outlays not requiring formal analysis.[a] Generally, firms operating under critical time constraints with respect to production often find it necessary to provide exceptions to a strict dollar-outlay scheme. In such cases the plant manager is often given the power to make decisions necessary to keep the production line moving, even though the outlays entailed are larger than he or she would normally be allowed to authorize.
Implementation	Once a proposal has been approved and funding has been made available,[b] the implementation phase begins. For minor outlays, implementation is relatively routine; the expenditure is made and payment is rendered. For major expenditures, greater control is required to ensure that what has been proposed and approved is acquired at the budgeted costs. Often the expenditures for a single proposal may occur in phases, with each outlay requiring the signed approval of company officers.
Follow-up	Involves monitoring the results during the operating phase of a project. The comparisons of actual outcomes in terms of costs and benefits with those expected and those of previous projects are vital. When actual outcomes deviate from projected outcomes, action may be required to cut costs, improve benefits, or possibly terminate the project.

[a] There is a certain dollar limit beyond which outlays are *capitalized* (i.e., treated as a fixed asset) and *depreciated* rather than *expensed*. This dollar limit depends largely on what the U.S. Internal Revenue Service will permit. In accounting, the issue of whether to expense or capitalize an outlay is resolved using the *principle of materiality*, which suggests that any outlays deemed material (i.e., large) relative to the firm's scale of operations should be capitalized, whereas others should be expensed in the current period.

[b] Capital expenditures are often approved as part of the annual budgeting process, although funding will not be made available until the budget is implemented—frequently as long as six months after approval.

CAPITAL BUDGETING ANALYST:
The Art of Spending Wisely

In a corporation as large as the one Ron works for, every division has a proposal for investing corporate funds in order to make more money. For example, a new processing plant close to the source of a raw material could save hundreds of thousands in transportation costs. Or a new product line could complement an existing line and increase sales by a significant amount. It takes money to build new processing plants, add new product lines, or do any of the many things that can put more money into the company's treasury. All of these proposals come to Ron's department—capital budgeting—before they're recommended.

As a capital budgeting analyst, Ron and the others in the department evaluate all projects and decide which of them would have the most favorable financial impact on the company. Ron says "even though large companies like mine have big capital budgets, the capital proposals always exceed the funds available. We must choose to do the things that will bring the best financial return. That means other things will not get done at all or will be delayed. My

job is to study the dollars involved and help decide what *will* get done."

Right now, Ron is working on an analysis of two big projects: one is the construction of a warehouse; the other, the purchase of a machine that would increase production of one of the company's best-selling products. Other people in the department are working on other projects at the same time. In order to study the building project, Ron traveled to the proposed site, met with the contractor, and learned the construction costs. He also met city officials to learn what taxes would be levied on this new facility. The next step was to work with company people to discover maintenance and personnel costs for running the warehouse as well as—and this is most important—the savings the company would realize as a result of owning its own warehouse rather than renting space.

When Ron's financial analysis is complete, he will go over it with his manager just to be sure all factors have been included in the analysis. If everything looks accurate, they will present

their recommendation to the vice president of finance, who will continue to consult with them as the final decision is made. Even after the project is approved, Ron is not finished with it. He then oversees the financial arrangements that will bring the project to completion. "It's my final test," says Ron. "In my projection I said it would take so-many dollars to implement it. Now I find out exactly how accurate my analysis was. If I was wrong, I have to live with my mistake and do my best to minimize its financial harm to the company."

"This job has variety. Every project is different and I have to learn something new with each one. And the travel is just enough to be stimulating but not tiring. Salary? Right now I make $34,500. If I get to be manager of the department some day, the opportunities really begin to open up. I could even work my way into the upper levels of the financial management of this company."

ment; the acceptance of one *does not eliminate* the others from further consideration. If a firm has unlimited funds to invest, all the independent projects that meet its minimum investment criteria can be implemented. **Mutually exclusive projects** are projects that have the same function and therefore compete with one another. The acceptance of one of a group of mutually exclusive projects *eliminates* all other projects in the group from further consideration. For example, if a firm is considering three ways to achieve its goal of increasing productive capacity, the three alternatives would be considered mutually exclusive. Acceptance of the "best" alternative will eliminate the need for either of the other two.

mutually exclusive projects Projects that compete with one another, so that the acceptance of one eliminates the others from consideration.

unlimited funds The financial situation in which a firm is able to accept all independent projects that provide an acceptable return.

Unlimited Funds versus Capital Rationing

The availability of funds for capital expenditures affects the firm's decision environment. If a firm has **unlimited funds** for investment, making capital budgeting decisions is quite

capital rationing The financial situation in which a firm has only a fixed number of dollars for allocation among competing capital expenditures.

simple. All independent projects that will provide returns greater than some predetermined level can be accepted. Typically, firms are not in such a situation; they instead operate under **capital rationing.** This means that they have only a fixed number of dollars available for capital expenditures and that numerous projects will compete for these limited dollars. The firm must therefore ration its funds by allocating them to projects that will maximize share value. Procedures for dealing with capital rationing are presented in Chapter 10. The discussions that follow assume unlimited funds.

Accept-Reject versus Ranking Approaches

accept-reject approach The evaluation of capital expenditure proposals to determine whether they meet the firm's minimum acceptance criterion.

ranking approach The ranking of capital expenditure projects on the basis of some predetermined measure such as the rate of return.

Two basic approaches to capital budgeting decisions are available. The **accept-reject approach** involves evaluating capital expenditure proposals to determine whether they meet the firm's minimum acceptance criterion. This approach can be used when the firm has unlimited funds, as a preliminary step when evaluating mutually exclusive projects, or in a situation in which capital must be rationed. In these cases only acceptable projects should be considered. The second method, the **ranking approach,** involves ranking projects on the basis of some predetermined measure such as the rate of return. The project with the highest return is ranked first, and the project with the lowest return is ranked last. Only acceptable projects should be ranked. Ranking is useful in selecting the "best" of a group of mutually exclusive projects and in evaluating projects with a view to capital rationing.

Conventional versus Nonconventional Cash Flow Patterns

conventional cash flow pattern An initial outflow followed by a series of inflows.

nonconventional cash flow pattern A pattern in which an initial outlay is *not* followed by a series of inflows.

Cash flow patterns associated with capital investment projects can be classified as *conventional* or *nonconventional.* A **conventional cash flow pattern** consists of an initial outflow followed by a series of inflows. This pattern is associated with many types of capital expenditures. For example, a firm may spend $10,000 today and as a result expect to receive cash inflows of $2,000 each year for the next eight years. This conventional pattern is diagrammed in Figure 9.1. A **nonconventional cash flow pattern** is any pattern in which an initial outlay is *not* followed by a series of inflows. For example, the purchase of a machine may require an initial cash outflow of $20,000 and may generate cash inflows of $5,000 each year for four years. In the fifth year after purchase, an outlay of $8,000 may be required to overhaul the machine, after which it generates inflows of $5,000 each year for five years. This nonconventional pattern is illustrated in Figure 9.2.

Figure 9.1
A Conventional Cash Flow Pattern

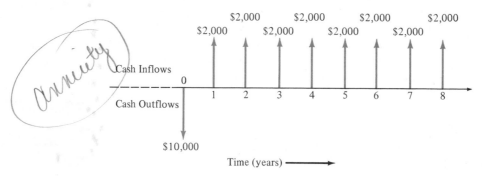

Figure 9.2
A Nonconventional Cash Flow Pattern

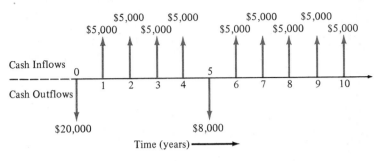

Difficulties often arise in evaluating projects involving a nonconventional pattern of cash flows. The discussions in the remainder of this chapter and in the following chapter are therefore limited to the evaluation of conventional patterns.

Annuity versus Mixed Stream Cash Flows

As pointed out in Chapter 6, an **annuity** is a stream of equal annual cash flows. A series of cash flows exhibiting any pattern other than an annuity is a **mixed stream** of cash flows. The cash inflows of $2,000 per year (for eight years) in Figure 9.1 are inflows from an annuity, whereas the unequal pattern of inflows in Figure 9.3 (page 296) represents a mixed stream. As pointed out in Chapter 6, the techniques required to evaluate cash flows are much simpler to use when the pattern of flows is an annuity.

annuity A stream of equal annual cash flows.

mixed stream A series of cash flows exhibiting any pattern other than that of an annuity.

The Relevant Cash Flows

To evaluate capital expenditure alternatives, the **relevant cash flows,** which are the *incremental after-tax cash outflow (investment) and resulting subsequent inflows,* must be determined. The **incremental cash flows** represent the *additional* cash flows—outflows or inflows—expected to result from a proposed capital expenditure. As noted in Chapter 3, cash flows, rather than accounting figures, are used because it is these flows that directly affect the firm's ability to pay bills and purchase assets. Furthermore, accounting figures and cash flows are not necessarily the same, due to the presence of certain noncash expenditures on the firm's income statement. The remainder of this chapter is devoted to the procedures for measuring the relevant cash flows associated with proposed capital expenditures.

relevant cash flows The incremental after-tax cash outflow (investment) and resulting subsequent inflows associated with a proposed capital expenditure.

incremental cash flows The *additional* cash flows— outflows or inflows— expected to result from a proposed capital expenditure.

Major Cash Flow Components

The cash flows of any project having the *conventional pattern* can include three basic components: (1) an initial investment, (2) operating cash inflows, and (3) terminal cash flow. All projects, whether for expansion, replacement, renewal, or some other purpose, have the first two components. Some, however, lack the final component, terminal cash flow.

Figure 9.3 depicts the cash flows for a project. Each of the cash flow components is labeled. The **initial investment,** which is the relevant cash outflow at time zero, is

initial investment The relevant cash outflow at time zero.

Figure 9.3
Major Cash Flow Components

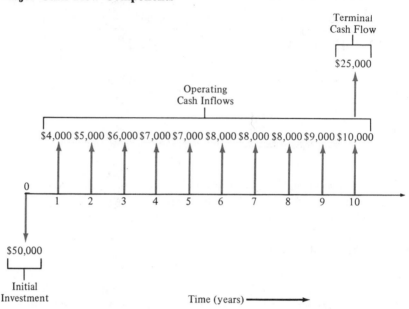

operating cash inflows The incremental after-tax cash inflows resulting from use of a project during its life.

terminal cash flow The after-tax nonoperating cash flow occurring in the final year of a project, usually attributable to liquidation of the project.

$50,000 for the proposed project. The **operating cash inflows,** which are the incremental after-tax cash inflows resulting from use of the project during its life, gradually increase from $4,000 in the first year to $10,000 in the tenth and final year of the project. The **terminal cash flow,** which is the after-tax nonoperating cash flow occurring in the final year of the project, usually attributable to liquidation of the project, is $25,000 received at the end of the project's ten-year life. Note that the terminal cash flow does *not* include the $10,000 operating cash inflow for year 10.

Expansion Versus Replacement Cash Flows

The development of relevant cash flows is most straightforward in the case of *expansion decisions.* In this case the initial investment, operating cash inflows, and terminal cash flow are merely the after-tax cash outflow and inflows associated with the proposed outlay. When making *replacement decisions,* the development of relevant cash flows is more complicated due to the need to find the *incremental* cash outflows and inflows that will result from the proposed replacement. The initial investment in this case would be found by subtracting any after-tax cash inflows expected from liquidation of the old asset being replaced from the initial investment needed to acquire the new asset. The operating cash inflows would be found by taking the difference between the operating cash inflows from the new asset and from the replaced asset. The terminal cash flow would be found by taking the difference between the after-tax cash flows expected upon termination of the new and the old assets.

Example
Column 1 of Table 9.3 shows the initial investment, operating cash inflows, and terminal cash flow for an *expansion decision* involving the acquisition of new asset A.

It can be seen that as a result of a $13,000 initial investment, the firm would expect operating cash inflows of $5,000 in each of the next five years and a terminal cash flow of $7,000 at the end of year 5.

If new asset A is being considered as a *replacement* for old asset A, the relevant cash flows would be found by subtracting the cash flows attributed to old asset A from the cash flows for new asset A. The expected after-tax cash inflows from liquidating old asset A and the current operating cash inflows and terminal cash flow from the old asset are shown in column 2 of Table 9.3. If old asset A is liquidated, $3,000 of after-tax cash inflows would result initially, in years one through five $3,000, $2,500, $2,000, $1,500, and $1,000 of operating cash inflows would be eliminated, and also, in year five, $5,000 of terminal cash flow would be eliminated. Therefore the relevant cash flows resulting from the replacement decision would be the difference in cash flows between new asset A and old asset A, as shown in column 3 of Table 9.3.

Table 9.3
Expansion and Replacement Cash Flows

	Expansion	Replacement	
	New Asset A (1)	Old Asset A (2)	Relevant cash flows [(1) − (2)] (3)
Initial investment	$13,000	$3,000[a]	$10,000
Year	Operating cash inflows		
1	$ 5,000	$3,000	$ 2,000
2	5,000	2,500	2,500
3	5,000	2,000	3,000
4	5,000	1,500	3,500
5	5,000	1,000	4,000
Terminal cash flow	$ 7,000	$5,000	$ 2,000

[a] After-tax cash inflows expected from liquidation.

Actually, all capital budgeting decisions can be viewed as replacement decisions. Expansion decisions are merely replacement decisions in which all cash flows from the old asset are zero. In light of this fact, the following discussions emphasize the more general replacement decisions.

Finding the Initial Investment

As previously stated, the term *initial investment* as used here refers to the relevant cash outflow to be considered in evaluating a prospective capital expenditure. It is calculated by subtracting all cash inflows occurring at time zero from all cash outflows occurring at time zero (the time the expenditure is made). Since our discussion of capital budgeting is concerned only with investments exhibiting conventional cash flows, the initial investment must occur at time zero.

The basic variables that must be considered in determining the initial investment associated with a capital expenditure are the cost of the new asset, the installation costs (if any), the proceeds (if any) from the sale of an old asset, the taxes (if any) resulting from the sale of an old asset, and the change (if any) in net working capital. The basic format for determining the initial investment is given in Table 9.4.

Table 9.4
The Basic Format for Determining Initial Investment

Cost of new asset
+ Installation costs
− Proceeds from sale of old asset
± Taxes on sale of old asset
± Change in net working capital
Initial investment

FACT OR FABLE?

3   The initial investment is calculated by subtracting installation costs and the after-tax proceeds from sale of an old asset from the cost of the new asset, and then adjusting for any change in net working capital. *(Fable)*

The initial investment is calculated by *adding installation costs* to and subtracting the after-tax proceeds from sale of an old asset from the cost of the new asset, and then adjusting for any change in net working capital.

The Cost of a New Asset

cost of a new asset The net outlay its acquisition requires.

The **cost of a new asset** is the net outlay it requires. Usually we are concerned with the acquisition of a fixed asset for which a definite purchase price is paid. If there are no installation costs and the firm is not replacing an existing asset, the purchase price of the asset adjusted for any change in net working capital is equal to the initial investment. Each capital expenditure decision should be checked to make sure installation costs have not been overlooked.

Installation Costs

installation costs Any added costs necessary to place an asset into operation.

Installation costs are any added costs necessary to place an asset into operation. They are considered part of the firm's capital expenditure. The Internal Revenue Service (IRS) requires the firm to add installation costs to the purchase price in order to determine the depreciable value of an investment, which is depreciated over a period of years.

Proceeds from the Sale of an Old Asset

proceeds from the sale of an old asset The net cash inflow resulting from the sale of an old asset.

If a new asset is intended to replace an existing asset that is being sold, the **proceeds from the sale of an old asset** are the net cash inflows it provides. The proceeds from the sale of the old asset are reduced by any costs incurred in the process of removing the old asset.

Proceeds received from the sale (liquidation) of an old asset decrease the firm's initial investment in the new asset.

Taxes

Taxes must be considered in calculating the initial investment whenever a new asset replaces an old asset that has been sold.[2] The proceeds from the sale of the replaced asset are normally subject to some type of tax. The amount of tax depends on the relationship between the sale price, initial purchase price, and book value of the asset being replaced. An understanding of (1) book value and (2) basic tax rules is necessary to determine the taxes on the sale of an asset.

Book Value

The **book value** of an asset is its strict accounting value. It can be calculated using the following equation:

$$\text{Book value} = \text{installed cost of asset} - \text{accumulated depreciation} \qquad (9.1)$$

book value The strict accounting value of an asset, calculated by subtracting its accumulated depreciation from installed cost.

Example

Hudson Industries acquired a machine tool with an installed cost of $100,000 two years ago. The asset was being depreciated under ACRS (see Chapter 3) using a five-year recovery period.[3] Table 3.6 (page 66) shows that under ACRS for a five-year recovery period, 20 percent and 32 percent of the installed cost would be depreciated in years 1 and 2, respectively. In other words, 52 percent (20 percent + 32 percent) of the $100,000 cost, or $52,000 (.52 × $100,000), would represent the accumulated depreciation at the end of year 2. Substituting into Equation 9.1, we get:

$$\text{Book value} = \$100,000 - \$52,000 = \$48,000$$

The book value of Hudson's asset at the end of year 2 is therefore $48,000.

Basic Tax Rules

Four potential tax situations can occur when selling an asset. These situations differ, depending upon the relationship between the asset's sale price, its initial purchase price, and its book value. The three key forms of taxable income and their associated tax treatments are defined and summarized in Table 9.5. The assumed tax rates used throughout this text are noted in the final column of the same table. The four possible tax situations resulting in one or more forms of taxable income are: (1) the asset is sold for more than its initial purchase price; (2) the asset is sold for more than its book value but less than its initial purchase price; (3) the asset is sold for its book value; and (4) the asset is sold for less than its book value. An example will illustrate.

---

[2] A brief discussion of the tax treatment of ordinary and capital gains income was presented in Chapter 2.

[3] Under the *Tax Reform Act of 1986* most manufacturing machinery and equipment has a 7-year recovery period as noted in Chapter 3 (Table 3.5). Using this recovery period results in 8 years of depreciation, which unnecessarily complicates examples and problems. To simplify, *machinery and equipment are treated as 5-year assets throughout this and the following chapters.*

Table 9.5
Tax Treatment on Sales of Assets

Type of taxable income	Definition	Tax treatment	Assumed tax rate
Capital gain	Portion of the sale price that is in excess of the initial purchase price.	Regardless of how long the asset has been held, the total capital gain is taxed as ordinary income.	40%
Recaptured depreciation	Portion of the sale price that is in excess of book value and represents a recovery of previously taken depreciation.	All recaptured depreciation is taxed as ordinary income.	40%
Loss on sale of asset	Amount by which sale price is *less than* book value.	If asset is depreciable and used in business, loss is deducted from ordinary income.	40% of loss is a tax savings
		If asset is *not* depreciable or is *not* used in business, loss is deductible only against capital gains.	40% of loss is a tax savings

Example

The old asset purchased two years ago for $100,000 by Hudson Industries has a current book value of $48,000. What will happen if the firm now decides to sell the asset and replace it? The tax consequences associated with sale of the asset depend upon the sale price. Let us consider each of the four possible situations.

The sale of the asset for more than its initial purchase price   If Hudson sells the old asset for $110,000, it realizes a capital gain of $10,000 (the amount by which the sale price exceeds the initial purchase price of $100,000) which is taxed as ordinary income.[4] The firm also experiences ordinary income in the form of **recaptured depreciation,** which is the portion of the sale price that is above book value and below the initial purchase price. In this case there is recaptured depreci-

recaptured depreciation
The portion of the sale price that is above book value and below the initial purchase price.

[4] Although the *Tax Reform Act of 1986* requires corporate capital gains to be treated as ordinary income, the structure for corporate capital gains is retained under the law in order to facilitate a rate differential in the likely event of future tax revisions. Therefore, this distinction is made throughout the text discussions.

ation of $52,000 ($100,000 − $48,000). The taxes on the total gain of $62,000 are calculated as follows:

	Amount (1)	Rate (2)	Tax [(1) × (2)] (3)
Capital gain	$10,000	.40	$ 4,000
Recaptured depreciation	52,000	.40	20,800
Totals	$62,000		$24,800

These taxes should be used in calculating the initial investment in the new asset, using the format in Table 9.4. In effect, the taxes raise the amount of the firm's initial investment in the new asset by reducing the proceeds from the sale of the old asset.

The sale of the asset for more than its book value but less than its initial purchase price.   If Hudson sells the old asset for $70,000, which is less than its original purchase price but more than its book value, there is no capital gain. However, the firm still experiences a gain in the form of recaptured depreciation of $22,000 ($70,000 − $48,000), which is taxed as ordinary income. Since the firm is assumed to be in the 40 percent tax bracket, the taxes on the $22,000 gain are $8,800. This amount in taxes should be used in calculating the initial investment in the new asset.

The sale of the asset for its book value.   If the asset is sold for $48,000, which is its book value, the firm breaks even. Since *no tax results from selling an asset for its book value,* there is no effect on the initial investment in the new asset.

The sale of the asset for less than its book value.   If Hudson sells the asset for $30,000, an amount less than its book value, it experiences a loss of $18,000 ($48,000 − $30,000). If this is a depreciable asset used in the business, the loss may be used to offset ordinary operating income. If the asset is *not* depreciable or *not* used in the business, the loss can be used only to offset capital gains. In both cases the loss will save the firm $7,200 ($18,000 × .40) in taxes. In either case, if current operating earnings or capital gains are not sufficient to offset the loss, the firm may be able to apply these losses to prior years' taxes or future years' taxes.[5]

---

4 When an asset held for a period of time is sold for more than its original purchase price, both a taxable capital gain and a taxable recapture of depreciation would result. (*Fact*)

FACT OR FABLE?

---

[5] The tax law provides detailed procedures for tax loss *carrybacks* and *carryforwards*. Coverage of such procedures is beyond the scope of this text, and they are therefore ignored in subsequent discussions.

Change in Net Working Capital

Net working capital, as noted in Chapter 3, is the amount by which a firm's current assets exceed its current liabilities. This topic is treated in depth in Part Five, especially in Chapter 13, but at this point it is important to note that changes in net working capital often accompany capital expenditure decisions, regardless of their motive. If a firm acquires new machinery to expand its level of operations, accompanying such expansion will be increased levels of cash, accounts receivable, inventories, accounts payable, and accruals. As long as the expanded operations continue, the increased investment in current assets (cash, accounts receivable, and inventories) and increased current liability financing (accounts payable and accruals) would be expected to continue. The difference between the change in current assets and the change in current liabilities would be the **change in net working capital.** Generally, current assets increase by more than current liabilities, resulting in an increased investment in net working capital, which would be treated as an initial outflow associated with the project.[6] If the change in net working capital were negative, it would be shown as an initial inflow associated with the project. The change in net working capital—regardless of whether an increase or a decrease—*is not taxable* because it merely involves a net build-up or reduction of current accounts.

change in net working capital The difference between a change in current assets and a change in current liabilities.

Example
Hanson Company is contemplating expanding its operations to meet the growing demand for its products. In addition to Hanson's acquiring a variety of new capital equipment, financial analysts expect that the changes in current accounts summarized in Table 9.6 will occur and be maintained over the life of the expansion. Current assets are expected to increase by $22,000, and current liabilities are expected to increase by $9,000, resulting in a $13,000 increase in net working capital. In this case the increase would represent an increased working capital investment and be treated as a cash outflow in calculating the initial investment.

**Table 9.6
Calculation of Change in Net Working Capital for
Hanson Company**

Current account	Change in balance	
Cash	+ $ 4,000	
Accounts receivable	+ 10,000	
Inventories	+ 8,000	
(1) Current assets		+ $22,000
Accounts payable	+ $ 7,000	
Accruals	+ 2,000	
(2) Current liabilities		+ 9,000
Change in net working capital [(1) − (2)]		+ $13,000

[6] When net working capital changes apply to the calculation of the initial investment associated with a proposed capital expenditure, they are for convenience assumed to be spontaneous and thereby occurring at time zero. In practice, frequently the change in net working capital will occur over a period of months as the capital expenditure is implemented.

Calculating the Initial Investment

It should be clear that a variety of tax and other considerations enter into the initial investment calculation. The following example illustrates how the basic variables described in the preceding discussion are used to calculate the initial investment according to the format in Table 9.4.[7]

Example

Powell Corporation is trying to determine the initial investment required to replace an old machine with a new, much more sophisticated model. The proposed machine's purchase price is $380,000, and an additional $20,000 will be required to install it. It will be depreciated under ACRS using a five-year recovery period. The old machine was purchased three years ago at a cost of $240,000 and was being depreciated under ACRS using a five-year recovery period. The firm has found a buyer willing to pay $280,000 for the old machine and remove it at the buyer's own expense. The firm expects that a $35,000 increase in current assets and an $18,000 increase in current liabilities will accompany the replacement; these changes will result in a $17,000 ($35,000 − $18,000) *increase* in net working capital. Both ordinary income and capital gains are taxed at a rate of 40 percent.

The only component of the initial investment required by the proposed purchase that is difficult to obtain is taxes. Since the firm is planning to sell the old machine for $40,000 more than its purchase price, it will realize a *capital gain of $40,000*. The book value of the old machine can be found using the depreciation percentages from Table 3.6 (page 66) of 20 percent, 32 percent, and 19 percent for years 1 through 3, respectively. The resulting book value is $69,600 ($240,000 − [(.20 + .32 + .19) × $240,000]). An *ordinary gain of $170,400* ($240,000 − $69,600) in recaptured depreciation is also realized on the sale. The total taxes on the gain are $84,160 [($40,000 + $170,400) × .40]. Substituting these taxes along with the purchase price and installation cost of the new machine, the proceeds from the sale of the old machine, and the change in net working capital, into the format in Table 9.4 results in an initial investment of $221,160. This represents the net cash outflow required at time zero:

Cost of new machine	$380,000	Depreciable
+ Installation costs	20,000	outlay
− Proceeds from sale of old machine	280,000	
+ Taxes on sale of old machine	84,160	
+ Change in net working capital	17,000	
Initial investment	$221,160	

[7] Throughout our discussions of capital budgeting, all assets evaluated as candidates for replacement are assumed to be depreciable assets that are directly used in the business, so any losses on the sale of these assets can be applied against ordinary operating income. The decisions are also structured so as to ensure that the usable life remaining on the old asset is just equal to the life of the new asset; this assumption permits the avoidance of the problem of unequal lives, which is discussed in Chapter 10.

FINANCE IN ACTION

A CAPITAL INVESTMENT THAT WON'T GO UP IN SMOKE

In the late 1970s, R.J. Reynolds Industries Inc. found itself saddled with old, ill-equipped production facilities and decided to build anew, designating as its crown jewel a factory-of-the-future in Tobaccoville, N.C. In the spring of 1980, facing the prospect of a no-growth market in cigarettes and a slipping market share, Reynolds decided to "revitalize" its tobacco operation. The goal: to catch up with technological advances already underway in the industry.

The unit's executives, armed with a corporate commitment of $2 billion in capital spending over eight years, developed a plan that included several retrofit projects. But anchoring the program was the $1 billion, two-million-square-foot factory in Tobaccoville, 12 miles from the company's Winston-Salem headquarters. "Our facilities were probably the oldest in the business. Consequently, we couldn't stand pat and do nothing," says Gerald H. Long, who became president of the tobacco unit in 1981. Many of

Reynolds's buildings were more than 50 years old, and remodeling the red brick, multistory buildings was considered impractical.

By early 1986, the plant began spewing out cigarettes, and by 1987 the high-tech facility was able to produce 20 million cigarettes an hour—twice as fast as the company's existing facilities, with a considerably smaller work force. (Reynolds declines to say exactly how many people are involved in the production of cigarettes and what the work force will decline to by 1990, when the capital-spending program ends.) Hand-in-hand with more efficient production is the promise of broader marketing flexibility. The new technology makes it a lot easier for Reynolds to move quickly in producing dozens of new brands and styles to compete in today's so-called niche market, where specific cigarettes are aimed at relatively small but profitable markets. Twenty years ago, Reynolds had nine types of cigarettes and other domestic producers a total of 59. Today, Reynolds has 55 and

the industry has crowded shelves with 291 different types.

Retooling used to be a long and complex process, making it difficult to react to a competitor's foray. But at Tobaccoville, producing new brands will sometimes be as easy as pushing a few buttons. There will be 72 modules of equipment that can take processed tobacco, roll it into cigarettes, wrap the cigarettes in a pack, slide the packs into cartons and push the cartons into shipping boxes. If necessary, the plant could produce 72 different brands and styles at the same time.

Reynolds already has had a taste of what the new plant will provide. The equipment in place at some of the retrofit plants has reversed the results of consumer blind taste tests, where loyal Winston smokers once often preferred competitors' cigarettes. And, the company says, consumer complaints have dropped 24 percent in the past five years.

SOURCE: Ed Bean, "From the Ground Up," *The Wall Street Journal*, September 16, 1985. Reprinted by permission of *The Wall Street Journal*, © Dow Jones & Company, Inc. 1985. All rights reserved.

Finding the Operating Cash Inflows

The benefits expected from a capital expenditure are measured by its *operating cash inflows*, which are *incremental after-tax cash inflows*. In this section we use the income statement format to develop clear definitions of the terms *after-tax, cash inflows,* and *incremental*.

Interpreting the Term *After-Tax*

Benefits expected to result from proposed capital expenditures must be measured on an after-tax basis, since the firm will not have the use of any benefits until it has satisfied the government's tax claims. These claims depend on the firm's taxable income, so the deduction of taxes *prior to* making comparisons between proposed investments is necessary for consistency. Consistency is required in evaluating capital expenditure alternatives, since the intention is to compare like benefits.

Interpreting the Term *Cash Inflows*

All benefits expected from a proposed project must be measured on a cash flow basis. Cash inflows represent dollars that can be spent, not merely "accounting profits," which are not necessarily available for paying the firm's bills. A simple technique for converting after-tax net profits into operating cash inflows was illustrated in Chapter 3. The basic calculation requires adding any *noncash charges* deducted as expenses on the firm's income statement back to net profits after taxes. Probably the most common noncash charge found on income statements is depreciation. It is the only noncash charge that will be considered in this section. The following example shows how after-tax operating cash inflows can be calculated for a present and a proposed project.

Example

Powell Corporation's estimates of its revenues and expenses (excluding depreciation), with and without the proposed capital expenditure described in the preceding example, are given in Table 9.7. Note that both the expected usable life of the proposed machine and the remaining usable life of the present machine is five years. The amount to be depreciated with the proposed machine is calculated by summing the purchase price of $380,000 and the installation costs of $20,000. Since the machine is to be depreciated under ACRS using a five-year recovery period, 20, 32, 19, 12, 12, and 5 percent would be recovered in years 1 through 6, respectively (see Chapter 3 and Table 3.6 on page 66 for more detail).[8] The resulting depreciation on this machine for each of the six years, as well as the remaining three years of depreciation on the old machine, are calculated in Table 9.8.[9]

The operating cash inflows in each year can be calculated using the following income statement format:

	Revenue
−	Expenses (excluding depreciation)
	Profits before depreciation and taxes
−	Depreciation
	Net profits before taxes
−	Taxes
	Net profits after taxes
+	Depreciation
	Operating cash inflows

Substituting the data from Tables 9.7 and 9.8 into this format and assuming a 40 percent tax rate, Table 9.9 demonstrates the calculation of operating cash inflows for each year for both the proposed and the present machine. Since the proposed machine will be depreciated over six years, the analysis must be performed over the six-year period in order to fully capture the tax effect of depreciation in year 6 for the new asset.

---

[8] As noted in Chapter 3, it takes $n + 1$ years to depreciate an n-year class asset under the provisions of the *Tax Reform Act of 1986*. Therefore, ACRS percentages are given for each of six years for use in depreciating an asset with a five-year recovery period.

[9] It is important to recognize that although both machines will provide five years of use, the proposed new machine will be depreciated over the six-year period, whereas the present machine—as noted in the preceding example—has been depreciated over three years and therefore has only its final three years (years 4, 5, and 6) of depreciation (i.e., 12, 12, and 5 percent, respectively, under ACRS) remaining.

The resulting operating cash inflows are shown in column 8 of the table. The year-6 cash inflow for the proposed machine of $8,000 results from the tax benefit of the year-6 depreciation deduction.

**Table 9.7
Powell Corporation's Revenue and
Expenses (Excluding Depreciation)
for Proposed and Present Machines**

Year	Revenue (1)	Expenses (excl. depr.) (2)
With proposed machine		
1	$2,520,000	$2,300,000
2	2,520,000	2,300,000
3	2,520,000	2,300,000
4	2,520,000	2,300,000
5	2,520,000	2,300,000
With present machine		
1	2,200,000	$1,990,000
2	2,300,000	2,110,000
3	2,400,000	2,230,000
4	2,400,000	2,250,000
5	2,250,000	2,120,000

**Table 9.8
Depreciation Expense for Proposed and Present Machines for
Powell Corporation**

Year	Cost (1)	Applicable ACRS depreciation percentages (from Table 3.6) (2)	Depreciation [(1) × (2)] (3)
With proposed machine			
1	$400,000	20%	$ 80,000
2	400,000	32	128,000
3	400,000	19	76,000
4	400,000	12	48,000
5	400,000	12	48,000
6	400,000	5	20,000
Totals		100%	$400,000
With present machine			
1	$240,000	12% (year-4 depreciation)	$ 28,800
2	240,000	12 (year-5 depreciation)	28,800
3	240,000	5 (year-6 depreciation)	12,000
4		Since the present machine is at the end of the third year of its cost	0
5		recovery at the time the analysis is performed, it has only the final	0
6		three years of depreciation (years 4, 5, and 6) yet applicable.	0
		Total	$69,600[a]

[a] The total of $69,600 represents the book value of the present machine at the end of the third year, which was calculated in the preceding example.

Table 9.9
Calculation of Operating Cash Inflows for Powell Corporation's Proposed and Present Machines

Year	Revenue[a] (1)	Expenses (excl. depr.)[b] (2)	Profits before depreciation and taxes [(1) − (2)] (3)	Depreciation[c] (4)	Net profits before taxes [(3) − (4)] (5)	Taxes [.40 × (5)] (6)	Net profits after taxes [(5) − (6)] (7)	Operating cash inflows [(4) + (7)] (8)
With proposed machine								
1	$2,520,000	$2,300,000	$220,000	$ 80,000	$140,000	$56,000	$ 84,000	$164,000
2	2,520,000	2,300,000	220,000	128,000	92,000	36,800	55,200	183,200
3	2,520,000	2,300,000	220,000	76,000	144,000	57,600	86,400	162,400
4	2,520,000	2,300,000	220,000	48,000	172,000	68,800	103,200	151,200
5	2,520,000	2,300,000	220,000	48,000	172,000	68,800	103,200	151,200
6	0	0	0	20,000	−20,000	−8,000	−12,000	8,000
With present machine								
1	$2,200,000	$1,990,000	$210,000	$ 28,800	$181,200	$72,480	$108,720	$137,520
2	2,300,000	2,110,000	190,000	28,800	161,200	64,480	96,720	125,520
3	2,400,000	2,230,000	170,000	12,000	158,000	63,200	94,800	106,800
4	2,400,000	2,250,000	150,000	0	150,000	60,000	90,000	90,000
5	2,250,000	2,120,000	130,000	0	130,000	52,000	78,000	78,000
6	0	0	0	0	0	0	0	0

[a] From column 1 of Table 9.7.

[b] From column 2 of Table 9.7.

[c] From column 3 of Table 9.8.

Interpreting the Term *Incremental*

The final step in estimating the operating cash inflows to be used in evaluating a proposed project is to calculate the *incremental (relevant)* cash inflows. Incremental operating cash inflows are needed, since our concern is *only* with how much more or less operating cash will flow into the firm as a result of the proposed project.

FACT OR FABLE?

5 In a replacement decision, the relevant operating cash inflows are the after-tax cash inflows expected to result from the new asset, without regard to the cash inflows from the old asset. *(Fable)*

In a replacement decision, the relevant operating cash inflows are the *incremental* after-tax cash inflows expected to result from the new asset.

Example
Table 9.10 demonstrates the calculation of Powell Corporation's incremental (relevant) operating cash inflows for each year. The estimates of operating cash inflows developed in Table 9.9 are given in columns 1 and 2. The column 2 values represent the amount of operating cash inflows that Powell Corporation will receive if it does not replace the present machine. If the proposed machine replaces the present machine, the firm's operating cash inflows for each year will be those shown in column 1. Subtracting the operating cash inflows with the present machine from the operating cash in-

flows with the proposed machine in each year results in the incremental operating cash inflows for each year, shown in column 3 of Table 9.10. These are the relevant inflows to be considered in evaluating the benefits of making a capital expenditure for the proposed machine.[10]

Table 9.10
Incremental (Relevant) Operating Cash Inflows
for Powell Corporation

	Operating cash inflows		
Year	Proposed machine[a] (1)	Present machine[a] (2)	Incremental (relevant) [(1) − (2)] (3)
1	$164,000	$137,520	$26,480
2	183,200	125,520	57,680
3	162,400	106,800	55,600
4	151,200	90,000	61,200
5	151,200	78,000	73,200
6	8,000	0	8,000

[a] From column 8 of Table 9.9.

Finding the Terminal Cash Flow

The cash flow resulting from termination and liquidation of a project at the end of its economic life is its *terminal cash flow*. It represents the after-tax cash flows, exclusive of operating cash inflows, occurring in the final year of the project. When applicable, it is important to recognize these flows because they could significantly affect the capital expenditure decision. Consideration of these flows also provides closure to the analysis,

---

[10] The following equation can be used to more directly calculate the incremental cash inflow in year t, ICI_t.

$$ICI_t = [\Delta PBDT_t \times (1 - T)] + [\Delta D_t \times T]$$

where: $\Delta PBDT_t$ = the change in profits before depreciation and taxes
[revenues − expenses (excl. depr.)] in year t
ΔD_t = the change in depreciation expense in year t
T = the firm's marginal tax rate

Applying this formula to Powell Corporation in Tables 9.7 and 9.8 for year 3, we get variable values of:

$$\Delta PBDT_3 = (\$2,520,000 - \$2,300,000) - (\$2,400,000 - \$2,230,000)$$
$$= \$220,000 - \$170,000 = \$50,000$$
$$\Delta D_3 = \$76,000 - \$12,000 = \$64,000$$
$$T = .40$$

Substituting into the equation, we get:

$$ICI_3 = [\$50,000 \times (1 - .40)] + [\$64,000 \times .40]$$
$$= \$30,000 + \$25,600 = \underline{\$55,600}$$

The $55,600 of incremental cash inflow for year 3 is the same value as that calculated for year 3 in column 3 of Table 9.10.

Table 9.11
The Basic Format for
Determining Terminal Cash
Flow

	Proceeds from sale of new asset
−	Proceeds from sale of old asset
∓	Taxes on sale of new asset
±	Taxes on sale of old asset
±	Change in net working capital
	Terminal cash flow

allowing the firm to return to its initial position in terms of the expenditures being considered. Terminal cash flow, which is most often positive, can be calculated for replacement projects using the basic format presented in Table 9.11.

Proceeds from Sale of Assets

The proceeds from sale of the new and old asset represent the amount *net of any removal costs* expected upon termination of the project. For replacement projects, proceeds from both the new asset and the old asset must be considered as noted. For expansion, renewal, and other types of capital expenditures, the proceeds from the old asset would be zero. Of course, it is not unusual for the values of assets to be zero at termination of the project.

Taxes on Sale of Assets

Like the tax calculation on sale of old assets (demonstrated earlier as part of finding the initial investment), taxes must be considered on the terminal sale of both the new and the old asset for replacement projects, and on only the new asset in other cases. The tax calculations apply whenever an asset is sold for a value different from its book value. If the net proceeds from the sale are expected to exceed book value, a tax payment shown as an *outflow* for the new asset and an *inflow* for the old asset would occur. When the net proceeds from the sale are below book value, a tax rebate shown as a cash *inflow* for the new asset and an *outflow* for the old asset would result.[11] Of course, for assets sold to net exactly their book value, no taxes would be due.

Change in Net Working Capital

The change in net working capital reflects the reversion to its original status of any net working capital investment reflected as part of the initial investment. Most often this will show up as a cash inflow attributed to the reduction in net working capital; with termination of the project, the need for the increased net working capital investment is assumed to end.[12] Since the net working capital investment is in no way consumed, the amount

[11] It is important to recognize that while the sign is negative for tax outflows on the new asset, it is positive for tax outflows on the old asset, and vice versa. This treatment is necessary to accomplish the proper netting of the *after-tax* sale proceeds of the new asset and the old asset measured at project termination.

[12] As noted earlier, the change in net working capital is, for convenience, assumed to occur spontaneously—in this case, upon termination of the project. In actuality, it may take a number of months for the original increase in net working capital to be worked down to zero.

recovered at termination will equal the amount shown in the calculation of the initial investment. Tax considerations are not involved because the change in net working capital results from an internal reduction or build-up of current accounts. Of course, occasionally net working capital will not be changed by the proposed investment and therefore will not enter into the analysis.

It should be clear that the terminal value calculation, when applicable, involves the same procedures as those used to find the initial investment. The following example demonstrates how the terminal cash flow is calculated for a replacement decision.

Example

Continuing with Powell Corporation, assume that the firm expects to be able to liquidate the new machine at the end of its five-year usable life to net $50,000 after paying removal costs. The old machine can be liquidated at the end of the five years to net $0 because it will then be completely obsolete. The firm expects to recover its $17,000 net working capital investment upon termination of the project. As noted earlier, both ordinary income and capital gains are taxed at a rate of 40 percent.

From the analysis of the operating cash inflows presented earlier, it can be seen that while the old machine will be fully depreciated and therefore have a book value of zero at the end of the five years, the new machine will have a book value of $20,000 (equal to the year-6 depreciation) at the end of five years. Since the sale price of $50,000 for the new machine is below its initial installed cost of $400,000 but greater than its book value of $20,000, taxes will have to be paid only on the recaptured depreciation of $30,000 ($50,000 sale proceeds − $20,000 book value). Applying the ordinary tax rate of 40 percent to the $30,000 results in a tax of $12,000 (.40 × $30,000) on the sale of the new machine. Since the old machine would net $0 at termination and its book value would be $0, no tax would be due on sale of the old machine. Substituting the appropriate values into the format in Table 9.11 results in the terminal cash inflow value of $55,000 derived below. This represents the after-tax cash flow, exclusive of operating cash inflows, occurring upon termination of the project at the end of year 5.

Proceeds from sale of new machine	$50,000
− Proceeds from sale of old machine	0
− Taxes on sale of new machine	12,000
+ Taxes on sale of old machine	0
+ Change in net working capital	17,000
Terminal cash flow	$55,000

FACT OR FABLE? 6 The terminal cash flow is most often an inflow representing the after-tax cash flows, exclusive of operating cash inflows, occurring in the final year of a project. *(Fact)*

Figure 9.4
Powell Corporation's Relevant Cash Flows with the New Machine

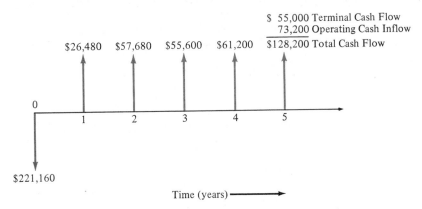

Summarizing the Relevant Cash Flows

The three cash flow components—the initial investment, operating cash inflows, and terminal cash flow—together represent a project's *relevant cash flows*. These cash flows can be viewed as the incremental after-tax cash flows attributable to the proposed project. They represent, in a cash flow sense, how much better or worse off the firm will be if it chooses to implement the proposal.

Example
The relevant cash flows for Powell Corporation's proposed replacement expenditure can now be presented. They are shown graphically in Figure 9.4. Note that because the new asset is assumed sold at the end of its five-year usable life, the year-6 incremental operating cash inflow calculated in Table 9.10 has no relevance; the terminal cash flow effectively replaces this value in the analysis. As the figure shows, the relevant cash flows follow a conventional pattern (an initial outlay followed by a series of inflows). Techniques for analyzing this type of pattern to determine whether to undertake a proposed capital investment are discussed in Chapter 10.

Summary

● Capital budgeting is the process used to evaluate and select capital expenditures consistent with the goal of owner wealth maximization. Capital expenditures are long-term investments made to expand, replace, or renew fixed assets or to obtain some other less tangible benefit.

● The capital budgeting process contains five distinct but interrelated steps: proposal generation, review and analysis, decision making, implementation, and follow-up.

● Capital expenditure proposals may be independent or mutually exclusive. Typically, firms have only limited funds for capital investments and must ration them among carefully selected projects. To make investment decisions when proposals are mutually exclusive or when capital must be rationed, projects must be ranked; otherwise, accept-reject decisions must be made.

● Conventional cash flow patterns consist of an initial outflow followed by a series of inflows; any other pattern is nonconventional. These patterns can be either annuities or mixed streams.

● The relevant cash flows necessary for making capital budgeting decisions are the initial investment, the operating cash inflows, and the terminal cash flow associated with a given proposal. For replacement decisions, these flows are found by determining the difference between the cash flows associated with the new asset and the old asset. Expansion decisions are viewed as replacement decisions in which all cash flows from the old asset are zero.

● The initial investment is the initial outlay required, taking into account the cost (including installation) of the new asset, proceeds from the sale of the old asset, taxes on the sale of the old asset, and any change in net working capital.

● The book value of an asset is its strict accounting value, which is used to determine what, if any, taxes are owed as a result of selling an asset. Any of three forms of taxable income—capital gain, recaptured depreciation, or a loss—can result from sale of an asset, depending upon whether it is sold (1) for more than its initial purchase price; (2) for more than book value but less than initially paid; (3) for book value; or (4) for less than book value.

● Incremental after-tax operating cash inflows are the additional cash flows received as a result of implementing a proposal. The income statement format can be conveniently used to estimate these ''relevant'' operating cash inflows.

● The terminal cash flow represents the after-tax cash flows, exclusive of operating inflows, expected to result from liquidation of the project at the end of its life.

Questions

9-1   What is *capital budgeting?* How do capital expenditures relate to the capital budgeting process? Do all capital expenditures involve fixed assets? Explain.

9-2   What are the basic motives described in the chapter for making capital expenditures? Discuss, compare, and contrast them.

9-3   Briefly describe each of the steps—proposal generation, review and analysis, decision making, implementation, and follow-up—involved in the capital budgeting process.

9-4   Define and differentiate between each of the following sets of capital budgeting terms.

  a. Independent versus mutually exclusive projects
  b. Unlimited funds versus capital rationing
  c. Accept-reject versus ranking approaches
  d. Conventional versus nonconventional cash flow patterns
  e. Annuity versus mixed stream cash flows

9-5   Why is it important to evaluate capital budgeting projects on the basis of *incremental after-tax cash flows?* How can expansion decisions be treated as replacement decisions? Explain.

9-6   Describe each of the following components of the initial investment and explain how the initial investment is calculated using them.

  a. Cost of new asset
  b. Installation costs
  c. Proceeds from sale of old asset
  d. Taxes on sale of old asset
  e. Change in net working capital

9-7   What is the *book value* of an asset, and how is it calculated? Describe the three key types of taxable income and their associated tax treatments.

9-8   What four tax situations may result from the sale of an asset that is being replaced? Describe the tax treatment in each situation.

9-9   Referring to the framework for calculating initial investment given in this chapter, explain how a firm would determine the *depreciable value* of the new asset.

9-10   How is the *Accelerated Cost Recovery System (ACRS)* used to depreciate an asset? How does depreciation enter into the operating cash inflow calculation?

9-11   Given the revenues, expenses (excluding depreciation), and depreciation associated with a present asset and a proposed replacement for it, how would the incremental (relevant) operating cash inflows associated with the decision be calculated?

9-12   What is the *terminal cash flow?* How is the value of this cash flow calculated for replacement projects?

9-13   Diagram and describe the three elements representing the *relevant cash flows* for a conventional capital budgeting project.

Self-Test Problems

(Solutions on page 322)

ST-1 Irvin Enterprises is considering the purchase of a new piece of equipment to replace the current equipment. The new equipment will cost $75,000 and require $5,000 in installation costs. It will be depreciated under ACRS using a five-year recovery period. The old piece of equipment was purchased for an installed cost of $50,000 four years ago; it was being depreciated under ACRS using a five-year recovery period. The old equipment can be sold today for $55,000 net of any removal costs. As a result of the proposed replacement the firm's investment in net working capital is expected to increase by $15,000. The firm pays taxes at a rate of 40 percent on both ordinary income and capital gains.

    a. Calculate the book value of the old piece of equipment.

    b. Determine the taxes, if any, attributable to the sale of the old equipment.

    c. Find the initial investment associated with the proposed equipment replacement.

ST-2 A machine currently in use was originally purchased two years ago for $40,000. The machine is being depreciated under ACRS using a five-year recovery period; it has three years of usable life remaining. The current machine can be sold today to net $42,000. A new machine, using a three-year ACRS recovery period, can be purchased at a price of $140,000. It will require $10,000 to install and has a three-year usable life. If the new machine is acquired, the investment in accounts receivable is expected to rise by $10,000, the inventory investment will increase by $25,000, and accounts payable will increase by $15,000. *Profits before depreciation and taxes* are expected to be $70,000 for each of the next three years with the old machine, and $120,000 in the first year and $130,000 in the second and third years with the new machine. At the end of three years, the market value of the old machine would equal zero, but the new machine could be sold to net $35,000 before taxes. Both ordinary corporate income and capital gains are subject to a 40 percent tax. (Table 3.6 on page 66 contains the applicable ACRS depreciation percentages.)

    a. Determine the initial investment associated with the proposed replacement decision.

    b. Calculate the incremental operating cash inflows for years 1 to 4 associated with the proposed replacement. (*Note:* Only depreciation cash flows must be considered in year 4.)

    c. Calculate the terminal cash flow associated with the proposed replacement decision. (*Note:* This is at the end of year 3.)

    d. Diagram the relevant cash flows found in **a, b,** and **c** associated with the proposed replacement decision assuming it is terminated at the end of year 3.

Problems

9-1 (**Classification of Expenditures**) Given the following list of outlays, indicate whether each would normally be considered a capital or a current expenditure. Explain your answers.

    a. An initial lease payment of $5,000 for electronic point-of-sale cash register systems.

    b. An outlay of $20,000 to purchase patent rights from the inventor.

    c. An outlay of $80,000 for a major research and development program.

d. An $80,000 investment in a portfolio of marketable securities.

e. A $300 outlay for an office machine.

f. An outlay of $2,000 for a new machine tool.

g. An outlay of $240,000 for a new building.

h. An outlay of $1,000 for a marketing research report.

9-2   **(Basic Terminology)** A firm is considering the following three separate situations.

Situation A: Build either a small office building or a convenience store on a parcel of land located in a high-traffic area. Adequate funding is available, and both projects are known to be acceptable. The office building will require an initial investment of $620,000 and is expected to provide operating cash inflows of $40,000 per year for 20 years. The convenience store is expected to cost $500,000 and provide a growing stream of operating cash inflows over its 20-year life. The initial operating cash inflow is $20,000 and will increase by 5 percent each year.

Situation B: Replace a machine with a new one requiring a $60,000 initial investment and providing operating cash inflows of $10,000 per year for the first five years. At the end of year 5, a machine overhaul costing $20,000 is required, and after it is completed, expected operating cash inflows are $10,000 in year 6; $7,000 in year 7; $4,000 in year 8; and $1,000 in year 9, at the end of which the machine will be scrapped.

Situation C: Invest in any or all of the four machines whose relevant cash flows are given in the following table. The firm has $500,000 budgeted to fund these machines, all of which are known to be acceptable. Initial investment for each machine is $250,000.

| Year | Operating cash inflows | | | |
	Machine 1	Machine 2	Machine 3	Machine 4
1	$ 50,000	$70,000	$65,000	$90,000
2	70,000	70,000	65,000	80,000
3	90,000	70,000	80,000	70,000
4	−30,000	70,000	80,000	60,000
5	100,000	70,000	−20,000	50,000

For each situation or project, indicate

a. Whether the *situation* is independent or mutually exclusive.

b. Whether the availability of funds is unlimited or if capital rationing exists.

c. Whether accept-reject or ranking decisions are required.

d. Whether each *project's* cash flows are conventional or nonconventional.

e. Whether each *project's* cash flow pattern is an annuity or mixed stream.

9-3 **(Expansion versus Replacement Cash Flows)** Edison Systems has estimated the cash flows over the five-year lives for two projects, A and B. These cash flows are summarized below:

	Project	
	A	**B**
Initial investment	$40,000	$12,000[a]
Year	**Operating cash inflows**	
1	$10,000	$6,000
2	12,000	6,000
3	14,000	6,000
4	16,000	6,000
5	10,000	6,000

[a] After-tax cash inflows expected from liquidation.

a. If project A were actually a *replacement* for project B and the $12,000 initial investment shown for B was the after-tax cash inflows expected from liquidating it, what would be the relevant cash flows for this replacement decision?

b. How can an *expansion decision* such as project A be viewed as a special form of a replacement decision? Explain.

9-4 **(Relevant Cash Flow Pattern Fundamentals)** For each of the following projects, determine the *relevant cash flows,* classify the cash flow pattern, and diagram the pattern.

a. A project requiring an initial investment of $120,000 that generates annual operating cash inflows of $25,000 for the next 18 years. In each of the 18 years, maintenance of the project will require a $5,000 cash outflow.

b. A new machine having an installed cost of $85,000. Sale of the old machine will yield $30,000 after taxes. Operating cash inflows generated by the replacement will exceed the operating cash inflows of the old machine by $20,000 in each year of a six-year period. At the end of year 6, liquidation of the new machine will yield $20,000 after taxes, which is $10,000 greater than the after-tax proceeds expected from the old machine had it been retained and liquidated at the end of year 6.

c. An asset requiring an initial investment of $2 million that will yield annual operating cash inflows of $300,000 for each of the next ten years. Operating cash outlays will be $20,000 for each year except year 6, when an overhaul requiring an additional cash outlay of $500,000 will be required. The asset's liquidation value at the end of year 10 is expected to be $0.

9-5   **(Book Value)** Find the book value for each of the assets below, assuming that ACRS depreciation is being used. (*Note:* See Table 3.6 on page 66 for the applicable depreciation percentages.)

Asset	Installed cost	Recovery period	Elapsed time since purchase
A	$ 950,000	5 years	3 years
B	40,000	3 years	1 year
C	96,000	5 years	4 years
D	350,000	5 years	1 year
E	1,500,000	7 years	5 years

9-6   **(Book Value and Taxes on Sale of Assets)** Troy Industries purchased a new machine three years ago for $80,000. It is being depreciated under ACRS with a five-year recovery period using the percentages given in Table 3.6 on page 66. Assume 40 percent ordinary and capital gains tax rates.

a. What is the book value of the machine?

b. Calculate the firm's tax liability if it sells the machine for the following: $100,000; $56,000; $23,200; $15,000.

9-7   **(Tax Calculations)** For each of the following cases, describe the various taxable components of the funds received through sale of the asset and determine the total taxes resulting from the transaction. Assume 40 percent ordinary and capital gains tax rates. The asset was purchased for $200,000 two years ago and is being depreciated under ACRS using a five-year recovery period. (See Table 3.6 on page 66 for the applicable depreciation percentages.)

a. The asset is sold for $220,000.

b. The asset is sold for $150,000.

c. The asset is sold for $105,600.

d. The asset is sold for $80,000.

9-8   **(Change in Net Working Capital Calculation)** Samuels Manufacturing is considering the purchase of a new machine to replace one they feel is obsolete. The firm has total current assets of $920,000 and total current liabilities of $640,000. As a result of the proposed replacement, the following *changes* are anticipated in the levels of the current asset and current liability accounts noted.

Account	Change
Accruals	+ $ 40,000
Marketable securities	0
Inventories	− 10,000
Accounts payable	+ 90,000
Notes payable	0
Accounts receivable	+ 150,000
Cash	+ 15,000

a. Using the information given, calculate the change, if any, in net working capital expected to result from the proposed replacement action.

b. Explain why a change in these current accounts would be relevant to the analysis of the proposed capital expenditure.

c. Would the change in net working capital enter into any of the other cash flow components comprising the relevant cash flows? Explain.

9-9 **(Initial Investment—Basic Calculation)** Cushing Corporation is considering the purchase of a new grading machine to replace the existing one. The existing machine was purchased three years ago at an installed cost of $20,000; it was being depreciated under ACRS using a five-year recovery period. (See Table 3.6 on page 66 for the applicable depreciation percentages.) The existing machine is expected to have a usable life of at least five more years. The new machine would cost $35,000 and require $5,000 in installation costs; it would be depreciated using a five-year recovery period under ACRS. The existing machine can currently be sold for $25,000 without incurring any removal costs. The firm pays 40 percent taxes on both ordinary income and capital gains. Calculate the *initial investment* associated with the proposed purchase of a new grading machine.

9-10 **(Initial Investment at Various Sale Prices)** Edwards Manufacturing Company is considering replacement of one machine with another. The old machine was purchased three years ago for an installed cost of $10,000. The firm is depreciating the machine under ACRS using a five-year recovery period. (See Table 3.6 on page 66 for the applicable depreciation percentages.) The new machine costs $24,000 and requires $2,000 in installation costs. Assume the firm is subject to a 40 percent tax rate on both ordinary income and capital gains. In each of the following cases, calculate the initial investment for the replacement.

a. Edwards Manufacturing Company (EMC) sells the old machine for $11,000.

b. EMC sells the old machine for $7,000.

c. EMC sells the old machine for $2,900.

d. EMC sells the old machine for $1,500.

9-11 **(Depreciation)** A firm is evaluating the acquisition of an asset that costs $64,000 and requires $4,000 in installation costs. If the firm depreciates the asset under ACRS using a five-year recovery period (see Table 3.6 on page 66 for the applicable depreciation percentages), determine the depreciation charge for each year.

9-12 **(Incremental Operating Cash Inflows)** A firm is considering renewing its equipment to meet increased demand for its product. The cost of equipment modifications will be $1.9 million plus $100,000 in installation costs. The firm will depreciate the equipment modifications under ACRS using a five-year recovery period. (See Table 3.6 on page 66 for the applicable depreciation percentages.) Additional sales revenue from the renewal should amount to $1.2 million per year, and additional operating expenses and other costs (excluding depreciation) will amount to 40 percent of the additional sales. The firm has an ordinary tax rate of 40 percent. (*Note:* Answer the following questions for each of the next *six* years.)

a. What incremental earnings before depreciation and taxes will result from the renewal?

b. What incremental earnings after taxes will result from the renewal?

c. What incremental operating cash inflows will result from the renewal?

9-13 **(Incremental Operating Cash Inflows—Expense Reduction)** Miller Corporation is considering replacement of a machine. The replacement will reduce operating expenses (i.e., increase revenues) by $16,000 per year for each of the five years the new machine is expected to last. Although the old machine has zero book value, it can be used for five more years. The depreciable value of the new machine is $48,000; the firm will depreciate the machine under ACRS using a five-year recovery period (see Table 3.6 on page 66 for the applicable depreciation percentages) and is subject to a 40 percent tax rate on ordinary income. Estimate the incremental operating cash inflows generated by the replacement. (*Note:* Be sure to consider the depreciation in year 6.)

9-14 **(Incremental Operating Cash Inflows)** Strong Tool Company has been considering purchasing a new lathe to replace a fully depreciated lathe that will last five more years. The new lathe is expected to have a five-year life and depreciation charges of $2,000 in year 1; $3,200 in year 2; $1,900 in year 3; $1,200 in both year 4 and year 5; and $500 in year 6. The firm estimates the revenues and expenses (excluding depreciation) for the new and the old lathes as shown in the following table. The firm has a 40 percent tax rate on ordinary income.

	New lathe		Old lathe	
Year	Revenue	Expenses (excl. depr.)	Revenue	Expenses (excl. depr.)
1	$40,000	$30,000	$35,000	$25,000
2	41,000	30,000	35,000	25,000
3	42,000	30,000	35,000	25,000
4	43,000	30,000	35,000	25,000
5	44,000	30,000	35,000	25,000

a. Calculate the operating cash inflows associated with each lathe. (*Note:* Be sure to consider the depreciation in year 6.)

b. Calculate the incremental (relevant) operating cash inflows resulting from the proposed lathe replacement.

c. Diagram the incremental operating cash inflows calculated in **b.**

9-15 **(Terminal Cash Flows—Various Lives and Sale Prices)** Looner Industries is currently analyzing the purchase of a new machine costing $160,000 and requiring $20,000 in installation costs. Purchase of this machine is expected to result in an increase in net working capital of $30,000 to support the expanded level of operations. The firm plans to depreciate the asset under ACRS using a five-year recovery period and expects to sell the machine to net $10,000 before taxes at the end of its usable life. The firm is subject to a 40 percent tax rate on both ordinary and capital gains income.

a. Calculate the terminal cash flow for a usable life of (1) three years, (2) five years, and (3) seven years.

b. Discuss the effect of usable life on terminal cash flows using your findings in **a.**

c. Assuming a five-year usable life, calculate the terminal cash flow if the machine were sold to net (1) $9,000 or (2) $170,000 (before taxes) at the end of the five years.

d. Discuss the effect of sale price on terminal cash flows using your findings in **c.**

9-16 **(Terminal Cash Flow—Replacement Decision)** Russell Industries is considering replacing a fully depreciated machine having a remaining useful life of ten years with a newer, more sophisticated machine. The new machine will cost $200,000 and require $30,000 in installation costs. It will be depreciated under ACRS using a five-year recovery period. A $25,000 increase in net working capital will be required to support the new machine. The firm plans to evaluate the potential replacement over a four-year period. They estimate that the old machine could be sold at the end of four years to net $15,000 before taxes; the new machine at the end of four years will be worth $75,000 before taxes. Calculate the terminal cash flow relevant to the proposed purchase of the new machine. The firm is subject to a 40 percent tax rate on both ordinary and capital gains income.

9-17 **(Relevant Cash Flows—No Terminal Value)** Central Laundry and Cleaners is considering replacing an existing piece of machinery with a more sophisticated machine. The old machine was purchased three years ago at a cost of $50,000, and this amount was being depreciated under ACRS using a five-year recovery period. The machine has five years of usable life remaining. The new machine being considered will cost $76,000 and requires $4,000 in installation costs. The new machine would be depreciated under ACRS using a five-year recovery period. The old machine can currently be sold for $55,000 without incurring any removal costs. The firm pays 40 percent taxes on both ordinary income and capital gains. The revenues and expenses (excluding depreciation) associated with the new and the old machine for the next five years are given in the table below. (Table 3.6 on page 66 contains the applicable ACRS depreciation percentages.)

	New machine		Old machine	
Year	Revenue	Expenses (excl. depr.)	Revenue	Expenses (excl. depr.)
1	$750,000	$720,000	$674,000	$660,000
2	750,000	720,000	676,000	660,000
3	750,000	720,000	680,000	660,000
4	750,000	720,000	678,000	660,000
5	750,000	720,000	674,000	660,000

a. Calculate the initial investment associated with replacement of the old machine by the new one.

b. Determine the incremental operating cash inflows associated with the proposed replacement. (*Note:* Be sure to consider the depreciation in year 6.)

c. Diagram the relevant cash flows found in **a** and **b** associated with the proposed replacement decision.

9-18 **(Integrative—Determining Relevant Cash Flows)** The Lombard Company is contemplating the purchase of a new high-speed widget grinder to replace the existing grinder. The existing grinder was purchased two years ago at an installed cost of $60,000; it was being depreciated under ACRS using a five-year recovery period. The existing grinder is expected to have a usable life of five more years. The new grinder would cost $105,000 and require $5,000 in installation costs; it has a five-year usable life and would be depreciated under ACRS using a five-year recovery period. The existing grinder can currently be sold for $70,000 without incurring any removal costs. To support the increased business resulting from purchase of the new grinder, accounts receivable would increase by $40,000, inventories by $30,000, and accounts payable by $58,000. At the end of five years, the existing grinder is expected to have a market value of zero; the new grinder would be sold to net $29,000 after removal costs and before taxes. The firm pays 40 percent taxes on both ordinary income and capital gains. The estimated *profits before depreciation and taxes* over the five years for both the new and existing grinder are given at the top of page 320. (Table 3.6 on page 66 contains the applicable ACRS depreciation percentages.)

Year	Profits before depreciation and taxes	
	New grinder	Existing grinder
1	$43,000	$26,000
2	43,000	24,000
3	43,000	22,000
4	43,000	20,000
5	43,000	18,000

a. Calculate the initial investment associated with the replacement of the existing grinder by the new one.

b. Determine the incremental operating cash inflows associated with the proposed grinder replacement. (*Note:* Be sure to consider the depreciation in year 6.)

c. Determine the terminal cash flow expected from the proposed grinder replacement.

d. Diagram the relevant cash flows associated with the proposed grinder replacement decision.

9-19 (**Integrative—Determining Relevant Cash Flows**) Atlantic Drydock is considering replacement of an existing hoist with one of two newer, more efficient pieces of equipment. The existing hoist is three years old, cost $32,000, and is being depreciated under ACRS using a five-year recovery period. Although the existing hoist has only three years (years 4, 5, and 6) of depreciation remaining under ACRS, it has a remaining usable life of five years. Hoist A, one of the two possible replacement hoists, costs $40,000 to purchase and $8,000 to install. It has a five-year usable life and will be depreciated under ACRS using a five-year recovery period. The other hoist, B, costs $54,000 to purchase and $6,000 to install. It also has a five-year usable life and it will be depreciated under ACRS using a five-year recovery period.

Increased investments in net working capital will accompany the decision to acquire hoist A or hoist B. Purchase of hoist A would result in a $4,000 increase in net working capital; hoist B would result in a $6,000 increase in net working capital. The projected *profits before depreciation and taxes* with each alternative hoist and the existing hoist are given in the following table.

Year	Profits before depreciation and taxes		
	With hoist A	With hoist B	With existing hoist
1	$21,000	$22,000	$14,000
2	21,000	24,000	14,000
3	21,000	26,000	14,000
4	21,000	26,000	14,000
5	21,000	26,000	14,000

The existing hoist can currently be sold for $18,000 and will not incur any removal costs. At the end of five years, the existing hoist can be sold to net $1,000 before taxes. Hoists A and

B can be sold to net $12,000 and $20,000 before taxes, respectively, at the end of the five-year period. The firm is subject to a 40 percent tax rate on both ordinary income and capital gains. (Table 3.6 on page 66 contains the applicable ACRS depreciation percentages.)

a. Calculate the initial investment associated with each alternative.

b. Calculate the incremental operating cash inflows associated with each alternative. (*Note:* Be sure to consider the depreciation in year 6.)

c. Calculate the terminal cash flow associated with each alternative. (*Note:* This is at the end of year 5.)

d. Diagram the relative cash flows associated with each alternative.

9-20   (**Integrative—Determining Relevant Cash Flows**) Clark Upholstery Company expects its *net profits after taxes* for the next five years to be as shown in the following table.

Year	Net profits after taxes
1	$100,000
2	150,000
3	200,000
4	250,000
5	320,000

Consideration is currently being given to the renewal of Clark's *only* depreciable asset, a machine originally costing $30,000, having a current book value of zero, and that can now be sold for $20,000. At the end of five years the existing machine can be sold to net $2,000 before taxes. The firm is subject to a 40 percent tax on both ordinary income and capital gains. The company uses ACRS depreciation. (See Table 3.6 on page 66 for the applicable depreciation percentages.)

Alternative 1: Renew the existing machine at a total depreciable cost of $90,000. The renewed machine would have a five-year usable life and be depreciated under ACRS using a five-year recovery period. Renewing the machine would allow the firm to achieve the following projected *profits before depreciation and taxes:*

Year	Profits before depreciation and taxes
1	$198,500
2	290,800
3	381,900
4	481,900
5	581,900

The renewed machine would result in an increase of $15,000 in net working capital. At the end of five years, the machine could be sold to net $8,000 before taxes.

Alternative 2: Replace the existing machine with a new machine costing $100,000 and requiring installation costs of $10,000. The new machine would have a five-year usable life and be depreciated under ACRS using a five-year recovery period. The firm's projected *profits before depreciation and taxes,* if it acquires the machine, are as follows:

Year	Profits before depreciation and taxes
1	$235,500
2	335,200
3	385,100
4	435,100
5	551,100

The new machine would result in an increase of $22,000 in net working capital. At the end of five years, the new machine could be sold to net $25,000 before taxes.

a. Calculate the initial investment associated with each alternative.

b. Calculate the incremental operating cash inflows associated with each alternative. (*Note:* Be sure to consider the depreciation in year 6.)

c. Calculate the terminal cash flow associated with each alternative. (*Note:* This is at the end of year 5.)

d. Diagram the relevant cash flows associated with each alternative.

Solutions to Self-Test Problems

ST-1 a. Book value = installed cost − accumulated depreciation
Installed cost = $50,000
Accumulated depreciation = $50,000 × (.20 + .32 + .19 + .12)
$$= \$50,000 \times .83 = \$41,500$$
Book value = $50,000 − $41,500 = $8,500

b. Taxes on sale of old equipment:

Capital gain = sale price − initial purchase price
$$= \$55,000 - \$50,000 = \$5,000$$
Recaptured depreciation = initial purchase price − book value
$$= \$50,000 - \$8,500 = \$41,500$$
Taxes = (.40 × $5,000) + (.40 × $41,500)
$$= \$2,000 + \$16,600 = \$18,600$$

c. Initial investment:

Cost of new equipment	$75,000
+ Installation costs	5,000
− Proceeds from sale of old equipment	55,000
+ Taxes on sale of old equipment	18,600
+ Change in net working capital	15,000
Initial investment	$58,600

ST-2 a. Initial investment:

Cost of new machine	$140,000
+ Installation costs	10,000
− Proceeds from sale of old machine	42,000
+ Taxes on sale of old machine[1]	9,120
+ Change in net working capital[2]	20,000
Initial investment	$137,120

[1] Book value of old machine = $40,000 − [(.20 + .32) × $40,000] = $40,000 − (.52 × $40,000) = $40,000 − $20,800 = $19,200
Capital gain = $42,000 − $40,000 = $2,000
Recaptured depreciation = $40,000 − $19,200 = $20,800
Taxes = (.40 × $2,000) + (.40 × $20,800) = $800 + $8,320 = $9,120

[2] Change in net working capital = +$10,000 + $25,000 − $15,000
  = $35,000 − $15,000 = $20,000

b. Incremental operating cash inflows:

Calculation of Depreciation Expense for New and Old Machine

Year	Cost (1)	Applicable ACRS depreciation percentages (from Table 3.6) (2)	Depreciation [(1) × (2)] (3)
With new machine			
1	$150,000	33%	$ 49,500
2	150,000	45	67,500
3	150,000	15	22,500
4	150,000	7	10,500
Totals		100%	$150,000
With old machine			
1	$40,000	19 (year-3 depreciation)	$ 7,600
2	40,000	12 (year-4 depreciation)	4,800
3	40,000	12 (year-5 depreciation)	4,800
4	40,000	5 (year-6 depreciation)	2,000
		Total	$ 19,200[a]

[a] The total of $19,200 represents the book value of the old machine at the end of the second year, which was calculated in part **a.**

(The solution to Problem ST-2 continues on the following page.)

Calculation of Operating Cash Inflows

Year	Profits before depreciation and taxes (1)	Depreciation[a] (2)	Net profits before taxes [(1) − (2)] (3)	Taxes [.40 × (3)] (4)	Net profits after taxes [(3) − (4)] (5)	Operating cash inflows [(2) + (5)] (6)
New machine						
1	$120,000	$49,500	$ 70,500	$28,200	$42,300	$ 91,800
2	130,000	67,500	62,500	25,000	37,500	105,000
3	130,000	22,500	107,500	43,000	64,500	87,000
4	0	10,500	−10,500	−4,200	−6,300	4,200
Old machine						
1	$ 70,000	$ 7,600	$ 62,400	$24,960	$37,440	$ 45,040
2	70,000	4,800	65,200	26,080	39,120	43,920
3	70,000	4,800	65,200	26,080	39,120	43,920
4	0	2,000	−2,000	−800	−1,200	800

[a] From column 3 of the preceding table.

Calculation of Incremental Operating Cash Inflows

Year	Operating cash inflows		
	New machine[a] (1)	Old machine[a] (2)	Incremental (relevant) [(1) − (2)] (3)
1	$ 91,800	$45,040	$46,760
2	105,000	43,920	61,080
3	87,000	43,920	43,080
4	4,200	800	3,400

[a] From column 6 of the preceding table.

c. Terminal cash flow (end of year 3):

Proceeds from sale of new machine	$35,000
− Proceeds from sale of old machine	0
− Taxes on sale of new machine[1]	9,800
− Taxes on sale of old machine[2]	800
+ Change in net working capital	20,000
Terminal cash flow	$44,400

[1] Book value of new machine at end of year 3
= $150,000 − [(.33 + .45 + .15) × $150,000] = $150,000 − (.93 × $150,000)
= $150,000 − $139,500 = $10,500
Tax on sale = .40 × ($35,000 sale price − $10,500 book value)
= .40 × $24,500 = $9,800

[2] Book value of old machine at end of year 3
= $40,000 − [(.20 + .32 + .19 + .12 + .12) × $40,000)] = $40,000 − (.95 × $40,000)
= $40,000 − $38,000 = $2,000
Tax on sale = .40 × ($0 sale price − $2,000 book value)
= .40 × (−$2,000) = −$800 (i.e., $800 tax saving)

d.

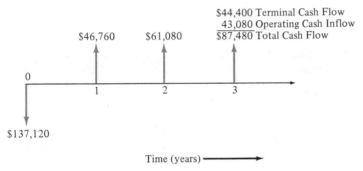

$$\begin{array}{r} \$44,400 \text{ Terminal Cash Flow} \\ \underline{43,080} \text{ Operating Cash Inflow} \\ \overline{\$87,480} \text{ Total Cash Flow} \end{array}$$

$46,760 $61,080

0

1   2   3

$137,120

Time (years) ⟶

Note: The year-4 incremental operating cash inflow of $3,400 is not directly included; it is instead reflected in the book values used to calculate the taxes on sale of the machines at the end of year 3 and therefore part of the terminal cash flow.

CHAPTER 10

Capital Budgeting Techniques: Certainty, Risk, and Some Refinements

FACT OR FABLE?
Are the following statements fact *(true)* or fable *(false)*?

1
Both the payback period and net present value (NPV) are considered sophisticated capital budgeting techniques since they explicitly consider the time value of money.

2
The internal rate of return (IRR) is the discount rate that causes the present value of a project's cash inflows to just equal the initial investment, thereby resulting in a net present value of $0.

3
Net present value (NPV) and internal rate of return (IRR) always give the same accept-reject decisions, but may disagree when ranking projects due to differences in the magnitude and timing of cash flows.

4
Sensitivity analysis is used to assess project risk by evaluating the impact on return of simultaneous changes in a number of variables, whereas scenario analysis considers only a single variable change.

5
In practice, risk-adjusted discount rates (RADRs) are the preferred method of capital budgeting risk adjustment in spite of the fact that certainty equivalents (CEs) are theoretically superior.

6
Annualized net present value (ANPV) is the most widely accepted approach for choosing the best project when the firm is operating under capital rationing.

Some investments are too staggering even for mighty General Motors. In 1985 the giant car-maker announced it would spend $3.5 billion to get its new subcompact—the Saturn—off the drawing board and into production at a super-sophisticated, state-of-the-art assembly plant at Spring Hill, Tenn. At that time Roger Smith, GM's CEO, referred to the inception and production of the Saturn as a "project of cosmic dimensions." But lower GM profits in 1986 apparently brought the Saturn down to earth. The budget was cut to $1.7 billion.

At that, the investment is a large one, and some observers think the fixed costs of the Saturn will make it too expensive to compete profitably. Others think GM is willing to take a bit of a whipping on the Saturn for several years because of what it will learn. GM expects not only to compete in earnest with the Japanese and Korean car imports but also to learn how to make cars less expensively in the United States—by carrying technology to new heights, by eliminating the costly and inefficient assembly line, by relying more on the computer, and by cutting labor costs.

The venerable assembly line worked when all cars were more or less alike. But since the days when options began to proliferate like buttons on a dashboard, assembly lines—which carry a car past every station, whether it needs the feature supplied there or not—have been wasteful. In addition, they move the vehicle so quickly past some critical stations that workers sometimes cannot maintain quality. The new Saturn plant will remedy these problems. Each automobile frame will ride a cart electronically guided by wires in the floor to the stations it needs to visit for work. And because the constant assembly-line speed will be eliminated, workers will have time to devote to operations that need extra time.

If GM's predictions are correct, the $1.7 billion dollar capital outlay will provide returns consistent with the high level of risk. GM's capital outlay surely was based on application of appropriate decision and risk analysis techniques to the project's expected cash flows. In this chapter the popular decision techniques that can be applied to the relevant cash flows (developed in the preceding chapter) under certainty and risk as well as a couple of refinements are presented.

Capital Budgeting Techniques

The relevant cash flows developed in Chapter 9 must be analyzed to assess whether a project is acceptable or to rank projects. A number of techniques are available for performing such analyses. The preferred approaches integrate time value procedures (Chapter 6), risk and return considerations (Chapter 7), and valuation concepts (Chapter 8) in order to select capital expenditures that are consistent with the firm's goal of maximizing owners' wealth. This and the following section focus on the use of these techniques to evaluate capital expenditure proposals for decision-making purposes.

We shall use the same basic problem to illustrate the application of all the techniques described in this chapter. The problem concerns the Bennett Company, which is currently contemplating two projects—project A, requiring an initial investment of $42,000, and project B, requiring an initial investment of $45,000. The projected incremental (relevant) operating cash inflows for the two projects are presented in Table 10.1.[1] It can be seen that the projects exhibit conventional cash flow patterns, which are assumed throughout the text. In addition, we continue to assume that all projects' cash flows have the same level of risk, that projects being compared have equal usable lives, and that the firm has unlimited funds. Since very few decisions are actually made under such conditions, these simplifying assumptions are relaxed in later sections of the chapter. Here we look at the three most popular capital budgeting techniques—payback period, net present value, and internal rate of return.

Table 10.1
Capital Expenditure Data for Bennett Company

	Project A	Project B
Initial investment	$42,000	$45,000
Year	Operating cash inflows	Operating cash inflows
1	$14,000	$28,000
2	14,000	12,000
3	14,000	10,000
4	14,000	10,000
5	14,000	10,000
Average	$14,000	$14,000

Payback Period

Payback periods are a commonly used criterion for evaluating proposed investments. The **payback period** is the exact amount of time required for the firm to recover its initial investment as calculated from *cash inflows*. In the case of an *annuity,* the payback period can be found by dividing the initial investment by the annual cash inflow; for a *mixed stream,* the yearly cash inflows must be accumulated until the initial investment is recovered. Although popular, the payback period is generally viewed as an *unsophisticated capital budgeting technique* since it does *not* explicitly consider the time value of money by discounting cash flows to find present value.

payback period The exact amount of time required for a firm to recover its initial investment as calculated from *cash inflows*.

The Decision Criterion

The decision criterion when payback is used to make accept-reject decisions is as follows: *If the payback period is less than or equal to the maximum acceptable payback period, accept the project; otherwise, reject the project.*

[1] For simplification, these five-year-lived projects with five years of cash inflows are used throughout this chapter. Projects with usable lives equal to the number of years of cash inflows are also included in the end-of-chapter problems. It is important to recall from Chapter 9 that under the *Tax Reform Act of 1986* ACRS depreciation results in $n + 1$ years of depreciation for an n-year class asset. This means that in actual practice projects will commonly have at least one year of cash flow beyond their recovery period.

Example

The data for Bennett Company's projects A and B presented in Table 10.1 can be used to demonstrate the calculation of the payback period. For project A, which is an annuity, the payback period is 3.00 years ($42,000 initial investment ÷ $14,000 annual cash inflow). Since project B generates a mixed stream of cash inflows, the calculation of the payback period is not quite as clear-cut. In year 1, the firm will recover $28,000 of its $45,000 initial investment. At the end of year 2, $40,000 ($28,000 from year 1 plus $12,000 from year 2) will be recovered. At the end of year 3, $50,000 ($40,000 from years 1 and 2 plus $10,000 from year 3) will be recovered. Since the amount received by the end of year 3 is greater than the initial investment of $45,000, the payback period is somewhere between two and three years. Only $5,000 ($45,000 − $40,000) must be recovered during year 3. Actually, $10,000 is recovered, but only 50 percent of this cash inflow ($5,000 ÷ $10,000) is needed to complete the payback of the initial $45,000. The payback period for project B is therefore 2.50 years (2 years plus 50 percent of year 3).

If Bennett's maximum acceptable payback period is 2.75 years, project A would be rejected and project B would be accepted. If the maximum payback were 2.25 years, both projects would be rejected. If the projects were being ranked, project B would be preferred over project A since it has a shorter payback period (2.50 years versus 3.00 years).

Pros and Cons of Payback Periods

The payback period is appealing in light of the fact that it considers cash flows rather than accounting profits; it also gives *some* implicit consideration to the timing of cash flows and therefore of the time value of money. Because it can be viewed as a measure of *risk exposure*, many firms use the payback period as a decision criterion or as a supplement to sophisticated decision techniques. The longer the firm must wait to recover its invested funds, the greater the possibility of a calamity, and vice versa. Therefore, the shorter the payback period, the lower the firm's exposure to such risk.

The major weakness of payback is that the appropriate payback period cannot be specified in light of the wealth maximization goal. A second weakness is that this approach fails to take *fully* into account the time factor in the value of money; by measuring how quickly the firm recovers its initial investment, it only implicitly considers the timing of cash flows.[2] A third weakness is the failure to recognize cash flows that occur *after* the payback period. This weakness can be illustrated by an example.

Example

Data for two investment opportunities—X and Y—are given in Table 10.2. The payback period for project X is two years; for project Y it is three years. Strict adherence to the payback approach suggests that project X is preferable to project Y. However, if we look beyond the payback period, we see that project X returns only an additional

---

[2] To consider differences in timing *explicitly* when using the payback method, the *present-value payback period* is sometimes used. It is found by first calculating the present value of the cash inflows at the appropriate discount rate and then finding the payback period using the present value of the cash inflows.

$1,200 ($1,000 in year 3, $100 in year 4, and $100 in year 5), whereas project Y returns an additional $7,000 ($4,000 in year 4 and $3,000 in year 5). Based on this information, it appears that project Y is preferable to X. The payback approach ignores the cash inflows in years 3, 4, and 5 for project X and in years 4 and 5 for project Y.[3]

Table 10.2
Calculation of the Payback Period for Two Alternative Investment Projects

	Project X	Project Y
Initial investment	$10,000	$10,000
Year	**Cash inflows**	
1	$5,000	$3,000
2	5,000	4,000
3	1,000	3,000
4	100	4,000
5	100	3,000
Payback period	2 years	3 years

Net Present Value (NPV)

Because *net present value* gives explicit consideration to the time value of money, it is considered a *sophisticated capital budgeting technique*. All such techniques in one way or another discount the firm's cash flows at a specified rate. This rate, which is often called the *discount rate, opportunity cost,* or *cost of capital* (the topic of Chapter 11), refers to the minimum return that must be earned on a project in order to leave the firm's market value unchanged.

net present value (NPV)
Found by subtracting a project's initial investment from the present value of the cash inflows discounted at a rate equal to the firm's cost of capital.

The **net present value (NPV),** as noted in Equation 10.1, is found by subtracting the initial investment *(II)* from the present value of the cash inflows *(CF$_t$)* discounted at a rate equal to the firm's cost of capital *(k).*

$$NPV = \text{present value of cash inflows} - \text{initial investment}$$

$$NPV = \sum_{t=1}^{n} \frac{CF_t}{(1 + k)^t} - II \tag{10.1}$$

Using NPV, both inflows and outflows are measured in terms of present dollars. Since we are dealing with conventional investments, the initial investment is automatically stated in terms of today's dollars. If it were not, the present value of a project would be found by subtracting the present value of outflows from the present value of inflows.

[3] To get around this weakness, some analysts add a desired dollar return to the initial investment and then calculate the payback period for the increased amount. For example, if the analyst wished to pay back the initial investment plus 20 percent for projects X and Y in Table 10.2, the amount to be recovered would be $12,000 [$10,000 + (.20 × $10,000)]. For project X, the payback period would be infinite because the $12,000 would never be recovered; for project Y, the payback period would be 3.50 years [3 years + ($2,000 ÷ $4,000 years)]. Clearly, project Y would be preferred.

SMALL BUSINESS

REAPING REWARD FROM NEW TECHNOLOGY: IBM Quit . . . He Did It!

"If I had inherited a billion dollars, I couldn't buy this feeling," says Sadeg M. Faris, president of startup Hypres Inc. The 41-year-old Libyan-born American is understandably proud: Early in 1987, he unveiled the world's first electronic system based on Josephson-junction chips. The superconducting chips are the heart of an ultrasensitive oscilloscope that analyzes very fast and faint electronic signals. "To introduce a product packed with many frontier technologies, all working together just like they're supposed to—that's the ultimate satisfaction," says Faris. "Most people would figure you'd be crazy just to try."

Indeed, Faris spent a lot of time convincing both potential employees and potential customers of his sanity. Before founding Hypres, he was an award-winning member of an International Business Machines Corp. research team trying to build a new generation of computers based on Josephson junctions. Although he tried to talk Big Blue out of it, the company scuttled the project in 1983. So Faris set up his own

shop in Elmsford, N.Y., to prove that JJ technology is the basis of the "Third Age of Electronics," the successor to vacuum tubes and transistors. "Here you've got giant IBM, which invested $300 million and 14 years in the technology and couldn't make it go. And then along comes me." Asks Faris with a grin: "Who would you believe?"

Armed only with his enthusiasm and licenses to IBM's JJ patents, Faris soon won believers. He sauntered uninvited into the offices of the three leading venture-capital firms—E. M. Warburg Pincus, Asset Management Associates, and Adler—plunked down a business plan, and within days won promises of support.

Not quite four years and $6 million later, in late February 1987, Hypres produced the system that IBM had, in effect, turned down: an analyzer that can plot electronic signals with unrivaled sensitivity and detail. "Ironically," says Faris, "one of our first machines went to IBM."

Faris's long-term goal is clearly to do what IBM couldn't. "Our strategy

will be to leverage out technology" by concentrating on the "brains" of tomorrow's computers, he says. With Hypres's limited resources and staff of 60, he can't afford to get bogged down in ordinary components. "That would be dumb. I want to build what nobody else knows how to make. That's where we will have a high return on investment."

So it seems likely that little Hypres will soon be shopping for a computer-company partner to help develop a number-cruncher at least 100 times faster than anything dreamed of with silicon transistors.

To hear Faris tell it, he is cutting Hypres from the same cloth as Polaroid, Texas Instruments, and Xerox. "They were like me—stubborn about going after their own private visions." And he predicts Hypres will crack the magic billion-dollar club "while I'm still young enough to enjoy it." IBM may have thought the risk too high, so Faris will gain the well-earned reward.

SOURCE: Otis Port, "He's Walking Tall Where IBM Wouldn't Tread," *Business Week*, May 4, 1987, p. 124.

The Decision Criterion

The criterion when NPV is used to make accept-reject decisions is as follows: *If NPV is greater than or equal to $0, accept the project; otherwise, reject the project.* If the NPV is greater than or equal to zero, the firm will earn a return greater than or equal to its cost of capital. Such action should enhance or maintain the wealth of the firm's owners.

Example
The net present value (NPV) approach can be illustrated using the Bennett Company data presented in Table 10.1. If the firm has a 10 percent cost of capital, the net present values for projects A (an annuity) and B (a mixed stream) can be calculated as in

Table 10.3. These calculations are based on the application of the techniques presented in Chapter 6. The results show that the net present values of projects A and B are, respectively, $11,074 and $10,914. Both projects are acceptable, since the net present value of each is greater than zero. If the projects were being ranked, however, project A would be considered superior to B since it has a higher net present value ($11,074 versus $10,914) than that of B.

Table 10.3
The Calculation of NPVs for Bennett Company's Capital Expenditure Alternatives

Project A	
Annual cash inflow	$14,000
×Present value annuity interest factor, $PVIFA^a$	3.791
Present value of cash inflows	$53,074
−Initial investment	42,000
Net present value (NPV)	$11,074

Project B			
Year	Cash inflows (1)	Present value interest factor, $PVIF^b$ (2)	Present value [(1) × (2)] (3)
1	$28,000	.909	$25,452
2	12,000	.826	9,912
3	10,000	.751	7,510
4	10,000	.683	6,830
5	10,000	.621	6,210
		Present value of cash inflows	$55,914
		−Initial investment	45,000
		Net present value (NPV)	$10,914

[a] From Table A-4, for 5 years and 10 percent.

[b] From Table A-3, for given year and 10 percent.

FACT OR FABLE?

[1] Both the payback period and net present value (NPV) are considered sophisticated capital budgeting techniques since they explicitly consider the time value of money. *(Fable)*

The *payback period* is an unsophisticated capital budgeting technique since it does not explicitly consider the time value of money; net present value (NPV) on the other hand is a sophisticated technique since it does explicitly consider time value.

Internal Rate of Return (IRR)

The internal rate of return (IRR), although considerably more difficult to calculate than NPV, is probably the most used *sophisticated capital budgeting technique* for evaluating investment alternatives. The **internal rate of return *(IRR)*** is defined as the discount rate that equates the present value of cash inflows with the initial investment associated with a project. The IRR, in other words, is the discount rate that equates the NPV of an investment opportunity with zero (since the present value of cash inflows equals the initial investment). Mathematically, the IRR is found by solving Equation 10.1 for the value of *k* that causes NPV to equal zero.

internal rate of return (IRR) The discount rate that equates the present value of cash inflows with the initial investment associated with a project, thereby causing NPV = $0.

$$\$0 = \sum_{t=1}^{n} \frac{CF_t}{(1 + IRR)^t} - II$$

$$\sum_{t=1}^{n} \frac{CF_t}{(1 + IRR)^t} = II \tag{10.2}$$

As will be demonstrated shortly, the actual calculation of the IRR from Equation 10.2 is no easy chore.

The Decision Criterion

The criterion, when the IRR is used in making accept-reject decisions, is as follows: *If the IRR is greater than or equal to the cost of capital, accept the project; otherwise, reject the project.* This criterion guarantees that the firm is earning at least its required return and assures that the market value of the firm will increase or at least remain unchanged.

Calculating the IRR

The IRR must be calculated using trial-and-error techniques. Calculating the IRR for an annuity is considerably easier than calculating it for a mixed stream of operating cash inflows.[4] The steps involved in calculating the IRR in each case are given in Table 10.4. The application of these steps can be illustrated by the example on pages 334–337.

---

[4] The ease of calculating the IRR for an annuity as well as the steps in the process results from an ability to simplify Equation 10.2. Since for annuities, $CF_1 = CF_2 = \ldots = CF_n$, the CF_t term can be factored from Equation 10.2. Doing this, we get

$$CF_t \sum_{t=1}^{n} \frac{1}{(1 + IRR)^t} = II$$

Dividing both sides of the equation by CF_t, we get

$$\sum_{t=1}^{n} \frac{1}{(1 + IRR)^t} = \frac{II}{CF_t}$$

Since the left side of the equation is equal to $PVIFA_{IRR,n}$ and the right side equals the payback period—the initial investment divided by the annual cash inflow—it is not difficult to estimate the IRR for annuities.

Table 10.4
Steps for Calculating the Internal Rates of Return (IRRs) of Annuities and Mixed Streams

---

FOR AN ANNUITY

Step 1: Calculate the payback period for the project.[a]

Step 2: Use Table A-4 (the present-value interest factors for a $1 annuity, *PVIFA*) to find, for the life of the project, the factor closest to the payback value. This is the internal rate of return (IRR) to the nearest 1 percent.

FOR A MIXED STREAM[b]

Step 1: Calculate the average annual cash inflow.

Step 2: Divide the average annual cash inflow into the initial investment to get an "average payback period" (or present-value interest factor for a $1 annuity, *PVIFA*). The average payback is needed to estimate the IRR for the average annual cash inflow.

Step 3: Use Table A-4 *(PVIFA)* and the average payback period in the same manner as described in step 2 for finding the IRR of an annuity. The result will be a *very rough* approximation of the IRR, based on the assumption that the mixed stream of cash inflows is an annuity.

Step 4:[c] Adjust subjectively the IRR obtained in step 3 by comparing the pattern of average annual cash inflows (calculated in step 1) to the actual mixed stream of cash inflows. If the actual cash flow stream seems to have higher inflows in the earlier years than the average stream, adjust the IRR up a few percentage points. If the actual cash inflows in the earlier years are below the average, adjust the IRR down a few percentage points. If the average cash inflows seem fairly close to the actual pattern, make no adjustment in the IRR.

Step 5: Using the IRR from step 4, calculate the net present value of the mixed-stream project. Be sure to use Table A-3 (the present-value interest factors for $1, *PVIF*), treating the estimated IRR as the discount rate.

Step 6: If the resulting NPV is greater than zero, subjectively raise the discount rate; if the resulting NPV is less than zero, subjectively lower the discount rate.

Step 7: Calculate the NPV using the new discount rate. Repeat step 6. Stop as soon as two *consecutive* discount rates that cause the NPV to be positive and negative, respectively, have been found.[d] Whichever of these two rates causes the NPV to be closer to zero is the IRR to the nearest 1 percent.

---

[a] The payback period calculated actually represents the interest factor for the present value of an annuity (*PVIFA*) for the given life discounted at an unknown rate, which, once determined, represents the IRR for the project.

[b] Note that subjective estimates are suggested in steps 4 and 6. After working a number of these problems, a "feel" for the appropriate subjective adjustment, or "educated guess," may result.

[c] The purpose of this step is to provide a more accurate first estimate of the IRR. This step can be skipped.

[d] A shortcut method is to find a discount rate that results in a positive NPV and another that results in a negative NPV. Using only these two values, one can interpolate between the two discount rates to find the IRR. This approach, which may be nearly as accurate as that described above, can guarantee an answer after only two NPV calculations. Of course, because interpolation involves a straight-line approximation to an exponential function, the wider the interpolation interval, the less accurate the estimate.

Example
The two-step procedure given in Table 10.4 for finding the IRR of an *annuity* can be demonstrated using Bennett Company's project A cash flows given in Table 10.1.

> **Step 1:** Dividing the initial investment of $42,000 by the annual cash inflow of $14,000 results in a payback period of 3.000 years ($42,000 ÷ $14,000 = 3.000).

Step 2: According to Table A-4, the *PVIFA* factors closest to 3.000 for five years are 3.058 (for 19 percent) and 2.991 (for 20 percent). The value closest to 3.000 is 2.991; therefore the IRR for project A, to the nearest 1 percent, is *20 percent*. The actual value, which is between 19 and 20 percent, could be found using a financial calculator or computer or by interpolation;[5] it is 19.87 percent. *(Note:* For our purposes, values rounded to the nearest 1 percent are acceptable.) Project A with an IRR of 20 percent is quite acceptable, since this IRR is above the firm's 10 percent cost of capital (20 percent IRR > 10 percent cost of capital).

The application of the seven-step procedure given in Table 10.4 for finding the internal rate of return of a *mixed stream* of cash inflows can be illustrated using Bennett Company's project B cash flows given in Table 10.1.

Step 1: Summing the cash inflows for years 1 through 5 results in total cash inflows of $70,000, which, when divided by the number of years in the project's life, results in an average annual cash inflow of $14,000 [($28,000 + $12,000 + $10,000 + $10,000 + $10,000) ÷ 5].

Step 2: Dividing the initial outlay of $45,000 by the average annual cash inflow of $14,000 (calculated in step 1) results in an "average payback period" (or present value of an annuity factor, *PVIFA*) of 3.214 years.

Step 3: In Table A-4, the factor closest to 3.214 for five years is 3.199, the factor for a discount rate of 17 percent. The starting estimate of the IRR is therefore 17 percent.

Step 4: Since the actual early-year cash inflows are greater than the average cash inflows of $14,000, a *subjective* increase of 2 percent is made in the discount rate. This makes the estimated IRR 19 percent.

Step 5: Using the present-value interest factors *(PVIF)* for 19 percent and the correct year from Table A-3, the net present value of the mixed stream is calculated as follows:

Year (t)	Cash inflows (1)	$PVIF_{19\%,t}$ (2)	Present value at 19% [(1) × (2)] (3)
1	$28,000	.840	$23,520
2	12,000	.706	8,472
3	10,000	.593	5,930
4	10,000	.499	4,990
5	10,000	.419	4,190
	Present value of cash inflows		$47,102
	−Initial investment		45,000
	Net present value (NPV)		$ 2,102

[5] *Interpolation* is a mathematical technique used to find intermediate or fractional values when only integer data are provided. Since interest factors for whole percentages are included in the financial tables in Appendix A, interpolation is required to calculate more precisely the internal rate of return. See footnote 12 in Chapter 6 for a demonstration of the use of interpolation to obtain better estimates of rates of return.

Steps 6 and 7: Since the net present value of $2,102, calculated in step 5, is greater than zero, the discount rate should be subjectively increased. Since the NPV is not close to zero, let's try an increase to 21 percent.

Year (t)	Cash inflows (1)	PVIF$_{21\%,t}$ (2)	Present value at 21% [(1) × (2)] (3)
1	$28,000	.826	$23,128
2	12,000	.683	8,196
3	10,000	.564	5,640
4	10,000	.467	4,670
5	10,000	.386	3,860
		Present value of cash inflows	$45,494
		−Initial investment	45,000
		Net present value (NPV)	$ 494

These calculations indicate that the NPV of $494 for an IRR of 21 percent is reasonably close to, but still greater than, zero. Thus a higher discount rate should be tried. Since we are so close, let's try 22 percent. As the following calculations show, the net present value using a discount rate of 22 percent is −$256.

Year (t)	Cash inflows (1)	PVIF$_{22\%,t}$ (2)	Present value at 22% [(1) × (2)] (3)
1	$28,000	.820	$22,960
2	12,000	.672	8,064
3	10,000	.551	5,510
4	10,000	.451	4,510
5	10,000	.370	3,700
		Present value of cash inflows	$44,744
		−Initial investment	45,000
		Net present value (NPV)	−$ 256

Since 21 and 22 percent are consecutive discount rates that give positive and negative net present values, the trial-and-error process can be terminated. The IRR we are seeking is the discount rate for which the NPV is closest to zero. For this project, 22 percent causes the NPV to be closer to zero than 21 percent, so 22 percent is the IRR we shall use. If we had used a financial calculator, a computer, or interpolation, the exact IRR would be 21.66 percent; as indicated earlier, for our purposes the IRR rounded to the nearest 1 percent will suffice. Therefore, the IRR of project B is approximately *22 percent*.

Project B is acceptable since its IRR of approximately 22 percent is greater than the Bennett Company's 10 percent cost of capital. This is the same conclusion reached using the NPV criterion. It is interesting to note that the IRR suggests that project B is preferable to A, which has an IRR of approximately 20 percent. This conflicts with the rankings of the projects obtained using NPV. Such conflicts are not unusual; *there is no guarantee that these two techniques (NPV and IRR) will rank projects in the same order. However, both methods should reach the same conclusion about the acceptability or nonacceptability of projects.*

---

2 **The internal rate of return (IRR) is the discount rate that causes the present value of a project's cash inflows to just equal the initial investment, thereby resulting in a net present value of $0.** *(Fact)*

FACT OR FABLE?

Comparing NPV and IRR Techniques

For conventional projects, net present value (NPV) and internal rate of return (IRR) will always generate the same accept-reject decision, but differences in their underlying assumptions can cause them to rank projects differently. To understand the differences and preferences surrounding these techniques, we need to look at net present value profiles, conflicting rankings, and the question of which approach is better.

Net Present Value Profiles

Projects can be compared graphically by constructing **net present value profiles** that depict the net present value for various discount rates. These profiles are useful in evaluating and comparing projects, especially when conflicting rankings exist. Their development and interpretation are best demonstrated via an example.

net present value profiles
Graphs that depict the net present value of a project for various discount rates.

Example
To prepare net present value profiles for Bennett Company's two projects, A and B, the first step is to develop a number of discount-rate–net-present-value coordinates. Three coordinates can easily be obtained for each project; they are at discount rates of 0 percent, 10 percent (the cost of capital, k), and the IRR. The net present value at a 0 percent discount rate is found by merely adding all the cash inflows and subtracting the initial investment. Using the data in Table 10.1, for project A we get ($14,000 + $14,000 + $14,000 + $14,000 + $14,000) − $42,000 = $28,000, and for project B we get ($28,000 + $12,000 + $10,000 + $10,000 + $10,000) − $45,000 = $25,000. The net present values for projects A and B at the 10 percent cost of capital were found to be $11,074 and $10,914, respectively, in Table 10.3. Since the IRR is the discount rate for which net present value equals zero, the IRRs of 20 percent for

project A and 22 percent for project B result in $0 NPVs. The three sets of coordinates for each of the projects are summarized in Table 10.5.

Plotting the data in Table 10.5 on a set of discount rate-NPV axes results in the net present value profiles for projects A and B plotted in Figure 10.1. An analysis of Figure 10.1 indicates that for any discount rate less than approximately 10.7 percent, the NPV for project A is greater than the NPV for project B. Beyond this point, the NPV for B is greater than that for A. Since the net present value profiles for projects A and B cross at a positive NPV, the IRRs for the projects cause conflicting rankings whenever they are compared to NPVs calculated at discount rates below 10.7 percent.

Table 10.5
Discount Rate-NPV Coordinates for Projects A and B

Discount rate	Net present value	
	Project A	Project B
0%	$28,000	$25,000
10	11,074	10,914
20	0	—
22	—	0

Conflicting Rankings

The possibility of *conflicting rankings* of projects by NPV and IRR should be clear from the Bennett Company example. Ranking is an important consideration when projects are mutually exclusive or when capital rationing is necessary. When projects are mutually

Figure 10.1
Net Present Value Profiles for Bennett Company's Projects A and B

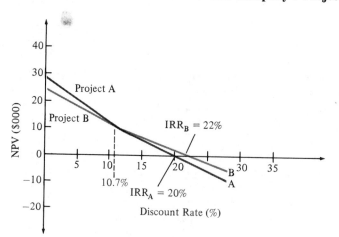

DAVID RODERICK:
A Financial Knack for Figuring Things Out

One might say David M. Roderick has fulfilled the American Dream. From modest beginnings, he has risen to a position of prominence in the industry that is synonymous with his hometown: steel. He has been chairman and chief executive officer of USX Corp. (formerly United States Steel Corp.), parent of the nation's biggest steel-maker, for seven years. In a poll conducted by a Pittsburgh newspaper, his fellow citizens named him second only to the mayor as the most influential man in their city. The son of a postal worker, Roderick grew up in a blue-collar neighborhood. After joining the Marines in World War II, he earned a degree in finance and economics at the University of Pittsburgh. Says Roderick, "I don't consider myself a financial expert. I've never closed a set of books in my life, nor been a general accountant, treasurer, or tax man. Most of my experience has been in the area of analyzing costs and finances. I've worked with engineers and production managers to find ways to improve productivity and to make divisions more profitable and products more saleable."

Roderick's reputation as a problem-solver began when, as a young financial analyst for one of U.S. Steel's railroad subsidiaries, he developed a cost-effective plan for transporting manganese ore from mines deep in the jungles of French Equatorial Africa.

Later, as assistant to U.S. Steel's director of statistics, he did a profitability study on the mine. In 1964, Roderick became vice president for international accounting. He was promoted to vice president-international in 1967 and named chairman of the finance committee in 1973. Monthly meetings of the finance committee gave Roderick the kind of exposure to the entire corporation that would be invaluable to him later, first on becoming president in 1975 and then on being elected chairman and CEO four years later.

"Two things have been tremendously helpful to me as chairman," he says. "The first is my 25 years of expe-

rience in objectively analyzing options and consequences in both long- and short-term situations. The other is my experience as chairman of the finance committee. We live in a financial world, and we're constantly dealing with acquisitions and with the sale and redeployment of assets. A financial background is helpful all the way up the line, but it's vital at the decision-making level."

Financial know-how, says Roderick, makes an executive more objective. But some Wall Street analysts questioned that objectivity when Roderick merged U.S. Steel with Texas Oil and Gas in 1986, a time when natural gas prices were declining. Roderick, however, viewed the merger as part of a long-term strategy to diversify the company so that its troubled steel-making operations would not depress earnings. USX's acquisition of Marathon Oil in 1982 was another step in the diversification process. Says Roderick, "I'd like to see us in three or four major lines of business—well managed, well funded, and worth top management's time."

In the future, Roderick's knack for problem-solving will be put to the test as he must decide among a host of strategies, which includes restructuring the company, how to accommodate and manage such diversity of businesses. One can bet he'll figure it out.

SOURCE: "David M. Roderick of USX Corporation: How to Become a CEO," by Barbara Ross. Reprinted by permission from *FE: the magazine for financial executives*, November 1986, copyright 1986 by Financial Executives Institute.

exclusive, ranking enables the firm to determine the best project from a financial viewpoint. When capital rationing is necessary, ranking projects may not determine the group of projects to accept, but it will provide a logical starting point.

conflicting rankings
Conflicts in the ranking of projects by NPV and IRR that result from differences in the magnitude and timing of cash flows.

intermediate cash inflows
Cash inflows received prior to the termination of a project.

Conflicting rankings using NPV and IRR result from *differences in the magnitude and timing of cash flows*. Although these two factors can be used to explain conflicting rankings, the underlying cause results from the implicit assumption concerning the reinvestment of **intermediate cash inflows**—cash inflows received prior to termination of the project. NPV assumes that intermediate cash inflows are reinvested at the cost of capital, whereas IRR assumes that intermediate cash inflows can be invested at a rate equal to the project's IRR.

In general, projects with similar-sized investments[6] and lower early-year cash inflows (lower cash inflows in the early years) tend to be preferred at lower discount rates. Projects having higher early-year cash inflows (higher cash inflows in the early years) tend to be preferred at higher discount rates. These behaviors can be explained by the fact that at high discount rates, later-year cash inflows tend to be severely penalized in present-value terms. Of course, annuities (projects with level cash inflows) cannot be characterized in this fashion; they can best be evaluated in comparison to other cash inflow streams. Table 10.6 summarizes the preferences associated with extreme discount rates and dissimilar cash inflow patterns.

Example

In an earlier example, the Bennett Company's projects A and B were found to have conflicting rankings at the firm's 10 percent cost of capital. This finding is depicted in Figure 10.1. If we review each project's cash inflow pattern as presented in Table 10.1, we see that although the projects require similar initial investments, they have dissimilar cash inflow patterns—project A has level cash inflows and project B has higher early-year inflows. Table 10.6 indicates that project B would be preferred over project A at high discount rates. Figure 10.1 shows that this is in fact the case. At a discount rate in excess of 10.7 percent, project B's NPV is above that of project A. Clearly the magnitude and timing of the cash inflows does affect their rankings.

Table 10.6
Preferences Associated with Extreme Discount Rates and Dissimilar Cash Inflow Patterns

Discount rate	Cash inflow pattern	
	Lower early-year cash inflows	Higher early-year cash inflows
Low	Preferred	Not preferred
High	Not preferred	Preferred

---

[6] Because differences in the relative sizes of initial investments can also affect conflicts in rankings, the initial investments are assumed to be similar. This permits isolation of the effect of differences in magnitude and timing of cash inflows on project rankings.

Although the classification of cash inflow patterns in Table 10.6 is useful in explaining conflicting rankings, differences in the magnitude and timing of cash inflows do not guarantee conflicts in ranking. In general, the greater the difference between the magnitude and timing of cash inflows, the greater the likelihood of conflicting rankings. Conflicts based on NPV and IRR can be reconciled computationally by creating and analyzing an incremental project reflecting the difference in cash flows between the two mutually exclusive projects. Because a detailed description of this procedure is beyond the scope of an introductory text, suffice it to say that IRR techniques can be used to generate consistently the same project rankings as would be obtained using NPV.

Which Approach Is Better?

The better approach for evaluating capital expenditures is difficult to determine because the theoretical and practical strengths of the approaches differ. It is therefore wise to view both NPV and IRR techniques in light of each of the following dimensions.

Theoretical View

On a purely theoretical basis, NPV is the better approach to capital budgeting. Its theoretical superiority is attributed to a number of factors. Most important is the fact that the use of NPV implicitly assumes that any intermediate cash inflows generated by an investment are reinvested at the firm's cost of capital. The use of IRR assumes reinvestment at the often high rate specified by the IRR. Since the cost of capital tends to be a reasonable estimate of the rate at which the firm could actually reinvest intermediate cash inflows, the use of NPV with its more conservative and realistic reinvestment rate is in theory preferable. In addition, certain mathematical properties may cause a project with nonconventional cash flows to have zero or more than one IRR; this problem does not occur with the NPV approach.

Practical View

Evidence suggests[7] that in spite of the theoretical superiority of NPV, *financial managers prefer to use IRR.* The preference for IRR is attributable to the general disposition of business people toward *rates of return* rather than actual *dollar returns.* Because interest rates, profitability, and so on are most often expressed as annual rates of return, the use of IRR makes sense to financial decision makers. They tend to find NPV more difficult to use because it does not really measure benefits *relative to the amount invested.* Because a variety of methods and techniques are available for avoiding the pitfalls of the IRR, its widespread use should not be viewed as reflecting a lack of sophistication on the part of financial decision makers.

---

3 Net present value (NPV) and internal rate of return (IRR) always give the same accept-reject decisions, but may disagree when ranking projects due to differences in the magnitude and timing of cash flows. *(Fact)*

FACT OR FABLE?

---

[7] For example, see Suk H. Kim, Trevor Crick, and Seung H. Kim, "Do Executives Practice What Academics Preach?" *Management Accounting* (November 1986), pp. 49–52, for a discussion of evidence with respect to capital budgeting decision-making practices in major U.S. firms.

Approaches for Dealing with Risk

Up to this point, the discussion of capital budgeting techniques has been based on the assumption that all projects' cash flows have the same level of risk as the firm. Project cash inflows were equally risky. In actuality, there are very few capital budgeting projects for which cash inflows have the same risk as the firm. Using the basic risk concepts presented in Chapter 7, here we present a few approaches for dealing with risk in capital budgeting: risk and cash inflows, sensitivity and scenario analysis, and simulation.

Risk and Cash Inflows

In the discussion of capital budgeting, *risk* refers to the chance that a project will prove unacceptable (i.e., NPV < $0 or IRR < cost of capital, *k*) or, more formally, to the degree of variability of cash flows. Projects with a small chance of being acceptable and a broad range of expected cash flows are more risky than projects having a high chance of acceptance and a narrow range of expected cash flows.

In the conventional capital budgeting projects assumed here, risk therefore stems almost entirely from *cash inflows,* since the initial investment is generally known with relative certainty. These inflows, of course, derive from a number of risky variables related to revenues, expenditures, and taxes. Examples would include the level of sales, cost of raw materials, labor rates, utility costs, and tax rates. We will concentrate on the risk in the cash inflows, but remember that this risk actually results from the interaction of these underlying variables. Therefore, to assess the risk of a proposed capital expenditure, the analyst needs to evaluate the probability that the cash inflows will be large enough to provide for project acceptance. This concept is best demonstrated by a simple example.

Example
Treadwell Tire Company is considering investing in either of two mutually exclusive projects, A and B, each requiring a $10,000 initial investment *(II)* and expected to provide equal annual cash inflows *(CF)* over their 15-year lives. For either project to be acceptable using the net present value technique, its NPV must be greater than or equal to zero. Letting *CF* equal the annual cash inflow and *II* equal the initial investment, the following condition must be met in order for projects with annuity cash inflows, such as A and B, to be acceptable.

$$NPV = CF \times (PVIFA_{k,n}) - II \geq \$0 \tag{10.3}$$

breakeven cash inflow
The level of cash inflow necessary for a project to be acceptable.

Substituting *k* = 10%, *n* = 15 years, and *II* = $10,000, the **breakeven cash inflow**—the level of cash inflow necessary for Treadwell's projects to be acceptable—can be found.

$$CF \times (PVIFA_{10\%,15yrs}) - \$10,000 \geq \$0$$

$$CF \times (7.606) \geq \$10,000$$

$$CF \geq \frac{\$10,000}{7.606} = \underline{\underline{\$1,315}}$$

In other words, for the projects to be acceptable, they must have annual cash inflows of at least $1,315.

Given this breakeven level of cash inflows, the risk of each project could be assessed by determining—using various statistical techniques beyond the scope of this text[8]—the probability that the firm's cash inflows will equal or exceed this breakeven level. Assume that such a statistical analysis results in the following:

Probability of $CF_A > \$1,315$ 100%

Probability of $CF_B > \$1,315$ 65%

Since project A is certain (100 percent probability) to have a positive net present value, while there is only a 65 percent chance that project B will have a positive NPV, project A is less risky than project B. Of course, the potential level of returns associated with each project must be evaluated in view of the firm's risk preference prior to selecting the preferred project.

The example clearly identifies risk as it relates to the chance that a project is acceptable, but it does not address the issue of cash flow variability. Even though project B has a greater chance of loss than project A, it might result in higher potential NPVs. Recall from Chapters 7 and 8 that it is the combination of risk and return that determines value. Similarly, the worth of a capital expenditure and its impact on the firm's value must be viewed in light of both risk and return. The analyst must therefore consider the *variability* of cash inflows and NPVs in order to assess project risk and return fully.

Sensitivity and Scenario Analysis

Two approaches for dealing with project risk to capture the variability of cash inflows and NPVs are sensitivity analysis and scenario analysis. **Sensitivity analysis,** as noted in Chapter 7, uses a number of possible values for a given variable, such as cash inflows, to assess its impact on the firm's return, measured here by NPV. This technique is often useful in getting a feel for the variability of return in response to changes in a key variable. In capital budgeting, one of the most common sensitivity approaches is to estimate the NPVs associated with pessimistic (worst), most likely (expected), and optimistic (best) cash inflow estimates. By subtracting the pessimistic-outcome NPV from the optimistic-outcome NPV, the *range* can be determined.

sensitivity analysis An approach that uses a number of possible values for a given variable in order to assess its impact on a firm's return.

Example

Continuing with Treadwell Tire Company, assume that the financial manager made pessimistic, most likely, and optimistic estimates of the cash inflows for each project. The cash inflow estimates and resulting NPVs in each case are summarized in Table 10.7. Comparing the ranges of cash inflows ($1,000 for project A and $4,000 for project B) and, more important, the range of NPVs ($7,606 for project A and $30,424 for project B) makes it clear that project A is less risky than project B. The assumed risk-averse decision maker will take project A, thereby eliminating the possibility of loss.

[8] Normal distributions are commonly used to develop the concept of the probability of success—that is, of a project's having a nonnegative NPV. The reader interested in learning more about this technique should see any second- or MBA-level managerial finance text.

Table 10.7
Sensitivity Analysis of Treadwell's Projects A and B

	Project A	Project B
Initial investment	$10,000	$10,000
	Annual cash inflows	
Outcome		
Pessimistic	$ 1,500	$ 0
Most likely	2,000	2,000
Optimistic	2,500	4,000
Range	$ 1,000	$ 4,000
	Net present values[a]	
Outcome		
Pessimistic	$ 1,409	−$10,000
Most likely	5,212	5,212
Optimistic	9,015	20,424
Range	$ 7,606	$30,424

[a] These values were calculated using the corresponding annual cash inflows. A 10 percent cost of capital and a 15-year life for the annual cash inflows were used.

scenario analysis An approach that evaluates the impact on return of simultaneous changes in a number of variables.

   Scenario analysis, which is similar to sensitivity analysis but broader in scope, is used to evaluate the impact of various circumstances on the firm's return. Rather than isolating the effect of a change in a single variable, scenario analysis is used to evaluate the impact on return of simultaneous changes in a number of variables, such as cash inflows, cash outflows, and the cost of capital, resulting from differing assumptions relative to economic and competitive conditions. For example, the firm could evaluate the impact of both high inflation (scenario 1) and low inflation (scenario 2) on a project's NPV. Each scenario will affect the firm's cash inflows, cash outflows, and cost of capital, thereby resulting in different levels of return. The decision maker can use these return estimates to roughly assess the risk involved with respect to the level of inflation. The widespread availability of computer-based spreadsheet programs (such as Lotus 1-2-3) has greatly enhanced the ease and popularity of use of scenario as well as sensitivity analysis.

FACT OR FABLE?

[4] Sensitivity analysis is used to assess project risk by evaluating the impact on return of simultaneous changes in a number of variables, whereas scenario analysis considers only a single variable change. *(Fable)*

Sensitivity analysis is used to assess project risk by evaluating the impact on return of changes in a *single variable;* scenario analysis considers *simultaneous changes in a number of variables.*

Simulation

Simulation is a statistically based approach used in capital budgeting to get a feel for risk by applying predetermined probability distributions and random numbers to estimate risky outcomes. By tying the various cash flow components together in a mathematical model and repeating the process numerous times, a probability distribution of project returns can be developed. Figure 10.2 presents a flowchart of the simulation of the net present value of a project. The process of generating random numbers and using the probability distributions for cash inflows and outflows allows values for each of these variables to be determined. Substituting these values into the mathematical model results in an NPV. By repeating this process perhaps a thousand times, a probability distribution of net present values is created.

Although only gross cash inflows and outflows are simulated in Figure 10.2, more sophisticated simulations using individual inflow and outflow components, such as sales volume, sales price, raw material cost, labor cost, maintenance expense, and so on, are quite common. From the distribution of returns, regardless of how they are measured (NPV, IRR, and so on), the decision maker can determine not only the expected value of the return but also the probability of achieving or surpassing a given return. The use of

simulation A statistically based approach used to get a feel for risk by applying predetermined probability distributions and random numbers to estimate risky outcomes.

Figure 10.2
Flowchart of a Net Present Value Simulation

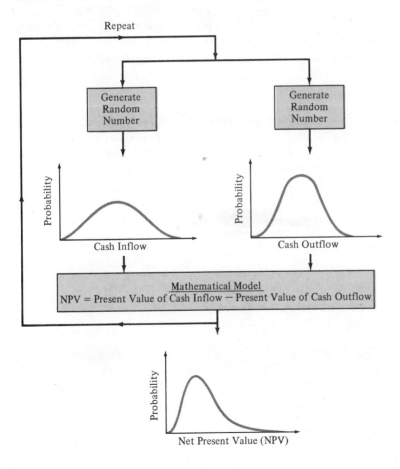

computers has made the simulation approach quite feasible. The output of simulation provides an excellent basis for decision making since it allows the decision maker to view a continuum of risk-return trade-offs rather than a single-point estimate.

Risk-Adjustment Techniques

The approaches for dealing with risk presented so far allow the financial manager to get a "feel" for project risk. Unfortunately, they do not really provide a straightforward basis for evaluating risky projects. We will now illustrate the two major risk-adjustment techniques using the net present value (NPV) decision method.[9] The NPV decision rule of accepting only those projects with NPVs $\geq$ \$0 will continue to hold. The basic equation for NPV was presented earlier in Equation 10.1. Close examination of that equation should make it clear that since the initial investment *(II)*, which occurs at time zero, is known with certainty, a project's risk is embodied in the present value of cash inflows:

$$\sum_{t=1}^{n} \frac{CF_t}{(1 + k)^t} \tag{10.3}$$

Two opportunities to adjust the present value of cash inflows for risk exist: (1) the cash inflows, CF_t, can be adjusted, or (2) the discount rate, k, can be adjusted. Here we describe and compare two techniques—the cash inflow adjustment process, using *certainty equivalents,* and the discount rate adjustment process, using *risk-adjusted discount rates.* In addition, we consider the portfolio effects of project analysis as well as the practical aspects of certainty equivalents and risk-adjusted discount rates.

Certainty Equivalents (CEs)

certainty equivalents (CEs) Risk-adjustment factors that represent the percent of estimated cash inflow that investors would be satisfied to receive for *certain* rather than the cash inflows that are *possible* for each year.

One of the most direct and theoretically preferred approaches for risk adjustment is the use of **certainty equivalents (CEs),** which represent the percent of estimated cash inflow that investors would be satisfied to receive *for certain* rather than the cash inflows that are *possible* for each year. Equation 10.4 presents the basic expression for NPV when certainty equivalents are used for risk adjustment.

$$NPV = \sum_{t=1}^{n} \frac{\alpha_t \times CF_t}{(1 + R_F)^t} - II \tag{10.4}$$

where

$$\alpha_t = \text{certainty equivalent factor in year } t \ (0 \leq \alpha_t \leq 1)$$
$$CF_t = \text{relevant cash inflow in year } t$$
$$R_F = \text{risk-free rate of return}$$

The equation shows that the project is adjusted for risk by first converting the expected cash inflows to certain amounts, $\alpha_t \times CF_t$, and then discounting the cash inflows at the

risk-free rate (R_F) The rate of return one would earn on a virtually riskless investment such as a U.S. Treasury bill.

risk-free rate, R_F.[10] The **risk-free rate (R_F)** is the rate of return one would earn on a

---

[9] The IRR could just as well have been used, but since NPV is theoretically preferable, it is used instead.

[10] Alternately, the internal rate of return could be calculated for the risk-adjusted cash inflows and then compared to the risk-free rate in order to make the accept-reject decision.

virtually riskless investment such as a U.S. Treasury bill. It is used to discount the certain cash inflows and is not to be confused with a risk-adjusted discount rate. (If a risk-adjusted rate were used, the risk would in effect be counted twice.) Although the process described here of converting risky cash inflows to certain cash inflows is somewhat subjective, the technique is theoretically sound.

Example

Bennett Company wishes to consider risk in the analysis of two projects, A and B. The basic data for these projects were initially presented in Table 10.1, and the analysis of the projects using net present value and assuming the projects had equivalent risks was presented in Table 10.3. Ignoring risk differences and using net present value, it was shown earlier that at the firm's 10 percent cost of capital, project A was preferred over project B since its NPV of $11,074 was greater than B's NPV of $10,914. Assume, however, that on further analysis the firm found that project A was actually more risky than project B. To consider the differing risks, the firm estimated the certainty equivalents for each project's cash inflows for each year. Columns 2 and 7 of Table 10.8 show the estimated values for projects A and B, respectively. Multiplying the risky cash inflows (given in columns 1 and 6) by the corresponding certainty equivalents (CEs) (columns 2 and 7, respectively) gives the certain cash inflows for projects A and B shown in columns 3 and 8, respectively.

Upon investigation, Bennett's management estimated the prevailing risk-free rate of return, R_F, to be 6 percent. Using the 6 percent risk-free rate to discount the certain cash inflows for each of the projects results in the net present values of $4,541 for project A and $10,141 for project B, as calculated in Table 10.8. Note that as a result of the risk adjustment, project B is now preferred. The usefulness of the certainty equivalent approach for risk adjustment should be quite clear; the only difficulty lies in the need to make subjective estimates of the certainty equivalents.

Risk-Adjusted Discount Rates (RADRs)

A more practical approach for risk adjustment involves the use of risk-adjusted discount rates (RADRs). Instead of adjusting the cash inflows for risk, as was done using the certainty equivalent approach, this approach adjusts the discount rate.[11] Equation 10.5 presents the basic expression for NPV when risk-adjusted discount rates are used.

$$\text{NPV} = \sum_{t=1}^{n} \frac{CF_t}{(1 + \text{RADR})^t} - II \qquad (10.5)$$

The **risk-adjusted discount rate (RADR)** is the rate of return that must be earned on a given project in order to compensate the firm's owners adequately, thereby resulting in the maintenance or improvement of share price. The higher the risk of a project, the higher the RADR and therefore the lower the net present value for a given stream of cash inflows. Because the logic underlying the use of RADRs is closely linked to the capital

risk-adjusted discount rate (RADR) The rate of return that must be earned on a given project to compensate the firm's owners adequately, thereby resulting in the maintenance or improvement of share price.

---

[11] The risk-adjusted discount rate approach can be applied when using the internal rate of return as well as net present value. If the IRR is used, the risk-adjusted discount rate becomes the cutoff rate that must be equaled or exceeded by the IRR for the project to be accepted. When using NPV, the projected cash inflows are merely discounted at the risk-adjusted discount rate.

Table 10.8
Analysis of Bennett Company's Projects A and B Using Certainty Equivalents

	Project A				
Year *(t)*	Cash inflows (1)	Certainty equivalent factors[a] (2)	Certain cash inflows [(1) × (2)] (3)	$PVIF_{6\%,t}$ (4)	Present value [(3) × (4)] (5)
1	$14,000	.90	$12,600	.943	$11,882
2	14,000	.90	12,600	.890	11,214
3	14,000	.80	11,200	.840	9,408
4	14,000	.70	9,800	.792	7,762
5	14,000	.60	8,400	.747	6,275
			Present value of cash inflows		$46,541
			−Initial investment		42,000
			Net present value (NPV)		$ 4,541

	Project B				
Year *(t)*	Cash inflows (6)	Certainty equivalent factors[a] (7)	Certain cash inflows [(6) × (7)] (8)	$PVIF_{6\%,t}$ (9)	Present value [(8) × (9)] (10)
1	$28,000	1.00	$28,000	.943	$26,404
2	12,000	.90	10,800	.890	9,612
3	10,000	.90	9,000	.840	7,560
4	10,000	.80	8,000	.792	6,336
5	10,000	.70	7,000	.747	5,229
			Present value of cash inflows		$55,141
			−Initial investment		45,000
			Net present value (NPV)		$10,141

NOTE: The basic cash flows for these projects were presented in Table 10.1, and the analysis of the projects using NPV and assuming equal risk was presented in Table 10.3.

[a] These values were estimated by management; they reflect the risk managers perceive in the cash inflows.

asset pricing model developed in Chapter 7, we will review some of its basic constructs before demonstrating the development and use of RADRs.

RADR and CAPM

In Chapter 7, the *capital asset pricing model (CAPM)* was used to link the *relevant* risk and return for all assets traded in *efficient markets*. In the development of the CAPM, the *total risk* of an asset was defined as

$$\text{Total risk} = \text{nondiversifiable risk} + \text{diversifiable risk} \qquad (10.6)$$

For assets traded in an efficient market, the *diversifiable risk,* which results from uncontrollable or random events, can be eliminated through diversification. The relevant risk is therefore the *nondiversifiable risk*—the risk for which owners of these assets are rewarded. Nondiversifiable risk for securities is commonly measured using *beta*, which is an index of the degree of movement of an asset's return with the market return.

Using beta, b_j, to measure the relevant risk of any asset j, the CAPM is

$$k_j = R_F + [b_j \times (k_m - R_F)] \tag{10.7}$$

where

$$k_j = \text{required return on asset } j$$

$$R_F = \text{risk-free rate of return}$$

$$b_j = \text{beta coefficient for asset } j$$

$$k_m = \text{return on the market portfolio of assets}$$

In Chapter 7 we demonstrated that the required return on any asset, j, could be determined by substituting values of R_F, b_j, and k_m into the CAPM—Equation 10.7. Any security expected to earn in excess of its required return would be acceptable, and those expected to earn an inferior return would be rejected.

If we assume for a moment that real corporate assets such as computers, machine tools, and special-purpose machinery are traded in efficient markets, the CAPM could be redefined as noted in Equation 10.8.

$$k_{\text{project } j} = R_F + [b_{\text{project } j} \times (k_m - R_F)] \tag{10.8}$$

The security market line (SML), which is a graphic depiction of the CAPM, is shown for Equation 10.8 in Figure 10.3. As noted, any project having an IRR falling above the SML would be acceptable since its IRR would exceed the required return, k_{project}, while any project j with an IRR below k_{project} would be rejected. In terms of NPV, any project falling above the SML would have a positive NPV and any project falling below the SML a negative NPV.[12]

Figure 10.3
CAPM and SML in Capital Budgeting Decision Making

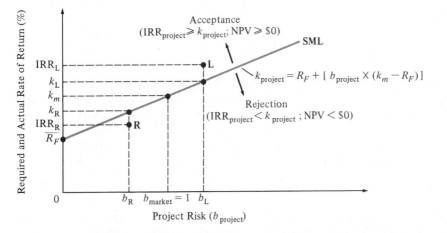

[12] As noted earlier, whenever the IRR is above the cost of capital or required return (IRR > k), the NPV is positive, and whenever the IRR is below the cost of capital or required return (IRR < k), the NPV is negative. Since by definition the IRR is the discount rate that causes NPV to equal zero and the IRR and NPV always agree on accept-reject decisions, the relationship noted in Figure 10.3 logically follows.

Example

Two projects, L and R, are shown in Figure 10.3. Project L has a beta, b_L, and generates an internal rate of return, IRR_L. The required return for a project with risk b_L is k_L. Since project L generates a return greater than that required ($IRR_L > k_L$), project L would be acceptable. Project L would have a positive NPV when its cash inflows are discounted at its required return, k_L. Project R, on the other hand, generates an IRR below that required for its risk, b_R ($IRR_R < k_R$). This project would have a negative NPV when its cash inflows are discounted at its required return, k_R. Project R should be rejected.

Applying RADRs

Because the CAPM cannot be directly applied in order to make real corporate asset decisions, attention is typically devoted to assessing the total risk of a project as measured by its standard deviation or coefficient of variation. Relating these measures (described in Chapter 7) to the required level of return would then result in a risk-adjusted rate of return (RADR), which can be used in Equation 10.5 to find the NPV. To adjust the discount rate, it is necessary to develop a function that expresses the return for each level of project risk required in order to at least maintain the firm's value.

market risk-return function A graph of the discount rates associated with each level of project risk.

Using the coefficient of variation (CV)[13] as a measure of project risk, the firm can develop some type of **market risk-return function**—a graph of the discount rates associated with each level of project risk. An example of such a function is given in Figure 10.4, which relates the risk-adjusted discount rate, RADR, to the project risk as measured by the coefficient of variation, CV. In a fashion similar to CAPM, the relationship is assumed to be linear. The risk-return function in Figure 10.4 indicates that project cash inflows associated with a riskless event $(CV = 0)$ should be discounted at a 6 percent rate. This rate of return therefore represents the risk-free rate, R_F (point a in the figure). For all levels of risk greater than certainty $(CV > 0)$, the associated required rate of return is indicated. Points b, c, and d indicate that rates of return of approximately 9, 11, and 14 percent will be required on projects with coefficients of variation of 0.6, 1.0, and 1.5, respectively.

Figure 10.4 is a *risk-return function*, which means that investors will discount cash inflows with the given levels of risk at the corresponding rates. Therefore, in order not to damage its market value, the firm must use the correct discount rate for evaluating a project. If a firm discounts a risky project's cash inflows at too low a rate and accepts the project, the firm's market price may drop as investors recognize that the firm itself has become more risky.[14] The amount by which the required discount rate exceeds the risk-free rate is called the **risk premium.** It of course increases with increasing project risk. A simple example will clarify the use of the risk-adjusted discount rate, RADR, in evaluating capital budgeting projects.

risk premium The amount by which the required discount rate for a project exceeds the risk-free rate.

---

[13] The coefficient of variation is used here since it provides a relative basis for comparing risk. Although it is a project-specific measure that embodies both diversifiable and nondiversifiable risk, it is assumed to represent a reasonable measure of the relative risk of real-asset projects.

[14] It is also true that if the firm discounts a project's cash inflows at too high a rate, resulting in the rejection of an acceptable project, the firm's market price may drop because investors believe it is being overly conservative and sell their stock, putting downward pressure on the firm's market value.

Figure 10.4
A Market Risk-Return Function

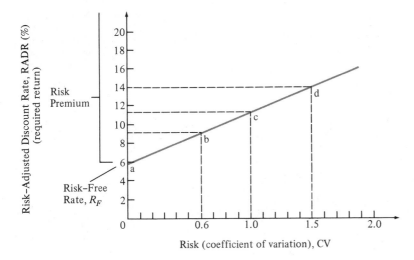

Example

Bennett Company wishes to use the risk-adjusted discount rate approach to determine, according to NPV, whether to implement project A or project B. In addition to the data presented earlier, Bennett's management has estimated the coefficient of variation for project A as 1.5 and for project B as 1.0. According to Figure 10.4, the RADR for project A is approximately 14 percent; for project B, it is approximately 11 percent. Due to the riskier nature of project A, its risk premium is 8 percent (14 percent–6 percent); for project B the risk premium is 5 percent (11 percent–6 percent). The net present value of each project, using its RADR, is calculated in Table 10.9. The results clearly show that project B is preferable, since its risk-adjusted net present value (NPV) of $9,802 is greater than the $6,062 risk-adjusted NPV for project A. This is the same conclusion that resulted using certainty equivalents in the preceding example. As noted earlier (see Table 10.3), when the discount rates are not adjusted for risk, project A would be preferred to project B. The usefulness of risk-adjusted discount rates should now be clear; the real difficulty of this approach lies in estimating the market risk-return function.

Portfolio Effects

As noted in Chapter 7, since investors are not rewarded for taking diversifiable risk, they should hold a diversified portfolio of securities. Since a business firm can be viewed as a portfolio of assets, is it similarly important that the firm maintain a diversified portfolio of assets?

By holding a diversified portfolio, the firm could reduce the variability of its cash flows. By combining two projects with negatively correlated cash inflows, the combined cash inflow variability—and therefore the risk—could be reduced. But are firms re-

Table 10.9
Analysis of Bennett Company's Projects A and B Using Risk-Adjusted Discount Rates

Project A		Project B			
		Year (t)	Cash inflows (1)	$PVIF_{11\%,t}$ (2)	Present value [(1) × (2)] (3)
Annual cash inflow	$14,000	1	$28,000	.901	$25,228
× $PVIFA_{14\%,5yrs}$	3.433	2	12,000	.812	9,744
PV of cash inflows	$48,062	3	10,000	.731	7,310
−Initial investment	42,000	4	10,000	.659	6,590
Net present value (NPV)	$ 6,062	5	10,000	.593	5,930
		PV of cash inflows			$54,802
		−Initial investment			45,000
		Net present value (NPV)			$ 9,802

NOTE: Using Figure 10.4 and the coefficients of variation of 1.5 and 1.0 for projects A and B, respectively, a discount rate of 14 percent is used for project A and 11 percent for project B.

warded for diversifying risk in this fashion? If they are, the value of the firm could be enhanced through diversification into other lines of business. Surprisingly, the value of the stock of firms whose shares are traded publicly in an efficient marketplace is generally *not* affected by diversification. In other words, diversification is not normally rewarded and therefore is generally not necessary.

The lack of reward for diversification results from the fact that investors themselves can diversify by holding securities in a variety of firms; they do not need to have the firm do it for them. And investors can diversify more readily due to the ease of making transactions and at a lower cost due to the greater availability of information and trading mechanisms. Of course, if as a result of acquiring a new line of business the firm's cash flows tend to respond more to changing economic conditions (i.e., greater nondiversifiable risk), greater returns would be expected. If, for the additional risk, the firm earned a return in excess of that required (IRR > k), the value of the firm could be enhanced. Also, other benefits such as increased cash, greater borrowing capacity, guaranteed availability of raw materials, and so forth could result from, and therefore justify, diversification in spite of any immediate cash flow impact.

In spite of the fact that a strict theoretical view supports the use of a technique that relies on the CAPM framework, the presence of market imperfections causes the market for real corporate assets to be inefficient. The relative inefficiency of this market coupled with difficulties associated with measurement of nondiversifiable project risk and the market risk-return function tend to favor the use of *total risk* to evaluate capital budgeting projects. Therefore, the use of total risk as an approximation for the relevant risk tends to have widespread practical appeal.

CE Versus RADR in Practice

Certainty equivalents (CEs) are the theoretically preferred approach for project risk adjustment. They are theoretically superior because they derive from utility theory and constitute a vehicle that accurately converts risky cash flows to certain cash flows. Risk-adjusted discount rates (RADRs), on the other hand, have a major theoretical problem: Because of the basic mathematics of compounding and discounting, they implicitly assume that risk is an increasing function of time. Rather than demonstrate this implicit assumption, suffice it to say that *CEs are theoretically superior to RADRs.*

Because of the complexity of developing CEs, *RADRs are most often used in practice.* Their popularity stems from two major facts: (1) They are consistent with the general disposition of financial decision makers toward rates of return,[15] and (2) they are easily estimated and applied. The first reason is clearly a matter of personal preference, but the second is based on the computational convenience and well-developed procedures involved in the use of RADRs. In practice, risk is often subjectively categorized rather than related to a continuum of RADRs associated with each level of risk, as illustrated by the market risk-return function in Figure 10.4. Firms often establish a number of *risk classes,* with an RADR assigned to each. Each project is then subjectively placed in the appropriate risk class, and the corresponding RADR is used to evaluate it. An example will help to illustrate this approach.

Example

Assume that the management of Bennett Company decided to use a more subjective but practical RADR approach to analyze projects. Each project would be placed in one of four risk classes according to its perceived risk. The classes were ranged from I for the lowest-risk projects to IV for the highest-risk projects. Associated with each class was an RADR appropriate to the level of risk of projects in the class. A brief description of each class, along with the associated RADR, is given in Table 10.10. It shows that lower-risk projects tend to involve routine replacement or renewal activities, whereas higher-risk projects involve expansion, often into new or unfamiliar activities.

The financial manager of Bennett has assigned project A to Class III and project B to Class II. The cash flows for project A would therefore be evaluated using a 14 percent RADR, and project B's would be evaluated using a 10 percent RADR.[16] The net present value of project A at 14 percent was calculated in Table 10.9 to be $6,062, and the NPV for project B at a 10 percent RADR was found to be $10,914 in Table 10.3. Clearly, with RADRs based on the use of risk classes, project B is preferred over project A. As noted earlier, this result is contrary to the findings in Table 10.3, where no attention was given to the differing risk of projects A and B.

---

[15] Recall that while NPV was the theoretically preferred evaluation technique, IRR was more popular in actual business practice due to the general preference of business people toward rates of return rather than pure dollar returns. The preference for RADRs over CEs is therefore consistent with the preference for IRR over NPV.

[16] Note that the 10 percent RADR for project B using the risk classes in Table 10.10 differs from the 11 percent RADR found earlier for project B using the market risk-return function. This difference is attributable to the less precise nature of the use of risk classes.

Table 10.10
Bennett Company's Risk Classes and RADRs

Risk Class	Description	Risk-adjusted discount rate, RADR
I	*Below-average risk:* Projects with low risk typically involve routine replacement without modernization of existing activities.	8%
II	*Average risk:* Projects similar to those currently implemented. Typically involve replacement or renewal of existing activities.	10%
III	*Above-average risk:* Projects with higher than normal, but not excessive, risk. Typically involve expansion of existing or similar activities.	14%
IV	*Highest risk:* Projects with very high risk. Typically involve expansion into new or unfamiliar activities.	20%

FACT OR FABLE?   **5** In practice, risk-adjusted discount rates (RADRs) are the preferred method of capital budgeting risk adjustment in spite of the fact that certainty equivalents (CEs) are theoretically superior. *(Fact)*

Capital Budgeting Refinements

Refinements must often be made in the analysis of capital budgeting projects in order to accommodate special circumstances. These adjustments permit the relaxation of certain simplifying assumptions presented earlier. Two areas where special forms of analysis are frequently needed are (1) comparison of mutually exclusive projects having unequal lives and (2) capital rationing caused by a binding budget constraint.

Comparing Projects with Unequal Lives

The financial manager must often select the best of a group of unequal-lived projects. If the projects are independent, the length of the project lives is not critical. But when unequal-lived projects are mutually exclusive, the impact of differing lives must be considered because the projects do not provide service over comparable time periods.

The Problem

A simple example will demonstrate the basic problem of noncomparability caused by the need to select the best of a group of mutually exclusive projects with differing usable lives.

Example

The AT Company is in the process of evaluating two projects, X and Y. The relevant cash flows for each project are given in the table. The applicable cost of capital for use in evaluating these equally risky projects is 10 percent.

	Project X	Project Y
Initial investment	$70,000	$85,000
Year	**Cash inflows**	
1	$28,000	$35,000
2	33,000	30,000
3	38,000	25,000
4	—	20,000
5	—	15,000
6	—	10,000

The net present value (NPV) of each project at the 10 percent cost of capital is found to be

$$NPV_X = [\$28,000 \times (.909) + \$33,000 \times (.826) + \$38,000 \times (.751)] - \$70,000$$
$$= (\$25,452 + \$27,258 + \$28,538) - \$70,000$$
$$= \$81,248 - \$70,000 = \underline{\underline{\$11,248}}$$

$$NPV_Y = [\$35,000 \times (.909) + \$30,000 \times (.826) + \$25,000 \times (.751)$$
$$+ \$20,000 \times (.683) + \$15,000 \times (.621)$$
$$+ \$10,000 \times (.564)] - \$85,000$$
$$= (\$31,815 + \$24,780 + \$18,775 + \$13,660 + \$9,315 + \$5,640)$$
$$- \$85,000$$
$$= \$103,985 - \$85,000 = \underline{\underline{\$18,985}}$$

The NPV for project X is $11,248, for project Y, $18,985. Ignoring the differences in project lives, it can be seen that both projects are acceptable (NPVs greater than zero) and that the project Y is preferred over project X. In other words, if the projects are independent and, due to limited funds, only one could be accepted, project Y, with the larger NPV, would be preferred. On the other hand, if the projects are mutually exclusive, their differing lives must be considered; project X provides three years of service, and project Y provides six years of service.

The analysis in this example is incomplete if the projects are mutually exclusive (which will be our assumption throughout the remaining discussions). To compare these unequal-lived, mutually exclusive projects correctly, the differing lives must be considered in the analysis; an incorrect decision could result from use of NPV to select the better project. While a number of approaches are available for dealing with unequal lives, here we present only the most efficient technique—the annualized net present value (ANVP) approach.

Annualized Net Present Value (ANPV) Approach

annualized net present value (ANPV) approach
An approach to evaluating unequal-lived projects that converts the net present value of unequal-lived, mutually exclusive projects into an equivalent (in NPV terms) annual amount.

The **annualized net present value (ANPV) approach** converts the net present value of unequal-lived projects into an equivalent (in NPV terms) annual amount that can be used to select the best project.[17] This net-present-value-based approach can be applied to unequal-lived, mutually exclusive projects using the following steps.

1. Calculate the net present value of each project j, NPV_j, over its life, n_j, using the appropriate cost of capital, k.

2. Divide the net present value of each project having a positive NPV by the present-value interest factor for an annuity at the given cost of capital and the project's life to get the annualized net present value for each project j, $ANPV_j$.

$$ANPV_j = \frac{NPV_j}{PVIFA_{k,n_j}} \tag{10.9}$$

3. The project having the highest ANPV would be the best, followed by the project with the next highest ANPV, and so on. Application of these steps can be illustrated using data from the preceding example.

Example

Using the AT Company data presented earlier for projects X and Y, the three-step ANPV approach can be applied as follows:

1. The net present values of projects X and Y discounted at 10 percent—calculated in the preceding example for a single purchase of each asset—are

$$NPV_X = \$11,248$$
$$NPV_Y = \$18,985$$

As noted earlier, based on these NPVs, which ignore the differing lives, project Y is preferred over project X.

2. Applying Equation 10.9 to the NPVs, the annualized net present value for each project can be calculated.

$$ANPV_X = \frac{\$11,248}{PVIFA_{10\%,3yrs}} = \frac{\$11,248}{2.487} = \underline{\underline{\$4,523}}$$

$$ANPV_Y = \frac{\$18,985}{PVIFA_{10\%,6yrs}} = \frac{\$18,985}{4.355} = \underline{\underline{\$4,359}}$$

3. Reviewing the ANPVs calculated in step 2, it can be seen that project X would be preferred over project Y. Given that projects X and Y are mutually exclusive, project X would be the recommended project because it provides the highest annualized net present value.

---

[17] The theory underlying this as well as other approaches for comparing projects with unequal lives assumes that each project can be replaced in the future for the same initial investment and each will provide the same expected future cash inflows. While changing technology and inflation will affect the initial investment and expected cash inflows, the lack of specific attention to them does not detract from the usefulness of this technique.

Capital Rationing

Firms commonly find a greater number of acceptable projects than they have the funds to undertake. The objective of *capital rationing* is to select the group of projects that provides the *highest overall net present value* and does not require more dollars than are budgeted. As a prerequisite to capital rationing, the best of any mutually exclusive projects must be chosen and placed in the group of independent projects. Two basic approaches to project selection under capital rationing are discussed here.

Internal Rate of Return Approach

The **internal rate of return approach** involves graphically plotting IRRs in descending order against the total dollar investment. This graph, which is discussed in some detail in Chapter 11, is called the **investment opportunities schedule (IOS).** By drawing the cost of capital line and then imposing a budget constraint, the group of acceptable projects can be determined. The problem with this technique is that it does not guarantee the maximum dollar return to the firm. It merely provides a satisfactory solution to capital rationing problems.

> **internal rate of return approach** An approach to capital rationing that involves the graphic plotting of project IRRs in descending order against the total dollar investment.
>
> **investment opportunities schedule (IOS)** The graph that plots project IRRs in descending order against total dollar investment.

Example

The Tate Company is confronted with six projects competing for the firm's fixed budget of $250,000. The initial investment and IRR for each project are as follows:

Project	Initial investment	IRR
A	$ 80,000	12%
B	70,000	20
C	100,000	16
D	40,000	8
E	60,000	15
F	110,000	11

The firm has a cost of capital of 10 percent. Figure 10.5 presents the investment opportunities schedule (IOS) resulting from ranking the six projects in descending order based on IRRs. According to the schedule, only projects B, C, and E should be accepted. Together they will absorb $230,000 of the $250,000 budget. Project D is not worthy of consideration since its IRR is less than the firm's 10 percent cost of capital. The drawback of this approach, however, is that there is no guarantee that the acceptance of projects B, C, and E will maximize *total dollar returns* and therefore owners' wealth.

Net Present Value Approach

The **net present value approach** is based on the use of present values to determine the group of projects that will maximize owners' wealth. It is implemented by ranking projects on the basis of IRRs and then evaluating the present value of the benefits from each potential project to *determine the combination of projects with the highest overall present value*. This is the same as maximizing net present value, since whether the entire budget is used or not, it is viewed as the total initial investment. The portion of the firm's budget

> **net present value approach** An approach to capital rationing that involves the use of present values to determine the group of projects that will maximize owners' wealth.

Figure 10.5
Investment Opportunities Schedule (IOS) for Tate Company Projects

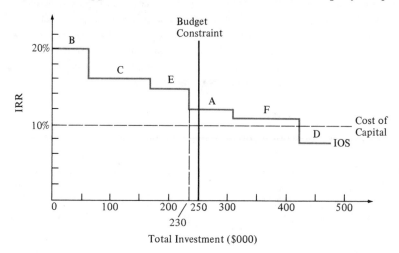

that is not used does not increase the firm's value. At best, the unused money can be invested in marketable securities or returned to the owners in the form of cash dividends. In either case the wealth of the owners is not likely to be enhanced.

Example

The group of projects described in the preceding example is ranked in Table 10.11 on the basis of IRRs. The present value of the cash inflows associated with the projects is also included in the table. Projects B, C, and E, which together require $230,000, yield a present value of $336,000. However, if projects B, C, and A were implemented, the total budget of $250,000 would be used and the present value of the cash inflows would be $357,000. This is greater than the return expected from selecting the projects on the basis of the highest IRRs. Implementing B, C, and A is preferable, since they maximize the present value for the given budget. *The firm's objective is to use its budget to generate the highest present value of inflows.* Assuming that any unused portion of the budget does not gain or lose money, the total NPV for projects B, C, and E would be $106,000 ($336,000 − $230,000), whereas for projects B, C, and A, the total NPV would be $107,000 ($357,000 − $250,000). Selection of projects B, C, and A will therefore maximize NPV.

Table 10.11
Rankings for Tate Company Projects

Project	Initial investment	IRR	PV of inflows at 10%	
B	$ 70,000	20%	$112,000	
C	100,000	16	145,000	
E	60,000	15	79,000	
A	80,000	12	100,000	
F	110,000	11	126,500	Cutoff point
D	40,000	8	36,000	(IRR < 10%)

---

6 Annualized net present value (ANPV) is the most widely accepted approach for choosing the best project when the firm is operating under capital rationing. *(Fable)*
Annualized net present value (ANPV) is the *most efficient technique for comparing mutually exclusive projects with unequal lives;* it is *not* used in capital rationing.

Summary

● The key formulas/definitions and decision criteria for capital budgeting techniques are summarized in Table 10.12.

● The payback period is an unsophisticated capital budgeting technique that measures the amount of time required for the firm to recover its initial investment from cash inflows. Shorter payback periods are generally preferred.

● Sophisticated capital budgeting techniques use the cost of capital to consider the time factor in the value of money. Two such techniques are the net present value (NPV) and internal rate of return (IRR). Both provide the same accept-reject decisions for a given project but often conflict when ranking projects.

● Net present value profiles are useful in comparing projects, especially when conflicting rankings exist between NPV and IRR. On a purely theoretical basis, NPV is preferred over IRR. In practice, the IRR is more commonly used by major firms.

● Risk in capital budgeting is concerned with either the chance that a project will prove unacceptable or, more formally, the degree of variability of cash flows. Finding the breakeven cash inflow and assessing the probability that it will be realized is one approach used to assess the chance of success.

● Sensitivity analysis and scenario analysis are two approaches for dealing with project risk to capture the variability of cash inflows and NPVs. Simulation is a statistically based approach that can also be applied in order to get a feel for project risk.

● The two major risk-adjustment techniques are certainty equivalents (CEs) and risk-adjusted discount rates (RADRs). The RADR technique is closely linked to the CAPM, but because real corporate assets, unlike securities, are generally not traded in an efficient market, the CAPM cannot be applied directly to capital budgeting. Instead, a market risk-return function can be used to determine the risk-adjusted discount rate.

● Although portfolio effects are relevant when evaluating securities investments, the ability of shareholders to diversify makes project diversification by the firm unnecessary. In spite of this, the use of total project risk as an approximation for the relevant risk tends to have widespread appeal.

● Certainty equivalents are the theoretically superior risk-adjustment technique. Risk-adjusted discount rates are more commonly used in practice because decision makers prefer rates of return and they are easier to calculate.

● The annualized net present value (ANPV) approach is the most efficient method of comparing mutually exclusive projects having unequal usable lives. Common techniques for solving capital rationing problems include the internal rate of return approach and the generally preferred net present value approach.

Table 10.12
Summary of Key Formulas/Definitions and Decision Criteria for Capital Budgeting Techniques

Technique	Formula/Definition	Decision criteria
Payback period[a]	For annuity: $\dfrac{\text{initial investment}}{\text{annual cash inflow}}$ For mixed stream: Calculate cumulative cash inflows on year-to-year basis until the initial investment is recovered.	*Accept* if ≤ maximum acceptable payback period; otherwise *reject*.
Net present value (NPV)[b]	present value of cash inflows − initial investment	*Accept* if ≥ $0; otherwise *reject*.
Internal rate of return (IRR)[b]	The discount rate that equates the present value of cash inflows with the initial investment, thereby causing NPV = $0.	*Accept* if ≥ the cost of capital; otherwise *reject*.

[a] Unsophisticated technique since it does not give explicit consideration to the time value of money.

[b] Sophisticated technique since it gives explicit consideration to the time value of money.

Questions

10-1 What is the *payback period?* How is it calculated? What weaknesses are commonly associated with the use of the payback period to evaluate a proposed investment?

10-2 What is the formula for finding the *net present value (NPV)* of a project with conventional cash flows? What is the acceptance criterion for NPV?

10-3 What is the *internal rate of return (IRR)* on an investment? How is it determined? What is its acceptance criterion?

10-4 Do the net present value (NPV) and internal rate of return (IRR) always agree with respect to accept-reject decisions? With respect to ranking decisions? Explain.

10-5 What is a *net present value profile?* How can it be used to compare projects when conflicting rankings exist? What causes conflicts in the ranking of projects using net present value (NPV) and internal rate of return (IRR)?

10-6 Explain how, on a purely theoretical basis, the assumption concerning the reinvestment of intermediate cash inflows tends to favor the use of net present value (NPV) over internal rate of return (IRR). In practice, which technique is preferred? Why?

10-7 Define *risk* in terms of the cash inflows from a project. How can determination of the *breakeven cash inflow* be used to gauge project risk? Explain.

10-8 Briefly describe, compare, and explain how each of the following can be used to deal with project risk:

a. Sensitivity analysis

b. Scenario analysis

c. Simulation

10-9 Explain the concept of *certainty equivalents (CEs)*. How are they used in the risk-adjustment process?

10-10 Describe the logic as well as the basic procedures involved in using *risk-adjusted discount rates (RADRs)*. How does this approach relate to the *capital asset pricing model (CAPM)?* Explain.

10-11 Explain why a firm whose stock is actively traded in the securities markets need not concern itself with diversification. In spite of this, how is the risk of capital budgeting projects frequently measured? Why?

10-12 Compare and contrast certainty equivalents (CEs) and risk-adjusted discount rates (RADRs) from both a theoretical and a practical point of view. In practice, how are risk classes often used to apply RADRs? Explain.

10-13 Explain why a mere comparison of the NPVs of unequal-lived mutually exclusive projects is inappropriate. Describe the *annualized net present value (ANPV)* approach for comparing unequal-lived mutually exclusive projects.

10-14 What is *capital rationing?* Is it unusual for a firm to ration capital? Compare and contrast the *internal rate of return approach* and *net present value approach* to capital rationing. Which is better? Why?

Self-Test Problems

(Solutions on page 375)

ST-1 Fitch Industries is in the process of choosing the better of two equal-risk, mutually exclusive capital expenditure projects—M and N. The relevant cash flows for each proposal are given below. The firm's cost of capital is 14 percent.

	Project M	Project N
Initial investment (II)	$28,500	$27,000
Year (t)	**Cash inflows (CF_t)**	
1	$10,000	$11,000
2	10,000	10,000
3	10,000	9,000
4	10,000	8,000

a. Calculate each project's payback period.

b. Calculate the net present value (NPV) for each project.

c. Calculate the internal rate of return (IRR) for each project.

d. Summarize the preferences dictated by each measure and indicate which project you would recommend. Explain why.

e. Draw the net present value profiles for each project on the same set of axes and explain the circumstances under which a conflict in rankings might exist.

ST-2 The market risk-return data and certainty equivalents applicable to the CBA Company's mutually exclusive projects A and B are given below.

Market risk-return data	
Coefficient of variation	**Market discount rate**
0.0 (risk-free rate, R_F)	7.0%
0.2	8.0
0.4	9.0
0.6	10.0
0.8	11.0
1.0	12.0
1.2	13.0
1.4	14.0
1.6	15.0
1.8	16.0
2.0	17.0

Certainty equivalents (α_t)		
Year (t)	**Project A**	**Project B**
0	1.00	1.00
1	.95	.90
2	.90	.85
3	.90	.70

The firm is considering two mutually exclusive projects, A and B. Project data is given below.

	Project A	Project B
Initial investment *(II)*	$15,000	$20,000
Project life	3 years	3 years
Annual cash inflow *(CF)*	$ 7,000	$10,000
Coefficient of variation	0.4	1.8

a. Ignoring any differences in risk and assuming the firm's cost of capital is 10 percent, calculate the net present value (NPV) of each project.

b. Use NPV to evaluate the projects using *certainty equivalents* to account for risk.

c. Use NPV to evaluate the projects using *risk-adjusted discount rates* to account for risk.

d. Compare, contrast, and explain your findings in **a, b,** and **c.**

Problems

10-1 **(Payback Period)** Jordan Enterprises is considering a capital expenditure that requires an initial investment of $42,000 and returns after-tax cash inflows of $7,000 per year for 10 years. The firm has a maximum acceptable payback period of eight years.

a. Determine the payback period for this project.

b. Should the company accept the project? Why, or why not?

10-2 **(Payback Comparisons)** Nova Products has a five-year maximum acceptable payback period. The firm is considering the purchase of a new machine and must choose between two alternative ones. The first machine requires an initial investment of $14,000 and generates annual after-tax cash inflows of $3,000 for each of the next seven years. The second machine requires an initial investment of $21,000 and provides an annual cash inflow after taxes of $4,000 for 20 years.

a. Determine the payback period for each machine.

b. Comment on the acceptability of the machines, assuming they are independent projects.

c. Which machine should the firm accept? Why?

d. Do the machines in this problem illustrate any of the criticisms of using payback? Discuss.

10-3 **(NPV)** Calculate the net present value (NPV) for the following 20-year projects. Comment on the acceptability of each. Assume that the firm has an opportunity cost of 14 percent.

a. Initial investment is $10,000; cash inflows are $2,000 per year.

b. Initial investment is $25,000; cash inflows are $3,000 per year.

c. Initial investment is $30,000; cash inflows are $5,000 per year.

10-4 **(NPV for Varying Required Returns)** Dane Cosmetics is evaluating a new fragrance-mixing machine. The asset requires an initial investment of $24,000 and will generate after-tax cash inflows of $5,000 per year for eight years. For each of the required rates of return listed, (1) calculate the net present value, (2) indicate whether to accept or reject the machine, and (3) explain your decision.

a. The cost of capital is 10 percent.

b. The cost of capital is 12 percent.

c. The cost of capital is 14 percent.

10-5 **(Net Present Value—Independent Projects)** Using a 14 percent cost of capital, calculate the net present value for each of the independent projects given in the table at the top of page 363 and indicate whether or not each is acceptable.

	Project A	Project B	Project C	Project D	Project E
Initial investment *(II)*	$26,000	$500,000	$170,000	$950,000	$80,000
Year *(t)*			Cash inflows *(CF$_t$)*		
1	$4,000	$100,000	$20,000	$230,000	$ 0
2	4,000	120,000	19,000	230,000	0
3	4,000	140,000	18,000	230,000	0
4	4,000	160,000	17,000	230,000	20,000
5	4,000	180,000	16,000	230,000	30,000
6	4,000	200,000	15,000	230,000	0
7	4,000		14,000	230,000	50,000
8	4,000		13,000	230,000	60,000
9	4,000		12,000		70,000
10	4,000		11,000		

10-6 **(NPV and Maximum Return)** A firm can purchase a fixed asset for a $13,000 initial investment. If the asset generates an annual after-tax cash inflow of $4,000 for four years:

a. Determine the net present value (NPV) of the asset, assuming that the firm has a 10 percent cost of capital. Is the project acceptable?

b. Determine the maximum required rate of return (closest whole-percentage rate) the firm can have and still accept the asset. Discuss this finding in light of your response in **a.**

10-7 **(NPV—Mutually Exclusive Projects)** Hook Industries is considering the replacement of one of its old drill presses. Three alternative replacement presses are under consideration. The relevant cash flows associated with each are given in the following table. The firm's cost of capital is 15 percent.

	Press A	Press B	Press C
Initial investment *(II)*	$85,000	$60,000	$130,000
Year *(t)*		Cash inflows *(CF$_t$)*	
1	$18,000	$12,000	$50,000
2	18,000	14,000	30,000
3	18,000	16,000	20,000
4	18,000	18,000	20,000
5	18,000	20,000	20,000
6	18,000	25,000	30,000
7	18,000	—	40,000
8	18,000	—	50,000

a. Calculate the net present value (NPV) of each press.

b. Using NPV, evaluate the acceptability of each press.

c. Rank the presses from best to worst using NPV.

10-8 **(Payback and NPV)** Neil Corporation has three projects under consideration. The cash flows for each of them are given in the table at the top of page 364. The firm has a 16 percent cost of capital.

	Project A	Project B	Project C
Initial investment *(II)*	$40,000	$40,000	$40,000
Year *(t)*	**Cash inflows *(CF_t)***		
1	$13,000	$ 7,000	$19,000
2	13,000	10,000	16,000
3	13,000	13,000	13,000
4	13,000	16,000	10,000
5	13,000	19,000	7,000

a. Calculate each project's payback period. Which project is preferred using this method?

b. Calculate each project's net present value (NPV). Which project is preferred using this method?

c. Comment on your findings in **a** and **b** and recommend the best project. Explain your recommendation.

10-9 (**Internal Rate of Return**) For each of the following projects, calculate the internal rate of return (IRR), and indicate for each project the maximum cost of capital the firm could have and find the IRR acceptable.

	Project A	Project B	Project C	Project D
Initial investment *(II)*	$90,000	$490,000	$20,000	$240,000
Year *(t)*	**Cash inflows *(CF_t)***			
1	$20,000	$150,000	$7,500	$120,000
2	25,000	150,000	7,500	100,000
3	30,000	150,000	7,500	80,000
4	35,000	150,000	7,500	60,000
5	40,000	—	7,500	—

10-10 (**IRR—Mutually Exclusive Projects**) Bell Manufacturing is attempting to choose the better of two mutually exclusive projects available for expanding the firm's warehouse capacity. The relevant cash flows for the projects are given. The firm's cost of capital is 15 percent.

	Project X	Project Y
Initial investment *(II)*	$500,000	$325,000
Year *(t)*	**Cash inflows *(CF_t)***	
1	$100,000	$140,000
2	120,000	120,000
3	150,000	95,000
4	190,000	70,000
5	250,000	50,000

a. Calculate the IRR to the nearest whole percent for each of the projects.

b. Assess the acceptability of each project based on the IRRs found in **a.**

c. Which project is preferred, based on the IRRs found in **a?**

10-11 (IRR, Investment Life, and Cash Inflows) Oak Enterprises accepts projects earning more than the firm's 15 percent cost of capital. Oak is currently considering a ten-year project that provides annual cash inflows of $10,000 and requires an initial investment of $61,450. *(Note:* All amounts are after taxes.)

a. Determine the IRR of this project. Is it acceptable?

b. Assuming that the cash inflows continue to be $10,000 per year, how many *additional years* would the flows have to continue to make the project acceptable (i.e., have an IRR of 15 percent)?

c. With the given life, initial investment, and cost of capital, what is the minimum annual cash inflow the firm should accept?

10-12 (NPV and IRR) Benson Designs has prepared the following estimates for a long-term project it is considering. The initial investment will be $18,250, and the project is expected to yield after-tax cash inflows of $4,000 per year for seven years. The firm has a 10 percent cost of capital.

a. Determine the net present value (NPV) of the project.

b. Determine the internal rate of return (IRR) for the project.

c. Would you recommend that the firm accept or reject the project? Explain your answer.

10-13 (Payback, NPV, and IRR) Rieger International is attempting to evaluate the feasibility of investing $95,000 in a piece of equipment having a five-year life. The firm has estimated the *cash inflows* associated with the proposal as follows:

Year *(t)*	Cash inflows *(CF_t)*
1	$20,000
2	25,000
3	30,000
4	35,000
5	40,000

The firm has a 12 percent cost of capital.

a. Calculate the payback period for the proposed investment.

b. Calculate the net present value (NPV) for the proposed investment.

c. Calculate the internal rate of return (IRR), rounded to the nearest whole percent, for the proposed investment.

d. Evaluate the acceptability of the proposed investment using NPV and IRR. What recommendation would you make relative to implementation of the project? Why?

10-14 (NPV, IRR, and NPV Profiles) Thomas Company is considering two mutually exclusive projects. The firm, which has a 12 percent cost of capital, has estimated its cash flows as shown in the table at the top of page 366.

	Project A	Project B
Initial investment (II)	$130,000	$85,000
Year (t)	Cash inflows (CF_t)	
1	$25,000	$40,000
2	35,000	35,000
3	45,000	30,000
4	50,000	10,000
5	55,000	5,000

a. Calculate the NPV of each project and assess its acceptability.

b. Calculate the IRR for each project and assess its acceptability.

c. Draw the NPV profile for each project on the same set of axes.

d. Evaluate and discuss the rankings of the two projects based on your findings in **a, b,** and **c.**

e. Explain your findings in **d** in light of the pattern of cash inflow associated with each project.

10-15 (All Techniques—Mutually Exclusive Investment Decision) Pound Industries is attempting to select the best of three mutually exclusive projects. The initial investment and after-tax cash inflows associated with each project are given in the table.

Cash flow	Project A	Project B	Project C
Initial investment (II)	$60,000	$100,000	$110,000
Cash inflow (CF), years 1–5	$20,000	$ 31,500	$ 32,500

a. Calculate the payback period for each project.

b. Calculate the net present value of each project, assuming that the firm has a cost of capital equal to 13 percent.

c. Calculate the internal rate of return for each project.

d. Draw the net present value profile for each project on the same set of axes and discuss any conflict in ranking that may exist between NPV and IRR.

e. Summarize the preferences and indicate which project you would recommend. Explain why.

10-16 (All Techniques with NPV Profile—Mutually Exclusive Projects) The following two proposals of equal risk have been made for the purchase of new equipment. The firm's cost of capital is 13 percent. The cash flows for each project are given in the table at the top of page 367.

	Project A	Project B
Initial investment *(II)*	$80,000	$50,000
Year *(t)*	Cash inflows *(CF_t)*	
1	$15,000	$15,000
2	20,000	15,000
3	25,000	15,000
4	30,000	15,000
5	35,000	15,000

a. Calculate each project's payback period.

b. Calculate the net present value (NPV) for each project.

c. Calculate the internal rate of return (IRR) for each project.

d. Draw a net present value profile for each project on the same set of axes and discuss any conflict in ranking that may exist between NPV and IRR.

e. Summarize the preferences dictated by each measure and indicate which project you would recommend. Explain why.

10-17 (Integrative—Complete Investment Decision) Wells Printing is considering the purchase of a new printing press. The total installed cost of the press would be $2.2 million. This outlay would be partially offset by the sale of an existing press. The old press has zero book value, cost $1 million ten years earlier, and can be sold currently for $1.2 million before taxes. As a result of the new press, sales in each of the next five years are expected to increase by $1.6 million, but product costs (excluding depreciation) will represent 50 percent of sales. The new press will not affect the firm's net working capital requirements. The press will be depreciated under ACRS using a five-year recovery period (see Table 3.6 on page 66). The firm is subject to a 40 percent tax rate on both ordinary income and capital gains. Wells Printing's cost of capital is 11 percent. *(Note:* Assume both the old and new press will have terminal values of $0 at the end of year 6.)

a. Determine the initial investment required by the new press.

b. Determine the operating cash inflows attributable to the new press. *(Note:* Be sure to consider the depreciation in year 6.)

c. Determine the payback period.

d. Determine the net present value and the internal rate of return related to the proposed new press.

e. Make a recommendation to accept or reject the new press and justify your answer.

10-18 (Integrative—Investment Decision) Norwich Tool is considering the replacement of an existing machine. The machine costs $1.2 million and requires installation costs of $150,000. The existing machine can be sold currently for $185,000 before taxes. It is two years old, cost $800,000 new, and has a $384,000 book value and a remaining useful life of five years. It was being depreciated under ACRS using a five-year recovery period (see Table 3.6 on page 66) and therefore has the final four years of depreciation remaining. If held until the end of five years, the machine's market value would be zero. Over its five-year life, the new machine should reduce operating costs by $350,000 per year. The new machine will be depreciated under ACRS using a five-year recovery period (see Table 3.6 on page 66). The new machine can be sold for $200,000 net of removal costs at the end of five years. An increased investment in net working capital of $25,000 will be needed to support operations if the new machine is acquired. Assume the firm has adequate operating income against which to deduct any loss experienced on the sale of the existing machine. The firm has a 9 percent cost of capital and is subject to a 40 percent tax rate on both ordinary income and capital gains.

a. Develop the relevant cash flows needed to analyze the proposed replacement.

b. Determine the net present value of the proposal.

c. Determine the internal rate of return on the proposal.

d. Make a recommendation to accept or reject the replacement proposal and justify your answer.

e. What is the highest cost of capital the firm could have and still accept the proposal? Explain.

10-19 (**Breakeven Cash Inflows and Risk**) Pueblo Enterprises is considering investment in either of two mutually exclusive projects, X and Y. Project X requires an initial investment of $30,000; project Y, $40,000. Each project's cash inflows are five-year annuities; project X's inflows are $10,000 per year; project Y's, $15,000. The firm has unlimited funds and, in the absence of risk differences, accepts the project with the highest NPV. The cost of capital is 15 percent.

a. Find the NPV for each project. Are the projects acceptable?

b. Find the *breakeven cash inflow* for each project.

c. The firm has estimated the probabilities of achieving various ranges of cash inflow for the two projects, as noted in the following table. What is the probability that each project will achieve the breakeven cash inflow found in **b?**

Range of cash inflows	Probability of achieving cash inflow in given range	
	Project X	Project Y
$0 to $5,000	0%	5%
$5,000 to $7,500	10	10
$7,500 to $10,000	60	15
$10,000 to $12,500	25	25
$12,500 to $15,000	5	20
$15,000 to $20,000	0	15
Above $20,000	0	10

d. Which project is more risky? Which project has the potentially higher NPV? Discuss the risk-return trade-offs of the two projects.

e. If the firm wished to minimize losses (i.e., NPV < $0), which project would you recommend? Which would you recommend if the goal, instead, was achieving the highest NPV?

10-20 (Basic Sensitivity Analysis) Murdock Paints is in the process of evaluating two mutually exclusive additions to their processing capacity. The firm's financial analysts have developed pessimistic, most likely, and optimistic estimates of the annual cash inflows associated with each project. These estimates are given in the following table.

	Project A	Project B
Initial investment *(II)*	$8,000	$8,000
Outcome	Annual cash inflows *(CF)*	
Pessimistic	$ 200	$ 900
Most likely	1,000	1,000
Optimistic	1,800	1,100

a. Determine the range of annual cash inflows for each of the two projects.

b. Assume that the firm's cost of capital is 10 percent and that both projects have 20-year lives. Construct a table similar to that above for the NPVs for each project. Include the *range* of NPVs for each project.

c. Do **a** and **b** provide consistent views of the two projects? Explain.

d. Which project would you recommend? Why?

10-21 (Sensitivity Analysis) James Secretarial Services is considering the purchase of one of two new word processors, P and Q. Both are expected to provide benefits over a ten-year period, and each has a required investment of $3,000. The firm uses a 10 percent cost of capital. Management has constructed the following table of estimates of probabilities and annual cash inflows for pessimistic, most likely, and optimistic results:

	Processor P	Processor Q
Initial investment *(II)*	$3,000	$3,000
Outcome	Annual cash inflows *(CF)*	
Pessimistic	$ 500	$ 400
Most likely	750	750
Optimistic	1,000	1,200

a. Determine the range of annual cash inflows for each of the two processors.

b. Construct a table similar to that above for NPVs associated with each outcome for both processors.

c. Find the range of NPVs and subjectively compare the risk of each processor.

10-22 (Simulation) Ogden Corporation has compiled the following information on a capital expenditure proposal:
(1) The projected cash *inflows* are normally distributed with a mean of $36,000 and a standard deviation of $9,000.
(2) The projected cash *outflows* are normally distributed with a mean of $30,000 and a standard deviation of $6,000.
(3) The firm has an 11 percent cost of capital.

(4) The probability distributions of cash inflows and cash outflows are not expected to change over the project's 10-year life.

a. Describe how the preceding data could be used to develop a simulation model for finding the net present value of the project.

b. Discuss the advantages of using a simulation to evaluate the proposed project.

10-23 (**Certainty Equivalents—Accept-Reject Decision**) Allison Industries has constructed a table, shown below, that gives expected cash inflows and certainty equivalents for these cash inflows. These measures are for a new machine that lasts five years and requires an initial investment of $95,000. The firm has a 15 percent cost of capital, and the risk-free rate is 10 percent.

Year (t)	Cash inflows (CF_t)	Certainty equivalent (α_t)
1	$35,000	1.0
2	35,000	.8
3	35,000	.6
4	35,000	.6
5	35,000	.2

a. What is the net present value (unadjusted for risk)?

b. What is the certainty equivalent net present value?

c. Should the firm accept the project? Explain.

d. Management has some doubts about the estimate of the certainty equivalent for year 5. There is some evidence that it may not be any lower than for year 4. What impact might this have on the decision you recommended in **c?** Explain.

10-24 (**Certainty Equivalents—Mutually Exclusive Decision**) Kent Manufacturing is considering investing in either of two mutually exclusive projects, C and D. The firm has a 14 percent cost of capital, and the risk-free rate is currently 9 percent. The initial investment, expected cash inflows, and certainty equivalents associated with each of the projects are presented in the following table.

	Project C		Project D	
Initial investment (II)	$40,000		$56,000	
Year (t)	Cash inflows (CF_t)	Certainty equivalent (α_t)	Cash inflows (CF_t)	Certainty equivalent (α_t)
1	$20,000	.90	$20,000	.95
2	16,000	.80	25,000	.90
3	12,000	.60	15,000	.85
4	10,000	.50	20,000	.80
5	10,000	.40	10,000	.80

a. Find the net present value (unadjusted for risk) for each project. Which is preferred using this measure?

b. Find the certainty equivalent net present value for each project. Which is preferred using this risk-adjustment technique?

c. Compare and discuss your findings in **a** and **b**. Which, if either, of the projects would you recommend that the firm accept? Explain.

10-25 (Risk-Adjusted Discount Rates—Basic) Country Wallpapers is considering investment in one of three mutually exclusive projects, E, F, and G. The firm's cost of capital is 15 percent, and the risk-free rate, R_F, is 10 percent. The firm has gathered the following basic cash flow and risk index data for each project.

	Project (j)		
	E	**F**	**G**
Initial investment (II)	$15,000	$11,000	$19,000
Year (t)	Cash inflows (CF_t)		
1	$ 6,000	$ 6,000	$ 4,000
2	6,000	4,000	6,000
3	6,000	5,000	8,000
4	6,000	2,000	12,000
Risk index (RI_j)	1.80	1.00	0.60

a. Find the net present value (NPV) of each project using the firm's cost of capital. Which project is preferred in this situation?

b. The firm uses the following equation to determine the risk-adjusted discount rate, $RADR_j$, for each project j.

$$RADR_j = R_F + RI_j \times (k - R_F)$$

where

$$R_F = \text{risk-free rate of return}$$
$$RI_j = \text{risk index for project } j$$
$$k = \text{cost of capital}$$

Substitute each project's risk index into this equation to determine its RADR.

c. Use the RADR for each project to determine its risk-adjusted NPV. Which project is preferable in this situation?

d. Compare and discuss your findings in **a** and **c**. Which project would you recommend that the firm accept?

10-26 (Integrative—Certainty Equivalents and Risk-Adjusted Discount Rates) After a careful evaluation of investment alternatives and opportunities, Masters School Supplies has determined the best estimate of the market risk-return function as shown in the table at the top of page 372.

Risk index	Appropriate discount rate
0.0	7.0% (risk-free rate, R_F)
0.2	8.0
0.4	9.0
0.6	10.0
0.8	11.0
1.0	12.0
1.2	13.0
1.4	14.0
1.6	15.0
1.8	16.0
2.0	17.0

The firm is faced with two mutually exclusive projects, A and B. The following are the data the firm has been able to gather about the projects:

	Project A	Project B
Initial investment (II)	$20,000	$30,000
Project life	5 years	5 years
Annual cash inflow (CF)	$ 7,000	$10,000
Risk index	0.2	1.4

	Certainty equivalents (α_t)	
Year (t)	Project A	Project B
0	1.00	1.00
1	0.95	0.90
2	0.90	0.80
3	0.90	0.70
4	0.85	0.70
Greater than 4	0.80	0.60

All the firm's cash inflows have already been adjusted for taxes.

a. Evaluate the projects using *certainty equivalents*.

b. Evaluate the projects using *risk-adjusted discount rates*.

c. Discuss your findings in **a** and **b** and explain why the two approaches are alternative techniques for considering risk in capital budgeting.

10-27 (Risk Classes and RADR) Moses Manufacturing is attempting to select the best of three mutually exclusive projects, X, Y, and Z. Though all the projects have five-year lives, they possess differing degrees of risk. Project X is in Class V, the highest-risk class; project Y is in Class II, the below-average-risk class; and project Z is in Class III, the average-risk class. The basic cash flow data for each project and the risk classes and risk-adjusted discount rates (RADRs) used by the firm are given in the tables at the top of page 373.

	Project X	Project Y	Project Z
Initial investment	$180,000	$235,000	$310,000
Year	Cash inflows		
1	$ 80,000	$ 50,000	$ 90,000
2	70,000	60,000	90,000
3	60,000	70,000	90,000
4	60,000	80,000	90,000
5	60,000	90,000	90,000

Risk Classes and RADRs

Risk Class	Description	Risk-adjusted discount rate, RADR
I	Lowest risk	10%
II	Below-average risk	13
III	Average risk	15
IV	Above-average risk	19
V	Highest risk	22

a. Find the risk-adjusted NPV for each project.

b. Which, if any, project would you recommend the firm undertake?

10-28 (Unequal Lives—ANPV Approach) Evans Industries wishes to select the best of three possible machines, each expected to fulfill the on-going need for additional aluminum extrusion capacity. The three machines—A, B, and C—are equally risky. The firm plans to use a 12 percent cost of capital to evaluate each of them. The initial investment and annual cash inflows over the life of each machine are as follows:

	Machine A	Machine B	Machine C
Initial investment (II)	$92,000	$65,000	$100,500
Year (t)	Cash inflows (CF_t)		
1	$12,000	$10,000	$ 30,000
2	12,000	20,000	30,000
3	12,000	30,000	30,000
4	12,000	40,000	30,000
5	12,000	—	30,000
6	12,000	—	—

a. Calculate the NPV for each machine over its life. Rank the machines in descending order based on NPV.

b. Use the *annualized net present value* approach to calculate the ANPV of each machine. Rank the machines in descending order based on the ANPV.

c. Compare and contrast your findings in **a** and **b**. Which machine would you recommend that the firm acquire? Why?

10-29 (Unequal Lives—ANPV Approach) Portland Products is considering purchase of one of three mutually exclusive projects for increasing production efficiency. The firm plans to use a 14 percent cost of capital to evaluate these equal-risk projects. The initial investment and annual cash inflows over the life of each project are summarized as follows:

	Project X	Project Y	Project Z
Initial investment (II)	$78,000	$52,000	$66,000
Year (t)	Cash inflows (CF_t)		
1	$17,000	$28,000	$15,000
2	25,000	38,000	15,000
3	33,000	—	15,000
4	41,000	—	15,000
5	—	—	15,000
6	—	—	15,000
7	—	—	15,000
8	—	—	15,000

a. Calculate the NPV for each project over its life. Rank the projects in descending order based on NPV.

b. Use the *annualized net present value (ANPV)* approach to evaluate and rank the projects in descending order based on ANPV.

c. Compare and contrast your findings in **a** and **b.** Which project would you recommend the firm purchase? Why?

10-30 (Capital Rationing—IRR and NPV Approaches) Valley Corporation is attempting to select the best of a group of independent projects competing for the firm's fixed capital budget of $4.5 million. The firm recognizes that any unused portion of this budget will earn less than its 15 percent cost of capital, thereby resulting in a present value of inflows that is less than the initial investment. The firm has summarized the key data to be used in selecting the best group of projects in the following table.

Project	Initial investment	IRR	Present value of inflows at 15%
A	$5,000,000	17%	$5,400,000
B	800,000	18	1,100,000
C	2,000,000	19	2,300,000
D	1,500,000	16	1,600,000
E	800,000	22	900,000
F	2,500,000	23	3,000,000
G	1,200,000	20	1,300,000

a. Use the *internal rate of return (IRR) approach* to select the best group of projects.

b. Use the *net present value (NPV) approach* to select the best group of projects.

c. Compare, contrast, and discuss your findings in **a** and **b.**

d. Which projects should the firm implement? Why?

10-31 (Capital Rationing—NPV Approach) A firm with a 13 percent cost of capital must select the optimal group of projects from those in the table, given its capital budget of $1 million.

Project	Initial investment	NPV at 13% cost of capital
A	$300,000	$ 84,000
B	200,000	10,000
C	100,000	25,000
D	900,000	90,000
E	500,000	70,000
F	100,000	50,000
G	800,000	160,000

a. Calculate the *present value of cash inflows* associated with each project.

b. Select the optimal group of projects, keeping in mind that unused funds are costly.

Solutions to Self-Test Problems

ST-1 a. Payback period:

Project M: $\dfrac{\$28,500}{\$10,000} = \underline{\underline{2.85 \text{ years}}}$

Project N:

Year (t)	Cash inflows (CF$_t$)	Cumulative cash inflows
1	$11,000	$11,000
2	10,000	21,000 ←
3	9,000	30,000
4	8,000	38,000

$$2 + \frac{\$27,000 - \$21,000}{\$9,000} \text{ years}$$

$$2 + \frac{\$6,000}{\$9,000} \text{ years} = \underline{\underline{2.67 \text{ years}}}$$

b. Net present value:

Project M: NPV $= (\$10,000 \times PVIFA_{14\%,4yrs}) - \$28,500$
$= (\$10,000 \times 2.914) - \$28,500$
$= \$29,140 - \$28,500 = \underline{\underline{\$640}}$

(The solution to Problem ST-1 continues on the following page.)

Project N:

Year (t)	CF_t (1)	$PVIF_{14\%,t}$ (2)	PV at 14% [(1) × (2)] (3)
1	$11,000	.877	$ 9,647
2	10,000	.769	7,690
3	9,000	.675	6,075
4	8,000	.592	4,736
		Present value inflows	$28,148
		−Initial investment	27,000
		Net present value (NPV)	$ 1,148

c. Internal rate of return:

Project M: $\dfrac{\$28,500}{\$10,000} = 2.850$

$PVIFA_{IRR,4yrs} = 2.850$

From Table A-4:

$PVIFA_{15\%,4yrs} = 2.855$

$PVIFA_{16\%,4yrs} = 2.798$

IRR = <u>15%</u> (2.850 is closest to 2.855)

Project N:

Average annuity $= \dfrac{\$11,000 + \$10,000 + \$9,000 + \$8,000}{4}$

$= \dfrac{\$38,000}{4} = \$9,500$

$PVIFA_{k,4yrs} = \dfrac{\$27,000}{\$9,500} = 2.842$

$k \approx 15\%$

Try 16% since more cash inflows in early years.

Year (t)	CF_t (1)	$PVIF_{16\%,t}$ (2)	PV at 16% [(1) × (2)] (3)	$PVIF_{17\%,t}$ (4)	PV at 17% [(1) × (4)] (5)
1	$11,000	.862	$ 9,482	.855	$ 9,405
2	10,000	.743	7,430	.731	7,310
3	9,000	.641	5,769	.624	5,616
4	8,000	.552	4,416	.534	4,272
		Present value inflows	$27,097		$26,603
		−Initial investment	27,000		27,000
		(NPV)	$ 97		−$ 397

IRR = <u>16%</u> (rounding to nearest whole percent)

d.

	Project	
	M	**N**
Payback period	2.85 years	2.67 years*
NPV	$640	$1,148*
IRR	15%	16%*

*Preferred project.

Project N is recommended since it has the shorter payback period and the higher NPV, which is greater than zero, and the larger IRR, which is greater than the 14 percent cost of capital.

e. Net present value profiles:

Data		
	NPV	
Discount rate	**Project M**	**Project N**
0%	$11,500[a]	$11,000[b]
14	640	1,148
15	0	—
16	—	0

[a] ($10,000 + $10,000 + $10,000 + $10,000) − $28,500
   $40,000 − $28,500 = $11,500

[b] ($11,000 + $10,000 + $9,000 + $8,000) − $27,000
   $38,000 − $27,000 = $11,000

From the NPV profile below it can be seen that in the event the firm has a cost of capital below approximately 6 percent (exact value is 5.75 percent), conflicting rankings of the projects would exist using the NPV and IRR decision techniques. Since the firm's cost of capital is 14 percent, it can be seen in part **d** that no conflict exists.

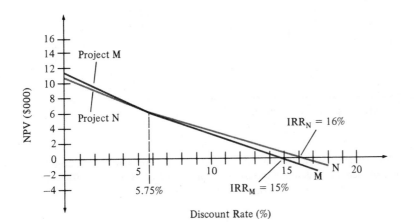

ST-2 a. $NPV_A = (\$7,000 \times PVIFA_{10\%,3yrs}) - \$15,000$
$= (\$7,000 \times 2.487) - \$15,000$
$= \$17,409 - \$15,000 = \underline{\underline{\$2,409}}$

$NPV_B = (\$10,000 \times PVIFA_{10\%,3yrs}) - \$20,000$
$= (\$10,000 \times 2.487) - \$20,000$
$= \$24,870 - \$20,000 = \underline{\underline{\$4,870*}}$

*Preferred project since higher NPV.

b. Project A:

Year (t)	CF_t (1)	Certainty equivalents (α_t) (2)	Certain CF_t [(1) × (2)] (3)	$PVIF_{7\%,t}$ (4)	PV at 7% [(3) × (4)] (5)
1	$7,000	.95	$6,650	.935	$ 6,218
2	7,000	.90	6,300	.873	5,500
3	7,000	.90	6,300	.816	5,141
			Present value inflows		$16,859
			−Initial investment		15,000
			(NPV)		$ 1,859*

Project B:

Year (t)	CF_t (1)	Certainty equivalents (α_t) (2)	Certain CF_t [(1) × (2)] (3)	$PVIF_{7\%,t}$ (4)	PV at 7% [(3) × (4)] (5)
1	$10,000	.90	$9,000	.935	$ 8,415
2	10,000	.85	8,500	.873	7,421
3	10,000	.70	7,000	.816	5,712
			Present value inflows		$21,548
			−Initial investment		20,000
			(NPV)		$ 1,548

*Preferred project since higher NPV.

c. From the market risk-return data, the risk-adjusted discount rate for project A which has a coefficient of variation of 0.4 is *9 percent;* for project B with a coefficient of variation of 1.8 the risk-adjusted discount rate is *16 percent.*

$$NPV_A = (\$7,000 \times PVIFA_{9\%, 3yrs}) - \$15,000$$
$$= (\$7,000 \times 2.531) - \$15,000$$
$$= \$17,717 - \$15,000 = \underline{\underline{\$2,717^*}}$$

$$NPV_B = (\$10,000 \times PVIFA_{16\%, 3yrs}) - \$20,000$$
$$= (\$10,000 \times 2.246) - \$20,000$$
$$= \$22,460 - \$20,000 = \underline{\underline{\$2,460}}$$

*Preferred project since higher NPV.

d. When the differences in risk were ignored in **a,** project B is preferred over project A, but when the higher risk of project B is incorporated in the analysis using either certainty equivalents **(b)** or risk-adjusted discount rates **(c),** *project A is preferred over project B.* Clearly, project A should be implemented.

Lasting Impressions Company

Lasting Impressions (LI) Company is a medium-sized commercial printer of promotional advertising brochures, booklets, and other direct mail pieces. Their major clients are New York- and Chicago-based ad agencies. The typical job is characterized by production runs of over 50,000 units and high quality. LI has not been able to compete effectively with larger printers due to its existing older, inefficient presses. LI is currently having problems cost effectively meeting run length requirements as well as meeting quality standards.

The general manager has proposed the purchase of one of two large six-color presses designed for long, high-quality runs. The purchase of a new press would enable LI to reduce its cost of labor and therefore the price to the client, putting the firm in a more competitive position.

The key financial characteristics of the existing press and the two proposed presses are summarized below.

Old press: Originally purchased three years ago at an installed cost of $400,000, it is being depreciated under ACRS using a five-year recovery period. The old press has a remaining economic life of five years. It can be sold today to net $420,000 before taxes; if it is retained, it can be sold to net $150,000 before taxes at the end of five years.

Press A: This highly automated press can be purchased for $830,000 and will require $40,000 in installation costs. It will be depreciated under ACRS using a five-year recovery period. At the end of the five years, the machine could be sold to net $400,000 before taxes. If this machine is acquired, it is anticipated that the following current account changes would result.

Cash	+$ 25,400
Accounts receivable	+ 120,000
Inventories	− 20,000
Accounts payable	+ 35,000

Press B: This press is not as sophisticated as press A. It costs $640,000 and requires $20,000 in installation costs. It will be depreciated under ACRS using a five-year recovery period. At the end of five years, it can be sold to net $330,000 before taxes. Acquisition of this press will have no effect on the firm's net working capital investment.

The firm estimates that its earnings before depreciation and taxes with the old press and with press A or press B for each of the five years would be as shown in Table 1 at the top of page 381. The firm is subject to a 40 percent tax rate on both ordinary income and capital gains. The firm's cost of capital, *k,* applicable to the proposed replacement is 14 percent.

Table 1
Earnings Before Depreciation and Taxes for
Lasting Impressions Company's Presses

Year	Old press	Press A	Press B
1	$120,000	$250,000	$210,000
2	120,000	270,000	210,000
3	120,000	300,000	210,000
4	120,000	330,000	210,000
5	120,000	370,000	210,000

Required

1. For each of the two proposed replacement presses, determine:
   a Initial investment.
   b Operating cash inflows (*Note:* Be sure to consider the depreciation in year 6).
   c Terminal cash flow (*Note:* This is at the end of year 5).

2. Using the data developed in **1,** find and diagram the relevant cash flow stream associated with each of the two proposed replacement presses assuming each is terminated at the end of five years.

3. Using the data developed in **2,** apply each of the following decision techniques:
   a Payback period.
   b Net present value (NPV).
   c Internal rate of return (IRR).

4. Draw net present value profiles for the two replacement presses on the same set of axes and discuss conflicting rankings of the two presses, if any, resulting from use of NPV and IRR decision techniques.

5. Recommend which, if either, of the presses the firm should acquire if the firm has (a) unlimited funds and (b) capital rationing.

6. What is the impact on your recommendation of the fact that the operating cash inflows associated with press A are characterized as very risky in contrast to the low-risk operating cash inflows of press B?

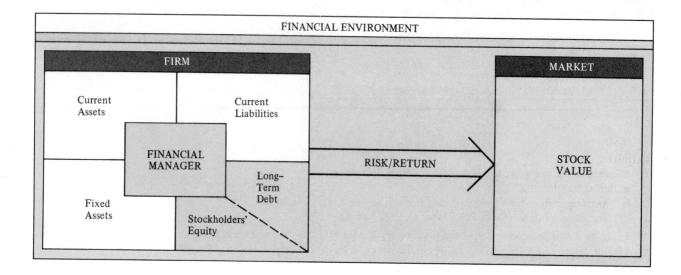

PART FOUR

Cost of Capital, Leverage, and Capital Structure

CHAPTER 11

The Cost of Capital

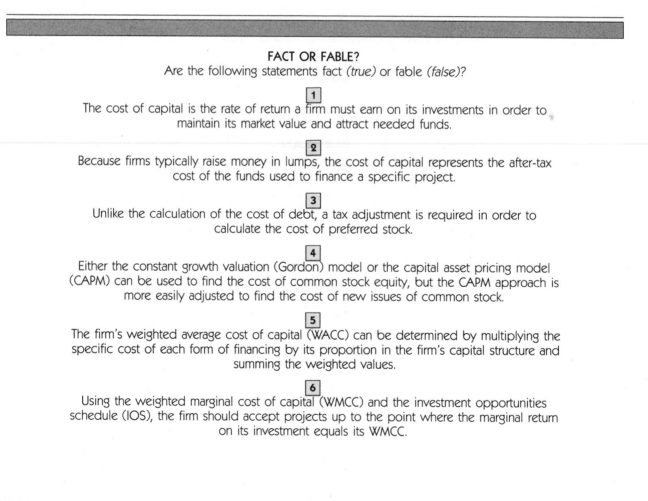

FACT OR FABLE?
Are the following statements fact *(true)* or fable *(false)?*

1
The cost of capital is the rate of return a firm must earn on its investments in order to maintain its market value and attract needed funds.

2
Because firms typically raise money in lumps, the cost of capital represents the after-tax cost of the funds used to finance a specific project.

3
Unlike the calculation of the cost of debt, a tax adjustment is required in order to calculate the cost of preferred stock.

4
Either the constant growth valuation (Gordon) model or the capital asset pricing model (CAPM) can be used to find the cost of common stock equity, but the CAPM approach is more easily adjusted to find the cost of new issues of common stock.

5
The firm's weighted average cost of capital (WACC) can be determined by multiplying the specific cost of each form of financing by its proportion in the firm's capital structure and summing the weighted values.

6
Using the weighted marginal cost of capital (WMCC) and the investment opportunities schedule (IOS), the firm should accept projects up to the point where the marginal return on its investment equals its WMCC.

ewspaper stories about bond ratings are not generally considered to be "big news." Despite this lack of attention, bond ratings can have a huge impact on a company's overall financial performance.

Moody's Investors Service Inc. is a subscription advisory service that deals with a wide variety of financial matters, like rating the debt of large companies. Their determinations are made on a number of financial criteria, and the highest rating they assign for bonds and other debts is Aaa. In mid-1987, Moody's considered raising the credit rating on $6.8 million of debt held by Atlantic Richfield Co. (Arco), a large oil company. Under consideration were the various single-A and double-A debts issued or guaranteed by Arco.

The reasons Moody's was reviewing the ratings were numerous. First, oil prices had improved and stabilized in comparison with past fluctuations, allowing Arco to improve its profitability. In addition, debt was reduced by ridding the company of unprofitable assets. Capital expenditures were also cut. Despite this, Arco's operating performance and capital structure had been somewhat unstable in 1985 and 1986. According to a July 7, 1987, article in *The Wall Street Journal*, this instability was due to "a big common stock buyback program, last year's oil price collapse, and a series of large asset charges." However, because Arco had set aside sufficient money to pay off some of its issues, Moody's favorable review was made possible.

If Arco's rating does go up, the result will be a decrease in the cost of debt. This change will allow Arco to issue bonds at a lower interest rate in the future. Ultimately, this decrease in the cost of debt will result in a decrease in the cost of capital.

Like Arco, most firms attempt to obtain financing on favorable terms that result in a low overall cost of funds. Here we discuss the costs of various forms of long-term financing and their relationship to the firm's overall cost of capital, the level of which, as will be shown in Chapter 12, can significantly impact stock value.

An Overview of the Cost of Capital

The cost of capital is an extremely important financial concept. It acts as a major link between the firm's long-term investment decisions (discussed in Part Three) and the wealth of the owners as determined by investors in the marketplace. It is in effect the "magic number" used to decide whether a proposed corporate investment will increase or decrease the firm's stock price. Clearly, only those investments expected to increase stock price [NPV (at cost of capital) $\geq$ $0, or IRR $\geq$ cost of capital] would be recommended. Due to its key role in financial decision making, the importance of the cost of capital cannot be overemphasized.

The **cost of capital** can be defined as the rate of return a firm must earn on its project investments in order to maintain the market value of its stock. It can also be thought of as

cost of capital The rate of return a firm must earn on its investments in order to maintain its market value and attract needed funds.

385

the rate of return required by the market suppliers of capital in order to attract their funds to the firm. Holding risk constant, the implementation of projects with a rate of return below the cost of capital will decrease the value of the firm, and vice versa.

FACT OR FABLE?   1 **The cost of capital is the rate of return a firm must earn on its investments in order to maintain its market value and attract needed funds.** *(Fact)*

Basic Assumptions

The cost of capital is a dynamic concept affected by a variety of economic and firm factors. In order to isolate the basic structure of the cost of capital, key assumptions relative to risk and taxes need to be clarified:

business risk The risk to the firm of being unable to cover operating costs.

financial risk The risk to the firm of being unable to cover required financial obligations.

1. **Business risk**—the risk to the firm of being unable to cover operating costs—*is assumed unchanged*. This assumption means that the acceptance of a given project by the firm leaves its ability to meet operating costs unchanged.

2. **Financial risk**—the risk to the firm of being unable to cover required financial obligations (interest, lease payments, preferred stock dividends)—*is assumed unchanged*. This assumption means that the projects are financed in such a way that the firm's ability to meet required financing costs is unchanged.

3. **After-tax costs** are considered relevant. In other words, *the cost of capital is measured on an after-tax basis*. Note that this assumption is consistent with the framework used to make capital budgeting decisions.

Risk and Financing Costs

Regardless of the type of financing employed, the following equation can be used to explain the general relationship between risk and financing costs.

$$k_l = r_l + bp + fp \tag{11.1}$$

where

$$k_l = \text{the specific (or nominal) cost of the various types of long-term financing, } l$$

$$r_l = \text{the risk-free cost of the given type of financing, } l$$

$$bp = \text{the business risk premium}$$

$$fp = \text{the financial risk premium}$$

Equation 11.1 indicates that the cost of each type of capital depends on the risk-free cost of that type of funds, the business risk of the firm, and the financial risk of the firm.[1] We can evaluate the equation in either of two ways:

1. *Time-series comparisons* are made by comparing the firm's cost of each type of

---

[1] Although the relationship between r_l, bp, and fp is presented as linear in Equation 11.1, this is only for simplicity; the actual relationship is likely to be much more complex mathematically. The only definite conclusion that can be drawn is that the cost of a specific type of financing for a firm is somehow functionally related to the risk-free cost of that type of financing adjusted for the firm's business and financial risks [i.e., that $k_l = f(r_l, bp, fp)$].

financing *over time*. Here the differentiating factor is the risk-free cost of the given type of financing.

2. *Comparisons between firms* are made by comparing the cost of each type of capital to a given firm with its cost *to another firm*. In this case the risk-free cost of the given type of funds would remain constant[2] while the cost differences would be attributable to the differing business and financial risk of each firm.

An example may help to clarify these two comparisons.

Example
The Hobson Company's cost of long-term debt two years ago was 8 percent. This 8 percent was found to represent a 4 percent risk-free cost of long-term debt, a 2 percent business risk premium, and a 2 percent financial risk premium. Currently, the risk-free cost of long-term debt is 6 percent. How much would you expect the company's cost of long-term debt to be today, assuming that its business and financial risk have remained unchanged? The previous business risk premium of 2 percent and financial risk premium of 2 percent will still prevail, since neither has changed. Adding the 4 percent total risk premium (the 2 percent business risk premium plus the 2 percent financial risk premium) to the 6 percent risk-free cost of long-term debt results in a cost of long-term debt to Hobson Company of 10 percent. In this *time-series comparison,* where business and financial risk are assumed to be constant, the cost of the long-term funds changes only in response to changes in the risk-free cost of the given type of funds.

Another company, Raj Company, which has a 2 percent business risk premium and a 4 percent financial risk premium, can be used to demonstrate *comparisons between firms*. Although Raj and Hobson are in the same type of business (and thus have the same business risk premium of 2 percent), the cost of long-term debt to Raj Company is 12 percent (the 6 percent risk-free cost plus a 2 percent business risk premium plus a 4 percent financial risk premium). This is greater than the 10 percent cost of long-term debt for Hobson. The difference is attributable to the greater financial risk associated with Raj.

The Basic Concept

The cost of capital is measured at a given point in time. It reflects the cost of funds over the long run, based on the best information available. This view is consistent with the use of the cost of capital to make long-term financial investment decisions. Although firms typically raise money in lumps, the cost of capital should reflect the interrelatedness of financing activities. For example, if a firm raises funds with debt (borrowing) today, it is likely that some form of equity, such as common stock, will have to be used next time. Most firms maintain a deliberate, optimal mix of debt and equity financing. This mix is commonly called a **target capital structure**—a topic that will be discussed in greater

target capital structure
The desired optimal mix of debt and equity financing that most firms attempt to achieve and maintain.

[2] The risk-free cost of each type of financing, r_l, may differ considerably. In other words, at a given point in time the risk-free cost of long-term debt may be 6 percent while the risk-free cost of common stock may be 9 percent. The risk-free cost is expected to be different for each type of financing, l. The risk-free cost of different *maturities* of the same type of debt may differ, since, as discussed in Chapter 2, long-term issues are generally viewed as more risky than short-term issues.

detail in Chapter 12. It is sufficient here to say that although firms raise money in lumps, they tend toward some desired *mix of financing* in order to maximize owner wealth.

To capture the interrelatedness of financing assuming the presence of a target capital structure, we need to look at the *overall cost of capital* rather than the cost of the specific source of funds used to finance a given expenditure. The importance of such a view can be illustrated by a simple example.

Example

A firm is *currently* faced with an opportunity. Assume the following:

> Best project available
> Cost = $100,000
> Life = 20 years
> IRR = 7 percent
> Cost of least-cost financing source available
> Debt = 6 percent

Since it can earn 7 percent on the investment of funds costing only 6 percent, the firm undertakes the opportunity. Imagine that *one week later* a new opportunity is available:

> Best project available
> Cost = $100,000
> Life = 20 years
> IRR = 12 percent
> Cost of least-cost financing source available
> Equity = 14 percent

In this instance the firm rejects the opportunity, since the 14 percent financing cost is greater than the 12 percent return expected.

The firm's actions were not in the best interests of its owners. It accepted a project yielding a 7 percent return and rejected one with a 12 percent return. Clearly, there is a better way. Due to the interrelatedness of financing decisions, the firm must use a combined cost, which over the long run would provide for better decisions. By weighting the cost of each source of financing by its target proportion in the firm's capital structure, a *weighted average cost* that reflects the interrelationship of financing decisions can be obtained. Assuming that a 50–50 mix of debt and equity is desired, the weighted average cost above would be 10 percent [(.50 × 6% debt) + (.50 × 14% equity)]. Using this cost, the first opportunity would have been rejected (7% IRR < 10% weighted average cost), and the second one would have been accepted (12% IRR > 10% weighted average cost). Such an outcome would clearly be more desirable.

FACT OR FABLE? **2** Because firms typically raise money in lumps, the cost of capital represents the after-tax cost of the funds used to finance a specific project. *(Fable)*

Because firms typically raise money in lumps, the cost of capital is a *weighted average* of funds' costs that reflects the interrelatedness of financing activities.

The Cost of Specific Sources of Capital

The ultimate objective of this chapter is to analyze specific sources to show the basic inputs for determining the weighted average cost of capital. Our concern is only with the long-term sources of funds available to a business firm, since these sources supply the permanent financing. Long-term financing supports the firm's fixed-asset investments,[3] which, we assume, are selected using appropriate techniques.

There are four basic sources of long-term funds for the business firm: long-term debt, preferred stock, common stock, and retained earnings. The right-hand side of a balance sheet can be used to illustrate these sources.

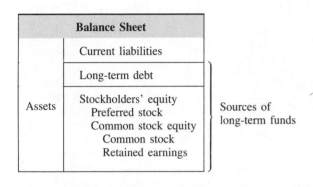

Although not all firms will use each of these methods of financing, each firm is expected to have funds from some of these sources in its capital structure. The *specific cost* of each source of financing is the *after-tax* cost of obtaining the financing *today,* not the historically based cost reflected by the existing financing on the firm's books. Techniques for determining the specific costs of each source of long-term funds are presented on the following pages. Although these techniques tend to develop precisely calculated values of specific as well as weighted average costs, the resulting values are at best *rough approximations* due to the numerous assumptions and forecasts that underlie them.

The Cost of Long-Term Debt (Bonds)

The **cost of long-term debt (bonds),** k_i, is the after-tax cost today of raising long-term funds through borrowing. For convenience we typically assume that the funds are raised through issuance and sale of bonds. In addition, consistent with Chapter 8, we assume that the bonds pay *annual*—rather than *semiannual*—interest.

cost of long-term debt (bonds), k_i The after-tax cost today of raising long-term funds through borrowing.

Net Proceeds

Most corporate long-term debts are incurred through the sale of bonds. The **net proceeds** from the sale of a bond are the funds actually received from the sale. **Flotation costs**—the total costs of issuing and selling a security—reduce the net proceeds from the sale of a bond, whether sold at a premium, at a discount, or at its par (face) value.

net proceeds Funds actually received from the sale of a security.

flotation costs The total costs of issuing and selling a security.

[3] The role of both long-term and short-term financing in supporting both fixed and current asset investments is addressed in Chapter 13. Suffice it to say that long-term funds are at minimum used to finance fixed assets.

PROFILE

CHARLES EXLEY, JR.: Curing a Company's Ills

Do you want to be chief executive officer? Many business experts agree that one sure way to the top of any company is to find and implement a cure for the company's most critical problem; be the one responsible for bringing an ailing business back to health and prosperity.

Charles Exley, Jr., is one of two such saviors-turned-CEO who rescued the NCR Corporation of Dayton, Ohio, from the brink of obsolescence in the 1970's. NCR, a 102-year-old company built on the production and sale of cash registers, had fallen desperately behind the times. Its old-fashioned, electro-mechanical cash boxes could not compete with new lines of computerized equipment. NCR competitors, from Singer to the Japanese, were rapidly stealing both prospective and long-standing customers.

NCR headquarters called in William Anderson, chairman of NCR Japan, the company's largest and most successful international division. His solution was the obvious: bring NCR into the computer age. Within three years, he completely replaced the old, outdated product with the latest in microprocessor-based machines. NCR was safe but not particularly profitable. In 1976, Anderson recruited Charles Exley to succeed him as CEO.

Exley joined NCR with an MBA from Columbia and twenty-two years experience as a financial executive with Burroughs Corporation, an NCR competitor. His remedy to restore the company to health involved more than financial measures. First, reorganize the

outmoded marketing structure; second, decentralize research and development operations; and third, control costs.

Exley divided the sales staff into two groups: "solution" and "tool" salespeople. Solution salespeople continued to supply small businesses with the right products to "solve" their problems, while tool salespeople sold stripped-down computers to larger companies that used them as a "tool" to run programs they created themselves. For example, Citibank purchased 300 NCR Towers. The Tower, a series of microcomputers that tie into a company's mainframe and can run software written for machines made by others, allowed Citibank to develop its own program for the automation of branch tellers.

Exley than extended decision-

making to the local level. He gave plant managers authority to spend millions of dollars on new product development. The NCR Tower, for example, was conceived and created by the Columbia, South Carolina, plant. Says Exley, "We decentralized decision-making by evolving as many genuine profit centers as we could."[1]

With these two major modifications, Exley added tight cost controls. He avoided borrowing money, believing a company should finance its own growth. States Exley, "We start with a growth objective, we establish what we consider to be a suitable balance sheet ratio, and from that we know how much money we have to make."[2] The strategy increased NCR's cash flow 51.8 percent in 1985 and has since enabled it to finance its research and development.

Today, NCR is one of the industry's most powerful, innovative leaders. To what does Exley attribute his success? He admits his rise to CEO with a background in finance is unusual in a high-tech industry. Most executives are likely to have technical backgrounds or marketing experience. "However," says Exley, "there is now broader recognition of the financial officer's function in most businesses. Responsibility for information technology, as well as understanding the regulatory climate and the complex options for financing, have increased the CFO's role. The rate of change today is so remarkable that technical education quickly becomes obsolete."[3]

---

[1] Barbara Ross, "Charles E. Exley, Jr.," *FE: the magazine for financial executives,* April 1986, pp. 22–25.

[2] Fred V. Guteri, "The Transformation of NCR Corp.," *Dun's Business Month,* August 1986, pp. 32–35.

[3] Barbara Ross, p. 25.

Example

Duchess Corporation is contemplating selling $10 million worth of 20-year, 9 percent coupon (stated *annual* interest rate) bonds, each with a par value of $1,000. Since similar-risk bonds earn returns greater than 9 percent, the firm must sell the bonds for $980 to compensate for the lower coupon interest rate. The flotation costs paid to the investment banker are 2 percent of the par value of the bond (2% × $1,000), or $20.[4] The net proceeds to the firm from the sale of each bond are therefore $960 ($980 − $20).

Before-Tax Cost of Debt

The before-tax cost of debt, k_d, for a bond can be obtained in any of three ways—quotation, calculation, or approximation.

Using Cost Quotations

When the net proceeds from sale of a bond equal its par value, the before-tax cost would just equal the coupon interest rate. For example, a 10 percent coupon interest rate bond that nets proceeds equal to the bond's $1,000 par value would have a before-tax cost, k_d, of 10 percent. A second quotation sometimes used would be the *yield to maturity (YTM)* (see Chapter 8) on a similar-risk bond.[5] For example, if a similar-risk bond has a YTM of 9.7 percent, this value can be used as the before-tax cost of debt, k_d.

Calculating the Cost

This approach finds the before-tax cost of debt by calculating the internal rate of return on the bond cash flows. From the issuer's point of view, this value can be referred to as the *cost to maturity* of the cash flows associated with the debt. The cost to maturity is calculated using the techniques presented in Chapter 10. It represents the annual before-tax percentage cost of the debt to the firm.

Example

In the preceding example the net proceeds of a $1,000, 9 percent coupon interest rate, 20-year bond were found to be $960. Although the cash flows from the bond issue do not have a conventional pattern, the calculation of the annual cost is quite simple. Actually, the cash flow pattern is exactly the opposite of a conventional pattern in that it consists of an initial inflow (the net proceeds) followed by a series of annual outlays (the interest payments). In the final year, when the debt is retired, an outlay representing the repayment of the principal also occurs. The cash flows associated with the

---

[4] As noted in Chapter 2, investment bankers are often hired by firms to find buyers for new security issues, regardless of whether they are privately placed or sold through a public offering. The flotation cost includes compensation to the investment banker for marketing the issue. Detailed discussion of the functions, organization, and cost of investment banking is included in Chapter 16.

[5] Generally, the yield to maturity of bonds with a similar "rating" is used. Bond ratings, which are published by independent agencies, are discussed in Chapter 16.

Duchess Corporation's bond issue are as follows:

End of year(s)	Cash flow
0	$ 960
1–20	−$ 90
20	−$1,000

The initial $960 inflow is followed by annual interest outflows of $90 (9% coupon interest rate × $1,000 par value) over the 20-year life of the bond. In year 20 an outflow of $1,000, representing the repayment of the principal, occurs. The before-tax cost of the debt can be determined by finding the discount rate that equates the present value of the outflows with the initial inflow. Applying the trial-and-error internal rate of return techniques of Chapter 10 and using interpolation[6] results in before-tax cost, or cost to maturity, k_d, of 9.47 percent.

Approximating the Cost

The before-tax cost of debt, k_d, for a bond with a $1,000 par value can be approximated using the following equation:

$$k_d = \frac{I + \dfrac{\$1,000 - N_d}{n}}{\dfrac{N_d + \$1,000}{2}} \tag{11.2}$$

where

$$I = \text{annual interest in dollars}$$
$$N_d = \text{net proceeds from the sale of debt (bond)}$$
$$n = \text{number of years to the bond's maturity}$$

Example

Substituting the appropriate values from the Duchess Corporation example into Equation 11.2 results in an approximate before-tax debt cost, k_d, of 9.39 percent:

$$k_d = \frac{\$90 + \dfrac{\$1,000 - \$960}{20}}{\dfrac{\$960 + \$1,000}{2}} = \frac{\$90 + \$2}{\$980}$$

$$= \frac{\$92}{\$980} = 9.39\%$$

[6] In Chapter 6, footnote 12, an explanation was given of how to approximate interest or growth rates using *interpolation,* a simple technique for finding intermediate or fractional values when only integer data are available.

After-Tax Cost of Debt

As indicated earlier, the *specific cost* of financing must be stated on an after-tax basis. Since interest on debt is tax-deductible, a tax adjustment is required. The before-tax debt cost, k_d, can be converted to an after-tax debt cost, k_i, by the following equation:

$$k_i = k_d \times (1 - T) \tag{11.3}$$

The T represents the firm's tax rate.

> **Example**
> We can use the 9.39 percent before-tax debt cost approximation for Duchess Corporation, which has a 40 percent tax rate, to demonstrate the after-tax debt cost calculation. Applying Equation 11.3 results in an after-tax cost of debt of 5.63 percent [9.39% × (1 − .40)]. Typically, the explicit cost of long-term debt is less than the explicit cost of any of the alternative forms of long-term financing, which is due primarily to the tax-deductibility of interest.

The Cost of Preferred Stock

Preferred stock represents a special type of ownership interest in the firm. Preferred shareholders must receive their *stated* dividends prior to the distribution of any earnings to common shareholders. Since preferred stock is a form of ownership, the proceeds from the sale of preferred stock are expected to be held for an infinite period of time. A complete discussion of the various characteristics of preferred stock is presented in Chapter 18. However, the one aspect of preferred stock that requires clarification at this point is dividends.

Preferred Stock Dividends

Most preferred stock dividends are stated as a *dollar amount*—"x dollars per year." When dividends are stated this way, the stock is often referred to as "x dollar preferred stock." Thus a $4 preferred stock is expected to pay preferred shareholders $4 in dividends each year on each share of preferred stock owned. Sometimes preferred stock dividends are stated as an *annual percentage rate;* this rate represents the percentage of the stock's par, or face, value that equals the annual dividend. For instance, an 8 percent preferred stock with a $50 par value would be expected to pay an annual dividend of $4 a share (.08 × $50 par = $4). Before calculating the cost of preferred stock, any dividends stated as percentages should be converted to annual dollar dividends.

Calculating the Cost of Preferred Stock

The **cost of preferred stock, k_p,** is found by dividing the annual preferred stock dividend, D_p, by the net proceeds from the sale of the preferred stock, N_p. The net proceeds represent the amount of money to be received net of any flotation costs required to issue and sell the stock. Equation 11.4 gives the cost of preferred stock, k_p, in terms of the

cost of preferred stock, k_p
The annual preferred stock dividend, D_p, divided by the net proceeds from the sale of the preferred stock, N_p.

annual dollar dividend, D_p, and the net proceeds from the sale of the stock, N_p:

$$k_p = \frac{D_p}{N_p} \tag{11.4}$$

Since preferred stock dividends are paid out of the firm's *after-tax* cash flows, a tax adjustment is not required.

> **Example**
> Duchess Corporation is contemplating issuance of a 9 percent preferred stock expected to sell for its $85 per share par value. The cost of issuing and selling the stock is expected to be $3 per share. The firm would like to determine the cost of the stock. The first step in finding this cost is to calculate the dollar amount of preferred dividends, since the dividend is stated as a percentage of the stock's $85 par value. The annual dollar dividend is $7.65 (.09 × $85). The net proceeds from the proposed sale of stock can be found by subtracting the flotation costs from the sale price. This gives a value of $82 per share. Substituting the annual dividend, D_p, of $7.65 and the net proceeds, N_p, of $82 into Equation 11.4 gives the cost of preferred stock, 9.33 percent ($7.65 ÷ $82).

Comparing the 9.33 percent cost of preferred stock to the 5.63 percent cost of long-term debt (bonds) shows that the preferred stock is more expensive. This difference results primarily because the cost of long-term debt—interest—is tax deductible.

FACT OR FABLE?   3 Unlike the calculation of the cost of debt, a tax adjustment is required in order to calculate the cost of preferred stock. *(Fable)*

Unlike the calculation of the cost of preferred stock and other forms of equity financing, a tax adjustment is required to calculate the cost of *long-term debt*.

The Cost of Common Stock

The *cost of common stock* is the return required on the stock by investors in the marketplace. There are two forms of common stock financing: (1) new issues of common stock and (2) retained earnings. As a first step in finding each of these costs we must estimate the cost of common stock equity.

cost of common stock equity, k_s The rate at which investors discount the expected dividends of the firm in order to determine its share value.

Finding the Cost of Common Stock Equity

The **cost of common stock equity, k_s,** is the rate at which investors discount the expected dividends of the firm in order to determine its share value. Two techniques for measuring the cost of common stock equity capital are available. One uses the constant growth valuation model; the other relies on the capital asset pricing model (CAPM).

Using the Constant Growth Valuation (Gordon) Model

The **constant growth valuation model**—the **Gordon model**—was presented in Chapter 8. It is based on the widely accepted premise that the value of a share of the stock is equal to the present value of all future dividends it is expected to provide over an infinite time horizon. The key expression derived in Chapter 8 and presented as Equation 8.9 is restated in Equation 11.5:

$$P_0 = \frac{D_1}{k_s - g} \tag{11.5}$$

constant growth valuation (Gordon) model Assumes that the value of a share of stock equals the present value of all future dividends (assumed to grow at a constant rate) it will provide over an infinite time horizon.

where

P_0 = value of common stock

D_1 = per-share dividend expected at the end of year 1

k_s = required return on common stock

g = constant rate of growth in dividends

Solving Equation 11.5 for k_s results in the following expression for the *cost of common stock equity:*

$$k_s = \frac{D_1}{P_0} + g \tag{11.6}$$

Equation 11.6 indicates that the cost of common stock equity can be found by dividing the dividend expected at the end of year 1 by the current price of the stock and adding the expected growth rate. Since common stock dividends are paid from after-tax income, no tax adjustment is required.

Example
Duchess Corporation wishes to determine its cost of common stock equity capital, k_s. The market price, P_0, of its common stock is $50 per share. The firm expects to pay a dividend, D_1, of $4 at the end of the coming year, 1989. The dividends paid on the outstanding stock over the past six years (1983–1988) are as follows:

Year	Dividend
1988	$3.80
1987	3.62
1986	3.47
1985	3.33
1984	3.12
1983	2.97

Using the table for the present-value interest factors, *PVIF* (Table A-3), in conjunction with the technique described for finding growth rates in Chapter 6, the annual growth rate of dividends, g, can be calculated. It turns out to be approximately 5 percent. Substituting $D_1 = \$4$, $P_0 = \$50$, and $g = 5$ percent into Equation 11.6 results in the cost of common stock equity:

$$k_s = \frac{\$4}{\$50} + .05 = .08 + .05 = .13 = \underline{\underline{13\%}}$$

The 13 percent cost of common stock equity capital represents the return required by *existing* shareholders on their investment in order to leave the market price of the firm's outstanding shares unchanged.

Using the Capital Asset Pricing Model (CAPM)

capital asset pricing model (CAPM) Describes the relationship between the required return, or cost of common stock equity capital, k_s, and the nondiversifiable risk of the firm as measured by the beta coefficient, b.

The **capital asset pricing model (CAPM)** was developed and discussed in Chapter 7. It describes the relationship between the required return, or cost of common stock equity capital, k_s, and the nondiversifiable risk of the firm as measured by the beta coefficient, b. The basic CAPM is given in Equation 11.7:

$$k_s = R_F + [b \times (k_m - R_F)] \tag{11.7}$$

where

$$R_F = \text{risk-free rate of return}$$

$$k_m = \text{required return on the market portfolio}$$

Using CAPM, the cost of common stock equity is the return required by investors as compensation for the firm's nondiversifiable risk, which is measured by beta, b.

Example

Duchess Corporation, which calculated its cost of common stock equity capital, k_s, using the constant growth valuation model in the preceding example, also wishes to calculate this cost using the capital asset pricing model. From information provided by the firm's investment advisers and its own analyses, it is found that the risk-free rate, R_F, equals 7 percent; the firm's beta, b, equals 1.50; and the market return, k_m, equals 11 percent. Substituting these values into Equation 11.7, the company estimates the cost of common stock equity capital, k_s, as follows:

$$k_s = 7\% + [1.50 \times (11\% - 7\%)] = 7\% + 6\% = \underline{\underline{13\%}}$$

The 13 percent cost of common stock equity capital, which is the same as that found using the constant growth valuation model, represents the required return of investors in Duchess Corporation common stock.

Comparing the Constant Growth and CAPM Techniques

Use of CAPM differs from the constant growth valuation model in that it directly considers the firm's risk as reflected by beta in order to determine the *required* return or cost of common stock equity capital. The constant growth model does not look at risk; it uses the market price, P_0, as a reflection of the *expected* risk-return preference of investors in the marketplace. Although both techniques are theoretically sound, the use of the constant growth valuation model is often preferred because the data required are more readily available.

Another difference lies in the fact that when the constant growth valuation model is used to find the cost of common stock equity capital, it can easily be adjusted for flotation costs to find the cost of new common stock; the CAPM does not provide such an adjustment mechanism. The difficulty in adjusting the cost of common stock equity capital calculated using CAPM for these costs stems from the fact that the model does not include the market price, P_0, a variable that is needed to make such an adjustment. Because of its computational appeal, the traditional constant growth valuation model is used throughout this text to measure common stock costs.

The Cost of New Issues of Common Stock

Our purpose in finding the firm's overall cost of capital is to determine the after-tax cost of *new* funds required for financing projects. Attention must therefore be given to the **cost of a new issue of common stock, k_n.** This cost is determined by calculating the cost of common stock after considering both the amount of underpricing and the associated flotation costs. Normally, in order to sell a new issue it will have to be **underpriced**—sold at a price below the current market price, P_0. In addition, flotation costs paid for issuing and selling the new issue will reduce proceeds.

The cost of new issues can be calculated by determining the net proceeds after underpricing and flotation costs, using the constant growth valuation model expression for the cost of existing common stock, k_s, as a starting point. If we let N_n represent the net proceeds from the sale of new common stock after allowing for underpricing and flotation costs, the cost of the new issue, k_n, can be expressed as follows:[7]

$$k_n = \frac{D_1}{N_n} + g \qquad (11.8)$$

Since the net proceeds from sale of new common stock, N_n, will be less than the current market price, P_0, the cost of new issues, k_n, will always be greater than the cost of existing issues, k_s. The cost of new common stock is normally greater than any other long-term financing cost. Since common stock dividends are paid from after-tax cash flows, no tax adjustment is required.

cost of a new issue of common stock, k_n
Determined by calculating the cost of common stock after considering both the amount of underpricing and the associated flotation costs.

underpriced Stock sold at a price below its current market price, P_o.

> **Example**
> In the example using the constant growth valuation model, an expected dividend, D_1, of \$4; a current market price, P_0, of \$50; and an expected growth rate of dividends, g, of 5 percent were used to calculate Duchess Corporation's cost of common stock equity capital, k_s, which was found to be 13 percent. To determine its cost of *new* common stock, k_n, Duchess Corporation, with the aid of its advisers, has estimated that, on average, new shares can be sold for \$49. The \$1 per share underpricing is necessary due to the competitive nature of the market. A second cost associated with a new issue is an underwriting fee of \$.80 per share that would be paid to cover the costs of issuing

---

[7] An alternative, but computationally less straightforward, form of this equation is

$$k_n = \frac{D_1}{P_0 \times (1 - f)} + g \qquad (11.8a)$$

where f represents the *percentage* reduction in current market price expected as a result of underpricing and flotation costs. Simply stated, N_n in Equation 11.8 is equivalent to $P_0 \times (1 - f)$ in Equation 11.8a. For convenience, Equation 11.8 is used to define the cost of a new issue of common stock, k_n.

and selling the new issue. The total underpricing and flotation costs per share are therefore expected to be $1.80.

Subtracting the $1.80 per share underpricing and flotation cost from the current $50 share price, P_0, results in expected net proceeds, N_n, of $48.20 per share ($50.00 − $1.80). Substituting $D_1 = \$4$, $N_n = \$48.20$, and $g = 5$ percent into Equation 11.8 results in a cost of new common stock, k_n, as follows:

$$k_n = \frac{\$4.00}{\$48.20} + .0500 = .0830 + .0500 = .1330 = \underline{\underline{13.30\%}}$$

Duchess Corporation's cost of new common stock, k_n, is therefore 13.30 percent. This is the value to be used in the subsequent calculation of the firm's overall cost of capital.

FACT OR FABLE?

4 Either the constant growth valuation (Gordon) model or the capital asset pricing model (CAPM) can be used to find the cost of common stock equity, but the CAPM approach is more easily adjusted to find the cost of new issues of common stock. *(Fable)*
Either the constant growth valuation (Gordon) model or the capital asset pricing model (CAPM) can be used to find the cost of common stock equity, but *the Gordon model is more easily adjusted to find the cost of new issues of common stock.*

The Cost of Retained Earnings

cost of retained earnings, k_r The same as the cost of an equivalent fully subscribed issue of additional common stock, which is measured by the cost of common stock equity, k_s.

If earnings were not retained, they would be paid out to the common stockholders as dividends. Thus the **cost of retained earnings, k_r,** to the firm is the same as the cost of an *equivalent fully subscribed issue of additional common stock*. This means that retained earnings increase the stockholders' equity in the same way as a new issue of common stock. Stockholders find the firm's retention of earnings acceptable only if they expect it will earn at least their required return on the reinvested funds.

Viewing retained earnings as a fully subscribed issue of additional common stock, the firm's cost of retained earnings, k_r, can be set equal to the cost of common stock equity as given by Equations 11.6 and 11.7.[8]

$$k_r = k_s \qquad (11.9)$$

It is not necessary to adjust the cost of retained earnings for either underpricing or flotation costs. By retaining earnings, the firm bypasses these costs and still raises the equity capital.

---

[8] Technically, if a stockholder received dividends and wished to invest them in additional shares of the firm's stock, he or she would have to first pay personal taxes on the dividends and then pay brokerage fees prior to acquiring additional shares. Using *pt* as the average stockholder's personal tax rate and *bf* as the average brokerage fees stated as a percentage, the cost of retained earnings, k_r, can be specified as: $k_r = k_s \times (1 - pt) \times (1 - bf)$. Due to the difficulty in estimating *pt* and *bf*, only the simpler definition of k_r given in Equation 11.9 is used here.

Example

The cost of retained earnings for Duchess Corporation was actually calculated in the preceding examples, since it is equal to the cost of common stock equity when underpricing and flotation costs are ignored. Thus k_r equals 13 percent. The cost of retained earnings is always lower than the cost of a new issue of common stock, which in this case is 13.30 percent. This difference is due to the absence of underpricing and flotation costs in financing projects with retained earnings.

The Weighted Average Cost of Capital (WACC)

Now that methods for calculating the cost of specific sources of financing have been reviewed, we can present techniques for determining the overall cost of capital. As noted earlier, the **weighted average cost of capital (WACC), k_a,** is found by weighting the cost of each specific type of capital by its proportion in the firm's capital structure. Let us look at the common weighting schemes and the procedures and considerations involved.

weighted average cost of capital (WACC), k_a Determined by weighting the cost of each specific type of capital by its proportion in the firm's capital structure.

Weighting Schemes

Weights can be calculated as *book value* or *market value* and as *historic* or *target*.

Book Value versus Market Value

Book value weights use accounting values to measure the proportion of each type of capital in the firm's financial structure. **Market value weights** measure the proportion of each type of capital at its market value. Market value weights are appealing, since the market values of securities closely approximate the actual dollars to be received from their sale. Moreover, since the costs of the various types of capital are calculated using prevailing market prices, it seems reasonable to use market value weights. *Market value weights are clearly preferred over book value weights.*

book value weights Use accounting values to measure the proportion of each type of capital in the firm's structure; used in calculating the weighted average cost of capital.

market value weights Use market values to measure the proportion of each type of capital in the firm's structure; used in calculating the weighted average cost of capital.

Historic versus Target

Historic weights can be either book or market weights based on *actual data*. For example, past as well as current book proportions would constitute a form of historic weighting. Likewise, past or current market proportions would represent a historic weighting scheme. Such a weighting scheme would therefore be based on real—rather than desired—proportions. **Target weights,** which can also be based on either book or market values, reflect the firm's *desired* capital structure proportions. Firms using target weights establish such proportions on the basis of the "optimal" capital structure they wish to achieve. When one considers the somewhat approximate nature of the calculations, the choice of weights may not be critical. However, from a strictly theoretical point of view the *preferred weighting scheme is target market value proportions,* and these will be used throughout this chapter.

historic weights Either book or market value weights based on actual capital structure proportions; used in calculating the weighted average cost of capital.

target weights Either book or market value weights based on *desired* capital structure proportions; used in calculating the weighted average cost of capital.

FINANCE IN ACTION

COST OF CAPITAL PRACTICES OF LEADING FIRMS

A relatively recent survey examined the cost of capital practices of the nation's leading firms. Findings of the study were based upon 177 usable responses received from a questionnaire mailed to all firms in the *Fortune* 1000 list.

The companies were asked to indicate the approximate level of their cost of capital on October 15, 1980. Their responses are summarized in the first table. The mean cost of capital for the respondents was 14.3 percent.

The responses relative to weighting schemes used to calculate the weighted average cost of capital for the same sample are summarized in the second table. It can be seen that the majority of respondents used some type of weighted average when determining their cost of capital. Somewhat surprising is the fact that nearly 16 percent of the respondents used the cost of the specific source of funds employed as a cutoff rate for making financial decisions. Such an approach clearly runs counter to theory. Of the firms using a weighted average, the majority appear to use target capital structure weights. Second most popular are market value weights, followed by book value weighting schemes.

Cost of Capital (Oct. 15, 1980)

Range of overall cost of capital	Percentage of respondents
Less than 5%	1.7%
5% to 7%	0.6
7% to 9%	3.4
9% to 11%	10.1
11% to 13%	20.9 ⎤
13% to 15%	21.5 ⎬ 65%
15% to 17%	22.6 ⎦
17% to 19%	12.3
19% to 21%	4.0
21% to 23%	0.6
23% to 25%	0.6
Greater than 25%	1.7
Total	100.0%

Weighting Schemes

Approach or weighting scheme	Percentage of respondents
Use the cost of the specific source of financing planned for funding the alternative	16%
Use a weighted average cost of capital based on:	
Book value weights	16
Target capital structure weights	40
Market value weights	27
Other weighting scheme	1
Total	100%

Calculating the Weighted Average Cost of Capital (WACC)

Once the cost of the specific sources of financing and the appropriate weighting schemes have been determined, the weighted average cost of capital (WACC) can be calculated. This calculation is performed by multiplying the specific cost of each form of financing by its proportion in the firm's capital structure and summing the weighted values. As an equation, the weighted average cost of capital, k_a, can be specified as follows:

$$k_a = (w_i \times k_i) + (w_p \times k_p) + (w_s \times k_{r \text{ or } n}) \tag{11.10}$$

where

w_i = proportion of long-term debt in capital structure

w_p = proportion of preferred stock in capital structure

w_s = proportion of common stock equity in capital structure

$w_i + w_p + w_s = 1$

Two important points should be noted in Equation 11.10:

1. *The sum of weights must equal 1.* Simply stated, all capital structure components must be accounted for.

2. The firm's common stock equity weight, w_s, is multiplied by either the cost of retained earnings, k_r, or the cost of new common stock, k_n. The specific cost used in the common stock equity term depends on whether the firm's common stock equity financing will be obtained using retained earnings, k_r, or new common stock, k_n.

Example

Earlier in the chapter, the costs of the various types of capital for Duchess Corporation were found to be as follows:

Cost of debt, $k_i = 5.63$ percent
Cost of preferred stock, $k_p = 9.33$ percent
Cost of new common stock, $k_n = 13.30$ percent
Cost of retained earnings, $k_r = 13.00$ percent

The company has determined what it believes to be the optimal capital structure. Duchess Corporation uses this target capital structure, based on market values, to calculate the weighted average cost of capital. The target market value proportions are as follows:

Source of capital	Target market value proportions
Long-term debt	40%
Preferred stock	10
Common stock equity	50
Total	100%

Because the firm expects to have a sizable amount of retained earnings available ($300,000), it plans to use its cost of retained earnings, k_r, as the cost of common stock equity. Using this value along with the other data presented, Duchess Corporation's weighted average cost of capital is calculated in Table 11.1. The resulting weighted average cost of capital for Duchess is 9.685 percent. In view of this cost of capital and assuming an unchanged risk level, the firm should accept all projects that earn a return greater than or equal to 9.685 percent.

---

5 The firm's weighted average cost of capital (WACC) can be determined by multiplying the specific cost of each form of financing by its proportion in the firm's capital structure and summing the weighted values. *(Fact)*

FACT OR FABLE?

Table 11.1
Calculation of the Weighted Average Cost of Capital for Duchess Corporation

Source of capital	Target proportion (1)	Cost (2)	Weighted cost [(1) × (2)] (3)
Long-term debt	40%	5.63%	2.252%
Preferred stock	10	9.33	.933
Common stock equity	50	13.00	6.500
Totals	100%		9.685%
Weighted average cost of capital = 9.685%			

The Marginal Cost and Investment Decisions

The firm's weighted average cost of capital is a key input to the investment decision-making process. As demonstrated earlier in the chapter, the firm should make only those investments for which the expected return is greater than the weighted average cost of capital. Of course at any given time the firm's financing costs and investment returns will be affected by the volume of financing/investment undertaken. The concepts of a *weighted marginal cost of capital* and an *investment opportunities schedule* provide the mechanisms whereby financing and investment decisions can be made simultaneously at any point in time.

The Weighted Marginal Cost of Capital (WMCC)

weighted marginal cost of capital (WMCC) A schedule or graph relating the firm's weighted average cost of capital to the level of new financing.

The weighted average cost of capital may vary at any time depending on the volume of financing the firm plans to raise. As the volume of financing increases, the costs of the various types of financing will increase, raising the firm's weighted average cost of capital. A schedule or graph relating the firm's weighted average cost of capital to the level of new financing is called the **weighted marginal cost of capital (WMCC).** These increasing costs are attributable to the fact that suppliers of capital will require greater returns in the form of interest, dividends, or growth to compensate for the increased risk introduced as larger volumes of *new* financing are incurred.

A second factor relates to the use of common stock equity financing. The portion of new financing provided by common stock equity will be taken from available retained earnings until exhausted and then obtained through new common stock financing. Since retained earnings are a less expensive form of common stock equity financing than the sale of new common stock, it should be clear that once retained earnings have been exhausted, the weighted average cost of capital will rise with the addition of more expensive new common stock.

breaking point The level of *total* financing at which the cost of one of the financing components rises, thereby causing an upward shift in the *weighted marginal cost of capital (WMCC).*

Finding Breaking Points

In order to calculate the WMCC, the **breaking points,** which reflect the level of *total* financing at which the cost of one of the components rises, must be calculated. The following general equation can be used to find breaking points:

$$BP_j = \frac{AF_j}{w_j} \qquad (11.11)$$

where

BP_j = breaking point for financing source j

AF_j = amount of funds available from financing source j at a given cost

w_j = capital structure proportion (historic or target) for financing source j

Example
When Duchess Corporation exhausts its $300,000 of available retained earnings, (k_r = 13.00%), it must use the more expensive new common stock financing (k_n = 13.30%) to meet its common stock equity needs. In addition, the firm expects that it can borrow only $400,000 of debt at the 5.63 percent cost; additional debt will have an after-tax cost (k_i) of 7.10 percent. Two breaking points therefore exist—(1) when the $300,000 of retained earnings costing 13.00 percent is exhausted and (2) when the $400,000 of long-term debt costing 5.63 percent is exhausted. The breaking points can be found by substituting these values and the corresponding capital structure proportions given earlier into Equation 11.11. We get:

$$BP_{\text{common equity}} = \frac{\$300,000}{.50} = \$600,000$$

$$BP_{\text{long-term debt}} = \frac{\$400,000}{.40} = \$1,000,000$$

Calculating the WMCC

Once the breaking points have been determined, the weighted average cost of capital over the range of total financing between breaking points must be calculated. First, the weighted average cost of capital for a level of total new financing between zero and the first breaking point is found. Next, the weighted average cost of capital for a level of total new financing between the first and second breaking points is found, and so on. By definition, for each of the ranges of total new financing between breaking points, certain component capital costs will increase, causing the weighted average cost of capital to increase to a higher level than over the preceding range.

Example
Table 11.2 summarizes the calculation of the weighted average cost of capital for Duchess Corporation over the three total new financing ranges created by the two breaking points—$600,000 and $1,000,000. Comparing the costs in column 3 of the table for each of the three ranges, we can see that the costs in the first range ($0 to $600,000) are those calculated in earlier examples and used in Table 11.1. In the second range ($600,000 to $1,000,000), the increase in the common equity cost to 13.30 percent is reflected. In the final range the increase in the long-term debt cost to 7.10 percent is introduced.

The weighted average costs of capital (WACC) for the three ranges created by the two breaking points are summarized in Table 11.3. This schedule represents the weighted marginal cost of capital (WMCC). The increasing nature of this relationship should be evident from the data presented. Figure 11.1 presents the WMCC graphically. Graph (a) shows a plot of the actual data; graph (b) presents a smoothed function that more realistically depicts the firm's WMCC. Again, it is clear that the WMCC is an increasing function of the amount of total new financing raised.

Table 11.2
Weighted Average Cost of Capital for Ranges of Total New Financing for Duchess Corporation

Range of total new financing	Source of capital (1)	Target proportion (2)	Cost (3)	Weighted cost [(2) × (3)] (4)
$0 to $600,000	Debt	40%	5.63%	2.252%
	Preferred	10	9.33	.933
	Common	50	13.00	6.500
		Weighted average cost of capital		9.685%
$600,000 to $1,000,000	Debt	40%	5.63%	2.252%
	Preferred	10	9.33	.933
	Common	50	13.30	6.650
		Weighted average cost of capital		9.835%
$1,000,000 and above	Debt	40%	7.10%	2.840%
	Preferred	10	9.33	.933
	Common	50	13.30	6.650
		Weighted average cost of capital		10.423%

Table 11.3
Weighted Marginal Cost of Capital for Duchess Corporation

Range of total new financing	WACC
$0 to $600,000	9.685%
$600,000 to $1,000,000	9.835
$1,000,000 and above	10.423

Figure 11.1
Weighted Marginal Cost of Capital (WMCC) for Duchess Corporation

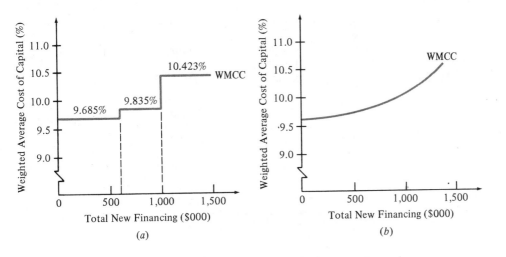

The Investment Opportunities Schedule (IOS)

At any given time a firm has certain investment opportunities available to it. These opportunities differ with respect to the size of investment anticipated, risk, and return. (For convenience, we assume all opportunities have equal risk similar to the firm's risk.) The firm's **investment opportunities schedule (IOS)** is a ranking of investment possibilities from best (highest returns) to worst (lowest returns). As the cumulative amount of money invested in a firm's capital projects increases, its return (IRR) on the projects will decrease, since generally the first project selected will have the highest return, the next project the second highest, and so on. In other words, the return on investments will *decrease* as the firm accepts additional projects.

investment opportunities schedule (IOS) A ranking of investment possibilities from best (highest returns) to worst (lowest returns).

Example
Duchess Corporation's current investment opportunities schedule (IOS) lists the best (highest return) to the worst (lowest return) investment possibilities in column 1 of Table 11.4. In column 2 of the table, the initial investment required by each project is shown, and in column 3 the cumulative total invested funds required to finance all projects better than and including the corresponding investment opportunity are given. Plotting the project returns against the cumulative investment (column 1 against column 3 in Table 11.4) on a set of total new financing or investment–weighted average cost of capital and IRR axes results in the firm's investment opportunities schedule (IOS). A graph of the IOS for Duchess Corporation is given in Figure 11.2.

Table 11.4
Investment Opportunities Schedule (IOS) for Duchess Corporation

Investment opportunity	Internal rate of return (IRR) (1)	Initial investment (2)	Cumulative investment[a] (3)
A	13.0%	$100,000	$ 100,000
B	12.5	200,000	300,000
C	12.0	400,000	700,000
D	11.0	100,000	800,000
E	10.0	200,000	1,000,000
F	9.5	300,000	1,300,000
G	9.0	100,000	1,400,000

[a] The cumulative investment represents the total amount invested in projects with higher returns plus the investment required for the given investment opportunity.

Making Financing/Investment Decisions

As long as a project's internal rate of return[9] is greater than the weighted marginal cost of new financing, the project should be accepted by the firm. Although the return will decrease with the acceptance of more projects, the weighted marginal cost of capital will

Figure 11.2
Using the IOS and WMCC to Select Projects

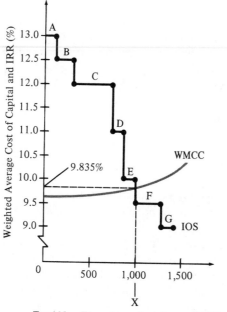

Total New Financing or Investment ($000)

---

[9] Although net present value could be used to make these decisions, the internal rate of return is used here because of the ease of comparison it offers.

increase because greater amounts of financing will be required. The firm would therefore *accept projects up to the point where the marginal return on its investment equals its weighted marginal cost of capital*. Beyond that point its investment return will be less than its capital cost.[10] This approach is consistent with achievement of the goal of owner wealth maximization. Returning to the Duchess Corporation example, we can demonstrate the application of this procedure.

| 6 | Using the weighted marginal cost of capital (WMCC) and the investment opportunities schedule (IOS), the firm should accept projects up to the point where the marginal return on its investment equals its WMCC. *(Fact)* | **FACT OR FABLE?** |

Example
Figure 11.2 shows Duchess Corporation's WMCC and IOS on the same set of axes. Using these two functions in combination, the firm's optimal capital budget (''X'' in Figure 11.2) is determined. By raising $1 million of new financing and investing these funds in projects A, B, C, D, and E, the wealth of the firm's owners should be maximized, since the 10 percent return on the last dollar invested (in project E) *exceeds* its 9.835 percent weighted average cost. Investment in project F is not feasible because its 9.5 percent return is *less* than the 10.423 percent cost of funds available for investment. The importance of the WMCC and IOS for investment decision making should now be quite clear.

Summary

- The key cost of capital definitions and formulas are given in Table 11.5.

- The cost of capital is the rate of return a firm must earn on its investments in order to maintain its market value and attract needed funds. To capture the interrelatedness of financing, an overall or weighted average cost of capital should be used.

- The specific costs of the basic sources of capital (long-term debt, preferred stock, common stock, and retained earnings) can be calculated individually. Only the cost of debt must be adjusted for taxes. The cost of each is affected by business and financial risks, which are assumed unchanged, and the risk-free cost of the given type of financing.

- The cost of long-term debt is the after-tax cost today of raising long-term funds through borrowing. It can be approximated using a formula and a tax-adjustment calculation.

- The cost of preferred stock is the stated annual dividend expressed as a percentage of the net proceeds from the sale of preferred shares.

- The cost of common stock equity can be calculated using the constant growth valuation model or the capital asset pricing model (CAPM). An adjustment in the cost of common stock equity to reflect underpricing and flotation costs is required to find the cost of new issues of common stock. The cost of retained earnings is equal to the cost of common stock equity.

- A firm's weighted average cost of capital (WACC) can be determined by combining the costs of specific types of capital after weighting each cost using historical book or market value weights or target book or market value weights. The theoretically preferred approach uses target weights based on market values.

---

[10] So as not to confuse the discussion presented here, the fact that the use of the IRR for selecting projects may not provide optimum decisions is ignored. The problems associated with the IRR and its use in capital rationing were discussed in greater detail in Chapter 10.

● A firm's weighted marginal cost of capital (WMCC) function can be developed by finding the weighted average cost of capital for various levels of total new financing. The function relates the weighted average cost of capital to each level of total new financing.

● The investment opportunities schedule (IOS) presents a ranking of currently available investments from those with the highest returns to those with the lowest returns. It is used in combination with the WMCC to find the level of financing/investment that maximizes owners' wealth.

Table 11.5
Summary of Key Definitions and Formulas for Cost of Capital

Variable definitions
k_d = before-tax cost of debt
I = annual interest in dollars
N_d = net proceeds from the sale of debt (bond)
n = number of years to the bond's maturity
k_i = after-tax cost of debt
T = firm's tax rate
k_p = cost of preferred stock
D_p = annual preferred stock dividend (in dollars)
N_p = net proceeds from the sale of preferred stock
k_s = required return on common stock
D_1 = per-share dividend expected at the end of year 1
P_0 = value of common stock
g = constant rate of growth in dividends
R_F = risk-free rate of return
b = beta coefficient or measure of nondiversifiable risk
k_m = required return on the market portfolio
k_n = cost of a new issue of common stock
N_n = net proceeds from sale of new common stock
k_r = cost of retained earnings
k_a = weighted average cost of capital
w_i = proportion of long-term debt in capital structure
w_p = proportion of preferred stock in capital structure
w_s = proportion of common stock equity in capital structure
BP_j = breaking point for financing source j
AF_j = amount of funds available from financing source j at a given cost
w_j = capital structure proportion (historic or target) for financing source j

Cost of capital formulas
Before-tax cost of debt

$$k_d = \frac{I + \frac{\$1,000 - N_d}{n}}{\frac{N_d + \$1,000}{2}}$$ [Eq. 11.2]

After-tax cost of debt

$$k_i = k_d \times (1 - T)$$ [Eq. 11.3]

Cost of preferred stock

$$k_p = \frac{D_p}{N_p}$$ [Eq. 11.4]

Cost of common stock equity

Using constant growth valuation model: $k_s = \frac{D_1}{P_0} + g$ [Eq. 11.6]

Using capital asset pricing model (CAPM): $k_s = R_F + [b \times (k_m - R_F)]$ [Eq. 11.7]

Cost of new issues of common stock

$$k_n = \frac{D_1}{N_n} + g$$ [Eq. 11.8]

Cost of retained earnings

$$k_r = k_s$$ [Eq. 11.9]

Weighted average cost of capital (WACC)

$$k_a = (w_i \times k_i) + (w_p \times k_p) + (w_s \times k_{r \text{ or } n})$$ [Eq.11.10]

Breaking point

$$BP_j = \frac{AF_j}{w_j}$$ [Eq. 11.11]

Questions

11-1 What is the *cost of capital?* What role does it play in making long-term investment decisions? Why is use of a weighted average cost rather than the specific cost recommended?

11-2 Why are business and financial risk assumed unchanged when evaluating the cost of capital? Discuss the implications of these assumptions on the acceptance and financing of new projects.

11-3 Why is the cost of capital most appropriately measured on an after-tax basis? What effect, if any, does this have on specific cost components?

11-4 You have just been told, "Since we are going to finance this project with debt, its required rate of return must exceed the cost of debt." Do you agree or disagree? Explain.

11-5 What is meant by the *net proceeds* from the sale of a bond? In which circumstances is a bond expected to sell at a discount or at a premium?

11-6 What sort of general approximation is used to find the before-tax cost of debt? How is the before-tax cost of debt converted into the after-tax cost?

11-7 How would you calculate the cost of preferred stock? Why do we concern ourselves with the net proceeds from the sale of the stock instead of the sale price?

11-8 What premise about share value underlies the constant growth valuation (Gordon) model used to measure the cost of common stock equity, k_s? What does each component of the equation represent?

11-9 If retained earnings are viewed as a fully subscribed issue of additional common stock, why is the cost of financing a project with retained earnings technically less than the cost of using a new issue of common stock?

11-10 Describe the logic underlying the use of *target capital structure weights,* and compare and contrast this approach with the use of historic weights.

11-11 What does the *weighted marginal cost of capital (WMCC)* function represent? Why does this function increase?

11-12 What is the *investment opportunities schedule (IOS)?* Is it typically depicted as an increasing or decreasing function of the level of investment at a given point in time? Why?

11-13 Use a graph to show how the weighted marginal cost of capital (WMCC) and the investment opportunities schedule (IOS) can be used to find the level of financing/investment that maximizes owners' wealth.

Self-Test Problem

(Solution on page 418)

ST-1 Humble Manufacturing is interested in measuring its overall cost of capital. Current investigation has gathered the following data. The firm is in the 40 percent marginal tax bracket.

Debt. The firm can raise an unlimited amount of debt by selling $1,000, 10 percent, 10-year bonds on which annual interest payments will be made. To sell the issue, an average discount of $30 per bond would have to be given. The firm must also pay flotation costs of $20 per bond.

Preferred Stock. The firm can sell 11 percent preferred stock at its $100-per-share par value. The cost of issuing and selling the preferred stock is expected to be $4 per share. An unlimited amount of preferred stock can be sold under these terms.

Common Stock. The firm's common stock is currently selling for $80 per share. The firm expects to pay cash dividends of $6 per share next year. The firm's dividends have been growing at an annual rate of 6 percent, and this rate is expected to continue in the future. The stock will have to be underpriced by $4 per share, and flotation costs are expected to amount to $4 per share. The firm can sell an unlimited amount of new common stock under these terms.

Retained Earnings. When measuring this cost, the firm does not concern itself with the tax bracket or brokerage fees of owners. It expects to have available $225,000 of retained earnings in the coming year; once these retained earnings are exhausted, the firm will use new common stock as the form of common stock equity financing.

a. Calculate the specific cost of each source of financing. (Round to the nearest .10.)

b. The firm's target capital structure proportions used in calculating its weighted average cost of capital are given below. (Round to the nearest .01 in this part.)

Source of capital	Target capital structure proportion
Long-term debt	40%
Preferred stock	15
Common stock equity	45
Total	100%

(1) Calculate the single breaking point associated with the firm's financial situation. (*Hint:* This point results from the exhaustion of the firm's retained earnings.)

(2) Calculate the weighted average cost of capital associated with total financing below the breaking point calculated in (1).

(3) Calculate the weighted average cost of capital associated with total financing above the breaking point calculated in (1).

c. Using the results of **b** along with the information at the top of page 411 on the available investment opportunities, draw the firm's weighted marginal cost of capital (WMCC) function and investment opportunities schedule (IOS) on the same set of total new financing or investment (*x*-axis)–weighted average cost of capital and IRR (*y*-axis) axes.

Investment opportunity	Internal rate of return (IRR)	Initial investment
A	11.2%	$100,000
B	9.7	500,000
C	12.9	150,000
D	16.5	200,000
E	11.8	450,000
F	10.1	600,000
G	10.5	300,000

d. Which, if any, of the available investments would you recommend the firm accept? Explain your answer.

Problems

11-1 **(Cost of Debt—Risk Premiums)** Mulberry Printing's cost of long-term debt last year was 10 percent. This rate was attributable to a 7 percent risk-free cost of long-term debt, a 2 percent business risk premium, and a 1 percent financial risk premium. The firm currently wishes to obtain a long-term loan.

a. If the firm's business and financial risk are unchanged from the previous period and the risk-free cost of long-term debt is now 8 percent, at what rate would you expect the firm to obtain a long-term loan?

b. If, as a result of borrowing, the firm's financial risk will increase enough to raise the financial risk premium to 3 percent, how much would you expect the firm's borrowing cost to be?

c. One of the firm's competitors has a 1 percent business risk premium and a 2 percent financial risk premium. What is that firm's cost of long-term debt likely to be?

11-2 **(Concept of Cost of Capital)** Wren Manufacturing is in the process of analyzing its investment decision-making procedures. The two projects evaluated by the firm during the past month were projects 263 and 264. The basic variables surrounding each project analysis using the IRR decision technique and the resulting decision actions are summarized in the following table.

Basic variables	Project 263	Project 264
Cost	$64,000	$58,000
Life	15 years	15 years
IRR	8%	15%
Least-cost financing		
Source	Debt	Equity
Cost (after-tax)	7%	16%
Decision		
Action	Accept	Reject
Reason	8% IRR > 7% cost	15% IRR < 16% cost

a. Evaluate the firm's decision-making procedures and explain why the acceptance of project 263 and rejection of project 264 may not be in the owners' best interest.

b. If the firm maintains a capital structure containing 40 percent debt and 60 percent equity, find its weighted average cost using the data in the table.

c. Had the firm used the weighted average cost calculated in **b,** what actions would have been taken relative to projects 263 and 264?

d. Compare and contrast the firm's actions with your findings in **c.** Which decision method seems most appropriate? Explain why.

11-3 **(Cost of Debt Using Both Methods)** Currently Warren Industries can sell 15-year, $1,000 par-value bonds paying annual interest with a 12 percent coupon. As a result of current interest rates, the bonds can be sold for $1,010 each; flotation costs of $30 per bond will be incurred in this process. The firm is in the 40 percent marginal tax bracket.

a. Find the net proceeds from sale of the bond, N_d.

b. Show the cash flows from the firm's point of view over the maturity of the bond.

c. Use the *IRR approach* with interpolation (see footnote 6) to estimate the before-tax and after-tax cost of debt.

d. Use the *approximation formula* to estimate the before-tax and after-tax cost of debt.

e. Compare and contrast the cost of debt calculated in **c** and **d.** Which approach do you prefer? Why?

11-4 **(Cost of Debt Using the Approximation Formula)** For each of the following $1,000 bonds, assuming annual interest payment and a 40 percent marginal tax rate, calculate the *after-tax* cost to maturity using the *approximation formula*.

Bond	Life	Underwriting fee	Discount (−) or premium (+)	Coupon interest rate
A	20 years	$25	$−20	9%
B	16	40	+10	10
C	15	30	−15	12
D	25	15	Par	9
E	22	20	−60	11

11-5 **(Cost of Preferred Stock)** Taylor Systems has just issued preferred stock. The stock has a 12 percent annual dividend and a $100 par value and was sold at $97.50 per share. In addition, flotation costs of $2.50 per share must be paid.

a. Calculate the cost of the preferred stock.

b. If the firm had sold the preferred stock with a 10 percent annual dividend and a $90.00 net price, what would its cost have been?

11-6 **(Cost of Preferred Stock)** Determine the cost for each of the following preferred stocks.

Preferred stock	Par value	Sale price	Flotation cost	Annual dividend
A	$100	$101	$9.00	11%
B	40	38	$3.50	8%
C	35	37	$4.00	$5.00
D	30	26	5% of par	$3.00
E	20	20	$2.50	9%

11-7 **(Cost of Common Stock Equity)** Ross Textiles wishes to measure its cost of common stock equity. The firm's stock is currently selling for $57.50. The firm expects to pay a $3.40 dividend at the end of the year. The dividends for the past five years were as follows:

Year	Dividend
1988	$3.10
1987	2.92
1986	2.60
1985	2.30
1984	2.12

After underpricing and flotation costs, the firm expects to net $52 per share on a new issue.

a. Determine the growth rate of dividends.
b. Determine the net proceeds, N_n, the firm actually receives.
c. Using the constant growth valuation model, determine the cost of new common stock equity, k_n.
d. Using the constant growth valuation model, determine the cost of retained earnings, k_r.

11-8 **(New Common Stock Versus Retained Earnings)** Using the data for each firm in the following table, calculate the cost of new common stock and the cost of retained earnings using the constant growth valuation model.

Firm	Current market price per share	Dividend growth rate	Projected dividend per share next year	Underpricing per share	Flotation cost per share
A	$50.00	8%	$2.25	$2.00	$1.00
B	20.00	4	1.00	0.50	1.50
C	42.50	6	2.00	1.00	2.00
D	19.00	2	2.10	1.30	1.70

11-9 **(Cost of Equity—CAPM)** J&M Corporation common stock has a beta, b, of 1.2. The risk-free rate is 6 percent and the market return is 11 percent.

a. Determine the risk premium on J&M common stock.

b. Determine the required return J&M common stock should provide.

c. Determine J&M's cost of common equity using the CAPM.

11-10 **(WACC—Book Weights)** Ridge Tool has on its books the following amounts and specific (after-tax) costs for each source of capital:

Source of capital	Book value	Specific cost
Long-term debt	$700,000	5.25%
Preferred stock	50,000	12.00
Common stock equity	650,000	16.00

a. Calculate the firm's weighted average cost of capital using book value weights.

b. Explain how the firm can use this cost in the investment decision-making process.

11-11 **(WACC—Book Weights and Market Weights)** The Webster Company has compiled the following information:

Source of capital	Book value	Market value	After-tax cost
Long-term debt	$4,000,000	$3,840,000	6.00%
Preferred stock	40,000	60,000	13.00
Common stock equity	1,060,000	3,000,000	17.00
Totals	$5,100,000	$6,900,000	

a. Calculate the weighted average cost of capital using book value weights.

b. Calculate the weighted average cost of capital using market value weights.

c. Compare the answers obtained in **a** and **b.** Explain the differences.

11-12 **(WACC and Target Weights)** After careful analysis, Dexter Brothers has determined that its optimal capital structure is composed of the following sources and target market value proportions:

Source of capital	Target market value proportions
Long-term debt	30%
Preferred stock	15
Common stock equity	55
Total	100%

The cost of debt is estimated to be 7.2 percent; the cost of preferred stock is estimated to be 13.5 percent; the cost of new common stock is estimated to be 16.5 percent; and the cost of retained earnings is estimated to be 16 percent. All these are after-tax rates. Currently, the company's debt represents 25 percent, the preferred stock represents 10 percent, and the common stock equity represents 65 percent of the capital structure based on market values of the three components. The company expects to have a significant amount of retained earnings available and does not expect to sell any new common stock.

a. Calculate the weighted average cost of capital based on market value weights.

b. Calculate the weighted average cost of capital based on target weights.

11-13 (Calculation of Specific Costs, WACC, and WMCC) Dillon Labs has asked its financial manager to measure the cost of each specific type of capital as well as the weighted average cost of capital. The weighted average cost is to be measured using the firm's target capital structure weights. The firm wishes to finance projects using 40 percent long-term debt, 10 percent preferred stock, and 50 percent common stock equity (retained earnings, new common stock, or both). The firm's marginal tax rate is 40 percent.

Debt. The firm can sell a 10-year, $1,000-par-value bond having a 10 percent annual coupon interest rate for $980. A flotation cost of 3 percent of the par value would be required in addition to the discount of $20 per bond.

Preferred Stock. Eight percent preferred stock having a par value of $100 can be sold for $65. An additional fee of $2 per share must be paid to the underwriters.

Common Stock. The firm's common stock is currently selling for $50 per share. The dividend expected to be paid at the end of the coming year (1989) is $4. Its dividend payments, which have been approximately 60 percent of earnings per share of each in the past five years, were as follows:

Year	Dividend
1988	$3.75
1987	3.50
1986	3.30
1985	3.15
1984	2.85

It is expected that, to sell, new common stock must be underpriced $3 per share and the firm must also pay $2 per share in flotation costs. Dividend payments are expected to continue at 60 percent of earnings.

a. Calculate the specific cost of each source of financing. (Assume that $k_r = k_s$.)

b. If earnings available to common shareholders are expected to be $7 million, what is the breaking point associated with the exhaustion of retained earnings?

c. Determine the weighted average cost of capital between zero and the breaking point given in **b.**

d. Determine the weighted average cost of capital just beyond the breaking point calculated in **b.**

11-14 (Calculation of Specific Costs, WACC, and WMCC) Lang Enterprises, is interested in measuring its overall cost of capital. Current investigation has gathered the following data. The firm is in the 40 percent tax bracket.

Debt. The firm can raise an unlimited amount of debt by selling $1,000, 8 percent coupon interest rate, 20-year bonds on which annual interest payments will be made. To sell the issue, an average discount of $30 per bond would have to be given. The firm also must pay flotation costs of $30 per bond.

Preferred Stock. The firm can sell 8 percent preferred stock at its $95-per-share par value. The cost of issuing and selling the preferred stock is expected to be $5 per share. An unlimited amount of preferred stock can be sold under these terms.

Common Stock. The firm's common stock is currently selling for $100 per share. The firm expects to pay cash dividends of $7 per share next year. The firm's dividends have been growing at an annual rate of 6 percent, and this is expected to continue into the future. The stock will have to be underpriced by $3 per share, and flotation costs are expected to amount to $5 per share. The firm can sell an unlimited amount of new common stock under these terms.

Retained Earnings. When measuring this cost, the firm does not concern itself with the tax bracket or brokerage fees of owners. It expects to have available $100,000 of retained earnings in the coming year; once these retained earnings are exhausted, the firm will use new common stock as the form of common stock equity financing.

a. Calculate the specific cost of each source of financing. (Round answers to the nearest .10 percent.)

b. The firm's target capital structure proportions used in calculating its weighted average cost of capital are given. (Round answer to the nearest .01 percent in this part.)

Source of capital	Target capital structure proportion
Long-term debt	30%
Preferred stock	20
Common stock equity	50
Total	100%

(1) Calculate the single breaking point associated with the firm's financial situation. (*Hint:* This point results from exhaustion of the firm's retained earnings.)

(2) Calculate the weighted average cost of capital associated with total financing below the breaking point calculated in (1).

(3) Calculate the weighted average cost of capital associated with total financing above the breaking point calculated in (1).

11-15 (Integrative—WACC, WMCC, and IOS) Cartwell Products has compiled the data given in the table at the top of page 417 relative to the current costs of its three basic sources of external capital—long-term debt, preferred stock, and common stock equity—for various ranges of financing.

Source of capital	Range of new financing	After-tax cost
Long-term debt	$0 to $320,000 $320,000 and above	6% 8
Preferred stock	$0 and above	17
Common stock equity	$0 to $200,000 $200,000 and above	20 24

The company's target capital structure proportions used in calculating its weighted average cost of capital are as follows:

Source of capital	Target capital structure
Long-term debt	40%
Preferred stock	20
Common stock equity	40
Total	100%

a. Determine the breaking points and ranges of *total* new financing associated with each source of capital.

b. Using the data developed in **a,** determine the breaking points (levels of *total* new financing) at which the firm's weighted average cost of capital will change.

c. Calculate the weighted average cost of capital for each range of total new financing found in **b.** (*Hint:* There are three ranges.)

d. Using the results of **c** along with the following information on the available investment opportunities, draw the firm's weighted marginal cost of capital (WMCC) function and investment opportunities schedule (IOS) on the same set of total new financing or investment (*x*-axis)–weighted average cost of capital and IRR (*y*-axis) axes.

Investment opportunity	Internal rate of return (IRR)	Initial investment
A	19%	$200,000
B	15	300,000
C	22	100,000
D	14	600,000
E	23	200,000
F	13	100,000
G	21	300,000
H	17	100,000
I	16	400,000

e. Which, if any, of the available investments would you recommend the firm accept? Explain your answer.

Solution to Self-Test Problem

ST-1 a. Cost of debt, k_i (using approximation formula)

$$k_d = \frac{I + \dfrac{\$1,000 - N_d}{n}}{\dfrac{N_d + \$1,000}{2}}$$

$I = .10 \times \$1,000 = \$100$
$N_d = \$1,000 - \$30 \text{ discount} - \$20 \text{ flotation cost} = \$950$
$n = 10 \text{ years}$

$$k_d = \frac{\$100 + \dfrac{\$1,000 - \$950}{10}}{\dfrac{\$950 + \$1,000}{2}} = \frac{\$100 + \$5}{\$975} = .1077$$

$k_i = k_d \times (1 - T)$
$T = .40$

$k_i = .1077 \times (1 - .40) = .0646 = .065 \text{ or } \underline{6.5\%}$

Cost of preferred stock, k_p

$$k_p = \frac{D_p}{N_p}$$
$D_p = .11 \times \$100 = \$11$
$N_p = \$100 - \$4 \text{ flotation cost} = \$96$

$$k_p = \frac{\$11}{\$96} = .1146 = .115 \text{ or } \underline{11.5\%}$$

Cost of new common stock, k_n

$$k_n = \frac{D_1}{N_n} + g$$
$D_1 = \$6$
$N_n = \$80 - \$4 \text{ underpricing} - \$4 \text{ flotation cost} = \$72$
$g = .06$

$$k_n = \frac{\$6}{\$72} + .06 = .0833 + .06 = .1433 = \underline{14.3\%}$$

Cost of retained earnings, k_r

$$k_r = k_s = \frac{D_1}{P_0} + g$$

$$= \frac{\$6}{\$80} + .06 = .075 + .06 = .1350 = \underline{13.5\%}$$

b. (1) Breaking point, BP

$$BP_{\text{common equity}} = \frac{AF_{\text{common equity}}}{w_{\text{common equity}}}$$

$$AF_{\text{common equity}} = \$225,000$$

$$w_{\text{common equity}} = .45$$

$$BP_{\text{common equity}} = \frac{\$225,000}{.45} = \$500,000$$

(2) WACC for total new financing < $500,000

Source of capital	Target proportion (1)	Cost (2)	Weighted cost [(1) × (2)] (3)
Long-term debt	40%	6.50%	2.60%
Preferred stock	15	11.50	1.73
Common stock equity	45	13.50	6.08
Totals	100%		10.41%

Weighted average cost of capital = 10.41%

(3) WACC for total new financing > $500,000

Source of capital	Target proportion (1)	Cost (2)	Weighted cost [(1) × (2)] (3)
Long-term debt	40%	6.50%	2.60%
Preferred stock	15	11.50	1.73
Common stock equity	45	14.30	6.44
Totals	100%		10.77%

Weighted average cost of capital = 10.77%

c. IOS data for graph

Investment opportunity	Internal rate of return (IRR)	Initial investment	Cumulative investment
D	16.5	$200,000	$ 200,000
C	12.9	150,000	350,000
E	11.8	450,000	800,000
A	11.2	100,000	900,000
G	10.5	300,000	1,200,000
F	10.1	600,000	1,800,000
B	9.7	500,000	2,300,000

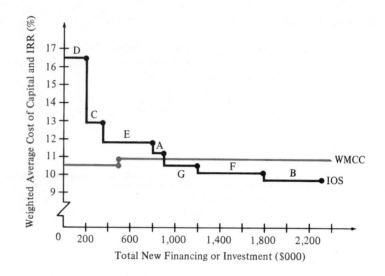

d. Projects D, C, E, and A should be accepted because their respective IRRs exceed the WMCC.

CHAPTER 12

Leverage and Capital Structure

FACT OR FABLE?
Are the following statements fact *(true)* or fable *(false)*?

1

The operating breakeven point will decrease as a result of an increase in either fixed or variable operating costs, or a decrease in the sales price.

2

Financial leverage results from the existence of fixed financial costs and magnifies the effects of changes in earnings before interest and taxes (EBIT) on the firm's earnings per share (EPS).

3

The degree of total leverage (DTL) can be found by adding the degree of operating leverage (DOL) to the degree of financial leverage (DFL).

4

The traditional approach to capital structure suggests that an optimal capital structure exists and that it occurs at the point where the firm's weighted average cost of capital is minimized.

5

The EBIT–EPS approach to capital structure involves selecting the capital structure that maximizes earnings per share (EPS) over the expected range of earnings before interest and taxes (EBIT).

6

Selecting the capital structure that maximizes profits typically results in a structure consistent with achievement of the firm's wealth maximization goal.

Communications king Rupert Murdoch rules an international media empire which compares in size to Time, Inc., and Gannett. This global empire is better known in business circles as News Corporation, a portfolio of over 100 newspapers, magazines, and broadcast stations—among them Twentieth Century Fox, Reuters, and the *Times of London*.

What began modestly in 1954 as two small Australian newspapers has ballooned into a multinational corporation with assets of over $3 billion. The man who made it all happen is an Australian who is willing to gamble for high stakes. The visionary Murdoch has been characterized by *Forbes* as "the quintessential late-twentieth-century man, a sardonic figure who understands in his gut what modern communications, modern finance, and modern politics are all about."

Indeed, Murdoch's 1986 financing of the $2.6 billion global acquisition blitz could have been engineered only by a financial wizard. Part of the financing was arranged through a $1.15 billion issue of preferred stock of Fox Television Stations. The prospectus filed with the Securities and Exchange Commission was a 470-page document which took seven months, five law firms, and three accounting firms to prepare. It is to date the longest document of its kind ever filed with the SEC—topping even AT&T's mammoth prospectus.

Even more notable is the state of News Corporation's balance sheet following the acquisition binge. In 1987, debt exceeded $3 billion, resulting in a debt-equity ratio of 3.4. If the preferred stock is considered with the debt, the debt-equity ratio is a whopping 11.6. Although hardly a textbook example of a recommended capital structure, News Corporation's creditors are gambling that Murdoch is building asset value and that the $300-million-plus yearly interest payments will be met.

As Rupert Murdoch's News Corporation demonstrates, the creation of a highly leveraged capital structure can generate attractive results, but not without risk. In this chapter the concepts of leverage and capital structure and their linkage to the cost of capital and stock value are thoroughly examined.

Leverage

leverage Results from the use of fixed-cost assets or funds to magnify returns to the firm's owners.

capital structure The mix of long-term debt and equity maintained by the firm.

Leverage and capital structure are closely related concepts linked to cost of capital (Chapter 11) and therefore capital budgeting decisions (Chapters 9 and 10). **Leverage** results from the use of fixed-cost assets or funds to magnify returns to the firm's owners. Changes in leverage result in changes in level of return and associated risk. Generally, increases in leverage result in increases in return and risk, whereas decreases in leverage result in decreased return and risk. The amount of leverage in the firm's **capital structure**—the mix of long-term debt and equity maintained by the firm—can significantly

Table 12.1
General Income Statement Format and Types of Leverage

	Sales revenue	
Operating leverage	Less: Cost of goods sold	
	Gross profits	
	Less: Operating expenses	Total leverage
	Earnings before interest and taxes (EBIT)	
Financial leverage	Less: Interest	
	Net profits before taxes	
	Less: Taxes	
	Net profits after taxes	
	Less: Preferred stock dividends	
	Earnings available for common stockholders	
	Earnings per share (EPS)	

affect its value by affecting return and risk. Because of its effect on value, the financial manager must understand how to measure and evaluate leverage when attempting to create the best capital structure.

The three basic types of leverage can best be defined with reference to the firm's income statement. In the general income statement format in Table 12.1, the portions related to the firm's operating leverage, financial leverage, and total leverage are clearly labeled. *Operating leverage* is concerned with the relationship between the firm's sales revenue and its earnings before interest and taxes, or EBIT (EBIT is a descriptive label for *operating profits*). *Financial leverage* is concerned with the relationship between the firm's earnings before interest and taxes (EBIT) and its earnings per share of common stock. *Total leverage* is concerned with the relationship between the firm's sales revenue and the earnings per share of common stock. In subsequent sections we will develop the three leverage concepts separately in detail, but first it is important to understand various aspects of breakeven analysis.

Breakeven Analysis

Breakeven analysis, which is sometimes called **cost-volume-profit analysis,** is used by the firm (1) to determine the level of operations necessary to cover all operating costs and (2) to evaluate the profitability associated with various levels of sales. The firm's **operating breakeven point** is the level of sales necessary to cover all operating costs. At the operating breakeven point, earnings before interest and taxes, or EBIT, equals zero.[1] The first step in finding the operating breakeven point is to divide the cost of goods sold and operating expenses into fixed and variable operating costs. (*Fixed costs* are a function of time, not sales, and are typically contractual; *variable costs* vary directly with sales and are a function of volume, not time.) The top portion of Table 12.1 can then be recast as shown in the left-hand side of Table 12.2. Using this framework, the firm's operating breakeven point can be developed and evaluated.

breakeven analysis (cost-volume-profit analysis)
Used (1) to determine the level of operations necessary to cover all operating costs and (2) to evaluate the profitability associated with various levels of sales.

operating breakeven point
The level of sales necessary to cover all operating costs; the point at which EBIT = $0.

[1] Quite often the breakeven point is calculated so that it represents the point where *all operating and financial costs* are covered. Our concern in this chapter is not with this overall breakeven point.

Table 12.2
Operating Leverage, Costs, and Breakeven Analysis

	Item	Algebraic representation
Operating leverage	Sales revenue	$(P \times Q)$
	Less: Fixed operating costs	$-\quad FC$
	Less: Variable operating costs	$-(VC \times Q)$
	Earnings before interest and taxes	EBIT

The Algebraic Approach

Using the following variables, the operating portion of the firm's income statement can be represented as shown in the right-hand portion of Table 12.2.

$$Q = \text{sales quantity in units}$$
$$P = \text{sale price per unit}$$
$$FC = \text{fixed operating cost per period}$$
$$VC = \text{variable operating cost per unit}$$

Rewriting the algebraic calculations in Table 12.2 as a formula for earnings before interest and taxes yields Equation 12.1:

$$\text{EBIT} = (P \times Q) - FC - (VC \times Q) \qquad (12.1)$$

Simplifying Equation 12.1 yields

$$\text{EBIT} = Q \times (P - VC) - FC \qquad (12.2)$$

As noted above, the operating breakeven point is the level of sales at which all fixed and variable operating costs are covered—that is, the level at which EBIT equals zero. Setting EBIT equal to zero and solving Equation 12.2 for Q yields

$$Q = \frac{FC}{P - VC} \qquad (12.3)$$

Q is the firm's operating breakeven volume. Let us look at an example.

> **Example**
> Assume that a firm has fixed operating costs of $2,500, the sale price per unit of its product is $10, and its variable operating cost per unit is $5. Applying Equation 12.3 to these data yields
>
> $$Q = \frac{\$2,500}{\$10 - \$5} = \frac{\$2,500}{\$5} = 500 \text{ units}$$
>
> At sales of 500 units the firm's EBIT should just equal zero.

In the example, the firm will have positive EBIT for sales greater than 500 units and negative EBIT, or a loss, for sales less than 500 units. We can confirm this by substituting values above and below 500 units, along with the other values given, into Equation 12.1.

Figure 12.1
Graphic Operating Breakeven Analysis

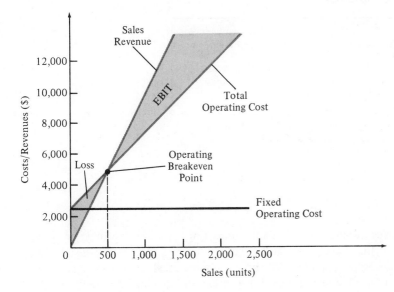

The Graphic Approach

Figure 12.1 presents in graph form the breakeven analysis of the data in the example above. The firm's operating breakeven point is the point at which its *total operating cost,* or the sum of its fixed and variable operating costs, equals sales revenue. At this point EBIT equals zero. The figure shows that a loss occurs when the firm's sales are *below* the operating breakeven point. In other words, for sales of less than 500 units, total operating costs exceed sales revenue and EBIT is less than zero. For sales levels *greater than* the breakeven point of 500 units, sales revenue exceeds total operating costs and EBIT is greater than zero.

Changing Costs and the Operating Breakeven Point

A firm's operating breakeven point is sensitive to a number of variables: fixed operating costs *(FC),* the sale price per unit *(P),* and the variable operating cost per unit *(VC).* The effects of increases or decreases in each of these variables can be readily assessed by referring to Equation 12.3. The sensitivity of the breakeven sales volume *(Q)* to an *increase* in each of these variables in summarized in Table 12.3. As might be expected, the table indicates that an increase in cost *(FC* or *VC)* tends to increase the operating breakeven point, whereas an increase in price per unit *(P)* will decrease the operating breakeven point.

☐ 1   The operating breakeven point will decrease as a result of an increase in either fixed or variable operating costs, or a decrease in the sales price. *(Fable)*
The operating breakeven point will *increase* as a result of an increase in either fixed or variable operating costs, or a decrease in the sales price.

FACT OR FABLE?

Table 12.3
Sensitivity of Operating Breakeven Point to Increases in Key Breakeven Variables

Increase in variable	Effect on operating breakeven point
Fixed operating cost *(FC)*	Increase
Sale price per unit *(P)*	Decrease
Variable operating cost per unit *(VC)*	Increase

NOTE: Decreases in each of the variables shown would have the opposite effect from that indicated on the breakeven point.

Example
Assume that the firm wishes to evaluate the impact of (1) increasing fixed operating costs to $3,000, (2) increasing the sales price per unit to $12.50, (3) increasing the variable operating cost per unit to $7.50, and (4) simultaneously implementing all three of these changes. Substituting the appropriate data into Equation 12.3 yields the following:

$$(1) \text{ Operating breakeven point} = \frac{\$3,000}{\$10 - \$5} = 600 \text{ units}$$

$$(2) \text{ Operating breakeven point} = \frac{\$2,500}{\$12.50 - \$5} = 333\tfrac{1}{3} \text{ units}$$

$$(3) \text{ Operating breakeven point} = \frac{\$2,500}{\$10 - \$7.50} = 1,000 \text{ units}$$

$$(4) \text{ Operating breakeven point} = \frac{\$3,000}{\$12.50 - \$7.50} = 600 \text{ units}$$

Comparing the resulting operating breakeven points to the initial value of 500 units, we can see that, as noted in Table 12.3, the cost increases (actions 1 and 3) raise the breakeven point (600 units and 1,000 units, respectively), whereas the revenue increase (action 2) lowers the breakeven point to $333\tfrac{1}{3}$ units. The combined effect of increasing all three variables (action 4) results in an increased breakeven point of 600 units.

Operating Leverage

operating leverage The potential use of fixed operating costs to magnify the effects of changes in sales on earnings before interest and taxes (EBIT).

Operating leverage results from the existence of *fixed operating costs* in the firm's income stream. Using the structure presented in Table 12.2, **operating leverage** can be defined as the potential use of fixed operating costs to magnify the effects of changes in sales on earnings before interest and taxes (EBIT). The following example illustrates how operating leverage works.

Example

Using the data presented earlier (sales price, $P = \$10$ per unit; variable operating costs, $VC = \$5$ per unit; fixed operating costs, $FC = \$2,500$), Figure 12.2 on page 428 presents the operating breakeven chart originally shown in Figure 12.1. The additional notations on the chart indicate that as the firm's sales increase from 1,000 to 1,500 units (Q_1 to Q_2), its EBIT increases from \$2,500 to \$5,000 ($EBIT_1$ to $EBIT_2$). In other words, a 50 percent increase in sales (1,000 to 1,500 units) results in a 100 percent increase in EBIT. Table 12.4 includes the data for Figure 12.2 as well as relevant data for a 500-unit sales level. Using the 1,000-unit sales level as a reference point, two cases can be illustrated.

Case 1 A 50 percent *increase* in sales (from 1,000 to 1,500 units) results in a 100 percent *increase* in earnings before interest and taxes (from \$2,500 to \$5,000).

Case 2 A 50 percent *decrease* in sales (from 1,000 to 500 units) results in a 100 percent *decrease* in earnings before interest and taxes (from \$2,500 to \$0).

Table 12.4
The EBIT for Various Sales Levels

	Case 2		Case 1
	-50%		$+50\%$
Sales (in units)	500	1,000	1,500
Sales revenue[a]	\$5,000	\$10,000	\$15,000
Less: Variable operating costs[b]	2,500	5,000	7,500
Less: Fixed operating costs	2,500	2,500	2,500
Earnings before interest and taxes (EBIT)	\$ 0	\$ 2,500	\$ 5,000
	-100%		$+100\%$

[a] Sales revenue = \$10/unit × sales in units.

[b] Variable operating costs = \$5/unit × sales in units.

From the above example we see that operating leverage works in both directions. When a firm has fixed operating costs, operating leverage is present. An increase in sales results in a more than proportional increase in earnings before interest and taxes; a decrease in sales results in a more than proportional decrease in earnings before interest and taxes.

Measuring the Degree of Operating Leverage (DOL)

The **degree of operating leverage (DOL)** is the numerical measure of the firm's operating leverage. It can be derived using the following equation:[2]

$$DOL = \frac{\text{percentage change in EBIT}}{\text{percentage change in sales}} \quad (12.4)$$

degree of operating leverage (DOL) The numerical measure of the firm's operating leverage.

[2] The degree of operating leverage also depends on the base level of sales used as a point of reference. The closer the base sales level used is to the operating breakeven point, the greater the operating leverage. *Comparison of the degree of operating leverage of two firms is valid only when the base level of sales used for each firm is the same.*

Figure 12.2
Breakeven Analysis and Operating Leverage

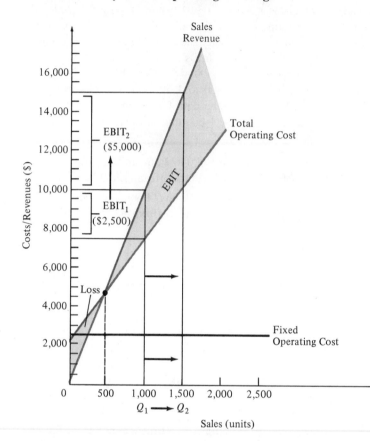

Whenever the percentage change in EBIT resulting from a given percentage change in sales is greater than the percentage change in sales, operating leverage exists. This means that as long as DOL is greater than 1, there is operating leverage.

Example

Applying Equation 12.4 to Cases 1 and 2 in Table 12.4 yields the following results:[3]

$$\text{Case 1: } \frac{+100\%}{+50\%} = 2.0$$

$$\text{Case 2: } \frac{-100\%}{-50\%} = 2.0$$

Since the result is greater than 1, operating leverage exists. For a given base level of sales, the higher the value resulting from applying Equation 12.4, the greater the degree of operating leverage.

[3] Because the concept of leverage is *linear*, positive and negative changes of equal magnitude will always result in equal degrees of leverage when the same base sales level is used as a point of reference. This relationship holds for all types of leverage discussed in this chapter.

A more direct formula for calculating the degree of operating leverage at a base sales level, Q, is shown in Equation 12.5, using the symbols given earlier.[4]

$$\text{DOL at base sales level } Q = \frac{Q \times (P - VC)}{Q \times (P - VC) - FC} \qquad (12.5)$$

Example
Substituting $Q = 1{,}000$, $P = \$10$, $VC = \$5$, and $FC = \$2{,}500$ into Equation 12.5 yields the following result:

$$\text{DOL at 1,000 units} = \frac{1{,}000 \times (\$10 - \$5)}{1{,}000 \times (\$10 - \$5) - \$2{,}500} = \frac{\$5{,}000}{\$2{,}500} = 2.0$$

The use of the formula results in the same value for DOL (2.0) as that found using Table 12.4 and Equation 12.4.[5]

Fixed Costs and Operating Leverage

Changes in fixed operating costs affect operating leverage significantly. This effect can be best illustrated by continuing our example.

Example
Assume that the firm discussed earlier is able to exchange a portion of its variable operating costs for fixed operating costs. This exchange results in a reduction in the variable operating cost per unit from $5 to $4.50 and an increase in the fixed operating costs from $2,500 to $3,000. Table 12.5 presents an analysis similar to that given in Table 12.4 using these new costs. Although the EBIT of $2,500 at the 1,000-unit sales level is the same as before the shift in operating cost structure, Table 12.5 shows that by shifting to greater fixed operating costs, the firm has increased its operating leverage.

With the substitution of the appropriate values into Equation 12.5, the degree of operating leverage at the 1,000-unit base level of sales becomes

$$\text{DOL at 1,000 units} = \frac{1{,}000 \times (\$10 - \$4.50)}{1{,}000 \times (\$10 - \$4.50) - \$3{,}000} = \frac{\$5{,}500}{\$2{,}500} = 2.2$$

Comparing this value to the DOL of 2.0 before the shift to more fixed costs, it is clear that the higher the firm's fixed operating costs relative to variable operating costs, the greater the degree of operating leverage.

---

[4] Technically, the formula for DOL given in Equation 12.5 should include absolute value signs because it is possible to get a negative DOL when the EBIT for the base sales level is negative. Since we assume that the EBIT for the base level of sales is positive, the absolute value signs are not included.

[5] When total sales in dollars—instead of unit sales—are available, the following equation in which TR = dollar level of base sales and TVC = total variable operating costs in dollars can be used:

$$\text{DOL at base dollar sales } TR = \frac{TR - TVC}{TR - TVC - FC}$$

This formula is especially useful for finding the DOL for multiproduct firms. It should be clear that since in the case of a single-product firm $TR = P \times Q$ and $TVC = VC \times Q$, substitution of these values into Equation 12.5 results in the equation given here.

CAREERS IN FINANCE

COMMERCIAL LOAN OFFICER: Evaluating and Responding to Business Loan Requests

"If people really want to know how the local economy is doing, they should talk to people like me." says Bob Haines. As a commercial loan officer for a statewide banking system, Bob, age 30, handles loan requests from small- to medium-size businesses in a large metropolitan area. He knows how much money they need and why they need it: Do they want to borrow to expand their facilities to handle increased business, or do they want to borrow because their sales haven't been as high as anticipated?

Bob's job is to service the bank's commercial customers' financing needs. He evaluates the loan application, helps decide whether to approve the loan, works out the price of the loan, and establishes the repayment schedule. During the term of the loan, Bob may act as informal consultant for a small business client, reviewing its financial health on a regular basis. At the same time, Bob tries to cross sell other bank services.

If Bob has judged correctly, the client complies with the terms of the loan and the stockholders of the bank make money. If Bob's confidence in the business is misplaced, however, the bank may lose funds as well as income. Despite the risk, Bob likes his job. "Every day I'm thinking about committing hundreds of thousands of the bank's dollars," he says, "but I like knowing that my decision counts."

Bob is getting better and better at his specialty, and he's gaining the confidence he needs to sell his loan recommendations to his superiors. "I examine financial statements from businesses all the time," he says. "Most are audited statements prepared by the company's finance department. One of the trickiest parts of my job is getting all the raw data I need to make a decision and then arranging these data so they give a true picture of the company's financial position."

Although Bob has a specialty, he doesn't feel his job is narrow. "I meet lots of people and I call on a variety of businesses. This morning I went to a small publisher, this afternoon I visited a meat packer, and tomorrow morning I'm meeting the officers of a company that launders and cleans uniforms. They all need money for different reasons. That variety keeps my job from becoming routine."

Bob entered the banking world eight years ago when he graduated from college with a finance degree. An entry-level trainee, he eventually worked his way up to the position of manager of a small suburban branch, and then into commercial lending.

What's next in Bob's career? After several years he could become a senior commercial loan officer, and after a number of years, he could become a vice president. Most people at Bob's present level earn between $25,000 and $35,000 a year. With experience, that figure could rise to between $35,000 and $65,000.

What was the hardest thing to learn about his job? Bob thinks it was the need to reserve judgment about a company's loan application until he had all the facts. "A finance degree prepares you for only so much. After that, it's a matter of composure and intuition."

Table 12.5
Operating Leverage and Increased Fixed Costs

	Case 2		Case 1
	−50%		+50%
Sales (in units)	500	1,000	1,500
Sales revenue[a]	$5,000	$10,000	$15,000
Less: Variable operating costs[b]	2,250	4,500	6,750
Less: Fixed operating costs	3,000	3,000	3,000
Earnings before interest and taxes (EBIT)	−$250	$ 2,500	$ 5,250
	−110%		+110%

[a] Sales revenue was calculated as indicated in Table 12.4.

[b] Variable operating costs = $4.50/unit × sales in units.

Financial Leverage

Financial leverage results from the presence of fixed *financial costs* in the firm's income stream. Using the framework in Table 12.1, **financial leverage** can be defined as the potential use of fixed financial costs to magnify the effects of changes in earnings before interest and taxes (EBIT) on the firm's earnings per share (EPS). The two fixed financial costs normally found on the firm's income statement are (1) interest on debt and (2) preferred stock dividends. These charges must be paid regardless of the amount of EBIT available to pay them. The following example illustrates how financial leverage works.

financial leverage The potential use of fixed financial costs to magnify the effects of changes in earnings before interest and taxes (EBIT) on earnings per share (EPS).

Example
A firm expects earnings before interest and taxes of $10,000 in the current year. It has a $20,000 bond with a 10 percent (annual) coupon rate of interest and an issue of 600 shares of $4 (annual dividend per share) preferred stock outstanding. It also has 1,000 shares of common stock outstanding. The annual interest on the bond issue is $2,000 (.10 × $20,000). The annual dividends on the preferred stock are $2,400 ($4.00/ share × 600 shares). Table 12.6 presents the levels of earnings per share resulting from levels of earnings before interest and taxes of $6,000, $10,000, and $14,000 assuming the firm is in the 40 percent tax bracket. Two situations are illustrated in the table.

Case 1 A 40 percent *increase* in EBIT (from $10,000 to $14,000) results in a 100 percent *increase* in earnings per share (from $2.40 to $4.80).

Case 2 A 40 percent *decrease* in EBIT (from $10,000 to $6,000) results in a 100 percent *decrease* in earnings per share (from $2.40 to $0).

Table 12.6
The EPS for Various EBIT Levels

	Case 2		Case 1
	−40%	+40%	
EBIT	$6,000	$10,000	$14,000
Less: Interest (*I*)	2,000	2,000	2,000
Net profits before taxes	$4,000	$ 8,000	$12,000
Less: Taxes (*T* = .40)	1,600	3,200	4,800
Net profits after taxes	$2,400	$ 4,800	$ 7,200
Less: Preferred stock dividends (PD)	2,400	2,400	2,400
Earnings available for common (EAC)	$ 0	$ 2,400	$ 4,800
Earnings per share (EPS)	$\dfrac{\$0}{1,000} = \$0$	$\dfrac{\$2,400}{1,000} = \$2.40$	$\dfrac{\$4,800}{1,000} = \$4.80$
	−100%	+100%	

The effect of financial leverage is such that an increase in the firm's EBIT results in a greater-than-proportional increase in the firm's earnings per share, while a decrease in the firm's EBIT results in a more-than-proportional decrease in EPS.

FACT OR FABLE?   2 Financial leverage results from the existence of fixed financial costs and magnifies the effects of changes in earnings before interest and taxes (EBIT) on the firm's earnings per share (EPS). *(Fact)*

Measuring the Degree of Financial Leverage (DFL)

degree of financial leverage (DFL) The numerical measure of the firm's financial leverage.

The **degree of financial leverage (DFL)** is the numerical measure of the firm's financial leverage. It can be computed in a fashion similar to that used to measure the degree of operating leverage. The following equation presents one approach for obtaining DFL.[6]

$$\text{DFL} = \frac{\text{percentage change in EPS}}{\text{percentage change in EBIT}} \qquad (12.6)$$

Whenever the percentage change in EPS resulting from a given percentage change in EBIT is greater than the percentage change in EBIT, financial leverage exists. This means that whenever DFL is greater than 1, there is financial leverage.

> **Example**
> Applying Equation 12.6 to cases 1 and 2 in Table 12.6 yields
>
> $$\text{Case 1: } \frac{+100\%}{+40\%} = 2.5$$
>
> $$\text{Case 2: } \frac{-100\%}{-40\%} = 2.5$$
>
> In both cases, the quotient is greater than 1, and financial leverage exists. The higher this value, the greater the degree of financial leverage.

A more direct formula for calculating the degree of financial leverage at a base level of EBIT is given by Equation 12.7, using the notation from Table 12.6.[7]

$$\text{DFL at base level EBIT} = \frac{\text{EBIT}}{\text{EBIT} - I - \left(PD \times \dfrac{1}{1 - T}\right)} \qquad (12.7)$$

---

[6] This approach is valid only when the base level of EBIT used to calculate and compare these values is the same. In other words, *the base level of EBIT must be held constant to compare the financial leverage associated with different levels of fixed financial costs.*

[7] Using the formula for DFL in Equation 12.7, it is possible to get a negative value for the DFL if the EPS for the base level of EBIT is negative. Rather than show absolute value signs in the equation, it is instead assumed that the base-level EPS is positive.

Example
Substituting EBIT = $10,000, I = $2,000, PD = $2,400, and the tax rate (T = .40) into Equation 12.7 yields the following result:

$$\text{DFL at \$10,000 EBIT} = \frac{\$10,000}{\$10,000 - \$2,000 - \left(\$2,400 \times \dfrac{1}{1 - .40}\right)}$$

$$= \frac{\$10,000}{\$4,000} = 2.5$$

Notice that the formula given in Equation 12.7 provides a more direct method for calculating the degree of financial leverage than the approach illustrated using Table 12.6 and Equation 12.6.

Total Leverage: The Combined Effect

The combined effect of operating and financial leverage on the firm's risk can be assessed using a framework similar to that used to develop the individual concepts of leverage. This combined effect, or **total leverage,** can be defined as the potential use of fixed costs, both operating and financial, to magnify the effect of changes in sales on the firm's earnings per share (EPS). Total leverage can therefore be viewed as the total impact of the fixed costs in the firm's operating and financial structure.

total leverage The potential use of fixed costs, both operating and financial, to magnify the effect of changes in sales on the firm's earnings per share (EPS).

Example
A firm expects sales of 20,000 units at $5 per unit in the coming year and must meet the following: variable operating costs at $2 per unit; fixed operating costs of $10,000; interest of $20,000; and preferred stock dividends of $12,000. The firm is in the 40 percent tax bracket and has 5,000 shares of common stock outstanding. Table 12.7 presents the levels of earnings per share (EPS) associated with the expected sales of 20,000 units and with sales of 30,000 units.

The table illustrates that as a result of a 50 percent increase in sales (20,000 to 30,000 units), the firm would experience a 300 percent increase in earnings per share (from $1.20 to $4.80). Although not shown in the table, a 50 percent decrease in sales would, conversely, result in a 300 percent decrease in earnings per share. The linear nature of the leverage relationship accounts for the fact that sales changes of equal magnitude in opposite directions result in earnings per share changes of equal magnitude in the corresponding direction. At this point it should be clear that whenever a firm has fixed costs—operating or financial—in its structure, total leverage will exist.

Table 12.7
The Total Leverage Effect

		+50%			
Sales (in units)		20,000	30,000	DOL =	
Sales revenue[a]		$100,000	$150,000		
Less: Variable operating costs[b]		40,000	60,000	$\dfrac{+60\%}{+50\%} = 1.2$	
Less: Fixed operating costs		10,000	10,000		
Earnings before interest and taxes (EBIT)		$ 50,000	$ 80,000		DTL =
			+60%		
Less: Interest		20,000	20,000		$\dfrac{+300\%}{+50\%} = 6.0$
Net profits before taxes		$ 30,000	$ 60,000		
Less: Taxes ($T = .40$)		12,000	24,000		
Net profits after taxes		$ 18,000	$ 36,000	DFL =	
Less: Preferred stock dividends		12,000	12,000		
Earnings available for common		$ 6,000	$ 24,000	$\dfrac{+300\%}{+60\%} = 5.0$	
Earnings per share (EPS)	$\dfrac{\$6{,}000}{5{,}000} = \$1.20$		$\dfrac{\$24{,}000}{5{,}000} = \$4.80$		
		+300%			

[a] Sales revenue = $5/unit × sales in units.

[b] Variable operating costs = $2/unit × sales in units.

Measuring the Degree of Total Leverage (DTL)

degree of total leverage (DTL) The numerical measure of the firm's total leverage.

The **degree of total leverage (DTL)** is the numerical measure of the firm's total leverage. It can be obtained in a fashion similar to that used to measure operating and financial leverage. The following equation presents one approach for measuring DTL.[8]

$$\text{DTL} = \frac{\text{percentage change in EPS}}{\text{percentage change in sales}} \tag{12.8}$$

Whenever the percentage change in EPS resulting from a given percentage change in sales is greater than the percentage change in sales, total leverage exists. This means that as long as the DTL is greater than 1, there is total leverage.

Example
Applying Equation 12.8 to the data in Table 12.7 yields

$$\text{DTL} = \frac{+300\%}{+50\%} = 6.0$$

Since this result is greater than 1, total leverage exists. The higher the value, the greater the degree of total leverage.

---

[8] This approach is valid only when the base level of sales used to calculate and compare these values is the same. In other words, *the base level of sales must be held constant in order to compare the total leverage associated with different levels of fixed costs.*

A more direct formula for calculating the degree of total leverage at a given base level of sales, Q, is given by Equation 12.9,[9] which uses the same notation presented earlier:

$$\text{DTL at base sales level } Q = \frac{Q \times (P - VC)}{Q \times (P - VC) - FC - I - \left(PD \times \dfrac{1}{1 - T}\right)} \quad (12.9)$$

Example

Substituting $Q = 20{,}000$, $P = \$5$, $VC = \$2$, $FC = \$10{,}000$, $I = \$20{,}000$, $PD = \$12{,}000$, and the tax rate ($T = .40$) into Equation 12.9 yields the following result:

DTL at 20,000 units

$$= \frac{20{,}000 \times (\$5 - \$2)}{20{,}000 \times (\$5 - \$2) - \$10{,}000 - \$20{,}000 - \left(\$12{,}000 \times \dfrac{1}{1 - .40}\right)}$$

$$= \frac{\$60{,}000}{\$10{,}000} = 6.0$$

Clearly, the formula used in Equation 12.9 provides a more direct method for calculating the degree of total leverage than the approach illustrated using Table 12.7 and Equation 12.8.

The Relationship of Operating, Financial, and Total Leverage

Total leverage reflects the combined impact of operating and financial leverage on the firm. High operating and high financial leverage will cause total leverage to be high. The opposite will also be true. The relationship between operating and financial leverage is *multiplicative* rather than *additive*. The relationship between the degree of total leverage (DTL) and the degrees of operating (DOL) and financial (DFL) leverage is given by Equation 12.10.

$$\text{DTL} = \text{DOL} \times \text{DFL} \quad (12.10)$$

Example

Substituting the values calculated for DOL and DFL, shown on the right-hand side of Table 12.7, into Equation 12.10 yields

$$\text{DTL} = 1.2 \times 5.0 = 6.0$$

The resulting degree of total leverage (6.0) is the same value as was calculated directly in the preceding section.

---

[9] Using the formula for DTL in Equation 12.9, it is possible to get a negative value for the DTL if EPS for the base level of sales is negative. For our purposes, rather than show absolute value signs in the equation, we instead assume that the base-level EPS is positive.

The Firm's Capital Structure

Capital structure is one of the most complex areas of financial decision making due to its interrelationship with other financial decision variables. In order to achieve the firm's goal of owner wealth maximization, the financial manager must be able to assess the firm's capital structure and understand its relationship to risk, return, and value. This section links together the concepts presented in Chapters 4, 7, 8, and 11 and the discussion of leverage in this chapter.

Types of Capital

capital The long-term funds of the firm; all items on the right-hand side of the firm's balance sheet, excluding current liabilities.

The term **capital** denotes the long-term funds of the firm. All of the items on the right-hand side of the firm's balance sheet, excluding current liabilities, are sources of capital. The simplified balance sheet on page 437 illustrates the basic breakdown of total capital into its two components—debt capital and equity capital.

debt capital All long-term borrowing incurred by the firm.

Debt capital includes all long-term borrowing incurred by the firm. The various types and characteristics of long-term debt will be discussed in detail in Chapter 16. In Chapter 11 the cost of debt was found to be less than the cost of other forms of financing. The relative inexpensiveness of debt capital is due to the fact that the lenders take the least risk of any long-term contributors of capital. Their risk is less than that of others because (1) they have a higher priority of claim against any earnings or assets available for payment, (2) they have a far stronger legal pressure against the company to make payment than do preferred or common stockholders, and (3) the tax-deductibility of interest payments lowers the debt cost to the firm substantially.

equity capital The long-term funds provided by the firm's owners, the stockholders.

Equity capital consists of the long-term funds provided by the firm's owners, the stockholders. Unlike borrowed funds that must be repaid at a specified future date, equity capital is expected to remain in the firm for an indefinite period of time. The two basic sources of equity capital are (1) preferred stock and (2) common stock equity, which includes common stock and retained earnings. As demonstrated in Chapter 11, common stock is typically the most expensive form of equity, followed by retained earnings and preferred stock, respectively. The characteristics of common stock and retained earnings are discussed in Chapter 17; preferred stock is discussed further in Chapter 18.

Our concern here is the relationship between debt and equity capital. Key differences between these two types of capital relative to voice in management, claims on income and assets, maturity, and tax treatment are summarized in Table 12.8. It should be clear that due to its secondary position relative to debt, suppliers of equity capital take greater risk and therefore must be compensated with higher expected returns than suppliers of debt capital.

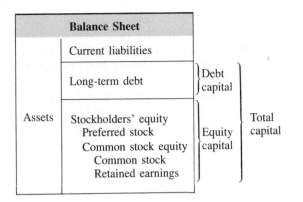

An Agency Problem: Owners Versus Lenders

As noted in Chapter 1, the managers of firms typically act as *agents* of the owners. The owners hire the managers and give them the authority to manage the firm for the owners' benefit. The *agency problem* created by this relationship extends not only to the relationship between owners and managers, but also to the relationship between owners and lenders. This latter problem is due to the fact that lenders provide funds to the firm based upon their expectations for the firm's current and future capital expenditures and capital structure. These factors determine the firm's business and financial risk.

When a lender provides funds to a firm, the interest rate charged is based upon the lender's assessment of the firm's risk. The lender-borrower relationship, therefore, depends on the lender's expectations for the firm's subsequent behavior. If unconstrained, this arrangement creates incentives for the firm to increase its risk without increasing current borrowing costs. The borrowing rates are, in effect, locked-in when the loans are negotiated. After obtaining a loan at a certain rate from a bank or through the sale of bonds, the firm could increase its risk by investing in risky projects or by incurring additional debt. Such action could weaken the lender's position in terms of its claim on the cash flow of the firm. From another point of view, if these risky investment strategies paid

Table 12.8
Key Differences Between Debt and Equity Capital

	Type of Capital	
Characteristic	Debt	Equity
Voice in management[a]	No	Yes
Claims on income and assets	Senior to equity	Subordinate to debt
Maturity	Stated	None
Tax treatment	Interest deduction	No deduction

[a] In default, debtholders and preferred stockholders *may* receive a voice in management; otherwise, only common stockholders have voting rights.

off, the stockholders would benefit since their payment obligations to the lender remain unchanged; the excess cash flows generated by a positive outcome from the riskier action would enhance the value of the firm to its owners. In other words, if the risky investments pay off, the owners receive all the benefits, but if the risky investments do not pay off, the lenders share in the costs.

Clearly, an incentive exists for the managers acting on behalf of the stockholders to "take advantage" of lenders. In order to avoid this type of situation, lenders have developed a variety of techniques for monitoring and controlling the firm's actions. The most

Table 12.9
Debt Ratios for Selected Industries and Lines of Business
(Fiscal Years Ended 6/30/85 through 3/31/86)

Industry or line of business	Debt ratio	Times interest earned ratio
Manufacturing industries		
Books: publishing and printing	63.5%	2.7
Dairy products	62.5	2.9
Electronic computing equipment	52.6	2.6
Fertilizers	61.1	1.7
Iron and steel foundries	58.1	2.8
Jewelry, precious metals	63.2	2.2
Motor vehicles	69.4	2.2
Wines, distilled liquors, liqueurs	66.0	1.6
Women's dresses	53.0	2.9
Wholesaling industries		
Furniture	65.3	3.1
General groceries	66.8	2.3
Hardware and paints	61.8	2.4
Men's and boys' clothing	64.2	2.8
Petroleum products	67.4	2.6
Retailing industries		
Autos, new and used	72.8	3.0
Department stores	57.8	2.2
Radio, television, record players	66.0	2.9
Restaurants	72.2	2.0
Shoes	64.2	2.2
Service industries		
Accounting, auditing, bookkeeping	49.9	7.1
Advertising agencies	73.6	4.4
Auto-repair shops	66.8	2.4
Insurance agents and brokers	80.1	3.4
Physicians	59.4	3.3
Travel agencies	72.9	1.8

SOURCE: *Annual Statement Studies, 1986* (fiscal years ended 6/30/85 through 3/31/86) (Philadelphia: Robert Morris Associates, 1986) Copyright © 1986 by Robert Morris Associates.

NOTE: Robert Morris Associates recommends that these ratios be regarded only as general guidelines and not as absolute industry norms. No claim is made as to the representativeness of their figures.

obvious strategy is to deny subsequent loan requests or to increase the cost of future loans to the firm. Because this strategy is an after-the-fact approach, other controls must be included in the loan agreement. Lenders typically protect themselves by including provisions that limit the firm's ability to significantly alter its business or financial risk. These loan provisions tend to center on issues such as the level of net working capital, asset acquisitions, executive salaries, and dividend payments. (Typical loan provisions are discussed in Chapter 16.) By including appropriate provisions in the loan agreement, the lender can both monitor and control the risk of the firm. The lender thus can protect itself against the adverse consequences of this agency problem and assure itself adequate compensation for risk. Of course, the owners benefit from loan provisions, since by agreeing to constrain their behavior, they can obtain funds at a lower cost.

External Assessment of Capital Structure

Earlier it was shown that *financial leverage* results from the use of fixed-payment financing, such as debt and preferred stock, to magnify return and risk. Debt ratios, which measure, directly and indirectly, the firm's degree of financial leverage were presented in Chapter 4. The direct measures of the degree of indebtedness are the *debt ratio* and the *debt-equity ratio:* The higher these ratios, the greater the firm's financial leverage. The measures of the firm's ability to meet fixed payments associated with debt include the *times interest earned ratio* and the *fixed-payment coverage ratio.* These ratios provide indirect information on leverage. The smaller these ratios, the less able the firm is to meet payments as they come due. In general, low-debt-payment ratios are associated with high degrees of financial leverage. The more risk a firm is willing to take, the greater will be its financial leverage. In theory, the firm should maintain financial leverage consistent with a capital structure that maximizes owners' wealth.

An acceptable degree of financial leverage for one industry or line of business can be highly risky in another due to differing operating characteristics between industries or lines of business. Table 12.9 presents the debt and times interest earned ratios for selected industries and lines of business. Significant industry differences can be seen in these data. For example, the debt ratio for electronic computing equipment manufacturers is 52.6 percent, whereas for auto retailers it is 72.8 percent. Of course, differences in debt positions are also likely to exist *within* an industry or line of business.

The Optimal Capital Structure

A firm's capital structure is closely related to its cost of capital. Many debates over whether an "optimal" capital structure exists are found in the financial literature. This controversy began in the late 1950s, and there is as yet no resolution. Those who believe that an optimal capital structure exists follow the **traditional approach,** while those who believe such a structure does *not* exist are supporters of the **M and M approach,** named for its initial proponents, Franco Modigliani and Merton H. Miller.

To provide some insight into what is meant by an optimal capital structure, we will

traditional approach The theory that an optimal capital structure exists, and that the value of the firm is maximized when the cost of capital is minimized.

M and M approach Named for its initial proponents, Franco Modigliani and Merton H. Miller, the theory that an optimal capital structure does *not* exist.

examine the traditional approach.[10] In the traditional approach to capital structure, *the value of the firm is maximized when the cost of capital is minimized.* Using a simple zero growth valuation model (see Equation 8.7 in Chapter 8), the value of the firm, V, can be defined by Equation 12.11, where EBIT equals earnings before interest and taxes and k_a is the weighted average cost of capital:

$$V = \frac{\text{EBIT}}{k_a} \qquad (12.11)$$

Clearly, if we assume that EBIT is constant, the value of the firm, V, is maximized by minimizing the weighted average cost of capital, k_a.

Cost Functions

Figure 12.3 plots three cost functions—the cost of debt, k_i; the cost of equity, k_s; and the weighted average cost of capital, k_a—as a function of financial leverage measured by the debt ratio (debt-to-total assets). The *cost of debt*, k_i, remains constant as financial leverage increases from zero up to the point where lenders begin to raise interest rates to compensate for the increasing risk. At that point, the cost of debt will increase. The *cost of equity*, k_s, also increases with increasing financial leverage, but much more rapidly than the cost of debt. The faster increase in the cost of equity occurs because, in order to compensate for the higher degree of financial risk, the firm's earnings are discounted at a higher rate as leverage increases.

The *weighted average cost of capital*, k_a, results from a weighted average of the firm's debt and equity capital. At a debt ratio of zero, the firm is 100 percent equity-financed. As debt is substituted for equity and as the debt ratio increases, the weighted average cost of capital declines because the debt cost is less than the equity cost ($k_i < k_s$). As the debt ratio continues to increase, the increased debt cost eventually causes the weighted average cost of capital to rise (after point M in Figure 12.3). This behavior results in a U-shaped, or saucer-shaped, weighted average cost of capital function, k_a.

A Graphic View of the Optimal Structure

optimal capital structure
Under the *traditional approach* to capital structure, the capital structure at which the weighted average cost of capital is minimized, thereby maximizing the firm's value.

Since the maximization of value, V, is achieved when the overall cost of capital, k_a, is at a minimum (see Equation 12.11), the **optimal capital structure** is therefore that at which the weighted average cost of capital, k_a, is minimized. In Figure 12.3 the point M represents the minimum weighted average cost of capital—the point of optimal financial leverage and hence of optimal capital structure for the firm.[11] Generally, the lower the firm's weighted average cost of capital, the greater the difference between the return on a project and this cost, and therefore the greater the owners' return. These increased returns of course contribute to an increase in the firm's value.

---

[10] You may wonder why attention is given only to the traditional approach and not to the Modigliani and Miller approach. The chief reason is that the M and M model is algebraically somewhat rigorous, and it is more important at this level to become familiar with the key concepts that affect managerial decisions than to delve deeply into the theory of finance. Business people tend to believe the traditional as opposed to the M and M approach.

[11] In the Modigliani and Miller approach, the firm's overall cost of capital, when plotted on a graph similar to Figure 12.3, is represented by a horizontal line parallel to the *x*-axis. In other words, *the M and M approach suggests that there is no optimal capital structure* since the method by which the firm finances itself has no effect on its overall cost of capital. These conclusions are logically sound, given M and M's assumptions, but their assumptions are highly unrealistic.

Figure 12.3
The Traditional Approach to Capital Structure

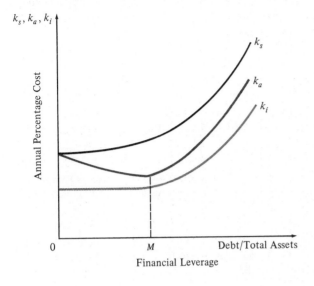

Risk and Capital Structure

A firm's capital structure must be developed with an eye toward risk because it is a direct link to value. Risk comes into play in two ways: (1) The capital structure must be consistent with the business risk, and (2) the capital structure results in a certain level of financial risk. In other words, the prevailing business risk tends to act as an input into the capital structure decision process, the output of which is a certain level of financial risk.

Business Risk

In Chapter 11, *business risk* was defined as the risk to the firm of being unable to cover its operating costs. In general, the greater the firm's operating leverage—the use of fixed operating costs—the higher its business risk. Although operating leverage is an important factor affecting business risk, two other factors also affect it—revenue stability and cost stability. *Revenue stability* refers to the relative variability of the firm's sales revenues. Firms with reasonably stable levels of demand and products with stable prices have stable revenues that result in low levels of business risk. Firms with highly volatile product demand and price have unstable revenues that result in high levels of business risk. *Cost stability* refers to the relative predictability of input prices such as those for labor and materials. The more predictable and stable these input prices are, the lower is the business risk, and vice versa.

Business risk varies among firms, regardless of line of business, and is not affected by capital structure decisions. The level of business risk must be taken as given. The higher a firm's business risk, the more cautious the firm must be in establishing its capital structure. Firms with high business risk therefore tend toward less highly levered capital structures, and vice versa. Here, as in Chapter 11, we will hold business risk constant throughout the discussions that follow. Let us look at an example.

Example

Cooke Company, in preparing to make a capital structure decision, has obtained estimates of sales and the associated levels of EBIT. The firm's forecasting group feels there is a 25 percent chance that sales will total $400,000, a 50 percent chance that sales will total $600,000, and a 25 percent chance that sales will total $800,000. Fixed operating costs total $200,000 and variable operating costs equal 50 percent of sales. These data are summarized and the resulting earnings before interest and taxes (EBIT) calculated in Table 12.10.

The table shows that there is a 25 percent chance that EBIT will be zero, a 50 percent chance that it will be $100,000, and a 25 percent chance that it will equal $200,000. The financial manager must accept as given these levels of EBIT and their associated probabilities when developing the firm's capital structure. These EBIT data effectively reflect a certain level of business risk that captures the firm's sales variability, cost variability, and operating leverage.

Table 12.10
Sales and Associated EBIT Calculations for Cooke Company ($000)

Probability of sales	0.25	0.50	0.25
Sales	$400	$600	$800
Less: Fixed operating costs	200	200	200
Less: Variable operating costs (50% of sales)	200	300	400
Earnings before interest and taxes (EBIT)	$ 0	$100	$200

Financial Risk

The firm's capital structure directly affects its *financial risk,* which is the risk to the firm of being unable to cover required financial obligations. The more fixed-cost financing—debt (including financial leases) and preferred stock—a firm has in its capital structure, the greater its financial leverage and risk. Since the level of this risk and the associated level of return (EPS) are key inputs to the valuation process, the financial manager must estimate the potential impact of alternative capital structures on these factors and, ultimately, on value in order to select the best capital structure. Fund suppliers will, of course, raise the cost of funds as the firm's financial leverage increases.

Example

Cooke Company's current capital structure is as shown:

Current capital structure	
Long-term debt	$ 0
Common stock equity (25,000 shares at $20)	500,000
Total capital	$500,000

Let us assume that the firm is considering seven alternative capital structures. If we measure these structures using the debt ratio, they are associated with ratios of 0, 10, 20, 30, 40, 50, and 60 percent. If (1) the firm has no current liabilities, (2) its capital structure currently contains all equity as shown, and (3) the total amount of capital remains constant[12] at $500,000, the mix of debt and equity associated with the debt ratios just stated would be as noted in Table 12.11. Also shown in the table is the number of shares of common stock remaining outstanding under each alternative.

Associated with each of the debt levels in column 3 of Table 12.11 would be an interest rate that is expected to increase with increases in financial leverage, as reflected in the debt ratio. The level of debt, the associated interest rate (assumed to apply to *all* debt), and the dollar amount of annual interest associated with each of the alternative capital structures is summarized in Table 12.12. Since both the level of debt and the interest rate increase with increasing financial leverage (debt ratios), the annual interest increases as well.

Table 12.11
Capital Structures Associated with Alternative Debt Ratios

Debt ratio (%) (1)	Capital structure ($000)			Shares of common stock outstanding (000) [(4) ÷ $20][b] (5)
	Total assets[a] (2)	Debt [(1) × (2)] (3)	Equity [(2) − (3)] (4)	
0%	$500	$ 0	$500	25.00
10	500	50	450	22.50
20	500	100	400	20.00
30	500	150	350	17.50
40	500	200	300	15.00
50	500	250	250	12.50
60	500	300	200	10.00

[a] Because the firm, for convenience, is assumed to have no current liabilities, its total assets equal its total capital of $500,000.

[b] The $20 value represents the book value per share of common stock equity noted earlier.

[12] This assumption is needed to permit the assessment of alternative capital structures without having to consider the returns associated with the investment of additional funds raised. Concern here will be given only to the *mix* of capital rather than to its investment.

Table 12.12
Level of Debt, Interest Rate, and Dollar Amount of Annual Interest Associated with Cooke Company's Alternative Capital Structures

Capital structure debt ratio (%)	Debt ($000) (1)	Interest rate on *all* debt (%) (2)	Interest ($000) [(1) × (2)] (3)
0%	$ 0	0.0%	$ 0.00
10	50	9.0	4.50
20	100	9.5	9.50
30	150	10.0	15.00
40	200	11.0	22.00
50	250	13.5	33.75
60	300	16.5	49.50

Table 12.13 uses the levels of earnings before interest and taxes (EBIT) and associated probabilities developed in Table 12.10, the number of shares of common stock found in column 5 of Table 12.11, and the interest values calculated in column 3 of Table 12.12 to calculate the earnings per share (EPS) for debt ratios of 0, 30, and 60 percent. A 40 percent tax rate is assumed. Also shown are the resulting expected EPS, the standard deviation of EPS, and the coefficient of variation of EPS associated with each debt ratio.

The resulting statistics from the calculations in Table 12.13, along with the same statistics for the other debt ratios (10, 20, 40, and 50 percent—calculations not shown), are summarized for the seven alternative capital structures in Table 12.14. Because the coefficient of variation measures the risk relative to the expected EPS, it is the preferred risk measure for use in comparing capital structures. As the firm's financial leverage increases, so does its coefficient of variation of EPS. As expected, an increasing level of risk is associated with increased levels of financial leverage.

The relative risk of two of the capital structures evaluated in Table 12.13 (debt ratio = 0% and 60%) can be illustrated by showing the probability distribution of EPS associated with each of them. Figure 12.4 shows these two distributions. While the expected level of EPS increases with increasing financial leverage, so does risk, as reflected in the relative dispersion of each of the distributions. Clearly, the uncertainty of the expected EPS, as well as the chance of experiencing negative EPS, is greater when higher degrees of leverage are employed.

The nature of the risk-return trade-off associated with the seven capital structures under consideration can clearly be observed by plotting the EPS and coefficient of variation relative to the debt ratio. Plotting the data obtained from Table 12.14 results in Figure 12.5. An analysis of the figure shows that as debt is substituted for equity (as the debt ratio increases), the level of earnings per share rises and then begins to fall (graph *a*). The graph demonstrates that the peak earnings per share occur at a debt ratio of 50 percent. The decline in earnings per share beyond that ratio results from the fact that the significant increases in interest are not fully offset by the reduction in the number of shares of common stock outstanding.

Table 12.13
Calculation of EPS for Selected Debt Ratios ($000)

Debt ratio = 0%			
Probability of EBIT	**0.25**	**0.50**	**0.25**
EBIT (Table 12.10)	$ 0.00	$100.00	$200.00
Less: Interest (Table 12.12)	0.00	0.00	0.00
Net profits before taxes	$ 0.00	$100.00	$200.00
Less: Taxes ($T = .40$)	0.00	40.00	80.00
Net profits after taxes	$ 0.00	$ 60.00	$120.00
EPS (25.0 shares, Table 12.11)	$ 0.00	$ 2.40	$ 4.80
Expected EPS[a]		$2.40	
Standard deviation of EPS[a]		$1.70	
Coefficient of variation of EPS[a]		0.71	

Debt ratio = 30%			
Probability of EBIT	**0.25**	**0.50**	**0.25**
EBIT (Table 12.10)	$ 0.00	$100.00	$200.00
Less: Interest (Table 12.12)	15.00	15.00	15.00
Net profits before taxes	($15.00)	$ 85.00	$185.00
Less: Taxes ($T = .40$)	(6.00)[b]	34.00	74.00
Net profits after taxes	($ 9.00)	$ 51.00	$111.00
EPS (17.50 shares, Table 12.11)	($ 0.51)	$ 2.91	$ 6.34
Expected EPS[a]		$2.91	
Standard deviation of EPS[a]		$2.42	
Coefficient of variation of EPS[a]		0.83	

Debt ratio = 60%			
Probability of EBIT	**0.25**	**0.50**	**0.25**
EBIT (Table 12.10)	$ 0.00	$100.00	$200.00
Less: Interest (Table 12.12)	49.50	49.50	49.50
Net profits before taxes	($49.50)	$ 50.50	$150.50
Less: Taxes ($T = .40$)	(19.80)[b]	20.20	60.20
Net profits after taxes	($29.70)	$ 30.30	$ 90.30
EPS (10.00 shares, Table 12.11)	($ 2.97)	$ 3.03	$ 9.03
Expected EPS[a]		$3.03	
Standard deviation of EPS[a]		$4.24	
Coefficient of variation of EPS[a]		1.40	

[a] The procedures used to calculate the expected value, standard deviation, and coefficient of variation were presented in equations 7.2, 7.3, and 7.4, respectively, in Chapter 7.

[b] It is assumed that the firm receives the tax benefit from its loss in the current period as a result of applying the tax loss carryback procedures specified in the tax law.

If we look at the risk behavior as measured by the coefficient of variation, we can see that risk increases with increasing leverage (graph *b*). As noted, a portion of the risk can be attributed to business risk, while that portion changing in response to increasing financial leverage would be attributed to financial risk. Clearly, a risk-return trade-off exists relative to the use of financial leverage. How to combine these risk-return factors into a valuation framework will be addressed later in the chapter. The key point to recognize here is that as a firm introduces more leverage into its capital structure, it will experience increases in both the expected level of return and the associated risk.

Table 12.14
Expected EPS, Standard Deviation, and Coefficient of Variation for Alternative Capital Structures

Capital structure debt ratio (%)	Expected EPS ($) (1)	Standard deviation of EPS ($) (2)	Coefficient of variation of EPS [(2) ÷ (1)] (3)
0%	$2.40	$1.70	0.71
10	2.55	1.88	0.74
20	2.72	2.13	0.78
30	2.91	2.42	0.83
40	3.12	2.83	0.91
50	3.18	3.39	1.07
60	3.03	4.24	1.40

The EBIT–EPS Approach to Capital Structure

EBIT–EPS approach
Involves selecting the capital structure that maximizes earnings per share (EPS) over the expected range of earnings before interest and taxes (EBIT).

The **EBIT–EPS approach** to capital structure involves selecting the capital structure that maximizes earnings per share (EPS) over the expected range of earnings before interest and taxes (EBIT). Here the main emphasis is on the effects of various capital structures on

Figure 12.4
Probability Distribution of EPS for Debt Ratios of 0 and 60 Percent

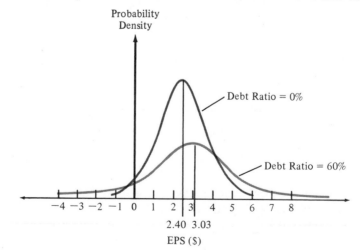

Figure 12.5
Expected EPS and Coefficient of Variation of EPS for Alternative Capital Structures for Cooke Company

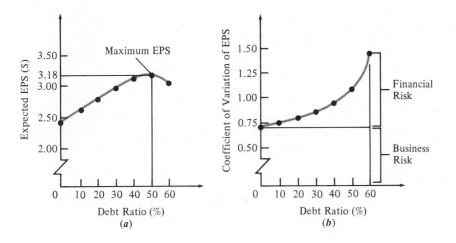

owners' returns. Since one of the key variables affecting the market value of the firm's shares is its earnings, EPS can be used to measure the effect of various capital structures on shareholders' investment.[13]

---

5 The EBIT–EPS approach to capital structure involves selecting the capital structure that maximizes earnings per share (EPS) over the expected range of earnings before interest and taxes (EBIT). *(Fact)*	**FACT OR FABLE?**

Presenting a Financing Plan Graphically

To analyze the effects of a firm's capital structure on the owners' returns, we consider the relationship between earnings before interest and taxes (EBIT) and earnings per share (EPS). A constant level of EBIT—constant business risk—is assumed in order to isolate the impact on returns of the financing costs associated with alternative capital structures (financing plans). EPS is used to measure the owners' returns, which are expected to be closely related to share price.[14]

---

[13] If investors did not require risk premiums (additional returns) as the firm increased the proportion of debt in its capital structure, a strategy involving maximizing earnings per share would also maximize owners' wealth. Since risk premiums increase with increases in financial leverage, the maximization of EPS does *not* assure owners' wealth maximization.

[14] The relationship expected to exist between earnings per share and owners' wealth is not one of cause and effect. As was indicated in Chapter 1, the maximization of profits does not necessarily assure the firm that owners' wealth is also being maximized. Nevertheless, it is expected that the movement of earnings per share will have some effect on owners' wealth since EPS data constitute one of the few pieces of information investors receive, and they often bid the firm's share price up or down in response to the level of these earnings.

The Data Required

To graph a financing plan, at least two EBIT–EPS coordinates are required. The approach for obtaining coordinates can be illustrated by the following simple example.

> **Example**
> Cooke Company data developed earlier can be used to illustrate the EBIT–EPS approach. The EBIT–EPS coordinates can be found by assuming two EBIT values and calculating the EPS associated with them.[15] Such calculations for three capital structures—debt ratios of 0, 30, and 60 percent—for Cooke Company were presented in Table 12.13. Using the EBIT values of $100,000 and $200,000, the associated EPS values calculated there are summarized in Table 12.15.

Plotting the Data

The data summarized for Cooke Company in Table 12.15 can now be plotted on a set of EBIT–EPS axes, as shown in Figure 12.6. Since our concern is only with positive levels of EPS, the graphs have not been extended below the *x*-axis. The figure shows the level of EPS expected for each level of EBIT. For levels of EBIT below the *x*-axis intercept—known as the **financial breakeven point,** where EBIT just covers required financial obligations (EPS = $0)—a loss (negative EPS) would result.

financial breakeven point
The level of EBIT necessary to cover required financial obligations; the level of EBIT at which EPS = $0.

Comparing Alternative Capital Structures

The graphic display of financing plans in a fashion similar to Figure 12.6 can be used to compare alternative capital structures. The following example illustrates this procedure.

> **Example**
> Cooke Company's capital structure alternatives were plotted on the EBIT–EPS axes in Figure 12.6. An analysis of this figure discloses that over certain ranges of EBIT, each capital structure reflects superiority over the others in terms of maximizing EPS. The zero-leverage capital structure (debt ratio = 0 percent) would be superior to either of the other capital structures for levels of EBIT between $0 and $50,000; between $50,000 and $95,500 of EBIT, the capital structure associated with a debt ratio of 30 percent would be preferred; and at a level of EBIT in excess of $95,500, the capital structure associated with a debt ratio of 60 percent would provide the highest earnings per share.[16]

---

[15] A convenient method for finding one EBIT–EPS coordinate is to calculate the *financial breakeven point,* the level of EBIT for which the firm's EPS just equals zero. It is the level of EBIT needed to satisfy all fixed charges—interest *(I)* and preferred stock dividends *(PD)*. The equation for the financial breakeven point is

$$\text{Financial breakeven point} = I + \frac{PD}{1 - T}$$

where *T* is the tax rate. It can be seen that when *PD* = 0, the financial breakeven point is equal to *I*, the annual interest payment.

[16] Algebraic techniques are available for finding the *indifference points* between the capital structure alternatives. These techniques involve expressing each capital structure as an equation stated in terms of earnings per share, setting the equations for two capital structures equal to each other, and solving for the level of EBIT that causes the equations to be equal. Instead of demonstrating these techniques, emphasis here is given to the visual estimation of these points from the graph.

Table 12.15
EBIT–EPS Coordinates for Cooke
Company Selected Capital Structures
(from Table 12.13)

	EBIT	
	$100,000	**$200,000**
Capital structure debt ratio (%)	**Earnings per share (EPS)**	
0%	$2.40	$4.80
30	2.91	6.34
60	3.03	9.03

Considering Risk in EBIT–EPS Analysis

When interpreting EBIT–EPS analysis, it is important to consider the risk of each capital structure alternative. Graphically, the risk of each capital structure can be viewed in light of the *financial breakeven point* (EBIT-axis intercept) and the *degree of financial leverage* reflected in the slope of the capital structure line. The higher the financial breakeven point and the steeper the slope of the capital structure line, the greater the financial risk.[17] Further assessment of risk can be performed using ratios. With increased financial leverage, as measured using the debt ratio, we would expect a corresponding decline in the firm's ability to make scheduled interest payments, as measured using the times interest earned ratio.

Figure 12.6
A Graphic Comparison of Selected Capital Structures for Cooke Company

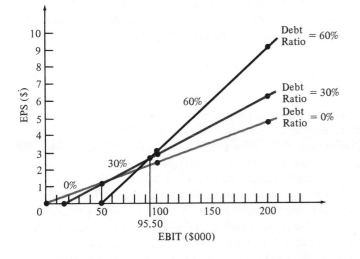

[17] The degree of financial leverage (DFL) is reflected in the slope of the EBIT–EPS function. The steeper the slope, the greater the degree of financial leverage since the change in EPS (*y*-axis) resulting from a given change in EBIT (*x*-axis) will increase with increasing slope, and vice versa.

Example

Reviewing the three capital structures plotted for Cooke Company in Figure 12.6, we can see that as the debt ratio increases, so does the financial risk of each alternative. Both the financial breakeven point and the slope of the capital structure lines increase with increasing debt ratios. If we use the $100,000 EBIT value, the times interest earned ratio (EBIT ÷ interest) for the zero-leverage capital structure is infinity ($100,000 ÷ $0); for the 30 percent debt case it is 6.67 ($100,000 ÷ $15,000); and for the 60 percent debt case it is 2.02 ($100,000 ÷ $49,500). Since lower times interest earned ratios reflect higher risk, these ratios support the earlier conclusion that the risk of the capital structures increases with increasing financial leverage. The capital structure for a debt ratio of 60 percent is more risky than that for a debt ratio of 30 percent, which in turn is more risky than the capital structure for a debt ratio of 0 percent.

Basic Shortcoming of EBIT–EPS Analysis

The most important point to recognize when using EBIT–EPS analysis is that this technique tends to concentrate on *maximization of earnings rather than maximization of owners' wealth*. Although there may be a positive relationship between these two objectives, the use of an EPS-maximizing approach ignores risk. To select the best capital structure, both return (EPS) and risk (via the required return, k_s) must be integrated into a valuation framework in a fashion consistent with the capital structure theory presented earlier.

Choosing the Optimal Capital Structure

Creating a wealth maximization framework for use in making capital structure decisions is not easy. While the two key factors—return and risk—can be used separately to make capital structure decisions, integration of them into a market value context should provide the best results. This section describes the procedures for linking the return and risk associated with alternative capital structures to market value in order to select the best capital structure.

Linkage

To determine its value under alternative capital structures, the firm must find the level of return that must be earned in order to compensate investors and owners for the risk being incurred. That is, the risk associated with each structure must be linked to the required rate of return. Such a framework is consistent with the overall valuation framework developed in Chapter 8 and applied to capital budgeting decisions in Chapter 10.

The required return associated with a given level of financial risk can be estimated in a number of ways. Theoretically, the preferred approach would be to first estimate the beta associated with each alternative capital structure and then use the CAPM framework presented in Chapter 7 (see Equation 7.6) to calculate the required return, k_s. Another approach would involve linking the financial risk associated with each capital structure alternative directly to the required return. Such an approach is similar to the market risk-return function presented in Chapter 10 (see Figure 10.4). It would require estimation

---

PROFILE

FRANK LORENZO:
Empire Builder Flying High

Frank Lorenzo has always been interested in two things: airplanes and investments. As a boy, he decorated his room with airplane models and posters. He bought his first stock at age 15—in TWA. At 32, he became the youngest airline president ever. From small, unprofitable Texas International Airlines, Lorenzo built the largest airline holding company in the nation.

How has he done it? By restructuring corporate entities to his advantage, exacting concessions from workers, slashing costs, exploiting faltering takeover targets, and taking some very big risks.

With friend Robert Carney, Lorenzo formed Jet Capital Corporation in 1969 and began looking for an airline they could afford. In 1971 they bought debt-ridden Texas International. By 1973 they had made TI profitable. Then the ground employees union struck. With characteristic flintiness, Lorenzo drew the costly confrontation out for over four months, during which time planes remained on the ground and nearly all employees were furloughed. When the strike ended on Lorenzo's terms, bitterness lingered. The experience became a pattern.

Deregulation became law in 1978, ending an era of protected routes and guaranteed rates. The cut-throat competition to come would favor the large and the highly efficient. Lorenzo decided to expand quickly. The debt-financed, hostile takeover was born.

In 1980, Lorenzo won a bitter fight with leadership and unions for Continental Airlines. When he gained control, Continental's losses were $100 million per year. Drastic measures were needed. Lorenzo gambled everything, taking the airline into Chapter 11 bankruptcy. His purpose: to get the courts to revoke union contracts and thus cut labor costs up to 50 percent. By the end of 1984, he had won, and Continental was making a profit.

Then came financially troubled Eastern. Lorenzo stepped in during a stalemated contract negotiation between Eastern chairman Frank Borman and union president Charles Bryan. Lorenzo demanded $20 million for making an offer. Then he bid a low $600 million, fixed a 48-hour deadline, and reaped victory in a 2 a.m. voting session. Soon Lorenzo had also acquired Rocky Mountain Airlines and People Express.

Frank Lorenzo did what he set out to do—consolidating separate organizations into a mega-airline to serve many markets. He had also put himself into his most difficult position ever—coping with labor problems, bankruptcy, and a corporate debt of $4.5 billion.

---

of the required return associated with each level of financial risk, as measured by a statistic such as the coefficient of variation of EPS. Regardless of the approach used, one would expect that the required return would be greater the greater the financial risk involved. An example will illustrate.

Example
Cooke Company, using the coefficients of variation of EPS associated with each of the seven alternative capital structures (see column 3 of Table 12.14) as a risk measure, estimated the associated required returns, k_s. These are shown in Table 12.16. As expected, the estimated required return, k_s, increases with increasing risk, as measured by the coefficient of variation of EPS.

Table 12.16
Required Returns for Cooke Company's
Alternative Capital Structures

Capital structure debt ratio (%)	Coefficient of variation of EPS (from column 3 of Table 12.14) (1)	Estimated required return, k_s (%) (2)
0%	0.71	11.5%
10	0.74	11.7
20	0.78	12.1
30	0.83	12.5
40	0.91	14.0
50	1.07	16.5
60	1.40	19.0

Estimating Value

The value of the firm associated with alternative capital structures can be estimated using one of the standard valuation models. If, for simplicity, we assume that all earnings are paid out as dividends, a zero growth valuation model such as that developed in Chapter 8 can be used. The model, originally stated in Equation 8.7, is restated here with EPS substituted for dividends, since in each year the dividends would equal EPS.

$$P_0 = \frac{\text{EPS}}{k_s} \tag{12.12}$$

By substituting the estimated level of EPS and the associated required return, k_s, into Equation 12.12, the value of the firm, P_0, can be estimated.

Example
Returning again to Cooke Company, we can now estimate the value of its stock under each of the alternative capital structures. Substituting the expected EPS (from column 1 of Table 12.14) and the required returns, k_s (from column 2 of Table 12.16), into Equation 12.12 for each of the alternative capital structures results in the share values given in column 3 of Table 12.17. Plotting the resulting share values against the associated debt ratios as shown in Figure 12.7 clearly illustrates that the maximum share value occurs at the capital structure associated with a debt ratio of 30 percent.

Maximizing Value Versus Maximizing EPS

Throughout this text, for a variety of reasons, the goal of the financial manager has been specified as maximizing owners' wealth, not profit. Although there is some relationship

Table 12.17
Calculation of Share Value Estimates Associated with Alternative
Capital Structures for Cooke Company

Capital structure debt ratio (%)	Expected EPS ($) (from column 1 of Table 12.14) (1)	Estimated required return, k_s (from column 2 of Table 12.16) (2)	Estimated share value ($) [(1) ÷ (2)] (3)
0%	$2.40	.115	$20.87
10	2.55	.117	21.79
20	2.72	.121	22.48
30	2.91	.125	23.28
40	3.12	.140	22.29
50	3.18	.165	19.27
60	3.03	.190	15.95

between the level of expected profit and value, there is no reason to believe that profit-maximizing strategies necessarily result in wealth maximization. It is therefore the wealth of the owners as reflected in the estimated share value that should act as the criterion for selecting the best capital structure. A final look at Cooke Company will help to highlight the point.

Figure 12.7
Estimated Share Value and EPS for Alternative Capital Structures
for Cooke Company

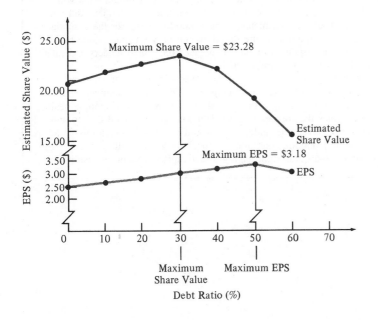

Table 12.18
Additional Factors to Consider When Making Capital Structure Decisions

Factor	Description
Cash flow	The key concern of the firm when considering a new capital structure must center on its ability to generate the necessary cash flows to meet obligations. Cash forecasts reflecting an ability to service debts (and preferred stock) must support any capital structure shift.
Revenue stability	Firms having stable and predictable revenues can more safely undertake highly levered capital structures than can firms with volatile patterns of sales revenue. Firms with increasing revenues (growing sales) tend to be in the best position to benefit from added debt because they can reap the positive benefits of leverage, which tends to magnify the effect of these increases.
Control	A management concerned about control may prefer to issue debt rather than (voting) common stock to raise funds. Of course, if market conditions are favorable, a firm that wanted to sell equity could issue *nonvoting shares* or make a *preemptive offering* (see Chapter 17), allowing each shareholder to maintain proportionate ownership. Generally, only in closely held firms or firms threatened by takeover does control become a major concern in the capital structure decision process.
Contractual obligations	A firm may be contractually constrained with respect to the type or form of funds it subsequently raises. For example, a contract describing conditions of an earlier bond issue might prohibit the firm from selling additional debt except where the claims of holders of such debt are made subordinate to the existing debt. Contractual constraints on the sale of additional stock as well as the ability to distribute dividends on stock might also exist.
Management preferences	Occasionally a firm will impose an internal constraint on the use of debt to limit the firm's risk exposure to a level deemed acceptable to its management. In other words, due to risk aversion, the firm's management constrains the firm's capital structure at a certain level, which may or may not be the true optimum.
External risk assessment	The firm's ability to raise funds quickly and at favorable rates will clearly depend on the external risk assessments of lenders and bond raters. The financial manager must therefore consider the potential impact of capital structure decisions not only on share value but also on published financial statements from which lenders and raters tend to assess the firm's risk.
Timing	At certain points in time, when the general level of interest rates is low, the use of debt financing might be more attractive; when interest rates are high, the sale of stock may become more appealing. Sometimes the sources of both debt and equity capital dry up and become unavailable under what would be viewed as reasonable terms. General economic conditions—especially those of the capital market—can thus significantly affect capital structure decisions.

Example
Further analysis of Figure 12.7 clearly shows that while the firm's profits (EPS) are maximized at a debt ratio of 50 percent, share price is maximized at a 30 percent debt ratio. In this case, the preferred capital structure would be the 30 percent debt ratio. The failure of the EPS-maximization approach to provide a similar conclusion stems from its lack of consideration of risk. Based solely on the quantitative analysis presented, Cooke Company should employ the capital structure resulting in a 30 percent debt ratio.

---

6 | Selecting the capital structure that maximizes profits typically results in a structure consistent with achievement of the firm's wealth maximization goal. *(Fable)*
The capital structure that maximizes profits typically is *not* the same structure that maximizes the owners' wealth since profit maximization does not consider risk.

FACT OR FABLE?

Some Other Important Considerations

Any quantitative analysis of capital structure must be tempered with other important considerations. A nearly endless list of additional factors relative to capital structure decisions could be created; some of the more important of these factors are summarized in Table 12.18.

Summary

- Breakeven analysis is used to measure the level of sales necessary to cover total operating costs. The breakeven point may be calculated algebraically or determined graphically. It is sensitive to changes in fixed costs, selling price, and variable costs.

- Operating leverage is the potential use of fixed operating costs by the firm to magnify the effects of changes in sales on earnings before interest and taxes (EBIT). The higher the fixed operating costs, the greater the operating leverage.

- Financial leverage is the potential use of fixed financial costs by the firm to magnify the effects of changes in earnings before interest and taxes (EBIT) on earnings per share (EPS). The higher the fixed financial costs—typically interest on debt and preferred stock dividends—the greater the financial leverage.

- The total leverage of the firm is the potential use of fixed costs—both operating and financial—to magnify the effects of changes in sales on earnings per share. Total leverage reflects the combined effect of operating and financial leverage.

- A firm's capital structure is determined by the mix of long-term debt and equity it uses in financing its operations. Debt and equity capital differ with respect to voice in management, claims on income and assets, maturity, and tax treatment.

- Lenders typically include appropriate provisions in loan agreements in order to protect against the potential agency problem caused by the relationship between owners and lenders. Capital structure can be externally assessed using the debt ratio, the debt-equity ratio, the times interest earned ratio, and the fixed-payment coverage ratio.

- Under the traditional approach to capital structure, as financial leverage increases, the cost of debt remains constant and then rises, whereas the cost of equity always rises. The optimal capital structure is that for which the weighted average cost of capital is minimized, thereby maximizing share value.

- A firm's capital structure must be consistent with its business risk and results in a certain level of financial risk. In general, the higher the business risk, the lower the financial risk—the less highly levered is the firm's capital structure—and vice versa.

- The EBIT–EPS approach can be used to evaluate various capital structures in light of the returns they provide the firm's owners and their degree of financial risk. Using the EBIT–EPS approach, the preferred capital structure would be the one expected to provide maximum EPS over the firm's expected range of EBIT. Graphically, this approach reflects risk in terms of the financial breakeven point and the slope of the capital structure line.

● The optimal capital structure can be selected by using a valuation model to link return and risk factors. The preferred capital structure would be the one that results in the highest estimated share value—not the highest profits (EPS). Of course, other important nonquantitative factors must also be considered when making capital structure decisions.

Questions

12-1 What is meant by the term *leverage?* How do operating leverage, financial leverage, and total leverage relate to the income statement?

12-2 What is the *operating breakeven point?* How do changes in fixed operating costs, the sale price per unit, and the variable operating cost per unit affect it?

12-3 What is meant by *operating leverage?* What causes it? How is the *degree of operating leverage (DOL)* measured?

12-4 What is meant by *financial leverage?* What causes it? How is the *degree of financial leverage (DFL)* measured?

12-5 What is the general relationship among operating leverage, financial leverage, and the total leverage of the firm? Do these types of leverage complement each other? Why or why not?

12-6 What is a firm's *capital structure?* How do *debt* and *equity* capital differ?

12-7 Briefly describe the *agency problem* that exists between owners and lenders, and explain how this problem is typically resolved. Do all firms agree on the amount of financial leverage that is optimal? Explain.

12-8 Under the traditional approach to capital structure, what happens to the cost of debt and the cost of equity as the firm's financial leverage increases? Describe the resulting weighted average cost of capital. Is there an *optimal capital structure* under this approach?

12-9 Define *business risk* and discuss the three factors that affect it. What is the influence of business risk on a firm's capital structure?

12-10 Explain the *EBIT–EPS approach* to capital structure. Include in your answer a graph indicating the financial breakeven point; label the axes.

12-11 Do *maximizing value* and *maximizing EPS* lead to the same conclusion about the optimal level of financial leverage? If the conclusions are different, what is the cause?

12-12 How might a firm go about determining its optimal capital structure?

12-13 In addition to quantitative considerations, what other factors should a firm consider when making capital structure decisions?

Self-Test Problems

(Solutions on page 464)

ST-1 TOR most recently sold 100,000 units at $7.50 each; its variable operating costs are $3.00 per unit, and its fixed operating costs are $250,000. Annual interest charges total $80,000, and the firm has 8,000 shares of $5 (annual dividend) preferred stock outstanding. It currently has 20,000 shares of common stock outstanding. Assume that the firm has a 40 percent tax rate.

   a. At what level of sales (in units) would the firm break even on operations (i.e., EBIT = $0)?

   b. Calculate the firm's earnings per share (EPS) in tabular form at (1) the current level of sales and (2) a 120,000-unit sales level.

   c. Using the current *$750,000 level of sales as a base,* calculate the firm's degree of operating leverage (DOL).

   d. Using the EBIT *associated with the $750,000 level of sales as a base,* calculate the firm's degree of financial leverage (DFL).

   e. Use the degree of total leverage (DTL) concept to determine the effect (in percentage terms) of a 50 percent increase in TOR's sales from the $750,000 base level on its earnings per share.

ST-2 Newlin Electronics is considering additional financing of $10,000. It currently has $50,000 of 12 percent (annual interest) bonds and 10,000 shares of common stock outstanding. The firm can obtain the financing through a 12 percent (annual interest) bond issue or the sale of 1,000 shares of common stock. The firm has a 40 percent tax rate.

a. Calculate two EBIT–EPS coordinates for each plan.

b. Plot the two financing plans on a set of EBIT–EPS axes.

c. Based on your graph in **b,** at what level of EBIT does the bond plan become superior to the stock plan?

ST-3 The Hawaiian Macadamia Nut Company has collected the following data with respect to its capital structure, expected earnings per share, and required return.

Capital structure debt ratio (%)	Expected earnings per share ($)	Required return, k_s (%)
0%	$3.12	13%
10	3.90	15
20	4.80	16
30	5.44	17
40	5.51	19
50	5.00	20
60	4.40	22

a. Compute the estimated share value using the simplified method described in this chapter (see Equation 12.12).

b. Determine the optimal capital structure based on (1) maximization of expected earnings per share and (2) maximization of share value.

c. Which capital structure do you recommend? Why?

Problems

12-1 **(Breakeven Point—Algebraic)** Kate Rowland wishes to estimate the number of flower arrangements she must sell at $24.95 in order to break even. She has estimated fixed operating costs of $12,350 per year and variable operating costs of $15.45 per arrangement. How many flower arrangements must Kate sell in order to break even on operating costs?

12-2 **(Breakeven Comparisons—Algebraic)** Given the following price and cost data for each of the three firms F, G, and H, answer the questions below.

	F	G	H
Sales price per unit	$ 18.00	$ 21.00	$ 30.00
Variable operating cost per unit	6.75	13.50	12.00
Fixed operating cost	45,000	30,000	90,000

a. What is the operating breakeven point in units for each firm?

b. How would you rank these firms in terms of their risk?

12-3 **(Breakeven Point—Algebraic and Graphic)** Fine Leather Enterprises sells its single product for $129.00 per unit. The firm's fixed operating costs are $473,000 annually and its variable operating costs are $86.00 per unit.

a. Find the firm's operating breakeven point.

b. Label the x-axis "Sales (units)" and the y-axis "Costs/Revenues ($)" and then graph the firm's sales revenue, total operating cost, and fixed operating cost functions on these axes. In addition, label the operating breakeven point and the areas of loss and profit (EBIT).

12-4 **(Breakeven Analysis)** Barry Carter is considering opening a record store. He wants to estimate the number of records he must sell in order to break even. The records will be sold for $6.98 each, variable operating costs are $5.23 per record, and fixed operating costs are $36,750.

a. Find the operating breakeven point.

b. Calculate the total operating costs at the breakeven volume found in **a.**

c. If Barry estimates that at a minimum he can sell 2,000 records *per month,* should he go into the record business?

d. How much EBIT would Barry realize if he sells the minimum 2,000 records per month noted in **c**?

12-5 **(Breakeven Point—Changing Costs/Revenues)** JSG Company publishes *Creative Crosswords.* Last year the book of puzzles sold for $10 with variable operating cost per book of $8 and fixed operating costs of $40,000. How many books must be sold this year to achieve the breakeven point for the stated operating costs, given the following different circumstances?

a. All figures remain the same as last year.

b. Fixed operating costs increase to $44,000; all other figures remain the same as last year.

c. The selling price increases to $10.50; all costs remain the same as last year.

d. Variable operating cost per book increases to $8.50; all other figures remain the same.

e. What conclusions about the operating breakeven point can be drawn from your answers?

12-6 **(EBIT Sensitivity)** Stewart Industries sells its finished product for $9 per unit. Its fixed operating costs are $20,000 and the variable operating cost per unit is $5.

a. Calculate the firm's earnings before interest and taxes (EBIT) for sales of 10,000 units.

b. Calculate the firm's EBIT for sales of 8,000 and 12,000 units, respectively.

c. Calculate the percentage change in sales (from the 10,000-unit base level) and associated percentage changes in EBIT for the shifts in sales indicated in **b.**

12-7 **(Degree of Operating Leverage)** Grey Products has fixed operating costs of $380,000, variable operating costs per unit of $16, and a selling price of $63.50 per unit.

a. Calculate the operating breakeven point in units and sales dollars.

b. Calculate the firm's EBIT at 9,000, 10,000, and 11,000 units, respectively.

c. Using 10,000 units as a base, what are the percentage changes in units sold and EBIT as sales move from the base to the other sales levels used in **b**?

d. Use the percentages computed in **c** to determine the degree of operating leverage (DOL).

e. Use the degree of operating leverage formula to determine the DOL at 10,000 units.

12-8 **(Degree of Operating Leverage—Graphic)** Levin Corporation has fixed operating costs of $72,000, variable operating costs of $6.75 per unit, and a selling price of $9.75 per unit.

a. Calculate the operating breakeven point in units.

b. Compute the degree of operating leverage (DOL) for the following unit sales levels: 25,000, 30,000, 40,000. Use the formula given in the chapter.

c. Graph the DOL figures you computed in **b** (on the *y*-axis) against sales levels (on the *x*-axis).

d. Compute the degree of operating leverage at 24,000 units; add this point to your graph.

e. What principle is illustrated by your graph and figures?

12-9 **(EPS Calculations)** Southland Industries has $60,000 of 16 percent (annual interest) bonds outstanding, 1,500 shares of preferred stock paying an annual dividend of $5 per share, and 4,000 shares of common stock outstanding. Assuming the firm has a 40 percent tax rate, compute earnings per share (EPS) for the following levels of EBIT:

a. $24,600

b. $30,600

c. $35,000

12-10 **(Degree of Financial Leverage)** Northwestern Savings and Loan has a current capital structure consisting of $250,000 of 16 percent (annual interest) debt and 2,000 shares of common stock. The firm pays taxes at the rate of 40 percent.

a. Using EBIT values of $80,000 and $120,000, determine the associated earnings per share (EPS).

b. Using $80,000 of EBIT as a base, calculate the degree of financial leverage (DFL).

c. Rework parts **a** and **b** assuming the firm has $100,000 of 16 percent (annual interest) debt and 3,000 shares of common stock.

12-11 **(DFL and Graphic Display of Financing Plans)** Wells and Associates has EBIT of $67,500. Interest costs are $22,500 and the firm has 15,000 shares of common stock outstanding. Assume a 40 percent tax rate.

a. Use the degree of financial leverage (DFL) formula to calculate the DFL for the firm.

b. Using a set of EBIT–EPS axes, plot Wells and Associates' financing plan.

c. Assuming the firm also has 1,000 shares of preferred stock paying a $6.00 annual dividend per share, what is the DFL?

d. Plot the financing plan including the 1,000 shares of $6.00 preferred stock on the axes used in **b.**

e. Briefly discuss the graphs of the two financing plans.

12-12 **(Integrative—Multiple Leverage Measures)** Play-More Toys produces inflatable beach balls, selling 400,000 balls a year. Each ball produced has a variable operating cost of $.84

and sells for $1.00. Fixed operating costs are $28,000. The firm has annual interest charges of $6,000, preferred dividends of $2,000, and a 40 percent tax rate.

a. Calculate (1) the operating breakeven point in units and (2) the total (including both operating and financial costs) breakeven point in units.

b. Use the degree of operating leverage (DOL) formula to calculate DOL.

c. Use the degree of financial leverage (DFL) formula to calculate DFL.

d. Use the degree of total leverage (DTL) formula to calculate DTL. Compare this to the product of DOL and DFL calculated in **b** and **c**.

12-13 **(Integrative—Leverage and Risk)** Firm R has sales of 100,000 units at $2.00 per unit, variable operating costs of $1.70 per unit, and fixed operating costs of $6,000. Interest is $10,000 per year. Firm W has sales of 100,000 units at $2.50 per unit, variable operating costs of $1.00 per unit, and fixed operating costs of $62,500. Interest is $17,500 per year. Assume that both firms are in the 40 percent tax bracket.

a. Compute the degree of operating, financial, and total leverage for firm R.

b. Compute the degree of operating, financial, and total leverage for firm W.

c. Compare the relative risks of the two firms.

d. Discuss the principles of leverage illustrated in your answers.

12-14 **(Various Capital Structures)** Charter Enterprises currently has $1 million in total assets and is totally equity-financed. It is contemplating a change in capital structure. Compute the amount of debt and equity that would be outstanding if the firm were to shift to one of the following debt ratios: 10; 20; 30; 40; 50; 60; and 90 percent. (The amount of total assets would not change.) Is there a limit to the debt ratio's value?

12-15 **(EPS and Debt Ratio)** Tower Interiors has made the following forecast of sales. Also given is the probability of each level of sales.

Sales	Probability
$200,000	.20
300,000	.60
400,000	.20

The firm has fixed operating costs of $75,000 and variable operating costs of 70 percent of the sales level. The company pays $12,000 in interest per period. The tax rate is 40 percent.

a. Compute the earnings before interest and taxes (EBIT) for each level of sales.

b. Compute the expected earnings per share (EPS), standard deviation of the EPS, and the coefficient of variation of EPS for each level of forecast sales, assuming that there are 10,000 shares of common stock outstanding.

c. Tower has the opportunity to reduce leverage to zero and pay no interest. This will require that the number of shares outstanding be increased to 15,000. Repeat **b** under this assumption.

12-16 (EPS and Optimal Debt Ratio) Williams Glassware has estimated, at various debt ratios, the expected earnings per share and the standard deviation of the earnings per share as follows:

Debt ratio (%)	Earnings per share (EPS)	Standard deviation of EPS
0%	$2.30	$1.15
20	3.00	1.80
40	3.50	2.80
60	3.95	3.95
80	3.95	5.53

a. Estimate the optimal debt ratio based on the relationship between earnings per share and the debt ratio. You will probably find it helpful to graph the relationship.

b. Graph the relationship between the coefficient of variation and the debt ratio. Label the areas associated with business risk and financial risk.

12-17 (EBIT–EPS and Structure) Data-Check is considering two capital structures. The key information follows. Assume a 40 percent tax rate.

Source of capital	Structure A	Structure B
Long-term debt	$100,000 at 16%	$200,000 at 17%
Common stock	4,000 shares	2,000 shares

a. Calculate two EBIT–EPS coordinates for each of the structures by selecting any two EBIT values and finding their associated EPS.

b. Plot the two capital structures on a set of EBIT–EPS axes.

c. Indicate over what EBIT range, if any, each structure is preferred.

d. Discuss the leverage and risk aspects of each structure.

e. If the firm is fairly certain its EBIT will exceed $75,000, which structure would you recommend? Why?

12-18 (EBIT–EPS and Preferred Stock) Litho-Print is considering two possible capital structures, A and B:

Source of capital	Structure A	Structure B
Long-term debt	$75,000 at 16% coupon rate	$50,000 at 15% coupon rate
Preferred stock	$10,000 with an 18% annual dividend	$15,000 with an 18% annual dividend
Common stock	8,000 shares	10,000 shares

a. Calculate two EBIT–EPS coordinates for each of the structures.

b. Graph the two capital structures on the same set of EBIT–EPS axes.

c. Discuss the leverage and risk associated with each of the structures.

d. Over what range of EBIT would each structure be preferred?

e. Which structure would you recommend if the firm expects its EBIT to be $35,000? Explain.

12-19 **(Integrative—Optimal Capital Structure)** Nelson Corporation has made the following forecast of sales, with the associated probability of occurrence noted.

Sales	Probability
$200,000	.20
300,000	.60
400,000	.20

The company has fixed operating costs of $100,000 per year, and variable operating costs represent 40 percent of sales. The existing capital structure consists of 25,000 shares of common stock that have a $10 per share book value. No other capital items are outstanding. The marketplace has assigned the following discount rates to risky earnings per share.

Coefficient of variation of EPS	Estimated required return, k_s (%)
.43	15%
.47	16
.51	17
.56	18
.60	22
.64	24

The company is contemplating *shifting its capital structure* by substituting debt in the capital structure for common stock. Three different debt ratios are under consideration, given here with the estimate of the required interest rate on *all* the debt.

Debt ratio (%)	Interest rate on *all* debt
20%	10%
40	12
60	14

The tax rate is 40 percent. The market value of the equity for a levered firm can be found using the simplified method (see Equation 12.12).

a. Calculate the expected earnings per share (EPS), the standard deviation of EPS, and the coefficient of variation of EPS for the three proposed capital structures.

b. Determine the optimal capital structure, assuming (1) maximization of earnings per share and (2) maximization of share value.

c. Construct a graph (similar to Figure 12.7) showing the relationships in **b.** (*Note:* You will probably have to sketch the lines, since you have only three data points.)

12-20 (Integrative—Optimal Capital Structure) Country Textiles, which has fixed operating costs of $300,000 and variable operating costs equal to 40 percent of sales, has made the following three sales estimates, with their probabilities noted.

Sales	Probability
$ 600,000	.30
900,000	.40
1,200,000	.30

The firm wishes to analyze five possible capital structures—0, 15, 30, 45, and 60 percent debt ratios. The firm's total assets of $1 million are assumed constant. Its common stock is valued at $25 per share, and the firm is in the 40 percent tax bracket. The following additional data has been gathered for use in analyzing the five capital structures under consideration.

Capital structure debt ratio (%)	Cost of debt, k_i (%)	Required return, k_s (%)
0%	0.0%	10.0%
15	8.0	10.5
30	10.0	11.6
45	13.0	14.0
60	17.0	20.0

a. Calculate the level of EBIT associated with each of the three levels of sales.

b. Calculate the amount of debt, the amount of equity, and the number of shares of common stock outstanding for each of the capital structures being considered.

c. Calculate the annual interest on the debt under each of the capital structures being considered. (*Note:* The cost of debt, k_i, is the interest rate applicable to *all* debt associated with the corresponding debt ratio.)

d. Calculate the EPS associated with each of the three levels of EBIT calculated in **a** for each of the five capital structures being considered.

e. Calculate the (1) expected EPS, (2) standard deviation of EPS, and (3) coefficient of variation of EPS for each of the capital structures, using your findings in **d.**

f. Plot the EPS and coefficient of variation of EPS against the capital structures (*x*-axis) on separate sets of axes and comment on the return and risk relative to capital structure.

g. Using the EBIT–EPS data developed in **d,** plot the 0, 30, and 60 percent capital structures on the same set of EBIT–EPS axes and discuss the ranges over which each is preferred. What is the major problem with the use of this approach?

h. Using the valuation model given in Equation 12.12 and your findings in **e,** estimate the share value for each of the capital structures being considered.

> **i.** Compare and contrast your findings in **f** and **h.** Which structure is preferred if the goal is to maximize EPS? Which structure is preferred if the goal is to maximize value? Which capital structure do you recommend? Explain.

Solutions to Self-Test Problems

ST-1 **a.** $Q = \dfrac{FC}{P - VC}$

$$= \frac{\$250,000}{\$7.50 - \$3.00} = \frac{\$250,000}{\$4.50} = \underline{\underline{55,556 \text{ units}}}$$

b.

			+20%	
Sales (in units)		100,000		120,000
Sales revenue (units × $7.50/unit)		$750,000		$900,000
Less: Variable operating costs (units × $3.00/unit)		300,000		360,000
Less: Fixed operating costs		250,000		250,000
Earnings before interest and taxes (EBIT)		$200,000		$290,000
Less: Interest		80,000	+45%	80,000
Net profits before taxes		$120,000		$210,000
Less: Taxes (T = .40)		48,000		84,000
Net profits after taxes		$ 72,000		$126,000
Less: Preferred dividends (8,000 shares × $5.00/share)		40,000		40,000
Earnings available for common		$ 32,000		$ 86,000
Earnings per share (EPS)	$32,000/20,000 = $1.60/share		$86,000/20,000 = $4.30/share

+169%

c. $\text{DOL} = \dfrac{\% \text{ change in EBIT}}{\% \text{ change in sales}} = \dfrac{+45\%}{+20\%} = \underline{\underline{2.25}}$

d. $\text{DFL} = \dfrac{\% \text{ change in EPS}}{\% \text{ change in EBIT}} = \dfrac{+169\%}{+45\%} = \underline{\underline{3.76}}$

e. $\text{DTL} = \text{DOL} \times \text{DFL}$
$$= 2.25 \times 3.76 = 8.46$$

Using other DTL formula:

$$\text{DTL} = \frac{\% \text{ change in EPS}}{\% \text{ change in sales}}$$

$$8.46 = \frac{\% \text{ change in EPS}}{+50\%}$$

% change in EPS = 8.46 × .50 = 4.23 = $\underline{\underline{+423\%}}$

ST-2

	Data Summary for Alternative Plans	
Source of Capital	**Plan A (Bond)**	**Plan B (Stock)**
Long-term debt	$60,000 at 12% annual interest	$50,000 at 12% annual interest
Annual interest =	.12 × $60,000 = $7,200	.12 × $50,000 = $6,000
Common stock	10,000 shares	11,000 shares

a.

	Plan A (Bond)		**Plan B (Stock)**	
EBIT*	$30,000	$40,000	$30,000	$40,000
Less: Interest	7,200	7,200	6,000	6,000
Net profits before taxes	$22,800	$32,800	$24,000	$34,000
Less: Taxes ($T = .40$)	9,120	13,120	9,600	13,600
Net profits after taxes	$13,680	$19,680	$14,400	$20,400
EPS (10,000 shares)	$1.37	$1.97		
(11,000 shares)			$1.31	$1.85

* Values were arbitrarily selected; other values could have been utilized.

	Coordinates	
	EBIT	
	$30,000	**$40,000**
Financing plan	**Earnings per share (EPS)**	
A (Bond)	$1.37	$1.97
B (Stock)	1.31	1.85

b.

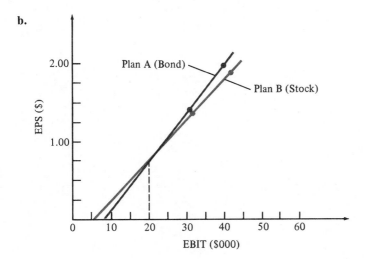

c. The bond plan (Plan B) becomes superior to the stock plan (Plan A) at *around $20,000* of EBIT as represented by the dashed vertical line in the figure in **b** above. (*Note:* The actual point is $19,200 which was determined algebraically using techniques not described in this text.)

ST-3 a.

Capital structure debt ratio (%)	Expected EPS ($) (1)	Required return, k_s (2)	Estimated share value ($) [(1) ÷ (2)] (3)
0%	$3.12	.13	$24.00
10	3.90	.15	26.00
20	4.80	.16	30.00
30	5.44	.17	32.00
40	5.51	.19	29.00
50	5.00	.20	25.00
60	4.40	.22	20.00

b. Using the table in **a** above:
  (1) Maximization of EPS: *40 percent debt ratio*, EPS = $5.51/share (see column 1).
  (2) Maximization of share value: *30 percent debt ratio*, share value = $32.00 (see column 3).

c. Recommend *30 percent debt ratio* since it results in the maximum share value and is therefore consistent with the firm's goal of owner wealth maximization.

O'Grady Apparel Company

O'Grady Apparel Company was founded 135 years ago when an Irish merchant named Garrett O'Grady landed in Los Angeles with an inventory of heavy canvas, which he hoped to sell for tents and wagon covers to miners headed for the California goldfields. Instead, however, he turned to the sale of harder-wearing clothing.

Today, the O'Grady Apparel Company is a small manufacturer of fabrics and clothing whose stock is traded on the over-the-counter exchange. In 1988, the Los Angeles-based company experienced sharp increases in both domestic and European markets resulting in record earnings. Sales rose from $15.9 million in 1987 to $18.3 million in 1988 with earnings per share of $3.28 and $3.84, respectively.

The European sales represented 29 percent of total sales in 1988, up from 24 percent the year before and only 3 percent in 1983, one year after foreign operations were launched. Although foreign sales represent nearly one-third of total sales, the growth in the domestic market is expected to affect the company most markedly. In 1989 management expects sales to surpass $21 million, while earnings per share are expected to rise to $4.40. (Selected income statement items are presented in Table 1.)

Because of the recent growth, Margaret Jennings, the corporate treasurer, is concerned that available funds are not being used to their fullest. The projected $1,300,000 of internally-generated 1989 funds are expected to be insufficient to meet the company's expansion needs. Management has set a policy to maintain the current capital structure proportions of 25 percent long-term debt, 10 percent preferred stock, and 65 percent common stock equity for at least the next three years. In addition, it plans to pay out about 40 percent of its earnings as dividends. Total capital expenditures are yet to be determined.

Ms. Jennings has been presented several competing investment opportunities by division and product managers. However, since funds are limited, choices of which projects to accept must be made. The investment opportunities schedule (IOS) is shown in Table 2. In order to analyze the effect of the increased financing requirements on the weighted average cost of capital (WACC), Ms. Jennings contacted a leading investment banking firm which provided the financing cost information given in Table 3. The firm is in the 40 percent tax bracket.

Table 1
Selected Income Statement Items

	1986	1987	1988	Projected 1989
Net sales	$13,860,000	$15,940,000	$18,330,000	$21,080,000
Net profits after taxes	1,520,000	1,750,000	2,020,000	2,323,000
Earnings per share (EPS)	2.88	3.28	3.84	4.40
Dividends per share	1.15	1.31	1.54	1.76

Table 2
Investment Opportunities Schedule (IOS)

Investment opportunity	Internal rate of return (IRR)	Initial investment
A	21%	$400,000
B	19	200,000
C	24	700,000
D	27	500,000
E	18	300,000
F	22	600,000
G	17	500,000

Table 3
Financing Cost Data

Long-term debt: The firm can raise $700,000 of additional debt by selling 10-year, $1,000, 12 percent annual interest rate bonds to net $970 after flotation costs. Any debt in excess of $700,000 will have a before-tax cost, k_d, of 18 percent.
Preferred stock: Preferred stock, regardless of the amount sold, can be issued with a $60 par value, 17 percent annual dividend rate, and will net $57 per share after flotation costs.
Common stock equity: The firm expects its dividends and earnings to continue to grow at a constant rate of 15 percent per year. The firm's stock is currently selling for $20 per share. The firm expects to have $1,300,000 of available retained earnings. Once the retained earnings have been exhausted the firm can raise additional funds by selling new common stock, netting $16 per share after flotation costs.

Required
1. Over the relevant ranges noted in the following table, calculate the after-tax cost of each source of financing needed to complete the table.

Source of capital	Range of new financing	After-tax cost (%)
Long-term debt	$0–$700,000	—
	$700,000 and above	—
Preferred stock	$0 and above	—
Common stock equity	$0–$1,300,000	—
	$1,300,000 and above	—

2. **a.** Determine the breaking points associated with each source of capital.
   b. Using the breaking points developed in **a,** determine each of the ranges of *total* new financing over which the firm's weighted average cost of capital (WACC) remains constant.
   c. Calculate the weighted average cost of capital for each range of total new financing.

3. **a.** Using your findings in **2.c** above with the investment opportunities schedule (IOS), draw the firm's weighted marginal cost of capital (WMCC) function and IOS on the same set of total new financing or investment (x-axis)–weighted average cost of capital and IRR (y-axis) axes.

    b. Which, if any, of the available investments would you recommend the firm accept? Explain your answer.

4. **a.** Assuming the specific financing costs do not change, what effect would a shift to a more highly levered capital structure consisting of 50 percent long-term debt, 10 percent preferred stock, and 40 percent common stock have on your findings above? (Note: Rework **2** and **3** above using these capital structure weights.)

    b. Which capital structure—the original one or this one—seems better? Why?

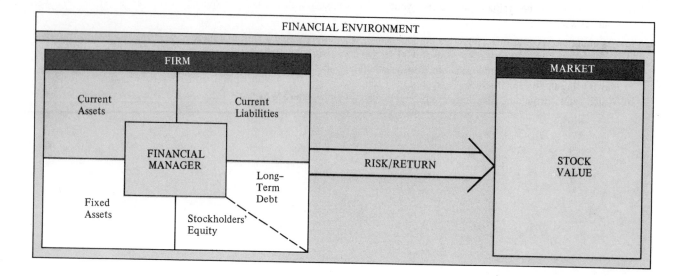

The Management of Working Capital

CHAPTER 13

Working Capital and Short-Term Financing

FACT OR FABLE?

Are the following statements fact *(true)* or fable *(false)?*

1

In addition to its common definition of current assets minus current liabilities, net working capital can be defined as the portion of current assets financed with short-term funds.

2

Holding the level of total assets constant, an increase in the ratio of current liabilities to total assets would result in a decrease in both profit and risk.

3

Using the high-cost, low-risk conservative financing strategy, the firm finances all projected funds requirements with long-term funds and uses short-term funds to meet unexpected cash needs.

4

When the cost of forgoing a cash discount is greater than the cost of short-term bank borrowing, the firm should take the cash discount.

5

Banks lend unsecured short-term funds through a single-payment note, a line of credit, or a revolving credit agreement—all of which charge interest on a floating-rate basis tied to the prime rate of interest.

6

The use of accounts receivable or inventory as collateral for short-term loans makes them less risky than unsecured loans, thereby resulting in a lower rate of interest.

Many lending institutions look at assets when determining credit limits, but who would consider charcoal briquets or automotive parts as assets? Only an asset-based lender. An asset-based lender (ABL) can provide a unique type of loan to a company unable to get financing from more conventional sources.

While many ABLs have been bought out by banks, some have remained independent. Foothill Capital Corporation is one of the largest independent ABLs. Foothill has made deals with companies like the Los Angeles Lakers and MacGregor's Sporting Goods, both with unique assets as collateral. Foothill may also use receivables as collateral to make a deal more secure.

ABLs also assign low appraisal values to collateral that might be hard to move, such as the baseball hats that MacGregor's offered as collateral. An agreement may be made in advance with someone like concession stand owners to buy the goods at a bargain price in the event of liquidation.

Clearly, these debts carry a large risk, and the ABLs like Foothill charge accordingly. Their fee is usually several percent over the prime rate, including large fees for origination, collateral management, and other services.

Foothill has also assisted many companies in and out of reorganization proceedings under the bankruptcy laws. By lending money to firms that had poor financial outlooks and were unable to secure conventional loans, Foothill gave them an opportunity to reorganize. This was the case with United Press International, Inc. (UPI). As a major creditor, Foothill had the option to liquidate the failing company and recover their money. However, confident of the new management and the company's prospect for a turnaround, Foothill stood by the company when it filed for reorganization. With the new financing from Foothill, UPI experienced an amazing cash-flow reversal.

While ABLs are clearly an important and interesting type of lender, they are only one of many possible sources of short-term financing available to firms in need of funds to support seasonal working capital needs. This chapter presents the fundamentals of working capital management and describes the role and sources of short-term financing available to the firm.

Working Capital Fundamentals

An important responsibility of the financial manager is overseeing the firm's day-to-day financial activities. This area of finance, known as **working capital management,** is concerned with management of the firm's current accounts, which include current assets and current liabilities. In U.S. manufacturing firms, current assets account for about 40 percent of total assets; current liabilities represent about 25 percent of total financing. It is therefore not surprising that managing working capital is one of the most important and time-consuming activities of the financial manager.

working capital management Management of the firm's current accounts, which include current assets and current liabilities.

473

The goal of the financial manager is to achieve a balance between profit and risk that maximizes the firm's value by managing each of the firm's current assets (cash, marketable securities, accounts receivable, and inventory) and current liabilities (accounts payable, notes payable, and accruals). Current liabilities represent the firm's **short-term financing** since they include all debts of the firm that come due (must be paid) in one year or less. Here attention is first given to the basic relationship between current assets and current liabilities, and then the key features of the major sources of short-term financing are described. Subsequent chapters consider the management of current assets.

short-term financing All debts of the firm that come due (must be paid) in one year or less.

net working capital Current assets minus current liabilities; alternatively, the portion of a firm's current assets financed with *long-term funds*.

long-term funds The sum of the firm's long-term debt and stockholders' equity.

Net Working Capital

As noted in Chapter 4, **net working capital** is commonly defined as the difference between the firm's current assets and its current liabilities. Alternatively it can be defined as the portion of the firm's current assets financed with **long-term funds**—the sum of long-term debt and stockholders' equity. Since current liabilities represent the firm's sources of short-term funds, as long as current assets exceed current liabilities, the amount of the excess must be financed with long-term funds.

FACT OR FABLE?

1 In addition to its common definition of current assets minus current liabilities, net working capital can be defined as the portion of current assets financed with short-term funds. *(Fable)*

In addition to its common definition of current assets minus current liabilities, net working capital can be defined as the portion of current assets financed with *long-term funds*.

When current assets exceed current liabilities, the firm has *positive net working capital*. In general, the greater the margin by which a firm's current assets cover its short-term obligations (current liabilities), the better able it will be to pay its bills as they come due. This relationship results from the fact that current assets are sources of *cash inflow*, whereas current liabilities are sources of *cash outflow*. The cash outflows resulting from payment of current liabilities are relatively predictable. What is difficult to predict are the cash inflows. The more predictable its cash inflows, the less net working capital a firm may require. Because most firms are unable to match cash inflows to outflows, sources of inflow (current assets) that more than cover outflows (current liabilities) are necessary. Let us look at an example.

Example
For Nicholson Company, which has the current position given in Table 13.1, the following situation may exist. All $600 of the firm's accounts payable, plus $200 of its notes payable and $100 of accruals, are due at the end of the current period. The $900 in outflows is certain; how the firm will cover these outflows is not certain. The firm can be sure that $700 will be available since it has $500 in cash and $200 in marketable securities, which can easily be converted into cash. The remaining $200 must come from the collection of accounts receivable, the sale of inventory for cash, or both.[1]

---

[1] A sale of inventory for credit would show up as a new account receivable, which could not be easily converted into cash. Only a *cash sale* will guarantee the firm that its bill-paying ability during the period of the sale has been enhanced.

However, the firm cannot be sure when either the collection of an account receivable or a cash sale will occur. Generally, the more accounts receivable and inventories on hand, the greater the probability that some of these items will be converted into cash.[2] Thus a certain level of net working capital is often recommended to ensure the firm's ability to pay bills. Nicholson Company has $1,100 of net working capital (current assets minus current liabilities, or $2,700 − $1,600), which will most likely be sufficient to cover its bills. Its current ratio of 1.69 (current assets divided by current liabilities, or $2,700 ÷ $1,600) should provide sufficient liquidity as long as its accounts receivable and inventories remain relatively active.

Table 13.1
The Current Position of Nicholson Company

Current assets		Current liabilities	
Cash	$ 500	Accounts payable	$ 600
Marketable securities	200	Notes payable	800
Accounts receivable	800	Accruals	200
Inventories	1,200	Total	$1,600
Total	$2,700		

The Trade-Off Between Profitability and Risk

A trade-off exists between a firm's profitability and its risk. **Profitability,** in this context, is the relationship between revenues and costs. A firm's profits can be increased in two ways: (1) by increasing revenues or (2) by decreasing costs. **Risk** is the probability that the firm will be unable to pay its bills as they come due. A firm that cannot pay its bills is said to be **technically insolvent.** The risk of becoming technically insolvent is commonly measured using either the current ratio or the amount of net working capital. In this chapter the latter measure will be used. It is assumed that the *greater the amount of net working capital a firm has, the less at risk the firm is.* In other words, the more net working capital, the more liquid the firm, and therefore the less likely it is to become technically insolvent.

In evaluating the profitability-risk trade-off, we assume (1) that the firm under consideration is a *manufacturing firm,* (2) that the firm *earns more from its fixed, or earning, assets than from its current assets,* and (3) that *current liabilities are a cheaper form of financing than long-term funds,* which are costly. Using these assumptions, the impact of changes in current assets and changes in current liabilities on the profitability-risk trade-off can be demonstrated.

profitability The relationship between revenues and costs.

risk The probability that a firm will be unable to pay its bills as they come due.

technically insolvent The inability of a firm to pay its bills as they are due.

Changes in Current Assets

The effects of changing the level of the firm's current assets on its profitability-risk trade-off can be demonstrated using the ratio of current assets to total assets. This ratio indicates the *percentage of total assets* that is current. Assuming that the level of total

---

[2] It should be recognized that levels of accounts receivable or inventory can be too high, reflecting certain management inefficiencies. Acceptable levels for any firm can be calculated. The efficient management of accounts receivable and inventory is discussed in Chapter 15.

Table 13.2
Effects of Changing Ratios on Profits and Risk

Ratio	Change in ratio	Effect on profit	Effect on risk
Current assets / Total assets	Increase Decrease	Decrease Increase	Decrease Increase
Current liabilities / Total assets	Increase Decrease	Increase Decrease	Increase Decrease

assets remains unchanged,[3] the effects on both profitability and risk of an increase or decrease in this ratio are summarized at the top of Table 13.2. When the ratio increases, profitability decreases because current assets are less profitable than fixed assets. In turn, however, the risk of technical insolvency decreases because the increase in current assets increases net working capital. The opposite effects on profit and risk result from a decrease in the ratio.

Changes in Current Liabilities

The effects of changing the level of the firm's current liabilities on its profitability-risk trade-off can be demonstrated using the ratio of current liabilities to total assets. This ratio indicates the percentage of total assets that has been financed with current liabilities. Assuming that total assets remain unchanged, the effects on both profitability and risk of an increase or decrease in the ratio are summarized at the bottom of Table 13.2. When the ratio increases, profitability increases because the firm uses more of the less expensive current-liability financing and less long-term financing. The risk of technical insolvency also increases because the increase in current liabilities in turn decreases net working capital. The opposite effects on profit and risk result from a decrease in the ratio.

FACT OR FABLE?   2 Holding the level of total assets constant, an increase in the ratio of current liabilities to total assets would result in a decrease in both profit and risk. *(Fable)*
Holding the level of total assets constant, an increase in the ratio of current liabilities to total assets would result in an *increase in both profit and risk.*

Working Capital Strategies

One of the most important decisions that must be made with respect to current assets and liabilities is how current liabilities will be used to finance current assets. The amount of current liabilities available is limited by the dollar amount of purchases in the case of accounts payable, by the dollar amount of accrued liabilities in the case of accruals, and

---

[3] The level of total assets is assumed *constant* in this and the following discussion in order to isolate the effect of changing asset and financing mixes on the firm's profitability and risk.

by the amount of seasonal borrowing considered acceptable by lenders in the case of notes payable. Lenders make short-term loans to allow a firm to finance seasonal buildups of accounts receivable or inventory. *They generally do not lend short-term money for long-term uses.*[4]

There are two basic strategies—the aggressive strategy and the conservative strategy—for determining an appropriate mix of short-term (current liability) and long-term financing. Before discussing the cost and risk considerations of each of these strategies, it is helpful to consider the permanent and seasonal components of the firm's financing need. In these discussions the alternate definition that defines *net working capital* as *the portion of current assets financed with long-term funds* is applied.

The Firm's Financing Need

The firm's financing requirements can be separated into a permanent and a seasonal need. The **permanent need,** which consists of fixed assets plus the permanent portion of the firm's current assets, remains unchanged over the year; the **seasonal need,** which is attributable to the existence of certain temporary current assets, varies over the year. The relationship between current and fixed assets and permanent and seasonal funds requirements can be illustrated graphically with the aid of a simple example.

permanent need Financing requirements for the firm's fixed assets plus the permanent portion of the firm's current assets; these requirements remain unchanged over the year.

seasonal need Financing requirements for temporary current assets, which vary throughout the year.

Example

Nicholson Company's estimate of current, fixed, and total asset requirements on a monthly basis for the coming year is given in columns 1, 2, and 3 of Table 13.3. Note that the relatively stable level of total assets over the year reflects, for convenience, an absence of growth by the firm. Columns 4 and 5 present a breakdown of the total requirement into its permanent and seasonal components. The permanent component (column 4) is the lowest level of total funds required during the period; the seasonal portion is the difference between the total funds requirement (i.e., total assets) for each month and the permanent funds requirement.

By comparing the firm's fixed assets (column 2) to its permanent funds requirement (column 4), it can be seen that the permanent funds requirement exceeds the firm's level of fixed assets. This result occurs because *a portion of the firm's current assets are permanent,* since they are apparently always being replaced. The size of the permanent component of current assets is $800 for Nicholson Company. This value represents the base level of current assets that remains on the firm's books throughout the entire year. This value can also be found by subtracting the level of fixed assets from the permanent funds requirement ($13,800 − $13,000 = $800). The relationships presented in Table 13.3 are depicted graphically in Figure 13.1.

An Aggressive Financing Strategy

The **aggressive financing strategy** requires that the firm finance its seasonal needs with short-term funds and its permanent needs with long-term funds. Short-term borrowing is geared to the actual need for funds. In other words, the aggressive strategy involves a

aggressive financing strategy Plan by which the firm finances its seasonal needs with short-term funds and its permanent needs with long-term funds.

---

[4] The rationale for, techniques of, and parties to short-term business loans are discussed in detail later in this chapter. The primary sources of short-term loans to businesses, commercial banks, make these loans *only for seasonal or self-liquidating purposes* such as temporary buildups of accounts receivable or inventory.

Table 13.3
Estimated Funds Requirements for Nicholson Company

Month	Current assets (1)	Fixed assets (2)	Total assets[a] [(1) + (2)] (3)	Permanent funds requirement (4)	Seasonal funds requirement [(3) − (4)] (5)
January	$4,000	$13,000	$17,000	$13,800	$3,200
February	3,000	13,000	16,000	13,800	2,200
March	2,000	13,000	15,000	13,800	1,200
April	1,000	13,000	14,000	13,800	200
May	800	13,000	13,800	13,800	0
June	1,500	13,000	14,500	13,800	700
July	3,000	13,000	16,000	13,800	2,200
August	3,700	13,000	16,700	13,800	2,900
September	4,000	13,000	17,000	13,800	3,200
October	5,000	13,000	18,000	13,800	4,200
November	3,000	13,000	16,000	13,800	2,200
December	2,000	13,000	15,000	13,800	1,200
Monthly average[b]				$13,800	$1,950

[a] This represents the firm's total funds requirement.

[b] Found by summing the monthly amounts for 12 months and dividing the resulting totals by 12.

Figure 13.1
Nicholson Company's Estimated Funds Requirements

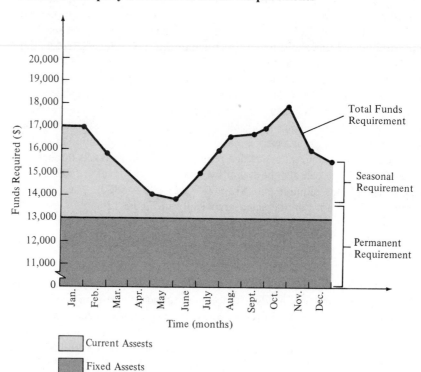

process of *matching* maturities of debt with the duration of each of the firm's financial needs. This approach can be illustrated graphically.

Example

Nicholson Company's estimate of its total funds requirements (i.e., total assets) on a monthly basis for the coming year is given in Table 13.3, column 3. Columns 4 and 5 divide this requirement into permanent and seasonal components.

The aggressive strategy requires that the permanent portion of the firm's funds requirement ($13,800) be financed with long-term funds and that the seasonal portion (ranging from $0 in May to $4,200 in October) be financed with short-term funds. The application of this financing strategy to the firm's total funds requirement is illustrated graphically in Figure 13.2.

Cost Considerations

Under the aggressive strategy, Nicholson's average short-term borrowing (seasonal funds requirement) is $1,950, and average long-term borrowing (permanent funds requirement) is $13,800 (see columns 4 and 5 of Table 13.3). If the annual cost of short-term funds needed by Nicholson is 3 percent and the annual cost of long-term financing is 11 percent,

Figure 13.2
Applying the Aggressive Strategy to Nicholson Company's Funds Requirements

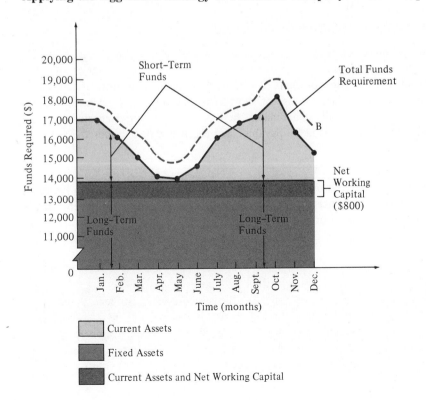

the total cost of the financing strategy is estimated as follows:

$$\text{Cost of short-term financing} = 3\% \times \$1,950 = \$\quad 58.50$$
$$\text{Cost of long-term financing} = 11\% \times 13,800 = \underline{\quad 1,518.00}$$
$$\text{Total cost} \qquad\qquad\qquad \underline{\underline{\$1,576.50}}$$

The total annual cost of $1,576.50 will become more meaningful when compared to the cost of the conservative financing strategy.

Risk Considerations

The aggressive strategy operates with minimum net working capital since only the permanent portion of the firm's current assets is being financed with long-term funds. For Nicholson Company, as noted in Figure 13.2, the level of net working capital is $800, which is the amount of permanent current assets ($13,800 permanent funds requirement − $13,000 fixed assets = $800).

The aggressive financing strategy is risky not only from the standpoint of low net working capital but also because the firm must draw as heavily as possible on its short-term sources of funds to meet seasonal fluctuations in its requirements. If its total requirement turns out to be, say, the level represented by dashed curve B in Figure 13.2, the firm may find it difficult to obtain longer-term funds quickly enough to satisfy short-term needs. This aspect of risk associated with the aggressive strategy results from the fact that a firm has only a limited amount of short-term borrowing capacity. If it draws too heavily on this capacity, unexpected needs for funds may become difficult to satisfy.

conservative financing strategy Plan by which the firm finances all projected funds needs with long-term funds and uses short-term financing only for emergencies or unexpected outflows.

A Conservative Financing Strategy

The most **conservative financing strategy** should be to finance all projected funds requirements with long-term funds and use short-term financing in the event of an emergency or an unexpected outflow of funds. It is difficult to imagine how this strategy could actually be implemented, since the use of short-term financing tools, such as accounts payable and accruals, is virtually unavoidable. In illustrating this approach, the spontaneous short-term financing provided by payables and accruals will be ignored.

FACT OR FABLE?   3 Using the high-cost, low-risk conservative financing strategy, the firm finances all projected funds requirements with long-term funds and uses short-term funds to meet unexpected cash needs. *(Fact)*

Example
Figure 13.3 shows graphically the application of the conservative strategy to the estimated funds requirements for Nicholson Company given in Table 13.3. Long-term financing of $18,000, which equals the firm's peak need (during October) is used under this strategy. Therefore all the funds required over the one-year period, including the entire $18,000 forecast for October, are financed with long-term funds.

Figure 13.3
Applying the Conservative Strategy to Nicholson Company's Funds
Requirements

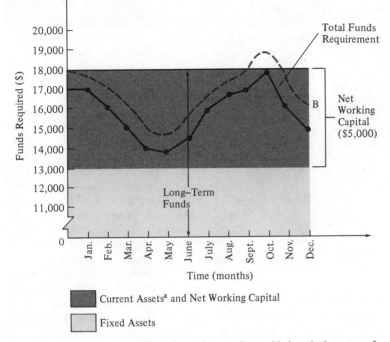

Current Assets[a] and Net Working Capital

Fixed Assets

[a] The current assets above the total funds requirement line and below the long-term funds line are excess current assets created by investment of the excess long-term funds in marketable securities.

Cost Considerations

In the preceding example the annual cost of long-term funds was 11 percent per year. Since the average long-term financing balance under the conservative financing strategy is $18,000, the total cost of this plan is $1,980 or (11% × $18,000). Comparing this figure to the total cost of $1,576.50 using the aggressive strategy indicates the greater expense of the conservative strategy. The reason for this higher expense is apparent if we examine Figure 13.3. The area above the Total Funds Requirement curve and below the long-term funds, or borrowing, line represents the level of funds not actually needed but for which the firm is paying interest. In spite of the fact that the financial manager will invest these excess available funds in some type of marketable security so as partially to offset their cost, it is highly unlikely that the firm can earn more on such funds than their interest cost.

Risk Considerations

The $5,000 of net working capital ($18,000 long-term financing − $13,000 fixed assets) associated with the conservative strategy should mean a very low level of risk for the

PROFILE

KAREN HORN: From Public to Private Sector Banking

As the first woman president of a Federal Reserve Bank, Karen Horn learned many things. She came to the job as a qualified economist, and she left it with the experience of a lifetime.

Horn was the president of the Federal Reserve Bank of Cleveland from May 1982 to April 1987. The biggest challenge during that time was Ohio's savings and loan crisis of 1985. This was triggered by the failure of E.S.M. Government Securities Inc. in Florida, which left the Cincinnati-based Home State Savings Bank with potential losses of $145 million. The Ohio Depositor Guaranty Fund of $130 million that was supposed to cover Home State, as well as many other banks, was insufficient. In the panic that swept through Ohio, depositors withdrew their funds at an alarming rate.

One dilemma Horn faced was the limited legal authority of the Federal Reserve Board in situations of this kind. The state had the power to call the shots. Horn and her staff did act as crucial advisers to Governor Richard Celeste, however. By gathering data and making recommendations, they were able to assist the governor in mak-

ing the decision that ultimately resolved the crisis. Horn became a nationally respected figure for her performance under pressure and the effectiveness of her arbitration. She was also involved in the buy-out of the failed Home State Savings Bank, which was permitted because of the crisis.

In April of 1987, however, Karen Horn opted for a change and became the chief executive officer of Bank One in Cleveland. This represented a major

change from the public to the private sector. Horn had always intended to return to the private sector. She feels that she works best under private sector conditions, despite the satisfaction she derives from public service. The private sector stresses a competitive market environment which is lacking in public work. This is particularly true for Bank One. While it is the leading bank holding company in Ohio, it trails National City Corporation, AmeriTrust Corporation, and Society Corporation in the local Cleveland area. Part of Horn's new job responsibility is to change this to make Bank One number one there. She is looking forward to achieving this goal through her own management expertise. One disadvantage of her work for the Federal Reserve Bank was the process of decision making by committee.

The future success of Karen Horn is almost guaranteed by her past experience. She has a knowledgeable background and the motivation to excel. Most importantly, she has shown that she has what it takes to cope with the heat of the high-pressure banking world.

firm.[5] The firm's risk should also be lowered by the fact that the plan does not require the firm to use any of its limited short-term borrowing capacity. In other words, if total required financing actually turns out to be the level represented by the dashed line B in Figure 13.3, sufficient short-term borrowing capacity should be available to cover the unexpected needs and avoid technical insolvency.

Conservative Versus Aggressive Strategy

Unlike the aggressive strategy, the conservative strategy requires the firm to pay interest on unneeded funds. The lower cost of the aggressive strategy therefore makes it more

---

[5] The level of net working capital is constant throughout the year since the firm has $5,000 in current assets that will be fully financed with long-term funds. Because the portion of the $5,000 in excess of the scheduled level of current assets is assumed to be held as marketable securities, the firm's current asset balance will increase to this level.

profitable than the conservative strategy; however, the aggressive strategy involves much more risk. For most firms a trade-off between the extremes represented by these two strategies should result in an acceptable financing strategy.

Spontaneous Sources of Short-Term Financing

Spontaneous financing arises from the normal operations of the firm. The two major spontaneous sources of short-term financing are accounts payable and accruals. As the firm's sales increase, accounts payable increases in response to the increased purchases required to produce at higher levels. Also in response to increasing sales, the firm's accruals increase as wages and taxes rise due to greater labor requirements and the increased taxes on the firm's increased earnings. There is normally no explicit cost attached to either of these current liabilities, although they do have certain implicit costs. In addition, both are forms of **unsecured short-term financing**—short-term financing obtained without pledging specific assets as collateral. The firm should take advantage of these often ''interest-free'' sources of unsecured short-term financing whenever possible.

spontaneous financing Financing that arises from the normal operations of the firm, the two major short-term sources of which are accounts payable and accruals.

unsecured short-term financing Short-term financing obtained without pledging specific assets as collateral.

Accounts Payable

Accounts payable is the major source of unsecured short-term financing for business firms. They result from transactions in which merchandise is purchased but no formal note is signed evidencing the purchaser's liability to the seller. The purchaser, by accepting merchandise, in effect agrees to pay the supplier the amount required in accordance with the terms of sale. The credit terms extended in such transactions are normally stated on the supplier's invoice. The discussion of accounts payable here is presented from the viewpoint of the purchaser rather than the supplier of ''trade credit.''[6]

Credit Terms

The supplier's credit terms state the credit period, the size of the cash discount offered (if any), the cash discount period, and the date the credit period begins. Each of these aspects of a firm's credit terms is concisely stated in such expressions as ''2/10 net 30 EOM.'' These expressions are a kind of shorthand containing the key information about the length of the credit period (30 days), the cash discount (2 percent), the cash discount period (10 days), and the time the credit period begins, which is the end of each month (EOM).

Credit Period. The **credit period** of an account payable is the number of days until payment in full is required. Regardless of whether a cash discount is offered, the credit period associated with any transaction must always be indicated. Credit periods usually range from zero to 120 days, although in certain instances longer times are provided. Most credit terms refer to the credit period as the ''net period.'' The word *net* indicates that the full amount of the purchase must be paid within the number of days indicated from the beginning of the credit period. For example, ''net 30 days'' indicates that the firm must make *full payment* within 30 days of the beginning of the credit period.

credit period The number of days until full payment of an account payable is required.

Cash Discount. A **cash discount,** if offered as part of the firm's credit terms, is a percentage deduction from the purchase price if the buyer pays within a specified time

cash discount A percentage deduction from the purchase price if the buyer pays within a specified time shorter than the credit period.

---

[6] An account payable of a purchaser is an account receivable on the supplier's books. Chapter 15 highlights the key strategies and considerations involved in extending credit to customers.

shorter than the credit period. Cash discounts normally range from between 1 and 5 percent. A 2 percent cash discount indicates that the purchaser of $100 of merchandise need pay only $98 if payment is made within the specified shorter interval. Techniques for analyzing the benefits of taking a cash discount or paying at the end of the full credit period are discussed later.

cash discount period The number of days after the beginning of the credit period during which the cash discount is available.

Cash Discount Period. The **cash discount period** is the number of days after the beginning of the credit period during which the cash discount is available. Typically the cash discount period is between 5 and 20 days. Often large customers of smaller firms use their position as key customers as a form of leverage, enabling them to take cash discounts far beyond the end of the cash discount period. This strategy, although ethically questionable, is common practice.

date of invoice Indicates that the beginning of the credit period is the date on the invoice for the purchase.

end of month (EOM) Indicates that the credit period for all purchases made within a given month begins on the first day of the month immediately following.

Beginning of the Credit Period. The beginning of the credit period is stated as part of the supplier's credit terms. One of the most common designations for the beginning of the credit period is the **date of invoice.**[7] Both the cash discount period and the net period are then measured from the invoice date. **End of month (EOM)** indicates that the credit period for all purchases made within a given month begins on the first day of the month immediately following. These terms simplify record keeping on the part of the firm extending credit. The following example may help to clarify the differences between credit period beginnings.

Example

Simpson Corporation made two purchases from a certain supplier offering credit terms of 2/10 net 30. One purchase was made on September 10 and the other on September 20. The payment dates for each purchase, based on date of invoice and end of month (EOM) credit period beginnings are given in Table 13.4. The payment dates if the firm takes the cash discount and if it pays the net amount are shown. From the point of view of the recipient of trade credit, a credit period beginning at the end of the month is preferable in both cases since purchases can be paid for without penalty at a later date than otherwise would have been possible.

Table 13.4
Payment Dates for the Simpson Corporation
Given Various Assumptions

Beginning of credit period	September 10 purchase		September 20 purchase	
	Discount taken	Net amount paid	Discount taken	Net amount paid
Date of invoice	Sept. 20	Oct. 10	Sept. 30	Oct. 20
End of month (EOM)	Oct. 10	Oct. 30	Oct. 10	Oct. 30

In order to maintain their competitive position, firms within an industry generally offer the same terms. In many cases, stated credit terms are not the terms actually given to a customer. Special arrangements, or "deals," are made to provide certain customers

[7] Occasionally firms receive invoices prior to receiving the actual merchandise purchased. In these situations the beginning of the credit period is not tied to the invoice date, which could be 30 days prior to the receipt of goods.

with more favorable terms. The prospective purchaser is wise to look closely at the credit terms of suppliers when making a purchase decision. In many instances, concessions may be available.

Analyzing Credit Terms

The credit terms offered a firm by its suppliers allow it to delay payments for its purchases. Since the supplier's cost of having its money tied up in merchandise after it is sold is probably reflected in the purchase price, the purchaser is already indirectly paying for this benefit. The purchaser should therefore carefully analyze credit terms in order to determine the best trade credit strategy.

Taking the Cash Discount. If a firm is extended credit terms that include a cash discount, it has two options. Its first option is to *take the cash discount*. If a firm intends to take a cash discount, it should pay on the last day of the discount period. There is no cost associated with taking a cash discount.

> **Example**
> Lawrence Industries purchased $1,000 worth of merchandise on February 27 from a supplier extending terms of 2/10 net 30 EOM. If the firm takes the cash discount, it will have to pay $980 [$1,000 − .02($1,000)] on March 10, thereby saving $20.

Forgoing the Cash Discount. The second option open to the firm is to *forgo the cash discount* and pay on the final day of the credit period. Although there is no direct cost associated with forgoing a cash discount, there is an implicit cost. The **cost of forgoing a cash discount** is the implied rate of interest paid in order to delay payment of an account payable for an additional number of days. This cost can be illustrated by a simple example. The example assumes that if the firm takes a cash discount, payment will be made on the final day of the cash discount period, and if the cash discount is forgone, payment will be made on the final day of the credit period.

cost of forgoing a cash discount The implied rate of interest paid in order to delay payment of an account payable for an additional number of days.

> **Example**
> As in the preceding example, Lawrence Industries has been extended credit terms of 2/10 net 30 EOM on $1,000 worth of merchandise. If it takes the cash discount on its February 27 purchase, payment will be required on March 10. If the cash discount is forgone, payment can be made on March 30. To keep its money for an extra 20 days (from March 10 to March 30), the firm must forgo an opportunity to pay $980 for its $1,000 purchase. In other words, it will cost the firm $20 to delay payment for 20 days. Figure 13.4 shows the payment options open to the corporation.
>
> To calculate the cost of forgoing the cash discount, the *true purchase price* must be viewed as the discounted cost of the merchandise. For Lawrence Industries, this discounted cost would be $980. To delay paying the $980 for an extra 20 days, the firm must pay $20 ($1,000 − $980). The annual percentage cost of forgoing the cash discount can be calculated using Equation 13.1.[8]

---

[8] Equation 13.1 and the related discussions are based on the assumption that there is only one discount period. In the event that multiple discount periods are offered, calculation of the cost of forgoing the discount must be made for each alternative.

Figure 13.4
Payment Options for Lawrence Industries

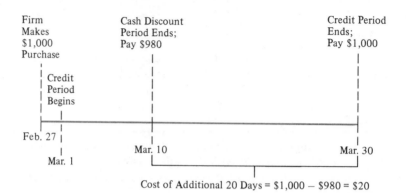

Cost of Additional 20 Days = $1,000 − $980 = $20

$$\text{Cost of forgoing cash discount} = \frac{CD}{100\% - CD} \times \frac{360}{N} \qquad (13.1)$$

where

CD = the stated cash discount in percentage terms

N = the number of days payment can be delayed by forgoing the cash discount

Substituting the values for CD (2%) and N (20 days) into equation 13.1 results in a cost of forgoing the cash discount of 36.73 percent [(2% ÷ 98%) × (360 ÷ 20)]. A 360-day year is assumed.

A simple way to *approximate* the cost of a forgone discount is to use the stated cash discount percentage, CD, in place of the first term of Equation 13.1.

$$\text{Approximate cost of forgoing cash discount} = CD \times \frac{360}{N} \qquad (13.2)$$

The smaller the cash discount, the closer the approximation to the actual cost of forgoing the cash discount. Using this approximation, the cost of forgoing the cash discount for Lawrence Industries is 36 percent [2% × (360 ÷ 20)].

Using the Cost of Forgoing a Cash Discount in Decision Making. The financial manager must determine whether it is advisable to take a cash discount.

Example

Mason Products has four possible suppliers, each offering different credit terms. Except for the differences in credit terms, their products and services are identical. Table 13.5 presents the credit terms offered by suppliers A, B, C, and D, respectively, and the cost of forgoing the cash discounts in each transaction. The approximation method of calculating the cost of forgoing a cash discount has been used to simplify the analysis. The cost of forgoing the cash discount from supplier A is 36 percent; from supplier B, 8 percent; from supplier C, 21.6 percent; and from supplier D, 28.8 percent.

If the firm needs short-term funds, which are currently available from its bank at an interest rate of 13 percent, and if each of the suppliers (A, B, C, and D) is viewed *separately,* which (if any) of the suppliers' cash discounts will the firm forgo? To answer this question, each supplier's terms must be evaluated as they would be if it were the firm's sole supplier. In dealing with supplier A, the firm will take the cash discount since the cost of forgoing it is 36 percent. The firm will then borrow the funds it requires from its commercial bank at 13 percent interest. In dealing with supplier B, the firm will do better to forgo the cash discount since the cost of this action is less than the cost of borrowing money from the bank (8 percent as opposed to 13 percent). In dealing with either supplier C or supplier D, the firm should take the cash discount since in both cases the cost of forgoing the discount is greater than the 13 percent cost of borrowing from the bank.

Table 13.5
Cash Discounts and Associated Costs
for Mason Products

Supplier	Credit terms	Approximate cost of forgoing cash discount
A	2/10 net 30 EOM	36.0%
B	1/10 net 55 EOM	8.0
C	3/20 net 70 EOM	21.6
D	4/10 net 60 EOM	28.8

$$\frac{2\%}{100-2} \times \frac{360}{10}$$

The example shows that the cost of forgoing a cash discount is relevant when evaluating a single supplier's credit terms in light of certain *bank borrowing costs*. In comparing various suppliers' credit terms, the cost of forgoing the cash discount may not be the most important factor in the decision process. Other factors relative to payment strategies may also need to be considered.

FACT OR FABLE?

4 **When the cost of forgoing a cash discount is greater than the cost of short-term bank borrowing, the firm should take the cash discount.** *(Fact)*

Effects of Stretching Accounts Payable

A strategy often employed by a firm is **stretching accounts payable**—that is, paying bills as late as possible without damaging its credit rating. Such a strategy can reduce the cost of forgoing a cash discount. Although this strategy is financially attractive, it raises an important ethical issue: It may cause the firm to violate the agreement it entered into with its supplier when it purchased merchandise. Clearly, a supplier would not look kindly on a customer who regularly and purposely postponed paying for purchases.

stretching accounts payable Paying bills as late as possible without damaging one's credit rating.

> **Example**
> Lawrence Industries was extended credit terms of 2/10 net 30 EOM. The cost of forgoing the cash discount, assuming payment on the last day of the credit period, was found to be approximately 36 percent [2% × (360 ÷ 20)]. If the firm were able to stretch its account payable to 70 days without damaging its credit rating, the cost of forgoing the cash discount would be only 12 percent [2% × (360 ÷ 60)]. Stretching accounts payable reduces the implicit cost of forgoing a cash discount.

Accruals

accruals Liabilities for services received for which payment has yet to be made.

The second spontaneous source of short-term financing for a business is accruals. **Accruals** are liabilities for services received for which payment has yet to be made. The most common items accrued by a firm are wages and taxes. Since taxes are payments to the government, their accrual cannot be manipulated by the firm. However, the accrual of wages can be manipulated to some extent. This is accomplished by delaying payment of wages, thereby receiving an interest-free loan from employees who are paid sometime after they have performed the work. The pay period for employees who earn an hourly rate is often governed by union regulations or by state or federal law. However, in other cases the frequency of payment is at the discretion of the company's management.

> **Example**
> The Tenney Company currently pays its employees at the end of each work week. The weekly payroll totals $400,000. If the firm were to extend the pay period so as to pay its employees one week later throughout an entire year, the employees would in effect be loaning the firm $400,000 for a year. If the firm could earn 10 percent annually on invested funds, such a strategy would be worth $40,000 per year (.10 × $400,000). By delaying payment of accruals in this way, the firm could save this amount of money.

Unsecured Sources of Short-Term Loans

Businesses obtain unsecured short-term loans from two major sources—banks and commercial paper. Unlike the spontaneous sources of *unsecured short-term financing,* these sources are negotiated and result from deliberate actions taken by the financial manager. Bank loans are more popular because they are available to firms of all sizes; commercial paper tends to be available only to large firms.

Bank Loans

short-term self-liquidating loan An unsecured short-term loan in which the borrowed funds provide the mechanism through which the loan itself is repaid.

Banks are a major source of unsecured short-term loans to businesses. The major type of loan made by banks to businesses is the **short-term self-liquidating loan.** Self-liquidating loans are intended merely to carry the firm through seasonal peaks in financing needs attributable primarily to buildups of accounts receivable and inventory. It is expected that as receivables and inventories are converted into cash, the funds needed to retire these loans will automatically be generated. In other words, the use to which the borrowed money is put provides the mechanism through which the loan is repaid (hence the term *self-liquidating*). Banks lend unsecured short-term funds in three basic ways: through single-payment notes, lines of credit, and revolving credit agreements.

Single-Payment Notes

A **single-payment note** can be obtained from a commercial bank by a creditworthy business borrower. This type of loan is usually a ''one-shot'' deal made when a borrower needs additional funds for a short period but does not believe this need will continue. The resulting instrument is a *note,* which must be signed by the borrower. The note states the terms of the loan, which include the length of the loan (the maturity date) and the interest rate charged. This type of short-term note generally has a maturity of 30 days to 9 months or more. The interest charged on the note is generally tied in some fashion to the prime rate of interest.

Prime Rate of Interest. The **prime rate of interest (prime rate)** is the lowest rate of interest charged by the nation's leading banks on business loans to the most important and reliable business borrowers. The prime rate fluctuates with changing supply-and-demand relationships for short-term funds.[9] Banks generally determine the rate charged on loans to various borrowers by adding some type of premium to the prime rate to adjust it for the borrower's ''riskiness.'' The premium may amount to 4 percent or more, although most unsecured short-term notes carry premiums of less than 2 percent. In general, commercial banks do not make short-term unsecured loans to businesses that are believed to be questionable risks.

Fixed- and Floating-Rate Notes. Notes can have either fixed or floating interest rates. On a **fixed-rate note** the rate of interest is determined as a set increment above the prime rate and remains unvarying at that rate until maturity. On a **floating-rate note** the increment above the prime rate is initially established and the rate of interest is allowed to ''float,'' or vary, above prime *as the prime rate varies* until maturity. Generally the increment above the prime rate on a floating-rate note will be *lower* than on a fixed-rate note of equivalent risk because the lender bears less risk with a floating-rate note. The highly volatile nature of the prime rate in recent years, coupled with the widespread use of computers by banks to monitor and calculate loan interest, has been responsible for the *current dominance of floating-rate notes and loans.* Let us look at an example.

single-payment note A short-term, one-time loan payable as a single amount at its maturity.

prime rate of interest (prime rate) The lowest interest rate charged by leading banks for business loans to their most important and reliable business borrowers.

fixed-rate note A note whose rate of interest is determined as a set increment above the prime rate and remains unvarying at that rate until maturity.

floating-rate note A note whose rate of interest is established as an increment above the prime rate and is allowed to ''float,'' or vary, above prime *as the prime rate varies* until maturity.

Example

Gordon Manufacturing recently borrowed $100,000 from each of two banks—bank A and bank B. The loans were incurred on the same day, when the prime rate of interest was 9 percent. Each loan involved a 90-day note. The interest rate was set at 1.5 percent above the prime rate on bank A's fixed-rate note. This means that over the 90-day period the rate of interest will remain at 10.5 percent (9 percent prime rate + 1.5 percent increment) regardless of fluctuations in the prime rate. The interest rate

---

[9] From 1975 through the third quarter of 1978 the prime rate was generally below 9 percent. From the end of 1978 until June of 1985 the prime rate remained above 9.5 percent. In late December 1980 the prime rate reached a record high, 21.5 percent. The prime rate slowly dropped from 9.5 percent in June 1985 to 7.5 percent in late August 1986, and in March 1987 it began a slow rise to 9.00 percent by November of 1987. At that time the general expectation was a reasonably stable prime rate.

was set at 1 percent above the prime rate on bank B's floating-rate note. This means that the rate charged over the 90 days will vary directly *with* the prime rate. Initially the rate will be 10 percent (9 percent + 1 percent), but when the prime rate changes, so will the rate of interest on the note. For instance, if after 30 days the prime rate rises to 9.5 percent and after another 30 days drops to 9.25 percent, the firm would be paying 10 percent interest for the first 30 days, 10.5 percent for the next 30 days, and 10.25 percent for the last 30 days. Depending upon fluctuations in the prime rate over the 90 days, Gordon could pay more or less interest on the floating-rate loan from bank B than on the fixed-rate loan from bank A.

Lines of Credit

line of credit An agreement between a commercial bank and a business specifying the amount of unsecured short-term borrowing the bank will make available to the firm over a given period of time.

A **line of credit** is an agreement between a commercial bank and a business that states the amount of unsecured short-term borrowing the bank will make available to the firm over a given period of time. A line of credit agreement is typically made for a period of one year and often places certain constraints on the borrower. A line of credit agreement is *not a guaranteed loan* but indicates that if the bank has sufficient funds available, it will allow the borrower to owe it up to a certain amount of money. The amount of a line of credit is *the maximum amount the firm can owe the bank* at any point in time.

In applying for a line of credit the borrower may be required to submit such documents as its cash budget, its pro forma income statement, its pro forma balance sheet, and its recent financial statements. If the bank finds the customer acceptable, the line of credit will be extended. The major attraction of a line of credit from the bank's point of view is that it eliminates the need to examine the creditworthiness of a customer each time it borrows money. A few characteristics of lines of credit require further explanation.

Interest Rates. As with single-payment notes, the interest charge on a line of credit is normally stated as a floating rate—the *prime rate plus a percent*. If the prime rate changes, the interest rate charged on new *as well as outstanding* borrowing will automatically change. The amount a borrower is charged in excess of the prime rate depends on its creditworthiness. The more creditworthy the borrower, the lower the interest increment above prime, and vice versa.

effective rate of interest The actual rate of interest paid on a loan as opposed to the stated rate.

Method of Computing Interest. Once the rate of interest charged a given customer has been established, the method of computing interest should be determined. Interest can be paid either when a loan matures or in advance. If interest is paid at maturity, the **effective rate of interest**—the actual rate of interest paid—is equal to the stated interest rate. The effective rate of interest is found by dividing the dollar amount of interest paid by the amount of loan proceeds available to the borrower. When interest is paid in advance, it is deducted from the loan so that the borrower actually receives less money than it requested. Paying interest in advance therefore raises the effective rate of interest above the stated rate. Let us look at an example.

Example

The Wooster Company wants to borrow $10,000 at a stated rate of 10 percent interest for one year. If the interest on the loan is paid at maturity, the firm will pay $1,000 (.10 × $10,000) for the use of the $10,000 for the year. The effective rate of interest will therefore be

$$\frac{\$\ 1,000}{\$10,000} = 10.0 \text{ percent}$$

If the money is borrowed at the same *stated* rate but interest is paid in advance, the firm will still pay $1,000 in interest, but it will receive only $9,000 ($10,000 − $1,000). Thus the effective rate of interest in this case is

$$\frac{\$1,000}{\$9,000} = 11.1 \text{ percent}$$

Paying interest in advance thus makes the effective rate of interest greater than the stated rate. Loans on which interest is paid in advance are often called **discount loans.** Most commercial bank loans to businesses require the interest payment at maturity.

discount loans Loans on which interest is paid in advance.

Operating Change Restrictions. In a line of credit agreement, a bank may impose **operating change restrictions,** thereby retaining the right to revoke the line if any major changes occur in the firm's financial condition or operations. The firm is usually required to submit for review periodically—quarterly or semiannually—up-to-date and, preferably, audited financial statements. In addition, the bank typically needs to be informed of shifts in key managerial personnel or in the firm's operations prior to changes taking place; such changes may affect the future success and debt-paying ability of the firm and thus could alter its credit status. If the bank does not agree with the proposed changes and the firm makes them anyway, the bank has the right to revoke the line of credit agreement.

operating change restrictions Contractual restrictions that a bank may impose on a firm as part of a line of credit agreement.

Compensating Balances. To ensure that the borrower will be a good customer, most short-term unsecured bank loans—single-payment notes and lines of credit—often require the borrower to maintain a **compensating balance** in a demand deposit account (checking account) equal to a certain percentage of the amount borrowed.[10] Compensating balances of 10 to 20 percent are normally required. A compensating balance not only forces the borrower to be a good customer of the bank but may also raise the interest cost to the borrower, thereby increasing the bank's earnings. An example will illustrate.

compensating balance A required checking account balance equal to a certain percentage of the borrower's short-term unsecured loan.

Example

A company has borrowed $1 million under a line of credit agreement. It must pay a stated interest charge of 10 percent and maintain a compensating balance of 20 percent of the funds borrowed, or $200,000, in its checking account. Thus it actually receives the use of only $800,000. To use the $800,000 for a year, the firm pays $100,000 (.10 × $1,000,000). The effective rate of interest on the funds is therefore 12.5 percent ($100,000 ÷ $800,000), 2.5 percent more than the stated rate of 10 percent.

If the firm normally maintains a balance of $200,000 or more in its checking account, the effective interest cost will equal the stated interest rate of 10 percent because none of the $1 million borrowed is needed to satisfy the compensating balance requirement. If the firm normally maintains a $100,000 balance in its checking ac-

---

[10] Sometimes the compensating balance will be stated as a percentage of the amount of the line of credit rather than the amount borrowed. In other cases the compensating balance will be linked to both the amount borrowed and the amount of the line of credit.

count, only an additional $100,000 will have to be tied up, leaving it with $900,000 ($1,000,000 − $100,000) of usable funds. The effective interest cost in this case would be 11.1 percent ($100,000 ÷ $900,000). Thus a compensating balance raises the cost of borrowing *only* if it is larger than the firm's normal cash balance.

Annual Cleanups. To ensure that money lent under a line of credit agreement is actually being used to finance seasonal needs, many banks require an **annual cleanup.** This means that the borrower must have a loan balance of zero—that is, owe the bank nothing—for a certain number of days during the year. Forcing the borrower to carry a zero loan balance for a certain period of time ensures that short-term loans do not turn into long-term loans.

> **annual cleanup** The requirement that for a certain number of days annually borrowers under a line of credit carry a zero loan balance (i.e., owe the bank nothing).

All the characteristics of a line of credit agreement are negotiable to some extent. Today, banks bid competitively to attract large, well-known firms. A prospective borrower should attempt to negotiate a line of credit with the most favorable interest rate, for an optimal amount of funds, and with a minimum of restrictions. Lenders will often accept fees instead of deposit balances, and vice versa, as compensation for loans and other services rendered to their commercial customers. The lender will attempt to get a good return with maximum safety. These negotiations should produce a line of credit suitable to both borrower and lender.

Revolving Credit Agreements

> **revolving credit agreement** A line of credit guaranteed to the borrower by the bank for a stated time period and regardless of the scarcity of money.

A **revolving credit agreement** is nothing more than a *guaranteed line of credit*. It is guaranteed in the sense that the commercial bank making the arrangement assures the borrower that a specified amount of funds will be made available regardless of the scarcity of money. The interest rate and other requirements for a revolving credit agreement are similar to those for a line of credit. It is not uncommon for a revolving credit agreement to be for a period greater than one year.[11] Since the bank guarantees the availability of funds to the borrower, a **commitment fee** is normally charged on a revolving credit agreement.[12] This fee often applies to the average unused balance of the line of credit. It is normally about .5 percent of the *average unused portion* of the funds. An example will clarify the nature of the commitment fees.

> **commitment fee** The fee normally charged on a revolving credit agreement, often based on the average unused balance of the borrower's credit line.

> **Example**
> The REH Company has a $2 million revolving credit agreement with its bank. Its average borrowing under the agreement for the past year was $1.5 million. The bank charges a commitment fee of .5 percent. Since the average unused portion of the committed funds was $500,000 ($2 million − $1.5 million), the commitment fee for the year was $2,500 (.005 × $500,000). Of course, REH also had to pay interest on

[11] Many authors classify the revolving credit agreement as a form of *intermediate-term financing,* defined as having a maturity of one to seven years. In this text, the intermediate-term financing classification is not used; only short-term and long-term classifications are made. Since many revolving credit agreements are for more than one year, they can be classified as a form of long-term financing; however, they are discussed here because of their similarity to line of credit agreements.

[12] Some banks not only require payment of the commitment fee but also require the borrower to maintain, in addition to the compensating balance against actual borrowings, a compensating balance of 10 percent or so against the unused portion of the commitment.

the actual $1.5 million borrowed under the agreement. Although more expensive than a line of credit, a revolving credit agreement can be less risky from the borrower's viewpoint, since the availability of funds is guaranteed by the bank.

---

5 Banks lend unsecured short-term funds through a single-payment note, a line of credit, or a revolving credit agreement—all of which charge interest on a floating-rate basis tied to the prime rate of interest. *(Fact)*

FACT OR FABLE?

Commercial Paper

Commercial paper is a form of financing that consists of short-term, unsecured promissory notes issued by firms with a high credit standing. Generally, only quite large firms of unquestionable financial soundness and reputation are able to issue commercial paper. Most commercial paper has maturities ranging from 3 to 270 days. Although there is no set denomination, it is generally issued in multiples of $100,000 or more. A large portion of the commercial paper today is issued by finance companies; manufacturing firms account for a smaller portion of this type of financing. As will be noted in Chapter 14, businesses often purchase commercial paper, which they hold as marketable securities, to provide an interest-earning reserve of liquidity.

commercial paper A form of financing consisting of short-term, unsecured promissory notes issued by firms with a high credit standing.

Interest on Commercial Paper

The interest paid by the issuer of commercial paper is determined by the size of the discount and the length of time to maturity. Commercial paper is sold at a discount from its *par*, or *face, value,* and the actual interest earned by the purchaser is determined by certain calculations. These can be illustrated by the following example.

> **Example**
> Bertram Corporation has just issued $1 million worth of commercial paper that has a 90-day maturity and sells for $980,000. At the end of 90 days the purchaser of this paper will receive $1 million for its $980,000 investment. The interest paid on the financing is therefore $20,000 on a principal of $980,000. This is equivalent to an annual interest rate for the Bertram Corporation commercial paper of 8.2 percent [($20,000 ÷ $980,000) × (360 days ÷ 90 days)].

An interesting characteristic of commercial paper is that it *normally* has a yield of 1 to 2 percent below the prime bank lending rate. In other words, firms are able to raise funds through the sale of commercial paper more cheaply than by borrowing from a commercial bank. The reason is that many suppliers of short-term funds do not have the option of making low-risk business loans at the prime rate.[13] They can invest only in marketable securities such as Treasury bills and commercial paper.

---

[13] Commercial banks are legally prohibited from lending an amount greater than 15 percent (plus an additional 10 percent for loans secured by readily marketable collateral) of their unimpaired capital and surplus to any one borrower. This restriction is intended to protect depositors by forcing the commercial bank to spread its risk across a number of borrowers. In addition, smaller commercial banks do not have many opportunities to lend to high-quality business borrowers.

CAREERS IN FINANCE

SENIOR BANKING ANALYST:
Negotiating and Maintaining Sound Banking Relationships

Doris always suspected she'd grow up to hold a responsible financial position. She was the high school student who was so good in math that she ranked second in the state in a scholarship exam. Now Doris, 39, is the senior banking analyst for a large corporation. Hers is a job that demands skills in accounting, statistics, and financial analysis as well as the desire to manage the company's money more carefully than she manages her own.

As senior banking analyst, Doris's main responsibilities are to handle short-term assets and short-term debt so that the company realizes the greatest financial advantage. She reports directly to the manager of financial services and provides financial data when it is requested by various departments in the company. Most large companies need short-term loans to finance purchases or special business activities. Doris's job is to examine ways to finance these needs through the twenty or so banks with which she works. Of course, she borrows the money on

terms that are best for the company. Occasionally, the company has funds to invest for a short time. Doris cautions, "This is the time to be especially careful. The temptation is to think you're in clover since you're the lender. Actually that's the time to look for the best deals."

When her boss approves Doris's recommendation about where to borrow or where to invest, Doris handles the transfer of funds from bank to bank or from account to account. It's an important detail since bank regulations and state laws can add many complications. "I also have to resolve problems that develop in various accounts," says Doris. "Usually these are minor. There may be a misunderstanding about the time when an account begins drawing interest, for example. Handling these issues brings me into contact with banking officials in several cities. I must be careful not to jeopardize our relationship with the banks."

Like most other people with management responsibilities, Doris has

continuing paperwork. "I don't think there's a job that doesn't demand report writing, and I certainly have my share," she says. "I prepare weekly updates on changes in the company's cash position, including the purchase and sale of securities during that time. The report I like least is the one requiring me to predict how much service we'll probably need from the banks in the coming quarters: either borrowing or investing. Since interest rates vary from week to week, I can never be exactly on target. Estimates are essential, however, to make a business run smoothly."

Doris has grown tremendously in her understanding of finance since she began in the accounting department fifteen years ago. Her big step into the position of senior banking analyst five years ago at an annual salary of $35,000 was an indication of that growth. At the same time, Doris is trying to plan when she will be able to go back to school and earn an MBA degree.

Although the cost of borrowing through the sale of commercial paper is usually lower than the prime bank loan rate, it must be remembered that a firm needs to maintain a good working relationship with its bank. Therefore even if it is slightly more expensive to borrow from a commercial bank, it may at times be advisable to do so in order to establish the necessary rapport with a particular institution. This strategy ensures that when money is tight, funds can be obtained promptly and at a reasonable interest rate.

Sale of Commercial Paper

Commercial paper is *directly placed with investors* by the issuer or is *sold by commercial paper dealers*. For performing the marketing function, the commercial paper dealer is paid a fee. Regardless of the method of sale, most commercial paper is purchased from a firm by other businesses, banks, life insurance companies, pension funds, and money market mutual funds.

Secured Sources of Short-Term Loans

Once a firm has exhausted its unsecured sources of short-term financing, it may be able to obtain additional short-term loans on a secured basis. **Secured short-term financing** has specific assets pledged as collateral.[14] The **collateral** commonly takes the form of an asset, such as accounts receivable or inventory. The lender obtains a security interest in the collateral through the execution of a contract (security agreement) with the borrower. The **security agreement** specifies the collateral held against the loan. In addition, the terms of the loan against which the security is held are attached to, or form part of, the security agreement. They specify the conditions required for the security interest to be removed, along with the interest rate on the loan, repayment dates, and other loan provisions. A copy of the security agreement is filed in a public office within the state—typically a county or state court. Filing provides subsequent lenders with information about which assets of a prospective borrower are unavailable for use as collateral. The filing requirement protects the lender by legally establishing the lender's security interest.

secured short-term financing Short-term financing (loans) obtained by pledging specific assets as collateral.

collateral The security offered the lender by the borrower, usually in the form of an asset such as accounts receivable or inventory.

security agreement The agreement between the borrower and the lender that specifies the collateral held against a secured loan.

Characteristics of Secured Short-Term Loans

Although many people believe that holding collateral as security reduces the risk of the loan, lenders do not usually view loans in this way. Lenders recognize that by having an interest in collateral they can reduce losses if the borrower defaults, but *as far as changing the risk of default, the presence of collateral has no impact*. A lender requires collateral to ensure recovery of some portion of the loan in the event of default. What the lender wants above all, however, is to be repaid as scheduled. In general, lenders prefer to make less risky loans at lower rates of interest than to be in a position in which they are forced to liquidate collateral.

Collateral and Terms

A number of factors relative to the characteristics desirable in collateral and the basic terms of secured short-term loans need to be examined.

Collateral. Lenders of secured short-term funds prefer collateral that has a life, or duration, closely matched to the term of the loan. This assures the lender that the collateral can be used to satisfy the loan in the event of a default. Current assets—accounts receivable and inventories—are the most desirable short-term loan collateral since they normally convert into cash much sooner than do fixed assets. Thus the short-term lender of secured funds generally accepts only liquid current assets as collateral.

Terms. Typically, the lender determines the desirable **percentage advance** to make against the collateral. This percentage advance constitutes the principal of the secured loan and is normally between 30 and 100 percent of the book value of the collateral. It varies not only according to the type and liquidity of collateral but also according to the type of security interest being taken.

The interest rate charged on secured short-term loans is typically *higher* than the rate

percentage advance The percent of the book value of the collateral that constitutes the principal of a secured loan.

---

[14] The terms *security* and *collateral* are used interchangeably to refer to the items used by a borrower to back up a loan. Loan security or collateral may be any assets against which a lender, as a result of making a loan, has a legal claim that is exercisable if the borrower defaults on some provision of the loan. If the borrower defaults, the lender can sell the security or collateral to satisfy the claim against the borrower. Some of the more technical aspects of loan defaults are presented in Chapter 19.

on unsecured short-term loans. Commercial banks and other institutions do not normally consider secured loans less risky than unsecured loans and therefore require higher interest rates on them. In addition, negotiating and administering secured loans is more troublesome for the lender than negotiating and administering unsecured loans. The lender therefore normally requires added compensation in the form of a service charge, a higher interest rate, or both. The higher cost of secured as opposed to unsecured borrowing is attributable to the greater risk of default and to the increased administration costs involved. (Remember that firms typically borrow on a secured basis only after exhausting less costly unsecured sources of short-term funds.)

Institutions Extending Secured Short-Term Loans

The primary sources of secured short-term loans to businesses are commercial banks and commercial finance companies. Both institutions deal in short-term loans secured primarily by accounts receivable and inventory. The operations of commercial banks have already been described. **Commercial finance companies** are lending institutions that make *only* secured loans—both short-term and long-term—to businesses. Unlike banks, finance companies are not permitted to hold deposits.

> **commercial finance companies** Lending institutions that make *only* secured loans—both short- and long-term—to businesses.

Only when its unsecured and secured short-term borrowing power from the commercial bank is exhausted will a borrower turn to the commercial finance company for additional secured borrowing. Because the finance company generally ends up with higher-risk borrowers, its interest charges on secured short-term loans are usually higher than those of commercial banks. The leading U.S. commercial finance companies include the Commercial Investors Trust (CIT) Corporation and Westinghouse Credit Corporation, Industrial Division.

The Use of Accounts Receivable as Collateral

Two commonly used means of obtaining short-term financing with accounts receivable are pledging accounts receivable and factoring accounts receivable. Actually, only a pledge of accounts receivable creates a secured short-term loan; factoring really entails the *sale* of accounts receivable at a discount. Although factoring is not actually a form of secured short-term borrowing, it does involve the use of accounts receivable to obtain needed short-term funds.

Pledging Accounts Receivable

> **pledge of accounts receivable** The use of a firm's accounts receivable as security, or collateral, to obtain a short-term loan.

A **pledge of accounts receivable** is often used to secure a short-term loan. Because accounts receivable are normally quite liquid, they are an attractive form of short-term collateral. Both commercial banks and commercial finance companies extend loans against pledges of accounts receivable.

When a firm approaches a prospective lender for a loan against accounts receivable, the lender will first evaluate the receivables to assess their desirability as collateral. Next, the dollar value of the acceptable accounts is adjusted by the lender for expected returns on sales and other allowances. Then, the percentage advanced against the adjusted collateral·is determined by the lender based on its evaluation of the quality of the acceptable receivables and the expected cost of their liquidation. This percentage represents the principal of the loan and typically ranges between 50 and 90 percent of the face value of acceptable accounts receivable. Finally, to protect its interest in the collateral the lender will file a **lien,** which is a publicly disclosed legal claim on the collateral.

> **lien** A publicly disclosed legal claim on collateral.

Pledges of accounts receivable are normally made on a **nonnotification basis.** This means that a customer whose account has been pledged as collateral is not notified of this action. Under the nonnotification arrangement, the borrower still collects the pledged account receivable and the lender trusts that the borrower will remit these payments as they are received. If a pledge of accounts receivable is made on a **notification basis,** the customer is notified to remit payment directly to the lender.

The stated cost of a pledge of accounts receivable is normally 2 to 5 percent above the prime interest rate offered by banks. In addition to the stated interest rate, a service charge of up to 3 percent may be levied. Although the interest payment is expected to compensate the lender for making the loan, the service charge is needed to cover the administrative costs incurred by the lender.

Factoring Accounts Receivable

Factoring accounts receivable involves their outright sale at a discount to a factor or other financial institution. A **factor** is a financial institution that purchases accounts receivable from businesses. There are 15 to 20 firms currently operating in the United States that deal solely in factoring accounts receivable. Some commercial banks and commercial finance companies also factor accounts receivable. Although not actually the same as obtaining a short-term loan, factoring accounts receivable is similar to borrowing with accounts receivable as collateral. Factoring constitutes approximately one-third of the total financing secured by accounts receivable (including factoring) and inventory in the United States currently.

A factoring agreement normally states the exact conditions, charges, and procedures for the purchase of an account. The factor, like a lender against a pledge of accounts receivable, chooses accounts for purchase, selecting only those that appear to be acceptable credit risks. Where factoring is to be on a continuing basis, the factor will actually make the firm's credit decisions, since this will guarantee the acceptability of accounts.[15] Factoring is normally done on a *notification basis,* and the factor receives payment of the account directly from the customer. In addition, most sales of accounts receivable to a factor are made on a **nonrecourse basis.** This means that the factor agrees to accept all credit risks. Thus if a purchased account turns out to be uncollectible, the factor must absorb the loss.

Typically the factor is not required to pay the firm until the account is collected or until the last day of the credit period, whichever occurs first. The factor sets up an account similar to a bank deposit account for each customer. As payment is received or as due dates arrive, the factor deposits money into the seller's account, from which the seller is free to make withdrawals as needed. In many cases, if the firm leaves the money in the account, a *surplus* will exist on which the factor will pay interest. In other instances, the factor may make *advances* to the firm against uncollected accounts that are not yet due. These advances represent a negative balance in the firm's account, on which interest is charged.

Factoring costs include commissions, interest levied on advances, and interest earned on surpluses. The factor deposits in the firm's account the face value of the accounts

nonnotification basis The basis on which a borrower, having pledged an account receivable, continues to collect the account payments without notifying the account customer.

notification basis The basis on which an account customer whose account has been pledged or factored is notified to remit payments directly to the lender or factor rather than to the borrower.

factoring accounts receivable The outright sale of accounts receivable at a discount to a factor or other financial institution in order to obtain funds.

factor A financial institution that specializes in purchasing accounts receivable from businesses.

nonrecourse basis The basis on which accounts receivable are sold to a factor with the understanding that the factor accepts all credit risks on the purchased accounts.

---

[15] The use of credit cards such as MasterCard, VISA, and Discover by consumers has some similarity to factoring, since the vendor accepting the card is reimbursed at a discount for purchases made using the card. The difference between factoring and credit cards is that the cards are nothing more than a line of credit extended by the issuer, which charges the vendors a fee for accepting the cards. In factoring, the factor does not analyze credit until after the sale has been made; in many cases (except where factoring is done on a continuous basis) the initial credit decision is the responsibility of the vendor, not the factor who purchases the account.

purchased by the factor, less the commissions. The commissions are typically stated as a 1 to 3 percent discount from the face value of factored accounts receivable. The *interest levied on advances* is generally 2 to 4 percent above the prime rate. It is levied on the actual amount advanced. The interest paid on surpluses or positive account balances left with a factor is generally around .5 percent per month. Although its costs may seem high, factoring has certain advantages that make it quite attractive to many firms. One is the ability it gives the firm to *turn accounts receivable immediately into cash* without having to worry about repayment. Another advantage of factoring is that it ensures a *known pattern of cash flows*. In addition, if factoring is undertaken on a continuous basis, the firm *can eliminate its credit and collection departments*.

The Use of Inventory as Collateral

Inventory is generally second to accounts receivable in desirability as short-term loan collateral. Inventory is attractive as collateral since it normally has a market value greater than its book value, which is used to establish its value as collateral. A lender securing a loan with inventory will probably be able to sell it for at least book value if the borrower defaults on its obligations.

The most important characteristic of inventory being evaluated as loan collateral is *marketability*, which must be considered in light of its physical properties. A warehouse of *perishable* items, such as fresh peaches, may be quite marketable, but if the cost of storing and selling the peaches is high, they may not be desirable collateral. *Specialized items* such as moon-roving vehicles are not desirable collateral either, since finding a buyer for them could be difficult. In evaluating inventory as possible loan collateral, the lender looks for items with very stable market prices that have ready markets and that lack undesirable physical properties.

FACT OR FABLE?

[6] The use of accounts receivable or inventory as collateral for short-term loans makes them less risky than unsecured loans, thereby resulting in a lower rate of interest. *(Fable)* **The use of accounts receivable or inventory as collateral for short-term loans *does not reduce the risk of default, and therefore does not lower the rate of interest below that on unsecured short-term loans.***

Floating Inventory Liens

floating inventory lien
A lender's claim on the borrower's general inventory as collateral for a secured loan.

A lender may be willing to secure a loan under a **floating inventory lien,** which is a claim on inventory in general. This arrangement is most attractive when the firm has a stable level of inventory that consists of a diversified group of relatively inexpensive merchandise. Inventories of items such as auto tires, screws and bolts, and shoes are candidates for floating-lien loans. Since it is difficult for a lender to verify the presence of the inventory, the lender will generally advance less than 50 percent of the book value of the average inventory. The interest charge on a floating lien is 3 to 5 percent above the prime rate. Floating liens are often required by commercial banks as extra security on what would otherwise be an unsecured loan. A floating-lien inventory loan may also be available from commercial finance companies.

Trust Receipt Inventory Loans

A **trust receipt inventory loan** can often be made against relatively expensive automotive, consumer-durable, and industrial equipment that can be identified by serial number. Under this agreement, the borrower keeps the inventory and the lender may advance 80 to 100 percent of its cost. The lender files a lien on all the items financed. The borrower is free to sell the merchandise but is trusted to remit the amount lent against each item along with accrued interest to the lender immediately after the sale. The lender then releases the lien on the appropriate item. The lender makes periodic checks of the borrower's inventory to make sure that the required amount of collateral remaining is still in the hands of the borrower. The interest charge to the borrower is normally 2 percent or more above the prime rate.

> **trust receipt inventory loan** An agreement under which the lender advances 80 to 100 percent of the cost of the borrower's salable inventory items in exchange for the borrower's promise to immediately repay the loan, with accrued interest, upon the sale of each item.

Trust receipt loans are often made by manufacturers' wholly-owned financing subsidiaries, known as *captive finance companies,* to their customers.[16] *Floor planning* of automobile or equipment retailers is done under this arrangement. For example, General Motors Acceptance Corporation (GMAC), the financing subsidiary of General Motors, grants these types of loans to its dealers. Trust receipt loans are also available through commercial banks and commercial finance companies.

Warehouse Receipt Loans

A **warehouse receipt loan** is an arrangement whereby the lender, who may be a commercial bank or commercial finance company, receives control of the pledged collateral, which is stored, or warehoused, in the lender's possession. After selecting acceptable collateral, the lender hires a warehousing company to act as its agent and take possession of the inventory. Two types of warehousing arrangements are possible: terminal warehouses and field warehouses. A *terminal warehouse* is a central warehouse used to store the merchandise of various customers. Such a warehouse is normally used by the lender when the inventory is easily transported and can be delivered to the warehouse relatively inexpensively. Under a *field warehouse* arrangement, the lender hires a field warehousing company to set up a warehouse on the borrower's premises or to lease part of the borrower's warehouse as a repository for the pledged collateral. Regardless of whether a terminal or field warehouse is established, the warehousing company places a guard over the inventory. Only upon written approval of the lender can any portion of the secured inventory be released.

> **warehouse receipt loan** An arrangement in which the lender receives control of the pledged collateral, which is warehoused by a designated agent in the lender's behalf.

The actual lending agreement specifically states the requirements for the release of inventory. As in the case of other secured loans, the lender accepts only collateral believed to be readily marketable and advances only a portion—generally 75 to 90 percent—of the collateral's value. The specific costs of warehouse receipt loans are generally higher than those of any other secured lending arrangements due to the need to hire and pay a third party (the warehousing company) to guard and supervise the collateral. The basic interest charged on warehouse receipt loans is higher than that charged on unsecured loans, generally ranging from 3 to 5 percent above the prime rate. In addition to the interest charge, the borrower must absorb the costs of warehousing by paying the warehouse fee, which is generally between 1 and 3 percent of the amount of the loan. The borrower is normally also required to pay the insurance costs on the warehoused merchandise.

---

[16] Captive finance companies are especially popular in industries manufacturing consumer durable goods because they provide the manufacturer with a useful sales tool as well as certain tax and borrowing advantages.

Table 13.6
Summary of Key Features of Common Sources of Short-Term Financing

Type of short-term financing	Source	Cost or conditions	Characteristics
I. Spontaneous sources			
Accounts payable	Suppliers of merchandise	No stated cost except when a cash discount is offered for early payment.	Credit extended on open account for 0 to 120 days. The largest source of short-term financing.
Accruals	Employees and government	Free.	Result from the fact that wages (employees) and taxes (government) are paid at discrete points in time after the service has been rendered. Hard to manipulate this source of financing.
II. Unsecured sources of loans			
Bank sources			
(1) Single-payment notes	Commercial banks	Prime plus 0% to 4% risk premium—fixed or floating rate.	A single-payment loan used to meet a funds shortage expected to last only a short period of time.
(2) Lines of credit	Commercial banks	Prime plus 0% to 4% risk premium—fixed or floating rate. Often must maintain 10% to 20% compensating balance and clean up the line.	A prearranged borrowing limit under which funds, if available, will be lent to allow the borrower to meet seasonal needs.
(3) Revolving credit agreements	Commercial banks	Prime plus 0% to 4% risk premium—fixed or floating rate. Often must maintain 10% to 20% compensating balance and pay a commitment fee of approximately .5% of the average unused balance.	A line of credit agreement under which the availability of funds is guaranteed. Often for a period greater than one year.
Commercial paper	Other businesses, banks, life insurance companies, pension funds, and money market mutual funds	Generally 1% to 2% below the prime rate of interest	An unsecured short-term promissory note issued by the most financially sound firms. May be placed directly or sold through commercial paper dealers.

III. Secured sources of loans

Accounts receivable collateral

Type	Source	Cost or terms	Description
(1) Pledging	Commercial banks and commercial finance companies	2% to 5% above prime plus up to 3% in fees. Advance 50% to 90% of collateral value.	Selected accounts receivable are used as collateral. The borrower is trusted to remit to the lender upon collection of pledged accounts. Done on a non-notification basis.
(2) Factoring	Factors, commercial banks, and commercial finance companies	1% to 3% discount from face value of factored accounts. Interest levied on advances of 2% to 4% above prime. Interest earned on surplus balances left with factor of about .5% per month.	Selected accounts are sold—generally without recourse—at a discount. All credit risks go with the accounts. Factor will loan (make advances) against uncollected accounts that are not yet due. Factor will also pay interest on surplus balances. Typically done on a notification basis.

Inventory collateral

Type	Source	Cost or terms	Description
(1) Floating liens	Commercial banks and commercial finance companies	3% to 5% above prime. Advance less than 50% of collateral value.	A loan against inventory in general Made when firm has stable inventory of a variety of inexpensive items.
(2) Trust receipts	Manufacturers' captive financing subsidiaries, commercial banks, and commercial finance companies	2% or more above prime. Advance 80% to 100% of cost of collateral.	Loan against relatively expensive automotive, consumer-durable, and industrial equipment that can be identified by serial number. Collateral remains in possession of borrower who is trusted to remit proceeds to lender upon its sale.
(3) Warehouse receipts	Commercial banks and commercial finance companies	3% to 5% above prime plus a 1% to 3% warehouse fee. Advance 75% to 90% of collateral value.	Inventory used as collateral is placed under control of the lender by putting it in a terminal warehouse or through a field warehouse. A third party—a warehouseing company—guards the inventory for the lender. Inventory is released only upon written approval of the lender.

Summary

● Net working capital is defined either as the difference between current assets and current liabilities or as the portion of a firm's current assets financed with long-term funds. Firms maintain net working capital to provide a cushion between cash outflows and inflows.

● Net working capital is often used as a measure of the risk of technical insolvency by the firm. The more liquid a firm is, the more net working capital it has and the less likely that it will be unable to satisfy its current obligations as they come due.

● The higher a firm's ratio of current assets to total assets, the less profitable the firm, and the less risky it is. The converse is also true. The higher a firm's ratio of current liabilities to total assets, the more profitable and more risky the firm is. The converse of this statement is also true.

● The aggressive working capital strategy is a high-profit, high-risk financing strategy whereby seasonal needs are financed with short-term funds and permanent needs are financed with long-term funds. At the other extreme, the conservative strategy results in low profit and low risk since all funds requirements are financed with long-term funds and short-term funds are saved for emergencies.

● Spontaneous sources of short-term financing include accounts payable, which are the primary source of short-term funds, and accruals. The key features of these forms of financing are summarized in part I of Table 13.6.

● Credit terms may differ with respect to the credit period, cash discount, cash discount period, and beginning of the credit period. The cost of forgoing cash discounts is a factor in deciding whether to take or forgo a cash discount. Stretching accounts payable can lower the cost of forgoing a cash discount.

● Banks are the major source of unsecured short-term loans to businesses. The interest rate on these loans may be fixed or may float and is tied to the prime rate of interest by a risk premium. The key features of the various types of bank loans as well as commercial paper are summarized in part II of Table 13.6.

● Secured short-term loans are those for which the lender requires collateral—typically, current assets such as accounts receivable or inventory. These loans are more expensive than unsecured loans since the presence of collateral does not lower the risk of default. The key features of the popular forms of these loans are summarized in part III of Table 13.6.

Questions

13-1 Why is working capital management considered so important by stockholders, creditors, and the firm's financial manager? What are the two definitions of *net working capital?*

13-2 What relationship would you expect there to be between the predictability of a firm's cash flows and its required level of net working capital? How are net working capital, liquidity, technical insolvency, and risk related?

13-3 Why is an increase in the ratio of current to total assets expected to decrease both profits and risk as measured by net working capital? How can changes in the ratio of current liabilities to total assets affect profitability and risk?

13-4 Describe both the *aggressive strategy* and the *conservative strategy* for meeting a firm's funds requirements. Compare and contrast the effects of each of these strategies on the firm's profitability and risk.

13-5 What are the two key sources of spontaneous short-term financing for a firm? Why are these sources considered spontaneous, and how are they related to the firm's sales? Do they normally have a stated cost?

13-6 Is there a cost associated with taking a cash discount? Is there any cost associated with forgoing a cash discount? How is the decision to take a cash discount affected by the firm's cost of borrowing short-term funds?

13-7 What are the basic terms and characteristics of a single-payment note? How is the prime interest rate relevant to the cost of short-term bank borrowing? What is a *floating-rate note?*

13-8 What is a *line of credit?* Describe each of the following features often included in these agreements.

  a. Operating change restrictions

  b. Compensating balance

  c. Annual cleanup

13-9 What is meant by a *revolving credit agreement?* How does this arrangement differ from the line of credit agreement? What is a *commitment fee?*

13-10 How is commercial paper used to raise short-term funds? Who can issue commercial paper? Who buys commercial paper? How is it sold?

13-11 In general, what kind of interest rates and fees are levied on secured short-term loans? Why are these rates generally *higher* than the rates on unsecured short-term loans?

13-12 Compare, contrast, and describe the basic features of:

    a. Pledging accounts receivable

    b. Factoring accounts receivable

Be sure to mention the institutions offering each of them.

13-13 Describe the basic features and compare each of the following methods of using *inventory* as short-term loan collateral.

    a. Floating lien

    b. Trust receipt loan

    c. Warehouse receipt loan

Self-Test Problems

(Solutions on page 508)

ST-1 Santo Gas has forecast its total funds requirements for the coming year as follows:

Month	Amount	Month	Amount
Jan.	$7,400,000	July	$5,800,000
Feb.	5,500,000	Aug.	5,400,000
Mar.	5,000,000	Sept.	5,000,000
Apr.	5,300,000	Oct.	5,300,000
May	6,200,000	Nov.	6,000,000
June	6,000,000	Dec.	6,800,000

    a. Divide the firm's monthly funds requirement into a *permanent* and a *seasonal* component and find the monthly average for each of these components.

    b. Describe the amount of long-term and short-term financing used to meet the total funds requirement under (1) an *aggressive strategy* and (2) a *conservative strategy*.

    c. Assuming short-term funds cost 10 percent annually and long-term funds cost 16 percent annually, use the averages found in **a** to calculate the total cost of each of the strategies described in **b**.

    d. Discuss the profitability-risk trade-offs associated with the aggressive strategy and the conservative strategy.

ST-2 The credit terms for each of three suppliers are as follows:

Supplier	Credit terms
X	1/10 net 55 EOM
Y	2/10 net 30 EOM
Z	2/20 net 60 EOM

    a. Determine the *approximate* cost of forgoing the cash discount from each supplier.

    b. Assuming that the firm needs short-term financing, recommend whether it would be better to forgo the cash discount or take the discount and borrow from a bank at 15 percent annual interest. Evaluate each supplier separately using your findings in **a**.

    c. What impact, if any, would the fact that the firm could stretch its accounts payable (net period only) by 20 days from supplier Z have on your answer in **b** relative to this supplier?

Problems

13-1 **(Permanent versus Seasonal Funds Requirements)** Manchester Industries' current, fixed, and total assets for each month of the coming year are summarized in the table below:

Month	Current assets (1)	Fixed assets (2)	Total assets [(1) + (2)] (3)
January	$15,000	$30,000	$45,000
February	22,000	30,000	52,000
March	30,000	30,000	60,000
April	18,000	30,000	48,000
May	10,000	30,000	40,000
June	6,000	30,000	36,000
July	9,000	30,000	39,000
August	9,000	30,000	39,000
September	15,000	30,000	45,000
October	20,000	30,000	50,000
November	22,000	30,000	52,000
December	20,000	30,000	50,000

a. Divide the firm's monthly total funds requirements (total assets) into a permanent and a seasonal component.

b. Find the monthly average (1) permanent and (2) seasonal funds requirements using your findings in **a.**

13-2 **(Annual Loan Cost)** What is the average loan balance and the annual loan cost, given an annual interest rate on loans of 15 percent, for a firm with total monthly borrowings as follows?

Month	Amount	Month	Amount
Jan.	$12,000	July	$6,000
Feb.	13,000	Aug.	5,000
Mar.	9,000	Sept.	6,000
Apr.	8,000	Oct.	5,000
May	9,000	Nov.	7,000
June	7,000	Dec.	9,000

13-3 **(Aggressive versus Conservative Financing Strategy)** Dynabase Tool has forecast its total funds requirements for the coming year as follows:

Month	Amount	Month	Amount
Jan.	$2,000,000	July	$12,000,000
Feb.	2,000,000	Aug.	14,000,000
Mar.	2,000,000	Sept.	9,000,000
Apr.	4,000,000	Oct.	5,000,000
May	6,000,000	Nov.	4,000,000
June	9,000,000	Dec.	3,000,000

a. Divide the firm's monthly funds requirement into a *permanent* and a *seasonal* component and find the monthly average for each of these components.

b. Describe the amount of long-term and short-term financing used to meet the total funds requirement under (1) an *aggressive strategy* and (2) a *conservative strategy*.

c. Assuming short-term funds cost 12 percent annually and the cost of long-term funds is 17 percent annually, use the averages found in **a** to calculate the total cost of each of the strategies described in **b**.

d. Discuss the profitability-risk trade-offs associated with the aggressive strategy and the conservative strategy.

13-4 **(Payment Dates)** Determine when a firm must make payment for purchases made and invoices dated on November 25 under each of the following credit terms.

a. net 30   c. net 45 date of invoice

b. net 30 EOM   d. net 60 EOM

13-5 **(Cost of Forgoing Cash Discounts)** Determine the cost of forgoing cash discounts under each of the following terms of sale.

a. 2/10 net 30   e. 1/10 net 60

b. 1/10 net 30   f. 3/10 net 30

c. 2/10 net 45   g. 4/10 net 180

d. 3/10 net 45

13-6 **(Cash Discount Versus Loan)** Erica Stone works in an accounts payable department. She has attempted to convince her boss to take the discount on the 3/10 net 45 credit terms most suppliers offer, but her boss argues that forgoing the 3 percent discount is less costly than a short-term loan at 14 percent. Prove that either Erica or her boss is incorrect.

13-7 **(Cash Discount Decisions)** Prairie Manufacturing has four possible suppliers, each offering different credit terms. Except for the differences in credit terms, their products and services are virtually identical. The credit terms offered by each supplier are as follows:

Supplier	Credit terms
J	1/10 net 30 EOM
K	2/20 net 80 EOM
L	1/20 net 60 EOM
M	3/10 net 55 EOM

a. Calculate the *approximate* cost of forgoing the cash discount from each supplier.

b. If the firm needs short-term funds, which are currently available from its commercial bank at 16 percent, and if each of the suppliers is viewed *separately*, which, if any, of the suppliers' cash discounts should the firm forgo? Explain why.

c. What impact, if any, would the fact that the firm could stretch its accounts payable (net period only) by 30 days from supplier M have on your answer in **b** relative to this supplier?

13-8 **(Changing Payment Cycle)** Upon accepting the position of chief executive officer and chairman of Reeves Machinery, Frank Cheney changed the firm's weekly payday from Monday afternoon to the following Friday afternoon. The firm's weekly payroll was $10 million, and the cost of short-term funds was 13 percent. If the effect of this change was to delay check clearing by one week, what *annual* savings, if any, were realized?

13-9 (Cost of Bank Loan) Data Back-up Systems has obtained a 90-day bank loan at an annual interest rate of 15 percent. If the loan is for $10,000, how much interest (in dollars) will the firm pay?

13-10 (Effective Rate of Interest) A financial institution lends a firm $10,000 for one year at 10 percent on a discounted basis and requires compensating balances of 20 percent of the face value of the loan. Determine the effective annual rate of interest associated with this loan.

13-11 (Integrative—Comparison of Loan Terms) Cumberland Furniture wishes to establish a prearranged borrowing agreement with its local commercial bank. The bank's terms for a line of credit are 3.30 percent over the prime rate, and the borrowing must be reduced to zero for a 30-day period. For an equivalent revolving credit agreement, the rate is 2.80 percent over prime with a commitment fee of .50 percent on the average unused balance. With both loans, the compensating balance is 20 percent of the amount borrowed. The prime rate is currently 8 percent. The revolving credit agreement is for $1 million. The firm expects on average to borrow $500,000 during the year no matter which loan agreement it decides to use.

a. What is the effective annual rate of interest under the line of credit?

b. What is the effective annual rate of interest under the revolving credit agreement? (*Hint:* Compute the ratio of the dollars the firm will pay in interest and commitment fees to the dollars the firm will effectively have use of.)

c. If the firm does expect to borrow an average of half the prearranged funds, which arrangement would you recommend for the borrower? Explain why.

13-12 (Cost of Commercial Paper) Commercial paper is usually sold at a discount. Fan Corporation has just sold an issue of 90-day commercial paper with a face value of $1 million. The firm has received $978,000.

a. What effective *annual* interest rate will the firm pay for financing with commercial paper?

b. If a brokerage fee of $9,612 was paid from the initial proceeds to an investment banker for selling the issue, what effective annual interest rate will the firm pay?

13-13 (Accounts Receivable as Collateral) Springer Products wishes to borrow $80,000 from a local bank using its accounts receivable to secure the loan. The bank's policy is to accept as collateral any accounts that are normally paid within 30 days of the end of the credit period so long as the average age of the account is not greater than the customer's average payment period. Springer's accounts receivable, their average ages, and the average payment period for each customer are given in the following table. The company extends terms of net 30 days.

Customer	Account receivable	Average age of account	Average payment period of customer
A	$20,000	10 days	40 days
B	6,000	40	35
C	22,000	62	50
D	11,000	68	65
E	2,000	14	30
F	12,000	38	50
G	27,000	55	60
H	19,000	20	35

a. Calculate the dollar amount of acceptable accounts receivable collateral held by Springer Products.

b. The bank reduces collateral by 10 percent for returns and allowances. What is the level of acceptable collateral under this condition?

c. The bank will advance 75 percent against the firm's acceptable collateral (after adjusting for returns and allowances). What amount can Springer borrow against these accounts?

13-14 (Factoring) Blair Finance factors the accounts of the Holder Company. All eight factored accounts are listed, with the amount factored, the date due, and the status as of May 30. Indicate the amounts Blair should have remitted to Holder as of May 30 and the dates of those remittances. Assume that the factor's commission of 2 percent is deducted as part of determining the amount of the remittance.

Account	Amount	Date Due	Status on May 30
A	$200,000	May 30	Collected May 15
B	90,000	May 30	Uncollected
C	110,000	May 30	Uncollected
D	85,000	June 15	Collected May 30
E	120,000	May 30	Collected May 27
F	180,000	June 15	Collected May 30
G	90,000	May 15	Uncollected
H	30,000	June 30	Collected May 30

13-15 (Inventory Financing) Raymond Manufacturing faces a liquidity crisis—it needs a loan of $100,000 for 30 days. Having no source of additional unsecured borrowing, the firm must find a secured short-term lender. The firm's accounts receivable are quite low, but its inventory is considered liquid and reasonably good collateral. The book value of the inventory is $300,000, of which $120,000 is finished goods.

(1) City-Wide Bank will make a $100,000 trust receipt loan against the finished goods inventory. The annual interest rate on the loan is 12 percent on the outstanding loan balance plus a .25 percent administration fee levied against the $100,000 initial loan amount. Because it will be liquidated as inventory is sold, the average amount owed over the month is expected to be $75,000.

(2) Sun State Bank is willing to lend $100,000 against a floating lien on the book value of inventory for the 30-day period at an annual interest rate of 13 percent.

(3) Citizens' Bank and Trust will loan $100,000 against a warehouse receipt on the finished goods inventory and charge 15 percent annual interest on the outstanding loan balance. A .5 percent warehousing fee will be levied against the average amount borrowed. Because the loan will be liquidated as inventory is sold, the average loan balance is expected to be $60,000.

a. Calculate the cost of each of the proposed plans for obtaining an initial loan amount of $100,000.

b. Which plan do you recommend? Why?

c. If the firm had made a purchase of $100,000 for which it had been given terms of 2/10 net 30, would it increase the firm's profitability to forgo the discount and not borrow as recommended in **b**? Why or why not?

Solutions to Self-Test Problems

ST-1   **a.**

Month	Total funds requirement (1)	Permanent funds requirement[a] (2)	Seasonal funds requirement [(1) − (2)] (3)
January	$7,400,000	$5,000,000	$2,400,000
February	5,500,000	5,000,000	500,000
March	5,000,000	5,000,000	0
April	5,300,000	5,000,000	300,000
May	6,200,000	5,000,000	1,200,000
June	6,000,000	5,000,000	1,000,000
July	5,800,000	5,000,000	800,000
August	5,400,000	5,000,000	400,000
September	5,000,000	5,000,000	0
October	5,300,000	5,000,000	300,000
November	6,000,000	5,000,000	1,000,000
December	6,800,000	5,000,000	1,800,000
Monthly average[b]		$5,000,000	$ 808,333

[a] Represents the lowest level of total funds required over the 12-month period.

[b] Found by summing the monthly amounts for 12 months and dividing the resulting totals by 12. For the permanent funds requirement, $60,000,000/12 = $5,000,000 and for the seasonal funds requirement, $9,700,000/12 = $808,333.

b. (1) *Aggressive strategy*—Applying this strategy would result in a perfect matching of long-term financing with the permanent funds requirement and short-term financing with the seasonal funds requirement. Therefore $5,000,000 of long-term financing and average monthly short-term financing of $808,333 would be used.

     (2) *Conservative strategy*—Applying this strategy, enough long-term financing to meet all projected funds requirements would be used; short-term financing would be used only to meet emergency or unexpected financial needs. In this case, $7,400,000 of long-term financing would be used to meet the peak funds requirement (during January) and no short-term financing would be used.

c. (1) *Aggressive strategy*

Total cost = ($5,000,000 × .16) + ($808,333 × .10)
            = $800,000 + $80,833 = $880,833

     (2) *Conservative strategy*

Total cost = ($7,400,000 × .16) + ($0 × .10)
            = $1,184,000 + $0 = $1,184,000

d. The *aggressive strategy is most profitable* since as noted in **c** its total cost is $880,833 as compared to the total cost of $1,184,000 under the conservative strategy. This difference results because the aggressive strategy uses as much of the less expensive short-term (current liability) financing as possible, whereas the conservative strategy finances all needs with the more expensive long-term financing. Also, under the aggressive strategy interest is paid only on necessary financing; under the conservative strategy interest is paid on unneeded funds. (For example, under the conservative strategy, in July interest is paid on $7,400,000 while only $5,800,000 of financing is needed.)

     The *aggressive strategy, on the other hand, is more risky* since it relies heavily on the *limited* short-term financing, while the conservative strategy reserves short-term borrowing for emergency or unexpected financial needs. In addition, the aggressive strategy results in lower net working capital than the conservative strategy, thereby resulting in lower liquidity and a higher risk of technical insolvency.

ST-2 a.

Supplier	Approximate cost of forgoing cash discount
X	$1\% \times [360/(55 - 10)] = 1\% \times 360/45 = 1\% \times 8\ \ = 8\%$
Y	$2\% \times [360/(30 - 10)] = 2\% \times 360/20 = 2\% \times 18 = 36\%$
Z	$2\% \times [360/(60 - 20)] = 2\% \times 360/40 = 2\% \times 9\ \ = 18\%$

b.

Supplier	Recommendation
X	8% cost of forgoing discount < 15% interest cost from bank; therefore, *forgo discount.*
Y	36% cost of forgoing discount > 15% interest cost from bank; therefore, *take discount and borrow from bank.*
Z	18% cost of forgoing discount > 15% interest cost from bank; therefore, *take discount and borrow from bank.*

c. Stretching accounts payable for supplier Z would change the cost of forgoing the cash discount to:

$$2\% \times [360/((60 + 20) - 20)] = 2\% \times 360/60 = 2\% \times 6 = 12\%$$

In this case, in light of the 15 percent interest cost from the bank, the recommended strategy in **b** would be to *forgo the discount* since the 12 percent cost of forgoing the discount would be less than the 15 percent bank interest cost.

CHAPTER 14

Cash and Marketable Securities

1

Basic strategies for the efficient management of cash include (1) paying accounts payable as late as possible, (2) turning inventory as quickly as possible, and (3) collecting accounts receivable as quickly as possible.

2

For a given level of total outlays, the firm's operating cash can be minimized by maximizing the cash cycle and thereby minimizing cash turnover.

3

Popular collection techniques, which include the use of concentration banking, lockboxes, and direct sends, are employed in order to maximize collection float.

4

Firms sometimes play the float by consciously anticipating the resulting float associated with the payment process in order to earn an additional return on the delay in withdrawal of funds from their accounts.

5

Marketable securities not only must have a ready market, but also should exhibit good safety of principal, which means that there is little or no likelihood of loss in value over time.

6

Commercial paper is an unsecured short-term note representing the deposit of a certain number of dollars in a commercial bank and providing a yield typically above that on a Treasury bill.

There used to be a saying "When E.F. Hutton talks, people listen." After a recent scandal on Wall Street, some people began saying "When E.F. Hutton talks, the feds listen."

E.F. Hutton, then the nation's fifth largest stock brokerage firm prior to its merger with Shearson Lehman Brothers, found itself involved in a scandal that led to its indictment on 2,000 counts of mail and wire fraud violations. It was accused of having engaged in a check-kiting scheme during the early 1980s that allowed Hutton to profit from check-clearing delays that involved the interest-free use of as much as $25 million dollars a day.

The indictment charged that Hutton used two cash management techniques to carry out its check-kiting scheme, "chaining" and "crossing." The process called "chaining" enables its users to maximize profits by making deposits and withdrawals in various regional banks that would create delays in the collection and payment system. Through the process called "crossing," a firm uses smaller banks to make check withdrawals of deposits that were not actually available, depositing those checks in a larger bank, and eventually cross-depositing checks drawn on the large bank in the small bank.

Hutton was accused of using a cash management technique called "playing the float." The firm supposedly wrote checks on funds that did not exist because it knew there would be a delay between the time that the check was received and that when the actual withdrawal would take place. However, when the checks were drawn on insufficient funds, Hutton is said to have carried the technique outside the limits of the law by purposely exploiting the use of funds it never had and taking advantage of deficiencies in the banking system, particularly with respect to small banks. The practice is one many cash managers would love to take advantage of, but today's technology allowed the law to catch up with Hutton. "Playing the float" is a cash management technique that can be used effectively as long as it's practiced within the boundaries of the law.

Clearly, the activities E.F. Hutton stood indicted of during the early 1980s demonstrate the benefits and consequences of overly aggressive and illegal cash management. Here we concentrate on important concepts and generally accepted—and legal—practices that can be employed in order to efficiently manage cash and liquid reserves held in marketable securities.

The Efficient Management of Cash

Cash and marketable securities are the most liquid of the firm's assets. Together they act as a pool of funds that can be used to pay bills as they come due and to meet any unexpected outlays. **Cash** is the ready currency to which all liquid assets can be reduced. **Marketable securities** are short-term, interest-earning, money market instruments used by the firm to obtain a return on temporarily idle funds. Because the rate of interest

cash The ready currency to which all liquid assets can be reduced.

511

marketable securities Short-term, interest-earning, money market instruments used by the firm to obtain a return on temporarily idle funds.

applied by banks to checking accounts is relatively low, firms tend to use excess bank balances to purchase marketable securities.

The basic strategies that should be employed by the business firm to manage cash are as follows:

1. Pay accounts payable as late as possible without damaging the firm's credit rating, but take advantage of any favorable cash discounts.[1]

2. Turn over inventory as quickly as possible, avoiding stockouts (depletions of stock) that might result in a loss of sales.

3. Collect accounts receivable as quickly as possible without losing future sales due to high-pressure collection techniques. Cash discounts, if they are economically justifiable, may be used to accomplish this objective.

The overall implications of these strategies for the firm can be demonstrated by looking at cash cycles and cash turnovers.[2]

FACT OR FABLE?   **1** Basic strategies for the efficient management of cash include (1) paying accounts payable as late as possible, (2) turning inventory as quickly as possible, and (3) collecting accounts receivable as quickly as possible. *(Fact)*

The Cash Cycle and Cash Turnover

cash cycle The amount of time elapsed from the point when an outlay is made to purchase raw materials to the point when cash is collected from the sale of the finished product using the raw material.

cash turnover The number of times per year the firm's cash is turned into a marketable product and then back into cash.

The **cash cycle** of a firm is defined as the amount of time that elapses from the point when the firm makes an outlay to purchase raw materials to the point when cash is collected from the sale of the finished product using the raw material. **Cash turnover** refers to the number of times each year the firm's cash is actually turned into a marketable product and then back into cash. The concept of the cash cycle and cash turnover can be illustrated using a simple example.

> **Example**
> MAX Company currently purchases all its raw materials on a credit basis and sells all its merchandise on credit. The credit terms extended the firm currently require payment within 30 days of a purchase, while the firm currently requires its customers to pay within 60 days of a sale. The firm's calculations of the average payment period and average collection period indicate that it is taking, on the average, 35 days to pay its accounts payable and 70 days to collect its accounts receivable. Further calculations reveal that, on the average, 85 days elapse between the purchase of a raw material and the sale of a finished good. In other words, the average age of the firm's inventory is 85 days.

---

[1] A discussion of the variables to consider in determining whether to take cash discounts appears in Chapter 13. A cash discount is often an enticement to pay accounts payable early to reduce the purchase price of goods. Strategies for the use of accruals as a free source of short-term financing are also discussed in Chapter 13.

[2] The conceptual model used in this part to demonstrate basic cash management strategies was developed by Lawrence J. Gitman in "Estimating Corporate Liquidity Requirements: A Simplified Approach," *The Financial Review,* 1974, pp. 79–88, and refined and operationalized by Lawrence J. Gitman and Kanwal S. Sachdeva in "A Framework for Estimating and Analyzing the Required Working Capital Investment," *Review of Business and Economic Research,* Spring 1982, pp. 35–44.

The firm's cash cycle can be shown by a simple graph, as in Figure 14.1. There are 120 days between the *cash outflow* to pay the account payable (on day 35) and the *cash inflow* from the collection of the account receivable (on day 155). During this period the firm's money is tied up. The firm's cash cycle is calculated by finding the average number of days that elapse between the cash outflows associated with paying accounts payable and the cash inflows associated with collecting accounts receivable. Stated as an equation, the cash cycle (CC) is

$$CC = AAI + ACP - APP \qquad (14.1)$$

where

$$AAI = \text{average age of inventory}$$
$$ACP = \text{average collection period}$$
$$APP = \text{average payment period}$$

Substituting AAI = 85 days, ACP = 70 days, and APP = 35 days into Equation 14.1, MAX's cash cycle is found to be 120 days (85 days + 70 days − 35 days). This result can be seen in Figure 14.1.

A firm's cash turnover (CT) is calculated by dividing the cash cycle into 360:

$$CT = \frac{360}{CC} \qquad (14.2)$$

MAX Company's cash turnover is currently 3 (360 days ÷ 120 days). The higher a firm's cash turnover, the less cash the firm requires. Cash turnover, like inventory turnover, should be maximized.

Figure 14.1
MAX Company's Cash Cycle

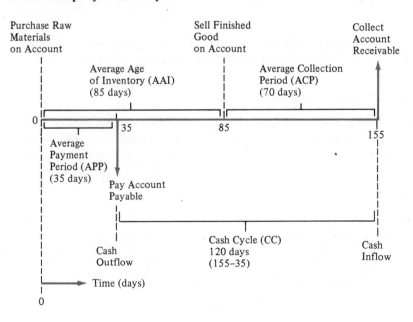

Determining Minimum Operating Cash[3]

A primary objective of corporate cash management should be to operate the firm *in a fashion that requires minimum cash*. This will in turn allow the availability of surplus cash funds for various investments and for repayment of debts. On the other hand, the more cash required for the firm's operation, the more investment opportunities (and potential returns) the firm must forgo. In other words, the fewer interest-earning assets a company can acquire, due to cash needed elsewhere, the higher the **opportunity cost** of the failure to make such investments.

opportunity cost The cost to the firm of forgone returns due to its failure to undertake available investment opportunities.

Establishing an optimal minimum cash level depends on both expected and unexpected receipts and disbursements. One simple approach is to set the minimum level as a *percentage of sales*. For example, a firm that wishes to maintain a cash balance equal to 8 percent of $2 million annual sales would set a balance of $160,000 (.08 × $2,000,000).

Using another simple technique, the minimum operating cash (MOC) needed by a firm can be estimated by *dividing the firm's total annual outlays (TAO)* by its *cash turnover (CT)*:

$$MOC = \frac{TAO}{CT} \tag{14.3}$$

The minimum operating cash can be multiplied by the opportunity cost in order to estimate the cost of these funds. The following example demonstrates this process.

> **Example**
> If MAX Company spends approximately $12 million annually on operating outlays (TAO) and has a cash turnover, CT, of 3, its minimum operating cash (MOC) is $4 million ($12,000,000 ÷ 3.00). This means that if it begins the year with $4 million in cash, it should have sufficient cash to pay bills as they come due. If the firm could earn at best 10 percent on investments or loan repayments, its opportunity cost of holding cash is 10 percent. Using this value, the cost of maintaining a $4 million cash balance will be $400,000 (.10 × $4,000,000) per year.

Note that while the corporate cash budget (discussed in Chapter 5) is a useful tool in cash planning, it does not deal with establishing the appropriate cash balance.

Cash Management Strategies

The effects of implementing each of the cash management strategies mentioned earlier are described in the following paragraphs, using the MAX Company data. The costs of implementing each proposed strategy are ignored, whereas in practice these costs would be measured against the calculated savings in order to make the appropriate strategy decision.

---

[3] The expression *minimum operating cash* as used throughout this part of the chapter can more correctly be viewed as the *net working capital investment required to support a specified level of operations*. Although minimum operating cash would be held in a variety of forms—cash, marketable securities, accounts receivable, or inventory—the expression is used here for pedagogical convenience. In other words, this model illustrates key concepts of cash management rather than its operational characteristics.

Stretching Accounts Payable

One strategy available to MAX is to *stretch accounts payable*—that is, as noted in Chapter 13, to pay its bills as late as possible without damaging its credit rating. Although this approach is financially attractive, it raises an important ethical issue; clearly, a supplier would not look favorably on a customer who purposely postponed payments.[4]

> **Example**
> If MAX Company can stretch the payment period from the current average of 35 days to an average of 45 days, its cash cycle will be reduced to 110 days (CC = 85 days + 70 days − 45 days = 110 days). By stretching its accounts payable 10 additional days, the firm increases its cash turnover rate from 3.00 to 3.27 (CT = 360 days ÷ 110 days = 3.27). This increased cash turnover rate results in a decrease in the firm's minimum operating cash requirement from $4,000,000 to approximately $3,670,000 (MOC = $12,000,000 ÷ 3.27 = $3,670,000). The reduction in required operating cash of approximately $330,000 ($4,000,000 − $3,670,000) represents an *annual savings* to the firm of $33,000 (.10 × $330,000), which is the opportunity cost of tying up that amount of funds. This savings clearly demonstrates the potential benefits of stretching accounts payable.

Efficient Inventory-Production Management

Another means of minimizing required cash is to increase inventory turnover. This can be achieved by increasing raw materials turnover, shortening the production cycle, or increasing finished goods turnover. Regardless of which of these approaches is used, the result will be a reduction in the amount of operating cash required.

> **Example**
> If MAX manages to increase inventory turnover by reducing the average age of inventory from the current level of 85 days to 70 days—a reduction of 15 days—the effects on its minimum operating cash will be as follows: There will be a reduction of 15 days in the cash cycle, from 120 days to 105 days (CC = 70 days + 70 days − 35 days = 105 days). The decreased average age of inventory for MAX increases the annual cash turnover rate from the initial level of 3.00 to 3.43 (CT = 360 days ÷ 105 days = 3.43). The increased cash turnover rate, in turn, results in a decrease in the firm's minimum operating cash requirement from $4 million to approximately $3.5 million (MOC = $12,000,000 ÷ 3.43 = $3,500,000). The reduction in required operating cash of approximately $500,000 ($4,000,000 − $3,500,000) represents an *annual savings* to the firm of $50,000 (.10 × $500,000). This savings clearly indicates the importance of efficiency in inventory and production management.

---

[4] The resolution of this ethical issue is not further addressed in this text. Suffice it to say that although the use of various techniques to slow down payments is widespread due to its financial appeal, it may not be justifiable on purely ethical grounds.

CAREER

CASH MANAGER:
Balancing Cash Deficits and Surpluses

Ten years ago Maria was a currency trader making split second million-dollar decisions at a major international bank in Canada. Recently she joined a *Fortune* 1000 company as the cash manager reporting to the treasurer.

Maria's responsibilities have changed, but she still finds herself on daily deadlines. Her job is to forecast the firm's daily, weekly, and monthly cash deficit or surplus. If the cash position is projected to be a surplus, Maria must decide in which of many investments to park the cash until the firm needs it. She has to decide not only which marketable securities will maximize her return but also the length of time the money can be invested. If, on the other hand, the firm is in a deficit cash position, Maria must decide where to get the funds at the best rate.

On this particular Monday morning, Maria begins the week meeting with her boss, the treasurer. They go over the computer printouts of maturing loans, cash disbursements, and cash collected from receivables in order to size up the need for cash. They estimate that, the firm needs to borrow $9.5 million today. They have three basic options: to dip into the firm's compensating balances (the amount left on deposit with the bank as a requirement of borrowing), to borrow under their established credit line, or to tap the commercial paper market.

They agree to attempt issuing commercial paper (actually an unsecured loan to the company) because its cost is lower than the interest rate charged on the credit line. It is Maria's job to organize and secure the sale of the issue by noon.

She meets with the commercial paper staff at 10 a.m. to set an interest rate which will be competitive and attractive to purchasers. Since commercial paper is sold at discount, the inter-est rate is implicit in the price rather than boldly stated. They also must decide on the maturity (how long they will need the funds, anywhere from 3 to 270 days). Once the interest rate and maturity are determined, the staff sets out to telemarket the issue to their favorite investors. Their phone list may include big insurance companies, pension fund managers, banks, or other corporations. Whoever they call, they must sell the issue before lunch. Should they fall short in this mission, Maria will have to either raise the interest rate and try again or pursue another source of financing. Today Maria decides to increase the interest rate (lower the price) of the paper. Her decision pays off—the needed financing is secured—at least for today. Maria's afternoon can now be spent on longer range planning—at a slower pace. At least until tomorrow, when it all starts over again.

Accelerating the Collection of Accounts Receivable

A third means of reducing the operating cash requirement is to speed up, or accelerate, the collection of accounts receivable. Accounts receivable, like inventory, tie up dollars that could otherwise be invested in earning assets. Let us consider the following example.

Example

If MAX Company, by changing its credit terms, is able to reduce the average collection period from the current level of 70 days to 50 days, it will reduce its cash cycle by 20 days (70 days − 50 days) to 100 days (CC = 120 days − 20 days = 100 days). The decrease in the collection period from 70 to 50 days raises the annual cash turnover rate from the initial level of 3.00 to 3.60 (CT = 360 days ÷ 100 days = 3.60). The increased cash turnover results in a decrease in the firm's minimum operating cash requirement from $4,000,000 to approximately $3,330,000 (MOC = $12,000,000 ÷ 3.60 = $3,330,000). The reduction in required operating cash of approximately $670,000 ($4,000,000 − $3,330,000) represents an *annual savings* to the firm of approximately $67,000 (.10 × $670,000). The $67,000 annual earnings represents the amount the firm can earn at its 10 percent opportunity cost on the $670,000 reduction in operating cash.

Combining Cash Management Strategies

Firms typically do not attempt to implement just one cash management strategy; they attempt to use them all to reduce their operating cash requirement. Of course, when implementing these policies, care should be taken not to damage the firm's credit rating by overstretching accounts payable, to avoid having a large number of inventory stock-outs, or to avoid losing sales due to the use of high-pressure collection techniques. Using a combination of these strategies would have the following effects on MAX Company.

Example
If MAX simultaneously increased the average payment period by 10 days, decreased the average age of inventory by 15 days, and sped the collection of accounts receivable by 20 days, its cash cycle would be reduced to 75 days, as shown here.

Initial cash cycle		120 days
Reduction due to:		
1. Increased payment period		
35 days to 45 days =	10 days	
2. Decreased inventory age		
85 days to 70 days =	15 days	
3. Decreased collection period		
70 days to 50 days =	20 days	
Less: Total reduction in cash cycle		45 days
New cash cycle		75 days

MAX's annual cash turnover rate increases from 3.00 to 4.80 (CT = 360 days ÷ 75 days = 4.80). The increased cash turnover reduces the minimum operating cash requirement from $4 million to approximately $2.5 million (MOC = $12,000,000 ÷ 4.80 = $2,500,000). The reduction in required operating cash of approximately $1.5 million ($4,000,000 − $2,500,000) represents an annual savings to the firm of $150,000 (.10 × $1,500,000). This savings represents a sizable decrease in the firm's opportunity costs, from an initial level of $400,000 (.10 × $4,000,000) to $250,000 (.10 × $2,500,000).

---

2 For a given level of total outlays, the firm's operating cash can be minimized by maximizing the cash cycle and thereby minimizing cash turnover. *(Fable)*
For a given level of total outlays, the firm's operating cash can be minimized by *minimizing* the cash cycle and thereby *maximizing* cash turnover.

FACT OR FABLE?

Cash Management Techniques

Financial managers have at their disposal a variety of cash management techniques that can provide additional savings. These techniques are aimed at minimizing the firm's cash requirements by taking advantage of certain imperfections in the collection and payment systems. Assuming that the firm has done all it can to select vendors offering the most attractive and flexible credit terms and to stimulate customers to pay promptly, certain techniques can further speed collections and slow disbursements. These procedures take advantage of the ''float'' existing in the collection and payment systems.

Float

float Funds dispatched by a payer that are not yet in a form that can be spent by the payee.

In the broadest sense, **float** refers to funds that have been dispatched by a payer (the firm or individual *making* payment) but are not yet in a form that can be spent by the payee (the firm or individual *receiving* payment). Float also exists when a payee has received funds in a spendable form but these funds have not been withdrawn from the account of the payer. Delays in the collection-payment system resulting from the transportation and processing of checks are responsible for float. With electronic payments systems as well as deliberate action by the Federal Reserve system, it seems clear that in the foreseeable future float will virtually disappear. Until that time, however, financial managers must continue to understand and take advantage of float.

Types of Float

collection float The delay between the time when a payer or customer deducts a payment from the checking account ledger and the time when the payee or vendor actually receives the funds in a spendable form.

disbursement float The lapse between the time when a firm deducts a payment from its checking account ledger (disburses it) and the time when funds are actually withdrawn from its account.

Currently business firms and individuals can experience both collection and disbursement float as part of the process of making financial transactions. **Collection float** results from the delay between the time when a payer or customer deducts a payment from the checking account ledger and the time when the payee or vendor actually receives these funds in a spendable form. Thus collection float is experienced by the payee and is a delay in the receipt of funds. **Disbursement float** results from the lapse between the time when a firm deducts a payment from its checking account ledger (disburses it) and the time when funds are actually withdrawn from its account. Disbursement float is experienced by the payer and is a delay in the actual withdrawal of funds.

Components of Float

mail float The delay between the time when a payer mails a payment and the time when the payee receives it.

processing float The delay between the receipt of a check by the payee and its deposit in the firm's account.

clearing float The delay between the deposit of a check by the payee and the actual availability of the funds.

Both collection float and disbursement float have the same three basic components:

1. **Mail float:** The delay between the time when a payer places payment in the mail and the time when it is received by the payee.
2. **Processing float:** The delay between the receipt of a check by the payee and the deposit of it in the firm's account.
3. **Clearing float:** The delay between the deposit of a check by the payee and the actual availability of the funds. This component of float is attributable to the time required for a check to clear the banking system.[5]

[5] Currently, on checks cleared through the Federal Reserve banking system, clearing time of less than two days is guaranteed to the collecting bank, but, of course, this does not assure the depositor (payee) that the bank will make the money available within two days.

Figure 14.2
Float Resulting from a Check Issued and Mailed by the Payer Company to the Payee Company

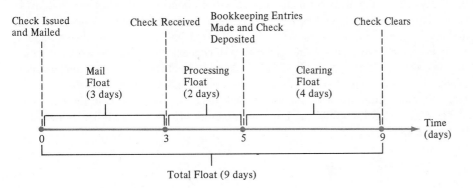

Figure 14.2 illustrates the key components of float resulting from the issuance and mailing of a check by the payer company to the payee company on day zero. The entire process required a total of nine days: three days' mail float; two days' processing float; and four days' clearing float. To the payer company, the delay is disbursement float; to the payee company, the delay is collection float.

Collection Techniques

The firm's objective is not only to stimulate customers to pay their accounts as promptly as possible but also to convert their payments into a spendable form as quickly as possible—in other words, to *minimize collection float*. A variety of techniques aimed at *speeding up collections,* and thereby reducing collection float, are available.

Concentration Banking

Firms with numerous sales outlets throughout the country often designate certain offices as collection centers for given geographic areas. Customers in these areas remit their payments to these sales offices, which in turn deposit the receipts in local banks. At certain times, or on a when-needed basis, funds are transferred by wire from these regional banks to a concentration, or disbursing, bank, from which bill payments are dispatched.[6]

Concentration banking is used to reduce collection float by shortening the mail and clearing float components. Mail float is reduced because regionally dispersed collection centers bring the collection point closer to the point from which the check is sent. Clearing float should also be reduced, since the payee's regional bank is likely to be in the same Federal Reserve district or the same city as the bank on which the check is drawn; it may even be the same bank. A reduction in clearing float will, of course, make funds available to the firm more quickly.

concentration banking Reduces collection float by shortening mail and clearing float. Payments are made to regionally dispersed collection centers, then deposited in local banks for quick clearing.

[6] Most large firms disburse funds, or pay bills, only from certain banks. Normally, separate payroll and general expense accounts are maintained.

Example

Suppose a firm could go to concentration banking and reduce its collection period by three days; if the company normally carried $10 million in receivables and that level equaled a 30-day supply, cutting three days from the collection process would result in a $1 million drop in receivables [(3 ÷ 30) × $10,000,000]. Given a 10 percent opportunity cost, the gross annual benefits (profits) of concentration banking would amount to $100,000 (.10 × $1,000,000). Clearly, assuming no change in risk, so long as total annual costs—*incremental* administrative costs and bank service fees, and the opportunity cost of holding specified minimum bank balances—are less than the expected annual benefits of $100,000, the proposed program of concentration banking should be implemented.

Lockboxes

lockbox system Reduces collection float by having the payer send the payment to a nearby post office box that is emptied by the firm's bank several times daily, thus accelerating the deposit process.

Another method used to reduce collection float is the **lockbox system,** which differs from concentration banking in several important ways. Instead of mailing payment to a collection center, the payer sends it to a post office box that is emptied by the firm's bank one or more times each business day. The bank opens the payment envelopes, deposits the checks in the firm's account, and sends a deposit slip (or, under certain arrangements, a computer tape) indicating the payments received, along with any enclosures, to the collecting firm. Lockboxes normally are geographically dispersed, and the funds, when collected, are wired from each lockbox bank to the firm's disbursing bank.

The lockbox system is superior to concentration banking because it reduces processing float as well as mail and clearing float. The receipts are immediately deposited in the firm's account by the bank so that processing occurs after, rather than before, funds are deposited in the firm's account. This allows the firm to use the funds almost immediately for disbursing payments. Additional reductions in mail float may also result since payments do not have to be delivered but are picked up by the bank at the post office.

Direct Sends

direct send Reduces clearing float by allowing the payee to present payment checks directly to the banks on which they are drawn, thus avoiding the delay of the clearing process.

To reduce clearing float, firms that have received large checks drawn on distant banks, or a large number of checks drawn on banks in a given city, may arrange to present these checks directly for payment to the bank on which they are drawn. Such a procedure is called a **direct send.** Rather than depositing these checks in its collection account, the firm arranges to present the checks to the bank on which they are drawn and receive immediate payment. The firm can use Express Mail or private express services to get the checks into a bank in the same city or to a sales office where an employee can take the checks to the bank and present them for payment. In most cases the funds will be transferred via wire into the firm's disbursement account.

Deciding whether to use direct sends is relatively straightforward. If the benefits from the reduced clearing time are greater than the cost, the checks should be sent directly for payment rather than cleared through normal banking channels.

Example
If a firm with an opportunity to earn 10 percent on its idle balances can, through a direct send, make available $1.2 million three days earlier than would otherwise be the case, the benefit of this direct send would be $1,000 [.10 × (3 days ÷ 360 days) × $1,200,000]. If the cost of achieving this three-day reduction in float is less than $1,000, the direct send would be recommended.

Other Techniques

A number of other techniques can be used to reduce collection float. One method commonly used by firms that collect a fixed amount from customers on a regular basis, such as insurance companies, is the preauthorized check. A **preauthorized check (PAC)** is a check written against a customer's checking account for a previously agreed-upon amount by the firm to which it is payable. Because the check has been legally authorized by the customer, it does not require the customer's signature. The payee merely issues and then deposits the PAC in its account. The check then clears through the banking system just as though written by the customer and received and deposited by the firm.

A method used by firms with multiple collection points to move funds is the depository transfer check. A **depository transfer check (DTC)** is an unsigned check drawn on one of the firm's bank accounts and deposited into its account at another bank—typically a concentration or major disbursing bank. Once the DTC has cleared the bank on which it is drawn, the actual transfer of funds is completed. Most firms currently transmit deposit information via telephone rather than by mail to their concentration banks, which then prepare and deposit DTCs into the firm's accounts.

Firms also frequently use wire transfers to reduce collection float by quickly transferring funds from one bank account to another. **Wire transfers** are telegraphic communications that, via bookkeeping entries, remove funds from the payer's bank and deposit them into the payee's bank. Wire transfers can eliminate mail and clearing float and may provide processing float reductions as well. They are sometimes used instead of DTCs to move funds into key disbursing accounts.

preauthorized check (PAC) A check written by the payee against a customer's checking account for a previously agreed-upon amount. Due to prior legal authorization, the check does not require the customer's signature.

depository transfer check (DTC) An unsigned check drawn on one of the firm's bank accounts and deposited into its account at a concentration or major disbursement bank, thereby avoiding clearance delays.

wire transfers Telegraphic communications that, via bookkeeping entries, remove funds from the payer's bank and deposit them in the payee's bank, thereby reducing collection float.

---

3 Popular collection techniques, which include the use of concentration banking, lockboxes, and direct sends, are employed in order to maximize collection float. *(Fable)*
Popular collection techniques, which include the use of concentration banking, lockboxes, and direct sends, are employed in order to *minimize* collection float.

FACT OR FABLE?

Disbursement Techniques

The firm's objective relative to accounts payable is not only to pay its accounts as late as possible but also to slow down the availability of funds to suppliers and employees once the payment has been dispatched—in other words, to *maximize disbursement float.* A variety of techniques aimed at *slowing down disbursements,* and thereby increasing disbursement float, are available.

Controlled Disbursing

controlled disbursing The strategic use of mailing points and bank accounts to lengthen mail float and clearing float, respectively.

Controlled disbursing involves the strategic use of mailing points and bank accounts to lengthen mail float and clearing float, respectively. When the date of postmark is considered the effective date of payment by the supplier, the firm may be able to lengthen the mail time associated with disbursements.[7] This is done by placing payments in the mail at locations from which it is known they will take a considerable amount of time to reach the supplier. Typically, small towns not close to major highways and cities provide excellent opportunities to increase mail float.

The widespread availability of computers and data on check clearing times allows firms to develop disbursement schemes that maximize clearing float on their payments. These methods involve assigning payments going to vendors in certain geographic areas to be drawn on specific banks from which maximum clearing float will result.

Data on clearing time among banks located in various cities can be developed by the firm itself; it can be obtained from a major bank's cash management service department; or it can be purchased from a firm such as Phoenix-Hecht Cash Management Services, a Chicago-based firm that sells information to banks and other firms. Firms that are attempting to assign checks to be drawn on banks providing maximum float to the vendor city will typically run a computer program each payment cycle. The program will draw on the clearing-time database and assign the checks to be drawn on the bank account providing maximum clearing float to each vendor. The number of potential bank accounts considered will depend on the economics of the system. Once the computer has assigned payments to banks, the computer will print the checks on blank check forms, and the checks will then be sorted and mailed from remote points, as mentioned earlier. Although such controlled disbursement systems are commonly used today, their cost must be justified by the additional earnings achieved by the firm on the disbursement float created.

Playing the Float

playing the float A method of consciously anticipating the resulting float, or delay, associated with the payment process.

Playing the float is a method of consciously anticipating the resulting float, or delay, associated with the payment process. Firms often play the float by writing checks against funds not currently in their checking accounts. They are able to do this because they know a delay will occur between the receipt and the deposit of checks by suppliers and the actual withdrawal of funds from their checking accounts. It is likely that the firm's bank account will not be drawn down by the amount of the payments for a few additional days. Although the ineffective use of this practice could result in problems associated with ''bounced checks,'' many firms use float to stretch out their accounts payable.[8]

Firms play the float in a variety of ways—all of which are aimed at keeping funds in an interest-earning form for as long as possible. For example, one way of playing the float is to deposit a certain proportion of a payroll or payment into the firm's checking account on several successive days *following* the actual issuance of a group of checks. If the firm

---

[7] A supplier's credit terms as well as any penalties associated with late payment are typically stated in the invoice that accompanies the shipment of merchandise. Of course, depending on the supplier, the terms of the invoice may or may not be enforced. Knowledge of the strictness of suppliers' credit terms is often useful for developing the firm's accounts payable strategies.

[8] Issuing checks against nonexistent funds can be prosecuted only if the check is drawn on insufficient funds. The fact that a check bounces is viewed as prima facie—but not irrefutable—evidence of fraud. The burden of proof that the act causing insufficient funds was not willful is placed on the issuer. If such proof cannot be given, the issuer will be convicted of fraud. Prosecution rarely results, since the issuer usually obtains sufficient funds to satisfy the obligation prior to the filing of any criminal charges.

can determine from historic data that only 25 percent of its payroll checks are cashed on the day immediately following the issuance of the checks, then only 25 percent of the value of the payroll needs to be in its checking account one day later. The amount of checks cashed on each of several succeeding days can also be estimated, until the entire payroll is accounted for. Normally, however, to protect itself against any irregularities a firm will place slightly more money in its account than is needed to cover the expected withdrawals.

Another way of playing the float is to use payable-through drafts, rather than checks, to pay large sums of money like the payroll. A **payable-through draft** is similar to a check in that it is drawn on the payer's checking account and is payable to a given payee. Unlike a check, however, it is not payable on demand; approval of the draft by the payer is required before the bank pays the draft. The advantage of these drafts to the payer is that money does not have to be placed on deposit until the draft clears the bank; instead, the firm can invest it in short-term money market vehicles. As the drafts are cleared for payment by the payer, the investments can be liquidated and the funds used to cover the drafts. Banks may charge a modest fee for processing the drafts, but this technique enables the firm to keep its money more fully invested for a longer period of time.

payable-through draft
A draft drawn on the payer's checking account, payable to a given payee but not payable on demand; approval of the draft by the payer is required before the bank pays the draft.

Example
Assume that by using payable-through drafts in place of checks to meet its payroll, a firm can increase disbursement float by five days. If its monthly payroll is $12 million, this increase in float will translate into profits of $200,000 per year given an opportunity cost of 10 percent. That is the amount of profit the firm would realize by keeping $12 million invested at 10 percent (per year) for five additional days each month for an entire year [$.10 \times (5 \text{ days} \div 360 \text{ days}) \times \$12,000,000 \times (12 \text{ months/} \text{year}) = \$200,000$].

But note that many vendors will not accept payable-through drafts as payment for the goods or services provided, and in some states the use of these drafts is prohibited by law.

---

4 Firms sometimes play the float by consciously anticipating the resulting float associated with the payment process in order to earn an additional return on the delay in withdrawal of funds from their accounts. *(Fact)*

FACT OR FABLE?

Overdraft Systems and Zero-Balance Accounts

Firms that aggressively manage cash disbursements will often arrange for some type of overdraft system or a zero-balance account. Under an **overdraft system,** if the firm's checking account balance is insufficient to cover all checks presented against the account, the bank will automatically lend the firm enough money to cover the amount of the overdraft. The bank, of course, will charge the firm interest on the funds lent and will limit the amount of overdraft coverage. Such an arrangement is important for a business that actively plays the float.

Firms can also establish **zero-balance accounts**—checking accounts in which zero balances are maintained. Under this arrangement, each day the bank will notify the firm of the total amount of checks presented against the account. The firm then transfers only that

overdraft system Automatic coverage by the bank of all checks presented against the firm's account, regardless of the account balance.

zero-balance account A checking account in which a zero balance is maintained and the bank requires the firm to deposit funds to cover checks drawn on the account only as they are presented.

amount—typically from a master account or through liquidation of a portion of its marketable securities—into the account. Once the corresponding checks have been paid, the account balance reverts to zero. The bank, of course, must be compensated for this service.

The Role of Strong Banking Relationships

Establishing and maintaining strong banking relations is one of the most important elements in an effective cash management system. Banks have become keenly aware of the profitability of corporate accounts and in recent years have developed a number of innovative services and packages designed to attract various types of businesses. No longer are banks simply a place to establish checking accounts and secure loans; instead, they have become the source of a wide variety of cash management services. For example, in addition to providing advice and assistance with government securities portfolios, banks are selling sophisticated information-processing packages to commercial clients; these packages deal with everything from basic accounting and budgeting to complex multinational disbursement and centralized cash control. All are designed to help financial managers maximize day-to-day cash availability and facilitate short-term investing.

Today most bank services are offered to corporations on a direct-fee basis, but some of the depository functions are still paid for with deposit balances rather than direct charges. Banks prefer the "compensating balance" approach—giving credit against bank service charges for amounts maintained in the customer's checking account, since it fosters deposit growth and provides a foundation for the future growth of bank earnings. Bank services available to cash managers should be used only if the benefits to be derived from their use are greater than their costs.

Example

A firm has been offered a cash management service that should eliminate "excess" cash on deposit and reduce certain administrative and clerical costs. Assume that the service, which costs $50,000 per year, involves the collection, movement, and reporting of corporate cash. The purported benefits are these: (1) The firm should be able to reduce the cash required to support operations by some $600,000 (as a result of tighter control over the cash flow), and (2) administrative and clerical costs should drop by about $1,000 per month (since the bank will be taking on administrative and clerical duties as part of the service). Using a 10 percent opportunity cost, the benefits and costs would be as follows:

Benefits (annual)	
Extra returns from reduced cash on hand (.10 × $600,000)	$60,000
Reduced administrative and clerical costs ($1,000 × 12)	12,000
Total annual benefits	$72,000
Less: Costs (annual)	
Bank service charges	50,000
Net annual benefits	$22,000

From a benefit-cost perspective, the proposal looks promising; the major risk, of course, is that the purported benefits will fall far short of the mark. Management, however, can at least get an idea of such risk. A simple calculation, for example, may be used to estimate the minimum reduction in cash or opportunity cost required to generate a sufficient level of total benefits. On the other hand, some positive risk reductions may result from adoption of the bank's program, such as less exposure to volatile interest rates, and these should obviously also be considered.

Marketable Securities Fundamentals

Marketable securities are short-term, interest-earning, money market instruments that can easily be converted into cash.[9] Marketable securities are classified as part of the firm's liquid assets.

Motives for Holding Marketable Securities

There are three motives for holding marketable securities, which act as a storehouse of liquidity. Each motive is based on the premise that the firm should attempt to earn a return on temporarily idle funds. The type of marketable security purchased will depend on the motive for its purchase.

Transactions Motive

A firm that must make various planned payments in the near future may already have the cash with which to make these payments. In order to earn some return on these funds, the firm invests them in a marketable security that matures or can be easily liquidated on or just before the required payment date. These marketable securities are held for **transactions motives.**

Safety Motive

Marketable securities held for **safety motives** are used to service the firm's cash account. These securities must be very liquid, since they are bought with funds that will be needed at some unknown future time. Such securities protect the firm against being unable to satisfy unexpected demands for cash.

Speculative Motive

Marketable securities held because the firm currently has no other use for certain funds are said to be held for **speculative motives.** Although this motive is the least common, some firms occasionally have excess cash. Until the firm finds a suitable use for this money, it invests it in marketable securities as well as in long-term instruments.

Characteristics of Marketable Securities

The basic characteristics of marketable securities affect the degree of their salability. To be truly marketable, a security must have two basic characteristics: (1) a ready market and (2) safety of principal (no likelihood of loss in value).

transactions motives Reasons for which marketable securities are held to earn a temporary return and then liquidated in order to make various planned payments.

safety motives Reasons for which marketable securities are held to earn returns and liquidated as needed in order to service the firm's cash account.

speculative motives Reasons for which marketable securities are held to earn returns until the firm finds a suitable use for the excess cash.

[9] As explained in Chapter 2, the *money market* results from a financial relationship between the suppliers and demanders of short-term funds, that is, marketable securities.

A Ready Market

breadth of a market
Determined by the number
of participants (buyers).

depth of a market
Determined by its ability to
absorb the purchase or sale
of a large dollar amount of
a particular security.

The market for a security should have both breadth and depth in order to minimize the amount of time required to convert it into cash. The **breadth of a market** is determined by the number of participants (buyers). A broad market is one that has many participants. The **depth of a market** is determined by its ability to absorb the purchase or sale of a large dollar amount of a particular security. It is therefore possible to have a broad market that has no depth. Thus 100,000 participants each willing to purchase 1 share of a security is less desirable than 1,000 participants each willing to purchase 2,000 shares. Although both breadth and depth are desirable, in order for a security to be salable, it is much more important for a market to have depth.

Safety of Principal (No Likelihood of Loss in Value)

safety of principal The ease
of salability of a security for
close to its initial value.

There should be little or no loss in the value of a marketable security over time. Consider a security recently purchased for $1,000. If it can be sold quickly for $500, does that make it marketable? No. According to the definition of marketability, the security must not only be salable quickly but must also be salable for close to the $1,000 initially invested. This aspect of marketability is referred to as **safety of principal.** Only securities that can be easily converted into cash without experiencing any appreciable reduction in principal are candidates for short-term investment.

FACT OR FABLE?
    5   Marketable securities not only must have a ready market, but also should exhibit good safety of principal, which means that there is little or no likelihood of loss in value over time. *(Fact)*

Making Purchase Decisions

A major decision confronting the business firm is when to purchase marketable securities.[10] This decision is difficult because it involves a trade-off between the opportunity to earn a return on idle funds during the holding period and the brokerage costs associated with the purchase and sale of marketable securities.

> **Example**
> Assume that a firm must pay $35 in brokerage costs to purchase and sell $4,500 worth of marketable securities yielding an annual return of 8 percent that will be held for one month. Since the securities are to be held for $\frac{1}{12}$ of a year, the firm will earn interest of .67 percent ($\frac{1}{12} \times 8\%$) or $30 (.0067 × $4,500). Since this is less than the $35 cost of the transaction, the firm should not make the investment. This trade-off between interest returns and brokerage costs is a key factor in determining when and whether to purchase marketable securities.

---

[10] Numerous quantitative models for determining the optimum amounts of marketable securities to hold in certain circumstances have been developed. One of the most popular of these models is based on the inventory theory underlying the EOQ model, which is briefly described in Chapter 15. A discussion of these cash–marketable security models is beyond the scope of this text.

JOSHUA SMITH:
A Vision for Becoming a *Fortune* 500 Company

There was a time when most minority businesses were small ventures with little need for the rules of corporate finance. But times are changing, and Joshua Smith is leading the way. In 1978, he took $15,000 and started a small business, located in a single room with a borrowed typewriter. The business was the MAXIMA Corporation, a full service, integrated information processing corporation, which had revenues of $54.3 million in fiscal year 1987.

After qualifying for participation in the Small Business Administration's (SBA) 8(a) set-aside program in 1979, MAXIMA began to receive government contracts. Contracts obtained through the 8(a) set-aside program were one source of steady income that provided MAXIMA's sustained growth. As a participant of the 8(a) program, MAXIMA was able to engage in a limited competitive bidding process with other 8(a) participants and rely heavily on personal contacts. This process suited Smith's style as a superb salesman.

Another source of income for MAXIMA was the 1984 purchase of 18 percent of MAXIMA by Martin-Marietta. This gave Smith an additional $1 million in expansion and equity capital, which was used to acquire several information-related businesses.

The future looked bright for Smith and MAXIMA at the start of 1987. However, because of their enormous success within the SBA program, the company was now too large to qualify. It would have to begin entering into competitive bidding for government work or look into commercial ventures. Smith had expected to have plenty of time to prepare the company for this change, but the end came sooner than he expected.

MAXIMA's strategy began to look foggy. In less than one year, the company made six acquisitions in various information-related fields. The previously tight management system began to strain at the task of effectively coordinating all of these new operations. In February 1987, senior vice president and acquisitions planner Paul Jones resigned. Other problems included Smith's exhausting schedule and the failure of one of MAXIMA's commercial ventures.

Over the past two fiscal years since its last 8(a) contract, MAXIMA has doubled its revenues and was profitable. In the competitive arena, MAXIMA won over 30 percent of all contracts it bid and was in the best and finals in almost 90 percent of all proposals submitted.

Despite all of this, MAXIMA still has the benefit of Joshua Smith's superb salesmanship and the strong support of a new management team. This support is due in part to Smith's friendly management style and also to the fact that the employees own 13 percent of the company through a profit sharing plan.

Clearly, MAXIMA is a company at a major turning point. Joshua Smith envisions MAXIMA becoming a Black Fortune 500 company. However, guaranteed to be a rough one. Smith, himself may be the only one who can determine the fate of the MAXIMA Corporation.

The Popular Marketable Securities

The securities most commonly held as part of a firm's marketable securities portfolio are divided into two groups: (1) government issues and (2) nongovernment issues. Table 14.1 presents the July 17, 1987, yields for the marketable securities described in the sections that follow.

Government Issues

The short-term obligations issued by the federal government and available as marketable security investments are Treasury bills, Treasury notes, and federal agency issues.

Table 14.1
Yields on Popular Marketable Securities for the Week
Ended July 17, 1987

Security	Maturity period	Yield
Banker's acceptances	3 months	6.52%
Certificates of deposit	3 months	6.64
Commercial paper	3 months	6.59
Eurodollar deposits	3 months	6.84
Federal agency issues[a]	3 months	5.71
Money market mutual funds[b]	approx. 30 days	6.16
Treasury bills	3 months	5.58
Treasury notes	1 year	6.53

[a] A Federal Home Loan Bank (FHLB) issue maturing in October 1987 is used here in the absence of any average-yield data.

[b] A Scudder Cash Investment Fund with an average maturity of 30 days is used here in the absence of any average-yield data.

Treasury Bills

Treasury bills U.S. Treasury obligations issued weekly on an auction basis, having varying maturities, generally under a year, and virtually no risk.

Treasury bills are obligations of the U.S. Treasury that are issued weekly on an auction basis. The most common maturities are 91 and 182 days, although bills with one-year maturities are occasionally sold. Treasury bills are sold by competitive bidding. Because they are issued in bearer form, there is a strong *secondary (resale) market*. The bills are sold at a discount from their face value, the face value being received at maturity. The smallest denomination of a Treasury bill currently available is $10,000. Since Treasury bills are issues of the United States government, they are considered to be virtually risk-free. For this reason, and because of the strong secondary market for them, Treasury bills are one of the most popular marketable securities. The yields on Treasury bills are generally lower than those on any other marketable securities due to their virtually risk-free nature.

Treasury Notes

Treasury notes U.S. Treasury obligations with initial maturities of between one and seven years, paying interest at a stated rate semiannually, and having virtually no risk.

Treasury notes have initial maturities of between one and seven years, but due to the existence of a strong secondary market, they are quite attractive marketable security investments. They are generally issued in minimum denominations of $5,000, carry a coupon interest rate, and pay interest semiannually. A firm that purchases a Treasury note that has less than one year left to maturity is in the same position as if it had purchased a marketable security with an initial maturity of less than one year. Due to their virtually risk-free nature, Treasury notes generally have a relatively low yield.

Federal Agency Issues

federal agency issues Low-risk securities issued by government agencies but not guaranteed by the U.S. Treasury, having generally short maturities and offering slightly higher yields than comparable Treasury issues.

Certain agencies of the federal government issue their own debt. These **federal agency issues** are not part of the public debt, are not a legal obligation of the U.S. Treasury, and are not guaranteed by the U.S. Treasury. Regardless of their lack of direct government backing, the issues of government agencies are readily accepted as low-risk securities, since most purchasers feel they are implicitly guaranteed by the federal government.

Agency issues generally have minimum denominations of $5,000 and are issued either with a coupon interest rate or at a discount. Agencies commonly issuing short-term instruments include the Bank for Cooperatives (BC), the Federal Home Loan Banks (FHLB), the Federal Intermediate Credit Banks (FICB), the Federal Land Banks (FLB), and the Federal National Mortgage Association (FNMA). Most agency issues have short maturities and offer slightly higher yields than Treasury issues having similar maturities. Agency issues have a strong secondary market, which is most easily reached through government security dealers.

Nongovernment Issues

A number of additional marketable securities are issued by banks or businesses. These nongovernment issues typically have slightly higher yields than government issues due to the slightly higher risks associated with them. The principal nongovernment marketable securities are negotiable certificates of deposit, commercial paper, banker's acceptances, Eurodollar deposits, money market mutual funds, and repurchase agreements.

Negotiable Certificates of Deposit (CDs)

Negotiable certificates of deposit (CDs) are negotiable instruments representing the deposit of a certain number of dollars in a commercial bank. The amounts and maturities are normally tailored to the investor's needs. Average maturities of 30 days are quite common. A good secondary market for CDs exists. Normally the smallest denomination for a negotiable CD is $100,000. The yields on CDs are initially set on the basis of size, maturity, and prevailing money market conditions. They are typically above those on Treasury bills and comparable to or slightly above the yield on commercial paper.

Commercial Paper

Commercial paper is a short-term, unsecured promissory note issued by a corporation with a very high credit standing.[11] These notes are issued, generally in multiples of $100,000, by all types of firms and have initial maturities of anywhere from 3 to 270 days.[12] They can be directly placed by the issuer or sold through dealers. The yield on commercial paper typically is comparable to or slightly below that available on negotiable CDs but above that paid on government issues with similar maturities.

negotiable certificates of deposit (CDs) Negotiable instruments representing specific cash deposits in commercial banks, having varying maturities and yields based on size, maturity, and prevailing money market conditions. Yields are generally comparable to or a bit above those of commercial paper.

commercial paper A short-term, unsecured promissory note issued by a corporation with a very high credit standing, having a yield slightly below that of negotiable CDs but above that of comparable government issues.

---

6 | Commercial paper is an unsecured short-term note representing the deposit of a certain number of dollars in a commercial bank and providing a yield typically above that on a Treasury bill. *(Fable)*
Commercial paper is an unsecured short-term note *issued by a corporation with a very high credit standing* and providing a yield typically above that on a Treasury bill.

---

[11] The role of commercial paper from the point of view of the issuer is included in the discussion of the various sources of short-term financing available to business in Chapter 13.

[12] The maximum maturity is 270 days because the Securities and Exchange Commission (SEC) requires formal registration of corporate issues having maturities greater than 270 days.

Banker's Acceptances

banker's acceptances Short-term, low-risk marketable securities arising from bank guarantees of business transactions; they are sold by banks at a discount from their maturity value and provide yields competitive with negotiable CDs and commercial paper.

Banker's acceptances arise from a short-term credit arrangement used by businesses to finance transactions, especially those involving firms in foreign countries or firms with unknown credit capacities. The purchaser, to assure payment to the seller, requests its bank to issue a *letter of credit* on its behalf, authorizing the seller to draw a *time draft*—an order to pay a specified amount at a specified time—on the bank in payment for the goods. Once the goods are shipped, the seller presents a time draft along with proof of shipment to its bank. The seller's bank then forwards the draft with appropriate shipping documents to the buyer's bank for acceptance and receives payment for the transaction. The buyer's bank may either hold the acceptance to maturity or sell it at a discount in the money market. If sold, the size of the discount from the acceptance's maturity value and the amount of time until the acceptance is paid determine the purchaser's yield.

As a result of its sale, the banker's acceptance becomes a marketable security that can be traded in the marketplace. The initial maturities of banker's acceptances are typically between 30 and 180 days, 90 days being most common. A banker's acceptance is a low-risk security because at least two, and sometimes three, parties may be liable for its payment at maturity. The yields on banker's acceptances are similar to those on negotiable CDs and commercial paper.

Eurodollar Deposits

Eurodollar deposits Deposits denominated in U.S. dollars and deposited in banks outside the United States, having varying maturities, and having yields above nearly all other marketable securities.

Eurodollar deposits are deposits denominated in U.S. dollars and deposited in banks located outside the United States. The nationality of the bank makes no difference. It might be a foreign bank or the foreign branch of an American bank. The deposit is always a time deposit or negotiable CDs in large denominations, typically in units of $1 million. London is the center of the Eurodollar market. Other important centers are Paris, Frankfurt, Zürich, Nassau (Bahamas), Singapore, and Hong Kong. The maturities of Eurodollar deposits range from overnight to several years, with most of the money held in the one-week to six-month maturity range. Because of the added foreign exchange risks, Eurodollar deposits tend to provide yields above nearly all other marketable securities, government or nongovernment. An active secondary market allows Eurodollar deposits to be used to meet both transactions and safety motives.

Money Market Mutual Funds

money market mutual funds Portfolios (groups) of various popular marketable securities, having instant liquidity, competitive yields, and low transactions costs.

Money market mutual funds, often called *money funds,* are portfolios of marketable securities such as those described earlier. Shares or interests in these funds can be easily acquired—often without paying any brokerage commissions. A minimum initial investment of as low as $500, but generally $1,000 or more, is required. Money funds provide instant liquidity in much the same fashion as a checking or savings account. In exchange for investing in these funds, investors earn returns that are comparable to or higher than—especially during periods of high interest rates—those obtainable from most other marketable securities. Due to the high liquidity, competitive yields, and often low transactions costs, these funds have achieved significant growth in size and popularity in recent years.

Repurchase Agreements

repurchase agreement An agreement whereby a bank or security dealer sells a firm specific securities and agrees to repurchase them at a specific price and time.

A **repurchase agreement** is not a specific security. It is an arrangement whereby a bank or security dealer sells specific marketable securities to a firm and agrees to repurchase the securities at a specific price at a specified point in time. In exchange for the tailor-made maturity date provided by this arrangement, the bank or security dealer provides the purchaser with a return slightly below that obtainable through outright purchase of similar marketable securities. The benefit to the purchaser is the guaranteed repurchase, and the tailor-made maturity date ensures that the purchaser will have cash at a specified point in time. The actual securities involved may be government or nongovernment issues. Repurchase agreements are ideal for marketable securities investments made to satisfy the transactions motive.

Summary

● Cash and marketable securities act as a pool of liquid assets, providing the firm with funds for paying bills as they come due and for meeting any unexpected outlays.

● The efficient management of cash is based on three basic strategies: (1) paying accounts payable as late as possible; (2) turning inventory as quickly as possible; and (3) collecting accounts receivable as quickly as possible.

● Although the cash budget is useful for cash planning, decisions on the appropriate cash balance for the firm depend on the magnitude of both expected and unexpected cash receipts and cash disbursements.

● Financial managers can use a variety of techniques to manipulate certain imperfections in the collection and payment system to take advantage of float in order to minimize the firm's cash requirements.

● Popular collection techniques include concentration banking, lockboxes, direct sends, preauthorized checks (PACs), depository transfer checks (DTCs), and wire transfers. Disbursement techniques include controlled disbursing, playing the float, overdraft systems, and zero-balance accounts.

● Establishing and maintaining strong banking relationships is crucial for effective cash management.

● Marketable securities allow the firm to earn a return on temporarily idle funds. They are held for three primary reasons: the transactions motive, the safety motive, and the speculative motive.

● For a security to be considered marketable, it must have a ready market that has both breadth and depth. Furthermore, the risks associated with the safety of the principal must be quite low.

● The decision to purchase marketable securities depends on the trade-off between the return earned during the holding period and the brokerage costs associated with purchasing and selling the securities.

● The most popular marketable securities include government issues—Treasury bills, Treasury notes, and federal agency issues—and nongovernment issues—negotiable certificates of deposit (CDs), commercial paper, banker's acceptances, Eurodollar deposits, money market mutual funds, and repurchase agreements.

Questions

14-1 What is the objective of the financial manager in cash management? What conditions must be satisfied in meeting this objective?

14-2 What are the *key strategies* with respect to accounts payable, inventory, and accounts receivable for the firm that wants to manage its cash efficiently?

14-3 What is a firm's *cash cycle?* How are the cash cycle and cash turnover of a firm related? What should a firm's objective with respect to cash cycle and cash turnover be?

14-4 If a firm reduces the average age of its inventories, what effect might this action have on the cash cycle? On the firm's total sales? Is there a trade-off between average inventory and sales? Give reasons for your answer.

14-5 Define *float* and describe its three basic components. Compare and contrast collection and disbursement float and cite the financial manager's goal with respect to each of these types of float.

14-6 Briefly describe the key features of each of the following collection techniques.

    a. Concentration banking

    b. Lockboxes

    c. Direct sends

    d. Preauthorized checks (PACs)

    e. Depository transfer checks (DTCs)

    f. Wire transfers

14-7 Briefly describe the key features of each of the following disbursement techniques.

  a. Controlled disbursing

  b. Playing the float

  c. Overdraft systems

  d. Zero-balance accounts

14-8 Describe the role of strong banking relationships in the cash management process. How should available bank services be evaluated?

14-9 What are the possible motives for holding marketable securities? What two characteristics are essential for a security to be deemed ''marketable''?

14-10 For each of the following government-based marketable securities, give a brief description emphasizing maturity, liquidity, risk, and return.

  a. Treasury bill

  b. Treasury note

  c. Federal agency issue

14-11 Describe the basic features—including maturity, liquidity, risk, and return—of each of the following nongovernment marketable securities.

  a. Negotiable certificate of deposit (CD)

  b. Commercial paper

  c. Banker's acceptance

  d. Eurodollar deposit

14-12 Briefly describe the basic features of the following marketable securities and explain how they both involve other marketable securities.

  a. Money market mutual fund

  b. Repurchase agreement

Self-Test Problems

(Solutions on page 537)

ST-1 The Hurkin Manufacturing Company pays accounts payable on the tenth day after purchase. The average collection period is 30 days, and the average age of inventory is 40 days. Total annual cash outlays are approximately $18 million. The firm is considering a plan that would stretch its accounts payable by 20 days. If the firm can earn 12 percent on equal-risk investments, what annual savings can it realize by this plan? Assume no discount for early payment of trade credit and a 360-day year.

ST-2 A firm that has an opportunity cost of 9 percent is contemplating installation of a lockbox system at an annual cost of $90,000. The system is expected to reduce mailing time by $2\frac{1}{2}$ days and reduce check clearing time by $1\frac{1}{2}$ days. If the firm collects $300,000 per day, would you recommend the system? Explain.

Problems

14-1 (**Cash Cycle and Minimum Operating Cash**) American Products is concerned about managing cash in an efficient manner. On the average, accounts receivable are collected in 60 days, and inventories have an average age of 90 days. Accounts payable are paid approximately 30 days after they arise. The firm spends $30 million each year, at a constant rate. Assuming a 360-day year:

  a. Calculate the firm's cash cycle.

  b. Calculate the firm's cash turnover.

c. Calculate the minimum operating cash balance the firm must maintain to meet its obligations.

14-2 **(Cash Cycle and Minimum Operating Cash)** Harris & Company has an inventory turnover of 12, an average collection period of 45 days, and an average payment period of 40 days. The firm spends $1 million per year. Assuming a 360-day year:

a. Calculate the firm's cash cycle.

b. Calculate the firm's cash turnover.

c. Calculate the minimum operating cash balance the firm must maintain to meet its obligations.

14-3 **(Comparison of Cash Cycles)** A firm collects accounts receivable, on the average, after 75 days. Inventory has an average age of 105 days, and accounts payable are paid an average of 60 days after they arise. Assuming a 360-day year, what changes will occur in the cash cycle and cash turnover with each of the following circumstances?

a. The average collection period changes to 60 days.

b. The average age of inventory changes to 90 days.

c. The average payment period changes to 105 days.

d. The circumstances in **a, b,** and **c** occur simultaneously.

14-4 **(Changes in Cash Cycles)** A firm is considering several plans that affect working capital accounts. Given the five plans and their probable results in the following table, which one would you favor? Explain.

	Change		
Plan	Average age of inventory	Average collection period	Average payment period
A	+30 days	+20 days	+5 days
B	+20 days	−10 days	+15 days
C	−10 days	0 days	−5 days
D	−15 days	+15 days	+10 days
E	+5 days	−10 days	+15 days

14-5 **(Changing Cash Cycle)** Camp Manufacturing turns its inventory eight times each year, has an average payment period of 35 days, and has an average collection period of 60 days. The firm's total annual outlays are $3.5 million.

a. Calculate the firm's minimum operating cash, assuming a 360-day year.

b. Assuming that the firm can earn 14 percent on its short-term investments, how much would the firm earn annually if it could *favorably change* its current cash cycle by 20 days?

14-6 **(Multiple Changes in Cash Cycle)** Garrett Industries turns its inventory six times each year, has an average payment period of 30 days, and has an average collection period of 45 days. The firm's total annual outlays are $3 million.

a. Calculate the firm's minimum operating cash, assuming a 360-day year.

b. Find the firm's minimum operating cash in the event that it makes the following changes simultaneously.
(1) Extends average payment period by 10 days.
(2) Shortens the average age of inventory by 5 days.
(3) Speeds the collection of accounts receivable by an average of 10 days.

c. If the firm can earn 13 percent on its short-term investments, how much, if anything, could it earn annually as a result of the changes in **b**?

d. If the annual cost of achieving the savings in **c** is $35,000, what action would you recommend to the firm? Why?

14-7 **(Float)** Simon Corporation has daily cash receipts of $65,000. A recent analysis of its collections indicated that customers' payments were in the mail an average of $2\frac{1}{2}$ days. Once received, the payments are processed in $1\frac{1}{2}$ days. After payments are deposited, it takes an average of 3 days for these receipts to clear the banking system.

a. How much collection float (in days) does the firm currently have?

b. If the firm's opportunity cost is 11 percent, would it be economically advisable for the firm to pay an annual fee of $16,500 in order to reduce collection float by three days? Explain why or why not.

14-8 **(Concentration Banking)** Mead Enterprises sells to a national market and bills all credit customers from the New York City office. Using a continuous billing system, the firm has collections of $1.2 million per day. Under consideration is a concentration banking system that would require customers to mail payments to the nearest regional office to be deposited in local banks.

Mead estimates that the collection period for accounts will be shortened an average of $2\frac{1}{2}$ days under this system. The firm also estimates that *annual* service charges and administrative costs of $300,000 will result from the proposed system. The firm can earn 14 percent on equal-risk investments.

a. How much cash will be made available for other uses if the firm accepts the proposed concentration banking system?

b. What savings will the firm realize on the $2\frac{1}{2}$-day reduction in the collection period?

c. Would you recommend the change? Explain your answer.

14-9 **(Concentration Banking—Range of Outcomes)** Pet-Care Company markets its products through widely dispersed distributors in the United States. It currently takes between six and nine days for cash-receipt checks to become available to the firm once they are mailed. Through use of a concentration banking system, the firm estimates that the collection float can be reduced to between two and four days. Daily cash receipts currently average $10,000. The firm's minimum opportunity cost is 5.5 percent—the rate paid on passbook savings accounts.

a. Use the data given to determine the minimum and maximum annual savings from implementing the proposed system.

b. If the annual cost of the concentration banking system is $7,500, what recommendation would you make?

c. What impact, if any, would the fact that the firm's opportunity cost is 12 percent have on your analysis? Explain.

14-10 (Lockbox System) Eagle Industries feels a lockbox system can shorten its accounts receivable collection period by three days. Credit sales are $3,240,000 per year, billed on a continuous basis. The firm has other equally risky investments with a return of 15 percent. The cost of the lockbox system is $9,000 per year.

a. What amount of cash will be made available for other uses under the lockbox system?

b. What net benefit (cost) will the firm receive if it adopts the lockbox system?

14-11 (Direct Send—Single) Ocean Research of San Diego, California, just received a check in the amount of $800,000 from a customer in Bangor, Maine. If the firm processes the check in the normal manner, the funds will become available in six days. To speed up this process, the firm could send an employee to the bank in Bangor on which the check is drawn to present it for payment. Such action will cause the funds to become available after two days. If the cost of the direct send is $650 and the firm can earn 11 percent on these funds, what recommendation would you give them? Explain.

14-12 (Direct Sends—Multiple) Delta Company just received four sizable checks drawn on various distant banks throughout the United States. The data on these checks is summarized in the following table. The firm, which has a 12 percent opportunity cost, can lease a small business jet with pilot to fly the checks to the cities of the banks on which they are drawn and present them for immediate payment. This task can be accomplished in a single day—thereby reducing to one day the funds availability from each of the four checks. The total cost of leasing the jet with pilot and other incidental expenditures is $4,500. Analyze the proposal and make a recommendation as to the proposed action.

Check	Amount	Number of days until funds are available
1	$ 600,000	7 days
2	2,000,000	5
3	1,300,000	4
4	400,000	6

14-13 (Controlled Disbursing) A large Texas firm has annual cash disbursements of $360 million made continuously over the year. Although annual service and administrative costs would increase by $100,000, the firm is considering writing all disbursement checks on a small bank in Oregon. The firm estimates this will allow an additional $1\frac{1}{2}$ days of cash usage. If the firm earns a return on other equally risky investments of 12 percent, should it change to the distant bank? Why, or why not?

14-14 (Playing the Float) Clay Travel, Inc., routinely funds its checking account to cover all checks when written. A thorough analysis of its checking account discloses that the firm could maintain an average account balance 25 percent below the current level and adequately cover all checks presented. The average account balance is currently $900,000. If the firm can earn 10 percent on short-term investments, what, if any, annual savings would result from maintaining the lower average account balance?

14-15 **(Payroll Account Management)** Cord Products has a weekly payroll of $250,000. The payroll checks are issued on Friday afternoon each week. In examining the check-cashing behavior of its employees, it has found the following pattern:

Number of business days[a] since issue of check	Percentage of checks cleared
1	20%
2	40
3	30
4	10

[a] Excludes Saturday and Sunday.

Given this information, what recommendation would you give the firm with respect to managing its payroll account? Explain.

14-16 **(Zero-Balance Account)** Union Company is considering establishment of a zero-balance account. The firm currently maintains an average balance of $420,000 in its disbursement account. As compensation to the bank for maintaining the zero-balance account, the firm will have to pay a monthly fee of $1,000 and maintain a $300,000 noninterest-earning deposit in the bank. The firm currently has no other deposits in the bank. Evaluate the proposed zero-balance account and make a recommendation to the firm assuming it has a 12 percent opportunity cost.

14-17 **(Marketable Securities Purchase Decisions)** To purchase and sell $25,000 in marketable securities, a firm must pay $800. If the marketable securities have a yield of 12 percent annually, recommend whether or not to purchase if:

a. The securities are held for one month.

b. The securities are held for three months.

c. The securities are held for six months.

d. The securities are held for one year.

14-18 **(Marketable Securities—Comparison and Selection)** Steve Perry is cash manager for Patient Services Corporation. The cash budget indicates that excess cash of $20,000 will be available for the next 90 days. He is considering an investment of this sum in one of the instruments listed below. Ignoring taxes, calculate the expected rate of return (for the next quarter) for each and select the best investment. Explain your choice.

a. Common stock costing $40 per share and paying a $2 annual dividend ($.50 each quarter); the stock price is expected to increase by $1 next quarter.

b. Preferred stock that pays a $6 annual dividend ($1.50 each quarter), currently selling for $50 a share. No increase in price is anticipated.

c. Municipal bonds issued by the city of Phoenix, Arizona, maturing in 2005. Currently and in the near future, these are expected to sell at par. They have an 8 percent annual coupon (2 percent per quarter).

d. A 90-day certificate of deposit paying 12 percent annual interest (3 percent per quarter).

e. Ninety-day commercial paper selling at 97 percent of face value (commercial paper sells at a discount).

f. A money market mutual fund expected to yield 11.8 percent per year.

Solutions to Self-Test Problems

ST-1

Basic data		
Time component	Current	Proposed
Average payment period (APP)	10 days	30 days
Average collection period (ACP)	30 days	30 days
Average age of inventory (AAI)	40 days	40 days

Cash cycle (CC) = AAI + ACP − APP

$$CC_{current} = 40 \text{ days} + 30 \text{ days} - 10 \text{ days} = 60 \text{ days}$$
$$CC_{proposed} = 40 \text{ days} + 30 \text{ days} - 30 \text{ days} = 40 \text{ days}$$

Cash turnover (CT) = 360/CC

$$CT_{current} = \frac{360 \text{ days}}{60 \text{ days}} = 6$$

$$CT_{proposed} = \frac{360 \text{ days}}{40 \text{ days}} = 9$$

Minimum operating cash (MOC) = TAO/CT

TAO = Total annual outlays = $18,000,000

$$MOC_{current} = \frac{\$18,000,000}{6} = \$3,000,000$$

$$MOC_{proposed} = \frac{\$18,000,000}{9} = \$2,000,000$$

Reduction in minimum operating cash = $3,000,000 − $2,000,000 = $1,000,000
Annual savings on minimum operating cash reduction = .12 × $1,000,000 = $120,000

ST-2 Time reduction

Mailing time	$2\frac{1}{2}$ days
Clearing time	$1\frac{1}{2}$ days
Total time reduction	4 days

Float reduction

4 days × $300,000/day = $1,200,000

Earnings (annual) on float reduction

.09 × $1,200,000 = $108,000

Since the annual earnings from the float reduction of $108,000 exceed the annual cost of $90,000, *the proposed lockbox should be implemented*. It will result in a net annual savings of $18,000 ($108,000 earnings − $90,000 cost).

CHAPTER 15

Accounts Receivable and Inventory

FACT OR FABLE?
Are the following statements fact *(true)* or fable *(false)*?

1
When a firm relaxes its credit standards, its sales volume, investment in accounts receivable, and bad debt expenses all would be likely to increase.

2
Credit analysis is performed by obtaining and analyzing relevant credit information in order to determine customer creditworthiness and the maximum amount of credit the customer is capable of supporting.

3
If the firm manipulates its credit terms by increasing the cash discount, increasing the cash discount period, or increasing the credit period, bad debt expenses are expected to decrease.

4
The likely effects of increasing collection expenditures would be an increased sales volume, increased investment in accounts receivable, and decreased bad debt expenses.

5
Because inventory is an investment in the sense that it requires the firm to tie up its money, the financial manager typically has direct control over the inventory management process.

6
The EOQ model is an inventory management technique used to find the optimal order quantity that minimizes the total cost which includes order cost and carrying cost.

538

Accounts receivable collection is a problem that every company faces. After a sale has been made and the product has been delivered, the actual collection of payment can drag on for months. As these late payments stretch out over time, they may cause a company to experience a substantial drop in its profit margin. By making its salespeople act as collection supervisors, Macke Business Products, Inc., in New York has devised a creative solution to this problem.

Macke, a large office furniture and supply company, links salespeoples' commissions to collection requirements by reducing commissions as the aging of overdue accounts increases. A salesperson's commission is reduced by 5 percent if an account is sixty days past due and by 10 percent if it is ninety days past due; the commission is completely lost at 120 days. In light of the large amount of money lost on overdue accounts, Macke believes this novel approach is indeed necessary.

Macke's idea is to make the routine business transaction of collection easier for both the client and the salesperson. This approach is effective because it allows the client to work with a familiar salesperson rather than with a distant collections department. The client is less likely to feel annoyed or intimidated and more likely to clear the account—and that's the goal of the whole process.

In addition, Macke's approach forces the salesperson to be more aware of the company's overall concerns. The firm feels it is essential for the salesperson to understand that accounts receivable can be very expensive. Although selling is important, it is certainly not the *only* part of a business transaction.

Both the management and salespeople at Macke Business Products recognize the importance of effective management of accounts receivable. This chapter places primary emphasis on the key strategies and techniques for effectively managing accounts receivable and briefly discusses inventory—a costly current asset over which the financial manager has only limited control.

Credit Policy

In order to keep current customers and attract new ones, most manufacturing firms extend credit. *Accounts receivable* represent the extension of credit by the firm to its customers. For the average manufacturer they account for over 37 percent of *current assets* and nearly 16 percent of *total assets*. Generally, the firm's financial manager directly controls accounts receivable through involvement in the establishment and management of credit policy, credit terms, and collection policy. Here we discuss credit policy; in the following sections credit terms and collection policy are discussed.

A firm's **credit policy** provides guidelines for determining whether to extend credit to a customer, and how much credit to extend. The firm must establish *credit standards* to use in making these decisions. Appropriate *sources of credit information* and *methods of*

credit policy Guidelines for determining whether to extend credit to a customer and how much credit to extend.

credit analysis must be developed. Each of these aspects of credit policy is important to the successful management of accounts receivable. A brief look at credit scoring will help place credit policy in proper perspective.

Credit Scoring

credit scoring The ranking of an applicant's overall credit strength, derived as a weighted average of scores on key financial and credit characteristics.

Consumer credit decisions, because they involve a large group of similar applicants, each representing a small part of the firm's total business, can be handled using impersonal, computer-based credit decision techniques. One popular technique is **credit scoring**—a procedure resulting in a score reflecting an applicant's overall credit strength, derived as a weighted average of the scores obtained on a variety of key financial and credit characteristics. Credit scoring is often used by large credit card operations such as oil companies and department stores. This technique can best be illustrated by an example.

Example

Haller's Stores uses a credit scoring model to make its consumer credit decisions. Each credit applicant fills out and submits a credit application to the company. The application is reviewed and scored by one of the company's credit analysts and then entered into the computer; the rest of the process, including making the credit decision, generating a letter of acceptance or rejection to the applicant, and dispatching the preparation and mailing of a credit card, is automated.

Table 15.1 demonstrates the calculation of Barb Buyer's credit score. The firm's predetermined credit standards are summarized in Table 15.2. The cutoff credit scores were developed to accept the group of credit applicants that will result in a positive contribution to the firm's share value. In evaluating Barb Buyer's credit score of 80.25 in light of the firm's credit standards, the decision would be to *extend standard credit terms* to her (80.25 > 75).

Table 15.1
Credit Scoring of Barb Buyer by Haller's Stores

Financial and credit characteristics	Score (0 to 100) (1)	Predetermined weight (2)	Weighted score [(1) × (2)] (3)
Credit references	80	.15	12.00
Home ownership	100	.15	15.00
Income range	70	.25	17.50
Payment history	75	.25	18.75
Years at address	90	.10	9.00
Years on job	80	.10	8.00
Total		1.00	Credit score 80.25

KEY: Column 1: Scores assigned by analyst and computer using company guidelines on the basis of data presented in credit application. Scores range from 0 (lowest) to 100 (highest). Column 2: Weights based on the company's analysis of the relative importance of each financial and credit characteristic in predicting whether or not a customer will pay an account. These weights must sum to 1.00.

Table 15.2
Credit Standards for Haller's Stores

Credit score	Action
Greater than 75	Extend standard credit terms.
65 to 75	Extend limited credit; if account is properly maintained, convert to standard credit terms after one year.
Less than 65	Reject application.

The attractiveness of credit scoring should be clear from the above example. Unfortunately, most manufacturers sell to a diversified group of different-sized businesses, not to individuals. The statistical characteristics necessary for applying credit scoring to decisions regarding *mercantile credit*—credit extended by business firms to other business firms—rarely exist. In the following discussion we concentrate on the basic concepts of mercantile credit decisions, which cannot easily be expressed in quantifiable terms.

Credit Standards

The firm's **credit standards** are the minimum criteria for the extension of credit to a customer. Our concern here is with the restrictiveness or nonrestrictiveness of a firm's overall policy. Understanding the key variables that must be considered when a firm is contemplating relaxing or tightening its credit standards will give a general idea of the kinds of decisions involved.

credit standards The minimum criteria for the extension of credit to a customer.

Key Variables

The major variables that should be considered in evaluating proposed changes in credit standards are (1) sales volume, (2) the investment in accounts receivable, and (3) bad debt expenses.[1] Let us examine each in more detail.

Sales Volume. Changing credit standards can be expected to change the volume of sales. If credit standards are relaxed, sales are expected to increase; if credit standards are tightened, sales are expected to decrease. Generally, increases in sales affect profits positively, whereas decreases in sales affect profits negatively.

Investment in Accounts Receivable. Carrying, or maintaining, accounts receivable involves a cost to the firm. This cost is attributable to the forgone earnings opportunities resulting from the necessity to tie up funds in accounts receivable. Therefore, the higher the firm's investment in accounts receivable, the greater the carrying cost, and vice versa. If the firm relaxes its credit standards, the volume of accounts receivable increases and so does the firm's carrying cost (investment). This change results from increased sales and longer collection periods due to slower payment on average by credit customers.[2] The

---

[1] A relaxation of credit standards would be expected to add to the *clerical costs* as a result of the need for a larger credit department, whereas a tightening of credit standards might save clerical costs. Because these costs are assumed to be included in the variable cost per unit, they are not explicitly isolated in the analyses presented in this chapter.

[2] Due to the forward-looking nature of accounts receivable analysis, certain items such as sales, collections, and bad debts resulting from changes in the management of accounts receivable must be estimated. The need to estimate these future values may introduce a great deal of uncertainty into the decision process. Some of the techniques discussed in Chapter 10, such as sensitivity and scenario analysis and simulation, can be applied to these estimates to adjust them for uncertainty.

opposite occurs if credit standards are tightened. Thus a relaxation of credit standards is expected to affect profits negatively due to higher carrying costs, whereas tightening credit standards would affect profits positively as a result of lower carrying costs.

Bad Debt Expenses. The probability, or risk, of acquiring a bad debt increases as credit standards are relaxed. The increase in bad debts associated with relaxation of credit standards raises bad debt expenses and impacts profits negatively. The opposite effects on bad debt expenses and profits result from a tightening of credit standards.

The basic changes and effects on profits expected to result from the *relaxation* of credit standards are tabulated as follows:

Variable	Direction of change	Effect on profits
Sales volume	Increase	Positive
Investment in accounts receivable	Increase	Negative
Bad debt expenses	Increase	Negative

If credit standards were tightened, the opposite effects would be expected.

FACT OR FABLE?   **1** When a firm relaxes its credit standards, its sales volume, investment in accounts receivable, and bad debt expenses all would be likely to increase. *(Fact)*

Determining Values of Key Variables

The way in which the key credit standard variables are determined can be illustrated by the following example.[3]

Example

Dodd Tool is currently selling a product for $10 per unit. Sales (all on credit) for last year were 60,000 units. The variable cost per unit is $6, and the average cost per unit, given a sales volume of 60,000 units, is $8. The difference of $2 between the average cost per unit and the variable cost per unit represents the contribution of each of the 60,000 units toward the firm's fixed costs. Working backward, since each of the 60,000 units sold contributes $2 to fixed costs, the firm's total fixed costs must be $120,000.

The firm is currently contemplating a *relaxation of credit standards* that is expected to result in a 5 percent increase in unit sales to 63,000 units, an increase in the average collection period from its current level of 30 days to 45 days, and an increase

---

[3] Because various credit policy decisions tend to commit the firm to long-run behaviors, a number of authors have suggested that credit policy decisions should be made using a present-value framework. See Yong H. Kim and Joseph C. Atkins, "Evaluating Investments in Accounts Receivable: A Maximizing Framework," *Journal of Finance* 33 (May 1978), pp. 402–412. Although their suggestions are valid, a more recent article by Kanwal S. Sachdeva and Lawrence J. Gitman, "Accounts Receivable Decisions in a Capital Budgeting Framework," *Financial Management* 10 (Winter 1981), pp. 45–49, has shown that single-period decision rules similar to those applied throughout this chapter will provide correct accept-reject decisions without the computational rigor of the present-value approach.

in bad debt expenses from the current level of 1 percent of sales to 2 percent. The firm's required return on equal-risk investments, which is the opportunity cost of tying funds up in accounts receivable, is 15 percent.

To determine whether Dodd Tool should implement the proposed relaxation in credit standards, the effect on the firm's additional profit contribution from sales, the cost of the marginal investment in accounts receivable, and the cost of marginal bad debts must be calculated.

Additional profit contribution from sales The additional profit contribution from sales expected to result from the relaxation of credit standards can be calculated easily. Because fixed costs are "sunk" and thereby unaffected by a change in the sales level, the only cost relevant to a change in sales would be out-of-pocket or variable costs. Sales are expected to increase by 5 percent, or 3,000 units. The profit contribution per unit will equal the difference between the sale price per unit ($10) and the variable cost per unit ($6). The profit contribution per unit will therefore be $4. Thus the total additional profit contribution from sales will be $12,000 (3,000 units × $4 per unit).

Cost of the marginal investment in accounts receivable The cost of the marginal investment in accounts receivable can be calculated by finding the difference between the cost of carrying receivables before and after the introduction of the relaxed credit standards. The average investment in accounts receivable can be calculated using the following formula:

Average investment in accounts receivable

$$= \frac{\text{cost of annual sales}}{\text{turnover of accounts receivable}} \quad (15.1)$$

where

$$\text{Turnover of accounts receivable}^4 = \frac{360}{\text{average collection period}}$$

The cost of annual sales under the proposed and present plans can be found as noted below.

Cost of annual sales:

Under proposed plan: ($8 × 60,000 units) + ($6 × 3,000 units)
$480,000 + $18,000 = $498,000
Under present plan: ($8 × 60,000 units) = $480,000

The calculation of the sales cost for the present plan involves the straightforward use of the average cost per unit of $8. The cost under the proposed plan is found by adding the marginal cost of producing an additional 3,000 units at $6 per unit to the total cost of producing 60,000 units. With implementation of the proposed plan, the cost of annual sales will increase from $480,000 to $498,000.

The turnover of accounts receivable refers to the number of times each year the

---

[4] The turnover of accounts receivable can also be calculated by *dividing annual sales by accounts receivable*. For the purposes of this chapter, only the formula transforming the average collection period to a turnover of accounts receivable is emphasized.

firm's accounts receivable are actually turned into cash. In each case it is found by dividing the average collection period into 360—the number of days in a year.

Turnover of accounts receivable:

$$\text{Under proposed plan: } \frac{360}{45} = 8$$

$$\text{Under present plan: } \frac{360}{30} = 12$$

With implementation of the proposed plan, the accounts receivable turnover would drop from 12 to 8.

Substituting the cost and turnover data just calculated into Equation 15.1 for each case, the following average investments in accounts receivable result:

Average investment in accounts receivable:

$$\text{Under proposed plan: } \frac{\$498,000}{8} = \$62,250$$

$$\text{Under present plan: } \frac{\$480,000}{12} = \$40,000$$

The marginal investment in accounts receivable as well as its cost are calculated as follows:

Cost of marginal investment in accounts receivable:

Average investment under proposed plan	$62,250
− Average investment under present plan	40,000
Marginal investment in accounts receivable	$22,250
× Required return on investment	.15
Cost of marginal investment in A/R[5]	$ 3,338

The cost of investing an additional $22,250 in accounts receivable was found by multiplying it by 15 percent (the firm's required return on investment). The resulting value of $3,338 is considered a cost because it represents the maximum amount that could have been earned on the $22,250 had it been placed in the best equal-risk investment alternative available.

Cost of marginal bad debts The cost of marginal bad debts is found by taking the difference between the level of bad debts before and after the relaxation of credit standards, as shown here.

Cost of marginal bad debts:

Under proposed plan: (.02 × $10/unit × 63,000 units)	=	$12,600
Under present plan: (.01 × $10/unit × 60,000 units)	=	6,000
Cost of marginal bad debts		$ 6,600

Thus the resulting cost of marginal bad debts is $6,600.

---

[5] Throughout the text, A/R will frequently be used interchangeably with *accounts receivable*.

SMALL BUSINESS

SOME GUIDELINES FOR MANAGING ACCOUNTS RECEIVABLE

Most small business managers face the same problem: raising capital for any of the many reasons a company needs money—new equipment, plant expansion, more personnel. Their first thought is to borrow money, but doing so adds to the debt load. For many, the next step is to cut inventory, but that doesn't raise as much money as selling the product, which brings in the full price of the goods.

Most companies have another source of capital close at hand: their own accounts receivable. By implementing a plan to manage its accounts receivable in a consistent, businesslike fashion, a company can often generate a large part of the capital it needs. The first question a small business manager must ask is whether credit should even be offered to prospective customers. While credit is a valuable service option, it can create many problems such as waiting for payment and managing collections. If these obstacles outweigh the advantages of offering credit, the manager should consider doing a cash-only business.

If credit is extended, the manager can do several things to improve collections. The first is to invoice properly. Document all shipments to the customer with shipping and receiving papers. Send invoices to customers the same day the order is shipped—certainly no later than the following day. State all pertinent information such as terms, discounts, and net amount due clearly on the invoice. The next step is the processing of incoming funds. Everyone working in accounts receivable should be familiar with the terms of payment so there is no confusion.

The attitude of administrative and marketing personnel is crucial in the collection process. Without the support of top management, any attempts by accounts receivable will be limited. Sometimes though, it is necessary to waive company policy.

Finally, there is the problem of delinquent accounts. This is a tricky area because of the delicate customer-supplier relationship. All communications should be very professional. Viewing collections as a part of a business transaction allows the collection agent to be cordial yet firm. Generally the ratio of cordiality to firmness can be reduced as the period of delinquency increases. Often, the best way to prompt a customer to pay on delinquent accounts is through motivational tactics. Phrases like "as we had agreed upon earlier" and "in order to prevent future problems" can be effective in making the customer want to clear the account. Another way to reinforce the urgency of the situation is by sheer repetition. Polite telephone calls mixed with several letters a week can push the issue to a resolution. The last result of collection efforts is often to refer the account to a professional collection agency. This provides for a more removed and experienced firm to deal with the problem.

An organized plan can help make accounts receivable a source of even greater revenue for many companies. The starting point is to establish a set of clearly stated procedures and follow them.

Making the Credit Standard Decision

To decide whether the firm should relax its credit standards, the additional profit contribution from sales must be compared to the sum of the cost of the marginal investment in accounts receivable and the cost of marginal bad debts. If the additional profit contribution is greater than marginal costs, credit standards should be relaxed; otherwise, present standards should remain unchanged. Let us look at an example.

Example
The results and key calculations relative to Dodd Tool's decision to relax its credit standards are summarized in Table 15.3. Since the additional profit contribution from the increased sales would be $12,000, which exceeds the sum of the cost of the marginal investment in accounts receivable and the cost of marginal bad debts, the firm *should* relax its credit standards as proposed. The net addition to total profits resulting from such an action will be $2,062 per year.

Table 15.3
The Effects of a Relaxation of Credit Standards on Dodd Tool

Additional profit contribution from sales		
[3,000 units $\times$ ($10 $-$ $6)]		$12,000
Cost of marginal investment in A/R[a]		
Average investment under proposed plan:		
$$\frac{(\$8 \times 60,000) + (\$6 \times 3,000)}{8} = \frac{\$498,000}{8}$$	$62,250	
Average investment under present plan:		
$$\frac{(\$8 \times 60,000)}{12} = \frac{\$480,000}{12}$$	40,000	
Marginal investment in A/R	$22,250	
Cost of marginal investment in A/R (.15 $\times$ $22,250)		($3,338)
Cost of marginal bad debts		
Bad debts under proposed plan (.02 $\times$ $10 $\times$ 63,000)	$12,600	
Bad debts under present plan (.01 $\times$ $10 $\times$ 60,000)	6,000	
Cost of marginal bad debts		($6,600)
Net profit from implementation of proposed plan		$2,062

[a] The denominators 8 and 12 in the calculation of the average investment in accounts receivable under the proposed and present plans are the accounts receivable turnovers for each of these plans (360/45 = 8 and 360/30 = 12).

The technique described here for making a credit standard decision is commonly used for evaluating other types of changes in the management of accounts receivable as well. If the firm in the preceding example had been contemplating more restrictive credit standards, the cost would have been a reduction in the profit contribution from sales, and the return would have been reductions in the cost of the marginal investment in accounts receivable and in bad debts. Another application of this analytical technique is described later in the chapter.

Credit Analysis

credit analysis The evaluation of a credit applicant to estimate creditworthiness and the maximum amount of credit to extend.

line of credit The maximum amount a customer can owe the firm at any time.

Once the firm has established its credit standards, it must develop procedures for **credit analysis**—the evaluation of credit applicants. Often the firm must not only determine the creditworthiness of a customer but it must also estimate the maximum amount of credit the customer is capable of supporting. Once this is done, the firm can establish a **line of credit,** the maximum amount the customer can owe the firm at any time. Lines of credit are established to eliminate the necessity of checking a major customer's credit each time a purchase is made.

Whether the firm's credit department is evaluating the creditworthiness of a customer desiring credit for a specific transaction or that of a regular customer in order to establish a line of credit, the basic procedures are the same. The only difference is in the depth of the analysis. A firm would be unwise to spend $50 to investigate the creditworthiness of a customer making a one-time $40 purchase, but $50 for a credit investigation may be a good investment in the case of a customer who is expected to make credit purchases of $60,000 annually. The two basic steps in the process are (1) obtaining credit information and (2) analyzing the information.

Obtaining Credit Information

When a business is approached by a customer desiring credit terms, the credit department typically begins the evaluation process by requiring the applicant to fill out various forms requesting financial and credit information and references. Working from the application, the firm obtains additional information from other sources. If the firm has previously extended credit to the applicant, it will have its own information on the applicant's payment history. The major external sources of credit information are as follows:

Financial Statements. By requiring the credit applicant to provide financial statements for the past few years, the firm can analyze the applicant firm's liquidity, activity, debt, and profitability positions.

Dun & Bradstreet, Inc. **Dun & Bradstreet** is the largest mercantile credit-reporting agency in the United States. It provides subscribers with a copy of a reference book containing credit ratings and keyed estimates of overall financial strength for approximately 3 million U.S. and Canadian firms. The key to the D & B ratings is shown in Figure 15.1. For example, a firm rated 2A3 would have estimated financial strength (net worth) in the range of $750,000 to $999,999 and would have a *fair* credit rating. For an additional charge, subscribers can obtain detailed reports on specific companies.

Dun & Bradstreet The largest mercantile credit-reporting agency in the United States.

Credit Interchange Bureaus. Firms can obtain credit information through the National Credit Interchange System, a national network of local credit bureaus that exchange information on a reciprocal basis. The reports obtained through these exchanges contain factual data rather than analyses. A fee is usually levied for each inquiry.

Figure 15.1
The Key to Dun & Bradstreet's Ratings

Key to Ratings

Estimated Financial Strength			Composite Credit Appraisal			
			High	Good	Fair	Limited
5A	$50,000,000	and over	1	2	3	4
4A	$10,000,000 to	49,999,999	1	2	3	4
3A	1,000,000 to	9,999,999	1	2	3	4
2A	750,000 to	999,999	1	2	3	4
1A	500,000 to	749,999	1	2	3	4
BA	300,000 to	499,999	1	2	3	4
BB	200,000 to	299,999	1	2	3	4
CB	125,000 to	199,999	1	2	3	4
CC	75,000 to	124,999	1	2	3	4
DC	50,000 to	74,999	1	2	3	4
DD	35,000 to	49,999	1	2	3	4
EE	20,000 to	34,999	1	2	3	4
FF	10,000 to	19,999	1	2	3	4
GG	5,000 to	9,999	1	2	3	4
HH	Up to	4,999	1	2	3	4

DUN & BRADSTREET
Credit Services
DB a company of
The Dun & Bradstreet Corporation

Direct Credit Information Exchanges. Another means of obtaining credit information is through local, regional, or national credit associations. Often, an industry association maintains certain credit information that is available to members. Another method is to contact other suppliers selling to the applicant and ask what its payment patterns are like.

Bank Checking. It may be possible for the firm's bank to obtain credit information from the applicant's bank. However, the type of information obtained will most likely be vague, unless the applicant aids the firm in obtaining it. Typically, an estimate of the firm's cash balance is provided. For instance, it may be found that a firm maintains a "high five-figure" balance.

Analyzing Credit Information

A credit applicant's financial statements and accounts payable ledger can be used to calculate its "average payment period." This value can then be compared to the credit terms currently extended the firm. For customers requesting large amounts of credit or lines of credit, a thorough ratio analysis of the firm's liquidity, activity, debt, and profitability should be performed using the relevant financial statements. A time-series comparison (discussed in Chapter 4) of similar ratios for various years should uncover any developing trends. The *Dun & Bradstreet Reference Book* can be used for estimating the maximum line of credit to extend. Dun & Bradstreet itself suggests 10 percent of a customer's "estimated financial strength" (see Figure 15.1).

One of the key inputs to the final credit decision is the credit analyst's *subjective judgment* of a firm's creditworthiness. Experience provides a "feel" for the nonquantifiable aspects of the quality of a firm's operations. The analyst will add his or her knowledge of the character of the applicant's management, references from other suppliers, and the firm's historic payment patterns to any quantitative figures developed to determine creditworthiness. The analyst will then make the final decision as to whether to extend credit to the applicant, and possibly what amount of credit to extend. Often these decisions are made not by one individual but by a credit review committee.

FACT OR FABLE?　　　2 | Credit analysis is performed by obtaining and analyzing relevant credit information in order to determine customer creditworthiness and the maximum amount of credit the customer is capable of supporting. *(Fact)*

Credit Terms

credit terms Specification of the repayment terms required of a firm's credit customers.

A firm's **credit terms** specify the repayment terms required of all its credit customers.[6] Typically, a type of shorthand is used. For example, credit terms may be stated as *2/10 net 30,* which means that the purchaser receives a 2 percent cash discount if the bill is paid within 10 days after the beginning of the credit period; if the customer does not take the cash discount, the full amount must be paid within 30 days after the beginning of the credit period. Credit terms cover three things: (1) the cash discount, if any (in this case 2

---

[6] An in-depth discussion of credit terms as viewed by the customer is presented in Chapter 13. In this chapter our concern is with credit terms from the point of view of the seller.

percent); (2) the cash discount period (in this case 10 days); and (3) the credit period (in this case 30 days). Changes in any aspect of the firm's credit terms may have an effect on its overall profitability. The positive and negative factors associated with such changes, and quantitative procedures for evaluating them, are presented in this section.

Cash Discounts

When a firm initiates or *increases* a cash discount, the following changes and effects on profits can be expected:

Variable	Direction of change	Effect on profits
Sales volume	Increase	Positive
Investment in accounts receivable	Decrease	Positive
Bad debt expenses	Decrease	Positive
Profit per unit	Decrease	Negative

As shown in the table above, the sales volume should increase because if a firm is willing to pay by day 10, the unit price decreases. The decreased accounts receivable investment results from the fact that some customers who did not previously take the cash discount will now take it. The bad debt expenses should decline since, as customers on the average will pay earlier, the probability of their not paying at all will decrease.[7] Both the decrease in the receivables investment and the decrease in bad debt expenses should result in increased profits. The negative aspect of an increased cash discount is a decreased profit per unit as more customers take the discount and pay the reduced price.

Decreasing or eliminating a cash discount would have opposite effects. The quantitative effects of changes in cash discounts can be evaluated by a method similar to that used to evaluate changes in credit standards.

Example

Assume that Dodd Tool is considering initiating a cash discount of 2 percent for payment prior to day 10 after a purchase. The firm's current average collection period is 30 days [turnover = (360/30) = 12], credit sales of 60,000 units are made, the variable cost per unit is $6, and the average cost per unit is currently $8. The firm expects that if the cash discount is initiated, 60 percent of its sales will be on discount, and sales will increase by 5 percent to 63,000 units. The average collection period is expected to drop to 15 days [turnover = (360/15) = 24]. Bad debt expenses are expected to drop from the current level of 1 percent of sales to .5 percent of sales. The firm's required return on equal-risk investments remains at 15 percent.

The analysis of this decision is presented in Table 15.4. It can be seen that the calculations are similar to those presented for the credit standard decision in Table

---

[7] This contention is based on the fact that the longer a person has to pay, the less likely it is that the person will pay. The more time that elapses, the more opportunities there are for a customer to become technically insolvent or fail. Therefore, the probability of a bad debt is expected to increase directly with increases in the credit period.

15.3[8] except for the final entry, "Cost of cash discount." This cost of $7,560 reflects the fact that *profits will be reduced* as a result of a 2 percent cash discount being taken on 60 percent of the new level of sales. Dodd Tool can increase profit by $10,178 by initiating the proposed cash discount. Such an action therefore seems advisable. This type of analysis can also be applied to decisions concerning the elimination or reduction of cash discounts.

Table 15.4
The Effects of Initiating a Cash Discount on Dodd Tool

Additional profit contribution from sales		
$[3{,}000 \text{ units} \times (\$10 - \$6)]$		$12,000
Cost of marginal investment in A/R		
Average investment under proposed plan:		
$\dfrac{(\$8 \times 60{,}000) + (\$6 \times 3{,}000)}{24} = \dfrac{\$498{,}000}{24}$	$20,750	
Average investment under present plan:		
$\dfrac{(\$8 \times 60{,}000)}{12} = \dfrac{\$480{,}000}{12}$	40,000	
Marginal investment in A/R	($19,250)	
Cost of marginal investment in A/R $(.15 \times \$19{,}250)$		$2,888[a]
Cost of marginal bad debts		
Bad debts under proposed plan $(.005 \times \$10 \times 63{,}000)$	$ 3,150	
Bad debts under present plan $(.01 \times \$10 \times 60{,}000)$	6,000	
Cost of marginal bad debts		$2,850[a]
Cost of cash discount[b] $(.02 \times .60 \times \$10 \times 63{,}000)$		($7,560)
Net profit from implementation of proposed plan		$10,178

[a] This value is positive since it represents a savings rather than a cost.

[b] This calculation reflects the fact that a 2 percent cash discount will be taken on 60 percent of the new level of sales—63,000 units at $10 each.

Cash Discount Period

The net effect of changes in the cash discount period is quite difficult to analyze due to the nature of the forces involved. For example, if the cash discount period were *increased,* the changes noted in the table at the top of the next page could be expected.

[8] The calculation of the average investment in accounts receivable presented for both the present and proposed plans is not entirely correct. Whenever a change in credit terms or some other aspect of accounts receivable is expected to change the payment pattern of existing customers, formal analysis should recognize that the firm's pattern of receipt of both cost *and* profit from these customers is being altered. Therefore, the average investment in receivables for existing customers whose payment patterns have been altered should be measured at the sale price, not cost. For an excellent discussion of this point, see Edward A. Dyl, "Another Look at the Investment in Accounts Receivable," *Financial Management* (Winter 1977), pp. 67–70. To convey the key concepts throughout the remainder of this chapter without confusing the reader, the average accounts receivable investment is calculated at cost regardless of whether or not existing customers' payment patterns are altered by the proposed action.

Variable	Direction of change	Effect on profits
Sales volume	Increase	Positive
Investment in accounts receivable due to nondiscount takers now paying earlier	Decrease	Positive
Investment in accounts receivable due to discount takers still getting cash discount but paying later	Increase	Negative
Bad debt expenses	Decrease	Positive
Profit per unit	Decrease	Negative

The problems in determining the exact results of changes in the cash discount period are directly attributable to the two forces affecting the firm's *investment in accounts receivable*. If the firm were to shorten the cash discount period, the effects would be the opposite of those described above.

Credit Period

Changes in the credit period also affect the firm's profitability. The following effects on profits can be expected from an *increase* in the credit period:

Variable	Direction of change	Effect on profits
Sales volume	Increase	Positive
Investment in accounts receivable	Increase	Negative
Bad debt expenses	Increase	Negative

Increasing the credit period should increase sales, but both the investment in accounts receivable and bad debt expenses are likely to increase as well. Thus the net effect on profits of the sales increase is positive, while the increases in accounts receivable investment and bad debt expenses will negatively affect profits. A decrease in the credit period is likely to have the opposite effect. The credit period decision is analyzed in the same ways as the credit standard decision illustrated earlier in Table 15.3.

FACT OR FABLE?

3 If the firm manipulates its credit terms by increasing the cash discount, increasing the cash discount period, or increasing the credit period, bad debt expenses are expected to decrease. *(Fable)*

If the firm manipulates its credit terms by increasing the cash discount, increasing the cash discount period, or *decreasing* the credit period, bad debt expenses are expected to decrease.

Collection Policies

collection policies The procedures for collecting a firm's accounts receivable when they are due.

The firm's **collection policies** are the procedures for collecting accounts receivable when they are due. The effectiveness of these policies can be partly evaluated by looking at the level of bad debt expenses. This level depends not only on collection policies, but also on

Figure 15.2
Collection Expenditures and Bad Debt Losses

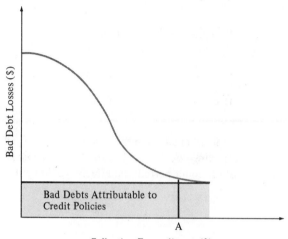

the policies on which the extension of credit is based. If one assumes that the level of bad debts attributable to credit policies is relatively constant, increasing collection expenditures can be expected to reduce bad debts. This relationship is depicted in Figure 15.2. As the figure indicates, beyond point A, additional collection expenditures will not reduce bad debt losses sufficiently to justify the outlay of funds. Popular approaches used to evaluate credit and collection policies include the *average collection period ratio* (presented in Chapter 4) and *aging accounts receivable*.

Aging Accounts Receivable

aging A technique for providing information concerning the proportion of the accounts receivable balance that has been outstanding for a specified period of time.

Aging is a technique that provides the analyst with information concerning the proportion of the accounts receivable balance that has been outstanding for a specified period of time. By highlighting irregularities, it allows the analyst to pinpoint the cause of credit and/or collection problems. Aging requires that the firm's accounts receivable be broken down into groups based on the time of origin. This breakdown is typically made on a month-by-month basis, going back three or four months. Let us look at an example.

Example

Assume that Dodd Tool extends 30-day credit terms to its customers. The firm's December 31, 1988, balance sheet shows $200,000 of accounts receivable. An evaluation of the $200,000 of accounts receivable results in the following breakdown:

Days	Current	0–30	31–60	61–90	Over 90	
Month	December	November	October	September	August	Total
Accounts receivable	$60,000	$40,000	$66,000	$26,000	$8,000	$200,000
Percentage of total	30	20	33	13	4	100

Since it is assumed that Dodd Tool gives its customers 30 days after the end of the month in which the sale is made to pay off their accounts, any December receivables still on the firm's books are considered current. November receivables are between zero and 30 days overdue, October receivables still unpaid are 31 to 60 days overdue, and so on.

The table shows that 30 percent of the firm's receivables are current, 20 percent are one month late, 33 percent are two months late, 13 percent are three months late, and 4 percent are more than three months late. While payment seems generally slow, a noticeable irregularity in these data is the high percentage represented by October receivables. This indicates that some problem may have occurred in October. Investigation may find that the problem can be attributed to the hiring of a new credit manager, the acceptance of a new account that has made a large credit purchase it has not yet paid for, or ineffective collection policies. When accounts are aged and such a discrepancy is found, the analyst should determine its cause.

Basic Trade-Offs

The basic trade-offs expected to result from an *increase* in collection efforts are as follows:

Variable	Direction of change	Effect on profits
Sales volume	None or decrease	None or negative
Investment in accounts receivable	Decrease	Positive
Bad debt expenses	Decrease	Positive
Collection expenditures	Increase	Negative

Increased collection expenditures should reduce the investment in accounts receivable and bad debt expenses, increasing profits. The costs of this strategy may include lost sales in addition to increased collection expenditures if the level of collection effort is too intense. In other words, if the firm pushes its customers too hard to pay their accounts, they may be angered and may take their business elsewhere. The firm should therefore be careful not to be overly aggressive. The basic collection policy trade-offs can be evaluated quantitatively in a manner similar to that used to evaluate the trade-offs for credit standards and cash discounts.

FACT OR FABLE?

4 The likely effects of increasing collection expenditures would be an increased sales volume, increased investment in accounts receivable, and decreased bad debt expenses. *(Fable)*

The likely effects of increasing collection expenditures would be *no change or a decrease* in sales volume, *decreased* investment in accounts receivable, and decreased bad debt expenses.

CREDIT MANAGER:
Analyzing, Extending, and Monitoring Customer Credit

Frank has been credit manager for Bettman's Men's Stores for three years. A chain of five stores located in three mid-size cities, Bettman's sells the best lines of clothing and furnishings to professionals who are dressing for success.

Frank's main responsibilities are to evaluate credit applications and to supervise the collection of accounts receivable. "I try to go over every application, review the applicant's credit history, note how much credit we can extend and on what terms. If a customer gets behind in his payments, I call him up and determine a mutually agreeable repayment. In this job," Frank says, "you really need the ability to analyze a situation, to use sound judgment, tact, and diplomacy—all very quickly. Just yesterday a man called me to ask why a finance charge was levied on his late payment. He felt he shouldn't have to pay it since the suit he bought had alterations and he didn't receive it until after the end of the billing cycle. I pointed

out that our policy is that the sale is considered complete on the day goods are sold, not when they're received. The man agreed to pay the finance charge to protect his good credit rating, but threatened to close his account. Fortunately, I had his customer history on my desktop computer while I was talking to him. Since he had been a long-standing customer, I waived the finance charge of $2.63. I could have been hard-nosed, but Bettman's would have lost a customer who spends $500 a year." Frank's decision shows how aware he is of the marketing objectives of his company. "We want to keep the steady, reliable, long-time customers. We can offer them personal service in our credit department as well as in the suit department."

Recently Frank received a job offer to become credit manager of a manufacturer of metal clamps. The clamps are sold to other manufacturers who use them on the products they make. As

credit manager, Frank would be analyzing the credit standing of companies placing orders. "It would be similar to what I'm doing now," says Frank, "but the stakes are different. Presently we look at the credit of applicants who are a small part of our total business. Actually the computer does most of the analysis, applying a certain number of points for each item on the application. As credit manager for a company that sells to other companies, I would analyze each application individually using financial analysis techniques. Each customer would require more study since each account involves a sizable amount of credit."

The new job would pay $30,000. That's $5,000 more than Frank earns now at Bettman's. At 28 and with two children, he thinks he'll make the move. "It's a step up," he says, "and I'll still have the people contact I like so much."

Types of Collection Techniques

A number of collection techniques are employed. As an account becomes more and more overdue, the collection effort becomes more personal and more strict. The basic techniques are presented in the order typically followed in the collection process.

Letters

After an account receivable becomes overdue a certain number of days, the firm normally sends a polite letter reminding the customer of its obligation. If the account is not paid within a certain period of time after the letter has been sent, a second, more demanding letter is sent. This letter may be followed by yet another letter, if necessary. Collection letters are the first step in the collection process for overdue accounts.

Telephone Calls

If letters prove unsuccessful, a telephone call may be made to the customer to personally request immediate payment. If the customer has a reasonable excuse, arrangements may be made to extend the payment period. A call from the seller's attorney may be used if all other discussions seem to fail.

Personal Visits

This technique is much more common at the consumer credit level, but it may be effectively employed by industrial suppliers. Sending a local salesperson, or a collection person, to confront the customer can be a very effective collection procedure. Payment may be made on the spot.

Using Collection Agencies

A firm can turn uncollectible accounts over to a collection agency or an attorney for collection. The fees for this service are typically quite high; the firm may receive less than 50 cents on the dollar from accounts collected in this way.

Legal Action

Legal action is the most stringent step in the collection process. It is an alternative to the use of a collection agency. Not only is direct legal action expensive, but it may force the debtor into bankruptcy, thereby reducing the possibility of future business without guaranteeing the ultimate receipt of the overdue amount.

Computerization of Accounts Receivable Management

The use of computers in the billing and collection of accounts is widespread. A computer is used to bill credit customers at the appropriate time following a purchase. As payments are received, a record of them is keyed into the computer. A computer can be programmed to monitor accounts receivable after a customer has been billed. Periodic checks are automatically made at certain points in time after billing to see if the accounts have been paid. If payment has not been received at certain predetermined points, collection letters are sent. After a prescribed number of these letters have been sent without any receipt of payment, a special notice will be generated, probably as part of a report to the credit manager. At this point, the collection efforts become more directly personal. Actions such as telephone calls, personal visits, and use of a collection agency will then be taken. Legal action is also a possibility.

Currently, computers are being used not only to monitor accounts but also to aid in the credit decision process. Data on each customer's payment patterns are maintained and can be called forth to evaluate requests for renewed or additional credit. A computer can also be used to monitor the effectiveness of the collection department by generating data on the status of outstanding accounts. Although the computer cannot carry out the entire accounts receivable management function, it will continue to reduce the amount of paperwork required.

Inventory Management

Inventory, or goods on hand, is a necessary current asset that permits the production-sale process to operate with a minimum of disturbance. Like accounts receivable, inventory represents a significant monetary investment on the part of most firms. For the average manufacturer, it accounts for over 42 percent of *current assets* and nearly 18 percent of *total assets*. Chapter 14 illustrated the importance of turning over inventory quickly in order to minimize investment. The financial manager generally acts as a ''watchdog'' and advisor in matters concerning inventory; he or she does not have direct control over inventory, but does provide input into the inventory management process.

Inventory Fundamentals

Two aspects of inventory require some elaboration. One is the *types of inventory;* the other concerns differing viewpoints as to the *appropriate level of inventory*.

Types of Inventory

raw materials inventory
Items purchased by the firm for use in the manufacture of a finished product.

work-in-process inventory
All items currently in production.

finished goods inventory
Items that have been produced but not yet sold.

The three basic types of inventory are raw materials, work in process, and finished goods. **Raw materials inventory** consists of items purchased by the firm—usually basic materials such as screws, plastic, raw steel, or rivets—for use in the manufacture of a finished product. If a firm manufactures complex products with numerous parts, its raw materials inventory may consist of manufactured items that have been purchased from another company or from another division of the same firm. **Work-in-process inventory** consists of all items currently in production. These are normally partially finished goods at some intermediate stage of completion. **Finished goods inventory** consists of items that have been produced but not yet sold.

Differing Viewpoints about Inventory Level

Differing viewpoints concerning appropriate inventory levels commonly exist among the finance, marketing, manufacturing, and purchasing managers of a company. Each sector views inventory levels in light of its own objectives. The *financial manager's* general disposition toward inventory levels is to keep them low. The financial manager must police the inventories, making sure that the firm's money is not being unwisely invested in excess resources. The *marketing manager,* on the other hand, would like to have large inventories of each of the firm's finished products. This would ensure that all orders could be filled quickly, thus eliminating the need for backorders due to stockouts.

The *manufacturing manager's* major responsibility is to make sure that the production plan is correctly implemented and that it results in the desired amount of finished goods. In fulfilling this role, the manufacturing manager would keep raw materials inventories high to avoid production delays and would favor high finished goods inventories by making large production runs for the sake of lower unit production costs. The *purchasing manager* is concerned solely with the raw materials inventories. He or she is responsible for seeing that whatever raw materials are required by production are available in the correct quantities at the desired times and at a favorable price. Without proper control, the purchasing manager may purchase larger quantities of resources than are actually needed in order to get quantity discounts or in anticipation of rising prices or a shortage of certain materials.

Inventory as an Investment

Inventory is an investment in the sense that it requires that the firm tie up its money, thereby forgoing certain other earnings opportunities. In general, the higher a firm's average inventories, the larger the dollar investment and cost required, and vice versa. In evaluating planned changes in inventory levels, the financial manager should consider such changes from a benefit-versus-cost standpoint.

Example
A firm is contemplating making larger production runs in order to reduce the high setup costs associated with the production of its only product. The total *annual* reduction in setup costs that can be obtained has been estimated at $20,000. As a result of the larger production runs, the average inventory investment is expected to increase from $200,000 to $300,000. If the firm can earn 25 percent per year on equal-risk investments, the *annual* cost of the additional $100,000 ($300,000 − $200,000) inventory investment will be $25,000 (.25 × $100,000). Comparing the annual $25,000 cost of the system with the annual savings of $20,000 shows that the proposal should be rejected since it results in a net annual *loss* of $5,000.

---

5 Because inventory is an investment in the sense that it requires the firm to tie up its money, the financial manager typically has direct control over the inventory management process. *(Fable)*
Although inventory is an investment in the sense that it requires the firm to tie up its money, *the financial manager only provides input to, but has no control over, the inventory management process.*

FACT OR FABLE?

The Relationship Between Inventory and Accounts Receivable

The level and the management of inventory and accounts receivable are closely related. Generally in the case of manufacturing firms, when an item is sold, it moves from inventory to accounts receivable and ultimately to cash. Because of the close relationship between inventory and accounts receivable, management of them should not be viewed independently. For example, the decision to extend credit to a customer can result in an increased level of sales, which can be supported only by higher levels of inventory and accounts receivable. The credit terms extended will also affect the investment in inventory and receivables, since longer credit terms may allow a firm to move items from inventory to accounts receivable. Generally there is an advantage to such a strategy, since the cost of carrying an item in inventory is greater than the cost of carrying an account receivable. This is true because the cost of carrying inventory includes, in addition to the required return on the invested funds, the costs of storing, insuring, and otherwise maintaining the physical inventory. This relationship can be shown using a simple example.

Example
Mills Industries estimates that the annual cost of carrying $1 of merchandise in inventory for a one-year-period is 25 cents, whereas the annual cost of carrying $1 of receivables is 15 cents. The firm currently maintains average inventories of $300,000 and an average *investment* in accounts receivable of $200,000. The firm believes that

by altering its credit terms, it can cause its customers to purchase in larger quantities on the average, thereby reducing its average inventories to $150,000 and increasing the average investment in accounts receivable to $350,000. The altered credit terms are not expected to generate new business but will result only in a shift in purchasing and payment patterns. The costs of the present and proposed inventory–accounts receivable systems are calculated in Table 15.5.

Table 15.5 shows that by shifting $150,000 of inventory to accounts receivable, Mills Industries is able to lower the cost of carrying inventory and accounts receivable from $105,000 to $90,000—a $15,000 ($105,000—$90,000) addition to profits. This profit is achieved without changing the level of average inventory and accounts receivable investment from its $500,000 total. Rather, the profit is attributed to a shift in the mix of these current assets so that a larger portion of them is held in the form of accounts receivable, which is less costly to hold than inventory.

Table 15.5
Analysis of Inventory–Accounts Receivable Systems for Mills Industries

		Present		Proposed	
Variable	Cost/return (1)	Average investment (2)	Cost [(1) × (2)] (3)	Average investment (4)	Cost [(1) × (4)] (5)
Average inventory	25%	$300,000	$ 75,000	$150,000	$37,500
Average receivables	15	200,000	30,000	350,000	52,500
Total		$500,000	$105,000	$500,000	$90,000

The inventory–accounts receivable relationship is affected by decisions made in all areas of the firm—finance, marketing, manufacturing, and purchasing. The financial manager should consider the interactions between inventory and accounts receivable when developing strategies and making decisions related to the production-sale process. This interaction is especially important when making credit decisions, since the required as well as actual levels of inventory will be directly affected.

Techniques for Managing Inventory

Techniques commonly used in managing inventory are (1) the ABC system, (2) the basic economic order quantity (EOQ) model, and (3) the reorder point. Although these techniques are not strictly financial, it is helpful for the financial manager to understand them.

The ABC System

ABC system Divides inventory into three categories of descending importance, based on the dollar investment in each.

A firm using the **ABC system** divides its inventory into three groups, A, B, and C. The *A group* includes those items that require the largest dollar investment. In the typical distribution of inventory items, this group consists of the 20 percent of inventory items that account for 80 percent of the firm's dollar investment. The *B group* consists of the items accounting for the next largest investment. The *C group* typically consists of a large number of items accounting for a relatively small dollar investment. Dividing its inventory into A, B, and C items allows the firm to determine the level and types of inventory control procedures needed. Control of the A items should be most intensive due to the high dollar investment involved, while the B and C items would be subject to correspondingly less sophisticated control procedures.

The Basic Economic Order Quantity (EOQ) Model

One of the most commonly cited sophisticated tools for determining the optimal order quantity for an item of inventory is the **economic order quantity (EOQ) model.** This model could well be used to control the firm's A items. It takes into account various operating and financial costs and determines the order quantity that minimizes total inventory costs.

economic order quantity (EOQ) model A technique for determining the optimal order quantity of an inventory item, based on the trade-off between various operating and financial inventory costs.

Basic Costs

Excluding the actual cost of the merchandise, the costs associated with inventory can be divided into three broad groups: order costs, carrying costs, and total cost. Each has certain key components and characteristics.

Order Costs. **Order costs** include the fixed clerical costs of placing and receiving an order—the cost of writing a purchase order, of processing the resulting paperwork, and of receiving an order and checking it against the invoice. Order costs are normally stated as dollars per order.

order costs The fixed clerical costs of placing and receiving an inventory order.

Carrying Costs. **Carrying costs** are the variable costs per unit of holding an item in inventory for a specified time period. These costs are typically stated as dollars per unit per period. Carrying costs include storage costs, insurance costs, the cost of deterioration and obsolescence, and most important, the opportunity, or financial, cost of tying up funds in inventory. A commonly cited rule of thumb suggests that the cost of carrying an item in inventory for one year is between 20 and 30 percent of the cost (value) of the item.

carrying costs The variable costs per unit of holding an item in inventory for a specified time period.

Total Cost. The **total cost** of inventory is defined as the sum of the order and carrying costs. Total cost is important in the EOQ model, since the model's objective is to determine the order quantity that minimizes it.

total cost The sum of the order and carrying costs of inventory.

A Graphic Approach

The stated objective of the EOQ model is to find the order quantity that minimizes the firm's total inventory cost.[9] The economic order quantity can be found graphically by plotting order quantities on the *x*, or horizontal, axis and costs on the *y*, or vertical, axis. Figure 15.3 shows the general behavior of these costs. The total cost line represents the sum of the order costs and carrying costs for each order quantity. The minimum total cost occurs at the point labeled EOQ, where the order cost line and the carrying cost line intersect.

[9] The EOQ methodology is also applied to situations in which the firm wishes to minimize a total cost with fixed and variable components. It is commonly used to determine optimal production quantities when there is a fixed setup cost and a variable operating cost. The EOQ methodology has also been used in the financial cash–marketable security decision process.

Figure 15.3
A Graphic Presentation of an EOQ

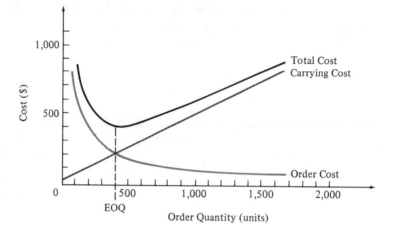

A Mathematical Approach

A formula can be developed for determining the firm's EOQ for a given inventory item. By letting

$$S = \text{usage in units per period}$$
$$O = \text{order cost per order}$$
$$C = \text{carrying cost per unit per period}$$
$$Q = \text{order quantity in units}$$

the firm's total cost equation can be developed. The first step in deriving the total cost equation is to develop an expression for the order cost function and the carrying cost function. The order cost can be expressed as the product of the cost per order and the number of orders. Since the number of orders equals the usage during the period divided by the order quantity (S/Q), the order cost can be expressed as follows:

$$\text{Order cost} = O \times S/Q \tag{15.2}$$

The carrying cost is defined as the cost of carrying a unit per period multiplied by the firm's average inventory. The average inventory is defined as the order quantity divided by 2 $(Q/2)$, since inventory is assumed to be depleted at a constant rate. Thus the carrying cost can be expressed as follows:

$$\text{Carrying cost} = C \times Q/2 \tag{15.3}$$

Analyzing Equations 15.2 and 15.3 shows that as the order quantity, Q, increases, the order cost will decrease while the carrying cost increases proportionately.

The total cost equation is obtained by combining the order cost and carrying cost expressions in Equations 15.2 and 15.3, as follows:

$$\text{Total cost} = (O \times S/Q) + (C \times Q/2) \tag{15.4}$$

Since the EOQ is defined as the order quantity that minimizes the total cost function, Equation 15.4 must be solved for the EOQ.[10] The following formula results:

$$EOQ = \sqrt{\frac{2 \times S \times O}{C}} \qquad (15.5)$$

Example
Assume that a firm uses 1,600 units of an item annually; its order costs are $50 per order and carrying costs are $1 per unit per year. Substituting $S = 1,600$, $O = \$50$, and $C = \$1$ into Equation 15.5 yields an EOQ of 400 units:

$$EOQ = \sqrt{\frac{2 \times 1,600 \times \$50}{\$1}} = \sqrt{160,000} = \underline{\underline{400 \text{ units}}}$$

If the firm orders in quantities of 400 units, it will minimize its total inventory cost. This solution is depicted in Figure 15.3.

Although even the simple EOQ model has weaknesses, it certainly provides decision makers with better grounds for a decision than subjective observations. Although the financial manager is normally not directly associated with the use of the EOQ model, he or she must be aware of its utility. The financial manager must also provide certain financial inputs, specifically with respect to inventory carrying costs, to enable the firm to use the EOQ model.

| **6** The EOQ model is an inventory management technique used to find the optimal order quantity that minimizes the total cost which includes order cost and carrying cost. *(Fact)* | **FACT OR FABLE?** |

The Reorder Point

Once the firm has calculated its economic order quantity, it must determine when to place orders. A reorder point is required that considers the lead time needed to place and receive orders. Assuming a constant usage rate for inventory, the **reorder point** can be determined by the following equation:

> **reorder point** The point at which to reorder inventory, expressed equationally as: lead time in days × daily usage.

$$\text{Reorder point} = \text{lead time in days} \times \text{daily usage} \qquad (15.6)$$

[10] The solution can be found by taking the first derivative of Equation 15.4 with respect to Q or by setting the order cost equal to the carrying cost and solving for Q, the EOQ, as demonstrated below.

(1) Multiply both sides by Q	$O \times \dfrac{S}{Q}$	$= C \times \dfrac{Q}{2}$
(2) Multiply both sides by 2	$O \times S$	$= C \times \dfrac{Q^2}{2}$
(3) Divide both sides by C	$2 \times O \times S$	$= C \times Q^2$
(4) Take the square root of both sides	$\dfrac{2 \times O \times S}{C}$	$= Q^2$
	$\sqrt{\dfrac{2 \times S \times O}{C}}$	$= Q = EOQ$

For example, if a firm knows that it requires 10 days to receive an order once the order is placed, and if it uses five units of inventory daily, the reorder point would be 50 units (10 days × 5 units per day). Thus as soon as the firm's inventory level reaches 50 units, an order will be placed for an amount equal to the economic order quantity. If the estimates of lead time and daily usage are correct, the order will be received exactly when the inventory level reaches zero.

Summary

- Accounts receivable and inventory represent sizable investments by the firm. The management of accounts receivable centers on credit policies, credit terms, and collection policies. Inventory management is generally not the direct responsibility of the financial manager.

- Credit policies involve establishing credit standards and performing credit analysis in order to make credit decisions. Consumer credit decisions are often made using impersonal techniques, such as credit scoring.

- At the mercantile level, credit standards must be set by considering the trade-offs between the profit contribution from sales, the cost of investment in accounts receivable, and the cost of bad debts.

- Credit analysis is devoted to the collection and evaluation of credit information on credit applicants in order to determine whether they can meet the firm's standards. The subjective judgment of the credit analyst is an important input to the credit decision.

- Credit terms have three components: (1) the cash discount, (2) the cash discount period, (3) and the credit period. Changes in each of these variables affect the firm's sales, investment in accounts receivable, bad debt expenses, and profit per unit.

- Collection policies determine the type and degree of effort exercised to collect overdue accounts. In addition to looking at the average collection period ratio, accounts receivable are often aged to evaluate the effectiveness of the firm's credit and collection policies. The procedures used to evaluate changes in collection policy are similar to those used to evaluate credit policies and credit terms.

- The basic collection techniques include letters, telephone calls, personal visits, the use of collection agencies, and, as a last resort, legal action.

- The respective viewpoints held by marketing, manufacturing, and purchasing managers relative to the appropriate levels of various types of inventory (raw materials, work in process, and finished goods) tend to conflict with that of the financial manager. The financial manager views inventory as an investment that should be kept at a low level.

- The financial manager, who views inventory as an investment that consumes dollars, must consider the interrelationship between inventory and accounts receivable when making decisions related to the production-sale process.

- Several techniques are used to manage inventory. The ABC system determines which inventories require the most attention according to dollar investment. One of the most common techniques for determining optimal order quantities is the economic order quantity (EOQ) model. Once the optimal order quantity has been determined, the firm can set a reorder point, the level of inventory at which an order will be placed.

Questions

15-1 What do the *accounts receivable* of a firm typically represent? What is meant by a firm's *credit policy?*

15-2 Describe *credit scoring* and explain why this technique is typically applied to consumer credit decisions rather than to mercantile credit decisions.

15-3 What key variables should be considered in evaluating possible changes in a firm's credit standards? What are the basic trade-offs in a *tightening* of credit standards?

15-4 What is *credit analysis?* Describe the two basic steps in the credit investigation process and summarize the basic sources of credit information.

15-5 Discuss what is meant by *credit terms*. What are the three components of credit terms? How do credit terms affect the firm's accounts receivable?

15-6 What are the expected effects of a *decrease* in the firm's cash discount on sales volume, investment in accounts receivable, bad debt expenses, and per-unit profits, respectively?

15-7 What are the expected effects of a *decrease* in the firm's credit period? What is likely to happen to sales volume, investment in accounts receivable, and bad debt expenses, respectively?

15-8 What is meant by a firm's *collection policy?* Explain how *aging accounts receivable* can be used to evaluate the effectiveness of both the credit policy and the collection policy.

15-9 Describe the basic trade-offs involved in collection policy decisions, and describe the popular types of collection techniques.

15-10 What is the financial manager's role with respect to the management of inventory? What are likely to be the viewpoints of each of the following managers, respectively, about the levels of the various types of inventory?

    a. Finance

    b. Marketing

    c. Manufacturing

    d. Purchasing

15-11 Explain the relationship between inventory and accounts receivable. Assuming the total investment in inventory and accounts receivable remains constant, what impact would lengthening the credit terms have on the firm's profits? Why?

15-12 What is the *ABC system* of inventory control? On what key premise is this system based?

15-13 What is the *EOQ model?* To which group of inventory items is it most applicable? What costs does it consider? What financial cost is involved?

Self-Test Problems

(Solutions on page 568)

ST-1 The Regency Rug Repair Company is attempting to evaluate whether it should ease collection efforts. The firm repairs 72,000 rugs per year at an average price of $32 each. Bad debt expenses are 1 percent of sales, and collection expenditures are $60,000. The average collection period is 40 days, the average cost per unit is $29 at the current sales level, and the variable cost per unit is $28. By easing the collection efforts, Regency expects to save $40,000 per year in collection expense. Bad debts will increase to 2 percent of sales, and the average collection period will increase to 58 days. Sales will increase by 1,000 repairs per year. If the firm has a required rate of return on equal-risk investments of 24 percent, what recommendation would you give the firm? Use your analysis to justify your answer.

ST-2 The Thompson Paint Company uses 60,000 gallons of pigment per year. The cost of carrying the pigment in inventory is $1 per gallon per year, and the cost of ordering pigment is $200 per order. The firm uses pigment at a constant rate every day throughout the year.

    a. Calculate the EOQ.

    b. Calculate the total cost of the plan suggested by the EOQ.

    c. Determine the total number of orders suggested by this plan.

    d. Assuming that it takes 20 days to receive an order once it has been placed, determine the reorder point in terms of gallons of pigment. (*Note:* Use a 360-day year.)

Problems

15-1 **(Credit Scoring)** Clemens Department Store uses credit scoring to evaluate retail credit applications. The financial and credit characteristics considered and weights indicating their relative importance in the credit decision are given in the table at the top of page 564. The firm's credit standards are to accept all applicants with credit scores of 80 or more; to extend limited credit on a probationary basis to applicants with scores of greater than 70 and less than 80; and to reject all applicants with scores below 70.

Financial and credit characteristics	Predetermined weight
Credit references	.25
Education	.15
Home ownership	.10
Income range	.10
Payment history	.30
Years on job	.10

The firm currently needs to process three applications recently received and scored by one of its credit analysts. The scores for each of the applicants on each of the financial and credit characteristics are summarized in the following table:

Financial and credit characteristics	Applicant		
	A	B	C
	Score (0 to 100)		
Credit references	60	90	80
Education	70	70	80
Home ownership	100	90	60
Income range	75	80	80
Payment history	60	85	70
Years on job	50	60	90

a. Use the data presented to find the credit score for each of the applicants.

b. Recommend the appropriate action for each of the three applicants.

15-2 (Accounts Receivable and Costs) Randolph Company currently has an average collection period of 45 days and annual credit sales of $1 million. Assume a 360-day year.

a. What is the firm's average accounts receivable balance?

b. If the average cost of each product is 60 percent of sales, what is the average investment in accounts receivable?

c. If the equal-risk opportunity cost of the investment in accounts receivable is 12 percent, what is the total opportunity cost of the investment in accounts receivable?

15-3 (Changes in Credit Policy Without Bad Debts) Tara's Textiles currently has credit sales of $600 million per year and an average collection period of 60 days. Assume that the price of Tara's products is $100 per unit, the variable costs are $55 per unit, and the average costs are $85 per unit at the current level of sales. The firm is considering changing its credit policy. This will result in a 20 percent increase in sales and an equal 20 percent increase in the average collection period. No change in bad debts is expected. The firm's equal-risk opportunity cost on its investment in accounts receivable is 14 percent.

a. What are the firm's total fixed costs with and without the policy change?

b. Calculate the additional profits from new sales the firm will realize if it changes its credit policy.

c. What marginal investment in accounts receivable will result?

d. Calculate the cost of the marginal investment in accounts receivable.

e. Should the firm change its credit policy? What other information would be helpful in your analysis?

15-4 (Bad Debt Policy) A firm is evaluating a credit policy change that would increase bad debts from 2 percent to 4 percent of sales. Sales are currently 50,000 units, the selling price is $20 per unit, variable cost per unit is $9, and average cost per unit is $11 at the current level of sales. As a result of the change in accounts receivable policy, sales are forecast to increase to 60,000 units.

a. What are bad debts in dollars under the present and proposed plans?

b. Calculate the cost of the marginal bad debts to the firm.

c. Ignoring the profitability from increased sales, if the policy saves $3,500 and causes no change in the average investment in accounts receivable, would you recommend the policy change? Explain.

d. Considering *all* changes in costs and benefits, would you recommend this policy change? Explain.

e. Compare and discuss your answers in **c** and **d**.

15-5 (Tightening Credit Standards—Bad Debt Losses) Michael's Menswear feels its credit costs are too high. By tightening its credit standards, bad debts will fall from 5 percent of sales to 2 percent. However, sales will fall from $100,000 to $90,000 per year. If the variable cost per unit is 50 percent of the sale price, fixed costs are $10,000, and the average investment in receivables does not change,

a. What cost will the firm face in a reduced contribution to profits from sales?

b. Should the firm tighten its credit standards? Explain your answer.

15-6 (Relaxation of Credit Standards) Lewis Enterprises is considering relaxing its credit standards in order to increase its currently sagging sales. As a result of the proposed relaxation, sales are expected to increase by 10 percent from 10,000 to 11,000 units during the coming year, the average collection period is expected to increase from 45 to 60 days, and bad debts are expected to increase from 1 percent to 3 percent of sales. The sale price per unit is $40, the variable cost per unit is $31, and the average cost per unit at the current 10,000-unit sales volume is $36. If the firm's required return on equal-risk investments is 25 percent, evaluate the proposed relaxation and make a recommendation to the firm.

15-7 (Initiating a Cash Discount) Gardner Company currently makes all sales on credit and offers no cash discount. The firm is considering a 2 percent cash discount for payment within 15 days. The firm's current average collection period is 60 days, sales are 40,000 units, selling price is $45 per unit, variable cost per unit is $36, and average cost per unit is $40 at the current sales volume. The firm expects that the change in credit terms will result in an increase in sales to 42,000 units, that 70 percent of the sales will take the discount, and that the average collection period will fall to 30 days. If the firm's required rate of return on equal-risk investments is 25 percent, should the proposed discount be offered?

15-8 (Credit Term Change—Shortening the Credit Period) A firm is contemplating *shortening* its credit period from 40 to 30 days and believes that as a result of this change its average collection period will decline from 45 to 36 days. Bad debt expenses are expected to decrease from 1.5 percent to 1 percent of sales. The firm is currently selling 12,000 units but believes that as a result of the proposed change, sales will decline to 10,000 units. The sale price per unit is $56, its variable cost per unit is $45, and the average cost per unit at the 12,000-unit volume is $53. The firm has a required return on equal-risk investments of 25 percent. Evaluate this decision and make a recommendation to the firm.

15-9 (Credit Term Change—Lengthening the Credit Period) Parker Tool is considering lengthening its credit period from 30 to 60 days. All customers will continue to pay on the net date. The firm currently bills $450,000 for sales, has $345,000 in variable costs, and has $45,000 in fixed costs. The change in credit terms is expected to increase sales to $510,000. Bad debt expense will increase from 1 percent to 1.5 percent of sales. The firm has a required rate of return on equal-risk investments of 20 percent. (*Hint:* Calculate the contribution margin $\left[1 - \dfrac{\text{variable costs}}{\text{sales revenue}}\right]$ and use it along with the total fixed costs to find the additional profit contribution and the marginal investment in accounts receivable.)

a. What additional profit contribution from sales will be realized from the change?

b. What changes in the cost of financing the investment in accounts receivable and bad debts will the firm face?

c. Do you recommend this change in credit terms? Why or why not?

15-10 (Aging Accounts Receivable) Burnham Services' accounts receivable totaled $874,000 on August 31, 1988. A breakdown of these outstanding accounts on the basis of the month in which the credit sale was initially made is given below. The firm extends 30-day credit terms to its credit customers.

Month of credit sale	Accounts receivable
August 1988	$320,000
July 1988	250,000
June 1988	81,000
May 1988	195,000
April 1988 or before	28,000
Total (August 31, 1988)	$874,000

a. Prepare an aging schedule for Burnham Services' August 31, 1988, accounts receivable balance.

b. Using your findings in **a**, evaluate the firm's credit and collection activities.

c. What are some probable causes of the situation discussed in **b**?

15-11 (Inventory Investment) Paterson Products is considering leasing a computerized inventory control system in order to reduce its average inventories. The annual cost of the system is $46,000. It is expected that with the system the firm's average inventory will decline by 50 percent from its current level of $980,000. The level of stockouts is expected to be unaffected by this system. The firm can earn 20 percent per year on equal-risk investments.

a. How much of a reduction in average inventory will result from the proposed installation of the computerized inventory control system?

b. How much, if any, annual savings will the firm realize on the reduced level of average inventory?

c. Should the firm lease the computerized inventory control system? Explain why or why not.

15-12 (Inventory versus Accounts Receivable Costs) Hamilton Supply estimates the annual cost of carrying a dollar of inventory is $.27, while the annual carrying cost of an equal investment in accounts receivable is $.17. The firm's current balance sheet reflects its average inventory of $400,000 and average investment in accounts receivable of $100,000. If the firm can convince its customers to purchase in large quantities, the average level of inventory can be reduced by $200,000 and the average investment in receivables increased by the same amount. Assuming no change in annual sales, what addition to profits will be generated from this shift? Explain your answer.

15-13 (Inventory—The ABC System) Newton, Inc., has 16 different items in its inventory. The average number of units held in inventory and the average unit cost are listed below for each item. The firm wishes to introduce the ABC system of inventory control. Suggest a breakdown of the items into classifications of A, B, and C. Justify your selection and point out items that could be considered borderline cases.

Item	Average number of units in inventory	Average cost per unit
1	1,800	$ 0.54
2	1,000	8.20
3	100	6.00
4	250	1.20
5	8	94.50
6	400	3.00
7	80	45.00
8	1,600	1.45
9	600	0.95
10	3,000	0.18
11	900	15.00
12	65	1.35
13	2,200	4.75
14	1,800	1.30
15	60	18.00
16	200	17.50

15-14 (Graphic EOQ Analysis) Knoll Manufacturing uses 10,000 units of raw material per year on a continuous basis. The firm estimates the cost of carrying one unit in inventory at 25 cents per year. Placing and processing an order for additional inventory costs $200 per order.

a. What are annual order costs, carrying costs, and total costs of inventory if the firm orders in quantities of 1,000; 2,000; 3,000; 4,000; 5,000; 6,000; and 7,000 units, respectively?

b. Graph order costs and carrying costs (*y*-axis) relative to quantity ordered (*x*-axis). Label the EOQ.

c. Based on your graph, in what quantity would you order? Is this consistent with the EOQ equation? Explain why or why not.

15-15 (EOQ Analysis) Tiger Corporation purchases 1,200,000 units per year of one component. Annual carrying costs of the item are 27 percent of the item's $2 cost. Fixed costs per order are $25.

a. Determine the EOQ under the following conditions: (1) no changes, (2) carrying cost of zero, (3) order cost of zero.

b. What do your answers illustrate about the EOQ model? Explain.

15-16 (Reorder Point) Beeman Gas and Electric (BG&E) is required to carry a minimum of 20 days' average coal usage, which is 100 tons of coal. It takes 10 days between order and delivery. At what level of coal would BG&E reorder?

15-17 (EOQ, Reorder Point, and Safety Stock) A firm uses 800 units of a product per year on a continuous basis. The product has carrying costs of $2 per unit per year and fixed costs of $50 per order. It takes 5 days to receive a shipment after an order is placed, and the firm wishes to hold in inventory 10 days' usage as a safety stock.

   a. Calculate the EOQ.

   b. Determine the average level of inventory.

   c. Determine the reorder point.

   d. Which of the following variables change if the firm does not hold the safety stock: (1) carrying costs, (2) order costs, (3) reorder point, (4) total inventory cost, (5) average level of inventory, (6) number of orders per year, (7) economic order quantity? Explain.

Solutions to Self-Test Problems

ST-1 Tabular Calculation of the Effects of Easing Collection Efforts on Regency Rug Repair Company.

Additional profit contribution from sales [1,000 rugs × ($32 avg. sale price − $28 var. cost)]		$ 4,000
Cost of marginal investment in accounts receivable Average investment under proposed plan:		
$\dfrac{(\$29 \times 72,000 \text{ rugs}) + (\$28 \times 1,000 \text{ rugs})}{360/58} = \dfrac{\$2,116,000}{6.21}$	$340,741	
Average investment under present plan:		
$\dfrac{(\$29 \times 72,000 \text{ rugs})}{360/40} = \dfrac{\$2,088,000}{9}$	232,000	
Marginal investment in A/R	$108,741	
Cost of marginal investment in A/R (.24 × $108,741)		($26,098)
Cost of marginal bad debts		
Bad debts under proposed plan (.02 × $32 × 73,000 rugs)	$ 46,720	
Bad debts under present plan (.01 × $32 × 72,000 rugs)	23,040	
Cost of marginal bad debts		($23,680)
Annual savings in collection expense		$40,000
Net loss from implementation of proposed plan		($ 5,778)

Recommendation: Since a net loss of $5,778 is expected to result from easing collection efforts, *the proposed plan should not be implemented.*

ST-2 a. *Data:*

   S = 60,000 gallons
   C = $1 per gallon per year
   O = $200 per order

Calculation:

$$\text{EOQ} = \sqrt{\frac{2 \times S \times O}{C}} = \sqrt{\frac{2 \times 60,000 \times \$200}{\$1}} = \sqrt{24,000,000} = \underline{4,899 \text{ gallons}}$$

b. Total cost = $(O \times S/Q) + (C \times Q/2)$
Q = EOQ = 4,899 gallons
Total cost = [$200 × (60,000/4,899)] + [$1 × (4,899/2)]
= ($200 × 12.25) + ($1 × 2,449.5)
= $2,450 + $2,449.5 = $\underline{\$4,899.50}$

c. Number of orders = S/Q
= 60,000/4,899 = $\underline{12.25 \text{ orders}}$

d. *Data:*

Lead time = 20 days
Daily usage = 60,000 gallons/360 days
= 166.67 gallons/days

Calculation:

Reorder point = lead time in days × daily usage
= 20 days × 166.67 gallons/day
= $\underline{3,333.4 \text{ gallons}}$

Casa de Diseño

In January 1989, Teresa Leal was named treasurer of Casa de Diseño. She decided that she could best orient herself by systematically examining each area of the company's financial operations. She began by studying the firm's short-term financial activities.

Casa de Diseño is located in southern California and specializes in a furniture line called "Ligne Moderna." Of high quality and contemporary design, the furniture appeals to the customer who wants something unique for his or her home or apartment. Most Ligne Moderna furniture is built by special order since a wide variety of upholstery, accent trimming, and colors is available. The product line is distributed through exclusive dealership arrangements with well-established retail stores. Casa de Diseño's manufacturing process virtually eliminates the use of wood. Plastic and metal provide the basic framework and wood is used only for decorative purposes.

Casa de Diseño entered the plastic furniture market in late 1983. The company markets its plastic furniture products as indoor-outdoor items under the brand name "Futuro." Futuro plastic furniture emphasizes comfort, durability, and practicality and is distributed through wholesalers. The Futuro line has been very successful, accounting for nearly 40 percent of the firm's sales and profits in 1988. Casa de Diseño anticipates some additions to the Futuro line and also some limited change of direction in its promotion in an effort to expand the applications of the plastic furniture.

Ms. Leal has decided to study the firm's cash mangement practices. To determine the effects of these practices, she must first determine the current cash cycle and cash turnover. In her investigations she found that Casa de Diseño purchases all of its raw materials and production supplies on open account. The company is operating at production levels that preclude volume discounts. Most suppliers do not offer cash discounts, and Casa de Diseño usually receives credit terms of net 30. An aging of Casa de Diseño's accounts payable showed that since the company pays within its credit terms, the average payment period is 30 days. Leal consulted industry data and found that the industry average payment period was 39 days. Investigation of six California furniture manufacturers revealed that their average payment period was also 39 days.

Next, Leal studied the production cycle and inventory policies. Casa de Diseño tries not to hold any more inventory in either raw materials or finished goods than necessary. The average inventory age was 110 days. Leal determined that the industry standard as reported in a survey done by *Furniture Age,* the trade association journal, was 83 days.

Casa de Diseño sells to its customers on a net 60 basis, in line with the general trend to grant such credit terms on specialty furniture. Leal discovered that, by aging the accounts receivable, the average collection period for the firm was 75 days. Investigation of the trade association's and California manufacturers' averages showed that the same collection period existed where net 60 credit terms were given. Where cash discounts were offered, the collection period was significantly shortened. Leal believed that if Casa de Diseño were to offer credit terms of 3/10 net 60, the average collection period could be reduced by 40 percent.

Casa de Diseño was spending an estimated $26,500,000 per year for operations, excluding capital outlays, which were $3,000,000 per year. Leal considered these expenditure levels to be the minimum she could expect the firm to disburse during 1989. Her concern was whether the firm's cash management was as efficient as it could be. She knew that the company faced an investment opportunity cost (required return) of 15 percent on every dollar of inefficient investment. For this reason, she was concerned about the cost of any excess cash balances caused by inefficiency in Casa de Diseño's operations.

Required

1. Assuming a constant rate for purchases, production, and sales throughout the year, what are Casa de Diseño's existing cash cycle, cash turnover, and minimum operating cash requirements?

2. If Leal can optimize Casa de Diseño's operations according to industry standards, what would Casa de Diseño's cash cycle, cash turnover, and minimum operating cash requirements be under these more efficient conditions?

3. In terms of cash balance requirements, what is the cost of Casa de Diseño's operational inefficiency?

4. **a.** If in addition to achieving industry standards for payables and inventory, the firm can reduce the average collection period by offering 3/10 net 60 credit terms, what additional savings would result from the shortened cash cycle, assuming that the level of sales remains constant?

   b. If the firm's sales (all on credit) are $40,000,000 and 45 percent of the customers are expected to take the cash discount, how much will the firm's annual revenues be reduced by as a result of the discount?

   c. If the firm's average cost of the $40,000,000 in sales is 80 percent, determine the reduction in the average investment in accounts receivable and the annual savings resulting from this reduced investment assuming that sales remain constant. (Assume a 360-day year.)

   d. If the firm's bad debt expenses decline from 2 percent of sales to 1.5 percent of sales, what annual savings would result, assuming sales remain constant?

   e. Use your findings in parts **b** through **d** to assess whether offering the cash discount can be justified financially. Explain why or why not.

5. Based upon your analysis in questions 1 through 4, what recommendations would you offer Teresa Leal?

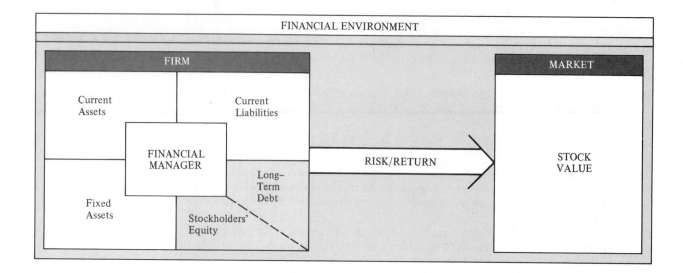

PART SIX

Sources of Long-Term Financing

CHAPTER 16

Long-Term Debt and Investment Banking

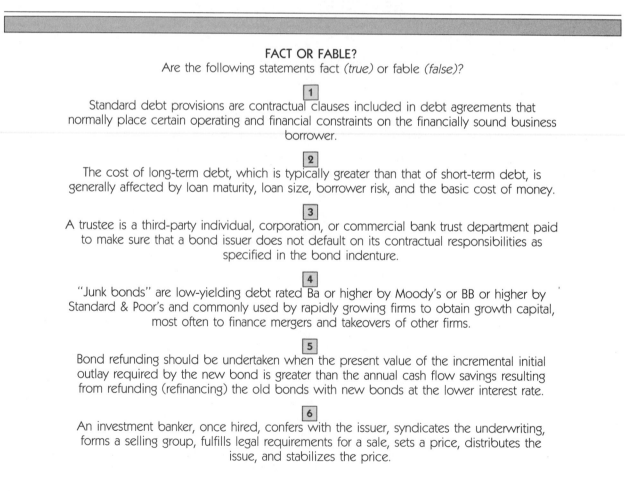

FACT OR FABLE?

Are the following statements fact *(true)* or fable *(false)*?

1

Standard debt provisions are contractual clauses included in debt agreements that normally place certain operating and financial constraints on the financially sound business borrower.

2

The cost of long-term debt, which is typically greater than that of short-term debt, is generally affected by loan maturity, loan size, borrower risk, and the basic cost of money.

3

A trustee is a third-party individual, corporation, or commercial bank trust department paid to make sure that a bond issuer does not default on its contractual responsibilities as specified in the bond indenture.

4

"Junk bonds" are low-yielding debt rated Ba or higher by Moody's or BB or higher by Standard & Poor's and commonly used by rapidly growing firms to obtain growth capital, most often to finance mergers and takeovers of other firms.

5

Bond refunding should be undertaken when the present value of the incremental initial outlay required by the new bond is greater than the annual cash flow savings resulting from refunding (refinancing) the old bonds with new bonds at the lower interest rate.

6

An investment banker, once hired, confers with the issuer, syndicates the underwriting, forms a selling group, fulfills legal requirements for a sale, sets a price, distributes the issue, and stabilizes the price.

The terms "taking a company public" and "going public" refer to the initial public offering of a company's common and/or preferred stock. A strict set of procedures for this process has been determined by the Securities and Exchange Commission. When Bill Gates took Microsoft public in March 1986, he experienced the arduous process of conforming to SEC regulations. Despite Gates's fears that going public would disrupt his business, a public offering was becoming inevitable. Gates had issued many stock options and shares of stock to attract new people into the organization, and companies with a large number of stockholders are required to register with the SEC. Once registered, Gates figured that he might as well go public to broaden what was in effect an already public market and to make this market more liquid. When the deal was done, he had made millions of dollars.

The first step in going public was to choose an investment banker to underwrite the offering. The investment banker manages the sale of the company's stock. The major criteria for Microsoft's investment bankers were experience in high technology finance and overall rapport with the software company. The prestigious Wall Street firms Goldman Sachs and Alex. Brown & Sons were selected.

Next, a prospectus, a security registration document which is issued to potential buyers, had to be written. The prospectus for Microsoft had to be worded carefully to comply with SEC regulations. Finally, the price of the common stock had to be set. Microsoft's work on pricing strategy went on for months and was made difficult in part by Gates's ultraconservative outlook. Eventually, a price range of $16 to $19 was agreed upon, but as the offering grew nearer, the market was surging and the range was raised to $20 to $22.

Microsoft stock was publicly traded on the over-the-counter market for the first time on March 13, 1986. It opened at $25.75 and stood at $27.75 by the end of the first day, with millions of shares being traded. Veteran Wall Street observers called the initial offering a triumph for everyone involved.

Some firms, like Microsoft, obtain needed long-term financing through public sale, typically with the aid of an investment banker, of long-term debt (bonds) or equity (stock). Other firms negotiate or use private placements to obtain long-term funds. Here we discuss the major provisions, types, and costs of long-term debt and the functions, organization, and costs of investment banking services.

Characteristics of Long-Term Debt Financing

Long-term debt is an important form of **long-term financing**—financing with an initial maturity of more than one year. It can be obtained with a *term loan,* which is negotiated from a financial institution, or through the sale of *bonds,* which are marketable debt sold

long-term financing
Financing with an initial maturity of more than one year.

575

to a number of institutional and individual lenders. The process of selling bonds, as well as stock, is generally accomplished using an *investment banker*—an institution that can assist in private placements and take a lead role in public offerings. Long-term debt provides financial leverage and is a desirable component of capital structure (see Chapter 12) since it tends to lower the weighted average cost of capital[1] (see Chapter 11).

The long-term debts of a business typically have maturities of between 5 and 20 years.[2] When a long-term debt is within one year of its maturity, accountants will show the balance of the long-term debt as a current liability because at that point it becomes a short-term obligation. Similar treatment is given to portions of long-term debts payable in the coming year. These entries are normally labeled "current portion of long-term debt." Here we discuss long-term debt provisions and costs. In subsequent sections attention is given to term loans, corporate bonds, and investment banking.

Standard Debt Provisions

standard debt provisions
Provisions in long-term debt agreements specifying certain criteria of satisfactory record keeping and reporting, tax payment, and general business maintenance on the part of the borrowing firm.

A number of **standard debt provisions** are included in long-term debt agreements. These provisions specify certain criteria of satisfactory record keeping and reporting, tax payment, and general business maintenance on the part of the borrowing firm. Standard debt provisions do not normally place a burden on the financially sound business. Commonly included standard provisions are listed below.

1. The borrower is required to *maintain satisfactory accounting records* in accordance with generally accepted accounting principles (GAAP).

2. The borrower is required to periodically *supply audited financial statements* which are used by the lender to monitor the firm and enforce the debt agreement.

3. The borrower is required to *pay taxes and other liabilities when due*.

4. The borrower is required to *maintain all facilities in good working order*, thereby behaving as a "going concern."

FACT OR FABLE?

1 Standard debt provisions are contractual clauses included in debt agreements that normally place certain operating and financial constraints on the financially sound business borrower. *(Fable)*

Standard debt provisions are contractual clauses included in debt agreements that *do not normally place a burden* on the financially sound business borrower.

Restrictive Debt Provisions

restrictive covenants
Contractual clauses in long-term debt agreements that place certain operating and financial constraints on the borrower.

Long-term debt agreements, whether resulting from a term loan or a bond issue, normally include certain **restrictive covenants,** contractual clauses that place certain operating and financial constraints on the borrower. Since the lender is committing funds for a long

[1] Long-term debt tends to lower the WACC primarily because of the tax-deductibility of interest, which causes the explicit cost of long-term debt to be quite low. Of course, as noted in Chapter 12, the introduction of large quantities of debt into the firm's capital structure can result in high levels of financial risk, which can cause the weighted average cost of capital to rise.

[2] Some texts classify debts with maturities of one to seven years as *intermediate-term debt*. This text uses a strict short-term–long-term classification. Debts with maturities of less than one year are considered short-term, and debts with maturities greater than one year are considered long-term. This classification is consistent with the firm's balance sheet classification of current liabilities and long-term debts.

period, it of course seeks to protect itself. Restrictive covenants, coupled with standard debt provisions, allow the lender to monitor and control the borrower's activities in order to protect itself against the *agency problem* created by the relationship between owners and lenders (described in Chapter 12). Without these provisions the borrower could "take advantage" of the lender by acting to increase the firm's risk while not being required to pay the lender an increased return (interest).

Restrictive covenants remain in force for the life of the debt agreement. The most common restrictive covenants are listed below.

1. The borrower is required to *maintain a minimum level of net working capital*. Net working capital below the minimum is considered indicative of inadequate liquidity, a common precursor to loan default and ultimate failure.

2. Borrowers are *prohibited from selling accounts receivable* to generate cash, since using proceeds to meet current obligations could cause a long-run cash shortage.

3. Long-term lenders commonly impose *fixed-asset restrictions* on the firm. These constrain the firm with respect to the liquidation, acquisition, and encumbrance of fixed assets, since any of these actions could damage the firm's ability to repay its debt.

4. Many debt agreements *constrain subsequent borrowing* by prohibiting additional long-term debt, or by requiring that additional borrowing be *"subordinated"* to the original loan. **Subordination** means that all subsequent or less important creditors agree to wait until all claims of the *senior debt* are satisfied prior to having their claims satisfied.

    subordination In a long-term debt agreement, the stipulation that subsequent or less important creditors agree to wait until all claims of the *senior debt* are satisfied before having their claims satisfied.

5. Borrowers may be *prohibited from entering into certain types of leases* in order to limit additional fixed-payment obligations.

6. Occasionally the lender *prohibits combinations* by requiring the borrower to agree not to consolidate, merge, or combine in any way with another firm, since such an action could significantly change the borrower's business and financial risk.

7. To prevent liquidation of assets through large salary payments, the lender may *prohibit or limit salary increases* for specified employees.

8. The lender may include *management restrictions* requiring the borrower to maintain certain "key employees" without whom the future success of the firm would be uncertain.

9. Occasionally the lender includes a covenant *limiting the borrower's security investment* alternatives. This restriction protects the lender by controlling the risk and marketability of the borrower's security investments.

10. Occasionally a covenant specifically requires the borrower to *spend the borrowed funds on a proven financial need*.

11. A relatively common provision *limits the firm's annual cash dividend payments* to a maximum of 50 to 70 percent of its net earnings or a specified dollar amount.

In the process of negotiating the terms of long-term debt, borrower and lender must ultimately agree to acceptable restrictive covenants. A good financial manager will know in advance the relative impact of proposed restrictions and will "hold the line" on those that may have a severely negative or damaging effect. The violation of any standard or restrictive provision by the borrower gives the lender the right to demand immediate repayment of the debt. Generally the lender will evaluate any violation in order to determine whether it is serious enough to jeopardize the loan. On the basis of such an evaluation the lender may demand immediate repayment of the loan, waive the violation and continue the loan, or waive the violation but alter the terms of the initial debt agreement.

Cost of Long-Term Debt

The cost of long-term debt is generally greater than that of short-term borrowing. In addition to standard and restrictive provisions, the long-term debt agreement specifies the interest rate, the timing of payments, and the dollar amount of payments. The major factors affecting the cost, or interest rate, of long-term debt are loan maturity, loan size, and more importantly, borrower risk and the basic cost of money.

Loan Maturity

Generally long-term loans have higher interest rates than short-term loans. The longer the term of a loan, the less accuracy there is in predicting future interest rates and therefore the greater the risk of forgoing an opportunity to loan money at a higher rate. In addition, the longer the term, the greater the repayment risk associated with the loan. To compensate for both of these factors, the lender typically charges a higher interest rate on long-term loans.

Loan Size

The size of the loan affects the interest cost of borrowing in an inverse manner. Loan administration costs per dollar borrowed are likely to decrease with increasing loan size. On the other hand, the risk to the lender increases since larger loans result in less diversification. The size of the loan sought by each borrower must therefore be evaluated to determine the net administrative cost–risk trade-off.

Borrower Risk

As noted in Chapter 12, the higher the firm's operating leverage, the greater its business risk. Also, the higher the borrower's debt ratio or debt-equity ratio (or the lower its times interest earned ratio or fixed-payment coverge ratio), the greater its financial risk. The lender's main concern is with the ability of the borrower to repay the loan. The overall assessment of the borrower's business and financial risk, along with information on past payment patterns, is used by the lender in setting the interest rate on any loan.

Basic Cost of Money

The cost of money is the basis for determining the actual interest rate charged. Generally the rate on U.S. Treasury securities with *equivalent maturities* is used as the basic standard for the risk-free cost of money. To determine the actual interest rate to be charged, the lender will add premiums for loan size and borrower risk to this basic cost of money for the given maturity. Alternatively, some lenders determine a prospective borrower's risk class[3] and find the rates charged on similar maturity loans to firms believed to be in the same risk class. Instead of having to determine a risk premium, the lender can use the risk premium prevailing in the marketplace for similar loans.

---

[3] A *risk class* reflects the firm's overall risk profile. One must envision a continuum of risk, break it into discrete classes, and place the firm in an appropriate class. Looking at other firms perceived to be in the same risk class will help the lender make certain decisions with respect to the appropriate rate of interest. For publicly traded firms, betas (see Chapter 7) are often used to classify firms into homogeneous risk classes.

FINANCE IN ACTION

DEBT'S DOWNSIDE MAKES WINN A LOSER

Once there were three bright young brothers who built a billion-dollar company in no time at all, and then lived to preside over its rapid demise. Starting with a little cash flow, tax-loss carry-forwards, ambitious plans, and some eager bankers, the trio built Winn Enterprises' sales from $26.5 million in 1982 to $1.1 billion by December 1985, at which time Winn's assets were $749 million.

Less than a year later, Winn was in a shambles. Its shares traded at less than $1, down from a high of nearly $5. Assets were on the auction block. The company was effectively in bankruptcy. What was the brothers' problem? They pyramided assets on a pile of borrowed money, serviced by the assets' cash flow. A fine strategy—unless the cash flow slows, which is what happened to Winn. "They ran very close to the edge with cash flow," says Scott Gillespie, an analyst with Drake Capital, of Winn's troubles. "Any problems went right to Winn's ability to service debt."

The brothers decided to enter the dairy business with an acquisition of Knudsen Corp. for $78 million in May 1983. For a while the brothers looked pretty smart. In fiscal 1984 Winn's food operations, consisting almost entirely of Knudsen, earned $16.8 million pretax, on sales of $411 million. In a cyclical world, good times usually give way to bad. Milk price wars broke out. As Knudsen's chief competitor, Foremost Dairy, kept hammering prices, Winn's food operations' profit margins began to fall. The brothers' solution was to buy Foremost, which they accomplished by paying $50 million—all borrowed from Citicorp Industrial Credit—and assuming $80 million in debt in June 1985.

The plan was to merge the two operations. But both the inexperienced brothers and the so-called experts missed the point that the consolidation was impractical. A dismal record of mishaps and mismanagement followed: failure to pass a federal sanitation in-

spection, a decrease in milk from suppliers because of federal herd reduction, and a plant shut-down caused by discovery of a deadly bacteria. All these problems reduced sales, lowered profits, and slowed cash flow to a trickle. Nearly a year later, Knudsen's Modesto plant produced less than it did before the operations merged.

As Winn's cash flow ebbed, the company's debt burden—over $300 million, 20 times shareholders' equity—became unsupportable. The dominoes began to topple. In April 1986, the company began to sell off pieces of Winn to raise cash. "We quickly realized we couldn't operate our way out of our debt problems," said a company spokesman.

But, again, this is not only a tale of what went wrong for Winn Enterprises' young founders. It is also a general reminder that cash can ebb as well as flow—and that debt has the power both to create and to destroy wealth.

SOURCE: Adapted from Lisa Gubernick, "Debt's Downside," *Forbes*, September 8, 1986, pp. 40–48.

---

2 The cost of long-term debt, which is typically greater than that of short-term debt, is generally affected by loan maturity, loan size, borrower risk, and the basic cost of money. *(Fact)*   FACT OR FABLE?

Term Loans

A **term (long-term) loan** is a loan made by a financial institution to a business and having an initial maturity of more than one year. These loans generally have maturities of 5 to 12 years; shorter maturities are available, but minimum five-year maturities are common. Term loans are often made to finance *permanent* working capital needs, to pay for machinery and equipment, or to liquidate other loans.

term (long-term) loan
A loan made by a financial institution to a business and having an initial maturity of more than one year.

Characteristics of Term Loan Agreements

term loan agreement
A formal contract, ranging from a few to a few hundred pages, specifying the conditions under which a financial institution has made a long-term loan.

The actual **term loan agreement** is a formal contract ranging from a few to a few hundred pages. The following items are commonly specified in the document: the amount and maturity of the loan; payment dates; interest rate; standard provisions; restrictive provisions; collateral (if any); purpose of the loan; action to be taken in the event the agreement is violated; and stock-purchase warrants. Of these, only payment dates, collateral requirements, and stock-purchase warrants require further discussion.

Payment Dates

Term loan agreements generally require monthly, quarterly, semiannual, or annual payments. Generally these equal payments fully repay the interest and principal over the life of the loan. Occasionally a term loan agreement will require periodic payments over the life of the loan followed by a large lump-sum payment at maturity. This so-called **balloon payment** represents the entire loan principal if the periodic payments represent only interest.

balloon payment At the maturity of a loan, a large lump-sum payment representing the entire loan principal if the periodic payments represent only interest.

Collateral Requirements

Term lending arrangements may be unsecured or secured in a fashion similar to that for short-term loans. Whether collateral is required depends on the lender's evaluation of the borrower's financial condition. Common types of collateral include machinery and equipment, plant, pledges of accounts receivable, and pledges of securities. Any collateral required and its disposition under various circumstances are specifically described in the term loan agreement.

Stock-Purchase Warrants

stock-purchase warrants
Warrants allowing the holder to purchase a certain number of shares of the firm's common stock at a specified price over a certain period of time.

A trend in term lending is for the corporate borrower to give the lender certain financial perquisites in addition to the payment of interest and repayment of principal. **Stock-purchase warrants** are warrants that allow the holder to purchase a certain number of shares of the firm's common stock at a specified price over a certain period of time. These are used to entice institutional lenders to make long-term loans, possibly under more-than-normally-favorable terms. Stock-purchase warrants are discussed in greater detail in Chapter 18.

Term Lenders

The primary financial institutions making term loans to businesses are commercial banks; insurance companies; pension funds; regional development companies; the Small Business Administration; small business investment companies; commercial finance companies; and equipment manufacturers' financing subsidiaries. Although the characteristics and provisions of term lending agreements made by these institutions are similar, a number of basic differences exist. Table 16.1 summarizes the key characteristics and types of loans offered.

Corporate Bonds

corporate bond
A certificate indicating that a corporation has borrowed a certain amount of money from an institution or an individual and promises to repay it in the future under clearly defined terms.

A **corporate bond** is a certificate indicating that a corporation has borrowed a certain amount of money from an institution or an individual and promises to repay it in the future under clearly defined terms. Most bonds are issued with maturities of 10 to 30 years and

Table 16.1
Characteristics and Types of Term Loans Made by Major Financial Institutions

Institution	Characteristics	Types of loans
Commercial bank	Makes some term loans to businesses.	Generally less than 12-year maturity except for real estate. Often participates in large loans made by a group of banks since banks are legally limited[a] in the amount they can loan a single borrower. Loans typically secured by collateral.
Insurance company	Life insurers are most active lenders.	Maturities of 10 to 20 years. Generally to larger firms and in larger amounts than commercial bank loans. Both unsecured and secured loans.
Pension fund	Invests a small portion of its funds in term loans to businesses.	Generally mortgage loans to large firms. Similar to insurance company loans.
Regional development companies	An association generally attached to local or regional governments. Attempts to promote business development in a given area by offering attractive financing deals. Obtains funds from various governmental bodies and through sale of tax-exempt bonds.	Term loans are made at competitive rates.
Small Business Administration (SBA)	An agency of the federal government that makes loans to "eligible" small and minority-owned businesses.	Joins with private lender and lends or guarantees repayment of all or part of the loan. Most loans are made for less than $500,000 at or below commercial bank interest rates.
Small business investment company (SBIC)	Licensed by the government. Makes both debt and equity investments in small firms.	Makes loans to small firms with high growth potential. Term loans with 5- to 20-year maturities and interest rates above those on bank loans. Generally receives, in addition, an equity interest in the borrowing firm.
Commercial finance company (CFC)	Involved in financing equipment purchases. Often a subsidiary of the manufacturer of equipment.	Makes secured loans for purchase of equipment. Typically installment loans with less-than-10-year maturities at higher-than-bank interest rates.
Equipment manufacturers' financing subsidiary	A type of "captive finance company" owned by the equipment manufacturer.	Makes long-term installment loans on equipment sales. Similar to commercial finance companies.

[a] Commercial banks are legally prohibited from loaning amounts in excess of 15 percent of the bank's unimpaired capital and surplus to a single borrower.

with a par, or face, value of $1,000. The coupon interest rate on a bond represents the percentage of the bond's par value that will be paid annually, typically in two equal semiannual installments. The bondholders, who are the lenders, are promised the semiannual interest payments and, at maturity, the principal amount (par value) loaned.

Legal Aspects of Corporate Bonds

Since a corporate bond issue may be for millions of dollars obtained by selling portions of the debt to numerous unrelated persons, certain legal arrangements are required to protect purchasers. Bondholders are protected legally primarily through the indenture and the trustee.

Bond Indenture

bond indenture A complex and lengthy legal document stating the conditions under which a bond has been issued.

A **bond indenture** is a complex and lengthy legal document stating the conditions under which a bond has been issued. It specifies both the rights of the bondholders and the duties of the issuing corporation. In addition to specifying the interest and principal payments and dates, and containing various standard and restrictive provisions, it frequently contains sinking-fund requirements and provisions with respect to a security interest (if the bond is secured).

Sinking-Fund Requirements. The standard and restrictive provisions for long-term debt and for bond issues have already been described in an earlier section of this chapter. However, an additional restrictive provision often included in a bond indenture is a **sinking-fund requirement** A restrictive provision often included in a bond indenture providing for the systematic retirement of bonds prior to their maturity.

sinking-fund requirement A restrictive provision often included in a bond indenture providing for the systematic retirement of bonds prior to their maturity. **sinking-fund requirement.** Its objective is to provide for the systematic retirement of bonds prior to their maturity. To carry out this requirement, the corporation makes semiannual or annual payments to a *trustee,* who uses these funds to retire bonds by purchasing them in the marketplace. This process is simplified by inclusion of a *call feature,* which permits the issuer to repurchase bonds at a stated price prior to maturity. The trustee will "call" bonds only when sufficient bonds cannot be purchased in the marketplace or when the market price of the bond is above the stated (call) price.

Security Interest. The bond indenture is similar to a loan agreement in that any collateral pledged against the bond is specifically identified in the document. Usually, the title to the collateral is attached to the indenture, and the disposition of the collateral in various circumstances is specifically described. The protection of bond collateral is crucial to increase the safety and thereby enhance the marketability of a bond issue.

Trustee

trustee A paid individual, corporation, or commercial bank trust department that acts as the third party to a bond indenture in order to ensure that the issuer does not default on its contractual responsibilities to the bondholders.

A **trustee** is a third party to a bond indenture. The trustee can be an individual, a corporation, or, most often, a commercial bank trust department. The trustee, whose services are paid for, acts as a "watchdog" on behalf of the bondholders, making sure that the issuer does not default on its contractual responsibilities. The trustee is empowered to take specified actions on behalf of the bondholders if the terms of the indenture are violated.

FACT OR FABLE?   **3** A trustee is a third-party individual, corporation, or commercial bank trust department paid to make sure that a bond issuer does not default on its contractual responsibilities as specified in the bond indenture. *(Fact)*

General Features of a Bond Issue

Three common features of a bond issue are (1) a conversion feature, (2) a call feature, and (3) stock-purchase warrants. These features provide both the issuer and the purchaser with certain opportunities for replacing, retiring, and (or) supplementing the bond with some type of equity issue.

Conversion Feature

The **conversion feature** of certain so-called *convertible bonds* allows bondholders to change each bond into a stated number of shares of stock. Bondholders will convert their bonds only when the market price of the stock is greater than the conversion price, hence providing a profit for the bondholder. Chapter 18 discusses convertible bonds in detail.

conversion feature
A feature of so-called *convertible bonds* allowing bondholders to change each bond into a stated number of shares of stock.

Call Feature

The **call feature** is included in almost all corporate bond issues. It gives the issuer the opportunity to repurchase bonds prior to maturity. The **call price** is the stated price at which bonds may be repurchased prior to maturity. Sometimes the call privilege is exercisable only during a certain period. As a rule, the call price exceeds the par value of a bond by an amount equal to one year's interest. For example, a $1,000 bond with a 10 percent coupon interest rate would be callable for around $1,100 [$1,000 + (10% × $1,000)]. The amount by which the call price exceeds the bond's par value is commonly referred to as the **call premium.**

The call feature is generally advantageous to the issuer, since it enables the issuer to retire outstanding debt prior to maturity. Thus when interest rates fall, an issuer can call an outstanding bond and reissue a new bond at a lower interest rate. When interest rates rise, the call privilege will not be exercised, except possibly to meet sinking-fund requirements. Of course, to sell a callable bond the issuer must pay a higher interest rate than on noncallable bonds of equal risk in order to compensate bondholders for the risk of having the bonds called away from them.

call feature A feature included in almost all corporate bond issues giving the issuer the opportunity to repurchase bonds prior to maturity at a stated price.

call price The stated price at which a bond may be repurchased, by use of a call feature, prior to maturity.

call premium The amount by which a bond's call price exceeds its par value.

Stock-Purchase Warrants

Like term loans, warrants are occasionally attached to bonds as "sweeteners" to make them more attractive to prospective buyers. As noted earlier, a stock-purchase warrant gives its holder the right to purchase a certain number of shares of common stock at a specified price over a certain period of time. An in-depth discussion of stock-purchase warrants is included in Chapter 18.

Bond Ratings

The riskiness of publicly traded bond issues is assessed by independent agencies such as Moody's and Standard & Poor's. Moody's has 9 ratings; Standard & Poor's has 12. The ratings are derived by these agencies using financial ratio and cash flow analyses. Table 16.2 summarizes these ratings. There is normally an inverse relationship between the quality or rating of a bond and the rate of return it must provide bondholders. High-quality (high-rated) bonds provide lower returns than lower-quality (low-rated) bonds. This reflects the risk-return trade-off for the lender. When considering bond financing, the financial manager must therefore be concerned with the expected ratings of the firm's bond issue since these ratings can significantly affect salability and cost.

Table 16.2
Moody's and Standard & Poor's Bond Ratings

Moody's	Interpretation	Standard & Poor's	Interpretation
Aaa	Prime quality	AAA	Bank investment quality
Aa	High grade	AA	
A	Upper medium grade	A	
Baa	Medium grade	BBB	
Ba	Lower medium grade	BB	Speculative
	or speculative	B	
B	Speculative		
Caa	From very speculative	CCC	
Ca	to near or in default	CC	
C	Lowest grade	C	Income bond
		DDD	In default (rating
		DD	indicates the relative
		D	salvage value)

SOURCE: Moody's Investors Service, Inc., and Standard & Poor's N.Y.S.E. Reports.

Popular Types of Bonds

Bonds can be classified in a variety of ways. The popular types of bonds are summarized in terms of key characteristics and priority of lender's claim in Table 16.3. Note that the first three types—debentures, subordinated debentures, and income bonds—are unsecured; the next three—mortgage bonds, collateral trust bonds, and equipment trust certificates—are secured; and the last three—deep discount bonds, floating rate bonds, and "junk bonds"—can take either form, although they are most commonly unsecured. Deep discount and floating rate bonds are relatively new innovations in bond financing. They were developed to meet the needs of investors for tax deferral and as protection against changing interest rates. In addition, junk bonds have become extremely popular vehicles used to finance mergers and takeovers. New innovations in bond financing are expected to continue, in order to more effectively raise debt financing at a reasonable cost.

FACT OR FABLE?   **4** "Junk bonds" are low-yielding debt rated Ba or higher by Moody's or BB or higher by Standard & Poor's and commonly used by rapidly growing firms to obtain growth capital, most often to finance mergers and takeovers of other firms. *(Fable)*

"Junk bonds" are *high-yielding* debt rated Ba or *lower* by Moody's or BB or *lower* by Standard & Poor's and commonly used by rapidly growing firms to obtain growth capital, most often to finance mergers and takeovers of other firms.

Bond-Refunding Options

A firm that wishes to retire or refund a bond prior to maturity has two options. Both require some foresight on the part of the issuer.

Table 16.3
Summary of Characteristics and Priority of Claim of Popular Types of Bonds

Bond type	Characteristics	Priority of lender's claim
Debentures	Only creditworthy firms can issue debentures. Convertible bonds are normally debentures.	Claims are same as those of any general creditor. May have other unsecured bonds subordinated to them.
Subordinated debentures	Claims are not satisfied until those of the creditors holding certain (senior) debts have been fully satisfied.	Claim is that of a general creditor but not as good as a senior debt claim.
Income bonds	Payment of interest is required only when earnings are available from which to make such payment. Commonly issued in reorganization of a failed or failing firm.	Claim is that of a general creditor. Not in default when interest payments are missed since they are contingent only on earnings being available.
Mortgage bonds	Secured by real estate or buildings. Can be *open-end* (other bonds issued against collateral), *limited open-end* (a specified amount of additional bonds can be issued against collateral), or *closed-end;* may contain an *after-acquired clause* (property subsequently acquired becomes part of mortgage collateral).	Claim on proceeds from sale of mortgaged assets; if not fully satisfied, lender becomes a general creditor. The *first-mortgage* claim must be fully satisfied prior to distribution of proceeds to *second-mortgage* holders, and so on. A number of mortgages can be issued against the same collateral.
Collateral trust bonds	Secured by stock and (or) bonds that are owned by the issuer. Collateral value is generally 25 percent to 35 percent greater than bond value.	Claim on proceeds from stock and (or) bond collateral; if not fully satisfied, becomes a general creditor.
Equipment trust certificates	Used to finance "rolling stock"—airplanes, trucks, boats, railroad cars. A mechanism whereby a trustee buys equipment with funds raised through the sale of trust certificates and then leases the asset to the firm, which, after the final scheduled lease payment, receives title to the asset. A type of leasing.	Claim is on proceeds from sale of asset; if proceeds do not satisfy outstanding debt, trust certificate holders become general creditors.
Deep discount (and zero coupon) bonds	Issued with very low or no (zero) coupon (stated interest) rate and sell at a large discount from par. A significant portion (or all) of the investor's return therefore comes from gain in value (i.e., par value minus purchase price). Generally callable at par value.	Claims vary, depending on the other features of the bonds. Can be unsecured or secured.
Floating rate bonds	Stated interest rate is adjusted periodically within stated limits in response to changes in specified money or capital market rates. Popular when future inflation and interest rates are uncertain. Tend to sell at close to par as a result of the automatic adjustment to changing market conditions.	Claims vary, depending on the other features of the bonds. Can be unsecured or secured.
Junk bonds	Debt rated Ba or lower by Moody's or BB or lower by Standard & Poor's. Traditionally issued by troubled companies, but now commonly used by rapidly growing firms to obtain growth capital, most often as a way to finance mergers and takeovers of other firms. High-risk bonds with high yields— typically yielding 3 percent or more than the best quality corporate debt.	Claims vary, depending on the other features of the bonds. Can be unsecured or secured.

PROFILE

IVAN BOESKY:
A Tale of Life on the Inside

It's the classic American dream: The poor kid from the Midwest attends the local university, earns a law degree, marries, and heads for New York City to make his fortune. He takes on the East Coast establishment that runs Wall Street and succeeds so well that he buys a 200-acre estate in Westchester County. He makes large donations to American Ballet Theater, the Metropolitan Museum of Art, and Harvard University. The latter philanthropy even wins him membership in New York's prestigious Harvard Club. For most people it would be enough, but for Ivan Boesky the American dream became the American nightmare.

The law he broke is the restriction against insider trading in securities. When a company is being sought for acquisition, the value of its stock usually rises quickly. Anyone who knows that a company is a takeover target could buy large amounts of stock, wait for the takeover attempt to be announced, watch the value of the stock rise dramatically, sell the stock, and invest the profit in the next takeover opportunity that appears. It's a way to make a lot of money in a hurry, and investment banking firms have merger

and acquisition departments that follow that practice daily.

The legality or illegality of the process is determined by how the trader learns about the acquisition attempt. If the trader learns that a company is ripe for a takeover through research and study of company earnings and other records that are publicly available, that's completely legal. If, however, the information could not have been acquired without information from someone within a company or its bank,

that's insider trading, and it's illegal.

Say your friend is controller at the Glo-All Corporation. She hears that Big Bulb is about to buy out Glo-All and she calls you with the information. You pawn the family jewels, borrow on your life insurance, and buy as much Glo-All stock as you can. In a week the stock shoots up and you make a big profit. To show your appreciation, you buy your friend a new cashmere coat and stuff the pockets with $100 bills. Your friend says you're too kind and promises to keep an ear to the ground concerning other mergers and acquisitions.

Ivan Boesky was accused of having friends like this in several investment firms in the New York financial community. In late 1986 the Securities and Exchange Commission (SEC) charged Boesky with insider trading that took place between February 1985 and February 1986. Boesky agreed to pay a fine of $50 million. In addition, he consented to set aside another $50 million to pay investors and companies who won lawsuits against him. In December 1987 Boesky was sentenced to three years in prison for his confessed insider-trading activities.

Serial Issues

serial bonds An issue of bonds of which a certain proportion matures each year.

The borrower can issue **serial bonds,** a certain proportion of which matures each year. When serial bonds are issued, a schedule showing the interest rate associated with each maturity is given. An example would be a $30 million, 20-year bond issue for which $1.5 million of the bonds ($30 million ÷ 20 years) mature each year. The interest rates associated with shorter maturities would, of course, differ from the rates associated with longer maturities. Although serial bonds cannot necessarily be retired at the option of the issuer, they do permit the issuer to systematically retire the debt.

Refunding Bonds by Exercising a Call

If interest rates drop following the issuance of a bond, the issuer may wish to refund (refinance) the debt with new bonds at the lower interest rate. If a call feature has been included in the issue, the issuer can easily retire the issue. The desirability of such an action is not necessarily obvious but can be determined using present-value techniques. The process used in making these decisions can be illustrated by a simple example. However, a few tax-related points should be clarified first.

Call Premiums. The amount by which the call price exceeds the par value of the bond is the *call premium*. It is paid by the issuer to the bondholder to buy back outstanding bonds prior to maturity. The call premium is treated as a tax-deductible expense in the year of the call.

Bond Discounts and Premiums. When bonds are sold at a discount or at a premium, the firm is required to amortize (write off) the discount or premium in equal portions over the life of the bond. The amortized discount is treated as a tax-deductible expenditure, whereas the amortized premium is treated as taxable income. If a bond is retired prior to maturity, any unamortized portion of a discount or premium is deducted from or added to pre-tax income at that time.

Flotation or Issuance Costs. Any costs incurred in the process of issuing a bond must be amortized over the life of the bond. The annual write-off is therefore a tax-deductible expenditure. If a bond is retired prior to maturity, any unamortized portion of this cost is deducted from pre-tax income at that time.

Example

Halda Industries is contemplating calling $30 million of 30-year, $1,000 bonds issued five years ago with a coupon interest rate of 14 percent. The bonds have a call price of $1,140 and initially netted proceeds of $29.1 million due to a discount of $30 per bond. The initial flotation cost was $360,000. The company intends to sell $30 million of 12 percent coupon interest rate, 25-year bonds in order to raise funds for retiring the old bonds.[4] The firm intends to sell the new bonds at their par value of $1,000. The flotation costs on the new issue are estimated to be $440,000. The firm is currently in the 40 percent tax bracket and estimates its after-tax cost of debt to be 8 percent.[5] It expects a two-month period of overlapping interest, during which interest must be paid on both the old and the new bonds.

The first step is to calculate the incremental initial outlay, or initial investment, involved in implementing the proposed refunding. Table 16.4 presents the calculations required, which indicate that Halda Industries must pay out $2,960,000 now in order to implement the refunding plan. The second step is to determine the annual cash flow

[4] To simplify this analysis, the maturity of the new bonds has been set equal to the number of years to maturity remaining on the old bonds. A procedure using annualized net present value (ANPV) techniques as presented in Chapter 10 would be required in comparing bonds having unequal maturities remaining.

[5] Ignoring any flotation costs, the firm's after-tax cost of debt would be 7.2 percent [12 percent debt cost × (1 − .40 tax rate)]. To reflect the flotation costs associated with selling new debt, the use of an after-tax debt cost of 8 percent was believed to be the applicable discount rate. A more detailed discussion of techniques for calculating a firm's after-tax cost of debt can be found in Chapter 11.

savings that will result from issuing the new bond. The annual cash flow savings each year will be the same, since the old bond has 25 years remaining to maturity and the life of the new bond is 25 years. Table 16.5 shows how the annual cash flow savings are calculated by subtracting the annual cash outflows with the new bond from the annual cash outflows with the old bond. The new bond results in cash flow savings of $350,240 per year.

The final step in the analysis is to compare the initial outlay of $2,960,000 required to retire the old bond and issue the new bond to the annual cash flow savings of $350,240 resulting from the new bond. Due to the difference in the timing of these cash flows, the present value of the 25-year annuity of $350,240 must be found using the after-tax cost of debt. The *after-tax cost of debt* is used because the decision involves very low risk.[6] The present value of the $350,240, 25-year annuity discounted at 8 percent is $3,738,812 ($350,240 × 10.675). Subtracting the incremental initial outlay of $2,960,000 from the present value of the cash savings ($3,738,812) yields a net present value of $778,812. Since a positive net present value results, the proposed refunding plan is recommended.

Table 16.4
Calculating the Incremental Initial Outlay for Halda Industries

Initial cash outflows	
Cost of calling old bonds ($1,140 × 30,000 bonds)	$34,200,000
Cost of issuing new bonds	440,000
Interest on old bonds during overlap period	
(.14 × 2/12 × $30,000,000)	700,000
(1) Total cash outflows	$35,340,000

Initial cash inflows	
Proceeds from new bond	$30,000,000
Tax shields[a]	
Call premium (.40 × $140 × 30,000 bonds)	1,680,000
Unamortized discount on old bond	
($900,000 × 25/30 × .40)	300,000
Unamortized issue cost of old bond	
($360,000 × 25/30 × .40)	120,000
Overlapping interest	
(.14 × 2/12 × $30,000,000 × .40)	280,000
(2) Total cash inflows	$32,380,000
Incremental initial outlay [(1) − (2)]	$ 2,960,000

[a] These are treated as a cash inflow, although they actually represent a negative cash outflow.

[6] Because the refunding decision involves the choice between retaining an existing debt or substituting a new, lower-cost debt, it is viewed as a low-risk decision that will not significantly affect the firm's financial risk. The low-risk nature of the decision warrants the use of a very low rate, such as the firm's after-tax cost of debt.

Table 16.5
Calculating the Annual Cash Flow Savings for Halda Industries

Old bond	Annual cash outflow
Annual interest (.14 × $30,000,000)	$4,200,000
Less: Tax savings[a]	
Interest (.14 × $30,000,000 × .40)	(1,680,000)
Amortization of discount [($900,000 ÷ 30) × .40]	(12,000)
Amortization of issuing cost [($360,000 ÷ 30) × .40]	(4,800)
(1) Annual cash outflows with old bond	$2,503,200
New bond	
Annual interest (.12 × $30,000,000)	$3,600,000
Less: Tax savings[a]	
Interest (.12 × $30,000,000 × .40)	(1,440,000)
Amortization of issuing cost [($440,000 ÷ 25) × .40]	(7,040)
(2) Annual cash outflows with new bond	$2,152,960
Annual cash flow savings from new bond [(1) − (2)]	$ 350,240

[a] Tax savings are treated as cash inflows because of the tax shield they provide.

FACT OR FABLE?

5 Bond refunding should be undertaken when the present value of the incremental initial outlay required by the new bond is greater than the annual cash flow savings resulting from refunding (refinancing) the old bonds with new bonds at the lower interest rate. *(Fable)*

Bond refunding should be undertaken when the *present value of the annual cash savings from the new bond* is greater than the *incremental initial outlay required* in order to refund (refinance) the old bonds with the new bonds at the lower interest rate.

Investment Banking

Investment banking plays an important role in helping firms raise long-term financing—both debt and equity—in the capital markets. It is the investment banker's job to find buyers for new security issues. As noted briefly in Chapter 2, investment bankers are neither investors nor bankers; they neither make long-term investments nor guard the savings of others. Instead, acting as a broker between the issuer and the buyer of new security issues, the **investment banker** purchases securities from corporations and governments and sells them to the public. In the United States, for example, Salomon Brothers and Merrill Lynch Capital Markets are two of the largest investment banking firms. Many investment banking firms operate in other areas as well; for example, Merrill Lynch is also the nation's leading securities brokerage firm.

investment banker An individual that, acting as a broker, purchases securities from corporations and governments and sells them to the public.

Functions of the Investment Banker

The investment banker's primary function is underwriting security issues. A secondary function is advising clients.

Underwriting

underwriting An investment banker's guarantee to the issuer that it will receive at least a specified minimum amount from the issue.

When **underwriting** a security issue, an investment banker guarantees the issuer that it will receive at least a specified minimum amount from the issue. The banker buys the securities at a lower price than he or she plans to sell them for, thereby making a profit. The investment banker therefore bears the risk of price changes and a market collapse between the time of purchase and the time of sale of securities. There is always the possibility that the banker will be ''stuck'' with a large amount of the securities. In some instances, he or she may be able to sell the securities only at a price lower than the initial purchase price.

Example
Gigantica Corporation has agreed to underwrite a new $50 million common stock issue for Leader Electronics. It has agreed to purchase the stock for $48 million. Since Gigantica must pay Leader $48 million for the stock, it must attempt to sell the stock for net proceeds of at least $48 million. Actually, it will attempt to sell the stock for at least $50 million, thereby obtaining a $2 million commission. If it is unable to raise $50 million, the investment banking firm will not realize the full $2 million commission and will possibly lose part of the $48 million initially paid for the stock. In some cases, a security issue can be sold in a few days; in other situations, months are required to negotiate a sale. The investment banker therefore bears the risk of unfavorable price changes before the issue is sold as well as the risk of being unable to sell the issue at all.

Many security issues are not underwritten but rather are *privately placed* or sold on a *best efforts* basis. These functions are also handled by investment bankers.

private placement The direct sale of a new security issue to one or more purchasers.

Private Placement. **Private placement** occurs when an investment banker arranges for the direct sale of a new security issue to an individual, several individuals, a firm, or a group of firms. The investment banker is then paid a commission for acting as an intermediary in the transaction.

best efforts basis A public offering in which the investment banker uses his or her resources to sell the security issue without taking on the risk of underwriting and is compensated on the basis of the number of securities sold.

Best Efforts. In the case of some public offerings, the investment banker may not actually underwrite the issue; rather, the banker may use his or her resources to sell the securities on a **best efforts** basis. In this case, the banker does not take on the risk associated with underwriting, and compensation is based on the number of securities sold.

Advising

The investment banker performs an advisory function by analyzing the firm's financial needs and recommending appropriate means of financing. Since an investment banker has a feel for the pulse of the securities markets, he or she can provide useful advice on mergers, acquisitions, and refinancing decisions.

CAREERS IN FINANCE

INVESTMENT BANKER: Big Rewards For Those Who Can Make It

Amanda is a 28-year-old associate at a large New York investment banking firm. The words "investment banker," however, do not accurately describe her work. Amanda is neither an investor nor a banker. Rather, investment banking firms have two major lines of business: corporate finance and trading. Corporate finance includes the traditional work of planning and underwriting issues of securities, as well as merger and acquisition deal-making. Trading is simply buying and selling securities for profit.

Amanda, who is in her firm's merger and acquisitions group, sees the glamour of the job: high-stakes deals, fast-paced decision making, late-evening meetings, midnight rides home in a company-paid limo.

"In large firms," she says, "investment bankers work out deals like U.S. Steel's acquisition of Marathon Oil for six billion dollars in 1981. They are rewarded with quick promotion and big pay raises. Some become managing

directors at thirty, with six-figure annual earnings. Gaining expertise in investing helps them build personal fortunes, too."

"The work," says Amanda, "is grueling. Sixty- or eighty-hour workweeks are standard. Our main duty is service to corporate clients. They expect attention to their needs, and they don't pay fees unless a deal is closed. Investment bankers may manage fifteen deals at a time. The job tends to fill all waking hours. Then there are unpredictable travel schedules, tough meetings, and the anxiety of managing multi-million-dollar deals."

Those investment bankers who buy and sell securities for their firm's profit are called traders. They also have very difficult jobs. Traders get evenings and weekends off, but work feverishly during the day, without perks or comforts. On the trading floor there are no offices, secretaries, or moments of calm. Traders tend to burn out after a few years.

Is investment banking for you? First, consider that a blue chip MBA is necessary to gain entrance to the most prestigious firms. Those who make it, especially in New York City, may earn in the range of $100,000 the first year. Elsewhere, salaries are lower. In general, entry-level salaries average from $30,000 to $50,000. Upper-level salaries reach about $250,000.

Second, consider the personal commitment required. Because of demanding schedules, investment bankers have trouble making relationships and marriages work. Women bankers admit that the job leaves little time for motherhood. Friendships and outside interests suffer. You must like the work and you must like working intensely. No matter how generous the compensation, it is difficult to pour your whole life into a job you don't like.

What about Amanda? "I like it," she says. "I like the prestige, the work, and the money. I like the excitement."

Organization of Investment Banking Activity

The investment banker's functions of underwriting security issues and advising clients come into play as a result of a logical sequence of events. The process begins when a firm in need of additional financing selects an investment banking firm, which then confers with the issuer, syndicates the underwriting, forms a selling group, fulfills legal requirements for a sale, sets a price, distributes the issue, and stabilizes the price.

Selecting an Investment Banker

A firm that needs additional financing through the capital markets initiates the fundraising process by selecting an investment banker to underwrite the new issue and provide advice. The investment banker may be selected through **competitive bidding** or chosen by the issuing firm. In the case of competitive bidding, the investment banker or group of

competitive bidding
A method of choosing an investment banker, in which the banker that bids the highest price for a security issue is awarded the issue.

negotiated offering
A security issue for which the investment banker is merely hired rather than awarded the issue through competitive bidding.

bankers that bids the highest price for the issue is awarded it. If the investment banker is merely hired by the issuing firm, the security issue is called a **negotiated offering.**

Conferring with the Issuer

Once selected, the investment banker helps the firm determine how much capital should be raised and in what form, debt or equity. The banker analyzes the firm's financial position and proposed disposition of the funds to be raised to make sure that the firm is financially sound and that the proposed expenditures are justifiable. After an examination of certain legal aspects of the firm and its proposed offering, a tentative underwriting agreement is drawn up.

Syndicating the Underwriting

underwriting syndicate
A group of investment banking firms, each of which will underwrite a portion of a large security issue, thus lessening the risk of loss to any single firm.

Due to the size of many new security issues, it is often necessary for the investment banker to form an **underwriting syndicate,** which is a group of investment banking firms. The use of an underwriting syndicate lessens the risk of loss to any single firm. Each underwriter in the syndicate must sell its portion of the issue. This is likely to result in a wider distribution of the new securities.

Forming a Selling Group

selling group A group of investment bankers and brokerage firms, each of which will sell a portion of a security issue and be paid for each security sold.

The originating underwriter with the assistance of syndicate members puts together a **selling group,** which is responsible for distributing the new issue to the investing public. The selling group is normally made up of a large number of brokerage firms, each of which accepts the responsibility for selling a certain portion of the issue. Members of the selling group are paid a certain amount for each security sold.[7] Figure 16.1 depicts the selling process for a new security issue.

Fulfilling Legal Requirements

Through the Securities and Exchange Commission, the federal government regulates the initial and subsequent trading of securities. Initial regulation tends to center on the registration of new issues; subsequent regulation is concerned with the securities exchanges and markets.

prospectus A portion of a security registration statement filed with the SEC which details the firm's operating and financial position.

red herring On a prospectus, a statement, printed in red, indicating the tentative nature of a security offer while the offer is being reviewed by the SEC.

Registration Requirements. Before a new security can be issued, the issuer must obtain the approval of the Securities and Exchange Commission (SEC). According to the Securities Act of 1933, which was passed to ensure the full disclosure of information with respect to new security issues and prevent a stock market collapse similar to the one that occurred in 1929–1932, the issuer is required to file a registration statement with the SEC. The firm cannot sell the security until the SEC approves the registration statement. This procedure usually requires 20 days.

One portion of the registration statement is called the **prospectus.** This prospectus may be issued to potential buyers during the waiting period between filing the registration statement and its approval as long as a **red herring,** which is a statement indicating the tentative nature of the offer, is printed in red on the prospectus. Once the registration statement has been approved, the new security can be offered for sale if the prospectus is

---

[7] The selling group is usually compensated in the same fashion as the underwriter. In other words, the selling group buys the securities at a discount from the sale price and profits from the *spread* between the price at which it purchases and the price at which it sells the security.

Figure 16.1
The Selling Process for a New Security Issue

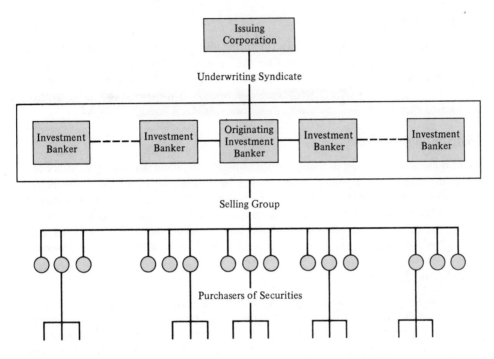

made available to all interested parties. If the registration statement is found to be fraudulent, the SEC will not only reject the issue but can also sue the directors and others responsible for the misrepresentation. Approval of the registration statement by the SEC does not mean that the security is a good investment; it indicates only that the facts presented in the statement accurately reflect the firm's operating and financial position.

As an alternative to filing a lengthy registration statement and awaiting SEC approval, firms can use a procedure known as **shelf registration.** This procedure allows a firm to file a "master registration statement"—a single document summarizing planned financing—covering a two-year period. At any time during the two years, the firm, after filing a "short statement," can sell securities already approved under the master statement. Using this procedure, the approved securities are effectively warehoused and kept "on the shelf" until the need exists or market conditions are appropriate for selling the securities. The use of shelf registration is especially popular with large firms that frequently need access to the capital markets to raise debt or equity funds. Although some firms using shelf registration can reduce their reliance on investment bankers, the investment banker continues to be the key link between the firm and the capital markets.

Trading Requirements. Another important piece of legislation regulating the securities markets is the Securities Exchange Act of 1934, which is aimed at controlling the secondary trading of securities by providing for the regulation of securities exchanges, listed securities, and the general activities of the securities markets. The act provides for the disclosure of information on and accurate representation of securities traded. This piece of legislation and the Securities Act of 1933 are the key laws protecting participants in the capital markets. Many states also have laws aimed at regulating the sale of securities

shelf registration An SEC procedure that allows firms to file a master statement for a two-year period and then during that period sell securities already approved under the master statement.

blue sky laws State laws aimed at regulating the sale of securities within the state and thereby protecting investors.

within their borders. These **blue sky laws** protect investors by preventing the sale of securities that provide "nothing but blue sky."

Pricing the Issue

Underwriting syndicates generally wait until the end of the registration period to price securities so that they will have a feel for the current mood of the market. The pricing decision is important because it affects the ease with which the issue can be sold and also the issuer's proceeds. The investment banker's "feel" for the market should result in a price that achieves the optimum mix of marketability and financial return.

Distributing the Issue

oversubscribed issue A security issue that is sold out.

undersubscribed issue A security issue whose shares are not immediately sold.

Prior to the actual offering of a new security for sale, the issue is publicized. This can be done only after the registration statement has been approved by the SEC. Publicity is obtained by advertising and personal contacts through the brokerage firms handling the issue. When the security is formally placed on the market, orders are accepted from the selling groups and from outsiders. If the issue is sold out, it is considered **oversubscribed;** if all shares are not sold immediately, it is said to be **undersubscribed.**

Stabilizing the Price

price pegging When an underwriting syndicate places orders to buy an underwritten security in order to keep the demand for the issue, and therefore the price, at the desired level.

Once an issue has been offered for sale, the underwriting syndicate attempts to stabilize its price so that the entire issue can be sold at the initial offering price. By placing orders to buy the security, the underwriting syndicate can keep the demand for the issue, and therefore the price, at the desired level. This activity, sometimes referred to as **price pegging,** is legal as long as the intent is disclosed in the registration statement filed with the SEC. Price pegging is in the best interests of both the issuer and the underwriting syndicate in that it reduces the syndicate's risk, thereby lowering the underwriting discount charged to the issuer.

FACT OR FABLE?   6 An investment banker, once hired, confers with the issuer, syndicates the underwriting, forms a selling group, fulfills legal requirements for a sale, sets a price, distributes the issue, and stabilizes the price. *(Fact)*

Cost of Investment Banking Services

spread The difference between the price paid for a security by the investment banker and the sale price.

The investment banker is compensated by purchasing the security issue at a discount from the proposed sale price. On an individual per-bond or per-share basis, the difference between the price paid for a security by the investment banker and the sale price is referred to as the **spread.** The size of the spread depends on the cost of investigations, printing, and registration, the discount to the underwriting syndicate, and the discount given to the selling group. The cost of an issue is a function of two basic components—administrative cost and underwriting cost. Generally, the larger the issue, the lower the overall cost in percentage terms. It is also generally true that the overall flotation cost for common stock is highest, preferred stock and bonds following in that order. The overall flotation cost ranges from as little as 0.5 percent of the total proceeds on a large bond issue to as much as 20 percent on a small common stock issue. The type of security issued affects the cost because it affects the ease with which large blocks can be placed with one purchaser. A firm that is contemplating a security issue must therefore weigh the cost of public sale against the cost and feasibility of private placement.

Private Placement

As an alternative to a public offering, a firm can sometimes negotiate private (or direct) placement of a security issue. Ordinarily, private placements are used only for bonds or preferred stock. Common stock is sometimes directly placed when the firm believes that the existing shareholders might purchase the issue through an arrangement known as a *rights offering,* which is described in detail in Chapter 17.

Private placement usually reduces issuance and administrative costs and provides the issuer with a great deal of flexibility, since the firm need not file registration statements and is not required to obtain the approval of the Securities and Exchange Commission. In addition, private placement is often advantageous because the issuer has more flexibility in tailoring covenants and later renegotiating them should the need arise than it does with a public offering. On the other hand, private placement poses a disadvantage to the buyer who at some future date may wish to sell the securities on the open market, because prior to public sale, registration and approval by the Securities and Exchange Commission is required. In the case of private placements, an investment banker is usually employed to assist in finding a buyer and provide pricing advice.

Direct placement of common stock is sometimes achieved through stock options or stock-purchase plans. **Stock options** are generally extended to management and permit the purchase of a certain number of shares of the firm's common stock at a specified price over a stated period of time. These options are intended to stimulate managerial actions that increase the long-run success of the firm. **Stock-purchase plans** are a fringe benefit offered to a firm's employees. They allow the employees to purchase the firm's stock at a discount or on a matching basis whereby the firm absorbs part of the cost. Both plans provide equity capital and at the same time increase employee motivation and interest in the company.

stock options Options that permit the purchase of a firm's common stock at a specified price over a stated period of time.

stock-purchase plans A fringe benefit that allows the purchase of a firm's stock at a discount or on a matching basis with a part of the cost absorbed by the firm.

Summary

● Standard and restrictive provisions are included in long-term debt agreements in order to protect the lender. Standard debt provisions do not ordinarily place a burden on a financially sound business. Restrictive covenants tend to place certain operating and financial constraints on the borrower.

● The cost (interest rate) of long-term debt is normally higher than the cost of short-term borrowing. Major factors affecting the cost of long-term debt are loan maturity, loan size, and more importantly, borrower risk and the basic cost of money.

● The conditions of a term (long-term) loan are specified in the term loan agreement. Term loans generally require periodic installment payments; may be either unsecured or secured; and may sometimes be accompanied by stock-purchase warrants. Term loans can be obtained from a number of types of major financial institutions.

● Corporate bonds are certificates indicating that a corporation has borrowed a certain amount that it promises to repay in the future under clearly defined terms. Most bonds are issued with maturities of 10 to 30 years and a par value of $1,000. All conditions of the bond issue are detailed in the indenture, which is enforced by the trustee.

● A bond may include a conversion feature, a call feature, or stock-purchase warrants. Bond ratings by independent agencies indicate the risk of a bond issue. A variety of unsecured, secured, and innovative bonds are available.

● Firms sometimes retire or refund (refinance) bonds prior to their maturity. When serial bonds are issued, retirement is on a planned basis. Bonds are refunded (refinanced) when there is a drop in interest rates sufficient to result in a positive net present value from calling the old bonds and replacing them with new lower-interest-rate bonds.

● Investment bankers underwrite or sell total issues of securities, receiving compensation in the form of a spread between the price paid the issuer and the sale price. They also assist in private placements and can be hired to sell new issues on a best efforts basis. Investment bankers provide advice to issuers in addition to underwriting.

● Once selected, the investment banker confers with the issuer, syndicates the underwriting, forms a selling group, fulfills legal requirements relative to registration and trading, prices and distributes the issue, and stabilizes the price.

● An alternative to public offerings is private (or direct) placement of securities—especially bonds and preferred stocks. In private placements, an investment banker is usually employed to assist in finding a buyer and to provide pricing advice.

Questions

16-1   What are the two key methods of raising long-term debt financing? What motives does the lender have for including certain *restrictive covenants* in a debt agreement? How do these covenants differ from so-called *standard debt provisions?*

16-2   What sort of negotiation process is required in settling on a set of restrictive loan covenants? What are the consequences of violation of a standard or restrictive provision by the borrower?

16-3   What is the general relationship between the cost of short-term and long-term debt? What are the major factors affecting the cost, or interest rate, of long-term debt?

16-4   What types of payment dates are generally required in a term (long-term) loan agreement? What is a *balloon payment?*

16-5   What role do commercial banks, insurance companies, pension funds, regional development companies, the Small Business Administration, small business investment companies, commercial finance companies, and equipment manufacturers play in lending long-term funds to businesses?

16-6   What types of maturities, denominations, and interest payments are associated with a typical corporate bond? Describe the role of the *bond indenture* and the *trustee.*

16-7   What does it mean if a bond has a *conversion feature?* A *call feature? Stock-purchase warrants?* How are bonds rated, and why?

16-8   Describe the basic characteristics of each of the following popular types of bonds.

   a. Debentures
   b. Subordinated debentures
   c. Income bonds
   d. Deep discount (and zero coupon) bonds
   e. Floating rate bonds
   f. Junk bonds

16-9   Describe, compare, and contrast the basic features of the following secured bonds.

   a. Mortgage bond
   b. Collateral trust bond
   c. Equipment trust certificate

16-10 What two options may be available to a firm that wants to retire or refund an outstanding bond issue prior to maturity? Must these options be provided for in advance of issuance? Why might the issuer wish to retire or refund a bond prior to its maturity?

16-11 Describe the role and functions performed by the *investment banker.* Explain the sequence of events involved in the investment banking activity.

16-12 How is the investment banker compensated for its services? How are underwriting costs affected by the size and type of an issue? What, if any, role does an investment banker play in private placements?

Self-Test Problem

(Solution on page 600)

ST-1 Torbert Manufacturing is considering refunding $20 million of outstanding bonds (20,000 bonds at $1,000 par value) as a result of recent declines in long-term interest rates. The plan would involve calling the $20 million in outstanding bonds and issuing $20 million of new bonds at the lower interest rate. The details of both bond issues are outlined at the top of the next page. The firm is in the 40 percent tax bracket.

Old bonds: Torbert's old bonds were initially issued 10 years ago with a 30-year maturity and a 13 percent coupon rate of interest. The bonds were initially sold at a $12 discount from their $1,000 par value, flotation costs were $150,000, and their call price is $1,130.

New bonds: The new issue is expected to sell at its $1,000 par value, have an 11 percent coupon interest rate, have a 20-year maturity, and require $400,000 in flotation costs. The firm will have a 3-month period of overlapping interest while it retires the old bond.

a. Calculate the incremental initial outlay required to issue the new bonds.

b. Calculate the annual cash flow savings, if any, expected from the proposed bond refunding.

c. If the firm uses its 7 percent after-tax cost of debt to evaluate low-risk decisions, would you recommend refunding? Explain your answer.

Problems

16-1 **(Bond Discounts or Premiums)** The initial proceeds per bond, the size of the issue, the initial maturity of the bond, and the years remaining to maturity are given for a number of bonds. In each case the firm is in the 40 percent tax bracket and the bond has a $1,000 par value.

Bond	Proceeds per bond	Size of issue	Initial maturity of bond	Years remaining to maturity
A	$ 980	20,000 bonds	25 years	20
B	1,020	14,000 bonds	20 years	12
C	1,000	10,500 bonds	10 years	8
D	950	9,000 bonds	30 years	21
E	1,030	3,000 bonds	30 years	15

a. Indicate whether each bond was sold at a discount, at a premium, or at its par value.

b. Determine the total discount or premium for each issue.

c. Determine the annual amount of discount or premium amortized for each bond.

d. Calculate the unamortized discount or premium for each bond.

e. Determine the after-tax cash flow associated with the retirement now of each of these bonds, using the values developed in **d.**

16-2 **(Cost of a Call)** For each of the callable bond issues in the table, calculate the after-tax cost of calling the issue. Each bond has a $1,000 par value; the various issue sizes and call prices are summarized in the following table. The firm is in the 40 percent tax bracket.

Bond	Size of issue	Call price
A	8,000 bonds	$1,080
B	10,000 bonds	1,060
C	6,000 bonds	1,010
D	3,000 bonds	1,050
E	9,000 bonds	1,040
F	13,000 bonds	1,090

16-3 **(Amortization of Issue Cost)** The initial issuance cost, the initial maturity, and the number of years remaining to maturity are given for a number of bonds. The firm is in the 40 percent tax bracket.

Bond	Initial issuance cost	Initial maturity of bond	Years remaining to maturity
A	$500,000	30 years	24
B	200,000	20 years	5
C	40,000	25 years	10
D	100,000	10 years	2
E	80,000	15 years	9

a. Calculate the annual amortization of the issuance cost for each bond.

b. Determine the after-tax cash inflow, if any, expected to result from the unamortized issuance cost if the bond were called today.

16-4 **(Interest Overlap Cost and Tax Shield)** The principal, coupon interest rate, and interest overlap period are given for a number of bonds.

Bond	Principal	Coupon interest rate	Interest overlap period
A	$ 2,000,000	12.0%	2 months
B	60,000,000	14.0	4 months
C	40,000,000	10.0	3 months
D	10,000,000	11.0	4 months
E	25,000,000	9.5	1 month

a. Calculate the dollar amount of interest that must be paid for each bond during the interest overlap period.

b. Calculate the tax shield resulting from the overlapped interest for each bond if the firm is in the 40 percent tax bracket.

16-5 **(Refunding Decision—No Interest Overlap)** The North Company is contemplating calling an outstanding $30 million bond issue and replacing it with a new $30 million bond issue. The firm wishes to do this to take advantage of the decline in interest rates that has occurred since the initial bond issuance. The old and new bonds are described below. The firm is in the 40 percent tax bracket.

Old bonds: The outstanding bonds have a $1,000 par value and a 14 percent coupon interest rate. They were issued 5 years ago with a 25-year maturity. They were initially sold for their par value of $1,000, and the firm incurred $250,000 in issuance costs. They are callable at $1,140.

New bonds: The new bonds would have a $1,000 par value and a 12 percent coupon interest rate. They would have a 20-year maturity and could be sold at their par value. The issuance cost of the new bonds would be $400,000. The firm does not expect to have any overlapping interest.

a. Calculate the after-tax cash inflow expected from the unamortized portion of the old bonds' issuance cost.

b. Calculate the annual after-tax cash inflow from the issuance cost of the new bonds, assuming the 20-year amortization.

c. Calculate the after-tax cash outflow from the call premium required to retire the old bonds.

d. Determine the incremental initial outlay required to issue the new bonds.

e. Calculate the annual cash flow savings, if any, expected from the bond refunding.

f. If the firm has a 7 percent after-tax cost of debt, would you recommend the proposed refunding and reissue? Why or why not?

16-6 **(Refunding Decision—With Interest Overlap)** Rubens Paper Company is considering calling an outstanding bond issue of $10 million and replacing it with a new $10 million issue. The firm wishes to do this to take advantage of the decline in interest rates that has occurred since the original issue. The two bond issues are described below; the firm is in the 40 percent tax bracket.

Old bonds: The outstanding bonds have a $1,000 par value and a 17 percent coupon interest rate. They were issued 5 years ago with a 20-year maturity. They were initially sold at a $20 per-bond discount and a $120,000 issuance cost was incurred. They are callable at $1,170.

New bonds: The new bonds would have a 15-year maturity, a par value of $1,000, and a 14 percent coupon interest rate. It is expected that these bonds can be sold at par for a flotation cost of $200,000. The firm expects the two issues to overlap by two months.

a. Calculate the incremental initial outlay required to issue the new bonds.

b. Calculate the annual cash flow savings, if any, expected from the bond refunding.

c. If the firm uses its after-tax cost of debt of 8 percent to evaluate low-risk decisions, would you recommend refunding? Explain your answer.

16-7 **(Refunding Decision—With Interest Overlap and Sensitivity Analysis)** L-D Hauling is considering the calling of an outstanding bond issue of $14 million and replacing it with a new $14 million issue. The details of both bond issues are outlined below. The firm is in the 40 percent tax bracket.

Old bonds: The firm's old issue has a coupon interest rate of 14 percent, was issued 6 years ago, and had a 30-year maturity. The bonds sold at a $15 discount from their $1,000 par value, flotation costs were $120,000, and their call price is $1,140.

New bonds: The new issue is expected to sell at par ($1,000), have a 24-year maturity, and have a flotation cost of $360,000. The firm will have a one-month period of overlapping interest while it retires the old bond.

a. What is the incremental initial outlay required to issue the new bonds?

b. What are the annual cash flow savings, if any, from refunding and reissuing if (1) the new bonds have a 12.5 percent coupon interest rate; and (2) the new bonds have a 13 percent coupon interest rate?

c. Construct a table showing the net benefits of refunding under the two circumstances given in **b,** when (1) the firm has an after-tax cost of debt of 6 percent; and (2) the firm has an after-tax cost of debt of 8 percent.

d. Discuss the set(s) of circumstances (described in **c**) when the refunding would be favorable and when it would not.

e. If the four circumstances summarized in **d** were equally probable (each had .25 probability), would you recommend the refunding? Why or why not?

16-8 **(Underwriting Spread)** Hildreth Recycling is interested in selling common stock to raise capital for plant expansion. The firm has consulted the First Atlanta Company, a large underwriting firm, which believes the stock can be sold for $80 per share. The underwriter, on investigation, has found that its administrative costs will be 2 percent of the sale price and its selling costs will be 1.5 percent of the sale price. If the underwriter requires a profit of 1 percent of the sale price, how much will the *spread* have to be *in dollars* to cover the underwriter's costs and profit?

16-9 **(Bond Underwriting Analysis)** RM International wishes to sell $100 million of bonds whose net proceeds will be used in the acquisition of Little Books. The company has estimated that the net proceeds after paying the underwriter costs should provide an amount sufficient to make the acquisition. The underwriter believes the 100,000 bonds can be sold to the public at their $1,000 par value. The underwriter estimates that its administrative costs will be $3.5 million. It also must sell the bonds at a .75 percent discount from their par value to members of the selling group. The underwriting commission (in addition to recovery of its administrative costs) is 1 percent of the par value of the offering.

a. Calculate the per-bond spread required by the underwriter to cover its costs.

b. How much will RM International net from the issue?

c. How much will the selling group receive? How much will the underwriter receive?

d. Assuming that this is a public offering, describe the nature of the underwriter's risk.

Solution to Self-Test Problem

ST-1 a. Tabular Calculation of the Incremental Initial Outlay for Torbert Manufacturing

Initial cash outflows	
Cost of calling old bonds ($1,130 × 20,000 bonds)	$22,600,000
Cost of issuing new bonds	400,000
Interest on old bonds during overlap period	
(.13 × 3/12[a] × $20,000,000)	650,000
(1) Total cash outflows	$23,650,000
Initial cash inflows	
Proceeds from new bond	$20,000,000
Tax shields	
Call premium (.40 × $130 × 20,000 bonds)	1,040,000
Unamortized discount on old bond	
($240,000[b] × 20/30[c] × .40)	64,000
Unamortized issue cost of old bond	
($150,000 × 20/30[c] × .40)	40,000
Overlapping interest	
(.13 × 3/12[a] × $20,000,000 × .40)	260,000
(2) Total cash inflows	$21,404,000
Incremental initial outlay [(1) − (2)]	$ 2,246,000

[a] 3 months overlapping interest ÷ 12 months per year
[b] 20,000 bonds × $12 per-bond discount
[c] 20 years to maturity ÷ 30 years initial maturity

b. Tabular Calculation of the Annual Cash Flow Savings for Torbert Manufacturing

Old bond	Annual cash outflow
Annual interest (.13 × $20,000,000)	$2,600,000
Less: Tax savings	
Interest (.13 × $20,000,000 × .40)	(1,040,000)
Amortization of discount [($240,000[a] ÷ 30) × .40]	(3,200)
Amortization of issuing cost [($150,000 ÷ 30) × .40]	(2,000)
(1) Annual cash outflows with old bond	$1,554,800

New bond	
Annual interest (.11 × $20,000,000)	$2,200,000
Less: Tax savings	
Interest (.11 × $20,000,000 × .40)	(880,000)
Amortization of issuing cost [($400,000 ÷ 20) × .40]	(8,000)
(2) Annual cash outflows with new bond	$1,312,000
Annual cash flow savings from new bond [(1) − (2)]	$ 242,800

[a] 20,000 bonds × $12 per-bond discount

c. Present value of annual cash flow savings from new bond = $242,800 × $PVIFA_{7\%, 20yrs}$ = $242,800 × 10.594 = $2,572,223.

Since the present value of the annual cash flow savings of $2,572,223 exceeds the incremental initial outlay of $2,246,000, *the proposed refunding should be undertaken*. It should yield a net present value of $326,223 ($2,572,223 − $2,246,000).

CHAPTER 17

Common Stock
and
Dividend Policy

FACT OR FABLE?
Are the following statements fact *(true)* or fable *(false)?*

1

The claims of holders of equity capital with respect to both income and assets are senior to the claims of debtholders, since the stockholders are the true owners of the firm.

2

Minority shareholders prefer a cumulative voting system over majority voting since it provides them with a better opportunity to elect at least some corporate directors.

3

Rights offerings allow stockholders to maintain their proportionate ownership in the corporation, and typically allow the corporation to raise new equity capital less expensively.

4

Modigliani and Miller argue that dividend policy is relevant since current dividend payments reduce investor uncertainty, thereby causing investors to place a higher value on the firm's stock.

5

A dividend policy that allows stockholders to get their share of the profits by always paying out a fixed percentage of earnings tends to be preferred over one that regularly pays a stable or increasing dividend.

6

The repurchase of common stock for retirement is similar to the payment of cash dividends since it involves the distribution of cash to the firm's owners, who are the sellers of the shares.

No one was more surprised than Paul Fireman, president and chief executive of Reebok International Ltd., when his line of women's designer sneakers became the hottest footwear fad in the country. What started as an attempt to tap the fitness market with the introduction of soft leather shoes for aerobic exercise, bloomed overnight into a $2 billion business.

Fireman founded Reebok in 1979 in order to acquire a license for the exclusive use of the Reebok name in North America. He had discovered the hand-sewn athletic shoe, made originally for elite runners around the world, at a trade show. Comfort, performance, and a selection of brilliant colors made them an overnight success. Sales exploded from $66 million in 1984 to $307 million in 1985. In July 1985 Reebok made its first public offering of 12,000,000 common shares at $17 a share. Two years later shares had climbed to $41. Although Reebok's profits grew steadily with sales during its nine-year history, Reebok did not pay any dividends to its stockholders until 1987. Even the 1987 dividend was nothing to cheer about at 30 cents per share (less than 10 percent of net profits). Reebok needed all of its cash to fund its growth, to repay short-term debt and interest-bearing accounts payable, and to finance accounts receivable and inventory.

Contrast the dividend policy of this young growth company with four stalwart companies which are among the 30 stocks monitored in the Dow Jones Industrial Average. DuPont, General Electric, Sears, Roebuck & Company, and Westinghouse all have generous policies, paying dividends ranging from 30 percent to 60 percent of net profits. And none has skipped a dividend in the last fifty-two years.

Rapidly growing firms like Reebok often publicly sell common stock to raise needed capital; rather than paying large dividends they retain earnings in order to finance continued growth. In this chapter the role and use of common stock as a form of long-term financing and the related dividend policy issues are discussed.

The Nature of Equity Capital

A firm needs to maintain an equity base large enough to allow it to take advantage of low-cost debt and build an optimal capital structure (see Chapter 12). Equity capital can be raised *internally* through retained earnings, which are significantly affected by dividend policy, or *externally* by selling common or preferred stock. Although preferred stock, which is discussed in Chapter 18, is a less costly form of financing than common stock or retained earnings, it is not frequently used. Here we discuss the key features of equity capital, followed by discussions of common stock, stock rights, and dividends.

The key differences between debt and equity were summarized in Chapter 12 (see specifically Table 12.8). These differences relate to ownership rights, claims on the firm's income and assets, maturity, and tax treatment.

Ownership Rights

Unlike creditors (lenders), holders of equity capital (common and preferred stockholders) are owners of the firm. Holders of equity capital often have voting rights that permit them to select the firm's directors and to vote on special issues. In contrast, debtholders may receive voting privileges only when the firm has violated the conditions of a *term loan agreement* or *bond indenture*.

Claims on Income and Assets

Holders of equity capital receive claims on both income and assets that are secondary to the claims of creditors.

Claims on Income

The claims of equity holders on income cannot be paid until the claims of all creditors have been satisfied. These claims include both interest and scheduled principal payments. Once these claims have been satisfied, the firm's board of directors can decide whether to distribute dividends to the owners. Of course, as explained later in this chapter, a firm's ability to pay dividends may be limited by legal, contractual, or internal constraints.

Claims on Assets

The claims of equity holders on the firm's assets are secondary to the claims of creditors. When the firm becomes bankrupt[1], assets are sold and the proceeds distributed in this order: to employees and customers; to the government; to secured creditors; to unsecured creditors; and finally to equity holders. Because equity holders are the last to receive any distribution of assets during bankruptcy proceedings, they expect greater compensation in the form of dividends or rising stock prices.

As noted in Chapter 11, the costs of the various forms of equity financing are generally higher than debt costs. This is partially explained by the fact that the suppliers of equity capital take more risk as a result of their claims on income and assets being subordinate to those of debtholders. Despite its being more costly, equity capital is necessary for the firm to grow and mature. All firms must initially be financed with some common stock equity.

Maturity

Unlike debt, equity capital is a permanent form of financing. It does not "mature," and therefore repayment of the initial amount paid in is not required. Since equity does not mature and will be liquidated only during bankruptcy proceedings, the owners must recognize that although a ready market may exist for the firm's shares, the price that can be realized may fluctuate. This potential fluctuation of the market price of equity makes the overall returns to a firm's owners even more risky.

Tax Treatment

As noted in Chapter 2, interest payments to debtholders are treated as tax-deductible expenses on the firm's income statement, whereas dividend payments to common and

---

[1] The procedures followed when a firm becomes bankrupt are described in Chapter 19.

preferred stockholders are not tax-deductible. The tax-deductibility of interest, as pointed out in Chapter 11, primarily accounts for the fact that the explicit cost of debt is generally less than the explicit cost of equity.

---

1 The claims of holders of equity capital with respect to both income and assets are senior to the claims of debtholders, since the stockholders are the true owners of the firm. *(Fable)*

The claims of holders of equity capital with respect to both income and assets are *secondary* to the claims of debtholders, since the stockholders are the true owners of the firm.

Common Stock Fundamentals

The true owners of business firms are the common stockholders, who invest their money in the firm because of their expectation of future returns. A common stockholder is sometimes referred to as a *residual owner,* since in essence he or she receives what is left after all other claims on the firm's income and assets have been satisfied. As a result of this generally uncertain position, the common stockholder expects to be compensated with adequate dividends and, ultimately, capital gains. Here we discuss the fundamental aspects of common stock: ownership; par value; authorized, outstanding, and issued stock; voting rights; dividends; and the distribution of earnings and assets.

Ownership

The common stock of a firm can be **privately owned** by a single individual, **closely owned** by a small group of investors, such as a family, or **publicly owned** by a broad group of unrelated individual and (or) institutional investors. Typically, small corporations are privately or closely owned, and if their shares are traded this occurs privately or on the over-the-counter exchange (see Chapter 2). Large corporations, which are emphasized in the following discussions, are publicly owned, and their shares are generally actively traded on the organized or over-the-counter exchanges, which were briefly described in Chapter 2.

Par Value

Common stock may be sold with or without a par value. A **par value** is a relatively useless value arbitrarily placed on the stock in the firm's corporate charter. It is generally quite low, somewhere in the range of $1. Firms often issue stock with **no par value,** in which case they may assign it a value or place it on the books at the price at which it is sold. A low par value may be advantageous in states where certain corporate taxes are based on the par value of stock; if a stock has no par value, the tax may be based on an arbitrarily determined per-share figure. The accounting entries resulting from the sale of common stock can be illustrated by a simple example.

privately owned (stock) All common stock of a firm owned by a single individual.

closely owned (stock) All common stock of a firm owned by a small group of investors such as a family.

publicly owned (stock) Common stock of a firm owned by a broad group of unrelated individual and (or) institutional investors.

par value A relatively useless value arbitrarily placed on stock in the corporate charter.

no par value Used to describe stock issued without a par value, in which case the stock may be assigned a value or placed on the books at the price at which it is sold.

> **Example**
> Bubble Soda Company has issued 1,000 shares of $2 par-value common stock, receiving proceeds of $50 per share. This results in the following entries on the firm's books:
>
> | | |
> |---|---|
> | Common stock (1,000 shares at $2 par) | $ 2,000 |
> | Paid-in capital in excess of par | 48,000 |
> | Common stock equity | $50,000 |
>
> Sometimes the entry labeled "paid-in capital in excess of par" may be labeled "capital surplus." This value is important because firms are usually prohibited by state law from distributing any paid-in capital as dividends.

authorized (stock) The shares of common stock that a firm is allowed (authorized) to issue, the number of which is stated in the corporate charter.

outstanding (stock) Shares of common stock currently under ownership of the firm's shareholders.

issued (stock) Shares of common stock put forth into circulation, which may be more in number than shares of outstanding stock.

treasury stock Issued stock that has been repurchased and is held by the firm.

nonvoting common stock Common stock that carries no voting rights; typically designated as class A common stock.

proxy statement A statement conferring the votes of a stockholder or stockholders to another party or parties.

proxy battle The attempt by a nonmanagement group to gain control of the management of a firm through the solicitation of a sufficient number of corporate votes.

Authorized, Outstanding, and Issued Stock

A corporate charter must state the number of shares of common stock the firm is **authorized** to issue. Not all authorized shares will necessarily be **outstanding**—that is, currently under ownership of the firm's shareholders. Since it is often difficult to amend the charter to authorize the issuance of additional shares, firms generally attempt to authorize more shares than they plan to issue. It is possible for the corporation to have **issued** more shares of common stock than are currently outstanding if it has repurchased stock. Repurchased stock is called **treasury stock.** The amount of treasury stock is therefore found by subtracting the number of outstanding shares from the number of shares issued.

Voting Rights

Generally, each share of common stock entitles the holder to one vote in the election of directors and in other special elections. Votes are generally assignable and must be cast at the annual stockholders' meeting. Occasionally, **nonvoting common stock** is issued when the firm's present owners wish to raise capital through the sale of common stock but do not want to give up any voting power. When this is done, the common stock will be classed. Class A common is typically designated as nonvoting; class B common would have voting rights. Because class A shares are not given voting rights, they generally are given preference over class B shares in the distribution of earnings and assets. Treasury stock, which resides within the corporation, generally *does not* have voting rights. Three aspects of voting require special attention—proxies, majority voting, and cumulative voting.

Proxies

Since most small stockholders do not attend the annual meeting to vote, they may sign a **proxy statement** giving their votes to another party. The solicitation of proxies from shareholders is closely controlled by the Securities and Exchange Commission, since there is a possibility that proxies will be solicited on the basis of false or misleading information. The existing management generally receives the stockholders' proxies, since it is able to solicit them at company expense. Occasionally, when the ownership of the firm is widely disseminated, outsiders may attempt to gain control by waging a **proxy battle.** This requires soliciting a sufficient number of votes to unseat the existing manage-

SMALL BUSINESS

BOSE CORPORATION DOES NOT WANT TO GO PUBLIC

Amar Bose, founder, Chairman, and CEO of the Bose Corporation, refuses to take his company public. ''We win only by staying on the cutting edge of the technology, and that can't be done just by following short-run goals,'' Bose says.

Bose shares the opinion of many entrepreneurs that going public forces companies to put more emphasis on quarterly financials than on the long-term strategies they desire to pursue.

Bose Corporation makes and markets premium quality, technologically innovative audio speaker systems in several markets worldwide. Based in Massachusetts, the company had sales of $130 million in 1985. Annual sales worldwide have increased 30 percent on the average, and the firm now employs over 1,100 people, still much smaller than the giant multinationals that market more traditional audio equipment.

In the past ten years, Bose has successfully developed a large Japanese

market. He also turned a $13 million investment into a working relationship with General Motors, for whom he developed a new car stereo system. GM's Delco division now offers the system as an option on certain autos. The potential for success for either venture might have been reduced had Bose had stockholders to satisfy. As it was, neither project was an overnight success.

The Japanese venture began in 1970, but despite all marketing efforts, fewer than 100 pairs of speakers had been sold three years later. Bose pulled out of Japan for a couple of years but went back in 1975. Sales by 1980 were still less than $300,000 annually. However, Bose was determined to save the operation, and with the help of a new Japanese manager, sales had reached $16 million four years later. The GM car stereo venture, begun in 1980, achieved no sales until 1982, but regained its $13 million investment by 1985. ''It would have been impossible

as a public company. I certainly would have lost my job,'' Bose says of the project.

For some companies, going public provides a needed source of equity capital. More paperwork is required, and annual reporting to the SEC is an event to be reckoned with. Some individuals who have founded companies have lost their positions of authority, or in some cases been fired. In addition, the inner workings of a company are subject to public scrutiny and analysis. Many entrepreneurs take these factors into account, weigh them against the need for capital, and decide against a public offering.

It is possible that a windfall amount of money could fund larger projects for Bose Corporation, but Amar Bose has decided that having control of his company and keeping it private is in the firm's best interests. And he is, after all, the boss.

ment. To win a corporate election, votes from a majority of the shares voted are required. Proxy battles generally occur when the existing management is performing poorly; however, the odds of a nonmanagement group winning a proxy battle are generally slim.

Majority Voting

In the **majority voting system,** each stockholder is entitled to one vote for each share of stock owned. The stockholders vote for each position on the board of directors separately, and each stockholder is permitted to vote all of his or her shares for *each* director he or she favors. The directors receiving the majority of the votes are elected. It is impossible for minority interests to select a director, since each shareholder can vote his or her shares for as many of the candidates as he or she wishes. As long as management controls a majority of the votes, it can elect all the directors. An example will clarify this point.

majority voting system
The system whereby, in the election of the board of directors, each stockholder is entitled to one vote for each share of stock owned, and he or she can vote all shares for *each* director.

Example

Merritt Company is in the process of electing three directors. There are 1,000 shares of stock outstanding, of which management controls 60 percent. The management-backed candidates are A, B, and C; the minority candidates are D, E, and F. By voting its 600 shares (60 percent of 1,000) for *each* of its candidates, management can elect A, B, and C; the minority shareholders, with only 400 votes for each of their candidates, cannot elect any directors. Management's candidates will receive 600 votes each, and other candidates will receive 400 votes each.

Cumulative Voting

cumulative voting system
The system under which each share of common stock is allotted a number of votes equal to the total number of corporate directors to be elected and votes can be given to *any* director.

Some states require, and others permit, the use of a **cumulative voting system** to elect corporate directors. This system gives a number of votes equal to the number of directors to be elected to each share of common stock. The votes can be given to *any* director(s) the stockholder desires. The advantage of this system is that it provides the minority shareholders with an opportunity to elect at least some directors.

Example

Dearing Company, like the Merritt Company, is in the process of electing three directors. In this case, however, each share of common stock entitles the holder to three votes, which may be voted in any manner desired. Again, there are 1,000 shares outstanding and management controls 600. It therefore has a total of 1,800 votes (3 × 600), while the minority shareholders have 1,200 votes (3 × 400). In this situation, the majority shareholders can elect only two directors, and the minority shareholders can elect at least one director. The majority shareholders can split their votes evenly among the three candidates (give them 600 votes each); but if the minority shareholders give all their votes to one of their candidates, he or she will win.

A commonly cited formula for determining the number of shares necessary to elect a certain number of directors, *NE,* under cumulative voting is given by Equation 17.1:

$$NE = \frac{O \times D}{T + 1} + 1 \tag{17.1}$$

where

NE = number of shares needed to elect a certain number of directors

O = total number of shares of common stock outstanding

D = number of directors desired

T = total number of directors to be elected

Example

Substituting the values in the preceding example for O (1,000) and T (3) into Equation 17.1 and letting D = 1, 2, and 3 yields values of NE equal to 251, 501, and 751. Since the minority stockholders control only 400 shares, they can elect only one director.

The advantage of cumulative voting from the viewpoint of minority shareholders should be clear from the example. However, even with cumulative voting, certain election procedures such as staggered terms for directors can be used to prevent minority representation on a board. Also, the majority shareholders may control a large enough number of shares or the total number of directors to be elected may be small enough to prevent minority representation.

---

2 Minority shareholders prefer a cumulative voting system over majority voting since it provides them with a better opportunity to elect at least some corporate directors. *(Fact)*   FACT OR FABLE?

Dividends

The payment of corporate dividends is at the discretion of the board of directors. Most corporations pay dividends quarterly. Dividends may be paid in cash, stock, or merchandise. Cash dividends are the most common; merchandise dividends are the least common. The common stockholder is not promised a dividend, but he or she grows to expect certain payments based on the historical dividend pattern of the firm. Before dividends are paid to common stockholders, the claims of all creditors, the government, and preferred stockholders must be satisfied. Because of the importance of the dividend decision to the growth and valuation of the firm, discussion of dividends is included in detail later in this chapter.

Distribution of Earnings and Assets

As mentioned in previous sections, holders of common stock have no guarantee of receiving any periodic distribution of earnings in the form of dividends, nor are they guaranteed anything in the event of liquidation. However, one thing they are assured of is that they cannot lose any more than they have invested in the firm. Moreover, the common stockholder can receive unlimited returns through dividends and through the appreciation in the value of his or her holdings. In other words, although nothing is guaranteed, the *possible* rewards for providing risk capital can be considerable and even great.

Stock Rights and Other Considerations

In addition to common stock fundamentals, stock rights, selling common stock, and the advantages and disadvantages of common stock are important considerations.

Stock Rights

Stock rights provide stockholders with the privilege to purchase additional shares of stock based on their number of owned shares. Rights are an important tool of common stock financing without which shareholders would run the risk of losing their proportionate control of the corporation.

stock rights Provide stockholders with the privilege to purchase additional shares of stock based on their number of owned shares.

Preemptive Rights

preemptive rights Allow common stockholders to maintain their *proportionate* ownership in the corporation when new issues are made.

Many issues of common stock provide shareholders with **preemptive rights,** which allow stockholders to maintain their *proportionate* ownership in the corporation when new issues are made. Most states permit shareholders to be extended this privilege in the corporate charter. Preemptive rights allow existing shareholders to maintain their voting control and protect against the dilution of their ownership and earnings. **Dilution of ownership** usually results in the dilution of earnings, since each present shareholder will have a claim on a *smaller* part of the firm's earnings than previously. Of course, if total earnings simultaneously increase, the long-run effect may be an overall increase in earnings per share.

dilution of ownership Occurs when a new stock issue results in each present stockholder having a claim on a *smaller* part of the firm's earnings than previously.

From the firm's viewpoint, the use of rights offerings to raise new equity capital may be cheaper than a public offering of stock. An example may help clarify the use of rights.

Example

The Patrick Company currently has 100,000 shares of common stock outstanding and is contemplating issuing an additional 10,000 shares through a rights offering. Each existing shareholder will receive one right per share, and each right will entitle the shareholder to purchase one-tenth of a share of new common stock (10,000 ÷ 100,000), so 10 rights will be required to purchase one share of the stock. The holder of 1,000 shares of existing common stock will receive 1,000 rights, each permitting the purchase of one-tenth of a share of new common stock, for a total of 100 shares of new common stock. If the shareholder exercises the rights, he or she will end up with a total of 1,100 shares of common stock, or 1 percent of the total number of shares outstanding (110,000). Thus the shareholder maintains the same proportion of ownership as he or she had prior to the rights offering.

Mechanics of Rights Offerings

date of record (rights) The last date on which the recipient of a right must be the legal owner shown in the company's stock ledger.

When a company makes a rights offering, the board of directors must set a **date of record,** which is the last date on which the recipient of a right must be the legal owner indicated in the company's stock ledger. Due to the time needed to make bookkeeping entries when a stock is traded, stocks usually begin selling **ex rights**—without the rights being attached to the stock—four *business days* prior to the date of record.

ex rights The condition under which stock is sold for a period without announced rights being attached to the stock.

The issuing firm sends rights to **holders of record**—owners of the firm's shares on the date of record, who are free to exercise their rights, sell them, or let them expire. Rights are transferable, and many are traded actively enough to be listed on the various securities exchanges. They are exercisable for a specified period of time, generally not more than a few months, at a price, called the **subscription price,** set somewhat below the prevailing market price. Since fractions of shares are not always issued, it is sometimes necessary to purchase additional rights or sell any extra rights. The value of a right depends largely on the number of rights needed to purchase a share of stock and the amount by which the right's subscription price is below the current market price. If the rights have a very low value and an individual owns only a small number of shares, the rights may be allowed to expire.

holders of record Owners of the firm's shares on the date of record, who may exercise their rights, sell them, or let them expire.

subscription price The price, below the prevailing market price, at which stock rights may be exercisable for a specified period of time.

Management Decisions

A firm's management must make two basic decisions when preparing for a rights offering. The first is the price at which the rights holders can purchase a new share of common stock. The subscription price must be set *below* the current market price, but how far below depends on management's evaluation of the sensitivity of the market demand to a price change, the degree of dilution in ownership and earnings expected, and the size of the offering. Management will consider the rights offering successful if approximately 90 percent of the rights are exercised.

Once management has determined the subscription price, it must determine the number of rights required to purchase a share of stock. Since the amount of funds to be raised is known in advance, the subscription price can be divided into this value to get the total number of shares that must be sold. Dividing the total number of shares outstanding by the total number of shares to be sold will give management the number of rights required to purchase a share of stock.

Example

Ingram Company intends to raise $1 million through a rights offering. The firm currently has 160,000 shares outstanding, which have been most recently trading for $53 to $58 per share. The company has consulted an investment banking firm, which has recommended setting the subscription price for the rights at $50 per share. It believes that at this price the offering will be fully subscribed. The firm must therefore sell an additional 20,000 shares ($1,000,000 ÷ $50 per share). This means that 8 rights (160,000 ÷ 20,000) will be needed to purchase a new share at $50. Each right will entitle its holder to purchase one-eighth of a share of common stock.

Value of a Right

Theoretically, the value of a right should be the same if the stock is selling *with rights* or *ex rights*. In either case, the market value of a right may differ from its theoretical value.

With Rights. Once a rights offering has been declared, shares will trade with rights for only a few days. Equation 17.2 is used to find the theoretical value of a right when the stock is trading with rights, R_w:

$$R_w = \frac{M_w - S}{N + 1} \qquad (17.2)$$

where

R_w = theoretical value of a right when stock is selling with rights

M_w = market value of the stock with rights

S = subscription price of the stock

N = number of rights needed to purchase one share of stock

Example

Ingram Company's stock is currently selling with rights at a price of $54.50 per share, the subscription price is $50 per share, and 8 rights are required to purchase a new share of stock. According to Equation 17.2, the value of a right is $.50 [($54.50 − $50.00) ÷ (8 + 1)]. A right should therefore be worth $.50 in the marketplace.

Ex Rights. When a share of stock is traded ex rights, meaning that the value of the right is no longer included in the stock's market price, the share price of the stock is expected to drop by the value of a right. Equation 17.3 is used to find the market value of the stock trading ex rights, M_e. The same notation is used as in Equation 17.2:

$$M_e = M_w - R_w \qquad (17.3)$$

The theoretical value of a right when the stock is trading ex rights, R_e, is given by Equation 17.4:

$$R_e = \frac{M_e - S}{N} \qquad (17.4)$$

The use of these equations can be illustrated by returning to the Ingram Company example.

Example
According to Equation 17.3, the market price of the Ingram Company stock selling ex rights is $54 ($54.50 − $.50). Substituting this value into Equation 17.4 gives the value of a right when the stock is selling ex rights, which is $.50 [($54.00 − $50.00) ÷ 8]. The theoretical value of the right when the stock is selling with rights or ex rights is therefore the same.

Market Behavior of Rights

As indicated earlier, stock rights are negotiable instruments, often traded on securities exchanges. The market price of a right will generally differ from its theoretical value. The extent to which it will differ will depend on how the firm's stock price is expected to behave during the period when the right is exercisable. By buying rights instead of the stock itself, investors can achieve much higher returns on their money when stock prices rise.

Under- and Oversubscribed Offerings

Rights offerings may be made through an investment banker or directly by the issuing company. Most rights offerings are made through investment bankers, who underwrite and issue the rights. In most underwriting agreements, the investment banker agrees to a **standby arrangement,** which is a formal guarantee that any shares not subscribed or sold publicly will be purchased by the investment banker. This guarantee assures the firm that the entire issue will be sold; it will not be *undersubscribed*. The investment banker, of course, charges a higher fee for making this guarantee.

Most rights offerings include an **oversubscription privilege,** which provides for the distribution of shares for which the rights were not exercised to interested shareholders on a pro rata basis at the stated subscription price. This privilege is a method of restricting ownership to the same group, although ownership proportions may change slightly. Shares that cannot be sold through the oversubscription privilege may be offered to the public. If an investment banker is used, the disposition of unsubscribed shares may be left up to the banker.

standby arrangement
A formal guarantee that any shares not subscribed or sold publicly will be purchased by the investment banker.

oversubscription privilege
Provides for distribution of shares for which rights were not exercised to interested shareholders on a pro rata basis.

3 Rights offerings allow stockholders to maintain their proportionate ownership in the corporation, and typically allow the corporation to raise new equity capital less expensively. *(Fact)*

Selling Common Stock

Aside from the sale of new common stock through a rights offering, the firm may be able to sell new shares of common stock directly through some type of stock option or stock-purchase plan. **Stock options** are generally extended to management and permit it to purchase a certain number of shares of their firm's common stock at a specified price over a certain period of time. **Stock-purchase plans** are fringe benefits occasionally offered to employees that allow them to purchase the firm's stock at a discount or on a matching basis, with the firm absorbing part of the cost.

New issues of common stock, like bonds, can also be sold publicly through an *investment banker*. Of course, these sales are closely regulated by the *Securities and Exchange Commission (SEC)* as well as by state securities commissions. Public sale is commonly used in situations in which rights offerings are not required or are unsuccessful. As noted in Chapter 16, the *public offering* of common stock through an investment banker is generally more expensive than any type of *private placement*, but the investment banker provides useful advice as well as a convenient forum for selling new common stock. For large public stock offerings, the total cost—administrative cost plus underwriting cost—ranges between 3 and 10 percent of the amount of funds raised. (A detailed discussion of the role of the investment banker was presented in Chapter 16.)

stock options Privileges generally extended to management permitting the purchase of a certain number of shares of their firm's common stock at a specified price over a certain period of time.

stock-purchase plans Fringe benefits occasionally offered to employees, allowing the purchase of the firm's stock at a discount or on a matching basis, with the firm absorbing part of the cost.

Advantages and Disadvantages of Common Stock

A number of key advantages and disadvantages of common stock are often cited.

Advantages

The basic advantages of common stock stem from the fact that it is a source of financing that places a *minimum of constraints* on the firm. Since dividends do not *have* to be paid on common stock and their nonpayment does not jeopardize the receipt of payment by other security holders, common stock financing is quite attractive. The fact that common stock has *no maturity*, thereby eliminating a future repayment obligation, also enhances its desirability as a form of financing. Another advantage of common stock over other forms of long-term financing is its *ability to increase the firm's borrowing power*. The more common stock a firm sells, the larger its equity base and therefore the more easily and cheaply long-term debt financing can be obtained.

Disadvantages

The disadvantages of common stock financing include the *potential dilution of ownership and earnings*. Only when rights are offered and exercised by their recipients can this be avoided. Of course, the dilution of ownership and earnings resulting from new issues of common stock may go unnoticed by the small shareholder. Another disadvantage of common stock financing is its *high cost*. In Chapter 11 common stock equity was shown to be, normally, the most expensive form of long-term financing. The reason is that dividends are not tax-deductible and common stock is a riskier security than either debt or preferred stock.

Dividend Fundamentals

Expected cash dividends are the key return variable from which owners and investors determine share price (see Chapter 8). They represent a source of cash flow to stockholders and provide them with information about the firm's current and future performance. Because **retained earnings**—earnings not distributed as dividends—are a form of *internal* financing, the dividend decision can significantly affect the firm's *external* financing requirements. In other words, if the firm needs financing, the larger the cash dividend paid, the greater the amount of financing that must be raised externally through borrowing or through the sale of common or preferred stock. To provide an understanding of the fundamentals of dividend policy, we discuss the procedures for paying cash dividends, dividend reinvestment plans, the residual theory of dividends, and the key factors affecting dividend policy.

retained earnings Earnings not distributed as dividends.

Cash Dividend Payment Procedures

The payment of cash dividends to corporate stockholders is decided by the firm's board of directors. The directors normally hold a quarterly or semiannual dividend meeting at which they evaluate the past period's financial performance and future outlook to determine whether and in what amount dividends should be paid. The payment date of the cash dividend, if one is declared, must also be established.

Amount of Dividends

Whether dividends should be paid and, if they are, how large they should be are important decisions that depend largely on the firm's dividend policy. Most firms pay some cash dividends each period. The amount is generally fixed, although significant increases or decreases in earnings may justify changing it. Most firms have a set policy with respect to the amount of the periodic dividend, but the firm's directors can change this amount at the dividend meeting.

Relevant Dates

date of record (dividends) The date, set by the firm's directors, on which all persons whose names are recorded as stockholders will at a specified future time receive a declared dividend.

If the directors of the firm declare a dividend, they will also indicate the record and payment dates associated with the dividend. Typically, the directors issue a statement indicating their dividend decision, the record date, and the payment date. This statement is generally quoted in *The Wall Street Journal, Barron's,* and other financial news media.

Record Date. All persons whose names are recorded as stockholders on the **date of record,** which is set by the directors, will at a specified future time receive a declared dividend. These stockholders are often referred to as *holders of record.* Due to the time needed to make bookkeeping entries when a stock is traded, the stock will begin selling **ex dividend** four *business days* prior to the date of record. A simple way to determine the first day on which the stock sells ex dividend is to subtract four from the date of record; if a weekend intervenes, subtract six days. Purchasers of a stock selling ex dividend do not receive the current dividend.

ex dividend Period beginning four business days prior to the date of record during which a stock will be sold without paying the current dividend.

Payment Date. The payment date is also set by the directors. It is generally set a few weeks after the record date. The **payment date** is the actual date on which the company will mail the dividend payment to the holders of record. An example will clarify the various dates and accounting entries.

payment date The actual date on which the company will mail the dividend payment to the holders of record.

Example

At the quarterly dividend meeting of the Rudolf Company, held June 10, the directors declared an $.80 per share cash dividend for holders of record on Monday, July 1. The firm had 100,000 shares of common stock outstanding. The payment date for the dividend was August 1. Before the dividend was declared, the key accounts of the firm were as follows:

Cash	$200,000	Dividends payable	$ 0
		Retained earnings	1,000,000

When the dividend was announced by the directors, $80,000 ($.80 per share × 100,000 shares) of the retained earnings was transferred to the dividends payable account. The key accounts thus became

Cash	$200,000	Dividends payable	$ 80,000
		Retained earnings	920,000

The Rudolf Company's stock began to sell ex dividend four *business days* prior to the date of record, which was June 25. This date was found by subtracting six days (since a weekend intervened) from the July 1 date of record. Purchasers of Rudolf's stock on June 24 or earlier received the rights to the dividends; those purchasing the stock on or after June 25 did not. When the August 1 payment date arrived, the firm mailed dividend checks to the holders of record as of July 1. This produced the following balances in the key accounts of the firm:

Cash	$120,000	Dividends payable	$ 0
		Retained earnings	920,000

The net effect of declaration and payment of the dividend was to reduce the firm's total assets (and stockholders' equity) by $80,000.

Dividend Reinvestment Plans

A growing number of firms offer **dividend reinvestment plans,** which enable stockholders to use dividends to acquire shares—even fractional shares—at little or no transaction (brokerage) cost. Especially popular between 1982 and 1985 were the plans of public utilities, such as electric companies, telephone companies, and natural gas distributors, because participating shareholders received a special tax break that ended December 31, 1985. Today, cash dividends (or the value of the stocks received through a dividend reinvestment plan) from all plans are taxed as ordinary income. In addition, when the acquired shares are sold, if the proceeds are in excess of the original purchase price, the capital gain will also be taxed as ordinary income.

Dividend reinvestment plans can be handled by a company in either of two ways.

dividend reinvestment plans Plans offered by firms that enable stockholders to use dividends to acquire full or fractional shares at little or no transaction (brokerage) cost.

Both allow the stockholder to elect to have dividends reinvested in the firm's shares. In one approach, a third-party trustee is paid a fee to buy the firm's *outstanding shares* in the open market on behalf of the shareholders who wish to reinvest their dividends. This type of plan benefits participating shareholders by allowing them to use their dividends to purchase shares generally at a lower transaction cost than they would otherwise pay. The second approach involves buying *newly issued shares* directly from the firm without paying any transaction costs. This approach allows the firm to raise new capital while at the same time permitting owners to reinvest their dividends, frequently at about 5 percent below the current market price. Clearly, the existence of dividend reinvestment plans may enhance the appeal of a firm's shares.

The Residual Theory of Dividends

residual theory of dividends A theory that suggests that the dividend paid by a firm should be the amount left over after all acceptable investment opportunities have been undertaken.

One school of thought—the **residual theory of dividends**—suggests that the dividend paid by a firm should be viewed as a *residual*—the amount left over after all acceptable investment opportunities have been undertaken. Using this approach, the firm would treat the dividend decision in three steps as follows:

1. Determine its optimum level of capital expenditures, which would be the level generated by the point of intersection of the investment opportunities schedule (IOS) and weighted marginal cost of capital (WMCC) function (see Chapter 11).

2. Using the optimal capital structure proportions (see Chapter 12), it would estimate the total amount of equity financing needed to support the expenditures generated in step 1.

3. Because the cost of retained earnings, k_r, is less than the cost of new common stock, k_n (see Chapter 11), retained earnings would be used to meet the equity requirement determined in step 2. If retained earnings are inadequate to meet this need, new common stock would be sold. If the available retained earnings are in excess of this need, the surplus amount would be distributed as dividends.

According to this approach, as long as the firm's equity need is in excess of the amount of retained earnings, no cash dividend would be paid. If an excess of retained earnings exists, the residual amount would then be distributed as a cash dividend. This view of dividends tends to suggest that the required return of investors, k_s, is *not* influenced by the firm's dividend policy—a premise that in turn suggests that dividend policy is irrelevant. Let us look at an example.

Example
Overbrook Industries has available from the current period's operations $1.8 million that can be retained or paid out in dividends. The firm's optimal capital structure is at a debt ratio of 30 percent, which represents 30 percent debt and 70 percent equity. Figure 17.1 depicts the firm's weighted marginal cost of capital (WMCC) function along with three investment opportunities schedules, IOS_1, IOS_2, and IOS_3. For each IOS, the level of total new financing or investment determined by the point of intersection of the WMCC and the IOS has been noted. For IOS_1 it is $1.5 million, for IOS_2 it is $2.4 million, and for IOS_3 it is $3.2 million. While only one IOS will actually exist, it is useful to look at the dividend decisions generated by applying the residual theory in each of the three cases. Table 17.1 summarizes this analysis.

Figure 17.1
WMCC and IOSs for Overbrook Industries

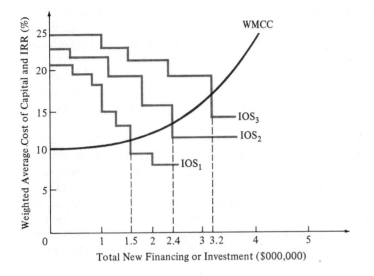

Table 17.1 shows that if IOS$_1$ exists, the firm would pay out $750,000 in dividends, since only $1,050,000 of the $1,800,000 of available earnings is needed. A 41.7 percent payout ratio results. For IOS$_2$, dividends of $120,000 (a payout ratio of 6.7 percent) results. Should IOS$_3$ exist, the firm would pay no dividends (a zero payout ratio), since its retained earnings of $1,800,000 are less than the $2,240,000 of earnings needed. In this case the firm would have to obtain additional new common stock financing to meet the new requirements generated by the intersection of the IOS$_3$ and WMCC. Depending on which IOS exists, the firm's dividend would in effect be the residual, if any, remaining after financing all acceptable investments.

Table 17.1
Applying the Residual Theory of Dividends to Overbrook Industries for Each of Three IOSs (shown in Figure 17.1)

	Investment opportunities schedules		
Item	IOS$_1$	IOS$_2$	IOS$_3$
(1) New financing or investment (Fig. 17.1)	$1,500,000	$2,400,000	$3,200,000
(2) Retained earnings available (given)	$1,800,000	$1,800,000	$1,800,000
(3) Equity needed [70% × (1)]	1,050,000	1,680,000	2,240,000
(4) Dividends [(2) − (3)]	$ 750,000	$ 120,000	$ 0[a]
(5) Dividend payout ratio [(4) ÷ (2)]	41.7%	6.7%	0%

[a] In this case additional new common stock in the amount of $440,000 ($2,240,000 needed − $1,800,000 available) would have to be sold; no dividends would be paid.

The Irrelevance of Dividends

clientele effect The theory
that a firm will attract
stockholders whose
preferences with respect to
the payment and stability of
dividends correspond to the
payment pattern and stability
of the firm itself.

informational content The
information provided by the
dividends of a firm that
causes owners to bid up the
price of the stock based on
future earnings expectations.

The residual theory of dividends suggests that dividends are irrelevant—that the value of the firm is not affected by its dividend policy. The major advocates of this view are Franco Modigliani and Merton H. Miller (commonly referred to as M and M). They argue that the way a firm splits its earnings between dividends and reinvestment has no direct effect on value. Modigliani and Miller suggest the existence of a **clientele effect:** A firm will attract stockholders whose preferences with respect to the payment and stability of dividends correspond to the payment pattern and stability of the firm itself. Since the shareholders get what they expect, M and M argue that the value of the firm's stock is unaffected by changes in dividend policy.

However, recognizing that dividends do somehow affect stock prices, M and M suggest that the positive effects of dividend increases are attributable not to the dividend itself but to the **informational content** of dividends with respect to future earnings. The information provided by the dividends causes owners to bid up the price of the stock based on future expectations. M and M argue that when acceptable investment opportunities are not available, the firm should distribute the unneeded funds to the owners, who can invest the money in other firms that have acceptable investment alternatives. They conclude that since dividends are irrelevant to the firm's value, the firm does not need to have a dividend policy.

The Relevance of Dividends

The key argument of those supporting dividend relevance is that because current dividend payments reduce investor uncertainty, investors will discount the firm's earnings at a lower rate, k_s, thereby placing a higher value on the firm's stock. If dividends are not paid, investor uncertainty will increase, raising the required rate of return, k_s, and lowering the stock's value.

The dividend relevance school's leading proponent, Myron J. Gordon, suggests that stockholders prefer current dividends and that there is, in fact, a direct relationship between the dividend policy of a firm and its market value. Gordon's "bird-in-the-hand" argument suggests that investors are generally risk averters and attach less risk to current as opposed to future dividends or capital gains.

In practice, the actions of financial managers and stockholders alike support the belief that dividend policy affects stock value.[2] Since our concern is with the day-to-day behavior of business firms, the remainder of this chapter is consistent with the widely held belief that dividends *are relevant*—that each firm must develop a dividend policy that fulfills the goals of owners and maximizes their wealth in the long run.

FACT OR FABLE?   **4** Modigliani and Miller argue that dividend policy is relevant since current dividend payments reduce investor uncertainty, thereby causing investors to place a higher value on the firm's stock. *(Fable)*

Modigliani and Miller argue that dividend policy is *irrelevant* since the way a firm splits its earnings between dividends and reinvestment has *no direct effect on value.*

---

[2] A common exception is small firms since they frequently treat dividends as a residual remaining after all acceptable investments have been initiated. This occurs because small firms do not normally have ready access to capital markets. The use of retained earnings therefore acts as a key source of financing for growth, which is generally an important goal of a small firm.

DIVIDENDS—"MANNA FROM HEAVEN"

Investors were expected to receive a treat—fatter dividends—as a result of the 1986 tax law changes. A Salomon Brothers, Inc., study of the effects of the Tax Reform Act of 1986 on the financial market concluded that "companies are likely to raise dividend payout ratios and dividend growth will accelerate." These changes would probably be made at the expense of other uses of corporate cash flow such as boosting retained earnings, financing share buyback programs, or financing mergers and acquisitions, the study said.

The new tax bill was to shift the major tax burden to corporations and away from individuals over the next five years. The fact that corporations would be roughly $25 billion poorer each year, however, might not be readily apparent from reported earnings of concerns, said economists at Salomon Brothers.

Some analysts saw the greatest promise of dividend growth in the shares of companies already having well-defined dividend policies, high cash flow, and good earnings streams. Free cash flow is one of the most important factors influencing corporate dividend policies. Companies whose cash flow is not affected by changes in the tax laws would be better positioned to raise dividends, analysts said.

The increased likelihood that some corporations would boost their dividends or start paying one because of increased investor preference for current income probably added more fuel to an old debate of whether dividends affect stock prices. Academicians, such as Professor Merton H. Miller at the University of Chicago and Nobel prize-winner Franco Modigliani at the Massachusetts Institute of Technology, have argued for more than twenty years that a company's earnings rather than its dividend policy determine its stock price.

They say that investors historically have not paid a premium for the shares of concerns adopting generous dividend policies and should not be expected to. But corporate officials and investment bankers insist dividends matter a great deal and often cite many examples of companies whose stock prices jump after announcing a resumption of a regular dividend or after a greater-than-expected dividend increase.

And with the new tax code, Prof. Miller said, "the balance of (corporate) incentives has shifted toward interest payments and dividends and away from plowing profits back (into the company) to generate lower-taxed capital gains." Regardless of their impact, or lack of it, on stock prices, the professor wasn't about to throw dividend checks away. "Dividends have a very good connotation," he said. "We think of them as manna from heaven."

Factors Affecting Dividend Policy

Before discussing the basic types of dividend policies, we should consider the factors involved in formulating dividend policy. These include legal constraints, contractual constraints, internal constraints, the firm's growth prospects, owner considerations, and market considerations.

Legal Constraints

Most states prohibit corporations from paying out as cash dividends any portion of the firm's "legal capital," which is measured by the par value of common stock. Other states define legal capital to include not only the par value of the common stock but also any paid-in capital in excess of par. These "capital impairment restrictions" are generally established to provide a sufficient equity base to protect creditors' claims. An example will clarify the differing definitions of capital.

Example

The Miller Flour Company's stockholders' equity account is presented below.

Miller Flour Company's Stockholders' Equity

Common stock at par	$100,000
Paid-in capital in excess of par	200,000
Retained earnings	140,000
Total stockholders' equity	$440,000

In states where the firm's legal capital is defined as the par value of its common stock, the firm could pay out $340,000 ($200,000 + $140,000) in cash dividends without impairing its capital. In states where the firm's legal capital includes all paid-in capital, the firm could pay out only $140,000 in cash dividends.

An earnings requirement limiting the amount of dividends to the sum of the firm's present and past earnings is sometimes imposed. In other words, the firm cannot pay more in cash dividends than the sum of its most recent and past retained earnings. However, *the firm is not prohibited from paying more in dividends than its current earnings.*[3]

Example

Assume the Miller Flour Company, presented in the preceding example, in the year just ended has $30,000 in earnings available for common stock dividends. An analysis of the stockholders' equity account above indicates that the firm has past retained earnings of $140,000. Thus it could legally pay dividends of up to $170,000.

If a firm has overdue liabilities or is legally insolvent or bankrupt (if the fair market value of its assets is less than its liabilities), most states prohibit its payment of cash dividends. In addition, the Internal Revenue Service prohibits firms from accumulating earnings in order to reduce the owners' taxes. A firm's owners must pay income taxes on dividends when received, but the owners are not taxed on capital gains in market value until the stock is sold. A firm may retain a large portion of earnings in order to delay the payment of taxes by the owners. If the IRS can determine that a firm has accumulated an excess of earnings in order to allow owners to delay paying ordinary income taxes, it may levy an **excess earnings accumulation tax** on any retained earnings above $250,000—the amount currently exempt from this tax for all firms except personal corporations.

excess earnings accumulation tax The tax levied by the IRS on retained earnings above $250,000, when it has determined that the firm has accumulated an excess of earnings in order to allow owners to delay paying ordinary income taxes.

Contractual Constraints

Often the firm's ability to pay cash dividends is constrained by certain restrictive provisions in a loan agreement. Generally, these constraints prohibit the payment of cash dividends until a certain level of earnings has been achieved or limit the dividends paid to

[3] A firm having an operating loss in the current period could still pay cash dividends as long as sufficient retained earnings were available and, of course, as long as it had the cash with which to make the payments.

a certain dollar amount, or percentage, of earnings. Constraints on dividend payments help to protect creditors from losses due to insolvency on the part of the firm. The violation of a contractual constraint is generally grounds for a demand of immediate payment by the funds supplier affected.

Internal Constraints

The firm's ability to pay cash dividends is generally constrained by the amount of excess cash available. Although it is possible for a firm to borrow funds to pay dividends, lenders are generally reluctant to make such loans since they produce no tangible or operating benefits that will help the firm repay the loan. Although a firm may have high earnings, its ability to pay dividends may be constrained by a low level of liquid assets (cash and marketable securities).

> **Example**
> The Miller Flour Company's stockholders' equity account presented earlier indicates that if the firm's legal capital is defined as all paid-in capital, the firm can pay $140,000 in dividends. If the firm has total liquid assets of $50,000 ($20,000 in cash plus marketable securities worth $30,000) and $35,000 of this is needed for operations, the maximum dividend the firm can pay is $15,000 ($50,000 − $35,000).

Growth Prospects

The firm's financial requirements are directly related to the degree of asset expansion anticipated. If the firm is in a growth stage, it may need all the funds it can get to finance capital expenditures. A growing firm also requires funds to maintain and improve its assets. High-growth firms typically find themselves constantly in need of funds. Their financial requirements may be characterized as large and immediate. Firms exhibiting little or no growth may periodically need funds to replace or renew assets.

A firm must evaluate its financial position from the standpoint of profitability and risk in order to develop insight into its ability to raise capital externally. It must determine not only its ability to raise funds but also the cost and speed with which financing can be obtained. Generally, a large, mature firm has adequate access to new capital, whereas the funds available to a rapidly growing firm may not be sufficient to support the numerous acceptable projects. A growth firm is likely to have to depend heavily on internal financing through retained earnings to take advantage of profitable projects, and is likely to pay out only a very small percentage of its earnings as dividends. A more stable firm that needs capital funds only for planned outlays is in a better position to pay out a large proportion of its earnings, especially if it has ready sources of financing.

Owner Considerations

In establishing a dividend policy, the primary concern of the firm should be to maximize owners' wealth. Although it is impossible to establish a policy that will maximize each owner's wealth, the firm must establish a policy that has a favorable effect on the wealth of the *majority* of owners.

One consideration is the *tax status of a firm's owners*. If a firm has a large percentage of wealthy stockholders who are in a high tax bracket, it may decide to pay out a *lower* percentage of its earnings in order to allow the owners to delay the payment of taxes until they sell the stock.[4] Of course, when the stock is sold, if the proceeds are in excess of the original purchase price, the capital gain will be taxed as ordinary income. Lower-income shareholders, however, who need dividend income, will prefer a *higher* payout of earnings.

A second consideration is the *owners' investment opportunities*. A firm should not retain funds for investment in projects yielding lower returns than the owners could obtain from external investments of equal risk. The firm should evaluate the returns expected on its own investment opportunities and, using present-value techniques, determine whether greater returns are obtainable from external investments such as government securities or other corporate stocks. If it appears that the owners would have better opportunities externally, the firm should pay out a higher percentage of its earnings. If the firm's investment opportunities are at least as good as similar-risk external investments, a lower payout is justifiable.

A final consideration is the *potential dilution of ownership*. If a firm pays out a higher percentage of earnings, new equity capital will have to be raised with common stock, which may result in the dilution of both control and earnings for the existing owners. By paying out a low percentage of its earnings, the firm can minimize such possibility of dilution.

Market Considerations

Since the wealth of the firm's owners is reflected in the market price of the firm's shares, an awareness of the market's probable response to certain types of policies is helpful in formulating a suitable dividend policy. Stockholders are believed to value a *fixed or increasing level of dividends* as opposed to a fluctuating pattern of dividends. In addition, stockholders are believed to value a policy of *continuous dividend payment*. Since regularly paying a fixed or increasing dividend eliminates uncertainty about the frequency and magnitude of dividends, the earnings of the firm are likely to be discounted at a lower rate. This should result in an increase in the market value of the stock and therefore increased owners' wealth.

A final market consideration is the *informational content* of dividends. Shareholders often view the firm's dividend payments as an indicator of future success. A stable and continuous dividend conveys to the owners that the firm is in good health and that there is no reason for concern. If the firm skips a dividend payment in a given period due to a loss or to very low earnings, shareholders are likely to react unfavorably. The nonpayment of the dividend creates uncertainty about the future, and this uncertainty is likely to result in lower stock values. Owners and investors generally construe a dividend payment during a period of losses as an indication that the loss is merely temporary.

Types of Dividend Policies

dividend policy The firm's plan of action to be followed whenever a decision concerning dividends must be made.

The firm's **dividend policy** represents a plan of action to be followed whenever the dividend decision must be made. The dividend policy must be formulated with two basic objectives in mind: maximizing the wealth of the firm's owners and providing for suffi-

[4] The consideration of the owners' tax status in making dividend policy decisions is illegal, although it is difficult for the IRS to police this law. Rather, the IRS will look for high retained earnings and high liquidity. Firms in this situation are penalized through an excess earnings accumulation tax. It is quite difficult, if not impossible, to determine the extent to which the tax status of a firm's owners affects dividend policy decisions.

cient financing. These two objectives are interrelated. They must be fulfilled in light of a number of factors—legal, contractual, internal, growth, owner-related, and market-related—that limit the policy alternatives. Three of the more commonly used dividend policies are described below. A particular firm's cash dividend policy may incorporate elements of each.

Constant-Payout-Ratio Dividend Policy

One type of dividend policy occasionally adopted by firms is the use of a constant payout ratio. The **dividend payout ratio,** calculated by dividing the firm's cash dividend per share by its earnings per share, indicates the percentage of each dollar earned that is distributed to the owners in the form of cash. With a **constant-payout-ratio dividend policy,** the firm establishes that a certain percentage of earnings will be paid to owners in each dividend period. The problem with this policy is that if the firm's earnings drop or if a loss occurs in a given period, the dividends may be low or even nonexistent. Since dividends are often considered an indicator of the firm's future condition and status, the firm's stock may thus be adversely affected by this type of action. An example will clarify the problems stemming from a constant-payout-ratio policy.

dividend payout ratio Calculated by dividing the firm's cash dividend per share by its earnings per share, thereby indicating the percentage of each dollar earned that is distributed to the owners in the form of cash.

constant-payout-ratio dividend policy A dividend policy based on the payment of a certain percentage of earnings to owners in each dividend period.

Example

Peachtree Power & Light has a policy of paying out 40 percent of earnings in cash dividends. In periods when a loss occurs, the firm's policy is to pay no cash dividends. Peachtree's earnings per share, dividends per share, and average price per share for the past six years were as follows:

Year	Earnings/share	Dividends/share	Average price/share
1988	$-0.50	$0.00	$42.00
1987	3.00	1.20	52.00
1986	1.75	0.70	48.00
1985	-1.50	0.00	38.00
1984	2.00	0.80	46.00
1983	4.50	1.80	50.00

Dividends increased in 1985–1986 and in 1986–1987 and decreased in 1983–1984, 1984–1985, and 1987–1988. The data show that in years of decreasing dividends, the firm's stock price dropped; when dividends increased, the price of the stock increased. Peachtree's sporadic dividend payments appear to make its owners uncertain about the returns they can expect from their investment in the firm and therefore tend to generally depress the stock's price. Although a constant-payout-ratio dividend policy is used by some firms, it is *not* recommended.

Regular Dividend Policy

Another type of dividend policy, the **regular dividend policy,** is based on the payment of a fixed-dollar dividend in each period. The *regular dividend policy* provides the owners with generally positive information, indicating that the firm is okay and thereby minimiz-

regular dividend policy A dividend policy based on the payment of a fixed-dollar dividend in each period.

ing their uncertainty. Often, firms using this policy will increase the regular dividend once a *proven* increase in earnings has occurred. Under this policy, dividends are almost never decreased.

Example

Woodward Laboratories' dividend policy is to pay annual dividends of $1.00 per share until per-share earnings have exceeded $4.00 for three consecutive years, at which time the annual dividend is raised to $1.50 per share and a new earnings plateau is established. The firm does not anticipate decreasing its dividend unless its liquidity is in jeopardy. Woodward's earnings per share, dividends per share, and average price per share for the past 12 years were as follows:

Year	Earnings/share	Dividends/share	Average price/share
1988	$4.50	$1.50	$47.50
1987	3.90	1.50	46.50
1986	4.60	1.50	45.00
1985	4.20	1.00	43.00
1984	5.00	1.00	42.00
1983	2.00	1.00	38.50
1982	6.00	1.00	38.00
1981	3.00	1.00	36.00
1980	0.75	1.00	33.00
1979	0.50	1.00	33.00
1978	2.70	1.00	33.50
1977	2.85	1.00	35.00

It can be seen that regardless of the level of earnings, Woodward Labs paid dividends of $1.00 per share through 1985. In 1986 the dividend was raised to $1.50 per share, since earnings of $4.00 per share had been achieved for three years. In 1986 the firm would also have had to establish a new earnings plateau for further dividend increases. Woodward Laboratories' average price per share exhibited a stable, increasing behavior in spite of a somewhat volatile pattern of earnings.

target dividend-payout ratio A policy under which the firm attempts to pay out a certain percentage of earnings as a stated dollar dividend adjusted toward a target payout as proven earnings increases occur.

Often, a regular dividend policy is built around a **target dividend-payout ratio.** Under this policy the firm attempts to pay out a certain percentage of earnings, but rather than let dividends fluctuate, it pays a stated dollar dividend and adjusts it toward the target payout as proven increases in earnings occur. For instance, Woodward Laboratories appears to have a target payout ratio of around 35 percent. The payout was about 35 percent ($1.00 ÷ $2.85) when the dividend policy was set in 1977, and when the dividend was raised to $1.50 in 1986, the payout ratio was about 33 percent ($1.50 ÷ $4.60).

low-regular-and-extra dividend policy A dividend policy based on paying a low regular dividend, supplemented by an additional dividend when earnings warrant it.

Low-Regular-and-Extra Dividend Policy

Some firms establish a **low-regular-and-extra dividend policy,** paying a low regular dividend, supplemented by an additional dividend when earnings warrant it. If earnings are higher than normal in a given period, the firm may pay this additional dividend, which will be designated an **extra dividend.** By designating the amount by which the dividend exceeds the regular payment as an extra dividend, the firm avoids giving shareholders

extra dividend An additional dividend optionally paid by the firm if earnings are higher than normal in a given period.

false hopes. The use of the "extra" designation is especially common among companies that experience cyclical shifts in earnings.

By establishing a low regular dividend that is paid each period, the firm gives investors the stable income necessary to build confidence in the firm, and the extra dividend permits them to share in the earnings if the firm experiences an especially good period. Firms using this policy must raise the level of the regular dividend once proven increases in earnings have been achieved. The extra dividend should not be a regular event, or it becomes meaningless. The use of a target dividend-payout ratio in establishing the regular dividend level is advisable.

FACT OR FABLE?

5 A dividend policy that allows stockholders to get their share of the profits by always paying out a fixed percentage of earnings tends to be preferred over one that regularly pays a stable or increasing dividend. *(Fable)*

A dividend policy that allows stockholders to get their share of the profits by always paying out a fixed percentage of earnings *is not preferred* over one that regularly pays a stable or increasing dividend.

Other Forms of Dividends

A number of other forms of dividends are available to the firm. Here, we will discuss two other methods of paying dividends—stock dividends and stock repurchases—as well as a closely related topic, stock splits.

Stock Dividends

A **stock dividend** is the payment of a dividend in the form of stock to existing owners. Often, firms pay stock dividends as a replacement for or a supplement to cash dividends. Although stock dividends do not have a real value, stockholders may perceive them to represent something they did not have before and therefore to have value.

stock dividend The payment of a dividend by the firm in the form of stock to existing owners.

Accounting Aspects

In an accounting sense, the payment of a stock dividend is a shifting of funds between capital accounts rather than a use of funds. When a firm declares a stock dividend, the procedures with respect to announcement and distribution are the same as those described earlier for a cash dividend. The accounting entries associated with the payment of stock dividends are given in the following example.

Example
Garrison Corporation's current stockholders' equity on its balance sheet is as follows:

Preferred stock	$ 300,000
Common stock (100,000 shares at $4 par)	400,000
Paid-in capital in excess of par	600,000
Retained earnings	700,000
Total stockholders' equity	$2,000,000

If Garrison declares a 10 percent stock dividend and the market price of its stock is $15 per share, $150,000 (10% × 100,000 shares × $15 per share) of retained earnings will be capitalized. The $150,000 will be distributed between common stock and paid-in capital in excess of par accounts based on the par value of the common stock. The resulting account balances are as follows:

Preferred stock	$ 300,000
Common stock (110,000 shares at $4 par)	440,000
Paid-in capital in excess of par	710,000
Retained earnings	550,000
Total stockholders' equity	$2,000,000

Since 10,000 (10 percent of 100,000) new shares have been issued and the prevailing market price is $15 per share, $150,000 ($15 per share × 10,000 shares) has been shifted from retained earnings to the common stock and paid-in capital accounts. A total of $40,000 ($4 par × 10,000 shares) has been added to common stock, and the remaining $110,000 [($15 − $4) × 10,000 shares] has been added to the paid-in capital in excess of par. The firm's total stockholders' equity has not changed; funds have only been *redistributed* among stockholders' equity accounts.

The Shareholder's Viewpoint

The shareholder receiving a stock dividend receives nothing of value. After the dividend is paid, the per-share value of the shareholder's stock will decrease in proportion to the dividend in such a way that the market value of his or her total holdings in the firm will remain unchanged. The shareholder's proportion of ownership in the firm will also remain the same, and as long as the firm's earnings remain unchanged, so will his or her share of total earnings. A continuation of the preceding example will clarify this point.

Example
Ms. X owned 10,000 shares of Garrison Corporation's stock. The company's most recent earnings were $220,000, and earnings are not expected to change in the near future. Before the stock dividend, Ms. X owned 10 percent (10,000 shares ÷ 100,000 shares) of the firm's stock, which was selling for $15 per share. Earnings per share were $2.20 ($220,000 ÷ 100,000 shares). Since Ms. X owns 10,000 shares, her earnings were $22,000 ($2.20 per share × 10,000 shares). After receiving the 10 percent stock dividend, Ms. X has 11,000 shares, which again is 10 percent (11,000 shares ÷ 110,000 shares) of the ownership. The market price of the stock can be expected to drop to $13.64 per share [$15 × (1.00 ÷ 1.10)], which means that the market value of Ms. X's holdings will be $150,000 (11,000 shares × $13.64 per share). This is the same as the initial value of her holdings (10,000 shares × $15 per share). The future earnings per share will drop to $2 ($220,000 ÷ 110,000 shares), since the same $220,000 in earnings must now be divided among 110,000 shares. Since Ms. X still owns 10 percent of the stock, her share of total earnings is still $22,000 ($2 per share × 11,000 shares). In summary, if the firm's earnings remain constant and total cash dividends do not increase, a stock dividend will result in a lower per-share market value for the firm's stock.

The Company's Viewpoint

Stock dividends are more costly to issue than cash dividends, but the advantages generally outweigh these costs. Firms find the stock dividend a means of giving owners something without having to use cash. Generally, when a firm is growing rapidly and needs internal financing to perpetuate this growth, a stock dividend is used. As long as the stockholders recognize that the firm is reinvesting its earnings in a manner that should tend to maximize future earnings, the market value of the firm should at least remain unchanged. If the stock dividend is paid so that cash can be retained to satisfy past-due bills, a decline in market value may result.

Stock Splits

Although not a type of dividend, *stock splits* have an effect on a firm's share price similar to that of stock dividends. A **stock split** is a method commonly used to lower the market price of a firm's stock by increasing the number of shares belonging to each shareholder. Quite often, a firm believes that its stock is priced too high and that lowering the market price will enhance trading activity. Stock splits are often made prior to new issues of a stock to enhance the marketability of the stock and stimulate market activity.

A stock split has no effect on the firm's capital structure. It commonly increases the number of shares outstanding and reduces the stock's per-share par value. In other words, when a stock is split, a specified number of new shares are exchanged for a given number of outstanding shares. In a 2-for-1 split, two new shares are exchanged for each old share; in a 3-for-2 split, three new shares are exchanged for each two old shares, and so on.

stock split
A method commonly used to lower the market price of a firm's stock by increasing the number of shares belonging to each shareholder.

Example
Delphi Company had 200,000 shares of $2 par-value common stock and no preferred stock outstanding. Since the stock is selling at a high market price, the firm has declared a 2-for-1 stock split. The total before- and after-split stockholders' equity is given below.

Before split	
Common stock (200,000 shares at $2 par)	$ 400,000
Paid-in capital in excess of par	4,000,000
Retained earnings	2,000,000
Total stockholders' equity	$6,400,000

After 2-for-1 split	
Common stock (400,000 shares at $1 par)	$ 400,000
Paid-in capital in excess of par	4,000,000
Retained earnings	2,000,000
Total stockholders' equity	$6,400,000

The insignificant effect of the stock split on the firm's books is obvious.

reverse stock split
A method used to raise the market price of a firm's stock by exchanging a certain number of outstanding shares for one new share of stock.

Stock can be split in any way desired. Sometimes a **reverse stock split** is made: a certain number of outstanding shares are exchanged for one new share. For example, in a 1-for-2 split, one new share is exchanged for two old shares; in a 2-for-3 split, two new shares are exchanged for three old shares, and so on. Reverse stock splits are initiated when a stock is selling at too low a price to appear respectable.[5]

It is not unusual for a stock split to cause a slight increase in the market value of the stock. This is attributable to the informational content of stock splits and the fact that *total* dividends paid commonly increase slightly after a split.

Stock Repurchases

stock repurchase The repurchasing by the firm of outstanding shares of its common stock in the marketplace.

In the recent past, firms have increased their repurchasing of shares of outstanding common stock in the marketplace. A **stock repurchase** is made for a number of reasons: to obtain shares to be used in acquisitions, to have shares available for employee stock option plans, to achieve a gain in the book value of equity when shares are selling below their book value, or merely to retire outstanding shares. This section is concerned with the repurchase of shares for retirement, since this type of repurchase is similar to the payment of cash dividends.

Accounting Entries

The accounting entries that result when common stock is repurchased are a reduction in cash and the establishment of a contra capital account called "treasury stock," which is shown as a deduction from stockholders' equity. The label *treasury stock* is used to indicate the presence of repurchased shares on the balance sheet. The repurchase of stock can be viewed as a cash dividend, since it involves the distribution of cash to the firm's owners, who are the sellers of the shares.

Motives for the Retirement of Shares

When common stock is repurchased for retirement, the underlying motive is to distribute excess cash to the owners. Retiring stock means that the owners receive cash for their shares. The general rationale for this action is that as long as earnings remain constant, the repurchase of shares reduces the number of outstanding shares, raising the earnings per share and therefore the market price per share. In addition, certain owner tax benefits may result from the use of stock repurchases. The retirement of common stock can be viewed as a type of reverse dilution, since the earnings per share and the market price of stock are increased by reducing the number of shares outstanding. A simple example will clarify this point.

> **Example**
> The Benton Company has released the following financial data:
>
> | | |
> |---|---|
> | Earnings available for common stockholders | $1,000,000 |
> | Number of shares of common outstanding | 400,000 |
> | Earnings per share ($1,000,000 ÷ 400,000) | $2.50 |
> | Market price per share | $50 |
> | Price/earnings (P/E) ratio ($50 ÷ $2.50) | 20 |

[5] If a firm's stock is selling at a low price—possibly less than a few dollars—many investors are hesitant to purchase it because they believe it is "cheap." These somewhat unsophisticated investors correlate cheapness and quality, and they feel that a low-priced stock is a low-quality investment. A reverse stock split raises the stock price and increases per-share earnings.

The firm is contemplating using $800,000 of its earnings either to pay cash dividends or to repurchase shares. If the firm pays cash dividends, the amount of the dividend would be $2 per share ($800,000 ÷ 400,000 shares). If the firm pays $52 per share to repurchase stock, it could repurchase approximately 15,385 shares ($800,000 ÷ $52 per share). As a result of this repurchase, 384,615 shares (400,000 shares − 15,385 shares) of common stock would remain outstanding. Earnings per share (EPS) would rise to $2.60 ($1,000,000 ÷ 384,615). If the stock still sold at 20 times earnings (P/E = 20), applying the price/earnings (P/E) multiples approach presented in Chapter 8, its market price would rise to $52 per share ($2.60 × 20). In both cases the stockholders would receive $2 per share—a $2 cash dividend in the dividend case or a $2 increase in share price ($50 per share to $52 per share) in the repurchase case.

The advantages of stock repurchases are an increase in per-share earnings and certain owner tax benefits. The tax advantage stems from the fact that if the cash dividend is paid, the owners will have to pay ordinary income taxes on it, whereas the $2 increase in the market value of the stock due to the repurchase will not be taxed until the owner sells the stock. Of course, when the stock is sold, if the proceeds are in excess of the original purchase price, the capital gain will be taxed as ordinary income. The IRS allegedly watches firms that regularly repurchase stock and levies a penalty if it believes the repurchases have been made to delay the payment of taxes by the stockholders. Enforcement in this area appears to be relatively lax.

---

6 The repurchase of common stock for retirement is similar to the payment of cash dividends since it involves the distribution of cash to the firm's owners, who are the sellers of the shares. *(Fact)*

FACT OR FABLE?

The Repurchase Process

When a company intends to repurchase a block of outstanding shares, it should make shareholders aware of its intentions. Specifically, it should advise them of the purpose of the repurchase (acquisitions, stock options, gain in book value, retirement, and so forth) and the disposition (if any) planned for the repurchased shares (traded for shares of another firm, distribution to executives, held in the treasury, and so forth).

Three basic methods of repurchase are commonly used. One is to purchase shares on the *open market*. This places upward pressure on the price of shares if the number of shares being repurchased is reasonably large in comparison with the total number outstanding. The second method is through tender offers.[6] A **tender offer** is a formal offer by the firm to purchase a given number of shares at a specified price. The price at which a tender offer is made is set above the current market price in order to attract sellers. If the number of shares desired cannot be repurchased through the tender offer, open-market purchases can be used to obtain the additional shares. Tender offers are preferred when large numbers of shares are repurchased since the company's intentions are clearly stated and each stockholder has an opportunity to sell his or her shares at the tendered price. The third method sometimes used to repurchase shares involves arranging to purchase on a

tender offer A formal offer by a firm to purchase a given number of its shares at a specified price.

---

[6] Tender offers are discussed in greater detail in Chapter 19. The motive for these offers may be to acquire control of another firm rather than to tender the firm's own shares.

negotiated basis a large block of shares from one or more major stockholders. Again, in this case the firm would have to state its intentions and make certain that the purchase price is fair and equitable in view of the interests and opportunities of the remaining shareholders.

Summary

● Holders of equity capital (common and preferred stock) are owners of the firm. They have claims on income and assets that are secondary to the claims of creditors, have no maturity date, and do not receive tax benefits similar to those given debtholders.

● The common stock of a firm can be privately owned, closely owned, or publicly owned. It can be sold with or without a par value. Not all shares authorized in the corporate charter will be outstanding. If the firm has treasury stock, it will have issued more shares than are outstanding.

● Some firms issue both voting and nonvoting common stock. Proxies can be used to transfer voting rights from one party to another. Either majority voting or cumulative voting may be used by the firm to elect its directors.

● Holders of common stock may receive stock rights which give them an opportunity to purchase new common stock at a reduced price on a pro rata basis. Rights may be exercised, sold, purchased, or allowed to expire. In addition to rights offerings, new common stock can be sold directly through stock options or a stock-purchase plan, or publicly through an investment banker.

● Basic advantages of common stock include the minimum of constraints it places on the firm, its lack of a maturity date, and its ability to increase the firm's borrowing power. Disadvantages include the potential dilution of ownership and earnings and its high cost.

● The cash dividend decision is normally a quarterly decision made by the corporate board of directors which establishes the record date and payment date. Because the dividend decision affects the level of retained earnings, it can significantly affect the firm's external financing requirements.

● Some firms offer dividend reinvestment plans that allow stockholders to acquire shares in lieu of cash dividends, often at an attractive price. A company offering such a plan can either have a trustee buy outstanding shares on behalf of participating shareholders or it can issue new shares to plan participants.

● The residual theory of dividends suggests that dividend policy does not affect the value of the firm and therefore is irrelevant. However, the more widely accepted school of thought maintains that dividend policy is relevant since paying dividends reduces the owners' uncertainty, causing them to discount earnings at a lower rate and thereby raise the market value of the firm's stock.

● Certain legal, contractual, and internal constraints as well as growth prospects, owner considerations, and certain market considerations affect a firm's dividend policy, which should maximize the wealth of its owners while providing for sufficient financing. Commonly used dividend policies include a constant-payout-ratio, regular dividends, or low-regular-and-extra dividends.

● Occasionally firms may pay stock dividends as a replacement or supplement to cash dividends. Stock splits are sometimes used to enhance trading activity in a firm's shares. Stock repurchases can be made in lieu of cash dividend payments in order to retire outstanding shares and delay the payment of taxes.

Questions

17-1 How do debt and equity capital differ? What are the key differences between them with respect to ownership rights, claims on income and assets, maturity, and tax treatment?

17-2 Why is the common stockholder considered the true owner of a firm? What risks do common stockholders take that other suppliers of long-term capital do not?

17-3 What are *proxies?* How are they used? How do majority and cumulative voting systems differ? Which of these voting systems would be preferred by the minority shareholders? Why?

17-4 What are *stock rights?* Compare the theoretical value of rights when a stock is selling *with rights* with its *ex rights* value. Do these values typically equal their market price? Why?

17-5 How are *stock options* and *stock-purchase plans* used to sell new common stock directly? How is new common stock sold publicly?

17-6 What are the key advantages and disadvantages of using common stock financing as a source of new capital funds?

17-7 How do the date of record and the holders of record relate to the payment of cash dividends? What does the term *ex dividend* mean? Who sets the dividend payment date?

17-8 What is a *dividend reinvestment plan?* What benefit is available to plan participants? Describe the two ways companies can handle such plans.

17-9 Describe the *residual theory of dividends*. Would following this approach lead to a stable dividend? What are the two key positions with respect to the relevance of dividend policy? Explain.

17-10 Briefly describe each of the following factors affecting dividend policy:

    a. Legal constraints

    b. Contractual constraints

    c. Internal constraints

    d. Growth prospects

    e. Owner considerations

    f. Market considerations

17-11 What are (1) a constant-payout-ratio dividend policy, (2) a regular dividend policy, and (3) a low-regular-and-extra dividend policy? What are the effects of these policies?

17-12 What is a *stock dividend?* If it is more costly to issue stock than to pay cash dividends, why do firms issue stock dividends? Compare a *stock split* with a stock dividend.

17-13 What is the logic behind *repurchasing shares* of common stock to distribute excess cash to the firm's owners? How might this raise the per-share earnings and market price of outstanding shares?

Self-Test Problems

(Solutions on page 638)

ST-1 Bulah Gas wishes to raise $1 million in common equity financing using a rights offering. The company has 500,000 shares of common stock outstanding that have recently traded for $25 to $28 per share. The firm believes that if the subscription price is set at $25, the shares will be fully subscribed.

    a. Determine the number of new shares the firm must sell to raise the desired amount of capital.

    b. How many shares will each right entitle a holder of one share to purchase?

    c. If Candy Lopez, who holds 5,000 shares of Bulah Gas, exercises her rights, how many additional shares can she purchase?

    d. What is the theoretical value of a right if the current market price is $27 *with rights* and the subscription price is $25? Answer for both stock selling *with rights* and stock selling *ex rights*.

    e. Approximately how much could Candy get for her rights immediately after the stock goes *ex rights?*

ST-2 The Off-Shore Steel Company has earnings available for common stockholders of $2 million and 500,000 shares of common stock outstanding at $60 per share. The firm is currently contemplating the payment of $2 per share in cash dividends.

    a. Calculate the firm's current earnings per share (EPS) and price/earnings (P/E) ratio.

    b. If the firm can repurchase stock at $62 per share, how many shares can be purchased in lieu of making the proposed cash dividend payment?

    c. How much will the EPS be after the proposed repurchase? Why?

    d. If the stock will sell at the old P/E ratio, what will the market price be after repurchase?

    e. Compare and contrast the earnings per share before and after the proposed repurchase.

    f. Compare and contrast the stockholders' position under the dividend and repurchase alternatives.

Problems

17-1 (**Accounting for Common Stock**) What accounting entries on the firm's balance sheet would result from the following cases?

a. A firm sells 10,000 shares of $1-par common stock at $13 per share.

b. A firm sells 20,000 shares of $2-par common and receives $100,000.

c. A firm sells 200,000 shares of no-par common stock for $8 million.

d. A firm sells 14,000 shares of common stock for the par value of $5 per share.

17-2 (**Majority versus Cumulative Voting**) Mountain Products is electing five new directors to the board. The company has 1,000 shares of common stock outstanding. The management, which controls 54 percent of the common shares outstanding, backs candidates A through E; the minority shareholders are backing candidates F through J.

a. If the firm uses a *majority voting system,* how many directors will each group elect?

b. If the firm uses a *cumulative voting system,* how many directors will each group elect?

c. Discuss the differences between these two approaches and the resulting election outcomes.

17-3 (**Majority versus Cumulative Voting**) Determine the number of directors that can be elected by the *minority shareholders* using (1) majority voting and (2) cumulative voting in each of the following cases:

Case	Number of shares outstanding	Percentage of shares held by minority	Number of directors to be elected
A	140,000	20%	3
B	100,000	40	7
C	175,000	30	4
D	880,000	40	5
E	1,000,000	18	9

17-4 (**Number of Rights**) Indicate (1) how many shares of stock one right is worth and (2) the number of shares a given stockholder, X, can purchase in each of the following cases:

Case	Number of shares outstanding	Number of new shares to be issued	Number of shares held by stockholder X
A	900,000	30,000	600
B	1,400,000	35,000	200
C	800,000	40,000	2,000
D	60,000	12,000	1,200
E	180,000	36,000	1,000

17-5 **(Theoretical Value of Rights)** Determine the theoretical value of the right when the stock is selling (1) *with rights* and (2) *ex rights* in each of the following cases:

Case	Market value of stock *with rights*	Subscription price of stock	Number of rights needed to purchase one share of stock
A	$20.00	$17.50	4
B	56.00	50.00	3
C	41.00	30.00	6
D	50.00	40.00	5
E	92.00	82.00	8

17-6 **(Value of a Right)** Your sister-in-law is a stockholder in a corporation that recently declared a rights offering. In need of cash, she has offered to sell you her rights for 30 cents each. The key data relative to the stock and associated rights are as follows:

Current stock price *with rights*	$37.25/share
Subscription price of stock rights	$36.00/share
Number of rights needed to purchase one share of common stock	4

a. Determine the theoretical value of the rights when the stock is trading *with rights*.

b. Determine the theoretical value of the rights when the stock is trading *ex rights*.

c. Discuss your findings in **a** and **b**. Would it be desirable to accept your sister-in-law's offer?

17-7 **(Sale of Common Equity—Rights)** Ziegler Manufacturing is interested in raising $600,000 of new equity capital through a rights offering. The firm currently has 300,000 shares of common stock outstanding. It expects to set the subscription price at $25 and anticipates that the stock will sell for $29 *with rights*.

a. Calculate the number of new shares the firm must sell to raise the desired amount of funds.

b. How many rights will be needed to purchase one share of stock at the subscription price?

c. Willie Jones holds 48,000 shares of Ziegler common stock. If he exercises his rights, how many additional shares can he purchase?

d. Determine the theoretical value of a right when the stock is selling (1) *with rights* and (2) *ex rights*.

e. Approximately how much could Jones get for his rights immediately after the stock goes *ex rights?*

f. If the date of record for Ziegler Manufacturing was Monday, March 15, on what dates would the stock sell (1) *with rights* and (2) *ex rights?*

17-8 **(Dividend Payment Procedures)** Wood Shoes, at the quarterly dividend meeting, declared a cash dividend of $1.10 per share for holders of record on Monday, July 10. The firm has

300,000 shares of common stock outstanding and has set a payment date of July 31. Prior to the dividend declaration, the firm's key accounts were as follows:

Cash	$500,000	Dividends payable	$ 0
		Retained earnings	2,500,000

a. Show the entries after the meeting adjourned.

b. When is the ex dividend date?

c. After the July 31 payment date, what values would the key accounts have?

d. What effect, if any, will the dividend have on the firm's total assets?

17-9 **(Residual Dividend Policy)** As president of Young's of California, a large clothing chain, you have just received a letter from a major stockholder. The stockholder asks about the company's dividend policy. In fact, the stockholder has asked you to estimate the amount of the dividend you are likely to pay next year. You have not yet collected all the information about the expected dividend payment, but you do know the following:

(1) The company will follow a residual dividend policy.

(2) The total capital budget for next year is likely to be one of three amounts, depending on the results of capital budgeting studies currently under way. The capital expenditure amounts are $2 million, $3 million, and $4 million.

(3) The forecasted level of potential retained earnings next year is $2 million.

(4) The target or optimal capital structure is a debt ratio of 40 percent.

You have decided to respond by sending the stockholder the best information available to you.

a. Describe a residual dividend policy.

b. Compute the amount of the dividend (or the amount of new equity needed) and the dividend payout ratio for each of the three capital expenditure amounts.

c. Compare, contrast, and discuss the amount of dividends (calculated in **b**) associated with each of the three capital expenditure amounts.

17-10 **(Dividend Constraints)** The Howe Company's stockholders' equity account is as follows:

Common stock (400,000 shares at $4 par)	$1,600,000
Paid-in capital in excess of par	1,000,000
Retained earnings	1,900,000
Total stockholders' equity	$4,500,000

The earnings available for common stockholders from this period's operations are $100,000, which have been included as part of the $1.9 million retained earnings.

a. What is the maximum dividend per share the firm can pay? (Assume that legal capital includes *all* paid-in capital.)

b. If the firm has $160,000 in cash, what is the largest per-share dividend it can pay without borrowing?

c. Indicate the accounts and changes, if any, that will result if the firm pays the dividends indicated in **a** and **b.**

d. Indicate the effects of an $80,000 cash dividend on stockholders' equity.

17-11 **(Dividend Constraints)** A firm has $800,000 in paid-in capital, retained earnings of $40,000 (including the current year's earnings), and 25,000 shares of common stock outstanding. In the most recent year it has $29,000 of earnings available for the common stockholders.

a. What is the most the firm can pay in cash dividends to each common shareholder? (Assume that legal capital includes *all* paid-in capital.)

b. What effect would a cash dividend of $.80 per share have on the firm's balance sheet entries?

c. If the firm cannot raise any new funds from external sources, what do you consider the key constraint with respect to the magnitude of the firm's dividend payments? Why?

17-12 (Alternative Dividend Policies) A firm has had the earnings per share over the past 10 years shown in the following table.

Year	Earnings per share
1988	$4.00
1987	3.80
1986	3.20
1985	2.80
1984	3.20
1983	2.40
1982	1.20
1981	1.80
1980	−0.50
1979	0.25

a. If the firm's dividend policy was based on a constant payout ratio of 40 percent for all years with positive earnings and a zero payout otherwise, determine the annual dividend for each year.

b. If the firm had a dividend payout of $1.00 per share, increasing by $.10 per share whenever the dividend payout fell below 50 percent for two consecutive years, what annual dividend did the firm pay each year?

c. If the firm's policy was to pay $.50 per share each period except when earnings per share exceed $3.00, when an extra dividend equal to 80 percent of earnings beyond $3.00 would be paid, what annual dividend did the firm pay each year?

d. Discuss the pros and cons of each dividend policy described in **a** through **c**.

17-13 (Alternative Dividend Policies) Given the following earnings per share over the period 1981–1988, determine the annual dividend per share under each of the policies set forth in **a** through **d**.

Year	Earnings per share
1988	$1.40
1987	1.56
1986	1.20
1985	−0.85
1984	1.05
1983	0.60
1982	1.00
1981	0.44

a. Pay out 50 percent of earnings in all years with positive earnings.

b. Pay $.50 per share and increase to $.60 per share whenever earnings per share rise above $.90 per share for two consecutive years.

c. Pay $.50 per share except when earnings exceed $1.00 per share, when there would be an extra dividend of 60 percent of earnings above $1.00 per share.

d. Combine policies in **b** and **c**. When the dividend is raised (in **b**), raise the excess dividend base (in **c**) from $1.00 to $1.10 per share.

e. Compare and contrast each of the dividend policies described in **a** through **d**.

17-14 (Stock Dividend—Firm) Columbia Paper has a stockholders' equity account, given here. The firm's common stock has a current market price of $30 per share.

Preferred stock	$100,000
Common stock (10,000 shares at $2 par)	20,000
Paid-in capital in excess of par	280,000
Retained earnings	100,000
Total stockholders' equity	$500,000

a. Show the effects on Columbia Paper of a 5 percent stock dividend.

b. Show the effects of (1) a 10 percent and (2) a 20 percent stock dividend.

c. In light of your answers to **a** and **b**, discuss the effects of stock dividends on stockholders' equity.

17-15 (Cash versus Stock Dividend) Milwaukee Tool has a stockholders' equity account as given. The firm's common stock currently sells for $4 per share.

Preferred stock	$ 100,000
Common stock (400,000 shares at $1 par)	400,000
Paid-in capital in excess of par	200,000
Retained earnings	320,000
Total stockholders' equity	$1,020,000

a. Show the effects on the firm of a $.01, $.05, $.10, and $.20 per-share *cash* dividend.

b. Show the effects on the firm of a 1 percent, 5 percent, 10 percent, and 20 percent *stock* dividend.

c. Compare the effects in **a** and **b**. What are the significant differences in the two methods of paying dividends?

17-16 (Stock Dividend—Investor) Sarah Warren currently holds 400 shares of Nutri-Foods. The firm has 40,000 shares outstanding. The firm most recently had earnings available for common stockholders of $80,000, and its stock has been selling for $22 per share. The firm intends to retain its earnings and pay a 10 percent stock dividend.

a. How much does the firm currently earn per share?

b. What proportion of the firm does Sarah Warren currently own?

c. What proportion of the firm will Ms. Warren own after the stock dividend? Explain your answer.

d. At what market price would you expect the stock to sell after the stock dividend?

e. Discuss what effect, if any, the payment of stock dividends will have on Ms. Warren's share of the ownership and earnings of Nutri-Foods.

17-17 (Stock Dividend—Investor) Security Data Company has outstanding 50,000 shares of common stock currently selling at $40 per share. The firm most recently had earnings available for common stockholders of $120,000, but it has decided to retain these funds and is considering either a 5 percent or a 10 percent stock dividend in lieu of a cash dividend.

a. Determine the firm's current earnings per share.

b. If Sam Waller currently owns 500 shares of the firm's stock, determine his proportion of ownership currently and under each of the proposed dividend plans. Explain your findings.

c. Calculate and explain the market price per share under each of the stock dividend plans.

d. For each of the proposed stock dividends, calculate the earnings per share after payment of the stock dividend.

e. How much would the value of Sam Waller's holdings be under each of the plans? Explain.

f. As Mr. Waller, would you have any preference with respect to the proposed stock dividends? Why or why not?

17-18 (Stock Split—Firm) Growth Industries' current stockholders' equity account is as follows:

Preferred stock	$ 400,000
Common stock (600,000 shares at $3 par)	1,800,000
Paid-in capital in excess of par	200,000
Retained earnings	800,000
Total stockholders' equity	$3,200,000

a. Indicate the change, if any, expected if the firm declares a 2-for-1 stock split.

b. Indicate the change, if any, expected if the firm declares a 1-for-1½ *reverse* stock split.

c. Indicate the change, if any, expected if the firm declares a 3-for-1 stock split.

d. Indicate the change, if any, expected if the firm declares a 6-for-1 stock split.

e. Indicate the change, if any, expected if the firm declares a 1-for-4 *reverse* stock split.

17-19 (Stock Split—Firm) Mammoth Corporation is considering a 3-for-2 stock split. It currently has the stockholders' equity position shown below. The current stock price is $120 per share. The most recent period's earnings available for common is included in retained earnings.

Preferred stock	$ 1,000,000
Common stock (100,000 shares at $3 par)	300,000
Paid-in capital in excess of par	1,700,000
Retained earnings	10,000,000
Total stockholders' equity	$13,000,000

a. What effects on Mammoth would result from the stock split?

b. What change in stock price would you expect to result from the stock split?

c. What is the maximum cash dividend *per share* the firm could pay on common stock before and after the stock split? (Assume that legal capital includes *all* paid-in capital.)

d. Contrast your answers to **a** through **c** with the circumstances surrounding a 50 percent stock dividend.

e. Explain the differences between stock splits and stock dividends.

17-20 (Stock Repurchase) The following financial data on the Boyd Recording Company are available:

Earnings available for common stockholders	$800,000
Number of shares of common outstanding	400,000
Earnings per share ($800,000 ÷ 400,000)	$2
Market price per share	$20
Price/earnings (P/E) ratio ($20 ÷ $2)	10

The firm is currently contemplating using $400,000 of its earnings to pay cash dividends of $1 per share or repurchasing stock at $21 per share.

a. Approximately how many shares of stock can the firm repurchase at the $21-per-share price using the funds that would have gone to pay the cash dividend?

b. Calculate earnings per share (EPS) after the repurchase. Explain your calculations.

c. If the stock still sells at 10 times earnings, how much will the market price be after the repurchase?

d. Compare and contrast the pre- and post-repurchase earnings per share. Discuss the tax implications of this action.

e. Compare and contrast the stockholders' position under the dividend and repurchase alternatives.

Solutions to Self-Test Problems

ST-1 a. Number of new shares $= \dfrac{\$1,000,000 \text{ to be raised}}{\$25 \text{ subscription price}} = \underline{\underline{40,000 \text{ shares}}}$

b. Number of shares per right $= \dfrac{40,000 \text{ new shares}}{500,000 \text{ shares outstanding}} = \underline{\underline{.08 \text{ shares}}}$

c. Candy Lopez's additional shares $= .08$ shares/right $\times 5,000$ rights (1 right/share)
$$= \underline{\underline{400 \text{ shares}}}$$

d. *Variables:*
$M_w = \$27$ market value of stock with rights
$S = \$25$ subscription price
$N = \dfrac{1}{.08} = 12.5$ rights needed to purchase one share of stock

Theoretical Value of Right With Rights, R_w:
$$R_w = \frac{M_w - S}{N + 1} = \frac{\$27 - \$25}{12.5 + 1} = \frac{\$2}{13.5} = \underline{\underline{\$.148}}$$

Theoretical Value of Right Ex Rights, R_e:
$M_e = M_w - R_w = \$27 - .148 = \$26.852$ market value of stock trading ex rights
$$R_e = \frac{M_e - S}{N} = \frac{\$26.852 - \$25}{12.5} = \frac{\$1.852}{12.5} = \underline{\underline{\$.148}}$$

e. Candy should receive at least the theoretical value of $.148 per right—a total of $740 for her 5,000 rights ($.148 × 5,000 = $740). If investors expect the price of Bulah Gas to rise during the period the rights are exercisable, the market value of the rights would be above their theoretical value.

ST-2 a. Earnings per share (EPS) = $\dfrac{\$2{,}000{,}000 \text{ earnings available}}{500{,}000 \text{ shares of common outstanding}} = \underline{\underline{\$4.00/\text{share}}}$

Price/earnings (P/E) ratio = $\dfrac{\$60 \text{ market price}}{\$4.00 \text{ EPS}} = \underline{\underline{15}}$

b. Proposed dividends = 500,000 shares × $2 per share = $1,000,000

Shares that can be repurchased = $\dfrac{\$1{,}000{,}000}{\$62} = \underline{\underline{16{,}129 \text{ shares}}}$

c. *After proposed repurchase:*
Shares outstanding = 500,000 − 16,129 = 483,871

EPS = $\dfrac{\$2{,}000{,}000}{483{,}871} = \underline{\underline{\$4.13/\text{share}}}$

d. Market price = 15 × $4.13/share = $\underline{\underline{\$61.95/\text{share}}}$

e. The earnings per share (EPS) are higher after the repurchase since there are fewer shares of stock outstanding (483,871 shares versus 500,000 shares) to divide up the firm's $2,000,000 of available earnings.

f. In both cases the stockholders would receive $2 per share—a $2 cash dividend in the dividend case or an approximately $2 increase in share price ($60.00 per share to $61.95 per share) in the repurchase case. [*Note:* The $.05 per share ($2.00 − $1.95) difference is due to rounding.]

CHAPTER 18

Other Sources: Preferred Stock, Leasing, Convertibles, Warrants, and Options

FACT OR FABLE?
Are the following statements fact *(true)* or fable *(false)*?

1
Preferred stock is typically issued in large quantities, is noncumulative with respect to dividends passed, and provides for participation with common stockholders in the receipt of dividends beyond a specified amount.

2
Financial (or capital) leases are long-term, noncancelable leases requiring total payments greater than the lessor's cost of the leased asset, whereas operating leases are cancelable, short-term agreements under which total payments are less than cost.

3
Lease-versus-purchase decisions can be made by first finding the present value of the after-tax cash outflows associated with both leasing and purchasing, and then selecting the alternative with the higher present value.

4
The market value of a convertible security typically is greater than its straight or conversion value as a result of positive investor expectations concerning future stock price movements.

5
While both convertible bonds and stock-purchase warrants when converted or exercised shift capital structure to a less highly levered position, a much greater reduction typically results from conversion of convertibles.

6
Call and put options are extremely popular investment vehicles that play an important role in the fund-raising activities of the firms that issue them.

American Airlines and Northwest Airlines in early 1987 leased a total of eight new jets for their fleets in deals totaling $350 million. U.S. Steel leased a $690 million plant. Thousands of businesses take advantage of leasing as a popular financial arrangement for obtaining the use of equipment without commiting the large blocks of capital required by purchasing.

Virtually any kind of business equipment or facility can be leased, and the leasing business itself has grown to an estimated $100 billion industry in recent years. Some leasing arrangements provide maintenance service and stipulate the return of the equipment at the end of the period. Furthermore, lease payments, which are tax-deductible expenses, do not always appear as a liability on the company's balance sheet.

At the time U.S. Steel made its arrangements, an industry-wide recession prompted the firm's decision not to go to the capital markets for funding. The General Electric Credit Corporation, a major industrial and commercial leasing firm, structured a complex leasing deal involving over fifteen banks and several foreign countries. Bell Atlantic TriCon, another large equipment lessor, arranged the airliner deals for McDonnell-Douglas and Boeing planes. In that instance the leasing company shared the purchase price of the planes and set up a ''leveraged lease'' for TriCon's portion of the ownership.

While such complex arrangements are becoming more common, most leases are smaller and much simpler to arrange. Companies can shop among various lessors to obtain a service and pricing arrangement tailored to their needs for nearly any piece of equipment for traditional business use. Most experts agree that the many bottom-line advantages to leasing will continue to make it a popular means of financing capital equipment.

Leasing, as used by American Airlines, Northwest Airlines, and U.S. Steel, is just one of a number of available financing techniques providing an alternative to the use of straight long-term debt or common stock. Here we look at the key roles, features, costs, and advantages and disadvantages of other sources of long-term financing including preferred stock, leasing, convertible securities, stock-purchase warrants, and options.

Preferred Stock

Preferred stock gives its holders certain privileges that make them senior to common stockholders. Because of this, firms generally do not issue large quantities of preferred stock. Preferred stockholders are assured a fixed periodic return, which is stated either as a percentage or as a dollar amount. In other words, a 5 percent preferred stock or a $5 preferred stock can be issued. The way the dividend is stated depends on whether the preferred stock has a par value. **Par-value preferred stock** has a stated face value. The annual dividend is stated as a percentage on par-value preferred stock and in dollars on **no-par preferred stock,** which does not have a stated face value. Thus a 5 percent preferred stock with a $100 par value is expected to pay $5 (5 percent of $100) in dividends per year, and a $5 preferred stock with no par value is also expected to pay its $5 stated dividend each year.

par-value preferred stock
Preferred stock with a stated face value that is used with the stated dividend percentage to determine the annual dollar dividend.

no-par preferred stock
Preferred stock that has a stated annual dollar dividend, but no stated face value.

adjustable-rate (or floating-rate) preferred stock (ARPS) Preferred stock whose dividend rate is tied to interest rates on specific government securities.

Most preferred stock has a fixed dividend, but some firms issue **adjustable-rate (or floating-rate) preferred stock (ARPS).** Such stocks have a dividend rate tied to interest rates on specific government securities. Rate adjustments are commonly made quarterly, and typically the rate must be maintained within certain preset limits. The appeal of ARPS is the protection offered investors against sharp rises in interest rates, since the dividend rate on ARPS will rise with interest rates. From the firm's perspective, adjustable-rate preferreds have appeal since they can be sold at an initially lower dividend rate and the scheduled dividend rate will fall if interest rates decline.

Basic Rights of Preferred Stockholders

The basic rights of preferred stockholders with respect to the distribution of earnings, the distribution of assets, and voting are somewhat more favorable than the rights of common stockholders. Because preferred stock is a form of ownership and has no maturity date, its claims on income and assets are secondary to those of the firm's creditors.

Distribution of Earnings

Preferred stockholders are given preference over common stockholders with respect to the distribution of earnings. If the stated preferred stock dividend is *passed* (not paid) by the board of directors, the payment of dividends to common stockholders is prohibited. It is this preference in dividend distribution that makes common stockholders the true risk takers with respect to receipt of periodic returns.

Distribution of Assets

Preferred stockholders are usually given preference over common stockholders in the liquidation of assets as a result of a firm's bankruptcy, although they must wait until all creditors have been satisfied. The amount of the claim of preferred stockholders in liquidation is normally equal to the par, or stated, value of the preferred stock. The preferred stockholder's preference over the common stockholder places the common stockholder in the more risky position with respect to recovery of investment.

Voting Rights

Preferred stock is often considered a *quasi-debt* since, much like interest on debt, it yields a fixed periodic (dividend) payment. Of course, as ownership preferred stock is unlike debt in that it has no maturity date. Because their claim on the firm's income is fixed and takes precedence over the claim of common stockholders, preferred stockholders are therefore not exposed to the same degree of risk as common stockholders. They are consequently *not* normally given the right to vote.

Features of Preferred Stock

A number of features are generally included as part of a preferred stock issue. These features, along with a statement of the stock's par value, the amount of dividend payments, the dividend payment dates, and any restrictive covenants, are specified in an agreement similar to a *term loan agreement* or *bond indenture* (see Chapter 16).

Restrictive Covenants

The restrictive covenants commonly found in a preferred stock issue are aimed at assuring the continued existence of the firm and, most important, regular payment of the stated dividend. These covenants include provisions related to passing dividends, the sale of senior securities, mergers, sales of assets, working capital requirements, and the payment of common stock dividends or common stock repurchases. The violation of preferred stock covenants usually permits preferred stockholders to force the retirement of their stock at or above its par, or stated, value.

Cumulation

Most preferred stock is **cumulative** with respect to any dividends passed. That is, all dividends in arrears must be paid prior to the payment of dividends to common stockholders. If preferred stock is **noncumulative,** passed (unpaid) dividends do not accumulate. In this case only the most recent dividend must be paid prior to paying dividends to common stockholders. Since the common stockholders, who are the firm's true owners, can receive dividends only after the dividend claims of preferred stockholders have been satisfied, it is in the firm's best interest to pay preferred dividends when they are due.[1] The following example will help clarify the distinction between cumulative and noncumulative preferred stock.

cumulative preferred stock Preferred stock for which all passed (unpaid) dividends in arrears must be paid prior to payment of dividends to common stockholders.

noncumulative preferred stock Preferred stock for which passed (unpaid) dividends do not accumulate.

Example
Zimmer Corporation currently has outstanding an issue of $6 preferred stock on which quarterly dividends of $1.50 are to be paid. Due to a cash shortage, the last two quarterly dividends were passed. The directors of the company have been receiving a large number of complaints from common stockholders, who have of course not received any dividends in the past two quarters either. If the preferred stock is cumulative, the company will have to pay its preferred shareholders $4.50 per share ($3.00 of dividends in arrears plus the current $1.50 dividend) prior to paying dividends to its common stockholders. If the preferred stock is noncumulative, however, the firm must pay only the current $1.50 dividend to its preferred stockholders prior to paying dividends to its common stockholders.

Participation

Most issues of preferred stock are **nonparticipating,** which means that preferred stockholders receive only the specified dividend payments. Occasionally, **participating preferred stock** is issued. This type provides for dividend payments based on certain formulas allowing preferred stockholders to participate with common stockholders in the receipt of dividends beyond a specified amount. This feature is included only when the firm considers it absolutely necessary in order to obtain badly needed funds.

nonparticipating preferred stock Preferred stock whose stockholders receive only the specified dividend payments.

participating preferred stock Preferred stock that provides for dividend payments based on certain formulas allowing preferred stockholders to participate with common stockholders in the receipt of dividends beyond a specified amount.

---

[1] Most preferred stock is cumulative since it is difficult to sell noncumulative stock. The common stockholders will obviously prefer noncumulative preferred to be issued, since it does not place them in quite as risky a position. But they must recognize that it is often in the best interest of the firm to sell *cumulative* preferred stock.

Call Feature

Preferred stock is generally *callable,* which means that the issuer can retire outstanding stock within a certain period of time at a specified price. The call option generally cannot be exercised until a period of years has elapsed since the issuance of the stock. The call price is normally set above the initial issuance price, but may decrease according to a predetermined schedule as time passes. Making preferred stock callable provides the issuer with a method of bringing the fixed-payment commitment of the preferred issue to an end.

conversion feature A provision permitting the holder of a preferred stock (or bond) to transfer it into a specified number of shares of common stock.

Conversion Feature

Preferred stock quite often contains a **conversion feature** that permits its transference into a specified number of shares of common stock. Sometimes the conversion ratio, or number of shares of common stock, changes according to a prespecified formula. A detailed discussion of conversion is presented later in this chapter.

FACT OR FABLE?

[1] Preferred stock is typically issued in large quantities, is noncumulative with respect to dividends passed, and provides for participation with common stockholders in the receipt of dividends beyond a specified amount. *(Fable)*

Preferred stock is typically *not issued in large quantities, is cumulative* with respect to dividends passed, and *does not provide for participation* with common stockholders in the receipt of dividends beyond a specified amount.

Advantages and Disadvantages of Preferred Stock

It is difficult to generalize about the advantages and disadvantages of preferred stock due to the variety of features that may be incorporated in a preferred stock issue. The attractiveness of preferred stock is also affected by current interest rates and the firm's existing capital structure. Nevertheless, some key advantages and disadvantages are often cited.

Advantages

One commonly cited advantage of preferred stock is its *ability to increase leverage.* Since preferred stock obligates the firm to pay only fixed dividends to its holders, its presence helps to increase the firm's financial leverage. (The effects of preferred stock on a firm's financial leverage were discussed in Chapter 12.) Increased financial leverage will magnify the effects of increased earnings on common stockholders' returns.

A second advantage is the *flexibility* provided by preferred stock. Although preferred stock provides added leverage in much the same way as bonds, it differs from bonds in that the issuer can pass a dividend payment without suffering the consequences that result when an interest payment is missed on a bond. Preferred stock allows the issuer to keep its levered position without running as great a risk of being forced out of business in a lean year as it might if it missed interest payments on actual debt.

A third advantage of preferred stock has been its *use in mergers.* Often preferred stock is exchanged for the common stock of an acquired firm, with the preferred dividend set at a level equivalent to the historic dividend of the acquired firm. This allows the acquiring firm to state at the time of the acquisition that only a fixed dividend will be paid.

All other earnings can be reinvested to perpetuate the growth of the merged enterprise. In addition, this permits the owners of the acquired firm to be assured of a continuing stream of dividends equivalent to that which may have been provided prior to acquisition.

Disadvantages

Two major disadvantages are often cited for preferred stock. One is the *seniority of the preferred stockholder's claim*. Since holders of preferred stock are given preference over common stockholders with respect to the distribution of earnings and assets, the presence of preferred stock in a sense jeopardizes common stockholders' returns. If a firm has preferred stockholders to pay, and if the firm's after-tax earnings are quite variable, its ability to pay at least token dividends to common stockholders may be seriously impaired.

A second disadvantage of preferred stock is cost. The *cost of preferred stock financing is generally higher than that of debt financing*. The reason is that, unlike the payment of interest to bondholders, the payment of dividends to preferred stockholders is not guaranteed. Since preferred shareholders are willing to accept the added risk of purchasing preferred stock rather than long-term debt, they must be compensated with a higher return. Another factor causing the cost of preferred stock to be significantly greater than that of long-term debt is the fact that interest on debt is tax-deductible, whereas preferred stock dividends must be paid from after-tax earnings.

Leasing

Leasing, like long-term debt, allows the firm to obtain the use of certain fixed assets for which it must make a series of contractual, periodic, tax-deductible payments. The **lessee** is the receiver of the services of the assets under the lease contract, whereas the **lessor** is the owner of the assets. Leasing can take a number of forms. Here we discuss the basic types of leases, leasing arrangements, legal requirements of a lease, the lease contract, the lease-versus-purchase decision, the effects of leasing on future financing, and the advantages and disadvantages of leasing.

leasing The process by which a firm can obtain the use of certain fixed assets through a series of contractual, periodic, tax-deductible payments.

lessee The receiver of the services of the assets under a lease contract.

lessor The owner of assets which are being leased.

Basic Types of Leases

The two basic types of leases available to a business are *operating* and *financial* leases, the latter of which are often called *capital leases* by accountants. Each is briefly described below.

Operating Leases

An **operating lease** is normally a contractual arrangement whereby the lessee agrees to make periodic payments to the lessor for five or fewer years in order to obtain an asset's services. Such leases are generally *cancelable* at the option of the lessee, who may be required to pay a predetermined penalty for cancellation. Assets leased under operating leases generally have a usable life *longer* than the term of the lease. Usually, however, they would become less efficient and technologically obsolete if leased for a longer period of years. Computer systems are prime examples of assets whose relative efficiency is expected to diminish with new technological developments. The operating lease is therefore a common arrangement for obtaining such systems, as well as for other relatively short-lived assets such as automobiles.

operating lease A *cancelable* contractual arrangement whereby the lessee agrees to make the periodic payments to the lessor for five or fewer years for an asset's services.

SMALL BUSINESS

PRACTICAL TIPS FOR SECURING THE BEST LEASE

Sources of financing for an expanding business are numerous. It will likely get its long-term money from one kind of lender, its working capital from another, and its equipment financing from a lessor. Here are some practical tips a company can use in order to secure the best lease.

How can a firm find the best leasing company for its needs?
Finding a leasing company is basically the same procedure as finding any other important vendor. The firm should get recommendations from business associates, a trade association, or a lease broker.

The next step is selection of equipment and getting written bids from dealers. Generally, the leasing company cannot be expected to provide much help in equipment selection. That's not their role. In leasing, it's up to the firm to select the equipment that's best for it—find a dealer, negotiate the purchase price and warranty, arrange for installation and maintenance, and so forth. That done, the firm then finds a lessor that will make it a deal.

Leasing proposals should specify security deposit, number of payments, balloon payment if any, renewal option, and purchase option. The proposal should additionally include the lease rate and tax effects.

Compare the terms. Overall, which offer best meets the firm's needs right now? The firm should call in the two or three lessors whose proposals were most attractive and negotiate to get the terms best for it now.

Evidently, there are many more variables in leasing than in straight financing.
That's one of the advantages of leasing. A firm can customize the financing to its particular needs much more than it can with the typical equipment loan.

Once the firm's negotiated the lease that is best for it, then what?
Before the firm negotiates or even calls for proposals, financial records should be prepared. No one is going to lease anything to a firm until its financial information has been approved by the lessor's credit manager.

What's the next step?
Gather all the leasing documents that are presented by the lessor and review them very thoroughly before signing. Everything that was in the proposal should be in the contract, plus any oral representations.

What should a company watch out for?
Legalisms and variable terms. Make sure the firm's legal counsel goes over them carefully. If necessary, this language can be changed, and often it is.

The terms are those parts applying just to the firm. Compare each with what had been agreed to earlier, and discuss them with colleagues to make sure everything is as expected.

There are often differences in interpretation of terms, so it pays to review the contract carefully. Once satisfied with the contract, sign it. The sooner it is signed, the sooner the lessor issues a purchase order for the equipment.

Given the additional range of options provided by leasing, it seems as if it is almost always better than buying.
No, it isn't. In some instances it is better, in others it is not. Which way to go is a management decision that has to be carefully costed out. Leasing is just a way to supplement instead of replace conventional financing. Ideally, it should be part of a comprehensive financing program, whereby leasing and purchasing are systematically compared against your needs. For the astute business executive, it is another valuable management tool.

SOURCE: "Lease Your Way to Corporate Growth," by Russell Hindin. Reprinted by permission from *FE: the magazine for financial executives,* May 1984, copyright 1984 by Financial Executives Institute.

If an operating lease is held to maturity, the lessee at that time returns the leased asset to the lessor, who may lease it again or sell the asset. Normally the asset still has a positive market value at the termination of the lease. In some instances, the lease contract will give the lessee the opportunity to purchase the leased asset. Generally the total payments made by the lessee to the lessor are *less* than the initial cost of the leased asset paid by the lessor.

Financial (or Capital) Leases

A **financial (or capital) lease** is a *longer-term* lease than an operating lease. Financial leases are *noncancelable* and therefore obligate the lessee to make payments for the use of an asset over a predefined period of time. Even if the lessee does not require the service of the leased asset, it is contractually obligated to make payments over the life of the lease contract. Financial leases are commonly used for leasing land, buildings, and large pieces of fixed equipment. The noncancelable feature of the financial lease makes it quite similar to certain types of long-term debt. The lease payment becomes a fixed, tax-deductible expenditure that must be paid at predefined dates over a definite period. Failure to make the contractual payments may in some instances mean bankruptcy for the lessee.

Another distinguishing characteristic of the financial lease is that the total payments over the lease period are *greater* than the cost of the leased asset to the lessor. Because the lease term is closely aligned with the economic life of the asset, the lessor must receive more than the asset's purchase price in order to earn its required return on the investment. The emphasis in this chapter is on financial leases, since they result in inescapable long-term financial commitments by the firm. Some financial leases give the lessee a purchase option at maturity.

financial (or capital) lease A *longer-term* lease than an operating lease that is *noncancelable* and obligates the lessee to make payments for the use of an asset over a predefined period of time.

---

2 Financial (or capital) leases are long-term, noncancelable leases requiring total payments greater than the lessor's cost of the leased asset, whereas operating leases are cancelable, short-term agreements under which total payments are less than cost. *(Fact)*

FACT OR FABLE?

Leasing Arrangements

Lessors use three primary techniques for obtaining assets to be leased. The method depends largely on the desires of the prospective lessee. A **direct lease** results when a lessor owns or acquires the assets that are leased to a given lessee. In other words, the lessee did not previously own the assets it is leasing. A second technique commonly used by lessors to acquire leased assets is to purchase assets already owned by the lessee and lease them back. A **sale-leaseback arrangement** is normally initiated by a firm that needs funds for operations. By selling an existing asset to a lessor and then *leasing it back,* the lessee receives cash for the asset immediately while at the same time obligating itself to make fixed periodic payments for use of the leased asset. Leasing arrangements that include one or more third-party lenders are leveraged leases. Unlike direct and sale-leaseback arrangements, under a **leveraged lease** the lessor acts as an equity participant, supplying only about 20 percent of the cost of the asset, and a lender supplies the balance. In recent years leveraged leases have become especially popular in structuring leases of very expensive assets.

A lease agreement normally specifies whether the lessee is responsible for maintenance of the leased assets. Operating leases normally include **maintenance clauses** requiring the lessor to maintain the assets and make insurance and tax payments. Financial leases almost always require the lessee to pay maintenance and other costs. The lessee is usually given the option to renew a lease at its expiration. **Renewal options,** which grant lessees the right to re-lease assets at expiration, are especially common in operating leases, since their term is generally shorter than the usable life of the leased assets.

direct lease A lease under which a lessor owns or acquires the assets that are leased to a given lessee.

sale-leaseback arrangement A lease under which the lessee sells an asset for cash to a prospective lessor and then leases back the same asset, making periodic payments for its use.

leveraged lease A lease under which the lessor acts as an equity participant, supplying only about 20 percent of the cost of the asset, while a lender supplies the balance.

maintenance clauses Provisions within an operating lease requiring the lessor to maintain the assets and make insurance and tax payments.

renewal options Provisions especially common in operating leases that grant the lessee the option to re-lease assets at their expiration.

The lessor can be one of a number of parties. In operating lease arrangements, the lessor is quite likely to be the manufacturer's leasing subsidiary or an independent leasing company. Financial leases are frequently handled by independent leasing companies or the leasing subsidiaries of large financial institutions such as commercial banks and life insurance companies. Life insurance companies are especially active in real estate leasing. Pension funds, like commercial banks, have also been increasing their leasing activities.

Legal Requirements of a Lease

To prevent firms from using a leasing arrangement as a disguise for what is actually an installment loan, the Internal Revenue Service specifies certain conditions under which lease payments are tax-deductible. If a lease arrangement does not meet these basic requirements, then the lease payments are not completely tax-deductible.[2] To conform with the IRS code, a leasing arrangement must meet the following major conditions:[3]

1. The lessor must own the property and anticipate earning a pretax profit from leasing it.
2. The lessor and lessee must agree that the transaction is a lease, the term of the lease must conform to IRS requirements, and the lessor must specify it as "designated lease property" on its income tax return.
3. The lease must be entered into within 90 days after the property is placed in service.
4. The lessee can be given the option to purchase the property, but the price must be equal to or greater than 10 percent of the original purchase price.

The Lease Contract

The key items of the lease contract normally include the term, or duration, of the lease, provisions for its cancellation, lease payment amounts and dates, renewal features, purchase options, maintenance and associated cost provisions, and other provisions specified in the lease negotiation process. Although some provisions are optional, the leased assets, the terms of the agreement, the lease payment, and the payment interval must all be clearly specified in every lease agreement. Furthermore, the consequences of the lessee missing a payment or the violation of any other lease provisions by either the lessee or lessor must be clearly stated in the contract.

The Lease-Versus-Purchase Decision

The lease-versus-purchase, or lease-versus-buy, decision is one that commonly confronts firms contemplating the acquisition of new fixed assets. The alternatives available are (1) lease the assets, (2) borrow funds to purchase the assets, or (3) purchase the assets using available liquid cash. Alternatives 2 and 3, although they differ, are analyzed in a similar fashion. Even if the firm has the liquid resources with which to purchase the assets, the use of these funds is viewed as equivalent to borrowing. Therefore, here we need to compare only the leasing and purchasing alternatives.

---

[2] The IRS's concern stems from the fact that the full lease payment is tax-deductible, whereas in the case of an installment loan, only the interest component of the payment is tax-deductible. To obtain high current tax deductions, the firm would lease the asset over a specified period, at the end of which it could purchase the asset for a nominal amount. Such a scheme would permit the firm to maximize its tax deductions and still ultimately own the asset.

[3] This is not an exhaustive listing of the conditions, but it reflects the most important and limiting requirements.

The lease-versus-purchase decision is made using basic present-value techniques. The following steps are involved in the analysis:

Step 1: Find the *after-tax cash outflows for each year under the lease* alternative. This step generally involves a fairly simple tax adjustment of the annual lease payments.

Step 2: Find the *after-tax cash outflows for each year under the purchase* alternative. This step involves adjusting the scheduled loan payments for the tax shields resulting from the tax deductions attributable to interest and depreciation.

Step 3: Calculate the *present value of the cash outflows* associated with the lease (from step 1) and purchase (from step 2) alternatives using the *after-tax cost of debt* as the discount rate. While some controversy surrounds the appropriate discount rate, the after-tax cost of debt is used to evaluate the lease-versus-purchase decision because the decision itself involves the choice between two financing alternatives having very low risk. If we were evaluating whether a given machine should be acquired, the appropriate risk-adjusted rate or cost of capital would be used, but in this type of analysis we are attempting only to determine the best *financing* technique—leasing or borrowing.

Step 4: Choose the alternative with the *lowest present value* of cash outflows from step 3. This will be the *least cost* financing alternative.

The application of each of these steps is demonstrated in the following example.

Example

Roberts Company is contemplating acquiring a new machine tool costing $24,000. Discussions with various financial institutions have shown that leasing or purchasing arrangements can be made to obtain the use of the machine. The firm is in the 40 percent tax bracket.

Leasing: The firm would obtain a five-year lease requiring annual end-of-year lease payments of $6,000.[4] All maintenance, insurance, and other costs would be borne by the lessee.

Purchasing: The firm would finance the purchase of the machine with a 9 percent, five-year loan requiring end-of-year installment payments of $6,170.[5] The machine would be depreciated under ACRS using a five-year recovery period, which means that six years of depreciation would result (see Chapter 3).

Using this data, we can apply the steps presented earlier.

Step 1: The after-tax cash outflow from the lease payments can be found by multiplying the before-tax payment of $6,000 by one minus the tax rate, *T*, of 40 percent.

---

[4] Lease payments are generally made at the beginning of the year. In order to simplify the following discussions, end-of-year lease payments have been assumed.

[5] The annual loan payment on the 9 percent, five-year loan of $24,000 is calculated using the loan amortization technique described in Chapter 6. Dividing the present-value interest factor for an annuity, *PVIFA,* from Table A-4 at 9 percent for five years (3.890) into the loan principal of $24,000 results in the annual loan payment of $6170. For a more detailed explanation of loan amortization, see Chapter 6.

Table 18.1
Determining the Interest and Principal Components of the Roberts Company Loan Payments

End of year	Loan payments (1)	Beginning-of-year principal (2)	Payments Interest $[.09 \times (2)]$ (3)	Payments Principal $[(1) - (3)]$ (4)	End-of-year principal $[(2) - (4)]$ (5)
1	$6,170	$24,000	$2,160	$4,010	$19,990
2	6,170	19,990	1,799	4,371	15,619
3	6,170	15,619	1,406	4,764	10,855
4	6,170	10,855	977	5,193	5,662
5	6,170	5,662	510	5,660	—[a]

[a] The values in this table have been rounded to the nearest dollar, which results in a slight difference ($2) between the beginning-of-year 5 principal (in column 2) and the year 5 principal payment (in column 4).

$$\text{After-tax cash outflow from lease} = \$6,000 \times (1 - T)$$
$$= \$6,000 \times (1 - .40) = \$3,600$$

Therefore, the lease alternative will result in annual cash outflows over the five-year lease of $3,600.

Step 2: The after-tax cash outflow from the purchase alternative is a bit more difficult to find. First, the interest component of each annual loan payment must be determined since the Internal Revenue Service allows the deduction of interest only—not principal—from income for tax purposes. Table 18.1 presents the calculations required to split the loan payments into their interest and principal components. Columns 3 and 4 show the annual interest and principal paid in each of the five years.

Next we find the annual depreciation write-off resulting from the $24,000 machine. Using the applicable ACRS five-year recovery period depreciation percentages—20 percent in year 1; 32 percent in year 2; 19 percent in year 3; 12 percent in years 4 and 5; and 5 percent in year 6—given in Table 3.6 on page 66, results in the annual depreciation for each year given in column 2 of Table 18.2.

Table 18.2 presents the calculations required to determine the cash outflows[6] associated with borrowing to purchase the new machine. Column 6 of the table presents the after-tax cash outflows associated with the purchase alternative. A few points should be clarified with respect to the calculations in Table 18.2. The major cash outflow is the total loan payment for each year given in column 1. This outflow is reduced by the tax savings from writing off the depreciation and interest associated with the new machine and its financing, respectively. The resulting cash outflows are the after-tax cash outflows associated with the purchasing alternative.

[6] Although other cash outflows such as maintenance, insurance, and operating expenses may be relevant here, they would be the same under the lease and the purchase alternatives and, therefore, would cancel out in the final analysis.

Table 18.2
After-Tax Cash Outflows Associated with Purchasing for Roberts Company

End of year (1)	Loan payments (1)	Depreci-ation (2)	Interest[a] (3)	Total deductions [(2) + (3)] (4)	Tax shields [.40 × (4)] (5)	After-tax cash outflows [(1) − (5)] (6)
1	$6,170	$4,800	$2,160	$6,960	$2,784	$3,386
2	6,170	7,680	1,799	9,479	3,792	2,378
3	6,170	4,560	1,406	5,966	2,386	3,784
4	6,170	2,880	977	3,857	1,543	4,627
5	6,170	2,880	510	3,390	1,356	4,814
6	0	1,200	0	1,200	480	(480)

[a] From Table 18.1, column 3.

Table 18.3
A Comparison of the Cash Outflows Associated with Leasing Versus Purchasing for Roberts Company

End of year	Leasing			Purchasing		
	After-tax cash outflows (1)	Present-value factors[a] (2)	Present value of outflows [(1) × (2)] (3)	After-tax cash outflows[b] (4)	Present-value factors[a] (5)	Present value of outflows [(4) × (5)] (6)
1	$3,600	.943	$ 3,395	$3,386	.943	$ 3,193
2	3,600	.890	3,204	2,378	.890	2,116
3	3,600	.840	3,024	3,784	.840	3,179
4	3,600	.792	2,851	4,627	.792	3,665
5	3,600	.747	2,689	4,814	.747	3,596
6	0	.705	0	(480)	.705	(338)
	PV of cash outflows		$15,163	PV of cash outflows		$15,411

[a] From Table A-3, *PVIF*, for 6 percent and the corresponding year.
[b] From column 6 of Table 18.2.

Step 3: The present value of the cash outflows associated with the lease (from step 1) and purchase (from step 2) alternatives are calculated in Table 18.3 using the firm's 6 percent after-tax cost of debt.[7] Applying the appropriate present-value interest factors given in columns 2 and 5 to the after-tax cash outflows in columns 1 and 4 results in the present values of lease and purchase cash outflows given in

[7] Ignoring any flotation costs, the firm's after-tax cost of debt would be 5.4 percent [9% debt cost × (1 − .40 tax rate)]. To reflect both the flotation costs associated with selling new debt and the need to sell the debt at a discount, the use of an after-tax debt cost of 6 percent was believed to be the applicable discount rate. A more detailed discussion of techniques for calculating the after-tax cost of debt can be found in Chapter 11.

> columns 3 and 6, respectively. The sum of the present values of the cash outflows for the leasing alternative is given in column 3 of Table 18.3, and the sum for the purchasing alternative is given in column 6 of Table 18.3.
>
> **Step 4:** Since the present value of cash outflows for leasing ($15,163) is lower than that for purchasing ($15,411), the leasing alternative is preferred. Leasing results in an incremental savings of $248 ($15,411 − $15,163) and is therefore the less costly alternative.

The techniques described here for comparing leasing and purchasing alternatives may be applied in different ways. The approach illustrated using the Roberts Company data is one of the most straightforward. It is important to recognize that the lower cost of one alternative over the other results from factors such as the differing tax brackets of the lessor and lessee, different tax treatments of leases versus purchases, and differing risks and borrowing costs for lessor and lessee. Therefore, when making a lease-versus-purchase decision the firm will find that inexpensive borrowing opportunities, high required lessor returns, and a low risk of obsolescence increase the attractiveness of purchasing. Subjective factors must also be included in the decision-making process. Like most financial decisions, the lease-versus-purchase decision requires a certain degree of judgment or intuition.

FACT OR FABLE?

3 Lease-versus-purchase decisions can be made by first finding the present value of the after-tax cash outflows associated with both leasing and purchasing, and then selecting the alternative with the higher present value. *(Fable)*

Lease-versus-purchase decisions can be made by first finding the present value of the after-tax cash outflows associated with both leasing and purchasing, and then selecting the alternative with the *lower* present value.

Effects of Leasing on Future Financing

Since leasing is considered a type of financing, it affects the firm's future financing. Lease payments are shown as a tax-deductible expense on the firm's income statement. Anyone analyzing the firm's income statement would probably recognize that an asset is being leased, although the actual details of the amount and term of the lease would be unclear. The following sections discuss the lease disclosure requirements established by the Financial Accounting Standards Board (FASB) and the effect of leases on financial ratios.

Lease Disclosure Requirements

After many years of debate and controversy, the *Financial Accounting Standards Board (FASB)* in November 1976, in Standard No. 13, ''Accounting for Leases,'' established requirements for the explicit disclosure of certain types of lease obligations on the firm's balance sheet. Standard No. 13 established criteria for classifying various types of leases and set reporting standards for each class. The standard defines a financial (capital) lease as one having *any* of the following elements:

1. The lease transfers ownership of the property to the lessee by the end of the lease term.

2. The lease contains an option to purchase the property at a "bargain" price.

3. The lease term is equal to 75 percent or more of the estimated economic life of the property.

4. At the beginning of the lease, the present value of the lease payments is equal to 90 percent or more of the fair market value of the leased property.

If a lease meets any of the above criteria, it is shown as a **capitalized lease,** meaning the present value of all its payments is included as an asset and corresponding liability on the firm's balance sheet. If a lease meets none of the above criteria it is an operating lease and need not be capitalized, but its basic features must be disclosed in a footnote to the financial statements. Standard No. 13, of course, establishes detailed guidelines to be used in capitalizing leases to reflect them as an asset and corresponding liability on the balance sheet. Subsequent standards have further refined lease capitalization and disclosure procedures. Let us look at an example.

capitalized lease
A *financial (capital) lease* that has the present value of all its payments included as an asset and corresponding liability on the firm's balance sheet, as required by *Financial Accounting Standards Board (FASB)* Standard No. 13.

Example

Lawrence Company is leasing an asset under a 10-year lease requiring annual end-of-year payments of $15,000. The lease can be capitalized merely by calculating the present value of the lease payments over the life of the lease. However, the rate at which the payments should be discounted is difficult to determine.[8] If 10 percent were used, the present, or capitalized, value of the lease would be $92,175 ($15,000 × 6.145). This value would be shown as an asset and corresponding liability on the firm's balance sheet, which should result in an accurate reflection of the firm's true financial position.

Leases and Financial Ratios

Since the consequences of missing a financial lease payment are the same as those of missing an interest or principal payment on debt, a financial analyst must view the lease as a long-term financial commitment of the lessee. With FASB No. 13, the inclusion of financial (capital) leases as an asset and corresponding liability (i.e., long-term debt) provides for a balance sheet that more accurately reflects the firm's financial status and thereby permits various types of financial ratio analyses to be performed directly on the statement by any interested party.

Advantages and Disadvantages of Leasing

Leasing has a number of commonly cited advantages and disadvantages that should be considered in making a lease-versus-purchase decision. Although not all these advantages and disadvantages hold in every case, it is not unusual for a number of them to apply in a given situation.

---

[8] The Financial Accounting Standards Board in Standard No. 13 established certain guidelines for the appropriate discount rate to use when capitalizing leases. Most commonly, the rate that the lessee would have incurred to borrow the funds to buy the asset with a secured loan under terms similar to the lease repayment schedule would be used. This simply represents the *before-tax cost of a secured debt.*

Advantages

The commonly cited advantages of leasing are listed below.

1. Leasing allows the lessee, in effect, to *depreciate land,* which is prohibited if the land were purchased. Since the lessee who leases land is permitted to deduct the *total lease payment* as an expense for tax purposes, the effect is the same as if the firm had purchased the land and then depreciated it.

2. Since it results in the receipt of service from an asset possibly without increasing the assets or liabilities on the firm's balance sheet, leasing may result in misleading *financial ratios*. With the passage of FASB No. 13, this advantage no longer applies to financial leases, although in the case of operating leases it remains a potential advantage.

3. The use of sale-leaseback arrangements may permit the firm to *increase its liquidity* by converting an *existing* asset into cash, which can then be used as working capital. A firm short of working capital or in a liquidity bind can sell an owned asset to a lessor and lease the asset back for a specified number of years.

4. Leasing provides *100 percent financing*. Most loan agreements for the purchase of fixed assets require the borrower to pay a portion of the purchase price as a down payment. As a result the borrower is able to borrow only 90 to 95 percent of the purchase price of the asset.

5. When a *firm becomes bankrupt* or is reorganized, the maximum claim of lessors against the corporation is three years of lease payments. If debt is used to purchase an asset, the creditors have a claim equal to the total outstanding loan balance.

6. In a lease arrangement, the firm may *avoid the cost of obsolescence* if the lessor fails to accurately anticipate the obsolescence of assets and sets the lease payment too low. This is especially true in the case of operating leases, which generally have relatively short lives.

7. A lessee *avoids many of the restrictive covenants* that are normally included as part of a long-term loan. Requirements with respect to minimum net working capital, subsequent borrowing, changes in management, and so on are *not* normally found in a lease agreement.

8. In the case of low-cost assets that are infrequently acquired, leasing—especially operating leases—may provide the firm with needed *financing flexibility*. That is, the firm does not have to arrange other financing for these assets and can somewhat conveniently obtain them through a lease.

Disadvantages

The commonly cited disadvantages of leasing are the following:

1. A lease does not have a stated interest cost. Thus in many leases the *return to the lessor is quite high,* so the firm might be better off borrowing to purchase the asset.

2. At the end of the term of the lease agreement, the *salvage value* of an asset, if any, is realized by the lessor. If the lessee had purchased the asset, it could have claimed its salvage value.

3. Under a lease, the lessee is generally *prohibited from making improvements* on the leased property or asset without the approval of the lessor. If the property were owned outright, this difficulty would not arise.

4. If a lessee leases (under a financial lease) an *asset that subsequently becomes obsolete,* it still must make lease payments over the remaining term of the lease. This is true even if the asset is unusable.

Convertible Securities

A **conversion feature** is an option included as part of a bond or a preferred stock issue that permits the holder to convert the security into a specified number of shares of common stock. The conversion feature typically enhances the marketability of an issue.

conversion feature An option included as part of a bond or a preferred stock issue permitting its holder to convert the security into a specified number of shares of common stock.

Types of Convertible Securities

Corporate bonds or preferred stocks may be convertible into common stock. The most common type of convertible security is the bond. Convertibles normally have an accompanying *call feature.* This feature permits the issuer to retire or encourage conversion of outstanding convertibles when appropriate.

Convertible Bonds

A **convertible bond** is a bond that at some future time can be converted into a specified number of shares of common stock. It is almost always a *debenture*—an unsecured bond—with a call feature. Because the conversion feature provides the purchaser of a convertible bond with the possibility of becoming a stockholder on favorable terms, convertible bonds are generally a less expensive form of financing than similar-risk nonconvertible or **straight bonds.** The conversion feature adds a degree of speculation to a bond issue, although the issue still maintains its value as a bond. Convertible bonds are normally convertible only for a specified period of years.

convertible bond A bond that at some future time can be converted into a specified number of shares of common stock.

straight bonds Bonds that are nonconvertible, having no conversion feature.

Convertible Preferred Stock

Convertible preferred stock can normally be sold with a lower stated dividend than a similar-risk nonconvertible or **straight preferred stock.** The reason is that the convertible preferred holder is assured of the fixed dividend payment associated with a preferred stock and also may receive the appreciation resulting from increases in the market price of the underlying common stock. Convertible preferred stocks are usually convertible over an unlimited time horizon. Although convertible preferred stock behaves in a fashion similar to convertible bonds, the following discussions will concentrate on the more popular convertible bonds.

convertible preferred stock Preferred stock that at some future time can be converted into a specified number of shares of common stock.

straight preferred stock Preferred stock that is nonconvertible, having no conversion feature.

General Features of Convertibles

The general features of convertible securities include the conversion ratio, the conversion period, and the conversion (or stock) value.

Conversion Ratio

The **conversion ratio** is the ratio at which a convertible security can be exchanged for common stock. The conversion ratio can be stated in two ways.

conversion ratio The ratio at which a convertible security can be exchanged for common stock.

conversion price The per-share price effectively paid for common stock as the result of conversion of a convertible security.

1. Sometimes the conversion ratio is stated by indicating that the security is convertible into a given number of shares of common stock. In this situation the conversion ratio is *given*. To find the **conversion price,** which is the per-share price effectively paid for common stock as the result of conversion, the par value (not the market value) of the convertible security must be divided by the conversion ratio.

> **Example**
> Western Wear Company has outstanding a bond with a $1,000 par value and convertible into 25 shares of common stock. The bond's conversion ratio is 25. The conversion price for the bond is $40 per share ($1,000 ÷ 25).

2. Sometimes, instead of the conversion ratio, the conversion price is given. The conversion ratio can be obtained by dividing the par value of the convertible by the conversion price.

> **Example**
> The Mosher Company has outstanding a convertible 20-year bond with a par value of $1,000. The bond is convertible at $50 per share into common stock. The conversion ratio is 20 ($1,000 ÷ $50).

The issuer of a convertible security normally establishes a conversion ratio or conversion price that sets the conversion price per share at the time of issuance above the current market price of the firm's stock. If the prospective purchasers do not expect conversion ever to be feasible, they will purchase a straight security or some other convertible issue. A predictable chance of conversion must be provided for in order to enhance the marketability of a convertible security.

Conversion Period

Convertible securities are often convertible only within or after a certain period of time. Sometimes conversion is not permitted until two to five years have passed. In other instances conversion is permitted only for a limited number of years, say for five or ten years after issuance of the convertible. Other issues are convertible at any time during the life of the security.

Conversion (or Stock) Value

conversion (or stock) value The value of the convertible security measured in terms of the market price of the common stock into which it can be converted.

The **conversion (or stock) value** is the value of the convertible measured in terms of the market price of the common stock into which it can be converted. The conversion value can be found simply by multiplying the conversion ratio by the current market price of the firm's common stock.

> **Example**
> McNamara Industries has outstanding a $1,000 bond that is convertible into common stock at $62.50 a share. The conversion ratio is therefore 16 ($1,000 ÷ $62.50). Since the current market price of the common stock is $65 per share, the conversion value is $1,040 (16 × $65). Since the conversion value is above the bond value of $1,000, conversion is a viable option for the owner of the convertible security.

Financing with Convertibles

Using convertible securities to raise long-term funds can help the firm achieve its cost of capital and capital structure goals (see Chapters 11 and 12, respectively). There are a number of more specific motives and considerations involved in evaluating convertible financing.

Motives for Convertible Financing

Convertibles can be used for a variety of reasons. One popular motive is their use as a form of *deferred common stock financing*. When a convertible security is issued, both issuer and purchaser expect the security to be converted into common stock at some point in the future. Since it is initially sold with a conversion price above the current market price of the firm's stock, conversion is initially not attractive. The issuer of a convertible could alternatively sell common stock, but only at or below its current market price. By selling the convertible, the issuer in effect makes a *deferred sale* of common stock. As the market price of the firm's common stock rises to a higher level, conversion may occur. By deferring the issuance of new common stock until the market price of the stock has increased, fewer shares will have to be issued, thereby decreasing the dilution of both ownership and earnings.

Another motive for convertible financing is its *use as a "sweetener" for financing*. Since the purchaser of the convertible is given the opportunity to become a common stockholder and share in the firm's future success, *convertibles can normally be sold with lower interest rates than nonconvertibles*. Therefore, from the firm's viewpoint, including a conversion feature reduces the effective interest cost of debt. The purchaser of the issue sacrifices a portion of his or her interest return for the potential opportunity to become a common stockholder in the future.

A final motive for using convertibles is to *raise temporarily cheap funds*. By using convertible bonds, the firm can temporarily raise debt, which is typically less expensive than common stock (see Chapter 11), to finance projects. Once such projects are on line, the firm may wish to shift its capital structure to a less highly levered position. A conversion feature gives the issuer the opportunity, through actions of convertible holders, to shift its capital structure at a future point in time.

Other Considerations

When the price of the firm's common stock rises above the conversion price, the market price of the convertible security will normally rise to a level close to its conversion value. When this happens, many convertible holders will not convert since they already have the market price benefit obtainable from conversion and can still receive fixed periodic interest payments. Because of this behavior, virtually all convertible securities have a *call feature* that enables the issuer to encourage or *"force"* conversion. The call price of the security generally exceeds the security's par value by an amount equal to one year's stated interest on the security. Although the issuer must pay a premium for calling a security, the call privilege is generally not exercised until the conversion value of the security is 10 to 15 percent *above the call price*. This type of premium above the call price helps to assure the issuer that when the call is made, the holders of the convertible will convert it instead of accepting the call price.

Unfortunately there are instances when the market price of a security does not reach a level sufficient to stimulate the conversion of associated convertibles. A convertible security that cannot be forced into conversion using the call feature is called an **overhanging**

overhanging issue
A convertible security that cannot be forced into conversion using the call feature.

issue. An overhanging issue can be quite detrimental to a firm. If the firm were to call the issue, the bondholders would accept the call price rather than convert the bonds and effectively pay an excessive price for the stock. In this case the firm would not only have to pay the call premium, but it would require additional financing to pay for the call itself. If the firm raised these funds through the sale of equity, a large number of shares would have to be issued due to their low market price. This, in turn, could result in the dilution of existing ownership. Another source of financing the call would be the use of debt or preferred stock, but this use would leave the firm's capital structure no less levered than prior to the call.

Determining the Value of a Convertible Bond

The key characteristic of convertible securities that greatly enhances their marketability is their ability to minimize the possibility of a loss while providing a possibility of capital gains. Here we discuss the three values of a convertible bond: (1) the straight bond value, (2) the conversion (or stock) value, and (3) the market value.

Straight Bond Value

straight bond value The price at which a convertible bond would sell in the market without the conversion feature.

The **straight bond value** of a convertible bond is the price at which it would sell in the market without the conversion feature. This value is found by determining the value of a nonconvertible bond with similar payments issued by a firm having the same risk. The straight bond value is typically the *floor,* or minimum, price at which the convertible bond would be traded. The straight bond value equals the present value of the bond's interest and principal payments discounted at the interest rate the firm would have to pay on a nonconvertible bond.

Example
Duncan Company has just sold a $1,000, 20-year convertible bond with a 12 percent coupon interest rate. The bond interest will be paid at the end of each year, and the principal will be repaid at maturity.[9] A straight bond could have been sold with a 14 percent interest rate, but the conversion feature compensates for the lower rate on the convertible. The straight bond value of the convertible is calculated as shown below.

Year(s)	Payments (1)	Present-value interest factor at 14 percent (2)	Present value [(1) × (2)] (3)
1–20	$ 120[a]	6.623[b]	$794.76
20	1,000	.073[c]	73.00
		Straight bond value	$867.76

[a] $1,000 at 12% = $120 interest per year.
[b] Present-value interest factor for an annuity, *PVIFA,* discounted at 14% for 20 years, from Table A-4.
[c] Present-value interest factor for $1, *PVIF,* discounted at 14% for year 20, from Table A-3.

[9] Consistent with Chapter 8, we continue to assume the payment of annual rather than semiannual bond interest. This assumption simplifies the calculations involved while maintaining the conceptual accuracy of the procedures presented.

This value, $867.76, is the minimum price at which the convertible bond is expected to sell. Generally, only in certain instances where the stock's market price is below the conversion price will the bond be expected to sell at this level.

Conversion (or Stock) Value

The *conversion (or stock) value* of a convertible security has been defined earlier as the value of the convertible measured in terms of the market price of the common stock into which the security can be converted. When the market price of the common stock exceeds the conversion price, the conversion (or stock) value exceeds the par value. An example will clarify the point.

Example

Duncan Company's convertible bond described earlier is convertible at $50 per share. This means each bond can be converted into 20 shares, since each bond has a $1,000 par value. The conversion values of the bond when the stock is selling at $30, $40, $50, $60, $70, and $80 per share are shown in the following table.

Market price of stock	Conversion value
$30	$ 600
40	800
50 (conversion price)	1,000 (par value)
60	1,200
70	1,400
80	1,600

It can be seen that when the market price of the common stock exceeds the $50 conversion price, the conversion value exceeds the $1,000 par value. Since the straight bond value (calculated in the preceding example) is $867.76, the bond will, in a stable environment, never sell for less than this amount, regardless of how low its conversion value is. If the market price per share were $30, the bond would still sell for $867.76— not $600—because its value as a bond would dominate.

Market Value

The market value of a convertible is likely to be greater than its straight value or its conversion value. The amount by which the market value exceeds its straight or conversion value is often called the **market premium.** The closer the straight value is to the conversion value, the larger the market premium. The premium is attributed to the convertible security purchaser's expectations relative to future stock price movements. The general relationship of the straight bond value, conversion value, market value, and market premium for Duncan Company's convertible bond is shown in Figure 18.1. The straight bond value acts as a floor for the security's value up to the point X, where the

market premium The amount by which the market value exceeds the straight or conversion value of a convertible security.

PROFILE

ROGER SMITH:
"There's No Easy Way to the Top"

Roger Smith, board chairman and chief executive officer of General Motors, is the financial executive par excellence. He started his GM career back in 1949 as a general accounting clerk at headquarters in Detroit. By 1970 he was corporate treasurer. The next year, he became vice president in charge of the financial staff. In 1974 he was made executive vice president in charge of the financial, public relations, and industry–government relations staffs. His only line management assignment—running GM's nonautomotive and defense products group—lasted but two years.

Smith credits his background in finance for his rise as much as anything else. "The common thread that holds all aspects of a business together is money," he points out. "And money is what accounting and finance are all about. Everything eventually comes down to dollars. If you're talking about people, you call it compensation. If you talk about sales, you call it price. If you talk about steel, you call it manufacturing cost. If you're working in the heart of dollar country, the way accounting and finance people are, you'll run across just about everything in your business."

Although starting out in finance may be an advantage in any big corporation, it is certainly no assurance of success. "Yes, I was a financial officer," says Smith. "But basically what I was doing was just working as hard as I could. When I started out at GM, I used to work on anything I could get my hands on, whether it was in my department or helping someone else out, because that's how you learn. I came here with what I thought was a good education (a bachelor's degree in accounting and an M.B.A. from the University of Michigan), but I soon found out there was a lot I didn't know. You can be the brightest finance guy in the world but you're not going to become a board chairman unless people are convinced you've got capabilities beyond finance."

The year before Smith took over, GM lost more than three-quarters of a billion dollars and was deep in trouble. He slashed costs and raised cash by closing factories and selling the GM building in New York. He kept costs down by consolidating and modernizing operations. He laid off thousands of workers and won wage concessions from hundreds of thousands more. As a result, Smith now rules a $60-billion-a-year (sales) enterprise that controls more than 60 percent of the U.S. automobile market and is the biggest manufacturing company in the world.

Yet, despite the honors, the powers of high corporate office, the seven-figure income, and the perquisites, Smith has a warning for finance people who would like to emulate him: "There's no easy way to the top. If you don't want to work hard, you shouldn't even start out to try to do it."

SOURCE: "Roger Smith of GM: How to Become a CEO," by M. Daniel Rosen. Reprinted by permission of *FE: the magazine for financial executives*, Jan./Feb. 1986, copyright 1986 by Financial Executives Institute.

share price is high enough to cause the conversion value to exceed the straight bond value. The market value of the convertible often exceeds both its straight and conversion values, thus resulting in a market premium.

FACT OR FABLE?   **4** The market value of a convertible security typically is greater than its straight or conversion value as a result of positive investor expectations concerning future stock price movements. *(Fact)*

Figure 18.1
The Values and Market Premium for Duncan Company's Convertible Bond

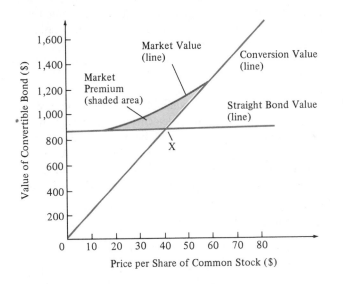

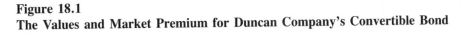

Stock-Purchase Warrants

Stock-purchase warrants are quite similar to stock rights, which were described in detail in Chapter 17. A **stock-purchase warrant** gives the holder an option to purchase a certain number of shares of common stock at a specified price over a certain period of time. Warrants also bear some similarity to convertibles in that they provide for the injection of additional equity capital into the firm at some future date.

stock-purchase warrant An instrument that gives its holder an option to purchase a certain number of shares of common stock at a specified price over a certain period of time.

Basic Characteristics

Some of the basic characteristics of stock-purchase warrants are discussed here.

Warrants as "Sweeteners"

Warrants are often attached to debt issues as "sweeteners," or added benefits. When a firm makes a large issue of debt, the attachment of stock-purchase warrants may add to the marketability of the issue while lowering the required interest rate. As sweeteners, warrants are similar to conversion features. Often, when a new firm is raising its initial capital, suppliers of debt will require warrants to permit them to share in whatever success the firm achieves.

Exercise Prices

The per-share price at which holders of warrants can purchase a specified number of shares of common stock is normally referred to as the **exercise price** or **option price.** This price is normally set at 10 to 20 percent above the market price of the firm's stock at the time of issuance. Until the market price of the stock exceeds the exercise price, holders of warrants would not be advised to exercise them, since they could purchase the stock more cheaply in the marketplace.

exercise price (option price) The per-share price at which holders of warrants can purchase a specified number of shares of common stock.

Life of a Warrant

Warrants normally have a life of no more than ten years, although some have infinite lives. While, unlike convertible securities, warrants cannot be called, their limited life stimulates holders to exercise them when the exercise price is below the market price of the firm's stock.

Warrant Trading

A warrant is usually *detachable*, which means that the bondholder may sell the warrant without selling the security to which it is attached. Many detachable warrants are listed and actively traded on organized securities exchanges and on the over-the-counter exchange. The majority of actively traded warrants are listed on the American Stock Exchange. Warrants, as demonstrated in a later section, often provide investors with better opportunities for gain (with increased risk) than the underlying common stock.

Comparison of Warrants and Rights

The similarity between a warrant and a right should be clear. Both result in new equity capital, although the warrant provides for *deferred* equity financing. The life of a right is typically not more than a few months; a warrant is generally exercisable for a period of years. Rights are issued at a subscription price below the prevailing market price of the stock; warrants are generally issued at an exercise price 10 to 20 percent above the prevailing market price.

Comparison of Warrants and Convertibles

The exercise of a warrant shifts the firm's capital structure to a less highly levered position because new common stock is issued without any change in debt. If a convertible bond were converted, the reduction in leverage would be even more pronounced, since common stock would be issued in exchange for a reduction in debt. In addition, the exercise of a warrant provides an influx of new capital; with convertibles the new capital is raised when the securities are originally issued rather than when converted. The influx of new equity capital resulting from the exercise of a warrant does not occur until the firm has achieved a certain degree of success that is reflected in an increased price for its stock. In this instance, the firm conveniently obtains needed funds.

FACT OR FABLE? **5** While both convertible bonds and stock-purchase warrants when converted or exercised shift capital structure to a less highly levered position, a much greater reduction typically results from conversion of convertibles. *(Fact)*

The Value of Warrants

warrant premium The difference between the theoretical and actual market values of a warrant.

Like a convertible security, a warrant has both a theoretical and a market value. The difference between these values, or the **warrant premium,** depends largely on investor expectations and the ability of the investors to get more leverage from the warrants than from the underlying stock.

Theoretical Value of a Warrant

The *theoretical value* of a stock-purchase warrant is the amount one would expect the warrant to sell for in the marketplace. Equation 18.1 gives the theoretical value of a warrant:

$$TVW = (P_o - E) \times N \qquad (18.1)$$

where

TVW = theoretical value of a warrant

P_o = current market price of a share of common stock

E = exercise price of the warrant

N = number of shares of common stock obtainable with one warrant

The use of Equation 18.1 can be illustrated by the following example.

Example
Dustin Electronics has outstanding warrants that are exercisable at $40 per share and entitle holders to purchase three shares of common stock. The warrants were initially attached to a bond issue to sweeten the bond. The common stock of the firm is currently selling for $45 per share. Substituting $P_o = \$45$, $E = \$40$, and $N = 3$ into Equation 18.1 yields a theoretical warrant value of $15 [($45 − $40) × 3]. Therefore, Dustin's warrants should sell for $15 in the marketplace.

Market Value of a Warrant

The market value of a stock-purchase warrant is generally above the theoretical value of the warrant. Only when the theoretical value of the warrant is very high are the market and theoretical values close. The general relationship between the theoretical and market values of Dustin Electronics' warrants is presented graphically in Figure 18.2. The market value of the warrants generally exceeds the theoretical value by the greatest amount when the stock's market price is close to the warrant exercise price per share.

Warrant Premium

The *warrant premium,* or amount by which the market value of Dustin Electronics' warrants exceeds the theoretical value of these warrants, is also shown in Figure 18.2. This premium results from a combination of positive investor expectations and the ability of the investor with a fixed sum to invest to obtain much larger potential returns (and risk) by trading in warrants rather than the underlying stock. An example will clarify the effect of expectations of stock price movements on warrant market values.

Example
Stan Buyer has $2,430 he is interested in investing in Dustin Electronics. The firm's stock is currently selling for $45 per share, and its warrants are selling for $18 per warrant. Each warrant entitles the holder to purchase three shares of Dustin's common stock at $40 per share. Since the stock is selling for $45 per share, the theoretical

warrant value, calculated in the preceding example using Equation 18.1, is $15 [($45 − $40) × 3].

The warrant premium is believed to result from positive investor expectations and leverage opportunities. Stan Buyer could spend his $2,430 in either of two ways. Ignoring brokerage fees, he could purchase 54 shares of common stock at $45 per share or 135 warrants at $18 per warrant. If Mr. Buyer purchases the stock, its price rises to $48, and if he then sells the stock, he will gain $162 ($3 per share × 54 shares). If instead of purchasing the stock he purchases the 135 warrants and the stock price increases by $3 per share, Mr. Buyer will make approximately $1,215. Since the price of a share of stock rises by $3, the price of each warrant can be expected to rise by $9, since each warrant can be used to purchase three shares of common stock. A gain of $9 per warrant on 135 warrants means a total gain of $1,215 on the warrants.

The greater leverage associated with trading warrants should be clear from the preceding example. Of course, since leverage works both ways it results in greater risk. If the market price fell by $3, the loss on the stock would be $162, while the loss on the warrants would be close to $1,215. Clearly, the use of warrants by investors is more risky.

Options

option An instrument that provides its holder with an opportunity to purchase or sell a specified asset at a stated price on or before a set *expiration date*.

In the most general sense, an **option** can be viewed as an instrument that provides its holder with an opportunity to purchase or sell a specified asset at a stated price on or before a set *expiration date*. Today the interest in options centers on options on common stock. The development of organized options exchanges has created markets in which to

Figure 18.2
The Values and Warrant Premium for Dustin Electronics' Stock-Purchase Warrants

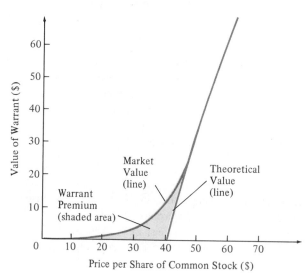

trade these options, which themselves are securities. Three basic forms of options are rights, warrants, and calls and puts. Rights were discussed in Chapter 17, and warrants have been described in the preceding section.

Calls and Puts

The two most common types of options are calls and puts. A **call option** is an option to *purchase* a specified number of shares (typically 100) of a stock on or before some future date at a stated price. Call options usually have initial lives of one to nine months, occasionally one year. The **striking price** is the price at which the holder of the option can buy the stock at any time prior to the option's expiration date; it is generally set at or near the prevailing market price of the stock at the time the option is issued. For example, if a firm's stock is currently selling for $50 per share, a call option on the stock initiated today would likely have a striking price set at $50 per share. To purchase a call option, a specified price of normally a few hundred dollars must be paid.

A **put option** is an option to *sell* a given number of shares (typically 100) of stock on or before a specified future date at a stated striking price. Like the call option, the striking price of the put is close to the market price of the underlying stock at the time of issuance. The lives and costs of puts are similar to those of calls.

How the Options Markets Work

There are two ways of making options transactions. The first involves making a transaction through one of twenty or so call and put options dealers with the help of a stockbroker. The other, more popular mechanism is the organized options exchanges. The main exchanges are the *Chicago Board Options Exchange (CBOE)* and the *American Stock Exchange (AMEX)*. Both exchanges provide organized marketplaces in which purchases and sales of both call and put options can be made in an orderly fashion. The options traded on the options exchanges are standardized and are considered registered securities. Each option is for 100 shares of the underlying stock. The price at which options transactions can be made is determined by the forces of supply and demand.

Logic of Options Trading

The most common motive for purchasing call options is the expectation that the market price of the underlying stock will rise by more than enough to cover the cost of the option and thereby allow the purchaser of the call to profit.

> **Example**
> Assume that Cindy Peters pays $250 for a three-month *call option* on Wing Enterprises at a striking price of $50. This means that by paying $250 Cindy is guaranteed that she can purchase 100 shares of Wing at $50 per share at any time during the next three months. Ignoring any brokerage fees or dividends, the stock price must climb $2.50 per share ($250 ÷ 100 shares) to $52.50 per share to cover the cost of the option. If the stock price were to rise to $60 per share during the period, Cindy's net profit would be $750 [(100 shares × $60/share) − (100 shares × $50/share) − $250]. Since this return would be earned on a $250 investment, it illustrates the high potential return on invest-

call option An option to *purchase* a specified number of shares (typically 100) of a stock on or before some future date at a stated price.

striking price The price at which the holder of a call option can buy (or holder of a put option can sell) a specified amount of stock at any time prior to the option's expiration.

put option An option to *sell* a given number of shares (typically 100) of stock on or before a specified future date at a stated striking price.

ment that options offer. Of course, had the stock price not risen above $50 per share, Cindy would have lost the $250 since there would have been no reason to exercise the option. Had the stock price risen to between $50 and $52.50 per share, Cindy probably would have exercised the option in order to reduce her loss to an amount less than $250.

Put options are purchased in the expectation that the share price of a given security will decline over the life of the option. Purchasers of puts commonly own the shares and wish to protect a gain they have realized since their initial purchase. By buying a put, they lock in the gain because it enables them to sell their shares at a known price during the life of the option. Investors gain from put options when the price of the underlying stock declines by more than the per-share cost of the option. The logic underlying the purchase of a put is exactly the opposite of that underlying the use of call options.

Role of Call and Put Options in Managerial Finance

Although call and put options are an extremely popular investment vehicle, they play *no* direct role in the fund-raising activities of the financial manager. These options are issued by investors, not businesses. *They are not a source of financing to the firm.* Corporate pension managers, whose job it is to invest and manage corporate pension funds, may use call and put options as part of their investment activities to earn a return or to protect or lock in returns already earned on securities. The presence of options trading in the firm's stock could—by increasing trading activity—stabilize the firm's share price in the marketplace, but the financial manager has no direct control over this. Buyers of options do not have any say in the firm's management or any voting rights; only stockholders are given these privileges. Despite the popularity of call and put options as an investment vehicle, the financial manager has very little need to deal with them, especially as part of fund-raising activities.

FACT OR FABLE?   **6** Call and put options are extremely popular investment vehicles that play an important role in the fund-raising activities of the firms that issue them. *(Fable)*
Call and put options *are issued by investors* **and although they are extremely popular investment vehicles** *they play no direct role in the fund-raising activities of the firm.*

Summary

● Preferred stockholders are given preference over common stockholders with respect to the distribution of earnings and assets, and as a result do not normally receive voting privileges. Preferred stock is similar to debt in that though some adjustable-rate (or floating-rate) issues exist, it generally has a fixed annual dividend.

● Preferred stock issues may have certain restrictive covenants,

cumulative dividends, participation in earnings, a call feature, and a conversion feature.

● The basic advantages for the use of preferred stock financing include its ability to increase the firm's leverage, the flexibility of the obligation, and its use in mergers. Disadvantages include the seniority of its claim over the common stockholders and its relatively high cost compared to debt financing.

● A lease, like long-term debt, allows the firm to make contractual, tax-deductible payments in order to obtain the use of fixed assets. Operating leases are generally short-term, cancelable, renewable, and provide for maintenance by the lessor. Financial leases are longer term, noncancelable, not renewable, and require the lessee to maintain the asset.

● A lessor can obtain assets to be leased through a direct lease, a sale-leaseback arrangement, or a leveraged lease. The IRS specifies conditions under which lease payments are tax-deductible. FASB Standard No. 13 requires firms to disclose in their financial statements the existence of leases.

● A lease-versus-purchase decision can be evaluated by calculating the after-tax cash outflows associated with the leasing and purchasing alternatives. The more desirable alternative is the one that has the lower present value of after-tax cash outflows. In addition, a number of commonly cited advantages and disadvantages should be considered in making lease-versus-purchase decisions.

● Corporate bonds and preferred stocks may both be convertible into common stock. The conversion ratio indicates the number of shares a convertible can be exchanged for and determines the conversion price. Convertibles are used to obtain deferred common stock financing, to "sweeten" bond issues, and to raise temporarily cheap funds. The call feature is sometimes used to encourage or "force" conversion, in the attempt to avoid an overhanging issue.

● Typically the minimum value at which a convertible bond will trade is its straight (nonconvertible) bond value. The market value of a convertible generally exceeds both its straight and conversion (stock) values, thereby creating a market premium.

● Stock-purchase warrants, like rights, provide their holders with the privilege of purchasing a certain number of shares of common stock at the specified exercise price. Warrants are often attached to debt issues as "sweeteners," generally have limited lives, are detachable, and may be listed and traded on securities exchanges.

● Warrants are similar to convertibles, but exercising them has a less pronounced effect on the firm's leverage and brings in new funds. The market value of a warrant usually exceeds it theoretical value, creating a warrant premium.

● An option provides its holder with an opportunity to purchase or sell a specified asset at a stated price on or before a set expiration date. Rights, warrants, and calls and puts are all options. Call and put options do not play a direct role in the fund-raising activities of the firm.

Questions

18-1 What is *preferred stock?* What claims do preferred stockholders have with respect to the distribution of earnings and assets? How are dividends on preferred stock typically stated? What is an *adjustable-rate (or floating-rate) preferred stock (ARPS)?*

18-2 What are *cumulative* and *noncumulative* preferred stock? Which form is more common? Why?

18-3 What is a *call feature* in a preferred stock issue? When and at what price does the call usually take place? What benefit does the call offer the issuer of preferred stock?

18-4 What are the key advantages and disadvantages of using preferred stock financing as a source of new capital funds?

18-5 What is *leasing?* Define, compare, and contrast *operating leases* and *financial (or capital) leases*. Describe three methods used by lessors to acquire assets to be leased.

18-6 Describe the four basic steps involved in the lease-versus-purchase decision process. Why must present-value techniques be used in this process?

18-7 According to FASB Standard No. 13, under what conditions must a lease be treated as a *capitalized lease* on the balance sheet? How does the financial manager capitalize a lease?

18-8 List and discuss the commonly cited advantages and disadvantages that should be considered in making a lease-versus-purchase decision.

18-9 What is the *conversion feature?* What is a *conversion ratio?* Briefly describe the motives for convertible financing.

18-10 When the market price of the stock rises above the conversion price, why may a convertible security *not* be converted? How can the *call feature* be used to force conversion in this situation? What is an *overhanging issue?*

18-11 Define *straight bond value, conversion value, market value,* and *market premium* associated with a convertible bond, and describe the general relationships among them.

18-12 What are *stock-purchase warrants?* What are the similarities and key differences between the effects of warrants and convertibles on the firm's capital structure and its ability to raise new capital?

18-13 What is the general relationship between the theoretical and market values of a warrant? In what circumstances are these values quite close? What is a *warrant premium?*

18-14 What is an *option?* Define *calls* and *puts*. What role, if any, do call and put options play in the fund-raising activities of the financial manager?

Self-Test Problems

(Solutions on page 674)

ST-1 The Hot Bagel Shop wishes to evaluate two plans, leasing and borrowing to purchase, for financing an oven.

Leasing: The shop could lease the oven under a five-year lease requiring annual end-of-year payments of $5,000. All maintenance, insurance, and other costs would be borne by the lessee.

Purchasing: The oven costs $20,000 and will have a five-year life. The asset will be depreciated under ACRS using a five-year recovery period, which means that six years of depreciation will result. (See Table 3.6 on page 66 for the applicable depreciation percentages.) The total purchase price will be financed by a five-year, 15 percent loan requiring equal annual end-of-year payments of $5,967. The firm is in the 40 percent tax bracket.

   a. For the leasing plan, calculate the following:
     (1) The after-tax cash outflows each year.
     (2) The present value of the cash outflows, using a 9 percent *discount* rate.

   b. For the purchase plan, calculate the following:
     (1) The annual interest expense deductible for tax purposes for each of the five years.
     (2) The after-tax cash outflows resulting from the purchase for each of the six years.
     (3) The present value of the cash outflows, using a 9 percent *discount* rate.

   c. Compare the present value of the cash-outflow streams from each plan and determine which would be preferable. Explain your answer.

ST-2 Mountain Mining Company has an outstanding issue of convertible bonds with a $1,000 par value. These bonds are convertible into 40 shares of common stock. They have an 11 percent annual coupon interest rate and a 25-year maturity. The interest rate on a straight bond of similar risk is currently 13 percent.

   a. Calculate the straight bond value of the bond.

   b. Calculate the conversion (or stock) values of the bond when the market prices of the common stock are $20, $25, $28, $35, and $50 per share, respectively.

   c. For each of the stock prices given in **b,** at what price would you expect the bond to sell? Why?

   d. What is the least you would expect the bond to sell for, regardless of the common stock price behavior?

Problems

18-1 **(Preferred Dividends)** Slater Lamp Manufacturing has an outstanding issue of preferred stock with an $80 par value and an 11 percent annual dividend.

   a. What is the annual dollar dividend? If it is paid quarterly, how much will be paid each quarter?

   b. If the preferred stock is *noncumulative* and the board of directors has passed the preferred dividend for the last three years, how much must be paid to preferred stockholders prior to paying dividends to common stockholders?

c. If the preferred stock is *cumulative* and the board of directors has passed the preferred dividend for the last three years, how much must be paid to preferred stockholders prior to paying dividends to common stockholders?

18-2 **(Preferred Dividends)** In each case in the table, how many dollars of preferred dividends per share must be paid to preferred stockholders prior to paying common stock dividends?

Case	Type	Par value	Dividend per share per period	Periods of dividends passed
A	Cumulative	$ 80	$5	2
B	Noncumulative	110	8%	3
C	Noncumulative	100	$11	1
D	Cumulative	60	8.5%	4
E	Cumulative	90	9%	0

18-3 **(Participating Preferred Stock)** Union Shipping Company has outstanding an issue of 3,000 shares of participating preferred stock that has a $100 par value and an 8 percent annual dividend. The preferred stockholders participate fully (on an equal per-share basis) with common shareholders in annual dividends of more than $9 per share for common stock. The firm has 5,000 shares of common stock outstanding.

a. If the firm pays preferred stockholders their dividends and then declares an additional $100,000 in dividends, how much will be the total dividend per share for preferred and common stock, respectively?

b. If the firm pays preferred stockholders their dividends and then declares an additional $40,000 in dividends, what is the total dividend per share for each type of shareholder?

c. If the firm's preferred stock is cumulative and the past two years' dividends have been passed, what dividends will be received by each type of shareholder if the firm declares a *total* dividend of $30,000?

d. Rework **c** assuming that the total dividend payment is $20,000.

e. Rework **a** and **b** assuming that the preferred stock is nonparticipating.

18-4 **(Lease Cash Flows)** Given the following lease payments and terms, determine the yearly after-tax cash outflows for each firm, assuming that lease payments are made at the end of each year and that the firm is in the 40 percent tax bracket.

Firm	Annual lease payment	Term of lease
A	$100,000	4 years
B	80,000	14 years
C	150,000	8 years
D	60,000	25 years
E	20,000	10 years

18-5   (**Loan Interest**) For each of the following loan amounts, interest rates, annual payments, and loan terms, calculate the annual interest paid each year over the term of the loan, assuming that the payments are made at the end of each year.

Loan	Amount	Interest rate	Annual payment	Term
A	$14,000	10%	$ 4,416	4 years
B	17,500	12	10,355	2 years
C	2,400	13	1,017	3 years
D	49,000	14	14,273	5 years
E	26,500	16	7,191	6 years

18-6   (**Loan Payments and Interest**) Schuyler Company wishes to purchase an asset costing $117,000. The full amount needed to finance the asset can be borrowed at 14 percent interest. The terms of the loan require equal end-of-year payments for the next six years. Determine the total annual loan payment and break it into the amount of interest and the amount of principal paid for each year. (*Hint:* Use techniques presented in Chapter 6 to find the loan payment.)

18-7   (**Lease versus Purchase**) JLB Corporation is attempting to determine whether to lease or purchase research equipment. The firm is in the 40 percent tax bracket, and its after-tax cost of debt is currently 8 percent. The terms of the lease and the purchase are as follows:

Lease: Annual end-of-year lease payments of $25,200 are required over the three-year life of the lease.

Purchase: The research equipment, costing $60,000, can be financed entirely with a 14 percent loan requiring annual end-of-year payments of $25,844 for three years. The firm in this case would depreciate the truck under ACRS using a three-year recovery period, which means that four years of depreciation will result. (See Table 3.6 on page 66 for the applicable depreciation percentages.)

a. Calculate the after-tax cash outflows associated with each alternative.

b. Calculate the present value of each cash outflow stream using the after-tax cost of debt.

c. Which alternative, lease or purchase, would you recommend? Why?

18-8   (**Lease versus Purchase**) Northwest Lumber Company needs to expand its facilities. To do so, the firm must acquire a machine costing $80,000. The machine can be leased or purchased. The firm is in the 40 percent tax bracket, and its after-tax cost of debt is 9 percent. The terms of the lease and purchase plans are as follows:

Lease: The leasing arrangement would require end-of-year payments of $19,800 over five years.

Purchase: If the firm purchases the machine, its cost of $80,000 would be financed with a five-year, 14 percent loan requiring equal end-of-year payments of $23,302. The machine would be depreciated under ACRS using a five-year recovery period, which means that six years of depreciation will result. (See Table 3.6 on page 66 for the applicable depreciation percentages.)

a. Determine the after-tax cash outflows of Northwest Lumber under each alternative.

b. Find the present value of the after-tax cash outflows using the after-tax cost of debt.

c. Which alternative, lease or purchase, would you recommend? Why?

18-9 (Capitalized Lease Values) Given the following lease payments, terms remaining until the leases expire, and discount rates, calculate the capitalized value of each lease, assuming that lease payments are made annually at the end of each year.

Lease	Lease payment	Remaining term	Discount rate
A	$ 40,000	12 years	10%
B	120,000	8 years	12
C	9,000	18 years	14
D	16,000	3 years	9
E	47,000	20 years	11

18-10 (Conversion Price) Calculate the conversion price for each of the following convertible bonds:

a. A $1,000-par-value bond convertible into 20 shares of common stock.

b. A $500-par-value bond convertible into 25 shares of common stock.

c. A $1,000-par-value bond convertible into 50 shares of common stock.

18-11 (Conversion Ratio) What is the conversion ratio for each of the following bonds?

a. A $1,000-par-value bond convertible into common stock at $43.75 per share.

b. A $1,000-par-value bond convertible into common stock at $25 per share.

c. A $600-par-value bond convertible into common stock at $30 per share.

18-12 (Conversion [or Stock] Value) What is the conversion (or stock) value for each of the following convertible bonds?

a. A $1,000-par-value bond convertible into 25 shares of common stock. The common stock is currently selling at $50 per share.

b. A $1,000-par-value bond convertible into 12.5 shares of common stock. The common stock is currently selling for $42 per share.

c. A $1,000-par-value bond convertible into 100 shares of common stock. The common stock is currently selling for $10.50 per share.

18-13 (Conversion [or Stock] Value) Find the conversion (or stock) value for each of the convertible bonds described in the following table.

Convertible	Conversion ratio	Current market price of stock
A	25	$42.25
B	16	50.00
C	20	44.00
D	5	19.50

18-14 (Straight Bond Values) Calculate the straight bond value for each of the bonds:

Bond	Par value	Coupon interest rate (paid annually)	Interest rate on equal-risk straight bond	Years to maturity
A	$1,000	10%	14%	20
B	800	12	15	14
C	1,000	13	16	30
D	1,000	14	17	25

18-15 (Determining Values—Convertible Bond) Craig's Cake Company has an outstanding issue of 15-year convertible bonds with a $1,000 par value. These bonds are convertible into 80 shares of common stock. They have a 13 percent annual coupon interest rate, whereas the interest rate on straight bonds of similar risk is 16 percent.

a. Calculate the straight bond value of this bond.

b. Calculate the conversion (or stock) values of the bond when the market price is $9, $12, $13, $15, and $20 per share of common stock, respectively.

c. For each of the common stock prices given in **b,** at which price would you expect the bond to sell? Why?

d. Graph the conversion value and straight value of the bond for each common stock price given. Plot the per-share common stock prices on the *x*-axis and the bond values on the *y*-axis. Use this graph to indicate the minimum market value of the bond associated with each common stock price.

18-16 (Warrant Values) Kent Hotels has warrants that allow the purchase of three shares of its outstanding common stock at $50 per share. The common stock price per share and the market value of the warrant associated with that stock price are summarized in the following table.

Common stock price per share	Market value of warrant
$42	$ 2
46	8
48	9
54	18
58	28
62	38
66	48

a. For each of the common stock prices given, calculate the theoretical warrant value.

b. Graph on a set of per-share common stock price (*x*-axis)–warrant value (*y*-axis) axes the theoretical and market values of the warrant.

c. If the warrant value is $12 when the market price of common stock is $50, does this contradict or support the graph you have constructed? Explain why or why not.

d. Specify the area of *warrant premium*. Why does this premium exist?

e. If the expiration date of the warrants is quite close, would you expect your graph to look different? Explain.

18-17 (Common Stock versus Warrant Investment) Susan Michaels is evaluating the Burton Tool Company's common stock and warrants in order to choose the best investment. The firm's stock is currently selling for $50 per share; its warrants to purchase three shares of common stock at $45 per share are selling for $20. Ignoring transactions costs, Ms. Michaels has $8,000 to invest. She is quite optimistic with respect to Burton because she has certain ''inside information'' about the firm's prospects with respect to a large government contract.

a. How many shares of stock and how many warrants can Ms. Michaels purchase?

b. Suppose Ms. Michaels purchased the stock, held it one year, then sold it for $60 per share. Ignoring brokerage fees and taxes, what total gain would she realize?

c. Suppose Ms. Michaels purchased warrants and held them for one year, and the market price of the stock increased to $60 per share. Ignoring brokerage fees and taxes, what would be her total gain if the market value of warrants increased to $45 and she sold out?

d. What benefit, if any, would the warrants provide? Are there any differences in the risk of these two alternative investments? Explain.

18-18 (Common Stock versus Warrant Investment) Tom Baldwin can invest $5,000 in the common stock or the warrants of Lexington Life Insurance. The common stock is currently selling for $30 per share; its warrants, which provide for the purchase of two shares of common stock at $28 per share, are currently selling for $7. The stock is expected to rise to a market price of $32 within the next year, so the expected theoretical value of a warrant over the next year is $8. The expiration date of the warrant is one year from the present.

a. If Mr. Baldwin purchases the stock, holds it for one year, and then sells it for $32, what is his total gain? (Ignore brokerage fees and taxes.)

b. If Mr. Baldwin purchases the warrant and converts to common stock in one year, what is his total gain if the market price of common shares is actually $32? (Ignore brokerage fees and taxes.)

c. Repeat **a** and **b** assuming that the market price of the stock in one year is (1) $30 and (2) $28.

d. Discuss the two alternatives and the trade-offs associated with them.

18-19 (Options Profits and Losses) For each of the following *100-share options,* use the underlying stock price at expiration and other information to determine the amount of profit or loss an investor would have had, ignoring brokerage fees.

Option	Type of option	Cost of option	Striking price per share	Underlying stock price per share at expiration
A	Call	$200	$50	$55
B	Call	350	42	45
C	Put	500	60	50
D	Put	300	35	40
E	Call	450	28	26

18-20 (Call Option) Carol Krebs is considering buying 100 shares of Sooner Products, Inc., at $62 per share. Because she has read that the firm will likely soon receive certain large orders from abroad, she expects the price of Sooner to increase to $70 per share. As an alternative, Carol is considering purchase of a call option for 100 shares of Sooner at a striking price of $60.

The 90-day option will cost $600. Ignore any brokerage fees or dividends.

a. What would Carol's profit be on the stock transaction if its price does rise to $70 and she sells?

b. How much would Carol earn on the option transaction if the underlying stock price rises to $70?

c. How high must the stock price rise in order for Carol to break even on the option transaction?

d. Compare, contrast, and discuss the relative profit and risk from the stock and the option transactions.

18-21 (Put Option) Ed Martin, the pension fund manager for Stark Corporation, is considering purchase of a put option in anticipation of a price decline in the stock of Carlisle, Inc. The option to sell 100 shares of Carlisle, Inc., at any time during the next 90 days at a striking price of $45 can be purchased for $380. The stock of Carlisle is currently selling for $46 per share.

a. Ignoring any brokerage fees or dividends, what profit or loss would Ed make if he buys the option and the lowest price of Carlisle, Inc. stock during the 90 days is $46, $44, $40, and $35, respectively?

b. What effect would the fact that the price of Carlisle's stock slowly rose from its initial $46 level to $55 at the end of 90 days have on Ed's purchase?

c. In light of your findings, discuss the potential risks and returns from using put options to attempt to profit from an anticipated decline in share price.

Solutions to Self-Test Problems

ST-1 a. (1) and (2) In tabular form—after-tax cash outflows in column 3 and present value of the cash outflows in column 5.

End of year (1)	Lease payment (1)	Tax adjustment $[(1 - .40) = .60]$ (2)	After-tax cash outflows $[(1) \times (2)]$ (3)	Present-value factors[a] (4)	Present-value of outflows $[(3) \times (4)]$ (5)
1	$5,000	.60	$3,000	.917	$ 2,751
2	5,000	.60	3,000	.842	2,526
3	5,000	.60	3,000	.772	2,316
4	5,000	.60	3,000	.708	2,124
5	5,000	.60	3,000	.650	1,950
			Present value of cash outflows		$11,667

[a] From Table A-3, *PVIF*, for 9 percent and the corresponding year.

b. (1) In tabular form—annual interest expense in column 3.

| End of year (1) | Loan payments (1) | Beginning-of-year principal (2) | Payments | | End-of-year principal [(2) − (4)] (5) |
			Interest [.15 × (2)] (3)	Principal [(1) − (3)] (4)	
1	$5,967	$20,000	$3,000	$2,967	$17,033
2	5,967	17,033	2,555	3,412	13,621
3	5,967	13,621	2,043	3,924	9,697
4	5,967	9,697	1,455	4,512	5,185
5	5,967	5,185	778	5,189	—a

a The values in this table have been rounded to the nearest dollar, which results in a slight difference ($4) between the beginning-of-year 5 principal (in column 2) and the year 5 principal payment (column 4).

(2) In tabular form—after-tax cash outflows in column 8.

End of year	Loan payments (1)	Cost of oven (2)	Depreciation percentagesa (3)	Depreciation [(2) × (3)] (4)	Interestb (5)	Total deductions [(4) + (5)] (6)	Tax shields [.40 × (6)] (7)	After-tax cash outflows [(1) − (7)] (8)
1	$5,967	$20,000	.20	$4,000	$3,000	$7,000	$2,800	$3,167
2	5,967	20,000	.32	6,400	2,555	8,955	3,582	2,385
3	5,967	20,000	.19	3,800	2,043	5,843	2,337	3,630
4	5,967	20,000	.12	2,400	1,455	3,855	1,542	4,425
5	5,967	20,000	.12	2,400	778	3,178	1,271	4,696
6	0	20,000	.05	1,000	0	1,000	400	(400)

a From Table 3.6 on page 66.
b From column 3 of table in b(1).

(3) In tabular form—present value of the cash outflows in column 3.

End of year	After-tax cash outflowsa (1)	Present-value factorsb (2)	Present-value of outflows [(1) × (2)] (3)
1	$3,167	.917	$ 2,904
2	2,385	.842	2,008
3	3,630	.772	2,802
4	4,425	.708	3,133
5	4,696	.650	3,052
6	(400)	.596	(238)
	Present value of cash outflows		$13,661

a From column 8 of table in b(2).
b From Table A-3, *PVIF,* for 9 percent and the corresponding year.

c. Because the present value of the lease outflows of $11,667 is well below the present value of the purchase outflows of $13,661, *the lease is preferred*. Leasing rather than purchasing the oven should result in an incremental savings of $1,994 ($13,661 purchase cost − $11,667 lease cost).

ST-2 a. In tabular form:

Year(s)	Payments (1)	Present-value interest factor at 13 percent (2)	Present value [(1) × (2)] (3)
1–25	$ 110[a]	7.330[b]	$806.30
25	1,000	.047[c]	47.00
		Straight bond value	$853.30

[a] $1,000 at 11% = $110 interest per year.

[b] Present-value interest factor for an annuity, *PVIFA*, discounted at 13 percent for 25 years, from Table A-4.

[c] Present-value interest factor for $1, *PVIF*, discounted at 13 percent for year 25, from Table A-3.

b. In tabular form:

Market price of stock (1)	Conversion ratio (2)	Conversion value [(1) × (2)] (3)
$20	40	$ 800
25 (conversion price)	40	1,000 (par value)
28	40	1,120
35	40	1,400
50	40	2,000

c. The bond would be expected to sell at the higher of the conversion value or straight value. In no case would it be expected to sell for less than the straight value of $853.30. Therefore, at a price of $20 the bond would sell for its straight value of $853.30, and at prices of $25, $28, $35, and $50, the bond would be expected to sell at the associated conversion values (calculated in **b**) of $1,000, $1,120, $1,400, and $2,000, respectively.

d. The straight bond value of $853.30.

Lonestar Enterprises

Lonestar Enterprises, located in Dallas, Texas, began as a small radio station and in 1973 used a sizable loan to purchase a much larger company involved in the exterminating business. Net earnings have risen continuously through 1988, 12 years since Lonestar Enterprises first went public. Then and now, the firm's equity base is quite small compared to the amount of debt financing currently on its books. The company is also doing well in its media, wallcovering, and burglary and fire protection systems businesses. And most important, the exterminating business—benefiting from wider markets, new customers, and higher fees—is performing magnificently. In the fiscal year ended June 30, 1988, gross income at Lonestar Enterprises rose 17 percent, while profits were held down somewhat by start-up costs in several new businesses.

The biggest factor in anticipating future gains is The Exterminator, Inc., the world's largest termite and pest control organization, which was acquired in September 1978. Sales have grown over the first decade from $37 million to $108 million, accounting for 65 percent of Lonestar's revenues and 64 percent of its profits in fiscal 1988.

The Exterminator is expanding its operations and expects eventually to have a national network capable of handling the needs of any client. If The Exterminator achieves the same degree of market penetration on a national basis as it has achieved in Louisiana and Florida, it would be a $500 million a year business.

The second largest contributor to Lonestar Enterprises' profits is the media division. Lonestar began as a small radio station, which provided its basis for expansion into other fields such as television stations and cable television.

Lonestar currently owns three television stations in Texas, all of which have provided substantial revenues in the past few years. It is also the leading dealer in cable television in the southwestern United States. The cable television market is specialized, and Lonestar's experience and reputation have secured the company's position as a frontrunner in this field.

Another source of revenue is the Textura subsidiary, currently the nation's largest distributor of wallcovering. Textura is 75 years old and operates in 34 states and in Mexico. Wallcovering demand for redecorating is not subject to the uncertainties of the building cycle and provides the stability of diversification.

Lonestar Enterprises also sells burglary and fire protection systems for houses and commercial establishments through its newest division. The firm's electronics background in the media division helped foster the growth of the burglary and fire protection division. This field is growing rapidly—the number of major markets served has expanded from 14 in December 1987 to 25 by September 1988, with 9 more to be added in 1989. This activity is expected to account for over 12 percent of total revenues within a few years, greatly enhancing the firm's profitability.

Capital outlays have approximated $11 million in each of the past two fiscal years, but higher expansion levels are likely in the near future and are expected to require an additional $23 million of financing.

Shortly after the acquisition of The Exterminator, long-term debt totaled $65 million, then equalling 85 percent of total capital, but debt has since been reduced to 70 percent of total capital. The debt carries a maximum interest rate of 7 percent after taxes. The debt reduction was partially financed through issuance of $7.7 million of 10-percent (annual dividend) preferred stock. On June 30, 1988, current assets were $55 million, current liabilities totaled $21 million, and net working capital was $34 million. Earnings before interest and taxes (EBIT) for the 1988 fiscal year amounted to $20 million. Because of the start-up costs of the expansion, the firm expects its EBIT to remain at the $20 million level for the next few years. The firm is in the 40 percent tax bracket.

Currently, the directors must decide upon a method of financing the $23 million expansion. The directors are primarily interested in an equity financing plan since funds could be obtained without incurring added mandatory interest payments that would result in greater risk. Additional equity would also allow Lonestar Enterprises to avoid restrictive covenants often tied to debt financing and would provide a more flexible foundation from which debt could be issued when interest rates fall. The decision, however, could result in lowering earnings per share (EPS) as well as diluting the current stockholders'

Table 1
Capital Structure Alternatives

Capital structures	Amount (millions)	Percent of total capital
Current Structure		
Long-term debt	$53.9	70%
Preferred stock	7.7	10
Common stock equity (906,000 shares)	15.4	20
Total capital	$77.0	100%
Structure A		
Long-term debt	$70.0	70%
Preferred stock	10.0	10
Common stock equity (998,000 shares)	20.0	20
Total capital	$100.0	100%
Structure B		
Long-term debt	$53.9	53.9%
Preferred stock	7.7	7.7
Common stock equity (1,366,000 shares)	38.4	38.4
Total capital	$100.0	100.0%
Structure C		
Long-term debt	$53.9	53.9%
Preferred stock	30.7	30.7
Common stock equity (906,000 shares)	15.4	15.4
Total capital	$100.0	100.0%
Structure D		
Long-term debt	$53.9	53.9%
Preferred stock	23.0	23.0
Common stock equity (1,060,000 shares)	23.1	23.1
Total capital	$100.0	100.0%

control of the company. Jonathon Marks, the chief financial officer, has developed a number of capital structure alternatives (shown in Table 1) and presented them to the executive committee. He expects additional debt to have an after-tax cost of 7 percent, and additional preferred stock will pay a 10 percent annual dividend. The committee must now weigh the advantages, costs, and risks of each plan.

Required

1. Discuss the level of financial leverage associated with each plan.

2. Discuss the overall advantages of equity financing for this firm at this time.

3. Discuss the advantages and disadvantages of selling preferred stock.

4. **a.** Discuss the advantages and disadvantages of selling common stock.
   b. Explain how the firm's dividend policy might affect is ability to sell new common stock.

5. **a.** Marks is also considering a rights offering to raise equity funds. With rights the price of the common stock is $50 per share, the subscription price per share is $43.50, and 9 rights are required to purchase a share of stock. Determine the theoretical value of a right.
   b. Discuss the advantages and disadvantages of the proposed rights offering versus the public sale of new common stock.

6. Recommend how Lonestar should finance its $23 million need. Justify your recommendation in light of the alternatives.

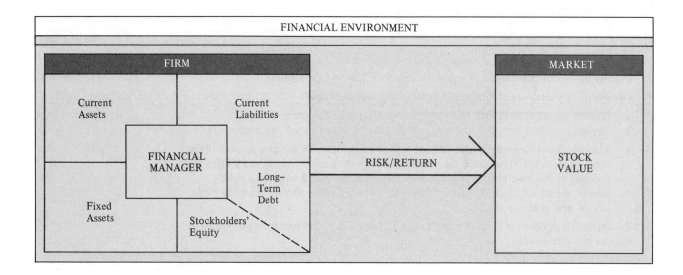

PART SEVEN

Special Managerial Finance Topics

CHAPTER 19

Expansion and Failure

FACT OR FABLE?
Are the following statements fact *(true)* or fable *(false)*?

1

Mergers are similar to consolidations except that when two firms are merged they are combined to form a completely new corporation rather than maintaining the identity of one of the firms.

2

Cash purchases of companies can be analyzed by applying present-value techniques in order to determine whether the proposed acquisition has a positive net present value, in which case it should be acquired.

3

If a firm in a stock-exchange acquisition pays a greater price/earnings (P/E) multiple than its current multiple, it will initially experience an increase in its earnings per share (EPS) while the acquired company's EPS will initially decrease.

4

An acquiring company initially experiencing a decrease in earnings per share (EPS) can experience higher future EPS than it would have without the merger if the acquired company's assets grow at a faster rate than that resulting from its premerger assets.

5

Voluntary settlements can be used to enable the debtor firm to continue to exist or to be liquidated in a manner that saves many of the costs involved in legal bankruptcy proceedings, thereby giving owners the greatest chance of recovering part of their investment.

6

When a firm is liquidated under the Bankruptcy Reform Act, taxes legally due and owed by the bankrupt firm must be paid prior to paying the expenses of administering the bankruptcy proceedings and allowable wages due workers.

You're one of the world's largest operators of offshore oil rigs. There's a worldwide shortage of oil and the market is willing to pay the price for the oil you find and extract from under the ocean floor.

But what happens to your business when agreements among Middle East nations to restrict oil production fall apart and these nations start pumping as much oil as they can? Of course, world oil prices fall, and few people want to buy the costlier oil you have to offer—the kind that depends on expensive oil rigs, expensive transportation, and expensive crews. To compete, you must lower your prices and sell your oil at close to cost.

Global Marine found itself in this spot back in 1984. Profits dropped to below zero, and the price of Global's stock fell from a high of $36 to a low of $1. Company management saw the handwriting on the wall and it read *bankruptcy*. Management's first step before declaring bankruptcy was to preserve as much of its cash as possible by announcing it would no longer make payments on the debt it had incurred. The plan was to look for alternative solutions and accumulate cash while still doing business. Global gambled that creditors would not foreclose, since most of the company's assets were tied up in offshore equipment that would have little comparative value until the oil industry turned around. Many lenders were counting on the price of oil to go up again so that Global Marine would start making its former huge profits and be able to pay its debts—with interest.

By preserving its cash and by filing for protection from creditors under Chapter 11 of the Bankruptcy Code in January 1986, Global Marine hoped to have enough cash flow to continue operating until oil prices recovered. Such a strategy is one way of buying time and avoiding going out of business when either product demand or price falls so low that the company is in a negative financial position.

While most firms attempt to expand either internally through increased production and sales or externally through business combinations (consolidations, mergers, or holding companies), some, like Global Marine, fail for any of a number of possible reasons. In this chapter we first discuss the fundamental concepts and procedures used to analyze and negotiate business combinations, and then we briefly describe the types, causes, and procedures involved in efficiently reorganizing or liquidating the failed firm.

Fundamentals of Business Combinations

Business combinations are sometimes used by firms to externally expand by acquiring control of other firms in order to rapidly increase productive capacity, liquidity, sales, earnings, or share price. Such combinations can be used to acquire a collection of needed assets or another going concern. A major boom in the use of business combinations as a form of external expansion began in 1980 and continues today. Unfortunately not all firms are able to sustain themselves indefinitely; many fail each year. Here we discuss business combination fundamentals. In subsequent sections attention is given to analyzing and negotiating business combinations, followed by discussion of business failure and its consequence—reorganization or liquidation.

Types of Business Combinations

The key forms of business combinations are *consolidations, mergers,* and *holding companies.* These arrangements have certain basic similarities and differences.

Consolidations

consolidation The combination of two or more companies to form a completely new corporation.

A **consolidation** involves the combination of two or more companies to form a completely new corporation. The new corporation normally absorbs the assets and liabilities of the companies from which it is formed. The former corporations cease to exist. Consolidations normally occur when the firms to be combined are of similar size. They are carried out by issuing to shareholders in the old firms a certain number (or fraction) of shares of stock in the new firm in exchange for each share of the old firm.

Mergers

merger Generally, the combination of two firms of unequal size, in which the identity of the larger of the two firms is maintained.

A **merger** is quite similar to a consolidation except that when two or more firms are merged, the resulting firm maintains the identity of one of the firms. Mergers are generally confined to combinations of two firms that are unequal in size; the identity of the larger of the two firms is normally maintained. Usually the assets and liabilities of the smaller firm are consolidated into those of the larger. The larger firm pays for its acquisition of the assets or common stock of the smaller firm with cash or with its preferred or common stock. Due to the similarity between consolidations and mergers, in the remainder of this chapter the term *merger* will be used to refer to both.

FACT OR FABLE?

$\boxed{1}$ Mergers are similar to consolidations except that when two firms are merged they are combined to form a completely new corporation rather than maintaining the identity of one of the firms. *(Fable)*

Mergers are similar to consolidations except that when two firms are merged *the resulting firm maintains the identity of one of the firms rather than forming a completely new corporation.*

Holding Companies

holding company A corporation that has voting control of one or more other corporations.

subsidiaries The companies controlled by a holding company.

A **holding company** is a corporation that has voting control of one or more other corporations. Having control in large, widely held companies generally requires ownership of between 10 and 20 percent of the outstanding stock. The companies controlled by a holding company are normally referred to as its **subsidiaries.** Control of a subsidiary is typically obtained by purchasing (generally for cash) a sufficient number of shares of its stock.

Motives for Combinations

Firms combine through mergers or holding company arrangements in order to fulfill certain objectives. The most common motives for combination include growth or diversification, synergistic effects, fund raising, increased managerial skills, tax considerations, and increased ownership liquidity.

Growth or Diversification

Companies that desire rapid growth in *size* or *market share* or diversification in *the range of their products* may find that some form of combination will fulfill this objective. Instead of going through the time-consuming process of internal growth or diversification, the firm may achieve the same objective in a short period of time by acquiring or combining with an existing firm. If a firm that wants to expand operations in existing or new product areas can find a suitable going concern, it may avoid many of the risks associated with the design, manufacture, and sale of additional or new products. Moreover, when a firm expands or extends its product line by acquiring another firm, it also removes a potential competitor.[1] Mergers and holding companies may be used to achieve horizontal, vertical, or congeneric growth, or conglomerate diversification. Each of these situations is briefly described in Table 19.1.

Table 19.1
Key Types of Growth or Diversification

Type of growth or diversification	Description
Horizontal growth	Results from combination of firms in the *same line of business*. For example, the merger of two machine-tool manufacturers. Used to expand operations in an existing product line and at the same time eliminate a competitor.
Vertical growth	When a firm *acquires a supplier or a customer*. For example, the merger of a machine-tool manufacturer with its supplier of castings. Economic benefit stems from greater control over the acquisition of raw materials or the distribution of finished goods.
Congeneric growth	Achieved by acquiring a firm in the *same general industry* but neither in the same line of business nor a supplier or customer. For example, the merger of a machine-tool manufacturer with the manufacturer of industrial conveyor systems. The benefit results from the ability to use the same sales and distribution channels to reach customers of both businesses.
Conglomerate diversification	Involves the combination of firms in *unrelated businesses*. For example, the merger of a machine-tool manufacturer with a chain of fast-food restaurants. The key benefit of conglomerates lies in their ability to *reduce risk* by combining firms with differing seasonal or cyclical patterns of sales and earnings.[a]

[a] A discussion of the key concepts underlying the portfolio approach to the diversification of risk was presented in Chapter 7. In the theoretical literature some questions exist relating to whether diversification by the firm is a proper motive consistent with shareholder wealth maximization. Many scholars argue that by buying shares in different firms investors can obtain the same benefits as they would from owning stock in the merged firms. It appears that other benefits need to be available to justify mergers.

[1] Certain legal constraints on growth—especially where the elimination of competition is expected—exist. The various antitrust laws, which are closely enforced by the Federal Trade Commission (FTC) and the Justice Department, prohibit business combinations that eliminate competition, especially when the resulting enterprise would be a monopoly.

Synergistic Effects

The *synergistic effects* of business combinations are certain economies of scale resulting from the combined firms' lower overhead. Synergistic effects are said to be present when a whole is greater than the sum of the parts ("1 plus 1 equals 3"). The economies of scale that generally result from combination lower combined overhead, thereby increasing earnings to a level greater than the sum of the earnings of each of the independent firms. Synergistic effects are most obvious when firms merge with other firms in the same line of business, since many redundant functions and employees can thereby be eliminated. Staff functions, such as purchasing and sales, are probably most greatly affected by this type of combination.

Fund Raising

Often firms combine to enhance their fund-raising ability. A firm may be unable to obtain funds for its own internal expansion but able to obtain funds for external business combinations. Quite often one firm may combine with another that has high liquid assets and low levels of liabilities. The acquisition of this type of "cash-rich" company immediately increases the firm's borrowing power by decreasing its financial leverage. This should enable the raising of funds externally at more favorable rates.

Increased Managerial Skills

Occasionally a firm will have good potential that it finds itself unable to develop fully due to deficiencies in certain areas of management. If the firm cannot hire the management it needs, it might combine with a compatible firm that has the needed managerial personnel. Of course any combination, regardless of the specific motive for it, should contribute to the maximization of owners' wealth.

Tax Considerations

tax loss carryforward In a combination or merger, the tax loss of one of the firms that can be applied against a limited amount of future income of the combined firm over the shorter of either 15 years or until the total tax loss has been exhausted.

Quite often tax considerations are a key motive for combination. In such a case the tax benefit generally stems from the fact that one of the firms has a **tax loss carryforward.** This means that the company's tax loss can be applied against a limited amount[2] of future income of the combined firm over the shorter of either 15 years or until the total tax loss has been exhausted. Two situations could actually exist. A company with a tax loss could acquire a profitable company in order to utilize the tax loss. In this case the acquiring firm would boost the combination's after-tax earnings by reducing the taxable income of the acquired firm. A tax loss may also be useful when a profitable firm acquires a firm that has such a loss. In either situation, however, the merger must be justified not only on the basis of the tax benefits but also on grounds consistent with the goal of owners' wealth maximization. Moreover, the tax benefits described are useful only in mergers—not in the formation of holding companies—since only in the case of mergers are operating results reported on a consolidated basis. An example will clarify the use of the tax loss carryforward.

---

[2] The *Tax Reform Act of 1986,* in order to deter firms from combining solely to take advantage of tax loss carryforwards, initiated an annual limit on the amount of taxable income against which such losses can be applied. The annual limit is determined by formula and is tied to the value of the loss corporation before the combination. While not fully eliminating this motive for combination, the act makes it more difficult for firms to justify combinations solely on the basis of tax loss carryforwards.

Example

The Bergen Company has a total of $450,000 in tax loss carryforwards resulting from operating tax losses of $150,000 a year in each of the past three years. To use these losses and to diversify its operations, the Hudson Company has acquired Bergen through a merger. Hudson expects to have *earnings before taxes* of $300,000 per year. We assume that these earnings are realized, that they fall within the annual limit legally allowed for application of the tax loss carryforward resulting from the merger (see footnote 2 on page 686), that the Bergen portion of the merged firm just breaks even, and that Hudson is in the 40 percent tax bracket. The total taxes paid by the two firms and their after-tax earnings without and with the merger are calculated as shown in the following table.

Total taxes and after-tax earnings without merger				
	Year			**Total for 3 years**
	1	**2**	**3**	
(1) Earnings before taxes	$300,000	$300,000	$300,000	$900,000
(2) Taxes [.40 × (1)]	120,000	120,000	120,000	360,000
(3) Earnings after taxes [(1) − (2)]	$180,000	$180,000	$180,000	$540,000
Total taxes and after-tax earnings with merger				
(4) Earnings before losses	$300,000	$300,000	$300,000	$900,000
(5) Tax loss carryforward	300,000	150,000	0	450,000
(6) Earnings before taxes [(4) − (5)]	$ 0	$150,000	$300,000	$450,000
(7) Taxes [.40 × (6)]	0	60,000	120,000	180,000
(8) Earnings after taxes [(4) − (7)]	$300,000	$240,000	$180,000	$720,000

With the merger the total tax payments are less—$180,000 (total of line 7) versus $360,000 (total of line 2). With the merger the total after-tax earnings are more—$720,000 (total of line 8) versus $540,000 (total of line 3). The combined firms are able to deduct the tax loss either for 15 years subsequently or until the total tax loss has been exhausted, whichever period is shorter. In this example the shorter is at the end of year 2.

Increased Ownership Liquidity

In the case of mergers the combination of two small firms or a small and a larger firm into a larger corporation may provide the owners of the small firm(s) with greater liquidity. This is due to the higher marketability associated with the shares of larger firms. Instead of holding shares in a small firm that has a very "thin" market, the owners will receive shares that are traded in a broader market and can thus be liquidated more readily. Not only does the ability to convert shares into cash quickly have appeal, but owning shares for which market price quotations are readily available provides owners with a better sense of the value of their holdings. Especially in the case of small, closely held firms, the improved liquidity of ownership obtainable through a merger with an acceptable firm may have considerable appeal.

Divestiture: A Related but Different Situation

operating unit A part of a business, such as a plant, division, or subsidiary, that contributes to the actual operations of the firm.

divestiture The selling of some of a firm's assets.

It is important to recognize that companies often achieve external expansion by acquiring an **operating unit**—plant, division, line of business, subsidiary, etc.—of another company. In such a case, the seller generally believes that the value of the firm would be enhanced by converting the unit into cash or some other more productive asset. The selling of some of a firm's assets is called **divestiture.** Unlike business failure, the motive for divestiture is often positive: to generate cash for expansion of other product lines; to get rid of a poorly performing operation; to streamline the corporation; to restructure the corporation's business consistent with its strategic goals.

There are a variety of methods by which firms divest themselves of operating units. One involves the *sale of a line of business to another firm*. These outright sales can be accomplished on a cash or stock-exchange basis using the procedures described later in this chapter. A second method that has become quite popular in recent years involves the *sale of the unit to existing management*. This sale is often achieved through the use of a *leveraged buyout (LBO),* a mechanism described later in this chapter. Sometimes divestiture is achieved through a **spin-off** which results in an operating unit becoming an independent company. This is accomplished by issuing shares in the operating unit being divested on a pro rata basis to the parent company's shareholders. Such an action allows the unit to be separated from the corporation and trade as a separate entity. Like outright sale, this approach achieves the divestiture objective although it does not bring additional cash or stock to the parent company. The final and least popular approach to divestiture involves *liquidation of the operating unit's individual assets*.

spin-off A form of divestiture in which an operating unit becomes an independent company by issuing shares of the new firm on a pro rata basis to the parent company's shareholders.

Regardless of the method used to divest a firm of an unwanted operating unit, the goal typically is to create a more lean and focused operation in order to enhance the efficiency as well as the profitability of the enterprise and create maximum value for shareholders. Recent divestitures seem to suggest that many operating units are worth much more to others than to the firm itself. Comparisons of post- and pre-divestiture market values have shown that the ''breakup value'' of many firms is significantly greater than their combined value. As a result of market valuations, divestiture often creates value in excess of the cash or stock received in the transaction. The use of acquisitions/ divestitures as part of corporate restructuring is expected to remain popular over the next few years, although the pace may slow somewhat as a result of the ''Stock Market Crash of 1987.''

Analyzing and Negotiating Business Combinations

This portion of the chapter describes the procedures used to analyze and negotiate business combinations. Initially attention is given to the analysis of mergers using cash purchases and stock-exchange acquisitions. Next, leveraged buyouts (LBOs) and the merger negotiation process are described. Finally, the major advantages and disadvantages of holding companies are reviewed.

Cash Purchases

When one firm acquires another firm for cash (debt is assumed to be the same as cash here), the use of simple capital budgeting procedures is required. Whether the second firm is being acquired for its assets or as a going concern, the basic approach is similar.

Acquisitions of Assets

In some instances a firm is acquired not for its income-earning potential but as a collection of assets (generally fixed assets) that are needed by the acquiring firm. The cash price paid for this type of acquisition depends largely on which assets are being acquired; consideration must also be given to the value of any tax losses. To determine whether the purchase of assets is financially justified, the firm must estimate both the costs and benefits of the assets. This is a capital budgeting problem (see Chapters 9 and 10) since an initial cash outlay is made to acquire assets and, as a result, future cash inflows are expected.

Example

Clark Company is interested in acquiring certain fixed assets of Noble Company. Noble, which has tax loss carryforwards from losses over the past five years, is interested in selling out, but it wishes to sell out entirely, not just get rid of certain fixed assets. A condensed balance sheet for Noble Company follows.

Balance Sheet for Noble Company			
Assets		**Liabilities and stockholders' equity**	
Cash	$ 2,000	Total liabilities	$ 80,000
Marketable securities	0	Stockholders' equity	120,000
Accounts receivable	8,000	Total liabilities and	
Inventories	10,000	stockholders' equity	$200,000
Machine A	10,000		
Machine B	30,000		
Machine C	25,000		
Land and buildings	115,000		
Total assets	$200,000		

Clark Company needs only machines B and C and the land and buildings. However, it has made some inquiries and has arranged to sell the accounts receivable, inventories, and machine A for $23,000. Since there is also $2,000 in cash, Clark will get $25,000 for the excess assets. Noble wants $20,000 for the entire company, which means that Clark will have to pay the firm's creditors $80,000 and its owners $20,000. The actual outlay required by Clark after liquidating the unneeded assets will be $75,000 [($80,000 + $20,000) − $25,000]. In other words, to obtain the use of the desired assets (machines B and C and the land and buildings) and the benefits of Noble's tax losses, Clark must pay $75,000. The *after-tax cash inflows* expected to result from the new assets and applicable tax losses are $14,000 per year for the next five years and $12,000 per year for the following five years. The desirability of this acquisition can be determined by calculating the net present value of this outlay using the Clark Company's 11 percent cost of capital, as shown in Table 19.2. Since the net present value of $3,072 is greater than zero, Clark's value should be increased by acquiring Noble Company.

Table 19.2
An Analysis of the Noble Company Acquisition by Clark Company

Year(s)	Cash inflow (1)	Present value factor at 11% (2)	Present value [(1) × (2)] (3)
1–5	14,000	3.696[b]	51,744
6	12,000	0.535[a]	6,420
7	12,000	0.482[a]	5,784
8	12,000	0.434[a]	5,208
9	12,000	0.391[a]	4,692
10	12,000	0.352[a]	4,224
	Present value of inflows		$78,072
	Less: Cash outlay required		75,000
	Net present value		$ 3,072

[a] The present-value interest factor, PVIF, for $1 discounted at 11 percent for the corresponding year obtained from Table A-3.

[b] The present-value interest factor for an annuity, PVIFA, with a five-year life discounted at 11 percent obtained from Table A-4.

Acquisitions of Going Concerns

Cash acquisitions of going concerns are best analyzed using capital budgeting techniques such as those described for asset acquisitions. The basic difficulty in applying the capital budgeting approach to the cash acquisition of a going concern is the *estimation of cash flows* and certain *risk considerations*. The methods of estimating expected cash flows from an acquisition are no different from those used in estimating cash flows in any capital budgeting decision. Whenever a firm considers acquiring for cash another firm that has different risk behaviors, it should adjust the cost of capital appropriately (see Chapter 10) prior to applying capital budgeting techniques. An example will clarify this procedure.

Example
The Square Company is contemplating the acquisition of the Circle Company, which can be purchased for $60,000 in cash. Square currently has a high degree of financial leverage, which is reflected in its 13 percent cost of capital. Because of the low financial leverage of the Circle Company, Square estimates that its overall cost of capital will drop to 10 percent after the acquisition. Since the effect of the less risky capital structure resulting from the acquisition of Circle Company cannot be reflected in the expected cash flows, the post-acquisition cost of capital (10 percent) must be used to evaluate the cash flows expected from the acquisition. The incremental cash inflows forecast from the proposed acquisition are expected over a 30-year time hori-

zon. These estimated inflows are $5,000 for years 1 through 10; $13,000 for years 11 through 18; and $4,000 for years 19 through 30. The net present value of the acquisition is calculated in Table 19.3.

Since the net present value of the acquisition is greater than zero ($2,357), the acquisition is acceptable. It is interesting to note that had the effect of the changed capital structure on the cost of capital not been considered, the acquisition would have been found unacceptable since the net present value *at a 13 percent cost of capital* is −$11,864, which is less than zero.

Table 19.3
An Analysis of the Square Company Acquisition of the Circle Company

Year(s)	Cash inflow (1)	Present value factor at 10%[a] (2)	Present value [(1) × (2)] (3)
1–10	5,000	6.145	30,725
11–18	13,000	(8.201 − 6.145)[b]	26,728
19–30	4,000	(9.427 − 8.201)[b]	4,904
		Present value of inflows	$62,357
		Less: Cash purchase price	60,000
		Net present value	$ 2,357

[a] Present-value interest factors for annuities, *PVIFA*, obtained from Table A-4.

[b] These factors are found using a shortcut technique that can be applied to annuities for periods of years beginning at some point in the future. By finding the appropriate interest factor for the present value of an annuity given for the last year of the annuity and subtracting the present-value interest factor of an annuity for the year immediately preceding the beginning of the annuity, the appropriate interest factor for the present value of an annuity beginning sometime in the future can be obtained. You can check this shortcut by using the long approach and comparing the results.

---

2 Cash purchases of companies can be analyzed by applying present-value techniques in order to determine whether the proposed acquisition has a positive net present value, in which case it should be acquired. *(Fact)*

FACT OR FABLE?

Stock-Exchange Acquisitions

Quite often a firm is acquired through the exchange of common stock. The acquiring firm exchanges its shares for shares of the firm being acquired according to a predetermined ratio. The *ratio of exchange* of shares is determined in the merger negotiations. This ratio affects the various financial yardsticks that are used by existing and prospective shareholders in valuing the merged firm's shares.

Ratio of Exchange

When one firm trades its stock for the shares of another firm, the number of shares of the acquiring firm to be exchanged for each share of the acquired firm must be determined. The first requirement, of course, is that the acquiring company have sufficient shares

PROFILE

T. BOONE PICKENS:
Making Millions Working for the Stockholders

Texas oilman, corporate raider, and the highest paid CEO in America are the phrases used most often in conjunction with the name T. Boone Pickens. As President and Chairman of the Board of the Mesa Petroleum Company, he engaged national attention, in the late 1970s and early 1980s, during a string of hostile takeover attempts in the oil industry. His attempts earned Mesa Petroleum stockholders dramatic gains and caused some corporate oil Goliaths to wonder if the contemporary David had arrived.

From its beginning in 1964, Mesa Petroleum focused primarily on oil exploration and production. Instead of adding pipelines, refineries, a fleet of tankers, and service stations, Mesa Petroleum was happy to drill and produce—and make a handsome profit. In the late 1970s, Mesa sold its Canadian and North Sea holdings just before Canada and Great Britain put costly restrictions on foreign producers. The sale left Pickens with a bundle of cash. Believing that oil prices were destined to go flat or even drop, Pickens decided to commit Mesa's extra dollars to acquisition rather than exploration.

Pickens targeted oil companies with domestic reserves and an undervalued trading price. After several unsuccessful takeover attempts, Pickens

took a shot at acquiring the fifth largest oil company in the United States—Gulf Oil. In 1983, Gulf Oil Corporation's stock was trading for less than $40 a share. The financial community had lost confidence in the stock because several decisions had put a dent in its financial reserves. Mesa, ninety-second among U.S. oil companies, began to acquire large amounts of stock in the giant Gulf Oil. By the end of January 1984, Pickens and his group held over 13 percent of Gulf stock. To gain control, they offered stockholders $55 per share.

Enter Atlantic Richfield, which

offered $70 per share. At this point, Gulf's Board of Directors began searching for a "white knight." Eventually, Standard Oil of California became that white knight by offering to buy Gulf stock for $80 per share. The merged companies became Chevron.

Although Pickens and his group did not ultimately acquire Gulf, they did make a profit of $760 million. Others made a profit too—the small investors in Gulf Oil who saw the value of their stock more than double.

T. Boone Pickens does not think he deserves to be called a corporate raider (the leader of a hostile takeover). He claims he is working for the stockholders of both Mesa and the companies Mesa tries to acquire. A poorly managed company, he believes, deserves new management approaches that will bring stockholders a higher return on investment.

Pickens feels he is trying to make chief executives more responsible to the stockholders of corporations. In fact, he would like to see executives own more stock. The separation of ownership and control has kept the owners of some companies from realizing a just return on their investment, he feels. As one of the highest paid executives in American business, Pickens's success is testimony to his outlook.

---

ratio of exchange The ratio of the amount *paid* per share of the acquired firm to the per-share market price of the acquiring firm.

available to complete the transaction. Often a firm's repurchase of shares, which was discussed in Chapter 17, is necessary to obtain sufficient shares for such a transaction. The acquiring firm generally offers more for each share of the acquired firm than the current market price of its publicly traded shares. The actual **ratio of exchange** is merely the ratio of the amount *paid* per share of the acquired firm to the per-share market price of the acquiring firm. It is calculated in this manner since the acquiring firm pays the acquired firm in stock, which has a value equal to its market price. An example will clarify the calculation.

Example

The Grand Company, whose stock is currently selling for $80 per share, is interested in acquiring the Small Company. To prepare for the acquisition, Grand has been repurchasing its own shares over the past three years. Small's stock is currently selling for $75 per share, but in the merger negotiations, Grand has found it necessary to offer Small $110 per share. Since Grand does not have sufficient financial resources to purchase the firm for cash, and it does not wish to raise these funds, Small has agreed to accept Grand's stock in exchange for its shares. As stated, Grand's stock currently sells for $80 per share and it must pay $110 per share for Small's stock. Therefore the ratio of exchange is 1.375 ($110 ÷ $80). This means that the Grand Company must exchange 1.375 shares of its stock for each share of Small's stock.

Effect on Earnings per Share

Ordinarily the resulting earnings per share differ from the premerger earnings per share for both the acquiring firm and the acquired firm. They depend largely on the ratio of exchange and the premerger earnings per share of each firm. It is best to view the initial and long-run effects of the ratio of exchange on earnings per share (EPS) separately.

Initial Effect. When the ratio of exchange is equal to 1 and both the acquiring and the acquired firm have the *same* premerger earnings per share, the merged firm's earnings per share will initially remain constant. In this rare instance, both the acquiring and the acquired firm would also have equal price/earnings (P/E) ratios. In actuality the earnings per share of the merged firm are generally above the premerger earnings per share of one firm and below the premerger earnings per share of the other, after making the necessary adjustment for the ratio of exchange. These differences can be illustrated by a simple example.

Example

The Grand Company is contemplating acquiring the Small Company by exchanging 1.375 shares of its stock for each share of Small's stock. The current financial data related to the earnings and market price for each of these companies are given in Table 19.4. Although Small's stock currently has a market price of $75 per share, Grand has offered it $110 per share. As seen in the preceding example, this results in a ratio of exchange of 1.375.

To complete the merger and retire the 20,000 shares of Small Company stock outstanding, Grand will have to issue and (or) use treasury stock totaling 27,500 shares (1.375 × 20,000 shares). Once the merger is completed, Grand will have 152,500 shares of common stock (125,000 + 27,500) outstanding. If the earnings of each of the firms remain constant, the merged company will be expected to have earnings available for the common stockholders of $600,000 ($500,000 + $100,000). The earnings per share of the merged company should therefore equal approximately $3.93 per share ($600,000 ÷ 152,500 shares).

It would appear at first that the Small Company's shareholders have sustained a decrease in per-share earnings from $5 to $3.93, but since each share of the Small Company's original stock is equivalent to 1.375 shares of the merged company, the

Table 19.4
Grand Company and Small Company Financial Data

Item	Grand Company	Small Company
(1) Earnings available for common stock	$500,000	$100,000
(2) Number of shares of common stock outstanding	125,000	20,000
(3) Earnings per share [(1) ÷ (2)]	$4	$5
(4) Market price per share	$80	$75
(5) Price/earnings (P/E) ratio [(4) ÷ (3)]	20	15

equivalent earnings per share are actually $5.40 ($3.93 × 1.375). In other words, as a result of the merger the Grand Company's original shareholders experience a decrease in earnings per share from $4 to $3.93 to the benefit of the Small Company's shareholders, whose earnings per share increase from $5 to $5.40. These results are summarized in Table 19.5

Table 19.5
Summary of the Effects on Earnings per Share of a Merger Between Grand Company and Small Company at $110 per Share

Stockholders	Earnings per share	
	Before merger	After merger
Grand Company	$4.00	$3.93[a]
Small Company	5.00	5.40[b]

[a] $\dfrac{\$500,000 + \$100,000}{125,000 + (1.375 \times 20,000)} = \$3.93$

[b] $3.93 × 1.375 = $5.40

The postmerger earnings per share for owners of the acquiring and acquired company can be explained by comparing the price/earnings (P/E) ratio paid by the acquiring company with its initial P/E ratio. This relationship is summarized in Table 19.6. By paying more than its current value per dollar of earnings to acquire each dollar of earnings (P/E paid > P/E of acquiring company), the acquiring firm transfers the claim on a portion of its premerger earnings to the owners of the acquired firm. Therefore, on a postmerger basis the acquired firm's EPS increases and the acquiring firm's EPS decreases. If the acquiring company were to pay less than its current value per dollar of earnings to acquire each dollar of earnings (P/E paid < P/E of acquiring company), the opposite effects would result. The P/E ratios associated with the Grand-Small merger can be used to explain the effect of the merger on earnings per share.

Table 19.6
Effect of Price/Earnings (P/E) Ratios on Earnings per Share (EPS)

Relationship between P/E paid and P/E of acquiring company	Effect on EPS	
	Acquiring company	Acquired company
P/E paid > P/E of acquiring company	Decrease	Increase
P/E paid = P/E of acquiring company	Constant	Constant
P/E paid < P/E of acquiring company	Increase	Decrease

---

3 If a firm in a stock-exchange acquisition pays a greater price/earnings (P/E) multiple than its current multiple, it will initially experience an increase in its earnings per share (EPS) while the acquired company's EPS will initially decrease. *(Fable)*

If a firm in a stock-exchange acquisition pays a greater price/earnings (P/E) multiple than its current multiple, it will initially experience a *decrease* in its earnings per share (EPS) while the acquired company's EPS will initially *increase*.

FACT OR FABLE?

Example
Grand Company's P/E ratio is 20, while the P/E ratio based on the share price paid Small Company was 22 ($110 ÷ $5). Since the P/E based on the share price paid for Small Company was greater than the P/E for Grand Company (22 versus 20), the effect of the merger was to decrease the EPS for original holders of shares in Grand Company (from $4.00 to $3.93) and to increase the effective EPS of original holders of shares in Small Company (from $5.00 to $5.40).

Long-Run Effect. The long-run effect of a merger on the earnings per share of the merged company depends largely on whether the earnings of the merged firm grow. Often, although a decrease in the per-share earnings of the stock held by the original owners of the acquiring firm is expected initially, the long-run effects of the merger on earnings per share are quite favorable. Since growth in earnings is generally expected by a business firm, the key factor enabling the acquiring company, which initially experiences a decrease in EPS, to experience higher future EPS than it would have without the merger is the fact that the earnings attributable to the acquired company's assets grow at a faster rate than those resulting from the acquiring company's premerger assets. An example will clarify this point.

Example
In 1988 Grand Company acquired Small Company by exchanging 1.375 shares of its common stock for each share of Small Company. Other key financial data and the effects of this exchange ratio were discussed in the preceding example. The total earnings of Grand Company were expected to grow at an annual rate of 3 percent

without the merger, while Small Company's earnings were expected to grow at a 7 percent annual rate without the merger. The same growth rates are expected to apply to the component earnings streams with the merger.[3] Table 19.7 shows the future effects on EPS for Grand Company without and with the proposed Small Company merger, based on these growth rates.

Table 19.7 indicates that the earnings per share without the merger will be greater than the EPS with the merger for the years 1988 through 1990. After 1990, however, the EPS will be higher than they would have been without the merger as a result of the faster earnings growth rate of Small Company (7 percent versus 3 percent). Although a few years are required for this difference in the growth rate of earnings to pay off, it can be seen that in the future Grand Company will receive an earnings benefit as a result of merging with Small Company at a 1.375 ratio of exchange. The relationships in Table 19.7 are graphed in Figure 19.1. The long-run earnings advantage of the merger is clearly depicted by this graph.[4]

Table 19.7
Effects of Earnings Growth on EPS for the Grand Company Without and With the Small Company Merger

Year	Without merger		With merger	
	Total earnings[a]	Earnings per share[b]	Total earnings[c]	Earnings per share[d]
1988	$500,000	$4.00	$600,000	$3.93
1989	515,000	4.12	622,000	4.08
1990	530,450	4.24	644,940	4.23
1991	546,364	4.37	668,868	4.39
1992	562,755	4.50	693,835	4.55
1993	579,638	4.64	719,893	4.72

[a] Based on a 3 percent annual growth rate.

[b] Based on 125,000 shares outstanding.

[c] Based on 3 percent annual growth in the Grand Company's earnings and 7 percent annual growth in the Small Company's earnings.

[d] Based on 152,500 shares outstanding [125,000 shares + (1.375 × 20,000 shares)].

FACT OR FABLE?   **4** An acquiring company initially experiencing a decrease in earnings per share (EPS) can experience higher future EPS than it would have without the merger if the acquired company's assets grow at a faster rate than that resulting from its premerger assets. *(Fact)*

[3] Sometimes, due to synergistic effects, the combined earnings stream is greater than the sum of the individual earnings streams. This possibility is ignored here.

[4] To discover properly whether the merger is beneficial, the earnings estimates under each alternative would have to be made over a long period of time, say 50 years, and then discounted at the appropriate rate. The alternative with the highest present value would be preferred. In the interest of simplicity, only the basic intuitive view of the long-run effect is presented here.

Figure 19.1
Future EPS Without and With the Grand-Small Merger

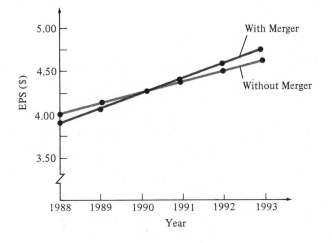

Effect on Market Price per Share

The market price per share does not necessarily remain constant after the acquisition of one firm by another. Adjustments occur in the marketplace in response to changes in expected earnings, the dilution of ownership, changes in risk, and certain other operating and financial changes. Using the ratio of exchange, a **ratio of exchange in market price** can be calculated. It indicates the market price per share of the acquiring firm *paid* for each dollar of market price per share of the acquired firm. This ratio, the *MPR*, is defined by Equation 19.1.

ratio of exchange in market price The ratio indicating the market price per share of the acquiring firm *paid* for each dollar of market price per share of the acquired firm.

$$MPR = \frac{MP_{acquiring} \times RE}{MP_{acquired}} \qquad (19.1)$$

where

MPR = market price ratio of exchange
$MP_{acquiring}$ = market price per share of the acquiring firm
$MP_{acquired}$ = market price per share of the acquired firm
RE = ratio of exchange

The following example can be used to illustrate the calculation of this ratio.

Example
In the Grand-Small example, the market price of the Grand Company's stock was $80 and that of the Small Company's was $75. The ratio of exchange was 1.375. Substituting these values into Equation 19.1 yields a ratio of exchange in market price of 1.47 [($80 × 1.375) ÷ $75]. This means that $1.47 of the market price of Grand Company is given in exchange for every $1.00 of the market price of Small Company.

The ratio of exchange in market price is normally always greater than 1, which indicates that to acquire a firm, a premium above its market price must be paid by the acquirer. Even so, the original owners of the acquiring firm may still gain because the merged firm's stock may sell at a price/earnings ratio above the individual premerger ratios. This results due to the improved risk and return relationship perceived by shareholders and other investors.

> **Example**
> The financial data developed earlier for the Grand-Small merger can be used to explain the market price effects of a merger. If the earnings of the merged company remain at the premerger levels, and if the stock of the merged company sells at an assumed multiple of 21 times earnings, the values in Table 19.8 can be expected. In spite of the fact that Grand Company's earnings per share decline from $4.00 to $3.93 (see Table 19.5), the market price of its shares will increase from $80.00 (see Table 19.4) to $82.53 as a result of the merger.

Although the kind of behavior exhibited in this example is not unusual, the financial manager must recognize that only with proper management of the merged enterprise can its market value be improved. If the merged firm cannot achieve sufficiently high earnings in view of its risk, there is no guarantee that its market price will reach the forecast value. Nevertheless, a policy of acquiring firms with low P/Es can produce favorable results for the owners of the acquiring firm. Acquisitions are especially attractive when the acquiring firm's stock price is high, since fewer shares must be exchanged to acquire a given firm.

Leveraged Buyouts (LBOs)

leveraged buyout (LBO)
An acquisition technique in which a large amount of debt is used to purchase a firm.

A popular technique currently used to make acquisitions is the **leveraged buyout (LBO)**, which involves the use of a large amount of debt to purchase a firm. Typically the debt represents 90 percent or more of the purchase price. A large part of the borrowing is secured by the acquired firm's assets, and the lenders, due to the high risk, take a portion of the firm's equity. The acquirers in LBOs are other firms or groups of investors that frequently include key members of existing management.

An attractive candidate for acquisition through leveraged buyout should possess three basic attributes:

1. It must have a good position in its industry with a solid profit history and reasonable expectations for growth.

Table 19.8
Postmerger Market Price of Grand Company Using a P/E Ratio of 21

Item	Merged company
(1) Earnings available for common stock	$600,000
(2) Number of shares of common stock outstanding	152,500
(3) Earnings per share [(1) ÷ (2)]	$3.93
(4) Price/earnings (P/E) ratio	21
(5) Expected market price per share [(3) × (4)]	$82.53

2. The firm should have a relatively low level of debt and a high level of "bankable" assets that can be used as loan collateral.

3. It must have stable and predictable cash flows that are adequate to meet interest and principal payments on the debt and provide adequate working capital.

Of course, a willingness on the part of existing ownership and management to sell the company on a leveraged basis is also needed.

The leveraged buyout of Gibson Greeting Cards by a group of investors and managers headed by William Simon, former secretary of the treasury, demonstrates the popularity of LBOs. In the early 1980s Simon's group, Wesray, purchased Gibson from RCA for $81 million. The group put up $1 million and borrowed the remaining $80 million, using the firm's assets as collateral. Within three years after Gibson had been acquired, Wesray had publicly sold 50 percent of the company for $87 million. Wesray still owned 50 percent of Gibson and had earned $87 million on a $1 million investment. While this success cannot be cited as the typical outcome of a leveraged buyout, it does point out the potential rewards from the use of LBOs to finance acquisitions.

The Merger Negotiation Process

Mergers are often handled by **investment bankers** hired by the prospective participants to find a suitable merger partner and assist in negotiations. A firm seeking a potential acquisition can hire an investment banker to find firms meeting its requirements. Once located, the investment banker negotiates with the management or the investment banker of the potential acquisition. Frequently, when management wishes to sell the firm or a division of the firm, it will hire an investment banker to seek out potential buyers.

In the event that attempts to negotiate with the management of an acquisition candidate break down, the firm, often with the aid of its investment banker, can make a direct appeal to shareholders by using *tender offers* (as explained below). The investment banker is typically compensated with a fixed fee, a commission tied to the transaction price, or with a combination of fees and commissions.

investment bankers Financial institutions hired by the prospective participants in a merger to find a suitable partner and assist in negotiations.

Management Negotiations

To initiate the negotiation process, the acquiring firm must make an offer either in cash or based on a certain ratio of exchange. The merger candidate must then review the offer and, in light of alternative offers, accept or reject the terms presented. A desirable merger candidate usually receives more than a single offer. Normally, certain nonfinancial issues relating to the disposition and compensation of the existing management, product-line policies, financing policies, and the independence of the acquired firm must be resolved. The key factor, of course, is the per-share price offered in cash or reflected in the ratio of exchange. Although the negotiations are generally based on the expectation of a merger, sometimes negotiations will break down.

Tender Offers

When management negotiations for an acquisition break down, *tender offers* may be used to negotiate a merger directly with the firm's stockholders. A **tender offer** is a formal offer to purchase a given number of shares of a firm's stock at a specified price. The offer is made at a premium above the market price to all the stockholders. The stockholders are advised of this proposal through announcements in financial newspapers or through direct

tender offer A formal offer to purchase a given number of shares of a firm's stock at a specified price, often in order to acquire the firm.

communications from the offering firm. Sometimes a tender offer is made in order to add pressure to existing merger negotiations. In other cases the tender offer may be made without warning as an attempt at an abrupt corporate takeover.

If the management of a firm does not favor a merger or considers the premium in a projected tender offer too low, it is likely to take certain defensive actions to ward off the tender offer. Common strategies include declaring an attractive dividend, informing stockholders of alleged damaging effects of being taken over, or attempting to sue the acquiring firm. These actions may deter or delay a tender offer. Deterring the tender offer by filing suit gives the management that is fearful of a takeover time to find and negotiate a merger with a firm it would prefer to be acquired by.

Holding Companies

As defined earlier, a *holding company* is a corporation that has voting control of one or more other corporations. The holding company may need to own only a small percentage of the outstanding shares to have this voting control. In the case of companies with a relatively small number of shareholders, as much as 30 to 40 percent of the stock may be required. In the case of firms with a widely dispersed ownership, 10 to 20 percent of the shares may be sufficient to gain voting control. A holding company desirous of obtaining voting control of a firm may use direct market purchases or tender offers to obtain needed shares.

Advantages of Holding Companies

The primary advantage of the holding company arrangement is the *leverage effect* that permits the firm to control a large amount of assets with a relatively small dollar investment. In other words, the owners of a holding company can *control* significantly larger amounts of assets than they could *acquire* through mergers. The following example may help illustrate the leverage effect.

Example

Carr Company currently holds voting control of two subsidiaries—company X and company Y. The balance sheets for Carr Company and its two subsidiaries are presented in Table 19.9. It owns approximately 17 percent ($10 ÷ $60) of company X and 20 percent ($14 ÷ $70) of company Y. It is assumed that these holdings are sufficient for voting control.

The owners of Carr Company's $12 worth of equity have control over $260 worth of assets (company X's $100 worth and company Y's $160 worth). This means that the owners' equity represents only about 4.6 percent ($12 ÷ $260) of the total assets controlled. From the discussions of ratio analysis, leverage, and capital structure in Chapters 4 and 12, you should recognize that this is quite a high degree of leverage. If an individual stockholder or even another holding company owns $3 of Carr Company's stock, which is assumed sufficient for its control, it will in actuality control the whole $260 of assets. The investment itself in this case would represent only 1.15 percent ($3 ÷ $260) of the assets controlled.

Table 19.9
Balance Sheets for Carr Company and Its Subsidiaries

Assets		Liabilities and stockholders' equity	
Carr Company			
Common stock holdings		Long-term debt	$ 6
Company X	$10	Preferred stock	6
Company Y	14	Common stock equity	12
Total	$24	Total	$24
Company X			
Current assets	$ 30	Current liabilities	$ 15
Fixed assets	70	Long-term debt	25
Total	$100	Common stock equity	60
		Total	$100
Company Y			
Current assets	$ 20	Current liabilities	$ 10
Fixed assets	140	Long-term debt	60
Total	$160	Preferred stock	20
		Common stock equity	70
		Total	$160

The high leverage obtained through a holding company arrangement greatly magnifies earnings and losses for the holding company. Quite often a **pyramiding** of holding companies occurs when one holding company controls other holding companies, thereby causing an even greater magnification of earnings and losses. The greater the leverage, the greater the risk involved. The risk-return trade-off is a key consideration in the holding company decision.

Another commonly cited advantage of the holding company arrangement is the *risk protection* resulting from the fact that failure of one of the companies (such as Y in the preceding example) does not result in the failure of the entire holding company. Since each subsidiary is a separate corporation, the failure of one company should cost the holding company, at maximum, no more than its investment in that subsidiary. Other advantages include the following: (1) certain state *tax benefits* may be realized by each subsidiary in its state of incorporation; (2) *lawsuits or legal actions* against a subsidiary will not threaten the remaining companies; and (3) it is *generally easy to gain control* of a firm since stockholder or management approval is not generally necessary.

pyramiding An arrangement among holding companies wherein one holding company controls other holding companies, thereby causing an even greater magnification of earnings and losses.

Disadvantages of Holding Companies

A major disadvantage of the holding company arrangement is the *increased risk* resulting from the leverage effect. When general economic conditions are unfavorable, a loss by one subsidiary may be magnified. For example, if subsidiary company X in Table 19.9 experiences a loss, its inability to pay dividends to Carr Company could result in Carr Company's inability to meet its scheduled payments.

Another disadvantage is *double taxation*. Prior to paying dividends a subsidiary must pay federal and state taxes on its earnings. Although an 80 percent tax exemption is allowed on dividends received by one corporation from another, the remaining 20 percent received is taxable. (In the event that the holding company owns 80 percent or more of the stock in the subsidiary, 100 percent of the dividends are tax exempt.) If a subsidiary were part of a merged company, double taxation would *not* exist.

A final disadvantage of holding companies is the generally *high cost of administration* resulting from maintaining each subsidiary company as a separate entity. A merger, on the other hand, would likely result in certain administrative economies of scale. The need for coordination and communication between the holding company and its subsidiaries may further elevate these costs.

Business Failure Fundamentals

A business failure is an unfortunate circumstance. Although the majority of firms that fail do so within the first year or two of life, other firms grow, mature, and fail much later. The failure of a business can be viewed in a number of ways and can result from one or more causes.

Types of Business Failure

A firm may fail because its *returns are negative or low*. A firm that consistently reports operating losses will probably experience a decline in market value. If the firm fails to earn a return greater than its cost of capital, it can be viewed as having failed. Negative or low returns, unless remedied, are likely to result eventually in one of the following more serious types of failure.

technical insolvency
Business failure that occurs when a firm is unable to pay its liabilities as they come due.

bankruptcy Business failure that occurs when a firm's liabilities exceed the fair market value of its assets.

A second type of failure, **technical insolvency,** occurs when a firm is unable to pay its liabilities as they come due. When a firm is technically insolvent, its assets are still greater than its liabilities, but it is confronted with a *liquidity crisis*. If some of its assets can be converted into cash within a reasonable period, the company may be able to escape complete failure. If not, the result is the third and most serious type of failure, **bankruptcy.** Bankruptcy occurs when a firm's liabilities exceed the fair market value of its assets. A bankrupt firm has a *negative* stockholders' equity.[5] This means that the claims of creditors cannot be satisfied unless the firm's assets can be liquidated for more than their book value. Although bankruptcy is an obvious form of failure, *the courts treat technical insolvency and bankruptcy in the same way*. They are both considered to indicate the financial failure of the firm.

Major Causes of Business Failure

The primary cause of business failure is *mismanagement,* which accounts for more than 50 percent of all cases. Numerous specific managerial faults can cause the firm to fail. Overexpansion, poor financial actions, an ineffective sales force, and high production costs can all singly, or in combination, cause the ultimate failure of the firm. Since all

---

[5] Since on a balance sheet the firm's assets equal the sum of its liabilities and stockholders' equity, the only way a firm that has more liabilities than assets can balance its balance sheet is to have a *negative* stockholders' equity.

FINANCE IN ACTION

PYRAMIDING:
How High Before it Starts to Get Shaky?

When ICH Corp., the $3.8 billion (in assets) life insurer, came to market in 1986 with a $600 million offering of preferred stock and debentures, it looked like a rock-solid opportunity for investors. After all, ICH itself had been a fabulous investment in recent years. Since 1981 revenues at the firm had grown at a 50 percent annual clip, earnings per share had climbed rapidly as well, and the stock had gone from a mere $1 per share to a value of about $23 at the time of the offering.

Did this make ICH a good deal? In fact, it made it a risky deal. It's the old story: Nothing grows to the sky. The very fact that the company had been compounding at 50 percent suggested strongly that it could not possibly keep this growth up.

During his twenty years as chairman and chief executive officer, Robert Shaw had built his company not by writing policies, but by acquiring ever-larger competitors, and then pledging them as collateral for loans to acquire yet more companies. This technique is

known as "pyramiding". Nearly all of that capital had been raised in the form of debt. The result was that ICH had emerged as far and away the most debt-burdened major life insurance company in the country. It had a debt-equity ratio of around 2.6, which is almost 25 times the industry average.

ICH's financial picture would have looked even worse were it not for some highly creative accounting on the company's balance sheet. Take the $322 million "asset" that appeared on its ledger as "present value of future profits of acquired businesses." In plain English, ICH was balancing its books by claiming as an "asset" $322 million worth of income that the company had not earned yet—and maybe never would. Or take another $250 million claimed for "excess cost of investments in subsidiaries over net assets acquired, net of accumulated amortization." That's "goodwill," meaning excess of price paid over assets acquired. The goodwill may or may not have been valid, but it is not the same thing as

cash or marketable securities—not under any conditions.

But too many investors rely more on trend lines on an earnings chart than concern themselves with what underlies the trend. As one broker said, "As long as the stock market kept providing Shaw with a window of opportunity to finance acquisitions, who cared how soft the balance sheet was?"

So the money kept pouring in. With the help of Kidder, Peabody and Little Rock, Arkansas's Stephens Inc., Shaw went to market twice in 1986, raising $121 million in May from a common stock offering and, in November, the $600 million in preferred stock and debentures.

ICH used that money, and more, to acquire four insurance businesses from Tenneco Inc. for around $1.273 billion. Many are now waiting to learn how successful the company will be with these new acquisitions. And will the pyramid continue to rise, or are there too many flaws in its structure?

SOURCE: Jill Andresky, "Demon Debt," *Forbes*, December 15, 1986, pp. 161–164. Excerpted by permission of *Forbes* magazine. © Forbes Inc., 1986.

---

major corporate decisions are eventually measured in terms of dollars, the financial manager may play a key role in avoiding or causing a business failure. It is his or her duty to monitor the firm's financial pulse.

Economic activity—especially economic downturns—can contribute to the failure of a firm.[6] If the economy goes into a recession, sales may decrease abruptly, leaving the firm with high fixed costs and insufficient revenues to cover them. In addition, rapid rises in interest rates during a recession can further contribute to cash flow problems and make

[6] The success of some firms runs countercyclical to economic activity, and other firms are unaffected by economic activity. For example, the sale of sewing machines is likely to increase during a recession since people are more willing to make their own clothes and less willing to pay for the labor of others. The sale of boats and other luxury items may decline during a recession, while sales of staple items such as electricity are likely to be unaffected. In terms of beta—the measure of nondiversifiable risk developed in Chapter 7—a negative-beta stock would be associated with a firm whose behavior generally is countercyclical to economic activity.

it more difficult for the firm to obtain and maintain needed financing. If the recession is prolonged, the likelihood of survival decreases even further.

A final cause of business failure is *corporate maturity*. Firms, like individuals, do not have infinite lives. Like a product, a firm goes through the stages of birth, growth, maturity, and eventual decline. The firm's management should attempt to prolong the growth stage through business combinations, research, and the development of new products. Once the firm has matured and has begun to decline, it should seek to be acquired by another firm or liquidate before it fails. Effective management planning should help the firm to postpone decline and ultimate failure.

Voluntary Settlements

voluntary settlement An arrangement between a technically insolvent or bankrupt firm and its creditors enabling it to bypass many of the costs involved in legal bankruptcy proceedings.

When a firm becomes technically insolvent or bankrupt, it may arrange with its creditors a **voluntary settlement,** which enables it to bypass many of the costs involved in legal bankruptcy proceedings. The settlement is normally initiated by the debtor firm, since such an arrangement may enable it to continue to exist or to be liquidated in a manner that gives the owners the greatest chance of recovering part of their investment. The debtor, possibly with the aid of a key creditor, arranges a meeting between itself and all its creditors. At the meeting a committee of creditors is selected to investigate and analyze the debtor's situation and recommend a plan of action. The recommendations of the committee are discussed with both the debtor and the creditors, and a plan for sustaining or liquidating the firm is drawn up.

FACT OR FABLE?

5 Voluntary settlements can be used to enable the debtor firm to continue to exist or to be liquidated in a manner that saves many of the costs involved in legal bankruptcy proceedings, thereby giving owners the greatest chance of recovering part of their investment. *(Fact)*

Voluntary Settlement to Sustain the Firm

extension An arrangement whereby the firm's creditors receive payment in full, although not immediately.

composition A pro rata cash settlement of creditor claims by the debtor firm; a uniform percentage of each dollar owed is paid.

creditor control An arrangement in which the creditor committee replaces the firm's operating management and operates the firm until all claims have been settled.

Normally the rationale for sustaining a firm is that it is reasonable to believe the firm's recovery is feasible. By sustaining the firm the creditor can continue to receive business from it. A number of strategies are commonly used. An **extension** is an arrangement whereby the firm's creditors receive payment in full, although not immediately. Normally when creditors grant an extension, they agree to require cash payments for purchases until all past debts have been paid. A second arrangement, called **composition,** is a pro rata cash settlement of creditor claims. Instead of receiving full payment of their claims, as in the case of an extension, creditors receive only a partial payment. A uniform percentage of each dollar owed is paid in satisfaction of each creditor's claim. A third arrangement is **creditor control.** In this case the committee may decide that the only circumstance in which maintaining the firm is feasible is if the operating management is replaced. The creditor committee may then take control of the firm and operate it until all claims have been settled. Sometimes, a plan involving some combination of extension, composition, and creditor control will result. An example of this would be a settlement whereby the debtor agrees to pay a total of 75 cents on the dollar in three equal annual installments of

25 cents on the dollar, while the creditors agree to sell additional merchandise to the firm on 30-day terms if the existing management is replaced by a new management acceptable to them.

Voluntary Settlement Resulting in Liquidation

After the situation of the firm has been investigated by the creditor committee, recommendations have been made, and talks among the creditors and the debtor have been held, the only acceptable course of action may be liquidation of the firm. Liquidation can be carried out in two ways—privately or through the legal procedures provided by bankruptcy law. If the debtor firm is willing to accept liquidation, legal procedures may not be required. Generally, the avoidance of litigation enables the creditors to obtain *quicker* and *higher* settlements. However, all the creditors must agree to a private liquidation in order for it to be feasible.

The objective of the voluntary liquidation process is to recover as much per dollar owed as possible. Under voluntary liquidation common stockholders, who are the firm's true owners, cannot receive any funds until the claims of all other parties have been satisfied. A common procedure is to have a meeting of the creditors at which they make an **assignment** by passing the power to liquidate the firm's assets to an adjustment bureau, trade association, or a third party, which becomes the *assignee*. The assignee's job is to liquidate the assets, obtaining the best price possible. The assignee is sometimes referred to as the *trustee,* since it is entrusted with the title to the company's assets and the responsibility to liquidate them efficiently. Once the trustee has liquidated the assets, it distributes the recovered funds to the creditors and owners (if any funds remain for the owners). The final action in a private liquidation is for the creditors to sign a release attesting to the satisfactory settlement of their claims.

assignment A voluntary liquidation procedure by which a firm's creditors pass the power to liquidate the firm's assets to an adjustment bureau, trade association, or a third party, which is designated the *assignee*.

Reorganization and Liquidation in Bankruptcy

If a voluntary settlement for a failed firm cannot be agreed upon, the firm can be forced into bankruptcy by its creditors. As a result of bankruptcy proceedings, the firm may be either reorganized or liquidated.

Bankruptcy Legislation

As already stated, *bankruptcy* in the legal sense occurs when the firm cannot pay its bills or when its liabilities exceed the fair market value of its assets. In either of these situations a firm may be declared legally bankrupt. However, creditors generally attempt to avoid forcing a firm into bankruptcy if it appears to have opportunities for future success.

The governing bankruptcy legislation in the United States today is the **Bankruptcy Reform Act of 1978,** which significantly modified earlier bankruptcy legislation. This law contains eight odd-numbered (1 through 15) and one even-numbered (12) chapters. A number of these chapters would apply in the instance of failure; the two key sections are Chapters 7 and 11. **Chapter 7** of the Bankruptcy Reform Act of 1978 details the procedures to be followed when liquidating a failed firm. This chapter typically comes into play once it has been determined that a fair, equitable, and feasible basis for the reorganization of a failed firm does not exist (although a firm may of its own accord choose not to

Bankruptcy Reform Act of 1978 The current governing bankruptcy legislation in the United States.

Chapter 7 The portion of the Bankruptcy Reform Act of 1978 that details the procedures to be followed when liquidating a failed firm.

Chapter 11 The portion of the Bankruptcy Reform Act of 1978 that outlines the procedures for reorganizing a failed (or failing) firm, whether its petition is filed voluntarily or involuntarily.

reorganize and may instead go directly into liquidation). **Chapter 11** outlines the procedures for reorganizing a failed (or failing) firm, whether its petition is filed voluntarily or involuntarily. If a workable plan for reorganization cannot be developed, the firm will be liquidated under Chapter 7.

Reorganization in Bankruptcy

There are two basic types of reorganization petitions—voluntary and involuntary. Any firm that is not a municipal or financial institution or a railroad can file a petition for **voluntary reorganization** on its own behalf.[7] **Involuntary reorganization** is initiated by an outside party, usually a creditor. An involuntary petition against a firm can be filed if one of three conditions is met:

voluntary reorganization
A petition filed by a failed firm on its own behalf for reorganizing its structure and paying its creditors.

involuntary reorganization
A petition initiated by an outside party, usually a creditor, for the reorganization and payment of creditors of a failed firm.

1. The firm has past-due debts of $5,000 or more.

2. Three or more creditors can prove they have aggregate unpaid claims of $5,000 against the firm. If the firm has fewer than 12 creditors, any creditor owed more than $5,000 can file the petition.

3. The firm is *insolvent,* which means (a) that is it not paying its debts as they come due, (b) that within the immediately preceding 120 days a custodian (a third party) was appointed or took possession of the debtor's property, or (c) that the fair market value of the firm's assets is less than the stated value of its liabilities.

Procedures

The procedures for the initiation and execution of corporate reorganizations entail five separate steps: filing; appointment; development and approval of a reorganization plan; acceptance of the plan; and payment of expenses.

Filing. A reorganization petition under Chapter 11 must be filed in a federal bankruptcy court. In the case of an involuntary petition, if it is challenged by the debtor, a hearing must be held to determine whether the firm is insolvent. If so, the court enters an "Order for Relief" that formally initiates the process.

Appointment. Upon the filing of a reorganization petition, the filing firm becomes the **debtor in possession (DIP)** of the assets. If creditors object to the filing firm being the debtor in possession, they can ask the judge to appoint a trustee.

debtor in possession (DIP)
The term assigned to a firm that files a reorganization petition under Chapter 11 and then develops, if feasible, a reorganization plan.

Reorganization Plan. After reviewing its situation, the debtor in possession submits a plan of reorganization to the court. The plan and a disclosure statement summarizing the plan are filed. A hearing is held to determine whether the plan is *fair, equitable,* and *feasible,* and whether the disclosure statement contains adequate information. The court's approval or disapproval is based on its evaluation of the plan in light of these standards. A plan is considered *fair and equitable* if it *maintains the priorities* of the contractual claims of the creditors, preferred stockholders, and common stockholders. The court must also find the reorganization plan *feasible,* meaning it must be *workable.* The reorganized corporation must have sufficient working capital, sufficient funds to cover fixed charges,

---

[7] Firms sometimes file a voluntary petition to obtain temporary legal protection from creditors or from prolonged litigation. Once they have straightened out their financial or legal affairs—prior to further reorganization or liquidation actions—they will have the petition dismissed. Although such actions are not the intent of the bankruptcy law, difficulty in enforcing the law has allowed this abuse to occur.

sufficient credit prospects, and sufficient ability to retire or refund debts as proposed by the plan.

Acceptance of the Reorganization Plan. Once approved, the plan, along with the disclosure statement, is given to the firm's creditors and shareholders for their acceptance. Under the Bankruptcy Reform Act, creditors and owners are separated into groups with similar types of claims. In the case of creditor groups, approval by holders of at least two-thirds of the dollar amount of claims as well as a numerical majority of creditors in the group is required. In the case of ownership groups (preferred and common stockholders), two-thirds of the shares in each group must approve the reorganization plan for it to be accepted. Once accepted and confirmed by the court, the plan is put into effect as soon as possible.

Payment of Expenses. After the reorganization plan has been approved or disapproved, all parties to the proceedings whose services were beneficial or contributed to the approval or disapproval of the plan file a statement of expenses. If the court finds these claims acceptable, the debtor must pay these expenses within a reasonable period of time.

Role of the Debtor in Possession (DIP)

Since reorganization activities are largely in the hands of the debtor in possession (DIP), it is useful to understand the DIP's responsibilities. The DIP's first responsibility is the valuation of the firm to determine whether reorganization is appropriate. To do this, the DIP must estimate both the *liquidation value* of the enterprise and its value as a *going concern.* If the DIP finds that its value as a going concern is less than its liquidation value, it will recommend liquidation. If the opposite is found to be true, the DIP will recommend reorganization. If the reorganization of the firm is recommended by the DIP, a plan of reorganization must be drawn up. The key portion of the reorganization plan generally concerns the firm's capital structure. Since most firms' financial difficulties result from high fixed charges, the company's capital structure is generally *recapitalized,* or altered, in order to reduce these charges. Under **recapitalization,** debts are generally exchanged for equity, or the maturities of existing debts are extended. The DIP, in recapitalizing the firm, places a great deal of emphasis on building a mix of debt and equity that will allow it to meet its debts and provide a reasonable level of earnings for its owners.

recapitalization The reorganization procedure under which a failed firm's debts are generally exchanged for equity or the maturities of existing debts are extended.

Once the optimal capital structure has been determined, the DIP must establish a plan for exchanging outstanding obligations for new securities. The guiding principle is to *observe priorities*. Senior claims (those with higher legal priority) must be satisfied prior to junior claims (those with lower legal priority). To comply with this principle, senior suppliers of capital must receive a claim on new capital equal to their previous claims. The common stockholders are the last to receive any new securities. (It is not unusual for them to receive nothing.) Security holders do not necessarily have to receive the same type of security they held before; often they receive a combination of securities. Once the debtor in possession has determined the new capital structure and distribution of capital, it will submit the reorganization plan and disclosure statement to the court as described.

Liquidation in Bankruptcy

The liquidation of a bankrupt firm usually occurs once the courts have determined that reorganization is not feasible. A petition for reorganization must normally be filed by the managers or creditors of the bankrupt firm. If no petition is filed, if a petition is filed and denied, or if the reorganization plan is denied, the firm must be liquidated. Three important aspects of liquidation in bankruptcy are the procedures, the priority of claims, and the final accounting.

Procedures

When a firm is adjudged bankrupt, the judge may appoint a *trustee* to perform the many routine duties required in administering the bankruptcy. The trustee takes charge of the property of the bankrupt firm and protects the interest of its creditors. Once the firm has been adjudged bankrupt, a meeting of creditors must be held between 20 and 40 days thereafter. At this meeting the creditors are made aware of the prospects for the liquidation. The meeting is presided over by the bankruptcy court clerk. The trustee is then given the responsibility to liquidate the firm, keep records, examine creditors' claims, disburse money, furnish information as required, and make final reports on the liquidation. In essence the trustee is responsible for the liquidation of the firm. Occasionally the court will call subsequent creditor meetings, but only a final meeting for closing the bankruptcy is required.

Priority of Claims

secured creditors Creditors who have specific assets pledged as collateral and in liquidation of the failed firm receive proceeds from the sale of those assets.

unsecured, or general, creditors Creditors having a general claim against all the firm's assets other than those specifically pledged as collateral.

It is the trustee's responsibility to liquidate all the firm's assets and to distribute the proceeds to the holders of *provable claims*. The courts have established certain procedures for determining the provability of claims. The priority of claims, which is specified in Chapter 7 of the Bankruptcy Reform Act, must be maintained by the trustee in distributing the funds from liquidation. It is important to recognize that any **secured creditors** have specific assets pledged as collateral and in liquidation receive proceeds from the sale of those assets. If these proceeds are inadequate to meet their claim, the secured creditors become **unsecured, or general, creditors** for the unrecovered amount since specific collateral no longer exists. These and all other unsecured creditors will divide up on a pro rata basis the funds, if any, remaining after all prior claims have been satisfied. If the proceeds from the sale of secured assets are in excess of the claims against them, the excess funds become available to meet claims of unsecured creditors. The complete order of priority of claims is as follows:

1. The expenses of administering the bankruptcy proceedings.
2. Any unpaid interim expenses incurred in the ordinary course of business between filing the bankruptcy petition and the entry of an Order for Relief in an involuntary proceeding. (This step is *not* applicable in a voluntary bankruptcy.)
3. Wages of not more than $2,000 per worker that have been earned by workers in the 90-day period immediately preceding the commencement of bankruptcy proceedings.
4. Unpaid employee benefit plan contributions that were to be paid in the 180-day period preceding the filing of bankruptcy or the termination of business, whichever occurred first. For any employee, the sum of this claim plus eligible unpaid wages (item 3) cannot exceed $2,000.
5. Claims of farmers or fishermen in a grain-storage or fish-storage facility, not to exceed $2,000 for each producer.
6. Unsecured customer deposits, not to exceed $900 each, resulting from purchasing or leasing a good or service from the failed firm.

7. Taxes legally due and owed by the bankrupt firm to the federal government, state government, or to any other governmental subdivision.

8. Claims of secured creditors, who receive the proceeds from the sale of collateral held, regardless of the priorities above. If the proceeds from the liquidation of the collateral are insufficient to satisfy the secured creditors' claims, the secured creditors become unsecured creditors for the unpaid amount.

9. Claims of unsecured creditors. The claims of unsecured, or general, creditors and unsatisfied portions of secured creditors' claims (item 8) are all treated equally.

10. Preferred stockholders, who receive an amount up to the par, or stated, value of their preferred stock.

11. Common stockholders, who receive any remaining funds, which are distributed on an equal per-share basis. If different classes of common stock are outstanding (see Chapter 17), priorities may exist.

In spite of the priorities listed in items 1 through 7, secured creditors have first claim on proceeds from the sale of their collateral. The claims of unsecured creditors, including the unpaid claims of secured creditors, are satisfied next and, finally, the claims of preferred and common stockholders. The application of these priorities by the trustee in bankruptcy liquidation proceedings can be illustrated by a simple example.

| 6 | When a firm is liquidated under the Bankruptcy Reform Act, taxes legally due and owed by the bankrupt firm must be paid prior to paying the expenses of administering the bankruptcy proceedings and allowable wages due workers. *(Fable)*
When a firm is liquidated under the Bankruptcy Reform Act, *expenses of administering the bankruptcy proceedings and allowable wages due workers must be paid prior to paying taxes legally due and owed by the bankrupt firm.*

FACT OR FABLE?

Example

Cambridge Company has the balance sheet presented in Table 19.10. The trustee, as was her obligation, has liquidated the firm's assets, obtaining the highest amounts she could get. She managed to obtain $2.3 million for the firm's current assets and $2 million for the firm's fixed assets. The total proceeds from the liquidation were therefore $4.3 million. It should be clear that the firm is legally bankrupt, since its liabilities of $5.6 million dollars exceed the $4.3 million fair market value of its assets.

The next step is to distribute the proceeds to the various creditors. The only liability not shown on the balance sheet is $800,000 in expenses for administering the bankruptcy proceedings and satisfying unpaid bills incurred between the time of filing the bankruptcy petition and the entry of an Order for Relief. The distribution of the $4.3 million among the firm's creditors is shown in Table 19.11. The table shows that once all prior claims on the proceeds from liquidation have been satisfied, the unsecured creditors get the remaining funds. The pro rata distribution of the $700,000 among the unsecured creditors is given in Table 19.12. The disposition of funds in the Cambridge Company liquidation should be clear from Tables 19.11 and 19.12. Since the claims of the unsecured creditors have not been fully satisfied, the preferred and common stockholders receive nothing.

Table 19.10
Balance Sheet for Cambridge Company

Assets		Liabilities and stockholders' equity	
Cash	$ 10,000	Accounts payable	$ 200,000
Marketable securities	5,000	Notes payable—bank	1,000,000
Accounts receivable	1,090,000	Accrued wages[a]	320,000
Inventories	3,100,000	Unpaid employee benefits[b]	80,000
Prepaid expenses	5,000	Unsecured customer deposits[c]	100,000
Total current assets	$4,210,000	Taxes payable	300,000
		Total current liabilities	$2,000,000
Land	$2,000,000		
Net plant	1,810,000	First mortgage[d]	$1,800,000
Net equipment	80,000	Second mortgage[d]	1,000,000
Total fixed assets	$3,890,000	Unsecured bonds	800,000
Total	$8,100,000	Total long-term debt	$3,600,000
		Preferred stock (5,000 shares)	$ 400,000
		Common stock (10,000 shares)	500,000
		Paid-in capital in excess of par	1,500,000
		Retained earnings	100,000
		Total stockholders' equity	$2,500,000
		Total	$8,100,000

[a] Represents wages of $800 per employee earned within 90 days of filing bankruptcy for 400 of the firm's employees.

[b] These unpaid employee benefits were due in the 180-day period preceding the firm's bankruptcy filing, which occurred simultaneously with the termination of its business.

[c] Unsecured customer deposits not exceeding $900 each.

[d] The first and second mortgages are on the firm's total fixed assets.

Table 19.11
Distribution of the Liquidation Proceeds of Cambridge Company

Proceeds from liquidation	$4,300,000
−Expenses of administering bankruptcy and paying interim bills	$ 800,000
−Wages owed workers	320,000
−Unpaid employee benefits	80,000
−Unsecured customer deposits	100,000
−Taxes owed governments	300,000
Funds available for creditors	$2,700,000
−First mortgage, paid from the $2 million proceeds from the sale of fixed assets	$1,800,000
−Second mortgage, partially paid from the remaining $200,000 of fixed asset proceeds	200,000
Funds available for unsecured creditors	$ 700,000

Table 19.12
Pro Rata Distribution of Funds Among Unsecured Creditors of Cambridge Company

Unsecured creditors' claims	Amount	Settlement at 25%[a]
Unpaid balance of second mortgage	$ 800,000[b]	$200,000
Accounts payable	200,000	50,000
Notes payable—bank	1,000,000	250,000
Unsecured bonds	800,000	200,000
Totals	$2,800,000	$700,000

[a] The 25 percent rate is calculated by dividing the $700,000 available for unsecured creditors by the $2.8 million owed unsecured creditors. Each is entitled to a pro rata share.

[b] This figure represents the difference between the $1 million second mortgage and the $200,000 payment on the second mortgage from the proceeds from the sale of the collateral remaining after satisfying the first mortgage.

Final Accounting

After the trustee has liquidated all the bankrupt firm's assets and distributed the proceeds to satisfy all provable claims in the appropriate order of priority, he or she makes a final accounting to the bankruptcy court and creditors. Once the court approves the final accounting, the liquidation is complete.

Summary

● Business combinations can be achieved through consolidations, mergers, and holding companies. Motives for them include growth or diversification, synergistic effects, fund raising, increased managerial skills, tax considerations, and increased ownership liquidity. Often firms acquire operating units that are being divested by other firms.

● Cash purchases of assets or going concerns can be evaluated using net present value techniques. In a stock-exchange acquisition, a ratio of exchange must be established. The resulting relationship between the price/earnings (P/E) ratio paid by the acquiring firm and its initial P/E ratio affects the merged firm's earnings per share and market price.

● A popular technique currently used in making acquisitions is the leveraged buyout, which involves the use of a large amount of debt to purchase a firm.

● Investment bankers are commonly hired by prospective participants to find a suitable merger partner and assist in negotiations. A merger can be negotiated with a firm's management or directly with the firm's stockholders by using tender offers to purchase their stock.

● A holding company can be created by one firm gaining control of other companies, often by owning as little as 10 to 20 percent of their stock. The chief advantages of holding companies are the leverage effect, risk protection, tax benefits, protection against lawsuits, and the fact that it generally is easy to gain control of a subsidiary. The disadvantages commonly cited include increased risk due to the magnification of losses, double taxation, and the high cost of administration.

● A firm may fail because it has negative or low returns, because it is technically insolvent, or because it is bankrupt. The major causes of business failure are mismanagement, downturns in economic activity, and corporate maturity.

● Voluntary settlements are initiated by the debtor and can result in sustaining the firm through an extension, a composition, creditor control of the firm, or a combination of these strategies. If creditors do not agree to a plan to sustain a firm, they may recommend voluntary liquidation, which bypasses many of the legal requirements of bankruptcy.

● A failed firm that cannot or does not want to arrange a voluntary settlement can voluntarily or involuntarily file in federal bankruptcy court for reorganization under Chapter 11 or liquidation under Chapter 7 of the Bankruptcy Reform Act of 1978. Under Chapter 11 the judge will appoint the debtor in possession, who with court supervision develops, if feasible, a reorganization plan.

● A firm that cannot be reorganized under Chapter 11 of the bankruptcy law or does not petition for reorganization is liquidated under Chapter 7. The responsibility for liquidation is placed in the hands of a court-appointed trustee, whose responsibilities include the liquidation of assets, the distribution of the proceeds, and making a final accounting.

Questions

19-1 Describe and differentiate between *consolidations, mergers,* and *holding companies.* How does the holding company arrangement differ from both consolidations and mergers? What is *divestiture?*

19-2 Briefly describe each of the four key types of growth or diversification. Why and in what situations may the acquisition of a firm with a *tax loss carryforward* be attractive?

19-3 Describe the procedures typically used when a firm is acquiring for cash either assets or a going concern.

19-4 What is the *ratio of exchange?* Is it based on the current market prices of the shares of the acquiring and acquired firm? Why, or why not?

19-5 What are the important considerations in evaluating the long-run impact of a merger on the combined firm's earnings per share? Why may a long-run view change a merger decision?

19-6 What is a *leveraged buyout (LBO)?* What are the three key attributes of an attractive candidate for acquisition using an LBO?

19-7 What role do *investment bankers* often play in the merger negotiation process? What is a *tender offer?* When and how is it used?

19-8 What are the key advantages and disadvantages cited for the holding company arrangement? What is *pyramiding,* and what are its consequences?

19-9 What are the three types of business failure? What is the difference between *technical insolvency* and *bankruptcy?* What are the major causes of business failure?

19-10 Define an *extension* and a *composition,* and explain how they might be combined to form a voluntary settlement plan to sustain the firm. How is a voluntary settlement resulting in liquidation handled?

19-11 What is the concern of Chapter 11 of the Bankruptcy Reform Act of 1978? How is the *debtor in possession (DIP)* involved in (1) the valuation of the firm, (2) the recapitalization of the firm, and (3) the exchange of obligations using the priority rule?

19-12 What is the concern of Chapter 7 of the Bankruptcy Reform Act of 1978? Under which conditions is a firm liquidated in bankruptcy? Describe the procedures (including the role of the trustee) involved in liquidating the bankrupt firm.

19-13 In which order would the following claims be settled in distributing the proceeds from liquidating a bankrupt firm?

    a. Claims of preferred stockholders

    b. Claims of secured creditors

    c. Expenses of administering the bankruptcy

    d. Claims of common stockholders

    e. Claims of unsecured, or general, creditors

    f. Taxes legally due

    g. Unsecured deposits of customers

    h. Certain eligible wages

    i. Unpaid employee benefit plan contributions

    j. Unpaid interim expenses incurred between the time of filing and the entry of an Order for Relief

    k. Claims of farmers or fishermen in a grain-storage or fish-storage facility

Self-Test Problems

(Solutions on page 721)

ST-1 Luxe Foods is contemplating acquisition of Valley Canning Company for a cash price of $180,000. Luxe currently has high financial leverage and therefore has a cost of capital of 14 percent. As a result of acquiring Valley Canning, which is financed entirely with equity, the firm expects its financial leverage to be reduced and its cost of capital therefore to drop to 11 percent. The acquisition of Valley Canning is expected to increase Luxe's cash inflows by $20,000 per year for the first three years and by $30,000 per year for the following 12 years.

a. Determine whether the proposed cash acquisition is desirable. Explain your answer.

b. If the firm's financial leverage would actually remain unchanged as a result of the proposed acquisition, would this alter your recommendation? Support your answer with numerical data.

ST-2 At the end of 1988, Lake Industries had 80,000 shares of common stock outstanding and had earnings available for common of $160,000. The Butler Company, at the end of 1988, had 10,000 shares of common stock outstanding and had earned $20,000 for common shareholders. Lake's earnings are expected to grow at an annual rate of 5 percent, while Butler's growth rate in earnings should be 10 percent per year.

a. Calculate earnings per share (EPS) for Lake Industries for each of the next five years, assuming there is no merger.

b. Calculate the next five years' earnings per share (EPS) for Lake if it acquires Butler at a ratio of exchange of 1.1.

c. Compare your findings in **a** and **b** and explain why the merger looks attractive when viewed over the long run.

ST-3 The Leto Company recently failed and was left with the following balance sheet.

Assets		Liabilities and stockholders' equity	
Cash	$ 80,000	Accounts payable	$ 400,000
Marketable securities	10,000	Notes payable—bank	800,000
Accounts receivable	1,090,000	Accrued wages[a]	500,000
Inventories	2,300,000	Unpaid employee benefits[b]	100,000
Prepaid expenses	20,000	Unsecured customer deposits[c]	50,000
Total current assets	$3,500,000	Taxes payable	250,000
		Total current liabilities	$2,100,000
Land	$1,000,000		
Net plant	2,000,000	First mortgage[d]	$2,000,000
Net equipment	1,500,000	Second mortgage[d]	800,000
Total fixed assets	$4,500,000	Unsecured bonds	500,000
Total	$8,000,000	Total long-term debt	$3,300,000
		Preferred stock (10,000 shares)	$ 300,000
		Common stock (5,000 shares)	300,000
		Paid-in capital in excess of par	1,500,000
		Retained earnings	500,000
		Total stockholders' equity	$2,600,000
		Total	$8,000,000

[a] Represents wages of $250 per employee earned within 90 days of filing bankruptcy for 2,000 of the firm's employees.

[b] These unpaid employee benefits were due in the 180-day period preceding the firm's bankruptcy filing, which occurred simultaneously with the termination of its business.

[c] Unsecured customer deposits not exceeding $900 each.

[d] The first and second mortgages are on the firm's total fixed assets.

The trustee liquidated the firm's assets, obtaining net proceeds of $2.2 million from the current assets and $2.5 million from the fixed assets. In the process of liquidating the assets, the trustee incurred expenses totaling $400,000. Because of the speed with which the Order for Relief was entered, no interim expenses were incurred.

    a. Prepare a table indicating the amount, if any, to be distributed to each claimant except unsecured creditors. Indicate the amount to be paid, if any, to the group of unsecured creditors.

    b. After all claims other than those of unsecured creditors have been satisfied, how much, if any, is still owed the second-mortgage holders? Why?

    c. Prepare a table showing how the remaining funds, if any, would be distributed to the firm's unsecured creditors.

Problems

19-1 **(Tax Effects of Acquisition)** The Connors Shoe Company is contemplating the acquisition of Salinas Boots, a firm that has shown large operating tax losses over the past few years. As a result of the acquisition, Connors believes the total pretax profits of the consolidation will not change from their present level for 15 years. The tax loss carryforward of Salinas is $800,000, while Connors projects annual earnings before taxes to be $280,000 per year for each of the next 15 years. These earnings are assumed to fall within the annual limit legally allowed for application of the tax loss carryforward resulting from the proposed acquisition (see footnote 2 on page 686). The firm is in the 40 percent tax bracket.

    a. If Connors does not make the acquisition, what are the company's tax liability and earnings after taxes each year over the next 15 years?

    b. If the acquisition is made, what are the company's tax liability and earnings after taxes each year over the next 15 years?

    c. If Salinas can be acquired for $350,000 in cash, should Connors make the acquisition, based on tax considerations? (Ignore present value.)

19-2 **(Tax Effects of Acquisition)** Trapani Tool Company is evaluating the acquisition of Sussman Casting. Sussman has a tax loss carryforward of $1.8 million. Trapani can purchase Sussman for $2.1 million. It can sell the assets for $1.6 million—their book value. Trapani expects earnings before taxes in the five years after the acquisition to be as follows:

Year	Earnings before taxes
1	$150,000
2	400,000
3	450,000
4	600,000
5	600,000

The expected earnings given above are assumed to fall within the annual limit legally allowed for application of the tax loss carryforward resulting from the proposed acquisition (see footnote 2 on page 686). Trapani is in the 40 percent tax bracket.

    a. Calculate the firm's tax payments and earnings after taxes for each of the next five years *without* the acquisition.

    b. Calculate the firm's tax payments and earnings after taxes for each of the next five years *with* the acquisition.

c. What are the total benefits associated with the tax losses from the acquisition? (Ignore present value.)

d. Discuss whether you would recommend the proposed acquisition. Support your decision with figures.

19-3 **(Tax Benefits and Price)** Hahn Textiles has a tax loss carryforward of $800,000. Two firms are interested in acquiring Hahn for the tax loss advantage. Reilly Investment Group has expected earnings before taxes of $200,000 per year for each of the next seven years and a cost of capital of 15 percent. Webster Industries has expected earnings before taxes for the next seven years as indicated:

Webster Industries	
Year	Earnings before taxes
1	$ 80,000
2	120,000
3	200,000
4	300,000
5	400,000
6	400,000
7	500,000

Both Reilly's and Webster's expected earnings are assumed to fall within the annual limit legally allowed for application of the tax loss carryforward resulting from the proposed acquisition (see footnote 2 on page 686). Webster has a cost of capital of 15 percent. Both firms are subject to 40 percent tax rates on ordinary income.

a. What is the tax advantage of the acquisition each year for Reilly?

b. What is the tax advantage of the acquisition each year for Webster?

c. What is the maximum cash price each interested firm would be willing to pay for Hahn Textiles? (*Hint:* Calculate the present value of the tax advantages.)

d. Use your answers in **a** through **c** to explain why an acquisition candidate can have different values to different potential acquiring firms.

19-4 **(Asset Acquisition Decision)** Zarin Printing Company is considering the acquisition of Freiman Press at a cash price of $60,000. Freiman Press has liabilities of $90,000. Freiman has a large press that Zarin needs; the remaining assets would be sold to net $65,000. As a result of acquiring the press, Zarin would experience an increase in cash inflow of $20,000 per year over the next ten years. The firm has a 14 percent cost of capital.

a. What is the effective or net cost of the large press?

b. If this is the only way Zarin can obtain the large press, should the firm go ahead with the acquisition? Explain your answer.

c. If the firm could purchase a press that would provide slightly better quality and $26,000 annual cash inflow for ten years for a price of $120,000, which alternative would you recommend? Explain your answer.

19-5 **(Cash Acquisition Decision)** Benson Oil is being considered for acquisition by Dodd Oil. The combination, Dodd believes, would increase its cash inflows by $25,000 for each of the next five years and $50,000 for each of the following five years. Benson has high financial leverage, and Dodd can expect its cost of capital to increase from 12 to 15 percent if the acquisition is made. The cash price of Benson is $125,000.

a. Would you recommend the acquisition?

b. Would you recommend the acquisition if Dodd could use the $125,000 to purchase equipment returning cash inflows of $40,000 per year for each of the next ten years?

c. If the cost of capital does not change with the acquisition, would your decision in **b** be different? Explain.

19-6 **(Ratio of Exchange and EPS)** Marla's Cafe is attempting to acquire the Victory Club. Certain financial data on these corporations are summarized as follows:

Item	Marla's Cafe	Victory Club
Earnings available for common stock	$20,000	$8,000
Number of shares of common stock outstanding	20,000	4,000
Market price per share	$12	$24

Marla's Cafe has sufficient authorized but unissued shares to carry out the proposed acquisition.

a. If the ratio of exchange is 1.8, what will be the earnings per share (EPS) based on the original shares of each firm?

b. If the ratio of exchange is 2.0, what will be the earnings per share (EPS) based on the original shares of each firm?

c. If the ratio of exchange is 2.2, what will be the earnings per share (EPS) based on the original shares of each firm?

d. Discuss the principle illustrated by your answers to **a** through **c**.

19-7 **(EPS and Merger Terms)** Cleveland Corporation is interested in acquiring the Lewis Tool Company by exchanging four-tenths shares of its stock for each share of Lewis stock. Certain financial data on these companies are given.

Item	Cleveland Corporation	Lewis Tool
Earnings available for common stock	$200,000	$50,000
Number of shares of common stock outstanding	50,000	20,000
Earnings per share (EPS)	$4.00	$2.50
Market price per share	$50.00	$15.00
Price/earnings (P/E) ratio	12.5	6

Cleveland has sufficient authorized but unissued shares to carry out the proposed acquisition.

a. How many new shares of stock will Cleveland have to issue in order to make the proposed acquisition?

b. If the earnings for each firm remain unchanged, what will the postmerger earnings per share be?

c. How much, effectively, has been earned on behalf of each of the original shares of Lewis stock?

d. How much, effectively, has been earned on behalf of each of the original shares of Cleveland Corporation's stock?

19-8 **(Ratio of Exchange)** Calculate the ratio of exchange (1) of shares and (2) in market price for each of the following cases. What does each ratio signify? Explain.

	Current market price per share		
Case	Acquiring firm	Acquired firm	Price per share offered
A	$50	$25	$ 30.00
B	80	80	100.00
C	40	60	70.00
D	50	10	12.50
E	25	20	25.00

19-9 **(Expected EPS—Merger Decision)** Graham & Sons wishes to evaluate a proposed merger into the RCN Group. Graham had 1988 earnings of $200,000, has 100,000 shares of common stock outstanding, and expects earnings to grow at an annual rate of 7 percent. RCN had 1988 earnings of $800,000, has 200,000 shares of common stock outstanding, and expects its earnings to grow at 3 percent per year.

a. Calculate the expected earnings per share (EPS) for Graham & Sons for each of the next five years without the merger.

b. What would Graham's stockholders earn in each of the next five years on each of their Graham shares converted into RCN shares at a ratio of (1) .6 and (2) .8 shares of RCN for one share of Graham?

c. Graph the pre- and postmerger EPS figures developed in **a** and **b** on a set of year (x-axis)–EPS (y-axis) axes.

d. If you were the financial manager for Graham & Sons, what would you recommend from **b,** (1) or (2)? Explain your answer.

19-10 **(EPS and Postmerger Price)** Data for the Henry Company and Mayer Services are given. Henry Company is considering the acquisition of Mayer by exchanging 1.25 shares of its stock for each share of Mayer stock. Henry Company expects to sell at the same price/earnings (P/E) multiple after the merger as before merging.

Item	Henry Company	Mayer Services
Earnings available for common stock	$225,000	$50,000
Number of shares of common stock outstanding	90,000	15,000
Market price per share	$45	$50

   a. Calculate the ratio of exchange of market prices.

   b. Calculate the earnings per share (EPS) and price/earnings (P/E) ratio for each company.

   c. Calculate the price/earnings (P/E) ratio used to purchase Mayer Services.

   d. Calculate the postmerger earnings per share (EPS) for the Henry Company.

   e. Calculate the expected market price per share of the merged firm. Discuss this result in light of your findings in **a.**

19-11 (Holding Company) Scully Corporation holds stock in company A and company B. A simplified balance sheet is presented for the companies. Scully has voting control over both company A and company B.

Assets		Liabilities and stockholders' equity	
Scully Corporation			
Common stock holdings		Long-term debt	$ 40,000
Company A	$ 40,000	Preferred stock	25,000
Company B	60,000	Common stock equity	35,000
Total	$100,000	Total	$100,000
Company A			
Current assets	$100,000	Current liabilities	$100,000
Fixed assets	400,000	Long-term debt	200,000
Total	$500,000	Common stock equity	200,000
		Total	$500,000
Company B			
Current assets	$180,000	Current liabilities	$100,000
Fixed assets	720,000	Long-term debt	500,000
Total	$900,000	Common stock equity	300,000
		Total	$900,000

   a. What percentage of the total assets controlled by Scully Corporation does its common stock equity represent?

   b. If another company owns 15 percent of the common stock of Scully Corporation and by virtue of this fact has voting control, what percentage of the total assets controlled does the outside company's equity represent?

   c. How does a holding company effectively provide a great deal of control for a small dollar investment?

   d. Answer questions **a** and **b** in light of the following additional facts.
   (1) Company A's fixed assets consist of $20,000 of common stock in company C. This provides voting control.
   (2) Company C, which has total assets of $400,000, has voting control of company D, which has $50,000 of total assets.
   (3) Company B's fixed assets consist of $60,000 of stock in both company E and company F. In both cases, this gives it voting control. Companies E and F have total assets of $300,000 and $400,000, respectively.

19-12 (Voluntary Settlements) Classify each of the following voluntary settlements as an extension, a composition, or a combination of the two.

    a. Paying all creditors 30 cents on the dollar in exchange for complete discharge of the debt.

    b. Paying all creditors in full in three periodic installments.

    c. Paying a group of creditors with claims of $10,000 in full over two years and immediately paying the remaining creditors 75 cents on the dollar.

19-13 (Voluntary Settlements) For a firm with outstanding debt of $125,000, classify each of the following voluntary settlements as an extension, a composition, or a combination of the two.

    a. Paying a group of creditors in full in four periodic installments and paying the remaining creditors in full immediately.

    b. Paying a group of creditors 90 cents on the dollar immediately and paying the remaining creditors 80 cents on the dollar in two periodic installments.

    c. Paying all creditors 15 cents on the dollar.

    d. Paying all creditors in full in 180 days.

19-14 (Voluntary Settlements—Payments) Jacobi Supply Company recently ran into certain financial difficulties that have resulted in the initiation of voluntary settlement procedures. The firm currently has $150,000 in outstanding debts and approximately $75,000 in liquidable short-term assets. Indicate, for each plan below, whether the plan is an extension, a composition, or a combination of the two. Also indicate the cash payments and timing of the payments required of the firm under each plan.

    a. Each creditor will be paid 50 cents on the dollar immediately, and the debts will be considered fully satisfied.

    b. Each creditor will be paid 80 cents on the dollar in two quarterly installments of 50 cents and 30 cents. The first installment is to be paid in 90 days.

    c. Each creditor will be paid the full amount of its claims in three installments of 50 cents, 25 cents, and 25 cents on the dollar. The installments will be made in 60-day intervals, beginning in 60 days.

    d. A group of creditors having claims of $50,000 will be immediately paid in full; the remainder will be paid 85 cents on the dollar, payable in 90 days.

19-15 (Unsecured Creditors) A firm has $450,000 in funds to distribute to its unsecured creditors. Three possible sets of unsecured creditor claims are presented. Calculate the settlement, if any, to be received by each creditor in each case.

Unsecured creditors' claims	Case I	Case II	Case III
Unpaid balance of second mortgage	$300,000	$200,000	$ 500,000
Accounts payable	200,000	100,000	300,000
Notes payable—bank	300,000	100,000	500,000
Unsecured bonds	100,000	200,000	500,000
Total	$900,000	$600,000	$1,800,000

19-16 (Liquidation and Priority of Claims) Keck Business Forms recently failed and was liquidated by a court-appointed trustee who charged $200,000 for her services. Between the time of filing of the bankruptcy petition and the entry of an Order for Relief, a total of $100,000 in unpaid bills was incurred and remain unpaid. The preliquidation balance sheet is as follows:

Assets		Liabilities and stockholders' equity	
Cash	$ 40,000	Accounts payable	$ 200,000
Marketable securities	30,000	Notes payable—bank	300,000
Accounts receivable	620,000	Accrued wages[a]	50,000
Inventories	1,200,000	Unsecured customer deposits[b]	30,000
Prepaid expenses	10,000	Taxes payable	20,000
Total current assets	$1,900,000	Total current liabilities	$ 600,000
Land	$ 300,000	First mortgage[c]	$ 700,000
Net plant	400,000	Second mortgage[c]	400,000
Net equipment	400,000	Unsecured bonds	300,000
Total fixed assets	$1,100,000	Total long-term debt	$1,400,000
Total	$3,000,000	Preferred stock (15,000 shares)	$ 200,000
		Common stock (10,000 shares)	200,000
		Paid-in capital in excess of par	500,000
		Retained earnings	100,000
		Total stockholders' equity	$1,000,000
		Total	$3,000,000

[a] Represents wages of $500 per employee earned within 90 days of filing bankruptcy for 100 of the firm's employees.

[b] Unsecured customer deposits not exceeding $900 each.

[c] The first and second mortgages are on the firm's total fixed assets.

a. Assume the trustee liquidates the assets for $2.5 million—$1.3 million from current assets and $1.2 million from fixed assets.
  (1) Prepare a table indicating the amount to be distributed to each claimant. Indicate if the claimant is an unsecured creditor.
  (2) Prior to satisfying unsecured creditor claims, how much is owed to first-mortgage holders and second-mortgage holders?
  (3) Do the firm's owners receive any funds? If so, in what amounts?

b. Assume the trustee liquidates the assets for $1.8 million—$1.2 million from current assets and $600,000 from fixed assets; rework your answers in **a.**

c. Compare, contrast, and discuss your findings in **a** and **b.**

Solutions to Self-Test Problems

ST-1 a. Net present value at 11%

Year(s)	Cash inflow (1)	Present value factor at 11%[a] (2)	Present value [(1) × (2)] (3)
1–3	$20,000	2.444	$ 48,880
4–15	30,000	(7.191 − 2.444)	142,410
		Present value of inflows	$191,290
		Less: Cash purchase price	180,000
		Net present value (NPV)	$ 11,290

[a] Present-value interest factors for annuities from Table A-4.

Since the NPV of $11,290 is greater than zero, *Luxe Foods should acquire Valley Canning.*

b. In this case the 14 percent cost of capital must be used.
Net present value at 14%

Year(s)	Cash inflow (1)	Present value factor at 14%[a] (2)	Present value [(1) × (2)] (3)
1–3	$20,000	2.322	$ 46,440
4–15	30,000	(6.142 − 2.322)	114,600
		Present value of inflows	$161,040
		Less: Cash purchase price	180,000
		Net present value (NPV)	($18,960)

[a] Present-value interest factors for annuities from Table A-4.

At the higher cost of capital, the *acquisition of Valley by Luxe cannot be justified.*

ST-2 a. Lake Industries' EPS without merger

	Earnings available for common				
Year	Initial value (1)	Future value factor at 5%[a] (2)	End-of-year value [(1) × (2)] (3)	Number of shares outstanding (4)	EPS [(3) ÷ (4)] (5)
1988	$160,000	1.000	$160,000	80,000	$2.00
1989	160,000	1.050	168,000	80,000	2.10
1990	160,000	1.102	176,320	80,000	2.20
1991	160,000	1.158	185,280	80,000	2.32
1992	160,000	1.216	194,560	80,000	2.43
1993	160,000	1.276	204,160	80,000	2.55

[a] Future-value interest factors, *FVIF*, from Table A-1.

b. Number of postmerger shares outstanding for Lake Industries

$$\text{Number of new shares issued} = \text{Initial number of Butler Company shares} \times \text{Ratio of exchange}$$

$$= 10{,}000 \times 1.1 = \qquad 11{,}000 \text{ shares}$$

Plus: Lake's premerger shares   80,000

Lake's postmerger shares   91,000 shares

	Earnings available for common						
	Butler Company			Lake Industries			
				Without merger	With merger		
Year	Initial value (1)	Future value factor at 10%[a] (2)	End-of-year value [(1) × (2)] (3)	End-of-year value[b] (4)	End-of-year value [(3) + (4)] (5)	Number of shares outstanding[c] (6)	EPS [(5) ÷ (6)] (7)
1988	$20,000	1.000	$20,000	$160,000	$180,000	91,000	$1.98
1989	20,000	1.100	22,000	168,000	190,000	91,000	2.09
1990	20,000	1.210	24,200	176,320	200,520	91,000	2.20
1991	20,000	1.331	26,620	185,280	211,900	91,000	2.33
1992	20,000	1.464	29,280	194,560	223,840	91,000	2.46
1993	20,000	1.611	32,220	204,160	236,380	91,000	2.60

[a] Future-value interest factors, *FVIF*, from Table A-1.

[b] From column 3 of table in part **a.**

[c] Calculated at beginning of this part.

c. Comparing the EPS without the proposed merger calculated in **a** (see column 5 of table in **a**) with the EPS with the proposed merger calculated in **b** (see column 7 of table in **b**), it can be seen that after 1990 the EPS *with* the merger rises above the EPS without the merger. Clearly, over the long-run the EPS with the merger will exceed those without the merger. This outcome is attributed to the higher rate of growth associated with Butler's earnings (10% versus 5% for Lake).

ST-3 a.

Proceeds from liquidation	$4,700,000
−Trustee's expenses	$ 400,000
−Wages owed workers	500,000
−Unpaid employee benefits	100,000
−Unsecured customer deposits	50,000
−Taxes owed governments	250,000
Funds available for creditors	$3,400,000
−First mortgage, paid from the $2.5 million proceeds from the sale of fixed assets	$2,000,000
−Second mortgage, partially paid from the remaining $500,000 of fixed assets proceeds	500,000
Funds available for unsecured creditors	$ 900,000

b. The second-mortgage holder is *still owed $300,000* since he has recovered from the sale of the fixed assets $500,000 of the $800,000 owed him.

c.

Unsecured creditors' claims	Amount	Settlement at 45%[a]
Unpaid balance of second mortgage	$ 300,000[b]	$135,000
Accounts payable	400,000	180,000
Notes payable—bank	800,000	360,000
Unsecured bonds	500,000	225,000
Totals	$2,000,000	$900,000

[a] The 45 percent rate is calculated by dividing the $900,000 available for unsecured creditors by the $2,000,000 owed unsecured creditors. Each is entitled to a pro rata share.

[b] Value calculated in part **b.**

International Finance

1

Although the U.S. government claims jurisdiction over all of the income, wherever earned, of U.S.-based multinational companies (MNCs), it may be possible for a multinational company to take foreign income taxes as a direct credit against its U.S. tax liabilities.

2

The rules in the United States require the full consolidation of financial statements of subsidiaries for financial reporting purposes whenever the parent has more than 20 percent beneficial ownership in the subsidiary.

3

Foreign exchange risk refers to the potential discontinuity or seizure of an MNC's operations in a host country due to the host's implementation of specific rules and regulations such as nationalization, expropriation, and confiscation.

4

Because repatriation of cash flows from a subsidiary may be totally or partially blocked by the host country, the returns and net present values associated with such projects can reflect good performance on the part of the subsidiary and yet mean no returns for the parent.

5

In appreciation-prone countries, intra-MNC accounts receivable are collected as late as possible, while intra-MNC accounts payable are paid as soon as possible.

6

The use of more local debt in a joint-venture subsidiary's capital structure provides protection by reducing potential threats from local authorities and thereby lessening the consequences of political risk.

Any suburban shopping district will show you that fast food in the United States is a mature business. With growth of only 1 percent a year, the U.S. market is saturated with burgers, fries, chicken, and shakes. The only way to keep growing is to look for markets that don't have American-style fast food. McDonald's Corporation has done just that. In fact, about 40 percent of all its new locations are overseas.

McDonald's finds a partner in the country it wants to penetrate. This local entrepreneur puts up a specified percentage of the capital to open the new franchise. Then the parent organization takes a percentage of the revenues. Experience has shown that he or she will dedicate complete attention and energy to succeeding. In addition, this entrepreneur knows local customs and business traditions. And the chance for success is good: most customers go to McDonald's because they can count on consistent quality in any location. Much of this quality results from McDonald's insistence that franchisees follow its management style and adhere to its meticulous food preparation guidelines.

There are risks involved in foreign investments, however, and they can result in lower profit margins for McDonald's. First, real estate, especially in countries with high-density populations, is expensive. And some products must be imported unless local suppliers can be found.

There's also a problem in imposing McDonald's Corporation values in some countries. For example, some cultures do not adapt to McDonald's rigid procedures for food preparation. Others don't accept McDonald's cleanliness standards. And when problems do arise, it's harder to replace a franchisee when he or she is 10,000 miles away and the laws of the land are very different from those of the United States. Still, international expansion is one way of developing new markets, and as long as the profits are there, the hamburger will undoubtedly continue its triumphant march around the world.

McDonald's, like other companies with international operations, faces additional challenges and opportunities when operating in today's complex international environment. In this chapter we look at the unique operating environment, accounting considerations, risks, and decision strategies that should be considered by the financial manager of an international company.

The Multinational Company and Its Environment

In recent years, as world markets have become significantly more interdependent, international finance has become an increasingly important element in the management of **multinational companies (MNCs).** These firms, being based in the United States, Western Europe, Japan, as well as many other countries, have international assets and operations in foreign markets and draw part of their total revenues and profits from such markets. The principles of managerial finance presented in this text are applicable to the manage-

multinational companies (MNCs) Firms that have international assets and operations in foreign markets and draw part of their total revenues and profits from such markets.

Table 20.1
The International Factors and Their Influence on MNCs' Operations

Factor	Firm A (Domestic)	Firm B (MNC)
Foreign ownership	All assets owned by domestic entities	Portions of equity of foreign investments owned by foreign partners, thus affecting foreign decision making and profits
Multinational capital markets	All debt and equity structures based on the domestic capital market	Opportunities and challenges arise from the existence of different capital markets where debt and equity can be issued
Multinational accounting	All consolidation of financial statements based on one currency	The existence of different currencies and of specific translation rules influences the consolidation of financial statements into one currency
Foreign exchange risks	All operations in one currency	Fluctuations in foreign exchange markets can affect foreign revenues and profits as well as the overall value of the firm

ment of MNCs. However, certain factors unique to the international setting tend to complicate the financial management of multinational companies. A simple comparison between a domestic U.S. firm (firm A) and a U.S.-based MNC (firm B), as illustrated in Table 20.1, can give an indication of the influence of some of the international factors on MNCs' operations.

In the present international environment, multinationals face a variety of laws and restrictions when operating in different nation-states. The legal and economic complexities existing in this environment are significantly different from those a domestic firm would face. Here we take a brief look at this environment. Subsequent sections discuss international financial statements, risks, and financial decisions.

Legal Forms of Business

In many countries outside the United States, operating a foreign business as a subsidiary or affiliate can take two forms, both similar to the U.S. corporation. In German-speaking nations, the two forms are the *Aktiengesellschaft* (A.G.) or the *Gesellschaft mit beschrankter Haftung* (GmbH); in many other countries the similar forms are a *Société Anonyme* (S.A.) or a *Société à Responsibilité Limitée* (S.A.R.L.). The A.G. or the S.A. is the most common form, but the GmbH or the S.A.R.L. enjoys much greater freedom and requires fewer formalities for formation and operation.

Although establishing a business in a form such as the S.A. can involve most of the provisions that govern a U.S.-based corporation, to operate in many foreign countries, especially in most of the less-developed nations, it is often essential to enter into joint-venture business agreements with private investors or with government-based agencies of the host country. A **joint venture** is a partnership under which the participants have contractually agreed to contribute specified amounts of money and expertise in exchange for stated proportions of ownership and profit. The governments of numerous countries,

joint venture A partnership under which the participants have contractually agreed to contribute specified amounts of money and expertise in exchange for stated proportions of ownership and profit.

such as Brazil, Colombia, Mexico, and Venezuela in Latin America, as well as Indonesia, Malaysia, the Philippines, and Thailand in Southeast Asia, have in recent years instituted new laws and regulations governing MNCs. The basic rule introduced by most of these nations requires that the majority ownership (i.e., at least 51 percent of the total equity) of MNCs' joint-venture projects be held by domestically based investors.

The existence of joint-venture laws and restrictions has certain implications for the operation of foreign-based subsidiaries. First of all, majority foreign ownership may result in a substantial degree of management and control by host-country participants; this in turn can influence day-to-day operations in a manner that is detrimental to the managerial policies and procedures normally pursued by MNCs. Next, foreign ownership may result in disagreements among the partners as to the exact distribution of profits and the portion to be allocated for reinvestment. Moreover, operating in foreign countries, especially on a joint-venture basis, can entail problems regarding the actual remission of profits. In the past, the governments of Argentina, Brazil, Nigeria, and Thailand, among others, have imposed ceilings not only on the repatriation (return) of capital by MNCs but also on profit remittances by these firms back to the parent companies. The shortage of foreign exchange is usually cited as the motivating factor by these governments. Finally, from a ''positive'' point of view, it can be argued that to operate in many of the less-developed countries, it would be beneficial for MNCs to enter into joint-venture agreements, given the potential risks stemming from political instability in the host countries. This issue will be addressed in detail later in this chapter.

International Taxes

Multinational companies, unlike domestic firms, have financial obligations—as well as opportunities—in foreign countries. One of their basic responsibilities is international taxation—a complex issue because national governments follow a variety of tax policies. In general, from the point of view of a U.S.-based MNC, several factors must be taken into account.

First, the *level* of foreign taxes needs to be examined. Certain countries are known for their ''low'' tax levels, including the Bahamas, Switzerland, Liechtenstein, Luxembourg, Panama, and Bermuda. These nations, unlike some of the major industrialized countries, typically have no withholding taxes on *intra-MNC dividends*. Next, there is a question as to the definition of *taxable income*. While some governments may regard profits to be taxable as received on a cash basis, others may treat the same profits as taxable as earned on an accrual basis. Differences can also exist on treatments of noncash charges, such as depreciation, amortization, and depletion.

Finally, the existence of tax agreements between the United States and other governments can influence not only the total tax bill of the parent MNC, but its international operations and financial activities as well. In mid-1987, for example, the U.S. Treasury stated that effective January 1, 1988, it will terminate a 1948 tax treaty with the Netherlands Antilles, affecting about $32 billion of debt issued by U.S.-based MNCs. Under this treaty, debt issued there was exempt from a 30 percent withholding tax imposed by the United States.

For a U.S.-based MNC, the U.S. government claims jurisdiction over *all* of its income, wherever earned. (Special rules apply to foreign corporations conducting business in the United States.) However, it may be possible for a multinational company to take foreign income taxes as a direct credit against its U.S. tax liabilities. For the tax credit to be applicable, the MNC must own at least 10 percent of the foreign corporation.

There can also be a pyramid effect, whereby the MNC parent can credit foreign income taxes paid by a subsidiary (subsidiary 2) owned by the foreign corporation (subsidiary 1) and the taxes paid by another subsidiary (subsidiary 3) owned by subsidiary 2. Each company must own at least 10 percent of the stock of the next lower firm, with the parent owning at least 5 percent (either directly or indirectly) of the stock of a subsidiary that paid taxes for it to be creditable. The overall technique is based on the **grossing up procedure:** The U.S. income is increased by the amount of foreign income (before the foreign taxes), and the U.S. tax calculation is then based on that higher level. The following example illustrates the procedure.

grossing up procedure
A taxation technique in which an MNC's U.S. income is increased by the amount of foreign income (before foreign taxes), and the U.S. tax calculation is based on that higher level.

Example

A U.S.-based MNC has three subsidiaries abroad as follows: subsidiary 1 (S1) is 40 percent owned by the MNC, with a taxable income of $20 million and local taxes of $10 million. The second subsidiary (S2) is 20 percent owned by S1 and has a taxable income of $48 million with local taxes of $16 million. The third subsidiary (S3) is 60 percent owned by S2 and has a taxable income of $15 million and local taxes of $9 million. In each case, the taxable income is the share belonging to the MNC. Assume a U.S. tax rate of 40 percent.

To calculate all the tax credits applicable to the MNC, the first part of the procedure is to establish the degree of ownership of each subsidiary by the MNC:

S1: 40 percent directly owned by the MNC

S2: (20 percent) × (40 percent) = 8 percent owned by the MNC

S3: (60 percent) × (20 percent) × (40 percent) = 4.8 percent owned by the MNC

Based on the regulations stated above, both S1 and S2 can be included in the calculation of tax credits, whereas S3, although more than 10 percent owned by S2, is still less than 5 percent owned by the parent MNC and is therefore not eligible. In terms of actual tax credits, if we assume that there are no withholding taxes in each of the local countries, the maximum credit against U.S. taxes would be 40 percent of the added income, or 40 percent of $68 million ($20 million from S1 and $48 million from S2), which is $27.2 million. Thus, the local taxes paid in foreign countries by S1 and S2—amounting to $26 million—can be applicable as a credit in the United States for the MNC.

FACT OR FABLE?

1 Although the U.S. government claims jurisdiction over all of the income, wherever earned, of U.S.-based multinational companies (MNCs), it may be possible for a multinational company to take foreign income taxes as a direct credit against its U.S. tax liabilities. *(Fact)*

Additional provisions apply to tax deferrals by MNCs on foreign income; to operations set up in American possessions, such as the U.S. Virgin Islands, Guam, and American Samoa; to capital gains from the sale of stock in a foreign corporation; and to withholding taxes. A final point to note is that as many as 24 individual state governments in the United States have in recent years introduced new measures—in the form of special

AUTOLATINA:
An International Venture Between Ford and VW

The endless flow of red ink from their subsidiaries in Brazil and Argentina is driving Ford Motor Co. and Volkswagen into each other's arms. The two giants have decided on a regional tie-up that, if all goes well, will result in the eleventh-largest car-maker in the world. It's a gusty, unorthodox move for two multinationals.

By lumping their problems together, the companies hoped for profits they could share later. In both countries they are up against government-imposed price controls. The major problem was in Brazil, where the two commanded 60 percent of the market. Despite Brazilians' eagerness to buy cars and trucks, the auto-makers lost close to $50 million each for 1986. By freezing prices, Brazil's anti-inflationary Cruzado Plan crimped the flow of auto parts and disrupted production.

Since they couldn't change government policy, Ford and VW could at least achieve greater efficiency and economies of scale in their 15 plants. In Brazil, the formation of a new holding company, Autolatina, Ltd., would be owned 51 percent by VW and 49 percent by Ford. It would engineer, finance, supply and manufacture some 700,000 autos and trucks annually, although marketing and export operations would continue to be run separately. The Argentine joint venture, Autolatina, Inc., would fully integrate all of Ford's and VW's operations and would replace the corporate names, perhaps even on new cars.

The merger was an important step toward a Latin American common market, a long-held dream of regional leaders. Ford's and VW's venture would benefit from recent steps by Brazil and Argentina to increase trade in manufactured goods and capital equipment.

Some saw the new venture as part of a broader trend in Latin America and other regions where individual companies are losing money. Said a São Paulo auto industry analyst, "Producers are seeing that it's very hard to show profits when operating in limited car markets with strong local-content requirements and where everybody has their own plant."

One immediate threat to the plan was the auto workers' unions. These strong unions have long called the shots among the companies' combined work force of 75,000. Union leaders in Brazil agreed to the idea of the merger if it meant no layoffs. But in strike-prone Argentina, where Ford has faced bitter disputes, union opposition was certain to be heated. Despite problems the two auto giants made the choice between two alternatives—try something daring or give up on two important markets.

SOURCE: Jeffrey Ryser, "Ford and VW: A Marriage of Convenience," *Business Week,* December 8, 1986, p. 53.

unitary tax laws—that tax the multinationals (American and foreign alike) on a percentage of their *total* worldwide income rather than, as is generally accepted elsewhere, on their earnings arising within the jurisdiction of each respective government. MNCs, meanwhile, may face overlapping taxation of income by states and by foreign governments, since U.S. federal tax treaties with other countries do not apply to state taxation of MNCs. As a part of their response to unitary tax laws, the multinationals have already pressured a number of state governments—including those of Colorado, Florida, Indiana, Massachusetts, and Oregon—into abolishing the laws, while many MNCs have in the last year relocated their investments away from those states which continue to apply such laws.

> **unitary tax laws** Laws in some U.S. states that tax multinationals (both American and foreign) on a percentage of their *total* worldwide income rather than the usual taxation of the MNCs' earnings within a given state.

International Financial Markets

During the last two decades the **Euromarket**—which provides for borrowing and lending currencies outside their country of origin—has grown quite rapidly. Its overall size is now estimated to be over $2.5 trillion. The Euromarket provides multinational companies with

> **Euromarket** The international financial market that provides for borrowing and lending currencies outside their country of origin.

an "external" opportunity to borrow or lend funds with the additional feature of less government regulation.

Growth of the Euromarket

Several reasons can be offered to explain why the Euromarket has grown to such a magnitude. First, beginning in the early 1960s, the Russians wanted to maintain their dollar earnings outside the legal jurisdiction of the United States, mainly due to the cold war. Second, the consistently large U.S. balance of payments deficits helped "scatter" dollars around the world. Third, the existence of specific regulations and controls on dollar deposits in the United States, including interest rate ceilings imposed by the government, helped send such deposits to places outside the United States.

These and other factors have combined and contributed to the creation of an "external" capital market whose size cannot be accurately determined, mainly because of lack of controls and regulations. Several sources that periodically estimate its size are the Bank for International Settlements (BIS), Morgan Guaranty Trust, the World Bank, and the Organization for Economic Cooperation and Development (OECD). The latest available estimate by BIS puts the overall size of the market at over $1.8 trillion *net* international lending.

offshore centers Certain cities around the world (including London, Singapore, Bahrain, Nassau, Hong Kong, and Luxembourg) that have achieved prominence as major offshore centers for Euromarket business.

One aspect of the Euromarket is the so-called **offshore centers.** Certain cities or states around the world—including London, Singapore, Bahrain, Nassau, Hong Kong, and Luxembourg—have achieved prominence and are considered major offshore centers for Euromarket business. The availability of communication and transportation facilities, along with the importance of language, costs, time zones, taxes, and local banking regulations, are among the main reasons for the importance of these centers.

Another important point to note is that in recent years a variety of new financial instruments have appeared in the international financial markets. Included are interest rate and currency swaps (with over $350 billion in total activity at year-end 1986), various combinations of forward and options contracts on different currencies, and new types of bonds and notes—along with an international version of U.S. commercial paper—with flexible characteristics in terms of currency, maturity, and interest rate. More details will be provided later in this chapter.

Major Participants

The Euromarket is still dominated by the U.S. dollar. However, activities in other major currencies, including Deutsche mark, Swiss franc, Japanese yen, British pounds sterling, French franc, and the European Currency Unit (ECU), have in recent years grown much faster than those denominated in the U.S. currency. Similarly, while American banks and other financial institutions continue to play a significant role in the global markets, financial giants from Japan and Europe have become major participants in Euromarkets in the 1980s. As of mid-1987, for example, the three largest banks in the world as measured in terms of total assets were based in Japan.

Following the oil price increases of 1973–1974 and of 1979–1980 by the Organization of Petroleum Exporting Countries (OPEC), massive amounts of dollars have been placed in various Euromarket financial centers. International banks, in turn, as part of the so-called *redistribution* of "oil money," have been lending to different groups of borrowers. At the end of 1985, for example, BIS reports that non-OPEC developing countries had total borrowings outstanding of over $350 billion, with OPEC members, a certain group of developed countries, and Eastern Europe having borrowed $110 billion, $100 billion, and $60 billion, respectively. (These figures can be contrasted with a *total* borrowing for the year 1974 of less than $30 billion.)

Although developing countries have become a major borrowing group in recent years, the industrialized nations continue to borrow actively in international markets. Included in the latter group's borrowings are the funds obtained by multinational companies. The multinationals use the Euromarket to raise additional funds as well as to invest excess cash. Both Eurocurrency and Eurobond markets are extensively used by MNCs. Further details on MNCs' Euromarket activities are given below.

International Financial Statements

Several features distinguish domestically oriented financial statements and internationally based reports. Among these are the issues of consolidation, translation of individual accounts within the financial statements, and overall reporting of international profits.

Consolidation

At the present time the rules in the United States require the consolidation of financial statements of subsidiaries according to the percentage of ownership by the parent of the subsidiary. Table 20.2 illustrates this point. As indicated, the regulations range from requiring a one-line income-item reporting of dividends, to a pro rata inclusion of profits and losses, to a full disclosure in the balance sheet and income statement. (When ownership is less than 50 percent, since the balance sheet and thus the subsidiary's financing do not get reported, it is possible for the parent MNC to have off-balance-sheet financing.)

FACT OR FABLE?

2 The rules in the United States require the full consolidation of financial statements of subsidiaries for financial reporting purposes whenever the parent has more than 20 percent beneficial ownership in the subsidiary. *(Fable)*

The rules in the United States require the full consolidation of financial statements of subsidiaries for financial reporting purposes whenever the parent has more than *50 percent* beneficial ownership in the subsidiary.

Table 20.2
United States Rules for Consolidation of Financial Statements

Percentage of beneficial ownership by parent in subsidiary	Consolidation for financial reporting purposes
0–19%	Dividends as received
20–49%	Pro rata inclusions of profits and losses
50–100%	Full consolidation[a]

[a] Consolidation may be avoided in the case of some majority-owned foreign operations if the parent can convince its auditors that it does not have control of the subsidiaries or if there are substantial restrictions on the repatriation of cash.

SOURCE: Rita M. Rodriguez and E. Eugene Carter, *International Financial Management*, 3rd ed. (Englewood Cliffs, NJ: Prentice-Hall, 1984), p. 492.

Translation of Individual Accounts

Unlike domestic items in financial statements, international items require translation back into U.S. dollars. Since December 1982 all financial statements of U.S. multinationals have to conform to Statement No. 52 issued by the Financial Accounting Standards Board (FASB). The basic rules of FASB No. 52 are given in Figure 20.1.

FASB No. 52 Statement issued by the FASB requiring U.S. multinationals first to convert the financial statement accounts of foreign subsidiaries into their *functional currency* and then to translate the accounts into the parent firm's currency using the *all-current-rate method.*

Under **FASB No. 52,** the *current rate method* is implemented in a two-step process. First, each entity's balance sheet and income statement are *measured* in terms of their functional currency by using generally accepted accounting principles (GAAP). In other words, various foreign-currency elements are translated by each subsidiary into the **functional currency**—the currency of the economic environment in which an entity primarily generates and expends cash, and in which its accounts are maintained—before financial statements are submitted to the parent for consolidation.

Through the second step, as shown in Figure 20.1, by using the **all-current-rate method** (which requires the translation of all balance sheet items at the closing rate and all income statement items at average rates), the functional currency-denominated financial statements are translated into the parent's currency.

functional currency The currency of the economic environment in which a financial entity primarily generates and expends cash, and in which its accounts are maintained.

Each of these steps can result in certain gains or losses. The first step can lead to transaction (cash) gains or losses, which, whether realized or not, are charged directly to net income. The completion of the second step can result in translation (accounting) adjustments, which are excluded from current income. Instead, they are disclosed and charged to a separate component of stockholders' equity.

all-current-rate method The method by which the *functional currency*-denominated financial statements of an MNC's subsidiary are translated into the parent company's currency.

International Profits

Prior to January 1976, the practice for most U.S. multinationals was to utilize a special account called the *reserve account* to show "smooth" international profits. Excess international profits due to favorable exchange fluctuations were deposited in this account. Withdrawals were made during periods of high losses stemming from unfavorable exchange movements. The overall result was to display a smooth pattern in an MNC's international profits.

Between 1976 and 1982, however, the existence of *FASB No. 8* required that both transaction gains or losses and translation adjustments be included in net income, with the separate disclosure of only the aggregate foreign exchange gain or loss. This requirement

Figure 20.1
Details of FASB No. 52

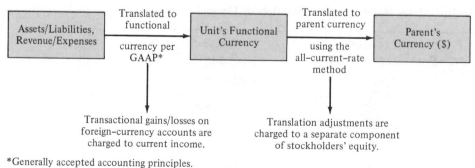

*Generally accepted accounting principles.

SOURCE: John B. Giannotti, "FAS 52 Gives Treasurers the Scope FAS 8 Denied Them," *Euromoney,* April 1982, pp. 141–151.

caused highly visible swings in the reported net earnings of U.S. multinationals. Under FASB No. 52, only certain transactional gains or losses are reflected in the income statement. Overall, assuming a positive income flow for a subsidiary, the income statement risk will be positive and will be similarly enhanced or reduced by an appreciation or depreciation of the functional currency.

International Risks

The concepts of risk and return discussed in earlier chapters of the text are applicable to international investments as well. However, additional factors must be taken into account, including both foreign exchange (economic) and political risks.

Foreign Exchange Risks

Since multinational companies operate in many different foreign markets, portions of these firms' revenues and costs are based on foreign currencies. In order to understand the **foreign exchange risk** caused by varying exchange rates between two currencies, we examine both the relationships that exist among various currencies and the impact of currency fluctuations.

foreign exchange risk The risk caused by varying exchange rates between two currencies.

Relationships Among Currencies

Since the mid-1970s, the major currencies of the world have had a *floating*—as opposed to *fixed*—relationship with respect to the U.S. dollar and to one another. Among the currencies regarded as being major (or "hard"), we have the British pound (£), the Swiss franc (Sf), the Deutsche mark (DM), the French franc (Ff), the Japanese yen (Y), the Canadian dollar (C$), and, of course, the U.S. dollar (US$). The value of two currencies with respect to each other, or their **foreign exchange rate,** is expressed as follows:

$$US\$ \ 1.00 = Sf \ 1.52$$
$$Sf \ 1.00 = US\$ \ .66$$

The usual exchange quotation in international markets is given as Sf 1.52/US$, where the unit of account is the Swiss franc and the unit of currency being priced is one U.S. dollar.

For the major currencies, the existence of a **floating relationship** means that the value of any two currencies with respect to each other is allowed to fluctuate on a daily basis. On the other hand, many of the nonmajor currencies of the world try to maintain a **fixed (or semi-fixed) relationship** with respect to one of the major currencies, a combination (basket) of major currencies, or some type of an international foreign exchange standard.

On any given day, the relationship between any two of the major currencies will contain two sets of figures, one reflecting the **spot exchange rate** (the rate on that day), and the other indicating the **forward exchange rate** (the rate at some specified future date). The foreign exchange rates given in Figure 20.2 can be used to illustrate these concepts. For instance, the figure shows that on Friday, June 26, 1987, the spot rate for the Swiss franc was Sf 1.5155/US$, while the forward (future) rate was Sf 1.5097/US$ for 30-day delivery. In other words, on June 26, 1987, one could take a contract on Swiss francs for 30 days hence at an exchange rate of Sf 1.5097/US$. *Forward delivery rates* are

foreign exchange rate The value of two currencies with respect to each other.

floating relationship The fluctuating relationship of the values of two currencies with respect to each other.

fixed (or semi-fixed) relationship The constant (or relatively constant) relationship of the values of two currencies with respect to each other.

spot exchange rate The rate of exchange between two currencies on any given day.

forward exchange rate The rate of exchange between two currencies at some specified future date.

Figure 20.2
Spot and Forward Exchange Rate Quotations

FOREIGN EXCHANGE

Friday June 26, 1987

The New York foreign exchange selling rates below apply to trading among banks in amounts of $1 million and more, as quoted at 3 p.m. Eastern time by Bankers Trust Co. Retail transactions provide fewer units of foreign currency per dollar.

Country	U.S. $ equiv. Fri.	Thurs.	Currency per U.S. $ Fri.	Thurs.
Argentina (Austral) ...	.5765	.5817	1.7345	1.7190
Australia (Dollar)	.7198	.7201	1.3893	1.3887
Austria (Schilling)	.07794	.07788	12.83	12.84
Belgium (Franc)				
Commercial rate	.02643	.02637	37.84	37.92
Financial rate	.02638	.02633	37.91	37.98
Brazil (Cruzado)	.02323	.02341	43.04	42.71
Britain (Pound)	1.6120	1.6130	.6203	.6199
30-Day Forward	1.6096	1.6106	.6213	.6209
90-Day Forward	1.6048	1.6058	.6231	.6227
180-Day Forward	1.5992	1.6004	.6253	.6248
Canada (Dollar)	.7505	.7522	1.3325	1.3295
30-Day Forward	.7498	.7515	1.3337	1.3307
90-Day Forward	.7484	.7499	1.3361	1.3334
180-Day Forward	.7463	.7477	1.3399	1.3374
Chile (Official rate) ...	.004565	.004576	219.07	218.51
China (Yuan)	.2686	.2693	3.722	3.7128
Colombia (Peso)	.004125	.004158	242.42	240.50
Denmark (Krone)	.1452	.1455	6.8850	6.8725
Ecuador (Sucre)				
Official rate	.005195	.005319	192.50	188.00
Floating rate	.006309	.006309	158.50	158.50
Finland (Markka)	.2255	.2251	4.4350	4.4425
France (Franc)	.1641	.1638	6.0930	6.1050
30-Day Forward	.1640	.1638	6.0985	6.1098
90-Day Forward	.1636	.1633	6.1130	6.1240
180-Day Forward	.1630	.1627	6.1360	6.1455
Greece (Drachma)	.007310	.007310	136.80	136.80
Hong Kong (Dollar) ...	.1281	.1281	7.8075	7.8065
India (Rupee)	.07740	.07758	12.91	12.89
Indonesia (Rupiah)	.0006064	.0006079	1649.00	1645.00
Ireland (Punt)	1.4680	1.4700	.6812	.6803
Israel (Shekel)	.6227	.6242	1.606	1.602
Italy (Lira)	.0007559	.0007559	1323.00	1323.00
Japan (Yen)	.006835	.006835	146.30	146.30
30-Day Forward	.006855	.006854	145.88	145.89
90-Day Forward	.006891	.006892	145.11	145.10
180-Day Forward	.006948	.006949	143.92	143.91
Jordan (Dinar)	2.9239	2.9499	.342	.339
Kuwait (Dinar)	3.5398	3.5474	.2825	.2819
Lebanon (Pound)	.007030	.007828	142.25	127.75
Malaysia (Ringgit)	.3971	.3962	2.5180	2.5240
Malta (Lira)	2.8571	2.8653	.3500	.3490
Mexico (Peso)				
Floating rate	.0007519	.0007519	1330.00	1330.00
Netherland (Guilder) ...	.4869	.4861	2.0540	2.0572
New Zealand (Dollar) ..	.5930	.5870	1.6863	1.7036
Norway (Krone)	.1497	.1494	6.6800	6.6925
Pakistan (Rupee)	.05750	.05780	17.39	17.30
Peru (Inti)	.06293	.06293	15.89	15.89
Philippines (Peso)	.04890	.04890	20.45	20.45
Portugal (Escudo)	.007052	.007013	141.80	142.60
Saudi Arabia (Riyal) ...	.2666	.2667	3.751	3.7500
Singapore (Dollar)	.4719	.4717	2.1193	2.1200
South Africa (Rand)				
Commercial rate	.4900	.4900	2.0408	2.0408
Financial rate	.2950	.2950	3.3898	3.3898
South Korea (Won)	.001232	.001231	811.70	812.50
Spain (Peseta)	.007927	.007905	126.15	126.50
Sweden (Krona)	.1571	.1569	6.3650	6.3750
Switzerland (Franc)	.6598	.6585	1.5155	1.5185
30-Day Forward	.6624	.6600	1.5097	1.5151
90-Day Forward	.6635	.6637	1.5072	1.5066
180-Day Forward	.6716	.6699	1.4890	1.4928
Taiwan (Dollar)	.03223	.03224	31.03	31.02
Thailand (Baht)	.03871	.03880	25.83	25.77
Turkey (Lira)	.001178	.001194	848.70	837.70
United Arab (Dirham) ..	.2723	.2723	3.673	3.673
Uruguay (New Peso)				
Financial	.004531	.004552	220.70	219.70
Venezuela (Bolivar)				
Official rate	.1333	.1333	7.50	7.50
Floating rate	.03503	.03390	28.55	29.50
W. Germany (Mark) ...	.5476	.5467	1.8263	1.8292
30-Day Forward	.5491	.5482	1.8211	1.8240
90-Day Forward	.5523	.5513	1.8107	1.8138
180-Day Forward	.5573	.5563	1.7945	1.7977

SOURCE: *The Wall Street Journal*, June 29, 1987, p. 32.

also available for 90-day and 180-day contracts. For all such contracts, the agreements and signatures are completed on, say, June 26, 1987, whereas the actual exchange of dollars and Swiss francs between buyers and sellers will take place on the future date, say, 30 days later.

Figure 20.2 can also be used to illustrate the differences between floating and fixed currencies. All the major currencies previously mentioned have spot and forward rates with respect to the U.S. dollar. Moreover, a comparison of the exchange rates prevailing on Friday, June 26, 1987, *versus* those on Thursday, June 25, 1987, indicates that the floating major currencies (or other currencies that also float in relation to the U.S. dollar, such as the Austrian schilling and the Indian rupee) experienced changes in rates. Other currencies, however, such as the United Arab dirham, do not exhibit relatively large fluctuations on a daily basis with respect to either the U.S. dollar or the currency to which they are pegged (i.e., they have very limited movements with respect to either the U.S. dollar or other currencies).

A final point to note is the concept of changes in the value of a currency with respect to the U.S. dollar or another currency. For the floating currencies, changes in the value of foreign exchange rates are called *appreciation* or *depreciation*. For example, referring to Figure 20.2, it can be seen that the value of the French franc has appreciated from Ff 6.1050/$ on Thursday to Ff 6.0930/$ on Friday. In other words, it takes fewer francs to buy one dollar. For the fixed currencies, changes in values are called official *revaluation* or *devaluation,* but these terms have the same meanings as appreciation and depreciation, respectively.

Impact of Currency Fluctuation

Multinational companies face foreign exchange risks under both floating and fixed arrangements. The case of the floating currencies can be used to illustrate these risks.

INTERNATIONAL FINANCIAL MANAGEMENT:
A Growing Field

Mark, 26, is a junior associate in the international finance group of a large East Coast financial services multinational corporation. He recently joined the firm after working in the international division of a large bank. In both positions Mark's fluency in French and master's degrees in business and economics were keys to his success.

Both large banks and multinational corporations need people with skills like Mark's in their overseas investments and currency trading activities. Recently Mark was involved with his firm's multimillion-dollar Eurobond placement. Currently he is working on a major deal with a European bank for the placement of Swiss bonds.

"When I worked at the bank," Mark says, "I spent most of my time on the telephone answering questions about the current exchange rate of the French franc, which was the currency I specialized in. I also transmitted buy-and-sell orders for that currency for some of our customers. I enjoyed it, but I decided to go into corporate work because I wanted to be more involved with the business side of things."

In his current position Mark still watches the franc, but he is also involved in the company's long-term international financial management. "We have to be concerned about foreign exchange. Sometimes millions of dollars can be lost or gained depending on the timing of a decision. In our group we have to be concerned about both short-term and long-term financial markets. What they always say is really true: decision-making is more of an art than a science, and it takes years to acquire the experience to know what to do."

It is because such decisions are so economically crucial and so difficult to assess correctly that the responsibility for planning in Mark's company, as in most comparable firms, rests with senior management. In Mark's case, a senior vice-president for the international group reports to the corporate treasurer. Both cash flow and foreign exchange planning go hand in hand and must be integrated into the annual as well as the strategic corporate plans.

In addition to academic backgrounds in business or economics, the people in Mark's group all speak at least one foreign language fluently and have an interest in other countries and their economies. Most who plan to advance, as Mark hopes to do, also expect to spend long hours keeping up with the current events in the world. At work much time is spent in meetings and planning sessions. Some foreign travel is necessary.

Average earnings for someone with Mark's education and experience begin in the $26,000–$36,000 range. Senior international financial officers make from $80,000 to over $100,000 in some companies. Because of the nature of the work, most jobs are in large metropolitan areas. Sometimes an overseas transfer to a branch or subsidiary is part of the career path. While in international banking, as in the banking industry generally, the salaries tend to be lower, international finance in both industry and banking is a growing field.

"More and more companies in the United States will be doing business with companies from all over the world," Mark says. "Seeing how other people operate in other countries has always fascinated me, and I've always liked business. Now I have a chance to do both. It's great!"

Returning to the U.S. dollar–Swiss franc relationship, we note that the forces of international supply and demand as well as internal and external economic and political elements help shape both the spot and the forward rates between these two currencies. Since the MNC cannot control much (or most) of these "outside" elements, the company faces potential changes in exchange rates in the form of appreciation or depreciation that can in turn affect its revenues, costs, and profits as measured in U.S. dollars. For currencies fixed in relation to each other, the risks come from the same set of elements indicated above. Again, these official changes, like the ones brought about by the market in the case of floating currencies, can affect the MNC's operations and its dollar-based financial position.

---

3 Foreign exchange risk refers to the potential discontinuity or seizure of an MNC's operations in a host country due to the host's implementation of specific rules and regulations such as nationalization, expropriation, and confiscation. *(Fable)*
Foreign exchange risk *is the risk created by the varying exchange rate between two currencies*. (Note: The definition given above is that of political risk.)

The risks stemming from changes in exchange rates can be illustrated by examining the balance sheet and income statement of MNC, Inc. We will focus on its subsidiary in Switzerland.

Example
MNC, Inc., has a subsidiary in Switzerland that at the end of 1988 has the financial statements shown in Table 20.3. The figures for the balance sheet and income statement are given in the local currency, Swiss francs (Sf). Using the foreign exchange rate of Sf 1.50/US$ for December 31, 1988, the statements have been translated into U.S. dollars. For simplicity it is assumed that all the local figures are expected to remain the same during 1989. As a result, as of January 1, 1989, the subsidiary expects to show the same Swiss franc figures on 12/31/89 as on 12/31/88. However, due to the change in the value of the Swiss franc relative to the dollar, from Sf 1.50/US$ to Sf 1.30/US$, it is clear that the translated dollar values of the items in the balance sheet, along with the dollar profit value on 12/31/89, are higher than those of the previous year, the changes being due only to fluctuations in foreign exchange.

There are additional complexities attached to each individual account in the financial statements. For instance, it is important whether a subsidiary's debt is all in the local currency, in U.S. dollars, or in several currencies. Moreover, it is important which currency (or currencies) the revenues and costs are denominated in. The risks exemplified so far relate to what is called the **accounting exposure.** In other words, foreign exchange fluctuations affect individual accounts in the financial statements. A different, and perhaps more important, risk element concerns **economic exposure,** which is the potential impact of exchange rate fluctuations on the firm's value. Given that all future revenues and thus net profits can be subject to exchange rate changes, it is obvious that the *present value* of the net profits derived from foreign operations will have, as a part of its total diversifiable risk, an element reflecting appreciation (revaluation) or depreciation (devaluation) of various currencies with respect to the U.S. dollar.

What can the management of MNCs do about these risks? The actions will depend on the attitude of the management toward risk. This attitude, in turn, translates into how aggressively management wants to hedge the company's undesirable positions and exposures. The money markets, the forward (futures) markets, and the foreign currency options markets can be used—either individually or in conjunction with one another—to hedge foreign exchange exposures. Further details on certain hedging strategies are described later in this chapter.

Political Risks

Another important risk facing MNCs is political risk. **Political risk** refers to the implementation by a host government of specific rules and regulations that can result in the

accounting exposure The risk resulting from the effects of changes in foreign exchange rates on the translated value of a firm's accounts denominated in a given foreign currency.

economic exposure The risk resulting from the effects of changes in foreign exchange rates on the firm's value.

political risk The potential discontinuity or seizure of an MNC's operations in a host country due to the host's implementation of specific rules and regulations (such as nationalization, expropriation, and confiscation).

Table 20.3
Financial Statements for MNC, Inc.'s, Swiss Subsidiary

Translation of Balance Sheet			
		12/31/88	12/31/89
Assets	Sf	US$	US$
Cash	8.00	5.33	6.15
Inventory	60.00	40.00	46.15
Plant and equipment (net)	32.00	21.33	24.61
Total	100.00	66.66	76.91
Liabilities and equity			
Debt	48.00	32.00	36.92
Paid-in capital	40.00	26.66	30.76
Retained earnings	12.00	8.00	9.23
Total	100.00	66.66	76.91
Translation of Income Statement			
Sales revenue	600.00	400.00	461.53
Cost of goods sold	550.00	366.66	423.07
Operating profits	50.00	33.34	38.46

NOTE: This example is simplified to show how the balance sheet and income statement are subject to exchange fluctuations. For the applicable rules on the translation of foreign accounts, review the discussion of international financial statements presented earlier.

discontinuity or seizure of the operations of a foreign company in that country. Political risk is usually manifested in the form of nationalization, expropriation, and confiscation. In general, the assets and operations of a foreign firm are taken over by the host government, usually without proper (or any) compensation.

Political risk has two basic paths: *macro* and *micro*. **Macro political risk** means that due to political change, revolution, or the adoption of new policies by a host government, *all* foreign firms in the country will be subjected to political risk. In other words, no individual country or firm is treated differently; all assets and operations of foreign firms are taken over wholesale. An example of macro political risk is China in 1949 or Cuba in 1959–1960. **Micro political risk,** on the other hand, refers to the case in which an individual firm, a specific industry, or companies from a particular foreign country will be subjected to takeover. Examples include the nationalization by a majority of the oil-exporting countries of the assets of the international oil companies in their territories.

Although political risk can take place in any country—even in the United States—the political instability of the Third World generally makes the positions of multinational companies most vulnerable there. At the same time, some of the countries in this group have the most promising markets for the goods and services being offered by MNCs. The main question, therefore, is how to engage in operation and foreign investment in such countries and yet avoid or minimize the potential political risk.

Table 20.4 shows some of the approaches that MNCs may be able to adopt to cope with political risk. The negative approaches are generally used by firms in extractive

macro political risk The subjection of *all* foreign firms to political risk (takeover) by a host country, due to political change, revolution, or the adoption of new policies.

micro political risk The subjection of an individual firm, a specific industry, or companies from a particular foreign country to political risk (takeover) by the host country.

Table 20.4
Approaches for Coping with Political Risks

Positive approaches		Negative approaches
Prior negotiation of controls and operating contracts Prior agreement for sale Joint venture with government or local private sector	} Direct	License or patent restrictions under international agreements Control of external raw materials
Use of locals in management Joint venture with local banks Equity participation by middle class Local sourcing Local retail outlets	} Indirect	Control of transportation to (external) markets Control of downstream processing Control of external markets
External approaches to minimize loss		

International insurance or investment guarantees
Thinly capitalized firms:
    Local financing
    External financing secured only by the local operation		

SOURCE: Rita M. Rodriguez and E. Eugene Carter, *International Financial Management,* 3rd ed. (Englewood Cliffs, NJ: Prentice-Hall, 1984), p. 512.

industries. The external approaches are also of limited use. The best policies MNCs can follow are the positive approaches, which have both economic and political aspects.

In recent years MNCs have been relying on a variety of complex forecasting techniques whereby "international experts," using available historical data, predict the chances for political instability in a host country and the potential effects on MNC operations. Events in Iran and Nicaragua, among others, however, point to the limited use of such techniques and tend to reinforce the usefulness of the positive approaches.

A final point to note relates to the introduction by most developed and developing "host" governments in the last two decades of comprehensive sets of rules, regulations, and incentives aimed at regulating inflows of *foreign direct investments* involving MNCs. Known as **national entry control systems,** they are designed to extract more benefits from MNCs' presence by regulating such flows in terms of a variety of factors, including local ownership, level of exportation, use of local inputs, number of local managers, internal geographic location, level of local borrowing, and the respective percentages of profits to be remitted and of capital to be repatriated back to parent firms. Host countries expect that as MNCs comply with these regulations, the potential for acts of political risk will decline, thus benefiting MNCs as well.

national entry control systems Comprehensive rules, regulations, and incentives aimed at regulating inflows of *foreign direct investments* involving MNCs and at the same time extracting more benefits from their presence.

International Financial Decisions

Most of the pertinent concepts covered earlier in the text are also applicable to multinational companies in terms of their international financial decisions. A number of unique factors, however, need to be emphasized here. In this final section of the chapter, we start our discussion by focusing on key aspects of MNCs' international long-term investments.

Next, we turn to international short-term financing, to be followed by a discussion of international cash management. Subsequently, issues related to international long-term debt will be examined. Finally, the last two segments will cover international equity capital and international business combinations, respectively.

International Long-Term Investments

Two specific topics will be covered in this segment. First, we will briefly examine some of the major reasons why MNCs undertake foreign direct investments (FDI). The coverage will include some data on U.S.-based MNCs' stock of FDI. Second, we will discuss some of the major aspects of international capital budgeting.

Foreign Direct (Long-Term) Investments (FDI)

Foreign direct investment (FDI) can be defined as the transfer, by a multinational firm, of capital, managerial, and technical assets from its home country to a host country. The equity participation on the part of an MNC can be 100 percent (resulting in a wholly-owned foreign subsidiary) or less (leading to a joint-venture project with foreign participants). As opposed to short-term, foreign portfolio investments undertaken by individuals and companies (e.g., internationally diversified mutual funds), FDI involves equity participation, managerial control, and day-to-day operational activities on the part of MNCs. Therefore, FDI projects will be subjected not only to business, financial, inflation, and foreign exchange risks (as would foreign portfolio investments), but also to the additional element of political risk. Consequently, the material presented earlier on political risks is applicable to the current discussion.

foreign direct investment (FDI) The transfer, by a multinational firm, of capital, managerial, and technical assets from its home country to a host country.

For a number of decades, U.S.-based MNCs had dominated the international scene in terms of both the *flow* and *stock* of FDI. The total FDI stock of U.S.-based MNCs over the last five decades, for instance, increased from $7.7 billion in 1929 to over $232.5 billion at the end of 1985. In the last fifteen years, though, their global presence is being challenged by MNCs based in Japan, Western Europe, and other developed and developing nations. In fact, even the "home" market of U.S. multinationals is being challenged by foreign firms. For instance, in 1960, FDI into the United States amounted to only 11.5 percent of American investment overseas. At the end of 1985, it had risen to about 78 percent.

International Capital Budgeting

Several factors unique to the international setting need to be examined. First, elements relating to a parent company's *investment* in a subsidiary and the concept of taxes must be considered. For example, in the case of manufacturing investments, questions may arise as to the value of the equipment a parent may contribute to the subsidiary. Is the value based on the market conditions in the parent country or the local host economy? In general, the market value in the host country is the relevant "price."

The existence of different taxes—as pointed out earlier here—can complicate measurement of the *cash flows* to be received by the parent because different definitions of taxable income can arise. There are still other complications when it comes to measuring the actual cash flows. From a parent firm's viewpoint, the cash flows are those repatriated from the subsidiary. In some countries, however, such cash flows may be totally or partially blocked. Obviously, depending on the life of the project in the host country, the returns and net present values (NPVs) associated with such projects can significantly vary from the subsidiary's and the parent's point of view. For instance, for a project of only five years' duration, if all yearly cash flows are blocked by the host government, the subsidiary may show a "normal" or even superior return and NPV, while the parent may show no return at all. On the other hand, for a project of longer life, even if cash flows are blocked for the first few years, the remaining years' cash flows can contribute toward the parent's returns and NPV.

FACT OR FABLE?

4 Because repatriation of cash flows from a subsidiary may be totally or partially blocked by the host country, the returns and net present values associated with such projects can reflect good performance on the part of the subsidiary and yet mean no returns for the parent. *(Fact)*

Finally, there is the issue of *risk* attached to international cash flows. The three basic types of risk categories are (1) business and financial risks, (2) inflation and foreign exchange risks, and (3) political risks. The first category relates to the type of industry the subsidiary is in as well as its financial structure (more details on financial risks are presented later). As for the other two categories, we have already discussed both the risks of having investments, profits, and assets/liabilities in different currencies, as well as the potential impacts of political risks and how MNCs can combat them.

The important point to note here is that the presence of such risks will influence the discount rate (or the cost of capital) to be used in evaluating international cash flows. The basic rule, however, is that the *local cost of equity capital* (applicable to the local business and financial environments within which a subsidiary operates) is the starting discount rate to which risks stemming from foreign exchange and political factors can be added, and from which benefits reflecting the parent's lower capital costs may be subtracted.

International Short-Term Financing

In international operations the usual domestic sources of short-term financing, along with other sources, are available to MNCs. Included are accounts payable as well as accruals, bank and nonbank sources in each subsidiary's local environment, and the Euromarket discussed earlier. Our emphasis here is on the "foreign" sources.

For a subsidiary of a multinational company, its local economic market is a basic source of both short- and long-term financing. Moreover, the subsidiary's borrowing and lending status, relative to a local firm in the same economy, can be superior, since the subsidiary can rely on the potential backing and guarantee of its parent MNC. One drawback, however, is that most local markets and local currencies are regulated by local authorities. Thus a subsidiary may ultimately choose to turn to the Euromarket and take advantage of borrowing and investing in an unregulated financial forum.

The Euromarket offers nondomestic financing opportunities for both the short term (Eurocurrency) and the long term (Eurobonds). (Eurobonds will be discussed later.) In the case of short-term financing, the forces of supply and demand are among the main factors determining exchange rates in **Eurocurrency markets,** with each currency's nominal interest rate being influenced by economic policies pursued by the respective "home" governments. In other words, the interest rates offered in the Euromarket on, for example, the U.S. dollar are greatly affected by the prime rate inside the United States, and the

Eurocurrency markets The portion of the Euromarket that provides short-term foreign-currency financing to subsidiaries of MNCs.

dollar's exchange rates with other major currencies are influenced by the supply and demand forces acting in such markets (and in response to interest rates).

Unlike borrowing in the domestic markets, where only one currency and a **nominal interest rate** is involved, financing activities in the Euromarket can involve several currencies and both nominal and effective interest rates. **Effective interest rates** are equal to nominal rates plus (or minus) any forecast appreciation (or depreciation) of a foreign currency relative to the currency of the MNC parent—say, the U.S. dollar. An example will illustrate the issues involved.

nominal interest rate In the international context, the stated interest rate charged on financing when only the MNC parent's currency is involved.

effective interest rates In the international context, the rates equal to nominal rates plus (or minus) any forecast appreciation (or depreciation) of a foreign currency relative to the currency of the MNC parent.

Example

A multinational company, MNC, Inc., has subsidiaries in Switzerland (local currency, Swiss franc, Sf) and Belgium (local currency, Belgian franc, Bf). Based on each subsidiary's forecast operations, the short-term financial needs of each (in equivalent U.S. dollars) are as follows:

Switzerland: $80 million excess cash to be invested (lent)

Belgium: $60 million funds to be raised (borrowed)

Based on all the available information, the parent firm has provided each subsidiary with the following figures regarding exchange rates and interest rates. (The figures for the effective rates shown are derived by adding the forecast percentage change numbers to the nominal rates.)

		Currency	
Item	**US$**	**Sf**	**Bf**
Spot exchange rates		Sf 1.52/US$	Bf 37.5/US$
Forecast % change		+2.2%	−1.5%
Interest rates			
Nominal			
Euromarket	7.9%	4.0%	8.7%
Domestic	7.5	3.6	9.2
Effective			
Euromarket	7.9%	6.2%	7.2%
Domestic	7.5	5.8	7.7

From the point of view of a multinational, the effective rates of interest, which take into account each currency's forecast percentage change (appreciation or depreciation) relative to the U.S. dollar, are the main items to be considered for investment and borrowing decisions. (It is assumed here that due to local regulations, a subsidiary is *not* permitted to use the domestic market of *any other* subsidiary.) The relevant question is, where should funds be invested and borrowed?

For investment purposes, the highest available rate of interest is the effective rate for the U.S. dollar in the Euromarket. Therefore, the Swiss subsidiary should invest the $80 million in the Euromarket. In the case of raising funds, the cheapest source *open* to the Belgian subsidiary is the 6.2 percent in the Sf Euromarket. The subsidiary should therefore raise the $60 million in Swiss francs. These two transactions will result in the most revenues and least costs, respectively.

Several points should be made with respect to the preceding example. First of all, this is a simplified case of the actual workings of the Eurocurrency markets. The example ignores taxes, intersubsidiary investing and borrowing, and periods longer or shorter than a year. Nevertheless, it shows how the existence of many currencies can provide both challenges and opportunities for MNCs. Next, the focus has been solely on accounting values; of greater importance would be the impact of these actions on market value. Finally, it is important to note the following details about the figures presented. The forecast percentage change (appreciation or depreciation) data are regarded as those normally supplied by the MNC's international financial managers. The management may have a *range of forecasts,* from the most likely to the least likely. In addition, the company's management is likely to take a specific position in terms of its response to any remaining foreign exchange exposures. If any action is to be taken, certain amounts of one or more currencies will be borrowed and then invested in other currencies in the hope of realizing potential gains to offset potential losses associated with the exposures.

International Cash Management

In its international cash management, a multinational can respond to foreign exchange risks by protecting (hedging) its undesirable cash and marketable securities exposures or by certain adjustments in its operations. While the former approach is more applicable in responding to *accounting exposures,* the latter is better suited against *economic exposures*. Each of these two approaches is examined here.

Hedging Strategies

hedging strategies
Techniques used to offset risk; in the international context, these include borrowing or lending in different currencies, undertaking contracts in the forward, futures, and/or options markets, and also swapping assets/liabilities with other parties.

Hedging strategies are techniques used to offset risk. In international cash management these strategies include actions such as borrowing or lending in different currencies, undertaking contracts in the forward, futures, and/or options markets, and also swapping assets/liabilities with other parties. Table 20.5 provides a brief summary of some of the major hedging tools available to MNCs.

Adjustments in Operations

In responding to exchange fluctuations, international cash flows can be given some protection through appropriate adjustments in assets and liabilities. Two routes are available to a multinational company. The first centers on the operating relationships that a subsidiary of an MNC maintains with *other* firms—*third parties*. Depending on management's expectation of a local currency's position, adjustments in operations would involve the reduction of liabilities if the currency is appreciating or the reduction of financial assets if it is depreciating. For example, if a U.S.-based MNC with a subsidiary in Mexico expects the Mexican currency to *appreciate* in value relative to the U.S. dollar, local customers' accounts receivable would be *increased* and accounts payable would be reduced if at all possible. Because the dollar is the currency in which the MNC parent will have to prepare consolidated financial statements, the net result in this case would be to favorably increase the Mexican subsidiary's resources in local currency. If the Mexican currency were, instead, expected to *depreciate,* the local customer's accounts receivable would be *reduced* and accounts payable would be increased, thereby reducing the Mexican subsidiary's resources in the local currency.

The second route focuses on the operating relationship a subsidiary has with its parent or with other subsidiaries within the same MNC. In dealing with exchange risks, a subsid-

Table 20.5
Foreign Exchange Risk Hedging Tools

Tool	Description	Impact on risk
Borrowing & lending	Borrowing/lending in different currencies to take advantage of interest rate differentials and foreign exchange appreciation/depreciation; can be either on a certainty basis with "up-front" costs or speculative.	Can be used to offset exposures in existing assets/liabilities and in expected revenues/ expenses.
Forward contract	"Tailor-made" contracts representing an *obligation* to buy/sell, with the amount, rate, and maturity agreed upon between the two parties; has little up-front cost.	Can eliminate downside risk but locks out any upside potential.
Futures contract	Standardized contracts offered on organized exchanges; same basic tool as a forward contract, but less flexible due to standardization; more flexibility due to secondary market access; has some up-front cost/fee.	Can also eliminate downside risk, plus position can be nullified, creating possible upside potential.
Options	Tailor-made or standardized contracts providing the *right* to buy or to sell an amount of the currency, at a particular price, during a specified time period; has up-front cost (premium).	Can eliminate downside risk and retain unlimited upside potential.
Interest rate swap	Allows the trading of one interest rate stream (e.g., on a fixed-rate U.S. dollar instrument) for another (e.g., on a floating-rate U.S. dollar instrument); fee to be paid to the intermediary.	Permits firms to change the interest rate structure of their assets/liabilities and achieves cost savings due to broader market access.
Currency swap	Two parties exchange principal amounts of two different currencies initially; they pay each other's interest payments, then reverse principal amounts at a pre-agreed exchange rate at maturity; more complex than interest rate swaps.	All the features of interest rate swaps, plus, it allows firms to change the currency structure of their assets/liabilities.
Hybrids	A variety of combinations of some of the above tools; may be quite costly and/or speculative.	Can create, with the right combination, a perfect hedge against certain foreign exchange exposures.

NOTE: The participants in the above activities include MNCs, financial institutions, and brokers. The organized exchanges include Amsterdam, Chicago, London, New York, Philadelphia, and Zurich, among others. It should be emphasized that while most of these tools can be utilized for short-term exposure management, some, such as swaps, are more appropriate for long-term hedging strategies.

iary can rely on *intra-MNC accounts*. Specifically, undesirable foreign exchange exposures can be corrected to the extent that the subsidiary can take the following steps:

1. In appreciation-prone countries, intra-MNC accounts receivable are collected as soon as possible, while payment of intra-MNC accounts payable is delayed as long as possible.

2. In devaluation-prone countries, intra-MNC accounts receivable are collected as late as possible, while intra-MNC accounts payable are paid as soon as possible.

Again using the example of a Mexican subsidiary, the net result of step 1 or step 2 would be the potential increase or decrease of that subsidiary's resources in the Mexican currency, depending on whether that currency is appreciating or depreciating relative to the parent MNC's main currency, the U.S. dollar.

FACT OR FABLE?   5 | In appreciation-prone countries, intra-MNC accounts receivable are collected as late as possible, while intra-MNC accounts payable are paid as soon as possible. *(Fable)*
In appreciation-prone countries, intra-MNC accounts receivable are collected *as soon as possible*, while payment of intra-MNC accounts payable is *delayed as long as possible.*

From a *global* point of view and as far as an MNC's consolidated intracompany accounts are concerned, the manipulation of such accounts by one subsidiary can produce the opposite results for another subsidiary or the parent firm. For example, if an MNC's subsidiaries in Brazil and Mexico are dealing with each other, the Brazilian subsidiary's manipulations of intra-MNC accounts—along the lines just discussed—in anticipation of an appreciation of that country's currency relative to that of Mexico can mean exchange gains for the Brazilian subsidiary but losses for the Mexican one. The exact degree and direction of the actual manipulations, however, may depend on the tax status of each country, the MNC obviously wanting to have the exchange losses in the country with the higher tax rate. Finally, changes in intra-MNC accounts can also be subject to restrictions and regulations put forward by the respective host countries of various subsidiaries.

International Long-Term Debt

Multinational companies, in conducting their global operations, have access to a variety of international financial instruments. International bonds are among the most widely used, so we will begin by focusing on them. Next, we discuss the role of international financial institutions in underwriting such instruments. Finally, emphasis is placed on the use of various techniques (such as swaps) by MNCs to change the structure of their long-term debts.

International Bonds

international bond A bond initially sold outside the country of the borrower and often distributed in several countries.

foreign bond An international bond sold primarily in the country of the currency of the issue.

In general, an **international bond** initially sold outside the country of the borrower is often distributed in several countries. When a bond is sold primarily in the country of the currency of the issue, it is called a **foreign bond.** For example, an MNC based in West Germany might float a bond issue in the French capital market underwritten by a French syndicate and denominated in French francs. When an international bond is sold primarily

---

SMALL BUSINESS

GOING PUBLIC ABROAD: CVD Inc.'s Experience

When sources of investment capital dry up, as they did in 1984, some businesses postpone their fund-raising. But there are always exceptions, as shown by CVD Inc. When times got tough in the United States, the small $3.3–million company pulled off a transatlantic initial public offering.

CVD, a producer of advanced materials for defense and industrial applications, was started in 1980 with an initial investment of $81,000 by the founders, Robert N. Donadio and Joseph F. Connolly, and a $275,000 bank loan guaranteed by the Small Business Administration (SBA). The demand for the company's two main products—zinc selenide and zinc sulfide started to heat up, and CVD suddenly began to feel pressure to expand.

In 1982 and 1983, the company's production capacity quadrupled. By the end of the fiscal year ending May 31, 1983, CVD had earned $393,000 (before taxes) on sales of $2.7 million. Meantime, however, debts soared. New furnaces were financed with new bank borrowings (also backed with SBA

guarantees), and much of the raw-material purchases were being funded by a key supplier. Indeed, by early 1984, CVD's debt-equity ratio was up around eight.

Donadio explored ways to expand CVD's equity base. Market conditions were not ripe for an initial public offering and venture capitalists were asking too much. "The venture guys wanted nearly 40 percent of the business for $2 million," Donadio notes. That made for a total valuation of around $5 million, barely eight times net income. Donadio contacted a London-based consultant he had hired to investigate financing possibilities in England. It seemed that CVD was a very plausible candidate for going public on London's Unlisted Securities Market of The Stock Exchange—its version of the U.S. over-the-counter market. The fact that CVD had a number of customers in the United Kingdom certainly didn't hurt.

It appeared that British investors were willing to value CVD significantly higher than U.S. venture funds. The prevailing market multiples, generally

higher in Britain for technology-oriented businesses, gave the company a market valuation of at least double and maybe triple the $5-million figure quoted by U.S. venture investors.

CVD spent a rigorous three months preparing for the public offering. Auditors on both sides of the ocean verified the accuracy of the company's financial records and testified to the veracity of CVD's business forecasts.

As it turned out, CVD ended up selling just 22 percent of its common shares for 3 million pounds—which converted into $3.7 million in late 1984. The market value of the total company was $16.7 million, or 51 times net income for fiscal-year 1984.

Even after the auditing, legal, and underwriting expenses, the company was well ahead of where it might have been had it stayed at home. "Last spring (1984) I didn't even know it was *possible* to do an offering in the U.K.," Donadio said. "I guess I just didn't know."

SOURCE: Adapted from Bruce G. Posner, "Adding Pounds," *INC.*, March 1985, pp. 140–142.

---

in countries other than the country of the currency in which the issue is denominated, it is called a **Eurobond.** Thus, an MNC based in the United States might float a Eurobond in several European capital markets, underwritten by an international syndicate and denominated in U.S. dollars.

The U.S. dollar dominated the Eurobond issues throughout the period 1982 to 1986, with the Japanese yen gaining popularity during 1985 and 1986. The importance of the U.S. currency in all aspects of international transactions, and thus its importance to MNCs, can explain this continued dominance. In the foreign bond category, the Swiss franc continues to be the major choice. Low levels of interest, the general stability of the currency, and the overall efficiency of the Swiss capital markets are among the primary reasons for the ongoing popularity of the Swiss franc. However, Eurobonds are much more widely used than foreign bonds. These instruments are heavily used, especially in

Eurobond An international bond sold primarily in countries other than the country of the currency in which the issue is denominated.

relation to Eurocurrency loans in recent years, by major market participants including U.S. corporations. During 1987, the so-called equity-linked Eurobonds (i.e., convertible to equity), especially those offered by a number of high-tech U.S. firms, found strong demand among Euromarket participants. It is expected that more of these innovative types of instruments will emerge on the international scene in the coming years.

A final point concerns the levels of interest rates in international markets. In the case of foreign bonds, interest rates are usually directly correlated with the domestic rates prevailing in the respective countries. For Eurobonds, several interest rates may be influential. For instance, for a Eurodollar bond, the interest rate will reflect the U.S. long-term rate, the Eurodollar rate, and long-term rates in other countries.

The Role of International Financial Institutions

For *foreign bonds,* the underwriting institutions are those that handle bond issues in the respective countries in which such bonds are issued. For *Eurobonds,* a number of financial institutions in the United States, Japan, and Western Europe form international underwriting syndicates. The underwriting costs for Eurobonds are comparable to those for bond flotation in the United States' domestic market. Although American institutions used to dominate the Eurobond scene, recent economic and financial strengths exhibited by some Japanese and Western European (especially German) financial firms have led to a change in that dominance. A number of Japanese and European firms held the top positions in terms of lead managing Eurobond issues during 1986 and again during the first four months of 1987.

In order to raise funds through international bond issues, many MNCs establish their own financial subsidiaries. Many American-based MNCs, for example, have created subsidiaries in the United States and Western Europe, especially in Luxembourg. Such subsidiaries can be used to raise large amounts of funds in "one move," with the funds redistributed wherever MNCs need them. (Special tax rules applicable to such subsidiaries also make them desirable to MNCs.)

Changing the Structure of Debt

In the earlier discussion of hedging strategies, it was emphasized that some of the tools, such as interest rate swaps and currency swaps, can be used by MNCs to change the structure/characteristics of their long-term assets and liabilities. For instance, multinationals can utilize interest rate swaps in order to obtain a desired stream of interest payments (e.g., fixed-rate) in exchange for another (e.g., floating-rate), and currency swaps for the purpose of exchanging an asset/liability denominated in one currency (e.g., U.S. dollar) for another (e.g., Swiss franc). The use of these instruments allows MNCs to gain access to a broader set of markets, currencies, and maturities, thus leading to both cost savings and a means of restructuring the existing assets/liabilities. Such use has experienced significant growth during the last few years, and this trend is expected to continue.

International Equity Capital

Here we emphasize two major aspects of international equity capital. First, we will look at international capital markets through which multinational companies can raise equity funds. Second, we will focus on the role of equity (versus debt) in the MNCs' foreign direct investment in international joint ventures.

International Equity Issues and Markets

One means of raising equity funds for MNCs is to have the parent's stock distributed internationally and owned by stockholders of different nationalities. In the 1980s, the world's equity markets have grown to be more "internationalized" (i.e., becoming more standardized and thus closer in character to the Eurobond market discussed earlier). In other words, while distinct *national* stock markets (such as New York, London, and Tokyo) continue to exist and grow, an *international* stock market has also emerged on the global financial scene.

In recent years, the terms **"Euro-equity market"** and "Euro-equities" have become widely known. While a number of capital markets—including New York, Tokyo, Zurich, and Paris—play major roles by hosting international equity issues, London has become *the* center of Euro-equity activity. As of mid-1987, for instance, London's *secondary market* activities on Euro-equities were estimated to have a daily turnover of between $1.6 billion and $2.0 billion. In terms of the *primary market,* the *Euromoney* magazine (May 1987) reported that in 1986, companies approached the international equity market 393 times, either through straight equity, convertible bonds, or equity warrant issues, raising a total of $33.38 billion. As for the nationality of the major issuers, the *Euromoney* report indicated that MNCs from at least 17 different countries took advantage of raising funds through Euro-equity issues. Companies based in Germany, followed by those domiciled in Italy, the United States, France, and the United Kingdom, led in terms of straight international equity issues during the period of January 1986–April 1987.

Euro-equity market The capital market that deals in international equity issues, the center of which is London.

International Joint Ventures

The basic aspects of foreign ownership of international operations were discussed earlier in this chapter. Worth emphasizing here is that certain laws and regulations enacted during the 1960s and 1970s by a number of host countries require MNCs to maintain less than 50 percent ownership in their subsidiaries in most of those countries. For a U.S.-based MNC, for example, establishing foreign subsidiaries in the form of joint ventures means that a certain portion of the firm's total international equity stock is (indirectly) held by foreign owners.

Some of the advantages and disadvantages of joint ventures have previously been highlighted. In establishing a foreign subsidiary, an MNC may wish to have as little equity and as much debt as possible, with the debt coming from local sources in the host country or the MNC itself. Each of these actions can be supported. The host country may allow *more local debt* for a subsidiary; this is a good protective measure in terms of lessening the potential impacts of political risk. In other words, since local sources are involved in the capital structure of a subsidiary, there may be fewer threats from local authorities in the event of changes in government or the enactment of new regulations on foreign business.

In support of the other action, having *more MNC-based debt* in a subsidiary's capital structure, it is true that many host governments are less restrictive—in terms of taxation and actual repatriation—toward intra-MNC interest payments than toward intra-MNC dividend remittances. The parent firm may therefore be in a better position if it has more MNC-based debt than equity in the capital structure of its subsidiaries.

---

6 The use of more local debt in a joint-venture subsidiary's capital structure provides protection by reducing potential threats from local authorities and thereby lessening the consequences of political risk. *(Fact)*

FACT OR FABLE?

International Business Combinations

The motives for domestic business combinations presented in Chapter 19—growth or diversification, synergistic effects, fund raising, increased managerial skills, tax considerations, and increased ownership liquidity—as well as the factors emphasized in earlier sections of this chapter, are all applicable to MNCs' international business combinations. Several additional points, nevertheless, need attention.

First, international joint ventures and acquisitions, especially those involving European firms acquiring assets in the United States, have increased significantly in the 1980s. MNCs based in Western Europe, Japan, and North America have made substantial contributions to this increase. Moreover, a fast-growing group of MNCs has emerged in the past two decades, based in the so-called newly-industrializing countries (which include, among others, Brazil, Argentina, Mexico, Hong Kong, Singapore, South Korea, Taiwan, India, and Pakistan). This growth has added further to the number and value of international acquisitions.

Foreign direct investments (i.e., *new* investments, *mergers,* and/or *acquisitions,* on the basis of either wholly-owned or joint venture) in the United States have gained popularity in the past few years. Most of the foreign direct investors in the United States come from seven countries: Britain, Canada, France, the Netherlands, Japan, Switzerland, and West Germany. The heaviest investments are concentrated in manufacturing, followed by the petroleum and trade/service sectors. British takeovers totaled $8.7 billion for the first nine months of 1986, compared to $4.3 billion for all of 1985. Another interesting trend is the current rise in the number of joint ventures between companies based in Japan and firms domiciled elsewhere in the industrialized world, especially U.S.-based MNCs. While Japanese authorities continue their discussions and debates with other governments regarding Japan's international trade surpluses as well as perceived trade barriers, joint ventures and other forms of business combinations, acquisitions, and agreements continue to take place. In the eyes of some U.S. corporate executives, such business ventures are viewed as a "ticket into the Japanese market" as well as a way to curb a potentially tough competitor.

Developing countries, too, have been attracting foreign direct investments in both horizontal and vertical industries. Meanwhile, during the last two decades a number of these nations have adopted specific policies and regulations aimed at controlling the inflows of foreign investments, a major provision being the 49 percent ownership limitation applied to MNCs. Of course, international competition among differently based MNCs has been of benefit to some developing countries in their attempts at extracting concessions from the multinationals. However, an increasing number of such nations have shown greater flexibility in their recent dealings with MNCs as the latter group has become more reluctant to form joint ventures under the stated conditions. Furthermore, given the present, as well as the expected, international economic and trade status, it is likely that as more Third World countries recognize the need for foreign capital and technology, they will show even greater flexibility in their agreements with MNCs.

A final point to note relates to the existence of international *holding companies*. Places such as Liechtenstein and Panama have long been considered favorable spots for forming holding companies due to their conducive legal, corporate, and tax environments. International holding companies control many business entities in the form of subsidiaries, branches, joint ventures, and other agreements. For international legal (especially tax-related) reasons, as well as anonymity, such holding companies have become increasingly popular in recent years.

Summary

● Setting up operations in foreign countries can entail special problems due to, among other things, the legal form of business organization chosen, the degree of ownership allowed by the host country, possible restrictions and regulations on the return of capital and profits, and international taxation.

● The existence and expansion of dollars held outside the United States have contributed in recent years to the development of a major international financial market, the Euromarket. The large international banks, developing and industrialized nations, and multinational companies participate as borrowers and lenders in this market.

● Certain regulations that apply to international operations tend to complicate the preparation of foreign-based financial statements. Included are rulings that pertain to consolidation, translation of accounts, and reporting international profits.

● Operating in international markets involves certain factors that can influence the risk and return characteristics of an MNC. Economic exposure from foreign exchange risk results from the existence of different currencies and the potential impact they can have on the value of foreign operations. Political risks stem mainly from political instability in a number of countries and from the associated implications for the assets and operations of MNCs with subsidiaries located in such countries.

● International cash flows can be subject to a variety of factors, including local taxes in host countries, host-country regulations that may block the return (repatriation) of MNCs' cash flow, the usual business and financial risks, risks stemming from inflation and different currency and political actions by host governments, and the application of a local cost of capital.

● The foreign exchange risks that complicate international cash management can be overcome through manipulations of accounts receivable and accounts payable from and to third parties and intra-MNC accounts. The existence of the Eurocurrency markets, in particular, allows multinationals to take advantage of unregulated financial markets to invest (lend) and raise (borrow) short-term funds in a variety of currencies and to protect themselves against foreign exchange risk exposures.

● International capital markets provide MNCs with an opportunity to raise long-term debt through the issuance of international bonds in various currencies. Foreign bonds are sold primarily in the country of the currency of issue, while Eurobonds are sold primarily in countries other than the country of the currency in which the issue is denominated.

● Multinational companies can use international capital markets to raise equity. In establishing foreign subsidiaries, it may be more advantageous to issue debt (either local or MNC-based) than MNC-owned equity.

● International business combinations—joint ventures and acquisitions, along with international holding companies—have come to exist for reasons similar to those leading to the creation of their domestic counterparts. Special factors affecting these combinations relate to international taxation and various regulations imposed on MNCs by host countries.

Questions

20-1 What is a *joint venture?* Why is it often essential to use this arrangement? What effect do joint-venture laws and restrictions have on the operation of foreign-based subsidiaries?

20-2 From the point of view of a U.S.-based MNC, what key tax factors need to be considered? What are *unitary tax laws?*

20-3 Discuss the major reasons for the growth of the Euromarket.

20-4 What is an *offshore center?* Name the major participants in the Euromarket.

20-5 State the rules for consolidation of foreign subsidiaries. Under *FASB No. 52,* what are the translation rules for financial statement accounts?

20-6 Define *spot* and *forward exchange rates.* Define and compare *accounting exposures* and *economic exposures* to exchange rate fluctuations.

20-7 Discuss *macro* and *micro political risk.* Describe some techniques for dealing with political risk.

20-8 Indicate how net present value (NPV) can differ if measured from the parent's point of view or from that of the foreign subsidiary when cash flows may be blocked by local authorities.

20-9 Discuss the steps to be followed in adjusting a subsidiary's accounts relative to *third parties* when that subsidiary's local currency is expected to appreciate in value in relation to the currency of the parent MNC.

20-10 Outline the changes to be undertaken in *intra-MNC accounts* if a subsidiary's currency is expected to depreciate in value relative to the currency of the parent MNC.

20-11 Describe the difference between *foreign bonds* and *Eurobonds*. Explain how each is sold and discuss the determinant(s) of their interest rates.

20-12 What are the long-run advantages of having more *local* debt and less MNC-based equity in the capital structure of a foreign subsidiary?

20-13 What are some of the major reasons for the rapid expansion in international business combinations of firms?

Self-Test Problem

(Solution on page 752)

ST-1 A U.S.-based MNC has three subsidiaries: S1 (40 percent owned by the MNC); S2 (40 percent owned by S1); and S3 (30 percent owned by S2). The taxable incomes and local taxes are, respectively: $175 million and $70 million; $225 million and $90 million; and $100 million and $50 million. Assume the MNC's tax rate is 40 percent.

a. Can the MNC apply all of the eligible local taxes as a credit against its U.S. taxes?

b. Based on the so-called *grossing up procedure*, calculate all the tax credits applicable to the MNC.

Problems

20-1 **(Tax Credits)** A U.S.-based MNC has three subsidiaries: S1 (50 percent owned by the MNC); S2 (35 percent owned by S1); and S3 (4 percent owned by the MNC). The taxable incomes and local taxes are, respectively: $190 million and $76 million; $160 million and $64 million; and $150 million and $60 million. Assume the MNC's tax rate is 40 percent.

a. Can the MNC apply all of the eligible local taxes as a credit against its U.S. taxes?

b. Based on the so-called *grossing up procedure*, calculate all the tax credits applicable to the MNC.

20-2 **(Translation of Financial Statements)** A U.S.-based MNC has a subsidiary in France. The balance sheet and income statement of the subsidiary are shown at the top of the next page. On 12/31/88, the exchange rate is: Ff 6.50/US$. Assume that the local (French franc, Ff) figures for the statements remain the same on 12/31/89. Calculate the U.S.-dollar-translated figures for the two ending time periods, assuming that between 12/31/88 and 12/31/89 the French currency has appreciated against the U.S. dollar by 6 percent.

Translation of Balance Sheet

	12/31/88		12/31/89
Assets	Ff	US$	US$
Cash	40.00		
Inventory	300.00		
Plant and equipment (net)	160.00	_____	_____
Total	500.00		

Liabilities and equity			
Debt	240.00		
Paid-in capital	200.00		
Retained earnings	60.00	_____	_____
Total	500.00		

Translation of Income Statement

Sales	3000.00		
Cost of goods sold	2750.00	_____	_____
Operating profits	250.00		

20-3 (**Euromarket Investment and Fund Raising**) A U.S.-based multinational company has two subsidiaries, in West Germany (local currency, Deutsche mark, DM) and in Switzerland (local currency, Swiss franc, Sf). Forecasts of business operations indicate the following short-term financing position for each subsidiary (in equivalent U.S. dollars):

W. Germany: $80 million excess cash to be invested (lent)

Switzerland: $60 million funds to be raised (borrowed)

The management gathered the following data:

		Currency	
Item	US$	DM	Sf
Spot exchange rates		DM 1.83/US$	Sf 1.58/US$
Forecast % change		+3.5%	+2.5%
Interest rates			
Nominal			
Euromarket	8.8%	5.4%	4.2%
Domestic	7.7	4.6	3.2
Effective			
Euromarket			
Domestic			

Determine the effective rates of interest for all three currencies in both the Euromarket and domestic market; then indicate where the funds should be invested and raised. (*Note:* Assume that due to local regulations, a subsidiary is not permitted to use the domestic market of *any other* subsidiary.)

Solution to Self-Test Problem

ST-1 a. The degree of ownership of each subsidiary can be determined as follows:

S1: 40% directly owned by the MNC

S2: (40% × 40%) = 16% owned by the MNC

S3: (30% × 40% × 40%) = 4.8% owned by the MNC

Based on these results, S1 and S2 can, but S3 cannot, be included in the calculation of tax credits. This occurs since, although all firms own more than 10 percent of the stock of the next lower firm, the parent MNC only owns more than the minimum 5 percent of the stock in S1 and S2. Its 4.8 percent ownership of S3 does not meet the 5 percent minimum.

b. The maximum credit against U.S. taxes would be 40 percent of the added income: 40% × ($175 million + $225 million) = $160 million. Thus, the total local taxes paid by S1 and S2, amounting to $70 million + $90 million = $160 million, can be used by the MNC as a credit in the United States.

Organic Solutions

Organic Solutions (OS), one of the nation's largest plant wholesalers in the Southeastern United States, was poised for expansion. Through strong profitability, a conservative dividend policy, and some recent realized gains in real estate, OS had a strong cash position and was searching for an acquisition candidate. The executive members on the acquisition search committee had agreed that they preferred to find a firm in a similar line of business rather than one that would provide broad diversification. This would be their first acquisition, and they preferred to stay in a familiar line of business. Jennifer Morgan, director of marketing, had identified through exhaustive market research the targeted lines of business.

Ms. Morgan had determined that the servicing of plants in large commercial offices, hotels, zoos, and theme parks would complement the existing wholesale distribution business. Frequently OS was requested by their large clients to bid on a service contract. However, Organic Solutions was neither manned nor equipped to enter this market. Ms. Morgan was familiar with the major plant service companies in the Southeast and had suggested Green Thumbs, Inc. (GTI) as an acquisition target because of its significant market share and excellent reputation.

GTI had successfully commercialized a market which had been dominated by small local contractors and in-house landscaping departments. By first winning a contract from one of the largest theme parks in the United States, GTI's growth in sales had compounded remarkably over its eight-year history.

GTI had also been selected because of its large portfolio of long-term service contracts with several major Fortune 500 companies. These contracted clients would provide a captive customer base for the wholesale distribution of OS's plant products.

At the National Horticultural meeting in Los Angeles the past March, Ms. Morgan and OS's chief financial officer, Jack Levine, had approached the owner of GTI (a closely-held corporation) to determine if a merger or acquisition offer would be welcomed. GTI's majority owner and president, Herb Merrell, had reacted favorably and subsequently provided financial data including GTI's earnings record and current balance sheet. These figures are presented in Tables 1 and 2.

Jack Levine had estimated that the incremental cash flow after taxes from the acquisition would be $18,750,000 for years 1 and 2; $20,500,000 for year 3; $21,750,000 for year 4; $24,000,000 for year 5; and $25,000,000 for years 6 through 30. He also estimated that the company should earn a rate of return of at least 16 percent on an investment of this type. Additional financial data for 1988 are available in Table 3 to analyze the acquisition potential of GTI.

Table 1
Green Thumbs, Inc., Earning Record

Year	EPS	Year	EPS
1981	$2.20	1985	$2.85
1982	2.35	1986	3.00
1983	2.45	1987	3.10
1984	2.60	1988	3.30

Table 2
Green Thumbs, Inc., Balance Sheet (December 31, 1988)

Assets		Liabilities and net worth	
Cash	$ 2,500,000	Current liabilities	$ 5,250,000
Accounts receivable	1,500,000	Mortgage payable	3,125,000
Inventories	7,625,000	Common stock	15,625,000
Land	7,475,000	Retained earnings	9,000,000
Fixed assets (net)	13,900,000	Total liabilities	
Total Assets	$33,000,000	and net worth	$33,000,000

Table 3
OS and GTI Financial Data (December 31, 1988)

Item	OS	GTI
Earnings available for common stock	$35,000,000	$15,246,000
Number of shares of common stock outstanding	10,000,000	4,620,000
Market price per share	$50	$30*

*Estimated by Organic Solutions

Required

1. What is the maximum price Organic Solutions should offer GTI for a cash acquisition? (*Note:* Assume the relevant time horizon for analysis is 30 years.)

2. **a.** What is the ratio of exchange in a stock-exchange acquisition if OS pays $30 per share for GTI? Explain why.
   b. What effect will this exchange of stock have on the EPS of the original shareholders of (1) Organic Solutions and (2) Green Thumbs, Inc.? Explain why.
   c. If the earnings attributed to GTI's assets grow at a much slower rate than those attributed to OS's pre-merger assets, what effect might this have on the EPS of the merged firm over the long run?

3. What other merger proposals could OS make to GTI's owners?

4. What impact would the fact that GTI is actually a foreign-based company have on the foregoing analysis? Describe the added regulations, costs, benefits, and risks likely to be associated with such an international business combination.

Appendixes

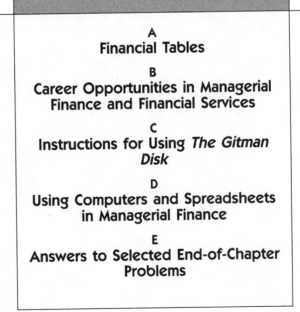

Financial
Tables

Table A-1 Future-Value Interest Factors for One Dollar Compounded at k Percent for n Periods: $FVIF_{k,n} = (1 + k)^n$

Period	1%	2%	3%	4%	5%	6%	7%	8%	9%	10%
1	1.010	1.020	1.030	1.040	1.050	1.060	1.070	1.080	1.090	1.100
2	1.020	1.040	1.061	1.082	1.102	1.124	1.145	1.166	1.188	1.210
3	1.030	1.061	1.093	1.125	1.158	1.191	1.225	1.260	1.295	1.331
4	1.041	1.082	1.126	1.170	1.216	1.262	1.311	1.360	1.412	1.464
5	1.051	1.104	1.159	1.217	1.276	1.338	1.403	1.469	1.539	1.611
6	1.062	1.126	1.194	1.265	1.340	1.419	1.501	1.587	1.677	1.772
7	1.072	1.149	1.230	1.316	1.407	1.504	1.606	1.714	1.828	1.949
8	1.083	1.172	1.267	1.369	1.477	1.594	1.718	1.851	1.993	2.144
9	1.094	1.195	1.305	1.423	1.551	1.689	1.838	1.999	2.172	2.358
10	1.105	1.219	1.344	1.480	1.629	1.791	1.967	2.159	2.367	2.594
11	1.116	1.243	1.384	1.539	1.710	1.898	2.105	2.332	2.580	2.853
12	1.127	1.268	1.426	1.601	1.796	2.012	2.252	2.518	2.813	3.138
13	1.138	1.294	1.469	1.665	1.886	2.133	2.410	2.720	3.066	3.452
14	1.149	1.319	1.513	1.732	1.980	2.261	2.579	2.937	3.342	3.797
15	1.161	1.346	1.558	1.801	2.079	2.397	2.759	3.172	3.642	4.177
16	1.173	1.373	1.605	1.873	2.183	2.540	2.952	3.426	3.970	4.595
17	1.184	1.400	1.653	1.948	2.292	2.693	3.159	3.700	4.328	5.054
18	1.196	1.428	1.702	2.026	2.407	2.854	3.380	3.996	4.717	5.560
19	1.208	1.457	1.753	2.107	2.527	3.026	3.616	4.316	5.142	6.116
20	1.220	1.486	1.806	2.191	2.653	3.207	3.870	4.661	5.604	6.727
21	1.232	1.516	1.860	2.279	2.786	3.399	4.140	5.034	6.109	7.400
22	1.245	1.546	1.916	2.370	2.925	3.603	4.430	5.436	6.658	8.140
23	1.257	1.577	1.974	2.465	3.071	3.820	4.740	5.871	7.258	8.954
24	1.270	1.608	2.033	2.563	3.225	4.049	5.072	6.341	7.911	9.850
25	1.282	1.641	2.094	2.666	3.386	4.292	5.427	6.848	8.623	10.834
30	1.348	1.811	2.427	3.243	4.322	5.743	7.612	10.062	13.267	17.449
35	1.417	2.000	2.814	3.946	5.516	7.686	10.676	14.785	20.413	28.102
40	1.489	2.208	3.262	4.801	7.040	10.285	14.974	21.724	31.408	45.258
45	1.565	2.438	3.781	5.841	8.985	13.764	21.002	31.920	48.325	72.888
50	1.645	2.691	4.384	7.106	11.467	18.419	29.456	46.900	74.354	117.386

Table A-1 Future-Value Interest Factors for One Dollar Compounded at k Percent for n Periods: $FVIF_{k,n} = (1 + k)^n$ (continued)

Period	11%	12%	13%	14%	15%	16%	17%	18%	19%	20%
1	1.110	1.120	1.130	1.140	1.150	1.160	1.170	1.180	1.190	1.200
2	1.232	1.254	1.277	1.300	1.322	1.346	1.369	1.392	1.416	1.440
3	1.368	1.405	1.443	1.482	1.521	1.561	1.602	1.643	1.685	1.728
4	1.518	1.574	1.630	1.689	1.749	1.811	1.874	1.939	2.005	2.074
5	1.685	1.762	1.842	1.925	2.011	2.100	2.192	2.288	2.386	2.488
6	1.870	1.974	2.082	2.195	2.313	2.436	2.565	2.700	2.840	2.986
7	2.076	2.211	2.353	2.502	2.660	2.826	3.001	3.185	3.379	3.583
8	2.305	2.476	2.658	2.853	3.059	3.278	3.511	3.759	4.021	4.300
9	2.558	2.773	3.004	3.252	3.518	3.803	4.108	4.435	4.785	5.160
10	2.839	3.106	3.395	3.707	4.046	4.411	4.807	5.234	5.695	6.192
11	3.152	3.479	3.836	4.226	4.652	5.117	5.624	6.176	6.777	7.430
12	3.498	3.896	4.334	4.818	5.350	5.936	6.580	7.288	8.064	8.916
13	3.883	4.363	4.898	5.492	6.153	6.886	7.699	8.599	9.596	10.699
14	4.310	4.887	5.535	6.261	7.076	7.987	9.007	10.147	11.420	12.839
15	4.785	5.474	6.254	7.138	8.137	9.265	10.539	11.974	13.589	15.407
16	5.311	6.130	7.067	8.137	9.358	10.748	12.330	14.129	16.171	18.488
17	5.895	6.866	7.986	9.276	10.761	12.468	14.426	16.672	19.244	22.186
18	6.543	7.690	9.024	10.575	12.375	14.462	16.879	19.673	22.900	26.623
19	7.263	8.613	10.197	12.055	14.232	16.776	19.748	23.214	27.251	31.948
20	8.062	9.646	11.523	13.743	16.366	19.461	23.105	27.393	32.429	38.337
21	8.949	10.804	13.021	15.667	18.821	22.574	27.033	32.323	38.591	46.005
22	9.933	12.100	14.713	17.861	21.644	26.186	31.629	38.141	45.923	55.205
23	11.026	13.552	16.626	20.361	24.891	30.376	37.005	45.007	54.648	66.247
24	12.239	15.178	18.788	23.212	28.625	35.236	43.296	53.108	65.031	79.496
25	13.585	17.000	21.230	26.461	32.918	40.874	50.656	62.667	77.387	95.395
30	22.892	29.960	39.115	50.949	66.210	85.849	111.061	143.367	184.672	237.373
35	38.574	52.799	72.066	98.097	133.172	180.311	243.495	327.988	440.691	590.657
40	64.999	93.049	132.776	188.876	267.856	378.715	533.846	750.353	1051.642	1469.740
45	109.527	163.985	244.629	363.662	538.752	795.429	1170.425	1716.619	2509.583	3657.176
50	184.559	288.996	450.711	700.197	1083.619	1670.669	2566.080	3927.189	5988.730	9100.191

Table A-1   Future-Value Interest Factors for One Dollar Compounded at k Percent for n Periods: $FVIF_{k,n} = (1 + k)^n$ (continued)

Period	21%	22%	23%	24%	25%	26%	27%	28%	29%	30%
1	1.210	1.220	1.230	1.240	1.250	1.260	1.270	1.280	1.290	1.300
2	1.464	1.488	1.513	1.538	1.562	1.588	1.613	1.638	1.664	1.690
3	1.772	1.816	1.861	1.907	1.953	2.000	2.048	2.097	2.147	2.197
4	2.144	2.215	2.289	2.364	2.441	2.520	2.601	2.684	2.769	2.856
5	2.594	2.703	2.815	2.932	3.052	3.176	3.304	3.436	3.572	3.713
6	3.138	3.297	3.463	3.635	3.815	4.001	4.196	4.398	4.608	4.827
7	3.797	4.023	4.259	4.508	4.768	5.042	5.329	5.629	5.945	6.275
8	4.595	4.908	5.239	5.589	5.960	6.353	6.767	7.206	7.669	8.157
9	5.560	5.987	6.444	6.931	7.451	8.004	8.595	9.223	9.893	10.604
10	6.727	7.305	7.926	8.594	9.313	10.086	10.915	11.806	12.761	13.786
11	8.140	8.912	9.749	10.657	11.642	12.708	13.862	15.112	16.462	17.921
12	9.850	10.872	11.991	13.215	14.552	16.012	17.605	19.343	21.236	23.298
13	11.918	13.264	14.749	16.386	18.190	20.175	22.359	24.759	27.395	30.287
14	14.421	16.182	18.141	20.319	22.737	25.420	28.395	31.691	35.339	39.373
15	17.449	19.742	22.314	25.195	28.422	32.030	36.062	40.565	45.587	51.185
16	21.113	24.085	27.446	31.242	35.527	40.357	45.799	51.923	58.808	66.541
17	25.547	29.384	33.758	38.740	44.409	50.850	58.165	66.461	75.862	86.503
18	30.912	35.848	41.523	48.038	55.511	64.071	73.869	85.070	97.862	112.454
19	37.404	43.735	51.073	59.567	69.389	80.730	93.813	108.890	126.242	146.190
20	45.258	53.357	62.820	73.863	86.736	101.720	119.143	139.379	162.852	190.047
21	54.762	65.095	77.268	91.591	108.420	128.167	151.312	178.405	210.079	247.061
22	66.262	79.416	95.040	113.572	135.525	161.490	192.165	228.358	271.002	321.178
23	80.178	96.887	116.899	140.829	169.407	203.477	244.050	292.298	349.592	417.531
24	97.015	118.203	143.786	174.628	211.758	256.381	309.943	374.141	450.974	542.791
25	117.388	144.207	176.857	216.539	264.698	323.040	393.628	478.901	581.756	705.627
30	304.471	389.748	497.904	634.810	807.793	1025.904	1300.477	1645.488	2078.208	2619.936
35	789.716	1053.370	1401.749	1861.020	2465.189	3258.053	4296.547	5653.840	7423.988	9727.598
40	2048.309	2846.941	3946.340	5455.797	7523.156	10346.879	14195.051	19426.418	26520.723	36117.754
45	5312.758	7694.418	11110.121	15994.316	22958.844	32859.457	46897.973	66748.500	94739.937	134102.187
50	13779.844	20795.680	31278.301	46889.207	70064.812	104354.562	154942.687	229345.875	338440.000	497910.125

Table A-1 Future-Value Interest Factors for One Dollar Compounded at k Percent for n Periods: $FVIF_{k,n} = (1 + k)^n$ (continued)

Period	31%	32%	33%	34%	35%	36%	37%	38%	39%	40%
1	1.310	1.320	1.330	1.340	1.350	1.360	1.370	1.380	1.390	1.400
2	1.716	1.742	1.769	1.796	1.822	1.850	1.877	1.904	1.932	1.960
3	2.248	2.300	2.353	2.406	2.460	2.515	2.571	2.628	2.686	2.744
4	2.945	3.036	3.129	3.224	3.321	3.421	3.523	3.627	3.733	3.842
5	3.858	4.007	4.162	4.320	4.484	4.653	4.826	5.005	5.189	5.378
6	5.054	5.290	5.535	5.789	6.053	6.328	6.612	6.907	7.213	7.530
7	6.621	6.983	7.361	7.758	8.172	8.605	9.058	9.531	10.025	10.541
8	8.673	9.217	9.791	10.395	11.032	11.703	12.410	13.153	13.935	14.758
9	11.362	12.166	13.022	13.930	14.894	15.917	17.001	18.151	19.370	20.661
10	14.884	16.060	17.319	18.666	20.106	21.646	23.292	25.049	26.924	28.925
11	19.498	21.199	23.034	25.012	27.144	29.439	31.910	34.567	37.425	40.495
12	25.542	27.982	30.635	33.516	36.644	40.037	43.716	47.703	52.020	56.694
13	33.460	36.937	40.745	44.912	49.469	54.451	59.892	65.830	72.308	79.371
14	43.832	48.756	54.190	60.181	66.784	74.053	82.051	90.845	100.509	111.119
15	57.420	64.358	72.073	80.643	90.158	100.712	112.410	125.366	139.707	155.567
16	75.220	84.953	95.857	108.061	121.713	136.968	154.002	173.005	194.192	217.793
17	98.539	112.138	127.490	144.802	164.312	186.277	210.983	238.747	269.927	304.911
18	129.086	148.022	169.561	194.035	221.822	253.337	289.046	329.471	375.198	426.875
19	169.102	195.389	225.517	260.006	299.459	344.537	395.993	454.669	521.525	597.625
20	221.523	257.913	299.937	348.408	404.270	468.571	542.511	627.443	724.919	836.674
21	290.196	340.446	398.916	466.867	545.764	637.256	743.240	865.871	1007.637	1171.343
22	380.156	449.388	530.558	625.601	736.781	866.668	1018.238	1194.900	1400.615	1639.878
23	498.004	593.192	705.642	838.305	994.653	1178.668	1394.986	1648.961	1946.854	2295.829
24	652.385	783.013	938.504	1123.328	1342.781	1602.988	1911.129	2275.564	2706.125	3214.158
25	854.623	1033.577	1248.210	1505.258	1812.754	2180.063	2618.245	3140.275	3761.511	4499.816
30	3297.081	4142.008	5194.516	6503.285	8128.426	10142.914	12636.086	15716.703	19517.969	24201.043
35	12719.918	16598.906	21617.363	28096.695	36448.051	47190.727	60983.836	78660.188	101276.125	130158.687
40	49072.621	66519.313	89962.188	121388.437	163433.875	219558.625	294317.937	393684.687	525508.312	700022.688

Table A-1 Future-Value Interest Factors for One Dollar Compounded at k Percent for n Periods: $FVIF_{k,n} = (1 + k)^n$ (continued)

Period	41%	42%	43%	44%	45%	46%	47%	48%	49%	50%
1	1.410	1.420	1.430	1.440	1.450	1.460	1.470	1.480	1.490	1.500
2	1.988	2.016	2.045	2.074	2.102	2.132	2.161	2.190	2.220	2.250
3	2.803	2.863	2.924	2.986	3.049	3.112	3.177	3.242	3.308	3.375
4	3.953	4.066	4.182	4.300	4.421	4.544	4.669	4.798	4.929	5.063
5	5.573	5.774	5.980	6.192	6.410	6.634	6.864	7.101	7.344	7.594
6	7.858	8.198	8.551	8.916	9.294	9.685	10.090	10.509	10.943	11.391
7	11.080	11.642	12.228	12.839	13.476	14.141	14.833	15.554	16.304	17.086
8	15.623	16.531	17.486	18.488	19.541	20.645	21.804	23.019	24.293	25.629
9	22.028	23.474	25.005	26.623	28.334	30.142	32.052	34.069	36.197	38.443
10	31.059	33.333	35.757	38.337	41.085	44.007	47.116	50.421	53.934	57.665
11	43.793	47.333	51.132	55.206	59.573	64.251	69.261	74.624	80.361	86.498
12	61.749	67.213	73.119	79.496	86.380	93.806	101.813	110.443	119.738	129.746
13	87.066	95.443	104.560	114.475	125.251	136.956	149.665	163.456	178.410	194.620
14	122.763	135.529	149.521	164.843	181.614	199.956	220.008	241.914	265.831	291.929
15	173.095	192.451	213.814	237.374	263.341	291.936	323.411	358.033	396.088	437.894
16	244.064	273.280	305.754	341.819	381.844	426.226	475.414	529.888	590.170	656.841
17	344.130	388.057	437.228	492.219	553.674	622.289	698.859	784.234	879.354	985.261
18	485.224	551.041	625.235	708.794	802.826	908.541	1027.321	1160.666	1310.236	1477.892
19	684.165	782.478	894.086	1020.663	1164.098	1326.469	1510.161	1717.785	1952.252	2216.838
20	964.673	1111.118	1278.543	1469.754	1687.942	1936.642	2219.936	2542.321	2908.854	3325.257
21	1360.188	1577.786	1828.315	2116.445	2447.515	2827.496	3263.304	3762.633	4334.188	4987.883
22	1917.865	2240.455	2614.489	3047.679	3548.896	4128.137	4797.051	5568.691	6457.941	7481.824
23	2704.188	3181.443	3738.717	4388.656	5145.898	6027.078	7051.660	8241.664	9622.324	11222.738
24	3812.905	4517.641	5346.355	6319.656	7461.547	8799.523	10365.934	12197.656	14337.258	16834.109
25	5376.191	6415.047	7645.289	9100.305	10819.242	12847.297	15237.914	18052.516	21362.508	25251.164
30	29961.941	37037.383	45716.496	56346.535	69348.375	85226.375	104594.938	128187.438	156885.438	191751.000

Table A-2   Future-Value Interest Factors for a One-Dollar Annuity Compounded at k Percent for n Periods: $FVIFA_{k,n} = \sum_{t=1}^{n} (1+k)^{t-1}$

Period	1%	2%	3%	4%	5%	6%	7%	8%	9%	10%
1	1.000	1.000	1.000	1.000	1.000	1.000	1.000	1.000	1.000	1.000
2	2.010	2.020	2.030	2.040	2.050	2.060	2.070	2.080	2.090	2.100
3	3.030	3.060	3.091	3.122	3.152	3.184	3.215	3.246	3.278	3.310
4	4.060	4.122	4.184	4.246	4.310	4.375	4.440	4.506	4.573	4.641
5	5.101	5.204	5.309	5.416	5.526	5.637	5.751	5.867	5.985	6.105
6	6.152	6.308	6.468	6.633	6.802	6.975	7.153	7.336	7.523	7.716
7	7.214	7.434	7.662	7.898	8.142	8.394	8.654	8.923	9.200	9.487
8	8.286	8.583	8.892	9.214	9.549	9.897	10.260	10.637	11.028	11.436
9	9.368	9.755	10.159	10.583	11.027	11.491	11.978	12.488	13.021	13.579
10	10.462	10.950	11.464	12.006	12.578	13.181	13.816	14.487	15.193	15.937
11	11.567	12.169	12.808	13.486	14.207	14.972	15.784	16.645	17.560	18.531
12	12.682	13.412	14.192	15.026	15.917	16.870	17.888	18.977	20.141	21.384
13	13.809	14.680	15.618	16.627	17.713	18.882	20.141	21.495	22.953	24.523
14	14.947	15.974	17.086	18.292	19.598	21.015	22.550	24.215	26.019	27.975
15	16.097	17.293	18.599	20.023	21.578	23.276	25.129	27.152	29.361	31.772
16	17.258	18.639	20.157	21.824	23.657	25.672	27.888	30.324	33.003	35.949
17	18.430	20.012	21.761	23.697	25.840	28.213	30.840	33.750	36.973	40.544
18	19.614	21.412	23.414	25.645	28.132	30.905	33.999	37.450	41.301	45.599
19	20.811	22.840	25.117	27.671	30.539	33.760	37.379	41.446	46.018	51.158
20	22.019	24.297	26.870	29.778	33.066	36.785	40.995	45.762	51.159	57.274
21	23.239	25.783	28.676	31.969	35.719	39.992	44.865	50.422	56.764	64.002
22	24.471	27.299	30.536	34.248	38.505	43.392	49.005	55.456	62.872	71.402
23	25.716	28.845	32.452	36.618	41.430	46.995	53.435	60.893	69.531	79.542
24	26.973	30.421	34.426	39.082	44.501	50.815	58.176	66.764	76.789	88.496
25	28.243	32.030	36.459	41.645	47.726	54.864	63.248	73.105	84.699	98.346
30	34.784	40.567	47.575	56.084	66.438	79.057	94.459	113.282	136.305	164.491
35	41.659	49.994	60.461	73.651	90.318	111.432	138.234	172.314	215.705	271.018
40	48.885	60.401	75.400	95.024	120.797	154.758	199.630	259.052	337.872	442.580
45	56.479	71.891	92.718	121.027	159.695	212.737	285.741	386.497	525.840	718.881
50	64.461	84.577	112.794	152.664	209.341	290.325	406.516	573.756	815.051	1163.865

Table A-2   Future-Value Interest Factors for a One-Dollar Annuity Compounded at k Percent for n Periods: $FVIFA_{k,n} = \sum\limits_{t=1}^{n}(1+k)^{t-1}$ (continued)

Period	11%	12%	13%	14%	15%	16%	17%	18%	19%	20%
1	1.000	1.000	1.000	1.000	1.000	1.000	1.000	1.000	1.000	1.000
2	2.110	2.120	2.130	2.140	2.150	2.160	2.170	2.180	2.190	2.200
3	3.342	3.374	3.407	3.440	3.472	3.506	3.539	3.572	3.606	3.640
4	4.710	4.779	4.850	4.921	4.993	5.066	5.141	5.215	5.291	5.368
5	6.228	6.353	6.480	6.610	6.742	6.877	7.014	7.154	7.297	7.442
6	7.913	8.115	8.323	8.535	8.754	8.977	9.207	9.442	9.683	9.930
7	9.783	10.089	10.405	10.730	11.067	11.414	11.772	12.141	12.523	12.916
8	11.859	12.300	12.757	13.233	13.727	14.240	14.773	15.327	15.902	16.499
9	14.164	14.776	15.416	16.085	16.786	17.518	18.285	19.086	19.923	20.799
10	16.722	17.549	18.420	19.337	20.304	21.321	22.393	23.521	24.709	25.959
11	19.561	20.655	21.814	23.044	24.349	25.733	27.200	28.755	30.403	32.150
12	22.713	24.133	25.650	27.271	29.001	30.850	32.824	34.931	37.180	39.580
13	26.211	28.029	29.984	32.088	34.352	36.786	39.404	42.218	45.244	48.496
14	30.095	32.392	34.882	37.581	40.504	43.672	47.102	50.818	54.841	59.196
15	34.405	37.280	40.417	43.842	47.580	51.659	56.109	60.965	66.260	72.035
16	39.190	42.753	46.671	50.980	55.717	60.925	66.648	72.938	79.850	87.442
17	44.500	48.883	53.738	59.117	65.075	71.673	78.978	87.067	96.021	105.930
18	50.396	55.749	61.724	68.393	75.836	84.140	93.404	103.739	115.265	128.116
19	56.939	63.439	70.748	78.968	88.211	98.603	110.283	123.412	138.165	154.739
20	64.202	72.052	80.946	91.024	102.443	115.379	130.031	146.626	165.417	186.687
21	72.264	81.698	92.468	104.767	118.809	134.840	153.136	174.019	197.846	225.024
22	81.213	92.502	105.489	120.434	137.630	157.414	180.169	206.342	236.436	271.028
23	91.147	104.602	120.203	138.295	159.274	183.600	211.798	244.483	282.359	326.234
24	102.173	118.154	136.829	158.656	184.166	213.976	248.803	289.490	337.007	392.480
25	114.412	133.333	155.616	181.867	212.790	249.212	292.099	342.598	402.038	471.976
30	199.018	241.330	293.192	356.778	434.738	530.306	647.423	790.932	966.698	1181.865
35	341.583	431.658	546.663	693.552	881.152	1120.699	1426.448	1816.607	2314.173	2948.294
40	581.812	767.080	1013.667	1341.979	1779.048	2360.724	3134.412	4163.094	5529.711	7343.715
45	986.613	1358.208	1874.086	2590.464	3585.031	4965.191	6879.008	9531.258	13203.105	18280.914
50	1668.723	2399.975	3459.344	4994.301	7217.488	10435.449	15088.805	21812.273	31514.492	45496.094

Table A-2 Future-Value Interest Factors for a One-Dollar Annuity Compounded at k Percent for n Periods: $FVIFA_{k,n} = \sum\limits_{t=1}^{n} (1 + k)^{t-1}$ (continued)

Period	21%	22%	23%	24%	25%	26%	27%	28%	29%	30%
1	1.000	1.000	1.000	1.000	1.000	1.000	1.000	1.000	1.000	1.000
2	2.210	2.220	2.230	2.240	2.250	2.260	2.270	2.280	2.290	2.300
3	3.674	3.708	3.743	3.778	3.813	3.848	3.883	3.918	3.954	3.990
4	5.446	5.524	5.604	5.684	5.766	5.848	5.931	6.016	6.101	6.187
5	7.589	7.740	7.893	8.048	8.207	8.368	8.533	8.700	8.870	9.043
6	10.183	10.442	10.708	10.980	11.259	11.544	11.837	12.136	12.442	12.756
7	13.321	13.740	14.171	14.615	15.073	15.546	16.032	16.534	17.051	17.583
8	17.119	17.762	18.430	19.123	19.842	20.588	21.361	22.163	22.995	23.858
9	21.714	22.670	23.669	24.712	25.802	26.940	28.129	29.369	30.664	32.015
10	27.274	28.657	30.113	31.643	33.253	34.945	36.723	38.592	40.556	42.619
11	34.001	35.962	38.039	40.238	42.566	45.030	47.639	50.398	53.318	56.405
12	42.141	44.873	47.787	50.895	54.208	57.738	61.501	65.510	69.780	74.326
13	51.991	55.745	59.778	64.109	68.760	73.750	79.106	84.853	91.016	97.624
14	63.909	69.009	74.528	80.496	86.949	93.925	101.465	109.611	118.411	127.912
15	78.330	85.191	92.669	100.815	109.687	119.346	129.860	141.302	153.750	167.285
16	95.779	104.933	114.983	126.010	138.109	151.375	165.922	181.867	199.337	218.470
17	116.892	129.019	142.428	157.252	173.636	191.733	211.721	233.790	258.145	285.011
18	142.439	158.403	176.187	195.993	218.045	242.583	269.885	300.250	334.006	371.514
19	173.351	194.251	217.710	244.031	273.556	306.654	343.754	385.321	431.868	483.968
20	210.755	237.986	268.783	303.598	342.945	387.384	437.568	494.210	558.110	630.157
21	256.013	291.343	331.603	377.461	429.681	489.104	556.710	633.589	720.962	820.204
22	310.775	356.438	408.871	469.052	538.101	617.270	708.022	811.993	931.040	1067.265
23	377.038	435.854	503.911	582.624	673.626	778.760	900.187	1040.351	1202.042	1388.443
24	457.215	532.741	620.810	723.453	843.032	982.237	1144.237	1332.649	1551.634	1805.975
25	554.230	650.944	764.596	898.082	1054.791	1238.617	1454.180	1706.790	2002.608	2348.765
30	1445.111	1767.044	2160.459	2640.881	3227.172	3941.953	4812.891	5873.172	7162.785	8729.805
35	3755.814	4783.520	6090.227	7750.094	9856.746	12527.160	15909.480	20188.742	25596.512	32422.090
40	9749.141	12936.141	17153.691	22728.367	30088.621	39791.957	52570.707	69376.562	91447.375	120389.375
45	25294.223	34970.230	48300.660	66638.937	91831.312	126378.937	173692.875	238384.312	326686.375	447005.062

Table A-2   Future-Value Interest Factors for a One-Dollar Annuity Compounded at k Percent for n Periods: $FVIFA_{k,n} = \sum\limits_{t=1}^{n} (1 + k)^{t-1}$ (continued)

Period	31%	32%	33%	34%	35%	36%	37%	38%	39%	40%
1	1.000	1.000	1.000	1.000	1.000	1.000	1.000	1.000	1.000	1.000
2	2.310	2.320	2.330	2.340	2.350	2.360	2.370	2.380	2.390	2.400
3	4.026	4.062	4.099	4.136	4.172	4.210	4.247	4.284	4.322	4.360
4	6.274	6.362	6.452	6.542	6.633	6.725	6.818	6.912	7.008	7.104
5	9.219	9.398	9.581	9.766	9.954	10.146	10.341	10.539	10.741	10.946
6	13.077	13.406	13.742	14.086	14.438	14.799	15.167	15.544	15.930	16.324
7	18.131	18.696	19.277	19.876	20.492	21.126	21.779	22.451	23.142	23.853
8	24.752	25.678	26.638	27.633	28.664	29.732	30.837	31.982	33.167	34.395
9	33.425	34.895	36.429	38.028	39.696	41.435	43.247	45.135	47.103	49.152
10	44.786	47.062	49.451	51.958	54.590	57.351	60.248	63.287	66.473	69.813
11	59.670	63.121	66.769	70.624	74.696	78.998	83.540	88.335	93.397	98.739
12	79.167	84.320	89.803	95.636	101.840	108.437	115.450	122.903	130.822	139.234
13	104.709	112.302	120.438	129.152	138.484	148.474	159.166	170.606	182.842	195.928
14	138.169	149.239	161.183	174.063	187.953	202.925	219.058	236.435	255.151	275.299
15	182.001	197.996	215.373	234.245	254.737	276.978	301.109	327.281	355.659	386.418
16	239.421	262.354	287.446	314.888	344.895	377.690	413.520	452.647	495.366	541.985
17	314.642	347.307	383.303	422.949	466.608	514.658	567.521	625.652	689.558	759.778
18	413.180	459.445	510.792	567.751	630.920	700.935	778.504	864.399	959.485	1064.689
19	542.266	607.467	680.354	761.786	852.741	954.271	1067.551	1193.870	1334.683	1491.563
20	711.368	802.856	905.870	1021.792	1152.200	1298.809	1463.544	1648.539	1856.208	2089.188
21	932.891	1060.769	1205.807	1370.201	1556.470	1767.380	2006.055	2275.982	2581.128	2925.862
22	1223.087	1401.215	1604.724	1837.068	2102.234	2404.636	2749.294	3141.852	3588.765	4097.203
23	1603.243	1850.603	2135.282	2462.669	2839.014	3271.304	3767.532	4336.750	4989.379	5737.078
24	2101.247	2443.795	2840.924	3300.974	3833.667	4449.969	5162.516	5985.711	6936.230	8032.906
25	2753.631	3226.808	3779.428	4424.301	5176.445	6052.957	7073.645	8261.273	9642.352	11247.062
30	10632.543	12940.672	15737.945	19124.434	23221.258	28172.016	34148.906	41357.227	50043.625	60500.207
35	41028.887	51868.563	65504.199	82634.625	104134.500	131082.625	164818.438	206998.375	259680.313	325394.688

Table A-2 Future-Value Interest Factors for a One-Dollar Annuity Compounded at k Percent for n Periods: $FVIFA_{k,n} = \sum_{t=1}^{n} (1 + k)^{t-1}$ (continued)

Period	41%	42%	43%	44%	45%	46%	47%	48%	49%	50%
1	1.000	1.000	1.000	1.000	1.000	1.000	1.000	1.000	1.000	1.000
2	2.410	2.420	2.430	2.440	2.450	2.460	2.470	2.480	2.490	2.500
3	4.398	4.436	4.475	4.514	4.552	4.592	4.631	4.670	4.710	4.750
4	7.201	7.300	7.399	7.500	7.601	7.704	7.807	7.912	8.018	8.125
5	11.154	11.366	11.581	11.799	12.022	12.247	12.477	12.710	12.947	13.188
6	16.727	17.139	17.560	17.991	18.431	18.881	19.341	19.811	20.291	20.781
7	24.585	25.337	26.111	26.907	27.725	28.567	29.431	30.320	31.233	32.172
8	35.665	36.979	38.339	39.746	41.202	42.707	44.264	45.874	47.538	49.258
9	51.287	53.510	55.825	58.235	60.743	63.352	66.068	68.893	71.831	74.887
10	73.315	76.985	80.830	84.858	89.077	93.494	98.120	102.961	108.028	113.330
11	104.374	110.318	116.586	123.195	130.161	137.502	145.236	153.383	161.962	170.995
12	148.168	157.651	167.719	178.401	189.734	201.752	214.497	228.007	242.323	257.493
13	209.916	224.865	240.837	257.897	276.114	295.558	316.310	338.449	362.062	387.239
14	296.982	320.308	345.397	372.372	401.365	432.514	465.975	501.905	540.471	581.858
15	419.744	455.837	494.918	537.215	582.980	632.470	685.983	743.819	806.302	873.788
16	592.839	648.288	708.732	774.589	846.321	924.406	1009.394	1101.852	1202.390	1311.681
17	836.903	921.568	1014.486	1116.408	1228.165	1350.631	1484.809	1631.740	1792.560	1968.522
18	1181.034	1309.625	1451.714	1608.626	1781.838	1972.920	2183.667	2415.974	2671.914	2953.783
19	1666.257	1860.666	2076.949	2317.421	2584.665	2881.461	3210.989	3576.640	3982.150	4431.672
20	2350.422	2643.144	2971.035	3338.084	3748.763	4207.926	4721.148	5294.422	5934.402	6648.508
21	3315.095	3754.262	4249.574	4807.836	5436.703	6144.566	6941.082	7836.742	8843.254	9973.762
22	4675.281	5332.047	6077.887	6924.281	7884.215	8972.059	10204.383	11599.375	13177.441	14961.645
23	6593.145	7572.500	8692.375	9971.957	11433.109	13100.195	15001.434	17168.066	19635.383	22443.469
24	9297.332	10753.941	12431.090	14360.613	16579.008	19127.273	22053.094	25409.730	29257.707	33666.207
25	13110.234	15271.582	17777.445	20680.270	24040.555	27926.797	32419.027	37607.387	43594.965	50500.316
30	73075.500	88181.938	106315.250	128058.125	154105.313	185273.000	222540.625	267055.375	320172.750	383500.000

Table A-3 Present-Value Interest Factors for One Dollar Discounted at k Percent for n Periods: $PVIF_{k,n} = \dfrac{1}{(1+k)^n}$

Period	1%	2%	3%	4%	5%	6%	7%	8%	9%	10%
1	.990	.980	.971	.962	.952	.943	.935	.926	.917	.909
2	.980	.961	.943	.925	.907	.890	.873	.857	.842	.826
3	.971	.942	.915	.889	.864	.840	.816	.794	.772	.751
4	.961	.924	.888	.855	.823	.792	.763	.735	.708	.683
5	.951	.906	.863	.822	.784	.747	.713	.681	.650	.621
6	.942	.888	.837	.790	.746	.705	.666	.630	.596	.564
7	.933	.871	.813	.760	.711	.665	.623	.583	.547	.513
8	.923	.853	.789	.731	.677	.627	.582	.540	.502	.467
9	.914	.837	.766	.703	.645	.592	.544	.500	.460	.424
10	.905	.820	.744	.676	.614	.558	.508	.463	.422	.386
11	.896	.804	.722	.650	.585	.527	.475	.429	.388	.350
12	.887	.789	.701	.625	.557	.497	.444	.397	.356	.319
13	.879	.773	.681	.601	.530	.469	.415	.368	.326	.290
14	.870	.758	.661	.577	.505	.442	.388	.340	.299	.263
15	.861	.743	.642	.555	.481	.417	.362	.315	.275	.239
16	.853	.728	.623	.534	.458	.394	.339	.292	.252	.218
17	.844	.714	.605	.513	.436	.371	.317	.270	.231	.198
18	.836	.700	.587	.494	.416	.350	.296	.250	.212	.180
19	.828	.686	.570	.475	.396	.331	.277	.232	.194	.164
20	.820	.673	.554	.456	.377	.312	.258	.215	.178	.149
21	.811	.660	.538	.439	.359	.294	.242	.199	.164	.135
22	.803	.647	.522	.422	.342	.278	.226	.184	.150	.123
23	.795	.634	.507	.406	.326	.262	.211	.170	.138	.112
24	.788	.622	.492	.390	.310	.247	.197	.158	.126	.102
25	.780	.610	.478	.375	.295	.233	.184	.146	.116	.092
30	.742	.552	.412	.308	.231	.174	.131	.099	.075	.057
35	.706	.500	.355	.253	.181	.130	.094	.068	.049	.036
40	.672	.453	.307	.208	.142	.097	.067	.046	.032	.022
45	.639	.410	.264	.171	.111	.073	.048	.031	.021	.014
50	.608	.372	.228	.141	.087	.054	.034	.021	.013	.009

Table A-3 Present-Value Interest Factors for One Dollar Discounted at k Percent for n Periods: $PV/F_{k,n} = \dfrac{1}{(1+k)^n}$ (continued)

Period	11%	12%	13%	14%	15%	16%	17%	18%	19%	20%
1	.901	.893	.885	.877	.870	.862	.855	.847	.840	.833
2	.812	.797	.783	.769	.756	.743	.731	.718	.706	.694
3	.731	.712	.693	.675	.658	.641	.624	.609	.593	.579
4	.659	.636	.613	.592	.572	.552	.534	.516	.499	.482
5	.593	.567	.543	.519	.497	.476	.456	.437	.419	.402
6	.535	.507	.480	.456	.432	.410	.390	.370	.352	.335
7	.482	.452	.425	.400	.376	.354	.333	.314	.296	.279
8	.434	.404	.376	.351	.327	.305	.285	.266	.249	.233
9	.391	.361	.333	.308	.284	.263	.243	.225	.209	.194
10	.352	.322	.295	.270	.247	.227	.208	.191	.176	.162
11	.317	.287	.261	.237	.215	.195	.178	.162	.148	.135
12	.286	.257	.231	.208	.187	.168	.152	.137	.124	.112
13	.258	.229	.204	.182	.163	.145	.130	.116	.104	.093
14	.232	.205	.181	.160	.141	.125	.111	.099	.088	.078
15	.209	.183	.160	.140	.123	.108	.095	.084	.074	.065
16	.188	.163	.141	.123	.107	.093	.081	.071	.062	.054
17	.170	.146	.125	.108	.093	.080	.069	.060	.052	.045
18	.153	.130	.111	.095	.081	.069	.059	.051	.044	.038
19	.138	.116	.098	.083	.070	.060	.051	.043	.037	.031
20	.124	.104	.087	.073	.061	.051	.043	.037	.031	.026
21	.112	.093	.077	.064	.053	.044	.037	.031	.026	.022
22	.101	.083	.068	.056	.046	.038	.032	.026	.022	.018
23	.091	.074	.060	.049	.040	.033	.027	.022	.018	.015
24	.082	.066	.053	.043	.035	.028	.023	.019	.015	.013
25	.074	.059	.047	.038	.030	.024	.020	.016	.013	.010
30	.044	.033	.026	.020	.015	.012	.009	.007	.005	.004
35	.026	.019	.014	.010	.008	.006	.004	.003	.002	.002
40	.015	.011	.008	.005	.004	.003	.002	.001	.001	.001
45	.009	.006	.004	.003	.002	.001	.001	.001	*	*
50	.005	.003	.002	.001	.001	.001	*	*	*	*

*PV/F is zero to three decimal places.

Table A-3   Present-Value Interest Factors for One Dollar Discounted at k Percent for n Periods: $PV/F_{k,n} = \dfrac{1}{(1+k)^n}$ (continued)

Period	21%	22%	23%	24%	25%	26%	27%	28%	29%	30%
1	.826	.820	.813	.806	.800	.794	.787	.781	.775	.769
2	.683	.672	.661	.650	.640	.630	.620	.610	.601	.592
3	.564	.551	.537	.524	.512	.500	.488	.477	.466	.455
4	.467	.451	.437	.423	.410	.397	.384	.373	.361	.350
5	.386	.370	.355	.341	.328	.315	.303	.291	.280	.269
6	.319	.303	.289	.275	.262	.250	.238	.227	.217	.207
7	.263	.249	.235	.222	.210	.198	.188	.178	.168	.159
8	.218	.204	.191	.179	.168	.157	.148	.139	.130	.123
9	.180	.167	.155	.144	.134	.125	.116	.108	.101	.094
10	.149	.137	.126	.116	.107	.099	.092	.085	.078	.073
11	.123	.112	.103	.094	.086	.079	.072	.066	.061	.056
12	.102	.092	.083	.076	.069	.062	.057	.052	.047	.043
13	.084	.075	.068	.061	.055	.050	.045	.040	.037	.033
14	.069	.062	.055	.049	.044	.039	.035	.032	.028	.025
15	.057	.051	.045	.040	.035	.031	.028	.025	.022	.020
16	.047	.042	.036	.032	.028	.025	.022	.019	.017	.015
17	.039	.034	.030	.026	.023	.020	.017	.015	.013	.012
18	.032	.028	.024	.021	.018	.016	.014	.012	.010	.009
19	.027	.023	.020	.017	.014	.012	.011	.009	.008	.007
20	.022	.019	.016	.014	.012	.010	.008	.007	.006	.005
21	.018	.015	.013	.011	.009	.008	.007	.006	.005	.004
22	.015	.013	.011	.009	.007	.006	.005	.004	.004	.003
23	.012	.010	.009	.007	.006	.005	.004	.003	.003	.002
24	.010	.008	.007	.006	.005	.004	.003	.003	.002	.002
25	.009	.007	.006	.005	.004	.003	.003	.002	.002	.001
30	.003	.003	.002	.002	.001	.001	.001	.001	*	*
35	.001	.001	.001	.001	*	*	*	*	*	*
40	*	*	*	*	*	*	*	*	*	*
45	*	*	*	*	*	*	*	*	*	*
50	*	*	*	*	*	*	*	*	*	*

*PV/F is zero to three decimal places.

Table A-3 Present-Value Interest Factors for One Dollar Discounted at k Percent for n Periods: $PVIF_{k,n} = \dfrac{1}{(1+k)^n}$ (continued)

Period	31%	32%	33%	34%	35%	36%	37%	38%	39%	40%
1	.763	.758	.752	.746	.741	.735	.730	.725	.719	.714
2	.583	.574	.565	.557	.549	.541	.533	.525	.518	.510
3	.445	.435	.425	.416	.406	.398	.389	.381	.372	.364
4	.340	.329	.320	.310	.301	.292	.284	.276	.268	.260
5	.259	.250	.240	.231	.223	.215	.207	.200	.193	.186
6	.198	.189	.181	.173	.165	.158	.151	.145	.139	.133
7	.151	.143	.136	.129	.122	.116	.110	.105	.100	.095
8	.115	.108	.102	.096	.091	.085	.081	.076	.072	.068
9	.088	.082	.077	.072	.067	.063	.059	.055	.052	.048
10	.067	.062	.058	.054	.050	.046	.043	.040	.037	.035
11	.051	.047	.043	.040	.037	.034	.031	.029	.027	.025
12	.039	.036	.033	.030	.027	.025	.023	.021	.019	.018
13	.030	.027	.025	.022	.020	.018	.017	.015	.014	.013
14	.023	.021	.018	.017	.015	.014	.012	.011	.010	.009
15	.017	.016	.014	.012	.011	.010	.009	.008	.007	.006
16	.013	.012	.010	.009	.008	.007	.006	.006	.005	.005
17	.010	.009	.008	.007	.006	.005	.005	.004	.004	.003
18	.008	.007	.006	.005	.005	.004	.003	.003	.003	.002
19	.006	.005	.004	.004	.003	.003	.003	.002	.002	.002
20	.005	.004	.003	.003	.002	.002	.002	.002	.001	.001
21	.003	.003	.003	.002	.002	.002	.001	.001	.001	.001
22	.003	.002	.002	.002	.001	.001	.001	.001	.001	.001
23	.002	.002	.001	.001	.001	.001	.001	.001	.001	*
24	.002	.001	.001	.001	.001	.001	.001	*	*	*
25	.001	.001	.001	.001	.001	*	*	*	*	*
30	*	*	*	*	*	*	*	*	*	*
35	*	*	*	*	*	*	*	*	*	*
40	*	*	*	*	*	*	*	*	*	*
45	*	*	*	*	*	*	*	*	*	*
50	*	*	*	*	*	*	*	*	*	*

*$PVIF$ is zero to three decimal places.

Table A-3 Present-Value Interest Factors for One Dollar Discounted at k Percent for n Periods: $PVIF_{k,n} = \dfrac{1}{(1 + k)^n}$ (continued)

Period	41%	42%	43%	44%	45%	46%	47%	48%	49%	50%
1	.709	.704	.699	.694	.690	.685	.680	.676	.671	.667
2	.503	.496	.489	.482	.476	.469	.463	.457	.450	.444
3	.357	.349	.342	.335	.328	.321	.315	.308	.302	.296
4	.253	.246	.239	.233	.226	.220	.214	.208	.203	.198
5	.179	.173	.167	.162	.156	.151	.146	.141	.136	.132
6	.127	.122	.117	.112	.108	.103	.099	.095	.091	.088
7	.090	.086	.082	.078	.074	.071	.067	.064	.061	.059
8	.064	.060	.057	.054	.051	.048	.046	.043	.041	.039
9	.045	.043	.040	.038	.035	.033	.031	.029	.028	.026
10	.032	.030	.028	.026	.024	.023	.021	.020	.019	.017
11	.023	.021	.020	.018	.017	.016	.014	.013	.012	.012
12	.016	.015	.014	.013	.012	.011	.010	.009	.008	.008
13	.011	.010	.010	.009	.008	.007	.007	.006	.006	.005
14	.008	.007	.007	.006	.006	.005	.005	.004	.004	.003
15	.006	.005	.005	.004	.004	.003	.003	.003	.003	.002
16	.004	.004	.003	.003	.003	.002	.002	.002	.002	.002
17	.003	.003	.002	.002	.002	.002	.001	.001	.001	.001
18	.002	.002	.002	.001	.001	.001	.001	.001	.001	.001
19	.001	.001	.001	.001	.001	.001	.001	.001	.001	*
20	.001	.001	.001	.001	.001	.001	*	*	*	*
21	.001	.001	.001	*	*	*	*	*	*	*
22	.001	*	*	*	*	*	*	*	*	*
23	*	*	*	*	*	*	*	*	*	*
24	*	*	*	*	*	*	*	*	*	*
25	*	*	*	*	*	*	*	*	*	*
30	*	*	*	*	*	*	*	*	*	*
35	*	*	*	*	*	*	*	*	*	*
40	*	*	*	*	*	*	*	*	*	*
45	*	*	*	*	*	*	*	*	*	*
50	*	*	*	*	*	*	*	*	*	*

*$PVIF$ is zero to three decimal places.

Table A-4 Present-Value Interest Factors for a One-Dollar Annuity Discounted at k Percent for n Periods: $PVIFA_{k,n} = \sum_{t=1}^{n} \frac{1}{(1+k)^t}$

Period	1%	2%	3%	4%	5%	6%	7%	8%	9%	10%
1	.990	.980	.971	.962	.952	.943	.935	.926	.917	.909
2	1.970	1.942	1.913	1.886	1.859	1.833	1.808	1.783	1.759	1.736
3	2.941	2.884	2.829	2.775	2.723	2.673	2.624	2.577	2.531	2.487
4	3.902	3.808	3.717	3.630	3.546	3.465	3.387	3.312	3.240	3.170
5	4.853	4.713	4.580	4.452	4.329	4.212	4.100	3.993	3.890	3.791
6	5.795	5.601	5.417	5.242	5.076	4.917	4.767	4.623	4.486	4.355
7	6.728	6.472	6.230	6.002	5.786	5.582	5.389	5.206	5.033	4.868
8	7.652	7.326	7.020	6.733	6.463	6.210	5.971	5.747	5.535	5.335
9	8.566	8.162	7.786	7.435	7.108	6.802	6.515	6.247	5.995	5.759
10	9.471	8.983	8.530	8.111	7.722	7.360	7.024	6.710	6.418	6.145
11	10.368	9.787	9.253	8.760	8.306	7.887	7.499	7.139	6.805	6.495
12	11.255	10.575	9.954	9.385	8.863	8.384	7.943	7.536	7.161	6.814
13	12.134	11.348	10.635	9.986	9.394	8.853	8.358	7.904	7.487	7.013
14	13.004	12.106	11.296	10.563	9.899	9.295	8.745	8.244	7.786	7.367
15	13.865	12.849	11.938	11.118	10.380	9.712	9.108	8.560	8.061	7.606
16	14.718	13.578	12.561	11.652	10.838	10.106	9.447	8.851	8.313	7.824
17	15.562	14.292	13.166	12.166	11.274	10.477	9.763	9.122	8.544	8.022
18	16.398	14.992	13.754	12.659	11.690	10.828	10.059	9.372	8.756	8.201
19	17.226	15.679	14.324	13.134	12.085	11.158	10.336	9.604	8.950	8.365
20	18.046	16.352	14.878	13.590	12.462	11.470	10.594	9.818	9.129	8.514
21	18.857	17.011	15.415	14.029	12.821	11.764	10.836	10.017	9.292	8.649
22	19.661	17.658	15.937	14.451	13.163	12.042	11.061	10.201	9.442	8.772
23	20.456	18.292	16.444	14.857	13.489	12.303	11.272	10.371	9.580	8.883
24	21.244	18.914	16.936	15.247	13.799	12.550	11.469	10.529	9.707	8.985
25	22.023	19.524	17.413	15.622	14.094	12.783	11.654	10.675	9.823	9.077
30	25.808	22.396	19.601	17.292	15.373	13.765	12.409	11.258	10.274	9.427
35	29.409	24.999	21.487	18.665	16.374	14.498	12.948	11.655	10.567	9.644
40	32.835	27.356	23.115	19.793	17.159	15.046	13.332	11.925	10.757	9.779
45	36.095	29.490	24.519	20.720	17.774	15.456	13.606	12.108	10.881	9.863
50	39.196	31.424	25.730	21.482	18.256	15.762	13.801	12.233	10.962	9.915

Table A-4   Present-Value Interest Factors for a One-Dollar Annuity Discounted at k Percent for n Periods: $PVIFA_{k,n} = \sum_{t=1}^{n} \dfrac{1}{(1+k)^t}$ (continued)

Period	11%	12%	13%	14%	15%	16%	17%	18%	19%	20%
1	.901	.893	.885	.877	.870	.862	.855	.847	.840	.833
2	1.713	1.690	1.668	1.647	1.626	1.605	1.585	1.566	1.547	1.528
3	2.444	2.402	2.361	2.322	2.283	2.246	2.210	2.174	2.140	2.106
4	3.102	3.037	2.974	2.914	2.855	2.798	2.743	2.690	2.639	2.589
5	3.696	3.605	3.517	3.433	3.352	3.274	3.199	3.127	3.058	2.991
6	4.231	4.111	3.998	3.889	3.784	3.685	3.589	3.498	3.410	3.326
7	4.712	4.564	4.423	4.288	4.160	4.039	3.922	3.812	3.706	3.605
8	5.146	4.968	4.799	4.639	4.487	4.344	4.207	4.078	3.954	3.837
9	5.537	5.328	5.132	4.946	4.772	4.607	4.451	4.303	4.163	4.031
10	5.889	5.650	5.426	5.216	5.019	4.833	4.659	4.494	4.339	4.192
11	6.207	5.938	5.687	5.453	5.234	5.029	4.836	4.656	4.486	4.327
12	6.492	6.194	5.918	5.660	5.421	5.197	4.988	4.793	4.611	4.439
13	6.750	6.424	6.122	5.842	5.583	5.342	5.118	4.910	4.715	4.533
14	6.982	6.628	6.302	6.002	5.724	5.468	5.229	5.008	4.802	4.611
15	7.191	6.811	6.462	6.142	5.847	5.575	5.324	5.092	4.876	4.675
16	7.379	6.974	6.604	6.265	5.954	5.668	5.405	5.162	4.938	4.730
17	7.549	7.120	6.729	6.373	6.047	5.749	5.475	5.222	4.990	4.775
18	7.702	7.250	6.840	6.467	6.128	5.818	5.534	5.273	5.033	4.812
19	7.839	7.366	6.938	6.550	6.198	5.877	5.584	5.316	5.070	4.843
20	7.963	7.469	7.025	6.623	6.259	5.929	5.628	5.353	5.101	4.870
21	8.075	7.562	7.102	6.687	6.312	5.973	5.665	5.384	5.127	4.891
22	8.176	7.645	7.170	6.743	6.359	6.011	5.696	5.410	5.149	4.909
23	8.266	7.718	7.230	6.792	6.399	6.044	5.723	5.432	5.167	4.925
24	8.348	7.784	7.283	6.835	6.434	6.073	5.746	5.451	5.182	4.937
25	8.422	7.843	7.330	6.873	6.464	6.097	5.766	5.467	5.195	4.948
30	8.694	8.055	7.496	7.003	6.566	6.177	5.829	5.517	5.235	4.979
35	8.855	8.176	7.586	7.070	6.617	6.215	5.858	5.539	5.251	4.992
40	8.951	8.244	7.634	7.105	6.642	6.233	5.871	5.548	5.258	4.997
45	9.008	8.283	7.661	7.123	6.654	6.242	5.877	5.552	5.261	4.999
50	9.042	8.304	7.675	7.133	6.661	6.246	5.880	5.554	5.262	4.999

Table A-4 Present-Value Interest Factors for a One-Dollar Annuity Discounted at k Percent for n Periods: $PVIFA_{k,n} = \sum_{t=1}^{n} \frac{1}{(1+k)^t}$ (continued)

Period	21%	22%	23%	24%	25%	26%	27%	28%	29%	30%
1	.826	.820	.813	.806	.800	.794	.787	.781	.775	.769
2	1.509	1.492	1.474	1.457	1.440	1.424	1.407	1.392	1.376	1.361
3	2.074	2.042	2.011	1.981	1.952	1.923	1.896	1.868	1.842	1.816
4	2.540	2.494	2.448	2.404	2.362	2.320	2.280	2.241	2.203	2.166
5	2.926	2.864	2.803	2.745	2.689	2.635	2.583	2.532	2.483	2.436
6	3.245	3.167	3.092	3.020	2.951	2.885	2.821	2.759	2.700	2.643
7	3.508	3.416	3.327	3.242	3.161	3.083	3.009	2.937	2.868	2.802
8	3.726	3.619	3.518	3.421	3.329	3.241	3.156	3.076	2.999	2.925
9	3.905	3.786	3.673	3.566	3.463	3.366	3.273	3.184	3.100	3.019
10	4.054	3.923	3.799	3.682	3.570	3.465	3.364	3.269	3.178	3.092
11	4.177	4.035	3.902	3.776	3.656	3.544	3.437	3.335	3.239	3.147
12	4.278	4.127	3.985	3.851	3.725	3.606	3.493	3.387	3.286	3.190
13	4.362	4.203	4.053	3.912	3.780	3.656	3.538	3.427	3.322	3.223
14	4.432	4.265	4.108	3.962	3.824	3.695	3.573	3.459	3.351	3.249
15	4.489	4.315	4.153	4.001	3.859	3.726	3.601	3.483	3.373	3.268
16	4.536	4.357	4.189	4.033	3.887	3.751	3.623	3.503	3.390	3.283
17	4.576	4.391	4.219	4.059	3.910	3.771	3.640	3.518	3.403	3.295
18	4.608	4.419	4.243	4.080	3.928	3.786	3.654	3.529	3.413	3.304
19	4.635	4.442	4.263	4.097	3.942	3.799	3.664	3.539	3.421	3.311
20	4.657	4.460	4.279	4.110	3.954	3.808	3.673	3.546	3.427	3.316
21	4.675	4.476	4.292	4.121	3.963	3.816	3.679	3.551	3.432	3.320
22	4.690	4.488	4.302	4.130	3.970	3.822	3.684	3.556	3.436	3.323
23	4.703	4.499	4.311	4.137	3.976	3.827	3.689	3.559	3.438	3.325
24	4.713	4.507	4.318	4.143	3.981	3.831	3.692	3.562	3.441	3.327
25	4.721	4.514	4.323	4.147	3.985	3.834	3.694	3.564	3.442	3.329
30	4.746	4.534	4.339	4.160	3.995	3.842	3.701	3.569	3.447	3.332
35	4.756	4.541	4.345	4.164	3.998	3.845	3.703	3.571	3.448	3.333
40	4.760	4.544	4.347	4.166	3.999	3.846	3.703	3.571	3.448	3.333
45	4.761	4.545	4.347	4.166	4.000	3.846	3.704	3.571	3.448	3.333
50	4.762	4.545	4.348	4.167	4.000	3.846	3.704	3.571	3.448	3.333

Table A-4 Present-Value Interest Factors for a One-Dollar Annuity Discounted at k Percent for n Periods: $PVIFA_{k,n} = \sum_{t=1}^{n} \dfrac{1}{(1+k)^t}$ (continued)

Period	31%	32%	33%	34%	35%	36%	37%	38%	39%	40%
1	.763	.758	.752	.746	.741	.735	.730	.725	.719	.714
2	1.346	1.331	1.317	1.303	1.289	1.276	1.263	1.250	1.237	1.224
3	1.791	1.766	1.742	1.719	1.696	1.673	1.652	1.630	1.609	1.589
4	2.130	2.096	2.062	2.029	1.997	1.966	1.935	1.906	1.877	1.849
5	2.390	2.345	2.302	2.260	2.220	2.181	2.143	2.106	2.070	2.035
6	2.588	2.534	2.483	2.433	2.385	2.339	2.294	2.251	2.209	2.168
7	2.739	2.677	2.619	2.562	2.508	2.455	2.404	2.355	2.308	2.263
8	2.854	2.786	2.721	2.658	2.598	2.540	2.485	2.432	2.380	2.331
9	2.942	2.868	2.798	2.730	2.665	2.603	2.544	2.487	2.432	2.379
10	3.009	2.930	2.855	2.784	2.715	2.649	2.587	2.527	2.469	2.414
11	3.060	2.978	2.899	2.824	2.752	2.683	2.618	2.555	2.496	2.438
12	3.100	3.013	2.931	2.853	2.779	2.708	2.641	2.576	2.515	2.456
13	3.129	3.040	2.956	2.876	2.799	2.727	2.658	2.592	2.529	2.469
14	3.152	3.061	2.974	2.892	2.814	2.740	2.670	2.603	2.539	2.478
15	3.170	3.076	2.988	2.905	2.825	2.750	2.679	2.611	2.546	2.484
16	3.183	3.088	2.999	2.914	2.834	2.757	2.685	2.616	2.551	2.489
17	3.193	3.097	3.007	2.921	2.840	2.763	2.690	2.621	2.555	2.492
18	3.201	3.104	3.012	2.926	2.844	2.767	2.693	2.624	2.557	2.494
19	3.207	3.109	3.017	2.930	2.848	2.770	2.696	2.626	2.559	2.496
20	3.211	3.113	3.020	2.933	2.850	2.772	2.698	2.627	2.561	2.497
21	3.215	3.116	3.023	2.935	2.852	2.773	2.699	2.629	2.562	2.498
22	3.217	3.118	3.025	2.936	2.853	2.775	2.700	2.629	2.562	2.498
23	3.219	3.120	3.026	2.938	2.854	2.775	2.701	2.630	2.563	2.499
24	3.221	3.121	3.027	2.939	2.855	2.776	2.701	2.630	2.563	2.499
25	3.222	3.122	3.028	2.939	2.856	2.776	2.702	2.631	2.563	2.499
30	3.225	3.124	3.030	2.941	2.857	2.777	2.702	2.631	2.564	2.500
35	3.226	3.125	3.030	2.941	2.857	2.778	2.703	2.632	2.564	2.500
40	3.226	3.125	3.030	2.941	2.857	2.778	2.703	2.632	2.564	2.500
45	3.226	3.125	3.030	2.941	2.857	2.778	2.703	2.632	2.564	2.500
50	3.226	3.125	3.030	2.941	2.857	2.778	2.703	2.632	2.564	2.500

Table A-4 Present-Value Interest Factors for a One-Dollar Annuity Discounted at k Percent for n Periods: $PVIFA_{k,n} = \sum_{t=1}^{n} \dfrac{1}{(1+k)^t}$ (continued)

Period	41%	42%	43%	44%	45%	46%	47%	48%	49%	50%
1	.709	.704	.699	.694	.690	.685	.680	.676	.671	.667
2	1.212	1.200	1.188	1.177	1.165	1.154	1.143	1.132	1.122	1.111
3	1.569	1.549	1.530	1.512	1.493	1.475	1.458	1.441	1.424	1.407
4	1.822	1.795	1.769	1.744	1.720	1.695	1.672	1.649	1.627	1.605
5	2.001	1.969	1.937	1.906	1.876	1.846	1.818	1.790	1.763	1.737
6	2.129	2.091	2.054	2.018	1.983	1.949	1.917	1.885	1.854	1.824
7	2.219	2.176	2.135	2.096	2.057	2.020	1.984	1.949	1.916	1.883
8	2.283	2.237	2.193	2.150	2.109	2.069	2.030	1.993	1.957	1.922
9	2.328	2.280	2.233	2.187	2.144	2.102	2.061	2.022	1.984	1.948
10	2.360	2.310	2.261	2.213	2.168	2.125	2.083	2.042	2.003	1.965
11	2.383	2.331	2.280	2.232	2.185	2.140	2.097	2.055	2.015	1.977
12	2.400	2.346	2.294	2.244	2.196	2.151	2.107	2.064	2.024	1.985
13	2.411	2.356	2.303	2.253	2.204	2.158	2.113	2.071	2.029	1.990
14	2.419	2.363	2.310	2.259	2.210	2.163	2.118	2.075	2.033	1.993
15	2.425	2.369	2.315	2.263	2.214	2.166	2.121	2.078	2.036	1.995
16	2.429	2.372	2.318	2.266	2.216	2.169	2.123	2.079	2.037	1.997
17	2.432	2.375	2.320	2.268	2.218	2.170	2.125	2.081	2.038	1.998
18	2.434	2.377	2.322	2.270	2.219	2.172	2.126	2.082	2.039	1.999
19	2.435	2.378	2.323	2.270	2.220	2.172	2.126	2.082	2.040	1.999
20	2.436	2.379	2.324	2.271	2.221	2.173	2.127	2.083	2.040	1.999
21	2.437	2.379	2.324	2.272	2.221	2.173	2.127	2.083	2.040	2.000
22	2.438	2.380	2.325	2.272	2.222	2.173	2.127	2.083	2.040	2.000
23	2.438	2.380	2.325	2.272	2.222	2.174	2.127	2.083	2.041	2.000
24	2.438	2.380	2.325	2.272	2.222	2.174	2.127	2.083	2.041	2.000
25	2.439	2.381	2.325	2.272	2.222	2.174	2.128	2.083	2.041	2.000
30	2.439	2.381	2.326	2.273	2.222	2.174	2.128	2.083	2.041	2.000
35	2.439	2.381	2.326	2.273	2.222	2.174	2.128	2.083	2.041	2.000
40	2.439	2.381	2.326	2.273	2.222	2.174	2.128	2.083	2.041	2.000
45	2.439	2.381	2.326	2.273	2.222	2.174	2.128	2.083	2.041	2.000
50	2.439	2.381	2.326	2.273	2.222	2.174	2.128	2.083	2.041	2.000

Career Opportunities in Managerial Finance and Financial Services

If you have an interest in the dollars and cents of running a business, like to follow the daily ups and downs of the financial markets, have a knack for numbers, and would like to land a job with a salary ranking among the highest of all business graduates, finance might be the career for you. Opportunities for the new graduate are abundant; there are over a million positions in the general field of finance. This appendix focuses on careers in finance—what they are, where to find them, and what they are paying.

What Are the Jobs?

There are two basic career paths in finance. The first is *managerial finance,* which involves managing the finance function for businesses in the manufacturing and trade industries. These industries make and sell consumer and commercial products. The second is a career in the *financial services* industry, which creates and sells intangible financial products or services. Banking, securities, real estate, and insurance are all financial service industries.

The job descriptions that follow are divided into two career paths: managerial finance and financial services. A mixture of entry-level positions available to the recent college graduate and advanced positions available after a number of years of work experience and/or an advanced degree are presented. Although many of the top positions in finance are not available to recent graduates, firms frequently hire new graduates as ''assistants'' to these positions. (Note: One * designates an entry-level position and two **s designate an advanced position.) A review of the job descriptions below should help you understand the many exciting career opportunities available in finance.

Career Path 1: Managerial Finance

A career in managerial finance can lead to the executive suite. According to a study of the chief executive officers (CEOs) of the nation's largest businesses, the majority have risen to the top after an average of 15 years in various financial management positions in the firm.[1] One explanation of why many CEOs are chosen from financial management may

[1] Louis E. Boone and James C. Johnson, ''Profiles of the 801 Men and 1 Woman at the Top,'' *Business Horizons,* February 1980, pp. 47–52.

be that the language of business is dollars, and those managing dollars generally have the full attention of a firm's top management. Exposure to these top policy makers can speed an effective financial manager's climb in the organization.

Capital Budgeting Analyst**/Manager**

The capital budgeting analyst/manager is responsible for the evaluation and selection of proposed projects and for the allocation of funds for these projects. In the evaluation process, the analyst compiles relevant data and makes cash flow projections about proposed projects. The analyst evaluates the project's acceptability based on the firm's return criteria and assesses the project's impact on the firm's asset structure. Upon selection of acceptable projects, the analyst/manager oversees the financial aspects of the implementation of the projects; this job sometimes includes analyzing and arranging the necessary financing.

> Salary: Junior analyst: $25,000–$30,000
> Manager: $30,000–$60,000

Cash Manager**

The cash manager is responsible for maintaining and controlling the daily cash balances of the firm. In a large company, this involves coordinating national or international banking relationships, compensating balances, lockbox arrangements, cash transfers, and establishing and maintaining lines of credit. An understanding of the business and cash cycles of the firm is essential in projecting the firm's daily cash surplus or deficit. The cash manager is responsible for investing surplus funds in short-term marketable securities, or, in the case of a deficit, arranging necessary short-term financing through trade credit, bank notes or lines, accounts receivable or inventory loans, factoring, commercial paper, or other sources.

> Salary: $40,000–$75,000

Property Manager**

A property manager acquires, finances, manages, promotes, and markets properties for a firm that is not otherwise in the real estate business. Real estate can be both a substantial source and use of cash to a firm. By developing existing property or refinancing property using various leasing techniques, the earnings performance of the firm can be significantly enhanced. Property managers are employed by large firms, insurance companies, pension funds, and banks.

> Salary: Entry-level: $20,000–$25,000
> Experienced corporate property manager: up to $70,000

Credit Analyst*/Manager**

The general credit analyst/manager administers the firm's credit policy by analyzing or managing two basic activities: the evaluation of credit applications and the collection of accounts receivable. Routine duties involve analyzing the financial condition of applicants, checking credit histories, and determining the appropriate amount of credit and credit terms to offer applicants. The manager also supervises the collection of current and past-due accounts receivable. By 1995, the demands for credit analysts and credit managers are expected to increase by about 41 percent and 33 percent, respectively.[2]

Salary: Analyst: $15,000–$20,000
             Manager: $25,000 and up

Financial Analyst*

A financial analyst may be responsible for a variety of financial tasks. Primarily, the analyst is involved in preparing and analyzing the firm's financial plans and budgets. This function requires a close working relationship with the accounting activity. Other duties may include financial forecasting, assisting in preparation of pro forma statements, and analyzing other aspects of the firm such as its liquidity, short-term borrowing, fixed assets, and capital structure. The degree of specialization of the analyst's duties is generally dependent upon the size of the firm. Larger firms tend to have specialized analysts, while smaller firms assign the analyst a number of areas of responsibility.

Many students headed for a career in managerial finance will begin as a financial, or "budget," analyst, doing financial planning and budgeting. According to the chief financial officers (CFOs) of firms in the *Fortune* 1000, financial planning and budgeting is the biggest career growth area in managerial finance.[3] In addition, these CFOs indicated it is also the most important and time-consuming managerial finance task. By 1995, the demand for financial analysts is expected to increase by about 37 percent.[4]

Salary: Entry-level: $15,000–$20,000
             MBA: $20,000–$40,000

Pension Fund Manager**

The pension fund manager is responsible for coordinating the management of the earning assets of the employees' pension fund. The fund may be managed by the firm or by a bank trust department, insurance company, or investment firm. If the pension fund is managed within the firm, the manager prudently assesses the suitability of investments, develops a diversified investment portfolio, monitors both the financial markets and the firm's portfolio, and administers all financial transactions involved in the investment management process. If all or part of the pension fund is managed outside the firm, the pension fund manager monitors the performance of the external fund managers and oversees the employee-related aspects of the fund.

Salary: $40,000 and up

[2] Steven S. Ross, "Careers: What's Hot, What's Not," *Business Week's Guide to Careers, Job Trak* (Special Edition), 1985, pp. 13–18.

[3] Lawrence J. Gitman and Charles E. Maxwell, "Financial Activities of Major U.S. Firms: Survey and Analysis of *Fortune's* 1000," *Financial Management*, Winter 1985, pp. 57–65.

[4] See note 2 above.

Project Finance Manager**

Project finance manager is a position that generally exists only at the largest firms. Responsibilities include arranging financing for capital expenditures that meet the firm's capital-structure objectives. The manager of project finance coordinates the activities of consultants, investment bankers, and legal counsel. An essential skill of this manager is the ability to evaluate and forecast financial market conditions and to assess their impact on future project financing.

Salary: $40,000–$50,000

Career Path 2: Financial Services

The financial services industry is the fastest-growing area in finance. It offers career opportunities in banking, securities, real estate, and insurance. Most of the jobs in the financial services industry can be obtained by qualified candidates upon graduation from college. To be successful in financial services, the graduate must understand the financial aspects of a product or service and also be able to sell that service. The majority of entry-level positions in this career path are sales-oriented.

Banking

Loan Officer**

A loan officer evaluates the credit of personal and business loan applicants. Loan officers may specialize in commercial, installment, or mortgage loans. The commercial loan officer develops and monitors the credit relationship between the business customer and the bank. Responsibilities include evaluation of the credit-worthiness of the business, negotiating credit terms, monitoring the firm's financial condition, cross-selling the bank's other corporate services, and acting as a financial adviser to smaller firms.

Salary: Entry-level: $20,000–$30,000
Experienced: $30,000–$50,000

Retail Bank Manager*

Retail banking involves the bank's branch offices, which deal directly with the public. The branch manager supervises the programs offered by the bank to its customers—installment loans, mortgages, checking, savings, retirement accounts, and other financial products. Due to the competitive nature of banking since the industry's deregulation, the successful retail banker must aggressively market the bank's new products as well as possess a certain degree of financial savvy.

The outlook for employment in the banking industry seems favorable over the next decade. Banks are hiring graduates with degrees in finance or accounting with a marketing emphasis as well as finance graduates with a technical background in management information systems and computers.[5] Many banks have management training programs that provide the entry-level trainee with experience in retail banking. According to *Business Week's Guide to Careers,* the bank-trainee position is one of the top 20 entry-level jobs in terms of ultimate salary potential and number of openings expected in the coming decade.

Salary: Entry-level: $14,000–$18,000
         MBA: $22,000–$30,000

Trust Officer**

Trust officers manage portfolios of investments for individuals, foundations, institutions, and corporate pension and profit-sharing plans. The trust officer and his or her staff research, analyze, and monitor both currently held and potential investment vehicles for retention or inclusion in the portfolios they manage.

Salary: $25,000–$50,000

Securities

Financial Planner*

A financial planner works in an advisory capacity to individuals. The planner advises the client about budgeting, securities, insurance, real estate, taxes, retirement and estate planning, and devises a comprehensive financial plan to meet the client's life objectives. This position has been included in the securities industry section but could as well have been in the banking, real estate, or insurance sections of this appendix. Eighty percent of all financial planners are employed by the financial services industry and serve as a complement to the sales function in their firm. The other 20 percent are self-employed and sell advice rather than financial products, such as securities, tax shelters, or insurance.

Salary: Entry-level: $18,000–$25,000
         Experienced: up to $100,000

Investment Banker**

Investment bankers are considered the financial ''movers and shakers'' on Wall Street. They act as brokers between the issuers and buyers of newly issued stocks and bonds. Generally, the investment banker purchases the security issue and then markets it to the public, bearing all the risk of selling the issue. Considerable experience and expertise are necessary to land a job in a Wall Street investment banking firm, but the rewards are worth the effort.

Salary: Entry-level MBA: $30,000–$50,000
         After 10 years' experience $250,000–$300,000

---

[5] John Stodden, ''Job Map,'' *Business Week's Guide to Careers, Job Trak* (Special Edition), 1985, pp. 4–9.

Securities Analyst**

Securities analysts are the financial experts on Wall Street who study stocks and bonds, usually in specific industries. They are specialists with respect to a particular firm or industry, and understand the economic impact of changes in the competitive, financial, and foreign markets on that firm or industry. They are employed by and act as advisers to securities firms, fund managers, and insurance companies.

Salary: Junior analyst with MBA: $25,000–$30,000
         Experienced analyst: up to $100,000

Stockbroker* or Account Executive*

A stockbroker or account executive's responsibilities include handling orders to buy and sell securities, counseling customers on financial matters, supplying the latest stock and bond quotations, and responding to customer inquiries. Stockbrokers are usually hired by brokerage firms, investment banks, mutual funds, and insurance companies. Job opportunities for brokers are also emerging in traditional financial institutions such as banks and savings and loans. Most firms offer a training program at the entry level that prepares the stockbroker to take the required standardized licensing examination. According to *Business Week's Guide to Careers,* the broker trainee position is one of the top 12 entry-level jobs in terms of ultimate salary potential and number of openings expected in the coming decade. Out of 200,000 people employed in the securities market, over one-half are stockbrokers or securities salespeople. However, the turnover rate—95 percent within the first two years—is very high among these positions.[6]

Salary: Trainee: $15,000–$20,000 plus commissions
         Experienced broker: $50,000–$100,000 or more

Real Estate

Real Estate Agent*/Broker*

Most property is sold or leased with the aid of a real estate agent who is generally employed by a broker. Some of the agent's and broker's duties include finding potential buyers and lessees for listed property, showing property, and negotiating sale or lease terms agreeable to both parties. Additionally, a broker is generally an independent businessperson experienced in the field of real estate; he or she supports the sales staff, providing office space and a budget for advertising and promoting listed properties. Many real estate agents and brokers are also certified property managers, real estate appraisers, and real estate developers. By 1995, the demand for real estate brokers is expected to increase by about 30 percent in economically developing regions of the country.[7]

Salary: Beginner: $10,000–$15,000
         Experienced: $25,000–$75,000

---

[6] Nicholas Basta, "Securities Industry," *Business Week's Guide to Careers,* February/March 1984, p. 75.

[7] See note 2 above.

Insurance

Insurance Agent*/Broker*

Insurance agents and brokers develop programs to fit customers' needs, interview insurance prospects, help with claims and settlements, and collect premiums. An agent is usually employed by a single insurance company, whereas a broker is independent and represents no particular company but can sell policies from many. Getting a job as an insurance agent is easy; being successful is much more difficult. The turnover rate is similar to that for stockbrokers; approximately 90 percent of the newly employed in this field leave after two years.[8]

Salary:	Trainee:	$15,000–$20,000
	Experienced agent:	$30,000–$60,000

Underwriter**

Underwriters appraise and select the risks their company will insure. This includes the appraisal of the risks of individuals after analyzing insurance applications, reports from loss-control consultants, medical reports, and actuarial studies. Commercial underwriting involves insuring a firm's major fixed assets, such as heavy equipment. When deciding whether an applicant is an acceptable risk, an underwriter may outline the terms of the contract, including the amount of the premium. By 1995, the demand for underwriters is expected to increase by about 21 percent.[9]

Salary: $25,000–$50,000

Where Are the Jobs?

Locating the fastest-growing job opportunities in managerial finance requires targeting the regions of the country where manufacturing and trade industries are flourishing. Figure B.1 shows where the jobs are. The best overall job markets in managerial finance currently are all in the southern half of the country. However, there are still many opportunities in the north.

The best job markets for first jobs in financial services are in New England, the Middle Atlantic, and the Pacific Southwest. In New England and the Middle Atlantic region, the growth in the service industry is resulting in the rapid expansion of opportunities in finance and insurance since most firms in these industries are headquartered in those regions. In the Pacific Southwest, demographics show that rising population and industrial activity are causing an increase in the demand for accountants, financial analysts, and associated managers and administrative staffs.[10] (See Figure B.1.)

[8] See note 6 above.
[9] See note 2 above.
[10] See note 5 above.

Figure B.1
Where Are the Jobs?

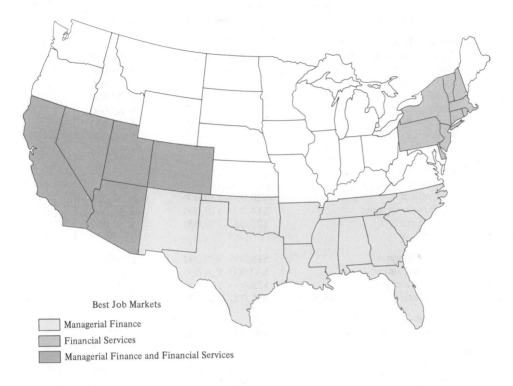

Best Job Markets

Managerial Finance

Financial Services

Managerial Finance and Financial Services

What Are the Jobs Paying?

The finance graduate can expect top salary offers among business graduates. In finance, entry-level job offers averaged $19,506 in 1985.[11] The best offers are going to business majors with a technical background. The salaries summarized in Table B.1 on page 786 are expressed in ranges and are only guidelines. Many factors may affect the salary level of a job: the geographic region, the employee's work experience and educational background, and the size of the company.

[11] John Shingleton and L. Patrick Scheetz, *Recruiting Trends, 1984–1985,* Placement Services, Michigan State University, East Lansing, Michigan.

Table B.1
Salaries of Various Career Opportunities in Finance

Job Title	Entry-level salary	Potential salary
Managerial Finance		
Capital budgeting analyst	$25,000–$30,000	$ 60,000
Cash manager	—	$ 75,000
Property manager	$20,000–$25,000	$ 70,000
Credit analyst	$15,000–$20,000	$ 30,000
Credit manager	$25,000–$40,000	$ 80,000
Financial analyst	$15,000–$20,000	$ 40,000
Pension fund manager	—	$100,000
Project finance manager	—	$ 50,000
Financial Services		
Banking		
Loan officer	$20,000–$30,000	$ 50,000
Retail bank manager	$14,000–$18,000	$ 30,000
Trust officer	$25,000–$30,000	$ 50,000
Securities		
Financial planner	$18,000–$25,000	$100,000
Investment banker	$30,000–$50,000	$300,000
Securities analyst	$25,000–$30,000	$100,000
Stockbroker or account executive	$15,000–$20,000	$100,000
Real Estate		
Real estate agent/broker	$10,000–$15,000	$ 75,000
Insurance		
Agent/broker	$15,000–$20,000	$ 60,000
Underwriter	$25,000–$30,000	$ 50,000

Instructions for Using
The Gitman Disk

Overview

The Gitman Disk is a collection of financial routines designed to accompany the fifth edition of *Principles of Managerial Finance*. The disk is available for use on Apple II and IBM PC microcomputers. All routines are written in BASIC and may be transferred easily to other computers with little or no modification.

The purpose of *The Gitman Disk* is to aid the student's learning and understanding of managerial finance by providing a fast and easy method for performing the often time-consuming mathematical computations required. The computer package does not eliminate the need for learning the various concepts, but assists in solving the problems once the appropriate formulas have been studied. It is important to recognize that the disk will not always directly compute answers to end-of-chapter problems; some problems require multiple steps, intermediate calculations, and/or noncomputer setup and work.

The routines on the disk are arranged in the same order as the text discussions. For convenience, text page references are shown on the screen for each associated computational routine. As noted in the text Preface and in Chapter 1, applicability of the disk throughout the text and study guide is always keyed to related text discussions and end-of-chapter problems by the printed disk symbol [disk symbol]. This should allow the user to integrate the procedures on the disk with the corresponding text discussions.

Technical Information

Because of differences in their operating systems, there are certain technical differences between the Apple II and IBM PC versions of *The Gitman Disk*.

Apple II Version

The Apple II version of *The Gitman Disk* is ready to use as supplied. It can be placed in the disk drive and booted without any reconfiguring. The disk contains the operating system and all necessary programs. Since the programs are written in Applesoft BASIC, those with earlier Apple IIs without autostart ROM will have to load Applesoft and then 'RUN HELLO' or transfer FPBASIC (Applesoft) to *The Gitman Disk* and then make the needed changes in the Hello program. (Refer to *Apple II Reference Manual*.) With all other Apple IIs (II+, IIe, and IIc), as well as most Apple compatibles, you will be able to place the disk in the disk drive, close the door, boot the disk (or turn on computer), and proceed with a session of interactive financial problem solving (i.e., homework).

The Gitman Disk contains a high-speed operating system called Diversi-DOS™, which is licensed for use with this program only. To legally use Diversi-DOS with other programs, you may send $30 directly to: DSR, Inc., 5848 Crampton Ct., Rockford, Illinois 61111. In return you will be sent a Diversi-DOS utility disk with documentation.

IBM PC Version

The IBM PC version of *The Gitman Disk* is written in IBM BASIC (DOS 2.1) and is as similar to the Applesoft version as possible. The main difference, from a user's point of view, is that the IBM version does not contain an operating system or the BASIC program (BASICA.COM). Before the financial programs can be accessed, PC DOS or a compatible operating system must be loaded into the computer. After DOS is loaded, BASIC must be loaded. When this process is complete, the main program (START.BAS) may be run. This is accomplished by typing RUN "START after BASIC is "up."

To simplify this process, copy all programs to a formatted system disk with BASICA.COM already installed. (Refer to DOS reference manual.) An autoboot procedure (AUTOEXEC.BAT) has been included to enable the IBM version to run in a "turnkey" fashion, as does the Apple version. This turnkey system will operate only if the programs are on a system disk that includes BASIC.

General Programming Conventions

The user should become familiar with several conventions employed in the display portion of the programs. These deal with the way responses to prompts or queries are answered. Keep in mind that answers to computer-generated prompts are basically of two types. These are single-character responses and multiple-character responses.

Most responses are of the multiple-character variety. That is, they require the user to enter one or more numbers or letters followed by the RETURN key. (*Note:* The RETURN key is used to refer to the *carriage return key*—often noted as ⟨CR⟩—which may be labeled RETURN, ENTER, or ⤶, depending on the specific microcomputer being used.) These responses usually involve entering data. The remainder of responses will be mainly for program control and choice of options. Where practical, responses have been reduced to single-character entries not requiring the use of the RETURN key. Therefore it is important not to be too quick to hit the RETURN key after answering a prompt that requires only a single-character response.

Responses that have been reduced to single characters involve such prompts as (Y/N), which means a yes-or-no answer is required. Press Y for Yes and N for No. In most instances, Y is the default answer that is assumed if no other answer is given. This default will usually mean "everything is OK, so continue." For example, at the end of a screen of data the user will be asked "Are all values correct (Y/N)" where the Y(es) response is assumed. If the user enters anything other than N, the program will continue as if a Y were entered. (*Note:* The ⟨CR⟩ response refers to the carriage return key described above. Also, on the IBM PC version, uppercase and lowercase letters are treated the same.)

The statement "Hit any key to continue ⟨ESC⟩ for menu" will be displayed at points where the program is pausing to permit the user to examine the screen. Almost any key stroke will allow the program to continue. Keys that do not have their own function codes will not allow the program to continue. Examples of these keys are the shift key and the control key. All other keys will allow the program to continue, but the ESCape key will bring up the current menu, thus permitting the user to return to the main menu or possibly end the session. (*Note:* Only at specified points in the program can escape be achieved using the ESC key.)

Procedures

The major procedures for using the start-up program, main menu, and a review of each of the main-menu items will acquaint you with the use of this user-friendly menu-driven disk. After the descriptions of each of the following routines, the file names for the given routine for both computers (Apple II and IBM PC) are given. These file names could prove helpful if program enhancements are desired. For those unfamiliar with programming, these file names need not be of concern.

Start-Up Program

This program will perform an initializing function. Here the user enters his or her name and is given the option of using a printer. If the printer option is used, there must be a printer attached to the system and it must be turned on. Otherwise a reboot of the disk may be necessary.

File Name
Apple II -- HELLO
IBM PC -- START.BAS

Main Menu

After answering the prompts in the start-up program, the main menu will be displayed. This menu controls *The Gitman Disk* and is used as the starting point for all of the financial routines. The main menu appears as follows:

```
*********** The Gitman Disk ***********
      Principles of Managerial Finance 5th ED

        (1)  Financial Ratios
        (2)  Cash Budget
        (3)  Pro Forma Statements
        (4)  Time Value of Money
        (5)  Stock & Bond Valuation
        (6)  Capital Budgeting Cash Flows
        (7)  Capital Budgeting Techniques
        (8)  Cost of Capital
        (9)  Breakeven Analysis
       (10)  Bond Refunding Decision
       (11)  Lease-Versus-Purchase Decision
        (0)  End Program
```

File Name
Apple II -- MENU
IBM PC -- MENU.BAS

Review of Main Menu Items

By entering one of the numbers within the parentheses followed by a return, the chosen routine is brought up. The next screen displayed will be a menu giving the options available in that routine. Each of the eleven menu routines is described below:

(1) Financial Ratios

Used for calculating financial ratios as described in Chapter 4. The menu is:

(1) Individual Ratios

Allows a single ratio to be calculated.

(2) Families of Ratios

Gives a choice of the four different groups of ratios: liquidity, activity, debt, and profitability.

(3) All Ratios

Gives all financial ratios as described in the text.

(4) Return to Main Menu

File Name
Apple II -- RATIO ANALYSIS
IBM PC -- RATIO.BAS

(2) Cash Budget
Used for creating cash budgets as described in Chapter 5. The menu is:

(1) Cash Budget
(2) Return to Main Menu

File Name
Apple II -- CASH BUDGET
IBM PC -- CASHBUDG.BAS

(3) Pro Forma Statements
Used for creating simple pro forma statements as described in Chapter 5. The menu is:

(1) Pro Forma Statements
(2) Return to Main Menu

File Name
Apple II -- PRO FORMA STATEMENTS
IBM PC -- PROFORMA.BAS

(4) Time Value of Money
Used for calculating present and future values as described in Chapter 6. The menu is:

(1) Present and Future Value of a Single Payment
(2) Present and Future Value of an Annuity
   Perpetuities may be calculated by entering any number of periods greater than or equal to 100.
(3) Present Value of a Mixed Stream
(4) Return to Main Menu

These routines may also be used to amortize or estimate growth rates. Enter known information as it is asked for, leaving one item blank. The blank item is the unknown calculated by the computer.

File Name
Apple II -- TIME VALUE OF MONEY
IBM PC -- TIMEVALU.BAS

(5) Stock & Bond Valuation
Used to determine the value of stocks and bonds as described in Chapter 8. The menu is:

(1) Bond Valuation
(2) Common Stock Valuation
(3) Return to Main Menu

File Name
Apple II -- STOCK BOND VALUATION
IBM PC -- STOCBOND.BAS

(6) Capital Budgeting Cash Flows

Used to determine the initial investment only or all relevant cash flows for capital budgeting projects as described in Chapter 9. The menu is:

(1) Determining Initial Investment
(2) Determining Relevant Cash Flows
(3) Return to Main Menu

File Name
Apple II -- CASH FLOW
IBM PC -- CASHFLOW.BAS

(7) Capital Budgeting Techniques

Used to compare multiple projects using capital budgeting techniques as described in Chapter 10. The menu is:

(1) Payback Period
    Net Present Value (NPV)
    Internal Rate of Return (IRR)
(2) Projects with Unequal Lives
(3) Return to Main Menu

File Name
Apple II -- CAPITAL BUDGETING
IBM PC -- CAPBUDG.BAS

(8) Cost of Capital

Calculates the costs of long-term debt (bonds), preferred stock, common stock, and the weighted average and weighted marginal costs of capital as described in Chapter 11. The menu is:

(1) Long-Term Debt (Bonds)
(2) Preferred Stock
(3) Common Stock
(4) Weighted Average Cost of Capital
(5) Weighted Marginal Cost of Capital
(6) Return to Main Menu

File Name
Apple II -- COST OF CAPITAL
IBM PC -- COSTCAP.BAS

(9) Breakeven Analysis

Used to determine the operating level at which a firm's breakeven point is reached, as described in Chapter 12. The menu is:

(1) Operating Breakeven Point
(2) Return to Main Menu

File Name
Apple II -- BREAKEVEN ANALYSIS
IBM PC -- BREAKEVN.BAS

(10) Bond Refunding Decision

Used to evaluate the option of retiring a bond issue with a new issue as described in Chapter 16. The menu is:

(1) Bond Refunding
(2) Return to Main Menu

File Name
Apple II -- BOND REFUNDING DECISION
IBM PC -- BONDRFND.BAS

(11) Lease-Versus-Purchase Decision

Used to compare the option of leasing an asset with the option of purchasing the asset as described in Chapter 18. The menu is:

(1) Lease-Versus-Purchase Decision
(2) Return to Main Menu

File Name
Apple II -- LEASE/PURCHASE DECISION
IBM PC -- LEASEPUR.BAS

Using Computers and Spreadsheets in Managerial Finance

Harnessing massive amounts of information is the challenge of every manager today. Fortunately, there are many tools available for gathering, storing, analyzing, and processing mounds of data. Here we will briefly discuss the two key components of a computer system—hardware and software—and some of the key features of electronic spreadsheets—an extremely popular type of software that is widely used by financial managers.

Hardware

Hardware refers to the physical components of a computer system. The basic components of a personal computer are a microprocessor (the "brain"), an input device (keyboard), a video display terminal, an output device (printer), and one or more storage devices (disk or tape drives). Critical to the decision of which type of computer is appropriate for the application software is the amount of memory available. Most general management applications programs (word processor, database management, and spreadsheets) require at least 256K of memory. Systems like the IBM PC, XT, and AT and the Macintosh 512, Plus, and SE are able to run the most popular management applications software available.

Software

Software consists of the programs that instruct the computer about the functions it is to perform. Without adequate software, the computer is useless. With the increased ownership of personal computers (PCs) has come a growing proliferation of software programs that cater to the financial manager. Moreover, PCs have become more "user friendly" (the user can communicate more easily with the computer and thus utilize it more fully), enabling managers to design programs to meet their objectives. The three basic tools of information management for use on the personal computer are word processing, database management, and spreadsheet software.

Word Processing Software

Word processing software is rapidly making the conventional typewriter obsolete. It allows text to be keyed into a computer and saved. While viewing the document on the display terminal, the user may easily edit, delete, or add more text. A variety of formats, type styles, and other features are available in most word processing programs to ease document preparation. (For a listing of popular word processing software, see Table D.1.)

Database Management Software

Database management software stores information in discrete ''parcels.'' These parcels may then be sorted in a variety of ways. Needed information can be easily extracted from the database by user-specified criteria. The parcel may contain only a single piece of data or hundreds of pieces of data. For example, some common applications of a database management program are storage of customer data (name, address, and city), inventory records, personnel data, and accounts receivable information. (For a listing of popular database management software, see Table D.1.)

Spreadsheet Software

Spreadsheet software facilitates extensive calculations based on models developed by the user. A spreadsheet appears on the screen divided into cells of rows and columns. Spreadsheet rows are generally numbered 1, 2, 3, etc., while columns are lettered A, B, C, etc. Some programs have as many as 16,000 rows and columns available. The user may enter text, numeric data, or program a formula into each cell. (For a listing of popular spreadsheet software, see Table D.1.)

Electronic Spreadsheets

A strength of electronic spreadsheets is the ability to customize formulas and to make automatic calculations using the desired model. Since the automatic calculation feature takes the drudgery out of the financial analysis of large amounts of data, the analyst may spend more time asking ''what if.'' The data or the formulas may be easily changed, often by a mere keystroke, to simulate various business conditions. (Table D.2 illustrates a spreadsheet with data and formulas.)

Additional Features

The most powerful spreadsheet software has several additional features beyond the basic calculating power: linking worksheets, using predefined functions, auditing of design logic, and the ability to use macros. These features are necessary for the serious ''number cruncher'' or ''power user.'' *Worksheet linking* allows the user to maintain multiple spreadsheets to support a final spreadsheet. For example, in developing a pro forma income statement, multiple supporting spreadsheets like sales, cost of goods sold, and

Table D.1
Popular Word Processing, Database Management, and Spreadsheet Software

Title	Hardware	Company
Word	IBM PC, XT, AT, and compatibles	Microsoft Corp. 16011 NE 36th Way Redmond, WA 98073
Word for the Macintosh	Macintosh 512, Plus, SE	
Word Perfect	IBM PC, XT, AT, and compatibles	Word Perfect Corp. 288 West Center St. Oren, UT 84057
Manuscript	IBM PC, XT, AT, and compatibles	Lotus Development Corp. 55 Cambridge Parkway Cambridge, MA 02142
Database Management		
dBase III	IBM PC, XT, AT, and compatibles	Ashton-Tate 20101 Hamilton Ave. Torrance, CA 90502
OverVUE	Macintosh 512, Plus, SE	ProVUE 2.0d 222 2nd St. Huntington Beach, CA 92648
Reflex	IBM PC, XT, AT, and compatibles	Borland International 4585 Scotts Valley Drive Scotts Valley, CA 95066
Rbase System V	IBM PC, XT, AT, and compatibles	Microrim 3925 159th Ave., NE P.O. Box 97022 Redmond, WA 98073
Spreadsheet		
Lotus 1-2-3	IBM PC, XT, AT, and compatibles	Lotus Development Corp. 55 Cambridge Parkway Cambridge, MA 02142
Multiplan	IBM PC, XT, AT, and compatibles	Microsoft Corp. 16011 NE 36th Way Redmond, WA 98073
Excel	Macintosh 512, Plus, SE, and compatibles IBM PC, AT, and compatibles	Microsoft Corp. 16011 NE 36th Way Redmond, WA 98073
SuperCalc4	IBM PC, XT, AT, and compatibles	Computer Assoc., Int'l Inc. Micro Products Division 2195 Fortune Drive San Jose, CA 95131
GoldSpread	IBM PC, XT, AT, and compatibles	Goldstein Software, Inc. 12520 Prosperity Dr. Silver Springs, MD 20904
VP Planner	IBM PC, XT, AT, and compatibles	Paperback Software Int'l 2830 Ninth Street Berkeley, CA 94710
Word & Figures	IBM PC, XT, AT, and compatibles	Lifetree Software, Inc. 411 Pacific St. Monterey, CA 93940

Table D.2
Illustration of a Spreadsheet with Data and Formulas

```
------------------------------------------------------------
  A        B        C        D        E        F
------------------------------------------------------------
  6 INPUT SECTION:
  7                        SUN VALLEY PRUNE COMPANY
  8                            INCOME STATEMENT
  9                     FOR THE YEAR ENDED DECEMBER 31
 10                                              19X8
 11                                           -----------
 12 SALES                                      $4,300,000
 13 COST OF GOODS SOLD:
 14      FIXED                                   $300,000
 15      VARIABLE                              $2,250,000
 16                                           -----------
 17    GROSS PROFIT                            $1,750,000
 18 GENERAL AND ADMIN. EXPENSES:
 19      FIXED                                   $100,000
 20      VARIABLE                                $333,000
 21                                           -----------
 22    EARNINGS BEFORE INT. AND TAX            $1,317,000
 23 INTEREST EXPENSES (ALL FIXED)                $150,000
 24                                           -----------
 25    EARNINGS BEFORE TAXES                   $1,167,000
 26 TAXES (40%)                                  $466,800
 27                                           -----------
 28    NET INCOME                                $700,200
 29                                           ===========
 30------------------------------------------------------------
 31 RESULTS SECTION:
 32                        SUN VALLEY PRUNE COMPANY
 33                      PRO FORMA INCOME STATEMENT
 34                       PERCENT-OF-SALES METHOD
 35                     FOR THE YEAR ENDED DECEMBER 31
 36                                              19X9
 37                                           -----------
 38 SALES                                      $4,750,000
 39 COST OF GOODS SOLD                          FORMULA A
 40                                           -----------
 41    GROSS PROFIT                             FORMULA B
 42 GENERAL AND ADMIN. EXPENSES                 FORMULA C
 43                                           -----------
 44    EARNINGS BEFORE INT. AND TAX             FORMULA D
 45 INTEREST EXPENSES                           FORMULA E
 46                                           -----------
 47    EARNINGS BEFORE TAXES                    FORMULA F
 48 TAXES (40%)                                 FORMULA G
 49                                           -----------
 50    NET INCOME                               FORMULA H
 51                                           ==========
```

FORMULA A:	+(F14+F15)/F12*F38	FORMULA B:	+F38−F39
FORMULA C:	+(F19+F20)/F12*F38	FORMULA D:	+F41−F42
FORMULA E:	+F23/F12*F38	FORMULA F:	+F44−F45
FORMULA G:	+F47*0.4	FORMULA H:	+F47−F48

general and administrative expense forecasts, among others, may be linked to produce the final summary pro forma spreadsheet. A *predefined function* is one that need not be programmed by the user. Some programs have predefined functions like depreciation calculation using the sum-of-the-years'-digits method, or net present value and internal rate of return calculation. The *auditing feature* is a simple check of the programmer's logic to ensure feasibility of the model. It does not, however, make the program design foolproof. *Macros* allow the user to program a sequence of operations to be used to manipulate data. For complicated manipulation, the recording of a frequently used sequence of operations reduces tedious duplication of effort.

Integrated Spreadsheet Systems

For the manager who not only wants to "crunch" the numbers but wants to communicate results with text or graphics, there are a variety of integrated systems on the market. The integrated spreadsheet system may have spreadsheet, graphics, database, and word processing features all in one system. In exchange for this versatility, generally the user must give up the computing power and convenience features found in the more basic packages. For instance, the word processing capabilities of an integrated spreadsheet program may be limited but still allow the user to do basic editing. For the casual user who would like to communicate financial forecasts or results with others in the firm, the integrated program may be best.

Spreadsheet Applications

For the financial manager the electronic spreadsheet can be customized to fit a range of financial tasks, from a simple return on investment calculation to a sophisticated merger analysis. The most common applications are forecasting models for preparation of cash budgets and pro forma income statements and balance sheets.

Pro Forma Balance Sheet Illustration

In the case of the pro forma balance sheet, the final spreadsheet may be supported by multiple spreadsheets that calculate various asset and liability values. For instance, the depreciation schedule for the existing fixed assets plus the projected purchases and sales of fixed assets might support the calculation of the net fixed asset account. Likewise, a supporting spreadsheet for the amortization of debt might take into account all existing loans, lines of credit, their payment terms and interest rates, and project the pro forma balance with no new borrowings. All other asset and liability account spreadsheets may then be linked to the final spreadsheet which has user-defined mathematical relationships common to balance sheets. The user may impose any type of restriction, such as a minimum cash balance or a desired current ratio.

Other Applications

There are a wide variety of financial analysis applications available to a user who is willing to spend the time to develop the model. Accounts receivable and inventory management can be achieved through the use of database software (for large amounts of data stored) and spreadsheets to analyze the data stored in the database. Capital budgeting analysis is made easier by many of the spreadsheet programs having predefined functions such as net present value and the internal rate of return formulas. Breakeven analysis and the WMCC and IOS analysis may be brought to life through the graphic abilities of an integrated spreadsheet program that translates the numerical data into a chart or graph. Other financial applications include cost of capital, lease-versus-purchase decisions, economic order quantity for inventory, and merger analysis among many others.

Spreadsheet Design

Designing a spreadsheet is as basic as the preparation of blueprints before building a house. Spreadsheets may contain four basic sections: the assumptions, the input data, the calculations, and the results summary. The *assumptions* are often grouped together at the top of the spreadsheet and are used as reference to drive the calculations section. If the user decides an assumption is not reasonable, it may be changed and the entire spreadsheet immediately recalculated. Stating the assumptions up front also aids the reader of the report. The *input data* section is the area where the data are to be manipulated and stored. For large sets of data, multiple spreadsheets are recommended. The data may then be imported from various other worksheets for manipulation. The *calculation* section sets forth the mathematical relationships among the data. The *results summary* section ends the spreadsheet and capsulizes the results. A spreadsheet divided into the four sections may more clearly communicate the what, how, and why of the report to its reader and allows for easy verification. Planning the layout of a spreadsheet is essential to its success.

Spreadsheet Errors

The ease with which a spreadsheet may be programmed and calculations performed may disguise the fact that errors are easy to make. Two independent Silicon Valley consulting firms, Input and Palo Alto Research, estimated that approximately one out of three business spreadsheets has some kind of error! The error to which these consulting firms refer is not a bug in the computer program; it is a programmer error—an illogical command or misplaced data. It is essential to test the program with simplified data and to verify the expected results with a hand-held calculator on the first pass. The results are only as good as the program.

Conclusion

Financial management applications for the computer are plentiful but, first, many decisions need to be made. The selection of hardware and software is one that must be investigated thoroughly to determine whether the capabilities of each meet the manager's needs. Requesting ''demo'' disks to ''test drive'' the software and actually using a computer at a dealer location is recommended. Talk with other professionals about the products they use and keep current on new products through computer periodicals. Once the hardware and software selection is made and the program mastered, the manager will be one step closer to conquering the massive amounts of information that complicates most business decisions.

Answers To Selected
End-of-Chapter Problems

The following list of answers to selected problems and portions of problems is included to provide "check figures" for use in preparing detailed solutions to end-of-chapter problems requiring calculations. For problems that are relatively straightforward, the key answer is given; for more complex problems, answers to a number of parts of the problem are included. Detailed calculations are not shown—only the final and, in some cases, intermediate answers, which should help to confirm whether the correct solution is being developed. For problems containing a variety of cases for which similar calculations are required, the answers for only one or two cases have been included. The only verbal answers included are simple yes-or-no or "choice of best alternative" responses; answers to problems requiring detailed explanations or discussions are not given.

The problems and portions of problems for which answers have been included were selected randomly; therefore, there is no discernible pattern to the choice of problem answers given. The answers given are based on what are believed to be the most obvious and reasonable assumptions related to the given problem; in some cases, other reasonable assumptions could result in equally correct answers.

2-1 **a.** Ms. Harper has unlimited liability; $60,000.
     c. Ms. Harper has limited liability.
2-2 **a.** $19,700
2-6 **a.** X $250
         Y $5,000
2-8 **b.** 11%
2-11 **a.** B   3%
         E   3.1%
2-13 **a.** C   11%
         E   14%
     c. C   13%
         E   15%

3-4 **b.** $21,460
3-5 **a.** $1.16
3-8 **a.** EPS = $1.9375
     b. Total assets $926,000
3-10 $80,000
3-15 **a.** Total sources $3,700
     c. Total sources $3,000
3-16 **a.** Total sources $90,800
     c. Total sources $72,900
4-2 **a.** Average age of inventory 97.6 days
4-6 **a.** 1987 Johnson ROE = 22.13%
             Industry ROE = 16.92%

4-8 a.

	Industry Average	Actual 1987	Actual 1988
Current ratio	1.80	1.84	1.04
Average collection period	37 days	36 days	56 days
Debt-Equity	50%	51%	40%
Net profit margin	3.5%	3.6%	4.1%
Return on equity	9.5%	8.0%	11.3%

5-3

	February	March	April
a. Ending cash	$37,000	$67,000	($22,000)
b. Required total financing			$37,000
Excess cash balance	$22,000	$52,000	

c. Line of credit should be at least $37,000 to cover borrowing needs for the month of April.

5-6 a. Net profit after taxes $216,857
b. Net profit after taxes $227,400

5-8 a. Accounts receivable $1,440,000
Net fixed assets $4,820,000
Total current liabilities $2,260,000
External funds required $ 775,000
Total assets $9,100,000

5-9 a. Net profits after taxes $67,500
b.

	Judgmental
Total assets	$697,500
External funds required	$ 11,250

6-3 A $530.60
     D $78,450

6-5 a. (1) Annual $8,810
        Semiannual $8,955
        Quarterly $9,030

6-9 A $3,862.50
     B $138,450.00
     C $6,956.80

6-12 $408
6-14 a. PV of stream A = $109,890
6-15 c. PV of stream C = $52,410
6-17 E $85,297.50
6-19 Future value of retirement home in 20 years = $272,595
Annual deposit = $4,759.49

6-21

Year	Interest	Principal
2	$1,489.61	$4,970.34

6-24 $PVIFA_{k,10}$ = 5.303
     $13\% < k < 14\%$
6-27 b. Deposit = $3,764.82
6-28 The corporation must make a $15,575.10 annual end-of-year deposit beginning in year 1 through year 12 in order to provide a retirement annuity of $42,000 per year in years 13 through 32.

7-1 a. X   12.5%
      Y   12.36%
7-2 A   25%
7-4 a. A   8 percentage points
      B   20 percentage points

7-5 a. R   10 percentage points
       S   20 percentage points
    b. R   25%
       S   25.5%
7-7 a. (4) Project 257 CV .366
           Project 432 CV .354
7-8 a. F   4%
    b. F   13.38%
    c. F   3.345
7-12 a. .18 increase
    b. .096 decrease
    c. .00 no change
7-15 A   8.9%
      D   15%
7-16 b. 10%
8-2 C $16,660
     E $14,112
8-4 a. $1,156.88
8-5 A $1,149.66
     D $450.80
8-9 a. 12.68%
    b. 12.58%
8-11 $841.15
8-14 b. Liquidation value per share = $42.40
8-15 A $18.60
8-17 a. $68.82
    b. $7.87
8-19 a. $37.75
    b. $60.40
8-20 $81.19
8-21 a. $40.94
    b. 22.24
    c. The equation is undefined.
8-24 2.67
8-25 a. 14.8%
    b. $29.55
9-1 a. Current expenditure
    d. Current expenditure
    f. Capital expenditure
9-5 A $275,500
     B $26,800
9-7 a. Total tax $49,600
    d. Total tax ($6,400)
9-9 Initial investment $22,680
9-10 a. Initial investment $18,240
    c. Initial investment $23,100
9-12 c. Cash inflow Year 3 $584,000
10-2 a. Machine 1: 4 years, 8 months
         Machine 2: 5 years, 3 months
10-4 a. (1) $2,675
       (2) accept
10-6 a. NPV = ($320); reject
10-8 a. Project A 3.08 years   Project C 2.39 years

10-9   Project A   17%
       Project D   21%

10-12 **a.** NPV = $1,222
      b. IRR = 12%
      c. Accept

10-14 **a.** Project A
         NPV = $15,245
      b. Project B
         IRR = 18%

10-17 **a.** Initial investment $1,480,000
      b.

Year	Cash Inflow
1	$656,000
2	761,600
3	647,200
4	585,600
5	585,600
6	44,000

      c. 3.2 years
      d. NPV = $959,289
         IRR = 35%

10-20 **a.** Range A $1,600
         Range B $200

10-23 **a.** NPV = $22,320
      b. NPV = ($5,596)

10-25 **a.** Project E   NPV = $2,130
         Project F   NPV = $1,678
         Project G   NPV = $1,144
      c. Project E   NPV = $834
         Project F   NPV = $1,678
         Project G   NPV = $2,138

10-29 **b.** X $920.04
         Y $1,079.54
         Z $772.80
         Y, X, Z

10-31 **b.** Projects C, F, and G

11-2 **b.** 12.4%

11-3 **a.** $980
      c. 12.31%
      d. 12.26%

11-4   A   5.66%
      E   7.10%

11-7 **c.** 16.54%
      d. 15.91%

11-11 **a.** Weighted cost 8.344%
      b. Weighted cost 10.848%

11-14 **a.** $k_i = 5.1\%$; $k_p = 8.4\%$; $k_n = 13.6\%$; $k_r = 13\%$
      b. (1) $200,000
         (2) 9.71%
         (3) 10.01%

12-4 **a.** $21,000
      d. $5,250

12-7 **a.** Q = 8,000 units
         D = $508,000
      e. 5.00

12-9 **a.** EPS = $0.375

12-11 **a.** DFL = 1.5

12-12 **a.** (1) 175,000 units
      d. DTL = 2.40

12-14

Debt ratio	Debt	Equity
40%	$400,000	$600,000

12-20 **a.** EBIT $60,000; $240,000; $420,000
      d. at 15% debt ratio, EPS = $0.85, $4.02, $7.20
      e. (1) at 15% debt ratio, expected EPS = $4.02
      g. $0 < EBIT < $80,000; choose 0%
         $80,001 < EBIT < $114,000; choose 15%
         $114,001 < EBIT < $163,000; choose 30%
         $163,001 < EBIT < $218,000; choose 45%
         $218,001 < EBIT < ∞; choose 60%
      h. at 15% debt ratio, share price = $38.29
      i. Maximize EPS at 60% debt ratio
         Maximize share value at 30% debt ratio

13-1 **b.** (1) $36,000
         (2) $10,333

13-2 Annual loan cost $1,200

13-4   a   December 25

13-6 Effective interest rate = 31.81%

13-8 $1,300,000

13-12 **a.** 9.0%
      b. 13.06%

13-14 Total $886,900

14-1 **a.** 120 days
      b. 3 times
      c. $10,000,000

14-2 **a.** 35 days
      c. $97,087

14-4 Plan E

14-7 **a.** 7 days
      b. $21,450

14-9 **a.** Maximum savings = $3,850
         Minimum savings = $1,100

14-14 $22,500 annual savings

14-18 **a.** 3.75%
      c. 2%
      f. 2.95%

15-1 **a.** Credit score applicant B   81.5

15-2 **b.** $75,000
      c. $9,000

15-4 **a.** Present plan: $20,000
         Proposed plan: $48,000

15-6 The credit standards should not be relaxed since the proposed plan results in a loss.

15-7 Net profit of the proposal $23,373

15-9 **a.** $14,000 additional profit
      b. $40,170 marginal investment in accounts receivable

15-11 **b.** $52,000 net savings

15-14 **c.** 4,000 units

15-17 **a.** 200 units   **b.** 122 units   **c.** 33 units

16-1 Bond A: **a.** Discount; **b.** $400,000; **c.** $16,000;
d. $320,000; **e.** $128,000

16-3 **b.** Bond B $20,000

16-4 **a.** Bond A $40,000
b. Bond A $16,000

16-5 **a.** $80,000
b. $8,000
c. $1,680,000

16-6 **a.** $1,294,000
b. $178,933
c. Net savings $237,666; bond refunding should be initiated.

16-8 $3.60 per share spread

17-1 **a.** Common stock (10,000 shares @ $1 par) $ 10,000
Paid in capital in excess of par   120,000
Common stock equity $130,000

17-2 **a.** Majority: A, B, C, D, E: (.54 × 1,000 = 540)
b. Majority can elect 3, and minority can elect 2.

17-5 Case E: (1) With rights $1.11
(2) Ex rights $1.11

17-7 **a.** 24,000 shares
b. 12.5 rights
c. 3,840 shares
d. (1) $R_w = \$0.296$
(2) $M_e = \$28.704$
$R_e = \$0.296$

17-10 **a.** $4.75/share
b. $0.40/share
d. A decrease in retained earnings and hence stockholder's equity by $80,000.

17-13 **a.** 1986 = $0.60
b. 1986 = $0.50
c. 1986 = $0.62
d. 1986 = $0.62

17-14 **a.** Retained earnings = $85,000
b. (1) Retained earnings = $70,000
(2) Retained earnings = $40,000

17-16 **a.** EPS = $2
b. 1%
c. 1%; stock dividends do not have a real value.

18-3 **a.** Preferred dividends = $14.875/share
Common dividends = $15.875/share
c. Preferred dividends = $10.00/share
Common dividends = $0.00/share

18-7 **b.** Lease–PV = $38,964
Purchase–PV = $39,754

18-9

Lease	Capitalized Value
A	$272,560
B	$596,160
E	$374,261

18-12 **a.** $1,250
b. $525
c. $1,050

18-15 **a.** $832.75
b. At $9: $720
c. At $9: $832.75

18-17 **a.** 160 shares, 400 warrants
b. 20%
c. 125%

18-20 **a.** $800 profit
b. $200
c. $68/share

19-1 **a.** Total tax liability = $1,680,000; per year = $112,000
b. Tax liability: Year 1 = $0
Year 2 = $0
Year 3 = $16,000
Years 4–15 = $112,000/year

19-3 **a.** Total tax advantage = $320,000; Years 1–4 = $80,000/year
b. Total tax advantage = $320,000
c. Reilly Investment Group: $228,400
Webster Industries: $205,288

19-5 **a.** Yes, the NPV = $42,150
b. Yes, the NPV = $101,000

19-6 **a.** EPS merged firm = $1.029
b. EPS Marla's = $1.00
c. EPS Victory = $2.139

19-8 Ratio of Exchange: (1) of shares; (2) market price
A: 0.60; 1.20
D: 0.25; 1.25
E: 1.00; 1.25

19-10 **a.** 1.125
b. Henry Co.: EPS = $2.50, P/E = 18
c. 16.89

19-15 Case II:
Unpaid balance of 2nd Mortgage $150,000
Accounts payable $ 75,000
Notes payable $ 75,000
Unsecured bonds $150,000

19-16 **b.** (1) 1st mortgage $661,539
2nd mortgage $246,154
Unsecured bonds $184,615

20-1 **a.** S1:50% directly owned by MNC
S1:17.5% owned by MNC
S1:4% owned by MNC

ABC system Divides inventory into three categories of descending importance, based on the dollar investment in each.

ability to service debts The ability of a firm to meet the contractual payments required on a scheduled basis over the life of a debt.

Accelerated Cost Recovery System (ACRS) System used to determine the depreciation of assets for tax purposes.

accept-reject approach The evaluation of capital expenditure proposals to determine whether they meet the firm's minimum acceptance criterion.

accounting exposure The risk resulting from the effects of changes in foreign exchange rates on the translated value of a firm's accounts denominated in a given foreign currency.

accrual method Method that recognizes revenue at the point of sale and recognizes expenses when incurred.

accruals Liabilities for services received for which payment has yet to be made.

activity ratios Ratios used to measure the speed with which various accounts are converted into sales or cash.

adjustable-rate (or floating-rate) preferred stock (ARPS) Preferred stock whose dividend rate is tied to interest rates on specific government securities.

agency costs Costs borne by stockholders to prevent or minimize agency problems and to contribute to the maximization of the owners' wealth. They include monitoring, bonding, and structuring expenditures and opportunity costs.

agency problem The likelihood that managers may place personal goals ahead of corporate goals.

aggressive financing strategy Plan by which the firm finances its seasonal needs with short-term funds and its permanent needs with long-term funds.

aging A technique for providing information concerning the proportion of the accounts receivable balance that has been outstanding for a specified period of time.

all-current-rate method The method by which the *functional currency*-denominated financial statements of an MNC's subsidiary are translated into the parent company's currency.

annual cleanup The requirement that for a certain number of days annually borrowers under a line of credit carry a zero loan balance (i.e., owe the bank nothing).

annual percentage rate (APR) In consumer finance, the effective interest rate which must be clearly stated to borrowers and depositors.

annualized net present value (ANPV) approach An approach to evaluating unequal-lived projects that converts the net present value of unequal-lived, mutually exclusive projects into an equivalent (in NPV terms) annual amount.

annuity A stream of equal annual cash flows. These cash flows can be inflows of returns earned on investments or outflows of funds invested in order to earn future returns.

articles of partnership The written contract used to formally establish a business partnership.

assignment A voluntary liquidation procedure by which a firm's creditors pass the power to liquidate the firm's assets to an adjustment bureau, trade association, or a third party, which is designated the *assignee*.

authorized (stock) The shares of common stock that a firm is allowed (authorized) to issue, the number of which is stated in the corporate charter.

average age of inventory Average length of time inventory is held by the firm.

average collection period The average amount of time needed to collect accounts receivable.

average payment period The average amount of time needed to pay accounts payable.

balance sheet Summary statement of the firm's financial position at a given point in time.

balloon payment At the maturity of a loan, a large lump-sum payment representing the entire loan principal if the periodic payments represent only interest.

banker's acceptances Short-term, low-risk marketable securities arising from bank guarantees of business transactions; they are sold by banks at a discount from their maturity value and provide yields competitive with negotiable CDs and commercial paper.

bankruptcy Business failure that occurs when a firm's liabilities exceed the fair market value of its assets.

Bankruptcy Reform Act of 1978 The current governing bankruptcy legislation in the United States.

bar chart The simplest type of probability distribution showing only a limited number of outcomes and associated probabilities for a given event.

best efforts basis A public offering in which the investment banker uses its resources to sell the security issue without taking on the risk of underwriting and is compensated on the basis of the number of securities sold.

beta coefficient (*b*) A measure of nondiversifiable risk. An index of the degree of movement of an asset's return in response to a change in the market return.

blue sky laws State laws aimed at regulating the sale of securities within the state and thereby protecting investors.

board of directors Group elected by the firm's stockholders and having ultimate authority to guide corporate affairs and make general policy.

bond Long-term debt instrument used by businesses and government to raise large sums of money, generally from a diverse group of lenders.

bond indenture A complex and lengthy legal document stating the conditions under which a bond has been issued.

book value The strict accounting value of an asset, calculated by subtracting its accumulated depreciation from installed cost.

book value per share The amount per share of common stock to be received if all assets are liquidated for their book value, and if the proceeds remaining after paying all liabilities (including preferred stock) are divided among the common stockholders.

book value weights Use accounting values to measure the proportion of each type of capital in the firm's structure; used in calculating the weighted average cost of capital.

breadth of a market Determined by the number of participants (buyers).

breakeven analysis (cost-volume-profit analysis) Used (1) to determine the level of operations necessary to cover all operating costs and (2) to evaluate the profitability associated with various levels of sales.

breakeven cash inflow The level of cash inflow necessary for a project to be acceptable.

breaking point The level of total financing at which the cost of one of the financing components rises, thereby causing an upward shift in the weighted marginal cost of capital (WMCC).

business risk The risk to the firm of being unable to cover operating costs.

call feature A feature included in almost all corporate bond issues giving the issuer the opportunity to repurchase bonds prior to maturity at a stated price.

call option An option to purchase a specified number of shares (typically 100) of a stock on or before some future date at a stated price.

call premium The amount by which a bond's call price exceeds its par value.

call price The stated price at which a bond may be repurchased, by use of a call feature, prior to maturity.

capital The long-term funds of the firm; all items on the right-hand side of the firm's balance sheet, excluding current liabilities.

capital asset pricing model (CAPM) The basic theory that links together risk and return for all assets; describes the relationship between the required return, or cost of common stock equity capital, k_s, and the nondiversifiable risk of the firm as measured by the beta coefficient, b.

capital budgeting The process of evaluating and selecting long-term investments consistent with the firm's goal of owner wealth maximization.

capital budgeting process Consists of five distinct but interrelated steps: proposal generation, review and analysis, decision making, implementation, and follow-up.

capital expenditure An outlay of funds by the firm that is expected to produce benefits over a period greater than one year.

capital gain The amount by which the price at which an asset was sold exceeds the asset's purchase price.

capitalized lease A financial (capital) lease that has the present value of all its payments included as an asset and corresponding liability on the firm's balance sheet, as required by Financial Accounting Standards Board (FASB) Standard No. 13.

capital market A financial relationship created by institutions and arrangements that allows suppliers and demanders of long-term funds to make transactions.

capital rationing The financial situation in which a firm has only a fixed number of dollars for allocation among competing capital expenditures.

capital structure The mix of long-term debt and equity maintained by the firm.

carrying costs The variable costs per unit of holding an item in inventory for a specified time period.

cash The ready currency to which all liquid assets can be reduced.

cash bonuses Bonus money paid to management for meeting stated performance goals.

cash budget (cash forecast) Financial projection of the firm's short-term cash surpluses or shortages.

cash cycle The amount of time elapsed from the point when an outlay is made to purchase raw materials to the point when cash is collected from the sale of the finished product using the raw material.

cash disbursements All cash outlays by the firm during a given financial period.

cash discount A percentage deduction from the purchase price if the buyer pays within a specified time shorter than the credit period.

cash discount period The number of days after the beginning of the credit period during which the cash discount is available.

cash method Method that recognizes revenues and expenses only with respect to actual inflows and outflows of cash.

cash receipts All items from which the firm receives cash inflows during a given financial period.

cash turnover The number of times per year the firm's cash is turned into a marketable product and then back into cash.

certainty equivalents (CEs) Risk-adjustment factors that represent the percent of estimated cash inflow that investors would be satisfied to receive for *certain* rather than the cash inflows that are *possible* for each year.

change in net working capital The difference between a change in current assets and a change in current liabilities.

Chapter 11 The portion of the Bankruptcy Reform Act of 1978 that outlines the procedures for reorganizing a failed firm, whether its petition is filed voluntarily or involuntarily.

Chapter 7 The portion of the Bankruptcy Reform Act of 1978 that details the procedures to be followed when liquidating a failed firm.

chief executive officer (CEO) See *president.*

clearing float The delay between the deposit of a check by the payee and the actual availability of the funds.

clientele effect The theory that a firm will attract stockholders whose preferences with respect to the payment and stability of dividends correspond to the payment pattern and stability of the firm itself.

closely owned (stock) All common stock of a firm owned by a small group of investors such as a family.

coefficient of variation (CV) A measure of relative dispersion used in comparing the risk of assets with differing expected returns.

collateral The security offered the lender by the borrower, usually in the form of an asset such as accounts receivable or inventory.

collection float The delay between the time when a payer or customer deducts a payment from the checking account ledger and the time when the payee or vendor actually receives the funds in a spendable form.

collection policies The procedures for collecting a firm's accounts receivable when they are due.

commercial finance companies Lending institutions that make *only* secured loans—both short- and long-term—to businesses.

commercial paper A form of financing consisting of a short-term, unsecured promissory note issued by a corporation with a very high credit standing, having a yield slightly below that of negotiable CDs but above that of comparable government issues.

commitment fee The fee normally charged on a revolving credit agreement, often based on the average unused balance of the borrower's credit line.

common-size income statement An income statement in which each item is expressed as a percentage of sales.

common stock Collectively, units of ownership interest, or equity, in a corporation.

compensating balance A required checking account balance equal to a certain percentage of the borrower's short-term unsecured loan.

competitive bidding A method of choosing an investment banker, in which the banker that bids the highest price for a security issue is awarded the issue.

composition A pro rata cash settlement of creditor claims by the debtor firm; a uniform percentage of each dollar owed is paid.

compounded interest When the amount earned on a given deposit has become part of the principal at the end of a specified period.

concentration banking Reduces collection float by shortening mail and clearing float. Payments are made to regionally dispersed collection centers, then deposited in local banks for quick clearing.

conflicting rankings Conflicts in the ranking of a given project by NPV and IRR that result from differences in the magnitude and timing of cash flows.

conservative financing strategy Plan by which the firm finances all projected funds needs with long-term funds and uses short-term financing only for emergencies or unexpected outflows.

consolidation The combination of two or more companies to form a completely new corporation.

constant growth model A widely cited dividend valuation approach that assumes dividends will grow at a constant rate that is less than the required return.

constant growth valuation (Gordon) model Model which assumes that the value of a share of stock equals the present value of all future dividends (assumed to grow at a constant rate) it will provide over an infinite time horizon.

constant-payout-ratio dividend policy A dividend policy based on the payment of a certain percentage of earnings to owners in each dividend period.

continuous compounding Compounding of interest an infinite number of times per year, at intervals of microseconds.

continuous probability distribution A probability distribution showing all the possible outcomes and associated probabilities for a given event.

controlled disbursing The strategic use of mailing points and bank accounts to lengthen mail float and clearing float, respectively.

controller The officer responsible for the firm's accounting activities, such as tax management, data processing, and cost and financial accounting.

conventional cash flow pattern An initial outflow followed by a series of inflows.

conversion feature A provision permitting the holder of a preferred stock (or bond) to transfer it into a specified number of shares of common stock.

conversion price The per-share price effectively paid for common stock as the result of conversion of a convertible security.

conversion ratio The ratio at which a convertible security can be exchanged for common stock.

conversion value The value of the convertible security measured in terms of the market price of the common stock into which it can be converted. Also called *stock value.*

convertible bond A bond that at some future time can be converted into a specified number of shares of common stock.

convertible preferred stock Preferred stock that at some future time can be converted into a specified number of shares of common stock.

corporate bond A certificate indicating that a corporation has borrowed a certain amount of money from an institution or an individual and promises to repay it in the future under clearly defined terms.

corporation An intangible business entity created by law (often called a "legal entity").

correlation A statistical measure of the relationship, if any, between series of numbers representing data of any kind.

correlation coefficient A measure of the degree of correlation between two series.

cost of a new asset The net outlay required to purchase a new asset.

cost of a new issue of common stock, k_n Determined by calculating the cost of common stock after considering both the amount of underpricing and the associated flotation costs.

cost of capital The rate of return a firm must earn on its investments in order to maintain its market value and attract needed funds.

cost of common stock equity, k_s The rate at which investors discount the expected dividends of the firm in order to determine its share value.

cost of forgoing a cash discount The implied rate of interest paid in order to delay payment of an account payable for an additional number of days.

cost of long-term debt (bonds), k_i The after-tax cost today of raising long-term funds through borrowing.

cost of preferred stock, k_p The annual preferred stock dividend, D_p, divided by the net proceeds from the sale of the preferred stock, N_p.

cost of retained earnings, k_r The same as the cost of an equivalent fully subscribed issue of additional common stock, which is measured by the cost of common stock equity, k_s.

coverage ratios Ratios that measure the firm's ability to meet certain fixed charges.

credit analysis The evaluation of a credit applicant to estimate creditworthiness and the maximum amount of credit to extend.

creditor control An arrangement in which a creditor committee replaces the firm's operating management and operates the firm until all claims have been settled.

credit period The number of days until full payment of an account payable is required.

credit policy Guidelines for determining whether to extend credit to a customer and how much credit to extend.

credit scoring The ranking of an applicant's overall credit strength, derived as a weighted average of scores on key financial and credit characteristics.

credit standards The minimum criteria for the extension of credit to a customer.

credit terms Specification of the repayment terms required of a firm's credit customers.

cross-sectional analysis The comparison of different firms' financial ratios at the same point in time.

cumulative preferred stock Preferred stock for which all passed (unpaid) dividends in arrears must be paid prior to payment of dividends to common stockholders.

cumulative voting system The system under which each share of common stock is allotted a number of votes equal to the total number of corporate directors to be elected and votes can be given to any director.

current assets Short-term assets, expected to be converted into cash within one year or less.

current expenditure An outlay of funds by the firm resulting in benefits received within one year.

current liabilities Short-term liabilities, expected to be converted into cash within one year or less.

current ratio A measure of liquidity calculated by dividing the firm's current assets by current liabilities.

date of invoice Indicates that the beginning of the credit period is the date on the invoice for the purchase.

date of record (dividends) The date, set by the firm's directors, on which all persons whose names are recorded as stockholders will at a specified future time receive a declared dividend.

date of record (rights) The last date on which the recipient of a right must be the legal owner shown in the company's stock ledger.

debt capital All long-term borrowing incurred by the firm.

debt-equity ratio Measures the ratio of long-term debt to stockholders' equity.

debtor in possession (DIP) The term assigned to a firm that files a reorganization petition under Chapter 11 and then develops, if feasible, a reorganization plan.

debt ratio Measures the proportion of total assets provided by the firm's creditors.

degree of financial leverage (DFL) The numerical measure of the firm's financial leverage.

degree of indebtedness Measures amount of debt against other significant balance sheet amounts.

degree of operating leverage (DOL) The numerical measure of the firm's operating leverage.

degree of total leverage (DTL) The numerical measure of the firm's total leverage.

Depository Institutions Deregulation and Monetary Control Act of 1980 (DIDMCA) Signaled the beginning of the "financial services revolution" by eliminating interest-rate ceilings on all accounts, permitting certain institutions to offer new types of accounts and services.

depository transfer check (DTC) An unsigned check drawn on one of the firm's bank accounts and deposited into its account at a concentration or major disbursement bank, thereby avoiding clearance delays.

depreciable life Time period over which an asset is depreciated.

depreciation The systematic charging of a portion of the cost of a fixed asset against the annual revenues generated by the asset.

depth of a market Determined by its ability to absorb the purchase or sale of a large dollar amount of a particular security.

dilution of ownership Occurs when a new stock issue results in each present stockholder having a claim on a smaller part of the firm's earnings than previously.

direct lease A lease under which a lessor owns or acquires the assets that are leased to a given lessee.

direct send Reduces clearing float by allowing the payee to present payment checks directly to the banks on which they are drawn, thus avoiding the delay of the clearing process.

disbursement float The lapse between the time when a firm deducts a payment from its checking account ledger (disburses it) and the time when funds are actually withdrawn from its account.

discount The amount by which a bond sells at a value that is less than its par, or face, value.

discounting cash flows The process of finding present values; the inverse of compounding interest.

discount loans Loans on which interest is paid in advance.

diversifiable risk The portion of an asset's risk attributable to firm-specific, random events that can be eliminated through diversification.

divestiture The selling of some of a firm's assets.

dividend payout ratio Calculated by dividing the firm's cash dividend per share by its earnings per share, thereby indicating the percentage of each dollar earned that is distributed to the owners in the form of cash.

dividend policy The firm's plan of action to be followed whenever a decision concerning dividends must be made.

dividend reinvestment plans Plans offered by firms that enable stockholders to use dividends to acquire full or fractional shares at little or no transaction (brokerage) cost.

dividends Periodic distributions of earnings to the owners of stock in a firm.

double taxation Occurs when the already once-taxed earnings of a corporation are distributed as dividends to the firm's stockholders, who are then taxed again on these dividends.

Dun & Bradstreet The largest mercantile credit-reporting agency in the United States.

DuPont formula Relates the firm's net profit margin and total asset turnover to its return on investment (ROI). The ROI is the product of the net profit margin and the total asset turnover.

DuPont system of analysis System used by management as a framework for dissecting the firm's financial statements and assessing its financial condition.

earnings per share (EPS) The total earnings available for a firm's common stockholders divided by the number of shares of common stock outstanding.

EBIT–EPS approach Involves selecting the capital structure that maximizes earnings per share (EPS) over the expected range of earnings before interest and taxes (EBIT).

economic exposure The risk resulting from the effects of changes in foreign exchange rates on the firm's value.

economic order quantity (EOQ) model A technique for determining the optimal order quantity of an inventory item, based on the trade-off between various operating and financial inventory costs.

effective (true) interest rate The rate of interest actually paid or earned; commonly called the *annual percentage rate (APR)*. In the international context, the rate equals the nominal rate plus (or minus) any forecast appreciation (or depreciation) of a foreign currency relative to the currency of the MNC parent.

efficient market An assumed "perfect" market in which there are many small investors, each having the same information with respect to securities; there are no restrictions on investment, no taxes, and no transaction costs; and all investors view securities similarly and prefer higher returns and lower risk.

efficient portfolio A portfolio that maximizes return for a given level of risk or minimizes risk for a given level of return.

ending cash The sum of the firm's beginning cash and its net cash flow for the period.

end of month (EOM) Indicates that the credit period for all purchases made within a given month begins on the first day of the month immediately following.

equity capital The long-term funds provided by the firm's owners, the stockholders.

equity multiplier The ratio of the firm's total assets to stockholders' equity.

Eurobond An international bond sold primarily in countries other than the country of the currency in which the issue is denominated.

Eurocurrency markets The portion of the Euromarket that provides short-term foreign-currency financing to subsidiaries of MNCs.

Eurodollar deposits Deposits denominated in U.S. dollars and deposited in banks outside the United States, having varying maturities, and having yields above nearly all other marketable securities.

Euro-equity market The capital market that deals in international equity issues, the center of which is London.

Euromarket The international financial market that provides for borrowing and lending currencies outside their country of origin.

excess cash balance The (excess) amount available for investment by the firm if the period's ending cash is greater than the minimum cash balance.

excess earnings accumulation tax The tax levied by the IRS on retained earnings above $250,000, when it has determined that the firm has accumulated an excess of earnings in order to allow owners to delay paying ordinary income taxes.

ex dividend Period beginning four business days prior to the date of record during which a stock will be sold without paying the current dividend.

exercise price (option price) The per-share price at which holders of warrants can purchase a specified number of shares of common stock.

expected value of a return (k) The most likely return on a given asset.

ex rights The condition under which stock is sold for a period without announced rights being attached to the stock.

extension An arrangement whereby the firm's creditors receive payment in full, although not immediately.

external forecast A sales forecast based on the relationships observed between the firm's sales and certain key external economic indicators.

external funds required ("plug" figure) Under the judgmental approach for developing a pro forma balance sheet, the amount of external financing needed to bring the statement into balance.

extra dividend An additional dividend optionally paid by the firm if earnings are higher than normal in a given period.

factor A financial institution that specializes in purchasing accounts receivable from businesses.

factoring accounts receivable The outright sale of accounts receivable at a discount to a factor or other financial institution in order to obtain funds.

FASB No. 52 Statement issued by the FASB requiring U.S. multinationals first to convert the financial statement accounts of foreign subsidiaries into their *functional currency* and then to translate the accounts into the parent firm's currency using the *all-current-rate method*.

federal agency issues Low-risk securities issued by government agencies but not guaranteed by the U.S. Treasury, having generally short maturities and offering slightly higher yields than comparable Treasury issues.

federal funds Loan transactions between commercial banks in which the Federal Reserve banks become involved.

fidelity bond A contract under which a bonding company agrees to reimburse a firm if a specified manager's dishonest act results in a financial loss to the firm.

finance The art and science of managing money.

Financial Accounting Standards Board (FASB) The accounting profession's rule-setting body, which authorizes generally accepted accounting principles (GAAP).

financial and legal flows Cash flows that include receipt and payment of interest, payment and refund of taxes, incurrence and repayment of debt, payment of dividends and stock repurchases, and cash inflow from sale of stock.

financial breakeven point The level of EBIT necessary to cover required financial obligations; the level of EBIT at which EPS = $0.

financial institution An intermediary that channels the savings of individuals, businesses, and governments into loans or investments.

financial lease A longer-term lease than an operating lease that is noncancelable and obligates the lessee to make payments for the use of an asset over a predefined period of time. Also called *capital lease*.

financial leverage The magnification of risk and return introduced through the use of more fixed-cost financing relative to the firm's total assets.

financial manager The officer who actively manages the financial affairs of any type of business, whether financial or nonfinancial, private or public, profit or not-for-profit.

financial markets Markets that provide a forum in which suppliers of funds and demanders of loans and investments can transact business directly.

financial planning process Planning that begins with long-run (strategic) financial plans that in turn guide the formulation of short-run (operating) plans and budgets.

financial risk The risk to the firm of being unable to cover required financial obligations.

financial services The area of finance concerned with design and delivery of advice and financial products to individuals, business, and government.

financial supermarket An institution at which the customer can obtain a full array of the financial services now allowed under the Depository Institutions Deregulation and Monetary Control Act of 1980 (DIDMCA).

finished goods inventory Items that have been produced but not yet sold.

fixed asset turnover Measures the efficiency with which the firm has been using its *fixed*, or earning, assets to generate sales.

fixed-payment coverage ratio Measures the firm's ability to meet all fixed-payment obligations.

fixed-rate note A note whose rate of interest is determined as a set increment above the prime rate and remains unvarying at that rate until maturity.

fixed (or semi-fixed) relationship The constant (or relatively constant) relationship of the values of two currencies with respect to each other.

float Funds dispatched by a payer that are not yet in a form that can be spent by the payee.

floating inventory lien A lender's claim on the borrower's general inventory as collateral for a secured loan.

floating-rate note A note whose rate of interest is established as an increment above the prime rate and is allowed to "float," or vary, above prime *as the prime rate varies* until maturity.

floating relationship The fluctuating relationship of the values of two currencies with respect to each other.

flotation costs The total costs of issuing and selling a security.

foreign bond An international bond sold primarily in the country of the currency of the issue.

foreign direct investment (FDI) The transfer, by a multinational firm, of capital, managerial, and technical assets from its home country to a host country.

foreign exchange rate The value of two currencies with respect to each other.

foreign exchange risk The risk caused by varying exchange rates between two currencies.

forward exchange rate The rate of exchange between two currencies at some specified future date.

functional currency The currency of the economic environment in which a financial entity primarily generates and expends cash, and in which its accounts are maintained.

funds Either cash or net working capital.

future value The value of a present sum at a future date found by applying compound interest over a specified period of time.

future-value interest factor The multiplier used to calculate at a specified interest rate the future value of a present amount as of a given time.

future-value interest factor for an annuity The multiplier used to calculate the future value of an annuity at a specified interest rate over a given period of time.

generally accepted accounting principles (GAAP) The practice and procedure guidelines used to prepare and maintain financial records and reports; authorized by the Financial Accounting Standards Board (FASB).

Gordon model A common name for the *constant growth model* widely used in dividend valuation.

government security dealer An institution that purchases for resale government securities and other money market instruments.

grossing up procedure A taxation technique in which an MNC's U.S. income is increased by the amount of foreign income (before foreign taxes), and the U.S. tax calculation is based on that higher level.

gross profit margin Indicates the percentage of each sales dollar left after the firm has paid for its goods.

hedging strategies Techniques used to offset risk; in the international context, these include borrowing or lending in different currencies, undertaking contracts in the forward, futures, and/or options markets, and also swapping assets/liabilities with other parties.

historic weights Either book or market value weights based on actual capital structure proportions; used in calculating the weighted average cost of capital.

holders of record Owners of the firm's shares on the date of record. For stock rights they may exercise their rights, sell them, or let them expire; for dividends, they are the recipients.

holding company A corporation that has voting control of one or more other corporations.

income statement Provides a financial summary of the firm's operating results during a specified period.

incremental cash flows The *additional* cash flows—outflows or inflows—expected to result from a proposed capital expenditure.

independent projects Projects that do not compete with one another for the firm's investment, so that the acceptance of one does not eliminate the others from further consideration.

informational content The information provided by the dividends of a firm that causes owners to bid up the price of the stock based on future earnings expectations.

initial investment The relevant cash outflow at time zero.

installation costs Any added costs necessary to place an asset into operation.

interest rate The compensation paid by a borrower of funds to the lender; from the borrower's point of view, the cost of borrowing funds.

intermediate cash inflows Cash inflows received prior to the termination of a project.

internal forecast A sales forecast based on a buildup, or consensus, of forecasts through the firm's own sales channels.

internal rate of return (IRR) The discount rate that equates the present value of cash inflows with the initial investment associated with a project, thereby causing NPV = \$0.

internal rate of return approach An approach to capital rationing that involves the graphic plotting of project IRRs in descending order against the total dollar investment.

international bond A bond initially sold outside the country of the borrower and often distributed in several countries.

inventory turnover Measures the activity, or liquidity, of a firm's inventory.

investment banker An individual engaged by a firm to solicit buyers for new security issues.

investment opportunities schedule (IOS) A ranking of investment possibilities from best (highest returns) to worst (lowest returns); the graph that plots project IRRs in descending order against total dollar investment.

involuntary reorganization A petition initiated by an outside party, usually a creditor, for the reorganization and payment of creditors of a failed firm.

issued (stock) Shares of common stock put forth into circulation, which may be more in number than shares of outstanding stock.

joint venture A partnership under which the participants have contractually agreed to contribute specified amounts of money and expertise in exchange for stated proportions of ownership and profit.

judgmental approach A method of developing the pro forma balance sheet in which the values of certain accounts are estimated while others are calculated, using the firm's external financing as a balancing, or ''plug,'' figure.

leasing The process by which a firm can obtain the use of certain fixed assets through a series of contractual, periodic, tax-deductible payments.

lessee The receiver of the services of the assets under a lease contract.

lessor The owner of assets which are being leased.

leverage Results from the use of fixed-cost assets or funds to magnify returns to the firm's owners.

leveraged buyout (LBO) An acquisition technique in which a large amount of debt is used to purchase a firm.

leveraged lease A lease under which the lessor acts as an equity participant, supplying only about 20 percent of the cost of the asset, while a lender supplies the balance.

lien A publicly disclosed legal claim on collateral.

limited partner A partner having limited liability and normally prohibited from active management participation in the firm.

limited partnership Business relationship in which one or more partners can be assigned to have limited liability but in which one partner must assume unlimited liability.

line of credit An agreement between a commercial bank and a business specifying the maximum amount of unsecured short-term borrowing the bank will make available to the customer over a given period of time.

liquidation value per share The *actual* amount per share of common stock to be received if all the firm's assets are sold, liabilities (including preferred stock) are paid, and the remaining proceeds divided among the common stockholders.

liquidity A firm's ability to satisfy its short-term obligations as they come due.

liquidity preferences General preferences of investors for shorter-term securities.

loan amortization The determination of the equal annual loan payments necessary to provide a lender with a specified interest return and repay the loan principal over a specified period.

loan amortization schedule A schedule of equal payments to repay a loan. It shows the allocation of each loan payment to interest and principal.

lockbox system Reduces collection float by having the payer send the payment to a nearby post office box that is emptied by the firm's bank several times daily, thus accelerating the deposit process.

long-run (strategic) financial plans Planned long-term financial actions and the anticipated financial impact of those actions.

long-term financing Financing with an initial maturity of more than one year.

long-term funds The sum of the firm's long-term debt and stockholders' equity.

low-regular-and-extra dividend policy A dividend policy based on paying a low regular dividend, supplemented by an additional dividend when earnings warrant it.

M and M approach Named for its initial proponents, Franco Modigliani and Merton H. Miller, the theory that an optimal capital structure does *not* exist.

macro political risk The subjection of *all* foreign firms to political risk (takeover) by a host country, due to political change, revolution, or the adoption of new policies.

mail float The delay between the time when a payer mails a payment and the time when the payee receives it.

maintenance clauses Provisions within an operating lease requiring the lessor to maintain the assets and make insurance and tax payments.

majority voting system The system whereby, in the election of the board of directors, each stockholder is entitled to one vote for each share of stock owned, and he or she can vote all shares for *each* director.

managerial finance The area of finance concerned with the duties of the financial manager in the business firm.

marginal analysis A type of analysis that states that financial decisions should be made and actions taken only when added benefits exceed added costs.

marginal tax rate The rate at which additional income is taxed.

marketable securities Short-term, interest-earning money market instruments issued by government, business, and financial institutions and purchased by others to obtain a return on temporarily idle funds.

market premium The amount by which the market value exceeds the straight or conversion value of a convertible security.

market return The return on the market portfolio of all traded securities.

market risk-return function A graph of the discount rates associated with each level of project risk.

market value weights Use market values to measure the proportion of each type of capital in the firm's structure; used in calculating the weighted average cost of capital.

merger Generally, the combination of two firms of unequal size, in which the identity of the larger of the two firms is maintained.

micro political risk The subjection of an individual firm, a specific industry, or companies from a particular foreign country to political risk (takeover) by the host country.

mixed stream A series of cash flows exhibiting any pattern other than that of an annuity.

modified DuPont formula Relates the firm's return on investment (ROI) to its return on equity (ROE) using the *equity multiplier*.

money market A financial relationship created between suppliers and demanders of *short-term funds*.

money market mutual funds Portfolios (groups) of various popular marketable securities, having instant liquidity, competitive yields, and low transactions costs.

multinational companies (MNCs) Firms that have international assets and operations in foreign markets and draw part of their total revenues and profits from such markets.

mutually exclusive projects Projects that compete with one another, so that the acceptance of one eliminates the others from consideration.

national entry control systems Comprehensive rules, regulations, and incentives aimed at regulating inflows of foreign direct investments involving MNCs and at the same time extracting more benefits from their presence.

negatively correlated Descriptive of two series that move in opposite directions.

negotiable certificates of deposit (CDs) Negotiable instruments representing specific cash deposits in commercial banks, having varying maturities and yields based on size, maturity, and prevailing money market conditions. Yields are generally comparable to or a bit above those of commercial paper.

negotiated offering A security issue for which the investment banker is merely hired rather than awarded the issue through competitive bidding.

net cash flow The mathematical difference between the firm's cash receipts and its cash disbursements in each period.

net present value (NPV) Found by subtracting a project's initial investment from the present value of the cash inflows discounted at a rate equal to the firm's cost of capital.

net present value approach An approach to capital rationing that involves the use of present values to determine the group of projects that will maximize owners' wealth.

net present value profiles Graphs that depict the net present value of a project for various discount rates.

net proceeds Funds actually received from the sale of a security.

net profit margin Measures the percentage of each sales dollar left after all expenses, including taxes, have been deducted.

net working capital A measure of liquidity calculated by subtracting total current liabilities from total current assets; alternatively, the portion of a firm's current assets financed with long-term funds.

nominal (stated) interest rate The rate of interest, agreed upon contractually, charged by the supplier of funds and paid by the demander. In the international context, the stated interest rate charged on financing when only the MNC parent's currency is involved.

noncash charges Expenses deducted on the income statement that do not involve an actual outlay of cash during the period.

nonconventional cash flow pattern A pattern in which an initial outlay is *not* followed by a series of inflows.

noncumulative preferred stock Preferred stock for which passed (unpaid) dividends do not accumulate.

nondiversifiable risk The relevant portion of an asset's risk attributable to factors that affect all firms; it cannot be eliminated through diversification.

nonnotification basis The basis on which a borrower, having pledged an account receivable, continues to collect the account payments without notifying the account customer.

nonparticipating preferred stock Preferred stock whose stockholders receive only the specified dividend payments.

nonrecourse basis The basis on which accounts receivable are sold to a factor with the understanding that the factor accepts all credit risks on the purchased accounts.

nonvoting common stock Common stock that carries no voting rights; typically designated as class A common stock.

no-par preferred stock Preferred stock that has a stated annual dollar dividend, but no stated face value.

no par value Used to describe stock issued without a par value, in which case the stock may be assigned a value or placed on the books at the price at which it is sold.

normal probability distribution A symmetrical probability distribution whose shape resembles a bell-shaped curve.

notification basis The basis on which an account customer whose account has been pledged or factored is notified to remit payments directly to the lender or factor rather than to the borrower.

offshore centers Certain cities around the world (including London, Singapore, Bahrain, Nassau, Hong Kong, and Luxembourg) that have achieved prominence as major offshore centers for Euromarket business.

operating breakeven point The level of sales necessary to cover all operating costs; the point at which EBIT = \$0.

operating cash inflows The incremental after-tax cash inflows resulting from use of a project during its life.

operating change restrictions Contractual restrictions that a bank may impose on a firm as part of a line of credit agreement.

operating lease A cancelable contractual arrangement whereby the lessee agrees to make the periodic payments to the lessor for five or fewer years for an asset's services.

operating leverage The potential use of fixed operating costs to magnify the effects of changes in sales on earnings before interest and taxes (EBIT).

operating profit margin Measures the percentage of profit earned on each sales dollar before interest and taxes.

operating unit A part of a business, such as a plant, division, or subsidiary, that contributes to the actual operations of the firm.

opportunity cost The cost to the firm of forgone returns due to its failure to undertake available investment opportunities.

optimal capital structure Under the *traditional approach* to capital structure, the capital structure at which the weighted average cost of capital is minimized, thereby maximizing the firm's value.

option An instrument that provides its holder with an opportunity to purchase or sell a specified asset at a stated price on or before a set expiration date.

order costs The fixed clerical costs of placing and receiving an inventory order.

ordinary income Income earned through the sale of a firm's goods or services.

organized securities exchanges Tangible organizations on whose premises outstanding securities are resold.

outstanding (stock) Shares of common stock currently under ownership of the firm's shareholders.

overdraft system Automatic coverage by the bank of all checks presented against the firm's account, regardless of the account balance.

overhanging issue A convertible security that cannot be forced into conversion using the call feature.

oversubscribed issue A security issue that is sold out.

oversubscription privilege Provides for distribution of shares for which rights were not exercised to interested shareholders on a pro rata basis.

over-the-counter (OTC) exchange Not an organization, but an intangible market for the purchasers and sellers of securities not listed by the organized exchanges.

paid-in capital in excess of par The amount of proceeds in excess of the par value received from the original sale of common stock.

participating preferred stock Preferred stock that provides for dividend payments based on certain formulas allowing preferred stockholders to participate with common stockholders in the receipt of dividends beyond a specified amount.

partnership A business owned by two or more persons and operated for profit.

par value Per-share value arbitrarily assigned to an issue of common stock primarily for accounting purposes.

par-value preferred stock Preferred stock with a stated face value that is used with the stated dividend percentage to determine the annual dollar dividend.

payable-through draft A draft drawn on the payer's checking account, payable to a given payee but not payable on demand; approval of the draft by the payer is required before the bank pays the draft.

payback period The exact amount of time required for a firm to recover its initial investment as calculated from cash inflows.

payment date The actual date on which the company will mail the dividend payment to the holders of record.

percentage advance The percent of the book value of the collateral that constitutes the principal of a secured loan.

percent-of-sales method A method for developing the pro forma income statement that expresses the cost of goods sold, operating expenses, and interest expense as a percentage of projected sales.

perfectly negatively correlated Describes two negatively correlated series having a correlation coefficient of -1.

perfectly positively correlated Describes two positively correlated series having a correlation coefficient of $+1$.

performance shares Shares of stock given to management as a result of meeting stated performance goals.

permanent need Financing requirements for the firm's fixed assets plus the permanent portion of the firm's current assets; these requirements remain unchanged over the year.

perpetuity An annuity with an infinite life, making continual annual payments.

playing the float A method of consciously anticipating the resulting float, or delay, associated with the payment process.

pledge of accounts receivable The use of a firm's accounts receivable as security, or collateral, to obtain a short-term loan.

political risk The potential discontinuity or seizure of an MNC's operations in a host country due to the host's implementation of specific rules and regulations (such as nationalization, expropriation, and confiscation).

portfolio A collection, or group, of assets.

positively correlated Descriptive of two series that move in the same direction.

preauthorized check (PAC) A check written by the payee against a customer's checking account for a previously agreed-upon amount. Due to prior legal authorization, the check does not require the customer's signature.

preemptive rights Rights that allow common stockholders to maintain their proportionate ownership in the corporation when new issues are made.

preferred stock A special form of stock having a fixed periodic dividend that must be paid prior to payment of any common stock dividends.

premium The amount by which a bond sells at a value that is greater than its par, or face, value.

present value The current dollar value of a future sum. The amount that would have to be invested today at a given interest rate over the period in order to equal the future sum.

present-value interest factor The multiplier used to calculate at a specified discount rate the present value of an amount to be received in a future period.

present-value interest factor for an annuity The multiplier used to calculate the present value of an annuity at a specified discount rate over a given period of time.

president or chief executive officer (CEO) Corporate official responsible for managing the firm's day-to-day operations and executing the policies established by the board of directors.

president's letter The first component of the annual stockholders' report, and the primary communication from management to the firm's owners.

price/earnings multiple approach A technique whereby the firm's expected earnings per share (EPS) are multiplied by the average price/earnings (P/E) ratio for the industry to estimate the firm's share value.

price/earnings (P/E) ratio Represents the amount investors are willing to pay for each dollar of the firm's earnings.

price pegging Placing orders to buy one's own underwritten security in order to keep the demand for the issue, and therefore the price, at the desired level.

primary market Financial market in which securities are initially issued; the only market in which the issuer is directly involved in the transaction.

prime rate of interest (prime rate) The lowest interest rate charged by leading banks for business loans to their most important and reliable business borrowers.

principal The amount of money on which interest is paid.

privately owned (stock) All common stock of a firm owned by a single individual.

private placement The direct sale of a new security issue, typically debt or preferred stock, to a selected investor or group of investors.

probability The *percentage chance* that a given outcome will occur.

probability distribution A model that relates probabilities to the associated outcomes.

proceeds from the sale of an old asset The net cash inflow resulting from the sale of an old asset.

processing float The delay between the receipt of a check by the payee and its deposit in the firm's account.

profitability The relationship between revenues and costs.

pro forma statements Projected, or forecast, financial statements: income statements and balance sheets.

prospectus A portion of a security registration statement filed with the SEC which details the firm's operating and financial position.

proxy battle The attempt by a nonmanagement group to gain control of the management of a firm through the solicitation of a sufficient number of corporate votes.

proxy statement A statement conferring the votes of a stockholder or stockholders to another party or parties.

publicly held corporations Corporations whose stock is traded on either an organized securities exchange or the over-the-counter exchange.

publicly owned (stock) Common stock of a firm owned by a broad group of unrelated individual and (or) institutional investors.

public offering A nonexclusive issue to the general public of either bonds or stock by a firm in order to raise funds.

put option An option to sell a given number of shares (typically 100) of stock on or before a specified future date at a stated striking price.

pyramiding An arrangement among holding companies wherein one holding company controls other holding companies, thereby causing an even greater magnification of earnings and losses.

quarterly compounding Compounding of interest over four periods within the year.

quick (acid-test) ratio A measure of liquidity calculated by dividing the firm's current assets minus inventory by current liabilities.

range The extent of an asset's risk, which is found by subtracting the pessimistic (worst) outcome from the optimistic (best) outcome.

ranking approach The ranking of capital expenditure projects on the basis of some predetermined measure such as the rate of return.

ratio analysis The calculation and interpretation of financial ratios to assess the firm's performance and status.

ratio of exchange The ratio of the amount paid per share of the acquired firm to the per-share market price of the acquiring firm.

ratio of exchange in market price The ratio indicating the market price per share of the acquiring firm paid for each dollar of market price per share of the acquired firm.

raw materials inventory Items purchased by the firm for use in the manufacture of a finished product.

real rate of interest That rate that creates an equilibrium between the supply of savings and the demand for investment funds in a perfect world, without inflation, where funds suppliers and demanders have no liquidity preference, and all outcomes are certain.

recapitalization The reorganization procedure under which a failed firm's debts are generally exchanged for equity or the maturities of existing debts are extended.

recaptured depreciation The portion of the sale price that is above book value and below the initial purchase price.

recovery period The appropriate depreciable life of a particular asset as determined by ACRS.

red herring On a prospectus, a statement, printed in red, indicating the tentative nature of a security offer while the offer is being reviewed by the SEC.

regular dividend policy A dividend policy based on the payment of a fixed-dollar dividend in each period.

relevant cash flows The incremental after-tax cash outflow (investment) and resulting subsequent inflows associated with a proposed capital expenditure.

renewal options Provisions especially common in operating leases that grant the lessee the option to re-lease assets at their expiration.

reorder point The point at which to reorder inventory, expressed equationally as: lead time in days × daily usage.

repurchase agreement An agreement whereby a bank or security dealer sells a firm specific securities and agrees to repurchase them at a specific price and time.

required return The level of return expected on an investment.

required total financing Amount of funds needed by the firm if the ending cash for the period is less than the minimum cash balance.

residual theory of dividends A theory that suggests that the dividend paid by a firm should be the amount left over after all acceptable investment opportunities have been undertaken.

restrictive covenants Contractual clauses in long-term debt agreements that place certain operating and financial constraints on the borrower.

retained earnings The cumulative total of all earnings retained and reinvested in the firm since its inception.

return The change in value of an asset plus any cash distribution, expressed as a percentage of the beginning-of-period investment value.

return on equity (ROE) Measures the return on the owners' (preferred and common stockholders') investment in the firm.

return on investment (ROI) Measures the overall effectiveness of management in producing profits from available assets.

reverse stock split A method used to raise the market price of a firm's stock by exchanging a certain number of outstanding shares for one new share of stock.

revolving credit agreement A line of credit guaranteed to the borrower by the bank for a stated time period and regardless of the scarcity of money.

risk The chance of financial loss or, more formally, the variability of returns associated with a given asset.

risk-adjusted discount rate (RADR) The rate of return that must be earned on a given project to compensate the firm's owners adequately, thereby resulting in the maintenance or improvement of share price.

risk-averse The attitude toward risk in which an increased return would be required for an increase in risk.

risk-free rate of interest, R_F The rate of return one would earn on a virtually riskless investment such as a U.S. Treasury bill.

risk-indifferent The attitude toward risk in which no change in return would be required for an increase in risk.

risk premium The amount by which the required discount rate for a project exceeds the risk-free rate.

risk-return trade-off The expectation that for accepting greater risk investors must be compensated with greater returns.

risk-taking The attitude toward risk in which a decreased return would be accepted for an increase in risk.

safety motives Reasons for which marketable securities are held to earn returns and liquidated as needed in order to service the firm's cash account.

safety of principal The ease of salability of a security for close to its initial value.

sale-leaseback arrangement A lease under which the lessee sells an asset for cash to a prospective lessor and then leases back the same asset, making periodic payments for its use.

sales forecast The prediction of the firm's sales over a given period, based on external and/or internal data, and used as the key input to the short-run financial planning process.

scenario analysis An approach that evaluates the impact on return of simultaneous changes in a number of variables.

S corporation A tax-reporting entity whose earnings are taxed not as a corporation but as the incomes of its shareholders, thus avoiding the usual double taxation on corporate earnings.

seasonal need Financing requirements for temporary current assets, which vary throughout the year.

secondary market Financial market in which preowned securities (those that are not new issues) are traded.

secured creditors Creditors who have specific assets pledged as collateral and in liquidation of the failed firm receive proceeds from the sale of those assets.

secured short-term financing Short-term financing (loans) obtained by pledging specific assets as collateral.

Securities and Exchange Commission (SEC) The federal regulatory body that governs the sale and listing of securities.

securities exchanges Provide the marketplace in which firms raise funds through the sale of new securities and in which purchasers can resell securities.

security agreement The agreement between the borrower and the lender that specifies the collateral held against a secured loan.

security market line (SML) The depiction of the capital asset pricing model (CAPM) as a graph.

selling group A group of investment bankers and brokerage firms, each of which will sell a portion of a security issue and be paid for each security sold.

semiannual compounding Compounding of interest over two periods within the year.

sensitivity analysis An approach in assessing risk that uses a number of possible values for a given variable in order to assess its impact on a firm's return.

serial bonds An issue of bonds of which a certain proportion matures each year.

shelf registration An SEC procedure that allows firms to file a master statement for a two-year period and then during that period sell securities already approved under the master statement.

short-run (operating) financial plans Planned short-term financial actions and the anticipated financial impact of those actions.

short-term financing All debts of the firm that come due (must be paid) in one year or less.

short-term self-liquidating loan An unsecured short-term loan in which the borrowed funds provide the mechanism through which the loan itself is repaid.

simulation A statistically based approach used to get a feel for risk by applying predetermined probability distributions and random numbers to estimate risky outcomes.

single-payment note A short-term, one-time loan payable as a single amount at its maturity.

sinking-fund requirement A restrictive provision often included in a bond indenture providing for the systematic retirement of bonds prior to their maturity.

sole proprietorship A business owned by one person and operated for his or her own profit.

speculative motives Reasons for which marketable securities are held to earn returns until the firm finds a suitable use for the excess cash.

spin-off A form of divestiture in which an operating unit becomes an independent company by issuing shares of the new firm on a pro rata basis to the parent company's shareholders.

spontaneous financing Financing that arises from the normal operations of the firm, the two major short-term sources of which are accounts payable and accruals.

spot exchange rate The rate of exchange between two currencies on any given day.

spread The difference between the price paid for a security by the investment banker and the sale price.

standard debt provisions Provisions in long-term debt agreements specifying certain criteria of satisfactory record keeping and reporting, tax payment, and general business maintenance on the part of the borrowing firm.

standard deviation (σ_k) The most common statistical indicator of an asset's risk, which measures the dispersion around the *expected* value.

standby arrangement A formal guarantee that any shares not subscribed or sold publicly will be purchased by the investment banker.

statement of changes in financial position Financial statement that provides a summary of the flow of funds over the period of concern, typically the past year.

statement of retained earnings Financial statement that reconciles the net income earned in a given year, and any cash dividends paid, with the change in retained earnings between the start and end of that year.

stock dividend The payment of a dividend by the firm in the form of stock to existing owners.

stockholders The true owners of the firm by virtue of their equity in the form of common and/or preferred stock.

stockholders' report Annual report required of publicly held corporations that summarizes and documents for stockholders the firm's financial activities of the past year.

stock options Privileges, generally extended to management, permitting the purchase of a certain number of shares of their firm's common stock at a specified price over a certain period of time.

stock-purchase plans A fringe benefit that allows the purchase of a firm's stock at a discount or on a matching basis with a part of the cost absorbed by the firm.

stock-purchase warrant An instrument that gives its holder an option to purchase a certain number of shares of common stock at a specified price over a certain period of time.

stock repurchase The repurchasing by the firm of outstanding shares of its common stock in the marketplace.

stock rights Rights that provide stockholders with the privilege to purchase additional shares of stock based on their number of owned shares.

stock split A method commonly used to lower the market price of a firm's stock by increasing the number of shares belonging to each shareholder.

straight bonds Bonds that are nonconvertible, having no conversion feature.

straight bond value The price at which a convertible bond would sell in the market without the conversion feature.

straight preferred stock Preferred stock that is nonconvertible, having no conversion feature.

stretching accounts payable Paying bills as late as possible without damaging one's credit rating.

striking price The price at which the holder of a call option can buy (or holder of a put option can sell) a specified amount of stock at any time prior to the option's expiration.

subordination In a long-term debt agreement, the stipulation that subsequent or less important creditors agree to wait until all claims of the senior debt are satisfied before having their claims satisfied.

subscription price The price, below the prevailing market price, at which stock rights may be exercisable for a specified period of time.

subsidiaries The companies controlled by a holding company.

target capital structure The desired optimal mix of debt and equity financing that most firms attempt to achieve and maintain.

target dividend-payout ratio A policy under which the firm attempts to pay out a certain percentage of earnings as a stated dollar dividend adjusted toward a target payout as proven earnings increases occur.

target weights Either book or market value weights based on desired capital structure proportions; used in calculating the weighted average cost of capital.

tax loss carryforward In a combination or merger, the tax loss of one of the firms that can be applied against a limited amount of future income of the combined firm over the shorter of either 15 years or until the total tax loss has been exhausted.

technical insolvency Business failure that occurs when a firm is unable to pay its liabilities as they come due.

tender offer A formal offer to purchase a given number of shares of a firm's stock at a specified price, often in order to acquire the firm.

terminal cash flow The after-tax nonoperating cash flow occurring in the final year of a project, usually attributable to liquidation of the project.

term loan A loan made by a financial institution to a business and having an initial maturity of more than one year. Also called a *long-term loan*.

term loan agreement A formal contract, ranging from a few to a few hundred pages, specifying the conditions under which a financial institution has made a long-term loan.

term structure of interest rates The relationship between the interest rate or rate of return and the time to maturity.

time-series analysis Evaluation of the firm's financial performance over time utilizing financial ratio analysis.

times interest earned ratio Measures the firm's ability to meet contractual interest payments.

total asset turnover Indicates the efficiency with which the firm uses all assets to generate sales.

total cost The sum of the order and carrying costs of inventory.

total leverage The potential use of fixed costs, both operating and financial, to magnify the effect of changes in sales on the firm's earnings per share (EPS).

total risk The combination of a security's nondiversifiable risk and diversifiable risk.

traditional approach (capital structure) The theory that an optimal capital structure exists, and that the value of the firm is maximized when the cost of capital is minimized.

transactions motives Reasons for which marketable securities are held to earn a temporary return and then liquidated in order to make various planned payments.

treasurer The officer responsible for the firm's financial activities, such as financial planning and fund raising, managing cash, capital expenditure decisions, managing credit activities, and managing the investment portfolio.

Treasury bills (T–bills) U.S. Treasury obligations issued weekly on an auction basis, having varying maturities, generally under a year, and virtually no risk.

Treasury notes U.S. Treasury obligations with initial maturities of between one and seven years, paying interest at a stated rate semiannually, and having virtually no risk.

treasury stock Issued stock that has been repurchased and is held by the firm.

trustee A paid individual, corporation, or commercial bank trust department that acts as the third party to a bond indenture in order to ensure that the issuer does not default on its contractual responsibilities to the bondholders.

trust receipt inventory loan An agreement under which the lender advances 80 to 100 percent of the cost of the borrower's salable inventory items in exchange for the borrower's promise to immediately repay the loan, with accrued interest, upon the sale of each item.

uncorrelated Descriptive of two series that lack any relationship or interaction and therefore have a correlation coefficient of zero.

underpriced Stock sold at a price below its current market price, P_0.

undersubscribed issue A security issue whose shares are not immediately sold.

underwriting An investment banker's guarantee to the issuer that it will receive at least a specified minimum amount from the issue.

underwriting syndicate A group of investment banking firms, each of which will underwrite a portion of a large security issue, thus lessening the risk of loss to any single firm.

unitary tax laws Laws in some U.S. states that tax multinationals (both American and foreign) on a percentage of their total worldwide income rather than the usual taxation of the MNCs' earnings within a given state.

unlimited funds The financial situation in which a firm is able to accept all independent projects that provide an acceptable return.

unlimited liability The condition imposed by a sole proprietorship (or general partnership) allowing the owner's total wealth to be taken to satisfy creditors.

unsecured creditors Creditors having a general claim against all the firm's assets other than those specifically pledged as collateral. Also called *general creditors*.

unsecured short-term financing Short-term financing obtained without pledging specific assets as collateral.

valuation The process that links risk and return in order to determine the worth of an asset.

variable growth model A dividend valuation approach that allows for a change in the dividend growth rate.

voluntary reorganization A petition filed by a failed firm on its own behalf for reorganizing its structure and paying its creditors.

voluntary settlement An arrangement between a technically insolvent or bankrupt firm and its creditors enabling it to bypass many of the costs involved in legal bankruptcy proceedings.

warehouse receipt loan An arrangement in which the lender receives control of the pledged collateral, which is warehoused by a designated agent in the lender's behalf.

warrant premium The difference between the theoretical and actual market values of a warrant.

weighted average cost of capital (WACC), k_a Determined by weighting the cost of each specific type of capital by its proportion in the firm's capital structure.

weighted marginal cost of capital (WMCC) A schedule or graph relating the firm's weighted average cost of capital to the level of new financing.

wire transfers Telegraphic communications that, via bookkeeping entries, remove funds from the payer's bank and deposit them in the payee's bank, thereby reducing collection float.

work-in-process inventory All items currently in production.

working capital management Management of the firm's current accounts, which include current assets and current liabilities.

yield curve A graph that shows the relationship between the yield to maturity of a security (y-axis) and the time to maturity (x-axis).

yield to maturity Annual rate of interest earned on a security purchased on a given day and held to maturity.

zero-balance account A checking account in which a zero balance is maintained and the bank requires the firm to deposit funds to cover checks drawn on the account only as they are presented.

zero growth model An approach to dividend valuation that assumes a constant, nongrowing dividend stream.